Jefferson Davis
Unconquerable Heart

SHADES OF BLUE AND GRAY SERIES

Edited by Herman Hattaway and Jon L. Wakelyn

The Shades of Blue and Gray Series will offer Civil War studies for the modern reader—Civil War buff and scholar alike. Military history today addresses the relationship between society and warfare. Thus biographies and thematic studies that deal with civilians, soldiers, and political leaders are increasingly important to a larger public. This series will include books that will appeal to Civil War Roundtable groups, individuals, libraries, and academics with a special interest in this era of American history.

Jefferson Davis
Unconquerable Heart

Felicity Allen

"relying on . . . our God, let us meet the foe with fresh defiance, with unconquered and unconquerable hearts"

—Jefferson Davis

To the People of the Confederate States of America, April 4, 1865

University of Missouri Press
Columbia and London

University of Missouri Press, Columbia, Missouri 65201
Printed and bound in the United States of America

5 4 3 2 1 04 03 02 01 00

Library of Congress Cataloging-in-Publication Data

Allen, Felicity, 1924–
Jefferson Davis, unconquerable heart / Felicity Allen.
p. cm.—(Shades of blue and gray series)
Includes bibliographical references (p.) and index.
ISBN 0-8262-1219-0 (alk. paper)
1. Davis, Jefferson, 1808–1889. 2. Presidents—Confederate States of America Biography. 3. Confederate States of America Biography. 4. Statesmen—United States Biography. I. Title. II. Series.
E467.1.D26A45 1999
973.7'13'092—dc21 99-39915
CIP

∞™ This paper meets the requirements of the American National Standard for Permanence of Paper for Printed Library Materials, Z39.48, 1984.

Designer: Stephanie Foley
Typesetter: BookComp, Inc.
Printer and binder: Thomson-Shore, Inc.
Typeface: Bookman

Frontispiece: *Jefferson Davis at Richmond, Va., Reviewing a Louisiana Regiment,* oil painting by L. M. D. Guillaume. Courtesy the R. W. Norton Art Gallery, Shreveport, Louisiana.

Publication of this book has been supported by a contribution from the Mary Nowell Kershaw Foundation.

This book is dedicated to

Maude Frizzell Hall,

my maternal grandmother,

a Confederate to the last

and to my husband,

Ward Sykes Allen,

who taught me all the rest

Contents

Preface

When Jeff Davis died in 1889, everyone in the South knew who he was, and what he was. In Europe and the North, most people knew something about him, even if it was bad. Yet by 1977, Frank Vandiver had picked up a phrase Communists were then using to obliterate their enemies and referred to him as "an historical nonperson." Beginning my research just before this, I had found indeed that ignorance like my own was a general state. My friends could not tell me anything except that Davis had been president of the Confederacy. So I read Dunbar Rowland's ten-volume collection of Davis's letters and papers, little by little, in order to answer the question: "What was he really like?"

This was what Sigrid Undset had asked in 1942 when Hudson Strode took her to see the daughters of Gen. and Mrs. Josiah Gorgas in Tuscaloosa, Alabama. They, whose parents had known Davis, told her, "He was noble! A man of impeccable integrity, with a truly warm and generous heart" and "a splendid soldier." The Nobel Prize winner in literature was puzzled. She knew that Robert E. Lee, her son's hero, was "glorified by both sides," and she could not understand why historians seemed to tell her only about Davis's faults. "Could anyone else have done so well, or held the Confederacy together so long with so little?" she asked. "Why is Jefferson Davis not given his due?"

Those four years as president will always be the ones of most interest, but that leaves seventy-seven more. "My whole life must speak for me," said Leonidas Polk. So must Davis's. Those other years are in this book, as detailed as space will allow, showing his youth, his careers of soldier, planter, statesman, executive, and lastly, writer. All the outward events of his life speak clearly but do not say enough. What a man is "really like" comes out in the thoughts of his heart—what he feels and thinks and, above all, believes. We discover these in this book through his own words, his prayers, what he chooses to read, and his relations with other people. His enemies speak their minds about him here, and we follow close friendships, some lasting throughout his life. The one with Lee is treated here more fully, I believe, than ever before. What emerges is the essential Davis, soldier and family man. His wife, Varina, and his six children were so important to him that this biography is really about them, too. We come to know Davis, as it were, from the inside out. The view we have of his times is largely the view he had. If all this weights the scales on his side, perhaps it produces a balance long overdue. He has been "strangely misconceived."

Dunbar Rowland expected to follow up his monumental collection of papers with a "Life" of Davis. He wanted to counter, he said, the prevailing "unscientific methods" and "bunk" about him. But he found that long acquaintance with Davis had "made me a hero-worshiper, and no hero-worshiper should attempt the biography of his hero." He gave all his papers to Robert McElroy. Walter Lynwood Fleming lighted up many new facets of Davis in scholarly articles and gathered all the material for "a definitive biography," but he died before he could write it. Using both his and Rowland's material, McElroy produced in 1937 the first full-scale scholarly biography, the two-volume *Jefferson Davis: The Unreal and the Real.* In it, as his subtitle hints, he tried to counter the "bunk."

Much of the "bunk" came from E. A. Pollard, Davis's wartime nemesis on the *Richmond Examiner.* During those years, he wrote a "multivolume diatribe," says Vandiver, which he "culled" finally into one volume called *The Lost Cause*—"lost by the perfidy of Jefferson Davis." In this and many other books, all containing many errors, Pollard not only blamed Davis for the loss of the Confederacy, but also vilified him and Varina personally. His picture of Davis as a flawed leader with a repellent and weak personality has come down to the present day in unending reprints of *The Lost Cause,* the last noted in 1995, advertised as "the Southern history of the War." No one thought to reprint McElroy until 1996, and the best biography before his, Frank Alfriend's, has never been reprinted, so far as I know.

Pollard's views were also perpetuated by others, notably by the scholar Hamilton J. Eckenrode in a 1923 book on the Davis presidency (also reprinted). From there, they passed directly into Allen Tate's narrative of the war (not a biography), *Jefferson Davis: His Rise and Fall,* and Andrew Lytle's book on Forrest, still reprinted and read. As Vandiver points out, Davis was such a nonperson that Eckenrode and Tate could use him "for their own purposes," advancing different theories of Confederate failure, in both of which the president was to blame. The hand of Pollard and Eckenrode is also seen in later works, surveyed by Vandiver in "Jefferson Davis—Leader without Legend," and more extensively in John Junior Jones's dissertation, "A Historiographical Study of Jefferson Davis" (1970), and Herman Hattaway's "Jefferson Davis and the Historians" (in *The Confederate High Command,* 1990).

Sigrid Undset inspired Hudson Strode to seek out Davis. This led him to unearth a treasure in family letters, which he was the first to use in his biography and to print collected. He was instrumental in having the originals donated to university libraries in Kentucky and Alabama, putting Davis scholars forever in his debt. Strode found other new clues to understanding Davis the man, but his three-volume biography has been overlooked because it lacks scholarly apparatus. Moreover, he took undue liberties in editing the letters. This became apparent as I read many of the manuscripts. Yet for those I could not read, I have had to rely on his printing. It has been estimated that there are fifty thousand Davis letters; one would have to start very young to read them all. Just in the years while I was writing, new donations piled up in the archives. I have had, unwillingly, to bypass several collections. For printings, I depend most, after Rowland, on *The Papers of Jefferson Davis*, a series still in progress.

Lee is still the great Southern hero, and people always want to know what he thought of Davis. He told a questioner after the war, "You can *always* say that few people could have done better than Mr. Davis. I knew of none that could have done as well." And "as a man," he said, Davis was "one of the purest and noblest that could be found in the world." Everyone knows Lee's piety; few know Davis's. Yet one eulogist said that his religious convictions were the "secret" of his character, that he was controlled by them, "not by caprice." According to Basil L. Gildersleeve, the noted professor of classics who fought for the Confederate States in his summer vacations, that whole "heroic generation" cannot be understood without its religion—"an historical element, like any other." It is treated so here. Sen. John Daniel said the South was fortunate to have for its leader the "true type of its honor, character, and history." That is the Davis of this book.

Probably there are people who still think of Davis as a nonperson because he owned slaves. If a certain obtuseness before the war allowed him to extol freedom without having them in mind, still, he honored blacks and Indians as he found them, and was honored by them. He thought European Americans were responsible for maintaining their own culture brought from the old country. Political structure was a part of this. Rowland well named his book *Jefferson Davis, Constitutionalist*. Many are beginning to see that Davis was the champion of constitutional, as opposed to consolidated, government.

If I had to characterize Davis, I would choose the words *simplicity, honesty, consistency*. The acquaintance who called him "direct, open and manly" had it about right. As Preston Johnston said about his father, Albert Sidney, Davis about Andrew Jackson, and Varina about him, absolute accuracy about his life is his finest tribute. Accuracy is what this book aims for.

Acknowledgments

My debt is total to my husband, Ward Sykes Allen, for help the whole way in every way. Support came from our children, Peter and Will Allen, Maude (Jeri) Earnest, and Mary Christine Bradshaw, and expert help from son-in-law David Bradshaw. My cherished friend Christine Langseth Benagh has nudged the book along from its very first thought, an informal and invaluable editor. I am grateful for various aid throughout the writing from other family members—Clare Allen, Jane Allen Gregory, the late Martha Hall McComas, Mary McComas McGavock, Jennifer Earnest and Guerry Clayton McComas. The help from our friends Walter and Jane Sullivan and Harold L. Weatherby deserves special note, but my gratitude goes out to many friends and acquaintances: Anne Amacher, Glenn Anderson, the Reverend Charles E. Baker, Wesley Baker, Thomas A. Belser, Col. (Ret.) Robert Bradshaw, Betty Jane and the late Bernard Breyer, Jonathan Buford, Robin Carter, Boyd Childress, Joanne and the late William Childers, Roger Cole, the late Helen Dick Davis, Billie Emert, the late Reverend George A. Fox, Emmalu Foy, Joseph Hobson Harrison, Jr., the Reverend John Harwell, David Holt, Sam and Jacque Hornsby, Sara Hudson, Edward and Karen Jacobs, Hutch Johnson, Madison and Shailah Jones, the late Andrew Lytle, Virgil and Louise LeQuire, Taylor Littleton, the Reverend Germain Marc'hadour, James Nicholson, the late Miriam Patrick, Hunter and Virginia Peak, Kaye Reyes, Col. (Ret.) Edward R. Schowalter, Forrest Shivers, Martha Solomon, John Sophocleus, Craig Thompson, Mills Thornton, Michelle Ladd Trimmier, James P. Warren, and Elly and Peter Welt. I owe an incalculable debt to my friends and mentors, the late Donald Davidson and Curtis Howe Walker, who taught me writing and historical research, and much else, at Vanderbilt University. Special thanks are due the late James Treadway, for many conversations that steered me right about the war. Doctors James P. Himmelwright, V. S. LeQuire, Emil Wright, and J. David Hagan, in person, and Harris D. Riley, Jr., in writing, provided much-appreciated medical information, but they are not responsible for my use of it.

On a more formal level, I am indebted to Charlene Alling; the late Sr. Aloysius, O. P.; Sr. Anne Odile, C. S. J.; the Reverend Jackson Biggers; David A. Bovenizer; the late Chester D. Bradley; Kathleen Bryson; Marie T. Capps; Cathy Carlson; Newton W. Carr, Jr.; Lynda Lasswell Crist; Thomas M. Czekanski; Shelby Foote; B. J. Gooch; Charles Goolsby; William Hanchett; Keith Hardison; Nancy S. Hartman; Michael Hennen; Jewel Horine; David J. Johnson; Kathy Joyner; Norwood A. Kerr; Judi Kincaid, James B. Lloyd; Joseph Dandridge Logan III; Margaret Prowse Mason; Deborah Nygren; John Oliver; Carolyn D. Palmgreen; Sheila Patterson; R. Cody Phillips; Richard Salvato; Virginia L. Smyers; Allen Stokes; Mrs. A. C. Tipton; James W. Thompson; Frank E. Vandiver; Lee Waldrip; Sr. Charlene Walsh, R. S. M.; Barbara Williamson; Melanie Yolles, David Zalik; and especially to Gordon Cotton, Pat Fulks, Julia Guice, Tucker Herrin Hill, Mary Lohrenz, John McGlone, Wilbur E. Meneray, Cameron Freeman Napier, and the host and hostesses at the First White House of the Confederacy.

Thanks for permission to quote excerpts from the following sources are due to: the Alabama Department of Archives and History, for the Jefferson Davis Papers and the Hardee Family Papers; Beauvoir, the Jefferson Davis Home and Presidential Library, for items in their possession; Brandt and Brandt, Literary Agents, for *First Lady of the South: The Life of Mrs. Jefferson Davis* by Ishbel Ross, published by HarperCollins; R. E. Canon of the Briars, for a Davis letter; the Casemate Museum at Fort Monroe, Virginia, for a note by Varina Davis; Columbia University Press, for *Braxton Bragg and Confederate Defeat* by Grady McWhiney, copyright 1969; Bertram Hayes-Davis, on behalf of the Davis Family Association, for Davis Family Papers in the Mississippi Archives, the University of Alabama, Transylvania University, and Tulane University; Nicholas T. Goldsborough, for the monograph, "Varina Howell Davis" by Anna Farrar Goldsborough; to Joseph H. Harrison, Jr., for a family letter; Dr. Jeanne T. Heidler, for her dissertation, "The Military Career of David Emanuel Twiggs"; to Ronald T. Hillhouse, for a family letter; Mark Hudson Mabry, for *Jefferson Davis: Private Letters, 1823–1889;* Wilbur E. Meneray, for the Louisiana Historical Association Collection at Howard-Tilton Memorial Library, Tulane University; Mercer University Press, for *"Fiction Distorting Fact": The Prison Life Annotated by Jefferson Davis* by Edward K. Eckert; Louisiana State University Press, for *The Papers of Jefferson Davis,* volumes 1 through 6; Mississippi Department of Archives and History, for their collections of Davis papers, for the Jefferson Davis Book Collection, Old Capitol Museum of Mississippi History (Jackson), and for "Jefferson Davis Recalls the Past; Notes of a Wartime Aide, William Preston Johnston," edited by Marilyn McAdams Sibley, *Journal of Mississippi History,* vol. 33 (May 1971); the Museum of the Confederacy, for "An Inventory of the Davis Family Artifacts" and inscriptions in a Davis Bible; Cameron F. Napier, Regent of the White

House Association of Alabama, for a Davis letter and other items; the National Society of the Sons of the American Revolution, for material in applications; the New Hampshire Historical Society, for Davis letters in the John Parker Hale Papers, 1822–1885, and the Franklin Pierce Papers, 1820–1946; the New York Public Library, for eleven items in the Walter L. Fleming Collection; Old Courthouse Museum, Vicksburg, for three Davis letters; the South Caroliniana Library of the University of South Carolina, for Mary Chesnut's Letterbook; Transylvania University, for Davis manuscripts; the University of Alabama, for Jefferson Davis Papers and Hudson Strode Papers; and the University of Memphis, for Jefferson Davis–Joel Addison Hayes, Jr., Family Papers in the Mississippi Valley Collection and Meriwether Papers of the West Tennessee Historical Society. For assistance in reproducing rare photographs, thanks go to Cameragraphics, Auburn, Alabama.

After more than twenty years of research and writing, I must have unintentionally overlooked someone who ought to be thanked. I can only beg forgiveness.

Editorial Note

Emendations

In allowing Davis and his contemporaries to speak for themselves, it has been my intention to present quotations in as clear and faithful a form as possible. Thus, original spelling, punctuation, and any lapses in grammar are reproduced here. Terminal punctuation has been added when necessary. In some cases editorial intervention has been required to avoid causing confusion or to provide essential information to the reader.

Davis Residences

In the long history of Davis's life, a number of residences are referred to. This list may be an aid to clarity:

1) Poplar Grove or Rosemont. The Jeff Davis boyhood home, a family farm established by his parents in 1811, about a mile and a half from Woodville, Mississippi, in Wilkinson County; kept in the family through Davis's sister Lucinda (Mrs. William Stamps) and her heirs until 1901; owned by Henry Johnson family until 1972; now open under private ownership as a place of historic pilgrimage.

2) Brierfield. Plantation with its house, first built by Davis in 1838, at Davis Bend (now Davis Island) on the Mississippi River, some twenty-five miles south of Vicksburg; home to him and Varina until 1861; seized by Union troops in 1863; subsequently returned to the Davis family; possession regained by Davis himself in 1881; never again his home, but frequently visited by him until his death in 1889; sold by Davis heirs in 1953; now a private hunting preserve; house burned 1931.

3) The Hurricane. Plantation and home of Davis's eldest brother, Joseph Emory, adjoining Brierfield; house burned by Union forces,

June 24, 1862; land confiscated; regained by Joseph after the war; now part of the Davis Island hunting preserve.

4) The Briars. Natchez, Mississippi, home of Varina Howell, where she and Davis were married in 1845; lost to Howell family in 1850; now privately owned and open to tourists.

5) Presidential mansions —
First White House of the Confederacy. Montgomery, Alabama; occupied for a few months in 1861; now a treasury of Davis memorabilia, given by Varina; owned by the First White House Association; open to the public.
White House of the Confederacy. Richmond, Virginia; a school after the war, then Museum of the Confederacy; now restored as a mid-nineteenth-century dwelling; many Davis items given by Varina in permanent display called "Victory in Defeat"; owned by the Confederate Memorial Literary Society; open to the public.

6) Beauvoir. House, originally on some six hundred acres, in Harrison County, Mississippi, on the Gulf of Mexico between Biloxi and Gulfport; purchased, then inherited, by Davis from Sarah Anne Ellis (Mrs. Samuel W.) Dorsey in 1879; home to him from 1878 until his death, and to Varina for several years after his death; sold in 1902 to the United Sons of Confederate Veterans (now Sons of Confederate Veterans) and still maintained by that group on reduced acreage as the Jefferson Davis Home and Presidential Library; repository of many Davis items; open to the public.

7) Houses in Memphis, Tennessee. At 129 East Court Street and 98 Court Street; rented in the 1870s; present status unknown.

Davis Children

Another aid to clarity may be the names and nicknames of the Davis children. They are, in order of birth:

1) Samuel Emory ("Sam," "Le Man")
2) Margaret Howell ("Maggie," "Pollie"; in the text, "Margaret" always means her aunt of this name)
3) Jefferson, Jr. (called in text "Jeff Jr.," and sometimes by Davis, "Big Boy")
4) Joseph Evan ("Little Man")
5) William Howell ("Billy" or "Billie")
6) Varina Anne ("Pie Cake," "Pie," "Li' Pie," "L. P.," "Winanne," "Winnie"; latter used for her exclusively in text, not as her mother's nickname, which it also was, except in quotations).

Jefferson Davis
Unconquerable Heart

I

Capture

> As the tug bore him away from the ship, he stood with bared head between the files of undersized German and other foreign soldiers on either side of him, and as we looked, as we thought, our last upon his stately form and knightly bearing, he seemed a man of another and higher race, upon whom "shame would not dare to sit."[1]

To one of the enemies waiting ashore, he appears "much wasted and very haggard"; to another, he seems to bear himself "with a haughty attitude." The latter is an assistant secretary of war for the United States, Charles A. Dana. By the death date of the man now his prisoner, Dana will have come to regard him as a "majestic soul" who "bore defeat and humiliation in the high Roman fashion." The other enemy is Bvt. Lt. Col. John J. Craven, M.D. He will attend the already ailing captive for seven months and prove, in the end, a friend.[2]

The man so variously looked upon is Jefferson Davis, until twelve days before, president of the Confederate States of America. The ship from which he is being borne away this May 22, 1865, is the *William P. Clyde,* an oceangoing, though barely seaworthy, side-wheeler. Escorted by the warship *Tuscarora,* it has brought Confederate prisoners up the coast from Port Royal, South Carolina, to Hampton Roads, Virginia. The "foreign soldiers" wear the uniform of the United States of America. They are a few of the thousands in the Northern army, many recruited surreptitiously abroad.[3] At Andersonville, Georgia, so many prisoners cannot speak English that the Catholic priest has had to send for an interpreter. Davis conveyed an informal protest to Pope Pius IX about this covert recruitment in Catholic regions of Europe. The pope "appeared to be touched" and "intimated . . . a salutary remedy," but no more came of it.[4]

The tug is bearing Davis toward the Engineer Wharf of Fortress Monroe, in the granite wall of which a gun casemate has been converted by concrete and iron bars into a cell to receive him. Night and day, soldiers will pace inside as well as in the guardroom that provides the only entrance to the cell. Against the thirty-foot walls of the encircling moat rise and fall the tides of Chesapeake Bay. Two casemates away, an almost identical cell and guardroom await Clement Claiborne Clay, who is with Davis in the tugboat. Dr. Craven, passing through the shore guard on his way to the wharf, hears, among excited speculations as to the ex-president's fate, "They'll hang Clem. Clay sure."[5]

Another "knightly" figure in his friends' eyes, Clay began his career after the University of Alabama as secretary to his father, the governor, who had been Alabama's first chief justice. After law school in Virginia, Clement practiced in Alabama, served in its legislature, and was then elected to the United States Senate, where he met the man standing in the boat beside him. Their comradeship was basically political, but it ripened into a friendship which both called "intimate" and which survived strong disturbance during the Confederate years.[6] Differences in temperament are apparent in their farewell addresses made to the Senate on the same day, January 21, 1861, as they quit that august body for an uncertain future with their seceded states. Davis's is a model of highly charged but restrained eloquence; Clay's is a passionate denunciation and defiance of the abolitionist foe.[7]

President Davis had sent Clay and others on a confidential mission to neutral Canada to feel out the Northern peace movement just prior to the 1864 elections. The agents tried to contact President Abraham Lincoln through newspaper editor Horace Greeley for informal peace talks, and they encouraged the copperhead C. L. Vallandigham and his Sons of Liberty. The secretive nature of the mission led to enormous flights of fancy in the Northern press as to what they were up to. Clay had been back in the South over two months before the assassination of Lincoln on April 14, 1865. But when it came out that some of those accused of it had been in Canada, people leapt to the conclusion (aided by false testimony) that the Confederate mission had instigated the murder. In the public mind, Clay is already condemned, which is why the soldier is "sure" "they" will hang him.[8]

There is very little doubt in anybody's mind that "they" will also hang Davis. Even his wife, Varina Howell Davis, leaning over the rail of the *Clyde,* believes that she and their children are looking their last upon him. With this belief piercing her heart, she still is able to bid farewell without a scene. His "eyes of quiet fortitude which shone [there]" and words whispered in their last embrace, have imparted to her his own courage. She is in herself a courageous woman, but she has feared the worst ever since their capture, especially since the Proclamation.[9]

Davis's route to capture and sites of military operations, 1861–1865

Gen. Robert Edward Lee telegraphed on April 2, 1865, that he could no longer protect Richmond from the troops of Gen. Ulysses Simpson Grant at Petersburg, Virginia, and Davis removed the whole Confederate government south to Danville, Virginia, that night. Varina was then in North Carolina. Against her wishes, he had sent her and their family out of Richmond a few days before. When Lee surrendered the Army of Northern Virginia on April 9, the dwindling governmental corps had to keep moving south and west. Davis and his wife pursued separate though similar routes, he nearly but never quite overtaking her.

From Danville, the president's party went to Greensboro, North Carolina, then Charlotte; from there, joined by several cavalry brigades, through South Carolina from Fort Mill to Abbeville; then across the Savannah River at Vienna to Washington-Wilkes in Georgia. Almost due south of there, by pressing relentlessly forward on horseback all one night "without drawing rein," Davis finally came up with his wife's wagons.[10]

Grant, knowing Lee's escape route from a paper found in captured Richmond, was able to hammer the sparse and starving Southern men at every point with massed troops, cut Lee off from Danville (where he and Davis planned to meet), and finally to trap him at Appomattox.[11]

Gen. Joseph Eggleston Johnston had command of the only other approximation of a Confederate army in the seaboard states. He wanted to surrender this too. He had for some time viewed resistance to the hordes of Generals Grant and William Tecumseh Sherman as hopeless. At Greensboro, he won Davis's reluctant consent to seek an armistice with Sherman, so that civilian officials could treat for peace. Should the armistice fail, Johnston was to follow Davis southwest with his cavalry, light artillery, and all the infantry he could mount, and they would join the Confederate troops in the Gulf states. They would then be in position, as belligerents, to exact favorable terms. As he traveled, Davis arranged for depots of supply "on the route [Johnston] had selected." Davis "never contemplated a surrender . . . as long as we were able to keep the field."[12]

Just as he anticipated, Sherman made it clear that "the United States did not acknowledge . . . a Southern Confederacy; nor, consequently, its civil authorities." They had, Davis said, "special dread" of seeming to recognize "the existence of a government which for four years they had been vainly trying to subdue." So Johnston proposed, citing Napoleon as precedent, that the generals themselves arrange the peace terms. The president, now in Charlotte, overlooked the presumption—"Heaven knows, I am not particular as to form"—and approved the terms that Sherman and Johnston worked out, since they "secured to our people the political rights and safety from pillage, to obtain which I proposed to continue the war."[13] The United States, however, rejected these terms. Then Johnston, "announcing to the Administration" that he was about to meet Sherman again, surrendered his army on April 26. Davis "had no part whatever in the transaction," getting his "first positive information" of it some ten days later, he says, when he found Augusta, Georgia, capitulating to Union troops. He wrote from Washington-Wilkes, "This Department has been surrendered without my knowledge and consent."[14]

It was not only the department. Sherman says Johnston thought that "further fighting would be *'murder'* " and that "we might arrange terms that would embrace *all* the Confederate armies . . . a universal surrender, embracing his own army, that of Dick Taylor, in Louisiana and Texas, and of Maury, Forrest and others, in Alabama and Georgia"—the very ones Davis was trying to reach (and all by now in Mississippi). Grant had tried to get Lee to "advise" this on the day after his own surrender, but Lee, though general-in-chief, had insisted he could not do it "without consulting the President first." This was impossible, and the proposal fell dead. Johnston, as he himself says, simply disobeyed his commander in chief's instructions to move his army south. Instead, he signed his own convention and strongly urged the other generals to follow suit—which they did. He assumed a presidential tone: "The pacification was announced by me to the States immediately concerned."[15]

Davis's reaction to the usurpation of his authority was mild, at least by the time he wrote *The Rise and Fall of the Confederate Government:* "something more than courtesy required that the Executive should have been advised if not consulted." He had "never expected a Confederate army to surrender while it was able either to fight or to retreat." To the end of his life, he thought, "General Lee was forced to surrender and General Johnston consented to do so."[16] Johnston obeyed his own feeling instead of his superiors, saying he wanted to "save the people" by surrender. Davis wanted to save them by fighting, to win "political rights of the states," which was not done by reunion "without condition." "Those who have endured the horrors of 'reconstruction,'" he later wrote, "a state of vindictive hostility" with "insult, robbery, and imprisonment without legal warrant . . . will probably think continued war not the greatest of evils."[17]

Varina Davis's reaction was passionate: "I cannot refrain from expressing my intense grief at the treacherous surrender of this Department." An outspoken friend of theirs in South Carolina, Mary Chesnut, wife of Brig. Gen. James Chesnut, was also incensed. She said that Joe Johnston, when asked if he had the government's consent, had answered he "was not aware that we had any government. No—nor has he ever been aware that he owed allegiance to any." "The women of Columbia weep & call *Joe* a traitor. Joe who makes a 'convention' to save the country from ruin—& leaves his country to ruin—the miserable demagogue. Intriguer." She even named him among "our base betrayers."[18]

If Johnston's action was a betrayal of Davis, it was the only one. The men who constituted the Confederate government as it left Richmond dropped away one by one, but each bade farewell and made his excuse for going. George Davis, the attorney general, a widower from North Carolina, was the first to leave. He wondered aloud at Charlotte whether his place was with the government or with his family. "By the side of your family" promptly responded the other Davis. Since this was a family of motherless children, the response was virtually certain. Jefferson Davis's devotion to his own children was well known. Not so obvious was the mutual attraction between him and every child he met. The last act of his life was to oblige a child.[19] Even now on the perilous road, Varina had with her Jim Limber, a mulatto orphan whom the Davises had rescued from a cruel guardian and informally adopted. At a stopping place, she wrote: "The children . . . play all day—Billy and Jim fast friends as ever."[20]

After settling his children, George Davis learned that Federal amnesty did not apply to civil officers. The hefty six-footer went penniless in disguise to Florida and hired on as a deckhand for passage to the Bahamas. But winds forced the small craft to Key West. He was arrested in October and sent to Fort Lafayette, New York harbor, where he was held prisoner for three months. A latecomer to the cabinet, he had originally been a political opponent of President Davis's but found that "the more you saw and heard him the greater he grew." He retained "unfailing confidence, esteem and love" for Jeff Davis until his death.[21]

George Trenholm, who had inherited the onerous duties of treasury secretary the year before, was the next to fall away. He had been ill the whole trip, and by the time the caravan reached South Carolina, could not go on. He addressed his regret to the president, saying: "I cannot retire without expressing the profound impression made upon me by your public and private virtues, and the grateful sense I entertain of the kindness and courtesy that I have received at your hands, in our official intercourse—." Davis in turn thanked him for the "kindness and wisdom" of his counsel through "many trying scenes." Trenholm was arrested at his home near Columbia and, despite his illness, imprisoned for four months at Fort Pulaski, Savannah harbor. In a letter written in 1870, his household sent Davis "undiminished respect and affection," and wanted to know "all about Mrs. Davis and the children."[22]

Judah Philip Benjamin went next. He had no taste for the noose or rigors of confinement that he saw ahead. He had managed to ride out of Greensboro in an ambulance (a small covered wagon) along with the aged and infirm, smoking his "cheerful cigar" and entertaining the company as he "rhythmically intoned" in his "silvery voice . . . verse after verse" of "Ode on the Death of the Duke of Wellington" by Alfred, Lord Tennyson. His figure was not made for the horseback riding to which he was reduced as the party crossed the Savannah River into Georgia.

Davis reassured someone worrying about this: "if one of us escapes it will be he." Indeed, Benjamin soon put to work the wits that later raised him to high rank at the English bar. He set off in a gig, disguised as a French traveler, aiming, said Davis, to reach the coast and then "join me in the Transmississippi Department whither he knew it was my fixed purpose to go." When he heard Davis was captured, however, he set out for the West Indies and eventually made it to England after terrible trials at sea. Thus escaped the secretary of state, who had also been attorney general and secretary of war.[23]

By this first week in May, only half the cabinet was left. Pleading family needs, Secretary of the Navy Stephen Russell Mallory resigned, not without noting Davis's "kindness, consideration and courtesy": "Language fails to give expression to my sense of your patriotic devotion to our common country. . . . Cheerfully would I follow you and share whatever fate may befall you, could I hope thereby in any degree to contribute to your safety or happiness." But he left Washington-Wilkes for LaGrange, on the western edge of Georgia.[24]

The last secretary of war, Maj. Gen. John Cabell Breckinridge, was also commander of the cavalry units, never more than three thousand men. Col. William Campbell Preston Breckinridge, his cousin, led one unit; the others were under Brigadier Generals Basil W. Duke, George Gibbs Dibrell, Samuel Wragg Ferguson, and John Crawford Vaughan. At the Savannah River, the troopers (number now uncertain) learned that Johnston had surrendered the department and they could be paroled at nearby Augusta and Macon. Breckinridge let each command decide its own course. He divided among them, with Davis's consent, $108,322.90 in silver coin from the Treasury wagons.[25]

Duke felt "the honor of the soldiery was involved" in the president's safety. Breckinridge led his men one way and sent Duke in another, trying to divert the Yankees. When he ran into a big Federal force, he left his officers to parley under a flag of truce and slipped into the forest with a few of his staff. But he lingered near, hoping to be of help to Davis. Not until he knew the president was captured would he go on to Florida. Eventually he made his way abroad. There was no time to resign or bid farewell.[26]

The only cabinet member left was John Henniger Reagan, postmaster general and acting secretary of the treasury. He had been with Davis since 1861, and he would be to the end. He and Col. Francis Richard Lubbock had "entered into a compact that we would never desert or leave him . . . [but] share his fortune, whatever might befall." Frank Lubbock was a latecomer to the president's staff. He had been governor of Texas from 1861 to 1863, then a lieutenant colonel in the army, until Davis called him to his side in 1864. He was to advise him on the Trans-Mississippi Department, which included not only Texas, but also Arkansas, Missouri, most of Louisiana, and the Indian, New

Mexico, and Arizona Territories. Neither of these two Texas politicians had known Davis well before. Both were attracted to him by what Lubbock called Davis's "winning, unaffected manners" and "his great heart."[27] The "maxim that distinguished men diminish in greatness as we get closer," said Reagan, "did not apply in his case." Lubbock agreed: "Constant attendance day by day" upon Davis "founded in my heart a strong love for the man." Something rang so true that it held both men, though so unlike—Lubbock the South Carolina gallant and Reagan the rugged East Tennessee mountain man. In the disaster now befalling the Confederacy, each could have made for Texas alone. Reagan had six motherless children as an excuse. But they made their compact.[28]

The other staff members were equally attached to the president. Davis had known the two other aides-de-camp all their lives. Col. William Preston Johnston was the son of his cherished friend Gen. Albert Sidney Johnston. Col. John Taylor Wood (who was also a naval commander) was a nephew of Davis's deceased first wife, Sarah Knox Taylor. The young men naturally felt bound to Davis by these ties, yet serving under him led to a personal devotion that never died.[29]

Then there was Burton Norvell Harrison. This Yale graduate was teaching mathematics at the University of Mississippi when war came. He was about to join the Washington Artillery of his native New Orleans, when he was called to be Davis's private secretary in March of 1862. He held something of a filial position in the Davis family, actually living in the executive mansion. His wife says that he might have avoided "his subsequent hard fate" except that he "loyally chose to follow [Davis]."[30] It was to Harrison that the president confided the safety of his family when he sent it out of Richmond on March 31, 1865. At the railroad station, he told Harrison to come right back, but by the time Varina and her large flock of dependents were settled in Charlotte, Davis had had to leave the capital. Harrison found him at Danville and went on with him to Greensboro and Charlotte.[31]

Varina Davis had by then left Charlotte, and on April 23, Davis sent Harrison out again to look for her. He found her at Abbeville, South Carolina, safely housed with her brood in the home of old friends, the Armistead Burts. Varina had thought Burt "simply an elegant man" when she knew him in Washington, D.C., but now he proved a heroic one.[32] She offered to leave after Yankees threatened to burn his home, only to have him insist, as Davis remembered, "there was no better use to which his house could be put." The Burts "have urged me to live with them . . . begged to have little Maggie—done everything in fact that relatives could do," she wrote Davis, calling it "their generous devotion to you."[33]

Her party now consisted of her younger sister, Margaret Graham Howell; the orphan, Jim Limber; James Jones, the hired mulatto coachman; two nursemaids, Ellen Bond (mulatto) and Catherine (white); and four Davis children: Margaret Howell, ten; Jefferson Jr., eight; William Howell, three and a half; and the ten-month-old baby, christened on March 19 as Varina Anne but known as Pie Cake or Li' Pie.[34]

Also at Abbeville was Jefferson Davis Howell, Varina's baby brother, named when Davis was thought mortally wounded at the battle of Buena Vista in the Mexican War. Jeffy D., as he was called, was now nineteen, a midshipman in the Confederate States Navy. At Richmond on April 2, his commandant, Capt. William Harwar Parker, had scuttled their training ship and formed the sixty middies into a guard for the Confederate treasury. They had escorted the gold and silver bullion and specie safely to Danville, where Davis noted his brother-in-law's arrival. From Charlotte on, Jeffy D. was escorting his two sisters as well, for Captain Parker persuaded Varina to follow him for protection.[35]

They went by rail to Chester, South Carolina, where the treasure had to be packed on wagons for passage to Newberry. This gave Varina time for a reunion with friends who were refugees there—Clement C. Clay, Mary and James Chesnut, John S. Preston of the Conscription Bureau, and Gen. John Bell Hood, headed for Texas "under orders to bring . . . all the troops that would follow me." He said, "If I have lost my leg and also lost my freedom, I am miserable indeed." Varina herself felt the misery of defeat that night, as she set out to follow the "treasure train" in an ambulance. "The ambulance was too heavily laden in the deep mud, and as my maid was too weak to walk and my nurse was unwilling, I walked five miles in the darkness in mud over my shoe tops, with my cheerful little baby in my arms." When they all stopped to rest at a church, a woman told Varina that they had saved the communion table for her bed; but the "additional comfort," she later wrote, "did not tempt one to commit sacrilege."[36]

At Newberry they took "the cars" for Abbeville, where Varina found comfort at the Burt home. Jeffy D. lay sick at the house of George Trenholm's son and could not go when Parker took the treasure and went looking for Davis. Unable to find the president, Parker finally went back to Abbeville and turned the treasure over to Reagan, who had replaced Trenholm.[37] He then disbanded the midshipmen, on Mallory's order, to Davis's "very great regret." When recovered, Jeffy D. went to Augusta and signed his parole not to take up arms against the United States, in return for which, he was "not to be disturbed." Varina left Abbeville on April 29 for Washington-Wilkes, and there her brother joined her.[38]

This was the home of Gen. Robert Toombs. Although an old enemy of Davis's, he "called with many kind offers of hospitality." Varina and the children were, however, being "entertained" elsewhere, says Harrison. He and Varina tried to form plans, hoping at first to meet Davis: "Mrs. Davis is very anxious to see him if she can do so without embarrassing [hindering] his movements." They thought of going west, but "our route was changed by the tidings of Genl. Johnston's surrender of the Department." Federal cavalry was suddenly deploying everywhere. They decided to head south for the coast.[39] Varina wanted to get to England, she wrote Davis, put Maggie and Jeff Jr. in "the best school I can find, and then with the two youngest join you in Texas—and that is the prospect which bears me up, to be once more with you—once more to suffer with you if need be—but God loves those who obey him, and I know there is a future for you." Besides, she had in her ears, from that voice, to her sweetest and most authoritative: "I charge you solemnly to leave when you hear the enemy are approaching; and if you cannot remain undisturbed in our own country, make for the Florida coast and take a ship there for a foreign country."[40]

It was on their last day together in Richmond that Davis had said this, as he showed her how to load, aim, and fire a handsome pistol given her by his aide, William Montague Browne. He had ordered Gen. Josiah Gorgas, the ordnance chief, to send him cartridges for "a small Colt pistol" as quickly as possible.[41] She was to use it, he said, "if you fear insult from our foes." He was, she recalled, "very apprehensive of our falling into the hands of the disorganized bands of troops, roving about the country, and said, 'You can at least, if reduced to the last extremity, force your assailants to kill you.'" The intensity of his fear for her may be measured by the ferocity of his proposal. It was a last desperate hope for souls to whom honor was dearer than life—upon whom, as Varina said, "shame would not dare to sit." It was perhaps the hope in his own heart for himself. Certainly he expected to die. He "almost gave way" when Jeff Jr. "begged to remain" and little Maggie "clung to him convulsively, for it was evident he thought he was looking his last upon us." He had already told Varina, "I do not expect to survive the destruction of constitutional liberty."[42]

All during Varina's travels, Davis the president was trying to maintain his government. He had issued a proclamation at Danville; he wrote military directives, transfers, and promotions; he requested saddles for Duke's command and artillery for the defense of Charlotte; he appointed Reagan acting secretary of the treasury when Trenholm resigned ("little money left to steal," he quipped); he asked for written reports from the cabinet; he told Maj. Gen. Howell Cobb how to recruit men for the defense of Macon, Georgia.[43]

All the while, his military props were being knocked out from under him. Maj. Gen. Wade Hampton, incensed at the idea of surrender, came to Davis at Greensboro, offering to take him to Texas with "many strong arms and brave hearts . . . and *I can get there.*" He soon found that Johnston had surrendered his troops in his absence. Alone, he tried to overtake Davis but finally gave up exhausted.[44]

To "cut loose" from everything "and ride at full speed to Forrest was [Davis's] only hope," said another cavalry leader, "if indeed there was any whatever after Appomat[t]ox." Davis postponed doing this, first because Johnston was parleying with Sherman, and then, because of his "scruple about moving until the truce had expired." His "impregnable" honor thus defeated his one chance to avoid capture.[45]

When he finally rode out of Charlotte on April 26, it was slowly, slowly, with the wagons of the civil corps and his large cavalry escort. After they reached Abbeville, he was finally convinced that military resistance in the area was hopeless. But he was still bent on reaching the troops remaining and rallying those beyond the Mississippi. Taking one company out of the cavalry brigades, which were beginning to disperse, he crossed the Savannah River into Georgia and reached Washington-Wilkes just after his wife had left. He then asked for ten men to go without question wherever he should lead them. The whole company volunteered. Capt. Given Campbell had to pick the ten himself.[46]

Jefferson Davis was finally doing—almost—what his wife had been frantically urging. She not infrequently had a more realistic grasp of people and events than he did. She saw, for example: "a stand cannot be made in this country." "I have seen a great many men who have gone through—not one has talked fight . . . do not be induced to try it." From Washington-Wilkes she had written: "May God grant you a safe conduct out of this maze of enemies—I do believe you are safer without the cavalry than with it." And again: "Why not cut loose from your escort? go swiftly and alone with the exception of two or three—Oh! may God in his goodness keep you safe, my own."[47]

They had kept in touch all along by a few letters and hurried notes confided to passing couriers, husband and wife never quite sure where or how the other was. The uncertainty and danger brought their mutual devotion to light. They fell into their pet names for each other: "My own precious Banny"; "My dear Winnie"; With a courier waiting at the door, he dashed off, "love to the children and Maggie [Howell]—God bless, guide and preserve you, ever prays / Your most affectionate / Banny." In Charlotte, he had time for a real letter:

> Dear children, I can say nothing to them, but for you and them my heart is full, my prayers constant, and my hopes are the trust I feel in the mercy of God.
>
> Farewell, my dear, there may be better things in store for us than are now in view, but my love is all I have to offer, and that has the value of a thing long possessed, and sure not to be lost.[48]

On her part, there was more frantic anxiety, more fervent expressions: "May God in his Mercy keep you safe and raise up defenders for our bleeding country prays your devoted wife—"; "Oh my dearest precious husband, the one absorbing love of my whole life may God keep you free from harm."[49]

In the midst of total collapse—the loss of worldly goods and a world—Davis cried out: "Dear Wife, this is not the fate to which I invited [you] when the future was rose colored to us both; but I know you will bear it even better than myself." Varina replied: "It is surely not the fate to which you invited me in brighter days, but you must remember that you did not invite me to a great Hero's home, but to that of a plain farmer, I have shared all your triumphs, been the *only* beneficiary of them, now I am but claiming the privilege for the first time of being all to you now these pleasures have past for me."[50]

They longed for one another: "Dear Winnie / I will come to you if I can—Everything is dark"; "My dear Old Banny . . . Where are you, how are you—what ought I to do with these helpless little unconscious charges of mine. . . . I am so at sea . . . I will come to you . . . if you cannot come to me." But as the danger of capture increased, Varina warned him repeatedly "not to calculate upon seeing me unless I happen to cross your shortest path to your bourne—be that what it may." She pleaded, "Do not try to meet me, I dread the Yankees getting news of you so much, you are the countrys only hope, and the very best intentioned do not calculate upon a stand this side of the river." It was then, as she was about to leave Washington-Wilkes, that she bade him "go swiftly and alone."[51]

Even after the president sent his baggage train south and gave up four of his escort to guard public papers, he still had roughly a dozen men instead of the two or three Varina had in mind. As for going swiftly, he was no more interested in that than in protection. He never considered himself in flight, only en route. Capt. Micajah H. Clark, Harrison's chief clerk, who had left Richmond with Davis, describes his progress:

> On that retreat (if so leisurely a retirement could be so called) . . . his great resources of mind and heart shone out most brilliantly. Still the head, he moved, calm, self-poised, giving way to no petulance of temper at discomfort, advising and consoling, laying aside all thought of self, planning and doing what was best, not only for our unhappy and despairing people, but uttering gentle, sweet words of consolation and wise advice to every family which he entered as guest.[52]

In Danville, he wrote a letter of thanks to the mayor and council for their hospitality. He refused, with tears in his eyes, a bag of gold that his hostess pressed on him, saying, "You will need it. I will not." "He was sure he would be killed," she said. He gave her a little gold pencil, which she treasured as "a sacred gift." He went to a community church service there on April 9, and to his own Episcopal church in Charlotte on April 23.[53] It was his habit. Doubtless he would have gone on April 16, Easter that year, but he was on the road to Salisbury, North Carolina. Arriving the next night, he stayed with the rector of St. Luke's Episcopal Church. "At tea and after tea [the evening meal], Mr. Davis was cheerful, pleasant, and inclined to talk." They sat late on the porch, "the President with an unlighted cigar in his mouth, talking of the misfortune of General Lee's surrender." Next morning at breakfast, when the host's little girl came crying that "old Lincoln's coming and going to kill us all," it was Davis who put down his fork and, turning the child's "tearful face toward his own," said, "Oh, no my little lady, you need not fear that. Mr. Lincoln is not such a bad man, he does not want to kill anybody, and certainly not a little girl like you."[54]

By the time the presidential party reached Washington-Wilkes, these easy stages were over. But Davis's manner was the same. Johnston's surrender had unleashed the Federal cavalry. Gen. George Stoneman ordered them to pursue the president "to the ends of the earth." They were less than twenty miles away, and "the citizens were anxious" for Davis to make his escape, says an eyewitness. "But Mr. Davis had not the remotest idea of going. . . . In the morning he was in no greater haste to depart. He was informed that Mrs. Davis was awaiting him at Raytown, but he must speak to the ladies who had called. He was informed that his horse was at the door, but he had to kiss the little children that were present. . . . At last . . . he walked in the most leisurely way down the front steps . . . saying something appropriate to everyone that approached him." He took time to shake the hand of each man in his escort company, expecting to meet them later and "rally on Forrest."[55]

If Davis seemed to be moving in a different time frame from others, it was partly because he was staggering from a heavy blow. General Duke had seen him "affable, dignified," "the very personification of high and undaunted courage," as he called his commanders to him at the Burt home in Abbeville to discuss the next move. "In a spirited and exceedingly eloquent speech [he] urged a continued prosecution of the war." But the cavalry leaders saw no hope of further resistance and said they were keeping their men together only to insure his escape.

> Mr. Davis declared that he wished to hear no plan which had for its object, only his safety—that twenty-five hundred men brave men were enough to prolong the war, until the panic had passed away, and they would then be a nucleus for thousands more. He urged us to accept his views. We were silent, for we could not agree with him, and respected him too much to reply. He then said, bitterly, that he saw all hope was gone—that all the friends of the South were prepared to consent to her degradation. When he arose to leave the room, he had lost his erect bearing, his face was pale, and he faltered so much in his step that he was compelled to lean upon General Breckinridge. It was a sad sight to men who felt toward him as we did.[56]

With "his whole soul" given to "the great end of Southern independence," says Duke, "an appearance of slackness . . . seemed to arouse his indignation . . . he at times exhibited some impatience and irascibility, but I never witnessed in any man a more entire abnegation of self." "I do not think he at all realized the situation."[57]

He did realize it. He told Varina that he had seen men "uncontrollably resolved to go home. . . . panic has seized the country." She had told him that no one would fight. At Charlotte he had asked his cabinet to assess the South's chances, and even Benjamin the optimist had said they were nil. Reagan alone said that if the armistice failed, "it will be our duty to continue the struggle as best we can . . . better and more honorable to waste our lives and substance in [an unequal] contest than to yield both to the mercy of a remorseless conqueror." "A gentleman may risk destruction," said the chivalric code, "but not dishonor."[58] Davis agreed; he had told his people how the "heroic devotion" of American Revolutionists made their reverses "but the crucible in which their patriotism was refined." To the cavalry leaders now, he held up the example of his hero, George Washington. Their desertion of the Cause shocked him so severely that he told Duke he failed "entirely to remember the conference at Abbeville."[59]

Gen. Braxton Bragg, though in North Carolina, had not surrendered with Johnston but had caught up with the president's party. At the Abbeville conference, reports General Dibrell, Davis's astonishment over Bragg's "unauthorized" furloughing of two cavalry regiments "twice brought Genl. Bragg to his feet to explain his reasons for so doing." Yet Davis always insisted that Bragg was not there.[60]

"I thought you were in error, in not acceding to our wishes [to escape the country]," Duke said later; "every Southern soldier would have exulted." He argued that it was not inconsistent with honor. Davis thought differently. In the United States Senate, he had voted against giving "the privileges of the floor" to the Hungarian leader Lajos Kossuth "because I did not believe a brave man or patriot would have abandoned his country with an army of 30,000 men in the field."[61] Davis had a soldier's "stern sense of duty," which made him determined now "to do and dare to the last extremity." He was not alone. About half the cavalrymen wanted to go with him to the Trans-Mississippi and refused to surrender. Colonel Breckinridge was ready to command his escort, and some sixty of John Hunt Morgan's men, now under Duke, offered their services. But General Breckinridge finally convinced Davis to head for Texas with very few men. Still, the president refused to go by way of the Gulf of Mexico: "I shall not leave Confederate soil while a Confederate regiment is on it."[62]

What got Davis finally to move fast was danger to his family. Mrs. Davis was *not* "awaiting him at Raytown." She was moving out of his way as rapidly as she could, "fearful that his uneasiness about our safety would cause him to keep near our train." She knew him well. He had written to her only two weeks before from Charlotte, in the throes of a "very painful" decision about whether to continue the fight:

> I think my judgment is undisturbed by any pride of opinion, I have prayed to our Heavenly Father to give me wisdom and fortitude equal to the demands of the position in which Providence has placed me. I have sacrificed so much for the cause of the Confederacy that I can measure my ability to make any further sacrifice required, and am assured there is but one to which I am not equal—My wife and my Children.[63]

Some fifty miles south of Washington-Wilkes, at Sandersville, Preston Johnston heard that Varina's wagon train, on a parallel road, was about to be attacked by a band of stragglers who wanted her horses and mules. Frank Lubbock advised him not to repeat the rumor to the president, saying "we had better not stop." But Johnston replied, "I know him better than you do. He would never forgive me. . . . He would say, 'It was your duty to give me the facts, and let me decide the course I should take.'" As soon as he heard it, Davis changed direction. He said to his men, "This move will probably cause me to be captured or killed. I do not feel that you are bound to go with me, but I must protect my family." Of course they all went.[64]

Davis moved so swiftly on "his fine bay horse," Kentucky, that he soon wore out the mounts of the few cavalrymen with him and left them behind. When Burton Harrison, guarding Varina's camp by moonlight, cried out, "Halt! Who comes there?" and was "astonished" to hear the president's voice answer "Friends," there were only seven with Davis—Preston Johnston, Reagan, Lubbock, John T. Wood, Col. Charles E. Thorburn, "his negro boy," and Robert Brown, a favorite servant who had come out of Richmond with Davis.[65]

It was near dawn of May 7, 1865. The rumored attack never came. The Davis parties traveled together all that day and night. On the eighth, after breakfast, "in deference to our earnest solicitations," says Harrison, the president, with his seven men and the escort, which had caught up, once again cut loose westward. They did not get far. Slowed by a driving rainstorm and made to double back by a flooded ford, they took shelter for the night a few miles ahead at the crossroads town of Abbeville, Georgia. Davis sent back a courier to tell Harrison to move on—Yankees were twenty-five miles away. Although he was sick with "dysentery and fever," Harrison managed to get in motion through the downpour his clumsy caravan of ambulance and wagons, loaded with women, children, and servants. As they passed this Abbeville, he went into the deserted house where his chief was and found him wrapped in a blanket on the bare floor. At Washington-Wilkes, Davis had taken to his bed in broad daylight, "almost as soon as he got into the house." He was "sick," says Johnston, "and a good deal exhausted, but was not the man to say anything about it." Mute witness to his illness is the fact that he, the most courteous of men, did not go out to see his wife, or even get up. He promised to follow when the horses were rested. Harrison pushed his caravan forward through dense woods, the lightning alone showing the way. Finally in "the midst of that storm and darkness, the President overtook us." During the next day, he took a little rest by riding with Varina in her ambulance. "He was still with us," says Harrison, "when, about five o'clock in the afternoon . . . I halted my party for the night, immediately after crossing the little creek just north of Irwinsville and went into camp."[66]

The aides were extremely unhappy about being entangled again with the slow wagon train. Davis promised to leave it "after taking tea with my family." But a new report reached camp that marauders intended to attack. Davis thought if they were ex-Confederates, they "would so far respect me as not to rob the encampment of my family. I[n] any event . . . it was my duty to wait the issue."

There was still his other duty, to the Confederacy, which he now embodied more than ever and meant to preserve. Wood and Thorburn had a boat ready in Florida, yet once more he refused to "leave the soil of the Confederacy, as long as there was an organized command displaying its flag." He insisted on his "original plan"—"if Taylor and Forrest were still maintaining themselves in the field to join them" (they were even then surrendering) or to reach the Trans-Mississippi.[67] The commander there, Gen. Edmund Kirby Smith, expected him. There was a rumor that Davis would lead his troops to Mexico, to help Maximilian, the French-supported emperor. (But Davis had only said privately that, if all else failed, "I can go to Mexico, and have the world from which to choose a location.") Davis had buoyed Smith in the "darkest hour" (July 1863): "May God guide and preserve you." After Appomattox, Smith was still exhorting his men to "sustain the holy cause," resist "invasion," and win "under the Providence of God . . . final success," or at least "terms that a proud people can with honor accept." These aims were identical with those of his commander in chief.[68]

"My horse was saddled to start," hitched near the road, "and my pistols were in their holsters," Davis says. "[I had on] my travelling dress, grey frock coat and trousers, the latter worn inside of heavy cavalry boots, on which remained a pair of conspicuous brass spurs of unusual size." "I lay down in my wife's tent with all my clothes on, to wait for the arrival of the marauders, but being weary fell into a deep sleep from which I was aroused by my coachman, James Jones, telling me that there was firing over the creek." Davis jumped up, thinking it was the marauders. (It was actually Union troopers firing at each other.) Stepping out of the tent, he saw horsemen deploying. "Though it was in the grey of morning their movement revealed more than sight could." As an old dragoon, he instantly recognized it and turned back to tell Varina that the United States cavalry was upon them. "She implored me to leave her at once. I hesitated, from unwillingness to do so, and lost a few precious moments. . . . My horse and arms were near the road . . . down which the cavalry approached. . . . I was compelled to start in the opposite direction." Quickly he told James to bring Kentucky to the "fringe of wood skirting the stream towards which I was going."[69]

> As it was quite dark in the tent, I picked up what was supposed to be my "raglan," a water-proof, light overcoat, without sleeves; it was subsequently found to be my wife's, so very like my own as to be mistaken for it; as I started, my wife thoughtfully threw over my head and shoulders a shawl. I had gone perhaps fifteen or twenty yards when a trooper galloped up and ordered me to halt and surrender, to which I gave a defiant answer, and, dropping the shawl and raglan from my shoulders, advanced toward him; he leveled his carbine at me, but I expected, if he fired, he would miss me, and my intention was in that event to put my hand under his foot, tumble him off on the other side, spring into his saddle, and attempt to escape. My wife . . . when she saw the soldier aim his carbine at me, ran forward and threw her arms around me. Success depended on instantaneous action, and, recognizing that the opportunity had been lost, I turned back, and, the morning being damp and chilly, passed on to a fire beyond the tent.[70]

It was May 10, 1865. In the cold drizzle, Preston Johnston went to find him. He knew how Davis had meant to unhorse the trooper, "for he had taught me the trick." Davis said he would have done it, "but she caught me around the arms." Johnston tried to console him with the truth that "it would have been useless." "Mr. Davis was dressed as usual," he says, and "had on a knit woolen visor, which he always wore at night for neuralgia. . . . He complained of chilliness, and said they had taken away his 'raglan.'" Having one "exactly similar . . . I went to look for it, and . . . he wore it afterwards. His own was not restored."[71]

Nor were ever restored any of the things snatched away that May morning: Preston Johnston's gold or the cherished horse and saddle, pistols and holsters that had been his father's at Shiloh; the privately owned mounts so prized by the other Southerners; Varina's carriage horses, returned to her by anonymous buyers after she had had to sell them in Richmond. All the prisoners were "subjected to petty pillage," says Davis, "and to annoyances such as military *gentlemen* never commit or permit."[72]

He thought "the *auri sacra fames*" had brought this on them. "The accursed thirst for gold" was certainly played upon by Maj. Gen. James H. Wilson, commanding the federal military district. On May 6 he had offered a reward "IN GOLD" to anyone who would "apprehend and deliver JEFFERSON DAVIS," adding, "Several millions of specie, reported to be with him, will become the property of the captors." This reflected both a proclamation by President Andrew Johnson and an order from War Secretary Edwin M. Stanton "to intercept the rebel chiefs and their plunder," estimated fantastically at between six and thirteen million dollars. Wilson's notice had not overtaken Col. Benjamin D. Pritchard and his Fourth Michigan Cavalry, however. They thought they had captured the Confederate treasure train and at first did not even know the president was there.[73]

They forced open Varina's trunks and strewed the campsite with a hoopskirt, children's clothes, Bibles, and Episcopal prayer books, looking for gold. Varina lost all of hers they could "ferret out and steal." The president had none. His last coin, a foreign gold piece, he had given away to a toddler whom he found named for him, at a farmhouse where he stopped for water. All he had left were Confederate bills, now worthless. Micajah Clark, in charge of specie, had forced some gold on Reagan for their use, but it was lost when his saddlebags were seized.[74]

Lubbock says the captors "stole the watches, jewelry, money, clothing, &c. I believe I was the only one of the party not robbed." He was the reason for that. Reagan saw him struggling with two soldiers trying to get his horse and saddlebags and threatening to shoot him. He heard Lubbock say "that they might shoot and be damned, but that they should not rob him while he was alive and looking on. I had my revolver cocked, and in my hand," Reagan says, "waiting to see if the shooting was to begin."[75] A major rode up, the troopers ran off, and Reagan, seeing the camp surrounded, gave up his revolver. Lubbock hung onto those saddlebags, gold and all, through his whole imprisonment, though he lost some other gold in his holsters when his horse was finally taken. "Freebooters," he called the Yankees. The officer in charge promised to return the stolen property, but he never did.[76]

The *auri sacra fames* stood one man in good stead. John T. Wood offered a Federal trooper gold to look the other way and escaped into the woods. As a former naval raider commanding the *Tallahassee,* Wood was afraid that, without his government to protect him, the United States just might hang him for piracy. They had tried this with others early in the war and been thwarted by Davis's strong reaction. Wood's civilian chief, Mallory, was in fact arrested for "setting on foot piratical expeditions," and treated with especial severity, but not, in the end, hanged.[77]

Wood invited Lubbock to escape with him, but Lubbock refused because of his pact with Reagan never to desert the chief.[78] In fact, he rushed to Davis's defense with typical ardor. He found him by the campfire, looking "in all respects more the ideal hero than in the hours of his greatest prosperity." "The man and patriot, who a few days before was at the head of a government, was treated by his captors with uncalled for indignity. . . . A private stepped up to him rudely and said: 'Well, Jeffy, how do you feel now?' I was so exasperated that I threatened to kill the fellow, and called upon the officers to protect their prisoner from insult." Lubbock was "completely unhinged" by this contemptuous treatment: "I cannot see how Mr. Davis could speak of Colonel Pritchard or his command with any degree of patience."[79]

Jefferson Davis's patience had not yet been made perfect. Prisoner though he was, he told the soldiers with some heat that he would not stand for their "violent language to Mrs. Davis." He was "chafed by the annoyances and petty thefts," and Preston Johnston found him "in altercation" with Colonel Pritchard. Seeing his children's breakfast snatched away "was the thieving which provoked my angry language." He told Pritchard "their conduct was not that of gentlemen, but of ruffians"; the colonel merely replied "in an offensive manner" and walked off.[80] For the most part, however, Davis held his usual air of quiet dignity, which people often mistook for haughtiness. Lubbock especially noticed this and reacted violently to the personal abuse precisely because Davis did not. Amidst the crying of the children, the howling of the servants, and Varina's "appeals," John Wood remarked that "the President was calm, his wife greatly excited."[81]

Varina was in extreme distress over his capture, not least because she had been the immediate cause. She had preferred his capture to his death, which perhaps he had not. But the surprise attack had caught him without his pistols. Asked if he had weapons, he answered, "If I had, you would not be alive to ask that question."[82] "Offensively declaring I would not surrender," he had advanced on the trooper. He knew this gave him the right to shoot but thought he could unhorse him, because in the Mexican War, a whole squadron armed with carbines had fired down on him, "and they all missed me."[83] Varina, running to share the danger "in accordance with her heroic nature," had spoiled his plan. That was escape or death, not surrender: "I had not asked 'for quarter.' " He was trapped and taken, meeting not "the violent death he expected to be his," but humiliation.[84]

Because his humility is already great, Jefferson Davis is not undone by this turn. In the moment of catastrophe—the fall of his hope, of his country, of his civilization—he remains upright. In deep anguish, he still soothes with his serenity Varina's wilder grief. She "threw her arms around my neck, that of course ended any possibility for my escape, and I said to her God's will be done, and turned back with her to the tent." These words, echoing Christ's in Gethsemane, were not chance but a continual refrain. They had been his when his son died and would be his in the prison to come. Even to Congress, he had said in his last message, "Let us bow submissively to the Divine will."[85]

This is the prayer of a humble man. It explains Davis's strange calm, even cheer, all the way from Richmond. He has refused to be hurried, moved more like a monarch than a fugitive, reminding one man of Robert the Bruce. At Greensboro, Mallory notes, with the fate of the country hanging, surrounded by an enemy "more powerful and exultant than ever," Davis, true to his "uniform habit," opens the cabinet meeting with light conversation. This is the more remarkable in that he is "not well" and is faced with two pretty open enemies of his, Generals J. E. Johnston and Pierre Gustave Toutant Beauregard. He has called them to assess the military situation after Lee's surrender, and everything they say is not what he wants to hear. Keeping his eyes on "a scrap of paper . . . folding and re-folding [it] abstractedly," he listens "without a change of position or expression" to Johnston's opinion, "jerked out" in a "tone and manner almost spiteful": "our people are tired of war, feel themselves whipped, and will not fight." Beauregard agrees. Although Davis believes "we can whip the enemy yet," he replies to Johnston's armistice proposal, "without raising his eyes from the slip of paper between his fingers, . . . 'Well, sir, you can adopt this course, though I confess I am not sanguine as to ultimate results.'" He even dictates, at Johnston's insistence, the galling note to Sherman. All with the utmost composure.[86]

Between Greensboro and Charlotte, the humility of the president passes an amusing test where his party stops for the night. A servant, sent to show the most honored guest to a private room, picks out Gen. Samuel Cooper (the sixty-six-year-old adjutant and inspector general) instead of him. Davis never says a word. Harrison reports "his cheerfulness" in Charlotte, "and I remember his there saying to me, 'I *cannot* feel like a beaten man!'" When they go to the Episcopal church, he tosses off "with a laugh" a sermon seeming "to fancy I had something to do with [Lincoln's] assassination" (a few days before). "The suggestion was preposterous," says Harrison; "No man ever carried on [war] . . . with less of disturbance of the nicest sense of perfect rectitude . . . his every utterance, act and sentiment was with the strictest regard for all the moralities," even while "passions" were making others "defiant" of them. Davis was actually made "very sad" by Lincoln's death: "I considered him a kind hearted man, and very much to be preferred by us to his successor Mr. Johnson."[87]

Davis's trust in God has only one weak spot: anxiety for his wife and children. For himself, as Duke attests, he has none. Mallory recalls how he enjoyed stretching out under a tree with his head pillowed on his saddle, talking pleasantly "under the inspiration of a good cigar." Harrison thinks him "entirely unable to apprehend the danger of capture." But the clue to his "quietest possible manner" is dropped by a Baptist preacher. Speaking "words of cheer and consolation" in Washington-Wilkes, he hears Davis say, "Though He slay me, yet will I trust in Him."

It is the reply of Job in affliction, total faith in total abandonment, the highest mystery.[88]

In the camp near Irwinville, Colonel Pritchard received orders to proceed to the headquarters of General Wilson in Macon, Georgia. Immediately, Davis tried to get his wife's party released (again echoing the scene in Gethsemane, which he knew so well): "I suppose, sir, your orders are accomplished in arresting me. You can have no wish to interfere with women and children; and I beg they may be permitted to pursue their journey." The men, he argued, had already signed their paroles (guaranteeing the right to go home). But the colonel's order said every person had to go prisoner to Macon.[89]

The president was put into the little covered-wagon ambulance with his family. An enemy account, which has many errors, says, "Mr. and Mrs. Davis were at times seen in tears. She read the Bible to him, and he regularly asked a blessing over their meals." The latter actions were indeed their habits. If, "exhausted and enfeebled" as he was, Davis did break down briefly in the overwhelming disaster, he was doubtless like the Southern soldier told of his child's death: "I took a good cry and gave her up to the Lord's will, I hope like a Christian ought to do." Varina says, "Only a firm belief in . . . an omnipresent and merciful Providence upheld us at this time, and Mr. Davis did not lose heart."[90]

It took the Michigan cavalry four days to move their prisoners the seventy-five miles north to Macon. On the second, Varina relates, "as we were about to get in the wagons, a man galloped into camp waving over his head a printed slip of paper."

> It was Mr. Johnson's proclamation of a reward for Mr. Davis's capture as the accessory to Mr. Lincoln's assassination. I was much shocked, but Mr. Davis was quite unconcerned, and said, "The miserable scoundrel who issued that proclamation knew . . . that it was false. Of course, such an accusation must fail at once; it may, however, render these people willing to assassinate me here." There was a perceptible change in the manner of the soldiers from this time, and the jibes and insults heaped upon us as they passed by, notwithstanding Colonel Pritchard's efforts to suppress the expression of their detestation, were hard to bear.

A regimental band "struck up 'Old John Brown,' the boys putting in the words; 'And we'll hang Jeff Davis on a sour-apple-tree,' with gusto,—which so affected him that he pulled down the curtain of his ambulance." But physical violence was not offered. "Within a short distance of Macon," Varina goes on, "we were halted and the soldiers drawn up in line on either side of the road. Our children crept close to their father, especially little Maggie, who put her arms about him and held him tightly, while from time to time he comforted her with tender words from the psalms of David, which he repeated as calmly and cheerfully as if he were surrounded by friends." The soldiers "expressed in words unfit for women's ears all that malice could suggest," showing "their belief in Mr. Davis's guilt."[91]

It was only the beginning. Davis's optimistic "at once" came from his own sense of innocence. He had no way of knowing the fury engendered in the North by Lincoln's murder. The false accusation, bolstered by Johnson's offer of $100,000 for his capture, turned the fury on Davis. Without the least evidence of his guilt, journalists and preachers began to demand his death. Belief in the lie helped to bring upon him some rough treatment now and later, but he left it largely to others to dwell upon this. It is Varina who says, "of the horrors and sufferings on that journey it is difficult to speak."[92]

In Macon, however, Davis remembers that as he entered Wilson's headquarters, the guard before the Lanier House "opened ranks, facing inward, and presented arms." He had met Wilson at West Point before the war. He found him "obliging" but was unable to get the paroled men released or any of the privately owned horses returned. "With the full expectation that it would be reported," he told Wilson that Andrew Johnson knew his accusation was false, "for *he* knows that I would a thousand times rather have Abraham Lincoln to deal with . . . than to have *him*."[93]

Varina tells of one bright moment at the hotel, when a black waiter slipped a bunch of flowers onto the supper tray. "With tears in his eyes he said, 'I could not bear for you to eat without something pretty from the Confederates.' I have one of the roses yet, and if he has gone to his reward, feel sure that this kind act was counted him for righteousness."[94]

Reagan heard they were to be kept in Macon and the president sent alone to Washington City (as the capital was called). He quickly asked to go with him, on the plea that "Davis was much worn down." Wilson, not knowing of the Reagan-Lubbock pact, found this a strange request and warned of the danger. His promise to see about it was obviated when the whole party was ordered to Washington City. Wilson courteously gave Davis a choice of routes. He chose, especially on the children's account, the easier one by water, from Port Royal on the Atlantic. First, however, they would have to go to Augusta and take a steamboat down the Savannah River. On the cars (the train), the Davises met other prisoners, such as Lt. Gen. Joseph Wheeler of the Confederate cavalry and their old friends Clement and Virginia Clay.[95]

The Clays had "refugeed" to Sterling Hall, the mansion of Confederate Sen. Benjamin Harvey Hill, at LaGrange, Georgia, near the Alabama border. In March, Hill had come here to tell Georgians for the president that defiance alone could save them from dishonorable terms. Also there were the Stephen Mallorys and Senators Thomas J. Semmes and Louis Trezevant Wigfall with their wives. Clay had been about to strike out with Wigfall for the Trans-Mississippi when Virginia arrived from town with Johnson's proclamation naming Clay along with Davis as an instigator of Lincoln's murder and putting a price on his head. Everyone rushed upstairs. There was Clay, Virginia relates, "sitting quietly, deep in the conning of a thick volume. It was Burton's 'Anatomy of Melancholy,' ever a favourite with him. It lay open on his knee," while one hand "was stroking his beard, absent-mindedly." As the towering Senator Hill read out the accusation, Semmes cried, " 'Fly for your life, Clay!' . . .'Fly?' he said, slowly . . .'from what?' Mr. Semmes's answer came drily. 'From death, I fear!' . . . I begged him hysterically to fly; I would join him anywhere if he would but escape. But my ever patient husband only answered . . .'Virginia! my wife! Would you have me fly like an assassin? As I am conscious of my innocence, my judgment is that I should at once surrender.' " Virginia felt he was signing "his own death warrant," but he wired General Wilson, and they started for Macon. As they passed through "pandemonium" in Atlanta, they heard on the cars that Davis was captured. " 'If that is true,' said Clay, 'my surrender was a mistake. We shall both perish!' " The mistake became apparent in Macon. Clay's voluntary surrender was called his "arrest." He and Virginia were sent to the cars with the prisoners.[96]

At the depot, Virginia saw the Davises coming under cavalry guard in a barouche, with "Miss Howell, the Davis little ones and nurses" in "a carryall" behind them. "Mr. Davis was dressed in a full suit of Confederate grey, including the hat, but his face was yet more ashen than was his garb." There were hoots of derision. "One heartless Union soldier . . . [called out] 'Hey, Johnny Reb, . . . we've got your President!' 'And the devil's got yours!' was the swift reply."

The Davises were put on the train first. Virginia recalled that when she entered, "Mr. Davis rose and embraced me. 'This is a sad meeting, Jennie!' he said." "I became aware that the car had filled up with soldiers," she goes on, "I heard the doors slam, and the command, 'Order arms!' and in the dull thud of their muskets as the butts struck the floor, I realized for the first time that we were indeed prisoners, and of the nation!"[97]

"Dawn found us haggard and ill," she says; "only the children slept." The foul air in the car, and other discomforts, made the trip "most trying to our invalids, of whom there now were three—Mr. Davis, Mr. Clay, and our venerable Vice-President, Mr. Stephens." Virginia Clay was mistaken. Alexander Hamilton Stephens had indeed been arrested at his home near Crawfordville, Georgia, on May 11, but he was not on this train. He had specifically asked to travel on a different one to avoid meeting Davis. This little man, of frail body and weighty mind, had been a center of civil discontent in the late Confederate States. He held secession to be "wrong," possibly "fatal," and he said, "[I] exerted my utmost power to prevent it." He managed to avoid Davis in Augusta, when the prisoners were transferred to the riverboat. Here the street was "thronged with ladies, all weeping bitterly," so that "even the President's Yankee guard seemed touched," said a witness, who was "glad some were there to testify that the feeling of the South is still with our fallen President and to shame with their tears the insulting cries of his persecutors."[98]

Stephens had to sleep on the deck of the "wretched little craft" on the Savannah River and was unable to hide when Davis came out the next morning. Although "I could but deeply sympathize with him," Stephens said, "I deplored the ruin which, I think, his acts helped to bring upon the whole country, as well as on himself." Davis's salutation was "not unfriendly, but . . . far from cordial." There were other reasons for reticence. Davis "suffered intensely during the trip from pain in his eye (for years a chronic disability)," and all night the ladies had been bathing "his temples with cologne in vain attempts to lessen his tortures."[99]

At 4 A.M. on May 16, 1865, the steamboat reached Savannah, and the prisoners took a "coast steamer" to Hilton Head, where they boarded the *William P. Clyde* for the trip to Washington. In the midst of his own woes, Davis typically cared for others. At Macon, he had tried to give Harrison, whose horse had been taken, a ride in his carriage, only to be forbidden. Now Jim Limber was on his mind. "He was about seven years old," observes Aleck Stephens, "and little Jeff's playfellow; they were always together."[100] Varina says Capt. Charles Y. Hudson "intended to take our poor little negro protégé as his own, and solicitude for the child troubled us more than Hudson's insults." Now at Port Royal harbor, when "a tug came out to us, bringing a number of jeering people to see Mr. Davis . . . we learned that our old friend, General Saxton, was there." They asked him "to look after . . . Jim's education," to save him from Hudson's "degrading influence." Brig. Gen. Rufus Saxton, "Inspector of Plantations and Settlements" (of freedmen on confiscated Sea Island estates) agreed to take the boy, and he was handed over to officers on the tugboat. When Jim realized he was to leave the Davises, "he fought like a little tiger." Stephens says he "screamed" and "had to be held to prevent his jumping overboard," and "at this, Jeff and Maggie and Billy screamed almost as loudly." Ellen and Varina wept. "Mrs. Clay threw Jimmy some money." He paid no attention "but kept on scuffling to get loose; he was wailing as long as he could be . . . seen by us."[101]

As the *Clyde* pushed into the Atlantic, the *Tuscarora* followed, its guns bearing "directly upon us, day and night." Mrs. Clay's "pocket-diary" tells why: fear "of the *Stonewall* or *Shenandoah*" (one an ironclad already surrendered, the other a raider in the Pacific or Indian Ocean). Davis called Virginia's attention to the fact that all the ship's axes were gone "from their usual positions. . . . 'Cowards!' he said, 'They're afraid of this handful of Confederate men!' "[102]

"Little Joe" Wheeler had in fact devised, on the riverboat, a plan to seize the guns of the guard and take over, but Davis would not allow it. His "fine sense of honor and propriety" made him refuse another Wheeler plan of escape. "Mr. Davis' noble courage never forsook him for a moment; he was perfectly calm and seemed to have no regard for himself or his fate." Wheeler thought he enjoyed "having a few days which he could so entirely devote to his family. He walked the deck with his baby, Winnie, in his arms, and frequently allowed me the same privilege."

It was not pure enjoyment. With Margaret and the two nursemaids all sick, Varina had the care of three invalids and four children on her hands. Davis was doing what he could to help, though coming down himself with malaria. He was restless and depressed, Virginia Clay says, but still called their attention to the beauty of sea and sky.[103]

The *Clyde* finally dropped anchor in Hampton Roads, under the guns of the strongest bastion on the east coast. Pritchard found he was not to take his prisoners to Washington after all. President Davis was not regarded as a head of state. Neither the Constitution, nor the intent of the founding fathers, nor the usage of years since had convinced those in power in the North of a state's right to secede. Southerners were merely rebels and their head, the "rebel chief." On him must fall the chief punishment for "the Southern rebellion."

> The Great Criminal is in our hands, what crime shall be laid to his charge? Guilty of treason, guilty of perjury, guilty of barbarity, guilty of murder—such is the indictment against Jefferson Davis. . . . If the Government shall not hang Jefferson Davis, then let it never hang another man while the world stands.[104]

Like this Northern editor, framing his indictment as a verdict, Joseph Holt, the judge advocate general of the United States Army, had condemned the Confederate leaders in April as "Iscariots of the human race": "May God in His eternal justice forbid that there should ever be shown mercy and forbearance." This was the man who had prepared the case for the United States military commission, now sitting, against the associates of Lincoln's presumed assassin, John Wilkes Booth. It was Holt who had named Jefferson Davis a coconspirator. Lubbock says this charge was "so preposterous to those of us who knew him that we were at a loss to account for its having been made until we became more fully acquainted with the blind rage that possessed the Northern people." With all this hanging over him, Davis "showed not the slightest trepidation, but reviewed the situation as calmly as if he had no personal interest in it," writes Wheeler.[105]

With Fortress Monroe looming ahead, Lubbock remembered his vow: "Mr. Davis did me the honor to request . . . that I should be permitted to share his prison with him. This was promptly refused." He and Wheeler and Preston Johnston were soon shipped off to Fort Delaware, on Delaware Bay, where Lubbock found that solitary confinement in an absolutely bare cell "tested my strength very severely." Reagan too was forced apart from Davis, remanded, with Alexander Stephens, to Fort Warren in Boston Harbor. At their parting, "Mr. Davis requested me to read often the 26th Psalm ["Be thou my judge, O Lord, for I have walked innocently"]. He said it gave him consolation to read it." The remembrance of this scene moved the bluff Tennessean to add: "I loved him as I have never loved any other man."[106]

Aleck Stephens had no love for Davis at all, but they had had a "friendly talk" and had perforce taken their meals together, where the president "bows his head and asks a blessing, but not audibly." "On my taking leave of Mr. Davis, he seemed more affected than I had ever seen him. He said nothing but good-bye, and gave my hand a cordial squeeze." Both must have known their danger: "If Jeff Davis and those who acted with him . . . do not deserve to be hung," said the Boston *Congregationalist*, "then surely 'the magistrate will bear the sword in vain.' "[107]

One by one, the Confederates were sent away, "we knew not whither." Varina saw Jeffy D. go over the side with a "cheery smile" (taken to Fort McHenry at Baltimore). The other young men of her party were "all incarcerated, in disregard of the protection promised when they surrendered," says Davis. Burton Harrison was dispatched to Old Capitol Prison in Washington City, then switched to the Arsenal, where those accused of Lincoln's murder were confined. He ended up at Fort Delaware in solitary confinement.[108]

At last only the Davises, their children, Margaret Howell, and the Clays were left on the *Clyde*. The maid and nurse, persuaded by the captors, had deserted. But Robert Brown remained faithful. Although newspapers depicted him as "happy to get rid of you and indifferent at parting," Varina wrote to Davis later, he was "entirely willing to be imprisoned with you." She quoted Robert: "He gave me charge of his family, and was too manly to make a scene, and I would not expose him and myself by showing what I suffered."[109]

The two casemates being converted into cells were at last ready. On May 22, in "a sultry, drizzling rain," Virginia Clay recalls, Clement came to their cabin "shortly after breakfast," saying, "There is no longer any doubt that this fort is the one destined for Davis and me! I have just been notified that we are expected to take a ride on a tug." Varina describes the Davises' response: "Our little Jeff ran to us pale with horror, and sobbed out, 'They say they have come for father, beg them to let us go with him.' Mr. Davis went forward, and returned with an officer, saying, 'It is true, I must go at once.' " There was no one "to whom I could say that he was quite ill; indeed suffering from fever." On deck, in their last embrace, he "whispered, 'No matter what proof is adduced by the North, remember that my dying testimony was to you that I had nothing to do with assassination. . . . Try not to weep, they will gloat over your grief,' and the desire to lessen his anguish enabled me to bid farewell quietly."[110]

This is the moment when Varina, looking down on them in the boat, sees her husband among the "German and other foreign soldiers" as "a man of another and higher race." The superiority she sees is not national—their Episcopal priest in Richmond, Dr. Charles Frederick Ernest Minnigerode, is also a German. The distinction is in her phrase "knightly bearing."[111]

Physically, Davis fits her allusion, except perhaps for his emaciation, and even in that he resembles a knight he admires, Don Quixote. His height is six feet, minus a half-inch. His long legs and military bearing, the carriage of his head and set of his shoulders, add to the impression of height, and he is always seen as tall. His broad, high brow dominates an aquiline nose and a firm mouth and chin. Deep-set eyes are "blue and very bright." Although the left one is blind, people remark on their keen and "very fearless" expression. Wrinkles at the corners attest frequent smiles. His cheeks are clean shaven, the only beard beneath the chin. The "very fine and abundant" blond hair is graying; cut short, it falls in "large soft curves—not curls."[112] Although a military man, he moves not stiffly, but with grace. In a society where every man is of necessity a cavalier, in the literal sense of horseman, Davis's worst enemy, said Mary Chesnut, "will allow that he is a consummate rider, graceful and easy in the saddle." Friend and foe alike note his native inborn dignity, "not to be acquired," as Varina says. To an English reporter, "He is like a gentleman."[113]

Yet Varina is looking past all this, to the man within. Her "higher race" is not physical, but spiritual—the *kalos kagathos* of the ancient world, the *honnête homme* of Europe, the chivalry of the South. Raphael Semmes saw Davis as "the 'Cavalier,' endowed by nature with the instincts and refinement" that to his captors "were offensive." It was at Jefferson Davis that Andrew Johnson had once aimed this phrase: "an illegitimate, swaggering, bastard, scrub aristocracy."[114] Even now, a Massachusetts preacher is calling "the boasted chivalry, the scum and refuse of humanity." Maj. Gen. David Hunter, presiding over the Lincoln murder trial, is pounding the table and denouncing the "humbug chivalry" of the South.[115]

To those who know it in their daily lives, however, Southern chivalry is real. To Davis, "fidelity, chivalry, honor and patriotism were realities, not words—entities, not abstractions." Virginia Clay says Clement possessed "the loftiest sense of honor, 'felt a stain like a wound,' and bore to his grave, despite slander and calumny, as unsullied an escutcheon as ever Knightly Crusader bore."[116] It is real even to Alonzo Quint, a Congregational preacher in New Bedford, Massachusetts, crying only a month before: "let Southern Chivalry be destroyed, root and branch, twig and leaf."[117]

What is the "Southern Chivalry"? The South has no king or liege lord or squire; but it has its knight in the Southern gentleman, "gentleman" and "chivalry" both indicating, historically, simply a good family and the right to bear arms. American society is civilian and becoming egalitarian, but in the South, military titles abound, the firearm is ever at hand—for the militia, the hunt, the duel—and family defines one's place. For the great seal of the Confederate States, Judah Benjamin chooses the equestrian statue of George Washington in Richmond, saying that a cavalier ("not only horseman, but gentleman, knight") will typify "chivalry, bravery, generosity, humanity." "The Southerners remain what their ancestors were—gentlemen. The Seal will typify this fact."[118]

If there is in the South no vigil of arms before the altar, there is at least the omnipresent Christian faith, witnessed in a thousand letters, diaries, speeches, and monuments. Ben Hill, a Methodist politician, sums it up: "I believe that God is a living God, and that Christ came into the world to save sinners, and he will save me." When three Episcopalians—Maj. Gen. Patrick Ronayne Cleburne, the Right Reverend Lt. Gen. Leonidas Polk, and the Reverend Charles Todd Quintard—create in 1863 a secret military order in the Army of Tennessee, they name it "Comrades of the Southern Cross." Among its ideals are these of Davis: not to abandon the South while it has an organized army and never to desert "a friend when surrounded by foes."[119]

Individuals may fail the chivalric ideal, but it pervades society. At Abbeville, it is the privates who hold it "a point of honor to secure the safety of Mr. Davis." Southern enlisted men, imprisoned and cajoled to join the enemy, form the "Order of the Seven Confederate Knights," open to anyone who will vow to suffer death "rather than sacrifice honor."[120]

Honor is what the gentleman demands of himself—an interior vow in the absence of accolade and investiture. In chivalry, the outward forms always did symbolize inner virtues: *"To speak the truth, to succour the helpless and oppressed, and never to turn back from an enemy";* indeed, *"the spirit was the Chivalry."* Truth is the underpinning; a gentleman's word is his bond, and to impugn it is to invite death on the field of honor. The duel itself recalls joust and trial by combat, all ruled by Providence, the will of God.[121] Even that distinctively Southern virtue, courtesy, is "a principal perfection in . . . the true knight." Grounded in Christian charity and humility—a sense of the honor due to others—it protects the weak and helpless, and in war, civilians, prisoners, and the wounded. A bishop of Alabama writes, "A true Southern man will not be unjust to his dog."[122]

The right to bear arms comes to full flower as Lincoln's troops invade the South. The Southern gentleman becomes the cavalier. The history of the Confederate States is a military history. At their head for the four years of their existence stands the military gentleman Jefferson Davis. A great niece recalls "his chivalrous manner." In politics, he is "our chivalric member of Congress," with his "nobleness of bearing," his "deep scorn of every thing little or deceptious." An early biographer sees "his personal courage . . . which in an age of chivalry would have sought the trophies of the tourney." Picturing Davis "in the midst of those chiefs whom he created"—Lee, the two Johnstons, Jackson—a eulogizer asks, "What grander knighthood could history assemble?"[123]

Not everyone sees him this way, of course. Robert Toombs thinks Davis not only incompetent but a scoundrel and resigns both a cabinet post and an army commission. But Toombs is also compelled by the rules of chivalry. When Davis reaches Washington-Wilkes in 1865, Toombs offers to escort him to the Chattahoochee River "at the risk of my life," and Davis remarks: "That is like Toombs; he always was a whole-souled man." Enemies may hate Davis's policies and despise his person, but very few dare to impugn his character. One of the Rhetts, whose *Charleston Mercury* excoriates Davis regularly, goes pretty far, calling him "conceited, wrong-headed, wranglesome, obstinate—a traitor"; to which Mary Chesnut retorts, "pernicious nonsense."[124]

Davis knows he can speak to his people about their "gallantry," of how "humanity to the wounded and captives" makes them "worthy descendants of chivalric sires," about offenses "of which a chivalrous people would be incapable." He can praise Beauregard at Fort Sumter for not "imposing any terms that could wound the sensibilities of the commander." As to unconditional surrender of himself, Davis finds "extermination preferable to dishonor."[125]

Davis believes "chivalry should be the star to light the pathway of war." He recalls that in Mexico, Zachary Taylor's "form, like the white plume of Henry [of Navarre], was a guide to point the bravest to the hottest of the fight." In the South, he sees in one army "that *preux* chevalier," Maj. Gen. William Henry Talbot Walker, and in the other, "the knightly Lee."[126] When the enemy's "savage" war against civilians seems to justify repudiating a prisoner exchange agreed upon, Davis tells Lee, "We shrink from the mere semblance of breaking faith, and do not resort to this extremity." When Lee's men invade the North, "their own self-respect," he says, "forbade their degenerating from Christian warriors into plundering ruffians."[127] In statecraft, it is the same: Benjamin, speaking for Davis, fears the Danish cabinet "may (as has happened to ourselves) fail to suspect in others a perfidy of which they themselves are incapable" and tells an envoy to use means "strictly legitimate, honorable, and proper. We rely on truth and justice alone."[128] Thus, fealty, purity, and valor are deeply ingrained in Davis's expectations of himself and others.

It is a plain case that the "knightly bearing" Varina sees is not in her eyes alone but intrinsic to the man she looks on. Soldiering is Davis's profession and his love. His place in the Confederacy has denied him the glory of active military command and brought criticism for military decisions. But after the war, the Association of the Army of Tennessee made him a member on his "military record": "entered the military service . . . as President and Commander-in-Chief, which position he filled with unswerving fidelity and patriotism—undismayed by disaster and unbeguiled by temporary success. . . . He met the obloquy of utter and final defeat, as he has the later shafts of detraction, with the patient, dignified bearing of a Christian gentleman and a hero."[129]

At his death, George Davis called him "a true prince in all that was most noble"; and an "old soldier," Bishop John Nicholas Galleher, bestowed at last his investiture: "as a soldier [Davis] was marked and fitted for more than fame, the Lord God having set on him the seal of a pure knighthood."[130]

II

Home

He was born Jefferson Davis on June 3, 1808. There is some dispute of the year, but he wrote to a friend on June 3, 1878, "This is my birth day, on which I fulfil the measure of three score and ten." Of this he was sure: "When I went to [West Point] in Sept. 1824 I reported my age 17 . . . but after graduation when I returned home my Mother corrected me, stating I was born in 1808." Nine children had already been born to Jane Cook and Samuel Emory Davis—Joseph Emory, Benjamin, Samuel A., Anna Eliza, Isaac Williams, Lucinda Farrar, Amanda, Matilda, and Mary Ellen.[1]

One biographer claims Jeff had the middle name of Finis (the End). His parents may have thus put a period to their long frontier statement about the goodness of life, but the "F." that occurs in his name off and on until 1839, when it is in his mother's will, is never spelled out. It is not even on his tombstone. That inscription begins: "Jefferson Davis / at rest / An American soldier."[2]

In any case, there were no more children. His mother was past forty-five when this tenth child was born.[3] She nearly died. Anna, the eldest daughter, then seventeen, took charge of her baby brother, and "Sister Anne" was forever after like a mother to him. More than forty years later, sending her a profile "cameo likeness" of himself, in lieu of the daguerreotype she wanted, Jefferson wrote: "It is set in a breastpin that it may be brought very near to you, and that in this manner I may have renewed the happy days of childhood when my sweet sister held me in her arms." Her granddaughter who quotes this letter says that this portrait brooch was Anna's "most cherished possession" and "the only ornament I ever saw her wear."[4]

When this last child was born, Samuel Davis had been raising food, tobacco, and horses on a farm in southwestern Kentucky for about fifteen years.[5] This was roughly half the time since the first permanent settlements—log stockades—had been built to the northeast by James Harrod and Daniel Boone. There were no Indian settlements. This was the hunting ground, roamed by many tribes who stalked the deer and bear and buffalo attracted to the salt licks, and also the human interlopers who wanted to make it home. A survivor remembered "when death was in almost every bush" and said, "[We] are but the remnant, the wreck, of large families lost." It was only after Kentucky became a state and sent a thousand men to help Gen. Anthony Wayne defeat the northwestern Indians near Lake Erie that the constant attacks on settlers dwindled to occasional bloody raids. This victory at Fallen Timbers in 1794 enabled Samuel and Jane Davis to raise their children in Kentucky instead of Georgia.[6]

Georgia had always been home to Samuel. His father, Evan Davis, born in Philadelphia of Welsh stock, had migrated first to a Baptist community in South Carolina, where he married the widow Mary Emory Williams, and then crossed the upper Savannah River to settle in Georgia.[7] Samuel Emory was born to them in 1856 or 1858.[8] Georgia was still an English colony, occupied largely by the natives, and Fort Augusta was merely a trading post. In the rich wilderness, the frontiersmen had no supports except themselves, each other, and God. Evan Davis proved himself equal to the challenge. Although he met death early, he left a fair estate. Samuel's share of it (presumably one-third) was two hundred acres. In this land, now Wilkes County, Georgia, Evan Davis still sleeps.[9]

The land was ruined, however, by the Revolutionary fury in those parts, and Samuel sold it in 1785. By then, he and Jane were planted on a farm near Augusta, with five children for roots. His services in the Revolution had been rewarded with a place as county court clerk and earned him more than a thousand acres in bounty land.[10]

Samuel's father had died soon after his birth. His mother—whose maiden name of Emory he bore and passed on to his eldest child—had two sons by her first marriage, Daniel and Isaac Williams, with whom he grew up. When the Revolutionary War began, these two older half-brothers went off with Col. Elijah Clarke, of newly formed Wilkes County, to fight the British and their Tory and Indian allies. Samuel withstood the war fever as long as he could; but when his mother sent him with supplies to the brothers in South Carolina, he joined up, and never got back home until the fighting was over.[11]

Clarke had been forced to lead his "mounted riflemen" out of Georgia because fierce devastation by Tories and reprisals by Whigs (the Revolutionists) had made Wilkes County into "the Hornet's Nest." Many colonists fled. "No part of the State suffered more," wrote Georgia's early historian, the Reverend George White.[12] Amidst that suffering, the twice widowed and now abandoned mother died, and the farm fell into ruin.

"My Father was impoverished by his losses in the War of the Revolution," Jefferson Davis was to say. What became of the half-brothers is not on record, but Samuel's affection for one is: he named his fourth son Isaac Williams.[13]

Samuel Davis proved a soldier. As a dragoon with Clarke, in Col. Andrew Pickens's command, he helped defeat a superior force near his own home, at the Battle of Kettle Creek, February 14, 1779. The British had to pull out of the region, though they still held Savannah and Augusta and harried the countryside for two more years.[14]

By the summer of 1779, Samuel was raising his own company. His son Jefferson says he served "first in the 'mounted gun-men,' and afterward as captain of infantry at the siege of Savannah" (September through October of that year). A descendant says that he was promoted there "for bravery," a family tradition preserved on the grave marker erected by the Sons of the American Revolution: "Samuel Emory Davis / Georgia / Major / Lincoln Co / Militia / Revolutionary War / 1756 1824."[15] The siege of Savannah was not successful. The British held it until they left voluntarily in 1782. By then the Georgians had gone back to confront those loyal to the Crown in their own region.[16]

Tory Lt. Col. Thomas Brown, who captured Augusta in 1780, made himself thoroughly hated in the vicinity by his cruelties, turning over prisoners to his Indian allies for torture, or ordering wounded ones hanged before his eyes. A British major massacred forty-six Americans after their surrender. Elijah Clarke's wife was run out and his house, as well as a hundred other settlements, burned. His second-in-command was murdered in his home with all his family. The frontiersmen were so incensed in their siege of Augusta that they killed the Tory commander of an outlying fort, Brown's right-hand man, after he surrendered. They would have "sacrificed every man taken" had not their officers stopped them. Lt. Col. Henry Lee said the officers tried "to detect the murderers" but never did. He noted that between Whigs and Tories "a spirit of hate and revenge had succeeded to those noble feelings of humanity and forgiveness which ought ever to actuate the soldier."[17]

Andrew Pickens had shown those feelings when he refused to set an enemy fort on fire because of "the unfortunate families within," and when he attended the dying British commander at Kettle Creek. He was now General Pickens, head of the forces in which Lee led the Continental cavalry. They forced the surrender of Augusta on June 5, 1781. Lee, knowing that the life of the notorious Colonel Brown was "sought with avidity," gave him security in his own quarters and an armed escort to Savannah.[18] Lee had learned military propriety from Gen. George Washington. While a major in Virginia, Lee had ordered a soldier hanged for desertion to be decapitated. He wanted the head passed around as an object lesson. Washington was "shocked" and said they must avoid even the "appearance of inhumanity." Lee, in his turn, found Lt. Col. Banastre Tarleton's butchery of an American command trying to surrender as "shocking" as the "roasting fire" of the Indians, and a "disgrace," not only to Tarleton, but also to Lord Cornwallis for not punishing "such barbarity." "I am persuaded that the commanding officer is as much bound . . . to punish the cruel, as the deserting soldier." There was no officer training school. Lee was merely expressing the code of the English gentleman, now becoming American, in a military mode. He wrote in his memoirs, he said, of "patriotic exertions and heroic exploits," so that later generations might be "vehemently excited to virtue." He and a major in the same command passed down to their sons—Robert E. Lee and Jefferson Davis—the same exalted concept of military honor.[19]

Jefferson Davis, with his father's example always before him, once warned the Senate that Southerners were not "degenerate sons of our glorious sires." He also spoke of his "hereditary attachment" to Georgia, as "the son of a Georgian, who fought through the first Revolution": "I would be untrue to myself if I should forget the State in her day of peril." This was the code of the frontier, which held desertion of a comrade in danger the one unforgivable trespass.[20] He was devoted to the Union, he said in 1853, because his father and uncles in 1776 had given "their youth, their blood, and their little patrimony to the constitutional freedom which I claim as my inheritance." He saw himself as "rocked in the cradle of Democracy [the Democratic party]" by his father, who was, he told a friend, "as you see by the name he gave, a friend of Thomas Jefferson, and an adherent to the states rights doctrine. I grew up in that faith."[21]

He described Samuel as "a silent, undemonstrative man of action" who "talked little, and never in general company, but what he said had great weight with the community in which he lived. His admonitions to his children were rather suggestive than dictatorial." "Grave and stoical," he had "such sound judgment that his opinions were a law to his children, and quoted by them long after he had gone to his final rest." He was "unusually handsome," with "a mass of black hair" and black eyes, the son said, and an "accomplished horseman." "The last time I saw my father he was sixty-four years of age. He was about to mount a tall and restless horse, so that it was difficult for him to put his foot in the stirrup. Suddenly he vaulted from the ground into the saddle without any assistance . . . a man of wonderful physical activity."[22]

This quality, and his strong spirit, enabled Samuel Davis to pick up and leave the old frontier for the new. It was 1792 or 1793 when he settled in Kentucky southwest of Green River. He wrested a farm homestead from six hundred acres of rolling land near the Tennessee border. He had a few slaves and his son Joseph to help. The other four children—Benjamin, Samuel, Anna, and Isaac—were all under ten. He raised a double log house, with a chimney at either end, which became a "wayfarers' rest"—that godsend for travelers in a sparsely settled region. He became known for his "open-handed hospitality," as the Bible recommended. "My father, who was a better man than I, was a Baptist," said Jefferson Davis, as he gave some of this land eighty years later to the Bethel Baptist Church of Fairview, Kentucky.[23]

Jane Cook Davis, who had met Samuel in South Carolina during the war and married him soon after, was apparently a niece of the Revolutionary War commander Maj. Gen. Nathanael Greene. Her son Jeff said she was "noted for her beauty and sprightliness of mind . . . a graceful poetic mind," and recalled her "loving care." Kentucky neighbors remembered her "ever-alert and sympathetic" succor to "the needy and afflicted around her," and especially one of her "works of the good Samaritan," raising along with her own five daughters a motherless girl named Mary Tillman. Mary was twelve when the last Davis baby came in 1808. She lived to be ninety-four and used to regale people with how she helped care for the infant "Little Jeff."[24]

Jane harbored many harborless children, and she must have passed along her proclivity for this corporal work of mercy to Jeff, for in him it was almost second nature. She also passed along her looks, "very fair with large blue eyes," and her "impetuosity of temper." The strong influence of both parents was well remembered to the second generation: "Grandmother was uncommon in looks and in intellect." Samuel was "a man of culture and strictly a religious governor of his large family. So also was grandmother who survived him many years. Honor and truth were the principles they instilled"—principles that filled to the full the soul of their youngest son. "Uncle Jeff . . . had no patience with any distortion of truth or facts."[25]

On the frontier, home was the nurturer of soul and body—the place of work and worship and healing and entertainment all in one. The home of Jane and Samuel Davis was quite remarkable for the absence of tiny graves nearby. All the children, except perhaps Matilda who was said to have "died young," grew up to remember "cow and horse and sheep bells, the forever ringing axes, thud of maul . . . whir of spinning wheel, thumpety bang of a loom, whispering scratch of flax or hemp running through the hackle," and, as little Jeff recollected, gathering "around a bonfire." Home in the wilderness required uncommon hardihood. Once Jane Davis, with her babies around her, plied a desperado with food until her menfolks, who had gone out in a posse to look for him, could get back and capture him.[26]

It took a hardy mind to hold the Christian faith where there was "scarcely one man and but few women who supported a creditable profession of religion," as a minister wrote in 1783. Even in 1805, Stephen Badin, a pioneer Roman Catholic priest, was saying, "Pretty near half the settlers do not affiliate with any religion but believe in a confused manner in revelation." Bibles he noticed "in almost every house, even among the Socinians and Skeptics, who are much multiplied here." The Davises found Baptists in their part of the state, however—probably knew of them beforehand, for the "Southern Kentucky Association" was formed in 1785. Just after the family's arrival, Baptists, Presbyterians, and Methodists joined in the Great Revival, a surge of religious fervor that began at a service near the Davis home and swept through Kentucky, cresting in a camp meeting at northeast Cane Ridge. There, in 1801, "hundreds were Knocked down by the Spirit at a time," and thousands were baptized.[27] This seems not to have touched the Samuel Davis family. Most of the children on record turned out in the end to be Episcopalians. All the Davises were "a very deeply religious people," thought a descendant—rather sternly so, but of "heroic mold, people of mystic and lofty spirituality."[28]

Slavery was not much questioned at this time. It was worldwide, and no country had yet condemned even the trade. The New World colonies of Catholic Spain and France, like the former colonies of England, depended on it for labor. In Kentucky slaves were "scarcely less numerous than the whites," and they were accepted as the servants of the time and place. Although Baptist preachers might disapprove, few condemned slavery outright. Their churches "had many negro members, and also many slave-holding adherents." Father Badin wondered, however, how these Calvinists who "predominate here, and who profess to put all men on the same level, can reconcile these [principles] without embarrassment, with the traffic in negroes whom they treat almost like animals; whose service they receive every day of the year without giving them either instruction or compensation, whom they feed with coarse food and dress meagerly." It was the trade, the neglect, and the inconsistency that Father Badin deplored. Slavery per se was not incompatible with a hierarchical view of human society or with that strict regard for holy scripture which Catholics and Protestants then shared. Catholics used slaves to work the church lands in the bluegrass region; Father Badin himself owned slaves.[29] The frontier, by its very nature, tempered the institution. Here were farms, not plantations, and "everybody worked." Usually "one or a half-dozen" servants lived and labored side by side with their masters. "Living in that close connection," Jeff Davis was to say one day, produces "the kindest relations which can possibly exist between master and dependent."[30]

Samuel Davis owned such a handful of family servants, two of whom were Samson and Aunt Charity. In 1810, he moved them along with his family from Kentucky to the Louisiana Territory.[31] Thomas Jefferson had risked his political fortune by purchasing the colony from Napoleon in 1803. The Spanish and French had been in Louisiana for a hundred years, and there were stories—both rumored and true—of fabulous fortunes made. On a lush semitropical waterway, Samuel Davis bought five hundred and sixty acres and built a home. It was quite a change from the Kentucky backcountry—too much so. "During my infancy my father removed to Bayou Têche, in Louisiana; but, as his children suffered from acclimatization, he sought a higher and healthier district. He found a place that suited him about a mile east of Woodville, in Wilkinson County, Miss. He removed his family there, and there my memories begin."[32]

It was 1811 when Samuel and Jane Davis finally settled for the last time. Once again, they had to conquer a primitive forest, but how different here, with vegetation ever green and the air soft! And in Woodville, where streets had just been laid out, they could attend an actual Baptist church, the one religious building in town. On the east and on the south, within easy reach, flowed the greatest highway on the continent, the Mississippi River. Thirty-six miles northwest was that cosmopolitan center Natchez, exceeded in elegant society only by New Orleans—if then. Ten miles south of Woodville was the Louisiana border. Below that spread the rich plantation parish of Feliciana, with its center at St. Francisville, and its port, Bayou Sara, on a back bend of the river.[33]

The frame house in the Davis clearing reflected the ease and cultivation of the place and perhaps a treasured memory from South Carolina or Georgia. Like Louisiana houses in their slender-columned galleries front and back, it suggests more strongly still the Greek Revival style in its classic proportions, its clear-glass lights framing the double doors in front and back, and its Palladian window in the pediment formed by the front gable. This window illuminates a large central area upstairs known as the reading room, with dormers to the bedrooms on either side echoing the Palladian shape. Downstairs, the wide hall runs between parlor and dining room, parents' and children's bedrooms, to the back porch. The panelled doors with their brass knobs, the jib doors beneath the front porch windows, the spacious square rooms, all speak of a house built for the delight and comfort of its owners. It was a home, not a mansion. The last Davis to live there found the memory of it in her old age "like dew on a parched and withered garden." At the end of a winding dirt road in wooded farmland, the house, now called "Rosemont," still sits much as the family always knew it.[34]

The Davises named it "Rosemont," but first called it "Poplar Grove," and usually referred simply to "Woodville." Jane Davis lined the walks with sweet pinks, and her flowers surrounded the house, "a comfortable brown cottage." Office and servants' quarters were in the yard, and in back, at the foot of the hill, a "crystal stream" from the "purest of springs" went "rippling through the forest." Jeff Davis viewed Wilkinson County with a farmer's eye: "The land near the river, although very hilly, was quite rich. Toward the east it fell off into easy ridges, the soil became thin, and the eastern boundary was a 'pine country.' My father's residence was at the boundary line between the two kinds of soil." Samuel established, along with crops of corn and cotton, that Davis

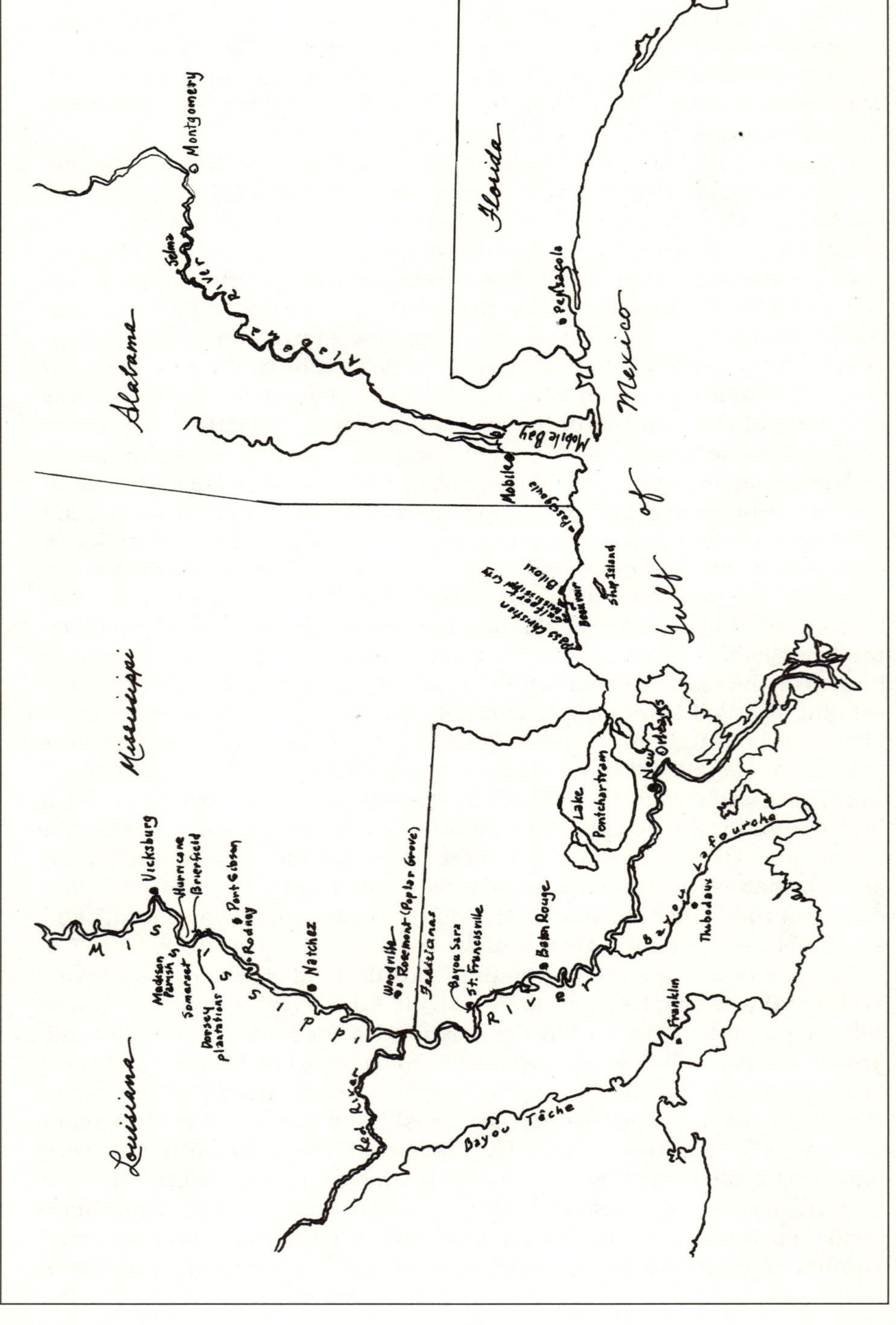
Alabama
Montgomery
Selma
Alabama River
Florida
Pensacola
Mobile Bay
Mobile
Pascagoula
Biloxi
Beauvoir
Ship Island
Pass Christian
Gulf of Mexico
Mississippi
New Orleans
Lake Pontchartrain
Vicksburg
Hurricane
Brierfield
Port Gibson
Rodney
Natchez
Madison Parish
Somerset
Dorsey plantations
Woodville
Rosemont (Poplar Grove)
Felicianas
Bayou Sara
St. Francisville
Baton Rouge
Mississippi River
Louisiana
Red River
Bayou Lafourche
Thibodaux
Franklin
Bayou Têche

hallmark, a stable of "blooded horses." In Kentucky, says his son, he had raised "some of the finest in the country" and brought to Wilkinson "many thoroughbred horses, the value of which was then unknown and unappreciated in that county." He would not allow racing, however. Jeff in later years liked to tell how his older brothers had secretly trained a mare who then beat "a famous local nag."[35]

"My elder brother, Joseph," wrote Jefferson, "remained in Kentucky when the rest of the family removed, and studied law at Hopkinsville in the office of Judge Wallace. He subsequently came to Mississippi, where he practised his profession for many years." Joseph was admitted to the Mississippi bar in 1812 and began his practice near home at Pinckneyville. Then he moved to Greenville, the plantation center for Jefferson County, just above Natchez, and seat of a venerable bar. Within five years, he was one of the men of "unmoving integrity and unsullied honor" chosen to draw up Mississippi's first constitution.[36]

Benjamin taught at the school supported by Woodville planters, until he decided to become a doctor and to practice in St. Francisville. This was surely prompted by another family move. In 1816, his sister Anna, little Jeff's second mother, married Luther Louisiana Smith, who was both a physician and a planter with large holdings in Feliciana Parish. The Smith plantation home, Locust Grove, was a mile and a half from St. Francisville, and it became a center of Davis family life. In due time, Anna and Luther and Benjamin were all laid to rest in "God's Acre" there—all that now remains of the once grand estate.[37]

The third and fourth sons, Isaac and Samuel A., fought in the War of 1812. The latter came home to help his father, and then in 1818 became one of the first settlers in Warren County, on land five miles north of Vicksburg, where he lived until his death in 1831.[38]

While baby Jefferson was passing from pinafores to pantaloons, Anna was still at home, as were plenty of other big sisters to amuse and tease him: Lucinda, Amanda, Matilda, and Mary Ellen, called "Pollie." Lucinda became almost as dear to Jeff as Anna. But it was Pollie who was his playmate and best friend. "She was two years older than he, but he thought he must take care of her." Before long, they were scholars at the one-room school where brother Benjamin taught and would walk there together through the woods with a basket of lunch. In the vicinity lived a chair-mender who used to carry his work home stacked up on his head. "He often got so drunk as to stagger aimlessly about," becoming "quarrelsome, not to say dangerous," writes Varina. "He was an object of terror to the children. One day they were in the thickest and loneliest of the woods on their way to school, and they saw him, as they supposed, with his load poised high above him, reeling along in the road, coming directly toward them. The five-year-old hero took his sister's hand and said, 'We will not run.'" They stood terrified, awaiting the drunkard, but soon saw "instead of the legs of chairs . . . the antlers of a splendid buck." It came close, "looked at them for some minutes, and turned off. They stood their ground; but it was a wild beast to them."[39]

Jeff's obstinate bravery went unnoticed by a schoolmate who could remember only that he was "a good little boy." Jeff's own recollection of the plantation school was that the chief duty of the teacher was to provide material for the scholar to copy in his copybook, "to prescribe the lesson and whip any boy who did not know it." He said, with his characteristic dry humor, "The very general opinion held by that class was that the oil of birch was the proper lubricator for any want of intelligence."[40]

About this time, something happened to educate Jeff far beyond the reach of copybooks or birch. The Davises had no Indian worries on their new frontier. The Choctaw nearby had settled down with their conquerors. "I have known them from my earliest days," recollected Jeff. "They never committed trespass or violence upon the white man . . . they were most marked for their peaceful habits, their proclivity to agriculture, the quiet with which they preserved their homes . . . and were remarkable for the morality and propriety of their conduct." It was their "traditionary boast . . . that they had never shed the blood of a white man." When war with England came in 1812, Mississippi Choctaw and Chickasaw were allies of their white neighbors.[41]

But the Creek in Georgia, and in the part of Mississippi Territory known as Alabama, were deeply divided over whether to accept or fight the European civilization. The British, at war with the United States since June 18, 1812, took advantage of this by inciting the Creek war party, the Red Sticks, in February of 1813, to an internecine war that soon involved the settlers. After a July battle in which American militia and both Creek factions were engaged, the farmers of south Alabama fled with their families to a militia stockade twenty miles north of Mobile, known as Fort Mims (or Mimms). When the Red Sticks attacked on August 30, the lax defenders, made up of militia and their Creek allies, found that their log gates were jammed open by drifted sand. The war party poured into the fort, killing soldiers and civilians indiscriminately. Of the five hundred and fifty-three men, women, and children at the fort, only thirty-six escaped. Some negroes were taken as captives, and the stockade was burned. The two militia companies, "drawn from the best population of the Mississippi Territory," had "bravely endeavored to drive the Indians from the gateway" but had all "perished in the first hours of the resistance." This heroism in defeat came home with peculiar force to a small boy in Woodville: "Among the earliest of my memories was the grief of our people because of the massacre at Fort Mimms, where many of our neighbors died in the fulfillment of that noblest motive of human action which causes one to give his life that others may live." It was only the luckiest chance that his brother Isaac was not among the slain. He held a commission as ensign in the regiment slaughtered at Fort Mims, but shortly before the attack, he had been ordered to command a different stockade at Hanson's Mill.[42]

The massacre electrified the South and brought open war with the rampaging half of the Creek nation. In September, the governor of Tennessee gave command of two thousand volunteers to his militia major general, Andrew Jackson. In the Mississippi Territory, five hundred more infantrymen signed up to serve alongside U.S. troops.[43] In the Natchez area, an elite corps took shape—the Mississippi Dragoons—made up of gentlemen riding their own horses and equipped at their own expense. Joseph Davis became an officer in the Jefferson County troop, which his neighbor Thomas Hinds had led since 1808. Samuel Davis the younger was apparently the other dragoon in the family. This corps of two hundred men, under the command of Major Hinds, became the nucleus of cavalry for the army forming to fight both the Indians and the British.[44]

Benjamin was about to go too, but the quota of Mississippi troops was filled, and he was drafted to defend the home front. Jeff, who turned six years old while the men were off fighting, remembered these days to the end of his life, the rush to arms "at the cry of the helpless," and his brothers who "bore arms in the War of 1812" under the "gallant Hinds."[45] The dragoons came home to rest and remount after the campaign against the Indians. They were recalled to arms in September of 1814 and rendezvoused near Woodville. Surely the proud father took Jeff to see his big brothers resplendent in "their dark blue uniforms, faced with scarlet, and [with] sabres slung within white belts," before they rode off at the call of Jackson, now U.S. major general commanding the whole American force, to aid in the defense of first Mobile, then New Orleans.[46]

The war, which had already seen the North embattled and Washington burned, finally reached the southern coast. The British sailed up from Jamaica to take the port cities. General Jackson, enforced by a Choctaw battalion, beat them off from Mobile. Then he chose the dragoons to lead the way to Pensacola, which the American army took by storm, driving the British back to sea. Their fleet headed for New Orleans as Jackson raced overland to prepare its defense.[47]

Once there, the Mississippi Dragoons won commendation from Jackson for their "daring manner" as they reconnoitered brilliantly. They would dash at full speed right up to the enemy lines, once jumping a trench full of British soldiers, over and then back, firing pistols as they went. Hinds commanded all Jackson's cavalry as colonel by the time the great victory came on January 8, 1815, at the Battle of New Orleans. In due time, the little brother now at home would make the general's praise for the dragoons resound in the United States House of Representatives. When Jackson died in 1845, Jeff Davis was chosen to deliver the eulogy in Vicksburg. With a dragoon holding the crepe-hung flag on its staff, he told how Jackson had called this troop the "admiration" of the American army and the "astonishment" of the British. And in 1853 he wrote: "Three of my brothers fought in the war of 1812, two of them were comrades of the Hero of the Hermitage, and received his commendation for gallantry at New Orleans."[48]

Soon the hero was to become more than a name, and the Hermitage too. The dragoons were mustered out of service in March 1815. Col. Thomas Hinds, now "preeminently the military hero of Mississippi," and his dragoon friend Joseph Davis went home to Jefferson County. With Joseph came Jeff, only three years older than his own daughter Florida. To this littlest brother, Joseph was the preeminent hero: "He was my beau ideal when I was a boy." A lawyer of rising repute, Joseph moved in the upper society of Natchez as well as Greenville. About this time he met a charming newcomer to Natchez, William Burr Howell, whose service in the war, as an officer in the Great Lakes theater, gave him an entrée into Southern society, even more than his father's position as governor of New Jersey. Joseph Davis introduced friends to him and later invited Howell to buy into the bottomlands he was acquiring for a plantation. Howell preferred to stay in town and was soon courting the daughter of the dragoon James Kempe, who had led the Adams County troop. He married Margaret Louisa Kempe in 1823 at Trinity Episcopal Church in Natchez, and Joseph Davis was his best man.[49]

Joseph had not yet moved to Natchez to live. Jeff grew up remembering "boyish days" in Jefferson County, where "all the endearing scenes of early life were fixed upon his mind." He recalled once to Joseph "the old Choctaw at Greenville." There was a county academy for him to go to, and a son about his own age on Colonel Hinds's plantation. Hinds's father-in-law, Thomas Marston Green, had befriended "the Hero of the Hermitage" in the days when he operated a trading post on the Mississippi River nearby. The young Tennessee lawyer had, in fact, married Rachel Donelson Robards (from a family that was literally one of the first in Nashville) while she was a guest at Green's plantation, Springfield, in 1791.[50]

This all led to the greatest adventure of Jefferson Davis's young life. Early in the summer of 1816, he and the Hinds boy, Howell, mounted their ponies and began a long trek up the Chickasaw Road, later known as the Natchez Trace.[51] Colonel Hinds was escorting his family and servants to Kentucky, "through what was then called 'The Wilderness.'" He planned to stop in Tennessee for a visit with his former commander. The party was in no danger from the Choctaw and Chickasaw they passed. They camped "wrapped in blankets in the open air," Jeff says, unless they stayed in one of the four log cabin "Stands" along the way.[52]

"When we reached Nashville," Jeff relates, "we went to the Hermitage." This was Andrew Jackson's plantation above the city, situated on a low, fertile bend of the Cumberland River. Here the idol of his country was trying to avoid the limelight created by his victory at New Orleans over the army that had defeated Napoleon. He and Rachel had made a homey retreat out of a two-story log blockhouse, expanding it with outbuildings to hold their growing family of nephews and friends' children (they had none of their own), as well as guests who came, like the Hinds party, to spend "several weeks." They were gaining a name for hospitality, and it was not lost on a small boy from Mississippi: "I found Mrs. Jackson amiable, unselfish, and affectionate to her family and guests, and just and mild toward her servants"—"in all the hospitable and womanly functions . . . she certainly was excelled by none."[53]

As for General Jackson, he said, "I had the opportunity a boy has to observe a great man—a standpoint of no small advantage . . . I have never forgotten the unaffected and well-bred courtesy. . . . Notwithstanding the many reports that have been made of his profanity, I remember that he always said grace at his table, and I never heard him utter an oath." This unusual view of Jackson through the honest eyes of a child is confirmed by the statements of others. "There was a deep-seated vein of piety in him," said Thomas Hart Benton, a man with least reason to think so. Jackson was holding a pistol against his breast when his brother Jesse gunned Jackson down in Nashville in 1813.[54] Saying grace was a minor but impressive example of Jackson's faith in that time and place. Some forty years later, in one of Virginia's foremost families, where they "used no form of prayer or grace," a young girl saw a dinner guest, "surrounded by a large and joyous crowd of gentlemen" clasp his hands and bow his head reverently. "It was the first silent grace I had ever witnessed, and his expression seemed to me the beauty of holiness." That man was Jefferson Davis. It is not too much to see the influence of example here; for Davis declared, "From my childhood I was attached to General Jackson. . . . My affection and admiration followed him to the grave, and cling to his memory."[55]

Jackson, so renowned in his own day for sternness and courage, was "remarked by court-trained diplomats," says Davis, for his courtesy and "very impressive bearing and manner." In New Orleans, he had completely charmed a famous hostess who was expecting a rough frontiersman. And he was then suffering from the long campaign in which, though crippled by a shattered shoulder and broken arm from the Benton street fight, chronic dysentery, and camp fatigue, he had whipped first the Creek, then the British. When the boy Jeff saw him, he was still recovering. An invincible will had sustained him, just as it had when he stood upright and shot Charles Dickinson dead on the field of honor after he had taken a bullet himself, close to the heart. A ward of his told Davis no one knew it until afterward: "I am shot thro', but I would not let the damned scoundrels have the satisfaction to know it." Yet what the little boy remembered about him was: "he was always very gentle and considerate."[56]

The context of this memory was the sporting contests at the Hermitage among Jeff Davis, Howell Hinds, and Andrew Jackson, Jr., Rachel's nephew, adopted at birth. The general boasted to his close friend, John Coffee, that when little Andrew's horse had run away, "he behaved like a soldier . . . stuck to him for half a mile," and even when finally thrown, "never hollowed." What would he have said, had he known that Jeff Davis at about the same age had stuck to his filly dashing bridleless and saddleless through the forest and over a fence and not only "never hollowed" but was never thrown? Jackson encouraged the boys in "pony-riding," and "all manly sports and recreations, joining their games and urging them to jump, run, and play." But, ironically, "he would not allow [them] to wrestle; for, he said, to allow hands to be put on one another might lead to a fight."[57]

It is no wonder that Davis, when near his death, still recalled leaving "the Hermitage with great regret" and said Jackson "inspired reverence and affection that has remained with me through my whole life." Reverence and affection, so integral to that life, were to be inspired again at this journey's end. Jeff and Howell were going to the College of St. Thomas Aquinas, near Springfield, Kentucky, operated by Dominican friars.[58]

III

School

It was a long way from the Hermitage to Springfield, Kentucky. The Hinds party finally came to the Bluegrass country, and their destination: the first Roman Catholic school west of the Appalachians. With it on a steep hill overlooking the rolling land were a little church and the first convent for men in British America, all built in the previous decade by Dominicans driven out of Bornheim, Belgium, during the French Revolution. Father Edward Fenwick, a native of Maryland, was one of them. He and three English Dominicans had established the priory, St. Rose's Church, and the school, which they named for their illustrious predecessor, St. Thomas Aquinas College.[1]

Here the Hinds family left Jeff Davis and Howell in the care of the white-robed fathers. Young Charles B. Green, a Mississippian studying law in Kentucky, was Jeff's guardian. For the next two years, the boy was grounded, so far as his age allowed, in a curriculum offering "Greek, Latin, French, English, Reading, Writing, Arithmetic, Algebra and Geometry . . . Geography, and the use of the Globes." In his autobiographical narrative, Davis does not say anything about that or about the lovely panorama of Kentucky countryside from that high hill. What he remembers is the people. "From whatever reason, the priests were particularly kind to me. . . . I was so small at this time that one of the good old priests had a little bed put in his room for me." One day, the other boys organized a revolt, against this priest especially.

> They persuaded me to promise to blow out the light which always burned in the room; so, after everything was quiet I blew it out; then the insurgents poured in cabbages, squashes, biscuits, potatoes, and all kinds of missiles. As soon as a light could be lit, search was made for the culprits, but they were all sound asleep and I was the only wakeful one. The priests interrogated me severely, but I

> declared that I did not know much and would not tell that. The one who had especial care of me then took me to a little room in the highest story of the monastery and strapped me down to a kind of cot, which was arranged to facilitate the punishment of the boys; but the old man loved me dearly and hesitated before striking me a blow, the first I should have received since I had been with the monks. He pleaded with me, "If you will tell me what you know, no matter how little, I will let you off." "Well," said I, "I know one thing, I know who blew out the light." The priest eagerly promised to let me off for that piece of information and I then said, "I blew it out." Of course I was let off, but with a long talk which moved me to tears and prevented me from co-operating with the boys again in their schemes of mischief.[2]

The impression made by his parents' lessons about honor and truth could not have wanted clearer evidence—neither could his mischievous bent and his sensitive nature. The influence of churchly surroundings on such a nature, with daily attendance at "religious exercises . . . for the sake of discipline," led Jeff to think "it would be well that I should become a Catholic," though, he says, "at that period of my life I knew, as a theologian, little of the true creed of Christianity." "I was the only Protestant boy." He sought out the prior "in his room partaking of his frugal meal, and stated to him my wish. He received me kindly, handed me a biscuit and a bit of cheese, and told me that for the present I had better take some Catholic food."[3]

This rebuff forever convinced him that Catholics were not proselytizers, and he remained prejudiced in their favor: "When I was a child the kindness of the Friars so won upon my affection that the impression has never been effaced, but has the rather extended from them to their whole church." He called it "mon premier amour [my first love]." All this he revealed to Varina in 1865 when she was somewhat anxious over sending their daughter to a convent school in Canada. He assured her that Maggie was in the right place. Faced with death or long imprisonment then, he gave a lot of thought to his children's education. Varina would have to see to it; and it was, they both thought, of the utmost importance.[4]

Surely his own training at St. Thomas speaks in this observation: "Discipline in childhood, can rarely be dispensed with, except at the cost of learning later in life and under harsher teachers the lessons which should have been early taught. Do not understand me as having become a convert to the use of harsh means. Uniformity and gentleness I still think to be better than severity." As for putting his boys "early at Latin": "It is the root of the languages of Southern Europe and enters largely into the etimology of our own; but the argument for it's study most conclusive with me is that it is the best exercise for the mind of which a small boy is capable." "Early associations are all important," he mused, summing up what he wanted for his children:

> Conscience, industry, perseverance, self denial are qualities which may be cultivated into fruitfulness or neglected to destruction. . . . To fill the heart with love for god and for man, to imbue the mind with a sense of justice, to surround it with an atmosphere of reason, to consume every prejudice by the concentrated rays of truth is the proper end of education. By instruction to direct the youthful mind towards that end, hic opus est.

His Latin phrase bespeaks his classical education—and Varina's too. He is quoting Virgil's *Aeneid*, knowing that she will recognize the line and supply the context: how easy the descent to the underworld, how difficult the escape to the upper air.[5]

After two years, an older and wiser little Jeff left the friars of St. Thomas because his mother wanted him home again. In the charge of Charles B. Green, he boarded his first steamboat, the *Aetna*—one of the very first on western waters. They got on at Louisville for the run to Natchez. Steamboats were still a novelty, Davis reports, and "many persons got on board to ride a few miles down the river," land, and "return in carriages." An old sailor was the captain of the *Aetna*, "and he always used a speaking-trumpet and spy-glass when landing the boat to take on wood." Jeff was met by his brother Isaac, who suggested, as they neared the Davis farm, that the ten-year-old go on alone and see if his parents recognized him.

> I found my dear old mother sitting near the door, and, walking up with an assumed air to hide a throbbing heart, I asked her if there had been any stray horses round there. She said she had seen a stray boy, and clasped me in her arms.
>
> After we had become somewhat calmer, I inquired for my father, and was told he was out in the field. I, impatient of the delay, went there to meet him. He was a man of deep feeling, though he sought to repress the expression of it whenever practicable; but I came to him unexpectedly. Greatly moved he took me in his arms with more emotion than I had ever seen him exhibit, and kissed me repeatedly. I remember wondering why my father should have kissed so big a boy.[6]

The parents soon sent Jeff off again, but only to the next county, Adams, where he attended Jefferson College, a good classical school in Washington, ten miles from Natchez. Here he formed "that strict friendship which, most of all, endures" with a Louisiana boy, John H. Harmanson. When he died in 1850, Davis called him " 'a true man' . . . generous to his enemies; frank and decided to all men." At Jefferson

College, Davis first suffered for principle: "The path along which I travelled to the school-house passed by the residence of an old dominie who had a great contempt for Latin. Why, he never told me; nor could he have told me, as he knew nothing about it; but whenever he saw me walking along the path, he would shout out, grinningly, 'How are you getting along with you [*sic*] hic, haec, hoc?' "[7]

He did not have to endure the "old dominie" long. The next year the Wilkinson County Academy opened, and he was able to live at home. At its head was "a scholarly man named John A. Shaw, from Boston. . . . He was a quiet, just man, and I am sure he taught me more in the time I was with him than I ever learned from any one else." Davis was especially glad that in him "a new class of teachers in our neighborhood" began—"classical scholars" instead of the "dominies whose sole method of tuition was to whip the boy when he was ignorant." Shaw believed in some kind of punishment. He threatened it when little Jeff could not master some memory work, which he had already complained of as too long. "I took my books and went to my father. He said, 'Of course, it is for you to elect whether you will work with head or hands; my son could not be an idler. I want more cotton-pickers and will give you work.' " Two days of being in the field "with a bag," having his cotton weighed at the end, "the heat of the sun and the physical labor, in conjunction with the implied equality with the other cotton-pickers, convinced me that school was the lesser evil."[8]

Life was not all work, whether of head or hands. Jeff swam and rode and fished and hunted like any Mississippi boy. Horses and cats and dogs were part of the household. He became the family expert on the latter: "The dogs being a pleasure to you are detained," his sister-in-law wrote in 1834, "twenty or thirty in & out of the house—the poor things will have to live untill you pass sentence upon them—when I expect at least half will be committed to the Waves."

His affection for dogs was great, said his daughter Winnie in later years, but for horses, even greater. "Each animal had a definite personality for him," remembered through the years. Preston Johnston bears her out: "A horse to him once seen is fixed on his mind. He remembers his points as we do the lineaments and forms of acquaintances." Davis taught Winnie that "the first rudiment of good riding [was] to sacrifice minor personal comforts to the well-being of [one's] steed"—ill-use was "a personal disgrace to the rider." "Born to the saddle," inheriting Samuel Davis's instinctive horsemanship (a "sixth sense," Winnie said) and having his fine stable, young Jeff perfected his riding into a thing of beauty that was to tax descriptive powers of women and call forth accolades from men: "A figure not to be forgotten"; "a fine rider—the finest, I think, I ever knew."[9] Part of the beauty came from the fluid, smooth, and rapid stride that he preferred: "His favorite gait is the running walk, which he soon teaches to any horse he rides." He told Preston

Johnston "he had learned to ride before he can remember." At this time, when he was eleven or twelve, he thought nothing of riding alone the twenty miles down to Locust Grove to visit Anna. All this brought him a high compliment from another expert in 1861: "Mr. Chesnut, who has talked horse with his father ever since he was born, owns that Mr. Davis knows more about horses than any man he met yet."[10]

Like many Southern boys, Davis took his "first lessons in field-sports" from black experts: "They fished, shot, and hunted together, eating the same bread, drinking from the same cup, sleeping under the same tree with their negro guide." Once, after Jeff was old enough to go without a guide, he and a friend named Bob Irion went hunting. They took separate paths, and late in the day they met. Jeff was out of shot and wanted to trade Bob powder for more. "Bob was unaccomodating and saucy—jeered at Davis, and finally told him he had a mind to shoot him any how, and made some threatening demonstration. . . . Davis jerked out a small pocket knife, dropped it down his gun on the load of powder and raised his gun and said: 'Now, sir, I'm ready for you; I dare you to shoot.'" Of course it was all more than half "foolishness"—they parted friends. "Bob told me this himself during the Mexican campaign," says the narrator, "as illustrating Davis' bravery and fertility of resources in emergencies."[11]

Davis kept hunting for many years, had a quiet passion for guns (Winnie speaks of "big game"), and was going on a "fishing expedition" in 1857. By 1879, however, he was referring to "those who fish, of whom I am not one" and had probably given up hunting too. He always forbade shooting near the house at Beauvoir because he "could never reconcile himself to the thought that any innocuous creature should be killed without some useful end, or on account of a misplaced trust in man," Winnie says. "He ceaselessly inculcated gentleness in his children as an integral part of the courage which was the first requisite in his estimation for all high character," echoing the chivalric ideal.[12]

When Jeff was almost fourteen, his father, through his own generosity, ran into financial trouble. Still owing some two thousand dollars on land he had bought in 1820, he went security for his daughter Pollie's husband, Robert Davis (no kin). The younger Davis defaulted, and the elder's debt became so great that Joseph, now living in Natchez, had to rescue his father by buying his "plantation near Woodville" in May of 1822. Jeff was busy studying Spanish with John Anthony Quitman, along with the "mainly [classical] languages and metaphysics that were considered desirable to know at that time." Probably he heard little about all this; for another brother-in-law, William Stamps, had to explain it to him in 1874.[13]

Samuel Davis did tell him why he had suddenly decided to visit Philadelphia in 1823. He wrote on June 25, "My dear Son Jefferson/ I have a few minutes past taken your letter out of the post office which has afforded me inexpressible satisfaction it being the only information which I have received since I left the Mississippi Country" (about May 1). In his sixties, he had gone to "the most beautiful city I ever Saw the place where my father drew his first breath" to seek his fortune, a family inheritance. Jeff was by then in Lexington, Kentucky, at the finest college west of the Appalachians, Transylvania University.[14]

Davis found that Mr. Shaw's predilection for "languages and metaphysics" had left him so deficient in mathematics that he was put with boys "much younger than myself." This offended his pride, since he had "usually been classed with boys beyond my age." He worked "for the balance of the session and through the [Christmas] vacation," first with a tutor and then by himself to overcome the handicap and had advanced to the junior class by the fall of 1823.[15]

This meant that he had passed "algebra, geometry and trigonometry," with "Mensuration of Superficies and Solids, [and] Navigation," as well as Latin composition and reading, "Adams's Roman Antiquities," ancient and modern geography, and history. He had read most of the *Collectanea Graeca Majora* (the *Minora* having been required for entrance). Now he was ready for Juvenal and Livy and the last of the *Excerpta Latina*, the rest of the Greek *Majora*, and "Exercises in writing Greek," as well as Latin verse; more history, "Natural Philosophy and Astronomy, Chemistry, Surveying, Lathrop on the Globes, Conic Sections," and "Chronology." French he got on his own with Monsieur and Madame Waldemard Mentelle—another Kentucky bonus from the French Revolution. The boy was settling into his lifelong enjoyment of literature and learning. "At that time," says George Wallace Jones, his classmate from Indiana, "young Davis was considered by the faculty and by his fellow-students as the first scholar, ahead of all his classes, and the bravest and handsomest of all the college boys." A Kentucky classmate, Belvard J. Peters, who became a judge, said he was "always prepared with his lessons, very respectful and polite to the President and professors."[16]

The president was Dr. Horace Holley from New England. Davis was only about thirty miles from his old school of St. Thomas, but he was at the other end of the world, religiously speaking. Transylvania University was in the hands of those "Socinians" (if not "Skeptics") that Father Badin had said were prevalent. Holley had graduated from Yale in theology and had been one of the first Unitarian preachers in Boston. He had come to head the school in 1818.[17] The Presbyterians who had started Transylvania as a seminary in 1789 had ousted a Baptist head who was suspected of skepticism, partly from his friendship with Thomas Jefferson. But by the time Holley came, his Arian religion of good works was evidently found acceptable, at least for a while. Like a good Socinian, Dr. Holley was interested mainly in education. He wanted to "send out lawyers, physicians, statesmen, poets, orators, and savants who will make the nation feel them."[18]

And he did. Holley raised Transylvania to preeminence in the West, turning out professional men the equal of graduates of Yale and Harvard. He built his student body up to rival the enrollment of those universities. "The very brilliant Horace Holly," Davis called him—but it is his only mention, and in a parenthesis. He probably never came under Holley's tutelage: "mental philosophy," which he taught, was a senior course, and Davis left at the end of his junior year. But the boy must have felt his cultural impact on this small town. His house, full of paintings and Greek statuary, Holley kept open to the young for "sumptuous entertainments," with "music, cards, and dancing." He patronized the Lexington theater, but he had to watch from backstage the "many good companies" perform, not daring to be seen in the audience. His "urbanity" was "distinguished," Albert Sidney Johnston thought. It was this, as much as his anti-Trinitarian, formless religion, that finally roused the legislature to cut off funds for Transylvania and force Holley to resign in 1827.[19]

Davis referred to the affair as "some sectarian troubles." He was aware of doctrinal issues boiling under the discontent with Holley through classes with the Reverend Robert H. Bishop. Although the boys had to be at prayers at daybreak and to hear preachers weekly in the chapel, religion had no place in their curriculum except where Dr. Holley touched on it in his "Philosophy of Mind" course. So when Davis speaks of learning "sacred history" as well as "profane," it was evidently under Mr. Bishop. This tall, gaunt Scotsman "of large attainments and very varied knowledge," was vice president of the university and a strict Presbyterian who did not hold with the loose views of the Holley faction. He resigned the year Davis left.

"In his lectures on the history of the Bible," Davis says, "his faith was that of a child, not doubting nor questioning, and believing literally as it was written." Mr. Bishop had no patience with a new trend that called certain "teachings of our Lord 'Eastern allegories,'" to the ruin of "valuable doctrines." Davis quotes him reading from the Bible, putting "the words 'Eastern allegories' where your learned friends think they occur. 'And all the Eastern allegories besought him, saying, Send us into the swine that we may enter into them. . . . And the Eastern allegories went out, and entered into the swine; and the herd ran violently down a steep place into the sea.'" When this raised a titter, Mr. Bishop "looked up astonished, and said, 'Sobriety becometh the house of God.'"

Davis was also amused with Mr. Bishop's way of greeting "a tall country boy, true-hearted and honest . . . but without grace or tact. The sight of him always seemed to suggest to Mr. Bishop the question of the Catechism, 'Who made ye, Dauvid?' to which Atchison always answered, 'Gaud,' and Mr. Bishop invariably responded, 'Quite right, Dauvid; quite right.'" When Davis met David Atchison in the Senate more than twenty years later, his first words were, "Who made ye, Dauvid?" Davis even enjoyed Mr. Bishop's application of the despised method of the old dominies. He was whipping "a vulgar boy" who had "committed some outrage," when "the culprit mumbled that it was against the law." "'Yes,' said the old gentleman . . .'but every rule has its exceptions, Toney.' Then he whacked him again."[20]

Clearly, Mr. Bishop, not Horace Holley, made the dominant impression on the young Davis. He obviously confirmed those orthodox and conservative views of the Bible and religion that Davis held for the rest of his life. Mr. Bishop later remarked how "unfavorable to religion and morals" Transylvania was, where "the majority of students were at all times from families which made no religious profession." This was, of course, not true of Davis, and he is said to have gone regularly to Christ Church with his best friends, who were Episcopalians. In spite of the general truth of Mr. Bishop's statement, more than twenty of his pupils became ministers. As "one turbulent student" explained, "We may respect Dr. Holley, but we love Mr. Bishop."[21]

Jeff's later religious tolerance, which some would trace to Holley, sprang from his charity, not from loose doctrinal views. He never doubted, as Holley did, that Jesus was the Savior. George Davis said, "His great and active intellect never exercised itself" with measuring the infinite by his own mind: his faith was "as the faith of a little child" (just as Jeff said Mr. Bishop's was). He had to read the New Testament as an entrance requirement—in Greek—and Mr. Bishop brought the texts alive for him.[22] The copy by Davis's bed in his old age, in the King James Version, was quite quite worn-out. Beside it was *The New Testament* by Constantine Tischendorf, comparing Greek texts, like the *Codex Sinaiticus* which he had discovered, with those used by King James's translators. Davis's Greek may have lapsed, but his intellectual curiosity and Bible reading, never.[23]

He never quoted Greek verbatim in after years, as he often did Latin; yet he made quite as many Greek references as Roman. Varina quoted to him in prison from a new translation of Homer, and he answered:

> It has been so long since I read the Iliad that its beauty remains to me indistinct, though the impression is yet enough to make all translations tame. The sound of the Greek is to Homer's verse a charm which no other language can borrow. Well read, it might move the heart of one who did not know the meaning of a single word, and tell its general tale like the music of an opera.[24]

Throughout his life, Davis's learning stirred comment. Frank Lubbock declared, "As a conversationalist he surpassed all I have ever met. His accurate observations and extensive reading made him . . . as a travelling companion the life of any party." His "great information" on "all subjects of discussion"—shipbuilding, animals, woodcraft, botany, Shakespeare, Scott, Burns—was "truly surprising." Lubbock and Davis were on a visit to Scotland then, and Davis pleased the Scots by speaking of "their heroes," doubtless influenced by Mr. Bishop, whose "hero of all the world" was William Wallace, or by Andrew Jackson, who spoke of Wallace to a nephew at Transylvania as the "best model for a young man."[25] As Davis entered public life, the *New York World* said that he was "intellectually . . . the best equipped man of his age in the United States . . . fluent in world history, economics, and political theory." A Confederate congressman called him "a close, industrious student" with "vast knowledge, which he could impart in the most felicitous manner." When he published *The Rise and Fall of the Confederate Government* in 1881, one reviewer found in the seventy-three-year-old author a "powerful intellect in full mastery of itself."[26]

The faculty of Transylvania recognized his scholarly bent. "As it was so long ago," he sheepishly said at the age of eighty-one, "I may say that I had taken an honor." It was awarded for scholarship and gave him the privilege of speaking at the junior class "Exhibition." Here first shone what his contemporaries saw as his foremost light—his oratory. Transylvanians were trained in it all four years and had to "declaim alternately in English and in one of the ancient languages, unless for special reasons, one of the modern be allowed." Jeff evidently had a flair for this, enhanced by what Peters called his "good form, indicating a good constitution." He was "attractive in appearance, a well-shaped head, and of manly bearing, especially for one of his age."[27]

Davis made a special study of Demosthenes. He told William Allen, a senator from Ohio, in 1840, that a speech of his was "the best English sample of the Demosthenean style," showing at the same time why one of John C. Calhoun's was not—"too sententious." Calhoun had to argue his points, whereas "the grecian orator," who addressed men already convinced, had merely to "lay bare . . . the true issue and excite them to action." Davis spoke at length about Demosthenes at the University of Mississippi in 1852 and also voiced approval of Cicero's dictum, "to be a perfect orator it is necessary to be also a good man" with "honesty of purpose and purity of heart."[28]

On June 18, 1824, he delivered "An Address on Friendship," which, the local paper said, "made friends of the hearers." It was the fruit of experience. The "cheerful, gentlemanly boy," with his "high moral tone and unswerving devotion to conscience," was very popular. George Jones said he "was considered the best-looking as he was the most intelligent and best loved student in the university." Jones and the Lexingtonians, Waller Bullock Redd and Henry Clay, Jr., were Davis's best friends, and he was close to Peters, Atchison, and Theodore Lewis. He also made friends of the family he boarded with, the Ficklins, and the three other boys who boarded there.[29]

Joseph Ficklin, postmaster and editor of the *Kentucky Gazette*, and his wife, Polly, were Lexington friends of the Davis family. Ficklin was old enough to remember Indian warfare—"perhaps the only man living who was in the early battles of the Kentucky 'Stations,'" said Davis, calling him "my friend and guardian." The Ficklins found Davis "usually so dignified, decorous and well-behaved" that they "fell into the way of treating him like a man of thirty." More than twenty years later, when Davis visited Lexington with Varina, he went to see them every day. When the aged couple entertained for them, Varina "saw Mr. Davis, across the supper room, take Mrs. Ficklin's hand and kiss it very respectfully. In a little while she came to me and said, 'Jeff is the same dear boy he was when he was sixteen.'"[30]

There was plenty of opportunity in Lexington for the students to run rather wild, what with the theater, cards and dancing, free-flowing bourbon, and the racetracks. Jeff had an especial entrée to the track at Ashland owned by the senior Henry Clay, father of his friend, and his natural attraction to horses must have led him there often. His friend Jones said the "young bloods" were notoriously free with their parents' money. He describes his own dress: "buff-colored buckskin boots," "shirt ruffled at the bosom and sleeves," with high-standing collar starched, by his order, stiff enough to "draw the blood from my ears." "No gentleman of that time or later was in good form in the ballroom without swallow-tail coat and dancing pumps." Davis was always a careful dresser, and he had learned ballroom dancing with the Mentelles. The convivial Jones insists that Jeff never got drunk and "never gambled." "At college, Mr. Davis was much the same as he was in after-life, always gay and buoyant of spirits, but without the slightest tendency to vice or immorality. He had the innate refinement and gentleness that distinguished him through life. He was always a gentleman in the highest sense of the word."[31]

Davis does not seem to have been in Jones's "cavalry troop," which Andrew Jackson reviewed in November 1823. He probably renewed his acquaintance with the general, however, for he knew Jackson's two Donelson nephews at Transylvania. Although Jones speaks of his friend as "the most active" boy in college, Peters says he did not often engage in "football" (soccer), which was the chief sport. Yet Davis speaks of the time when he, young Clay, and William Robertson McKee "mingled our sports together" at school, possibly meaning the field sports of hunting and fishing, or horseback riding and swimming. Always there was a certain reserve about the boy. Peters noticed that although he was "amiable, prudent, and kind . . . and beloved by teachers and students," he "was rather taciturn in disposition."[32]

Under the quiet manner was a taunting streak. "Poor Charles," wrote another friend in 1839, "I fail not to see his self sufficient tho, rather dull, yet good hearted personage . . . fretting at the geers and jibes and Mischeivious pranks of your identical self. Yet after the duel, he seemed to fill a better character, and . . . we all awarded to him a higher place in our esteem." Did Jeff fight the duel with Charles? He owned a brace of dueling pistols made in Lexington, and there was a Charles living at the Ficklins' named Morehead. He is perhaps the unnamed subject of Varina's story about a boarder, older than the boys, whose exaggerated self-esteem aroused their "indignation." One day a "card" appeared in the newspaper, urging this young man to run for sheriff, signed only "*Many Voters.*" Everyone wondered who had bought the ad. When the young man began to boast about it "with an air of superior dignity," Jeff's "crimson face and jerking muscles" finally gave him away as the perpetrator of the prank. Varina says nothing about a duel, but she makes here a poignant observation: "He was always fond of a joke, and very full of gay suggestions until the fall of the Confederacy; but never afterward."[33]

The incisive sorrows that were to chisel the man out of the youth began now. Jeff soon learned that the hopes of Samuel Emory Davis in Philadelphia had been quenched. His father wrote, "If I had applied some thirty year ago I might now have been immensely rich but I fear all is lost here by the lapse of time." He reminded Jeff of "the short lessons of instruction offered you before our parting use every possible means to acquire usefull knowledge as knowledge is power the want of which has brought mischiefs and misery on your father in old age." Between the receipt of this sobering letter and Jeff's address on "Friendship" came the shocking news of the death of his sister Mary Ellen, his own Pollie. She was eighteen.[34]

Jeff pulled himself through the examinations; then a second blow fell. His father, having returned to Mississippi, suddenly succumbed on July 4 to the scourge of the river country: "took the Fever on the River and died within five or six days after landing." This was on the property below Vicksburg owned jointly by his sons Joseph and Isaac. Isaac and his family were living there.[35] Isaac's wife, Susannah, wrote to Jeff. Back came the anguished cry of a sixteen-year-old far from home:

> You must imagine, I cannot describe the shock my feelings sustained, at that sad intelligence. In my Father I lost a parent ever dear to me, but rendered more so (if possible), by the disasters that attended his dclining years.
>
> When I saw him last, he told we would probably never see each other again, but I still hoped to meet him once more. But Heaven has refused my wish. This is the second time, I have been doomed to receive the heart rending intelligence of the *Death* of a *friend.*

> God only knows, whether or not it will be the last. If all the dear friends of my childhood are to be torn from earth, I care not how soon I may follow.

This is his only reference to his faith in those years—prayer answered in the negative. He contains his anguish, even this young, in discipline: "The formal manner of the letter he retained as long as he lived," comments Varina, quoting it. There is a stilted close—"the sincere regard of your brother Jefferson"—but a phrase slips in to show that the youthful spirits are not crushed: "Kiss the Children for Uncle Jeff." His father too had ended on a note of affection: "That you may be happy & shine in society when your father is beyond the reach of harm is the most ardent desire of his heart." A simple incident related by Varina reveals more surely than the adolescent rhetoric how deeply this loss cut: "When Mr. Davis was thirty-nine, he came accidentally upon a letter of his father's which he tried to read aloud, but handed it over unread and left the room unable to speak."[36]

There was something else going against the grain in 1824. Brother Joseph, become by parental death head of the Davis family, insisted that Jeff accept an "appointment as a cadet in the United States Military Academy" and "proceed at once to West Point." The boy did not like the idea of going down "from the head class in one institution to the lowest in another" or of leaving his humane studies for technical ones. "It was no desire of mine to go on," he wrote later to his sister Amanda, "but as Brother Joseph evinced some anxiety for me to do so, I was not disposed to object." "I yielded," he says—the first record of giving up his will to another, as he transferred filial piety to his brother. His own convictions, however, were by no means abandoned. He got a promise that after one year he could transfer and earn his academic degree at Thomas Jefferson's University of Virginia, "just beginning to attract attention" from afar.[37]

Jeff's friend Waller Redd was more prescient than he. On February 22, 1825, Lexington celebrated "the birth day of our illustrious WASHINGTON" with a military parade, prayers in Christ Church, and orations, one by another Davis friend, Gustavus Adolphus Henry. The Union Philosophical Society (literary and debating) took dinner at a confectionery shop, with Horace Holley himself among the guests. There were toasts to the Constitution and to Greek independence. Then Redd proposed this one: "To the health and prosperity of Jefferson Davis, late a Student of Transylvania University, now a Cadet at West Point—May he become the pride of our country, the idol of our army."[38]

IV

Army

Jefferson Davis began his army career when John C. Calhoun, secretary of war, issued his "commission of Cadet" on March 11, 1824. As Davis explained much later, cadets were warrant officers assigned to duty at the military academy and "in the service as much as they will ever be." But he was still very much the schoolboy when he returned a reluctant "I accept it" on July 7, adding, "am not able to go on before sept. for reasons I will explain to the superintendent on my arrival. Yours &C."[1] The term at West Point began unremittingly on June 25, with the summer encampment for drill and artillery practice. Classes began on September 1. When Cadet Davis arrived, he found the session under way and the superintendent, Lt. Col. Sylvanus Thayer, not at all interested in his explanation. Had it not been for Capt. Ethan Allen Hitchcock, who "had known my family" when on duty in Natchez, and the fact that the academic board was sitting in special session to examine a cadet with the magic name of Washington, he could not have gotten in.

Even so, barring the way was his old enemy, mathematics. Hitchcock got him a hearing "and told me that I would be examined, particularly in arithmetic. He asked, 'I suppose you have learned arithmetic?' To which I had to answer in the negative. . . . He was quite alarmed, and went off and got me an arithmetic, telling me to study as much as I could of fractions and proportion. I had hardly commenced when an order came to bring me before the staff." Davis muddled through the mathematics on his native wit and his knowledge of algebra. The French test he found easy, and the language professor, finding that Davis knew Greek, "launched into a discussion . . . as to the construction of Greek, with which he was so delighted that he kept on till the superintendent stopped him, and that broke up my examination." From then on, says

Davis, "I have never believed that an examination formed a very conclusive . . . test."[2]

The enemy had fallen to the power of humane letters, but it was an uneasy victory. Mathematics consumed all the academic work of the first year, except for French, and was the basis of the whole curriculum. Davis never pulled up to the top half of his class in it—not that year or any year. French he did well in, always. This was not unimportant. The textbooks, even in mathematics, were largely written in French. Thayer had modeled West Point on France's Ecole Polytechnique and had purchased America's first military library in Napoleon's country. But French earned only one credit, whereas math was worth three.[3]

The shift to scientific studies cramped the academic promise Davis had shown at Transylvania. Only in "rhetoric and moral philosophy" could he ever come near his French standing. In the end, he finished twenty-third among the thirty-three members of his graduating class. Still, the class had started at West Point with ninety-one members. It was something to have survived. Richard Stoddert Ewell's mother quoted a gentleman as saying "that West Point is decidedly the best college in the Union, that a boy cannot remain there unless he studies and that the examination is very strict." Only the "industrious and obedient" could stay, "and when a young man graduates there he is fit for anything." A lady told her that those who made it through "were the cleverest and most correct young men she knew."[4]

There was a lot more to being "ground in the Academy mill" than grades. The Mississippi cadet's flair for friendship grew and blossomed, if his scholarship did not. Indeed, his most frequent demerits in conduct came from visiting in other people's rooms or leaving the barracks during study hours or after taps; next came from sleeping through reveille. Once Cadet Davis was caught cooking in his room, once firing his musket out the window. But most of the aberrations that brought his academic standing down were careless—bad police, candlestick out of place, firescreen not up securely, inattention on parade—never "Gross disrespect" or "Ungentlemanly Conduct" or "Irreverence at church." Sunday church attendance was required. Davis missed only three times in his four years (the months he was hospitalized from a fall in 1826 did not count).[5]

The monthly list of those "distinguished for Correct Conduct" bore Davis's name only six times (two were while he was in the hospital). He was distinguished rather, along with fifteen others, for "having 'committed the greatest number of Offences' " (eleven) for the month of April 1825. Thirty offenses in his last year earned him one hundred and thirty-seven demerits. Two hundred would have meant dismissal. Although these seriously affected his academic standing, they did not hurt his soldierly standing. He was appointed a fourth sergeant, then sergeant of the color guard. A fellow cadet saw him as "distinguished in the corps for his manly bearing, his high-toned and lofty character. His figure was very soldier-like and rather robust."[6]

He struck a total stranger in much the same way at the end of his first year. This was Margaret Kempe, who had known Joseph Davis from girlhood and married his friend William Burr Howell. Their first baby, whom they had named for Joseph, was sickly and needed to get away from the Mississippi miasmas. Joseph Davis was also ailing in the winter of 1825 and wanted to go north for his health and to see his little brother. So the three friends, with baby and nurse, took carriage at Natchez and drove "through 'The Wilderness'" to the Ohio River. From there, traveling by public stage and steamboat, they finally reached West Point, New York, probably in the third week of July.[7]

Varina paints the scene, for the couple were her parents, the baby, her older brother. "As the boat neared the landing a very stout, florid, young fellow of about eighteen came running down to the landing-place and caught Mr. Joseph E. Davis in his arms. He said little, but my mother was struck by his beautiful blue eyes and graceful strong figure . . . [and] his open bright expression." Joseph may have wanted to see what Jeff had in mind to do. "I had consented to go to the Academy for one year, and then to the University of Virginia," wrote Davis later. "But at the end of the year, for various reasons, I preferred to remain." Doubtless the brother-guardian was relieved. The boy would at least have a profession.[8]

What made the academy unexpectedly congenial to the quiet but high-spirited Davis was a sense that he was in the right place. He spoke once of his son's "inheriting the [military] instincts of his ancestors and mine." There was also an inspiring friendship formed in his first year with a man he was to call "physically grand, intellectually great, morally sublime," a Kentuckian five years older than he, who had entered in 1822. Albert Sidney Johnston had also been at Transylvania but had left before Davis arrived. This nevertheless "formed a link between us, and inaugurated a friendship which grew as years rolled by, strengthened by after associations in the army. . . . [It] remains to me yet, a memory of one of the greatest and best characters I have ever known."[9]

The whole corps looked up to Sidney Johnston. W. H. C. Bartlett, who stood first in their class, said, "His nature was truly noble, and untainted by anything small or contracted." He was above all, a soldier. He was an exemplar of military excellence, selected as adjutant of cadets—"the most esteemed office in the corps." He looked his nobility, being a hefty six feet, two inches.[10] Leonidas Polk, arriving in 1823, told his mother how lucky he was to have Johnston as a roommate, with "his strict attention to duty and steadiness of character." Everyone "expected him to become a leader of men." Thirty years later, a young lieutenant, John Bell Hood, serving briefly under Sidney Johnston, remarked "the exalted character of this extraordinary man."[11]

"He did not have an enemy in the corps, or an unkind feeling to anyone, though he was select in his associates." He chose them, says Davis, for "congeniality of tastes." Yet the tastes of these two ran rather aslant. Johnston indeed loved the army and horses and guns, but he also excelled in mathematics and science and graduated eighth in his class.[12] Although he shared Davis's interest in history, he was not bookish and had little use for the poetry that Davis liked. At least, he later made fun of his wife's as "good prose spoiled."[13]

But both men had a hearty sense of humor. Both kept their ardent feelings so tightly reined that they appeared reserved, even severe. After the first boyish hug of his brother, Jeff Davis "said little," Margaret Howell noticed, and showed his emotion only by sitting close, with his hand through Joseph's arm. Johnston, even as a boy, was "grave and thoughtful in his deportment."[14] "He impressed me at first as an austere man," said someone who met him in 1834, "but I found him the kindest and gentlest of friends; a stoic, yet he had the tenderest nature, so mindful of others' feelings." Like Davis, he was mindful of even his horse's feelings. His son says he taught him not "to inflict upon any creature of God unnecessary pain." To show he was not morbidly sentimental, he hunted "moderately," but he still "would habitually turn aside from treading upon a worm in his path." Davis late in life turned Winnie from treading on a beetle, saying, "Is there not room in the world, little daughter, for you and that harmless insect too?"—a chuckling reference, really, to Uncle Toby and the fly in *Tristram Shandy,* a favorite Davis book.[15]

The discipline at the academy Polk found "very rigid" but "the quintessence of a well-regulated army." Its object was obedience to proper authority and the exact performance of duty, without regard to personal will or passions, all grounded in honor. A biographer sees that Davis "carried with him from West Point the high sense of honour and devotion to duty which is of the essence of the profession."[16] When Davis was president of the Confederate States and unconditional surrender was proposed, "duty and honor alike forbade," he said, his accepting what "our army, depleted as it was, would have rejected with disdain." He told veterans of the Mexican War that they "came back poorer than they went, except in that which is the true soldier's treasure—*honor, HONOR.*"[17]

Duty and honor are simple concepts, producing a simplicity of character that drew Sidney Johnston and Jeff Davis together far more surely than any outside interest could have done. "I believe I am very honest, and I would maintain my honor at the risk of my life," Johnston wrote his son Preston, "but I do not think there is anything else in my character worthy of imitation." "Unassuming and modest," a friend said, and "simple as a child," when being "a West Pointer was the grandest of earthly accidents." Children, in fact, felt a natural affinity for him, as they did for Davis, whom "all women and children seemed instinctively to love."[18]

Even in the glare of public life, Jefferson Davis was known for the "simplicity and loftiness" of his character. Dr. Minnigerode found him "unsophisticated," looking "for good in people rather than the evil," and "without guile" both in public and in private—"not a false fibre in him." "Pure in heart," the minister said. The sincerity of soldierly life pleased him: "I behold myself a member though an humble one of an honorable profession one in which sychophancy though it may be beneficial is not necessary to success."[19] Thirty years later, speaking of political platforms, he said, "If there be anything covert . . . no man yet has so far mistaken me as to make me a confidant of what he was doing, and I hope none ever will." One man wanted him to run for president of the United States because his "course" had always been "so decided and straight forward . . . free from ambiguity." Even a critical reporter saw in him "a simplicity that was sublime."[20]

As for duty, it would control both Davis and Johnston from now on. "Nothing could turn [Davis] from what he considered to be his duty," said Minnigerode; he was simply, as he like to call others, "a duty man." Davis told Mexican War veterans, "He who treads the path of duty for duty's sake walks under a shield which the slings and arrows of adversity cannot destroy, and has in the conscious rectitude of his own heart a balm for the worst wounds the world can inflict."[21] Even more telling, perhaps, is an offhand statement of Lt. Col. David E. Twiggs: "I do not know Mr. Davis' wishes on the Subject but he is so perfect a Soldier that he is ready for any duty." Davis said of Sidney Johnston at Shiloh, "his only thought was of his duty—he remembered not himself," a quality he had shown throughout life.[22]

To have become the friend of Sidney Johnston was no mean accomplishment. Postponing West Point in deference to a brother's wish, though he always wanted to be a soldier, had made Johnston older than most in his class. Nathaniel Eaton, a member of that class who revered him, never knew "exactly how I stood with him" because of his "reticence and dignity of manners," so they were not close socially. But Johnston received Davis, who was the same age as Eaton, "as an elder brother might do." They "belonged to the same 'set'" and knew each other "intimately through all the years of [their] manhood." All this says a great deal about Davis's gift for friendship.[23]

Probably one of the "introductory letters I brought on with me" from Transylvania friends had broken the ice. Davis was writing to Joseph in January of 1825 for some extra cash (against regulations): whether his pay (twenty-eight dollars a month) would prove sufficient "depends entirely upon the company I keep." His letters were not to "the Yankee part of the corps" (who lived on their pay) "nor are they such associates as I would at present select, enough of this as you have never been connected with them, you cannot know how pittiful they generally are." But Polk thought "not even the rigid economy of the Yankees can withstand" the pay stoppages; he never had enough.[24] "Yankees" then meant New Englanders. Two of Davis's best friends there, and till his death, were Northerners: Crafts J. Wright, a New Yorker transplanted to Ohio, and Alexander Dallas Bache from Philadelphia, first in the class of 1825, who stayed on to teach chemistry and engineering to cadets, Davis among them.[25]

It was largely the Southern boys, however, that he ran with. Some were in the habit of going to Benny Havens's tavern for comforts the mess hall did not provide. "As for your fear that I might be confined in the guard-house," Davis wrote to Joseph, "I trust ever to have enough prudence to keep from being confined." But pretty soon Davis was under arrest—not in the guardhouse, indeed, but confined to quarters. Down at Buttermilk Falls, Captain Hitchcock had caught him and boys from North Carolina, Virginia, and Tennessee (one an Andrew Jackson ward) at "a public house or place where spirituous liquors are sold, kept by one Benjamin Havens," their indictment read.[26]

Despite Davis's pleas that they had wandered away from the summer encampment because of flooded tents and that they were being tried under ex post facto laws, and his nice distinctions between spirituous and non-spirituous liquors, they were all convicted. Three of the five boys were dismissed. Because of previous good conduct, Davis and S. J. Hays (Rachel Jackson's nephew) had their sentences remitted. In conducting his own defense, Davis had called as witness the commandant of cadets, Maj. William J. Worth, who testified: "The prisoner's conduct and general deportment . . . has been marked by correct and strict attention to duty," and he had not before "committed any offence which called for animadversion. His deportment as a Gentleman has been unexceptionable." This must have soothed Davis's feelings, which had been violated, he said, by charges "so contrary to principles of a soldier & a man of honor."[27]

Nothing, however, could keep him from Benny Havens's. The next year, at the end of the summer encampment, he did not, like most, go home on furlough. He and a Louisiana friend, Emile LaSere, went to the tavern "on a little frolic," perhaps to celebrate Davis's appointment as sergeant of the color guard. Suddenly it was bruited that an officer was on the way.

> The two young men rushed off by a short cut to get back to barracks, and Cadet Davis fell over the bank, and as he afterward found, he had been precipitated sixty feet to the river bank. Fortunately he caught at a stunted tree, which broke the force of his fall, though it tore his hands dreadfully. Young Laserre looked over the face of the rock and called out, "Jeff, are you dead?" Mr. Davis

> said he was suffering too much to laugh, remembered the desire to do so, but could only move one hand. He lay ill many months afterward, and was expected to die for some weeks.[28]

Davis is listed as "Present; sick" on monthly returns from August 31 through November 30, 1826. The only time he ever mentioned this was during a greater trial, his imprisonment, when he said, as a comfort to his wife,

> I have tried and not without success to possess my soul in patience. A varied life has given me experience in most forms of trial: When a Cadet I lay for more than four months in Hospital and rarely saw any one save when it was thought I was about to die, then some of my friends were allowed to stay with me at night. I should have more resources to sustain me now than then.

He does not say what his injuries were or which friends sat with him—LaSere, Drayton, Wright, Polk, his roommate Walter Guion, or Robert E. Lee. Sidney Johnston had graduated July 1.[29]

Leonidas Polk had a new reason for the corporal work of mercy, visiting the sick. He had astounded the cadet corps in January by renouncing "the devil and all his works . . . the vain pomp and glory of the world" and being baptized right there in the cadet chapel, along with one other. "The service of adult baptism had never been witnessed there before," says the Reverend Charles P. McIlvaine. This Episcopal chaplain, on his arrival in 1825, had found no open Christian "among the officers, military or civil," and not one cadet who professed any interest in religion. Polk came to see the objective truth of Christianity through Dr. Olynthus Gregory's *Letters on the Evidences*, ordered for the post by McIlvaine, and his own sin through the chaplain's sermons and a tract "addressed to an unbeliever." Wanting to signify his newfound faith immediately, he had decided to kneel at chapel—something no one had ever done. "The cadets sat on benches without backs, and were so crowded together," says McIlvaine, that "when the confession in the service came, I could hear his movement to get space to kneel, and then his deep tone of response." "The whole corps was roused as by a thunder-clap" by Polk's conversion, Crafts J. Wright later recalled. He and others heard "that Polk was to lead a 'praying squad'" and they "stood on the stoop to see them go by and find out who they were." Soon McIlvaine was having nightly meetings for those who came to religion through Polk. "There was a veritable revolution." Even some professors came.[30]

Johnston and Davis do not appear to have been in Polk's "praying squad." Neither was baptized now. Johnston read Gregory's *Evidences* because his roommate Polk did, but he was not convinced. He never could confess the Apostle's Creed as Polk did at his christening. His faith, to his life's end, was simply: "*I trust in God.*" But "his piety was deep and sincere": "I never lay my head upon my pillow at night without returning thanks to God for his protecting care, and invoking his guidance in future."[31] Johnston's aloofness from the evangelical fervor probably influenced Davis, raised a Christian but still not a church member (so far as we know). But surely he was touched by Polk's example; he says their relations were "very near and affectionate." Not only did he honor and esteem the future priest, he later told Polk's son, "I loved him."[32]

During the long weeks of pain and solitude in the academy hospital, the conversion of so good a friend probably came to mind, along with images of his pious parents and days at St. Thomas school where the crucifix made Good Friday ever present. It was the first time that Davis had been seriously ill. The doctor's fears for him forced on him the thought of death and the other last things—judgment, heaven, and hell. Mr. McIlvaine, "a pronounced 'Evangelical,' " would not have missed the opportunity to speak of God, to pray, to leave a tract. Davis wrote to him many years later: "If the seed sown by you has not borne fruit in my case, I yet trust that the germ is not dead."[33]

Convalescence brought a new form of trial. Davis had missed almost all the class work for the fall term, and there was only a month left before the January exams. If he failed them, he would have to go back a whole year. He "declared he would quit the Academy before" he would do that. He proved he was a student after all. By intense concentration and the help after hours of a young instructor, W. F. Hopkins, he was ready in time. Instead of the usual twenty-minute examination before the board, he had to stand one of three hours. Hopkins thought he had passed; Superintendent Thayer said, "impossible." But after another three-hour grilling, Davis was "allowed his old stand." It was not only a triumph of pluck and intellect, it was achieved under a cloud.[34]

As Christmas of 1826 approached, the Southern boys were determined to celebrate with eggnog—a double offense at the academy but a custom long winked at. Before reveille on December 25 they were having a party in North Barrack, No. 5, with liquor from Benny Havens's. They had consumed one bucket of eggnog when Cadet Davis burst in, crying, "Put away that grog, boys, old Hitch is coming." Captain Hitchcock was in the room. Davis was ordered to quarters in the South Barrack, where he fell asleep; he was awakened by Walter Guion, coming in to look for his pistol. This was the first Davis knew of what became famous as the Eggnog Riot. North Barrack was loud with flying firewood crashing through windows. Finally the artillery unit stationed at the Point, called by cadets the "Bombadiers," had to be summoned to quell the disorder. Guion managed not to shoot anybody, but he soon found himself expelled, after a court-martial in which eighteen others were also tried. Davis was not one of them. His obedience to Hitchcock's order saved him from being charged—which he would have been had he been drunk, as he later pointed out. But he had to testify at the court of inquiry in January, and he remained under arrest and confinement. It was in the midst of this turmoil that he won his academic victory.[35]

His class standing, however, did not improve. Davis considered "the favorable verdict of his classmates of much more importance," says Varina. The instructor in "Pyrotechny" (making and handling explosives) had a dislike of Davis which he took out on him in class. He insinuated that because of a "mediocre mind" Davis would be "unstrung" in an emergency. Davis felt the insult but could not answer back. One day, while the class was learning to make "fire-balls," one ignited. "The room was a magazine of explosives." Davis "calmly asked of the doughty instructor, 'What shall I do, sir? This fire-ball is ignited.' The professor said, 'Run for your lives,' and ran for his. Cadet Davis threw it out of the window and saved the building and a large number of lives thereby."[36] Thomas Drayton was in that class and bears out the story. When asked "if he did not take a great risk," Davis replied, "No, I was very quick, and felt sure I had time to 'try him.'"

What made him show up the man who had abused him was his lifelong "horror of oppressing the weak." The man intrepid enough to toy with a fire-ball could not bear cruelty or injustice, even in a story. His wife tells how, when he was secretary of war, he begged her to stop reading to him "The Babes in the Wood" from "Percy's 'Relics'" because "if it is the truth, it is a cruel thing to perpetuate the story; if it is a fabrication, you may rely on it the man was a rascal who invented such a horror." The president of the Confederacy rose up from his sofa in clench-fisted indignation when someone in a novel Varina was reading to him struck an injured man. As for injustice, he said at his court-martial in 1825, "It is better a hundred guilty should escape than one rightuous person be condemned."[37]

Leaving West Point meant leaving behind good friends. Henry Clay, Jr., several years younger, was to graduate in 1831, second in his class. Robert E. Lee had another year to go. Lee was Davis's "friend in the military academy, and . . . until the hour of his death." It was "a warm personal friendship," said Lee's son. Davis seems to have been friendly too with Lee's crony from Virginia, Joseph E. Johnston, also in the class of 1829. The story of their having had a fistfight at the academy over a girl has been pronounced "a complete fabrication."[38] Lee's testimony against the Eggnog Rioters did not disturb his friendship with Davis. At the inquiry, Drayton testified against Davis, and Davis against Guion. There was no animosity involved, only the obligation to tell the truth—the hallmark of a gentleman, and the underpinning of the whole honor system at West Point.[39]

Polk was already gone. He stayed, only in deference to his father's wishes, long enough to graduate eighth in the class of 1827, then he resigned from the army. Thayer tried to keep him at the Point as quartermaster, but his heart was set on entering the Episcopal seminary at Alexandria, Virginia, which he did, to the "bitter disappointment" of both his parents, on November 4, 1828.[40]

Davis was to meet on army duty a few of the friends who graduated with him, like Drayton and John R. B. Gardenier, Theophilus Holmes, and James Izard. He saw the head of their class, Albert E. Church, in the 1850s at West Point, where he taught mathematics for over forty years. Crafts J. Wright soon resigned in favor of civilian life, lived in Cincinnati, and served in the Union army from 1861 to 1862. He and Davis revived their friendship after the war in lively letters.[41]

West Point gave Davis his style for life. As he said, a commission "conferred an undeniable cachet." "There always seemed to be something of the soldier about him," observed someone who knew him rather late. His parents' teaching about honor and truth had been confirmed, and to him, every West Pointer was a gentleman unless proven otherwise. He belonged to an elite corps, and his manner embodied that thought—the quick martial tread, the "erect military bearing of which not even death could rob him" (but "marvelously graceful"), the scrupulous care in dress ("delicately soigné," Varina says), the self-command, with its consequent air of being in control, whatever the situation. West Point gave him some of his happiest memories. They were on his mind when he died. He had been dictating an autobiography and said to Varina, "I have not told what I wish to say of my classmates Sidney Johnston and Polk. . . . I shall tell a great deal of West Point." But it was too late.[42]

It was July 1, 1828, when Jefferson Davis graduated from the military academy with a brevet as second lieutenant, assigned (temporarily) to the Sixth Regiment of Infantry. He left New York on leave of absence till October 30, when he was to report to Jefferson Barracks, Missouri. On August 26, however, he wrote from Lexington, Kentucky, asking an extension to December 31. He had been "unavoidably detained in the north," and "the sickly season" now made it "imprudent for me to return home (Mississippi)." It "would be unsafe" before October, and "after an absence of nearly six years I feel desirous of remaining some time with my relations." The granted extension was signed by Samuel Cooper, a man fated for close friendship with Davis.[43]

In Lexington with Jeff were his niece Florida, his new sister-in-law, Eliza Van Benthuysen Davis, and presumably her husband, Joseph. The two had wed the preceding October 5 and gone, with Joseph's three girls, to live at Davis Bend. They frequently spent the sickly season in Kentucky. Eliza was only seventeen, the same age as Florida, and Jeff was now twenty. The three became great friends, the girls showing their affection for Jeff through the years in letters full of feeling and banter.[44]

When the weather cooled, the Davis entourage went down to the Hermitage. It was an exciting fall for Tennesseans. Their own "Old Hickory" stood a good chance to be president of all the twenty-four United States. But the air was black with slander about the Jacksons' marriage years before. Rachel wrote to a friend: "The enemys of the Genls have dipt their arrows in wormwood and gall and sped them at me Almighty God was there ever aney thing to equal it." But he was still "The Hero of the Hermitage," his popularity greater than ever. He and Rachel lived now in a four-square brick dwelling, near the log house where Jeff had stayed as a boy.[45] Once more, the "kindness" of General Jackson "made a powerful impression" on Davis. He thought him "a great man in character unsurpassed." That character took a chisel blow after his election as president. Rachel, who had often said, "I had rather be a door-keeper in the house of God than to live in that palace [the White House]," suddenly died on December 22.[46]

The relations whom Lieutenant Davis wanted to see all lived fairly close to his mother's Poplar Grove. Sister Lucinda and William Stamps had a plantation nearby. Brother Samuel was still in Warren County. After their father's death, Isaac Davis had been driven from the river land in that county by a violent storm that swept away his improvements, broke his leg, and killed a little son. He had moved to a farm north of Canton, in Hinds County. Joseph had taken over the plantation and named it, defiantly, the Hurricane. Sister Anna and Luther Smith and their six children were just over the Louisiana border at Locust Grove. In God's Acre there, a stone told of brother Benjamin's death, October 22, 1827. In the same West Feliciana Parish lived sister Amanda, who had married David Bradford, planter and lawyer. They already had four of their eventual nine children, one of whom was to be named Jefferson Davis.[47]

On January 11, 1829, Lieutenant Davis reported to "the Infantry School of Practice" at Jefferson Barracks, taking a body servant, as officers were expected to do. Being "something of a martinet," as he says, straight from the spit and polish of West Point, "I arrayed myself in full uniform and made my way to the regimental headquarters." The commander, Maj. Bennet Riley, "was not in, and I was directed to the Commissary." There was Riley, "seated at a table with a pack of cards before him. . . . In response to my formal salute, he nodded, invited me to take a seat, and continued his game. Looking up after a few minutes, he inquired: 'Young man, do you play solitaire? Finest game in the world! You may cheat as much as you please and have nobody to detect it.' "[48]

Davis could soon amuse his friend Tom Drayton, and other classmates coming in, with this lackadaisical introduction to army life. Sidney Johnston was already here, as adjutant of the crack Sixth Infantry.

He had chosen this branch over the usually preferred engineers or artillery, to which his class standing entitled him, because he wanted the most active service, and there was no cavalry. He had even refused to be aide-de-camp to Brig. Gen. Winfield Scott in Washington. He and Davis took the word *service* literally. Johnston felt "born into the world not for himself, but for others." Davis termed being at the nadir of fortune in a prison cell, having "lost the power to serve."[49]

Johnston was now serving Bvt. Brig. Gen. Henry Atkinson, commandant of the post and head of the right wing of the army's Western Department. He and his wife were Southerners. They made Jefferson Barracks "a delightful and elegant home" for the young officers and introduced them in nearby St. Louis, though their commissions alone "accredited them to the best society." Here Sidney had met Henrietta Preston, visiting from Louisville, Kentucky, but originally from "the mountains of Virginia." They married on January 20. Johnston in later years told their son, Preston, of her "strong religious impulses" and of the "chivalric devotion" that she inspired, which forbade him "to cherish low views." These are the friends Davis was to describe as "pure gold."[50]

With his basic training over in March, Davis was ordered to the First Infantry on the northwestern frontier, in Michigan Territory. Headquarters was Fort Crawford, where the Wisconsin River met the Mississippi, but he reported farther east, to Maj. David Twiggs. Twiggs was building Fort Winnebago to protect "the Portage," between the Fox and Wisconsin Rivers, on the route from Lake Michigan's Green Bay settlement. Davis acted variously as ordnance officer, adjutant, or company commander. He was soon appointed commissary and quartermaster for the post. This meant getting materials and overseeing the construction—hiring "carts, wagons, and oxen to haul stone and lime" and sending squads into the forest to cut timber and then fashion it with whipsaws into logs and lumber. He was so successful that he was later put in charge of a sawmill near Fort Crawford. When president of the Confederacy, he rebuked the vanity of a man boasting of "the fine company he had kept" by saying he had once cut, sawed, and rafted timber for pay. He was much amused when the tale came back that he had hired out as a lumberjack; he "never explained the mistake." He himself amused a lady at the fort by making an outlandish combination wardrobe and china press that she promptly dubbed "a Davis." He would not be found wrong. He explained it was not designed for ladies: "the shelves were exactly the length of a gentleman's coat . . . made close together to hold each one separately."[51]

The lumbering days came close to being his last. Being "often wet to the skin for hours" in intense cold "brought on pneumonia." In those days, the chief medicine was endurance, whether in the wilds or no. The robust young man was soon frail and emaciated, but with his servant, James Pemberton, lifting him from bed to window, he still directed his men. Pemberton finally nursed him back to health. He "carried the arms, the money, and everything of value." He knew "he could be free with the simple ceremony of leave-taking; but he remained throughout the whole period of Mr. Davis's service on the frontier, as tender and faithful as a brother; and he was held nearly as dear as one."[52]

Lieutenant Davis, no longer "brevet" as of March 15, 1831, was sometimes sent out chasing deserters or recruiting enlisted men or on reconnaissance. His "file of soldiers" broke the trail from Fort Winnebago to Fort Dearborn, now Chicago. His ingenuity and daring saved him and his men more than once. Pursued in an open boat by furious Indians who were gaining on them, he took a chance of capsizing in a boisterous wind by improvising a sail from a blanket, and they outran the hostile canoes. Another time, on horseback, they met a sullen bunch who tried to misdirect them. One brave stationed himself right in their way. "Davis without further parley spurred his high-mettled horse . . . upon the Indian, seized him by the scalp-lock, and dragged him after him some distance. The attack was so quick that it disconcerted the rest, and the soldiers rode by without further molestation."[53]

Nor was his mettle tried only in the field. He was almost beardless still, and his "smooth face, fresh color, and gay laugh" prompted the bully of his work-gang, building Fort Winnebago, to announce "his intention of whipping that 'baby-faced Lieutenant if he attempted to direct him.'" The man was "immensely strong" and "a terror to everybody about him." One day, "with an insolent laugh," he repeatedly disobeyed orders. "Knowing that one blow from the soldier would fell him, Mr. Davis picked up a stout billet of wood, and as the man stooped he knocked him down and beat him until he cried for quarter." It was an unmilitary but effective solution. Davis acknowledged it as such: "This has been a fight between man and man and I shall not notice it officially." This won over the antagonist and the whole crew, who "from that day, required only to know his orders to obey." His inborn talent "for governing men," Varina says, came from "a sense of justice, personal dignity, self-denial, sympathy with the governed, and unflinching courage. He never had, with soldiers, children, or negroes, any difficulty to impress himself upon their hearts." He did not always come off so well with his superiors. When he returned to a quartermaster a letter he found insulting, the man got him reported for insubordination, but nothing came of it. Probably his commander, Twiggs, who thought highly of Davis, saw the matter dropped.[54]

The lieutenant found some children to care for even in the wilderness. He bought treats for an orphaned Indian boy named Tochonegra (the Otter), from his skill at diving after fish, and became his trusted friend. Davis once was called on to rescue a white boy stolen by Indians, which he did, though he said the child, dirty and sunburned, "seemed quite happy." The story of another orphan furnishes a remarkable instance of Davis's sense of justice, and of his humility, too, for he completely forgot about it. On the streets of a frontier village, Davis found a nurse whipping a little girl. He rescued the child and got the nurse dismissed. The girl never forgot her savior. When Davis was in a prison cell at Fortress Monroe in 1866, her son, a Union officer, reminded him of it.[55]

Davis was intrigued by the Indians among whom he lived while in the army. "He was at one time able to speak several Indian languages rather fluently, and knew a great deal of [their] traditions and customs." Responding to an example of Winnie's baby talk sent to him in prison by Varina, he wrote:

> The baby's mode of speech is the method of nature. The like is found in all languages which were spoken long before they were written. It has been regarded as one of the beauties of the Greek. I found it still more prominent in the Chippewa. By great freedom of abridgement a single word is formed out of many, and expresses the agent & his condition, the object, the action and it's effect. It is termed "*polysynthetic.*"

He was once—only once—persuaded to sing an Indian song at a party. But to his children he would regularly sing an Indian lullaby, and he loved to tell them "wild stories of Indian warfare, of hair-breadth escapes . . . or of horse fights and the wild dances of the red men."[56] Winnie thought it was her father's way of dignifying others that won "such devotion from the Indians in his early life." In the Confederacy, Burton Harrison once appeared in a charade wearing "a complete red man's outfit" given Davis "years ago by some Indian tribe" to whom he had shown kindness. He was, in fact, adopted as a brother, a relationship "so sacred" that only "the most absolute treachery" could break it. He was named "Little Chief."[57] This possibly distinguished him from Lt. Col. Zachary Taylor, who was "Big Chief," in honor of his excellence as Indian agent while commanding Fort Snelling in 1828 and 1829.[58]

In June 1831 construction duties at Fort Winnebago ended abruptly. Major Twiggs took his two companies to join Col. Willoughby Morgan and his men at Fort Crawford; all then proceeded down the Mississippi to Fort Armstrong on Rock Island. Gen. Edmund Pendleton Gaines, at the request of Illinois's governor, had ordered this show of force in the hope that Black Hawk would move his people across the river peaceably. The Sac and Fox, with six other tribes, had agreed two years before to sell the land between Lake Michigan and the Mississippi to the United States and to live west of the river. But Black Hawk had disputed the sale of his village, which was on the east bank near Rock Island, and refused to move.

The situation was serious, but Lieutenant Davis found something to engage his sense of humor when General Gaines took him to a parley with Indian warriors. An aged princess, known as the mother of the tribe, began haranguing and exciting the braves. The general said it was not right for a woman to interfere and that she really must keep quiet. "Does he call *me* a woman," she shrieked, "does he say *I* am to be *silent* in the councils of my people?" The warriors became menacing. Gaines and Davis had only two soldiers with them and were far from their base. But General Gaines, always calm "in moments of great danger," had an inspiration. In his deliberate, halting speech he brought forth: "Mr. Interpreter, a—tell her—a—that—my mother—was a woman." Somehow it mollified her and saved the day.

Finally Black Hawk was persuaded, more by Gaines's troops than his eloquence, to move to the western side of the river, promising never to return, but nursing his resentment. "It was the same old encroachment . . . of might against right," says Varina, doubtless reflecting her husband's opinion. Her whole write-up gives a sense of wrong done to the natives.[59]

Gaines's successful show of force became known later as the first campaign of the Black Hawk War. Davis was at Rock Island four days. This may be when Sidney Johnston gave him "one of a pair of pistols" (Davis says "in the 'Black Hawk' campaign," but not which one). He could also have heard about the birth of the Johnstons' first child; William Preston arrived on January 5.[60]

Between the first and second campaigns, Davis's company was stationed at Fort Crawford. This older fort, at the fur-trading village of Prairie du Chien, had a few more amenities of life than Winnebago, including "a small, but well-chosen library." Even on the frontier, Davis managed to read and study. He had told Lucinda from Winnebago about ordering some law books, to begin reading for that profession, hinting, for the only time in his life, some dissatisfaction with an army career.[61]

With his ear for language, Davis savored the French of Prairie du Chien villagers, who called the Chippewas "Sauteurs" (Leapers), and the Menominees "Folles Avoines" (Wild Oats); and equally the English of other settlers, who dealt cavalierly with French place-names—Roche Percé Creek became "Roosha Persia Creek" and Butte des Morts, "Betty Mores"—and coined words like "whang" for a strip of rawhide.[62]

Other officers relieved the tedium of the frontier fort by much card-playing, much gambling, and much drinking; but not Davis. He answered late in life a newspaper canard about playing draw poker by saying "I knew that many officers . . . played 'Brag' frequently, but [never heard] of 'Poker' while I was in the army"; in any case, he was "not a participant." When Davis's friend William Selby Harney heard Davis had been charged with gambling and drinking, he shouted, "It is an infamous, cowardly lie. Why, everybody who knows Jefferson Davis knows that he never gambled in his life. He always looked upon gaming with especial aversion. . . . and never was under the influence of liquor in his life. I wish I could find the man who told that story and I'd make him swallow it."[63] Even for the amateur theatricals and "gumbo balls" (fiddle music with a bowl of gumbo for refreshment) enjoyed by officers at Fort Crawford, Davis "had no liking" according to "those who knew him here," says an historian of the fort.[64]

All this makes highly dubious a tale of Davis's dancing wildly with an Indian maiden and avoiding a fight only by the intervention of Colonel Taylor. Its only basis is "A fragment of a memoir of a Pottawottomi Chief," which appeared in the Northern press in 1878, yet some have used it to explain the coolness that developed between the two men.[65]

Davis preferred more active diversions with Captain Harney. This professional soldier, born in Middle Tennessee, had been commissioned directly into the army in 1818, at age eighteen. Davis says, "he was, physically, the finest specimen of a man I ever saw. Tall, straight, muscular, broad chested and gaunt-waisted, he was one of the class which Trelawny describes as 'natures noblemen.' "[66] Their friendship, which was to last a lifetime, began at Fort Winnebago, where they had had a great time riding "crazy horses," hunting big game—wolves, bear, elk—and fighting their dogs against wolves. Davis once jumped clear of a rearing "crazy horse" as it fell, and then as it rose, "leapt into the saddle again." (Did he think of his father?) Harney told of chasing down a wolf on foot and having "a 'fist fight' with it, during which he choked it to death by main force." Rather incongruously, Harney also "was fond of gardening, and his vegetables were noted as the finest in the fort." Harney and Davis were known for not drinking hard liquor, one of "those rocks and shoals of life in a frontier garrison," as Davis said. The two friends, though anomalies among the officers, were not alone. Zachary Taylor, soon to be their colonel, was a teetotaler.[67]

Whatever morality frontier officers had they brought with them. There was no chapel in the detailed description Davis drew of Fort Winnebago. An "enthusiastic church-woman," coming as a bride in 1830, "vainly endeavoured" to start church services. She was told there was only one officer who was "religiously disposed": "when half tipsy . . . [he] takes his Bible and Newton's Works, and goes to bed and cries over them; he thinks in this way he is excessively pious." But Jefferson Davis found someone to talk to deeply about religion, evidently during trips on detached service. The Reverend Cutting Marsh was a Congregational missionary to the Stockbridge Indians, who had been driven from their native ground to the bank of the Fox River, just west of Lake Michigan. Davis often traversed this spot, going from Fort Winnebago to Fort Howard at Green Bay. He described in a report of 1831 the very portage where the minister had his mission. On July 25, 1831, Marsh wrote Davis a letter and recorded it in his diary by this précis:

> Wrote to Lieut. Davis Ft. Winnebago. Contents of t[he] letter. First the Bill of t[he] Bibles &c Se[co]nd urged t[he] importance of his inquiring whether he could not do something for t[he] moral renovation of t[he] soldiers at t[he] Ft. Love & gratitude to t[he] Sav[ior] sh[ou]d induce it. immediately. Altho' alone he sh[oul]d not feel a sufficient excuse for declining to make an effort. David went alone against his foe & t[he] defier of the army of Israel, but in t[he] name of t[he] Ld. of hosts, & he conquered. God has without doubt something for you to do in thus bringing you as you hope to t[he] knowledge & to t[he] acknowledgement. of t[he] truth as it is in Jesus.

Although Davis had left Winnebago for Fort Crawford, he probably received the letter, for there was much traffic between them. It gives concrete evidence of his faith in these years, which must otherwise be inferred from things like his charity, for he never preached to his comrades.[68]

The first Black Hawk campaign won David Twiggs a promotion and threw command of the First Infantry to Col. Willoughby Morgan. He first sent Davis up the Yellow River to superintend the sawmill, and next, down across the Mississippi, both to keep an eye on semihostile Indians "and to prevent trespassing on the Indian territory" by whites. The Sac had recently murdered some Sioux and, fearing punishment by United States forces, had fled, abandoning their lead mines west of the river. Named for the first developer, Julien Dubuque, these mines were being eyed covetously from the eastern side. Colonel Morgan was under orders to remove any unlawful settlers. "Loth to use force," he called on Davis, "a young Officer in whom I have much confidence," to "deter from intrusions."[69]

Davis was on duty at Dubuque's mines all that winter of 1831–1832. It was most likely at this time that he sought out George Wallace Jones, whom he had not seen since leaving Lexington. Jones was living at Sinsinawa Mound (now in Wisconsin), on the eastern side of the Mississippi River. He had settled there in a log cabin as farmer, merchant, and miner after graduating from Transylvania in 1825 and then reading law in Missouri. Davis rode up to the cabin one night to surprise him, and "We talked nearly all night of our college-boy days," says Jones.[70]

On March 26, 1832, Davis turned over his command to Lt. John Gardenier and started on a furlough. The steamboats that had been a novelty in his childhood were now running regularly up the Mississippi as high as Fort Crawford. He could easily ride all the way to Natchez. He may have seen Sidney and Henrietta Johnston and baby Willie, for he stopped at St. Louis. Varina says he "became much attached to Mrs. Johnston." By April 14, he was in Natchez, and by May 26, home in Woodville. He had an offer from a railroad and was tempted to resign his commission in favor of an engineering job, as many officers were doing given the stagnation of army promotions. Brother Joseph, though not wishing to influence him ("No One can judge for an other") said, "of this [local] Rail Road I have no high opinion." Before Jeff had to decide, duty called. News came that the second campaign of the Black Hawk War was in full cry, and he immediately cut short his furlough and left to rejoin his company.[71]

Black Hawk and his people had returned to the east side of the Mississippi River on April 6. The Sac warriors and their families crossed in full view of Fort Armstrong and proceeded to the northwest corner of Illinois, where they camped, planning to stay. At Stillman's Run on May 14 they ambushed and routed the body of militia attacking them. If these had been United States troops, the Indians "would have been removed back . . . without there being a gun fired." So thought General Atkinson's second-in-command, Zachary Taylor, who had become colonel of the First Infantry on the death of Willoughby Morgan and taken command of the two companies at Fort Armstrong. This militia attack, moreover, had "brought on the war," he said.[72]

And savage war it was. "A great excitement was created" by Black Hawk's braves. "Insolent" and greedy for "more saddlebags" after plundering at Stillman's Run, they "surprised and butchered solitary families and small parties." By June, "two hundred men, women and children had met death." But there was no further military clash until militia under Generals James Henry and Henry Dodge stumbled on Black Hawk's main force. At the Battle of Wisconsin Heights, the Indians were crippled. They headed for the Mississippi above Fort Crawford, trying only to retreat across the river. "That purpose was foiled," Davis tells us, by the "arrival of a steam-boat with a gun on board. The Indians took cover in a willow marsh, and there [August 2, 1832] was fought the battle of the 'Bad Axe.' The Indians were defeated, dispersed, and the campaign ended."[73]

Exactly when Davis arrived on the scene is not known, but he spoke of being on Taylor's staff in "June, July, and August, 1832." Augustus Caesar Dodge, aide-de-camp to his father, the militia general, and George W. Jones, also an aide, recall that Davis, Harney, and Taylor shared tents and rations with the ill-provisioned volunteers, apparently in the encampment that broke up June 30.[74] Davis was with General Henry at the Battle of Wisconsin Heights: "*We* were one day pursuing" the Indians, when their crossing of the river furnished "the most brilliant exhibition of military tactics that *I* ever witnessed [italics mine]." He may have been sent by Taylor as a guide, since this country was "almost totally unknown" to these militiamen, but well known to Davis. They were returning from Fort Winnebago when they discovered the trail of the Sac. Davis was evidently at Bad Axe, for he told Preston Johnston "he could not help feeling sorry for the Indians." But again he was only an observer: he spoke of Monterey, in the Mexican War, as his "baptism" of fire.[75]

On August 18, 1832, Davis joined his company at Fort Crawford. The rumor came that Black Hawk, who had escaped the scene of Bad Axe, was on an island in the Mississippi. Taylor dispatched Davis with some men to find him. They had beat the brush in vain for some time when Davis saw a white flag on the east bank. It was Black Hawk, in the custody of Winnebagoes who said that he "had surrendered to them, and that they wanted to take him to the fort and to see the Indian agent." Davis took them, but he told Taylor he did not believe the Winnebago story. "The grand old soldier merely replied, 'They want the credit of being friendly and to get a reward, let them have it.' "[76]

President Andrew Jackson had sent Winfield Scott with enough troops to secure the frontier. From Fort Armstrong, Scott sent Lt. Robert Anderson upriver to fetch the prisoners. But Scott's men had brought cholera with them, and by the time Anderson was ready to return from Fort Crawford, he and his command were down with it. Colonel Taylor put Davis in charge of a fresh detachment. Iron handcuffs had been riveted on Black Hawk for the steamboat ride, much to his mortification. On the order of Gen. Joseph M. Street, the Indian agent, Davis had them removed. On the way downriver, Davis allowed two prisoners dying of cholera to be put ashore, as they wished, "to go to the hunting-grounds together." Varina says "his heart ached" for them, but "he never knew their fate." Black Hawk said Davis "treated us all with much kindness." "He is a good and brave young chief, with whose conduct I was much pleased." At Galena, "people crowded to the boat to see us; but the war chief would not permit them to enter the apartment where we were—knowing [from] his own feelings . . . that we did not wish to have a gaping crowd around us."[77]

When they reached Jefferson Barracks, however, having skirted infectious Fort Armstrong, Davis "was directed by his commanding officers to show [the prisoners] to several gentlemen, among whom was Washington Irving. A little vexed, he remarked to one gentleman, 'Oh, Sirs! Gentlemen, here is the Grand Lama of Tustory, worshipped in foreign parts, and here is the real live lion stuffed with straw.' Irving overheard the remark, laughed heartily and pleasantly remarked, 'I see, Sir, you do not like the part of showman,' " and they had "some pleasant conversation."[78]

In appreciation of his care, Black Hawk presented Lieutenant Davis with a pipe, and they talked over the recent war. In time, the Sac leader was conveyed to Fortress Monroe, had his portrait painted, and toured eastern cities. He was released in June 1833 and returned to die in his lodge near the Des Moines River.[79]

While at Jefferson Barracks, Davis may have called on Henrietta Johnston, who had given birth to a daughter in April. Sidney was not there. He was at Rock Island, deathly ill with cholera, lying on the floor, "wrapped in heavy blankets, drenched with vinegar and salt, and then dosed with brandy and Cayenne pepper." Despite the treatment, he survived. Davis went on downriver to finish his interrupted furlough and was back at Fort Crawford by January 1833.[80]

Once again he was sent to Dubuque's mines. The Black Hawk War treaty had thrown open to pioneers a fifty-mile-wide strip west of the Mississippi, including the mines, which became the nucleus of the state of Iowa. Army officers had been sent to secure the strip to the Indians until treaty ratification, but they had failed, and whites had taken over the mines. Lieutenant Davis was given a larger force and told to evict them. He "thought seriously and long" about the situation, then went to confront them, taking only his orderly sergeant. He was met by "a dozen or more rugged and resolute-looking men, thoroughly armed." Their spokesman said, "if he knew when he was well off he had better leave honest men alone and quit showing partiality on the Indians." "Raising his voice over their murmurings," Davis "made his first public speech," explaining that their claims would be recognized once the treaty was valid, but now they must leave. One by one they grew quiet and listened. Going back after "some weeks," he found the same crew in "a drinking booth at the edge of the mines." His orderly entreated him not to go in: "They will be certain to kill you. I heard one of them say they would." "Lieutenant Davis entered the cabin at once, and . . . [said], 'My friends, I am sure you have thought over my proposition and are going to drink to my success. So I will treat you all.'" They cheered. He spent the next weeks going to their homes to explain, carefully registering their claims, and then helping them to move. "He induced all the men to leave," says George Jones, who lived in the area. But he allowed one woman to remain, "as the winter was excessively severe." From then on, "she never met me that she did not inquire for our mutual friend," and "on her dying bed, she sent her warmest regards" to him. Davis, writing to Jones in 1882, remembered her too and said it was "a happy memory" to him that "each miner in due time came into his own." "They all, *without exception,*" says Jones, "became the warm friends and admirers of Jefferson Davis."[81]

Congress established the first United States regiment of dragoons on March 2, 1833, and on March 4, President Jackson appointed to it from the First Infantry Lt. Jefferson Davis and Capt. Richard Barnes Mason. In accepting, Davis pointed out simply, without overt complaint or request, that the appointment as second lieutenant "places me subordinate to officers formerly much my juniors." Mason had been promoted to major in the transfer. He named Davis adjutant for the forming squadron; Henry Dodge, coming to take charge as colonel, made him adjutant of the whole regiment. Both of them recommended

Davis's promotion, and when his commission was finally approved, he was first lieutenant.[82]

Before reporting to the "rendezvous of the regiment" at Jefferson Barracks, Davis went on recruiting duty to Louisville and Lexington, Kentucky. The delight of familiar places and old friends was ruined by the presence of death. The Asiatic cholera had spread over the country, engulfing Lexington just when he was there. In the first eleven days of June 1833, 169 died; by August, 502 had succumbed. Everyone who could, fled. Davis, "true to his sense of duty," stayed at his post and even arranged rations for his recruits. A letter by Henry Clay, Sr., who was at Ashland, spoke of "a frightful gloom . . . no one moving in the streets except those concerned with the dead or the sick." Very few were left to bury the dead. A drunken ne'er-do-well known as "King" Solomon gained immortal fame in the town by his heroic labor as a grave digger. Davis performed this corporal work of mercy when he came upon "a poor old negro man who, with a white man, lay dead alone in a 'shanty.' " With difficulty he found a carpenter, helped him make two coffins, "took the corpses to the cemetery, and buried them decently." Mostly, "bodies were piled in heaps at the cemetery gates" and then laid in mass graves.[83]

Passing safely through this horror, Davis reported by July 11 to Jefferson Barracks, where he was posted for four months while his regiment was forming. Surely he was pleased to be a dragoon officer, following the tradition of his father and brothers. As adjutant, he was in a position of honor, entitled to two horses instead of one, as well as extra pay. As he rode through the parade ground one day on a favorite dark brown horse, in his blue "undress coat," trimmed with orange, and "white drill Pants, made quite narrow at the boot, and quite wide at the thigh," he struck one member of the corps as the very model of "a gallant and dashing Dragoon." Davis had left behind all thought of taking up law or engineering. The army was "my vocation for life."[84]

Davis still had James Pemberton with him. His mother sent word that "Jims wife and son are in good health also Aunt Charity and all his friends." Sidney Johnston was still at Jefferson Barracks, as General Atkinson's chief of staff. Late in September, Henrietta, who was expecting their third child, became so ill that Johnston had to take her to Louisville. The baby girl was born October 28; she lived only nine months. Henrietta's lungs were affected, and she went from bad to worse.[85]

On November 20, 1833, the First Dragoons, comprising five companies, left the St. Louis area headed for Fort Gibson, five hundred miles to the southwest. Three days out, in Missouri, they met the first snowstorm; by the time they reached Fort Gibson on December 14, they were suffering from exposure, fatigue, and hunger. "They found no comfortable quarters, but passed a severe winter" in tents, with the thermometer "more than one day" standing at eight below zero. It was the first of many trials on the plains. They produced in Davis energy and endurance equal to any challenge. Sometimes there was only cold flour to eat, sometimes only buffalo meat, which then became "the most distasteful of all food." Once on a desert march, his men pleaded to turn back when the water ran low. For answer, he gave them his own, and his grog too, and told them to march on. Discipline and duty first; after that, the tender heart might be allowed to show itself.[86]

When prevailing sickness caused the dragoons to move camp from the Cherokee Nation (near Fort Gibson) to the more healthful Creek Nation (some twenty miles away), the sergeant major, John Doran, was so ill that the surgeon forbade his removal. Davis, who visited the hospital every day, was pained to tell him he could not go, says Varina, and "the man begged so hard he had him wrapped up and took him with him." "I rapidly recovered," recalled Doran just before Davis's death in 1889:

> And I hope that your temporary removal from Beauvoir to New Orleans will result in a like benefit to your health; and that, when the long roll is sounded, you will find yourself in the camp of the Grand Commander.
>
> You have been my good friend on many occasions, and have shown that your friendship to me and others has not been measured by their rank or the size of their purse.[87]

These campaigns forever protected Davis against gluttony. "He said he had observed . . . how ill the gourmets fared." Varina says, "He never noticed the viands at our own table, but ate whatever was offered." He only insisted that he have his "little pones of hoecake." The campaigns probably fixed in Davis his contempt for selfishness in any form. Varina expressed "astonishment" in later life "at his undervaluation of rather an elegant man" who had been on a campaign with him. "He answered, 'You were not at the water-hole when he scooped out two tincups full of clear water and drank it off, leaving the muddy rest for us.' "

This was probably on a famous march of two hundred miles up the Red River, when the dragoons headed for a Pawnee Pict village to pacify all the tribes of the area and to rescue two white captives. They recovered one and met peacefully with the Indians, but on the way, 150 dragoons died of typhus and dysentery in the summer heat. Davis was one of 200 who reached their destination, led by Colonel Dodge. This was the sickness, brought back to Fort Gibson, that caused the removal to the Creek Nation.[88]

When Davis and Dodge were both in the Senate in 1850, Davis argued for a mounted regiment by recalling how they had pursued Comanche and brought "the wild men" to terms with a much smaller force, showing "we are their superiors in every way." Colonel Dodge often told George Jones of Davis's "studious habits" when a dragoon and of his never "neglecting a single duty as Adjutant." All the same, Davis resigned as adjutant in February of 1834. The colonel was soon writing to Jones of how Davis and Mason wanted "to Harrass me in Small Matters they dont want to fight if Mason would Say fight I would go to the field with him with Great pleasure"—the dueling field, not the battlefield; he complained of how "dull" it was, "no prospect of War with the Indians."[89]

By the next February, Mason had Davis before a court-martial. The matter might never have been tried, except that the lieutenant demanded justice. "An experienced officer," he said, tried "to save me the investigation." This was his commander, Bvt. Brig. Gen. Matthew Arbuckle, to whom General Gaines had suggested an "arrangement" instead of a trial. But this involved an apology, which Davis refused to offer. He felt falsely accused and thought "an examination into the charges should wipe away the discredit which belonged to my arrest." A subaltern's reputation, acquired by "years of the most rigid performance of his duty, is little worth in the wide world of Fame, but yet is something to himself." (His captain said he had never known him "to neglect his duty.")[90]

The "Specification" of the charge was that he stood in his tent on December 24, 1834, at reveille roll call, and when reprimanded for this, "did, in a highly disrespectful, insubordinate, and contemptuous manner abruptly turn upon his heel and walk off, saying at the same time, Hum!" When called back, he "stared Majr. Mason full in the face" and said, "Now are you done with me?" and had to be ordered three times to go to his quarters in arrest. Davis, conducting his own defense, contended that the rule allowed being in the tent in bad weather, and that Mason, not he, had disregarded "the 11th paragraph of the 2d Article Genl. Army Regulations," which forbade disobedience, but also improper conduct by a superior.[91]

He reduced to absurdity Mason's objection to his "Hum"—"an isolated meagre interjection as little expressive as any of it's class." As for looking him in the face: "can it be required of a Gentleman, is it part of the character of a soldier to humble him self beneath the haughty tone, or quail before the angry eye of any man?" The court asked Mason whether Davis's "usual manner" might not "be considered disrespectful or even contemptuous by one not well acquainted with him?" but Mason answered, "Far from it . . . the general conduct of the accused is that of a courteous gentleman." Davis, by the testimony of witnesses, including that of lieutenant friends Izard and Northrop, and his eloquent summation, convinced the court that Major Mason, rather than he, was guilty of "abusive or unbecoming language" and "capricious" conduct. The court found Davis guilty of the "Specification," excepting disrespectful conduct and involving "no criminality." As for "the *Charge,*" "conduct subversive of good order and Military discipline," it found him "*not Guilty* . . . and do therefore acquit *him.*" "He will resume his sword."[92]

The question to Mason, rather than his answer, has long been mistaken for the truth about Davis. But he did have a sarcastic streak and a habit of taking refuge in silence when afflicted, which led to such misunderstandings. He would not tell Major Mason why he did not stand in the cold rain that December morning because Mason had rebuffed his request for sick leave and was known to give "wounding reception" to explanations of conduct. The reason came out at the trial: "an affection of the lungs, a chronic complaint," which he had been suffering for several weeks. "Self respect," he said, caused him to be "silent under censure," rather than to plead his health again. A Davis descendant thought that this trait, so marked in him, infuriated his enemies more than anything else. In fact, Davis proved in the trial that his "calm, collected bearing" that morning had irritated Mason against him.[93] As long as his own conscience was satisfied, his justification to others could await the proper occasion. An astounding instance of this had just occurred.

Second Lieutenant Lucius Bellinger Northrop was being tried on charges by Mason before the same court as Davis. They testified for each other, and it was largely Davis's word that got Northrop acquitted on a charge of malingering. He was convicted on lesser charges, but the sentence was remitted. Northrop was in fact promoted to first lieutenant. Both men said, under oath, that they had met in the fall of 1833 (when Northrop joined the dragoons). So they did not meet, as is often claimed, at West Point (where Northrop graduated 1831).[94] Northrop, tall as Davis and "straight as an arrow," was from Charleston, South Carolina. He was a youth of "great courage and manliness," a Latin scholar, and crazy about horses. His maternal grandfather, known as "Jockey John" Bellinger, had a plantation stud farm. Northrop had been arrested when he and Davis left off supervising work details to watch a horse race. (Davis got off because he had left someone in charge.)[95]

Another of Mason's charges against Northrop was that while under arrest he had gone to get a book he was reading—another affinity with Davis, who forty-five years later recalled to him a quasi-literary occasion: "Even the weary days of our camp in the Creek Nation had their happy hours, especially when Bowman performed the part of Fadladeen to Trenor's Lala Rook." Lalla Rookh was the heroine of Irish poet Thomas Moore's enormously popular oriental tale of that name, much of which Davis knew by heart. Fadladeen was a comic character who spoke in the style of the *Edinburgh Review.* "I wish we could sit down together and remount the river of our years," Davis's letter went on. "When Kingsbury . . . told us how near he came to having his brains knocked out by his horse, do you recollect how angry he got at being told that he would thus have furnished to the world evidence of his having that article?"[96]

It was probably Davis who made the smart remark about the brains. "His sense of the ludicrous was intense," and his "incisive wit" and intelligence combined to produce satire, which sometimes got him into trouble. "Your haughty and sarcastic style of younger days," Northrop called it:

> I laugh now in thinking of your cruelty to old Col. Whistler who at Wilson's store one morning asked you to lend him your grey horse to ride to the Vindegres [*sic*], you replied, "Oh no Col. I am not going to lend you my horse to run away from home." Poor old fellow, he took it so humbly that I was sorry for him at the time,—I think, though enjoying it as much now while writing as formerly. You were terrible sometimes.

Northrop admitted, "My eyes dance with fun whenever I think of it."[97] He was taken aback when Davis replied:

> Poor old Col. I am very sorry to have said anything to him which others thought was offensive. I did not feel unkindly to him, and even at this remote time will explain the matter to you. I was sure if he had my horse he would go off and get drunk at some house in the [Creek] nation, and stay there until he was brought back. Just such a case had occurred at Green Bay, and he came near to being dismissed. His large family was dependent on his pay, and his wife would have expected me to keep him out of trouble, rather than to help him into it.[98]

"You acted very virtuously with old Whistler," Northrop answered; "Your humility surpasses his in making confession to me." The humility lay rather in Davis and his silence. He was willing to bear for forty-five years the stigma of "cruelty," rather than to put Whistler in a bad light by revealing his reason for what was an act of charity. No wonder Colonel Whistler paid him "a friendly visit" in the 1850s and Mrs. Whistler, when widowed, found his frequent calls "a great joy." Davis was glad Northrop implied that by this time, 1879, he had "lost hauteur and sarcasm." "If I have not acquired the 'greatest of all charity' better appreciation of my own weakness has probably given me more forbearance towards others, than existed in the pride and self confidence of youth."[99]

This letter also recalled a "controversy" with a different colonel, where Davis's manner affected his whole future. He was "right as to the principle," he said, "but impolitic in the manner of asserting it. A mean fellow misrepresented me, the Col. believed him and assailed me harshly, imputing to me motives the reverse of those by which I was actuated.

Then I became wrong as angry men are apt to be." This colonel was Zachary Taylor, and he was "highly incensed" too. Their only falling-out known was over whether a lieutenant would be excused from full uniform when sitting on a court-martial. Taylor was already angry with Maj. Thomas F. Smith, and when Davis and Smith voted against him on this issue, Taylor "swore, as an officer only in those days could swear, that no man who voted with 'Tom Smith' should ever marry his daughter."[100] This explosion was the remote reason when Davis resigned his commission as first lieutenant of dragoons, on March 2, 1835.

He asked General Arbuckle to "date and Transmit" his resignation if he did not return by the expiration of his leave, granted at the same time. Before he left Fort Gibson, he threw a "champagne treat" for his friends. Northrop recalled that after it, Davis tried to "infuse a little [theology] into me"—surely a spiritual work of mercy in the least likely place. The champagne, equally unlikely, probably celebrated not his departure, but his approaching marriage.[101]

V

Marriage

If Jefferson Davis had not become "the idol of the army," as Waller Redd hoped, he had made his mark. General Arbuckle, who held the resignation far past the deadline, finally sent it to General Gaines with the hope that he had received a countermanding letter from Davis, "a young officer of much intelligence and great promise."[1]

Col. Zachary Taylor, who knew Davis even better, said that he had for him "personally and officially the highest opinion of *respect and regard.*" That was when the lieutenant was "attentive to his daughter" (but doubtless before the affair of the court-martial uniform). Taylor's daughter Sarah Knox, who had been in school in Cincinnati, came to Fort Crawford only in 1832, when her parents returned from a furlough in Louisville. The elder Taylor daughter, Ann Mackall, had already married army surgeon Robert Crooke Wood and was living in the "wilderness surroundings of Fort Snelling" with two children when Jeff Davis came courting Knox (as the family called her). Her little sister Betty (Mary Elizabeth) was nine, and her only brother, Dick (Richard), was seven. Knox was nineteen and uncommonly pretty.[2]

Betty remembered her "great vivacity and charm of manner." Her best friend thought she resembled her father, with his "splendid hazel eye and strong even teeth," except that her figure was exquisitely small. A cousin spoke of "wavy brown hair and clear gray eyes" and called Knox "witty . . . clever . . . graceful as a nymph, and the best dancer in the State of Kentucky."[3]

Jeff and Knox had so little time together that it must have been love at first sight, and overwhelmingly strong. Nine days after he reached Fort Crawford, Davis was sent to bring in Black Hawk and then, a week later, to take him downriver. He returned from his interrupted leave in January 1833 and served through the winter at the Dubuque mines. In the spring he was appointed to the dragoons and was off to Lexington, Jefferson Barracks, and Fort Gibson. This itinerary alone bears mute witness to the suddenness and strength of their love. Her father had not at first opposed the match.[4]

Zachary Taylor was a soldier through and through, a man of great force, of great candor, born a Virginia gentleman and raised on the Kentucky frontier. His "simplicity and modesty," his "frank and unaffected bearing" were remarked, not only by Jefferson Davis, but by almost all who knew him. Even his bitterest enemy, Winfield Scott, who made fun of his simplicity as "childlike," admitted that he "had the true basis of a great character:—pure, uncorrupted morals, combined with indomitable courage."[5] These sound a lot like descriptions of Davis, and Taylor was like him in other ways too. A frequently stern aspect hid an affectionate nature that made him a favorite with children: "The bravest are, as a rule, the gentlest," Davis said in 1878. Long before that, on the Senate floor, he had contrasted Taylor's "eagle eye" in battle with its "mother's softness" toward the wounded (Davis among them) in the Mexican War. Under Taylor's warmth and cordiality ran a will like a steel spring, sensitive to pressure indeed, but strongly set. "When he had once formed a friendship, or adopted a resolution after due deliberation, no earthly power could make him desert the one or abate the other."[6]

At first Lieutenant Davis, with his "polished manners and . . . quiet, intellectual countenance," was welcome at the colonel's quarters at Fort Crawford, where Margaret (Peggy) Taylor happily kept house. His family was certainly acceptable, and maybe already known to Taylor, who was now a slave-holding planter. When stationed at Baton Rouge in 1823, he had purchased and worked land in Feliciana Parish, Louisiana, and had recently bought 137 acres next to it in Wilkinson County, Mississippi—all in the midst of similar Davis settlements. But when the young Davis asked for his daughter's hand in marriage, the colonel said no.[7]

This led to a persistent slander that Davis "stole away the lovely daughter of Genl. Taylor—his benefactor and, too, confiding friend." When George W. Jones read this insulting version in 1880, he was outraged: "I knew it was all a *lie.*" He went to Prairie du Chien (by then, Wisconsin) and asked Taylor's good friend, H. L. Dousman, about it. Dousman said Taylor had no objection to the marriage, "except that he already had a daughter married to an army officer." He would prefer a civilian "*only* because" of the "anxiety army officers' wives had."[8] Or, as the colonel more characteristically said to Maj. Stephen Watts Kearny: "I will be damned if another daughter of mine shall marry into the Army. . . . I know enough of the family life of officers. I scarcely know my own children or they me. I have no personal objections to Lieutenant Davis."[9]

The lovers were willing to wait, hoping for a change of heart. But then came the blowup over Tom Smith. Davis said it was "a dispute about a point of etiquette on a court martial" and caused "alienation . . . nothing more." But it was enough to throw the young people back on their own devices.[10]

Some of Zachary's fire flowed in Knox's veins—"a young woman of decided spirit," her cousin said. She was not rebellious. She simply declared that she would never marry anyone but Davis. "The time will come when you will see as I do all his rare qualities," she told her father. And she had her ways. She would take Betty and Dick on walks, where Jeff could find them. She would visit the house of Mary Street (who was in similar trouble over wanting to marry Lt. George Wilson) or the tent of Capt. and Mrs. Samuel MacRee and their children, knowing that Jeff would be there. Although she very much wanted her parents' approval, she did not wait for it. Before Jeff left Fort Crawford, he and Knox considered themselves engaged.[11]

For two whole years they remained steadfast, and so far as is known, with only letters to sustain them. All but one were lost when Union soldiers vandalized Davis's papers in 1863.[12] That one is to Knox, written from Fort Gibson, "Dec 16th 1834," and reads:

> Tis strange how superstitious intense feeling renders us. but stranger still what aids chance sometimes brings to support our superstition, dreams my dear Sarah we will agree are our weakest thoughts, yet by *dreams* have I been latly almost crazed, for they were of you and the *sleeping* imagination painted you not such as I left you, not such as I could like and see you, for you seemed a sacrifice to your parents desire the bride of a wretch that your pride and sense equally compelled you to despise . . . but last night the vision was changed you were at the house of an Uncle in Kentucky, Capt McCree was walking with you when I met you he left you and you told me of your Father and of yourself almost the same that I have read in your letter to night. Kind, dear letter, I have kissed it often and it has driven many mad notions from my brain. Sarah whatever I may be hereafter I will ascribe to you. Neglected by you I should be worse than nothing and if the few good qualities I possess shall under your smiles yield a fruit it will be your's as the grain is the husbandman's.
>
> It has been a source productive of regret with me that our union must seperate you from your earliest and best friends, a test to which the firmness of very few are equal, though giddy with passion or bouant by the hope of reconciliation there be many who brave it, from you I am prepared to expect all that intellect and dignified pride brings, the question as it has occured to you is truly startling Your own answer is the most grattifying to me, is that which I should expected from you, for as you are the first with whom I ever [s]ought to have one fortune so you would be

> the last from whom I would expect desertion. When I wrote to you I supposed you did not intend soon to return to Kentucky. I approve entirely of your preference to a meeting elsewhere than at Prarie-du-Chien and your desire to avoid any embarrassment might widen the breach made already cannot be greater than my own, did I know when you would be at St Louis I could meet you there. At all events we meet in Kentucky. Shall we not soon meet Sarah to part no more? oh! how I long to lay my head upon that breast which beats in unison with my own, to turn from the sickening sights of worldly duplicity and look in those eyes so eloquent of purity and love.

After some bantering answers to jealous inquiries about "Miss Bullitt" and "la belle Elvin" ("My dear girl I have no secrets from you") and assurance that the "'heart's ease'" she gave him is "bright as ever," he ends:

> The griefs over which we weep are not those to be dreaded. It is the little pains the constant falling of drops of care which wear away the heart, I join you in rejoicing that Mrs McCree is added to your society. I admire her more than any one else you could have had . . . My lines like the beggars days are dwindling to the shortest span. Write to me immediately My dear Sarah My betrothed No formality is proper between us. Adieu Ma chere tres chere amie adieu au Recrire
>
> Jeffn.[13]

A purity even in dreams surfaces; an undercurrent of sadness surprises. "Your Father . . ." may refer to her telling Taylor that since she had waited so long and "he had not alleged anything against Lieutenant Davis's character or honor, she would therefore marry him." The lovers seem already to have planned the wedding and Jeff's leaving the army. Eliza Davis was expecting them at the Hurricane "before Christmas," hoping the doors of Jeff's room would open "for yourself—& one equally as dear to you." "Bring Basto—as well as your pretty wild horse," her postscript reads: "*I* remind you of this—fearing a more precious charge Might occupy all your thoughts."[14]

Their plans had obviously changed before Jeff's arrest on Christmas Eve. But he had this secret reason, that cold, rainy morning, for not wanting to risk illness. Perhaps they decided to wait for Knox to turn twenty-one on March 6, or for her to be maid of honor in Mary Street's wedding to George Wilson on March 26. Betty Taylor said "there was never any estrangement between Gen. Taylor and his daughter" and that he had withdrawn his opposition. But Knox said she was marrying without her parents' "sanction," which seems to support Varina's story of her last futile attempt to win over her father as she left on the steamboat from Fort Crawford.[15] There was certainly no secrecy. She had been making her trousseau with her mother's help, and sister Ann, Dr. Wood, and the children went down to Louisville for the marriage. She may have gone down with them, for ladies did not travel alone.[16]

Lieutenant Davis stayed to testify in Northrop's trial on March 9, then he left for St. Louis. He wrote to Mrs. Taylor from there. Knox, he had told someone else, was already "in Kentucky with her aunt." He could not see the Johnstons at Jefferson Barracks this trip. Henrietta had been diagnosed as consumptive, and Sidney, after "a severe struggle," had resigned from the army, as she wanted, and bought a farm. They had visited many doctors and watering places and were spending "the few remaining months allotted her on earth" at the country house of her uncle, George Hancock, near Louisville.[17]

It is possible that Jeff saw them there, for he was headed to nearby Beechland, the home of Knox's aunt, Elizabeth Taylor. The colonel, seeing that Knox was going to have her way, had asked his widowed sister to have the wedding. He sent a "kind and affectionate letter" to Knox, and a "liberal supply of money." "My dear father," she called him, acknowledging these on the day of her marriage.[18]

It was June 17, 1835. She wore "a dark traveling dress" with a small bonnet to match. Jeff had "a long-tail cutaway coat, brocaded waistcoat, breeches tight-fitting and held under the instep with a strap, and a high stovepipe hat" (doffed for the ceremony). The Taylors had always been Episcopalian. The rector of Louisville's Christ Church read the prayer book service in the east parlor at Beechland. Hancock Taylor, Zachary's older brother, had gone with Jeff that morning to secure the marriage bond.[19] He gave the bride away. None of Jeff's family were there. Taylor cousins served as maid of honor and best man, and there was another Taylor aunt and plenty of children. One of them was John Taylor Wood, then almost five—the same who fled the scene of Davis's capture thirty years later. One recalled: "After the service everybody cried but Davis, and the Taylor children thought this most peculiar."[20]

The lower Mississippi valley had been spared its usual epidemic of yellow fever in 1835. This had altered the young couple's plans. On the day of the wedding, the bride wrote:

> You will be surprised, no doubt, my dear mother, to hear of my being married so soon; When I wrote to you last I had no idea of leaving here before fall; but hearing the part of the country to which I am going is quite healthy I have concluded to go down this summer and will leave here this afternoon at 4 o'clock.

The girl was deeply attached to her family. In addition to thanking the general for his gift in this letter, she sent "my best love to pa and Dick."

Having sister Ann there made her "feel not so entirely destitute" without her mother. She begged her to write, saying,

> You, my dearest Mother, I know will still retain some feelings of affection for a child who has been so unfortunate as to form a connection without the sanction of her parents, but who will always feel the deepest affection for them whatever may be their feelings toward her. . . . I send a bonnet by sister, the best I could get. I tried to get you some cherries to preserve, but could not. . . . Believe me always, your affectionate daughter,
>
> Knox[21]

As soon as the cake and wine were served in the west parlor at Beechland, the newly pronounced "Man and Wife" boarded an Ohio River steamboat, headed for the Hurricane. "All ashore" separated them from family and friends, and the "heavy steamboat bell toll[ed] for . . . all an adieu." Since Jeff's first trip at the age of ten, boats had become "floating palaces."

There were few stops on the passage down, except for isolated "wooding places," where the "coughing monster" would pause to take on thirty or more cords of cut timber to supply steam for the next stretch. In the leisurely pace forced by the Mississippi's meanderings, Jeff and Knox could see row upon row of cotton, stretching gray-green on either side, giving way to the dense cane of a semitropical climate, and then suddenly, around a big bend, Vicksburg—"a beautiful place" on a hill, said a traveler, with the houses "in clusters scattered here and there over the declivity. The streets are of good width and the people have considerable enterprise."[22]

At Vicksburg the couple might have left the riverboat and continued twenty-five miles overland to the Hurricane. If they went by water, they could get off at the Woods' Ursino Landing below or Palmyra Landing above, owned by the Turner-Quitman family. The mansion was meant to be approached from its own landing, but this was not always possible because of shifting currents and a big sandbar known as Hurricane Island.[23] However they came, this was Jeff's first sight of the Hurricane. Eliza had said in November, "Our House is unfinished—perhaps will get into it before March. . . . We have quite a Colony here—seven Carpenters two brick layers & one *Physician* so he calls himself." They also had mechanics from Cincinnati rigging up a tank in the attic that was to be pumped full every morning from three huge cisterns, giving the new house a rare convenience: bathrooms with running water.[24]

The long circular drive from Hurricane Landing led through the "many acres of splendid oaks," magnolias, and arching pecan trees, and near the house, past camellia bushes. The house was huge, with "galleries that ran nearly all around it, upstairs and down."[25] One entered through paneled doors into a wide hall, off which opened four

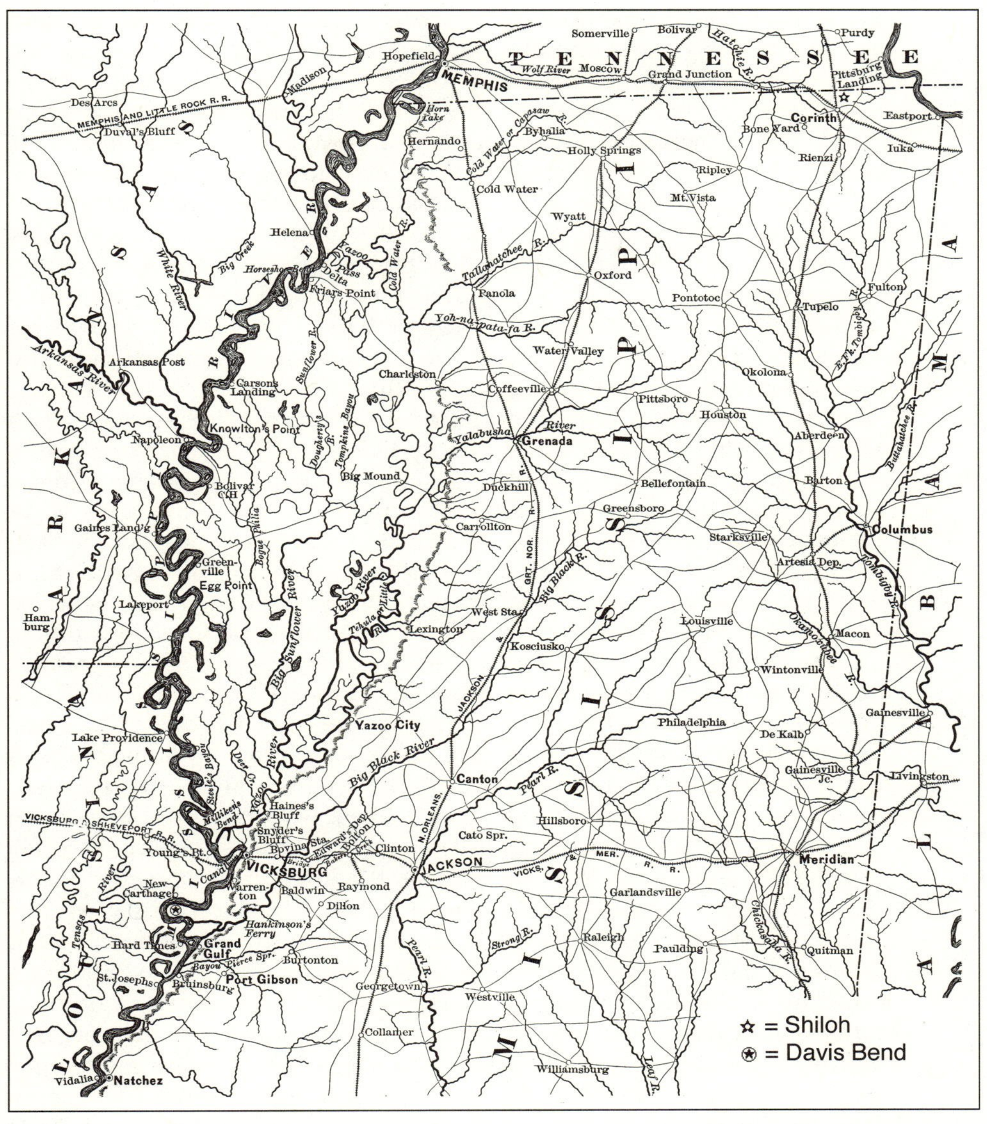

Mississippi (with southwest Tennessee), with Davis Bend and Shiloh indicated

rooms. As Varina remembered it: "On the right-hand side of the hall were the drawing-room and the 'tea-room,' where the ladies sat; on the other, was a bedchamber and the 'office.'" "The windows were small, the walls were thick," and the ceilings "low" (perhaps only compared to Brierfield's sixteen-foot ones). The second and third stories held four bedrooms each, to accommodate the never-ceasing flow of visitors. The first-floor chamber was Joseph's, and adjoining it was a storeroom, "out of which came . . . candy, negro shoes, field implements, new saddles and bridles, fancy plaid linsey or calico dresses for the negro women who needed consolation for a death in their families; guns and ammunition for hunting, pocket-knives, nails, and screws. This little closet was an ark, of which Mr. J. E. Davis kept the key, and made provision for the accidental needs of 'each one after his kind.'"[26]

Behind the house, covered walkways led to "a large annex of two rooms forty-three feet long and twenty-five wide. The lower one was a dining-room," says Varina, and the arched upper one was "the 'music-room,' where the young people sang and played, acted charades, gave mock concerts, and improvised games, while the family portraits looked stolidly down upon our antics."[27] One of these was of Joseph as a young man. He had had it done when he lived in Greenville, because a portraitist named William Edward West had fled the fever in Natchez and was doing prominent people in the area.[28] There was also a portrait of Eliza and perhaps one of the patriarch, Samuel Emory Davis.[29]

Joseph could show Knox through a virtual village: very large barn, stables for thirty-odd horses, coach house, combined commissary and overseer's apartment, the "Hall of Justice" (where slaves held court), the slaves' hospital, workshops where shoes, wagons, and plows were made, and "a small hamlet of whitewashed cabins"—the quarters for the field hands. Behind the "annex" was the kitchen and laundry, with "bedrooms above for the house servants." Beyond Eliza's garden was an eight-acre orchard. At Hurricane Landing stood the warehouse where cotton, ginned and baled on the place, was stored until loaded on boats bound for Vicksburg or New Orleans.[30] There was a "garden cottage," more fittingly called "Greek temple." The roof, sloping from a central chimney, was supported on all sides by square Doric columns twenty feet tall. Four "French windows" on each side opened into two rooms with brick floors and "huge fireplaces." They housed Joseph's treasured library as well as extra guests.[31]

A quarter mile from the house, within a wrought iron fence, Knox might look down upon a stone slab covering the remains of Samuel Davis and wonder how she and her father-in-law would have got on, had he not taken the fever on the river eleven years before. It was nearing the anniversary of his death, July 4. Other graves bespoke the great uncertainty of life and Joseph's kindly nature. There were a ten-year-old Bradford nephew and Isaac's child killed by the hurricane that gave the plantation its name. A "Mrs. Wallace" from Kentucky—most likely the wife of Joseph's mentor there—had died while visiting, leaving an orphaned granddaughter whom Joseph and Eliza then raised as their own.[32]

Joseph's self-contained community was so stable that even Independence Day 1835 could not shake it. In Mississippi, the Fourth of July meant that slaves could come together "from the different plantations, and enjoy themselves in uninterrupted feasting and festivity." Certain men saw in this the perfect moment for an uprising. Whites would have been massacred in 1835 on the Big Black River in Madison County, just northeast of Davis Bend, had the plot not been exposed. "The knife has been raised over us," wrote Samuel Gwin.[33] As authorized by the Mississippi constitution of 1832 in case of imminent peril,[34] a Committee of Safety was elected at Livingston. It had the powers of a court, and its trials, "if not formal at least *substantial*," forestalled lynchings (two of which had occurred), acquitted five whites, and on July 4 executed five, the chief culprit being a New Englander. The six black plotters were hanged by a committee elsewhere.[35]

Despite warnings, no one had been alarmed. The only police force, the civilian patrol of the roads, was not even operating. As Mary Chesnut said, "If they want to kill us, they can do it when they please. . . . But nobody is afraid of their own negroes." Even after servants had murdered a kinswoman, she "would go down on the plantation tomorrow and stay there, if there were no white person in twenty miles."[36] How could abolition writers understand? "Think of these holy New Englanders, forced to have a negro village walk through their houses whenever they saw fit." Blacks shared the feeling of security. The very pass one needed to go off the place was to show the road patrol (seldom in operation) that he or she belonged somewhere. The sense of belonging, of being needed, was strong. No one could get Andrew Jackson's servant Hannah to leave the room where he was dying: "I was born and raised on the place, and my place is here." "Shoo!" said the Chesnut servant Laurence, "I knew Mars Jeems could not do without me." "And indeed he cannot," agreed Mary.[37]

So, when abolitionists talked in 1858 of slaves revolting, Jefferson Davis was able to reply, in New York City: "Our doors are unlocked at night. . . . We lie down to sleep trusting to them for our defence, and the bond between the master and the slave is as near as that which exists between capital and labor anywhere." Of these relations, he said, the abolitionist "knows literally nothing." After the scare in 1835, though two whites accused of complicity lived in Davis Bend's Warren County, he borrowed money from Joseph and bought ten slaves.[38]

It was the only manual labor to be had.[39] He needed it to work more than a thousand acres next to the Hurricane.[40] This land was called "the Brierfield," from the "dense growth of briers . . . interlocked over the land." Joseph gave it to Jeff "in lieu of" his share "in his father's negroes." His only servant thus far had been James Pemberton.[41] Now he also took over the care of some servants he had known all his life: "Old Uncle Bob" and his wife, Farah, and others. He spoke in 1865 of "Tom. & Charley" as expressing "the feeling of all our family negroes, I hope their fidelity will be duly rewarded and regret that we are not in a situation to aid and protect them." Some planters called their workers their "black family."[42] The Davises generally said, "Our people." Property they may have been, technically, but living with them, providing for them, sharing joys and sorrows, made them first of all human beings to their owners.[43]

Southerners were never very good at seeing people abstractly. What Jefferson Davis saw abstractly was servitude: "Chattel slavery never existed in this country"—it was merely a term used "to excite prejudice."[44] He explained that only "a lifelong right to service and labor" could be purchased and that "life and person" were protected by laws making it "a crime to kill or maim a slave" as much as a white man. "Slaves were therefore not chattels."[45] Davis pointed out this protection and the double identity "as a person and as property" in the U.S. Senate. "Sympathy" with the slaves had been "somewhat suppressed, it is true, but not destroyed by the offensive and mischievous interference of our northern brethren with a domestic relation which they do not understand and cannot appreciate [i.e., evaluate justly]."[46]

Sarah Knox Taylor Davis was finding life happy among people who thought her "refined, intelligent, sincere, and very engaging in her manners." It showed as she answered an "affectionate letter" from her mother: "I imagine so often I can see you moving . . . down in the cellar skimming the milk or going to feed the chickens. . . . Tell Dick I have a beautiful colt, prettier than his, I expect." She asked about "dear little Betty" and sent "love to Pa and Dick . . . Sister [Ann] and the Doc. . . . Do not make yourself uneasy about me; the country is quite healthy." It was August 11, 1835.

The summer of 1820 had given Knox ample reason for reassuring her mother. They had been at Bayou Sara, Louisiana, then, when "a violent bilious fever" swept away the "sweet intelligent" three-year-old Octavia. The others, except Taylor, who was away on duty, had come down with it. Knox, who was six, her sister Ann, and her mother recovered. But the year-old baby, Margaret, died also. Now, in 1835, when "what is known on the Mississippi as 'the chill-and-fever season,'" approached, writes Varina, "it was thought advisable for the young couple to seek a more healthful place." What strange disquiet Knox must have felt when she learned they were going "to visit his sister, Mrs. Luther Smith, at her 'Locust Grove' plantation near Bayou Sara, La."[47]

Unaware that mosquitoes were carriers of malaria, people thought the danger lay in being "unacclimated" or in the swamps. It was generally believed that decaying vegetable matter produced fever: the "marsh miasm or malaria" (literally, "bad air").[48] Jeff and Knox were probably bitten by Anopheles mosquitoes before they ever reached Locust Grove.

> Very soon after their arrival Mr. Davis was taken very ill with malarial fever, and, the day after, Mrs. Davis became ill also. They were both suffering greatly, but he was considered very dangerously ill, and they were nursed in different rooms. He was too ill to be told of her peril, and delirium saved her from anxiety about him. Soon after the fever set in she succumbed to it, and hearing her voice singing loud and clear a favorite song, "Fairy Bells," he struggled up and reached her bedside—to find her dying. The poor young creature drew her last sigh September 15, 1835, and was buried in his sister's family burying-ground.

On her sarcophagus in "God's Acre" appear the simple words "Sarah Knox Davis / Wife of Jefferson Davis / Died 15th Sep. 1835 / Aged 21 years." There is no "Taylor" in the name—she belongs to the Davises.[49]

Quinine was already in use, and possibly it saved Jeff's life. Davis was to depend on this anti-periodic for the rest of his life; during "the season" in 1851, he took it daily as a preventive. In 1835, "his life was despaired of for a month." But at last, "when able to be lifted in his faithful James's arms, he returned to 'The Hurricane.'"[50]

Return can have brought only pain at the sight of Knox's trousseau and wedding gifts. He lovingly preserved them, and some remnants may be seen even today: her white kid gloves and embroidered sash, and a teacup in deep blue floral design. It is said that Jeff, coming upon Knox's slipper in a trunk years later, fainted. Her prayer book may have brought some consolation. After the committal, "earth to earth, ashes to ashes, dust to dust," came the words "looking for the general resurrection . . . and the life of the World to come." The prayers following assured him that "the souls of the faithful . . . are in joy and felicity" and looked for "perfect consummation and bliss, both in body and soul, in thy eternal and everlasting glory."[51] Jeff repeated many times in years to come the thought that the dead are the lucky ones, the survivors the losers.

Another early death tried Jeff's faith. Henrietta Johnston had passed away on August 12, leaving Sidney, too, a youthful widower. He at least had two children for comfort—William Preston and a daughter named for her mother, whom they called "Hennie." Although he had found it "hard to abandon his chosen career," he refused to use influence now to get back into the army. He was flopping disconsolately between Louisville and the Missouri farm, unsure of what he would do.[52]

Slowly, Jeff edged back toward normal life and was well enough in November to write to Fort Gibson, trying to settle some old quartermaster accounts. But he was emaciated and had a serious cough. Joseph and Eliza thought travel would help and packed him off to "the soft air" of Havana, Cuba, with James to look after him. Three weeks on a sailing vessel, with buckets of seawater dousing him for baths, started his recovery. This was his first voyage, and he took to the sea with a love that never left. On the island, he haunted the hills with sketchbook in hand, watching soldiers drill—a "clinging memory and affection" for his profession, so lately sacrificed. This nearly got him arrested. "Your bearing and walk proclaim you a soldier," an official warned; if he continued to watch drills and sketch fortifications he would be "put on the walls to break stones." This "espionage" against him made him "sick at heart," he told Varina later.[53]

Something else did too. In his bereavement, he sought out the dear associations of his childhood in the Catholic Church, easy enough in Spanish Cuba. He recalled in prison, years later, "the noble ceremonial of the High Mass, with all the brilliant surroundings which in the richly endowed Cathedrals are associated with it," and also his disillusion:

> My early impressions and continuing affection for the Priests of "Saint Thomas" led me to clothe all their brethren in a moral robe as white as the toga of my early friends. In Havanna I first learned how great was the mistake & elsewhere and subsequently was forced to believe that the vows which had seemed so well to fit the Roman Priest for the ministry of God, were in some places and with some, perhaps, in all places,—"cheap as custom-house oaths."

This disappointment may have prevented a renewed attempt to become Catholic, but he still called the Church his first love, still admired the clergy standing "between the despots and their victims, sublimely defying the rage of one and divinely bending to raise the other." He cherished the "heroic spirit" in which they cared for the suffering "in plague, pestilence and famine; in the wilderness and on fields of blood; in the prison, on the scaffold and among the deserted mourners"—"nobly have they maintained the glory of their order."[54]

Deprived of both spiritual solace and his one amusement in Cuba, still unwell, unhappy, Davis was "irritated into extreme nervousness." Seeing a ship making ready, he "suddenly decided to sail in her to New York." This he did, also touching New England and visiting Washington, where he met John C. Calhoun and John Tyler, then a Virginia senator.[55] He found in Tyler a kindred spirit. "I worship at the shrine of truth and honor," Tyler said. He had just decided to resign, rather than disobey either his conscience or the legislature which had elected him. When he made up his mind to "drain [this chalice] even to the dregs," not even Calhoun and Henry Clay could dissuade him from his "unnecessarily sacrificial" decision. (The other Virginia senator had simply disobeyed instructions and stayed.) Tyler may have inspired young Davis, who often weighed all advice against an unpleasant duty, and then did it anyway. The two men hit it off splendidly when they met again in 1845 and were finally united in the Confederacy.[56]

When he got home, Davis began again to clear his Brierfield acreage. In "late September," he went "to Esplanade street [New Orleans] to purchase slaves." By October 27, 1836, he owned twenty-three, on which he had to pay $14.75 in taxes.[57] He rewarded James Pemberton's years of loyal service by promoting him to plantation manager. He made a good one. Varina calls him "dignified," "of fine manly appearance, very silent, but what he said was always to the point." That propriety, mutually understood, which governed plantation life allowed Davis and him to be "devoted friends." James, for example, "never sat down without being asked, and his master always invited him to be seated, and sometimes fetched him a chair."[58]

It was not unusual for black men to be overseers. Andrew Jackson had Uncle Alfred, also a devoted friend. Black assistant overseers, called "drivers," were ubiquitous. Davis's slave Uncle Bob had been one "in General Washington's time." In old age, he "used to ride over Brierfield every day, and at the end of a nine months' session of Congress he could . . . tell the course of events on the place during our absence. . . . He could neither read nor write, but [his] memory was entirely accurate . . . and his word was unimpeachable."[59]

In clearing Brierfield, they found the cane "too thick to be uprooted or cut, and they burned it, and then dug little holes in the ground and put in the cotton-seed, which made an unusually fine crop." Varina tells this, saying the price of cotton eventually made the plantation "very remunerative." But until the mid-forties, the market was off, because of the panic of 1837 in America and hard times in Great Britain, a chief buyer. George Jones remembers that Davis was "pressed for money" when he visited Washington "in the early winter of 1837–38." He was again traveling for his health, going, as before, by way of Havana and New York. He visited Eliza Davis's brother, Watson Van Benthuysen, editor of the *New York American*, and went to a showing of George Catlin's Indian paintings, done on the dragoon expedition of 1834. Davis later said: "With pleasure I recognized the countenances of many a stalwart chief, and the shadowy record of many a scene of adventure, once a reality to my sight."[60]

On the way from New York, Davis became unwell and was attended to by an army surgeon at Baltimore. In Christmas week, he was confined to his Washington hotel "with a severe cough and considerable fever, which latter became intermittent [malarial]." On January 1, 1838, he ventured out to the traditional New Year's Day reception given by the president, now Martin Van Buren. But the White House was "closely crowded," and "being weak of body and luke warm of spirit," he wrote Joseph, "I hung like a poor boy at a frolick about the empty corners for a short time and left the House without being presented."

He described himself to George Jones as "pale and yellow" that winter. This sickness was not the only reason. After a champagne supper party, Ohio senator William Allen ("somewhat intoxicated") was to guide Davis ("perfectly sober") home through the Washington streets. Jones could hear Allen's "stentorian voice" as they came up Capitol Hill to Dowson's boardinghouse. Jones was in the room of Dr. Lewis Linn, one of Missouri's senators, and when the pair reached it, he saw blood "streaming down over [Davis's] face, and upon his white tie, shirt-front, and white waistcoat . . . from a deep cut in his head." "His clothes were drenched with water and stained with mud." Allen had missed the footbridge over the Tiber, and they had both fallen into the creek. Allen had landed on his feet and was still "repeating the speech which he had been delivering." Davis was becoming faint "from the loss of blood." Dr. Linn dressed the "severe wounds on his head" and got him to bed in the next room. The next morning, Jones found him unconscious. "After several hours' hard work," rubbing him with camphor and ether, he and Linn restored Davis. "Dr. Linn remarked that he would have been dead had I been five minutes later in reaching him."[61]

Davis now was staying with Jones at the boardinghouse, where he "messed," with forty-odd members of Congress, including Thomas Hart Benton, now a senator from Missouri, and Franklin Pierce, from New Hampshire. It was quite the fashion to board in Washington, with or without one's family. Joseph Davis had wished for his brother to visit Washington, so as "to form some acquaintan[c]e [with] the working of the machine of Govt." Now Jeff was living right among the cogs and wheels. He was soon invited to the "Executive Mansion" for breakfast. Van Buren, who, Varina says, had "refined taste" and was "*soigné*" in his person, was talking to Davis "of the army, of general politics," and so on, when he suddenly noticed Davis's feet "at their best in a pair of New Orleans shoes, and said, 'Where did you get your shoes, may I ask? I had a pair like that made in France, but have never seen that stitch since.' "[62]

While meeting President Van Buren may have seemed to the young Jacksonian Democrat to be the high point of his visit, it was really meeting the man who introduced him, for he and Franklin Pierce would become friends for life. Nathaniel Hawthorne, Pierce's college-mate at Bowdoin, remembered his "blue eyes and light curling hair, and a sweet expression of face" to go with his "generous and affectionate nature." Davis's description of him, said John Daniel, was "equally applicable" to himself: "Chivalrous, generous, amiable, true to his faith, frank and bold in the declaration of his opinions, he never deceived anyone. And, if treachery had ever come near him, it would have stood abashed in the presence of his truth, his manliness, and his confiding simplicity."[63]

As with Sidney Johnston, simplicity and spiritual affinity bound them together. But with Pierce, there was something more. Davis showed for the first time that he was deeply interested in politics. While an army officer, he had not been able to participate. Officers were in service to the whole country, he once explained, rather than to "the states in whose hands are all political power." "They took no part in political agitations"; "a proper delicacy forbade it." Zachary Taylor, for example, "never voted in his life." Davis's brother-in-law David Bradford had written to him, however, about the Louisiana politics in which he was embroiled, and Joseph Davis was big in "the Democracy" in Mississippi.[64]

Pierce, at thirty-three, was the youngest senator, a Yankee but a state rights Democrat. He argued and voted on principle, which Davis called the "cement of political parties." His new friend saw him as "a statesman and a patriot" at this time, discussing "those great principles on which the political schools of our country have always been divided." Pierce "knew no North, no South, no East, no West," said Davis, but steadily adhered "to the fundamental truths of" the Democratic Party, which guarded the interests of all sections by strict construction of the Constitution.[65]

Davis had held for a long time his basic belief in "our novel and admirable form of government, in which the States are independent though united, and the general government supreme in its functions, though devoid of all power except that which has been delegated to it by the States." At the height of the nullification crisis over the tariff, before its settlement in 1833, Lieutenant Davis had believed his regiment might be ordered to South Carolina "to enforce the execution of the laws."

> By education, by association, and by preference I was a soldier; then regarding that profession as my vocation for life. Yet, looking the issue squarely in the face, I . . . was prepared to resign my commission immediately . . . rather than be employed in the subjugation or coercion of a State of the Union.

He was to mention this in 1850, when Texas was threatened with coercion, saying he believed that it was "the sentiment of every portion" of the country: "You must raise a foreign army . . . when you attempt with sword and bayonet to enforce your laws upon the citizens of the United States. . . . This Union can never be preserved by force."[66]

In this "eventful session of 1837–8," Davis remembered two main issues: separating banks from government through an "independent treasury," and "Abolitionism, then in its infancy." An immediate end to slavery without compensation to the owners was pressed. This, as Davis pointed out, would simply "involve us in total ruin." William Lloyd Garrison's American Antislavery Society had launched a postal campaign in 1835, just after the "desperate phrenzy" of July 4 in Mississippi, flooding the South with tracts urging insurrection, causing a riot in Charleston. President Jackson had asked Congress to curb use of the mails for these "incendiary documents" to no avail.[67]

A flood of petitions to Congress began, especially to abolish slavery in the District of Columbia. The Democratic position was that Congress could not pass laws of any sort on slavery, since it was totally in the hands of the states, and that petitions only inflamed passions uselessly. Pierce had been on the House committee that agreed to table them. Davis held that they ought not even be received, but he recognized that this compromise avoided "a false issue" (the right of petition) and prevented "that agitation . . . which every patriot must deprecate." The whole House had approved the committee action. It voted 201 to 7 "that Congress has no constitutional authority to interfere with slavery in the States" and 163 to 47 that "Congress ought not to interfere with slavery in the District."[68] The latter would violate "the faith implied in the cessions" of land for it by Virginia and Maryland, would justly alarm the "slaveholding States," and would tend "to disturb and endanger the Union." Davis praised Pierce's "candor" in denouncing "the movements of Northern fanatics as fraught with incalculable mischief." It was Pierce who noted a "new phase of abolitionism, in which it had changed from religious fanaticism to political organization."[69]

The Congressional war of words over great constitutional issues spilled into the newspapers that were mere organs for the Democratic and Whig Parties. A newspaper quarrel drew Jonathan Cilley, Democratic senator from Maine who lived at Dowson's, into a duel that involved Jefferson Davis. Pierce and others failed to effect a settlement, and Cilley had to fight Kentucky representative William J. Graves. It was rifles at eighty paces on the dueling ground at Bladensburg, Maryland. George Jones was Cilley's second, and Davis "was by my side," Jones said, when "Cilley was killed at the second fire." The affair caused such an uproar that Jones was not reelected. His close friend, Van Buren, would not appoint him governor of Iowa Territory, for fear of hurting the Democratic Party, though he did make him surveyor general. To Davis, this was a revelation of what to expect from public life, and he wrote as much to Jones:

> Although I have seen on former occasions a man's best feelings used as weapons of assault against him, I had not conceived that the disinterested sacrifice you made to support Mr. Cilley and the pain and difficulty you encountered because of your connexion

> with that affair, could be arrayed against you, and I am glad to perceive that you have not recoiled with disgust from a constituency so little able to appreciate your motives.[70]

The affair of February 1838 may have prompted Davis to buy his own dueling pistols. They came in pairs (one kept ready for the second shot, if needed), in a specially fitted case with room for shot and powder and, ideally, a copy of the Code of Honor. Usually they were smoothbore muzzle-loaders with nine-inch barrels, and flintlocks, though by this time percussion firing was allowed. In March, Davis asked a Baltimore army surgeon to bring over "shooting Irons or rather Steels"—"the five pair of 11 inch pistols for *trial* . . . I think they might suit me." He added, "How long would the ajent for steel barrels require to execute an order for a pair of pistols?" Davis was taxed for two pistols in 1845—possibly these, or else the pair of double-barreled Staudenmayers that he had bought "when a Lieut. of Infantry" and used as "a Lieut. of Dragoons in the campaign against the nomadic Indians of the West."[71]

Davis was expected to be ready to defend his honor with pistols at "ten to twenty paces." No gentleman thought of using the law for redress of private grievance. Honor was personal. To refuse a challenge was to declare yourself no gentleman and allow the challenger to post you a coward—the ultimate insult. Thus gentlemen held each other accountable for words and deeds. Albert Sidney Johnston said once while writing a letter, "I never put on paper what I am not willing to answer for with my life."[72]

Abuses and tragedies occurred. Johnston had been a victim just the year before. After organizing and training the army for the new Republic of Texas as colonel and adjutant general, he was made commanding brigadier general. In February 1837 the jealous acting commander, Gen. Felix Huston (not to be confused with the president-elect of Texas, Sam Houston), challenged Johnston. The Texas army was mostly Southern and held many Huston adherents. Although Johnston had "but little respect" for dueling, he knew that "he could not have held the command an hour, if he had shown the least hesitation in meeting General Huston's challenge." He told Davis how, having no dueling set, they used Huston's "crook-handled" horse-pistols, "twelve inches in the barrel."[73]

Johnston was "a very good shot" but out of practice; Huston was a "dead-shot." Five times Johnston fired quickly, activating Huston's hair-trigger before he could aim. He thought it his only chance. But the sixth time, Huston's ball went through Johnston's hip. The surgeon in attendance expected him to die, but he slowly recovered. He was in New Orleans for treatment in the spring, when Davis could have gone down to see him. He heard the story from both him and Huston. The duel left Johnston with a slight limp and undisputed command of his army.[74]

Although Davis approved dueling as a last resort, he called it "irrational and immoral" and sought to "regulate" it "when it cannot be prevented." It was better than the all too common street fight and assassination, one of which had recently claimed David Bradford's life. Davis said this in May 1844, when he and Joseph and Thomas E. Robins were at the Vicksburg meeting of the Mississippi Anti-dueling Society. Robins's recent duel had helped prompt the society, which wanted to repudiate dueling entirely and set up in its place a "Board of Honor" (themselves) to hear disputes. A Democratic newspaper, the *Sentinel,* was incensed by this attempt of "a namby-pamby, milk and water pacificator mob" to "take the matter wholly out of the hands of chivalrous and fighting gentlemen."[75] It liked the "high-toned Southern sentiments and chivalry" of Capt. Walter Guion (Davis's West Point roommate) and "the main speaker, J[oseph] E. Davis Esq., who then in his sixtieth year, stood forth in a strain of pure, upright, manly and chivalric feeling." Joseph argued that the duel could not be abolished: "He said, no, Mr. Chairman! let us correct the abuses, but, sir, let us, for all gross insults not properly atoned for, make it imperative upon the agressed" to fight "or leave the country." Joseph was "the admitted arbiter of every question of honor," but neither he nor his brother ever fought a duel, though the younger came very near and the elder finally issued a futile challenge in his eighty-second year.[76]

Davis, for all his love of things military, hated strife so much that he "could not bear anyone to be inimical to him"; he always sought to soothe feelings and restore good humor. In regard to affairs of honor, he behaved more like the scorned pacificators than like his fire-eating brother. The duty of seconds was to prevent the duel by reconciliation, if possible. Even when not under obligation, Davis several times achieved this delicate victory. In 1845, he and John Quitman patched up a "difficulty" between two Mississippi editors, and in 1858 he three times saved friends from fighting.[77]

In Washington, Davis had "immediately won his way into the esteem of everybody," Jones says. The Van Benthuysens, who had named a son for him, wanted him in New York, where "we can take better care of you" (his bronchitis was already becoming chronic), and set out after him when he left Washington, "much startled to hear of your Serious accident." They gave up the chase but consoled themselves, Watson wrote, with the promise of seeing him again soon, "judging from What your friend Jones said." So another trip north was planned.[78]

These trips belie the usual picture of Davis as a recluse at Brierfield after Knox's death. Davis was perhaps to blame for the image: "seven years of almost entire separation from the external world engaged in clearing the fields in the primeval forests of the alluvium of the Mississippi." He enjoyed the separation. He seems not to have gone back to Washington, "that hot bed of heartlessness and home of the world's worldly." He had obviously not taken to the rough-and-tumble of politics.

The antithesis of "worldly" is "spiritual"—attention to eternal rather than temporal concerns, to principles rather than pragmatic pursuits. Jeff was known in the family for his "unworldly attitude": "He had no taste for fashionable life or frivolous people." Life among his books, horses, dogs, and guns, with leisure for thought, and conversation with a few intimates, suited his reserved temperament. The contrast with the bustling world of affairs, he felt deeply and made repeatedly. He told Jones: "the happiness you will find in the midst of your amiable family will greatly exceed all you could have hoped for at Washington."[79]

Yet, for all its seclusion, his plantation life was not isolation. He wrote to William Allen, "I am living as retired as a man on the great thoroughfare of the Mississippi can be." He rode the "thoroughfare" to Vicksburg and often to New Orleans on business. He spoke of riding it up to Wisconsin in the summer of 1839 to visit Jones. There were family visits back and forth. He offered to escort nieces to school in Kentucky. In 1843 he was seen setting out on horseback to visit Andrew Jackson. He attended Democratic Party meetings with Joseph. He helped organize the Vicksburg Jockey Club. The Turner-Quitman and Wood families lived on Davis Bend, and Joseph's "oldest and best friend," Judge John Perkins, "remarkable for a generous hospitality," lived just across the river on an enormous Louisiana plantation, Somerset. There was no lack of society if it was wanted.[80]

Besides, Davis lived in the midst of the forty slaves whom he had to feed, clothe, house, and tend in sickness. There was constant upkeep. When "the people seemed to be crowded," he planned improvements for quarters, storehouse, hospital, and corncrib. He had to repair or replace "the gin stands." He did not sit idly on the gallery and leave things to the overseer. Like his model, Joseph, who became "one of the wealthiest planters in Mississippi" by hard work ("overworking," Zachary Taylor thought), Jeff always showed "indomitable industry and energy."[81] He and James Pemberton, "with the help of the negroes," raised a "cat and clayed house" after their own fancy, with a brick-paved and latticed gallery. Varina poked fun at it. "Some miscalculation about the windows had placed the sills almost breast high," and the fireplaces "looked as though they had been built in Queen Elizabeth's time, to roast a sheep whole." The outer doors were six feet wide, to admit "plenty of cool air," and "when they were opened, the side of the house seemed to be taken down."[82]

Despite his solitary nature and the seclusion, this "abundant occupation," along with his stoic attitude toward suffering, kept Davis from brooding. He never alluded to his great loss. The few letters extant from this era show jovial spirits. He starts one to Jones: "If I were a 'whig'

I should begin this letter by a phillipic against Amos Kendall." This mock-dramatic coupling of Demosthenes and the postmaster general is his protest against the tardiness of the mails. To William Allen, he quotes Robert Burns: "I long hae thought my honored friend / A something to hae sent ye." This is the letter in which he discusses "the Demosthenean style," then mocks his own erudition: "perhaps like the Vicar of Wakefield said to the lecturer on Cosmogony you may say to me—however with this difference that instead of once you may have heard all this a dozen times before." A man "back in the hills" had praised Allen's speeches, prompting from Davis: "When Lord Byron saw an American edition of his works he said it seemed like to posthumous fame." In the letter to Jones, the planter again turns his wry humor on himself: "[President Van Buren] has sowed indecision, a plant not suited to the deep furrows ploughed by his predecessor. You perceive that when I write of Politics I am out of my element and naturally slip back to seeding and ploughing."[83]

Jeff was "an unusually observant and successful planter." Even when "unwell" at Baltimore in December of 1837, he went into the country "to see some late importations of the 'Short Horned Durhams' very superior to any I had seen before." In the forties, he talked crops and cows with John Tyler and Zachary Taylor. (In 1842, Taylor sold his other plantations and bought Cypress Grove, of almost two thousand acres, at Rodney, below Davis Bend.)[84] Joseph's letters were full of details of planting. Jeff identified "tillers of the ground and the breeders of stock" as "men of my own pursuit" and praised "the individuality, the sobriety, and self-reliance" of farmers.[85] He himself, Varina says, "gave great care to the details of cultivating cotton," and his "unremitting attention" to his crops and cattle "yielded him . . . a moderately large fortune."[86]

When Andrew Jackson died in 1845 and Davis delivered the Vicksburg eulogy, he said that Jackson had retired from politics "to the congenial shades of the 'Hermitage' " and "the more agreeable pursuit, the destiny of man, the tillage of the earth," and that his sayings then became "tempered by the calm of separation from worldly strife, and illumined by the light of a pure Christianity." This reflects not only Davis's own agrarian inclination, but also, in its allusion to Genesis, Cutting Marsh's "bill of the Bibles."[87] The Bible had crept into Davis's first political speech the year before. The biblical issues of life and death had stared him hard in the face of late. In addition to his young, beloved wife and Henrietta Johnston, he had lost "an intimate friend," Lt. James Izard, and his brother-in-law, David Bradford. His own brushes with death, first from malaria, then from the fall in Washington, were enough to focus his attention. Surely, with his Baptist upbringing, he had read the Bible all along, but he had seldom alluded to it. After this period of bereavement and retirement, he cited it continuously. In 1851 he stated there was only "one book in the world" that he would "endorse, wholesale, everything in it . . . and that was the Bible."[88]

The Bible was only a part of his omnivorous reading at this time. We have seen Demosthenes, Burns, and Byron fresh in his mind. An old millwright working at Brierfield took a notion to try Adam Smith's *Wealth of Nations* because he saw Davis "absorbed in" it. Joseph was also a great reader. His love was governmental law, and his vast library was full of works like the Constitution, *The Federalist*, and Elliott's *Debates*.[89] Brierfield's own library, distinct from Hurricane's, ranged from the poetry of Milton, Gray, and Collins, through the novels of Tobias Smollett and Sir Walter Scott, to an 1827 *View of South America and Mexico*. The first American edition of Charles Anthon's *Dictionary of Greek and Roman Antiquities* is signed "Jeffn. Davis." Night after night, the brothers "talked of books, of elementary law, of agricultural experiments," says Varina, and "made and perfected theories about everything in heaven and on earth."[90] Many of their theories were about government. One was about the government of their slaves.

Their type of government is reflected in their neighbors' jokes about "Mr. [Joseph] Davis's free negroes" and how he would have to widen the cotton rows to accommodate the pickers' hoopskirts. Even Jeff thought he let the negroes impose on him, just as Varina was to say they "took advantage" of Jeff. There was no whipping on Davis Bend (though there still was in the United States Navy), unless the slave jury in the Hall of Justice imposed it, and then the masters usually remitted it. Joseph was trying to teach his people basic American law, sometimes acting as judge, sometimes as defense lawyer. Jeff's sense of humor once got the better of his justice. He dismissed a case because he was so tickled by the thief's tale of how he had eaten a whole stolen pig.[91]

During Reconstruction, when the idea of court testimony by blacks was very unpopular in the South, Jeff was for it. He said he had learned "from Brother Joe" to let the jury judge "their credibility." "The change of relation diminishing protection, must increase the necessity. Truth only is consistent, and they must be acute and well trained, who can so combine as to make falsehood appear like truth when closely examined."[92]

A modern writer thinks Joseph was inspired by Robert Owen in the treatment of his slaves, but there is no hint of this in the 1825 stagecoach scene that she cites from Varina's book. On the contrary, Owen's utopian ideas are held up to ridicule by fellow passenger George Cruickshank, "the English caricaturist." The basis for the Davises' management of their people was not communal society and cooperative labor, but the Christian religion, with its teaching, "Be ye kind . . . tenderhearted." The monument that Joseph's grandchildren raised to him says: "He was just and generous to the sorrowful, a gentle and sympathizing friend to the poor, ever kind and charitable. Blessed are the meek for they shall inherit the earth."[93]

Everyone, bond and free, had to answer to the same master; all were slaves of Christ, "bought with a price." Therefore, "Servants, be obedient to them that are your masters according to the flesh. . . . With good will doing service, as to the Lord, and not to men," wrote St. Paul. "And, ye masters, do the same things unto them, forbearing threatening: knowing that your Master also is in heaven; neither is there respect of persons with him."[94]

In addition to the basic necessities, the Davis slave families had garden plots and peach trees and chickens, which they fed from the unlocked corncrib and were free to sell. Both brothers had literate slaves. Two of Joseph's, Benjamin Thornton Montgomery and his wife, Mary, taught their sons Thornton and Isaiah to read and write. Ben paid Joseph the equivalent of Mary's services so she could stay at home and raise the children in a house he had built on the riverbank. Isaiah became Joseph's secretary. Ben ran the plantation store for his own profit, selling to both blacks and whites. He marketed the Davis fruit and cotton crops and was really business manager for the Hurricane and, at times, for Brierfield. The Davises tried, in vain, to get him a patent on a steamboat propeller he invented.[95]

When Jeff surprised a Northerner by his "minute analysis and scientific description" of a remedy, he explained that he "had to learn something of medicine so as to take care of the negroes on my plantation." There was also a physician available, and Jeff sent a stubborn case down the river to Samuel A. Cartwright, who was his own doctor, as well as the Howells', and a specialist in "slave maladies."[96] A contemporary noted that planters generally had, along with "a knowledge of superiority . . . a high sense of moral responsibility," prompting them to care for their charges spiritually as well as physically. The Davises built their slaves a white frame church, which is now the King David Missionary Baptist Church at Letourneau, Mississippi. It was nothing like as grand as the brick Gothic Revival one on Leonidas Polk's estate, but it was more typical.[97]

Polk had married and become an Episcopal priest. He ministered to the slaves on Rattle and Snap, the huge Middle Tennessee tract owned by him and his three brothers, before he became missionary bishop of the Southwest in 1838. Charles P. McIlvaine, then bishop of Ohio, was one of his consecrators and told how he had baptized Cadet Polk before the whole corps at West Point. Just before Leonidas was elected to the newly created Diocese of Louisiana in 1841, the Polk brothers built St. John's Church on his part of the estate, called Ashwood. When a Northern visitor saw black members overflowing their gallery, joining the responses, and taking communion, he remarked how the scene "silenced the suspicion that a slaveholder values not the soul of his slave."[98]

While missionary bishop, Polk laid the cornerstone in Vicksburg for Christ Church, organized by the Reverend David Page from Trinity, Natchez. The Davis brothers were not members, but Eliza and Florida were, and Jeff at least attended. The brothers signed as witnesses when the rector came down to the Hurricane in 1842 to marry Joseph's youngest daughter, Caroline, to Tom Robins. When Joseph died, the priest from Christ Church buried him.[99]

Joseph "tried always to provide Religious instruction for his slaves," said his granddaughter, Lise Mitchell. The Episcopal priest who taught the children also "preached to the negroes," and "felt it a grievance," she remembered, that the master would then "allow them to hold their own meetings at night." Black preachers were often regarded as "great rascals." But Davis Bend was safe in the hands of Old Uncle Bob who was "eloquent in prayer," says Varina, and "fit to be, as he was, a shepherd of his people."[100]

Lise said, "My grandfather belonged to no church himself," but she was not born until 1842 and may not have known that he was one of the founding members, and a vestry man, of Trinity Church, Natchez, formed in 1822.[101]

Old Trinity was where Joseph had been best man for William Howell when he married Margaret Kempe. Their children called him "Uncle Joe," the Southern fashion with close friends. After the baby named for him, they had a girl, born May 7, 1826, and christened Varina Banks. When she was seventeen, Joseph and Eliza invited her to the Hurricane for Christmas. She was to take the steamboat up to Diamond Place, Florida and David McCaleb's plantation just above Davis Bend. Caroline and Tom Robins were in Vicksburg. Mary, the middle daughter, with her doctor husband, Charles Jouett Mitchell, lived across the river in Madison Parish, Louisiana, and the Bradford family was now on the plantation next to them. Probably all planned to converge on the Hurricane for the season.[102]

The Howells lived on the bluff south of Natchez at the Briars. This was really a town house, exquisite in proportion and detail, built by John Perkins around 1825 to give his stepdaughters entree to Natchez society. From the long gallery, with its three Palladian doorways and ten slender fluted columns, one could see the cotton flats across the river. Once the daughters married, Perkins sold the house and went back to Somerset. Varina had romped on the large acreage with the younger children and worked in the schoolroom beside the house, though studying at home, she said, "makes a child hate the very sight of books—I *speak* from long *experience*."[103]

She could not have had in mind her mentor, Judge George Winchester, of whom she was very fond, and for whom the fourth Howell son was named. He had come from Massachusetts in 1817 and was a faithful member of Old Trinity Church. He must have thought Varina especially bright; he had taken time from his law practice to tutor her in English and Latin.[104] When she was ten, she had gone to Madame Grelaud's school in Philadelphia, where her father's brother lived. Her aunt wrote to Margaret Howell that Varina "is a dear little affec[tion]ate girl . . . Miss Grelaud says she is very smart &n capable & improves fast."[105]

Varina's own letters showed even then "an original and independent mind." That would have appealed to Judge Winchester, who was "a strong thinker." He naturally made the little lady into a Whig like himself, her father, and "most of the gentlefolk of Natchez." The Whigs had found their reason for being in opposing Andrew Jackson's withdrawal of the deposits from their National Bank. The shell cameo brooch that Varina now wore symbolized that: it was carved with a tiny watchdog chained to a strongbox. But the influence of the judge went deeper than that. "The most valuable lessons I learned," says Varina, "were not from the Latin or English classics . . . but from [his] pure, high standard of right." He was for her "a saintly man . . . the realization of my childish ideal of 'Great-heart.'"[106]

It was the judge who escorted her up the river on the *Magnolia,* this December of 1843. Varina's own heart, of no meager dimensions, was strangely moved before long. A tall stranger who rode "with more grace than any man I have ever seen," appeared at Diamond Place plantation. That night she wrote to her mother:

> To-day Uncle Joe sent, by his younger brother (did you know he had one?), an urgent invitation to me to go at once to "The Hurricane." I do not know whether this Mr. Jefferson Davis is young or old. He looks both at times; but I believe he is old, for from what I hear he is only two years younger than you are. He impresses me as a remarkable kind of man, but of uncertain temper, and has a way of taking for granted that everybody agrees with him when he expresses an opinion, which offends me; yet he is most agreeable and has a peculiarly sweet voice and a winning manner of asserting himself. The fact is, he is the kind of person I should expect to rescue one from a mad dog at any risk, but to insist upon a stoical indifference to the fright afterward. I do not think I shall ever like him as I do his brother Joe. Would you believe it, he is refined and cultivated, and yet he is a Democrat!

Mary Jane Bradford (Amanda and David's daughter, just about Varina's age), known as "Malie," then came on horseback for her, with a servant leading her mount from the renowned Davis stables, complete "with a lady's side-saddle." "The old-fashioned high swung carriage and pair came also to bring my *impedimenta,* and 'all in the blue unclouded weather' we rode over the rustling leaves through the thick trees to 'The Hurricane.' "[107]

Soon Varina was noticing how that younger brother would "dash by the carriage so free and strong"—a horseman "incapable either of being unseated or fatigued." She found him "the strongest and most helpful of men . . . erect, well-proportioned, and active as a boy." When his eyes grew tired from reading the Congressional debates aloud to Joseph, she would take over for him, versed as she was in politics by Judge Winchester and the *National Intelligencer,* which, she says, "everybody took."[108] At night in the music room, while she and others played and sang, Jeff's eyes began to meet hers with those "answering looks which," as she later expressed it, "comfort while I am shone upon." "We fell in love in such an unreasoning way," she wrote to him later—she, an "anxious, loving girl, so little of use, yet so devoted to you"; he, her "first and only love."[109]

The Whig brooch with the little bloodhound discreetly disappeared. By the first week in January a large emerald surrounded by diamonds appeared on her left ring finger. Then there were "the long walks in the H[urricane] garden with their rose borders—and mockingbirds—and your sweet voice in my ear as we walked, and talked of our future when we should be married, and at home—and how I sneered at old married people when they told me I should even love you better than then." But she did. He was in prison when she wrote that. "Now I know," she went on, "that you are the dearest, the purest and best of men—and love you so much better than then that it seems to me wonderful to compare that feverish childish passion with this waking certainty."[110]

It was not all sweetness. He had to pass through trials for a whole year to win her, like the hero of some medieval romance. In fact, she saw him as one. "If I read a romaunt," she wrote to him in prison, "I find myself pausing to remember one more 'tender and true' than other woman ever knew." At this time, she told friends that he reminded her of one history's chivalric heroes.[111] Still, she would find fault, and he would answer back. "If after the unlimited declarations I have made to you of my love I could neglect you," he wrote, "it would not become you to give me another thought." And, "Don't cry out against prosing this time, and I will try to be less dull for the future." He assured her, "nothing could make me doubt your heart and I hope you will not believe that I could treasure up heedless expressions and elaborate from their harmlessness the poisons of suspicion and discontent."

It was obvious how deeply he cared for her: "Pray don't read at night, nor punish your angel eyes by keeping a light in your chamber all night . . . what pain shall I not suffer to know that you are sick, suffering, and that I cannot be with you . . . for my sake take care of your health. Bon soir, mon cher ange, Je suis votre—Jeffn. Davis." "You surely did not think how much it would cost me when you asked me to burn your letters, if the house was on fire those letters with the flowers you have made sacred by wearing and the lock of your hair, would be the first thing I should think of saving."[112]

She had left in February for Natchez, forbidding him to follow, though he was ready to leap on board the steamboat at the least signal. "But why shall I not come to see you[?] [I]n addition to the desire I have to be with you every day and all day, it seems to me but proper and necessary, to justify my writing to you that I should announce to your parents my wish to marry you." He paced the Hurricane thinking of her, and when a letter finally came, it answered "the longings of a love so selfish that it wished you to overcome your unwillingness to write to me . . . to gratify my feelings. When the weak cord is stretched it breaks, the strength of the strong one is proved by the trial." He could see now that her feelings were not "ephemeral passion or accidental preference": "You are always such as I wish you."[113]

Varina's mother had misgivings about the match, perhaps because Jeff was nearer her age than her daughter's. But a disparity of eighteen years was nothing unusual then, and he was still a young man. Varina's father was all for the marriage, and when the Whig Judge Winchester put in a good word for the Democrat Davis, objections melted away.[114]

At last Jeff got permission to visit. He began to call Varina "my wife," and to sign himself "Votre Mari" [Your Husband]. He spoke of the "reluctance with which I am ever apart from you" and sent "deepest truest purest love" all through the summer and fall. "Be prepared for the worst," he turned into a joke: "as blessed are they who expect nothing, for surely they shall not be disappointed—e.g. I did'nt expect of this pen with which I am writing *much*, therefore my disappointment is not *great*."[115]

Jeff's letters show how attentive to God he had become in the years alone. Varina's welfare, says a note written at the Hurricane, was "my first prayer this morning." He prayed in French: "ma chere, tres chere, plus chere Varina Dieu te benisse [my dear, very dear, most dear Varina God bless you]." In time, "Adieu" (good-bye) became "A Dieu" ([I commend you] to God). "Some day I hope it will be mine always to be with you and . . . to allay nervous excitement": "until then may God and your good sense preserve you."[116] Of their future—"if you will recall a small part of all that I have said to you on that subject you will not fail to perceive that we are controled by a master not likely to regard either your wishes or mine." (Was he recalling the plans he and Knox had made?) What he was to call the "superintending care of Providence" was already strong in his thought. In December, it looked as if Providence was about to call it all off. Going to New Orleans, Jeff wrote stiffly from the steamboat: "May God grant you a speedy restoration to health, and secure to you that happiness for which he has so highly qualified you—& this granted I am equal to any dispensation which may be confirmatory thereof."[117]

Perhaps the thought of losing him brought Varina around. He was joking with her by January and was soon on the steamboat bound from Brierfield to the Briars and for, he thought, his wedding. On board he met Col. Zachary Taylor. They had not seen each other since their joint bereavement. Taylor evidently did not hold Davis responsible, as he might have done, for his daughter's death. He approached his son-in-law "most cordially" and effected "an entire reconciliation."[118]

Despite this vivid reminder of Knox, Jeff soon took Varina Banks Howell to wife. Not then, for she became ill; "some three weeks afterward he came on a short visit and we concluded to marry then." It was February 26, 1845. As with his first marriage, it was in the parlor, with the prayer book ceremony, and informal, but "elaborate enough," Varina said, "for the bride of a farmer." She wore "a white embroidered Indian muslin with touches of lace, and a dark silk for her departure," with crystalline jewelry to set off her brunette good looks.[119]

After "a breakfast to our friends" in the large upper room of the Briars, Varina took leave of her beautiful home and her family, so dear to her. As in 1835, the newlyweds went off on a steamboat down the river, stopping first at Anna's Locust Grove—with what memories for him! But in the great realism of the day, when death was a large part of life, they went together to lay flowers on Knox's grave. Then Jeff took Varina up to Woodville to meet his mother and Lucinda. She found Jane Davis at eighty-five "still fair to look upon." "His sisters were both like him . . . spirited, intelligent women, with strong convictions of duty." What impressed her most about her new husband was "the tender love he evinced" for them all.[120]

Then it was on to New Orleans and the St. Charles—"decidedly the best . . . hotel in the United States." Varina met a real live poet, the Irish Richard Henry Wilde, now from Augusta, Georgia, who had grown famous on one poem, "My Life is like a Summer Rose." She found him "very refined in manner, with flashing black eyes, and a singular pallor." Jeff introduced Gen. E. P. Gaines, his old commander with the "very peculiar" manner of speaking, who immediately won her heart by pronouncing her husband "An—a—incomparable adjutant, and the most—a—fearless and—a—dashing young—a—soldier of—a—his day." The whole honeymoon of six weeks "seemed like a fairy tale or a dream."[121]

It was the start of a new life for Jeff, of life for Varina. Twenty years later, bereft by his imprisonment, and among women who were dubious, she wrote:

> I alone am a proud, and grateful Wife—honoring my choice even more than I love him, if there can be degrees in a superlative—I alone of the whole number can look back, and see no brighter,

fairer life which I would have accepted for this . . . I trust that my daughters may like their Mother find in their first love, the Husband of their choice, and then they will fully understand that "there's nothing half so sweet in life, as loves young dream" and that sanctified by marriage one never wakes, or if one does finds it only a waking certainty of bliss—I daily "arise" and "call" you "blessed."[122]

VI

Plantation and Politics

The long honeymoon went right on as Jeff brought Varina upriver in mid-April 1845 to Brierfield, the home whose proportions amused her so. She was not the fairylike beauty whom he had brought to the Hurricane ten years earlier. She was dark and statuesque—about as tall as he—and her beauty lay more in her laughing charm and the soul that looked out of her great eyes than in her features. Yet his love now was as strong as then, and even more humble. A courtship letter strikingly resembles his sole surviving one to Knox:

> I have felt as I have acknowledged to you my unworthiness of the love you bear me, yet never so deeply as when reading your kind, generous expressions towards me . . . I felt that you viewed me through the medium of your own noble nature, and ascribed to the object a brightness not it's own.
>
> When circumstances shall give you greater opportunities to instil into me goodness and purity I believe I shall be more worthy of [the] opinion you now have of me, incorrigible indeed would he be that could constantly drink at so sweet [a] fountain and not become fond of its properties . . .
>
> Your spirit is with me. I feel it's presence, my heart is yours, my dreams are of our union, they are not dreams, for I will not wake from them.
>
> Your own Jeff[1]

There was a fairy-tale cast to the Brierfield surroundings. "The land is so fertile," wrote Varina, "that golden-rod grows large enough for a strong walking-stick, and the heads of the bloom are like banks of gold on the sides of the road. . . . Nothing could be more pleasant than the dense shade through which we could ride for miles, in air redolent of the perfume of the moss, flowers, wild crabapple and plum blossoms. . . . We indulged in many races when the road was smooth [and] . . . our races were rather even." "Wild-geese, in great flocks, made fat by the waste corn in the fields; wild-ducks by the thousand, and white and blue cranes adorned almost every slough, standing on one leg among the immense lily-pads that yet cover the low places with lemon-colored flowers as large as coffee-cups."[2]

Being a Mississippian and a lover of guns, Jeff almost surely hunted the birds, as he did bear and deer. Varina's brother borrowed his rifle to shoot the ducks once. Jeff certainly shot the "immense" alligator that was killing his calves: "The negroes found its hole, and Mr. Davis put a long cane down it until the creature seized it in its mouth. He then put the gun on a line with the cane and shot the alligator in the mouth."[3]

The cat-and-clayed cottage was "a cool house, comfortably furnished," and "always seemed 'home'" to Varina, even after a finer Brierfield was built. "You know," she once wrote to Jeff, "I never loved a large house as you did. I fancied a small one with a large fireplace." In this informal dwelling of "a plain farmer," they "passed many happy days," recalls Varina, "looking after the sick negroes, reading and writing, and visiting our neighbors and the Hurricane every day."[4] Jeff's letter to Margaret Howell (only two years older, remember), beginning "My dear Mamma," gives the tone of these early days: "We are living so humbly that we may well expect happiness if it be true that it springs from a condition which changes for the better, in the mean time Varina seems as much occupied with the flowers and vines she is raising as though our situation was permanent, and we should not probably be more happy if the walls of a castle sheltered us, than we are beneath the protection of our rugged hut."[5]

Varina's gardens became her hallmark wherever she lived. She especially loved roses. She had stuck a white one in her raven hair for her wedding. The master of Brierfield was also "very fond of cultivating trees and of seeing roses and ornamental shrubs blooming about us." Varina reminded him in prison of a rose "near the gate of our home" called "Glory of France." If away, she would write back about care of the roses, the asparagus and strawberry beds, and the quinces (much prized for jelly). Her mother (whom Jeff was soon calling "Ma") sent vines and heliotrope and jasmine slips up by steamboat. "The cypress vines are beginning to run but the Madirra vine is not so flourishing—Jeff laughs at me a great deal about it—I said it would grow a foot in a night, and it has grown very little and has put out no runners yet."[6]

Laughter filled the air at Brierfield. Varina's silver ripple could be touched off by almost anything, as her writing attests. Her saddest letter will pick up suddenly with a comic turn. Jeff's sense of the ridiculous was as keen as hers. He entered into fun "with boyish zest" in these days. Between them they cherished many a private joke about people they knew—black and white, obscure and famous. Jeff's amusement with the world always had a wry twist to it, verging on satire. He wrote Ma:

> Varina . . . appears sometimes very languid, which latter effect might be well ascribed to the company she habitually keeps, being your corresponding son and a mongrel puppy in both of whom by a power of vision peculiarily her own she sees highly valuable and loveable qualities, but unless (which you will hardly believe to be possible) she is inclined to coquetry, your son has the honor of being first among her present visitors whilst she vows the Puppy to be second.[7]

Even the gap in age came in for ridicule. On the very eve of marriage, at the end of a solemn note telling her to "be calm and meet the contingencies of this important change as becomes you," he signs himself "Uncle Jeff." (Did she not call his brother, "Uncle Joe"?) Her nickname for him, "Banny," may even have been in similar vein, though no one really knows the origin. It often appears as "dear old Banny." Was it a teasing form of "Granny"? It was what their grandchildren would one day call Varina.[8]

Jeff's satiric bent led him to Lord Byron and Lawrence Sterne. Winnie, the youngest Davis child, thought Uncle Toby in *Tristram Shandy* was a real person, she heard him quoted so much. In these days, Jeff would repeat so often the bad puns from a foxhunting novel, running serially in *Spirit of the Times,* that Joseph swore if the story continued he would give up his subscription.[9]

There was always a book at hand, a poem on the tongue. The slightest literary allusion was instantly picked up. Jeff loved poetry and could recite a great deal by heart: lyrics of Burns, long stretches of *The Lady of the Lake* by Sir Walter Scott, reams of Tom Moore's *Lalla Rookh,* or Byron's *Childe Harold, The Giaour, Lara,* the satiric *English Bards and Scotch Reviewers,* "and especially the storm in 'Don Juan'," says Varina (though most of this poem was banned by "the guild of delicate-minded women"). "His voice was musical in the extreme," she says, and gave "new force to the verse."

Some thirty years later, Winnie would listen on his knee in the firelight to these same recitations "in his wonderful voice" that lent the lines "new music." She says Shakespeare and the Bible "held the foremost place." "His knowledge of the divine book was not exceeded by that of any clergyman I ever met." Varina tried to interest Jeff in contemporary poets like her own favorite, Alfred, Lord Tennyson, and Robert Browning, but he "had little sympathy with the latter." He also thought John Milton "a dreadful bore." His taste ran more to the "heroic songs," which he would quote for intimate friends: Varina "never saw anyone who could resist the charm of these recitations, when he was in the mood."[10]

The classical education of the young couple made another bond. "He never forgot his Greek and Latin," says Varina (a good Latinist herself), "was very familiar with Virgil, and loved to quote from him." Latin is forever appearing in their letters and his speeches. Husband and wife both mulled over niceties of English, and both were good French scholars, though Jeff's pronunciation irked Varina: he "pronounced it as though it were English." He also knew Spanish and German, not to mention Chippewa. Both Davises were great readers of history and biography. He much preferred books on "statecraft" to the novels that she enjoyed, except for Scott and Fenimore Cooper and *The Scottish Chiefs* by Jane Porter. But he would listen to lighter novels as "a means of driving out thoughts of more serious things," especially after his public duties became burdensome.[11]

Sometimes Jeff would sing the bittersweet lyrics of Tom Moore, who wrote "the fashionable songs," like "Had I the leisure to sigh," "The Minstrel Boy," and "The Harp that once in Tara's hall." "He had a lovely high baritone," Varina says, "no musical culture, but a fine ear; and if he heard a song rendered accurately, and well, sang it afterward very sweetly." *She* had the "musical culture." She missed her piano, though she could play the one at the Hurricane. That long elegant salon, scene of "mock concerts," remained forever in her memory. In the midst of the woes of 1865, she wrote to Jeff: "I oftenest now see you as you looked in the music room twenty-two years gone."[12]

Jeff gave her money to buy her own piano, but she offered it for her brother Billy's education instead. *"The money is my own,"* she wrote to Ma: "Don't consider it as anything from Jeff, and even if it were from him, he would send it with a son's affection. Jeff has always intended to educate Billy—*he wishes me* to send him to school. . . . He feels very anxious about him—and has spoken to me of him repeatedly."[13]

This is typical of their lifelong generosity, spreading out to nourish many. Children were raised, educated, and even rescued by it; grown-ups, supported and comforted. Jeff was even now allowing a sister's son to draw on his cotton factor in New Orleans for supplies. He gave the old millwright working on the cotton gin five hundred dollars (a very large sum then) to take his wife to a cancer specialist, saying, "Save your wife, and the knowledge that you have done so will satisfy your debt to me." All this was the natural expression of their warm hearts, but it was also the Christian virtue of liberality, embracing the corporeal and many spiritual works of mercy. When they had lost everything, and Jeff was threatened with a disgraceful death, Varina derived hope from that fact: "Don't take thought for the morrow . . . look upon the waters for your bread—your Mothers bread—mine—my Mothers—we cannot want. We have shared with many a Lazarus, freely and tenderly." She thanked him for "all the support and love showered upon my family and friends." "And you, dear old love," she said later, "how faithfully you helped my people in every way. The Lord has a blessing for you for all that you have done for others."[14]

Joseph was an example to them in this. Before they married, Jeff had written: "My dearest, my own one, I have just returned from the performance of a most painful and meloncholy duty. My Brother-in-law David Bradford was assassinated day before yesterday." The hot-tempered Bradford had been shot down on a street in Richmond, Louisiana, by a man with whom he had quarreled. Joseph's comment, bringing his body later to the Hurricane, was "poor David I could but think of his many good qualities his truth his freedom from envy, or petty malice, his generosity, his chivalry, with all his want of worldly wisdom he was man."[15] Joseph had sent Jeff to bring sister Amanda and all eight of her children to live at the Hurricane. Within the next two years, Joseph and Eliza also took in three grandchildren and an orphan. One of the Bradfords was Malie, who had fetched Varina from Diamond Place the December before. They were almost exactly the same age. With Varina's marriage they became niece and aunt and also fast friends.[16]

The benevolence extended to the black dependents. As long as Jeff "looked after his own plantation, there was no need of force with any of his laborers; they did their best for him," says Varina; but if he was gone, they "made no exertion." He insisted that they "should not be whipped, and that they should be kept healthy and satisfied, even if they made little crops." Naturally, "every year marked a decrease in our income," but naturally also, "to a man they loved him." One of them, William Samford, dropping tears over his dead body, said, "That I loved him this shows, and I can say that every colored man whom he ever owned loved him. He was a good, kind master." A niece saw Davis arriving home after a long absence: "[The slaves] came running to the house and without ceremony made their way to the room where we were and to my surprise threw themselves before him and embraced his knees at the risk of pulling him down. He must have been accustomed to such demonstrations for he very gently extricated himself and patiently answered their questions and asked kindly for their families."[17]

Varina thought she saw what made them so affectionate—his sense of humor, keeping everything in balance, and a "remarkable and invariable custom": "No matter who told him anything about his negroes, he said, 'I will ask him to give me his account of it.'" "He was a close observer," noticing "every shade of feeling" in others and "nothing could be more winning that his efforts to conciliate even his servants when he thought they were annoyed with him." This was perhaps his way of making up for what Varina calls "any little impatience," what Basil Duke later designated a "fiery" temper. A kinswoman said that his anger, though she never saw it, was known in the family as "cold, though quick" like a rapier soon sheathed. But he was "generally patient," says Varina, and "always just."[18]

"Merciful justice," said Winnie, was his characteristic. This tallies with what he once told Varina: "Uniformity and gentleness [are] better than severity. In the government of beasts or of men, I believe harshness is requisite in direct proportion to the incompetence of the ruler. Such at least has been my observation of overseers, Horse-breakers, school-masters, Parents & public-officers." In handling slaves, he said, the "relation of the races was one which could only incite to harshness in a very brutal nature."[19]

Davis tried to explain to the Senate in after years: so long as the number of slaves was not too large, the personal and "paternal character" of contact with them restrained even the "sordid and the vicious" who "in all countries" abuse their power over others. The slave's very position, "unlike that of the apprentice or the hired man," "awakens whatever there is of kindness or of nobility of soul in the heart of him who owns it." It was the chivalric duty of protecting the weak.[20] As another planter said, there were "some cases of brutality . . . yet we despise such men." Davis later spoke to Confederates of "Christianizing and improving" those "who have, by the will of Providence, been placed in our charge." Varina says he "literally suffered 'long and was kind' to all who depended on him."[21]

An outsider noticed this. "He is one of the purest and best of men, one of the kindest-hearted," said the Reverend William Wilberforce Lord, telling Mary Chesnut how Davis "attended his church" in Vicksburg, and how he also "knew him well at home on his plantation."[22] Davis was still not a communicant, but his mother was. In 1843, Bishop Polk had come out from St. Paul's, Woodville, and confirmed Jane Davis in the parlor at Poplar Grove.[23] "My saintly . . . sister, Lucinda," as Davis called her, probably arranged this. She and Williams Stamps were now living at the home place with their four children. By 1850, sister Anna was also an Episcopalian.[24]

Although Varina was born at Marengo, the plantation of her Kempe grandparents in Louisiana, she grew up in Natchez and was really a city girl at heart. At Brierfield she began to find out what hard work plantation life entailed. In a letter that told her mother, "Hagar has a baby, and has named it for you," she said, "you would be astonished to see the work I have got through—25 pairs of pantaloons since mondy . . . the negroes require constant attention—and that with the cotton book keeps me very busy." One morning she helped Jeff distribute "the negro clothes. I am so tired I can scarcely sit up."[25]

Varina's sense of humor always tempered her cares. She spent New Year's Day, 1847, in "undeniable hard work"—"entirely alone, putting down and stretching carpet," while singing "as loud as I could every thing I could, not forgetting the 'ni-ni-na'" She had made twelve pumpkin pies, but "a fraction ever so petite of the crust" would lay a sturdy man on the ground if "even gently struck." She was going to set "the negroes to Brick making," for the house Jeff "wants me to build," but right then she was trying to get the carpenter to work. "But all the negroes seem to try their best . . . and I cannot find fault."[26]

She described the "sliding-scale of duties" (a tariff phrase from her political tutelage) among the slaves: at a death, "the cerements were always furnished by us," and "a large quantity of flour, several pounds of sugar, the same quantity of coffee, a ham, a 'shote,' and a half a dozen or a dozen bottles of claret constituted the supper on which they felt they could be wakeful and watch the corpse"; for a baby, the levy was less; for a bride, more; "and these requests were never denied them."[27]

Jeff and Varina had no children as yet, but they were creating for themselves an ideal home. The city girl was soon as content "to dwell in happy obscurity" as her husband. They entertained and were entertained. Mint juleps and leisurely meals ("dinner" in the afternoon, "tea" at night) promoted that distinctively Southern art, conversation. "Geo. E. Payne . . . will dine with us to day," a note to Varina announced one Monday; "I told him to come around 4 1/2 oClock say—Dinner at 5—Family Dinner Your Husband." Walter Guion (whose older brother was Varina's godfather) was one old friend who came for a visit. He and Jeff were both very active in the state Democratic Party. "To the time of his death," wrote Jeff, Walter Guion was "near to me as a Brother." That time was close. Walter died on October 23, 1845, at the age of thirty-seven.[28]

By that time, Jeff was running for Congress, and the Davises' particular mold of the "cultured, patrician" life that typified the plantation South was about to be shattered. Caught up in a public career, he and Varina were never again to enjoy together their quiet home on the river for very long at a time, but it always floated visionlike before their eyes. During all the years when "public cares and frequent absence and preoccupation with disagreeable subjects" took Davis's attention, "that time so long looked for when we should be apart from the world, and quietly occupied with objects of common interest to us, seemed to rise before me like the 'convenient season' of the impenitent." This came from a prison cell in 1865, and Varina answered with her longing for "the real home life which has been the ignis fatuus which has lured me in cheerful submission through one political bog and then another, always looking for the sunny green bank upon which we might rest and pray, work and see its fruition. If I have loved and followed faithfully the soldier and statesman, it was because I first loved the man."[29]

When Jefferson Davis had stepped from obscurity into local fame, it was in a fashion typical of his whole career: "I was (in 1843) suddenly pressed into the service of the Democratic Party of the County." A candidate for the state legislature had resigned with the election a week off. Davis was asked to take his place. Warren County was heavily Whig; defeat was certain—"or at least so I regarded it," said Davis. But "our opponents must have thought otherwise," for they brought in as the Whig champion "the greatest popular orator in the State—it may be said of his day—Sargent S. Prentiss." Davis did lose the election, but he whittled down the Whig vote.[30]

The important thing was the impression he made. This verdict of the men sent to persuade him to run was later held up to schoolboys as an example: "a gentleman of pure thought, chaste language, profound convictions, conversant with all forms of present and past governments." "At this time," says Reuben Davis, a contemporary politician, "only a few intimate friends were aware of his wonderful powers and attainments." From the first debate, it was obvious that he "was master of the whole science of rhetoric" and "had made himself familiar with the subject in hand as it was possible for a man to be. Less brilliant in oratory than Prentiss, he was always fascinating and charming, and had much more strength as a debater. He was certainly more cautious and deliberate . . . from that time on, it was clearly seen that he was destined to play no small part in the history of his country."[31]

Why did he give up the quiet home life that he loved? It was because "man is not born for himself alone, or for his family only." In a land of self-government, "no one has a right to wholly withdraw himself from connection with public affairs." He revealed why he was willing to risk himself, then and later, in the picture he drew for students at the University of Mississippi in 1852. "A citizen's duty to his country" involved not only participating in, but understanding, the "complicated machinery" of "the best political organism which has ever existed among men."

> Perfectly to fulfil its mission, it must be controlled by those who adhere to truth for it's own sake, who through good and through evil report, through success and defeat, will tread with equal step the path of duty. It is to this noble, it may be self sacrificing course, I invite you by the proposition to become politicians, or to employ a less abused term, to be statesmen. . . . [T]ruth & honor beckon you on, and the path cannot fail to be attractive to those whose hearts feel a pride in the perilous ascents which conscience and patriotism require them to climb, [though it might lead] to the fate of him who falls wrapped in conscious rectitude, defeated but neither conquered or despised, and leaves his name connected with the eternal truth which may sleep for a day, but cannot die.

After he had himself fulfilled this fate, he still urged politics on a young namesake, assuring him: "Glory properly belongs to duty well performed and happiness only dwells with him whose conscience is at peace with itself."[32]

Andrew Jackson was a powerful exemplar. When Davis delivered his eulogy in Vicksburg in 1845, he told the large assembly that Old Hickory had "never hesitated between the promptings of self interest and the demands of honor and of duty" and that he died with "the cheerfulness of christian piety and hope." (He had made a good end, patiently linking his sufferings to Christ's and forgiving his enemies—even Rachel's.) Duty went beyond blind obedience. When Jackson floated his Tennessee infantry down to Natchez in 1813, only to be told to disband them and send his supplies to New Orleans, he sent the munitions, but he risked censure by keeping the wagons to transport his sick up the Natchez Trace home. When they were not enough, he gave up his own horses and marched on foot, and, said Davis, "from the ability with which he bore fatigue, above his apparent strength, received the soubriquet of 'Hickory.'" "His moral firmness" in doing the right as he saw it, and his "forecast and self-sacrificing temper" through life stamped him "emphatically 'a man who knew his duty, and knowing, dared perform it.'" Even the presidency that called him from "the repose of private life" was a duty. "Born for his country, it was enough for him to know his services were wanted. The spirit that even to his dying hour triumphed over physical infirmity, sustained him." Because Jackson measured "all things by the ru[l]e of rectitude," Davis concluded, his life was "a valuable text book to the statesman." It was all an unconscious prophecy of Davis's own future.[33]

Duty could lead one on strange paths. Davis said Jackson had a "duty to suppress" resistance even to a law he disapproved—a reference to the nullification crisis. The irony was that if Jackson had tried this, Davis would have resigned from the army. For him, invasion of a state was unthinkable, but so was disobedience. He agreed with John C. Calhoun that high protective tariffs violated the Constitution (imposts were for revenue only) and favored Northern industries while hurting the South's cotton market abroad, but he could not see defying the Union while still a part of it. Calhoun had devised nullification to avoid secession, the ultimate defense of the minority. Davis said in 1851, "I deny the power of Massachusetts to nullify the law and remain in the Union. But I concede to her the right . . . to take the 'extreme medicine,' secession." Only "mutual advantage," Davis believed, could ever keep the disparate states together.[34] Although he looked upon Calhoun as "the very embodiment of the doctrine of strict construction," duty to conscience made Davis oppose him as well when he called waterways "inland seas" in order to skirt the Constitution and get federal funds for internal improvement.[35]

Conscience had been involved in the Prentiss debates too. Whigs were still attacking Democrats over repudiation of a bond issue by the Union Bank. The ruling Democrats had granted a Mississippi charter to the bank in 1838 and then rescinded it. They declared the bond issue invalid and refused payment on it. Although "strongly convinced of the unconstitutionality of the Union Bank bonds," Davis defied his party by stating that if courts declared them "a debt of the state, I was in favor of levying a Tax to pay them." Democrats were willing to "merge" this difference with Davis, to get him to run, but he was never at ease with his party's stand. About 1848, duty came into play. He and his banker nephew, Tom Robins, "devised a plan" whereby Mississippians would pay off the bonds by "voluntary subscription." The holders were English creditors of the United States Bank of Pennsylvania, which had bought the bonds originally and sent them to England as collateral. Robins went to England but "failed in the attempted negotiation with the Bondholders, who probably," said Davis, "overestimated the legality of their claim, or underestimated the morality and pride of the people in whom they were invited to confide." Nonetheless, Davis's enemies repeatedly called him a repudiator, and in 1863 they used this "hypocrisy and falsehood," as he called it, to help destroy the European credit of the Confederate States of America.[36]

Davis's defeat by Prentiss had been a personal triumph—"our little David" against "the gigantic Goliath"—and had won him a seat in the state Democratic convention of January 8, 1844. Here his eloquence shone again. Warren County had instructed him to support Martin Van Buren for the presidential nomination. He praised the "magician" for backing the government's independent treasury policy when most unpopular, showing that he valued "truth and the good of his country above power and place." But then Davis spoke of Calhoun—what a great secretary of war he had been (1817–1824) and how his interests were their own: free trade, the annexation of Texas, and the defence of the Gulf Coast, which had been neglected while Northern ones were charted and fortified. Urging "a Southern President" so that "justice may be done" to Southern interests, he moved that, if Van Buren were not nominated, delegates to the national convention should vote for Calhoun. It passed unanimously. Davis was made an elector, "chosen as well for his great moral worth of character as for his talents."[37]

But when Davis stumped the state, it was for neither Van Buren nor Calhoun. Southerners had quashed Van Buren as unsafe on the tariff and the admission of Texas and run in James Knox Polk, a Tennessean born in North Carolina, a cousin to Leonidas. Polk and his running mate, George Mifflin Dallas, were Jacksonian Democrats for whom Davis could argue wholeheartedly. All that summer and fall, while his thoughts and letters went back to Varina in Natchez, he traveled with the other electors, striving to turn the state back to the Democrats after their loss to William Henry Harrison in 1840.[38]

Prentiss had called Polk "a blighted burr . . . from the mane of the warhorse of the Hermitage," and other Whigs ridiculed him as "a mere 'nobody' daring to run against the immortal 'Harry of the West'," Henry

Clay, but Davis was becoming as sure of his powers as of his politics. His speech for Calhoun had brought his colleagues to their feet, to make him elector by acclamation. People came out to see this new player in their favorite game, politics. A Whig editor, while admiring his "musical and well modulated voice," made fun of him—"a schoolboy declamation"— and quoted someone saying "that d—d fool Davis." Davis got off light. Henry Stuart Foote, campaigning with him, was called a "renowned political changeling" who had "the eloquent gestures of a galvanized frog."[39]

Foote was the criminal lawyer who had won acquittal for David Bradford's assassin. He was just the sort of stump speaker Davis was not—wisecracking, mocking, ready to turn his coat to suit the wind, telling Reuben Davis, "ignorance and impudence will succeed far better than intellect and modesty." He made a strange political bedfellow.[40] So did Gen. Felix Huston. Davis found himself speaking alongside the man who had shot his best friend. Huston was from Natchez and had come back to join the campaign for the annexation of Texas. This is probably when Davis heard his version of the duel with Sidney Johnston. The other Houston (Sam) had blocked Johnston's appointment as Texas major general, after his resignation as the Republic's secretary of war, and Johnston, now remarried, was living on a sugar plantation near Galveston.[41]

In contrast to Whig editors that summer, Democratic ones found Davis "an eloquent, calm, and deliberate speaker" whose "argumentative powers are of the first order," showing "a mind well disciplined and highly cultivated." One lamented that "he addresses the reason, the judgment, the intellect; but has no words for the passions"; if only he could "fire the heart with emotion," he would be one of the foremost orators. Still, on that day, June 13, 1844, "he enchained the attention of the assembly for nearly two hours. His exordium was as pure as a snow-wreath—as chastely beautiful as a lily." The veteran politician Reuben Davis, who heard him for the first time that summer, said, "From the moment he began to speak, with all the ease and eloquence of which he was so consummately master, he seemed to expand and etherealize into the very spirit of oratory." "Dignified and commanding, soft and persuasive," spinning his arguments from notes only, Jefferson Davis helped win the election for Polk. Reuben Davis said he was "even more popular than the great Prentiss."[42]

His success led Davis to seek the Democratic nomination for Congress from southwest Mississippi. (The state was undistricted as yet, but for convenience it was divided into four parts, with a representative elected from each.) He began to see what a tangled business politics could be. He had to run against a man who should have been, and later was, a political ally, Dr. William Gwin, graduate of Transylvania in medicine and protégé of Andrew Jackson's. Gwin had already served in Congress. Reuben Davis claimed there was "little trickery and no corruption" in Mississippi then, that a stuffed ballot box was unheard of, that the people demanded "honor and honesty." Jeff Davis's honesty almost ruined his chance for the nomination.[43]

John Isaac Guion, Walter's brother and a "dear friend," was a Whig, but Davis was supporting his amendment to the Briscoe Bill, in favor of fiscal responsibility. The Democratic Party had backed the original bill, which canceled debts owed to failed banks. Davis saw this as "a new phase of repudiation" and "against good morals and integrity." Old hands told him that supporting Guion was "political suicide," but Davis sat up all night getting his views printed in a pamphlet for distribution and took one personally to Briscoe. Varina reports his reaction: " 'Didn't you know I said I would not vote for any man holding these opinions?' 'Yes,' said my husband, "and therefore I thought you ought to know mine.' But Mr. Briscoe did vote for him nevertheless, and Mr. Davis was nominated."

"Most politicians . . . would have remained silent," the *Vicksburg Sentinel* declared. "Not so with him. . . . Doubly triumphant is the securing of such a man in public life. It is a triumph of straight forward frankness and honesty over the intriguing, non-committalism, and duplicity which we grieve to say has too much heretofore characterised our public men." A letter to the paper said: "Mr. Davis's chief virtue, his pearl of great price . . . is his spotless integrity."[44]

Davis discovered that campaigning came with a severe physical price. In itself, overland travel was arduous. The only railroad track in all of Mississippi ran from Vicksburg to Jackson and the six miles from Natchez to Washington. Politicians joggled in saddle or carriage over bumpy roads to speaking engagements, stopping at country houses. "Riding in the sun, and late in the dew, in midsummer, always gave him malarial fever," Varina tells us. "So these journeys were generally succeeded by long attacks of illness, and the fever affected his eyes greatly." She wrote to Ma, as Jeff left for a speaking tour in September, "He looks very badly, and has dreadfully inflamed eyes . . . he showed symptoms of sickness . . . and I fear he may be taken on the road." He had had trouble ever since "the snows of the Northwest had affected his eyes seriously." But "his mind dominated his body in so great a degree that he was able to endure nearly what he pleased." Even emotional anguish did not stop him. When he found his mother dead at Woodville, he was "much overcome," but after the funeral, he rode forty miles to see Varina "for an hour" in Natchez, then rode back and spoke in Woodville that night.[45]

Davis and the other Democratic nominees—Robert Roberts, Stephen Adams, and Jacob Thompson—easily won the Congressional seats. Varina wrote to her mother of Jeff's election: "I receive it as a just tribute to his merit—Am I not 'proper proud' of my good man?" Thompson, who had been elected to Congress three times before, got the most votes, but the freshman Davis was only three hundred behind him. It is a measure of his meteoric rise in Mississippi politics that "Major [*sic*] Jefferson Davis," and not Jacob Thompson, was chosen to make the "address of reception" that November when the great Calhoun visited Vicksburg.[46]

The South Carolina statesman was scheduled to stop on his way up the river from New Orleans to a commercial convention in Memphis. The Davises planned to meet him in Vicksburg and then go straight to Washington, taking Malie Bradford, but Varina, regretting the "inconvenience" to "that dear good Jeffy of mine," could just not get ready in time. Riding up alone, Davis found that a delayed steamboat gave Calhoun only time enough at Vicksburg to say "he would stop on his return." Davis went back to Brierfield chafed. He wanted to get to the House of Representatives in time to "vote for speaker and other officers." To save time, he dictated his Calhoun speech to Varina, instead of waiting as usual to write it out "for the reporters afterward." It was full of poetry and "pretty imagery," says Varina, and pointedly omitted any reference to "inland seas."

After more steamboat troubles, Calhoun finally arrived on November 18. At the Prentiss House hotel, Davis addressed several hundred people assembled for the reception and ball. He began rather slowly, Varina relates, as if trying to remember the written speech. Gradually, "his voice grew round and clearer until it filled the large hall to the echo. Without pausing for a word, he passed in rapid review" various political issues, and "came to the home-stretch with State rights sails all set and Mr. Calhoun at the helm." But "not one word had been repeated of all the very fine things I had indited in a fair hand." "We had no time to rewrite it, so the other was printed instead . . . very unlike the address, or any other Mr. Davis ever made afterward. . . . [His] speeches never read as they were delivered; he spoke fast, and thoughts crowded each other closely. . . . Only so much of his eloquence has survived as was indifferently reported." The "magnetism of manner and the exceeding beauty and charm of his voice" is lost.[47]

Davis's oratorical powers were not lost on Calhoun, who told Joe Howell "that I should be proud of my brother and sister": Davis's "talents were of the highest order," and he had never met a lady "with whose manners he was more pleased." "The old man indeed seemed quite struck with her, he walked with no one else talked with no one else, and seemed to have no use for his eyes except to look at her and Mr. Davis, thereby rendering Mrs Dr Gwin so jealous that I believe she would have fainted had she had a fair opportunity." Given her "Whig proclivities," Varina had meant to be "coolly civil . . . but when Mr. Calhoun, with head erect, cast his eagle eyes over the crowd, I felt like rising up to do homage to a king among men."

> [His] forehead . . . beetled squarely over the most glorious pair of yellow brown shining eyes, that seemed to have a light inherent in themselves. . . . He lowered them less than anyone I have ever seen. . . . He wore his thick hair all the same length, and rather long, combed straight back from his forehead. This, with his brilliant eyes and unflinching gaze, gave his head the expression of an eagle's. His mouth was wide and straight; he rarely smiled, and the firm, square chin and grave manner made a personality striking in the extreme.

Replying to her husband's welcome, Calhoun was "quick and alert," but his voice "was not musical; it was the voice of a professor of mathematics. . . . His language was plain to poverty . . . with no appeals to any emotion." "The duty of a citizen to the State was his theme; the reward he offered was the consciousness of having performed it faithfully. . . . He made few gestures, but those nervous, gentlemanly hands seemed to point the way to empire."

When he came to speak to her "without a trace of gallantry," she found that "though he was gray and much emaciated, the fire within made him seem hardly to have reached middle age . . . and his manner was so paternal and full of indulgent sympathy that I found myself telling him what a grief it was to contemplate my first separation from my mother. He in turn spoke of a daughter . . . who loved him better than any one else." Thus began a friendship that lasted until Calhoun's death five years later, "attested by long letters on governmental subjects" in a hand that "looked neat" but was "almost undecipherable." She sent one back for him to read, and "he responded, 'I know what I think on this subject, but cannot decipher what I wrote.' "[48]

The day after their encounter with greatness, the Davises and Malie Bradford set off for Washington on the "National Road," up the rivers to Wheeling, then overland. But they reached only "what the captain called the 'Norrows' " on the Ohio, where the ice "closed around us, and we remained on board nearly a week, hoping for a thaw." The steamboat pilot's wife wanted to know "what on airth that man was takin' them delicate, puny-lookin' gals through all the cold fur." Davis evaded an answer "in order to draw her out," says Varina. He had done this to "a Whig lady," who "bade me beware of poke berries" as he canvassed for Polk, and spoke of Jackson's "removing the depoe." He had told her, "I should fear to meet her on the stump." It was the gentlest mockery; he really savored odd uses of the English language, as he had on the frontier. But the pilot's wife, Mrs. McGruggy, thought he was not telling her "whar he is a goin' " because she was not "good enough," and she let him have an earful, ending with "Davis ain't a aristocratic name, no-how." More likely he was concealing the fact that he was now the Honorable Mr. Davis, so that she might not feel her less-exalted state. As Varina notes of George Dallas, "He considered the peculiarities of every one as worthy of his notice, and never mortified the sensibilities of the most uneducated." "With characteristic modesty he used to praise" the unlearned frontiersmen "for the great diversity of things they could accomplish and which he could not." His charm won back even Mrs. McGruggy. Before they parted, she gave Varina "some fine apricot seed, which grew and bore at Brierfield for nine years under the name of 'The Pilot's Wife.' "[49]

Finally a small boat got the Davis party to the south shore, where they parallelled the river "on a rough wood-sled with oaken runners." But they were "half-way up the side of a mountain," and "the sled slipped over," falling twenty feet, bruising Varina's head badly. To reach an inn took a whole day's journey, but here Varina had a curious comfort. The hostess, "stirred by some vague memory, asked my servant to tell her my maiden name; and then related how my father and mother, and Mr. Joseph E. Davis, had spent the night there, when 'going through the wilderness,' just nineteen years before. When my husband inquired why she remembered them so well, she answered, 'They were so beautiful and so cheerful, I have never forgotten them, and your voices are the same.' "

Varina calls this journey the survival of "the fittest." "When we reached Wheeling my husband's feet, of which he had not complained, were frozen." The stagecoach over the Alleghanies from Pittsburgh tossed them often to the ceiling and was always threatening to slip off an icy precipice.

> Under all these disadvantages Mr. Davis was cheerful; always ready with some pleasant story, making light of the discomforts, and sometimes singing "We'll tough it out till morning." When exhortations and jests failed, he went into the little wayside inns and bought candy and milk, and told us to "drink deep and forget our sorrows." Once, when hard-boiled eggs without salt were given us, as we were ruefully contemplating the luncheon he called out, theatrically, "What is the province of salt? 'Salt seasons dainties, blunts the sabre's edge,' " etc.
>
> So, half-dead with fatigue, but trying our best to command his respect by being stoical, though bruised black and blue, we arrived in Washington, and took temporary lodgings at the "National Hotel" on Pennsylvania Avenue.[50]

They saw Mr. Calhoun here, and many another famous man, but they soon moved into a "Congressional mess" with the other Mississippi representatives, Jake Thompson and Stephen Adams and Davis's dear old friend George Wallace Jones. Forty-three years later Jones told how Davis, hearing he was in debt, handed him a draft for a thousand dollars. "I drew my note for $1000 in his favor, at ten per cent. interest, and handed it to him. He tore the note into pieces, threw them under his feet, saying, 'When you get more money than you know what to do with, you may pay me, not before.' "[51]

Virginia Clay calls Jones "the pet of women and the idol of men." He had long, glossy, black hair and was an "indefatigable" party-goer. He styled himself "a natural-born mechanic, musician and dancer." This disguised a hardy soul. Hearing on the frontier that Indians had killed his brother-in-law, Jones "dashed into the country in hot pursuit," but found only the body "horribly mutilated." His special friends Gen. Henry Dodge and his son, Augustus Caesar, whom Davis also knew, boarded at the same "mess."[52]

There was plenty of other entrée to Washington society. Davis knew Senators William Allen and Henry Clay and, also from Kentucky days, Francis Preston Blair, who had just lost his influential place as editor of the Democratic *Washington Globe.* The wife of his son Montgomery became an intimate friend of Varina's. And there was Atchison, whom Davis greeted with "Who made ye, Dauvid?" Varina's description hints at the reason for Mr. Bishop's repeated question: "a solemn, literal, tender man of a tall ungainly figure."[53]

Even closer friends were the whole tribe of Baches, Emorys, and Walkers. Robert J. Walker had helped make Polk president and been rewarded with the second highest post in the cabinet, secretary of the treasury. He was a Pennsylvanian who had lived in Natchez many years, where his wife, Mary, had been Margaret Howell's "dear and intimate friend." Mary was a Bache, great-granddaughter of Benjamin Franklin, and niece to the newly elected vice president, George Mifflin Dallas. Her sister Matilda and Varina became inseparable. Matilda was married to William H. Emory of Maryland, a first lieutenant in the Topographical Engineers. The whole family, "well educated and thoroughly pleasant," furnished the sort of refined and witty society in which Varina shone. Four other sisters were married to men in public life, and two brothers were in the navy.

The genius in the family was Alexander Dallas Bache, Davis's particular friend from West Point days. He was a practical physicist with a knack for communicating his knowledge to others. "I believe he could explain the highest astronomical problems to any one of good understanding," Davis said. He had had a brilliant teaching career after leaving the academy staff, and in 1839 he established the first magnetic observatory in North America, when president of Girard College. He was now superintendent of the U.S. Coast and Geodetic Survey.[54]

Varina speaks of "the joy that used to pervade us" when asked to supper with the family at "the Coast Survey"—an "old-fashioned barrack of a house on the edge of Capitol Hill." The actual survey was under the Treasury Department, but it used army engineers. Davis felt so at home in this quasi-military group that he, Bache, and Emory "told stories of their West Point life," and "jested like boys." Varina recalls the delicate odor of the rose geraniums in the windows, the Rhine wine that Bache had brought back from his visit to the great Baron von Humboldt, and the "quip and jest that flew from one to another" as toasts were drunk. "Mr. Davis was the life of the party." One Christmas he "was persuaded to sing an Indian song, and Dallas Bache put on a fur coat to personate Santa Claus, and gave the presents in the most truly dreadful doggerel." Six months later, feeling "oppressed," Davis decided it was not the hot weather but the memory of that evening. He sighed, "I am sorry I did not make him sing, and do the rhyme myself." Varina comments: "As the Professor could not turn a tune, and Mr. Davis had no capacity for jocular rhyme, I thought they had reached their utmost limits as it was."[55]

The Honorable Jefferson Davis took his seat in the House of Representatives of the Twenty-ninth Congress on December 8, 1845. The literal seat was "a small mahogany desk & arm chair." Around rose twenty-two columns "of beautiful variegated marble," and above was a "magnificent" dome with "finely executed" paintings. At the front, behind elevated desks of Speaker and clerk, were "damask hangings," flanked by portraits of George Washington and the Marquis de Lafayette. Above the dais was "statuary representing Liberty," with an eagle and a serpent-wound column, while opposite, over the entrance, was "another group representing History recording passing events & the wheel of the car is made a clock." "All in all," said this visitor, "the room is a good one, and were members less careless where they spit tobacco juice the hall would be a neat one." Being fastidious in his dress, Davis was probably careful, but like many gentlemen of the day, he did chew.[56]

Davis was not in time to help organize the House as he had hoped, but he was in time to vote for admission of Texas as a state. He first rose to address the House on December 18, in reply to resolutions of the Massachusetts Whig Robert C. Winthrop who, in support of the Native American Party, wanted to "purify the ballot box" and change the naturalization laws. The party was forming to combat the Northern influx of immigrants, largely Roman Catholic. Davis "detested" its "sordid character" and "arrogant assumption"; only barbarians equated "foreign" with "enemy." He reminded the House of European help in the Revolutionary War and of "eight actual foreigners" who signed the Declaration of Independence. He rebuked the new party for claiming George Washington as patron, pointing out that he had welcomed the foreigners and was himself "born for no age and for no land . . . alone in his native grandeur . . . the boast and the property of the world." As for the ballot box, "regulating elections . . . was no concern of Congress": let the states see to it.

Another Massachusetts man had said that in "the whole history of the world . . . wherever a place was found for domestic slavery, there was a place for evil . . . where it was shut out . . . the freest play [was] afforded to moral principles and all right views." This was too much for a man brought up in the strictest morality and living in that very "prosperity and social happiness" that the Yankee denied was possible to his region. He contented himself at the moment with pointing out that Massachusetts had "tolerated slavery" in the day of "both the Adamses" and other patriots: "Would he deny to these men a high moral character?"

This may be the speech—it was one of Davis's first—that caused John Quincy Adams to remark, "That young man, gentlemen, is no ordinary man. He will make his mark yet, mind me." The ex-president usually voted against Davis, being one of the foremost abolitionists in the House, but he and Davis were on committees together and maintained "friendly relations," which "I am happy to remember," Davis wrote, "continued until the close of his life."[57]

Davis's first resolution was to put military schools at army bases. His first committee was the one to consider establishing the Smithsonian Institution. Robert Dale Owen (son of the Owen whom Cruikshank had squelched) introduced a bill to put to this use the bequest (to the United States of $508,318.46) from an Englishman, James Smithson. It was to be used "for the increase & diffusion of knowledge among men," and had been drawing interest at the Philadelphia mint since 1838. No one had known quite what to do with it. There was much protest over this bill from men as diverse as Adams and George W. Jones, but Davis and others argued for it, and President Polk signed it into law on August 10, 1846. Dallas Bache was one of the first regents, and Davis joined him on the board the next year.[58]

In April, Daniel Webster, Whig senator from Massachusetts, was charged by Charles J. Ingersoll, Democratic chairman of the House Committee on Foreign Affairs, with malfeasance when secretary of state in the Harrison-Tyler administration. "The hands of the public men of the time had been clean of plunder," Varina says, "and an imputation upon the honor of a senator startled his colleagues like 'a fire-bell in the night.'" The "effort to stain" Webster's "great reputation" left all Washington divided. Varina went to hear Webster speak in the Senate, not so much defending himself as "confiding his unexpected annoyance." In the House, Davis was put on a committee to determine whether Webster should be impeached.[59]

The committee called John Tyler before it to testify about his cabinet member, and he and others asserted Webster's innocence. The committee members on June 9 submitted to the House their report, drawn up by Davis. It completely exonerated Webster, and the matter was closed. Once more Davis's principles had superseded party loyalty. He was already being denounced for "whitewashing" an opposition leader when a Northern Democrat came to him on the evening of June 8 and implored him not to waste this opportunity to discredit the Whigs.

Nothing fired Davis's temper more quickly than an underhanded appeal to selfishness. "Mr. Davis told him with much heat that if Mr. Webster was to be entailed upon the country for life, 'and no one could deprecate his policy more than I do, I would not make a false and partizan report or parley with my sense of justice and honor, nor would the gentlemen associated with me.' "[60]

Whether Webster heard of this or not, he called on Davis "and expressed in warm terms," Varina says, "his sense of the manly manner in which he had defended him." "He was the most grateful man for any act of kindness or interest in him that I ever knew," said Davis. Later the Websters invited Varina to their home in Marshfield, Massachusetts. She does not say she went, but Davis did, in 1858. "Daniel Webster was very kind to me," he remarked, "and, though some of our political views were thoroughly antagonistic, we always met as friends."[61] This was not uncommon in the Washington of that day. An unspoken law forbade the intrusion of public matters into private society.

Varina was in her element. She loved the bustle and stir and hobnobbing with the great and near-great. Ingersoll, "notwithstanding his ill-made wig, great age, and prejudice against Mr. Webster," gave her "the most delightful evening of my early youth" at the Walkers' by talking to her and George Dallas about Byron, Dante, Virgil, Wordsworth, and Goethe. One day she went where the lines came in from Baltimore, "to see Mr. Morse's machine make the wires talk," and she wrote home, "I think it is a trick, but paid my two-bits (twenty-five cents) to get a message 'that it was a fine day.' " Jeff took her to the very first "National Exhibition" to see products from every state. No sooner had they been awed by the "sewing jenny," and Jeff amused by an old seamstress's disdain of it, than he had to catch an older gentleman to prevent his falling. It turned out to be John Tyler, in town for the Webster hearings. He and Jeff strolled along arm in arm, talking about Webster and agriculture, oblivious of "the young person who trotted beside them, ardently longing for a look at all the new and curious wares displayed."

After they had all had "a tin cup of unpleasantly warm but rich milk" from a fine Hereford of Tyler's, on exhibit from Sherwood Forest, his James River plantation, they sat on a bench in the Capitol grounds, and the men " 'talked above' me" for about an hour. "Mr. Tyler turned and said to me, in a wonderfully winning tone, 'Have I spoiled your morning, Madam, with my dull talk?' My husband, partly conscious that he had, and fearful lest I might not be able to cope with the emergency, answered quickly: 'Oh, no, my little wife is trying to be a statesman.' They both laughed."[62]

Evidently, Varina was already known for her sharp tongue. She was conscious of "that emb[ar]rased angry looking manner" which made her appear "to so much disadvantage," but she told her mother that she had "lost a great deal of" it and "my manners are much improved."

She could see "that Jeff's love is only to be retained by the practice of self-control, and that it is the only mode of gaining his esteem, and confidence."[63] She was maturing quickly into a popular social leader. After one impromptu evening entertainment when, despite a headache, she "played cotillions until I was tired," and "Jeff flirted to his hearts content," she wrote her mother, "I have [a] character you must know of giving the most delightful little hops of the season" (and in a boarding house!). Jeff's "elegant manners" that night left people smiling "wherever he went."

On another evening, however, late in January, she had written:

> Jeff had the hottest fever I ever felt in the next room to where it was all going on. I danced twice, and then went to him—but could not persuade myself to leave him again. I don't know which ached worst his dear head or my heart. . . . I feel so fearful—so uneasy—he has not been well since we arrived here—he has little fevers—cold constantly—severe earaches he sits up until two or three o'clock at night writing—until his eyes even lose their beauty to *me* they look so red and painful. I feel as if he would not stand it another year. I had fearful enough anticipations of what a public life would be but they were nothing like the reality Jeff is not away from me, but he is not so happy as he used to be—his mind wants rest.

She could do little to relieve him except "irritating his temple with volatile linament and rubbing behind his ear"; but "You know how patiently Jeffy always bears suffering."[64]

She tried to relieve his load of work by being secretary and helping to frank all the letters and documents to his constituents. He studied all night, "scrupulously attended" to "calls upon him for service," and went visiting with her "very little." One person he did visit, and that "frequently," was Calhoun. But that was business, preparing for sessions of the House. Calhoun's "conversation was always instructive and peculiarly attractive," Davis said. He discussed with him "the great question of the day": "giving notice to Great Britain of a termination of the joint occupation of Oregon. . . . There was great excitement in the country, and there was believed to be imminent danger of a war with Great Britain." Davis addressed this question in his first major speech, February 6, 1846.[65]

Rebuffed by the British on an offer to divide the vast Oregon country at the forty-ninth parallel, President Polk had led the United States into a belligerent stance by demanding all the land to fifty-four degrees and forty minutes. The country was fired up with the slogan "fifty-four-forty or fight." Calhoun had returned to the Senate expressly to prevent the threatened war. In the House, Davis enunciated, in his own way, Calhoun's position.[66]

Study had made him complete master of his subject. He gave in great detail geography, history (back to Sir Francis Drake), and relations with native tribes in the Pacific Northwest, with treaties and British parliamentary debates, to show that neither country had clear title to all of Oregon. Therefore, "no point of honor" would be involved in accepting a division at the forty-ninth parallel. He supported Polk's hope for more but argued that insistence would certainly mean a war for which the country was in no way prepared, "unarmed" as it was and unable to supply an army so far west. In the face of "war clamor," he would take his stand for peace and "be prepared to meet whatever censure might fall upon the act." He trusted the president to settle this affair by treaty.[67]

There was more at stake than territory. In this first speech are heard themes that would run through Davis's whole congressional career. "In our hearts, as in our history, are mingled the names" that speak "the common glory of our Union," he told the House members. "If envy, and jealousy, and sectional strife, are eating like rust in the bonds our fathers expected to bind us, they come from causes which our southern atmosphere has never furnished." "When ignorance, led by fanatic hate, and armed by all uncharitableness, assails a domestic institution of the South, I try to forgive, for the sake of the righteous among the wicked—our natural allies, the Democracy of the North." What he meant was, New England abolitionists were behind the drive to secure all of Oregon, as "a weight to balance Texas, whilst they attack others as governed by sectional considerations." They were making every issue into a slavery issue. "Public opinion" in the North "was slowly hardening," says an analyst, "and it would soon be impossible for Northern and Southern men to understand one another."[68]

Abolitionists, led in the House by Adams, had openly declared slavery the issue in Texas. They had blocked annexation earlier, saying it would destroy the Union. Adams had even presented a petition "praying for a peaceable dissolution." Now Davis charged that their real aim was to weaken the South. The British, under a similar cloak of philanthropy, had tried to gain control of Texas when it was a republic. Prime Minister Sir Robert Peel had plainly told the House of Commons "that the British Indies, since the emancipation of 1833, could not compete with areas in which slavery still existed, and intimated that British policy required the abolition of slavery in the rest of the Western Hemisphere to restore the balance." Abolition in Texas was to be "a preliminary" to it "in the United States." The American secretary of state had told Calhoun it was "worse than childish to suppose that she meditates this great movement simply from the impulse of philanthropy." It was to "create markets" and "destroy all competition."[69]

In his speech, Davis contrasted the British use of Oregon ("the home of fur-bearing beasts") for trade—a narrow and sordid policy—with the "restless spirit of adventure" that sent Americans there to create farm homesteads out of the wilderness. In the debate, still going on in April, he said it was a rich tribute to "our institutions" that the settlers wanted to come under "the restraints" of American law. In granting this, "most especially let us respect the rights of the more helpless occupant, and more rightful possessor—the savage—who originally held the country." In contrast to European governments, ours "had always recognized the usufruct of the Indians."

By now Texas was a state. Oregon was becoming one. On April 23, 1846, Davis voted to terminate the joint occupation with Great Britain. On June 18, Calhoun won his point; Oregon's southern boundary was set at the forty-ninth parallel. Only the organization of her government remained.[70]

Texas was only partly in the Union. She claimed her southern border was the Rio Grande. Mexico said it was the Neuces River, which ran at an angle to the Rio Grande, with its mouth more than a hundred miles farther north. The United States had sent John Slidell to settle the dispute, but the ever-unstable Mexican government had collapsed, and an anti-American strongman had taken over. Brig. Gen. Zachary Taylor, already near the Neuces mouth at Corpus Christi because of an earlier threat, had been told to move his little army to the Rio Grande. A strong naval force was ordered to patrol the Gulf. All this was in January of 1846.[71]

On May 4, Col. David Twiggs, from Point (now Port) Isabel, Taylor's supply port on the Gulf, wrote to Jefferson Davis

> We have war in earnest on the Rio Grande, an entire squadron of my Regiment (two comps) killed or captured, the army left Matamoros for this place on the 1[s]t of May, lea[v]ing the 7 Infanty & two companies of artr. to garrison a fort erected on the river bank, opposite Matamoros. yesterday morng we heard a vry heavy canonading in that direction, which continued all day & still continues, at intervals (now 4 ock), they have on this side of the river some 4000 men. 2100 light cavalry. We have to oppose that 2100 men. 200 only of cavalry—we have *five* regiments of infantry in the field & not a Single Colonel on duty with them, I am the only full Col. on duty with this army—cannot some thing be done by Congress, to get officers of rank in the field.

The two companies from Twigg's Second Dragoon Regiment had been ambushed on April 25 by Mexican cavalry. Eleven were killed and the captains, William Joseph Hardee and Seth Thornton, taken prisoner. General Taylor wired his government: "Hostilities may now be considered as commenced."[72] What Twiggs heard as he wrote was a day-and-night Mexican artillery barrage on Fort Texas. "Rapid and accurate fire" returned by the two American artillery companies, was all that prevented an assault on the fort. For this "gallant and meritorious conduct," the artillery's 1st Lt. Braxton Bragg was brevetted captain—the army's reward instead of a medal. Taylor had told his men to hold the post until he got back with supplies from Point Isabel. Surrounded and called on to surrender or die, the officers voted to a man to fight on. Just as they trusted, Taylor was coming. At Palo Alto and again at Resaca de la Palma he had to drive Mexican forces out of his path. These battles forced the United States to face the fact of war. At President Polk's call, Congress declared it, by votes of 174 to 14 in the House and 40 to 2 in the Senate. Calhoun abstained, opposing this war as he had one over Oregon. Obviously slavery was not the issue for him; his only colleagues were Whigs and abolitionists.[73]

In Woodville, Mississippi, "We are in great excitement, drums, beating, fifes, playing, flags flying, meetings holding, and 'To Arms, To arms,' in large Capitals stuck up at every corner of the streets." Woodville's son in Congress showed his excitement by pressing "for the vigorous prosecution of hostilities" and by telling his friend John Willis that "in the event of war I should like to command a Warren regiment." He explained to another friend: "My education and former practice would, I think, enable me to be of service to Mississippians who take the field. If they wish it, I will join them as soon as possible, wherever they may be." The editor of the *Vicksburg Sentinel and Expositor* printed part of this letter and urged the volunteers "UNANIMOUSLY" to choose Davis, the "gallant, glorious son of our soil—to lead you to your country's service." Davis still thought there would "probably" be war with England over Oregon, and he wanted peace made with Mexico quickly "by an Ambassador who cannot be refused"—"American cannon"—so as to be ready for "action on a larger scale."[74] While confessing his "strong desire" to go, Davis felt he had to remember "all which is due to those who sent me here." With volunteer companies forming all over Mississippi, he forcibly turned his attention to Congress.[75]

An issue as important as the war itself came to a head before Davis got to the battlefield. Democrats had a mandate to "restrict appropriations to objects which are clearly constitutional." Calhoun tried to get around this to allow internal improvements. When the Harbors and Rivers Bill came to the House floor, Davis argued that if the government were "permitted to take power from a connexion so remote and indirect" as that "to regulate commerce" ("Regulate is not synonymous with facilitate or create—the verb is derived from the substantive *regula*, a rule") it would "be no longer limited by the terms of its specific grants." It would be deciding its own powers "at discretion," rendering the reserved powers of the states "a bitter and delusive mockery." The bill passed.[76]

Calhoun was trying to draw together the West (the Mississippi Valley) and the South by this. Davis claimed it would not "cement our Union" but "will more probably generate disaffection and discord." "Cohesion" and the true interest of the West (with which he identified himself) lay rather in avoiding "the onerous taxation necessary" for "such a system," in strict governmental economy and in "rigid adherence to the Constitution."[77] By this bill, Calhoun got his improvements for the West (usually paid for by high tariffs) in return for support of the South's low tariff, formulated by Robert J. Walker. Davis preferred to have "the Democratic ship" stranded, rather than sacrifice "that rigid interpretation of the Constitution, by which alone we can hope for the maintenance of the Union." The South might have done well to heed Davis. Calhoun's astute move proved deadly. On August 3, as soon as Congress passed the Walker tariff, James K. Polk vetoed the Harbors and Rivers Bill. The West felt betrayed and "turned to the free states for an offer. The Northern price was the exclusion of slavery from the territories"—the issue that finally drove the South to secession.[78]

Davis had defended West Point and the army earlier, pleading successfully for two new regiments of infantry and one of mounted rifles to protect the route to Oregon. He had thwarted a Native American Party move to exclude foreigners from the regiments by citing an Englishman "who was the best dragoon he had ever seen."[79] Now he tried to get medals voted for everyone involved in the Texas battles, but only Taylor got one. In this debate, William Sawyer of Ohio urged Congress to abolish the United States Military Academy, saying nine-tenths of the graduates never served in the army, and it was "a blight, a mildew, a curse upon the nation." Davis leapt to defend it: most graduates were still in service, and it had furnished "a large majority" of officers in the recent battles. Let Sawyer consider why Fort Texas "stands unharmed by Mexican shot, whilst its guns have crumpled the stone walls in Matamoras to the ground, and then say whether he believes a blacksmith or a tailor could have secured the same results. He trusted the gentleman would be convinced that arms, like every occupation, requires to be studied."[80]

Davis had only named the trades at random, in contrast to trained soldiers, but Sawyer, a blacksmith, was outraged that Davis implied "a blacksmith or a tailor was not competent to take charge of our army." Davis replied that only Sawyer "could have so far misunderstood him," but a tailor was even more outraged, Andrew Johnson. Refusing to listen to Davis, he launched into a defense of his "class," which he called "mechanics"—Adam was a tailor, sewing fig leaves together, and "the Redeemer of mankind . . . the son of a carpenter." This was the occasion when Johnson railed against the "bastard, scrub aristocracy" that possessed "neither talents, information, nor a foundation on which you can rear a superstructure that would be useful."[81]

Armistead Burt seized the floor to keep Davis from replying, but the next day, the gentleman from Mississippi patiently explained his position again, saying that "he was incapable of wantonly wounding the feelings, or of making invidious reflections upon the origin or occupation of any man." Johnson paid no attention and went right on vindicating "the mechanical professions." The *Daily National Intelligencer* referred to this as a "colloquy of a personal and somewhat angry kind," and from it, says Varina, "arose all Mr. Johnson's subsequent animosity against Mr. Davis."[82]

Jefferson Davis knew perfectly well, even as Sawyer said, that formal training was not necessary to make a soldier. There were Washington, Jackson, and now Taylor to prove it, and he was recommending as brigadier general a lawyer who had been his Spanish tutor, John A. Quitman. Quitman wrote from Natchez of "highest excitement," with everyone "ready to volunteer." He was only afraid they would not be allowed to send as many troops as Louisiana. When William L. Marcy, secretary of war, allowed Mississippi only one regiment, the Pontotoc Dragoons felt it an insult to their "chivalry and devotion to country."[83]

Meanwhile, the trained Mississippi soldier, Jefferson Davis, was still detained in the capital by duty. He had to send Varina and Malie out of the heat to "the mountain air." "You asked me my dear Mother if I attend church," Varina had written; "I am not often well enough to sit up all day my health is very bad." When a "sweet letter . . . bearing on its face that ardent love you have always manifested" brought "sad tidings" that she was really ill, Jeff wrote, "Dear Wife Winnie," dating the letter "Morning in our room." "I may say as the great English poet said . . . 'and thou art sick and I not there.' " "Selfish as love must ever be, my first intention was to start in the morning and bring you back immediately." Then he remembered how "unhealthy" Washington was and how the vote on the tariff bill was pending. He trusted the servant Betsy to take care of her, but "if my presence is necessary to you all other things must yield." "May the Lord bless and protect my own sweet wife is the prayer of / Your 'Hubbin'. "[84]

There is no hint here of the "bitter" struggle over his volunteering, "though it was carried on in love between us." Varina had written Ma on June 6, "I found out last night accidentally that he had committed himself about going. I have cried until I am stupid, but you know there is 'no use crying, better luck next time.' " "Jeff promised me he would not volunteer, but he could not help it I suppose. . . . he is such a dear good fellow, I might quarrel a month and he would not get mad." To him, it was simple: "Having received a military education . . . I felt that my services were due to the country." Technically, he had not volunteered, only agreed to serve *if* there was war and *if* elected. Late in June, James Roach brought the news: he had been elected colonel of the First Mississippi Regiment.[85]

Davis wanted rifles for his regiment, and Polk promised him a direct order for them if he would only stay long enough for the vote on Walker's tariff.

> I made a requisition for a thousand Percussion Rifles of the model manufactured by Whitney at New Haven Connecticut, and the next day was requested by the Secretary [of War] to see General Scott. . . . [He] expressed a doubt as to the propriety of supplying a whole Regiment with percussion arms and positively insisted that at least six of the Companies should bear muskets, instead of rifles. I knew the confidence of the Men I was expecting to lead had in rifles, and their distrust of the musket then in use and therefore notwithstanding my reluctance to oppose the General insisted upon the thousand rifles and claimed from the Secretary the fulfillment of the President's promise to me.

Thus Davis commanded the first full rifle regiment, the unit he had urged on Congress as "the wanting bone to the skeleton of our army." Now he had only to defend Walker against "reviling as unjust as it was bitter" and vote for his tariff. Then, leaving Roach to see the rifles safely to New Orleans by sea, Col. and Mrs. Jefferson Davis set out for home, July 4, 1846.[86]

VII

Fame

In Col. Jeff Davis now rode the family pride in military service. It had slipped into his Oregon speech. He had thought someone slighted Mississippi's military record and cited Andrew Jackson's compliment to the dragoons of 1815: "the admiration of one army and the wonder of the other." And "whenever the honor of our country is assailed," he went on, "threatened with a cloud of banners that folded wait to gather on our sky, and darken it with the storm of war . . . [Mississippi's] sons will answer with defiance, and scornfully reply, 'Free be your banners flung, we're loth / Their silken folds should feed the moth.' "

These lines, taken from the dark protagonist of Sir Walter Scott's *Lady of the Lake*, sent Davis, as it were, on his way to Mexico. Taking the National Road home, he, Varina, and Malie found the mountainsides over which they had slipped so painfully last December "rosy with the blossoms of the laurel." "During the greater part of the journey Mr. Davis studied a little pocket edition of military tactics," Varina tells us, "and, when I remonstrated, explained agreeably the mysteries of enfilading, breaking column, hollow squares, and what not." One day "a rumbling noise in front of us" turned out to be a "battery going down to Mexico. Mr. Davis got out of the stage," and after "a few moments' eager conversation" with a cannoneer, "came back alert and flushed by the anticipation of his prospective campaign."[1]

She was still beside herself: "If Jeff was a cross bad husband, old, ugly, or stupid, I could better bear for him to go on a years campaign," she had written Ma, "but he is so tender, and good that I feel like he ought never to leave me." She had met her match: the army. Jeff had been willing to sacrifice his love for this rival for Knox Taylor. Now, he felt able to follow the siren call of the bugle and still hold close his new young wife. As their steamboat started down the Ohio, he tried to arrange for Varina's happiness in his absence by a letter to his saintly sister Lucinda. It shows the strains usual to the first year of marriage and speaks volumes about them both.

> I am on my way to Vicksburg as Colonel . . . and if occasion offers it may be that I will return with a reputation over which you will rejoice as my Mother would have done. . . . Varina [is] far from well. I wished to leave her in the North this summer, but she would not consent. If circumstances warranted it I would send her to you. To you and your family alone of all the world could I entrust her and rest assured that no waywardness would ever lessen kindness. . . .
>
> She will probably stay with her Mother most of the time. . . . With Eliza she could not be contented, nor would their residing together increase their good feeling for each other. This distresses me as you will readily imagine, but if you ever have an opportunity to understand Varina's character, you will see the propriety of the conclusion, and I feel that you will love her too much to take heed of the weaknesses which spring from a sensitive and generous temper.[2]

Varina did spend time with Eliza, with Anna Smith in Louisiana, and with her mother, but does not seem to have visited Lucinda. She insisted, in her independence, her strength of character, on spending a good bit of time at her own home, Brierfield, alone with the servants.[3]

When she and Jeff reached Brierfield now, they tried to arrange in one day for the expected absence of "a year or more." James Pemberton, given the choice, decided that he should stay and look after the place, especially as Varina "should need his protection"; so Jeff took one of Joseph's people, big Jim Green, with him. (Even most of the privates in the Mississippi regiment "took their servants to do the drudgery of the camp.") Choosing a stout horse for Jim and a temperamental Arabian named Tartar for himself, Colonel Davis set off to join his men.[4]

Made up of ten companies from all over Mississippi, the regiment had already gone to New Orleans under the second in command, Alexander Keith McClung. Aboard the steamboat *Star Spangled Banner* on July 13, 1846, Davis wrote to his constituents about the current political issues and said he hoped his experience "in the line of the army" might promote "the comfort, the safety and efficiency of the Mississippi Regiment." He promised to resign if the war was not over soon. Fifty-six-year-old Alexander B. Bradford (no kin to Malie) had first beat out Davis for colonel, but by only fifty from over nine hundred votes. He had graciously proposed another poll so that one of them might receive a majority, and Davis had won. Then Bradford had been elected major and McClung, lieutenant colonel.[5] The First Mississippi had chosen well; for eminently brave as they proved to be, Bradford was a flamboyant "Amateur of chivalry," and McClung, an eccentric. Neither had the training or the steadiness of Davis. When he got to New Orleans on July 17, he found that McClung had his men camping out in "inclement weather" and began the promised "comfort" by moving them to shelter.[6]

The regiment began to set sail piecemeal for the army concentration at the mouth of the Rio Grande. But the hard-won rifles had not arrived. Davis wrote to R. J. Walker, asking him to look into it. Perhaps Walker helped by getting use of the two revenue cutters of the Treasury Department by which James Roach sent the rifles, evading the slow quartermasters. The first ones got to Davis, however, only after he had reached the Rio Grande and was about to start for Zachary Taylor's base camp, some four hundred miles upriver at Camargo.[7]

He complained, as most others were doing, of "delay and detention at every turn," telling Walker that the New Orleans quartermasters were acting either "incompetently or maliciously." His men had "suffered much from disease, had transportation been furnished promptly we would have gone with a full Regt." With his usual acute observation, he spotted one of the troubles. "The mouth of this River has but little to invite one seeking the Land of promise," he said, "but the current meets the sea with such force as to keep the entrance generally smooth." He wondered why supplies were not landed there, "instead of being carried over the breakers at the Brozos [Brazos Island] in lighters & then brought in other lighters here."[8]

He had dashed off a "heart full of love to my own Winnie" in New Orleans, signing, "Your Hubbie." Now, "waiting for a lighter," he had time to write a real letter. He was "much gratified" that her "affectionate" one had shown her "engaged in useful and domestic things." "However unimportant in themselves each may be, it is the mass which constitutes the business of life, and as it is pursued so will it generally be found that a woman is happy and contented." He recommended "the cultivation of shrubs" because "no suspicion of ingratitude or faithfulness [*sic*] can exist towards them." His "extraordinarily quiet voyage" prompted this reflection: "Several times I have thought may it not be that the calm sea over which we are running is type of my fortune where agitation is to me of far greater moment than in the waters of the gulf—may God have preserved you as calm— . . . I ask that the season of our absence may be a season of reflection bearing fruits of soberness, and utility, and certainty of thought and of action." But he ends lightheartedly. After "Kiss Ma and the Children" comes, "Hubbin would kiss the paper . . . but is in the midst of the men, who though talking & whistling . . . have time to observe any thing the Col. does—I send a kiss upon the wires of love and feel earth, air & sea cannot break the connection." On August 16, still worrying, he offered her a surer help than shrubbery, out of his own devotional habits: "I have remembered your request on the subject of profanity and have improved— Have you remembered mine on the subject of prayer, and a steady reliance on the justice of one who sees through the veil of conduct to the motives of the heart. Be pious, be calm, be useful, and charitable and temperate in all things."[9]

He was still waiting "to ascend the River, much chafed by delay but in good health." Zachary Taylor, himself delayed for lack of a steamboat to take him from Matamoros to Camargo, wrote to Davis about "your excellent Regt.": "I am more than anxious to take you by the hand, and to have you & your command with or near me . . . but trust it will not be long before I shall have that pleasure." It was long. The general got to his upriver base and had started his army south from the Rio Grande by August 18, but his son-in-law could not follow until September 7. By that time, Taylor was almost halfway to Monterey.[10]

Davis met many old army friends in Mexico. Sidney Johnston was "on the march from Camargo," as colonel and acting inspector general in Maj. Gen. William O. Butler's "Field Division" of volunteer troops, in which the First Mississippi formed part of John A. Quitman's brigade. Johnston had brought down a Texas rifle regiment, but the volunteers had gone home when their enlistment term ran out, leaving their colonel high and dry. To keep him, Taylor had put him on his staff and then assigned him to Butler.[11] Davis's former commander, David Twiggs, had won a general's star by now, and he headed Taylor's First Division. Even old Whistler, sixty-six and colonel of the Fourth Infantry, had been on the Rio Grande, commanding the Third Brigade, but appears to have left before Davis arrived. Capt. George Crosman was there, and the lackadaisical Bennet Riley, a brevet colonel, said to Davis, "Good luck to you, my boy! As for me—six feet of Mexican soil or a [general's] yellow sash!"[12]

William Harney was in Mexico, but it would be a while before he and Davis met. He had been breveted colonel in 1840 for service in the Indian wars in Florida. As colonel of the Second Dragoons at San Antonio de Bexar, Texas, he had just been reprimanded by Brig. Gen. John E. Wool for dashing to the border, too anxious to fight. Wool was in charge of an expedition against Chihuahua, designed to cross the Rio Grande far above Taylor's men to secure their northwest flank. After that, the plan was uncertain. Meeting no opposition, Wool and his army went nine hundred gruelling miles into Mexico, never did take Chihuahua, and joined Taylor three months later near Saltillo. Laying the road before this force was the engineer officer, Capt. Robert E. Lee, but he and Davis just missed each other in Mexico.[13]

At Carmago, Davis may have first met William Joseph Hardee, who later became his good friend. Captain Hardee was rather notorious. In May he had requested a court of inquiry, to combat rumors about his conduct when captured in the Mexican foray that started the war. He was not actually charged with cowardice, but his fellow captain, Seth Thornton, was. Both were exonerated. Thornton was defended by

Braxton Bragg in court and by Jefferson Davis in Congress. Davis had followed every detail of this affair, which involved his own dragoons, and the early battles. Hardee, detained by sickness, got to the field just in time for the battle of Monterey and served under Taylor until transferred to Scott.[14]

The First Mississippi Regiment was made up of "the best-born, best-educated, and wealthiest young men of the State," says Reuben Davis (and he was later colonel of the *Second* Regiment). Davis's nephew Robert Hugh Davis and his brother-in-law Joe Howell were privates. His friend John Willis was captain of the Vicksburg Southrons. Lt. Amos Breckinridge Corwine later called Davis his "best Earthly friend and benefactor."[15] Capt. William P. Rogers and 1st Lt. Daniel R. Russell were not friends of Davis's, but they became so through his generous treatment of them. He was closest to Lt. Richard Griffith, his adjutant, who exemplified the diversity of Mississippi's society and its regiment. Born in Philadelphia, educated in Ohio, he had become a Vicksburg businessman. McClung and Bradford and at least sixteen others hailed from afar, three of them from Europe.[16]

Davis was "approachable to the lowest," said Sgt. William E. Estes, though he "carried with him into the camp and on the battle-field that native dignity which has [always] characterized him." It did not prevent him from laughing out loud at times, once when he saw two privates "playing cards while marching along," putting them "under the straps of the men in front." His manner in public dealings with men (never with women) was often severe, perhaps to cover up the tenderness and sensitivity that he felt as a fault. First Lt. Carnot Posey complained of his "repulsive and abrupt manner," contrasted to "that urbanity and courtesy which he can so easily assume." Posey thought, wrongly, that it was endangering "the affection . . . of his entire regiment."[17]

Davis made a point of knowing his enlisted men by first name as well as last. They never forgot it. They wrote to him ever after, wanting an appointment, a donation, a pension, or just to talk. One asked his help in getting out of the California penitentiary. One white-haired veteran decided to test him some forty years after the war. He moved from the periphery of a crowd that Davis had addressed to the speaker's platform, offered his hand, and asked if he knew him. "Mr. Davis fixed his eyes upon him for a moment, his mouth twitched, tears sprang into his eyes and he exclaimed: 'Ward, snow has fallen on your head since I last saw you.'"[18]

Even Davis's temper did not alienate his men. Sgt. Maj. Francis A. Wolff ran into it on this march. He was laying stones in a brook "for the infantry to cross over dryshod," but he was not fast enough. "The head of the column was pressing us closely. Col. Davis galloped up & reproved me harshly. . . . However, he increased my force of stone-rollers, and we kept ahead." Wolff wrote to Davis in 1848, reminding him of "his tone to me" that day. He had named a nephew for him and "intimated that he owed the child a coat." Calling him "My dear friend," Davis replied: "I have very often thought of you since we parted. . . . The incident you mention is wholly forgotten by me, I wish it were so by you, and yet I should then have lost the gratification it gives me to feel that my comrade in privation and danger remembers my infirmities only to forgive them." He hoped to "fulfill . . . the time-honored custom" of the coat. In the meantime, he would send "the young gentleman" what "will be his first book, I suppose . . . the new edition of the constitution . . . which I hope he will study early and well; that in after life, should the sacred compact of our Union be even less respected than now, he will stand its able and devoted champion" and "feel for it the reverence which impressed on childhood, age seldom obliterates."[19]

Stealing ears from a cornfield brought down his wrath, remembered one soldier: "I saw the Colonel coming and hid mine under a bush; but he was in such a tearing rage and asked me where the rest were that I pointed over the fence and made tracks for camp. That night he made us a speech, and told us that private rights must and should be respected. So he found out the owner of the corn and paid for the crop." In the midst of "diamonds, rubies, and emeralds" in the churches, and valuable Mexican stores, Davis allowed only one pair of shoes to be taken, and that was government, not private, property. This accorded with Taylor's directives and with his own sense of right.[20]

Part of his men's affection came from the unusual care Davis took of them. He personally saw to it that they had water, sought protection for them on the field, had his surgeon out giving "early relief to the wounded" and men bringing them in immediately after a battle, contrary to much practice then and later. His regiment had fewer casualties at Monterey than did others, and he boasted that they suffered only one amputation. Even Joe Howell, whose family feared his "six feet seven inches would make him a mark for the enemy," came safely through. The colonel "gave an attentive ear" to the grievances of privates and jealously guarded the interests of all.

His primary aim was to make a first-class fighting force, and he knew that discipline produced not only efficiency, but the true well-being of his men. The tactics book that Varina had seen him studying embraced formations and evolutions on the drill field and the use of small arms. Colonel Davis insisted on mastery of these. There was as yet no manual for rifles, so he wrote one himself. Estes says he "never relaxed the rigid military regulations in the least."[21]

"When we first went out," wrote Sergeant Wolff, "a few of the officers & men chafed under the necessary restraints of military usages & discipline." Joseph Davis wrote his brother: "Some complaints have been uttered against you for severity of training, but the battle I suppose will silence all murmurings, and the grumblers will hide their heads."

That was true. Wolff said: "After the first battle, & a little before, all these little 'cut-ups' & whimpers changed to the ecstacy of admiration; nor did their devotion ever falter to their beloved commander. To be with him was to tread the path of glory."[22]

As part of the Second Brigade, Davis's rifle regiment marched in Mexico to a junction with Gen. Thomas L. Hamer's First Brigade, made up of volunteers: the First Kentucky and First Ohio Regiments. At Cerralvo, Davis left two of his ten companies as a guard. From this point, their division commander, Butler, led the brigades to Marín, where the two divisions of regulars, Twiggs's First and William J. Worth's Second, were waiting. Just beyond Marín, Davis finally came up with Zachary Taylor. "On a hill, sat Gen. Taylor on 'Old Whitey,'" Frank Wolff reports. "Col. Davis galloped up to him with all the true bearing of a gallant Knight. They clasped hands, & the meeting was evidently warm & cordial." Gen. James Pinckney Henderson brought two regiments of mounted Texans to the rendezvous. Then the entire army advanced to within three miles of Monterey and camped at Walnut Springs.[23]

Taylor was heading for Saltillo, a mountain fastness some fifty miles southwest. He had met no resistance at all. At the strongly fortified city of Monterey, the Mexicans decided to make a stand. On September 20, 1846, Taylor began his assault. He had about six thousand men with which to attack a garrison of seven thousand who had "more than forty guns." Having "no proper siege train" of artillery with which to batter down the walls, he tried a pincer movement. He sent Worth to circle behind the city and enter from the northwest, while the other troops created a diversion on the east. The next day he changed this diversion into attack. His men got into the city but were pinned down by artillery and by small arms fire from the roofs and a bypassed fort, the Tenería. Bvt. Capt. Bragg found he could not maneuver his "horse artillery" in the narrow, twisted streets and never fired a shot that day. Taylor himself came in on foot with the Ohio regiment, only to meet the same incapacitating fire. Attempts to capture the galling Tenería had all been repulsed when the Mississippians and Tennesseans of General Quitman's brigade arrived before it.[24]

"I saw Col. Davis on his iron grey," says Wolff; "we felt the inspiration of his clarion voice." "The embrasures revealed cannon of large caliber & infantry well posted behind the parapets. . . . Already we had stepped over the bodies of . . . the young bloods of Tennessee." "Balls of all sorts sizes and descriptions were poured upon us from [the flanking forts]—killing and wounding a great many of our men," wrote Joe Howell. Davis ordered a "complicated evolution" meant to reduce the exposure of his men and give them better position: "Damn it why do not the men get nearer to the fort? why waste ammunition?" "Quietly and perfectly" they obeyed.[25] Then he told them "steadily to advance, firing." "Their fine rifles told upon the enemy so that in . . . say ten minutes, his fire was so reduced as to indicate the propriety of a charge. I had no instructions, no information as to the plan." Capt. John McManus heard him say, "Now is the time, Great God, if I had thirty men with knives I could take that fort."[26] Lieutenant Russell heard him "above the din of the battle shouting loudly for a charge" and saw him "50 yards before the general line . . . with your sword upraised waiving over your head Cheering on the Battalion." Lt. Col. McClung, not hearing Davis's order, had sprung before his old company, crying "Tombigbee boys, follow me!" He and Davis and a lieutenant leapt upon the wall together. The Mexicans were fleeing. McClung, "waving his sword in triumph, proclaimed the victory." A few minutes later, at another place, the "perfectly and powerfully formed" McClung fell with two fingers of his left hand shot off and a ball through his right hip.[27]

The Mexicans had run "hastily out of the redoubt to the stone building in the rear, and we pursued them," Davis relates. "I was so close behind . . . that as they closed the heavy door, I ran with all my force against it, before it could be barred and threw it open." A cry of surrender went up, and the officer there "delivered his sword." Davis shortly handed this prized trophy over to Sidney Johnston, who had arrived with other troops. Davis "followed the flying Mexicans with a large part of my regiment to attack the Fort el Diablo," to the west of La Tenería, and was soon complaining to Johnston that Quitman had ordered him back ("you were cursing bitterly," Lieutenant Russell said). The spot where they were standing was under artillery cross fire, which wounded General Butler. Davis asked his generals to let him move out and attack another fort. When they did not respond, Johnston told him to go ahead and try. He moved his men forward and was planning the attack with two regular army officers when they were all ordered back. Taylor was withdrawing his whole force from Monterey.

Davis was appointed rear guard for his division. Johnston and General Hamer, in place of the wounded Butler, were leading the way through a cornfield enclosed "by a high fence made of chaparral-bushes," when Mexican lancers leaped the fence and "commenced slaughtering stragglers and wounded men." Johnston, armed only with the captured sword, "felt that his hour was near." Then "he heard someone giving orders in tones welcome and familiar." Davis had halted his regiment, "formed line to the rear, and advanced on the enemy, firing." The lancers fled.[28]

The next day, September 22, while General Worth completed seizure of the western fortifications, Quitman's brigade was given the Tenería to hold. The enemy did not attack, though "he ought to have," Davis says, but his movements and rockets kept the Mississippians on the *qui vive* all day and all night. They were under "rain and a norther," and the blankets and food Davis ordered did not come. "Though the exposure was extremely severe," he wrote, "we remained at the breast work," and when he ordered a sortie at daybreak, the men "rushed forward with the same impetuosity as before."[29]

Then came their "heroic advance made into the very heart of danger" through lanes and gardens of the city, fighting from house to house. Under "a murderous fire," the men cheered when Captain Bragg, "galloping, fearlessly, at the head," "wheeled his artillery" and "commenced firing along the streets, & driving the enemy back upon the Plaza." Davis and Texans under General Henderson worked their way within sight of the Grand Plaza and planned to stay the night, firing into it; but when Davis sent for more men, he discovered, much to his disgust, that he had long since been ordered to retire.[30]

This was not easy. Davis learned "that the enemy was behind us, that all our other troops had been withdrawn, and that orders had three times been sent to me to return." It was late afternoon, ammunition was spent, the Mississippians had not eaten for thirty-six hours. They tried to slip back quietly but found themselves facing at the first square a battery of artillery "posted to command the street." Davis decided, "I should go first; if only one gun was fired at me, then another man should follow; and so on, another and another, until a volley should be fired, and then all of them should rush rapidly across before the guns could be reloaded. In this manner the men got across with little loss" and made their way out of the city.[31]

Worth had also attacked from the west and was shelling the Plaza. "Early next morning General Ampudia, commanding the Mexican force, sent in a flag and asked for a conference," wrote Davis. General Taylor "appointed General Worth, Governor Henderson, and myself, commissioners to arrange the terms of capitulation." The terms were written out, but Ampudia began "to delay and chaffer." Taylor told Davis to call for his copy early the next morning. "At dawn of day, I mounted my horse and started." As he passed the tents of Taylor and Sidney Johnston, they hailed him, and Johnston "proposed to go with me. General Taylor promptly said he wished he would do so." They rode through the streets towards Ampudia's headquarters in the Grand Plaza. Armed infantry lined the flat roofs; behind barricades was the Mexican artillery with "gunners in place, and the port-fires blazing." Raising white handkerchiefs, the two friends rode up to the battery. Three times they asked to see Ampudia; three times messengers were dispatched; but they never came back.

A crowd gathered. Johnston was wearing "a red-flannel shirt, blue-jean pants, a torn check coat, and a wide-awake hat," because his uniform had been ruined by seawater. His son relates how an "old hag . . . thrust out her skinny finger toward [him] and hissed out, 'Tejano!' [Texan]." "Immediately the aspect of the mob became more threatening," and the Americans "were probably saved from violence only by the opportune arrival of Ampudia's adjutant-general." The adjutant, however, merely tried to ride past them. Then, says Davis, with "that quick perception and decision which characterize the military genius," Johnston said to him, "'Had we not better keep him with us?' We squared our horses so as to prevent his passing," and he finally "turned back and conducted us to his chief." As Davis wrote: "The occasion may seem small to others; it was great to us. Together we had seen the sun rise; and the chances seemed to both, many to one, that neither of us would ever see it set." Ampudia received them effusively and offered breakfast. They declined, procured their document, and left. "After we had ridden, perhaps a mile," says Davis, "in leaping a ditch the flap of my holster flew up, and I discovered that the pistol"—the one Johnston had given him—"the best I ever owned"—had been stolen.[32]

The English copy of the capitulation, "done at Monterey sept. 24th 1846," is in Davis's hand. It proclaimed an eight-week armistice. Mexicans were to retire under arms to a line forty miles south; Americans were to occupy the city with its public stores and munitions. Congress had commended Taylor in July for "generosity to the vanquished"; now he was criticized. Even Joseph Davis asked his brother why "you had the Mexicans penned and let them go again." The government eventually "disapproved," but Davis always defended the lenient terms.[33]

The battle had tried the First Mississippi, and their colonel too. Davis's discipline showed its worth. He found that both the men and their rifles proved "equal to my highest expectations," as he evidently had to Taylor, who made him his envoy and commended him, among others, for "coolness and gallantry against the enemy." Joe Howell wrote home to Ma:

> Our Col, and our regiment wear the palm of honour for coolness courage and hard fighting, by universal acclamation. Brother Jeffs influence in the army here, and with Gen Taylor, is equalled by no other officer, the old Gen, calls us the striped tigers, from our uniforms being all striped, and says damn the boys, they make their little brass mounted rifles, do more execution in an hour than my regulars can do with musket and bayonet in a day—

Davis's "discretion" had also won him a "degree of power" in the army that "would hardly be believed at home. Everything difficult of decision is left to him."[34]

Many hoped the war was over, but Joe reported a proclamation by Santa Anna, the Mexican leader, as "anything but peaceful." He told Ma that if the enlistment time ran out, "and our Colonel even then thinks that we could be useful, there is not a man in his regiment who would not sacrifice his life to obey him, so much has his gallant conduct raised him in their estimation."

> I verily believe that if he should tell his men to jump into a cannon's mouth they would . . . all say, "Colonel Jeff," as they call him, "knows best, so hurrah, boys, let's go ahead." He is always in front of his men, and ready to be the first to expose himself . . . he has taken them into so many tight places, and got them out safely, that they begin to think if they follow him they will be sure to succeed. . . . I never wish to be commanded by a truer soldier than Colonel Davis.[35]

Colonel Jeff obviously enjoyed his command. It had proved him an organizer, a leader, and, above all, a fighter. He was soon telling the people of Vicksburg that the hour when he took their thanks back to the *"gentlemen"* of his command, whose "high spirit of honor" had added to "the chivalry of our State," would be "the proudest and happiest of my life."

If he had not obeyed Varina's behest about profanity, his surroundings were his excuse. "To swear like a trooper" was proverbial. Added to his ingrained habit and the stress of battle was the example of Zachary Taylor's "emphatic style of language," and "Old Davy" Twiggs was known as one of the best cussers in the army.[36] Davis's request to her about prayer met with more success. She wrote: "My darling Banny, . . . I have nothing to say, only to pray for you. . . . Dearest, best beloved, may God bring you these arms once more, and then at least for the time I clasp you I shall be happy. As God is your shield, and buckler may he shelter you, and bear you up, and give his angels charge over you is the prayer of your devoted Wife." Varina had not been well when he left, and "after the battle of Monterey my anxiety and depression were so great, and my health so much impaired" that Davis asked for a furlough. Leaving Major Bradford in charge, he started home on October 19. It took two months to get from Monterey to Davis Bend and back, and then he had only two weeks at Brierfield. Accompanied by John Willis, "he rode Tartar down, to take him home, for fear he might be shot in battle." The high-strung horse refused to leap from lighter to ship at Brazos, for all the sailors' blows, until Davis called him gently by name. Then, crouching "like a cat," and waiting for the proper moment, he "sprang lightly by his master's side, amid the cheers of the sailors."[37]

In New Orleans, Davis saw in the *Daily Picayune* a letter signed Balie Peyton, giving all the credit for capturing the Tenería to the First Tennessee Regiment. The colonel, William B. Campbell, claimed as much. Davis sent a note by John Willis asking Peyton to retract this "injustice to the Miss. Regt." but he refused. When Colonel Davis got home ("my ideas of military propriety prevented" an earlier statement), he wrote in the *Vicksburg Sentinel* that the claim was "improbable, unjust . . . and unnecessary": "the conduct of the whole was the property of each." He said that "commendation of the Tennesseans, our comrads in battle, could only give pleasure to me, & surely neither their gallantry, nor the character of their Colonel are issues which I have made." He again asked Peyton to retract, but he never did.[38]

Davis wrote "as a duty to my Regiment." Peyton, writing to Campbell (both Whigs), tried to reduce the matter to politics: Davis "only wished to make a little Locofoco [Democratic] capital at home" and "play the heroe at my expense." Davis's mind was not on politics. He had just resigned his seat in Congress, though some of his friends were "very much opposed." When he finally challenged someone over the regiment, in 1850, it was a Democrat, but the duel was avoided.[39]

In 1847, another Whig tried to tear down Davis. The crippled McClung, recovered and running for Congress, said that he, not Davis, had first ordered the attack on the Tenería. John Willis advised Davis not to answer "McClung's public card." William P. Rogers, captain of McClung's own company, told Davis not to imperil his "great popularity" by a reply, because McClung's "letter has fallen still born from the press."[40]

He did reply when a McClung newspaper insinuated that "sycophantic friends" and "public puffing" had gotten Davis elected colonel of the Second Mississippi Regiment. (He declined.) Davis had only to show the letter that said, "you are the *unanimous* choice of the whole regiment," but he indulged his sarcastic mode: he could not imagine "whose vanity has been wounded, whose envy excited, whose jealousy has prompted him to this misrepresentation." McClung indeed despised Davis. Before he turned his pistol on himself in 1855, he wanted to turn it on Davis in a duel "because I think the United States will be better off without him. . . . He is a dangerous and wily politician, loaded down with vanity and self conceit, wishing only for his own aggrandizement." But in those very years, Davis, urged by a Whig to be "magnanimous," twice recommended McClung for an army appointment, which he failed to receive.[41]

On the plantation Jeff found, as Joseph had written, that James Pemberton had "one hundred & seventy thousand pounds [of cotton] picked," enough for three hundred bales—"near as much as the Hurricane crop." While at Brierfield, Davis made out his will. He asked the manager "what he wished done in the matter of his liberty. James said he would prefer, in case of the death of his master, to take care of his mistress, but wanted his freedom if anything should happen to her." He was deeded "land or money, as he might choose." On November 10, when volunteers were feted in Vicksburg, Davis told some three hundred banqueters that others might have been first "in blazoning their deeds," but no one "beat the Mississippians in storming the enemy's ramparts." Taking Jim Green again as servant, he chose Richard, "a noble bay with black points," to replace Tartar, and started back.[42]

During a delay in New Orleans, he wrote to Robert Walker about a military idea, about the situation in Mexico, and about free trade. By December 10 he had reached the mouth of the Rio Grande and addressed "Dear Winnie," "sweetest wife." His arms were apparently all the medicine she needed. Joseph was soon sending "the most favorable account of Varina both mentally and bodily," and Jeff rejoined that if her "self command" should "restore her health and spirits it will be a boon cheaply purchased by all the sacrifices and inconveniences it costs me."[43]

Had he known of the delay, he could have spent more time with her, he told Varina. "But let us believe that all is ordered for the general good & tutor our minds . . . to feel as becomes creatures bound by many obligations to receive with gratitude whatever may be offered, and wait with patience and confidence the coming result." This early attention to the will of God may have contributed to his coolness, so remarked at the battle of Monterey.[44]

Jeff, out of his greater age and experience, was trying to smooth down a wilful young woman, to teach her the self-control he admired—in short, how to be his wife. "You have taken upon yourself in many respects the decision of your own course, and remember to be responsible for ones conduct is not the happy state which those who think they have been governed too much sometimes suppose it." She was evidently a good deal spoiled, yet it was Ma he depended on to help him in this. He did not want Varina a slave to convention, but he wanted her to avoid causing "remarks, the fear of which would render me as a *husband* unhappy."

He had just seen the lady whose company he had recommended to Knox Taylor, Mrs. MacRee, and pointedly told Varina, "Through our long acquaintance . . . I have never known her to do an improper act." He told of a letter "written when she was surrounded by annoyances especially disturbing." When he had delivered it to Major MacRee, "he said it put him in a good humor with all the world." "To rise superior to petty annoyances to pity and forgive the weakness in others which galls and incommodes us is a noble exhibition of moral philosophy and the surest indication of an elevated nature."

He hated strife so much that he said, even in the Tenería controversy: "I regret that I must notice things which it would never have been my choice to preserve or remember." Personal strife was unbearable. He freely admitted to Varina his "morbid sensibility." Fear that her conduct would provoke ridicule or detraction was "one of my many weaknesses." He tried now to smooth out one rough spot by telling Varina to "have such a house built as with [Joseph's] advice you desire, & endeavor to make your home happy to yourself and those who share it with you." The whole letter intimates that all is not well between them, but he ends, "ever with deepest love and fondest hope." And Varina's January letters are lighthearted.[45]

As he always did, Jeff told Varina what was going on: he expected to join General Taylor in a move to Tampico, and Santa Anna would probably attack. Taylor was, in fact, already leading Twiggs and his regulars south to Tampico. The navy had captured that city, halfway down the east coast of Mexico, as part of a new strategy. The United States had rejected Taylor's armistice signed at Monterey and had ordered him to occupy the Mexican province that included Tampico and Victoria. This was all to support General Scott's idea, lately approved by President Polk, of taking the port city of Vera Cruz, some three hundred miles south of Tampico, and invading Mexico from the sea. Taylor was marching to unite all the men he could safely spare with those that Bennet Riley and others were bringing down from the Rio Grande.[46]

When Colonel Davis arrived in camp on Christmas Day, 1846, Taylor had just received a "sugared letter." Major General Scott now needed more troops, and he had decided to take from Taylor, as he said, "most of [your] gallant officers and men," leaving him strictly on the defensive. Taylor and Davis both considered this an outrage. Taylor thought that Scott, Polk, and Marcy, the secretary of war, aimed either to destroy his army or to force his retirement "in disgust." "I shall disappoint them," he wrote, "as I have determined to remain and do my duty no matter under what circumstances."[47]

The circumstances were prickly. Taylor had already had to counter feints by Santa Anna. Scott was taking twice the number of soldiers Taylor had said he could spare with safety and "a large army of more than twenty thousand men is in my front." The converging American troops entered Victoria on January 4, 1847, and here Davis resumed command of his regiment. The others soon went off with Scott to battle and glory. Riley won the yellow sash at Cerro Gordo, and so did Harney. Taylor was allowed only an "escort" back to Monterey, but he carefully hand-picked it: a squadron of dragoons under Capt. Charles A. May, two batteries of light artillery under Captains Thomas W. Sherman and Braxton Bragg (who now held a brevet as major), and the Mississippi Rifles under Jefferson Davis.[48]

Colonel Davis was not exactly happy with this "high compliment." He wanted to go where the fighting was. He wrote to Joseph: "The desire to be in every battle fought during my term of service is strong, but I could not in the present condition of Genl. Taylor ask to leave him." He told how Scott had ruined Taylor's plan of advancing "by the interior line to make a junction of the two columns at the city of Mexico." "Genl. T. would have advanced without delay," if only Scott had left the number of men he had promised. "This opened to my hopes visions of constant confli[ct] . . . an invading force pressed by the enemy on every side and bristling to repel approach. But why dwell on a hope which has almost left me."[49]

Then General Wool sent for Taylor in great alarm. Santa Anna was coming from the south with his whole force against Saltillo. Taylor rushed from Monterey, ignoring Scott's order to hole up there, and began scouting for position. Saltillo was the key to the north-south route and the best spot to fight a battle. As Taylor stood poised at Agua Nueva, eighteen miles southwest, Colonel Davis complained again: "We came expecting a host and battle, have sound solitude and eternally peace."[50]

They began to think it was a false alarm. As they "whiled away the time," says Sergeant Estes of the Mississippi Rifles, they could "see the old General sitting under the fly of a tent," chatting with Davis. The whole army knew of "the former estrangement" and "now noticed the cordial intimacy." Davis was shortly to speak of his "warm personal attachment" to Taylor, a "man whose sacrifices are all of himself." Most of the general's soldiers treasured his "republican simplicity," his "benevolent smile," his decisiveness, his jocular coolness under fire. Dabney Maury says he "had won the unbounded confidence and love of us all."[51]

Only this kind of devotion could have nerved the tiny army to meet the fierce firestorm that broke upon them. "Old Zach" was ready for it. Some were saying Santa Anna would destroy him, but Sidney Johnston (now in Texas) said Taylor's strategy, which Maury called "silent, rapid, impetuous," was "the best under the circumstances." Davis was awed by "the immense responsibility" for men's lives resting "on him alone": "The struggle between the duties of the soldier . . . and the sympathies of the man, were terrible." Taylor might have retired to Monterey, "sheltering himself under his instructions . . . there to be invested and captured," said Davis. "He would not do it, but cast all upon the die to maintain his country's honor."[52]

As soon as Taylor found that the Mexicans were really coming, he fell back to a place cut by deep ravines, to impede their vaunted cavalry, and Santa Anna said this position was all that saved the American army. Taylor had less than five thousand with which to meet over twenty thousand. Drums beat "the signal for striking tents," says Estes, and "we took up the line of march" for the battlefield, just south of "the little hacienda" named Buena Vista. He saw Taylor with Colonels Davis and Henry Clay, Jr., and others riding over the field, "noting the topography . . . until dark and after." Troops took position and "slept on their arms," while Taylor led his escort six miles to the rear, to check the defense of his headquarters, stores, and ammunition at Saltillo.[53]

The next morning, Taylor brought the escort down to the field as his reserve force, while the strains of "Hail Columbia" and the watchword, "Honor of Washington," saluted the day, February 22. There was only light skirmishing on that day. Santa Anna, with his hordes now in view, invited Taylor to surrender unconditionally: "you . . . can not in any human probability avoid . . . being cut to pieces." Old Zach's words were said to be choice; Major Bliss, his chief of staff, translated them into a polite reply; Thomas Crittenden, a civilian aide, said "General Taylor never surrenders." That night, Taylor gave the Saltillo guard one of Bragg's guns and two companies from Davis's already diminished regiment, leaving less than three hundred Mississippians for the field.

One of Davis's captains, W. P. Rogers, had refused an order to stay at Saltillo that day. His diary shows how Davis handled his men. Instead of punishing him, the colonel came to him early on the twenty-third, saying he "hoped" he would not refuse this time. "He further said that he knew I had for him no kind feeling but that endangered as we were he hoped that might be forgotten. The post he assigned me he said was a post of honor and that he desired that I might have the glory of leading an independent command to action. . . . I could not again refuse." Rogers later wrote a glowing report of his action that day.[54]

Bragg now commanded the famous horse artillery of Maj. Samuel Ringgold, who had given his life at Palo Alto proving the worth of this "flying" battery. Bragg had to give up another gun to guard the wagons at Buena Vista ranch and so had only two when he took the "post of honor" on the far right, supporting the Second Kentucky, which was led by Davis's friends Clay and William R. McKee. These guns were "honey combed" (Scott had taken the replacements) and "deemed no longer safe," Davis tells us, but they "did good service . . . under the intrepid Captain Bragg."[55]

Breakfast on February 23, 1847, "was a solemn feast," says Sergeant Estes. Of six men wondering "who would return to partake of supper," only two came back. Before sunrise, the Mississippians, who had slept at Saltillo, were marching double-quick for the field, marching soon upon fire: the battle was on, and the far left, to which they were assigned, had been turned. As Davis approached his position, he saw American horsemen "running dispersed and confusedly from the field" and "a regiment of infantry flying disorganized." Riding forward "to examine the ground," Davis tried to rally the routed men of the Second Indiana, but only a few, with their colonel, turned and joined him. Their rout had left Bragg, who had crossed the whole field to get to the fighting, without support and nearly out of ammunition. Across a narrow plateau, framed by deep ravines, the Mexicans were "rapidly advancing." If they took the plateau, the American army would be trapped. The moment required, said Davis, "whatever sacrifice it might cost to check the enemy."[56]

With no support in sight, Davis gave the order to "fire advancing." His odds at this moment were about ten to one. His riflemen had to cross a "difficult chasm . . . under a galling fire," but they drove the enemy back, "the destruction great upon both sides." Their discipline told; there was no "high and wild shooting so common in battle." Colonel Davis "led the charge himself" and paid for it by taking a musket ball in the right foot. It passed through from the side, near the instep, driving pieces of brass spur, boot, and bone deep inside. "He sat on his horse, however," says

Estes, "and still commanded his regiment, witnessing the discomfiture of the enemy with evident satisfaction." He refused to retire for medical aid and sat Richard to the end of the day. His superb horsemanship came into play. At one point, with his wounded foot "thrown over the pommel of his saddle," he leapt a ravine so deep and wide that he could see a cart and horse beneath him.[57]

But now, says Estes, "we found ourselves almost surrounded," with an open plain behind, no support, and enemy cavalry beginning to flank them. "Our colonel, more by gestures than words, for he could not be heard," ordered the regiment back. The Mexicans shouted in triumph, and Major Bradford, not seeing Davis's command, cried out, "Kill me, kill me! the Mississippi regiment is running!" But Davis was only retiring some two hundred yards to reform his line. En route, he found "in person" the enemy cavalry moving up a ravine, called his nearest men, and "dispersed it." Now Captain Bragg emerged from the shelter of another ravine where he had been refilling his limber-boxes with ammunition. "I am happy to believe," he wrote, "that my rapid . . . fire, opened just at this time, held the enemy in check until Colonel Davis could . . . assume a stand." Lieutenant Kilburn's gun "opened a brisk and very effective fire," Davis reported. "The enemy immediately receded; we advanced, and he retired."[58]

The peril was by no means over. The flying artillery had gone to another part of the field, and the Third Indiana Volunteers had joined the Mississippians, when Davis saw "a large body of cavalry debouch from his cover . . . and advance rapidly upon us." Since they were "standing on the brink of a precipitous ravine," the foot soldiers "would have been absolutely secure," but the cavalry "could have dashed by" to the rear, endangering the artillery and opening the road to "our depot of ammunition." Davis felt "the safety of the army, the honor of their country" was in the keeping of the First Mississippi. He ordered "the Ordnance Sergeant to serve his men with more ammunition," for it was "entirely exhausted," says Estes. "The Mexican bugles were already sounding" the attack when the men discovered that the balls "were fully one size too large." Davis coolly gave directions. Every man spread his ammunition on the rocky ground, and "hammering away," reduced it to proper size.[59]

Davis called for artillery, but at the same moment, his whole line was "hotly engaged." Estes says, "We could look for no aid from any quarter, so we had to meet the charge. . . . Here Colonel Davis formed the celebrated V, which in reality was no V, but a re-entering angle." Davis put the Indiana men near the edge of a north-south ravine, with his own line meeting them at the north end, forming across the plain the long side of an obtuse angle, "so that we faced the approaching cavalry." "Colonel Davis, bleeding as he was," gave meticulous firing orders. "Confident of success," says he, "and anxious to obtain the full advantage of a cross fire at a short distance, I repeatedly called to the men not to shoot."[60]

Massed men on horses, outnumbering the Americans "more than ten to one," came around the ravines "in beautiful order," like "a huge serpent moving over the ground." These were the Lancers, the pride of the Mexican Army. "The sun shone on their lace covered breasts" and glinted from lance-heads adorned with tricolored streamers: "almost too pretty to shoot at," said a Mississippian. Their rush "like an avalanche" suddenly slowed as they got near and found a single line of infantry opposing them at a strange angle.[61] Probably fearing a ruse, they "had drawn up to a walk, and seemed about to halt" when the suspense got too much. Davis's orders were forgotten. Just as the horsemen passed the far right of the Indiana men, Sergeant Estes says, "the report of a solitary gun broke the stillness and was followed by a prolonged volley all along our line. I think I am safe in saying not a loaded gun was left in the whole command; but that one round did fearful execution. For the distance of nearly two hundred yards the riders lay thick, while their unharmed horses wheeled to the right and left . . . and mixed with the already demoralized lancers." Now the summoned field piece arrived. A twelve-pound howitzer, under Captain Sherman, began "to belch forth showers of grape and canister, and every effort of the Mexican officers to rally their men . . . was fruitless"; they "fled from the field in confusion."[62]

The army had been saved from entrapment, the left was secure, but there was no rest for the weary and wounded. Other Mexican cavalry reached the rear at Saltillo and the Buena Vista ranch but were beaten off, from the former by Captain Rogers and his men. With the terrible odds against him, Taylor's only hope lay in constant maneuver. Davis was almost immediately called to the central plateau, where Taylor had his command post. Santa Anna had launched a massive drive with all his remaining forces. He had struck the Second Kentucky and two Illinois regiments just as they were deploying and routed them by sheer numbers.[63]

At the sound of this clash, Bragg had rushed his jaded men and horses up as fast as he could. "Without any infantry to support him, and at the imminent risk of losing his guns," says Taylor's battle report, he whirled into position, and with the enemy "but a few yards from the muzzles of his pieces," began firing. "For the first time," Bragg later said, "I felt the imminent peril in which we stood." Davis could see it as he approached through a deep gully. His men began shooting as they came up on the plain, raking all three lines in front of Bragg from the Mexican right flank: "Our first fire . . . was eminently destructive. His right gave way and he fled in confusion," pursued hotly by the Mississippians. Seeing this, Taylor, who had been watching like a statue, with arms "calmly folded over his breast," disengaged his right leg "from the pommel of the saddle" and "fairly danced in the stirrups," weeping in relief; he had been told more than once that day that all was lost. Taylor cites the Mississippians in his report, but it was Bragg, he says, who "saved the day." This was immortalized in legend by Taylor's reported order, "A little more grape, Captain Bragg!" What he actually said, as Bragg whirled past his command post, was "Give 'em hell!"[64]

Both Taylor and Davis saw a divine hand in their marvelous victory. Each expressed the fact after his own fashion. Davis said, "So fortuitous was every event . . . that [the victory] must be assigned to the superintending care of Providence." Taylor said, "Nothing short of a miracle, saved us."[65]

By the time Jefferson Davis "retired to a tent upon the field for surgical aid," it was late afternoon. His leg was swollen in the boot, and the boot had filled with blood. The delay "had made it impossible" then to extract the "broken bones and foreign matter." Yet the wound, he wrote Varina, though painful, was "by no means dangerous."[66] He did not tell her then how, after he was removed to Saltillo by wagon about ten o'clock, Tom Crittenden had poured water through the wound all night to prevent lockjaw. He asked Tom to write in detail to Joseph, which he did, and said, "I have been with your brother almost daily for several months, and have formed for him a great personal attachment."[67]

The colonel was still giving orders. Even in these circumstances, he did not forget Captain Rogers. That very night he sent to Taylor the two companies that had guarded Saltillo, since they were "disappointed" to have missed the battle. Everyone expected to fight again the next day. Davis says the enemy's "numerical superiority over us would scarcely admit the supposition that he had finally retreated." But in the morning, while Davis was "waiting for the ambulance which was to take me to the field," the other Mississippians on the way down met General Taylor who "raised his hat," and announced, "Boys, they are gone." Santa Anna had decamped in the night.[68]

Taylor followed the enemy cautiously to Agua Nueva, but the fighting was over. In the hospital at Saltillo, Colonel Davis was "able to get about" on crutches and work on his battle report. He justified hurling himself at the enemy unsupported as he came on the field: "No one would have failed to perceive the hazard." It was "bold almost to rashness," a contemporary historian said. So were all his actions that day. Davis left them to "be best estimated" by the commanding general under whose eye "every part of the battle" was fought.[69]

The general's mind had certainly been on Davis. When told at first that he was killed, Taylor became very excited and sent courier after courier to get the truth. Davis used to speak of the "mother's softness" that came over Taylor's "eagle eye" when he looked on the wounded. There was none of that when he came to his son-in-law's cot: "I wish you had been shot in the body, you would have a better chance of recovering soon. I do not like wounds in the hand or feet, they cripple a soldier awfully." He was right. Davis was on crutches for two years, and "for eight or ten years the slightest misstep gave him pain." Taylor's solicitude, expressed over and over again in letters, signals their newfound intimacy, as well as the old soldier's tender heart.[70]

Taylor was "always most compassionate" in his care for all the wounded of both armies. The Mexicans, however, killed enemy wounded on the field. This came acutely to Davis's attention at Buena Vista. The Second Kentucky was overrun, and the regiment took refuge in a ravine. Mexican soldiers followed, and Davis's friends McKee and Clay, already wounded, were lanced to death before Davis could arrive with help.[71]

The rumor that Davis's own wound was mortal reached Natchez and caused a baby to be christened with his name. Margaret Howell had borne her eleventh child the year before, and she already called him "Jeff." He was now baptized "Jefferson Davis," becoming in time "Jeffy D." "None more worthy," his sister avows, ever bore the name. When the Iowa legislature heard the rumor of his death, it commended "the gallantry displayed" by Colonel Davis and "his brave Mississippi Riflemen."[72] Zachary Taylor did too:

> The Mississippi riflemen, under Colonel Davis, were highly conspicuous for their gallantry and steadiness, and sustained throughout the engagement the reputation of veteran troops. Brought into action against an immensely superior force, they maintained themselves for a long time unsupported, and with heavy loss, and held an important part of the field until reinforced. Colonel Davis, though severely wounded, remained in the saddle until the close of the action. His distinguished coolness and gallantry at the head of his regiment on this day, entitle him to the particular notice of the government.

Taylor's report, the "popular feeling in Mississippi," and some pressure from R. J. Walker made Davis a brigadier general.[73] Although Congress had authorized President Polk to appoint general officers for volunteers, Davis politely replied: "My opinions compel me to decline the proffered honor." Volunteers had "a constitutional right to be under" state officers. They would "lose their distinctive character of State troops," if the president appointed their generals. "Entertaining this opinion, my decision . . . was the necessary result." Logic, always logic, and always, the Constitution ruled him. What this decision cost him, loving the military life as he did—"I hope to [be] again in the field," he told Walker—his wife reveals: it was "his first sacrifice to State rights."[74]

This puts in a strange light remarks made by General Quitman, whom Davis had helped to the rank he himself refused: Davis was "a selfish and fiercely ambitious man, without one particle of generosity or magnanimity in his character. I am his superior. He is impatient of this, of the restraint of any superior, and full of envy & detraction." At the same time, Quitman was complaining of "injustice," Davis reported: "how? the members of the Regt. writing accounts of the battle had not mentioned *him*." Certainly Davis thought Quitman wrong to cancel his assault on the El Diablo fort at Monterey. He says in his memorandum that he obeyed "reluctantly . . . but cannot censure an order" designed "to save our men." This was scarcely "detraction." Neither was the mention of Quitman's "paltry excuses" for not answering Davis's inquiry in his quarrel with the Tennessee regiment. As for magnanimity, Davis would not use its own colonel's "condemnation" of that regiment, he told Joseph, because "I did not wish unless it became necessary to injure any one."[75]

There was enough glory drifting down to gild everyone, even, in time, Quitman. Taylor got the heaviest coating, naturally. Captain Bragg became brevet lieutenant colonel, and on his return from the war in 1848 was feted all the way from New Orleans to his home in Warrenton, North Carolina. He was extremely critical of everyone except Taylor and had real contempt for the volunteers, "With the exception of the Miss. regiment under Col. Davis."[76]

As for Davis, Taylor told Maj. A. H. Colquitt that "Napoleon never had a Marshal who behaved more superbly than did Colonel Davis to-day." He became "the Hero of Buena Vista."[77] He led what was left of his regiment—over half were casualties—home in June 1847. Cannon boomed a salute and wreaths fell from the balconies of New Orleans, as the First Mississippi Rifles moved through the streets. "One very pretty girl gratified" the colonel "by calling out, 'There goes our lion-hearted Davis.'" History, with delicate irony, made S. S. Prentiss the welcoming orator. Davis, leg propped on a chair, responded for the regiment.

They were "unconscious of having done any thing" to deserve such a reception; they had only done their duty. At the same time he claimed that "personal dignity" and character had exalted "the commonest man into the hero." He remembered the dead, especially Clay and McKee, "endeared to me" in youth, whose bodies were brought home by the Second Kentucky. Very typically, he remembered the forgotten—those dead of disease and the "unwritten heroes," those who had "a harder task than to die—to thirst for glory and not to realize it." "In the discharge of duty to be inactive, where action is glory—this is moral greatness." Surely this was meant especially for the ears of Captain Rogers, and they were not deaf. Rogers was soon writing Davis how he missed him at the dinners honoring Company K, and to pay no mind to McClung's attack. Davis in later years took occasion to praise Rogers's "gallantry."[78]

The regiment was honored with a luncheon on the Place d'Armes, where Davis's brothers had stood with Andrew Jackson in 1815. (It is now Jackson Square.) Then Davis took his mustered-out regiment by steamboat up the Mississippi River, stopping to let each man off nearest his home. At Natchez, militia companies escorted "the pride and glory of our chivalrous State" to the bluff, where officers and colors were crowned with wreaths and schoolchildren handed each veteran a bunch of flowers. Col. A. L. Bingaman's oration singled out Davis for defending "in the frank and fearless spirit of a true soldier" Taylor's terms at Monterey. Colonel Davis gave a "heart-thrilling response." With McClung's "mangled form" beside him, he recalled "with a flashing eye" how the lieutenant colonel had leapt first onto the wall at Monterey, exalting the action into epic with an allusion to the *Aeneid:* "and I speaking, saw it with my own eyes." Toasts "sped merrily around the board." The one to Taylor was, *"He never surrenders."*[79]

Varina was not present. "Mr. Davis—who was on crutches—came out in a barouche, nearly hidden with flowers," to the Howell home. Was it to have their reunion in private, or was there estrangement? He took her to the steamboat, with "bands playing their merriest tunes," and the upriver journey to Vicksburg "was one long ovation." After daylong festivities, they finally went home to Brierfield. They seemed about to achieve Davis's highest ambition. "God bless you, my dearest," he had written on May 27, "and preserve you in all things for the great end of our life, substantial, mutual happiness."[80] He reckoned without his newfound fame.

VIII

United States Senator

Sacrificing his desire for battle to duty and loyalty—"I could not in the present condition of Genl. Taylor ask to leave him"—had pitched Jeff Davis into the most glorious battle of the Mexican War. Americans tended to name their places Buena Vista rather than Cerro Gordo or Contreras or Churubusco or Chapultapec—the battles by which Scott went on to win Mexico City and the war. Buena Vista moved Capt. Albert Pike of the Arkansas cavalry to fifteen rhyming stanzas, in one of which "Gallant Davis drives the foe." It inspired the famous poem "The Bivouac of the Dead." Capt. Theodore O'Hara of Danville wrote it for the burial of Clay, McKee, and others in Kentucky soil, and in time it became a favorite for Civil War monuments:

> The muffled drum's sad roll has beat
> The soldier's last tattoo . . .
> Rest on, embalmed and sainted dead,
> Dear as the blood ye gave . . .
> Nor shall your glory be forgot
> While Fame her record keeps,
> Or Honor points the hallowed spot
> Where Valor proudly sleeps.[1]

Sacrificing high military honor, the generalship, to his constitutional creed led Davis to high civil honor, a seat in the Senate. Davis resented being ordered about, as Quitman said, if he thought the authority ill-used, like Quitman's, or questionable, like Jesse Speight's. When Davis went to Washington in 1845, Speight was a Mississippi senator. He was used to having great men like Clay come at his call. Early one snowy morning—never a good hour for Davis in the best of weather—he sent a summons to Davis's boarding house: "Come over. Speight." Davis, a freshman in Congress, ought to have hopped to it. Instead, "in no pacific mood," he wrote back: "Can't. Davis." The two had laughed about it later. Now Speight was dead. On August 10, 1847, Gov. Albert Gallatin Brown appointed Davis to take his place, until the legislature could elect someone in January to finish the term.[2]

Davis really wanted to go back to the field, but General Taylor had written: "Altho, I miss you very much . . . yet I could not . . . desire you to make so great a sacrifice; you have already gone far enough in that way, & . . . require some repose, at any rate until you get the entire use of your foot, ancle & leg as well as to set your affairs in order." This was when Davis was weighing the generalship, and Taylor advised against it. In fact, he told Dr. Wood it was "quite likely they gave him the appt of Br Genl under the expectation of keeping him out of the Senate." He assured Davis, "there is not an individual in the whole land I would have preferred having with me . . . had I advanced into the heart of Mexico, knowing I could rely to the utmost on both your head & heart in cou[n]sel, or in battle." But in northern Mexico the fighting now would be only "of the guerilla character where little of reputation can be gained." "I think you acted wisely in not accepting," he said, but from then on he almost always addressed Davis as "My Dear General." And Davis was "general" to many more, to the end of his life.[3]

Taylor advised that if Davis were offered the senatorship without his "electioneering . . . & it did not interfere too much with your private affairs, it seems to me you ought not to decline," but, as always, he told him to go by his own feelings.[4] The private affairs were running well enough under James Pemberton's management. Davis's 1,290 acres were assessed at $16,770. His "Negroes," who were "desirous to see and hear from you," Joseph wrote, had almost doubled in number since he began planting twelve years before. His taxable cattle were nearing fifty, and Joseph had written of "Some dozen colts," which he knew Jim Green "would be glad to hear of." The brothers, continuing in their father's footsteps, were raising a renowned pacing stock.[5]

There was the wounded foot to consider. Taylor wrote to Dr. Wood, "I deeply regret to learn from you that Col Davis wound is likely to prove so tedious in getting well." For several years, Varina says, "The bone exfoliated, and pieces that had been shattered worked out or were extracted by a surgeon, causing dreadful nervous disturbance, not to speak of the physical anguish." She learned to dress the wound: "I always imagine Dr. Mitchell hurts him. Jeff bandages it himself."[6] Davis referred to "the inconvenience and disagreeable exposure of hopping on crutches," in mid-July 1847, and admitted, "My foot has not improved much." Dr. Mitchell told Taylor how slowly it was healing: "sometime must elapse before he will be able to use it." This was a chief reason Davis refused the command of the Second Mississippi Regiment; he probably could not have resisted "had I been physically able, and free to accept."[7]

He did agree to be named senator. Joseph seemed anxious for it, and it was only for four and a half months. Taylor wrote: "I think there is but little doubt as to his election [to the unexpired term]; he appears however to be indifferent about it." Davis was indeed. When Jacob Thompson and Robert Roberts were found "barring the gates" to his advancement, Jeff wrote to Varina: "I am in no wise surprised; the public could not gain much if any thing from my labors." This is the man Quitman charged with vanity and ambition.[8]

In late September, Davis came down with fever. It was "a severe attack of sickness, which had very much effected his eyes," Taylor reported to Dr. Wood, "but he said nothing about his wounded foot." A newspaper said it had "never yet healed." Davis had to tell Governor Brown, "Ill health at last compels me to abandon the design" of writing "a history of our Campaign."[9] Varina was down with fever herself, at the Briars, and Jeff wrote, in his usual vein of ironic humor:

> Our family has changed since your departure, by . . . the introduction into the house of two kittens, and under of a slut with a litter of whelps. Eliza [a servant] is a little slow, somewhat dull and but a little neat or orderly. Tis strange that the great first law of God, *order*, a law written in all his works and by which animated creation on land and in water enjoys existence should so little impress itself upon the portion of his works made in his own image. This sermon to be concluded by yourself. . . .
>
> Mr. Phillips (miserabile dictu) has co[me] and interrupte[d] the progress of this valuable letter . . . talked me down quite prostrate, prevented me from doing any thing and thus rendered me as cross as a Bear.[10]

At some point, they visited Locust Grove, for Nannie Davis Smith, playing at her grandmother's door, saw "a strange gentleman approaching, who, though supported by a crutch, bore himself right soldierly." It was her first sight of "Uncle Jeff." His "invariable tenderness with children" soon won her undying affection. "I already adored 'Aunt Varina,'" who had often visited while he was in Mexico. Jeff's tenderness was even then giving a home to the bugler-boy of the First Mississippi, Ferdinand Carroll, whom he had brought back sick to Brierfield. Later, after the boy lost an appointment to the Naval Academy which Davis got him, he lived at Brierfield until he was eighteen.[11]

Jeff had signed his letter to Varina, "as ever, your husband in the bonds of affection," but the bonds were being stretched to the breaking point. The trouble centered about the new Brierfield house, designed to accommodate the widowed Amanda Bradford and her eight children. Although Varina was devoted to Malie, she had had the younger children throwing food "from one side of the room to the other" and ruining her carpets in the present house. She was not about to share command of the new one with Amanda.[12] Evidently Varina and Joseph had quarreled about this. In the summer, Varina had written to her mother:

> Jeff is not well, or like himself—he never complains, but he is quite feeble. This miserable business of Brother Joe's has given him more pain if possible than I expected, however I have determined to preserve perfect silence upon the subject until we can talk about it without it exciting either of us. The family and myself are upon as good terms as usual. I do not go there oftener than I can help, and they come down almost every day to see Jeff, and treat me with respect. . . . I beg that you will feel perfectly at rest concerning me, "all will be happy yet" I hope. . . . I do not think circumstances can make anyone happy; the heart at last, if it is well governed, makes the heaven.

In the fall, she wrote happily of Jeff's improvement: "He walks with one crutch pretty well." And he enjoyed having an officer of his regiment visit, when "they of course 'fought their battles o'er again.'" He and the other senator, Henry Foote, planned to go the "Southern Route"—up the Alabama River to Montgomery, by rail to Charleston, and then by sea to the nation's capital. But the river was too low. Jeff was too weak to "bear the stageing" overland anyway. His health was "still very bad," and "I felt what a comfort it was to us both to be together," Varina wrote Ma, calling him "my good man," saying "I had rather die than take leave of him." But as Jeff set off up the Mississippi by the National Road, headed for Washington, Varina was not with him.[13]

Sen. Jefferson Davis took his oath on December 6, 1847. He was soon appointed to the committees on military affairs, library, and pensions. He lived at Gadsby's Hotel, then at Mrs. Owner's boardinghouse. He found himself high in Democratic councils, talking politics with President Polk and dining at the White House. In January, the Mississippi legislature elected him to Speight's unexpired term by acclamation—an unprecedented action.[14]

Davis thought it "improper" to "canvass" for his own election; he would be "unworthy" to be senator if merely "representative of a party." He wrote to a Whig that he represented "the state sovereignty" and should serve "the whole people." Crittenden and Clay were Whig friends, and another, John Tyler, had boarded his steamboat on the way up, just to see him. Davis welcomed Whig support at home as an expression of "personal confidence" only, since "my principles and adherence to democratic measures are so well known." But he would never switch back and forth between parties.[15]

Henry Foote veered between Democrat and Whig so often, he was known as "General Weathercock." He had been elected Mississippi senator in 1847 as a Democrat. He was a lawyer, a newspaperman, and a politician: all three professions prone to violence in the South. David Bradford had been shot dead; editors were regular targets; Reuben Davis, criminal lawyer and Foote's good friend, had a bloody fight with a judge. Foote had been in four duels, two with S. S. Prentiss, and been wounded every time. At one of them, spectators were warned to get down out of the trees because, "General Foote shoots wild you know."[16] But no one was quite prepared for what happened on Christmas Day, 1847.

Six gentlemen in the sitting room of Mrs. Owner's boardinghouse were disputing "squatter sovereignty," a concept just introduced in the Senate, when Davis, inflamed by Foote's "offensive language," suddenly crossed the room and "whipped him until I was pulled off." It might have ended there (in the code of honor, blows were satisfaction for verbal assault), had not Foote turned as he was leaving the room and "said he struck first"—a delicate point of honor in the code.

> I went after him, calling him a liar, and shaking my fist in his face, told him, if he dared to say that I would beat him to death. He was silent, and I, though at the time a cripple, felt myself so much his superior that after a moment's delay I turned around to leave him and he struck me, whereupon I knocked him down, jumped on him and commenced beating him, when the gentlemen in the room again pulled me off. I then proposed that we go into my room and lock the door. He asked me if I had coffee and pistols for two. I told him I had no coffee, but pistols. He said it was an unfair . . . proposal. I thought he implied that I would not give him an equal chance, and was about to jump on him again, when he denied [this] . . . and after some such blarney as he always had on hand, it was urged by the friends present that the matter should be dropped as a Christmas frolic—it was the 25th of December, 1847—and the matter was, as I supposed, at an end.

A. W. Venable, coming in at this moment, was told of the fight but sworn to secrecy, as they all were: "the whole matter would . . . never be divulged by anyone." But Foote divulged it. He said, Davis wrote, "that he had struck me and I had not resented it"—which was the same as calling Davis a coward. Davis sent two notes demanding disavowal or duel. Foote would answer lengthily but inconclusively. Davis's friends, Walker and Brown, argued "that to push him farther would be [considered] ungenerous . . . by those who considered him unequal to me in a trial with deadly weapons. So the matter was permitted to rest."[17]

The Christmas scene shows, at the least, Davis's enormous vitality. Even if on only *one* crutch, how could he manage to fight? "I know your active disposition," Zachary Taylor wrote to him shortly before—how he would want to superintend "all the details & operations of your plantation [and] how inconvenient it is to do so with a lame foot." The frustrations of his wound and long animosity against Foote must have come together in rage at Mrs. Owner's. Davis was by nature a fighter. He used to repeat with glee what was said of the young Sir Walter Scott: "always the first in a row and the last out of it."[18] Never again would Davis's anger gain so much ascendancy over his self-control. But it would remain his besetting sin, calling for more and more patience.

A letter to Varina explains his flying off the handle that day, though he is talking about themselves. "Ill health" made him "less able to bear abuse." He had left with "body crippled, nerves shattered, and mind depressed." "The dread of constant strife . . . produced a necessity for separation at a time when a wifes kindness was most needed." She had written her resentment—he was neglecting her in favor of "grave and important matters" and meant for her "to *retire from the rest of the world.*" In reply, he told her why he had not taken her with him: "I will be frank with you. I cannot expose myself to such conduct as your's when with me here. I cannot bear constant harassment, occasional reproach, and subsequent misrepresentation. I have not forgotten . . . the multitude attracted by the servants of an angry woman."[19] Varina's own irascibility had finally overcome Jeff's patience with her, born of love. Gone were the days when she could say, "I might quarrel a month and he would not get mad." But she could not see what was happening. "We are all of us poor judges of our own case," he had told her, and another time quoted, "How little do we know that which we are."[20]

Varina was only twenty-one. Jeff had indulged her so long that she could not imagine a change. Even now he sent her a gold chain, a "gold pencil and pen altogether," and "a splendid cameo" in a "broad band of gold for my wrist. He looks beautiful in a cameo—it is exactly like him." At the same time she told Ma, seeming blind to the significance, "I have received no letters from him for a month." She was at Brierfield and sarcastically spoke of "some decision" about the disputed house: "as I am so little concerned it has not been thought proper to inform me. I always speak of it as if it were mine, and no one's else, so I suppose all will be straight." "In trying to do my whole duty, I am happy, and absolutely look upon Jeff's displeasure or pleasure as a minor consideration to my own duty. I have not been low spirited for two months or cross for I do not know how long."[21]

But she had been writing to Jeff in quite a different temper, as his answer shows: "You had an opportunity when I came to you crippled, so as to be confined to the house, to quarrel with me as much as would have satisfied any ordinary person, and I might have expected that you would have spared me from querulous letters, during my absence. . . . Your suspicions and threats are equally unjust and unnecessary." He was not trying to take away "your *rights as a woman and a wife.*" She was the one who proposed inviting "Sister Amanda to live with us, and I planned a house for that purpose. Now it becomes in your mind a source of *misery.*" Varina was often sick, unable to keep house, and "bitter to me" about the servants. He had thought this would bring "relief from domestic labors" and someone to care for her in his absence. "It did not occur to me that you were the unwilling party" in a plan "proposed by yourself."[22]

"Let there be peace and sincerity between us," he cried, but he exposed a deeper source of their trouble. "In vain have I striven to inspire you with confidence, until the conviction is forced upon me that you never trusted, that our union commenced in doubt." The words in her letter, even though she kissed the paper, renewed "the wounds your suspicion has so often inflicted." Varina seemed to have a lingering uneasiness over Sarah Knox Taylor. She knew Jeff was her "first and only love," and she was not his. As she sighed in 1859, "It saddens me to realize that there is so very much in one's being the first love of early youth."[23]

His letter said he might be coming "to Missi.": "I do not say home *for without hearts there is no home*"—a hollow echo of her "the heart . . . makes the heaven." "Henceforth I will not answer your assaults or your insults." But he did. They corresponded all winter, and through the acrimony peeped out a love that ran deeper than their emotions. "I had hoped that with cheerful friends and left in our separation to the full force of your affection for me, you would have enjoyed more equanimity than when we were together," he wrote in April. His health was "almost restored, very little lameness, and seldom any pain." But the interior pain was still there: "I cannot bear to be suspected or complained of, or misconstrued after explanation, *by you,*" yet her upbringing and "combativeness, render you prone to apply [these] tests."

> You do not wish to destroy my sensibility, or to drive me for relief to temporary stupefaction, and vicious associations; through these channels alone could I reach the condition suited to such treatment as I have received. We are apt by viewing our own heart, to construe our acts differently from others, and conscious of your love for me, you may not have understood how far your treatment of me was injurious . . . your course if continued would render it impossible for us *ever* to live together [italics mine].

He reveals his purity in denying its opposite. And either blind to, or very conscious of, his own temper, he urges self-control as "a moral obligation and a social duty," as well as "a line of conduct suited to the character of your husband, and demanded by your duties as a wife" (an unconscious rebuke to her self-satisfaction in doing "my whole duty").[24]

Varina's "anguish" was great over his stern warning, but she took it to heart. He invited her to come north for the summer: "I need not say that (because I love you) it would always make me happier to be with you, if kind and peaceful." She went, and in a few months, she was calling Jeff "sweetest, best husband," "my better life, my nobler self," and herself, "Your devoted Wife." His hope for "the great end of our life substantial, mutual happiness" was going to be realized after all.[25]

With all this turmoil in his soul, Davis had to turn his mind to Senate business. On the very day he wrote his devastating January letter to Varina, he made an eloquent plea for the ten temporary regiments that President Polk wanted, to insure victory in Mexico. The army's weakness, Davis pointed out, had "induced attacks," one of them at Buena Vista, and had cost "a fearful sacrifice" of blood when General Scott took Mexico City. "Sir, to insure a peace, we must show our power." He could not know that peace negotiations had begun the day before, January 2, 1848.[26]

Senator Davis argued for the regiments against Crittenden and John Bell of Tennessee, rebuked Webster for calling the war odious, and dared to lecture Calhoun on the Constitution. His formidable logic matched Calhoun's own and won from the leader grudging admission that Davis had presented a "strong view." Others said he gave "one of the most forceful speeches ever delivered in the Senate." The issue died when the Treaty of Guadalupe Hidalgo was ratified by the Senate on March 10 and by Mexico at the end of May. On August 1, the last American troops sailed home from Vera Cruz. The Mexican War was over.[27]

Davis dared to confront Calhoun again on the constitutionality of improvements to internal waterways for "the promotion of commerce": "a construction than which none was ever adopted more latitudinous in its nature, or tending to more flagrant abuse." He recognized, however, that "necessary" improvement could come under "the duty to provide for the common defense," and on this basis was able to vote with Calhoun for the appropriation in question.[28] On the other great issues of the day, Davis followed the party leader closely. Calhoun asked "the younger members" to state for him the South's position on slavery, and Davis did so on April 20, 1848.

Private citizens had just captured the sloop *Pearl,* which was taking runaway slaves north, and returned it to Washington. There was a small riot against the antislavery men there, and John P. Hale of New Hampshire, "the first avowed abolitionist to reach the Senate," asked Congress to indemnify them for their losses. "Is this Chamber to be the hot-bed in which plants of sedition are to be nursed?" asked Davis. Why should the subject of slavery, "so irritating always," be introduced "in this body, once looked to as the conservative branch of the Government" and "above the power of faction"? "Is this debatable ground? No!"

> We who represent the southern States are not here to be insulted on account of institutions which we inherit. And if civil discord is to be thrown from this Chamber upon the land—if the fire is to be kindled here with which to burn the temple of our Union—if this is to be made the centre from which civil war is to radiate, here let the conflict begin. I am ready, for one, to meet it with any incendiary, who, dead to every feeling of patriotism, attempts to introduce it.

Here the soldier speaks, almost prophetically, about a battle that is to rage through all his senatorial years—a battle to preserve the Union by preserving the Constitution, a battle forced by the enemy on one issue, slavery.

William Lloyd Garrison had seen very clearly that the document binding the states together protected slavery. This is why he called it "a covenant with death and an agreement with hell" and would not use political means to his end, abolition. In the prophecy of Isaiah, which he paraphrased, the "covenant" is "disannulled"; the "agreement . . . shall not stand." Just so, Garrison burned the Constitution in 1840, cried "No union with slaveholders," and called for Northern secession.[29]

Other abolitionists broke with Garrison over this, wanting to employ politics. In order to get around the covenant, which would not let them touch slavery where it existed, they planned to outlaw it in every territory and new state, overpower the Southern states by sheer numbers, and abolish slavery everywhere by Constitutional amendment. Ironically enough, the recent victory in a war regarded as the South's own was bringing on the crisis. Calhoun, almost alone, had seen the danger. While Taylor and Scott were subduing Mexico proper, other army and navy forces had been conquering Mexican territory from Texas to the Pacific. The Treaty of Guadalupe Hidalgo had ceded all this western land to the United States. In its organization, the antislavery men saw their chance.[30]

The battle had already begun in the Senate. While Davis was fighting in Mexico, Southerners had defeated David Wilmot's "Proviso" prohibiting slavery in the territories, only to have it reintroduced over and over again. Calhoun saw, his biographer says, that the real issue "was not the extension but the extinction of slavery," and that the "moral obloquy" thrown upon it "would soon make the position of the South in the Union intolerable." Attempts to exclude slavery had blocked so far organization of the Oregon Territory. Now, in June 1848, the Oregon Bill came up again. Hale attacked with an amendment barring slavery there forever.[31]

Abolitionists were never content to establish the frame of government; they always threw in the inflammatory question. Davis wanted impartiality: "We equally deny [to the federal government] the right to establish as to abolish slavery." His counteramendment would leave territories open to all comers. This would not "force slavery" on Oregon, he said, but restrain federal power. "Now, for the first time in our history," Congress aimed "to discriminate . . . against the citizens of one portion of the Union and in favor of another." For slaveholders already in Oregon, this bill would mean abolition by the federal government, "the exercise of a power not delegated." If Southerners did not resist now, they would "be dwarfed into helplessness and political dependence." Like Calhoun, he saw with horror where it all was leading:

> Shall jealousy, discord, and dissension . . . be permitted to undermine . . . our republican fabric . . . [and destroy] that fraternal feeling and mutual confidence on which alone can our institutions securely repose? Shall a discrimination against one section of the Confederacy, the palpable object of which is totally to destroy political equality . . . hasten its progress to the inevitable goal of such a principle—the disunion of the States?[32]

"The issue was joined for all the territories." Southern offers to abide by judicial decision (which Davis preferred to congressional action as "more just" and "more permanent") or to extend the Missouri Compromise line (though detrimental to the South) were to be refused. The South's stand was being warped into "extension" of slavery by "desire for political aggrandizement . . . and fanaticism," said Davis: "Non-interference with the subject of slavery is our main position, and is equally opposed to force for or against it."[33] To exclude it from territories had not "one point either of humanity or sound policy." This would simply perpetuate it where it was, "beyond its natural term," whereas, if its numbers were distributed, it could be ended "without injury to the progress of society." To suggest that a slave owner simply "dispose of his property" showed "inability to comprehend the attachment which generally subsists."[34]

If blacks were forced into "responsibilities" unprepared, Davis argued, then "instead of a blessing, liberty would be their greatest curse." He pointed to their "immense improvement" by "association with a more elevated race" and invited comparison "with recently-imported Africans" in the West Indies and "with the free blacks of the northern States"—"miserable, impoverished, loathsome from the deformity and disease which follows after penury and vice; covering the records of the criminal courts, and filling the penitentiaries."[35] He pointed out Northern hostility to blacks, and he recoiled "with surprise and horror" when Sen. John Dix of New York suggested that free blacks would "continue to be an inferior caste" and would simply die out. Davis, attached to blacks "from childhood," was shocked to hear "their extinction treated as a matter of public policy." Even if he believed a homogeneous population important, he said, or "slavery to be the moral, social, and political evil which it is described," he could never "be reconciled to such a policy for such a purpose."[36]

"And this is the moral teaching of those who assume to be our pastors, and offer their vicarious repentance for the sins of slavery." "If it be a sin," he said, "show, then, your repentance, if you feel any," for being "the importers of Africans; you sold them in the South." But, he argued, it was not a sin, it was "a common-law right to property in the service of man," going "back to the earliest Government of which we have any knowledge." "Its origin was Divine decree—the curse upon the graceless son of Noah. Slavery was regulated by the laws given through Moses to the Jews. Slaves were to be of the heathen, and with their offspring to descend by inheritance: thus, in the main particulars, being identical with the institution as it exists among us." The prophecy about the sons of Noah was "wonderfully" fulfilled when American "Indians" who were "sons of Shem . . . not doomed to bondage," proved "unprofitable" as slaves and were replaced by the descendants of Canaan, "the sons of Ham," who thus "came to their destiny." Slavery was "sanctioned everywhere" in the Bible, he showed later, in both Old and New Testaments, "in the prophecies, psalms, and the epistles of Paul," and it was seen in the Revelation to "exist until the end of time shall come." He believed the "happiness and usefulness" of the slaves "prove their present condition to be the accomplishment of an all-wise decree. It may have for its end the preparation of that race for civil liberty and social enjoyment."[37]

Neither "love for the African" (witness northern laws against him) nor revulsion from "property in persons" ("No, you imported Africans and sold them as chattels in the slave-markets") motivated the present-day agitators, argued Davis. "No, sir . . . the mask is off, the purpose is avowed. . . . It is a struggle for political power."[38]

This "crusade against the South . . . at war with justice, at war with the Constitution . . . will, if not checked . . . reach disunion tomorrow." "He must be blind indeed who does not see" the aim: "to amend the compact of our Union, and strip the South of the guarantees it gives." He warned:

> If the principles of the Constitution are to be disregarded by a self-sustaining majority, the days of the Confederation are numbered. The men who have encountered past wars for the maintenance of principle, will never consent to be branded . . . unworthy of further political growth. If such be your determination, it were better that we should part peaceably, and avoid staining the battlefields of the Revolution with the blood of civil war.

Citing Abraham and Lot, he pleaded, "If the folly, and fanaticism, and pride, and hate, and corruption of the day are to destroy the peace and prosperity of the Union, let the sections part like the patriarchs of old, and let peace and good will subsist among their descendants."[39]

Finally, on August 13, after an all-night debate, Congress passed a bill to organize the Territory of Oregon. At the last minute, Davis tried in vain to substitute the Clayton Compromise, which he thought "would have forever ended the quarrel between the North and the South" by throwing the question of Territorial slavery into the federal courts. He noted later that it had already been defeated in the House "by the treason of that *little pale star* from Georgia, Alexander Hamilton Stephens" and seven other Whigs. The Oregon Bill barred slavery forever. "At every step the South had lost."[40]

Davis had been speaking for strict constructionists, North and South. The slavery question was splitting the Democratic Party and drawing Southern Democrats and Whigs closer together. The whole Southern way of life faced extinction. Calhoun could see no hope except in dropping party labels and forming one massive Southern bloc to resist what Davis called "aggression." Calhoun wrote, "We must act in good faith, to save the Union if we can . . . but if not, to save ourselves."[41]

Publicly, the outlook for Davis was discouraging, but in private, things were looking up. Varina was making every effort to get along with her in-laws. One night at the Hurricane, she "got hold of a villainously long article . . . and Brother Joe said I read so well he could not let me go to bed until he did, so I waded with all my strength through it." Joseph and Eliza usually went at least as far as Kentucky in the summer. This year, they went to Washington, and they took Varina with them. Mary Bache Walker invited Varina to spend the Congressional recess with her, but Jeff was sick in August, and his wife evidently went home when he did, at the end of August, stopping in Kentucky, at Blue Lick Spring and Lexington, on the way. She did not return with him in December, but their estrangement was over.[42] She began a letter in January 1849, with "My own darling Husband," and called him "Jeff, my sweetest." She warned him about the cholera that was abroad:

> Take laudanum and camphor the *first* slight pain you feel. Only come back to me safe in person and I can bear all other evils. Much as I have loved and valued you it seems to me I never knew the vastness of my treasure until now. If you have no fear for yourself, have it for your Winnie, your thoughtless, dependent wife, and guard your health as you would my life. Sweetest, best husband, don't go out at night, don't drink wine, don't eat any fruit. If you feel any temptation to be imprudent just recall the question to your mind if you have any right to blast my life for your gratification of the moment. You were never selfish, then be yourself now, and think of your wife.[43]

Taylor had returned home the hero of the hour. On visits to his Mississippi plantation in March and April 1848, he stopped at the Hurricane. He told Jeff he had "spent a most delightful day," and said "your accomplished sister in law, while your brother was engaged, took me over the plantation." It was "handsomely arranged . . . a little paradise . . . with every comfort & I may say luxury." He regretted not buying land on the Bend instead of at Rodney, so that he could "have passed my spare time" with the Davises, "much more to my satisfaction than I could in the White H[ou]se where I never expect to get."[44] On July 10, while still speaking of Joseph, his health and wealth, he asked a favor of Jeff:

> My dear General,
> Owing to some cause either by accidents in the mails &c, I have not yet been notified by Govr. Morehead that I had been nominated by the National Whig Convention which recently assembled at Philadelphia as their candidate for the presidency at the coming election.

He had heard the news at his Baton Rouge plantation "by Telegraph to Memphis, & from there by the Steam Boat Genl. Taylor." Since he did not know Morehead's address, and because of the "great anxiety" of his friends, he wanted Davis to forward his request for an official notice.[45]

Although "highly gratified at the honor," Taylor went on, "I felt neither pride or exultation" at the news

> & if I know myself . . . my feelings would not be changed in the slightest degree was I to receive notice of my election . . . [or] to hear of the success of my adversary; for as the time approaches . . . I find my disinclination . . . greatly to increase. . . . That they should have nominated me an humble individual personally unknown to nearly the whole of them, as a suitable candidate for the first office in the gift of a great & free people, or I may say the first in the wor[l]d, . . . without requiring pledges or promises of any kind . . . [manifests] a confidence in my honesty, truthfulness & integrity never surpassed & rarely equalled since the days of the Father of his country, which confidence I hope to retain by continuing to merit it.[46]

Taylor had expressed his indifference many times. He disapproved of parties, had refused to be nominated by the Native Americans, and said even now he "would have accepted the Democratic nomination had it been tendered me in like manner, leaving me untrammeled and unpledged." (The Whig Party had adopted no platform.)[47] Davis had said, "he is no party man" (because an apolitical soldier), but if he were, his ideas on strict construction and state sovereignty, along "with his stern integrity and utter contempt for intrigue," would make him a Democrat, though he "probably would disagree with the ultra men of both parties."

As Taylor said, Davis "knows m[y] every thought in regard to political matters." When he finally declared, under party pressure, that he was a Whig, he added, "but not an ultra Whig," and "Taylor Democrats" helped to elect him.[48]

Taylor must have enjoyed beating out Winfield Scott, even more than Clay and Webster, for the Whig nomination. He admitted having some "hard feelings" about the man who, he thought, had tried to cut his throat in order to be president. He had said earlier, however, Scott's "duplicity to ward me has been rarely equalled; but let it all pass—" and had told Davis, "We must . . . bear & forbear, as well as to forgive as we expect to be forgiven." Davis was to use these very words about his own ill-usage many years later.[49]

Jeff Davis was not a Taylor Democrat. Not even his "confidence, admiration, and affection for the man" could make him bolt the Democratic Party. Taylor was "trusted and loved," but he "must draw his advisers from a party, the tenets of which I believed to be opposed to the interests of the country." Davis wanted "a Democratic President, with a Democratic Cabinet, and Democratic counselors in the two Houses of Congress." Replying to an army toast at a dinner for John J. Crittenden, who was leaving to run for governor of Kentucky, he called Taylor "a man of great wisdom and firmness of character." But that fall he campaigned for the Democratic nominees, Generals Lewis Cass and William Orlando Butler.[50]

Cass was an ancient by that day's standard, sixty-six, a militia major-general who had been secretary of war. Davis knew him well "as a scholar, a patriot and a statesman . . . and an honorable man," but privately he confided to a nephew that Cass did not merit being president. Neither Cass nor Butler, who had been Davis's division commander in Mexico, was "great," he said, and hinted a growing disillusion: "It has been my misfortune to witness in my political course but little of . . . elevated statesmanship."[51]

Canvassing in Mississippi "as fully as my physical condition would permit," Davis was severely hampered by what was known as the Nicholson Letter. Cass had written it in support of "squatter sovereignty," which allowed first settlers in a territory to decide for or against slavery. James K. Polk had proposed it as a middle way, where extremists on both sides of the slavery issue might walk. But even Davis, who was a moderate, thought it "absolutely wrong." It would give a territory the powers of a sovereign state, "demolishing the constitutional barriers which the fathers of the republic raised for our peace, protection, and fraternity." And, as Calhoun saw, it would not give slavery an even chance, but destroy it.[52]

Many Southern Democrats claimed that Cass did not mean to support popular sovereignty, but Davis was too honest. He said Cass did mean that, and his colleagues "well-nigh crucified me" for it. He had to admit, however, that their false reading of the letter "secured Mr. Cass the vote of Mississippi," where Cass beat Taylor by less than a thousand votes. Later, Davis's opinion, which had been "sneered at," saved Cass from the charge of having deceived the South. In spite of the letter, Davis argued for Cass because he was against the Wilmot Proviso. As president, Cass could veto the proviso if it came up, and Davis knew that Taylor would not.[53]

With cracks appearing in the Democratic Party, William Lowndes Yancey, in Alabama, had proposed a third-party ticket, to run Littleton W. Tazewell of Virginia and Davis. But before Yancey could even get their consent, the radicals of New York, known as Barnburners, had snatched away his third-party idea, bolting the Democratic convention and joining abolitionists to create a Free-Soil Party. They ran a lapsed Democrat, Martin Van Buren ("the most fallen man I have ever known," said Polk), and a "Conscience Whig," Charles Francis Adams, son of John Quincy Adams. To help them, John P. Hale withdrew as candidate of the totally abolitionist Liberty Party. The Free-Soil Party of the North was, as a member said, "wholly unhampered by a Southern wing." Thus began what Davis had called "for many years my dread, a division marked not by opinions, but by geographical lines." "The patriotic" would then have to "save the Republic" by "devotion to the principles of our federation." Calhoun thought the immediate result would be Taylor's election, which it was. He also, like Davis, saw that "the coming struggle for power would be along sectional rather than party lines."[54]

Davis's main interest was military. He delightedly recommended to the War Department, "at the request of Mr. Eli Whitney," the maker, the rifles he himself had made famous, praising "their neatness" and durability, their "greater certainty of fire and simplicity of construction." He told the ordnance chief, "In accuracy of fire they are equal to the finest sporting rifles." The First Mississippi were allowed to keep their rifles, and Davis helped assure that the "2d. Missi. Regt. and the Missi. Battalion" (which he had proposed) kept their arms too. The president asked his opinion on "the value of Colts revolving pistol for mounted troops." Davis approved but deferred to Harney and Ben McCulloch as having more experience.[55]

Davis used his new influence to help the men of his regiment, especially as a member of the Military Affairs Committee. He asked for army commissions, bounty lands, and pensions, and tried to get a marine hospital at New Orleans and his veterans into it. He sought an appointment as Mississippi marshal for Capt. William P. Rogers, whose enmity had turned to "high regard."[56] Davis recalled Twiggs cheering the men on at Monterey, thereby assuring his brevet as major general. Twiggs was put over the Eighth Military District in Texas and, subsequently, the whole Western Department. Davis also asked brevets for friends Bennet Riley, William Emory, and others.[57]

His old buddy in the First Dragoons, Lucius B. Northrop, needed help. Since their last meeting at Fort Gibson, whether because of Jeff's theology talk or not, he had become a Catholic and married one. Before that, he had accidentally shot himself in the knee while on arduous duty. The ball could not be extracted. With his active career in the dragoons ruined, he served in the Commissary Department, but soon his wound prevented even that. He was put on the disabled list, and he took a three-year leave to study medicine, with a view to supporting himself outside the army—"a delicacy of honor," said Davis, made him unwilling to draw pay "if unable to do duty." The only recourse then for the disabled was permanent sick leave, but Davis was trying to get a "retired list" for them. When he learned Northrop was dropped from army rolls in 1848, he worked to get him reinstated so he would be eligible for the list. Since he was from a prominent Charleston family, Davis got his senators, Calhoun and A. P. Butler, to sign a letter endorsing him. Northrop was not only restored to the dragoons, he was promoted to captain.[58]

The Democrats had lost the election, but they still had power in the Senate when Davis arrived for the second session of the Thirtieth Congress, which opened December 4, 1848. He had demonstrated a tough mind in debate, with ability to cut through complex questions to the root, and then to voice his conclusions in masterful English. His extensive and precise knowledge of the army was by now obvious. His party called him, freshman senator though he was, to the chair of the Military Affairs Committee, which Cass had vacated. He also served on the Library Committee and the Smithsonian Board of Regents. Davis later declined appointment to the West Point Board of Visitors.[59]

Calhoun was still the leader of the state rights men. Davis, who had the Senate seat next to him, said that on Calhoun's mind, "experience, and intensity of feeling and of thought, had shed more of prophetic light than I have ever found in any other individual." Calhoun hoped to direct the South to "unity of common purpose," and "thereby to avoid the extremes of giving in to the abolitionists or seceding from the Union." As the attack began now, Southerners of both parties called for a statement of their position, Davis being the first to sign the resolution and Calhoun, second. The elder statesman drew up a temperate "Southern Address." His call for approval before sending it out in January 1849 showed how deeply the South was divided. Over half the Democrats signed it, but only two Whigs. The Whig leaders, Toombs and Stephens of Georgia, were fearful of the effect on Taylor's coming administration. The Democrat Sam Houston would not sign, and Thomas Hart Benton was not even invited to. Calhoun barely got approval for his address.

He had doused the fire-eaters and stymied the compromisers, but only for the moment, and in the midst of the debate, on January 19, he collapsed—"the beginning of his final illness."[60]

Although a leader of the Democrats, Jeff Davis was friend and kinsman to the incoming Whig president. He was manager for the inaugural ball, on a select committee to examine electoral votes, and Senate teller to count them. He was on the committee to notify Zachary Taylor of his election and arrange for his reception by the Senate. The committee found Taylor "at 'Hurricane,' discussing with Joseph Davis his plans for Cabinet appointments." When the president-elect reached Washington in February, Davis addressed him on behalf of the Senate and went with him to call on President Polk. They dined together at the White House, and on March 5, Davis escorted Polk and Taylor to the inauguration.[61]

Davis was worried about Taylor politically. He tried to counter Henry Clay's "evil influence" by asking John J. Crittenden (now governor of Kentucky) to come advise the president about his cabinet. Crittenden advised Taylor only in Kentucky, telling him to rely on Toombs and Stephens in Washington. Davis soon was lamenting "the injury done the South" by two of Taylor's appointments.[62] Davis also talked to Crittenden about "My boy Tom" (whom Taylor was to make consul in Liverpool) and the older son, George, who had been cashiered for drunkenness. Davis had studied the court-martial and found him "unjustly treated." Davis's Military Affairs Committee reported serious flaws in the trial, and when Taylor came in, Maj. George Crittenden was reinstated.[63]

It was a short session. By the end of March, Davis was headed home. The idea of Whigs and Democrats making a common stand brought Mississippians together in May, and Davis addressed them. The South had remained supine under "wounding" assault for seventeen years; Northern assurances were but "the lulling of the vampire fawning the victim which he will destroy." When the North got its three-fourths "preponderance," in order to change the Constitution, "all that is now promised to the South will be forgotten." In an August letter from Brierfield, he wrote out his views fully. He quoted New York's Senator Seward, the Whig leader who had Taylor's ear, as saying recently in Ohio, "Slavery can and must be abolished, and you and I can do it." "The enemy has passed the outer gate," Davis announced, "we have to decide whether he shall be met at the threshold or on the hearth stone of our dwelling."[64]

He pointed out "the political heresy that ours is an union of the people" as a whole, rather than of states, and that the federal government has supreme, rather than delegated, power. Unless all are equals in the compact of states originally formed, having equal access to territories, "it ceases to be the Union," and becomes "despotism." The agitators who were calling it a sin even to associate with slaveholders had built their case on ignorance, he said, "the nurse of fiction and prejudice and passion." Some of the "fictions" he referred to were: no slave marriages, broken families, "fetters," and no Bible reading. "What could be more ridiculous than the idea of prohibiting the Bible to our slaves?" In its "sacred pages" they would learn "submission and faithful, not eye service, to masters," and to avoid novel teaching "whereof cometh envy, strife, railings, evils surmisings" (he cited "1 Tim. vi. 4, 5"). "We rely on the Bible as authority for the establishment of slavery among men, and on the Constitution for its recognition throughout the United States."[65]

"A truce to politics the meanest and most demoralizing pursuit which is followed," he cried to a friend. He thought Henry Foote and Quitman (now governor of Mississippi) would push him "as far north as possible." They would "form combinations which . . . I will never attempt"—probably meaning one between Democrats and Free-Soilers which he told another was "disgraceful" and would be "far worse than a party defeat." They would fault him for praising Taylor but hide "out of sight" how he had campaigned against him. "I wonder how many of my opponents standing in the relation I did to Gen Taylor would have endeavored to defeat him for d[em]ocracy's sake, & have refused to walk in the broad way and the open gate to self preferment." Even his political ideas were coming out in biblical terms. He had told state Democrats in June that the "creed" of their "political church," founded on truth, would stand "as the house which the wise man built on a rock." They should bring personal rivalries "as a peace offering, a sacrifice meet for the altar of principle," keeping "the holy fire alive" until they could "place it again on the democratic altar."[66]

Jeff and Varina had several months together at Brierfield. He was busy with new colts; she, with seeing to shelves for the library of the new house. In April, Davis Bend was festive for the wedding of Malie Bradford to David Brodhead, a member of Congress from Pennsylvania. In July the Bend was plunged into mourning when Joseph Davis's six-year-old grandson, Hugh Mitchell, was killed in a riding accident. Varina was sick in August, and Jeff refused all invitations until she was well. In October, he was "a little sick on the road," as he spoke for local candidates over the northern half of the state. But they were fine, Jeff's foot all well now, as they traveled to Washington together in November, taking two nieces with them. Jeff's happiness over their reconciliation was obvious in a note full of banter and allusion, inviting James Kingsbury for a visit and noting, "Mrs. Davis is with me." To Kingsbury, an army friend, he spoke of renewing "an association always remembered among the most pleasant of my life."[67]

By January 6, 1850, the Davises and William McWillies of Mississippi, the Armistead Burts of South Carolina (she was Calhoun's niece), and the Robert Toombses of Georgia had together rented a whole boardinghouse on Pennsylvania Avenue next to the United States Hotel. "I like to see the bustle," said Varina. They had "an elegant table, all sorts of nice French dishes," at the hotel, and "a right nice parlor" at the house. "I hired an excellent piano." She told Ma about "the most beautiful dinner I ever saw," with "an immense number of courses," lasting from seven to eleven, and described her dress in detail. "But I hate dinners, I declare I thought my back was broke before we got away."[68]

They had been to the New Year's reception at the White House. "But I did not enjoy it at all." The Taylors had been "very kind," but "Mrs. Bliss is, as I expected, less lovable than the rest of them, that is, she is not a cordial woman." There may have been a touch of jealousy in this, for Betty, who had married Col. W. W. S. Bliss on December 5, looked so like Sarah Knox that Jeff was startled when he saw her. They had not met since she was a child.[69]

William Seward, however, found Betty (acting hostess for Peggy Taylor, who was in Baton Rouge) "pretty, unaffected, and sensible," and her father "the most gentle-looking and amiable of men. Every word and look indicate sincerity of heart, even to guilelessness." Taylor had charmed Washington. Davis agreed with Seward for once, noting Taylor's habit of "cheerful, unaffected greeting," the "purity, the generosity, and unostentatious magnanimity of his private character." He knew more about this than most people.[70] Before the presidential campaign, Taylor had written: "I must beg you, my dear General . . . without regard to what concerns me, look to your interest; you are young . . . while my days are numbered, or nearly so, by the age allotted to man by his Creator; at any rate my days of ambition have passed away." And again: "I feel under my dear Genl. the greatest obligations for [your] continued interest . . . in my reaching the first office . . . in which you . . . take much more concern than I do . . . I have your own advancement more at heart than my own . . . it is sufficient to me to know that I possess your friendship, which is all I ask or wish."[71]

Politically, they were at odds. But Davis's fears about Henry Clay were ill-founded. Taylor predicted that Davis would end Clay's rule of Congress, amazing a friend, who said it showed "almost infatuation of admiration and esteem for Col. Davis." ("The time will come when you will see as I do all his rare qualities," Knox had said.) Taylor had fallen out with Clay over California. The gold rush had created chaos there, and the military governor, Bvt. Maj. Gen. Bennet Riley, had called a constitutional convention, even though California was not even a territory. Now Taylor irregularly offered immediate admission as a state (and it would be a free state), causing a furor. Henry Clay tried to calm the storm by offering resolutions that collectively became known as the "Compromise of 1850."[72]

Davis immediately asked: "Is a measure in which we of the minority are to receive nothing, a measure of compromise?" He fought Clay sharply, from a "stern sense of duty," yet reluctantly, because of "a tie of old memories . . . running back to boyhood's days" which "death alone can ever sever"—his friendship with the younger Clay. The elder once said, "My poor boy usually occupied about one half of his letters home in praising you."[73]

Clay privately tried to win Davis for his "Compromise" on the plea that it would put off trouble for thirty years. "I cannot consent to transfer to posterity a question which is as much ours as theirs," answered Davis; by then even greater "sectional inequality" would "render hopeless the attainment of justice." Clay saw that the North, risking nothing, had set a fire in the South that would destroy "social intercourse, habit, safety, property, life, everything." He said so in the Senate. Yet he claimed that by his compromise the North would yield "far more than she receives." Davis slashed at him:

> Where is the concession to the South? Is it in the admission, as a State, of California, from which we have been excluded by Congressional agitation? Is it in the announcement that slavery does not and is not to exist in the remaining Territories . . . ? Is it in denying the title of Texas to one-half of her territory? Is it in insulting her by . . . offering her [money for it]? Is it by declaring that it is inexpedient to abolish slavery in the District of Columbia, unless this Federal Government make compensation to the owners of the slaves—a class of property with which this Government has nothing more to do than with any other? . . . Can money be appropriated . . . for any other than those purposes indicated in the Constitution? And was this Constitution formed for the purpose of emancipation? Sir, it seems to me that this is a question which gives its own solution—needs no answer.[74]

Davis wanted real compromise, not one that would "merely change the issue and leave the contest open." He proposed extending to the Pacific Ocean the line of the Missouri Compromise, agreed on for so long by both sections, with slavery prohibited above it: "if the territory cannot be enjoyed in common, it should be divided." This would end "the controversy forever" and "stop the agitation which now disturbs and endangers the Union." But the North was feeling its power and would not listen. "Heretofore this [Missouri] compromise had always unequivocally operated against the South," cried Davis: "now, for the first time, it is a two sided question, and lo! the North rejects it. Who then, [is being] uncompromising, ultra, or selfish?"[75]

Congress rejected the "omnibus bill" that embodied Clay's resolutions, but by September 1850, it had passed virtually every one of its parts as separate laws—another bitter defeat for the South. The "Compromise" merely stirred up new animosity. Abolitionists in the Northeast denounced it. Yancey and Rhett, the fire-eaters, called for secession in

Alabama and South Carolina. The only "concession" to the South was a new Fugitive Slave Law, stronger than the one in force since 1793. But Davis pointed out the hypocrisy of this: "That law will be a dead letter in any State where the popular opinion is opposed to such rendition." And indeed, although the Constitution guaranteed the return of runaways, contradictory laws had already had been passed in fourteen states, and Northern mobs continually prevented extradition.[76]

With his elegant language filling more columns of print than any other senator's, Davis was expressing in this session not his opinion only, but that of the Southern bloc as he understood it. In February 1850, he stood in the place of Calhoun, who was too ill to speak, and for two days poured forth an address so eloquent that it saw print as a pamphlet. On March 4, the "ghostlike figure" of Calhoun appeared, feeble, but with "brilliant, flashing eyes" sweeping the floor "in the old lordly way." All Senate seats were filled as, wrapped in a long cloak, Calhoun heard James Mason read for him the speech of "cold, blunt realism" that he was too weak to pronounce.

Thomas Jefferson had seen agitation over slavery as "the speck on our horizon which is to burst on us as a tornado, sooner or later." Now, with agitation unchecked, Calhoun saw, "it can no longer be disguised or denied that the Union is in danger." The North dominated Congress, original equilibrium was destroyed, and the notion of consolidated government sought to swallow state sovereignty. No longer able to protect itself, the South could only plead. "If you, who represent the stronger portion, cannot agree" to settle the issues "on the broad principle of justice and duty, say so; and let the States . . . agree to separate and part in peace. If you are unwilling we should part in peace, tell us so, and we shall know what to do."[77]

On the next day, George Dallas got Varina a place on the Senate floor, and she saw Calhoun come in, "supported on each side . . . breathing in short gasps." "He gave me one burning hand as he passed," whispering, "My child, I am too weak to stop." Henry Foote "baited him for over an hour," until even Calhoun's deep enemy, Thomas Hart Benton, muttered, "No brave man could do this infamy. Shame, shame!" Davis and others wanted to answer for Calhoun, but he insisted on making his own replies in a weak voice, until he seemed about to die right there. His friends finally bore him away.

Daniel Webster, his admiring enemy, conferred with him for many hours the next day, and they agreed on a conciliatory appeal for union, which Calhoun dragged himself back to hear. But Webster's Seventh of March Speech gained him only the contempt of abolitionists like John Greenleaf Whittier (Garrison's protégé), who vilified him in his "shameful" poem, "Ichabod," and rejection by the Massachusetts electorate, who replaced him in 1851 with Charles Sumner, "a radical Free-Soiler and enemy of the compromise." "The olive branch withered and was trampled under foot."[78]

Calhoun came once more to the Senate on March 13, to deny categorically that he had advocated disunion: he had merely described the situation. Davis and A. P. Butler squelched Foote this time and hurried Calhoun away, feverish and exhausted. It was consumption, complicated by heart disease. He died on March 31. Webster, who had known Calhoun since 1813, spoke feelingly of his "unspotted integrity," his unselfishness, and his great courtesy. Davis was one of the senatorial guard of honor that took the body to Charleston in April and laid it to rest in St. Philip's churchyard. He wrote Varina particularly of the "Cloth of Gold" roses that covered the bier and "every available space."[79] Webster congratulated Davis for a speech in which he said Calhoun was taken away "Like a summer-dried fountain when our need was the sorest." Varina says, "Mr. Davis laughed and told him 'That was the only part of it that was not mine, that was Walter Scott's.' "[80]

Jeff and Varina still found time to read, as they always had. In this exceptionally long session, crammed with momentous business, Jeff checked out of the Library of Congress thirty-two octavo volumes, ranging from *Fabliaux, or Tales, 13th & 14th cents.* [*sic*] through *Pretty Woman,* and "Works of George Sand" to "Ure's Dictionary of Arts," "Bishop Heber's Sermons," and "Works of Josephus." Jeff also pleased Varina with a gift of "Dickens' pretty little Christmas Tales." "You admired the character of Milly, did you not?" she wrote—an innocent, noble character. She was busy with "Mrs. Ellis's Guide to Social Happiness," which "will help 'Winnie' to be 'Wife.' " If these remarks were a jab at his criticism of her the year before, she made up by calling him "my own bright love," and saying he could not help her illness "unless looking into your sweet eyes would be balm for all wounds."[81]

Varina grumblingly enjoyed Washington society. "I am invited to the President's to dine again," she wrote on May 18, "but I think I had rather take a whipping than go. The lilac silk has been to every party this winter, so I must get a new dress, and it hurts my conscience dreadfully." On May 20: "Well, darling sweet old Mammy doogle, I went to the President's in a sky blue silk ruffled up to the waist . . . with scarlet rosettes in my hair and bosom. . . . It is the only dinner party I have enjoyed in some time." She was not frivolous. Her kind heart took her upstairs at this very party to talk to the first lady, for Peggy Taylor had vowed to give up society if her husband came back safe from Mexico. Varina went to be with Malie Bradford Brodhead when her first child was born, since "she is so far from any of us." Her care for others soon had a real trial.[82]

"The great, the good, heroic Taylor," as Davis called him ("for a hero he was, not in the mere vulgar sense of animal courage, but by the higher and nobler attributes of generosity and clemency"), had his own hero, George Washington, who, he said, "had no parallel in history." On February 22, 1850, he helped lay the cornerstone for the statue on Richmond's Capitol Square. On July 4, already feeling ill, he went to the cornerstone-laying for the Washington Monument and sat for two hours in the broiling sun while "Henry Foote and others orated."[83] Varina described his ensuing illness for Ma on July 10. For two days, he would not have a physician, but "Sunday they sent [for one], whether he would or not. He continued hot, and cold by turns, and Tuesday (yesterday) congestion of the brain took place, and last night he died at half past eleven." Varina and Jeff had found

> his family round him, poor Mrs. Taylor on the bed chafing his hands, and telling him she had lived with him nearly forty years and he must talk to her. . . . Of course, he could neither see or speak. . . . And after a gentle breath he died like a child going to rest.
>
> Then the tearing Mrs. Taylor away from the body nearly killed me—she would listen to his heart . . . and insist he did not die without speaking to her. [The family's] grief, the bells tolling and the servants crying altogether I liked to have gone mad. . . . I went again this morning and stayed all day, and shall go again tomorrow and every day as long as they stay here. . . . The funeral takes place on Saturday. He is in a refrigerator until then, frozen, when he will be laid in state in the east room for a few hours. The last distinct words he said were to Jeff. He suddenly spoke, and said, "Apply the constitution to the measure, Sir, regardless of consequences."[84]

Taylor had succumbed at sixty-three to "cholera morbus," not to be confused (though perhaps it then was) with the contagious "Asiatic cholera" against which he had earlier asked the nation's fasting and prayer. The rector of St. John's, where he attended, had prayed over him, and he had declared himself prepared to die.[85]

On July 13, in an East Room jammed with dignitaries, Jeff sat with the men of the family. Taylor's only son, Richard, was on the Mississippi, managing the plantations, but the grandsons were there, Robert and John Taylor Wood (an Annapolis midshipman), and probably their little sister, Jeff's godchild, whom Taylor called "Dumple," but whose name was Sarah Knox. Millard Fillmore, sworn in as the new president, spoke of Taylor's "simplicity." The procession to the Congressional Burying Ground was everything he would have hated—a high silk-festooned bier drawn by eight caparisoned white horses with turbaned grooms, followed by a line of more than a hundred carriages, stretching nearly two miles, one hundred thousand spectators, and "Old Fuss and Feathers" himself, Winfield Scott, in uniformed splendor on a charger, wearing indeed a "towering plume of yellow feathers." Taylor's body was stored in a vault till it was taken to Kentucky and laid in the family graveyard near Louisville on November 1, All Saints Day.[86]

No sooner had the Davises lost the man who called Jeff "my most devoted & ardent friend," than they were stricken again with even less warning. Varina, teasing Jeff about the mail one day, opened the letter that Ma had addressed to him in hopes of softening the shock. The little brother named for her mentor, Judge Winchester, had died at the age of eleven. On July 18, Jeff wrote to "My dear Ma" of their grief over "our Dear little George." He said, Varina "has felt beneficially your christian example of resignation." Ma had already lost three children in infancy. Jeff too had had to ponder often the ways of death.

> I will not offer to you the mockery as to real grief it always appears, of words of consolation— The loss was great, and is irreparable. I mourn with you but am checked in its indulgence by the remembrance, that the loss is our's, not his. Though his life promised to be valuable to others, and his amiable elevated character must have been a blessing to his family, the trials and pains of its course would have been encountered without a possibility after lifes fitful fever was over of reaching a more desirable end— Happy indeed may those be considered whose mission is soon completed, of whom the creator requires but a brief probation.[87]

Jeff stayed home "all the time when not in the senate" to comfort her, but the rest of the session was dreary. They were in double mourning, the heat was oppressive, the Senate debates were either acrimonious or petty, and the nieces were visiting the Brodheads. There was no little one to cheer them, though they had been married five years. Varina was now twenty-four, and Jeff, forty-two.

On August 5, Jeff was fired up by "aspersions" cast on Zachary Taylor's memory to a full-fledged speech tracing his general's whole course in Mexico. In the routine petitioning, he was able to help Myra Clark Gaines (General E. P.'s widow) and the dragoons John Doran, David Hunter, and Bennet Riley as well as veterans, widows, and orphans in general.[88] He took up for half-breeds in Minnesota ("Let the Indians alone"), but argued against use of government money for "eleemosynary institutions" as loose construction, "the end of which no man can tell." He reported out the Library Committee bill to purchase Gilbert Stuart's "portraits of the first five Presidents . . . Provided, That they do not cost more than $500 each."[89]

Varina was startled one night during this session to find a swarthy stranger in the darkened parlor, his "glowing eyes and silvery hair" gleaming in the moonlight. It was Narcisco Lopez. He had come to recruit Colonel Davis as military head of his expedition to free Cuba from Spanish rule. Jeff politely refused the command as "inconsistent with my duty" and referred him to Bvt. Col. Robert E. Lee, in Baltimore. Lee came down to discuss it with Jeff and thus gave Varina her first glimpse of "the handsomest person I had ever seen." He too refused, which was well, for the filibustering expedition ended in disaster. Davis spoke of Lee's "extreme delicacy" of honor in this decision (but not his own).[90] He may have been tempted by the fortune and military fame promised by Lopez. On September 15, he was writing to Ma: "I am weary and more than ever before disgusted with political life."[91]

IX

Victory in Defeat

The long Congressional session finally ended September 30, 1850, and the Davises set out for Mississippi. Varina's heart must have been heavy, not only with grief, but with knowing her parents were no longer at the Briars. She had told Jeff, "I have been thinking constantly of Pa." "Kiss dear Father for me," she had written Ma, speaking of a "love I feel too deeply to write." She was to describe a man "so like my dear Father in his faith in men and his habitually soft and kind manner."[1] William Burr Howell, tall and blonde, fond of shooting and hunting, a favorite with everyone, could somehow never manage success. Sprague and Howell, the "large speculative concern" dealing in merchandizing and investments, went out of business when Sprague died in 1838. After failing to get the postmastership in Natchez, despite the efforts of Davis and others, Howell became a federal timber agent. Now he and Ma and five children (son Joe was off on a trading expedition to Oregon) had gone to Tunisberg, a suburb of New Orleans, where they started a dairy farm "optimistically called 'Betterdays.'"[2]

There was more woe waiting for the Davises at Brierfield. James Pemberton had died of pneumonia and was buried in the little cemetery southeast of the house. In the absence of this firm hand over the property, they met "the usual fate of absentees," says Varina. The housekeeper "told me, with friendly sympathy, 'Missis, 'taint't no use to talk; what isn't broke is crack, and what isn't crack is broke.'" Varina set about ordering the plantation as best she could while Jeff went off to stump for the state rights cause.[3]

They had stopped a week in Jackson, to prepare for his speaking tour. His distaste for politics expressed to Ma gave way to his sense of duty to the Democratic Party. There was considerable faction in it over the compromise measures, and Davis wanted his electors, the legislature, to instruct him in the face of the new developments—particularly the "utterly unconstitutional" prohibition of the slave trade in the District of Columbia and the "*fraud*" of the California admission. He had signed a protest against the latter in August because of no territorial organization, no census to count voters, and "odious discrimination" against the fifteen "slaveholding States." He now told the people that Southerners should "cease wrangling" and unite with Whigs on a common platform, that each Southern state should send delegates, "fresh from the people," to a convention that could "point out the guarantees and safe guards, which the South is entitled to." The similar Nashville Convention of June had had no effect, he knew, and if this one should fail, "the South would have no alternative" but to leave the Union. He insisted, however, echoing Calhoun, that the South should protect her honor "in the Union if she can and out of it if she must."[4]

What Davis called the "exigent demand for some attention to my private affairs" got short shrift. Having made eleven speeches since October 18, he headed back for Washington on November 22, leaving Varina to take care of Brierfield. Their marital happiness, and one basis for it, shows in the note he wrote back from Mrs. Hill's boardinghouse, "as you will not allow me to kiss you for an angel, be one now in the presence of Our God and the absence of Your Husband."

From the steamboat *General Scott* en route, he had analyzed for the citizens of Lowndes County, who had approved his course, how the Constitution had been violated covertly rather than openly, leaving them little hope for redress in the Supreme Court. There was none in the Congress, where the South was "reduced to a permanent minority." The "pseudo philanthropy of British teachers" (meaning abolitionists) had "entered like a wedge to rend our Union asunder." "The time has arrived when all who love the Union or the Constitution should unite to throw an adequate shield over the minority; before it is driven to seek in arms that protection against an aggressive majority which the existing forms of our government fail to afford."[5]

Davis took his seat on December 5, 1850, for the second session of the Thirty-first Congress, doubtless with the same "melancholy forebodings" he had brought to the first (that it might be the last). Although he had expressed a desire in January to take "a final leave of public station," he did not object to his election on February 12 to his own new six-year term as senator. He saw himself as "an accredited agent of Mississippi to the Federal Government"—rather like an ambassador—and "I have felt it due to her honor as well as my own" to observe the obligation of the station "faithfully." Allegiance to the Union "has been and will cheerfully be rendered." He made this point because his enemies were saying that he wanted disunion, a charge "slanderous and false." Should the Union change character so as to destroy the obligation of allegiance, his state, and not he, would say so. He was ready "to abide by the issue whenever Mississippi should make it."[6]

He was gratified on December 19 as a resolution from the state of Mississippi was read in the Senate. When the "attempt to adopt the 'Wilmot proviso' in another form," by admitting California as a free state, had risen earlier, the whole Congressional delegation had asked for instructions and been told by the legislature to "resist [the admission] by all honorable and constitutional means." Now its resolution stated that "the Hon. Jefferson Davis . . . [Representatives] A. G. Brown, William McWillie, W. S. Featherston, and Jacob Thompson" had obeyed and upheld the "rights and honor of Mississippi and the South." In contrast, "the Hon. Henry S. Foote" had not obeyed; rather he had rather supported "the miscalled compromise." "The Legislature does not consider the interests of the State . . . safe in his keeping."[7]

Thus secured, Davis felt free to tangle with Foote and Henry Clay over whether to create the rank of brevet lieutenant general for Winfield Scott. Foote said the "whole world" gave Scott the "preeminence . . . in the Mexican war," and Davis retorted, "I am not one of those who constitute the whole world." He showed in jealous replies that Taylor was the real victor. His "intimate acquaintance" with Scott for "some twenty-seven years" made him admire his "military attainments." He would never "wish to deprive him of any military honors," if "properly conferred," and would support creation of "a grade of full general of the Army, with the foreknowledge that it would be conferred upon him." What Davis opposed was brevets—an "injurious departure" from "our Army system"—which were causing much confusion.[8]

This was a brief session of Congress. During it, Davis stood up with Rep. S. W. Inge of Alabama as his second in a duel. Davis was reappointed to the Smithsonian board and he became chairman of the building committee. He was known as "a willing advocate" of "Religion & the Arts," but he tried to defend the Institution against gifts of a large art collection, "models from the Patent Office," and "the garden of plants" collected by "the Exploring Expedition." This would be rather like an elephant from the king of Siam, he told the Senate, a gift meant to ruin the recipient by the expense of feeding. Congress had already made the institution "erect an expensive building, with apartments for a museum and gallery of art." The regents, following Smithson's original intent, "only wish to explore fields which have not been trodden before." Davis had persuaded the Senate in 1849 not to buy George Catlin's Indian paintings. Although he had been with Catlin "in an expedition of great hardship and privation," when the artist created these scenes and portraits, and he thought them much more true-to-life than those of Charles Bird King, he did not want Congress to depart from "the simple republican character of the Government" by becoming "a patron of art." It had already commissioned decorations for the capitol, and "if we do not pause, I see no limit."[9]

Davis's prediction that the Fugitive Slave Law "was useless" had by now proven true in Boston, where a mob interfered with its execution. When this came up in the Senate, Davis pointed out that "the North did not pass" this law. Its Congressmen had not honored "their obligations to the Constitution," but had vacated their seats and "*allowed the southern minority* to pass the bill [italics mine]." "Was there, then, not reason to suppose that [it] . . . would be a failure?" The strength of our government was "moral, and moral only . . . It was not organized as one of force." "Whenever mobs can rule, and law is silenced beneath tumult, this is wholly an impracticable Government." If Massachusetts refused to enforce the law, "it can only be said" that "of her own free will and sovereign act," she "has dissolved the bonds that connected her to the other States." Let her go in peace, he said; we cannot use force against a state. When the Union "depends upon politicians to manufacture bonds to hold [it] together, it is gone—worthless as a rope of sand."[10]

"The South did not resist execution of the laws," Davis said—"a charge as untrue as it is common." Someone brought up the federal case against John A. Quitman. He had been urged to defy the right of the federal government to indict the governor of a sovereign state, even to defend himself by "a resort to arms." Instead he offered to stand trial when his term was up, and when this offer was refused, he simply resigned. Davis had this resignation of February 3, 1851, in hand as he said, "Offenders against this fugitive slave law have gone unpunished," and known Cuban filibusters "have remained unnoticed," but "the shaft unerring must be levelled [against] the State-rights Governor of Mississippi." Quitman was charged with "aiding and abetting an expedition," but, Davis pointed out, "from his public position he could not have been a participant."[11]

It was Narcisco Lopez again. When Davis and Lee had refused him, he had recruited General Quitman, first to back him with money and influence. Then if Lopez could establish a beachhead, Quitman was to come lead the full-fledged assault on Spanish troops. The cause of Cuban independence was strong in the South. Theodore O'Hara and John J. Crittenden's nephew William volunteered from Kentucky. From Tennessee came C. Roberdeau Wheat, son of an Episcopal priest, who had been an officer in the Mexican War and then in a failed Mexican revolution. But President Taylor had made it clear when Lopez first gathered forces in 1849 that he would not allow Americans to participate. The Lopez expedition of May 1850 had failed miserably. President Fillmore's government was now charging Quitman and fifteen others with violation of the Neutrality Law of 1818. The case against John

Henderson (a Mississippi state senator) was prepared as a test. If he could be convicted, they all could. In New Orleans, the district attorney, Horatio J. Harris (whose appointment Davis had helped procure), found himself stymied by three hung juries in succession. After the last one, on March 7, the suits were all dismissed; so Quitman was never tried. The conspirators were already planning a new expedition.[12]

Unconscious of how these events were to shape his future, Jefferson Davis arrived home on March 26, 1851, to a finer Brierfield, made from cypress "cut on our own swamp land." But it was still simple: a classic Southern house, eight balanced rooms on one floor with a hall between. There were galleries over a hundred feet long, with fluted Doric columns in front and plain square ones in back. The gleaming white whole was set off by dark green cypress louvers at the windows. One thing was finally settled: Varina and Amanda Bradford, equally unwilling "to be subordinate," had "mutually declined to live together." Varina had been seeing to the installation of marble mantel pieces, and ornate cornices over the parlor windows, ordering a "Shower Bath" and "Looking Glass & Shades," getting her piano repaired, and filling up the library. Jeff could only touch base before he was off again, down to New Orleans on business.[13]

He visited the Howells, of course, at Tunisburg. He had sent in William's application for bounty land, for which veterans of the War of 1812 were now eligible, but it was not acted on for over two years. "Hope hope I live upon hope," Ma wrote on April 7. Jeff promised to bring Varina soon to see her, but "I disliked to insist upon it, knowing how much he is away from home—and how much home requires him." "Jeff says your health is better than he ever saw it he thinks you *now* the finest woman he knows—you cannot know how gratified we felt—the *manner he said it*—was feeling and full of pride and affection—God grant you may continue to improve in all the christian graces—and I have no doubt your health will be good."[14]

Varina did go down to her parents. Jeff hastily wrote her on May 8 not to hurry home because "circumstances have pressed me immediately into service of the 'Southern Rights Democratic party' and I cannot return to you before the middle of June." "Could my heart decide," he assured her, "your claim on my time [is] first. . . . God bless you and keep you happy and well prays your Husband." He had need of her prayers instead; he was pressing himself very hard. With scarcely two weeks' rest, he had begun a speaking tour that took him to eighteen different places before he made his major address at the party convention in Jackson on June 16. Then, he had to take to his bed.[15]

Henry Foote was planning to run for governor, as an advocate of the Compromise of 1850, with the backing of a "Union party" of Whigs and Democrats. Spurning the legislature's rebuke, Foote claimed that he, not Davis, represented the opinion of the state. Reuben Davis tried to get the Democratic Party to nominate Davis: "The people had a confidence in his integrity and trustworthiness that surpasses anything I have ever known," and "much as [they] admired him, they loved him far more." Something about him "captivated the imagination, and exalted him into a hero." Reuben Davis's opinion is all the weightier from his being an intimate friend of Foote's. Adam Bingaman, a Whig leader, had told Margaret Howell in 1846 that Davis's support of Taylor in Congress "will immortalize him and that he will be Governor of this state if he chooses or anything else."

Reuben Davis says that during the convention Quitman's backers deviled Jeff Davis, "at his hotel, confined to his bed by severe illness," into agreeing not to run. The way Jeff tells it, Reuben's plan was to get him elected governor so he could appoint Quitman to the Senate. Davis seriously disagreed with Quitman on filibustering, nullification, and secession, but he felt obliged to compensate him for having to resign. He "left it to General Quitman" (the man who had said Davis lacked generosity) to decide who should run. "It is easier to fight for a man against his enemies than against himself," opined Reuben. Quitman wanted to be governor or nothing, and so he was chosen to run against Foote.[16]

To protect the party from Quitman's extremism, Davis sent the convention a resolution: "secession was the last alternative, the final remedy, and should not be resorted to under existing circumstances." Despite this, Foote kept saying his enemies were for disunion. Davis took it as a personal insult: "My own honor, as well as that of those whom I represented, forbade that whilst a Senator I should seek to destroy the post to which I was accredited." He had already told Foote in the Senate that if any man made such a charge, "I should answer him in monosyllables . . . tell him in his throat that he lied"—which would force a duel. As soon as he was up campaigning for Quitman, he confronted Foote: "Taking a chair into the aisle, I sat down before him prepared for equivocation and his habitual falsehoods." But Foote gave him no provocation. Davis spoke that night and "said what I thought of him and his traitorous course," but Foote was not there to hear it.[17] The attempt "to bring him to a settlement with deadly weapons" had failed again. Merciless mocking by Foote and heated rejoinders by Quitman led them to a fistfight, which ended their joint debates. Davis called Foote "as industrious as a bee and as reckless of truth as himself" for distorting the account of this fracas, as he had the one with Davis. Reuben Davis noted that Quitman was a "poor and flat" speaker, while Foote's "gorgeous imagery and splendid diction" was carrying "everything before him."[18]

Jeff Davis traveled the state, speaking every day or so, until he collapsed again, this time at Brierfield. Again he jumped up too soon and punished himself with eight more speeches in widely separated places until his disease prostrated him on August 18 at Pontotoc. Dr. John M. Dozier, a friend from Transylvania days, who lived nearby, took him home and cared for him. He was down for three weeks. Varina says that "exposure to the sun had its usual effect" of fever "which brought on acute inflammation of his left eye and threatened ulceration of the cornea" (probably from a concurrent viral infection, rather than the malaria). Finally, he dragged up to Memphis and took a steamboat home, suffering very much "from the glare, and varying light," only to find that Quitman had abandoned the race, and he was being called upon to replace him.[19]

There had been balloting in September for delegates to a meeting in protest of the compromise bills. "Thousands of Democrats, not fully understanding" the call, a Davis friend wrote, "refused to go to the polls; while the Whigs . . . turned out to a man." Foote's Union Party won, by more than seven thousand votes. Instead of condemning the compromise, the meeting declared "unalterable fealty to the Union." When Quitman saw he would be defeated for governor, he withdrew.[20]

What Davis thought of this defection is not on record, but he had said privately that Quitman's "vanity" was what had made him insist on running in the first place. His own rule was "to serve my party where they require me, not where my taste or ambition may indicate." Taking Quitman's place "was esteemed a forlorn hope," he said later. It was "therefore an obligation of honor not to decline," even though it meant losing his Senate seat, damaging his program in Congress and "my own reputation." "My health did not permit me to leave home . . . but, being assured that I was not expected to take any active part, and that the party asked only the use of my name, I consented to be announced [on September 17], and immediately resigned from the United States Senate."[21]

He had come home, Varina says, "a shadow of his former self, and not able to bear a ray of light upon either eye. For three weeks he slept all day, arose after sundown, and walked through the house all night." He wrote Dr. Cartwright in New Orleans on September 23 that

> the sight of that eye which was entirely blind has been partially restored. There is still great irritability in the nerve of the eye, and the cloud which had collected between the coatings of the cornea, and which entirely covered the pupil I am informed has receded so as now to appear like a clear drop of water which swells the cornea on one side (the outside,) and encroaches very little on the pupil, though it covers about a third of the iris. The eye has ceased to weep, and has rather an unnatural dryness, and heat, but without any engorgement of the bloodvessels.

This he called "the uni[n]telligible account" of an "unlearned patient." He was using "emollient washes" and taking "some quinine daily." He hoped to go down for consultation, but it is unclear whether he did.[22]

Varina must have penned the letter for him. He "could not see at all." Sitting in dimness that obscured the very "position of the furniture," Varina found she "could write, and even read large print." One night she was reading aloud a speech sent for him to sign when he seized a pen, crying "Oh, let me get at that," threw it away and dictated another. Quitman came to wish him success, saying, "I carry my State rights views to the citadel; you stop at the outworks." They had remained friends, since neither knew what the other had said about him. "Our own gallant Quitman," Davis had called him; and when he died, though noting his "love of popular esteem" and their differences, Davis stressed his "sincere devotion to Southern interests" and his loving relationship with family and friends.[23]

With only two weeks left, Davis, the good soldier, "took the field" on October 21, "contrary to his physician's advice." Still scarcely able to bear the light, with his left eye tied up, "and wearing [green] goggle-glasses," he set out after the adversary. But Foote gave him the slip and put out the rumor that Davis was dead. Davis said he did not intend to die before the election, and when he did, "he should die hard, clutching to the last the flag staff of the good old banner of Jackson and Jefferson and Madison Democracy." Davis "never thought he was defeated, till the votes were counted out," said one man. When they were, the Union Party's lead had been whittled down from seven thousand five hundred votes to nine hundred ninety-nine. But Foote won.[24]

As Davis told a friend, the news came as a "severe shock": a defeat "not of myself only but of the foundation principles of my political creed." He felt deserted by the very people whose instructions he had labored for so "zealously." Colonel Davis, fighting with words now, as once with rifles, said in the Senate:

> Can there be any duty more sacred, any obligation more imperious to an honest man than the maintenance of his principles? It is for that the martyr embraces the stake. It is for that the pure statesman sacrifices his political ambition. It is for that alone I esteem it honorable to live as a public man. To bow the suppliant knee to a majority . . . to change his course with every oscillation of the political needle, is a rule of conduct degrading to any man who claims to be a freeman, and disqualifying to a citizen of a representative Government like our own.[25]

It required courage to stand as "one of a minority." "The power of the majority has no terrors for me," Davis said. He confessed "small hope," however, when Southerners defected to the majority. He was rebuked in the Senate for calling this "recreancy." In Mississippi, he could call a spade a spade. "These same deserters—the very men that sacrificed and bartered away their rights," he said while campaigning, wanted now "to be supported in their unholy acts . . . to be again made leaders." If the people honored these "deceivers" and passed over "those who struggled for Southern rights, and justice . . . [few] would be willing again to represent them." After his sacrifices for "the great principle of his life," "what were his feelings when he found that" those (meaning Foote) who "went to Congress and sacrificed the South" were favored instead? "But he would not believe that Mississippi could so far stultify her own principles—(applause)." He wrote to David Yulee that unless the "Yankee influence" was "crushed" (the influx of immigrants to the South, largely Whig), "federalism will soon swallow up state rights and wholly change the nature of our government. I think Missi. will do enough to justify me in returning to the Senate, for I need hardly say to you that if she endorses the 'compromise' I will seek that post of honor which is found in a private station."[26]

He had "resigned the office, which of all others I preferred, to be a candidate for an office wholly undesirable to me, that I might thus serve my party—may I not say my State?" His course brought forth plaudits like this one from Wilkinson County: "We have seen you in every attack . . . surrounded by defection, stand up manfully . . . for our rights and honor" against the compromise, that "deceptious instrument for our destruction." And Lowndes County men, in "high admiration for your public and private virtue," praised his "manly maintenance of their rights . . . unawed by the fierceness of opposition."[27]

Support like this made his defeat all the more cutting. He took comfort in a sense of superiority. He wrote Whig Senator Clayton of Delaware (whose compromise he had urged), "Democrats who were rejected by their party have been put into power" by a "false issue": secession.

> Whigs gain the advantage to be derived from incompetent, or unprincipled officers for whom they are not, as a party, responsible—I know
>
> "a soul like thine would spurn
> The spoil from such foul foray borne":
>
> and therefore state the fact without circumlocution to you.

Davis conveyed, in these lines from Sir Walter Scott, his hurt and his disillusion with politics.[28]

But he never sulked. He was back as keynote speaker at the Democratic convention in Jackson on January 8, 1852 (the anniversary of the Battle of New Orleans), saying he did not regret his sacrifices for "the principles" without which "our Union . . . could never survive"; they were "offerings freely made upon the altar of his country." He only feared that his defeat "would long and deeply injure the cause of State rights." But "the mere demagogue"—obviously Foote—"has been thrown to the surface like dregs from the bottom of the pool, by such violent agitation as mingles heterogeneous elements, and like them must sink to the bottom whenever quiet is restored," though he would be "in all time an agitator still." ("Foote is in his element again & busy stirring up the embers of discord," a friend was to report next year.) The traditional party was "our best, if not our only hope," but he would not "excommunicate others from the Democratic church." He was trying to pull the party back together, drawing on his very real popularity.[29]

Reuben Davis said he would have won "by a grand majority" if nominated at the June convention "as he should have been." He told Jeff himself that the race had, all the same, elevated him even above "the noble height" he attained. As "a statesman and patriot . . . your friends now regard you with an admiration which no man has enjoyed since . . . Jackson. We are all anxious to fight, under your standard, another political battle. . . . [You are] emphatically the head and front of the Democracy in . . . the whole South; without a rival." Politically, Foote was "forever dead," and Quitman would "rise no more." Davis's future was "without a cloud . . . your course will be necessarily onwards and upwards, until you reach the Presidency." Such blandishment must have been hard to resist. But Davis made no move to recover his senatorship, though the acting governor reportedly offered it to him. Stephen Adams, a Union Democrat, was finally elected to his seat.[30]

Varina was immensely relieved not to be the governor's wife: "the outlay upon servants, silver, china, cutglass, table linen, bed linen, and carriage and horses would be *immense* for our fortune, to say nothing of the dinner parties," for which she had in her cellar only "six bottles of port wine, and a gallon of vinegar and one of brandy." Besides, "I doubt my power . . . to conciliate fools and busybodies, and [Jeff's] to bear with tiresome friends." Instead, she nurtured her many "beautiful plants." Jeff said, "the time passed pleasantly away . . . in cares for servants, in building, in rearing live stock, and the like." He laughed whenever he thought of the vegetable gardener's order: "Please send these seeds immediately, if not sooner." Varina wrote Ma "how agreeable" he was when he had "no political troubles." She and Jeff planted a little switch of live oak that, by the time she wrote in 1890, "shades ninety feet in all directions, and is over six feet in circumference." They ordered fruit trees, worked together in the garden, and established the roses that in time overran the fences around the house. They read or raced their horses on the dirt roads. Their marriage had been tried, "for better for worse," and they had been faithful "in sickness and in health." "We were very happy," says Varina.[31]

The spreading house, cooled by attic above and open space below, its galleries darkened by shade trees, was ideal for Jeff's recuperation. By March he was "quite well, and so busy at his field that I scarcely ever see him except when he is too tired to talk," says Varina. Obviously he was not, as Dr. M. W. Philips thought, one of those "parlor planters" who depended on overseers and did not know "the practical detail." He did use overseers, however, and when he left home again, he put another physician, George W. McElrath, in charge of everything.[32]

Foote was not exactly dead. He went to the Senate in December, never having resigned as he claimed, and, allied with the Whigs Toombs and Cobb, tried to get state righters read out of the Democratic Party. He failed, but he kept one of them out of the Senate by holding his seat until the eve of his inauguration. Foote had charged that Davis and Quitman had already been picked to head a Southern confederacy. This Davis denied in a temperate public letter. Foote's retaliation was printed, and Davis rejoined: "It is only to be regretted that the station which gives force to his vituperation cannot endow him with the dignity to abstain from it." He called him "an assassin of character and 'constitutionally a liar.'"[33] When this insult again failed to produce a challenge, Davis washed his hands of him: "I said . . . as much evil of Gov. Foote as my self respect would allow though much less than long and close observation of his depravity would have justified. Since then I have thought it due to myself to take no notice of him." Foote had the contempt of many besides Davis: "irritable, absurd and ridiculous personage" said one. Reuben Davis was right about Foote in Mississippi: he could never stabilize his shaky victory, lost a bid for senator in 1853, and soon after, left for California.[34]

He was wrong about Quitman, who rebounded and got elected to Congress in 1855 and 1857. Out of the whole affair, however, Davis emerged the strongest Democratic leader in Mississippi, perhaps in the South. Robert W. Barnwell of South Carolina wrote thanking him "in behalf of all true lovers of Southern rights, for your glorious self devotion in giving up the ease & dignity of yr senatorial office, to raise the falling standard of your state. . . . You are still my file leader as you were in Washington . . . and I look to your prudence & courage to mark out the course of our struggle." Davis was put up for vice president at the national Democratic convention of 1852, receiving votes from New York and Illinois. William Rufus King of Alabama prevailed; he ran with Franklin Pierce of New Hampshire.[35]

This was just the sort of state rights ticket Davis wanted, a truly national one, to draw North and South together. When the Democrats met in Jackson in June 1852, he tried to cement the party in Mississippi. He refused to avenge himself on those who had followed Foote out of it, and excused as best he could the national party's endorsement of the compromise as a cure-all for slavery agitation. He dwelt on the personal excellence of the presidential candidates. "Our experiment in the capacity of man to rule himself implied a belief in private and public virtue; without both, such a government could not be successful." Pierce and King would sweep away "misrule and corruption" and "restore the government to the purity which adorned its earlier years."[36]

He scored Millard Fillmore, the federalist incumbent, for threatening war on Texas over a border dispute while not enforcing the Fugitive Slave Law in Massachusetts and for a proclamation withdrawing "the protection of their own government" that had led to "the murder of the gallant Crittenden and his followers" the previous year. William Crittenden and fifty other filibusters, including Lopez, had been executed "on the Plaza of Havana," causing a riot in New Orleans. Speaking of how the Democrats and he had seen "adversity" together, Davis sounded a note that he would echo later, in many more serious battles: "to be successful was a merit not equal to that of deserving success. He would rejoice more with them when victorious, but he could never be more entirely theirs than he had been in the hour of gloom and defeat."[37]

In this speech, Davis had quoted Walter Scott and Francois Rabelais once and Shakespeare twice. His fame as a learned orator brought him invitations to speak to the literary societies at the universities of Alabama and Mississippi, both on the same day. Choosing his home state, he addressed the students on "the character proper to a citizen of the United States of America." Free from the senatorial necessity of argumentation, he could expound in his own "Demosthenean style" his underlying convictions, producing one of his finest and most characteristic utterances.[38]

He called on the young men, whatever their later pursuits, to "be remembered in the manner most worthy of a republican, as one who lived for his country's good." He cited the Southern linguist, John Fletcher, whose *Studies on Slavery* had come out that year, as one combating the "misconstruction" of the Bible, which had "produced the most dangerous agitation which has ever disturbed our Union." "Self canonized saints" had launched "an unholy crusade" against "that African slavery which has continued among us after it had ceased to be profitable among [them]." They proclaimed, Davis mockingly said, "all obligations social and political . . . annulled by the higher law revealed to them"—a reference to Seward's answer to Calhoun in 1850 that there was "a higher law than the Constitution" (meaning, God intended only free men to inhabit the territories). They would execute this "law," Davis went on, though it should bring ruin "upon a section" and "misery" to "both the happy races." "Religion has been perverted from its mission of peace, good will, and brotherly love to sanctify this unprovoked hostile aggression." He may have said here, "prompted by the enemy of mankind," an idea he had expressed earlier on the Senate floor: "these pious personages" scattering "the seeds of dissension and disunion" would more fittingly cry "Good devil" than "Good God."[39]

As his model good citizen, Davis chose Demosthenes, tracing the repeated but doomed efforts of this "pure patriot" of Greece to combat the power of Philip and Alexander of Macedon. He summed up his life this way: "From the beginning of his career Demosthenes strove to uphold a sinking state, his life was a long series of defeats, but he rose superior to his fate and nothing could be less just than to measure his greatness by the standard of success." Unconscious of the parallel to his own future, he went on to utter others. Could this "life of one who trod the path of duty, seeing it was not the high way to personal success," satisfy "a just ambition"? He answered that the fame of Demosthenes now "stands visible to all nations," linked forever with "the purpose for which he suffered," while "those who purchased security and reward by alliance with the invader . . . are seen only as creeping things which disturb but cannot destroy the beauty of the noble monument on which they climb." Quoting Demosthenes—"It is by design that the statesman is to be judged"—Davis said, "surely failure does not deprive exertion of the character of usefulness. It is enough that the cause is worthy of the effort, and the effort worthy of the cause."

He invited his young hearers' magnanimity for the Greek patriot's suicide: "He had lived for his country" and borne suffering "for her liberty . . . and when he shrunk from the task of surviving it, judge not his act by the moral philosophy and christian teachings which are of your time, but were not of his."[40]

Ignoring previous warnings, even though his eye had begun to bother him again, Davis set out from Oxford under the summer sun to campaign for Pierce and King. His zest for battle was sharpened by the fact that Gen. Winfield Scott was the adversary. At Holly Springs, he asserted that while Scott was an able commander, he was querulous and "utterly unfit to be president"; at Memphis, he said Scott's running mate was an honorable man "in very bad company" and that Seward's "higher-law gang, steeped in slime of treasonable designs have folded themselves about General Scott with the tenacious hug of the anaconda." At Vicksburg on July 24, he called Scott a self-serving "military man merely."[41]

Varina was writing, "I feel the want of you every hour, though I try not to be selfish. . . . My own precious second self . . . are you not turning your steps homeward even while I write? Your wife's courage is giving out about your staying away at such a time." Their first child was due any day. Jeff was "so dreadfully concerned" about Varina in March that he would not let her ride as far as the Hurricane, one and three-quarter miles away. She could not take the steamboat down to see Ma, though "it is the longest time I ever was away from you." Now Ma had come to her, bringing four children. "May God keep you my own sweetest Husband," Varina finished on July 25, "never were you more ardently longed for. . . . Your Winnie." Presumably Jeff made it down from Vicksburg in time. The baby was not born until July 30. It was a boy. They named him for his grandfather, Samuel Emory Davis.[42]

The Howell children kept asking for Davis and sent "their best love" to him in Varina's letter. Great was the affection between him and his friends' children too. But about Samuel he was absolutely foolish. Margaret Howell wrote her husband:

> Our dear little grandson continues healthy and is growing finely. . . . Jeff is the proudest, fondest father I ever saw—and the best husband. He is more like a woman about his "li' man," as he calls him, than any one I ever saw. He wishes you to purchase for his boy a little barouche with two seats—get it handsome lined. I mean a real little barouche for a child—such as the nice little children are pulled about in the city—stout, well made and good springs and wheels. This boy is to have nothing common.

Jeff and Ma, so near in age, were very close friends, so close that she could josh him about his aristocratic ways. When Varina was away once, she told Ma she was "anxious to see his old Lord ship"—meaning Jeff. In the midst of prison sufferings, Jeff wrote, "Remember me most affectionately to Ma. . . . Tell her that the old one hit Le Roy at last, but that his faith held out and he never cried 'quarter.'"[43]

Jeff suffered from "ophthalmic disease" all summer. By October, intense pain in his eye and head drove him down to see Dr. Cartwright at Pass Christian, on the Gulf Coast. Cartwright handed him this diagnosis "a misplaced malarial fever attacking those parts, which Rheumatism attacks." While fighting the malaria with "6 grs quinine 2 grs of solid opium & a tea spoon ful of colchicum wine" every four hours (with castor oil in between "if the pain increases"), Davis was to keep feet and legs in very "hot mustard water" and wrap his head in "towels, wrung out of water as hot as you can bear it," and then in dry "hot flannel." "These measures are to relieve the pain" which "itself is very hurtful." The wine prevented "the quinine from affecting the head." "You should use the flesh brush all over—or a coarse cloth, impregnated with vapor from burning rosemary, to rub your head with & all over—There is plenty of Rosemary on Ship island." For "pain any where," Davis was to "wet a piece of raw cotton in the Chloroform & apply it over the part" until numb. "In the event of severe pain, smell of the chloroform," not to "insensibility . . . but only to produce an intoxicated feeling." These measures, he said, were better than "the antiphlogistic treatment"—"bleeding, leeching, cupping, blistering, purgatives, cold applications, &c"—which "adds to the debility, the cause of the fever."[44]

This was the first instance of that "neuralgia" in the head and face that was to vex Davis ever after, an excruciating nerve pain whose unpredictable attacks were all but unbearable. The cause of it is unknown, but it can be triggered by an eye infection such as he had at this time, by emotional stress, and by other things. It may have been the "tic [douloureux]" that a reporter later called it. Certainly it was persistent, but the characteristic "tic," or muscle spasm, is noted only once, when Dr. Craven speaks of "painful twitching of the eyelids." Dr. Cartwright's treatment was about as good as any devised since. It evidently worked for Davis. He was able to keep a speaking engagement in New Orleans on October 29.[45]

In this parting shot before election, he warned the Whigs that their nominee, Scott, was not a Clay-and-Webster moderate, but an out-and-out Free-Soiler. His efforts in *this* campaign were rewarded. Pierce beat Scott 254 electoral votes to 42, winning all but four states. The popular majority, however, was less than fifty thousand. John P. Hale also ran, on a Free-Soil ticket, and in some states, more people voted against Pierce than for him. The Democratic Party seemed united behind him, but in truth its deep divisions remained. Pierce was sensible of his delicate position and hoped to select a cabinet that would reflect all the party elements. To represent the state rights faction, he had in mind Jefferson Davis.[46]

From his home in Concord, New Hampshire, the new president wrote to Davis on December 7: "My dear General, As the news of your illness filled with anxiety your friends in this northern region, so the intelligence of your convalescence has brought relief and joy. . . . I much desire to see you, and to avail myself . . . of your advice." Hinting at a post for Davis, he asked him to come to New England and discuss the cabinet, and "our party and the country." He felt sure "that whether our views coincide or not, from you I shall receive a friends free and useful suggestions." But Davis could not go. Pierce then offered the state rights cabinet position to R. M. T. Hunter, who declined.[47]

By the time Pierce wrote again, his wife, Jane, was "crushed to earth by the fearful bereavement" and he confessed to Davis: "How I shall be able to summon my manhood and gather up my energies for the duties before me it is hard for me to see." Their son Benjamin, the only one left of their three, "a fine boy 11 years old," whose nurture had absorbed them both, had been killed in a train wreck that spared the parents, though Pierce was injured. He was writing to Davis on January 12, 1853, of "the terrible catastrophe upon the rail road," six days after it happened. His own "desolate condition," he said, made him "tremble for you, my friend." (Davis had evidently reported sickness in the family.) Pierce noted that Davis's "noble spirited letter" had said "nothing of your own health, but I infer that it is fully restored and thank God for it." Their friendship was causing much comment: "It is pleasant to believe that they are unselfish and uncalculating relations not likely to be disturbed. I have no heart to write now. . . ." Not until February 13 did Davis agree to come, "if still desired," and then it was to Washington, for the inauguration. It was "not to take a seat in the Cabinet," he explained to his friend, Stephen Cocke, "but to prevent any misunderstanding as to the feeling I had towards the new administration." "Although warmly attached to Mr. Pierce," he later said, he had declined a cabinet post "for private and personal reasons."[48]

His health was not really restored. It was "much improved" in general, but his eye was about the same, he wrote Cartwright. The doctor told Margaret Howell that he should stay out of public life for a full year and just garden, ride, and eat to build himself up. Varina had mentioned back in May how thin he was—"scarcely eats enough for a child." This may have been brought on by a falling-out with Joseph that had even made Jeff think of moving away. Joseph had written a bitter letter, asking if he might be allowed to buy Brierfield. All this naturally upset Jeff, since he always regarded Joseph as his "nearest friend and best adviser."[49]

The cause of this upheaval is unknown, but it may stem from their involved monetary transactions with their cotton brokers, Edmund and William Laughlin, or from Joseph's dislike of Edmund, who married his daughter Florida after David McCaleb's death. Joseph especially resented the couple's adopting the four children of William who was killed in a knife fight in 1851. Jeff was especially close to Florida, and one of the Laughlin boys was named for him. Estrangement was evident by mid–1852, when Varina, speaking of people less than two miles away, wrote to Jeff: "The Hurricane family do not leave home at all this summer *so we hear*—all well *I believe* [italics mine]." It was still there in 1854, when Varina told Ma: "I think his Brother Joe's alienation preys upon his mind, but he never speaks of it."[50]

Or the cause may have been Ma. The tale came back to Jeff that "Mrs. Howell had abused [Joseph's] family, on the Steam Boat." Perhaps a critical remark was overheard, but abuse seems unlikely, judging from her expressions to Varina in January of 1852: "What is the matter with the Hurricane folks? . . . What a pity that a small community of relations like that cannot be at peace with one another—When will we all learn to do as we would be done by?" In February, Ma sent "Our love to Jeff and to your brother Joe" and others at the Hurricane. But on July 4 (of some year, perhaps this one) Joseph wrote that he "did not expect to see her again." Jeff firmly took Ma's part throughout, calling the story about her "a sheer fabrication." In discussing the affair, Joseph had delivered "the bitterest accusation and severest judgement which could have been inflicted on me," said Jeff. He scornfully endorsed Joseph's reply, "Bah" and "fudge." Many years later he spoke to Varina of "the painful controversy in which your Ma was involved," and in which "artful fanning" rendered "my Brother unjust to you and me."[51]

Davis was generally regarded as the obvious choice for secretary of war. Perhaps the quarrel, his "delicate state of health," or even his new son, were his "private" reasons for not wanting the post. But his main one was wanting "to re-argue before the people" of Mississippi the issues lost in 1851 by "false presentation." His political friends, however, both at home and in Washington, "assured me that it was necessary for the state's rights party that I should accept." Varina says he was "over-persuaded by his friends." He was so reluctant that he kept his acceptance secret until the Senate confirmed him and he was sworn in, both on March 7, 1853.[52]

It delighted the army. Amos B. Corwine had seen "quite a large number of officers" who "without a solitary exception" had told him "there would not be a solitary dissenting voice in the whole Army, but a hearty, unanimous approval of the appointment." Davis thanked a West Point graduate for his "favorable opinion of my fitness." A. G. Brown, a political rival, called Davis "the recognized leader . . . of the State Rights men of Mississippi," and said if Pierce appointed him to the cabinet, "*That will be glory enough*" for their party. From political defeat, Davis had come to one of his country's highest honors, amid great approbation, yet not without sacrifice.[53]

"I am paying dearly indeed for public honors," he wrote Varina, "worn out by incessant boring and seperated from all that brings freshness to my heart," and "my dear Le man has the whooping cough. Thank God he is at New Orleans not Washington . . . here it is cold and changeable." Varina was showing off little Sam to her parents and the Locust Grove family. Malie and David Brodhead were looking after Davis in the furnished house he had rented on 13th Street N.W., and their baby, Dick, was naming "every thing he values 'Little yam' [Sam]." Malie reported, "My dear Uncle . . . looks better than when he came on" but is "confined to his room for a day or two" with neuralgia in the head because he worked too hard. Jeff ended his letter: "Farewell my dear and let us hope that happier days will come when our trials have passed, but there can be none in which you will be dearer and nearer to the heart of your Husband."[54]

He had hoped to come for her, but his "eternal round of labor" proved unremitting. Finally an army major (though Brodhead and Col. Joseph Taylor had offered) escorted Varina and Sam to Washington by the southern route. In Mobile, General Twiggs came to see her, telling her that his adjutant, Colonel Bliss, was down with yellow fever. Betty Taylor Bliss's husband died on August 5 at his home in East Pascagoula, Mississippi, where Mrs. Taylor had died the year before.[55]

Davis warned Pierce that "I should have to leave his Cabinet," if elected to the Senate. He felt his first allegiance was "due to the state of which I was a citizen." He wanted to combat the "roar of the Northern majority" in Congress, which was destroying "the fraternity which should exist." And he wanted Mississippi to reclaim him after "the mortification at being beaten by such a man as Foote." "The state I love" had "weighed me against an empty demagogue and found me wanting."

He knew, however, that he was "especially odious to the 'Union men'" of his party, and "looking this question straight in the face, I see that it may be necessary to set me aside." After Mississippi's "abandonment" of principle in her embrace of the compromise, her "fame" demanded election of a state rights senator, whether him or another: "I ask of my friends to consider all personal feeling for me as but dust in the balance."[56]

He told a friend he "had resolved never to return to public life until called by the people of Missi." This explains his great reluctance to enter the cabinet. "I do not care for station . . . the emptiness of the honor which place can confer." His wish "which I have no power to suppress and will not disavow" was that Mississippians would exonerate him in some way before he died. He had told his probable rival, Albert Gallatin Brown, "before I left home . . . that if elected to the Senate I should accept."[57]

There was much feeling for Davis among Mississippians. Collin Tarpley, who had been "mainly instrumental" in getting him to resign the Senate, said, "I never shall feel that full justice has been done you, until you are restored." "We expect . . . to run you for the next Presidency." Reuben Davis wrote, "You are at this hour the *idol* of the state." Foote was running for senator while still governor, but he pulled out when he saw which way the wind was blowing. Brown, promising to support Davis in the next race (which he failed to do), let the rumor circulate that Davis would not resign the cabinet. So the Democratic caucus gave the nomination (tantamount to election), by two votes, to Albert Gallatin Brown.[58]

Luckily, Davis had said, "I will be content with any decision a state right's legislature may make, even though I should chafe at the assumption northern men make that I have been put in the same category with Foote and like him laid on the shelf." "I should be less devoted to Democracy than I believe myself to be if I could complain of being used as a sacrifice for the good of my party."[59]

X

War Department Days

While misunderstandings defeated him for the Senate, Jefferson Davis was finding himself "sufficiently content" in his post as secretary of war. His interest in his duties was increasing, his relations with other officials were "very agreeable," and he had "a field of usefulness wide enough to satisfy me, so far as I have any desire for public employment." "I have commenced many things in the War Dept. and have become more involved in the general administration than I expected," he told Stephen Cocke.[1]

He had to supervise the army, the military academy, and several large engineering projects as well: a survey of routes for a transcontinental railway, construction of an aqueduct to bring water to Washington, and additions to the post office, patent office, and capitol buildings.[2] In charge of the last four, he had Capt. Montgomery C. Meigs, to whom he gave absolutely free rein, "confident of the entire conscientiousness and propriety of your course."[3] Meigs appreciated Davis's "kindness and confidence," and as he later wrote, "became much attached to him": "Mr. Davis was a most courteous and amiable man in those days. . . . He was a man, too, of marked ability, and I quite looked up to him and regarded him as one of the great men of the time."[4] None of the building projects were finished while Davis was in office. He recommended Meigs to the next administration and later to the Senate, but he could not prevent his dismissal from the capitol project in 1860, over difficulties with the architect.[5]

For the capitol, Meigs was to "provide rooms suitable" for each house of Congress (the two wings, eventually) and to replace the low central dome with a much larger one. Davis worked closely with him on details of each project, down to the type of marble to use. Davis insisted on American artists for the capitol sculptures, but he preferred Italian

Carrara marble over American for the columns of the portico because it held "the sharpest edges in the flute."[6] For the figure of "Armed Liberty" (now called "Freedom"), designed to top the new dome, Davis suggested a helmet instead of a liberty bonnet, and in place of a wreath, "a circle of stars—expressive of endless existence and of heavenly birth." He deferred to the judgment of the sculptor, who approved "with much pleasure." Even Charles Sumner (a political foe and the artist's patron) said "No one ever yet has found [Davis's] judgment and taste at fault."[7]

Meigs designed and began building an aqueduct to carry water from the Great Falls of the Potomac to the capital. The Washington end was known as the Cabin John Bridge. During the war that severed Davis and Meigs, Davis's name was chiseled off this bridge, but President Theodore Roosevelt ordered it restored in 1908.[8]

In 1849, Davis had urged a railroad to the West Coast, to help bind settlers there "permanently to this Union." Now Congress had ordered a survey of possible routes, and since West Point furnished most of the country's engineers, the work fell to the War Department. For the first survey, Davis chose Isaac Stevens to push westward from Nebraska Territory while Bvt. Capt. George Brinton McClellan started eastward from Oregon. When the two men met in October 1853, they had traced the northernmost route. Davis had three other main lines mapped: a midcountry one, through Kansas and Utah Territories to Sacramento; and two southern ones, through Indian Territory, Texas, and New Mexico Territory, one terminating near Los Angeles and one at San Diego.[9] These surveys were in time the basis for congressional land grants to private companies which then ran the east-west rail lines. Davis had seen in 1851 that a strip of land south of the border was necessary to "a practicable route for waggon or rail road." He now persuaded Pierce to send James Gadsden to Mexico, and he made what became known as the Gadsden Purchase.[10]

Even more congenial duties were to engross Davis for the next four years, until his distinction rivaled that of his great predecessor in the office, John C. Calhoun. After McClellan had become a Union general, he said: "Colonel Davis was a man of extraordinary ability. . . . He was the best Secretary of War—and I use best in its widest sense—I have ever had anything to do with."[11]

In July of 1853, Varina Davis set foot in the nation's capital for the fourth time in her twenty-seven years. She had with her not only the baby, Samuel Emory Davis, but her brother Becket Kempe Howell (thirteen), her sister Margaret Graham Howell (eleven), and servants Betsy and Kate. The children were coming to live with the Davises and go to school. This would at once fit them for a genteel life, ease the strained finances of the Howells, and allow Jeff and Varina that exercise of benevolence that their very natures seemed to require.[12]

Charity, beginning at home, seemed to spread wherever Jefferson Davis was. In his new position, he tried to benefit army colleagues, with varying success. In his last annual report, he was still pleading for automatic grants, to sustain widows and orphans, and for the retired list, to take care of old and disabled soldiers. Twice he served briefly as acting secretary of the navy.[13] When navy reorganization forced many out, "he was most painfully depressed by the mortification and suffering of his old friends." One navy wife sent thanks for "your large heart" in speaking up for them. But the navy at least had a pension bill; Davis was never able to effect this for the army. It remained necessary for Congress to vote on each individual case.[14]

Davis was most instrumental in establishing, by 1853, old soldiers' homes, called military asylums, in Mississippi, Kentucky, and Washington. Taylor had asked for them, Scott had given Mexican tribute money for them, and Davis, while still in the Senate, had pushed a bill through. His "old and esteemed friend" Capt. Robert Anderson headed the Kentucky home until 1854. Then, under his own new rule forbidding "detached duty" for captains, Davis transferred him. There were so few inmates anyway that the Kentucky and Mississippi homes had to close. But Davis wanted the one in the capital to go on, and it did, till modern times.[15]

This was official benevolence. Personally, anyone sick or in need knew he had only to call upon the secretary of war to find relief. One man took it for granted that Davis would care for his sick son, in college at Georgetown, until he could get home. A postal clerk "desperately ill" asked him to look after his family. Young James Argyle Smith, traveling from Tennessee, was taken ill in Washington: "[I] thought I should die. I wrote to Mr. Davis and he came to see me, and engaged a nurse for me, and gave me the kindest and most tender attention for three or four weeks, until I was well enough to go on to West Point."[16]

Col. Archibald Campbell, the chief clerk in the War Office, tried to restrain Davis's almsgiving to beggars: "In anyone else it would be a mere yielding to importunity, but after they have left Mr. Davis grieves over their suffering, and it wears him very much." "Brave and honest men are not suspicious," said Davis. His lack of suspicion made him an easy gull for the unscrupulous. To one "poor disfigured creature" who sat outside his office winter and summer, knitting stockings, Davis sent out "a little cushion to prevent her taking cold," and every day his messenger had to take her money, though he declared that she was a "practised outlaw" and secretly rich. Then there was the capitol watchman named Smith. Davis had begun helping his family in 1845. In the fifties, he tried to get jobs for him and his son. Finally someone told him in 1857 that Smith was a known "rascal" who had kept his job by claiming to be "under your protection." Friendship in Jefferson Davis "was blind faith," said a friend: "you had 'no faults'" but if he found any, "woe betide you." When Smith was accused of improper conduct and refused to pay his bills, Davis told him to pay up or be discharged.[17]

Davis was never discouraged but went right on caring for those around him, especially underlings, as he always had. A stenographer in his Senate days recalled how Davis had known all the employees "personally," asked after their families, complimented their reports, tried to get them extra pay. Davis invited the secretary and sergeant-at-arms to sign his autograph book on the same page with Zachary Taylor and Millard Fillmore.[18] The secretary, Asbury Dickins, was devoted to him because of "your uniform friendship and kindness," and when Davis resigned the Senate, said, "I can ill spare so good a friend." It was the same in the War Department. One of his seven clerks, Maj. William B. Lee, who "knew him many years," said: "He was a good man . . . very considerate to serve under. I never heard a complaint. . . . Socially, he was a most charming man; officially, very pleasant. He was a warm friend and a bitter enemy." His messenger, Patrick Jordan, became "so attached" to him that when Davis left Washington in 1861, he entrusted to him a tiny, highly prized Japanese dog, and gave him a gold pencil case. When Jordan died, twenty-five years later, his wife, as he had requested, returned the case with a "loving message" that caused the former secretary's eyes to become "misty."[19]

Varina Davis never forgot two examples "of his tender consideration." About seven one morning, the wife of an army private came to the Davis house (before Mr. Secretary was up) seeking a pardon for her husband. Davis talked privately with her and then "came in to our breakfast-room with a soiled, yelling little boy by one hand, and followed by a frowsy young woman with a crying baby. He ordered a chair placed for her at the table . . . and led the child up to me, saying, 'My little man, there is a lady who comforts crying boys.'" Varina was left with the children while he took the suppliant to see President Pierce. In due time the young wife came back all smiles, with a note from Davis ordering a dollar for each child (a large sum in those days), an early dinner, and train tickets. The Davis butler was to see them safely off. "This was not an isolated instance," says Varina, "for hundreds could be cited."

The other seared on her memory involved a "dwarfish insane man" who had "expressed his intention to murder Mr. Clay."

> This little outcast came very often to see and levy upon Mr. Davis for contributions, and I said, "I do not know how you can bear with him, he is so intrusive." He looked troubled and said, "Perhaps if he were agreeable he would not care to call so often—it is a dreadful fate to be distraught and friendless." When the poor man was troublesome to others, and after he had been committed to the insane asylum, my husband sent supplies of letter paper and

> envelopes to him in order that he might follow his inclination to write long letters to everybody, and Mr. Davis personally answered those addressed to him.

Davis once pleaded that a different man not be put in the asylum, fearing that "confinement would convert partial insanity into madness."[20]

This attraction to the despised and outcast is one of the most striking and constant elements in Davis's character. It seemed to grow in proportion to the object's rejection by others—witness the "dwarfish insane man." He made it a rule, says his wife, "that no one should be turned away hungry, however undeserving or unattractive." His sensitivity made him feel what others were suffering, and his Christian upbringing led him to corporeal and spiritual works of mercy all through his life. The spiritual ones are the more difficult, and in these Davis was especially skilled. He unobtrusively gave comfort by simple encouragement, and by his friendship. Varina found his attempts to spread peace at home, however, sometimes clumsy.[21]

This pull toward those in trouble possibly had a part in his being such a good friend to Frank Pierce. Pierce was a pleasant, convivial man, but he was not a self-assured one; and when he buoyed his spirits with wine, the result was likely to be unfortunate. Davis was in Washington in 1836 when the future president brought momentary disgrace on himself by getting involved in a drunken fracas at a theater. His enemies brought up publicly his "alcoholic craving," as a biographer calls it, more than once. Davis never mentioned this, but he always stood up for Pierce, in public and private. He really admired him, and with good reason; he was an attractive man. But the early scandal and the threat of drunkenness, together with false accusations of cowardice in Mexico, where he served under Scott, were just the conditions that would rouse Davis's urge to protect the weak and endangered. Pierce admirably kept his resolve to abstain from strong drink all through his senatorial and presidential career. It was not until he had lost his wife and his best friend, Nathaniel Hawthorne, and was suffering isolation and disgrace in New England because of his friendship for Davis and the South, that he turned once more to the bottle for consolation.[22]

As for children, Davis's "anger against one who frightened or abused a child was appalling," his daughter Winnie says. Once when they were reading a book "on juvenile penology," he told her of visiting a reformatory in the North "many years before the war." "A small negro boy . . . caught him by the coat, with the plea, 'Please buy me, sir, and take me home wid you.' 'I tried to procure the little fellow's liberty and offered to take him and guarantee his freedom,' said my father, 'but he was in a free State, and I could not get him. It was bad enough to keep white children there, but it was inhuman to incarcerate that irresponsible negro child.'" Davis spoke in the Senate of the "suffering of the poor children" in "juvenile penitentiaries": "I thank my God, that . . . where I reside, we have no scenes so revolting as these."[23]

The black children at Brierfield knew his consideration. When leaving in 1857 he did not consult Old Uncle Bob about the work to be done, because a child was lying sick in his room. "The negroes" asked for a woman "who successfully treated a similar case and I stopped and asked her to go up." Davis's wrath was so roused against an overseer whose wife had dosed a black child almost to death with "Calomel and Quinine guess weight" that he fired him on the spot.[24]

The middle-aged father doted on his own first child. He had written to Varina before they arrived, "Tell Sam to run to his daddy as fast as he can." "Mr. Davis's first thought" as he came home in the evening was Sam, and he would find him, not yet two, waiting patiently at the door "to kiss his father first." Traveling, Jeff would write back: "How is Le man, you cannot tell how I wanted to run back and kiss the dear boy"; or, "If my dear Le man looks out for his Father our thoughts meet for there is little which does not associate itself in my mind with him."[25]

Varina was absorbed in him too. She wrote her mother: "Your little Sammy is the sweetest thing you ever saw. He calls his Father 'Boo.' . . . If Jeff speaks to him [when he is nursing] he lets go and goes to him. . . . [He] whistles when he is told and mocks the cows." On his first birthday they had "a little cake with Saml E. Davis on it" and "we all drank his health." When "I took him out in our Phaeton to drive," and Pierce, on horseback, stopped to talk to her, "Sam kept clicking his horse to go, and kissing his hand to him." She even took Sam house hunting (and Becket too), while Captain Northrop, who had two children of his own, kept Margaret busy. As Col. Archy Campbell showed Varina several homes for rent, a storm trapped them for over an hour. Campbell wrote Davis that "the best of the joke" was that Northrop was marooned with Margaret at the Smithsonian. She found a place just a block from the White House. The president's wife, still grieving over her Bennie, "constantly sent or called for [Sam] to drive with her." Becket and Margaret had made of this new nephew their "little pet."[26]

Although Sam could scream over having "his fine dresses put on him," and stamp his little foot in anger, he was still to Varina "the sweetest little boy you ever saw." She told Ma how, when chicken was set on the table, "he crows and flap his wings." Even after he began having mysterious swellings and sores and fevers, he still amused Varina by shaking his finger at her and saying, "Now mind, I say mind," and peeping around the chair when Pierce came to call, saying "Pretty man, pretty man." By the end of April the baby's head was "a perfect mat of scabs" and he had stopped walking, though he "sits up at table and hands his plate like a man." He "catches our faces and says, 'Kish nam' for kiss Sam. Jeff is absorbed in him to a fearful extent." In early June the anxious father consulted an eminent Washington physician. He also thanked his brother-in-law Dr. Robert Wood for "Kindness done to my little boy," sending "love to Sister Ann, Bettie, and the young folks." The diagnosis of the doctors is unknown.[27]

When Sam was first very sick, Varina said to Ma, "I felt as if the world was coming to an end." And suddenly it did. Samuel Emory Davis died on June 13, 1854. After a funeral at the residence, he was buried in Oak Hill Cemetery, Georgetown, with President Pierce and his cabinet in attendance.

> My dear Father and Mother
> I have made several efforts to write to you since our loss, but could not. My child suffered like a hero. A cry never escaped his lips until his death, but he would say, "Mamma, I tired, I wana walk, I wan bed". . . . We have had great sympathy shown us, and I am tortured with letters of condolence and it gives me nothing but unmitigated pain to see people, and hear the set forms of consolations.
> I thought I could write but cannot— . . .

William Howell felt "the severity with which our pride in him has been stricken down." Ma, who had been such an example when her George died, was "inconsolable," but she came as soon as she could, escorted by twenty-year-old Billy, bringing Jane and Jeffy D., now ten and eight.[28] The baby's parents grieved for him ever after, even though another offspring was already on the way. Margaret Howell Davis was born on February 25, 1855. Ten years later, Varina wrote, "That little grave . . . in Georgetown is ever fresh to me"; and she told Jeff that her new baby, Winnie, had "many traits of our angel Samuel." Fortunately, they had had a miniature painted of their first child and a little marble bust made. Even in old age, Jeff would refer to the strong arm he might have leaned on "had God so willed it." For the present, "a child's cry in the street well-nigh drove him mad." "For many months," he "walked half the night and worked fiercely all day."[29]

Jeff Davis had always been a hard worker. Joseph once said he tried to do too much on the plantation. In the army, Northrop had taken him to task for being too "rigidly military," meaning that he would never take time off like other officers but "confined himself to the Camp," ready for "any duty that might arise." By nature he was a perfectionist. He had to know everything about whatever interested him. This gained him a reputation for encyclopedic erudition. Whatever was done had to be done right, down the last detail, with attention to beauty as well as utility. He gave as much thought to the consequences of an action as to preparation and implementation. He labored in the War Office "with all his might," and it is no wonder he wore out his subordinates.[30]

Although he began work rather late in the day, he would sometimes work through till two in the morning, then bring home with him to dinner "his dear friend," Col. Samuel Cooper, the adjutant general of the army, "who, being much older than my husband," says Varina, "looked ready to faint." She would try to remedy this by sending "luncheon with wine" to the office, but Davis would forget to eat or to offer any to the colonel. Cooper had "the greatest affection and admiration" for Davis, but he said, "another four years would have killed me."

Davis leaned hard on Cooper. He had been in the army since 1813 and in the department since 1838, except for active service in Florida and Mexico. Scott had appointed him adjutant general in 1852. This was one place where Davis had no quarrel with the commanding general. Cooper, from New York state, had married Sarah Mason, sister to Davis's friend James, of Virginia. His "uniform courtesy" and "taste for elegant literature," as well as the fact that his father had fought in the Revolution, made him naturally congenial to the new secretary. He "habitually consulted him," Davis said, "as well because of the purity of his character as his knowledge of the officers and affairs of the army." He found him "calm" and "charitable," though "of great native force." Davis was impressed by a "rare virtue": "supremacy of judgment over feeling." "I never . . . saw Cooper manifest prejudice, or knew him to seek favors for a friend, or to withhold what was just," even from an enemy.[31]

So brilliantly seconded, Davis set his meticulous mind on improving what Varina called "the Army where his heart was." Ceaselessly appealed to for appointments, Davis tried to practice Cooper's "rare virtue." Northrop warned the mother of an applicant that Davis was "not a man to be influenced." He naturally did what he could for his friends, however, so long as it was justified. He apparently helped the son of Maj. George Crosman get into West Point but would not reverse a medical decision that kept him from a commission. He later recommended him for the Marine Corps. When his own namesake, J. D. Bradford, was dismissed from West Point for medical reasons, he would not appeal, saying "no true friend of the institution could desire an exception to be made for the gratification of his personal feelings."[32]

He had approved the refusal of Crosman, a quartermaster, to allow "forced contributions" on his clerks: he wanted "to keep the military branch . . . free from political influences." He rebuked as "unprofessional" an attempt to bring politics into his own assignments. Officers would be regarded, he assured one commander, "upon their military merits alone." He hired whatever clerks his bureau chiefs asked for, whether Whig or Democrat, not without criticism from his own party. Even government contracts were apolitical.[33]

Major Crosman was responsible for Davis's most bizarre innovation, the Camel Corps. Crosman had for years urged trying camels for American desert regions. In 1851 he and Maj. Henry Wayne had convinced

Davis to introduce the project to the Senate, where it was laughed at and rejected. Now Davis could propose it from an executive office. Asking Wayne for a written report, he himself translated a French work on military use of camels. He took to heart the history of the beast, its curiosity (there was dispute "as to its anatomical organization"), and its possibilities for burden-bearing and for pursuing "the wild Indians, who now escape our cavalry" nearly every time.[34]

Davis got a Senate appropriation and sent Wayne in the USS *Supply*, commanded by another camel fancier, naval lieutenant David Dixon Porter, to search the Near East for the best of each variety. They brought back thirty-four camels and dromedaries to Texas in spring of 1856 and Major Wayne took charge of the stables, sixty miles from San Antonio. Typically, Davis suggested that the animals be allowed to rest before being put to work. He sent Porter for a second load, especially the "swift kind" of dromedaries (thinking doubtless of those Indians), and the herd was increased by forty-one.[35]

The animals proved as adaptable and useful as hoped, but they were just too strange. Wherever they appeared, horses and mules reared and bolted and cattle stampeded; the soldiers who were their handlers came to hate them. General Twiggs was outraged to find camels in his department when he arrived in 1857. When Davis left office that same year, the beasts were thriving, and occasionally carrying large burdens long miles, but they were never used to chase Apaches. Capt. R. S. Ewell of the First Dragoons requested some for this very purpose after Davis had left, but he was ignored. No one ever seemed to know quite what to do with the creatures. They passed into Confederate hands in 1861 and back to Federal ones in 1865. Montgomery Meigs, who had become quartermaster general of the United States, ordered them sold in 1866 to the highest bidder. Circuses got a number, but very many were finally just turned loose to wander the western states.[36]

Davis thought the camel experiment would have succeeded, had it been followed through. The use of camels in the Crimean War confirmed his belief in their military value. His successor in office, John B. Floyd, asked for a thousand more in 1858. But war interfered, the corps was dissolved, and railroads made camels obsolete as carriers. But in 1889, Davis still listed the Camel Corps as one of his War Department achievements. His clerk Major Lee observed: "He was [a] regular bulldog when he formed an opinion, for he would never let go."[37]

Fortunately for the army, Davis pursued with equal doggedness his other achievements: "an improved system of infantry tactics"; the introduction of "rifled muskets and rifles and the use of Minié balls," as well as "substitution of iron for wood in gun carriages [for large guns]."[38] One artillery innovation was casting heavy guns "hollow, instead of boring them after casting." This process produced the famed Rodman gun, which the inventor had discussed with Davis.[39]

All these innovations came from constant consultation with army experts, followed by trial in the field. Davis, intensely interested in weaponry, had to decide which of hundreds of inventions should be tried. Having studied gun metals carefully, he was sure, from the design submitted, that one huge cannon would explode. When Congress ordered it cast, Davis told the inventor: "I cannot give you a man's life, and you must find someone else to fire it. I will not order a soldier to do so." The last Davis heard of the gun, it was lying in the navy yard, untested.[40]

To learn the latest techniques in all branches, he and President Pierce sent a commission to Europe, composed of Maj. Richard Delafield, specialist on coastal forts, Maj. Alfred Mordecai of the Ordnance Department, and George McClellan, now a captain of cavalry. They were to study the art of war, specifically as it was being practised in the Crimea, where rifled arms were already in use.[41]

Davis had, almost like a seer, insisted eight years before on percussion rifles for his regiment. Now he could point out officially "the superiority of the grooved or rifle barrel." He was testing a breechloader, but meanwhile working on "an elongated ball," to be muzzle-loaded. In tracing French inventions, Davis said success had been "attained by inserting into the rear part of the ball a conical iron cup, which, being driven into the lead by the explosion of the charge, acted as a wedge to expand the ball . . . the plan known by the name of the inventor, Captain Minié of the French army" (the famous Minié ball of the War between the States). He noted an English improvement on this and directed further experiments "both as to the proper shape of the ball and the best mode of grooving the barrel." Tests showed a rifle to be as effective as a musket "at three times the distance." Davis wanted no more arms on the "present pattern" until a report on the Crimean War and trials "in actual service" could determine the value of the rifle. By his next report, he was announcing: "The manufacture of smooth-bore arms has been brought to a close." He wanted all small arms in federal and state arsenals altered, with percussion instead of flintlock firing.[42] He also ordered trials of revolving pistols, a revolving carbine, and of "Beasley's Barrel Rolling Machines."[43] He asked for more breechloader trials but had not sufficient evidence to make a decision on this before he left office.[44]

In his fascination with firearms, Davis visited Enfield, Connecticut, where a fine rifle was made, and the Springfield Armory. He was enthusiastic about a Springfield "pistol of increased length of barrel [10 or 12 inches], furnished with an attachment to the stock which may be instantly applied, and which converts it into a carbine." He had his own pair of double-barrelled Staudenmayer pistols "changed from flint locks to percussion" and fitted with "a rectangular mortice to secure a movable stock, so that it might be fired from the shoulder like a shotgun."[45] He thought this weapon might replace the carbine, but "if not," then "the best breach loading carbine shd. be adopted"; and so it was. His pistol-carbine was not popular in army trials. His keen interest was rewarded, however, when his "valuable suggestions" moved the men at "Colt's Armory" to present him a pistol with the silver breech engraved, "To a brother inventor." His innovations in arms and equipment caused a modern writer to call him "the most progressive" secretary of war "since the office had been established."[46]

Davis had had to write his own book for rifles in 1846. The manual on infantry tactics then in use was Scott's 1835 revision of one from the twenties. Seeing that rifles now would prevail, Davis, with a new manual in mind, ordered Bvt. Lt. Col. William J. Hardee to Washington, November 2, 1853.[47] He had had his eye on Hardee for "good conduct and cool courage" ever since the Mexican War. He may have heard praise from his friends, Harney, Taylor, Twiggs, and Sumner, under all of whom Hardee had served. Davis had told the Senate that he was "one of the most accomplished soldiers in our army, whose education had been perfected abroad." On the new "system of tactics," Davis later said, "for a long time we daily worked together."[48]

Davis may have lent a hand with the translation of the French manual that Hardee and other officers used as the basis for an American one. He was translating the French work on camels and had a large French dictionary, while his department owned a six-volume *Bibliotèque historique et militaire.* On July 28, 1854, the manual in English was completed; it was published in 1855. Davis ordered West Point cadets to learn the drills, and in October, he watched them go through the new maneuvers. Hardee's *Rifle and Light Infantry Tactics,* in two pocket-sized volumes, became standard for the United States Army (and the Confederate States Army later). It virtually supplanted Scott's *Tactics* for "Heavy Infantry," with "emphasis on precision and mass," though Hardee referred the reader to it for "evolutions of the line." Hardee, dealing only with the regiment, taught rapid, fluid movement, perfected by the French in their Algerian wars, and, of crucial importance, "how to mass and increase firepower."[49] Scott countered with a new edition that included "Instructions for Light Infantry or Rifle." Davis had had Hardee's *Tactics* printed under the author's name, unusual for an army manual. He told the publisher in 1860 of the "frequent demand" upon him for it, suggesting that Lippincott put it on the market. He owned the edition of this date.[50]

Davis was at home with infantry, but his real love was the cavalry. When he was old, his daughter idly asked him, if he could live life over, "what would he best like to be?" He answered "without a moment's hesitation, 'I would be a cavalry officer, and break squares.'" Now he sent Edwin Sumner, lieutenant-colonel of the First Dragoons, to study the latest developments of this branch in Europe.[51] He knew that Hardee had spent a whole year at the French cavalry school at Saumur and had trained the Second Dragoons in the French method. As soon as *Light Infantry Tactics* was complete, Davis set him to revising the *Cavalry Tactics* of 1841. Both books were issued at the same time, though the latter does not bear Hardee's name. Hardee also served on the board that "virtually revolutionized American cavalry equipment," one innovation being the Hardee hat (a black shako with plume), also known as the Jeff Davis hat.[52]

Hardee was a lot like Davis—tall and thin, of soldierly bearing, with a "merry blue eye" showing the sense of humor behind his stern countenance. He too had a fiery temper, a love for the books of Sir Walter Scott, and courtly manners, which made him a great favorite with the ladies. He had grown up on Rural Felicity, a south Georgia plantation. But Hardee, sporting a modish French "imperial" and mustache (Davis was clean-shaven) had a more "convivial personality." He had been made one of the Aztec Club in Mexico City, created to while away the time after the fighting stopped, along with Harney, Lee, McClellan, Grant, and Pierce, who was its first president. Hardee was a recent widower with four young children—a sure appeal to Davis's heart. The two became fast friends.[53]

Davis had a "happy faculty" of seeing the merits of young officers, drawing them to him by "his charm of manner," and fostering their careers. George McClellan was one. Although McClellan was still under thirty, Davis appointed him to a commission to study the Crimean War, then in progress. His "gentle manner" and "modesty" pleased both the Davises. Varina tells of a dinner party she gave for the members of the Crimean Commission, the ambassadors of the countries they were to visit, and the general officers of the Army. General Scott was telling a French count how to cook terrapin ("wine with a judicious flavoring of spice, but no flour, sir—not a grain"), when catching something mistakenly that McClellan said across the table, he "set his fork rampant" and called across the table, "No, sir—*I say no,* . . . I have never heard of their being caught in a trap, sir." McClellan, who blushed easily, was meanwhile turning "a fine rosy purple."[54]

Captain McClellan was already distinguished. He now became, says a biographer, "a protegé" of Davis's, who had already sent him on a secret mission. The Crimean Commission studied European armies from 1855 to 1856, but arrived at the Russian battlefield too late to see the fighting. McClellan's report on this trip, written under Davis's eye, "fixed his reputation as an expert on the art of war." He also wrote a new cavalry manual, based on the Russian, which had been adopted by 1861.[55] His McClellan saddle was used "as long as there was horse cavalry."[56]

Davis had been recommending additions to the army since 1850. In his War Department reports, which read like literature, he reviewed each of the five departments (in place of eleven) that he had established: East, West, Texas, New Mexico, and Pacific. He showed that, to patrol an exterior and interior frontier (including routes to the West "which required constant protection") totalling over eighteen thousand miles, around which lay at least forty thousand "inimical" Indians, the army had at most an "effective force" of eleven thousand men.[57]

Congress finally saw his point. His third report announced: "The four additional regiments authorized by the act of March 3, 1855, have been recruited and organized." These included the first two actually called "cavalry." They were added to the two dragoon regiments and one of mounted riflemen already in service. The two new infantry regiments (the Ninth and Tenth) Davis made riflemen and sent immediately to places where Indians seemed hostile. Robert Davis, son of his brother Samuel, took the place of an officer who declined his appointment. Sanguine as usual, Jeff wrote to Joseph, "I hope for more than you probably expect." Two years later, Robert resigned.[58]

There were over thirteen hundred applications for commissions. Davis persuaded Pierce not to give them out as political rewards, but to let him appoint officers from the army, at least in the field grade (major and up). "The political pressure [on Davis] was very great," says Preston Johnston, "but no man was ever less amenable to such considerations." "In fact, I think it was detrimental in many instances," Cooper told Henry Heth, who wondered how he had gotten to be captain in the Tenth Infantry without it. Heth had not even known Davis's name, but Davis knew all about Heth. He and Cooper, through long acquaintance with the army, chose men "purely on their military record," never thinking about geography, until Pierce said there were far too many Southerners. They had to revise their list. "I am happy to remember," said Davis, that this was the only time when "my official action, while Secretary of War, was disturbed in any way by sectional or political considerations."[59]

Davis made the most of his chance to create crack units in his favorite branch. For his First Cavalry, he picked the veteran Sumner (of Massachusetts) as colonel and Joseph E. Johnston (of Virginia) as lieutenant colonel. Johnston had led, at this rank, a battalion of the short-lived Voltigeurs in the Mexican War, after serving as engineer captain. He had since been with the Topographical Engineers, in river improvement work, with Davis's support. Another distinguished "Topog," William H. Emory, Davis's "intimate friend," was named a major. McClellan was one of the eight captains. A first lieutenant was Robert Ransom, cavalry instructor at West Point, who soon became a personal friend of Davis's. Among the second lieutenants Davis appointed James Ewell Brown Stuart, known as Jeb.[60]

Davis was finally able to offer a proper place to Albert Sidney Johnston. Zachary Taylor had thought him "the best soldier he had ever commanded," and when president had appointed him army paymaster on the Texas frontier, with the staff rank of major. Now, on March 3, 1855, Davis named Johnston colonel of the Second Cavalry.[61]

For lieutenant colonel, Davis chose Robert E. Lee. Lee had written to Davis in 1850, and lately they had been in constant contact. Lee had been named superintendent of the United States Military Academy in 1852. There, Davis was known as Lee's "personal friend" and visited "often." Lee regretted leaving the Engineers, but he took the chance Davis offered for promotion. His line rank was still captain, held since 1838, despite three brevets in Mexico. Advancement in one's own corps had to wait for an opening in the rank above.[62] Lee asked (and got) a spot for his (and Cooper's) nephew, Fitzhugh Lee (known as Fitz). His wife had asked Davis to procure a cadetship at West Point for their second son, whom Lee confusingly called Fitzhugh, though most called him Rooney. For some reason, Davis failed, but Rooney was commissioned directly into the army in 1857.[63]

This elite Second Cavalry had majors William J. Hardee and George H. Thomas, and among the captains were Earl Van Dorn, Edmund Kirby Smith, George Stoneman, and Theodore O'Hara (author of "Bivouac of the Dead"). Fitz Lee and John Bell Hood were second lieutenants. Many years later, a French count wrote that Davis appointed his "creatures" to these regiments, instead of "regular officers whom he disliked." This was patently foolish, as "most of his nearest personal friends in Washington were army men," and he held his army associations "the dearest of my life." Jubal Early called it ludicrous to regard Johnston or Lee as anybody's "sycophants and parasites." Out of Davis's fifty-five appointments to the cavalry regiments, forty served in the war for Southern independence as generals (both sides) and the rest as field grade or staff officers: "Does the whole army besides," Early asked, "present such a brilliant record?" Still, in 1859, Davis had to defend in Congress both his appointments and the very existence of the regiments.[64]

Jeff Davis, "himself a soldier of distinguished merit," with "a perfect experience in the details and requirements," set about to improve "the organization and efficiency of all branches of the service." This is apparent in all his reports, especially that of 1854, and strikingly revealed in his 1858 analysis to the Senate of army needs, where he argues, with full historical reference, for the exact type of increase which will be most effective, down to the number in each company and the cost per man. He quoted there minutiae from recent general orders of the army, though he had left the War Department the year before.[65]

Davis has been called "innovative," and in details, he was, but he was also devoted to tradition and prerogative. To create an unattached post for an army doctor who had invented a new wigwag system, he called "utterly absurd in itself" and "utterly violative of every military principle." All military men looked on this as "improper." "Public necessities should govern," not rewards to individuals. "If this Doctor had been an educated soldier, trained to the usages of the Army, he would never have thought of such a reward."[66]

The commanding general himself was not more jealous of the army's prerogative. The Indian Bureau had been moved from the War to the Interior Department in 1849. In 1854, the commissioner of Indian affairs suggested that Lt. John Lawrence Grattan had caused a massacre and his own death by not letting the Indian agent handle the trouble. Scott called this "injustice to the Army," and Davis backed him up. He told Pierce that the commissioner was interfering and trying to effect "a radical change in the military system." The next year, Davis, rightly, as it turned out, objected to an Interior Department attempt to postpone an army parley with tribes of the Northwest.[67]

At the outset, Davis had argued for transfer of the bureau: the Indian wars were virtually over, and it would help prevent a relapse of "partially civilized" tribes "into barbarism." Obviously, he was wrong; in 1856, he reported "three Indian wars upon our hands." He wanted the natives back under the War Department, so the same hand could reward and punish. As he told the Senate in 1858, the Interior Department "sends arms and ammunition to the very Indian tribe whom the next month the War Department may send troops to subdue."[68] Davis took over in Florida in 1853 because the Interior Department had failed to remove "the few Seminoles remaining"; otherwise, he never got his wish. And the army there, even under Harney, could do no better. Davis's last report says efforts had "proved unavailing to effect the removal of the Seminole Indians."[69]

General Harney was more successful in chastising the Brulé Sioux—the ones who, some fifteen hundred strong, had wiped out Grattan's Sixth Infantry detachment of thirty men. Army patrols could simply not protect the vast routes to the West and settlements in Nebraska and Kansas, or even Texas (where Davis suggested reservations as a solution).[70] The only way "to stay the hand of violence" of the wild tribes was "to punish their repeated outrages." Davis summoned Harney from leave in Paris to lead this chastisement, and Harney reported to Scott, who had planned it, early in 1855. Civilians from Georgia to California offered to fight the Sioux, but the troops Harney led were all regulars, including the new First Cavalry and Henry Heth's company of the Tenth Infantry. Harney thrashed the culprits on September 3 at a battle called Blue Water (or Ash Hollow). Davis said it was "the most successful blow that was ever struck on that frontier for the preservation of its future peace." By November, Harney had driven all the Sioux to ask for a council.[71]

Pierce, through Davis, told Harney to make a treaty restoring "friendly relations." Harney tried in many ways to arrange peace with and among the Sioux, Pawnee, Cheyenne, and Arapaho, wanting to requite them "for their many sufferings, consequent to the domain of our people on the soil of this continent." He hoped to turn the Sioux to farming, but Henry Heth thought the braves would never do "squaw work." Harney did secure peace, at least until 1858, when Davis said that his work "stands as . . . a model for all treaties with Indian tribes."[72]

The Grattan massacre had taken place near Fort Laramie, one of the most isolated garrisons flung out to protect routes to the Pacific. Davis saw that these many small forts were costly, hard on their soldiers, and "nearly powerless." He wanted to revamp the whole system by concentrating in large garrisons on the fringe of the plains, from which troops could sally forth in spring and summer, along with the pioneer wagons. This would afford, he said, "the temporary dangers and toils" that "give zest to a soldier's life" and also a prospect of return to civilization. Through this plan, which he had learned from the French in Algeria, he hoped to render the service "attractive to persons of military spirit," and thus reduce the alarming rate of desertion and resignation. To this end also, he proposed increased pay (which more than tripled enlistment), bounties, and commissions for qualified noncommissioned officers. And still futilely, he urged the "retired list" and pensions for widows. He tried, but failed, to make merit, rather than seniority, the basis for promotion.[73]

His aim always was to create a trim and effective fighting force. He wanted to cut through the maze of brevets and staff and special appointments and make it known, "under all possible circumstances, who is the officer entitled to command." He was never able to win from Congress those "certain and permanent rules" on this, which he thought so necessary for "harmony and efficiency." The old structure was too firmly in place. But he did get a law giving "local rank" of colonel and lieutenant colonel to superintendent and commandant of cadets at West Point, so that a junior officer would never command a senior, as had just happened. When he tried to reform actual army units, he caused even more friction. His ideas on artillery, for instance, brought him straight up against an old comrade in arms, Braxton Bragg.[74]

Captain Bragg, brevet lieutenant-colonel, was a thoroughly military man. He had ranked fifth in his class at West Point. He had his own ideas about army reorganization, having published anonymously in the *Southern Literary Messenger,* 1844–1845, nine articles called "Notes on Our Army." Some ideas there, and in letters to his brother John in Congress, are markedly like Davis's 1854 report. But over his own Company C of the Third Artillery, their ideas clashed. After the Mexican War, Bragg had fought for it against Scott and the former secretary, but they saw fit to dismount the whole Third in 1851. When Davis came in, Bragg asked him to restore "my battery to 'Horse Artillery.'" But Davis was bent on trimming the corps to peacetime size. He refused the request and ordered Bragg to the frontier, which he detested. In April 1855, Bragg went on extended leave.[75]

"Cump" Sherman, a very good friend, said that Bragg "hated Davis bitterly" for sending him, as he expressed it, "to chase Indians with six-pounders." The truth was, Davis offered Bragg a line promotion to major in the First Cavalry, and Bragg turned it down. In December of 1855, he went to see Davis and tried to talk him into posting his battery somewhere besides the frontier. When Davis would not, Bragg resigned from the army. "He could drive me from the Army but not from my party," Bragg said next year, glad that Democrats had not pushed Davis for president. The War Department was "resolutely bent" on using long-range rifled guns instead of light artillery, Bragg grieved, and the "finest battery I ever saw was destroyed." "It was the duty of the department to carry out its own views, and mine to obey or quit."[76]

Others more truculent and highly placed than Bragg felt injured by Davis's policies. When army departments were reorganized, Twiggs took umbrage at having to serve at line instead of brevet rank.[77] John Ellis Wool, distinguished since 1812 and brevetted major general for Buena Vista, was sent by Davis in 1854 to command the Department of the Pacific. Davis welcomed his "cordial cooperation," but this was wishful thinking. Being honored at a dinner with Henry Foote was enough to show Wool's hostility. Then he misinterpreted or balked at orders, leading Davis to remind him that he owed "due respect and cheerful obedience" to the War Department. This did not sit well with the seventy-year-old career officer, and he soon took out his spleen in a newspaper attack.[78] Davis's friend S. W. Inge wrote from California: Wool's effort "to justify his . . . dissatisfaction," and to claim that praise for his "faultless" conduct was "most unjustly withheld," looked "frivolous and ridiculous in the extreme." Bragg had called Wool in Mexico "the weakest and most contemptible apology for a great man I have had the misfortune to meet."[79]

The War Department's loss of confidence in Wool, largely for disobedience, Davis termed "cause for regret rather than for complaint"—i.e., Wool's complaint against it. He sustained Wool militarily, especially in clashes with civil authority, but he tried to block Scott's reassignment of him to the East and was overruled by Pierce.[80] Wool publicly accused Davis, after he had left office, of spitefully withholding a sword voted to Wool by Congress. Davis, who had actually had the sword made, called this "palpable and pitiable falsehood." When Wool accused him of "Billingsgate language" suited only to "the filibuster, secessionist or disunionist," Davis answered that publishing "abusive, recriminating epithets," was "a remedy not recognized among Gentlemen . . . and one to the enjoyment of which I now dismiss him."[81]

Davis forgot that he was pretty good at recriminating epithets himself, as his concurrent embroilment with Winfield Scott showed. His letters, mainly cold appeals to the record, were warmed by some choice invective. Scott's were volcanic effusions, setting "my rights and feelings" against Davis's "the law and the facts." Each charged the other with egotism, arrogance, and slander. "I know your obstinacy," said Scott. There was certainly an obstinate streak in Davis, not necessarily bad. Although fatal in evil or error, obstinacy in truth is stability, and in virtue, fortitude. There is no martyr without it, probably no saint.[82] And Scott had his own obstinacy about a claim for pay that Davis "could not allow," Varina says. It was also about obedience. The army paymaster had sent Scott's tangled money claims to Davis, asking what to do. Davis was known to disallow a claim, even of Harney's, if it was out of line. In this case, he asked the view of Pierce and the attorney general, Caleb Cushing; yet Scott blamed him personally for every delay and disallowance and refused to obey any order unless Davis stated that it came directly from the president. Davis won this point in the end, but Scott won a large part of the money he asked for.[83]

Scott also won the palm for the most flamboyant insults. Davis conceded: "I shall leave you in the undisputed possession of a field of which I could not consent to be the victor." He could never come up to Scott's "Compassion is always due to an enraged imbecile," but he did pretty well: "The delay for which you make a hypocritical apology has strengthened you to resume the labor of vituperation" but having answered falsehood "by conclusive proof . . . I am gratified to be relieved from the necessity of further exposing your malignity and depravity."[84]

Scott whimpered that Davis was trying "to provoke a duel with an old soldier, known to be so lame in both arms" (not from wounds, as implied, but from falling on the sidewalk in New York to which he had moved his headquarters, to get away from Davis and Pierce). Davis blasted back that "when in the vigor of manhood" Scott had used religious scruples to duck out of a challenge from Andrew Jackson ("Vain, pompous nullity," Jackson had growled), thus giving "notice to the world that you would not act" as "a gentleman responsible to any one whom he assails." Davis could not allow this "to shield the slanderer from rebuke."[85]

In the midst of this dispute, Davis supported Scott where he thought him right, interceded for his protégé in trouble at West Point, entertained him at official dinners, and, to justify a ban on beards at West Point, cited Scott among "our most distinguished soldiers" who were beardless.[86] Scott had not attended the academy, but he loved to visit, and the young cadets thought his colossal six-feet-six figure embodied the glory of the old army. He rather thought so too. He told how, when promoted to major general, he "engaged a large parlor, with large mirrors at both ends, dressed himself in full uniform and strutted up and down the room half the day admiring himself."[87]

By contrast, a cadet who admired Scott, Morris Schaff, remembered Jeff Davis at West Point "in a dark blue flannel suit," with "his square shoulders, military walk, and lithe figure," his "spare, resolute, and rather pleading face." This was in 1860, as he loitered under the elms conversing with Colonel Hardee, whom he had appointed commandant of cadets four years before. He had made Delafield, of his Crimean Commission, superintendent when Lee left. Friends from his own day, Professors Bartlett, Mahan, and Church, were still teaching there, and ruled the academic board. But when he tried to break the exclusive hold of the Engineer Corps by opening the superintendency to other branches, Mahan defeated him.[88] The board backed him in one innovation: a fifth year of study, which was to include English literature, Spanish, history, geography, military law, and additional field instruction. He effected this in 1854 and successfully defended it in the Senate until 1861. When Schaff saw him, he was heading the Davis Commission from Congress, sent primarily to see how the five-year plan was working.[89]

For Davis it was always "relaxation from duty" to visit the post, where "all the professors" and most of the officers were his friends. In 1854, he had stayed with Superintendent Lee and his family, perhaps discussing the five-year course, which Lee also wanted. Davis always sustained Lee's decisions. Lee defended him when the *New York Times* attacked him in 1856, telling Mary he was "much pleased" with Davis's report. A new "confidence and respect" settled on the "old friendship."[90] So much alike in courtesy, truth, devotion to duty, love for children, a merciful and peace-making temperament, and a firm self-control that hid a lively temper and a warm heart, alike even in knowing much of *The Lady of the Lake* by heart, the two men remained friends to the end. The Scott affair might have strained it, but Lee, though he admired the general, recognized his egotism. Davis's affection embraced Mrs. Lee and the children, and theirs for him became greater as years went on. The eldest son, George Washington Custis Lee (called Custis), who was to become so close to Davis, graduated from West Point in 1854, leading his class every year.[91]

In spirituality, the likeness of Davis and Lee is striking. They used almost the same words about the will of God and the life to come, and they had the same favorite hymn, "How Firm a Foundation." Lee, like Varina baptized and raised in the Episcopal Church, was not confirmed until 1853.[92] Grief over Samuel seems to have deepened Varina's faith and sympathy. She showed her sympathy with a lady who had lost her third infant by sending her a color print of the Crucifixion. She and Jeff attended regularly the Church of the Epiphany in Washington. In November 1855, she autographed her own copy of the *Book of Common Prayer.* On the feast day of the church, January 6, 1856, Varina was confirmed. Now she, like Lee, could receive Holy Communion.[93]

Davis got the Connecticut-born rector of Epiphany, John William French, appointed chaplain and professor at West Point and assured the next president, James Buchanan, that he was "of the most exemplary piety." He owned "in the field of language, logic and ethics a larger mass of manuscript translations of the ancient authors than any one of my acquaintance," fitting him to teach in the five-year plan. Being "above sectional prejudices, and intellectually superior to fanaticism," French was also fit to train officers "in all circumstances to uphold the constitution." He taught until his death in 1871. When he left Washington, Davis wrote how "sadly" he and Varina missed "one we so much love." Their visiting minister, however, had given "a beautiful, and truly powerful discourse on community of the human race, and the obligation imposed upon us to bear the burthens one of another."[94]

This was November 1856. Davis had just seen French at West Point, on the way back from visiting the Springfield Armory with Hardee and Bartlett. Colonel Delafield had invited Varina to come too, but she evidently did not. She was expecting a baby in January.[95] She and Jeff had moved after Sam's death, renting a mansion two blocks west of the White House, near the War Department. Varina's little sister Margaret exulted in the "hot and cold water all through it" and "the largest dining room I ever saw in a private house." Varina furnished the twenty-three rooms with three sets of carved parlor furniture upholstered in crimson and blue, "Gilt-frame Pier Glass . . . Walnut Secretary . . . French China Dinner, Dessert, and Tea service." Some of this may have first belonged to the wife of Louisiana senator Judah Benjamin. He had richly furnished a house for her arrival, but she had returned to Paris to stay, and Varina had bought "lavishly" of her things at auction.[96]

Before Sam died, Varina had written her mother about her dinners, parties, and receptions: "I am so be-flattered and courted that I long for some good old home rudeness [plainness]. . . . I never led such an unsatisfactory life in all my days." Unsatisfactory or not, this was the life Varina was made for. Her home was a social center for the Pierce administration. She entertained the savants of the Coast Survey as well the many army officers. Her farewell reception was "the great success of the season." Ma, visiting in 1854, wrote home of the "delightful" society: "every body is well read . . . you are well entertained if you only sit still and listen. Talent makes the aristocracy here—money has its admirers too—but talent out ranks it."[97]

Talent included Professor Joseph Henry of Princeton, head of both the Smithsonian and the National Academy of Sciences. The Davis salon included the "extremely cultivated" John Perkins, Jr., the Clement Clays, the John Slidells, and Ambrose Dudley Mann, who had helped Perkins write a bill to reorganize the diplomatic corps.[98] Mann had just missed Davis at both Transylvania and West Point, having resigned the latter to become a career diplomat. He was now an assistant secretary of state. Varina said he had "every Christian virtue; with a detestation and scorn of wickedness he nevertheless grieved over the sinner, and was in his own life a shining exemplar of the Christian charity that 'suffereth long and is kind.' . . . Mr. Davis and he gravitated toward each other at once, and loved like David and Jonathan until extreme old age."[99]

As for talent outside the home, Varina gave a dinner party before a concert by Ole Bull, Maurice Strakosch, and "little Signorina Patti," the child soprano. Jeff's rapt attention to the music led a young guest to say that he "was a lover of art in all its forms and phases." He heard also, in 1855, a performance of Bellini's *Norma.*[100]

The whole Bache-Walker-Emory-Blair complex was still close, but Davis was beginning to be disillusioned with Walker and Blair, for their Free-Soil proclivities. While Blair presided over the first convention of the Republican Party, an abolitionist prayed that God would take Pierce away, so that a "God-fearing man might fill his place." The truth was that Frank Pierce, a strict Sabbath-keeper, held daily prayer in his home and went to the Presbyterian church.[101]

Ma found everyone "kind and polite . . . no one more so than Mr. and Mrs. Pierce." The families were almost inseparable. Jeff was seen with Pierce at the White House, on trips, at a piano concert. Varina was able to draw out the intelligent, reclusive Jane Pierce, who had "a keen sense of the ridiculous" but was "too ceremonious to indulge it often." The presidential couple could relax with these friends. One day at the Davises' summer house out from Washington, Frank was waxing "eloquent over the genius, the shy, tender ways . . . of his friend Hawthorne, and stuck his hands in his pockets as he paced up and down." He answered Jane's disapproving look with: "No; I won't take them out of my pockets, Jennie! I am in the country, and I like to feel the comfort of it."[102]

Varina loved Frank as Jeff did: "He was one of the most genuinely honest, upright men I have ever known. His wants were few, his personal habits were rather elegant." He "dearly loved to give, and gave much to the needy." When the first American ships ever to visit Japan returned laden with gifts for the president, Pierce soon came over, "glad as a boy to have something to give," and "burst out with, 'General, [as he always called Davis] I have a dog for you.' Mr. Davis said, 'What can I do with a dog in town?' 'Oh!,' said the President, 'you can put it in a tea-saucer, if it crowds your house' " (twenty-three rooms, remember). This was Bonin (born passing those islands, so not a gift from Japan), the tiny, jet-black dog that Patrick Jordan inherited. He was "Mr. Davis's pet and the scourge of the servants and of the family." Young lieutenants coming to call were forever tripping over him. If Varina complained, Jeff would bow and offer "to 'build a house for myself and my dog.' " But when Pierce invited Varina to take some of the Japanese presents, "as they belonged to no one," Jeff said, "In that case my wife knows they do not belong to her." He would not let her use the War Department messenger or stationery, either, or order flowers from the government greenhouse.[103]

Bonin may be the dog that little Maggie bit. Pierce, who "took a never-failing delight" in talking to her when she was not yet two, told the story: when the dog snapped at her, she did not cry, but lay down beside it, and when it went to sleep, bit it on the nose. The Davises doted on little Maggie as they had on Samuel. Jeff called her "Pollie," after the sister he had lost so long ago, and in old age was still calling her "my bright little angel Pollie," telling her, "you have been a joy and comfort from your birth." In prison he remembered her love in these days "when in lisping accents she welcomed my coming at evening and grieved at my going in the morning." Varina called her "the smartest thing I ever saw."[104]

Maggie soon had to share this adulation with a brother, Jeff Jr., born January 16, 1857, two days before the worst blizzard in Washington's history. Pierce arrived exhausted from floundering through waist-high drifts, coming to see about Varina. She was "ill unto death" for about two weeks from puerperal fever. Jeff, refusing to leave her until she was out of danger, worked at home. Her nurse could not get through to her until Senator Seward fetched her in his own sleigh. The Davises' gratitude for this outlived the many years of political bitterness.[105]

For Varina, the baby boy became "from the minute he was born . . . the 'friend of my bosom the balm of my life' . . . I pray to rear him every day." Sitting up for the first time, she wrote to her mother "to let you see I am not dead, though I have been very near it. . . . The baby . . . looks exactly like his Father, and I expect to call him Jeff though his Father is very much opposed to it." He was christened Jefferson (without Finis) on March 26. Soon after, the baby was himself "ill unto death" from pneumonia. He recovered after being treated by blistering and cupping (medical bleeding), but he was spared half of the latter because his father "got so frantic seeing the blood run down."[106] In a few months Davis was writing, "Kiss my dear Daughty and sweet little Boy for their old Tady who loves them 'too much.'" When about to leave office, he asked the president for copies of their letters as a legacy for his son, and the next year he wrote Pierce, "the little boy on whom his Mother inflicted my name [is] large . . . clumsey strong, and big boned . . . a promising child." But even Varina, who thought him "the best child on earth, and naturally the most upright loving little heart," soon admitted that he was "not at all precocious."[107]

This family happiness was offset somewhat by Pierce's political failure. Events in Kansas and Pierce's sweet nature cost him the Democratic nomination ("I never will take [it] if it is to be had by conflict with others"). It was James Buchanan and John C. Breckinridge who led the party to victory in 1856. Davis had been ignored at the national level, as Bragg said, but it was his own wish. Friends had mentioned him for vice president and even, "with more zeal than prudence," he said, for president. "The first office I would not have, the last is not to be thought of, and a man's friends should not make him ridiculous."[108]

In the first place, he wanted Pierce to run; and in the second, "Now, as heretofore I prefer the office of senator to any other," but "I could not attempt to affect it by personal solicitation." Campaigning for oneself for senator or president was still thought to be in bad taste. His friends secured the Senate seat for him on January 16, 1856, the Mississippi legislature giving him ninety-one votes, against thirty-three for eight other candidates combined.[109] His term was to begin when his cabinet post ended, March 4, 1857. When that day arrived, Pierce said, "I can scarcely bear the parting from you, who have been strength and solace to me for four anxious years and never failed me." He gave him a gold-headed walking stick. They were not to meet again for ten years, though they corresponded warmly. The Pierces left for Europe in the fall and did not come back till the country was about to split in two.[110]

Davis had proved his excellence as an executive, managing the minutiae of a department "most difficult and complex in its disbursements." His honesty was notorious, his oversight so scrupulous that no one could have cheated it "out of the value of a brass button."[111] He made a few enemies and a great many friends. A coast guard cutter, a lake steamer, and a fort and mountain range in Texas were all named after him. One of the clerks, forty years in the War Department, who worked with Davis daily, recalled the "hard feelings" roused by the Scott feud, but came to the conclusion that Davis "was one of the best Secretaries of War who ever served."[112]

XI

Struggles for Health and the South

On March 4, 1857, Jefferson Davis stepped to the Senate seat he had vacated at the call of his party six years before. Mississippi had vindicated him at last, wiping out his defeat by Foote. Much as he desired this, he had been as ready now as then "to offer up my political prospects." He was told to be present when the legislature voted or expect defeat. But he told his friend Cocke that he did not think "intrigue and importunity" very potent, and "I am quite well aware that I have no capacity, even if I had the will, to make much of such means." He could not ask for "consideration of my personal interest above that of the public good. This I know is sometimes called impracticable theory, and sometimes attributed to a vain assumption of superiority, but in my own case at least cannot be properly assigned to the latter cause." This is the sort of thing that led Davis's fellows to remark his "purity," and a twentieth-century writer to say, "He was very much the saint in politics."[1]

Davis was clear of a cabinet officer's "little carking cares" but plunged immediately into others. He was named chairman of the Senate Committee on Military Affairs—an unprecedented tribute to his earlier handling of this post and his "ability and propriety" as secretary of war. The high regard for him was general. To a political foe, Henry Wilson, he was "the clear-headed, practical, dominating Davis." William Hickling Prescott, a Northern historian then living, said that among all the great senators of that era, "Davis was the most accomplished."[2]

The incoming president, James Buchanan of Pennsylvania, knew Davis as a Southern leader of their party, and Davis had "affectionate regard" for him. Varina liked this older man, probably because he was "quick as a flash" in "polite repartee," as she was. His "fine presence"—very tall and blue-eyed—his "fair and delicate" complexion and perpetual "white cravat, faultlessly tied" prompted as her first thought, "how very clean he was."[3]

The much younger vice president, John C. Breckinridge, Davis had met three years before, when they unknowingly sparked political fires in Kansas, now raging out of control. Stephen A. Douglas had then headed the Senate Committee on Territories and was trying to organize Nebraska Territory, of which Kansas was the southern part. Unable to press his bill through Congress, he saw at the last minute that Pierce's support was crucial. But it was Sunday. The pious president did not discuss politics on Sunday. Douglas and Breckinridge came to his friend Davis for help. He argued Pierce out of his scruples; they got their support; and the Kansas-Nebraska Bill became history.

Non-fire-eating Southerners supported the bill, since it seemed at last to guarantee equal rights in a territory. It pronounced the Missouri Compromise "inoperative and void." Davis, Breckinridge, and Pierce all thought the compromise unconstitutional (as the Supreme Court was soon to declare) but better than nothing. Douglas's bill left settlers "perfectly free" to decide by their constitutions whether to have slavery or not. But settlers were not free from their passions or from outside influence. Northern Free-Soilers were not interested in equal rights; they wanted exclusive rights.[4] Davis said later, with his usual honesty, that if he had been in Congress then, he would have voted for the Kansas-Nebraska Bill, but he admitted, "its terms invited contending parties to meet on the plains of Kansas, and it well nigh eventuated in civil war."[5]

Using "equally irregular and extra-legal methods," men for and against slavery had set up rival governments in Kansas. The Southerners, having organized first, had the legitimate body. With approval of the governor, they had gone to Lawrence in May of 1856 to arrest their rivals for treason and had wrecked the Northerners' headquarters in an "almost bloodless" coup. In retaliation, abolitionists led by John Brown had hacked five proslavery men to death "in cold blood." Brown's settlement was then attacked, one of his sons was killed, and he was run out of Kansas. Col. E. V. Sumner and his First Cavalry were called from Fort Leavenworth to keep order.

Davis, as secretary of war, had told Sumner (of Northern sympathies) to be strictly impartial, and he was: he stopped raids by bands like David Atchison's "border ruffians," and he dispersed without "one drop of blood" a free-state meeting in Topeka that federal marshals had forbidden. This was in keeping with Davis's directive to use "moral force" if possible, yet Davis disapproved the latter more, because the meeting, though illegal, had committed no overt act. He hated troop use against civilians.[6] He called the disorder "bitter fruits of the substitution of expediency for principle" and the fallacy of "squatter sovereignty." He viewed the troop use "with sorrow, with humbled pride, and impaired confidence in the character of the American people." It cast doubt on their capacity for self-government, he said, and was "a melancholy evidence of the decadence of the political morals of our times."[7]

In the Senate, the attack on slavery had been stepped up when another Sumner, Charles, became the mouthpiece of abolition. He used words "as boys do stones [to] break windows and knock down flower pots," said a friend. Varina found this senator from Massachusetts "a handsome, unpleasing man." His physique was impressive (six feet, two inches; one hundred eighty-five pounds), and so was his conversation, except that it consisted mostly of "set pieces" on such topics as "the Indian mutiny, lace . . . Senaca's morals . . . the history of dancing."[8]

While Davis was still in the cabinet, Charles Sumner had excoriated the South with vile epithets and ridiculed Southern chivalry by calling the South Carolina senator A. P. Butler (in his absence) a Don Quixote whose mistress was "the harlot, Slavery." In Massachusetts, Sumner could get away with saying an opponent "told a lie." When he implied that Butler was a liar, the Southerner's young cousin, Rep. Preston Smith Brooks, knowing Sumner would not accept a challenge, watched two days for the right moment, then thrashed him severely with his gutta percha cane. This was a specified recourse in the code of honor, but it was not in the laws of the District. Brooks was fined for assault. A House attempt to expel him failed; he resigned, and was unanimously reelected. While searching recovery as far as Europe, Senator Sumner boasted that "to every sincere lover of civilization his vacant chair was a perpetual speech."[9]

What it spoke was the chasm of thought and feeling between North and South. Preston Brooks thought "the spirit of American freemen" would not let Sumner get away with slander. He told the House, if he had not called him "to a personal account . . . I should have forfeited my own self-respect." But few in the North could see Sumner's offense, and none, Brooks's obligation. In Massachusetts, Sumner was hailed as a martyr and compared to Christ, while Braxton Bragg, from his Louisiana plantation, exulted at seeing him "chastised": "You can reach the sensibilities of such dogs only through . . . their heads and a big stick." Quitman said Brooks was "incapable of a dishonorable act"; the North labeled him a sneak, a coward, and a bully.[10] Jefferson Davis declined a South Carolina invitation to speak at a testimonial dinner but expressed "high regard and esteem" for Brooks. When the young man died in Washington, January of 1857, he went to the funeral.[11]

The affair served as a new focus for Northern hatred of "slavery, & its political power." In 1856, opponents of the South combined to form one big antislavery party—the Republican. It was a plank of their platform that the South should never have Kansas, or any other new state.[12]

The verbal battle over Kansas was still going on as Davis returned to the Senate in 1857. Robert J. Walker, appointed governor of Kansas Territory in March, soon went back on his Southern commitments and, as Davis said, "struck hands with the Abolitionists"—a term which Southerners tended to use for anyone publicly opposed to slavery. Walker, who had turned coat before, was known as an unscrupulous manipulator, but Davis's great charity made him hope "for satisfactory explanations, though we may fail to perceive how they can possibly be made." They were not made, and Davis was once more disillusioned with politics.[13] Congressional debate was deadlocked on the issue until January 29, 1861, when Kansas became a free state in a Union of which Mississippi was no longer a part.[14]

Senator Davis managed Buchanan's inaugural ball and introduced department personnel to the new secretary of war, John B. Floyd, before this short special session of Congress ended on March 14, 1857. On the nineteenth, he dined at the White House. Then his troubles began. "On the score of economy," he and Varina had decided to give up their mansion, auction the furniture, and rent two rooms for the summer. The auction was held on March 27, but the rooms were not ready; so Matilda Bache Emory took in the whole family. Varina described what came next: "The house was heated to suffocation, and the weather very cold, and Jeff was the second day taken quite ill with an attack of his head, and his ear rose and broke [from an infection]." The servants, Betsy and Kate, quarreled; Betsy took to her bed, refusing to work; so Varina, still very weak from her childbed illness, had to climb the stairs "sometimes five or six times a day" from the ground floor to the garret, where the children were. Both of them had colds and fever. The baby's went into pneumonia, keeping everyone in "horrible suspense" for two weeks—"his little hands had death damp on them for four days."[15]

Still unwell, Jeff decided to go to Mississippi. The doctors "thought the change would be good for him," Varina said, and "I asked to come too." Still weak, she unpacked and repacked, with the help of friends, "and *then the cars left us.*" They had to go back and stay with Malie Brodhead for the night. By now, Maggie had chicken pox "dreadfully, and cried incessantly. Jeffy kept her company." Then he took it "and cried a little harder than usual—he could not have cried more constantly—until we landed at the Hurricane." What a relief it must have been to see the carriage Joseph had sent for them and to find when they reached the house "the parlor and tea room fitted up for us, and even a crib for the baby." The brothers were corresponding again, and Joseph had visited the year before: the alienation was over.

But the troubles of the younger Davises were not. They went to Brierfield the next day, "and the destruction I cannot speak of," wrote Varina: "all the locks spoilt," all the linens "swept from the land—nothing even to cook in—nothing but fruit trees which was not destroyed. I just sat down and cried. And so would Jeff I am sure if he could." But the sensible Varina soon set up her sewing machine and got to work "making pillow cases, sheets, towelling, and napkins—and tablecloths. . . . I have even got to furnish the negroes with summer clothes."[16]

By mid-May, everybody was well, and Jeff was speaking at a barbecue in Vicksburg about his love for the South. At Jackson later, he told some three thousand Mississippians how the Southern Democrats, by helping elect Buchanan, had defeated "the black republican faction," which was always "consolidating power in the federal head and verging the States to provincial degradation." They had "saved the Union of equal rights" by standing "like the old guard of Napoleon, with the inscription written upon their brows, 'the Old Guard knows how to die, but never surrenders!'"[17]

Between other speaking engagements in June and July, he would come home to see about the plantation. He fired one overseer for "mean and vicious" conduct and rejected another "because he had young children who had 'never lived on the low lands.'" He explained to the applicant that the "unhealthiness" had caused him to send his own away.[18] He had taken them and Varina "to the Sea coast" at Mississippi City "for the Summer." Returning to Brierfield, he wrote:

> Oh Winnie you cannot know how dreary the house seems. When busy in it some unexpected noise seems like that of the children and when coming back from the field or elsewhere every thing there is wanting which constituted the place's charm and made it home— . . .
>
> Farewell my dear Wife until a happier hour, but in all hours bright or gloomy you are the unclouded object of your husband's love and he prays for your welfare and our speedy reunion—God bless you all—

Varina was planning to sod "Bermuda Grass" on one of two lots they were buying on the coast, leaving trees and sweet bay "in a dense shade" on the other "to amuse you when you come down." As to the children: "Jeffy!!! bit boy, smart bit boy, grand old boy, big as him's Fader . . . and not a single tooth." Maggie was loving the ocean, "plays about like a fish." "Take care of yourself my own old Ban. . . . God bless you and keep you is the prayer of your devoted wife / W. D."[19]

But Jeff never took care of himself when duty called. Despite the experience of previous years, he set out on a speaking tour for the Democratic Party on September 1, after waiting in vain for a new overseer. "I leave home with extreme reluctance," he wrote Joseph from Jackson, "and if superstitious would believe that some strong necessity existed for my presence. . . . May God preserve you all." He got only as far as Holly Springs before illness, unnamed, came upon him and forced his return to Brierfield.[20]

Quoting Robert Burns, he had written Varina in August, "God . . . grant me soon again to have 'my arms about my dearie O.'" But it was not until daybreak on September 27 that he reached Mississippi City, after "beating about in an oyster boat" from New Orleans all night.

Varina wrote her father of how they went fishing right away, and while "the rest caught perch a foot long," she, in getting out of the boat, "lost my footing and fell in heels over head under the bath house. Jeff jumped in and fished me out." She wanted her parents to come over, especially as "Jeff speaks here Friday."[21]

That speech reviewed at length the peril of "the minority section." Their only ally was the "Northern Democracy." Its exemplar, Franklin Pierce, had "performed his duty" in the face of "fanatical excitement," and under "the bitter hostility of abolitionism, . . . had gone down with the constitution of his country in his hand and the flag of the Union flying over him, more dear to his friends in the hour of defeat" than any success "by a different course could have made him."

Davis insisted that slavery as they practiced it was the best "form of government" for "those who are morally and intellectually unable to take care of themselves." If it were "evil," as even some "Southern apologists" said, then "every honest man among us" would have to work for "its abatement." Doubtless it was "subject to abuse . . . but so, too, were even the tender relations of parent and child." By any "practicable and real" standard, it was a blessing, for "it had transferred the slave from a barbarian to a civilized master . . . and shed upon him the divine light of Christianity."

As to the new presidency, he said that if Buchanan should back Walker's referendum in Kansas, not required by the Constitution, "I will have done with him—have done with him!" Davis the soldier called the 1856 election "a truce for the next four years": it "could hardly be called a victory," since it "left our enemies upon the field with flag flying defiant and an army ready for attack."[22]

After visiting in New Orleans, the family returned to Brierfield. On November 4, A. G. Brown was reelected to the Senate by the legislature, and Davis reiterated his views. He "was not for a dissolution of the Union," but secession was part of "the vital principle of State rights," and if given up, would leave the states at the mercy "of a consolidated and omnipotent Federal Government." He "would stand as a sentinel on the watchtower, ready to sound the note of alarm," and to go "as far as the farthest," if Mississippi's rights or honor were assailed.[23]

Then, "fully relying on your Judgment," Davis asked his cotton factor to sell his crop for the best price and invest eleven thousand dollars of the proceeds in the "the lot of negroes offered by Mr. Christmas," sight unseen. With a new overseer, "Mr. Clarkson," finally in residence, he was about to leave for Washington. These new hands (perhaps needed for the land recently purchased in Arkansas) brought Davis near his 1860 total of one hundred and thirteen, which placed him in the top 6 percent of slaveholders in Mississippi.[24]

As they boarded a northbound steamboat late in November, the Davis family included four children instead of two. Margaret Howell was going back with them, and Becket's place was being taken by Jeffy D., now eleven. "Without even a suggestion Jeff offered to take [him], and educate him if you would let him go," Varina had written: "For God's sake, Ma, consider what a place New Orleans is to bring up a boy in, and don't refuse." They were in Washington by December 5. Renting a "small and badly arranged" house at 238 G Street, they settled in for the first session of the Thirty-fifth Congress.[25] To usher in 1858, Senator and Mrs. Davis gave the New Year's Day reception expected in governmental circles. They went to lectures on English songs. They dined with old Mississippi friends the William Gwins. Dr. Gwin, now senator from California, had put Davis on his select committee to iron out North-South difficulties about a railway to the Pacific, but nothing could be settled until the Kansas-Nebraska business was. Davis was busy enough with Democratic caucuses and Senate speeches.[26]

He spoke at great length in January and February for the increase of the army and defended Sidney Johnston, whom he had recommended to head forces sent to ensure United States authority over Mormons in the Utah Territory. Colonel Johnston was now "locked up in the mountains, unable to complete the campaign," but Davis said he was "equal to this or any other emergency," and "as a soldier, has not his superior in the army nor out of it." Johnston did get his army safely through a severe winter, and he did not have to fight the Mormons. For his "ability zeal energy and prudence," the army awarded him a brevet as brigadier general.[27]

Davis, not neglecting to praise "the great, the good, heroic Taylor," tried to convince fellow senators on February 11 that a plan proposed for the army was "the most economical and efficient." Despite his obvious command of his subject, he concluded: "If I am in error it is fortunate for me that the majority of the Senate will correct it. If I am right, the future will sustain my opinion. . . . I am, therefore, content with whatever fortune may befall the bill." It was three months before his voice was heard again on the Senate floor.[28]

A week later, Davis apologized to Buchanan for not seeing him because of an "indisposition," but to another he admitted that he had been "confined by a painful illness." His health had been generally good since Ma reported in 1854 that he had "escaped his usual attack of fever this fall for the first time since he has been in public life." "He looks well though thin."[29] This was his usual condition, but he seemed susceptible to ear and throat infection, and malaria was always a threat. Davis's eyesight had deteriorated ever since the ulcerated cornea of 1851. The work of the War Department was very taxing. At the end of the first year, he wrote of living "in the midst of interruption," unable to write to a friend because of "constant occupation . . . and my eyes do not permit me to write at night." By 1855 he had told Joseph, "At night I can neither read or write without such injury to my sight that I no longer attempt it," and "I find my sight failing rapidly under the labors of my present station." Early in 1856, David Atchison wrote him, "I am sorry to learn that your eyes still annoy you." Hearing of his sickness now, Thomas Drayton concluded: "Those four years of mental labor . . . have been I fear, a little too much for the physical man. . . . Had you toiled less, you might now be a stronger Senator."[30]

It began as "a very severe cold," Varina says. Soon he was speechless with laryngitis. The viral infection spread to his left eye, producing intense inflammation and, once more, an ulceration of the cornea, rendering him blind. He lay in a darkened room for four weeks, "only able to communicate his thoughts by feeling for the slate and writing them." Leeches were applied. Medication with atropine was tried. This perhaps prompted the secondary glaucoma, which, with the keratitis and accompanying photophobia, were all extremely painful. "My husband's fortitude and self-control had been so great that no one but I knew how much he suffered, and I only because one day I begged him to try to take nourishment, and he gave only one smothered scream and wrote, 'I am in anguish, I cannot.'" Finally a specialist, "Dr. Hayes, of Philadelphia," was brought in, and exclaimed, "I do not see why this eye has not burst." Varina says Jeff "felt for the slate and wrote, 'My wife saved it.' All the triumphs of my life were and are concentrated in and excelled by this blessed memory." The strong light required for Dr. Hayes's examination increased Davis's pain, yet he "sat patiently" without remonstrance. When he was led back to bed, "Dr. Hayes asked me if he was never irritable," says Varina, "and remarked such patience . . . is godlike."[31]

> There he lay, silent, uncomplaining, anxious to save everyone trouble, and most concerned about my little brother, Jefferson Davis Howell, who was ill with scarlet fever in the room above. As soon as Mr. Davis could speak he insisted on going up to him. When I objected because he had never had the disease, he watched the opportunity of my absence and had himself led upstairs.
>
> On my return he was sitting close by the child, whispering, for he could not speak yet aloud, bear stories to him with his arm under the little man's head, looking as happy as he.

Visits to the sickroom show the "personal affection most charming" that Davis inspired in "men of all politics." Lord Napier, the very popular British ambassador, used to come bringing "sunshine and cheer," says Varina. Lt. Col. Hardee "came very often, and sat reading, and writing for him," so that she could go out for an hour. Col. E. V. Sumner came to visit and announced that he was challenging General Harney to a duel. He had already chosen his second. In Varina's account, Davis says, "'You do not want to fight, of course, but to have this matter explained and the wrong acknowledged.' 'Well, I do not know,' said the old gentleman, 'I rather think I prefer fighting.' It was, however, happily settled without resort to violent measures."[32]

Another pacification involved George Jones. He recalled how Davis, confined by that "diseased eye, which was then giving you so much pain and trouble . . . forced our dearly beloved noble, brave and honest friend, Senator C. C. Clay Jr. and myself to make *friends,* the day after [we] had had high and angry words in the Senate." "The *ill feeling* was all on my side, *against* Clay," Jones said, and it would have ended "perhaps, in the shedding of blood but for your interposition, as '*peace maker*' . . . bloodthirsty and cruel as your enemies would make the world believe you are and have always been—d . . . n them I would say had I not ceased to swear."[33]

Clay had come to the Senate in 1853. "From their first meeting," says Virginia Clay, "Secretary Davis was the intimate friend of my husband." Davis gave her his *carte de visite,* and she wrote on the back, "handsome as this when I first knew him." Clay knew about sickness, being a victim of asthma, and "gave up many nights to the nursing of the invalid." He probably, like Hardee, read aloud to him, for he was as devoted as Davis to *belles lettres.* In 1861, inviting Clay to Montgomery, Alabama, Varina was still expressing "the affectionate gratitude I feel for all your sympathy during Mr. Davis's illness."[34]

A highly anomalous visitor was William Seward, "among the most prejudiced of [Davis's] antagonists." He came "for an hour daily, and sometimes oftener, to tell all the 'passing show'" in Congress. His "earnest, tender interest . . . was unmistakably genuine," Varina says; yet the Davises could not fathom Seward. He once told them that he never spoke to the senators around him but to the newspapers: "They have a larger audience than I, and can repeat a thousand times if need be what I want to impress upon the multitude outside." One day Varina asked how he could make "with a grave face, those piteous appeals for the negro . . . you were too long a schoolmaster in Georgia to believe the things you say?"

> He looked at me quizzically, and smilingly answered, "I do not, but these appeals . . . are potent to affect the rank and file of the North." Mr. Davis said, very much shocked . . . "But, Mr. Seward, do you never speak from conviction alone?" "Nev-er," answered he. Mr. Davis raised up his blindfolded head, and with much heat whispered, "As God is my judge, I never spoke from any other motive." Mr. Seward put his arm about him and gently laid down his head, saying, with great tenderness, "I know you do not—I am always sure of it."
>
> After this inscrutable human moral, or immoral, paradox left us, we sat long discussing him with sincere regret, and the hope that he had been making a feigned confidence to amuse us.

But it was not feigned: truth with Seward was "subsidiary to an end," and if something else would serve the end, he used it. "He said, again and again, that political strife was a state of war, and in war all stratagems were fair." But "he was thoroughly sympathetic with human suffering, and would do most unexpected kindnesses." It was this way Varina remembered him "when he lay wounded unto death" in 1865.[35]

"Mr. Seward and I both objected earnestly," Varina says, when on March 3, with speech and sight partially restored, Davis insisted on going to the Senate: "It is for the good of the country and for my boyhood's friend, Dallas Bache, and I must go if it kills me." Varina took him "in a close carriage." "He left me at the door of the waiting-room with beef-tea and wine in a little basket and went in—carried his point, then came almost fainting home." It was probably effort lost, because the Senate postponed the vote on this resolution regarding the coast survey.[36]

Davis threatened to go again on March 23 to vote on Kansas, until Simon Cameron offered to "pair off" with him—neither one would vote. Mississippi congressmen came to Davis's sickroom to discuss the "English bill," about to be brought out of a compromise committee. Its supporters in the House, Georgia's Alexander Stephens, asked for his vote. This would admit Kansas with the proslavery Lecompton constitution, but it would require a referendum on a land-grant provision. Two weeks later, Davis, "being still unable to write," said in a dictated letter that its importance "may be inferred from the fact that though an invalid . . . I went to the Senate for two days in succession [April 29–30], that I might have an opportunity to vote for the bill." He was recorded among the "Yeas" that brought it to the floor after long debate. But Kansas rejected the settlement.[37]

Now Davis "began to slide back into his accustomed place for an hour or two each day," and Seward said, "I think Mr. Davis must get sick again, I miss my daily walk." Davis was not the sentimentalist that Varina was; he could never have admitted "heartily liking" Seward. But he did help him prevent a duel in June between Senators Gwin and Wilson.[38] Back in 1849, Davis had called Seward "the very best authority" on "a wolf in sheep's clothing." After Seward's Rochester, New York, speech of October 25, 1858, Davis called him "the master mind of the so-called Republican party," a "dangerously powerful man" who believed "slave labor and free labor to be incompatible": "one or the other must disappear." Seward's famous phrase for this was "irrepressible conflict." Davis told his Mississippi audience that Seward said the founding fathers meant to destroy slavery and the South "meant to force slavery upon all the States of the Union." "Absurd as all this may seem to you, and incredulous as you may be" that anyone would believe it, "it has been inculcated to no small extent in the Northern mind." Seward described "slavery as degrading to labor, as intolerant and inhuman," and "the white laborer among us" as free "only because he cannot yet be reduced to bondage. Where he learned his lesson, I am at a loss to imagine; certainly not by observation."[39]

The eternal question was forever being agitated, and not by the South. "You have made it a political war," Davis had said in February; "How far are you to push us?" He wrote Pierce, still in Europe, of how little there was "to make the present pleasing, or to give the patriot hope for the future," but perhaps time "will enable the bubbling cauldron to purge itself." Davis returned to debate in May and stuck it out through June 16, "against the opinion of my physician." Although his "unimpaired eye cleared," he appeared to a reporter as "a pale, ghastly-looking figure, his [left] eye bandaged with strips of white linen passing over the head," his whole aspect "feebleness and debility." But his will was stronger than any lingering infirmity. He sounded anything but feeble when matching wits with Sam Houston or disputing details with Robert Toombs.[40]

There was even a near-duel with Judah Benjamin, the senior senator from Louisiana. In disputing money for army weapons—a topic on which Davis knew himself to be expert—both men lost their tempers. This was nothing unusual in the Senate, but next morning in the cloak room, Sen. James Bayard handed Davis a "direct challenge" from Benjamin. According to Bayard's son, Davis "read it and at once tore it up, and said, 'I will make this all right at once. I have been wholly wrong.' " Before he could rise to speak, Senator Pearce, in charge of the pending bill, explained the "misunderstanding." He had handed the men different papers: they had been arguing from two different sets of facts. Davis had used "asperity of tone," but "if he had known," he "would have been one of the last" to "wound the feelings" of another. Davis had not been wholly wrong, either. Benjamin, who accused him of "sneering reply," had himself sneered at Davis and suggested he was undermining the secretary of war. The "delicacy in my position" (as former secretary), said Davis, gave "some justification in a sensitiveness on my part," but "I am incapable of committing a wanton aggression on the feelings of any man." He felt "pained, nay, more, I feel humiliated, when I am involved in a personal controversy." He had respected Benjamin until "he exhibited anger." "Then, it is true, I intended to be offensive. Anger is contagious." Davis explained that he was not "trained to debate," and so usually rose simply to state his conviction, which made him appear sometimes "dogmatic and dictatorial." Against one "as skillful, as acute by nature, and as trained" in the law as Benjamin, "it is but natural that I should appear . . . the hasty man": "my manner implied more than my heart meant." Benjamin still thought himself the injured party but accepted Davis's statement "with great gratification" and assured him of his esteem and admiration.[41] And so the matter ended. Davis was not afraid to meet Benjamin with sarcasm the next year over the Pacific railroad bill, even alluding to "Sir Oracle at whom no man should bark."[42]

To another challenge, Davis responded even more humbly: "I was wrong; I am sorry for it, and in this chamber I beg his pardon and yours." "I am aware that I am very apt to be earnest, perhaps some would say excited, when I am speaking," he once admitted; "and it is due to myself that I should say now, once for all, that I do not intend ever to offer discourtesy to any gentleman, unless I manifest it in such a manner as renders it wholly unmistakable [i.e., meant to provoke a duel]."[43]

Jeff, still "quite unable to read, or to write," had dictated to Varina the chatty April letter to Pierce in which he said, "I am advised to take a sea voyage somewhere." He did not "feel at liberty" to go while Congress was in session, or "we should sail for the South of Europe, and probably see you there." They would not go home to "malarial exposure during the summer or fall." "Little Maggie" he reported "restless as a bird and singing quite as much, if not as sweetly," and "the little boy on whom his Mother inflicted my name" was "nearly as heavy" as she. ("Maggie was a beautiful child, of restless activity, and was the light of her father's eyes," says Varina.)[44]

Being "closely confined . . . under a painful illness . . . for more than seven weeks" in the "cramped" house on G Street with two baby children, however beloved, cannot have been easy. By May, he was pretty well except for the eye, but his frustrations began to depress him. In his June eulogy of Maj. Gen. Pinckney Henderson, he noted that the senator, though ill, had come to the session "when duty pointed the way . . . and the sacrifice of his life was the result." He recalled how they two, when surrounded at Monterey in 1846, "had decided, at whatever hazard," to obey the order to retire. "Superior to personal fear, [Henderson] was incapable of personal hate . . . quick, but too generous to bear malice . . . gentle as a lamb . . . in the midst of his friends, but bold as a lion . . . when confronted by an enemy." As his own qualities seem mirrored here, so does his situation in his melancholy conclusion: "we are warned how vain and transitory are the objects of our pursuit." They "prompt the public man to sacrifice his ease and private interest to the discharge of his public duty," yet "vanish like fleeting shadows."[45]

Davis gave the "feeble state of my health" as one reason he could not address the Democrats of Philadelphia on July 4, but "my prayers shall mingle with yours for . . . our common country." By then, he was on shipboard, "physically and mentally depressed, fearful that I should never again be able to perform my part," turning "away from my fellows" like a "wounded elk" that "seeks the covert to die alone." Not exactly alone: Varina and Maggie and Jeff sailed with him from Baltimore July 3. He picked up immediately, as he always did at sea. Before he reached Portland, Maine, "he was quite cheerful and able to dispense with the shade over his eyes for some hours toward twilight," though he still could not see to write.[46]

Out of "an unusually brilliant array of passengers," Davis was asked to make the shipboard Fourth of July oration. Despite his low state, he spoke with "singular felicity of diction," about "our common country . . . the only proper republic on earth." He rejoiced that the Senate "as one man" had repulsed Great Britain's "insulting claim" to search American ships, ostensibly to stop the slave trade ("against which the United States was the first nation to raise its voice"), but really to destroy our "lucrative commerce . . . in ivory and other products on the coast of Africa." He sounded his new theme: any insult "will find that we are not a divided people," but united by "common interest," "common sentiment of nationality," and "common memories."[47]

In Portland, a band serenade called for another speech (and he was to make five more before leaving Maine). "Vanity does not lead me," he told the cheering crowd, "to appropriate the demonstration to myself"; it was from Maine "to her sister Mississippi" in token of "that national sentiment and fraternity which made us, and which alone can keep us, one people." He meant to woo the people now, instead of politicians, as the only hope for unity. His touch was personal, and sad. Verging on self-pity, he spoke of the "waving elms" and "shaded walks" that gave comfort to the invalid, of the "deeper seclusion" of "the eternal mountains, frowning with brow of rock and cap of snow," which afforded "as much of wildness, and as much of solitude, as the pilgrim weary of the cares of life can desire." Or, he "may sit upon the quiet shore to listen to the murmuring wave until the troubled spirit sinks to rest, and in the little sail that vanishes on the illimitable sea, may find the type of the voyage which he is soon to take, when, his ephemeral existence closed, he embarks for that better state which lies beyond the grave."[48]

The melancholy tone sounded again, when he told the militia at Belfast that he could never see the laurel of victory "save through the solemn shade of the cypress." In his mind was the constant awareness of death, or, more accurately, death and resurrection, for he was an orthodox Christian believer. At a Portland dinner, he urged the necessity of a formal creed, against a celebrated "pulpit orator" who said that his own creed was "one-third democracy and two-thirds pluck." "Mr. Davis used often to cite this," says Varina, "to show how needful a written code of faith and dogmatic teaching was to Christians."[49]

Another sincere religionist, Dallas Bache, summoned the Davises from the clambakes and excursions of Portland to Mount Humpback and his "party of triangulation." (Davis explained this as "series of triangles" used to fix "a parallel of latitude.") After Pierce's alma mater, Bowdoin College, had given Davis an honorary degree, the family took a train to Bangor and then set out for the wilds. One dawn at an inn, Davis went into fits of laughter as he spied from the window a very large man in a "long, figured calico dressing-gown," mounted on a cart, tossing out shelled corn, and making a political speech to the assembled chickens, turkeys, geese, and ducks. This "merry mountebank," seeing Davis, made a deep bow and said to the fowl: "Fellow-citizens, allow me to present one more able and more eloquent than myself. Hear ye him." Illness had not quenched the Davis sense of humor.[50]

Varina tells how they took an elevated "natural road," past "lush green grass" and gigantic granite boulders, to the foot of Mount Humpback. Then an ox team drew the family on a sled up the steep side, with Davis rebuking the driver "many times" about goading the oxen. At white tents "on a plateau near the top," they found Bache, that "healthy and hearty lover of life" with "broad, perpetual humor in his countenance," and his wife, Nancy. He provided tenderloin steaks, his favorite Rhine wine, "the newest books," and "an exquisite and very large musical box which played 'Ah, che la morte,' and many other gems of the then new operas of Verdi."[51]

Searching out glacial deposits, Jeff and Varina "reasoned and wondered over" them—probably because of the controversy that had sprung up between geology and religion. (Varina once spoke of a time as long "as the Geologists say God's six days were.") The scientist Bache saw no conflict. There were merely new ideas about "the law which ministers the will of Him who made all things and us": "Who would be so indiscreet as to hinge his religious faith upon changeable, progressive science?" By day, Jeff would hike around with Maggie on his shoulder, or he would listen to Bache, who explained his methods as he worked. At night, he would read aloud to them, and they could perhaps see the "splendid comet that flaunted across the sky that summer." Jeff was supremely happy in this secluded place where "the fall of a leaf could be plainly heard." His health and sight improved every day—compensation, as it were, for his long support of Bache in the Senate and in the squabble over control of a New York observatory.[52]

By the time they reached Boston again on October 7, Jeff was well enough to plan a major speech, but Jeff Jr. was "dangerously ill" with "membranous croup." Many ladies called at the hotel to offer sympathy and help. After he began to mend, "the happiest hours I spent in Boston," Varina says, were in the library of Sen. Edward Everett (whose Washington mansion the Davises had earlier leased). She loved "looking over the editions de luxe in which it abounded, and hearing him talk about his travels." Everett had been the first American to receive a doctorate at Goettingen University (1817) and the first Eliot Professor of Greek at Harvard College, as well as minister to Great Britain. As president of the American Association for the Advancement of Science, he had heartily endorsed Bache's handling of the coast survey. Among the Davis well-wishers in Boston were other political elite, like Robert Winthrop and Col. Charles Greene of the *Boston Post,* who gave a reception.[53]

It was the erudite Caleb Cushing who introduced Davis when the Democrats of Boston packed their huge, storied Faneuil Hall to hear him on October 11. Cushing compared "General Davis," as reporters called him, to leaders of ancient Athens or Rome, combining "the highest military and civic qualities in the same person." He even claimed, to "tremendous applause," that Davis's famous formation at Buena Vista had "set the example" for the "two diverging lines" used by Sir Colin Campbell to meet a Russian cavalry charge at Sevastopol.

Davis, addressing a Northern audience uninfected by the bitterness prevalent in the Senate, pulled out the stops. He sounded love for the Union, hope that the people and the Democratic Party would save it, and favorite themes: everything from the "spirit of fraternity in which the Union began" to the protection of property, one end for which government was instituted. Some "with Pharisaical pretension" feel a "moral obligation" to destroy the slave property of the South: "I suppose . . . some sort of vicarious repentance for other men's sins." "How do they decide that it is a sin?" It was "the only agency through which Christianity has reached that inferior race."[54] (Social and political equality was not yet broached, even by most antislavery men.)[55] "Not one particle of good has been done to any man, of any color, by this agitation," he said, only evil. Its end was "the destruction of that Union on which our hopes of future greatness depend."[56]

Common interest bound people north and south together, said Davis, as the Constitution bound the states. There was no question of coercion. "Will anyone ask me, then, how a State is to be held to the fulfilment of its obligations? My answer is, by its honor." The tie was "the more sacred" precisely because "there is no power to enforce it." To swear to uphold the Constitution and retain "a mental reservation [to] war upon the institutions . . . of the States . . . is a crime too low to characterize as it deserves. . . . It is one . . . which a man with self-respect would never commit."

There was no need to name names. Boston's Charles Sumner had boasted on the Senate floor of just such a reservation—elected, said Stephen Douglas, "with a pledge to perjure himself." Douglas reminded the Senate that, when asked whether, if they repealed the Fugitive Slave Law as he wanted, he would honor the constitutional obligation to return runaways, Sumner had replied, "Is thy servant a dog that he should do this thing?" "A dog—to do what you swore you would do?" said Douglas; "A dog—to be true to the Constitution of your country?"[57]

Sumner's excuse was: "I swore to support the constitution *as I understood it.*" But this "wars upon every principle of Government," said Davis. He pointed out in 1860 that the tempter in the Garden of Eden "was the first teacher of that 'higher law' which sets the will of the individual above the solemn rule which he is bound . . . to observe." The "written Constitution"—"a fixed standard"—was one of America's "blessings." To let this go "involves both politics and morals in one ruinous confusion." To "construe the Constitution" subjectively, "I do not believe . . . is the path of safety; I am sure it is not the way of honor."[58]

Another Sumner theme (echoing Seward), the "incompatibility" of North and South because of "different systems of labor," Davis called elsewhere "palpably absurd" and, if pursued, "suicidal." At Faneuil Hall, Davis had just seen a petition saying that the Union had been tried long enough and that it was time to "get rid of those sections in which the curse of slavery existed." He wondered how these "criminal hearts" could come into that hall where voices of founding fathers had sounded and not fear that the sabres in their portraits "would leap from their scabbards to drive from this sacred temple those who desecrate it as did the money-changers who sold doves in the temple of the living God." This was fine rhetoric, but it did nothing to reverse the Republican control of Massachusetts, or, increasingly, of Congress. And Davis's clasp of the Union, though much admired outside, roused mutterings in the South.[59]

Before the Davises left Boston for Washington, Col. Samuel Cooper joined them. Colonel Hardee, who had named the summer encampment at West Point for Davis, invited the family to visit his home—"nothing could give me greater happiness . . . abundant room for your children, nurses etc." His own children were with him.[60] Apparently they did go. In New York City, Davis addressed another large Democratic rally, to repeated cheers and applause, even when he said: "This higher-law doctrine, it strikes me, is the most convenient one I ever heard of for the criminal." What security was there if every base man could find "in his own heart a higher law than . . . society, the Constitution and the Bible?" The "preachers" of it "should be tarred and feathered, and whipped" under a different "higher" law, which brought justice to "those who would otherwise escape" it—"called in good old revolutionary times, Lynch Law." If the Constitution of "our fathers" were not meticulously observed, "what do we see?" "A picture so black that if I could unveil it, I would not"—it would be "revolting to your patriotic hearts."[61]

When Davis went on alone to Mississippi "after the first frost," he found himself on the defensive. A newspaper that wanted a "Southern Union" said, "the Jefferson Davis that we loved to honor is no more"—with "such slavish sentiments," he could go to Boston and "stay there."[62] To the legislature on November 11 he justified himself. It would have been "inconsistent with the character of a gentleman" to assail people who had been hospitable, "and it was not in my nature to feel otherwise than grateful." He would not apologize for seeking "to allay sectional excitement, to cultivate sounder opinions [about the South] and a more fraternal feeling." If it aroused malice in some, "I have no reproaches for them, but cheerfully bear the burden [of] zeal in the cause to which my political life has been devoted, and in imitation of Job, would bless the State Rights Democracy of Mississippi, even if the object of its vengeance: 'Though he slay me, yet will I trust in him.' " But he wanted to correct "misrepresentation and calumny." He had never advocated disunion "except as the last alternative" and never approved Douglas's " 'squatter sovereignty' heresies." The Supreme Court had confirmed his position by the Dred Scott decision: the Constitution did guarantee protection in the territories. With anti-Southern forces about to gain control of the House, Davis made it clear that

> if an Abolitionist be chosen President of the United States, you will have presented to you the question of whether you will permit the government to pass into the hands of your avowed and implacable enemies . . . such a result would be a species of revolution by which the purposes of the Government would be destroyed and the . . . mere forms entitled to no respect. . . . Mississippi's patriotism will hold her to the Union as long as it is constitutional. . . . But if a disrespect for that instrument, a fanatical disregard of its purposes, should ever induce a majority . . . to seek by amending the Constitution, to pervert it from its original object, and to deprive you of . . . equality . . . I say let the star of Mississippi be snatched from the constellation to shine by its inherent light, if it must be so, through all the storms and clouds of war.[63]

(Both Seward and James A. Garfield also used the word *revolution* for the rise of the Republican Party; Karl Marx, then writing for the *New York Daily Tribune,* saw revolution in its aims, and the South's reaction as counterrevolution.) Davis reiterated that, like Calhoun, he regarded "the disruption of the Union as a great though not the greatest calamity": it was "the last remedy." Now he would go back to the duties of his "high trust," and should Providence "not permit me to return again, my last prayer will be for . . . Mississippi."[64]

In those duties, Davis "was a born leader," said E. V. Murphy, a Senate stenographer. He "spoke rapidly and forcibly . . . thoroughly in earnest" and "would always take the unpopular side" when "he believed he was right." The *New York World* admired "the purity of his style" and the "profundity of his learning":

> Tall, spare, ascetic, with a melancholy cast of countenance, . . . attired with the utmost care in the least obtrusive of colors, [he] was the most senatorial of them all. . . . His voice was low, clear and firm, he had all the grace of oratory without any of the tawdry clap-trap of the stump. He never stormed in debate, no matter how angry the sea around him; he was always cool, self-contained, a master of himself and of his subject.[65]

Always? Sen. James Hammond, one of the South Carolina hotheads who despised Davis as too moderate, thought him "the most irascible man I ever saw. Quick tempered, arbitrary, overbearing, he is lost when excited and he is easily excited." Kennedy of Maryland said he was "scrupulously polite to everybody, ordinarily, but cross and petulant when his health was bad." His replies were calm and quiet, however, when a senator broke into a speech of his several times. The other then apologized, and Davis said, "I do not feel in the least aggrieved. I was suffering at the time, and therefore was averse to any interruptions."[66]

Stenographer Murphy admitted "his quick, nervous temperament made him easily nettled," but he noted something others leave out, something the Benjamin fracas showed: after "a sharp retort," Davis "would apologize for it the next moment." After a run-in with Sen. J. P. Hale (against whom even Varina thought him "a little too violent"), he hastily wrote: "If I am unecessarily sensitive to reflection, I trust it is accompanied by an equal unwillingness to wound the feelings of another, and I wish to assure you of my regret at . . . harsh language towards you to-day." "He stood high in the estimation of senators on both sides of the chamber," said Murphy. An opponent noticed that his desk was "a rendezvous" for men of both parties because of "the delights of his conversation." To Northerner James Campbell, Davis was "in many respects one of the most lovable men whom I have ever seen"— "I may say, to know him was to love him."[67]

After his illness of 1858, Davis's manner became only more patient and conciliatory. He had already made his basic points in the Senate; there was nothing to do now except apply the same principles over and over again, with increasing despair, to new questions. He wrote to Frank Pierce from his Senate desk as someone read "a speech need I say on what, do we ever speak of any thing but that over which we have no control, slavery of the negro. The prospect for our country is not less gloomy than when you left . . . I will stand by the flag and uphold the constitution whilst there is possibility of effecting any thing . . . beyond that my duty binds me to Mississippi & her fortunes as she may shape them. I hope on for the kind providence that has preserved us heretofore."[68]

One new, though old, question was Cuba. Davis had hoped Pierce would buy it, but his try had failed; then the Senate had refused the money to Buchanan. Davis wanted Cuba, not only to increase slave-holding territory, but also to stop the international slave trade centered there, to prevent the island's seizure from Spain by a third power, to protect American shipping, and to replace tyranny with democracy. But he was against acquiring it by filibustering, to the disgust of some of his constituents.[69] That old would-be filibuster, John A. Quitman (rather ironically, since Pierce had ruined his last Cuban plans), was eulogized by Jeff Davis on January 5, 1859.

General Quitman had died at Monmouth, his Natchez mansion, having never really recovered from the National Hotel disease (probably caused by contaminated water) contracted at the time of Buchanan's inauguration. He had kept at his post in the House from a strong sense of duty. "Duty!" Davis proclaimed, "the first prerequisite of those who hold official trusts." Quitman had fallen "a victim to it; sadly impressing us with the fact that—'The paths of glory lead but to the grave.' . . . life's fitful fever was ended . . . He died leaving behind him that good name without which 'glory is but a tavern song.' "[70]

Events soon matched the mournful tone. On March 28, Davis was writing to Ma from Brierfield:

> The river here is high and rising rapidly . . . the excessive rains and transpiration water [through levees] have injured our prospect for a crop, and greatly embarrass us by destroying the pasturage. . . .
>
> My general health has improved. The eye of which the sight was almost lost has slowly recovered and hopes are entertained that by quiet and proper treatment during the approaching summer the sight may be restored so as to make it again useful for looking in two directions.

This was his quiet way of announcing the most disastrous flood on the Mississippi River in thirty years. His left eye was closed, a Vicksburg friend noted, saying he looked "very thin." Davis had continued weak after the New England trip, having to refuse invitations and to stop speaking several times in the Senate but still working usually till one o'clock in the morning.[71]

On the steamboat coming down, he was unable to make the speech requested of him. But Jeff was soon telling Pa, "My own health remains as good as usual, though I . . . can but feel the depressing circumstances by which we are surrounded." He wrote to Dr. Cartwright, never mentioning himself but discussing "defective principles in the construction of levees," and the health of a slave girl, Julia Ann, whom he was sending for treatment, via the Howells.[72] But Varina thought his letters showed he was more "distressed and broken down" than she had ever known him, and with reason: "We have lost *every thing.* Jeff gets into a boat at our steps at Brierfield and goes up all the way . . . through Sister Eliza's garden to the Hurricane back steps." Her own garden, the orchard, and the cotton crop were drowned. Joseph Davis hired a steamboat to take some four hundred cattle and five hundred sheep from Davis Bend to high ground at Grand Gulf.[73]

On April 24, Jeff told Pa the water was running "with strong current across the main ridge." He had sent off the rest of the stock and was "hastening to leave for Washington, as soon as due provision has been made for the negroes who I am unwilling to send away." "I accept thankfully your congratulations but my anxiety for Varina is so uncontrollable that the intelligence has caused me depression rather than joy." The Davises' fourth child, a boy, had been born April 18, and Varina was quite ill. It was May before Jeff could get away, and then Varina's condition—she spoke of "heart trouble"—kept him at their Washington home for several weeks. In June, he underwent an operation (perhaps two) on his diseased left eye.[74] They kept hoping to go to "some cool and healthy retreat," but Varina was "still too feeble to travel." Finally they made it to Oakland, Maryland, where the family spent the rest of the summer "near the crest of the blue ridge."[75]

Davis had to go back to Mississippi at the end of June to see about Brierfield and address a Democratic convention. Evidently he took Jeffy D., who had run away from school the year before, back to his parents. Ma reported in July that he was "gradually becoming tame" after she punished his "first act of disobedience." "He only wanted to be managed," she said pointedly.[76] Ma knew Davis's soft heart. Although hard on himself, and on soldiers, Davis was never able to discipline his children. He had written her how cute little Maggie was, getting people to unlock the gate for her and running to a neighbor's house "until a hue and cry detects her hiding place." Maggie's classic remark was: "I wish I could see my father, he would let me be bad." If Varina sent children from the table for misconduct, "he called them to kiss him before they went." He once sent Jeffy D. back to Varina without punishing him for truancy: "Brother Jeff knows how a man feels," said the boy.[77]

Ma reported that son Billy was happily married to Minnie Leacock, and daughter Jennie had been confirmed by Bishop Polk, "a great friend of mine." "He often talks of you with much affection . . . he is reading Cumming by my persuasion." This apocalyptic writer had convinced Ma that the end of time was near. She wanted Varina and Jeff, "my dear son, as dear to me as any child I have," to read "these books," so "we all may be found with our lamps trimmed and our wedding garments on—Oh Jeff dont say Ma is certainly crazy—." To prove she was not, she sent a collar she had made for Maggie, and was sending back Julia Ann, with directions for dressing her leg from Dr. Cartwright (who she also had reading Cumming).[78]

"The baby is a very fine one," Dr. Wood had pronounced. "The little fellow is a pretty boy—very Davis," Varina informed Ma, "enough like his Uncle Joe to be his child, small build, grey eyes, large nose, and black hair." This was appropriate enough, as he was to be named Joseph. But that fact was torture to Varina, who had wanted "to name it after my dear Father, and that it should be like him." She prayed the baby would "grow out of the resemblance," or that it would be "external only, unless

Howell & Kempe blood has run out." When Jeff had told her about the name, "I cried myself sick and had to take quinine." "Of course he had a perfect right" to name him that, but she could never willingly pay "the highest compliment in a woman's power" to a man whose name suggested only "injustice and unkindness." "I come so near hating him that I should hate mightily to be as near the edge of a precipice, for I am afraid I shall fall off." But Varina was a mercurial person, and her love for Jeff was stronger than anything else. By July, with him in Mississippi at the sickly season, she wrote: "May God keep you safe, my only love . . . so frightened when I think of your danger I am hardly coherent. . . . My little Joe seems blessed to me, and all the sweetness of our happiest hours seems to have returned with his birth."[79]

Both Varina and Joseph, who was leaving for Europe, warned Jeff to stay out of the sun and the night air, but he fell sick on the way home. His eye was again involved; his ophthalmologist had to come from Washington to treat him. From Oakland in September, Davis addressed "My dear friend" Pierce, back from Europe. "I . . . have been seriously ill, though now free of disease my strength has not been restored and there is therefore constant apprehension of a relapse."[80] "Frequent, though slight illness" dogged him as the family went back to the capital. Varina had to write for him in October. He went to Mississippi "without my health being entirely reestablished" and labored hard for the party and the plantation until Congress convened on December 5. It is small wonder that he never fully recovered his strength.[81]

In January of 1860, some new spectacles helped, but Davis had to have eye surgery again on March 31. The sight in his left eye was simply lost, never to be recovered. He could distinguish light from dark, nothing more. The eye was not disfigured, but it seemed to have a film over it.[82] He could no longer go out at night, but his heart was increasingly in his home anyway. Infirm through spring and summer, he worked just as usual. Sometimes he would have to stop short in a speech, or get Louis Wigfall or James Chesnut to read aloud material he wanted to insert.[83]

Clement Clay, who sat next to him, had read for him earlier. In debate, Davis was mildness itself compared to Clay, who once called Charles Sumner "a sneaking, sinuous, snakelike poltroon." Not since John Randolph, people said, had the Senate known such withering invective, such contemptuous fury, even to "the scornful shake of the finger." Clay did not spare his friends. When Davis's new son, Joseph Evan (middle name for his great grandfather), was christened in January 1860, Clay stood as godfather, but he had not failed to tell the proud parent that he hoped Joe would be an improvement over Jeff Jr. "in *manners & temper.*"[84]

Varina *would* pass over little Jeff's most obstreperous conduct with: "I do know [he] is the best child on earth, and naturally the most upright loving little heart." She admitted he was "heedless" and "provoking" but "never impudent, and if I can lay my hands on him, minds me." After all, he was two years old. There is no doubt he was loving. He took one of his father's letters, "opened it, and began 'dear Daddy, I love ou too moch.' He kissed it at least a dozen times."[85] Big Jeff told Ma he was "the most manly affectionate little fellow I ever saw." He told Pa how much the boy resembled him, how Maggie was "the general favorite," but Joe was "the beauty." These children were his solace when, as he wrote Pierce, "at evening I go home to forget the past and postpone the future."[86]

Postponing the future was really what Davis tried to do for the next year. He could see what was coming. It was foreshadowed in 1859 when John Brown, having roamed at large for three years, found financial backing from prominent Northern men known as the "Secret Six" and seized the United States arsenal at Harpers Ferry, Virginia, on October 16. He intended to lead slaves in an armed uprising, but, as Davis was to point out, their "only rebellion . . . was against the incendiaries . . . from whom they escaped to . . . their masters." Local militia and United States marines under Col. Robert E. Lee (in Virginia on leave) soon took both arsenal and raiders in custody. People were killed on both sides. Brown was tried in a Virginia court and died "a felon's death" on December 2. To those who hated the South, he died a "martyr." He had made treason "holy," said a Massachusetts preacher. Henry David Thoreau called Brown "a crucified hero."[87]

New England conservatives like Everett and Cushing had met at Faneuil Hall to disavow any connection with Brown. It was rumored that not only the Secret Six, but also United States senators had given him money. Davis was one of the select committee that met from December through June to investigate this. Seward, among others, proved to be guilty; but the senators all claimed ignorance of Brown's plans, and so were excused. Brown's raid excited the South. A Virginia lawyer, George Wythe Randolph, organized the Richmond Howitzers, to defend the city. A North Carolina Unionist said "the Harper's Ferry outrage" made him ready to embrace secession with "every possible evil . . . rather than submit any longer to Northern insolence."[88]

Jeff Davis's patience was stronger than that. He fought against breakup of the country as long as he could. But there was an irreducible minimum of protection that the minority section expected from the compact of Union, and Davis formulated this for the Senate in seven resolutions in February 1860 (revised on March 1). They won approval from Democrats, North and South, and passed the Senate in May. All they asked was what Davis had been asking for fifteen years: adherence to the Constitution, without which, the Union was nothing. He saw a "great battle" at hand "between the defenders of the constitutional government and the votaries of mob rule, fanaticism and anarchy."[89] His resolutions rested firmly on the Dred Scott decision: the Missouri

Compromise was unconstitutional; slaveholders could not be denied access to any territory. As he had pointed out, "The care of our fathers for the rights of minorities" had provided the Supreme Court as an "umpire . . . removed from the influence of public excitement." Everyone had agreed to accept its rulings. But when this one favored the South, the abolitionists, who more and more controlled the Republican Party, simply refused to obey it, just as they did the Constitution where it displeased them.[90]

For them, being antislavery was the test, not only of politics, but of right and wrong—the creed, in effect, of a new religion. If you believed in the evil of slavery, it mattered not what else you believed.[91] The Christian church had always tolerated every opinion on slavery. St. John Chrysostom, a church father who lived with it, called freedom and slavery neutral: only good or bad by "the use men make of them."[92] By 1837, the New England Anti-Slavery Society was asking members to secede from their church if it did not cast out slaveholders. The new morality, subjective, relative, rational, where the old was objective, stable, and revealed, was part of a groundswell that had long been rising against traditional religion, with its supernatural mysteries of Incarnation and Redemption. It rose from far-off tempests—eighteenth-century rationalism by which man, good by nature, could achieve heaven on earth, and Arianism out of the fourth century, enabling the chief abolitionists, Quakers and Unitarians (and liberal Protestants) to regard Christ as a man only, not God. This was humanitarianism in its primary meaning (only later did it mean the cult of humanity).[93]

Since Christianity did not condemn slavery, abolitionists tended to hold God unjust and the Bible "a fable." As Bishop William Meade of Virginia wrote Davis, they "abjured the Bible rather than give up their anti-slavery system."[94] Traditional churchmen who opposed slavery had to reason from general precepts like the Golden Rule or the assumption that Christianity was egalitarian. Northern Protestant churches began to resemble secular society and to see sin as political and social. When President Buchanan called for a day of prayer for personal repentance, he was denounced at the North because he did not mention slavery. The main scripture of the new religion was the Declaration of Independence, rooted in a Deism that rejected Christianity. All this may explain why another Episcopal bishop called abolitionism "that hateful and infidel pestilence."[95]

Davis and the others were fighting not just a political but an ideological battle. The turnabout in religion was made plain by Joshua R. Giddings of Ohio in the House of Representatives in 1856: those who opposed slavery were "religious" and those who did not were "infidel." The "religious truths [of] Jefferson" in the Declaration were "God's higher law," and the Republican Party had made them "the basis of its political action"—"a reformation more deep, more radical" than that of the sixteenth century. "The natural, Heaven-endowed rights of man" would produce happiness, "the ultimate object of human existence."[96] Laurence M. Keitt of South Carolina rebuked in the House this "horrid idol of northern contrivance," this "baleful spirit" that sought to correct "all the unseemly errors of the inconvenient law of God." These "willful falsifiers" repudiated Christ himself, who, with every occasion to do so, never even "hinted" that slavery violated "His Divine precepts." St. Paul told slaves to "honor" their masters. In the face of "words so plainly put together," the fact that slavery was neither sin nor abomination was "inconcussible." The "prostitution of religion to political and secular ends" showed contempt for Christ's words, especially, "My kingdom is not of this world."[97]

Giddings's "reformation," in trying to make abolition part of Christian doctrine, had already produced new denominations: the Methodist Episcopal Church, South, and Southern Baptist Convention in 1845, and the Christian Church in 1854. Presbyterians teetered precariously; Roman Catholics, free to believe as they liked on "polity and social order," never divided; Episcopalians and Lutherans did not until the schism split the country itself.[98]

The new religion explains how the Unitarian preacher Theodore Parker could call John Brown "a SAINT" and Charles Sumner ("vaguely Unitarian") could say he resembled an "early Christian martyr." Many new devotees denied God outright, but some, like Sumner, imagined Him after their own image and then claimed to be his agents. John Brown had. He came, as Mary Chesnut said, to "cut our throats in God's name."[99] The Secret Six backing Brown embraced Unitarianism or Transcendentalism (its pantheistic offshoot) or started their own private churches.[100]

Sumner enunciated the new faith as he harangued the Senate for four hours on June 4, 1860, in delayed revenge for his caning by Preston Brooks. He entitled this speech "The Barbarism of Slavery." With the freedom of thought he exemplified, he reversed language itself. Davis saw "the African captive" saved "from Sacrifice" through slavery and brought out of a barbaric society into a civilized one; Sumner said that slavery made Southern society itself "barbarous" and Southerners "Barbarians." Although well read in history, he ignored the slave-based civilizations of the ancient world and said that the South could not be civilized because slavery steeped it in evil, making any good impossible. Here was the new religion: slavery the criterion of wrong, evil not in personal disobedience to divine law but in society, and temporal well-being, not eternal salvation, the goal of life. Charles Frances Adams said Sumner raged "like a crazy man," when Seward suggested compromising with the evil South in the crisis confronting the nation.[101]

Jefferson Davis had long since seen this humanitarian religion used to justify "half the crimes defined by the Decalogue"—the Ten Commandments which he heard at every Communion service. He still thought the "patriotism and the sound sense of the people," if only they knew the truth, might overcome a "crusade" that was really "but a thirst for political dominion." On May 8, 1860, he told his fellow senators that in John Brown's raid, the slavery agitation of forty years had "reached the point of revolution and civil war." It was time "to ask seriously, solemnly, looking each other . . . in the face, what we should do to save our country." It would be a "sad fate . . . for this most minute cause, to destroy our Government."[102]

The Democrats had convened in Charleston in April. Davis had wanted them to nominate for president not Stephen A. Douglas, but Franklin Pierce. Pierce had wanted *him:* "Our people are looking for . . . one who is raised by all the elements of his character above the atmosphere ordinarily breathed by politicians." William Yancey said, "Davis was the favorite name with us."[103] Davis had been nominated in the Mississippi convention, but did not accept. Varina says he could have been president, if "recreant" to his political beliefs. Clement Clay, however, was "quite sure that Mr. Davis neither expected nor desired the nomination."[104]

Fearing trouble over the platform, Davis had wanted the Democrats to name their candidate first. Douglas men forced the vote in reverse order. They won approval of the minority platform report, backing squatter sovereignty, in place of the majority one, based on Davis's resolutions and Yancey's similar Alabama platform. When that happened, LeRoy Pope Walker led the Alabama delegates out of the hall, followed by those from Mississippi, Louisiana, South Carolina, Florida, Texas, and Arkansas (except two men). The rump convention took fifty-seven ballots, with Everett, Winthrop, and Benjamin F. Butler voting for Davis every time, but no one ever got the necessary two-thirds, and it adjourned.[105] In June, Davis deplored all this to Pierce, but "the darkest hour precedes the dawn and it may be that light will break upon us when most needed & least expected." He knew Southerners would not vote for "squatter sovereignty," and if the North insisted on Douglas, "we must be beaten." He was trying "to save our party from disintegration as the last hope of averting ruin from the country. . . . If our little grog drinking, electioneering Demagogue can destroy our hopes, it must be that we have been doomed to destruction."[106]

The convention reassembled in Baltimore on June 18, and now a complete split took place. Northern and border delegates joined Southern ones in another walkout, named themselves National or Constitutional Democrats, and nominated Breckinridge on the original majority platform. The rump convention nominated Douglas. Already the new Constitutional Union Party—largely Know-Nothing and Whig remnants —had nominated John Bell and Edward Everett, on a vaguely state rights platform with no slavery plank at all. Then Davis tried to get all three men to resign and everyone to settle on a compromise candidate—which he would never have done, Clay pointed out, had he himself been considered. Bell and Breckinridge were willing, but Douglas refused. Breckinridge told Varina, "I trust I have the courage to lead a forlorn hope."[107]

The Republican Party, named by Wendell Phillips "a party of the North, pledged against the South," rejected Seward in favor of a dark horse, Abraham Lincoln. Campaigning hard for Breckinridge, Davis called Lincoln "the 'rail-splitter,' aptly selected . . . for the accursed performance of rending the Union." Democrats quoted Davis; Republicans quoted Sumner's "Barbarism of Slavery." Lincoln was elected.[108]

Spokesmen for the Deep South states had said all along that this automatically meant the end of the Union. But Davis still tried to prevent Northern aggression by a solid front. He advised South Carolina, through Robert Barnwell Rhett, Jr., and "every Southern State . . . by telegrams and letters" to wait, to act in conjunction, not separately. He was called from home to advise Buchanan on his last State of the Union message, but it disappointed him, one of its results being the creation of compromise committees by Congress.[109]

The Senate one was called the Committee of Thirteen, and at first Davis refused to serve on it. He felt that "an appeal to the fraternity or moderation of the anti slavery party" was useless. The House committee did fail. On December 14, Davis joined in signing a letter "To Our Constituents," saying argument was "exhausted"; Republicans would "grant nothing"; the only recourse was "a Southern confederacy." He was finally persuaded to serve, along with Seward and Toombs, on the Committee of Thirteen, "the record of which shows," he said later, "who it was who opposed every effort at accom[m]odation."[110] Sidney Johnston, a staunch Unionist, saw even from afar "the persistent obstinacy of the Republican party, in refusing to concede anything whatever for the sake of the Union." Lincoln, president-elect, ordered Seward not to compromise on slavery extension, and so "spelled doom for the Committee of Thirteen."[111]

Davis had told Rhett that if his state did decide to go alone, she should do it before "the govt. has passed into hostile hands." On December 20, 1860, South Carolina passed her Ordinance of Secession. Davis met with Buchanan over and over about the crisis, until forced to conclude that "he has forfeited any claim" to Southern support: "I regard his treatment of So. Ca. as perfidious." (Davis was careful to say that the president's "evil deeds" came not from "a wicked purpose," but from fear of northern reprisal.)[112] Despite his promises not to reinforce the federal garrison at Fort Sumter, Buchanan sent troops and ammunition steaming toward the Charleston harbor, disguised in a merchant vessel. This *Star of the West* was fired upon by the South Carolinians and turned back, on January 9, 1861—the opening shot of the war, not recognized as such because not returned. Immediately, Davis went to Buchanan and tried to get him "to adopt a line of action" with "the best prospect for a peaceful solution."[113]

On that very day, Mississippi voted to resume its status as an independent sovereign state. By now, Davis believed this a necessity, as he had always believed it a right ("There was a time when none denied it"), but he felt no elation. He worked openly with others to form a Confederacy quickly, hoping to prevent attack, but there was no "conspiracy": "I did nothing secretly."[114] He had "the hard task" of telling Franklin Pierce that he was leaving "the United States, for the independence and Union of which my Father bled and in the service of which I have sought to emulate [him]." The constitutional Union no longer existed; the flag that, as he said publicly, had quickened his heart in battle, that he might have "claimed as my winding sheet," was now not his. He was severed from close friends and some family. What weighed him down most was the conviction that Southern states would never be allowed to go in peace. He told Pierce, "Civil war has only horror for me."[115]

Davis waited for official word before telling the Senate on January 21 that his occupation was gone. Florida and Alabama had also declared independence, and their senators were to speak farewells on the same day. Hearing a rumor that they would be charged with treason, Davis hoped "that he might be the person arrested," says Varina, wanting to test secession in the courts. But no one was. Although Davis's dyspepsia and neuralgia were so bad that his doctor thought he would not be able to speak, he did. The night before, he and Varina sat sleepless: "we felt blood in the air."

Next morning, Davis picked his way between hoopskirts crowding the Senate floor; spectators had come in droves. Varina wondered whether the dense crowd could see "beyond the cold exterior of the orator—his deep depression, his desire for reconciliation." "Graceful, grave, and deliberate," he delivered a spare but moving speech; within "the music of his voice," she says, were "unshed tears."[116]

He explained first how secession was the opposite of nullification; the United States could not use execution of the laws as an excuse for "coercion"; Mississippi was as separate now as a foreign country. She had resumed the powers granted to her "agent," because she was under attack. He sent a parting shot at "created equal" in the Declaration of Independence, showing with careful logic that it referred only to "the men of the political community" and meant "there was no divine right to rule" and no aristocracy in America. It had "no reference to the slave; else how happened it that" the same document arraigned George III for trying "to do just what the North has been endeavoring of late to do, to stir up insurrection among our slaves?" How could this be one of the "high crimes" that justified separation from England, if "the negroes were free and equal"? They were not so in the Constitution; it allowed them only three-fifths representation in Congress. "So stands the compact." "When you deny . . . the principles upon which our Government was founded . . . we but tread in the path of our fathers when we proclaim our independence and take the hazard."

The advantages of union were "known to be great." Mississippi gave them up, not to injure anyone or for "pecuniary benefit," but "from the high and solemn motive" of passing inherited rights "unshorn to our children." She wished for peace, but if other states wanted war, then "putting our trust in God and in our firm hearts and strong arms, we will vindicate the right as best we may."

For himself, "I am sure there is not one of you, whatever sharp discussion there may have been between us, to whom I can not now say, in the presence of my God, I wish you well." "Whatever of offense there has been to me, I leave here" and "offer you my apology for any pain which, in the heat of discussion, I have inflicted." Thus "making the only reparation in my power for any injury offered . . . it only remains for me to bid you a final adieu."

If Davis's tears were unshed, those of his audience were not: "there was scarcely a dry eye." The calm and conservative speech had such a "wonderful effect" that it caused the Virginia senators to decide on Davis as the proper man for a Southern president. It caused him, however, another sleepless night, in which Varina heard him over and over praying for peace and saying, "May God have us in His holy keeping."[117]

Sarah Knox Taylor Davis, first wife of Jefferson Davis. Courtesy Louisiana State Museum.

Jefferson and Varina Banks Howell Davis, about 1845. This is the earliest known picture of him, and he wears the 1835 "wedding vest" now at Beauvoir. From Francis Miller, *Photographic History of the Civil War,* 1912. Courtesy Auburn University Libraries.

Brierfield, built 1848–1849, second home on Jefferson Davis's plantation, Davis Bend, Warren County, Mississippi. Courtesy Old Courthouse Museum Collection, Vicksburg, Mississippi.

Rosemont, the Davis family home, as it appeared in 1904, when the Henry Johnson family lived there. Courtesy Percival T. Beacroft, Jr., Rosemont Plantation, Woodville, Mississippi.

Eliza van Bethuysen Davis, wife of Joseph E. Davis, portrait by unknown artist, at Rosemont. Courtesy Percival T. Beacroft, Jr., Davis Family Collection, Rosemont Plantation, Woodville, Mississippi.

Garden Cottage, or Library, on the Hurricane, Joseph E. Davis's plantation, Davis Bend, Warren County, Mississippi, undated. The people are probably indigents kept there by U.S. government after 1863, but they may be Davis slaves. Courtesy Old Courthouse Museum Collection, Vicksbury, Mississippi.

Joseph Emory Davis, portrait by William E. West, c. 1818, now at Rosemont. Courtesy Percival T. Beacroft, Jr., Davis Family Collection, Rosemont Plantation, Woodville, Mississippi.

Colonel ("General") Jeff Davis (center), age forty-one, watercolor on ivory miniature painted just after Mexican War by G. L. Saunders. Courtesy National Portrait Gallery, Smithsonian Institution.

(Clockwise from top right)

Leonidas Polk, West Point 1827, in his thirties. From William M. Polk, *Leonidas Polk, Bishop and General.*

Theophilus H. Holmes, C.S.A., West Point 1829. Courtesy Library of Congress, image LC-B816-2628.

William Selby Harney, U.S. Army 1818–1863, close friend of Davis's in First Infantry. Courtesy Library of Congress, image LC-B813-1323.

Alexander Dallas Bache, West Point 1825, late in life, a famous physicist. Photograph by Mathew Brady. Courtesy National Portrait Gallery, Smithsonian Institution.

Lucius Bellinger Northrop, West Point 1831, good friend of Davis's in First Dragoons. From Ezra J. Warner, *Generals in Gray.*

Robert E. Lee, West Point 1829, age thirty-one, detail of portrait by William E. West, 1838. Courtesy U.S. Army Military History Institute.

Thomas F. Drayton, C.S.A., West Point 1828. Courtesy Library of Congress, image LC-B8184-10642.

Albert Sidney Johnston, West Point 1826, Davis's best friend, engraving of bust by Edward V. Valentine. From Jefferson Davis, *The Rise and Fall of the Confederate Government.*

The Briars, Varina Howell's Natchez home, still standing, where she married Jeff Davis in 1845. Courtesy Museum of the Confederacy, Richmond, Virginia.

Margaret Graham Howell, later de Wechmar Stoess (1842–1930), Varina's younger sister. Courtesy Museum of the Confederacy, Richmond, Virginia.

Jefferson Davis (Jeffy D.) Howell (1846–1875), Varina's youngest brother, treated as son by Jeff Davis. From Varina Davis, *Jefferson Davis . . . A Memoir.*

Lt. Becket Howell, C.S. Marine Corps (1840–1882), Varina's younger brother (at far right), aboard CSS *Sumter* with Capt. Raphael Semmes (seated) and other officers, Gibraltar, 1862. Courtesy Museum of the Confederacy, Richmond, Virginia.

Bvt. Lt. Col. Braxton Bragg, U.S. Army, artillerist hero of Mexican War. Courtesy Library of Congress, image LC-USZ62-23254.

Zachary Taylor, major general in the Mexican War, U.S. president, 1849–1850, Davis's father-in-law and friend. Photograph by Mathew Brady. Courtesy National Archives.

Franklin Pierce, as brigadier general of volunteers, Mexican War; Davis's good friend for over thirty years; U.S. president 1853–1857. Courtesy New Hampshire Historical Society, image F4094.

Raising a column, 1860, for U.S. Capitol extension begun by Davis when secretary of war, 1853–1857; he is thought to be figure to right of column. Courtesy Library of Congress, image LC-USA7-5072.

Samuel Cooper (1798–1876), under Davis as adjutant general, U.S.A., and adjutant and inspector general, C.S.A. Courtesy National Archives.

Winfield Scott, a Davis antagonist from 1846 on, U.S. general-in-chief, 1861. Courtesy National Archives.

John Caldwell Calhoun, just as Varina described him. Photograph by Mathew Brady. Courtesy National Archives.

Howell Cobb, representative from Georgia, first in U.S., then in C.S., Congress. Courtesy Library of Congress, LC-BH832-1269 (cracked glass negative).

Henry Stuart Foote, Davis's political enemy throughout his career. Courtesy Mississippi Department of Archives and History.

XII

President

Jefferson Davis no more wanted to be president of the Confederate States of America now forming, than of the United States he was leaving. He already had what he wanted. On January 25, 1861, Gov. John J. Pettus commissioned him a major general and gave him command of the Army of Mississippi. "We both congratulated ourselves that he was to be in the field," says Varina. But others wanted him for president. An "experienced statesman, a man of the highest personal integrity, perfect courage, and absolute conviction, and an eloquent and attractive orator," wrote Basil Duke, Davis was at that time "the most prominent public man of the South, and generally esteemed the ablest." James Chesnut said, "He was regarded by nearly the whole South as the fittest man for the position. I certainly so regarded him."[1]

But Davis had seen enough of Pierce's troubles "behind the scenes" to make it "to me an office in no wise desirable. I thought myself better adapted to command in the field." His position as major general was now the one he "preferred to any other," and he tried to make himself secure by arranging (he does not say how) to have someone else elected, probably Howell Cobb. He did not feel himself "as well suited to the office as some others."[2] As he told a friend later, despite his years in politics, "I had no fondness for it and felt always a distaste for its belongings," whereas "a military training gave me some confidence in my ability to command troops." But it was Varina, not he, who said, "I thought his genius was military." She called "absurd" the "charge that Mr. Davis thought himself a military genius": "He was devoid of every kind of assumption." Neither was he "a party manager": "He did not know the arts of the politician, and would not practise them if understood." As if to confirm this, his attempt at wire-pulling failed.[3]

The Davises' return home with their three little children was like a triumphal progress. They could take the train the whole way now, but

Jeff was exhausted from having to address the crowd at every Southern stop. There was a threat of disorder at Chattanooga, in Unionist East Tennessee, but Varina heard "a rough man" say, "Jeff Davis ain't afraid. He will make his speech." And he did. In Jackson, Mississippi, General Davis began to organize his army and to order weapons—"We shall need . . . many more than we can get, I fear." Governor Pettus replied, "General, you overrate the risk."[4] Very few could believe Davis's predictions of war, though, fresh from the Senate, he was keenly aware of the Northern mood. He asked for three million dollars and got one hundred and fifty thousand. Still, he said of those spoiling for a fight, "God help us, war is a dreadful calamity even when it is made against aliens and strangers. They know not what they do." This was his temper always, expressed to Varina now and later: "Let us pray for that peace on earth and good-will to men that is needful for prosperity and happiness." As he stated long afterward, "The history of my public life bears evidence that I did all in my power to prevent the war."[5]

They went down to Brierfield finally, to prepare for his absence with the army, Davis telling one of the men: "You may have to defend your mistress and her children, and I feel I may trust you." Meanwhile, on February 4, delegates from the six seceded states—South Carolina, Mississippi, Alabama, Florida, Georgia, and Louisiana (Texas would not secede until March)—gathered at Montgomery, Alabama, to create a government. Howell Cobb was there, but he was made president only of the assembly that became the Provisional Congress.[6] Whatever the secret aspirations of Robert Barnwell Rhett and Robert Toombs, there was never any question that Davis was the choice.[7] In the Mississippi and Louisiana delegations, "No other man was spoken of"; "the claims of no one else were considered, or even alluded to." On February 9, 1861, Jefferson Davis was unanimously elected by the delegates as provisional president of the Confederate States of America.[8]

When a messenger brought the news, he found the general and his lady taking rose cuttings in the garden. From the look on her husband's face as he read the paper, Varina thought there had been a family tragedy. "After a few minutes' painful silence he told me, as a man might speak of a sentence of death." He spoke of the election to her later as "much more than I deserved and as you know far more of official honors than I desired."[9] But he had told Pierce, "Whatever circumstances demand shall be met as a duty," and "duty, not distinction," as someone said, was always his aim. He pointed out, in response to postwar slander about his election, "Had selfish considerations controlled my course, they would not have led me to sacrifice the results of a life's labor."[10] To another friend, he explained: "The trial was too great and the result too doubtful to justify one in declining any post to which he was assigned; therefore I accepted." It had become his rule of life by now to surrender his private wishes to a greater good. It caused John

Reagan to call him "the most devout Christian I ever knew, and the most self-sacrificing man." On February 12, Davis resigned his commission as "Major-General of the Army of Mississippi."[11]

Depressed, he set out alone for the provisional capital of the Confederacy. At least his office too was "provisional." He might be able to return to the army. His spirits picked up momentarily at the home of his old friend, Collin Tarpley, for the Tarpley children were there. Young Sue always found his coming "like sunshine to us all," his conversation "chaste and elegant." "He was a type of the Old South, bearing in his personality its culture and refinement. . . . To children he was lovely." He spent the day with the family, waiting for a train. "When the cannon boomed and the crowd gathered to escort him to the depot, Mr. Davis had a little boy on his knee trying to mend a broken toy." To Sue he gave his *carte de visite,* which she put with her jewels and later buried for safety. It was "my last day in private life," said Davis, "to-morrow I belong to the people."[12]

There were bonfires and enthusiastic crowds all along the rail trip north to Grand Junction, Tennessee, east to Chattanooga, down to Atlanta, then back southwest to Montgomery. Davis "insisted upon responding" to all. Yancey met him with an escort committee as he came into Alabama, and a few miles farther on, President Davis honored the Auburn Guards with his first military review.[13]

Yancey was the great orator of secession, a man of fine background and culture. Although "in no sense a demagogue," he had given up his congressional seat in 1846 in order to "fire the Southern heart" for separation, seeing that "destruction of slavery meant the destruction of society." Yet Davis had told the Senate correctly in 1860 that Yancey's "Southern League" was small, confined to Alabama, and no danger to the Union. The danger, rather, was in "consolidation" (centralization of power), which might "overwhelm the States."[14] Now Yancey's separate confederacy was real, but the laggard Davis, not he, was president. He had not even been a part of the convention. He was ready, like Davis, to deny himself for the Cause. When his friends had decided Davis was the best man, Yancey had cheerfully agreed. As the two arrived late at night in Montgomery, he warmly presented the president-elect to the people of his hometown with the ever-remembered words, "The man and the hour have met." "Bands played, drums beat, and cheers filled the air." Davis gave a brief, hoarse speech from the Exchange Hotel balcony, in which he warned that he might soon be returning to "the ranks as a soldier." Then he "shook hands with everyone present, not forgetting the children."[15]

It was well that he "valued fortitude . . . only a shade less than . . . honesty of purpose," for the courage he had proven on the field and in Congress was never more needed. His people had almost nothing but agriculture and their own courage to sustain them, and no one knew it better than he. As he told them in 1865, he embarked "on the cause with the full knowledge of the tremendous odds against us." "He not only acted without fear," said a contemporary, "but he had that fortitude of soul that bears the consequences of the course pursued without complaint." The wizened little man who stood beside him on February 18, Alexander Stephens, said it best: "I was not very friendly and in no ways chummy with Mr. Davis, but I wish to say he was the bravest and most courageous man I ever knew."[16]

They stood on the portico of the Alabama capitol between Corinthian columns, looking down the broad tree-lined avenue that stretched for half a mile to an artesian well and its basin.[17] Their open carriage had been drawn up the hill to a militia escort and the sound of a catchy minstrel tune, "Dixie," hastily arranged for the band. It was already spring in the Deep South and a fine day. On the table with a large Bible lay a "most beautiful wreath of Japonicas and hyacinths and small spring magnolias," made for the president by a matron that very morning, and "a large bunch of flowers for the Vice President." After the invocation by Dr. Basil Manly of the First Baptist church, and before the swearing-in on the Bible, held by Howell Cobb, President Davis gave his inaugural address.[18]

He spoke of his "difficult and responsible station," of the "toil and care and disappointment" that were "the price of official elevation," which "I neither sought nor desired." "I may disappoint your expectations. . . . You will see many errors to forgive, many deficiencies to tolerate; but you shall not find in me either a want of zeal or fidelity to the cause." He spoke of their constitution as a "judicial construction" of the old one. He spoke of "the rectitude of our conduct": "He who knows the hearts of men will judge." "We have entered upon the career of independence," and it must be inflexibly pursued." If "passion or the lust of dominion" should bring war, "the terrible responsibility would rest upon . . . the Government from which we have separated." "Reverently let us invoke the God of our fathers to guide and protect us. . . . With the continuance of His favor ever gratefully acknowledged, we may hopefully look forward to success, to peace, and to prosperity."[19]

"The inaugural pleased everybody," wrote Cobb's brother, who was not easy to please, and Davis's manner when taking the oath of office "was most impressive." Another eyewitness said that Davis, repeated "So help me God" in "a tone so loud and clear that he could have been heard by everyone present," then bent over and kissed the Bible. Howell Cobb handed him the floral wreath, "which he slipped on his arm." From the balconies and windows, ladies threw down "small bunches of flowers which the Pres. gathered and held in his hand." At the grand levee that night, he told the maker of the wreath how he wished he could take it "to his wife and children." Her husband asked if Davis remembered him. "He looked at him a moment and said 'Sampson Harris! Go on,

I can't talk to you now, come and see me and bring your wife.'" The remarkable Davis memory had recalled his face out of a scene where Harris lay near death four years before—the only time he had ever laid eyes on the man.[20]

It was two days before Davis had time to write Varina. "I was inaugurated on Monday. . . . The audience was large and brilliant. Upon my weary heart was showered smiles, plaudits, and flowers; but beyond them I saw troubles and thorns innumerable. We are without machinery, without means, and threatened by a powerful opposition; but I do not despond, and will not shrink from the task imposed upon me."[21]

The first task was to organize the executive department. More than once Davis had to give up his own ideas to those of others. He offered Yancey any post in the cabinet he wanted, but for some reason, Yancey declined. He finally agreed, against the advice of his diplomat brother, to head the commission to Europe that had already been created by Rhett's Foreign Relations Committee to seek, primarily, recognition for the new country. Davis wanted Robert Toombs for secretary of the treasury because his knowledge of finance had "attracted my notice." He got Christopher Memminger because Robert Barnwell, refusing to be secretary of state, asked for him to represent South Carolina in his stead. Davis felt, nonetheless, that Memminger "proved himself entirely worthy of the trust." He would have liked Clement Clay, incapacitated by asthma, to be secretary of war but appointed Leroy Pope Walker when Clay and Yancey put him forth as the cabinet member from Alabama.[22]

Davis argued the newly arrived Texan John Reagan into being postmaster general, after two other people had refused. He wanted and got Stephen Mallory of Florida for secretary of the navy, knowing his work in the Senate as head of the Naval Affairs Committee. Both these men, he said, could "always be relied on to the extent of their pledges." Both were at their posts when the Confederacy ended. Davis asked Benjamin, his former antagonist and a brilliant lawyer, to be attorney general and, on the recommendation of others, gave Toombs the highest cabinet post, secretary of state.[23]

The Davises and Toombses had lived together in Washington. Varina said Jeff was "very fond of" Julia, and "one could scarcely imagine a wittier and more agreeable companion" than Robert—"a university man" with "the personal habits of a fine gentleman." He was taking French with his daughters when she found him one day "roaring over" Moliere's *Médecin malgré lui,* with speeches in his other hand waiting correction, and he told her, "Whatever the Lord Almighty lets his geniuses create, He makes someone to enjoy; these plays take all the soreness out of me." There was plenty of "soreness" in him; his likes and dislikes were intense. His height ("over six feet") and fine physique gave him a lordly air, and when he spoke, tossing his "long, glossy black hair," he reminded Varina of Danton. His hands were beautiful as a woman's, and his "strong face" was marred only by a mouth that "was somewhat pendulous and subtracted." "His eyes were magnificent, dark and flashing, and they had a certain lawless way of ranging about that was indicative of his character."[24]

That probably says in a nutshell why he and Davis never hit it off. There was a wild streak in Toombs that would have made the quiet Davis nervous. He would not have minded the hard drinking, "exceedingly temperate" though he was; he had excused it in others. But Davis was proper and disciplined, though fervent; Toombs was extravagant in every way, brooking no restraint. Both spoke with elegant diction, but where Davis was guarded, deliberate, and wordy, Toombs was headlong, passionate, epigrammatic.[25] More often than not they had agreed politically, even when Toombs was a Whig, though they were almost always at loggerheads over the army.[26] In 1853 they had exchanged insults over whether Toombs, a strong compromise and Constitutional Union man, had called Davis a disunionist. A duel was narrowly averted, and it had taken their friends four years to patch things up. But lately they had supported each other in the Committee of Thirteen, and Toombs, veering completely, had led Georgia out of the Union, in defiance of his best friend, Aleck Stephens.[27]

Stephens was a curiosity: no bigger than a boy (67 inches; 94 pounds), with a piping voice and an old man's face, which had, Varina noted, "a fine, critical, deliberate expression." Stephens was widely admired for his intellect. He was one of those who hewed out the provisional constitution from the old one. He had voted against the secession of Georgia and had been elected vice president to placate the many reluctant secessionists. He was in favor of reconstruction (return to the Union). This put a wall between him and Davis, for once Davis had made up his mind to a course of action, there was no turning back. When he said in his first speech that independence was the goal of the South, he meant it. All through slanders to the contrary (immediately in Rhett's *Charleston Mercury*), pressure from others, and the terrible difficulties ahead, he obstinately held this purpose.[28]

For the State Department, Davis's only function was to name the members. Rhett (who felt he ought to be president) had set policy for it before it existed by getting Congress to create the commission to Europe and also one to the now foreign United States. To second Yancey, Davis picked Dudley Mann, "considered one of the best experts in European politics," and the French-born Louisiana judge Pierre A. Rost. Their credentials were addressed to England, France, Russia, and Belgium. They were to seek treaties of amity and commerce as well as recognition.[29]

To the United States, Davis quickly dispatched Martin J. Crawford of Georgia to get a note to Buchanan while he was still president. It was never delivered. The old man was unnerved by threats and dared not act. Another futile effort, the "Peace Convention" in Washington, called by Virginia, was already dissolving. Its leader, John Tyler, told Clement Clay with tears, "The end has come." He went home to advise Virginia's immediate secession. His sons Robert and John eventually became Confederate officials. Robert's teenage daughter, Letitia, had already raised the first Confederate flag, the "Stars and Bars," in Montgomery on March 4, 1861.[30]

On that same day, Buchanan turned over the presidency of the North to Abraham Lincoln. John Taylor Wood, still a naval lieutenant and instructor at Annapolis, termed his inaugural speech "a declaration of war against the South." Lincoln cajoled her, however, by insisting that there was no purpose to interfere with slavery "in the States where it exists," and that there would be "no bloodshed or violence . . . no using of force against or among the people anywhere." But he denied the obvious fact that Southerners had formed a separate nation by calling them "my dissatisfied fellow-countrymen." He tried to force the role of "aggressor" on them by saying, "the government will not assail you." This expressed the very autocracy that Davis and others had warned would come with "consolidation." Lincoln claimed he had sworn to preserve "the government," when in fact it was the Constitution. In his eyes, the block of states calling itself "United" *was* the government, and the Confederate States, merely destroyers. Seward, now secretary of state, saw only "a temporary and partisan excitement." This basic misunderstanding tainted all the relations of the two countries and worked against recognition of the Confederacy abroad. To work out all issues between them peaceably, including the right to forts in Southern territory, Davis sent A. B. Roman of Louisiana and John Forsyth of Alabama to join Crawford as commissioners. But Lincoln never received them. Neither would Seward see them but put them off from day to day.[31]

Under the Confederate Constitution, the Montgomery deputies had become the Provisional Congress, and provision was made for courts. With basic civil government in place, Davis could attend to his real interest, the army. He did not have a free hand, however. Congress had to give him authority to act. Men all over the South were volunteering; the only problem was to organize and arm them. All these hundreds of local companies had to become regiments, battalions, and brigades. States were to offer regiments (no larger units), or men might offer themselves directly to the provisional army.[32]

Fortunately for Davis, the greatest expert on organization in the United States Army came to the South. Col. Samuel Cooper resigned as its adjutant general even before his wife's state, Virginia, had seceded. Knowing his old friend's services to be "of incalculable value," Davis asked him in Montgomery to be adjutant and inspector general, at the highest rank then allowed, brigadier general. Davis loved "his self-sacrificing, duty-loving nature." He pointed out later how Cooper had left "his whole wealth" (his commission) and a service record of forty-six years to come with "the weaker party, because it was the party of law and right." Those who "*know* what he did . . . will not fail to place him among those who contributed most to whatever was achieved."[33]

Davis thought that arms purchases should be limited only by ability to pay. Congress was willing to appropriate money, though not enough, for many still could not believe that war would come. The big question was where to get the guns. There was not one arms factory in the South. Some states had seized federal forts, but this brought only a few military stores. Davis immediately sent out agents to buy weapons: Caleb Huse to Europe, and Raphael Semmes (whom he had known in Washington) back to the North, whence he had just come. The precise Davis made sure that Semmes had resigned as United States naval commander. Then he himself wrote out, three days after his inauguration, detailed instructions for Semmes on where to find, not only arms and ammunition, but machinery and the men to run it, for skilled workmen were as rare as armaments. There was absolutely no talk of "treason" yet, Semmes explains, so he was free to go North looking for these things. He sent some munitions South right away, but private contracts he made were canceled when war began. The charge that the president had not foreseen war or provided arms was, as Davis later said, an "absurdity."[34]

Morris Schaff, who went with the Union, said that Southern wives aside, it was Davis's "great personal charm" that caused certain men of the Northern army to break "natural bonds of home and blood" and fight for the Confederacy. He named Caleb Huse, who ended up in charge of all War Department purchases in Europe; Josiah Gorgas, whom Davis made chief of ordnance;[35] Charles Read Collins, colonel of the Fifteenth Virginia Cavalry; and Joseph Christmas Ives, Davis Commission secretary in 1860, who became a presidential aide-de-camp.[36]

Southern friends in the old army flocked to Davis. Hardee had left West Point in 1860 to be lieutenant colonel of the First Cavalry but never served: he was on leave then and resigned as soon as Georgia seceded. Davis made him a colonel of cavalry, in command of the Mobile Bay area, but by June of 1861, he was in Arkansas as brigadier general. Braxton Bragg, who had come from retirement to head the Army of Louisiana, became brigadier in the Provisional Army of the Confederate States on March 7, in charge of the coast from Pensacola to Mobile.[37]

The Davis "charm" certainly accounted for Robert Crooke Wood, Jr., who brooked the disapproval of his father, a surgeon in the United States Army. Rob came right away to offer his services to his uncle by marriage. He became adjutant on Bragg's staff. His uncle Richard Taylor was a "particular friend" of Bragg's and about to be his civilian aide. Both of them soon left for active duty—Taylor to be colonel of the

Louisiana Ninth Infantry and Wood to join the cavalry. Wood's older brother John had tried to be neutral. By October he found his "blood boiling over with indignation" at the Union military occupation of Maryland. He resigned the old navy for the Confederate one. His diary makes it clear that admiration for his Uncle Jeff helped to draw him South.[38]

Davis appointed as colonels old army acquaintances George Crittenden, John Bankhead Magruder, Gabriel J. Rains, and Earl Van Dorn (who had succeeded him as head of Mississippi forces), and, as lieutenant colonel, James Longstreet. Fitz Lee, resigning as tactics instructor at the military academy, came South at his same rank, first lieutenant. All these appointees except the Wood brothers became generals. Two sons of Davis's Iowa friend George W. Jones came to serve the Confederacy, obviously because of their father's warm feeling for Davis.[39]

Davis's West Point classmate Hugh Weedon Mercer was grandson of a general bayonetted to death in the Revolution as a "d—d Rebel" for refusing to ask for "quarters." He left off banking in Savannah to become colonel of a Georgia regiment. By fall he was a brigadier general. So was another classmate, Davis's particular friend, Thomas Drayton, a South Carolina planter and legislator. From the class of 1829 came the career soldier Theophilus Hunter Holmes. He resigned as major in the Eighth Infantry to come South in April, and he soon rose from colonel to major general.[40]

The first brigadier general had been Pierre Gustave Toutant Beauregard. He, like all these men, was extremely ardent for the South, and like most of them, gave up a promising army career for her. Bilked because Bragg instead of he had been named to head Louisiana state forces, he asked Davis for a Confederate appointment on February 10, 1861, and came to Montgomery. His cause was helped along by his brother-in-law, John Slidell, but he scarcely needed help. Davis had recommended him in 1858 to the secretary of war, John B. Floyd, as "an active officer of military habits and tastes and of high professional attainments" and forwarded his request for command of a new regiment, which he did not get. In November of 1860, Floyd had made him superintendent of West Point, a month before Floyd resigned, over Buchanan's failure to evacuate Fort Sumter. Beauregard had assumed office January 23, 1861, only to be summarily dismissed the next day by Floyd's acting successor, Joseph Holt, a highly vindictive anti-Southern man. Two days later, Louisiana had seceded, and Beauregard had left for home.[41]

The Fort Sumter situation was still most critical. Davis's close friend Maj. Robert Anderson had created the impasse by moving his Union troops from Fort Moultrie, altering the status quo ante secession, which had been guaranteed by both sides. Davis needed a firm military hand in Charleston, and he chose Beauregard. The Napoleonic Creole arrived in the city on March 3. He was an engineer officer, trained in the placement of guns, and he soon had Sumter ringed with firepower. The island was still being shipped mail and food, even cigars and wine, from Charleston. In the first week of April, Beauregard received orders to stop all that and conduct himself as if in the presence of the enemy.[42]

The change came because a secret naval force was about to leave Northern ports with "troops, munitions, and military supplies" for Sumter. The Confederate commissioners had learned of this from a newspaper. Seward had assured them in March that, on the advice of General Scott, the cabinet had decided to evacuate the island. Then at the end of the month, Lincoln decided "that supplies should be sent to Sumter, and issued confidential orders to that effect. All were gratified with this decision," says Secretary of the Navy Gideon Welles, "except Mr. Seward, who still remonstrated." Seward nonetheless cozened the commissioners while the ships were being loaded and was still assuring them on April 7: "Faith as to Sumter fully kept. Wait and see." Lincoln was pledged to notify them of any change. Instead, he notified the governor of South Carolina, late in the night of April 8, that the fleet was on the way with "provisions only." It was to arrive the next day, but "a heavy tempest" delayed it, giving Beauregard time to wire Montgomery for instructions. Six men-of-war lay "outside the *bar,*" and John Manning told Mary Chesnut in Charleston, "Madam, your country is invaded."[43]

The ships carried not "provisions only," but troops. "Thus disappeared the last vestige of the plighted faith and pacific pledges of the Federal Government," says Davis. If they waited, the Confederates would face "the simultaneous fire of the fleet and the fort." Beauregard was told to demand the evacuation of Sumter, and in the event of refusal, "reduce the fort." He dickered for two days with Major Anderson, who was opposed to the "relief expedition." Finally on April 12, 1861, after giving an hour's notice, Beauregard at 4:20 A.M. opened fire.

Anderson returned it. Thirty-three hours later, with his walls battered down and his fort on fire, Anderson surrendered. Miraculously, not a man on either side had been even injured. The chivalrous Beauregard allowed Anderson the "honors of war," including parade of his troops and a one-hundred–gun salute to his flag. The latter proved fatal, as one cannon exploded, killing one soldier and injuring five others. These were the first casualties of the war for Southern independence.[44]

"Scarcely had the President of the United States received intelligence of the failure of the scheme [to reinforce Sumter], when he issued a declaration of war against this Confederacy," Davis told his Congress on April 29. (He meant the call for troops was a virtual declaration: there was never a formal one.) "In this extraordinary production," Lincoln

> affects total ignorance of the existence of an independent Government, which, possessing the entire and enthusiastic devotion of

> its people, is exercising its functions without question over seven sovereign States . . . and over a territory whose area exceeds half a million of square miles. He terms sovereign States "combinations too powerful to be suppressed by the . . . powers vested in the marshals by law." He calls for an army of 75,000 men to act as a *posse comitatus* in aid of the . . . courts of justice.

But the "mandates" of courts in these states are all "cheerfully obeyed," said Davis, and Lincoln "avows that 'the *first* service to be assigned to the forces called out' will not be to execute the process of courts, but to capture forts. . . . He concludes by commanding 'the persons composing the combinations aforesaid'—to wit, the 5,000,000 inhabitants of these States—'to retire peaceably to their respective abodes within twenty days.'"

Lincoln had maneuvered Davis into firing the first shot, but the real "assault [was] made by sending a hostile fleet," said Davis later. "The attempt to represent us as the *aggressors* in the conflict which ensued is as unfounded as the complaint made by the wolf against the lamb in the familiar fable." On the contrary, "the forbearance of the Confederate Government," in not touching Sumter while those sent to arrange its peaceful transfer were being hoodwinked, "is perhaps unexampled in history." With "the hostile descent of the fleet, the reduction of Fort Sumter was a measure of defense rendered absolutely and immediately necessary."[45]

Lincoln's call for troops on April 15 united the South "almost to a man," said Aleck Stephens. Davis told Congress it was "a plain declaration of war which I was not at liberty to disregard." He had to take "active measures for our defense" because all did not imitate the border states and North Carolina "by denouncing [it] as an unconstitutional usurpation of power to which they refused to respond." Davis called for volunteers, and they "are constantly tendering service far in excess of our wants." Secretary Walker had manned coastal forts and sent sixteen thousand men "*en route* for Virginia," the point of expected attack. His aim was "an army of 100,000 men."[46]

Jeff had written Varina from Montgomery, "This is a gay and handsome town . . . and will not be an unpleasant residence. . . . I constantly wish to have you all with me." She came in early March to stay with him at the Exchange Hotel, leaving the children in New Orleans with her parents. When a two-story Italianate house at Bibb and Lee Streets (now on Washington Avenue) was chosen for the executive mansion, she went back for the children and some Brierfield furnishings. It was hard "to abandon all we had watched over for years," and "hardest to relinquish of all" was their "very large" collection of "fine and well-chosen English books." She brought a few favorites with her for the new library.

It was offset from the other rooms, giving Jeff a place to have crucial conferences at odd hours. His office was nearby (only Congress met at the hilltop capitol), and he was already back in his War Department habit of wearing out his colleagues with hard work.

The White House of the new nation was literally white, with dark green louvers framing floor-length windows on the front gallery. They looked in on bedrooms to the right and, on the left, double parlors, behind which was a commodious dining room. Varina immediately held a reception. As they always did for her entertainments, townspeople sent in "hampers of blossoms." Her style was typically Southern, with open doors, though a servant announced the callers. There was "no affectation of state or ceremony," said William Howard Russell, correspondent for the *London Times*. "Mrs. Davis, whom some of her friends call 'Queen Varina,' is a comely, sprightly woman . . . of good figure and manners, well-dressed, ladylike, and clever" (meaning, of obliging disposition). "She seemed a great favorite with those around her."[47]

Behind the house was the kitchen, the vegetable garden, and the all-important stable. The Davises could walk to church, however. St. John's Episcopal was only a few blocks away. The people of Montgomery remarked how they were in their pew every Sunday, near the back on the right side, and how the president walked in "with magnificent military bearing," carrying "his high silk hat in his hand." He "was very devout in his devotions," kneeling to pray as he entered, making all the Prayer Book responses audibly, and never leaving the church "until the benediction."[48]

Varina's great talent for entertaining was abetted by the presence of her sister, Margaret Howell, who was nineteen now, tall, "generously curved" and "fair like her father." She "was less striking than Varina but quite as witty, and sometimes as sharp." Varina's affectionate nature far outweighed her unguarded tongue, and made her a valued friend. She and Mary Chesnut, equally witty and affectionate, took up where they had left off in Washington: "Mrs. Jeff Davis . . . met me with open arms. What a chat that was, *two* hours. . . . We discussed the world & his wife & I could only get away by promising to come back every day."[49]

Virginia Clay came down to welcome her to Alabama, but Clement was nursing his asthma at "Cozy Cot," their home on Huntsville's Monte Sano. Varina wrote to him one day of the "much pleasure" they were expecting from "a night & day" with the Toombses and "C. Brown & his wife" at the Ben Fitzpatrick home. This would get them to the cooler hills north of Montgomery, away from the heat and mosquitoes near the Alabama River.[50] "C. Brown"—really William Montague Browne—had been dubbed "Constitution" by Mary Chesnut after the paper he edited in Washington. He was a wellborn Irishman, but such an ardent Southerner that he had been chosen to take Davis at Brierfield the message of his election. A social favorite, and a great friend of the

Davises', he was assistant secretary of state under Toombs until he joined the president's staff early in 1862.[51]

The Chesnuts were in Montgomery because James was a member of the Provisional Congress. While in South Carolina during its recess he had been an aide-de-camp to General Beauregard. Serving as an aide also was a friend of both the Chesnuts' and the Davises', Louis Wigfall. He went Toombs one better in wildness. In his youth, he had wounded Preston Brooks in a duel and killed Brooks's cousin in a street fight, and subsequently, in 1846, moved from South Carolina to Texas. His shock of black hair was unkempt. His eyes, "flashing, fierce, yet calm," reminded Russell, the newsman, of a Bengal tiger. It was rather as "a 'stormy petrel'" that Mary Chesnut saw him on the eve of the firing on Fort Sumter, the only person "thoroughly happy" over impending conflict. When the fort was blazing, he had had himself, on his own initiative, rowed out alone to invite Major Anderson to surrender, which he did.[52]

Varina had no sooner gotten settled than she had to start packing again. Lincoln's demand for troops had precipitated Virginia into the Confederacy, and the state offered her capital to the country. Against the president's wishes, Congress voted on May 21 to move to Richmond. By now, North Carolina, Arkansas, and Tennessee had also seceded, the latter waiting only a popular vote to become the eleventh Confederate state. There was much need for ampler space, both governmental and private, and Davis soon conceded that he needed to be in Richmond to direct Confederate defense. Federals seized Alexandria, Virginia, on May 24 (and the homes of R. E. Lee and Cooper, the latter destroyed) and began massing forces on the Potomac.[53]

"May 26th.—The President is sick to-day—having a chill I believe," but "he works incessantly, sick or well." (He had even ridden the cars to Charleston and Pensacola to inspect the military installations.)[54] He was prostrate when he left Montgomery the next day, in such secrecy that only Louis Wigfall (as informal aide-de-camp), Mrs. Wigfall, and Robert Toombs went with him. His family traveled on a separate train. He had been warned of a "desperado" released from prison and "sent to Montgomery to assassinate me," and a few days before, he had accosted and scared away a heavily armed man peering in the window of the White House. Davis traveled without stopping and reached Richmond in safety on May 29, well enough to ride with Gov. John Letcher in an open carriage to the Spotswood Hotel and make a balcony speech. He was "most rapturously received."[55]

The hilly city was the scene of great excitement, with people pouring in and army volunteers setting up camp on the outskirts. On June 3, as Davis turned fifty-three, his former protégé, George McClellan, now major general, led United States troops into Virginia mountains on the west. On the east, his fellow Democrat, Ben Butler, also major general, was at Fortress Monroe, gathering an invasion force to charge up Virginia's "Peninsula," formed by the York and James Rivers. War was close upon them. Mrs. Wigfall wrote to her daughter, "The President is to take the field . . . Your father of course will go with him."[56]

Both men would have liked nothing better. Wigfall was soon to be colonel of the First Texas Infantry and to become a brigadier general. But at the moment their hands were full. Wigfall had to organize Texas troops, and Davis, the whole army. "We had to create not only an army in the face of war itself, but also the military establishments necessary to equip and place it in the field." As he wrote to Governor Letcher, "Our line of defense is a long one, and my duty embraces all its parts." Even reluctant Virginians like Henry Heth were coming in now from the old army. His note to Davis read, "To you I owe more than any other man living; to the common cause you now represent, I offer my services." At the top Davis wrote: "Secty. of War—special attention, this is a first rate soldier and of the cast of man most needed."[57]

Military alliance with Virginia put her army under Confederate control. In it were Robert E. Lee and Joseph E. Johnston. Their state had first made them major generals, with Lee as head of its forces. When, to clarify the command, Virginia reduced Johnston to brigadier, he went to Montgomery, seeking a Confederate appointment. Davis could only make him a brigadier, as he did Lee, since it was the highest rank in the provisional army. Lee was perfectly happy with the lower rank; Johnston accepted it perforce. Davis at once sent Johnston to command the most threatened point, Harper's Ferry. He soon evacuated it, with great loss of matériel.[58] Davis left Lee in the overall command of forces in Virginia. This angered Johnston so much that he refused to "regard" Lee's orders, "because they are illegal." On each of his two dispatches about this, Davis endorsed one word: "Insubordinate." It was the first hint of trouble between them.[59] Davis commented after the war: "Lee in his generosity, magnanimity and self-abnegation, chose to overlook this insubordination. To him our cause was everything, and questions of rank were by him in comparison with our success, regarded as nothing." Davis kept Lee in Richmond as military advisor with "general direction of army affairs." Many called him chief of staff. When Mrs. Lee wrote of rumors that he was to be made commander in chief, the general responded: "President Davis holds that position."[60]

While chairman of the Military Affairs Committee in 1860, Davis had used "all my power and influence," against "serious opposition," to get J. E. Johnston confirmed as quartermaster general of the United States, having already gotten the Senate to keep staff rank of brigadier general for the post.[61] General Scott and Secretary Floyd, a kinsman of Johnston, had named him, over Sidney Johnston and Lee. Floyd had already awarded J. E. Johnston the brevet as colonel that he had been applying for ever since the Mexican War, and had made him acting inspector general, causing Lee to comment, "In proportion to his services [Johnston] has been advanced beyond anyone in the army and has thrown more discredit than ever on the system of favoritism and making brevets."[62]

Other colonels, claiming that the brevet had died along with Johnston's Voltigeur regiment, had asked Davis, then senator, to present their protest. While secretary of war, Davis had refused to reopen this case; but he had given Johnston the much more important line rank of lieutenant colonel in the First Cavalry. There Johnston was known to "foment discord," disobeying, undercutting, and criticizing his commander, Colonel Sumner. When Sumner seemed to be gaining the upper hand, Johnston had asked Floyd for the quartermaster appointment, which enabled him to leave the regiment. Lee congratulated his friend, but he had noted how Johnston was always pushing for his own advancement—something Lee knew himself incapable of doing. Johnston himself had said he desired promotion "more than any man in the army."[63]

Still, he was not the highest federal officer to come South. David Twiggs, brigadier general of the line since 1846, was brevet major general commanding in Texas when that state left the Union. He made no secret of his Southern leanings. He asked repeatedly for instructions, got none, and finally asked to be replaced. He had always said he would not fire on Americans. With Col. Ben McCulloch's eleven hundred Texans surrounding his one hundred and sixty men at San Antonio, Twiggs would still not surrender his guns—it would be "a disgrace." He persuaded the Texans to let him march his men out of the state under arms, leaving his military stores behind. Before he could start, the officer sent to relieve him finally arrived, criticized his arrangements, but then carried them out. Yet Joseph Holt, then acting secretary, called this Twiggs's "treachery" and got him dismissed from the service on March 1, 1861.

The seventy-year-old Twiggs, declining at first, finally agreed to take command in New Orleans (whose people loved him). As major general, the highest Confederate rank conferred thus far, he headed the First Military Department (the Gulf Coast). Hampered by shortages, quarrels, and his own failing health, he soon asked to be relieved, and Brig. Gen. Mansfield Lovell took over. Davis was probably relieved in another sense: he thought Twiggs was now inimical to him and had heard complaints of incapacity. Twiggs, remaining as ordnance officer, escaped at the last minute when New Orleans fell to the Yankees in 1862. He had to leave everything, and it was his silverware that gave the occupying Union general, Ben Butler, his nickname of "Spoons." Old Davey Twiggs got home in time to die where he was born, near Augusta, Georgia.[64]

E. V. Sumner had taken Twiggs's brigadier spot in March of 1861, and R. E. Lee had taken his as colonel of the First Cavalry. Lee ignored the offer about this time of a brigadier generalship in the new Confederacy. He did not believe in secession. He said his allegiance was due only to Virginia and the United States, in that order. He never actually took command of the First Cavalry, being home at Arlington on leave. He was told to report to Winfield Scott, who tried to keep him with the Union. (Twiggs said Scott thought "God Almighty had to spit on his hands to make Bob Lee.") Then Lincoln, through F. P. Blair, had offered Lee field command of the United States Army, under Scott. But Lee knew Virginia was on the brink of secession. He had refused, resigned his colonelcy on April 20, and offered his sword to his state.[65]

In May, another Virginian signing himself, "Your old friend," urged Jeff Davis to hurry to Richmond: there were "no means at hand to repel" an attack up the York River, but "the very fact of your presence will almost answer." This was William Nelson Pendleton, the fifty-one-year-old rector of Christ Episcopal Church in Lexington, who had decided that his West Point training ought to be at the service of his country. He was now captain of the Rockbridge Artillery (largely his parishioners). He was to serve under Lee as brigadier, chief of artillery, and then of reserve ordnance, all the way to Appomattox. The push from Fortress Monroe did not begin until June 10. Then Col. John B. Magruder, who had planned the peninsular defenses for the state of Virginia, handily repulsed it at Big Bethel, the first land battle of the war.[66]

About this time, another West Pointer turned cleric, Bishop Leonidas Polk, visited Louisiana troops in Virginia and dined with the president. "He is the best man we could have, and commands general confidence," he wrote to his wife, saying, "Davis will take the field in person." Gov. Isham G. Harris of Tennessee had asked Polk to plead for more big guns to defend the Mississippi Valley. Davis needed no appeal to protect his own home area. He promised artillery. Then he suggested that Polk take the command.[67]

Polk, quite sure that the South's cause was righteous, had taken his Louisiana diocese along with the state into independence then into the Confederacy. He and Bishop Stephen Elliott of Georgia had helped to form the Episcopal Church in the Confederate States, creating a separate jurisdiction under which seceded dioceses could continue the faith and order of the Church. He was not sure whether he should personally take up arms. Davis said once, speaking of Polk, "It is questionable whether war is ever justifiable except for defence, and then it is surely a duty." Polk did believe that the South was acting in "simple self-defense."[68]

His holy orders did not give Polk pause; he only wanted to be sure he was really needed. He thought and prayed; Bishop Meade of Virginia, who was "for a downright good fight," gave implicit approval. Finally Polk told Davis "that his calling required rather than excluded him from serving," since "he regarded the war as *pro aris et focis*" (for "our hearth-stones and our altars"—Polk's translation). He believed that his cabin at Sewanee, Tennessee, where he and other bishops had laid the cornerstone for a university, had just been burned to the ground, under the prompting of "Black Republican hate," while his wife and daughters were there. It showed that the South faced a war "of moral issues," of spoliation and outrage. He agreed to "buckle the sword over the gown," but only until he could be replaced. Davis made him a major general and sent him to command Department Number Two: both sides of the Mississippi River from the Kentucky-Tennessee border down to the Red River. "Like a Christian," Davis said, "he entered on a patriot's duty."[69]

Davis told Polk there was no immediate danger in his area. The threat was in northern Virginia. An enemy army assembled near Washington spilled over the Potomac in mid-July of 1861 toward the Confederate lines guarding Manassas, a rail junction twenty-five miles away. Beauregard had been brought up from Charleston to take charge here, and Davis planned for J. E. Johnston, still in the mountains, to hurry to his aid in case of attack.[70] Maj. Gen. Irvin McDowell led the Union forces (and a large entourage of sightseers). The watchword was "On to Richmond." Mary Chesnut said they had handcuffs for Jeff Davis and crew—"fit appendage of a policeman, but not of a soldier who came to meet his foeman hilt to hilt," said Davis. As they inched forward to Centreville, Confederates withdrew south of a small stream named Bull Run. They won a skirmish on July 18 at Blackburn's Ford, and Davis wired Beauregard, "God be praised for your successful beginning."[71]

Three days later, McDowell attacked in force. In a Richmond office, the restive old soldiers Davis and Lee, confined to telegraphic reports, itched to march on the firing. In fact, Davis had wired Beauregard, "I have tried to join you, but remain to serve you here as most useful for the time," funneling troops to him up the railroad. (And he had to address Congress on the twentieth.) Finally, Davis could stand it no longer. Pulling his rank on the twenty-first, he made Lee keep the office and, with his nephew Joseph Robert Davis, lieutenant colonel of the Tenth Mississippi, he mounted a train for the battlefield.[72]

Great was the confusion at Manassas Junction. Soldiers were crying that all was lost, and Davis could not go forward until he made the engineer uncouple his engine and take it on alone. At the field headquarters Davis found a horse, and soon found General Johnston, who told him "that we had won the battle." The Federals were dropping handcuffs, guns, and everything else in flight.[73] As planned, Johnston had come down when Beauregard sent the word, not without arguing and asking Cooper anxiously about his rank (the official order had not been published to the army). Davis had had to tell him again that he was a full general, Beauregard a brigadier, and he would be the senior on the field. Once there, Johnston had approved his junior's plans, but he later said he never relinquished operational command, as Beauregard and his adjutant, Col. Thomas Jordan, made it appear.[74]

Davis rode toward the front, only to be told by young Capt. John F. Lay that "he was much farther forward than he should be," that the enemy was "not entirely broken." Davis replied, "Surrounded as I am by so many brave and gallant hearts, I am in no danger." He called for an artillery piece, as Lay and James Chesnut (again aide to Beauregard) led a cavalry charge "upon the retreating army."[75] Davis continued to ride over the field, giving Col. Jubal Early asked-for military advice, even acting as his courier, but chiefly tending to the wants of the hungry and the wounded. Dismounting by an Alabama boy, he took him "by the hand and uttered words of deepest sympathy and kindness," and when he left, the boy "cheered him on" as he "rode off in the direction of the flying enemy."[76]

When Davis met the two commanders at headquarters late that night, he asked about pursuit of the broken federal forces. There was silence. There was silence again when he asked that the freshest brigade be sent. Then Colonel Jordan "asked if I would dictate the order, which was done." Davis says in his book, "It was of no consequence then or now as to who issued the order for pursuit, and, unless requested, I should not have dictated one, preferring that the generals [should do so]." Report of enemy panic had prompted him to insist on pursuit, but when he heard that it came from a captain known in the army as "Crazy Hill," he "laughed heartily, as did all."[77] He changed his order to read, "early dawn," but the plans were ruined before then by a very violent and prolonged downpour, and only cavalry followed the enemy. In fact, Davis's order was never sent. Jordan signed and sent one under Beauregard's name. Davis says it was "to the same effect," but it was not: it only ordered a small force to "scour the country" and send supplies and wounded back to headquarters. But, as Davis shortly said to Beauregard, "Enough was done for glory, and the measure of duty was full." He made him a full general on the spot.[78]

Davis admired a man who was a fighter like his heroes Andrew Jackson and Zachary Taylor; he was one himself. He was not called "The 'Game Cock' of the South" for nothing. Reuben Davis said his was "essentially a strong and forceful nature." He understood when Robert Toombs wanted to get out of the office and into the army. Even as troops converged on Bull Run, he had commissioned him a brigadier general and replaced him as secretary of state with Robert Mercer Talliaferro Hunter. Toombs had uncharacteristically said he wanted to resign as "quietly and inoffensively as possible." His reputation for obstreperousness caused the remark after the war that, while secretary, he was "impracticable and restless." Davis, with his usual honesty, countered: "Not so. When in the Cabinet he gave no cause for distrust or complaint" (making no comment, however, on the next assertion—that he was "an active malcontent" later). Accepting his resignation, Davis wrote an almost fatuous letter that suggested that he knew nothing of Toombs's continual carping against the government, especially him.[79]

The next cabinet member wanting an army commission told Davis that in his position "of great trial and enduring fortitude . . . I have been a daily witness of the singular power with which you have brought order out of chaos," while consulting "the popular heart." "You [are] the only man I have ever met whose greatness grew upon me the nearer I approached him." This was L. P. Walker, a fine gentleman lawyer but a haphazard administrator in bad health. One Sunday morning on his way to church, the president had stopped by the War Department in search of a letter, to find Secretary Walker gone home "quite ill." Davis and the one clerk on duty—John B. Jones, the diarist—dug through his file, "a large arm-chair" where correspondence was pitched "helter-skelter," Davis saying "with an impatient smile, 'it is always sure to be the last one.' And it was."

His health, and public complaint, led to Walker's resignation on September 16. Davis expressed "personal regard" and offered a diplomatic post, but Walker wanted to be a general. He was sent to Braxton Bragg, who eventually gave him recruiting duty, so "he can be of less harm." He resigned as brigadier in 1862 and finally found his niche as a military judge.[80] Judah Benjamin was shifted to the War Department, and to the emptied attorney general spot, Davis called Thomas Bragg, Braxton's brother, with whom he had served in the Senate.[81]

Scrappy though he was, Davis was essentially peace-loving. He resented the slander that he had wanted war. He had tried to withdraw his country quietly, but the Northern states had "refused even to listen to any proposals for a peaceful separation." Although the United States never declared war, the Confederate States had to recognize that "war exists"; for Lincoln's naval blockade of the South was universally regarded as an act of war. Having no navy at all, the Confederacy authorized its president to issue letters of marque and reprisal to private vessels. This time-honored right had specifically been recognized by the United States in the international agreement of 1856.[82] When Union blockaders captured one of these privateers, the *Savannah*, the crew was held "not as prisoners of war, but as criminals" and convicted of "piracy and treason." Fighting spirit and tender heart combined in Davis's message to Lincoln: "It is the desire of this Government so to conduct the war now existing as to mitigate its horrors as far as may be possible." The South had treated its prisoners with "the greatest humanity and leniency," furnishing them Confederate rations and paroling many, who could "remain at large" in the South or go home. Only since learning how the *Savannah* prisoners were being treated, Davis said, had he "been compelled to withdraw these indulgencies," and hold his own "in strict confinement."

> A just regard to humanity and to the honor of this Government now requires me to state explicitly that, painful as will be the necessity . . . if driven to the terrible necessity of retaliation by your execution of any of the officers or the crew of the Savannah, that retaliation will be extended so far as shall be requisite to secure the abandonment of a practice unknown to the warfare of civilized man, and so barbarous as to disgrace the nation which shall be guilty of inaugurating it. . . . I now renew the proposition . . . to exchange for the prisoners taken on the Savannah, an equal number of those now held by us, according to rank.[83]

"No answer ever came," but Lincoln got the message. The "pirates" became prisoners of war. Davis initiated the exchange policy that was worked out by cartel the next year and lasted until the Union repudiated it in 1863. It was lucky that Lincoln gave in; Davis could never have carried through on retaliation. He threatened it at other times, too, once for "such cruelties as are not permitted in warfare between Christian people." But it was all bluff. Even in the face of public clamor for it once, he told his cabinet, "If I could get [the culprit], I would hang him as high as Haman, but I have not the heart to [hang] these innocent soldiers."[84] His reaction to the execution of William B. Mumford, a citizen of New Orleans, was to brand Gen. Ben Butler "outlaw and common enemy of mankind." He named as felons white officers leading colored troops. But both these actions became dead letters. Butler was never taken, and when General Hood captured some of the officers, he paroled them.[85]

Personal peace was just as important to Davis. He once told the Senate, "I do not treasure disagreeable things . . . to excite a sentiment of hostility, of which we have too much." If he was attacked, his "sense of mortification and injustice" caused him "acute suffering," Varina says. She had opposed his being president because she foresaw what violent criticism his "supersensitive temperament" would have to bear. Her own carping had nearly caused their marriage to break up, but his strong stand, saying he simply could not put up with continual strife, had brought them out of their difficulty into a loving companionship of mutual respect and admiration. Varina, at present enjoying life at the Spotswood Hotel presidential suite, was expecting their fifth child. In Davis's eyes, he and Varina were "two persons combined into one."[86]

He wanted all his relationships so harmonious. He had "a sanguine temperament," always expecting the best, and said, "it is a part of my habit to forget, as soon as I can, disagreeable things." Dr. Minnigerode saw in him an "unsophisticated, guileless nature, which looked for the good in people rather than the evil," so much so that he was likely to be deceived, "at least for a time." Varina once reminded him of a man "with whom you unwillingly had unpleasant words, and who you told me was a useful and good man, and you would not willingly wound."[87] He assumed that other people had his own deep reserve of goodwill. He would have been appalled at the suspicion, rancor, and contempt gestating in the breasts of Beauregard and J. E. Johnston.

Beauregard had felt injured when Davis, as secretary of war, did not make him colonel of a new infantry regiment (though he was then chief engineer in a post he had much wanted) and thought of resigning the army. He pushed himself into the superintendency of West Point, deliberately to thwart Davis's wish to open it to other branches of the service. He expressed some confidence in Davis as president at first, but then Davis rejected his strategies—first a grand general one, and then one which he sent to Richmond verbally by Chesnut, involving an attack on Washington. Some of Beauregard's staff officers were heard calling Davis "a stupid fool."[88]

At the outset, wrote Davis, "few" had "a more favorable opinion of General Johnston as a soldier than I did." John Reagan confirms that they were "the best of friends" then, as were Lydia Johnston and Varina.[89] In 1855, Johnston had accepted a Davis invitation "with great pleasure." By 1860, there was a note of animosity: "I'll tell Davis nothing about Wood d—n him (D—n Wood, you understand)"—suggesting he might have meant Davis. Davis's 1861 letters to Johnston are almost chummy—July 10: "I know you will [do] whatever is possible, and . . . follow the dictates of your own good judgment and true patriotism. . . . I have tried for a week to get off and join you. . . . May God bless and direct you . . ."; July 13: "weary and heartsick over fruitless exertions to obtain the troops. . . . I need not assure you that my confidence and interest in you both as an officer and as a friend cause me to turn constantly to your position with deepest solicitude"; August 1: "With affectionate remembrance to Mrs. Johnston" closes a full, chatty letter.[90]

By contrast, the disdain that Johnston felt when Davis appeared at Manassas seethes in his own account. True, it was written later, but it shows seeds that soon sprouted. Davis had come "to control both general and army" (Varina says, to be sure the generals were not wrangling over the command). Davis had gotten there "after the last armed enemy had left" (contrary to the accounts of Captains Lay and Alexander). Johnston even faults Davis's natural question, "How has the battle gone?" He scorns the idea that Davis inspired the troops.[91] But there was the boy who cried "Hurrah for Jeff Davis" with his last breath, and the First Tennessee Regiment in which "Every boy snatched off his hat and saluted the President with the wild Rebel yell," as Davis went galloping past on a white horse.[92]

When strife pitted his generals against each other, Davis became alarmed for the army and the country. After Manassas, Johnston had not returned to the mountains of Virginia, being, in his own words, "unwilling to be removed to a much less important" service. Left in charge there, John B. Floyd and Henry A. Wise, brigadier generals, were fighting each other as much as the enemy. Davis picked Lee, whom he knew to be as peace-loving as himself, to soothe these politician-generals. He was to beat the enemy if possible, and then come back as adviser. Lee went, failed to achieve his objective, either social or military, and returned under a cloud. Davis recalled Wise for insubordination and joked, "General Wise, I think I will have to shoot you." Wise "started from his seat and said, 'Mr. President, shoot me, that is all right, but for God's sake let me see you hang that d— rascal Floyd first.'" Davis kept Floyd in Virginia and sent Wise to a North Carolina command.[93]

Lee confided to Davis why his attack at Cheat Mountain had failed, but he swore him to secrecy, in order to guard the man responsible. So in silence together the two friends endured newspaper taunts of "Granny Lee" and "President's pet."[94] As Davis said, "The blame was thrown jointly upon him and myself." It came chiefly from John Daniel of the *Richmond Examiner*, who was on Floyd's staff. Pollard, of the same paper, revealed the name Lee wanted secret.[95] Lee's repute was so low that when Davis next assigned him to improve the coastal defenses of South Carolina and Georgia, he felt compelled to write a letter "telling what manner of man he was." Davis's unshaken confidence in Lee after Cheat Mountain "was said to be a case of obstinate adherence to a personal friend." He adhered to that friend all the more obstinately as the enmity of others began to show itself.[96]

There had been a public outcry just after Manassas, when a Beauregard letter was read to the unicameral Provisional Congress, saying: "The want of food and transportation has made us lose all the fruits of our victory. We ought at this moment to be in or about Washington." Congressman R. B. Rhett's *Charleston Mercury* took this to mean that Davis had stopped Beauregard from pursuing the enemy. The *Richmond Daily Whig* praised what it thought was Davis's prudence, saying troops might have been "slaughtered" at Washington. Both show how little reporters really knew.[97]

Davis defended his supply chiefs, but he handled Beauregard with kid gloves: "you are unjust to yourself . . . it would have been extremely hazardous to have done more . . . let us rather show the untaught that their desires are unreasonable." Beauregard's official battle report (which the press had before Davis did) admitted, in fact, that pursuit after Manassas was "a military impossibility."[98] Then Beauregard said he was misunderstood. He had meant his strategic plan to regain Maryland, sent earlier by Chesnut, which Davis had rejected. Again public indignation was roused. Davis showed why it would not have worked and called on Lee and Chesnut for their recollection, telling the latter, "My confidence and friendship for Genl. Beauregard have been unmistakeably manifested, and none can regret more than myself the error he committed in bringing extraneous matter into his report of a battle." He could not think of any motive for it "consistent with the good opinion I entertained of him." He told Beauregard himself that he "was surprised": "it seemed to be an attempt to exalt yourself at my expense." To Chesnut's plea for "harmony," with advice to ignore "babbling" and "malice," Davis answered: "[I] can assure you that our cause is to me so far above any personal considerations that I can find no difficulty in fully co-operating with any one who can and will promote its success." That was his policy throughout the war.[99]

Always assuming goodwill in others, he asked Johnston "to say whether I obstructed the pursuit of the enemy," because the rumors were creating distrust of the government and making it hard to raise troops. Johnston answered plainly, "No." It was "obstructed" by "inadequate means" and the strength of federal positions. In his 1874 book, he even said failure to take Washington was "erroneously attributed . . . to the President's prohibition," but he never said Davis had ordered pursuit and actually charged that "he violated his duty and his oath" by failing to do so! Yet he told Bradley T. Johnson, a biographer, that he took all responsibility for nonpursuit and was always certain he had been right.[100] Early knew this and asked, "why, then, should an effort be made to shift it on any one else?" Yet the charge of interference after Manassas was revived by Lord Wolseley of the British army in 1887, and has pursued Davis to this day.[101]

In September 1861, Davis was still writing familiarly to Johnston (evidently after a bout of fever): "I am still weak, and seldom attempt to write even to you . . . May God protect and guide you." But he made two innocent mistakes. He spoke well of General Lee, and he reported, "I have just heard that Genl. A. S. Johnston is here."[102]

A. S. Johnston had resigned as brevet brigadier general in the United States Army, heading the Department of the Pacific, and had pursued a hard desert way overland from California to gladden Davis's heart by his step in the foyer of the Richmond White House. Lying sick above, Davis had said immediately: "That is Sidney Johnston's step. Bring him up." Even after he had resigned, Johnston, like Lee, had been offered command of United States forces, under Scott. Now he "simply offered himself to the cause," also like Lee, with no concern about rank. He found that Cooper, he, R. E. Lee, J. E. Johnston, and Beauregard were full generals, appointed by Davis, confirmed by Congress on August 31, and ranked in that order.[103]

For some time, J. E. Johnston had been styling himself "the ranking General of the Confederate Army." He told Dabney Maury in outrage: "I rank General Lee." Writing to Davis, he called himself "next in military place to yourself."[104] Imagine his fury when he discovered that not only Lee, but also Cooper and Sidney Johnston were before him on the list of full generals. He tore into Davis about "degrading" him "for the benefit of persons neither of whom has yet struck a blow for this Confederacy." Cooper was a staff officer, not expected to strike "a blow," which leaves, for the objects of jealousy, Sidney Johnston and Lee (and, as the letter shows later, Beauregard). Varina said that Johnston stabbed her husband continuously after "he found Genl. Lee ranked him in the army register." Despite the president and Congress, Johnston claimed: "I still rightfully hold the rank of first General in the armies of the Southern Confederacy."[105]

The five generals were exactly the same grade; the ranking, by date of commission, determined precedence only. This was dear to military men, as Davis well knew. He had had a great deal of experience in the War Department with the "jealousy, rancor, and insubordination" engendered by questions of rank and command.[106] The other Confederate generals might have objected to having first rank assigned to Cooper, a staff officer, but he *was* the senior colonel and had not left staff for line. No one else complained. What "conceit and folly" for Johnston "to snarl and sneer and quarrel," said a Chesnut cousin, because "not put ahead of General Lee!" But it all seemed to Johnston "a blow aimed at me only." In his letter to Davis, he laid out his claim rationally enough (but with suppressions and contradictions): he was the only brigadier general to come South (a staff position, and what about Twiggs?), while those now put above him had been colonels (his own *line* rank was *lieutenant colonel,* to which he reverted when he resigned the quartermaster staff). But then he allowed himself an emotional passage ending with his father's "revolutionary sword," which he would wield, if only as a private (would he resign or be degraded?), until freedom was won.[107]

Davis sounded more hurt than angry in his reply. He did not prepare, as was his wont, a long, minutely documented rebuttal. He simply said: "I have just received and read your letter of the 12th instant. Its language is, as you say, unusual; its arguments and statements, utterly one-sided, and its insinuations as unfounded as they are unbecoming." That was all; the relative rank stood. In his book, Johnston says he heard that Davis "freely expressed" his "irritation" about the letter. But Varina says if he thought that, he didn't know "the President's reticent temper. In the whole period of his official relation to General Johnston, in the confidence of family intercourse, I never heard him utter a word in derogation of General Johnston."[108]

Davis spent the rest of his life explaining why he ranked J. E. Johnston fourth. Varina was distressed that he "should feel annoyed, as he was a friend, and his wife was very dear to me." Jeff told her at the time:

> General Johnston does not remember that he did not leave the United States Army to enter the Confederate States Army, but that he entered the Army of Virginia, and when Virginia joined

> the Confederacy he came to the Confederate States; also that in the Virginia Army he was the subordinate of Lee, and that they were nominated to our Provisional Congress at the same time and with the same relative rank they had in Virginia. The Quartermaster-General had only assimilated or protective rank, and from it derived no right to command, but by law was prohibited from exercising command of troops.

No one mentioned that by the very law which he quoted to justify himself, Johnston had sworn "to obey the orders of the President of the Confederate States."[109] Jubal Early noted, in his usual trenchant manner, that Twiggs was "really the senior officer" in the old army: "According to General Johnston's theory, he (Twiggs) ought to have been commander-in-chief [meaning general-in-chief, a common error]."

> My view of the act of Congress (C. S.) is that officers could only claim their rank in their respective departments . . . if General Johnston had been made a Quarter-Master, he could have claimed the benefit of his former rank . . . when he went into the line, he could not claim the benefit of his rank as Quarter Master General. The principle contended for by General Johnston might have made a surgeon commander-in-chief of the army. . . . [It] was very absurd in General Johnston to make the complaint he did. He had the full command of a general, and was never under the command of any one except the President until he was [in 1865] nominally under the command of General Lee.[110]

In his book, General Johnston said that his letter (which he only excerpted there) caused "the animosity against me that [Davis] is known to have entertained ever since." The shoe was on the other foot. Nursing his hurt feelings, still claiming first rank, Johnston drew back from Davis and became as uncooperative and imperious as he dared. Years later, Gen. Marcus Wright, compiling Johnston's dispatches for the *Official Records*, wrote to Davis: "I can hardly conceive how you could so long have borne with the 'snarly tone' of his letters, which he wrote at all times and on all pretexts. . . . The official records when published will not add to, but greatly detract from, General Johnston's reputation."[111]

Both Joseph and Lydia Johnston vented their contempt and suspicion of Davis in private letters. They assumed that he hated them and did whatever he did to injure them. Davis never used the same sort of spiteful terms about them. His criticisms, prompted by events, were impersonal until after Johnston attacked him openly in his *Narrative* in 1874. And then he calmly wrote to Varina, "Johnston has more effectively than another could shown his selfishness and his malignity. He is skillful in suppression and his memory is very convenient."[112]

It was not Johnston's letter, but his deeds, that earned Davis's disapproval. He wrote all this out once in his tedious but telling way, dryly showing step by step his disappointment in Johnston's performance. This paper of his forbids the oversimplified view, that their feud was simply based on feelings. Davis, at least, denied that his decisions were so based, and Burton Harrison confirms this: "In public life, he was always disinterested." He would not even bend a minor rule for his West Point classmate Hugh Mercer. His alleged mistreatment of Johnston became the cause célèbre of the Confederacy.[113]

XIII

The Chief Executive

The Richmond White House was more imposing than the Montgomery one but not as homey. Its severe federal facade, three stories high, fronted Clay Street at the prow of a hill commanding a superb view. To the side ran Twelfth Street, and in the back was a splendid garden. Overlooking the garden was the most striking feature—a broad first-floor gallery with white columns. It perched atop a flight of steps with ground-floor entrances underneath. Its windows opening to the floor were doors into the formal rooms "over forty feet square"—parlor, drawing room, and dining room, behind an oval foyer. This porch followed the length of the house and turned the southeast corner where it was framed by a tall white balustrade. Beneath were the brick walks and courtyard that led to kitchen and stables.[1]

Maggie, Jeff Jr., and little Joe soon made the house home, kissing the marble goddesses on the mantel facings in the formal rooms, racing up and down the two sets of inside stairs, and romping in the garden. They had their own nursery running the whole length of the second floor. With their "ringing laughter," the "care-free and happy Davis children" naturally became pets of Richmond society, but also rather its caution.[2] Mary Chesnut gives the picture: "Drive with Mrs. Davis and all her infant family. Wonderfully clever and precocious children—but unbroken wills. At one time there was a sudden uprising. . . . They fought, screamed, laughed. It was bedlam broke loose. Mrs. Davis scolded, laughed, and cried." When Mary and James were paying a call in 1863, the president said the whole family had set out to visit them, "but the children became so troublesome they turned back. Just then little Joe rushed in and insisted on saying his prayer at his father's knee, then and there. He was in his nightclothes."[3]

Between the children's nursery and their parents' chamber (as bedrooms were called) was Davis's office, with a cubbyhole at the stair

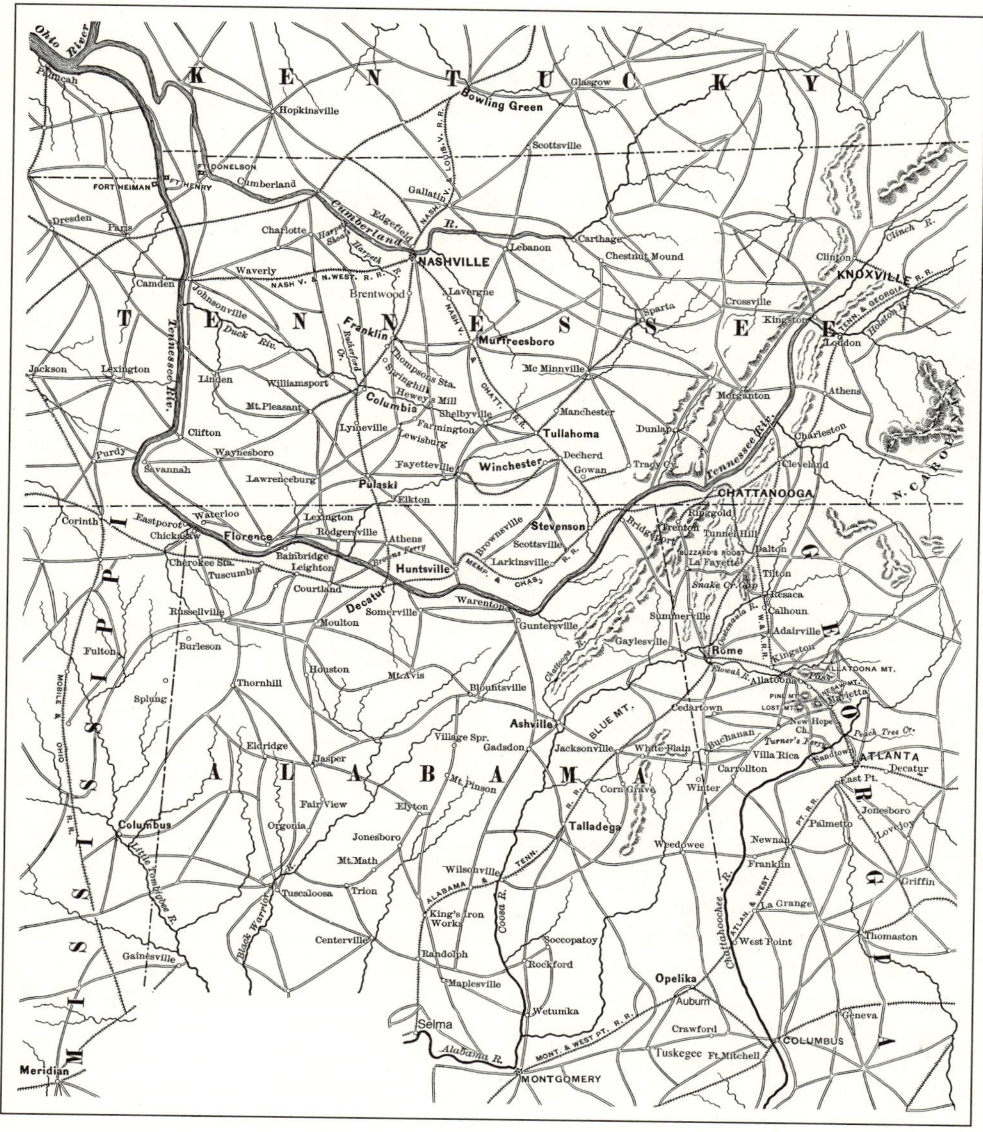

The first Confederate capital (Montgomery) and sites of military operations and Davis's travels, 1861–1864

end for Burton Harrison. This New Orleans native and Yale graduate became Davis's permanent private secretary in March of 1862, taking up residence on the third floor of the mansion. Thus the president, when too ill to get to the executive offices near the capitol, could carry on the business of the country at home.[4]

One night when Henry Heth was there, Davis gave him J. E. Johnston's letter to read, without comment. Heth had the feeling that Davis was just trying to hold him there as "some one to keep him company." He had said, "Don't go, I want to talk to you." About two o'clock in the morning, Davis was called out, and then reappeared "very nervous." It is some sort of tribute to the Davis reticence that Heth did not find out until the next day that a baby had been born. It was William Howell Davis. Varina finally had a son she could name for her father.[5]

Varina had come into her own. When she reached Richmond, she had written Ma, Jeff was "at the cars in the midst of hundreds of people," with "a carriage furnished us by the city with four horses, and open, with yellow satin lining. As we proceeded up the street bouquets were showered into the carriage, and hurrahs for the children. It is perfect man worship." She took command of her "very fine house" and its extensive ménage as if she were born to it. She had brought her own servants, and she hired others, notably the maid Ellen and Jim Jones, the coachman. She went in person to the Daughters of Charity and asked them for their prayers and "a practicing Catholic" to help in the nursery. They sent her an Irish girl named Catherine.[6] But this was by no means all the household. Margaret Howell was a permanent guest, as well as Harrison, and others continually came and went, keeping the third-floor rooms filled.[7]

Joseph and Eliza Davis were among the first visitors to the White House, along with their servants and five other family members. They were there for Varina's first big reception, which she gave for members of Congress in mid-August 1861. Eliza wrote home about the beautiful table appointments and the delicious punch, cake, and fruit; but also of how thin Jeff was, how he had cut his hair "close," how he hardly spoke to her and "rarely smiles": "I never saw a person so sadly changed."[8]

John Tyler was one of the Confederate congressmen. Varina was so stuck with the beauty of his young second wife that she just wanted to look at her without talking—a rare tribute. A few months later, this Julia Tyler and her seven children were left desolate when the venerable ex-president died in a Richmond hotel. Congress adjourned, Davis and Stephens spoke eulogies, the capitol bell "tolled all day," Bishop John Johns held the funeral at St. Paul's, and Virginia laid her "remarkable man" near President James Monroe in Hollywood Cemetery.[9]

The Davises at first entertained informally "almost nightly," but Jeff found this too much. Varina received alone once a week, and the *Richmond Examiner* attacked them for "parsimony" and "superior dignity."

Spiteful digs at Varina could not keep her from being a lively and popular hostess and guest. She and her friends, Mary Chesnut in particular, went on through the war years trying to uphold morale by a continual social whirl, even when reduced to ice water for refreshment. General Lee approved: his men needed this relaxation between battles.

The president enjoyed company, but little by little he withdrew from the frivolity. It seemed that bad news would invariably come during a party and upset both him and the guests. Also, chronic fatigue was setting in. Eliza noted, "He has so many callers he cannot take his meals in peace." He finally told Varina he could either entertain, or administer the government, but not both. So she limited herself to "informal dinners and breakfasts" and formal receptions. Constance Cary remembered Davis at the latter "always looking as if he bore the sorrows of a world," but "invariably courteous and sometimes playful in his talk with very young women," of whom she was one. Once, late in the war, he teased them about being reduced to eating rats—as good as mule meat, if fat, and less expensive.[10]

Throughout the war years, Davis, though "exhausted" at night, managed to attend certain notable affairs to benefit the army. One was a performance of *The Rivals* by Richard Brinsley Sheridan. Col. Joseph Ives had built a stage in his home, where he and his wife, née Cora Semmes, often entertained on behalf of Davis. The play drew three hundred people; Mallory declared it as good as Drury Lane; Mary Chesnut said Virginia Clay's Mrs. Malaprop was "beyond our wildest hopes."[11]

Charades and tableaux were popular. The president attended such a theatrical at the George Randolph home, and also the most memorable one at the home of Cora's brother, Sen. Thomas Jenkins Semmes, where characters in costume acted out words. Connie Cary almost missed her cue because of "a lively and pleasant conversation with the President." He had come to see Maggie in her stage debut. "She acted well" and moved gracefully, says the Chesnut diary, "and her splendid black eyes flashed." For the climax, the word *pilgrimage*, a shrine was set up, and a variety of people came worshipping. Burton Harrison was wearing a war bonnet that Indians had given Davis. "The gallant and joyous" Jeb Stuart, clad as a knight, advanced solemnly and offered his sword upon the altar beneath the cross. This was in January 1864; in "a few short months" he was dead.[12]

This brought the war home to the ladies, but the stark realities were always there for the president. As he wrote later, "We were involved in a great war without any preparations. Since Christians were thrown into the arena to fight unarmed with wild beasts there has not been a less equal conflict." He was too acutely aware of this to allow his personal feelings much play. At the end of September 1861, for example, he obeyed a summons from J. E. Johnston to come talk about strategy at his headquarters, though he thought it more proper for Johnston to come to him. He had already poured oil on jealousy-troubled waters there at Fairfax Court House, where Beauregard shared the command.[13] Beauregard, with Johnston and his "friend and protégé," Maj. Gen. Gustavus Woodson Smith (of whom Davis also thought highly), was pushing once again for an attack on Washington. Davis shared their desire for an offensive, but when he heard it would take ten or twenty thousand more men, he plainly said he could not supply them. The three generals had their answer ready: pull troops from every other spot. But every other spot was clamoring for protection. The enemy, in control of the coastal waters, might strike at any point on the whole periphery, and soon did. The main trouble was, not a single shipment of munitions had yet arrived from Europe. Davis had already told Johnston, "Had you arms to supply the 10,000 men you want, they could soon be had."[14]

Davis's War Department days had taught him much about disposing troops of inadequate force. He was perfectly aware that concentration was good military policy and urged it more than once. But he was responsible for the whole Confederacy, and he saw that giving up ground "seriously affected" morale. Hearing "the not uncommon mistake that I have chosen to carry on the war upon a 'purely defensive' system," he admitted "the error of my attempt to defend all the frontier, seaboard and inland; but . . . if we had received the arms and munitions which we had good reason to expect," it "would have been successful and the battlefields would have been on the enemy's soil." "For many months," he told another, "I have silently borne criticism on the supposition that I was opposed to offensive war, because to correct the error would have required the disclosure of facts which the public interest demanded should not be revealed."[15] Davis had even asked the Virginia legislature to send troops for Johnston. He told him then to curb "the natural impatience of the soldier" by "the devotion of the patriot." "[I] wish we could strike . . . a successful advance across the Potomac would relieve other places, but if not successful, ruin would befall us." It was the same now, and he had to say no to the wishes of his generals. To keep the troops active, he suggested small attacks on enemy communications, but they were not made.[16]

Smith wrote up this meeting, and the other two generals signed the account and kept copies. But Davis did not know this until 1880. Trusting people as usual, he had taken no one with him and had made no notes.[17] He now enlarged Johnston's command to embrace the three armies of the area as the Department of Northern Virginia.[18]

In coming months, he considered both Johnston and Smith for secretary of war and gave Smith the post briefly.[19] He still spoke soothingly to Beauregard: "My appreciation of you as a soldier and my regard for you as a man can not permit me willingly to wound your sensibility," "happy to receive your views and suggestions. . . . [With] prayers for your success, I am as ever / Your Friend." He even confided to the general his unhappiness in the presidency: "Others decided against my known desire and placed me where I am." He would "gladly exchange it" for any other, "if there I could better promote the end to which my life is devoted"—"the independence, and peace of the Confederacy." Not very subtly he added that his "best hope" was "that my co-laborers, purified and elevated by the sanctity of the cause they defend, would forget themselves in their zeal for the public welfare."

When Beauregard got into a dispute with Secretary of War Benjamin, Davis flattered him ("your genius and gallantry . . . among the smoke and blaze of battle"), and ended: "let me entreat you to dismiss this small matter from your mind" and contemplate instead, "the hostile masses before you. . . . My prayers always attend you; and with confidence I turn to you in the hour of peril." But the Creole was restive and resentful under J. E. Johnston. Davis finally sent him to second the command in the Department of the West. His friends thought he was being shelved, but he was ready "to do duty cheerfully wheresoever placed." He was a true patriot: he had asked to go to New Orleans. Before leaving Virginia, he did enough for glory again by designing the Confederate battle flag.[20]

The terrible discrepancy in manpower would plague the Confederacy to its end. Even now it was hampering Magruder at Yorktown.[21] It was trammeling Sidney Johnston. Davis had given his friend the first theater command, his innovative device for handling the vast areas involved in the South's defense. Called the Department of the West, it swept from the Kentucky mountains all the way to Indian Territory, and down the Mississippi (both sides) to the Red River. When Beauregard came, Sidney Johnston told him he had forty-five thousand men with which to defend this whole line. There was "feeble" response to his call for state troops. He could not convince the governors that "a decisive battle must probably be fought here for the freedom of the South."[22]

The left tip of the line was safe enough because President Davis had sent Douglas Hancock Cooper to secure relations, and Albert Pike to make treaties, with the various Indian Nations. Cooper, a captain in Davis's Mississippi Rifles, had been an Indian agent. He was to lead the First Choctaw and Chickasaw Mounted Rifles, one of many Indian units who fought for the Confederacy.[23]

The left center, Missouri, however, was in continual turmoil, all because William S. Harney had been repudiated by his government. In 1860, Harney had been one of only four generals of the line in the United States Army and had headed its Department of the West. He thought secessionists were "revolutionists" and traitors, but he did not believe in coercion. He had won a "bloodless victory" for the Union at St. Louis, he said, by agreeing with Sterling Price, head of the pro-Southern Missouri militia, that they would not attack each other. The Davises' erstwhile friends, the Blairs, held the political power in Missouri. Seeing they could not control the patronage with Harney there, they got him relieved of duty, intimating that he was disloyal. To his great rage, he was put on the shelf. In the real civil war that ensued in Missouri, Southerners were driven nearly out of the state; but their rump government voted to secede, creating a twelfth star for the Confederate flag.[24]

Gen. A. S. Johnston's new department enveloped Leonidas Polk's command. Polk was glad. He had asked Davis to appoint Johnston, planning to leave when he came. He had tried to resign in 1861, but Davis would not hear of it. He had gotten Bishops Meade and Otey and the layman Christopher Memminger to write to Polk. The latter argued: "both you and I are just as much *called and ordained* to the posts we occupy" as any "presbyter"; Davis was "the minister of God for the State," and when he appointed them, it was a sign "of Providence." Polk stayed. Now, in January 1862, he again tried to resign. This time, his friends John Perkins, Jr., and A. T. Bledsoe pleaded with him. Once more the bishop-general, who believing "resistance to tyrants is duty to God," stayed in his Mississippi River command.[25]

The president planned to woo his neutral native state into the Confederacy, but his beliefs, and Polk, got in the way. He had consistently refused to invade Kentucky, though under much pressure, unable to "violate the Cardinal principle . . . the guiding star of my political life"—state rights. Then General Grant was ordered to take Columbus and Paducah. His guns were in place across the river from Columbus, but Polk seized it first, September 3, 1861. When Gov. Beniah Magoffin complained, Polk said Kentucky had already violated neutrality by a camp for Northern recruits and congressional votes in support of war against the South. Davis told Polk to withdraw. Then Polk explained his military reasons, and Davis wired back: "The necessity must justify the action."[26] Grant beat Polk to Paducah, and then the whole Union force, poised for months, surged across the Ohio River into Kentucky. Sidney Johnston was just arriving, and Davis left further moves up to him. Polk had offered (as Johnston did later) to leave the state if the Federals would. This offer was not met, so Johnston said his troops "will not be withdrawn." Thus died Davis's hope of winning Kentucky by diplomacy.[27]

Johnston had to occupy Bowling Green, he said, "as an act of self-defense," to shield his strategic center, Tennessee, with its rail junctions. Its important base, Nashville, dispersed equipment, guns, and ammunition to the army as far away as Virginia. Brig. Gen. Simon Bolivar Buckner, a West Pointer who brought five hundred Kentucky State Guardsmen to the Confederacy, held Bowling Green until Johnston arrived on October 28, 1861. Hardee, now major general, brought well-drilled troops from Arkansas, and other small brigades came to

Johnston, one of them Floyd's, but the number was "kept down by disease" to "about 22,000," whereas Union troops in Kentucky numbered by early 1862, "between 75,000 and 100,000."

With one unit Johnston had specifically asked for, Terry's Texas Rangers, came the newly elected governor of Texas, F. R. Lubbock. He went on to Richmond and met Jefferson Davis for the first time. In 1900, he recalled thinking at the time "(which I still hold) that he was preeminently fitted" for the presidency.[28]

"Fully one-half" of the men under Johnston had no weapons. When he appealed to Davis in January of 1862, his helpless friend cried out to the messenger, "My God! why did General Johnston send you to me for arms and reinforcements when he must know that I have neither?" Col. Edward Munford said: "To those who ask why so able a man . . . *seemed* to fail, four words will answer, namely—*he had no army.*"[29]

Johnston had hoped to increase his strength by Kentucky recruits. He put his brother-in-law, William Preston, on his staff. There were Buckner and Humphrey Marshall, who was sent to the mountains as a brigadier general. Col. Ben Hardin Helm and Capt. John Hunt Morgan came, bringing their cavalry units. John C. Breckinridge, having resigned the Senate, fled to escape the military despotism descending on Kentucky.[30] The number disappointed Johnston, but enough came South to make up the First Kentucky "Orphan Brigade," of which Breckinridge took command. The presence of Southern troops enabled a Russellville convention to vote Kentucky into the Confederacy as its thirteenth state.[31]

General Johnston, with "little more than a 400-mile skirmish line," kept shifting troops so that the Union commander in Kentucky (Anderson, then Sherman, then Don Carlos Buell) would think he had more men than he did. The ruse worked: Sherman wondered later, as the Confederate Congress did now, why he did not take Louisville. Johnston weakened his own position to reinforce the back-to-back forts just below the Tennessee border—Henry on the Tennessee River and Donelson on the Cumberland. If he were not himself reinforced, he said, Nashville must fall.[32]

Winfield Scott had resigned and been replaced by George McClellan on November 1, 1861. The new general-in-chief was too smart to order attack at Bowling Green or Columbus, but Henry Halleck, the western commander, told him Columbus could be "turned, paralyzed, and forced to surrender." So flanking attacks began. In January, a tiny detached force on the Confederate right was defeated at Mill Springs (Fishing Creek), Kentucky.[33] Maj. Gen. George Crittenden, already suspect because his father and brother stayed with the Union, was accused of drunkenness. Once again, Davis defended the Kentuckian, just as he had in the old army.[34]

Johnston, "determined to fight for Nashville at Donelson," sent sixteen thousand more men to the Tennessee forts. But Halleck sent Grant with gunboats, of which Johnston had not one, and demolished his whole left flank. Fort Henry fell on February 6 and Fort Donelson on February 16. Grant could order gunboats up the Cumberland River the short distance to Nashville, and up the Tennessee, all the way to North Alabama.

Columbus was indeed turned, and Bowling Green too; both were abandoned; Polk withdrew his main force to Corinth, just south of the Mississippi border. Here Beauregard took command. Johnston, now in Nashville, termed the loss of the forts "indefensible." But he saw he had "no alternative" and ordered a retreat to Murfreesboro, thirty-two miles southeast. Here on February 23 he resumed command from Hardee, who brought the troops down from Bowling Green.

Some seven or eight thousand were captured at Fort Donelson, but not Col. Nathan Bedford Forrest, who got his cavalrymen out, and not the major generals, John B. Floyd and Gideon Pillow, who fled with some of their troops, leaving Buckner to surrender to "our ungenerous enemy." The unconditional terms and his subsequent confinement in solitary, he said, were not "civilized warfare."

At the same time, another Confederate flank was taken. The United States Navy, having destroyed a tiny fleet trying to defend it, seized Roanoke Island, North Carolina, the key to Albemarle Sound and its rivers.[35]

These were the "serious disasters" that Jefferson Davis felt bound to mention, when, on February 22, 1862, he became permanent (instead of provisional) president of the Confederate States. He and Alexander Stephens had been elected in November virtually by acclamation. Only Beauregard had been suggested for president, and he had refused to run.[36] Both the day and the place were in honor of George Washington, whom the whole South revered. Davis called him "the wisest, greatest of them all, the immortal." Georgia's T. R. R. Cobb had wanted to name the country after him. In the rotunda of the Richmond capitol stood his lifelike marble statue by the French sculptor Jean Antoine Houdon. On the lawn outside, above the figures of Virginia's other Revolutionary leaders, Washington sat in bronze, astride a prancing horse. This was the image chosen for the great seal. On a platform at the foot of this monument, Davis began his inaugural speech by referring to Washington's "heroic virtues."[37]

There were no spring flowers falling this time, but a wintry mixture of snow and rain. The president, in his "plain citizen's suit of black," stood addressing the "immense crowd" all unmindful that he had stepped from under the protecting canopy. (Someone put an umbrella over him.) He was absorbed in drawing from the people fervor equal to his own.

He told them that all hope of "a returning sense of justice" in the North was now "dispelled." Against "the tyranny of an unbridled majority . . . we are in arms to renew such sacrifices as our fathers made to the holy cause of constitutional liberty." This was also the anniversary of Buena Vista, and Davis warned that war cost "money and blood," but "nothing could be so bad as failure." Providence was perhaps teaching them the price of "our liberties." The struggle had awakened "the highest emotions and qualities of the human soul." "Instances of self-sacrifice and of generous devotion to the noble cause . . . are rife throughout the land."[38]

Varina had found him in his room that morning "on his knees in earnest prayer 'for the support I need so sorely.'" At the end of his speech, he confessed "unaffected diffidence" (even as Washington had done) and "humble gratitude and adoration" for the protection of Providence. Then, raising eyes and hands to the unpropitious heavens, he concluded, "To Thee, O God, I trustingly commit myself, and prayerfully invoke Thy blessing on my country and its cause."

> Thus Mr. Davis entered on his martyrdom. As he stood pale and emaciated, . . . evidently forgetful of everything but his sacred oath, he seemed to me a willing victim going to his funeral pyre, and the idea so affected me that making some excuse I regained my carriage and went home.[39]

Already a "recent severe indisposition" had given Davis a "pallor, painful to look upon," and cares invaded both "waking and sleeping hours." Now came the fires of spiritual trial, as Gen. Albert Sidney Johnston and the president who had appointed him suffered "anathema and denunciation."[40]

Davis was told that everyone thought Johnston had "culpably and inexcusably lost" the Mississippi Valley and could never reorganize his army. A newspaper called Davis "incompetent," "motionless as a clod," and "cold as ice" for retaining him. The new Congress voted to investigate. The Tennessee members came to Davis demanding Johnston's removal "because he is no general." "I paused under conflicting emotions," says Davis, knowing that Johnston's place "could not be filled by his equal," and "wounded by the injustice done to one I . . . believed to be one of the noblest men . . . and ablest soldiers I had ever seen." "After a time [I] merely answered: 'If Sidney Johnston is not a general, the Confederacy has none to give you.'" Such was the vibrant complexity behind a seemingly cold pronouncement.[41]

To cap Davis's agony came tempting appeals to his vanity: "Nothing but your presence here can save Tennessee. . . . For God's sake, come!" "The people now look to you as their deliverer . . . assume command, as you promised in a speech to take the field whenever it should become necessary." Davis ignored these telegrams. "He, almost alone, remained unmoved," says Preston Johnston, "and that intrepidity of intellectual conviction, characteristic of him, so often and so mistakenly called his obstinacy, saved the Confederacy, not only from a great injustice, but from a great mistake." But even Hardee was saying privately, "Nothing can save us except the presence of the President, who ought to come here, assume command, and call on people to rally to his standard."[42]

After enduring in virtual silence for a month, Davis finally expressed in a private letter to Johnston his "great anxiety," "not a little disturbed" by the "reflections" on him. The president had been looking for a full report on Fort Donelson.

> In the mean time I made for you such defense as friendship prompted and many years of acquaintance justified, but I needed facts to rebut the wholesale assertions made against you, to cover others, and to condemn my administration. The public, as you are aware, have no correct measure for military operations, and the journals are very reckless in their statements. Your force has been magnified . . . and the absence of an effective force at Nashville ignored. You have been held responsible for the fall of Donelson and the capture of Nashville. . . . [This has] undermined public confidence and damaged our cause. A full development of the truth is necessary. . . . I respect the generosity which has kept you silent, but would impress upon you, that the subject is not personal but public in its nature; that you and I might be content to suffer, but neither of us can willingly permit detriment to the country.

He planned to come out, simply to help bring "men to your standard." "We are deficient in arms, wanting in discipline, and inferior in numbers." "General Bragg [whom he had ordered to Corinth] brings you disciplined troops, and you will find in him the highest administrative capacity."

> With a sufficient force, the audacity which the enemy exhibits would no doubt give you the opportunity to cut some of his lines of communication, to break up his plan of campaign, and, defeating some of his columns, to drive him from the soil as well of Kentucky as of Tennessee. . . . I suppose the Tennessee or Mississippi river will be the object of the enemy's next campaign, and I trust you will be able to concentrate a force which will defeat either attempt.[43]

Two foreign officers at Bowling Green had pronounced Sidney Johnston "the very *beau-idéal* of a general." Polk, who thought him "high-toned, eminently honorable and just," had once sent him a cameo of George Washington because he was so much like him in character. Johnston magnanimously refused to blame Floyd and Pillow for the disaster at Fort Donelson, though everyone else did. He gave them new commands in his army. Davis refused to believe that the generals had "surrendered without a desperate effort to cut their way through investing forces," until he read their reports. Then he ordered both "relieved from command until further orders."[44]

Lt. Col. Randal McGavock of the Tenth Tennessee Regiment, surrendered at Fort Donelson, said its officers were "unanimously of the opinion . . . that President Davis did exactly right." Both officers and men held Floyd and Pillow in "universal execration . . . for their disertion, and unmilitary conduct." Davis never forgot the contrast to Brig. Gen. Lloyd Tilghman who, knowing Fort Henry was doomed, stayed firing his guns till the moment of surrender so that his two thousand men could escape to Donelson and fight the main battle: "For this soldierly devotion and self-sacrifice the gallant commander and his brave band must be honored while patriotism has an advocate and self-sacrifice for others has a votary."[45]

Sidney Johnston never showed his command of men more clearly than in this crisis. Perfectly calm in the ruins of his army, he reorganized it at Murfreesboro and slowly restored its morale, with the help of Hardee, as he led it down to the Tennessee River and across to Decatur, Alabama. From there, it could take the cars northwest to reach the other troops at Corinth, Mississippi. Once he had his men "in good order," and safely in motion south of the river, he took time for the full report on Fort Donelson that Davis wanted.[46]

"The blow was most disastrous," he admitted, "and almost without remedy." "Had I wholly uncovered my front" (by sending everyone to Donelson), Buell would have "marched directly on Nashville." He was deeply sensible that Davis's "friendship and confidence . . . have not been withdrawn from me in adversity." His own silence was not "generosity": it just seemed "the best way to serve the cause and the country." He addressed Davis as "My dear General" and urged him to come inspire the troops. If he decided to take command, "it would afford me the most unfeigned pleasure." Davis resisted this severe temptation. In the end, he did not even go.

"In conformity with my original design," Johnston was moving to join Beauregard "for the defense of the valley of the Mississippi." This "was deemed too hazardous by the most experienced members of my staff, but the object warranted the risk." The head of his column was already in Corinth. If all his troops arrived, he would have an army of over forty thousand, which "must be destroyed before the enemy can attain his object." "The test of merit in my profession with the people is success. It is a hard rule, but I think it right. If I join this corps to the forces of Beauregard . . . those who are now declaiming against me will be without an argument." He had said, if he could just get "where I can fight a battle . . . I think all will be well."[47]

Johnston's aide, who delivered this letter, watched, while talking with Lee, for Davis's reaction. "As his eye was raised from the paper, there seemed a tenderness in its expression, bordering on tears, surprising and pleasing." It was mostly relief. Davis dashed off a reply "in great haste."

> I hope the public will soon give me credit for judgment, rather than continue to arraign me for obstinacy . . . I breathe easier in the assurance that you will be able to make a junction of your two armies. If you can meet the division of the enemy [under Grant] moving from the Tennessee [River] before it can make a junction with that advancing from Nashville [under Buell], the future will be brighter. If [not] . . . our only hope is that the people . . . will rally *en masse* with their private arms, and thus enable you to oppose the vast army which will threaten the destruction of our country. . . . [It] would be worse than useless to point out to you how much depends upon you.
>
> May God bless you is the sincere prayer of your friend,
>
> Jefferson Davis.[48]

Braxton Bragg had retained his low opinion of Jeff Davis after their 1855 quarrel. He felt slighted as the Confederacy began. His wife, Elise, said to their friend William T. Sherman, "You know that my husband is not a favorite with the new president." Shortly after this, Davis commissioned Bragg. He came to admire his "generosity and self abnegation" and his training of raw troops. He told Bragg's brother Thomas that he was "the only General in command of an Army who had shewn himself equal to the management of Volunteers and at the same time commanded their love and respect." Davis promoted him to major general on September 12, 1861, and offered him command of the Trans-Mississippi. Benjamin's letter reveals Davis's method: "[we] anxiously scanned every name on our army list, and . . . we invariably fell back on yours." But Bragg did not want it. He told Benjamin, however, that "should the President decide on it," he would "offer myself (as a sacrifice, if necessary) to the great cause in which we are engaged." Davis did not insist. He sent Maj. Gen. Earl Van Dorn instead.[49]

Now Bragg had brought his "reputation for gallantry and efficiency" to Corinth, and Beauregard divided command of the "Army of the Mississippi" between him and Polk. Beauregard had had surgery on his throat before leaving Virginia and had been sick ever since. He wrote Bragg on March 17, 1862, "My physician tells me that I must stop talking altogether, and avoid any undue excitement. How in the world can that be done, at this critical moment?"[50]

Gen. Sidney Johnston arrived at Corinth on March 24. He made Bragg his chief of staff and commander of his second corps. Polk led the first corps, Hardee the third. George Crittenden had the fourth or reserve, until Bragg had him arrested (drunkenness again); then Breckinridge took it. Bragg struggled to organize "an heterogeneous mass": "new levies . . . all badly armed and equipped," with columns converging riskily from several directions. The task, he said later, "was simply appalling." But he had them ready for the fight when it came.[51]

As Davis had urged, Johnston planned to strike quickly, before the enemy could unite. Buell was marching through Middle Tennessee to meet Grant and take Corinth, which controlled rail traffic in all directions. Grant was camped some twenty miles northeast of Corinth, on the west bank of the Tennessee River, thinking that only Beauregard was before him, and in the town. He told Buell not to hurry.[52]

Johnston wired Davis on April 3, "*Hope engagement before Buell can form junction.*" Bragg was still organizing the troops, and Van Dorn had not arrived from Arkansas, but the army was already in lumbering motion toward Grant's camp at Pittsburgh Landing. The attempt at surprise was in so much danger from disorder, noise, and delay that Beauregard wanted to turn back. Johnston was adamant. On the eve of battle, he said to two different people, "I would fight them if they were a million." Bragg thought Johnston's "coolness, confidence, and determination" inspiring. His son says: "In the simple but sublime confidence of his creed—'in the great hand of God I stand'—he moved on to his fate."[53]

At dawn on April 6, Johnston went to the front to lead the troops, Hardee the first line, Bragg the second, leaving Beauregard at the command post. This was Shiloh Church, as soon as Sherman was driven out of it. Basil Duke, of Morgan's cavalry, said the infantry hit the Federals in their tents, "giving them no time to form, driving them in rapid panic." Fierce resistance developed, but "they never recovered from the stun of the surprise." As Hardee's attack slowed, "Bragg's disciplined tornado burst upon them." So it went all day until the Unionists were driven "from every position" on the field, to a last ridge above the landing on the riverbank.[54]

Before that, though, a stubborn stand had made one spot into "the Hornet's Nest." Johnston rode up there with his hat gone, his clothing torn by spent balls, and in his hand a little tin cup, which he wafted with more effect "than most men could have used a sword." He rode along, touching the men's bayonets. Saying "These must do the work," he wheeled his horse and cried, "I will lead you!" The onrush drove the Federals back almost a mile. His aide, the Tennessee governor-in-exile Isham G. Harris, said, "I had never in my life seen him looking more bright, joyous, and happy." Harris galloped off with an order and galloped back to find the general reeling in the saddle. When he finally got him to the ground, he kept looking for "a more serious wound than the one . . . bleeding profusely in the right leg; but I found no other." There was no other. A minié ball had severed an artery. Johnston had just sent his surgeon off to tend the wounded, friend and foe, and in a few minutes, he "ceased to breathe." His features were as "calm and natural" as in life. This is the way he appears today, lying above his grave in Austin, Texas, in marble sculpture by Elizabet Ney.[55]

William Preston wired the president: Johnston had died "gaining a brilliant victory." Staff members took his body immediately to New Orleans. Eighteen days later, the city fell to the Union navy, but the tomb in St. Louis Cemetery was always decorated with fresh flowers and a written tribute to Johnston's "sublime" simplicity ("His life was one long Sacrifice of Interest to Conscience") until Austin claimed the body in 1867. Both were occupied cities still, and the Union conquerors allowed no military honors. In New Orleans, eight generals were his pallbearers, but they were in mufti. As the body lay briefly in Houston, Davis though imprisoned in Fortress Monroe, was with his friend in a portrait above the coffin.[56]

On the night of April 6, Beauregard, too, wired Richmond: "thanks be to the Almighty, [we have] gained a complete victory." In the morning, victory was jarringly made incomplete. Buell had arrived and ferried his troops across the river all night. "Our wearied men found before them a fresh army," says Hardee. The fighting was "fierce and indecisive." Beauregard reported that Polk "made one of the most brilliant charges." "We fought them with varied success for eight hours," Bragg wrote to Elise, until "[we] retired in good order, though I must say because the enemy did not pursue." Breckinridge, with Forrest's cavalry, made sure of that. The army went back unmolested to Corinth, reduced by over ten thousand men.[57]

Hardee said that but for the "calamity" of Johnston's death, the triumph at Shiloh would have been "signal." General Polk too said this, and Beauregard's "order to retire," that followed it, were what "saved the Federals from capture or destruction" on the first day. When Bragg, "hotly pursuing" the enemy, heard the order, he said immediately, "The battle is lost." Up until then, he wrote Elise two days later, it was "a great victory." He always maintained that Johnston, executing "his general plan," was "eminently successful up to the moment of his fall. *The victory was won.*"[58]

In his report, though he mentioned this order, Bragg refrained from criticizing Beauregard. The two had become quite close. On the night of April 6, Beauregard had made Bragg second in command. He recommended that Bragg be "appointed to General A. S. Johnston's place." Davis at once appointed him full general, but, as even Bragg admitted, no one could take Johnston's place.[59]

What the death of Sidney Johnston meant to Davis is almost incalculable. His personal grief was so great that he dared not "trust myself" to express it, he told Congress, but "it may safely be asserted that our loss is irreparable." He still could not speak of it twenty-one years later, but simply said, "ruin stared before us." Although Davis advised "humble submission" to this "severe dispensation" of "an all-wise Creator," he believed quite simply that the cause of Confederate independence was lost.[60] Richard Taylor, Bragg, and others thought this, looking back. Davis thought it then. His aide, Preston Johnston, heard him say "not once, but many times: 'When Sidney Johnston fell, it was the turning-point of our fate; for we had no other hand to take up his work in the West' " (i.e., Beauregard, Bragg, and J. E. Johnston in succession failed to measure up). "How much his loss must have pierced your heart," Northrop wrote Davis after the war; "it was a terrible trial to your fortitude."[61]

Davis at least had another friend in Richmond who could sympathize, Robert E. Lee. He had called him back to his staff on March 2, 1862, with a typically deprecatory "order": "If circumstances will, in your judgment, warrant your leaving, I wish to see you here with the least delay." "Each man had prodigious talent and saw it in the other," says Frank Vandiver: "They made a powerful team." "He was my friend," Davis said, "and in that word is included all that I could say of any man." In Varina's words, Lee became, on Sidney Johnston's death, "his best friend."[62]

The rector of St. Paul's Episcopal Church, Dr. Minnigerode, christened William Howell Davis on March 4 at the executive mansion. On any Sunday, from his high white pulpit centered in the front of the church, where he preached in Germanic English, he could count on seeing Lee in his pew close down on his right, and farther back on his left, the Davis family. He said Davis "never failed to be there" unless sick or away from town. A British visitor noted the president showing little Jeff the place in the prayer book, to "guide him in the chants."[63]

Davis was constant in attendance but still not a member of the Episcopal church. Perhaps it was old Bishop Meade's letter in January: "like Washington . . . you look up to the great Ruler for guidance and support. May you not only be the instrument of great good . . . but be eternally saved yrself & yr whole household"; or Minnigerode's request that he avow his faith at the inauguration: "I reminded Mr. Davis that the character of the ruler was apt to become the guide or pattern of the people"; or the fact that Sidney Johnston had also gone with his wife but had died outside the church. Something was making Davis think about confirmation.[64]

But at the moment, those "thorns innumerable" that he had foreseen were springing up on every side. As if Shiloh were not enough, his former protégé McClellan was massing troops to thrust at Richmond, and Southern defense was still "limited by the supply of arms." Hopes for recognition by England, stemming from the *Trent* Affair, had been snuffed out when the Southern envoys, James Mason and John Slidell, who had been kidnapped off the British ship, were released by the North and sent on their way to London and Paris. The newly elected First Congress, which supplanted the provisional body, was showing opposition by refusing Davis's request to establish a supreme court. Military setbacks were bringing open assault.[65]

The president was still very popular; the people had returned his supporters to Congress. Howell Cobb, who called him "perverse and obstinate," and his brother, Thomas Reade Rootes Cobb, both about to leave for the army, had agreed with Robert Toombs (back during the winter lull in fighting) to "condemn [Davis's] errors" but support him "when he is right." "Stephens on the contrary, a poor selfish demagogue" was simply "factious," said T. R. R. Cobb, trying to create "an opposition party."[66]

Yancey, who had returned from England to become an Alabama senator, meant to sustain the government, but he fought Davis on certain issues. When he and Clay tried to tell Davis how many Alabama generals he should appoint (resenting the number of Virginians), Davis returned the letter, saying he would "respectfully" consider it, but "[I] do not recognize the fairness of the within statement of my course, and assumption as to what it should be." This made Yancey hostile.[67]

And Henry S. Foote was back in Davis's life, like a thorn in the flesh. Tennessee, where he now made his home, had sent him to the House of Representatives. It was he who had sparked the attack on Sidney Johnston. He never took the floor without castigating Davis and his administration. He had even led an attempt to depose him, backed by R. B. Rhett, who, unseated from Congress and back in Charleston, was flaying Davis regularly in the *Mercury*.[68]

Foote leapt at a chance to attack through Benjamin. He had angered Gen. T. J. ("Stonewall") Jackson by sending him a tactical order, and Gen. J. E. Johnston, by sending it over his head, and he was blamed for the loss of Roanoke Island. Before a congressional committee could report on the latter, Davis eased Benjamin out of the War Department and into the State Department, which R. M. T. Hunter had conveniently vacated to become senator from Virginia. Many wanted a military man to head the War Department, and Davis appointed Brig. Gen. George Randolph.[69]

In the midst of assault, Davis could always lean on Lee with "entire confidence." He gave him a specific task in March: creating a law to conscript soldiers. This went against the grain with Davis, a believer in patriotism and in state rights, but as president, he saw it as absolutely necessary. Lee and Maj. Charles Marshall drew up particulars, Benjamin shaped a bill, and Louis Wigfall led it through the Senate—the first conscription law in American history. There was bitter debate; the law was not popular; but Davis says it began to place the army in "a permanent and efficient condition." He asked for an overall commander for the South but then vetoed the bill Congress passed, because its provisions were vague and impinged on his constitutional prerogative as commander in chief. Despite reports of a storm in Congress over it, only one man opposed his veto.[70]

In place of this, he gave General Lee "the conduct of military operations in the armies of the Confederacy," under his own civilian control, as a general in chief would have been too. Some thought this a vacuous position, but T. R. R. Cobb said, "Lee is acting as commanding general and is doing good." Lee's adjutant, Walter H. Taylor, pointed out what real authority he had in this post. Lee could certainly order troops about; his doing so made J. E. Johnston so mad at one point that he asked to be relieved of "a merely nominal geographical command." Lee soothed Johnston and worked out with Jackson the brilliant valley campaign that kept reinforcements from reaching McClellan. Davis considered him "in command of all the armies of the Confederate States."[71]

Davis asked Lee's advice on all military questions from now on, even when he was in the field, and not only about Virginia. Having "entire harmony of purpose," Davis said, "we never disagreed." How could they? They vied in deferring to each other's judgment. If they were of two minds, they would discuss the issue until they were of one. Lee testified to a grand jury after the war that they "always finally reached the same conclusion." He told Burton Harrison that Davis "was the best military adviser he had ever consulted."[72]

Davis had, furthermore, put Lee's son Custis on his staff in 1861, along with his own nephew J. R. Davis. These "aides-de-camp," ranking as cavalry colonels, advised him, transmitted his wishes, gathered information, and sometimes signed commissions and wrote letters.[73] On April 19, 1862, Davis named four more: Joseph C. Ives (who came from Lee's staff), Preston Johnston (from the disbanded First Kentucky Infantry), William M. Browne (from the State Department), and James Chesnut, who joined the staff in October.[74]

Davis's main attention now was the army, not only by preference but by necessity. With twelve-month enlistments ending, the first draftees coming in, and state troops clamoring to be kept together, he had to direct reorganization in the face of a Yankee army building for attack.[75] J. E. Johnston had been disobeying the orders to reshuffle his command ever since winter. When Davis kept after him about it even into May, the general accused him of giving a "scolding to one whom he ought, for the public interest, to try to be on good terms with" and implied that Davis was no gentleman. Johnston's friend and biographer says, quite seriously: "He did not believe that Mr. Davis appreciated or understood at all the real conditions of the struggle. He believed that his large experience had qualified him far beyond the President to judge and decide as to proper measures and movements."[76]

Davis had written him in May, "While some have expressed surprise at my patience when orders to you were not observed, I have at least hoped that you would recognize the desire to aid and sustain you." But Johnston, still smarting from his "sense of cruel injustice . . . on the question of rank," had kept up a running battle against the administration, especially Benjamin, whom he privately termed "that miserable little Jew." He had quarreled continuously with him over army organization. When Stonewall Jackson had threatened to resign over a Benjamin order, Johnston had advised him not to, but had told him they should both ask to be relieved if not given a free hand. Johnston did ask relief from the valley command (not his other troops), but Davis kept him there and supported Benjamin (but no one interfered with Jackson again). When Gen. Chase Whiting wrote Benjamin an "insubordinate" letter, which Davis thought would excite "a mutinous and disorganizing spirit," Johnston admitted a share "in the wrong."[77]

After a February conference in Richmond, when people asked Johnston about a decision to retire from Centerville (which even his apologist saw as just a natural rumor), he took it as an information leak and decided never to tell Davis his plans again. Timing of this withdrawal was left to Johnston. He pulled back to Gordonsville without ever telling Davis, who had warned him repeatedly to send back his baggage and heavy guns beforehand. He burned tons of supplies and destroyed scarce rolling stock and a whole meat-packing plant because he fell back with unnecessary haste, so Davis and Robert Toombs thought.[78]

Brigadier General Toombs called his commander Johnston "a poor devil, small, arbitrary and inefficient," acting "from a mere fondness for power," though "polite and clever": "I never knew as incompetent [an] executive officer." He said about Johnston's "dying" army (often erroneously applied to Davis): "set down . . . its epitaph, '*died of West Point.*' " Toombs did say later: "The utter incompetency of Mr. Davis and his West Point generals have brought us to the verge of ruin." He was angry over Johnston's destruction of "millions of stores": "Never was any business worse managed. The enemy had no more idea of attacking us in Centreville than they had of attacking the Peaks of Otter."[79]

This was true, as it turned out, but at the time, even the Yankees were not sure which way they would come at Richmond. The effect of Johnston's retreat was to release the pressure on Washington City and free McClellan to move to the peninsula. Lincoln kept forty thousand men under McDowell to protect the capital, however, fearing Jackson, who pursued a vigorous campaign in the valley of Virginia.[80]

As soon as McClellan poured his troops ashore at Fortress Monroe late in March, Lee worked out a comprehensive plan for the peninsula, giving Magruder a defense line on the Warwick River below Yorktown. But Magruder had ten thousand men; McClellan soon had "nearly 112,000." This was the subject of an anxious conference on April 14,

1862. Johnston had by now brought most of his army down to Richmond and was to take command. Confederates were outnumbered at least two-to-one. The big question was whether to defend the peninsula. Secretary of War Randolph and Generals Lee, Johnston, Longstreet, and G. W. Smith talked, while President Davis mostly listened.[81]

Lee and Randolph thought they must hold the peninsula, especially since its loss meant loss of Norfolk, just opposite, and with it the only semblance of a navy the Confederacy had. The *Virginia* was there, that ironclad ship which had revolutionized naval warfare in March by sinking the wooden *Cumberland* and *Congress*, and fighting a drawn battle with the Federal ironclad *Monitor.* Fear of her was still keeping Union ships close to shore. Johnston and his partisans, Longstreet and Smith, proposed instead: 1) abandon the peninsula and Norfolk, and gather all troops from Virginia through Georgia to meet McClellan before Richmond; or 2) take all these troops and threaten Washington, leaving Magruder with a few to stand a siege of Richmond. Finally, past one o'clock the next morning, the president decided in favor of Lee's plan: defend the peninsula.[82]

Johnston believed that events "would soon compel the Confederate Government to adopt my method," and this "reconciled me somewhat to the necessity of obeying the President's order." Magruder's position was so weak, Johnston wrote Lee, that "No one but McClellan could have hesitated to attack." "The fight for Yorktown, as I said in Richmond, must be one of artillery, in which we cannot win. The result is certain; the time only doubtful." The heavier Union artillery could also destroy his guns guarding the river landings on either flank: "We must abandon the Peninsula soon." Again he urged his second plan: cross the Potomac with all the troops "while Beauregard, with all we have in the West, invades Ohio." To this fantasy, Lee answered calmly: "impracticable." Then Johnston did what he had wanted all along, pulled out of the Yorktown line. When his wire came that he was leaving the next night, Davis wired back: this "takes us by surprise, and must involve enormous losses including unfinished gun boats [at Norfolk]. Will the safety of your army allow more time?" Then there was silence until the rumor that Johnston was in full retreat up the peninsula reached Richmond on Sunday, May 4.[83]

This bombshell kept President Davis out of his pew at St. Paul's that day, even though he was supposed to be baptized and confirmed. Dr. Minnigerode says Davis had spoken "most humbly of needing the cleansing blood of Jesus and the power of the Holy Spirit." He felt "in his inmost soul" he was a Christian but was uncertain whether he had been baptized. Minnigerode went to the White House later in the day and christened Davis conditionally ("If thou art not already baptized"), pouring the blessed water over his head three times, in the name of the

Holy Trinity. The soldier Davis was entering the church militant. A cross was traced on his forehead in token that he should "not be ashamed to confess the faith of Christ crucified, and manfully to fight under his banner" as "Christ's faithful soldier . . . unto his life's end."[84]

Then on Tuesday, Bishop Johns completed Davis's initiation into the Church. There was a special confirmation service at St. Paul's, for him, Col. Josiah Gorgas and his wife, Amelia, and one other. Minnigerode says Davis showed his "resolute character" by leading the way to the altar rail. After "confirming" his baptismal vows, he knelt there, with the bishop's hands on his head, and heard the prayer, "Defend, O Lord, this thy Child with thy heavenly grace; that he may continue thine forever; and daily increase in thy Holy Spirit more and more, until he come unto thy everlasting kingdom. Amen." He might now, if believing, penitent, and in charity with all, receive the other great sacrament, the Holy Communion.[85]

Varina says "the joy of being received into the Church seemed to pervade his soul," and "a peace which passed understanding seemed to settle in his heart." He needed that; his faith merely goaded unbelievers to contempt. Edmund Ruffin told his diary: "To the morbid tenderness of conscience of a 'seeker of religion,' & a new convert [neither of which Davis was], I ascribe much of the imbecility of President Davis, in failing to punish military & political criminals—deserters, spies & traitors."[86] Wigfall wrote to Clay that with Richmond in danger, the government was "a dish of skimmed milk," and Davis "I suppose at this time engaged in prayer." The *Richmond Examiner,* under atheist John M. Daniel, pictured Davis "standing in a corner telling his beads, and relying on a miracle to save the country." Other enemies saw him as Cromwell or Richard III, using a show of religion to become a despot. One man gloated that at least baptism would estrange him from the Jew, Benjamin. Even Northrop was depressed; he had set his heart on his friend's becoming a Catholic.[87]

Davis's peace was also threatened by military fiascos and defecting political friends. Wigfall, now a Texas senator, was drinking a lot, abusing Davis in public places, and advising J. E. Johnston to disobey orders. The latter had again lost precious matériel in retreating up the peninsula, though much loss could not be helped. On Friday, May 16, Davis, obeying his own national summons, went to St. Paul's for a service of "humble supplication to Almighty God" for protection and blessing "on our beloved country"—the fourth of ten such days of prayer that he proclaimed, either for fasting and humiliation or for thanksgiving, during the life of the Confederacy.[88] He wrote to Varina that evening, making excuses for those who failed to come, speaking his heart:

> As the clouds grow darker, and when one after another of those who are trusted are detected in secret hostility, I feel like mustering

> clans were in me, and that cramping fetters had fallen from my limbs. The great temporal object is to secure our independence, and they who engage in strife for personal or party aggrandizement deserve contemptuous forgetfulness. I have no political wish beyond the success of our cause, no personal desire but to be relieved from further connection with office; opposition in any form can only disturb me insomuch as it may endanger the public welfare. . . . Be of good cheer and continue to hope that God will in due time deliver us from the hands of our enemies and "sanctify to us our deepest distress."[89]

He was quoting a favorite hymn, "How Firm a Foundation." Varina often heard him "with fervor" repeating to himself from it, "I'll strengthen thee, help thee, and cause thee to stand / Upheld by my righteous, omnipotent hand." Another line was, "When through the deep waters I call thee to go." These were rolling relentlessly in. New Orleans had fallen—the city that Davis preferred to all others. Adm. David Farragut had brushed aside the few Southern gunboats and steamed his flotilla past defending forts, to compel surrender on April 29. Blame fell on Confederate commanders and the Davis government. Maj. Gen. B. F. Butler landed an occupying force on May 1, but not before William Howell, naval agent in the suburb of Algiers, escaped upriver with daughters Jennie and Margaret (who was visiting from Richmond). Ma was away, but she joined them later, and they refugeed in Montgomery, Alabama. The whole Mississippi River, and Davis Bend with it, lay open to the enemy fleet. Farragut lost no time, seizing Baton Rouge and Natchez by May 13, and then shelling Vicksburg, fruitlessly, before retiring downriver.[90]

By then Joseph Emory Davis was also a refugee. The minute he heard that Farragut had passed the forts, he left the Hurricane, taking Eliza and Lise to the farm of his friend Owen B. Cox near Clinton. He had already sent two hundred bales of cotton, patriotically unsold, up the Big Black River for safety. Jeff Davis answered a newspaper charge that this was to keep from burning it, but it soon went up in flames when Gen. Martin Luther Smith, commanding at Vicksburg, ordered all cotton in the area burned. Although Joseph did not do it, Jeff had suggested sending cattle and slaves away too, feeling their land would be an object of "special malignity" and "an attraction to plunderers." That would come, but now his plantation, his brother, and his financial loss were added to his other worries.[91]

Varina herself was a refugee. Typically, a courier with bad news came during a Davis reception on May 9. Jeff whispered the message to her: "The enemy's gun-boats are ascending the river." They had kept right on being gracious hosts, but the very next day Jeff insisted that she take the four children and go to comparative safety in Raleigh, North Carolina. She wrote from there:

> Don't risk your precious life, my own noble Husband. . . . [The people] will be quite reassured if my St. George slays the Dragon gunboats. . . . Why go down while the gunboats are firing, you cant help & might be struck—May God have you in his Holy keeping & bear you up. . . . The peace which passeth all understanding I know you will receive, and it may be only in heaven that you will receive your reward, still it is sure.

He was lonely: "I have no attraction to draw me from my office now. . . . Those who stay behind have double pain . . . everything brings remembrance of the loss. . . . Kiss my dear children, may God preserve you and them for happier days and lives of love for each other and usefulness to the country."[92]

The Federals had slipped those dragon gunboats up the James River while the *Virginia* was busy holding "at bay a score of their most powerful vessels" near the mouth. But the formidable ironclad could not win alone. As Johnston's retreat caused the loss of Norfolk and its naval yard, her own crew had to blow her up, to save her from Yankee hands. One of these men was Lt. John Taylor Wood, who had brought the flags from her first Hampton Roads victories to his uncle, the president, in Richmond. He joined him there now. The crewmen hoisted their flag over the guns at Drewry's Bluff, below the city, and helped beat off an assault by the gunboats on May 15. It was a signal victory, for the *Monitor* was among the attackers, and the Federal commander had counted on taking Richmond as Farragut had taken New Orleans.[93]

Davis's main worry was McClellan, driving up the peninsula to take Richmond by land. Other old friends were with him: William Emory led a brigade, and E. V. Sumner, a corps. They had to be stopped. Capture of the capital would mean the end of the Confederacy. This was generally true in war and specifically true of Richmond. It was being equipped to make small arms and percussion caps, and by the end of the war, Tredegar Iron Works had furnished the Southern army all its field artillery.[94] Everyone was anxious to know Johnston's plan for saving Richmond. Lee pointedly asked where he meant to concentrate. "To you it is needless to say that the defense must be made outside of the city," Davis prompted him; "the question is where and how?" He should strike McClellan in motion, specifically if he tried to cross the Chickahominy, "which we can hardly hope." Virginians were saying their beloved capital should be battered down sooner than surrendered. " 'They lightly talk of scars who never felt a wound,' " wrote Jeff to Varina; in any case, "I could not allow the army to be penned up in a city." Lee said with tears, "Richmond must not be given up—it shall not be given up."[95]

Johnston had finally halted his army some fifteen miles northeast of the city, but before Davis knew it, he had crossed the Chickahominy southwest. "As on all former occasions, my design is to suggest not to direct," Davis had told him; "reposing confidently as well on your ability as your zeal, it is my wish to leave you with the fullest powers to exercise your judgment." He was probably sorry two days later, when he told Varina: "Gen. Johnston has brought his army back to the suburbs of Richmond, and I have been waiting all day for him to communicate his plans."[96] He had come up on part of the army less than two miles from the city when he thought Johnston was on the Chickahominy, ready to contest a crossing. Reagan, who was riding with Davis, said, "The look of surprise which swept over his face showed a trace of pain." Telling Varina, "We are uncertain of everything except that a battle must be near at hand," he sent her "the sword I wore for many years," his pistols from the Mexican War, "and my old dressing case" to keep for the boys.

But it was twelve days before battle was joined. Davis wanted McClellan hit before he could besiege Richmond. Johnston still would not reveal his plans. Lee said he "should of course advise you of what he expects or proposes to do. Let me go and see him." The only upshot was a plan of attack that was never carried out. Two corps of McClellan's army crossed the Chickahominy without opposition and entrenched near the crossroads known as Seven Pines.[97]

Always believing a general in the field was a better judge than he, Davis had patiently accepted Johnston's retreat. Not so Toombs, "in the trenches" with his brigade: "We could have whipped [McClellan] as easily there as anywhere else. But as usual we burnt up everything and fled," leaving behind casualties, "*after a decided victory* [rear-guard action at Williamsburg]. This is called generalship!!"[98] Davis revealed late in life that he was unhappy enough then to consider assuming active command of the army, "but the duties of the Executive office were many & important, and to whom could they have been entrusted?" Certainly not the vice president, with his "vagaries on Military matters." Davis fumed to Varina at the time: "It is hard to see incompetence losing opportunity and wasting hard-gotten means, but harder still to bear is the knowledge that there is no available remedy. I cultivate hope and patience, and trust to the blunders of our enemy and the gallantry of our troops for ultimate success."[99]

On May 31, though suffering "disease" (bodily discomfort), Davis was riding out to the army, when "I heard firing in the direction of Seven Pines." He found Lee, and they decided it was "at least a severe skirmish." "It is scarcely necessary to add that neither of us had been advised of a design to attack the enemy that day." He later believed that "there was no plan" (which was not quite true). He and Lee "rode to the field of battle." Seeing a chance for a flank attack on the left, Davis actually sent an order, but then countermanded it, as the general could not execute it quickly enough.[100] Johnston had McClellan at a classic disadvantage: the mass of one army against a portion of the other. But he was unable to win a clear victory, partly through command confusion and ignorance of the ground, and partly because General Sumner led his Union troops across the river at a crucial moment.[101]

Davis reported to Varina that "[we] suffered severely in attacking the enemy's entrenchments," some of which were known only "by receiving their fire." But "our troops behaved most gallantly," driving the enemy, capturing batteries, and marching "forward under fire more heavy than I had ever previously witnessed."

> Our loss was heavy . . . Gen. J. E. Johnston is severely wounded. The poor fellow bore his suffering most heroically. When he was about to be put into the ambulance . . . I dismounted to speak to him; he opened his eyes, smiled, and gave me his hand. . . . I saw him yesterday evening, his breathing was labored but he was free from fever and seemed unshaken in his nervous system. Mrs. Johnston is deeply distressed and very watchful. . . . I offered to share our house with them, but his staff obtained a whole house and seemed to desire such arrangement.[102]

Davis was soon able to assure Varina that Johnston was out of danger. Both men were chivalrously courteous for the occasion, but Davis was soon allowing himself a sarcasm on Johnston's loss of matériel: the enemy was using a rail line "which not being useful to our army nor paid for by our treasury, was of course not destroyed." And Johnston was rousing himself on an elbow to say "fiercely" how fortunate his wound was, since the president could now appoint a man in whom he had confidence. The last part of this bitter remark was true. Davis immediately made one of the most momentous decisions of his career. He appointed Robert E. Lee head of the Army of Northern Virginia.[103]

Davis rode out to tell this personally to G. W. Smith, commanding since Johnston's fall, "to relieve both him and General Lee from any embarrassment [hindrance]." It was said that Smith never forgave Davis for putting Lee in his stead. But he was suffering an attack of paralysis and was only a major general.[104] Davis did think a new head was needed. Seven Pines was indecisive, and Smith's "heavy skirmishing" since had brought "no important result." "The opportunity being lost we must try to find another. God will, I trust, give us wisdom to see and valor to execute, the measures necessary to vindicate the just cause."[105]

XIV

Commander in Chief

Gen. Robert E. Lee had been poring over the Virginia war maps for a full year. He could visualize the position of his whole army beyond Richmond—Ewell centered just north at Gordonsville with a reserve; to the east, a brigade watching Fredericksburg; Jackson northwest in the Shenandoah Valley. His new command also included North Carolina, where Wilmington, guarded by Fort Fisher, was a major entry for Southern blockade-runners.[1]

The president's view had to take in the strategic picture in the whole Confederate States. It was not encouraging. Beauregard had just given up Corinth, Mississippi, to the huge besieging army under Halleck. He slipped quietly south to Tupelo, saving his army, but losing Fort Pillow and Memphis. With Island No. 10 having already surrendered, this gave the Federals control of the river down to Vicksburg. Between there and New Orleans, they already held all but a hundred miles. It also gave them most of Tennessee, though Chattanooga and Knoxville on the eastern edge still secured the vital rail line through the mountains to Virginia. Beauregard's move had lost an equally vital link of "the Memphis & Charleston" from northeast Alabama to the Mississippi River (and with it Huntsville, the Clays' home).[2]

The Trans-Mississippi was quiescent. On the Gulf Coast, Federals in New Orleans always threatened Mobile and had caused evacuation of Pensacola. To the east, Charleston and Savannah were secure, thanks to Lee's fortifying of the year before. He had arrived just as the Union navy, nibbling away at the coast, was biting off a significant chunk between the two cities. Fort Pulaski near Savannah had fallen, and Commodore Samuel F. DuPont's fleet had taken the fine harbor of Port Royal as a base for the blockading Union squadron. Capt. Percival Drayton had helped to wrest their boyhood home, Hilton Head Island, from his brother, Brig. Gen. Thomas Drayton, Davis's friend. But Lee had closed this back door to Charleston and Savannah with quickly built defenses.[3]

After the battle of Seven Pines, there was a long lull while McClellan, caught by malarial fever, made up his mind to approach Richmond by regular siege operations. This gave Lee time to make his own plans and to fortify against attack. Southern soldiers resented digging shelter for themselves. Lee got the nickname "King of Spades." Some, notably Longstreet, resented him, thinking he would not be aggressive enough.[4] Col. Joseph Ives, echoing Davis, set Maj. E. P. Alexander straight about that: "Lee is audacity personified." Davis had been so delighted with a remark of Lee's that he often repeated it: Whiting, given a division by Johnston, had begun, like him, to calculate how McClellan's vast number of guns was sure to beat them, when Lee cried: "Stop, stop, if you go to ciphering we are whipped beforehand." It was precisely his daring and his pugnacious planning that spelled the difference between Lee and his predecessor in command. Alexander ended up thinking: "military critics will rank Gen. Lee as decidedly the most audacious commander who has lived since Napoleon." Militarily as well as personally, he was a man after Davis's own heart.[5]

As the "farseeing, dauntless" Lee (Davis's description) was looking to see how he could keep McClellan's big guns away from Richmond, Jeff Davis found himself again among thorns. He was ailing off and on through June. Preston Johnston thought he knew why: "He sits up late and smokes too much." But "he never complains, so that one cannot tell how he is except by his appearance." A niece visiting in May blamed "our reverses," and said "I fear he cannot live long, if he does not get some rest and quiet." Alexander Robert Lawton, leading his brigade through Richmond, thought Davis's health "seriously impaired." "Yet, still a splendid horseman . . . he rode along the lines . . . a figure not to be forgotten." Jeff told Varina on June 23, coming in from the "oppressive" heat and dust "around our main encampments," "I am nearly well again." Nothing was going to keep him from the battlefield: "With God's blessing [we] will beat the enemy as soon as *we* can get at him [italics mine]."[6]

All this time, he had to contend with other people's health as well. Visiting J. E. Johnston again, he found him "rapidly improving" and told Varina, with his usual candor, "I wish he were able to take the field. Despite the critics who know military affairs by instinct, he is a good soldier, never brags of what he did do, and could at this time render most valuable service." (Beauregard, whom Northrop called "the vainest man I ever met," had just bragged of his "brilliant and successful" retreat from Corinth.) No one could be more solicitous for the ill than Davis, and he would certainly have approved sick leave for Beauregard, if only he had asked. He simply announced (not to Davis) that he was going away for a rest, on doctor's orders. The president had meanwhile ordered Bragg away on temporary duty. Beauregard said Bragg could not go; he had to command for him at Tupelo, a clear case of interfering with command. Then the ailing general left.[7]

Davis had always been amused by Beauregard's pretension. Now he began to be disillusioned about his capacity, saying to Varina on June 13, "I fear he has been placed too high for his mental strength, as he does not exhibit the ability manifested in smaller fields." On the day Davis sent the order to Bragg, he sent Preston Johnston to Beauregard with a list of questions regarding abandonment of Memphis, Corinth, and "that most important" railroad.[8] Of course Beauregard was gone. Davis was so outdone with his highhandedness that he told Bragg to keep the command of the Western Department permanently. In his eyes, Beauregard's being away without leave—in the face of the enemy—was almost inexcusable. But good engineer officers were scarce. He was willing to send the general to Charleston, where he was still a hero, since Governor Pickens was dissatisfied with the resident major general, John Clifford Pemberton. Beauregard thought he deserved command of a whole army. He finally agreed to accept the Department of South Carolina, Georgia, and Florida, but he never forgave Davis.[9]

In the midst of all this, Jeff was writing, "My heart sunk within me at the news of the suffering of my angel baby." Billy "lay at the point of death" in Raleigh. Jeff sent his own physician with medicine. "It is hard that I cannot go." "God grant that my dear Baby may be relieved before the Doctor gets there." The separation already made the house "dreary at night" and the nursery like a "robbed nest." The lonesome father promised to ride horseback with Maggie when she returned, and he said that if there were such a thing as "miasmic power of communication," little Joe "must think of me very often." As for Varina: "I thought of you as though you were with me yesterday [Sunday] and the fire of the enemy's artillery did not prevent me from remembering that you were in the same hours praying for me and making sacramental communion with our Redeemer." "Again may God give you to my arms."[10]

His deep vein of sorrow was pricked: "unless God spares me another such trial, what is to become of me, I don't know" (was it little Samuel or Knox Taylor he thought of?). "My ease, my health, my property, my life I can give to the cause of my country. The heroism which could lay my wife and children on any sacrificial altar is not mine. Spare us, good Lord." Then, going right on about the military situation, he said, "I was out until late last night on the lines of the army." He also told about trying to keep a little boy who "looked something like Jeff" from "wading in the gutter"—"He raised his sunny face and laughed, but denied my conclusion." Happily, little Billy recovered.[11]

His property was another matter; it was good he was ready to lose it, for suddenly the "special malignity" he had foreseen materialized. Joseph had been able to move papers, books, some furniture, most of the stock, and nearly a hundred slaves to Cox's place near Clinton, Mississippi. But a shocking telegram came to Jeff on June 26 from Gen. M. L. Smith at Vicksburg: from the bluffs there throughout the night, the flames had been visible as Hurricane mansion burned. Admiral Farragut had come up the river again, and a Yankee raiding party had ravaged Davis Bend, stealing, smashing, and ripping up what was left of Joseph's personal effects, even family portraits. The little Greek-temple cottage survived, emptied of its books. The mansion was burnt to the ground. All the fences were burnt too, "laying open to everyone his fine yard with rare shrubbery, and garden with conservatory, choice plants, etc."[12]

Brierfield house, first reported burnt, was standing, but it was vandalized, "our fine library" destroyed. And "all the blooded stock" was lost. Jeff's only recorded reaction came in the midst of what Varina calls "a long letter about the army": "You will have seen a notice of the destruction of our home. If our cause succeeds we shall not mourn over any personal deprivation; if not, why, 'the deluge.' I hope I shall be able to provide for the comfort of the old negroes."[13] In August he sent Joseph three thousand borrowed dollars to help care for his people. Part went for down payment on a plantation to house them in Hinds County, where Joseph also bought one for himself. Many slaves stayed at their old home, but Joseph "could never again bring himself to set foot" on Davis Bend.[14]

On the very day of the direful telegram, Lee opened the battle for Richmond. He and Davis together had devised a classic plan to counter the weight of numbers—an attack in detail, the Confederate mass against a Union fragment—for McClellan's army was still straddling the Chickahominy, with the smaller right flank north of it. Lee was to make a great show of sending men north to Stonewall Jackson, then Jackson was to fall swiftly with this whole force on the enemy's right, while Lee attacked it at the same time. The great risk was that McClellan might rush the bulk of his command, south of the river, straight for Richmond. Lee gave Jeff Davis responsibility for the city: "If you will hold him as long as you can . . . I will be upon the enemy's heels before he gets there." Davis organized the defense; people thought he was in field command; but McClellan never made the lunge at Richmond. Lee's surprise assault was marred by faulty execution, but it worked. The battle of Mechanicsville began a domino series that fell against McClellan for seven days in a row, knocking him away from Richmond, down to the James River.[15]

Davis kept close to the fighting. "At the sound of guns," wrote Burton Harrison, "Mr. Davis was in the saddle and off, in a moment," riding

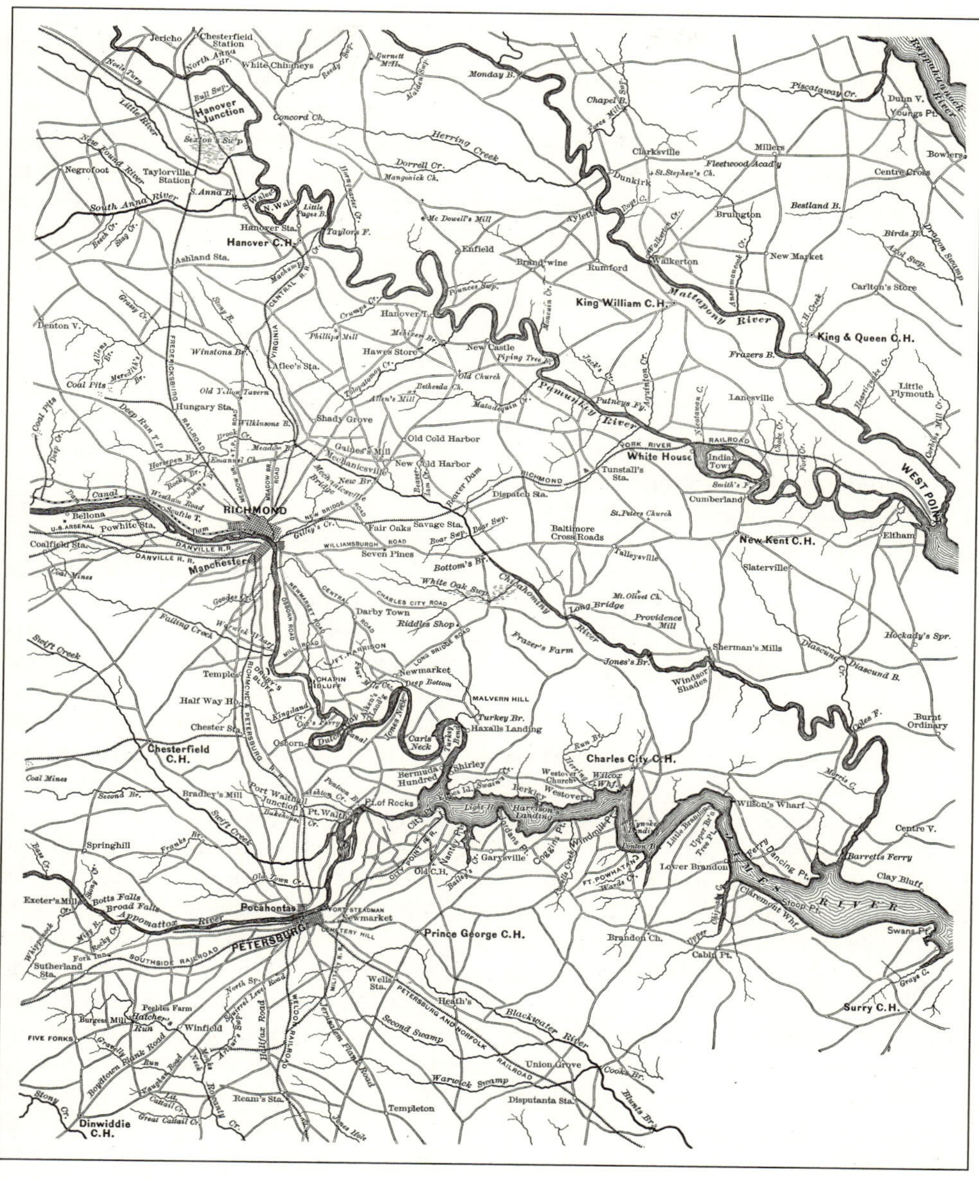

Richmond and the upper James River region

Kentucky, his "powerful and wellbred bay," and leading his staff a merry chase. Daniel Harvey Hill recalls him at the first battle "going 'to the sound of the firing'" and the next day giving an order along with Lee at Gaines's Mill. There, Davis watched the battle "for hours" with General Pendleton, who called it "awfully impressive as well as greatly exciting." E. P. Alexander remembers Davis "on the hills overlooking the Chickahominy" the first day, and again at Frayser's Farm. One man saw him going by himself "in the lanes and orchards."[16] He never took a guard. When one very young soldier insisted on escorting him, he conversed "in his kind and gentle way," as the boy told him how wrong he was to put himself in danger and got him to a safe place. Davis himself recounts many firsthand scenes of the fighting and recalled years later the prayers Pendleton offered as they lay down to sleep on the field after the last two battles, Frayser's Farm and Malvern Hill.[17]

The president, as Varina says, was exposed to enemy fire "on the field every day during the seven days' fight, and slept on it every night." Once, on Lee's warning, he left a house that was riddled by artillery fire a few minutes later. Reagan tells how Davis "jocularly remarked that he had supposed himself to be the Commander-in-Chief," before Lee ordered him off a field swept by shot and shell. At Frayser's Farm, Davis came under "a shower of metal and [tree] limbs" from a gunboat shell as he tried to rally some fleeing troops, while at the same time he "remonstrated with General Lee" about putting himself in danger. Earlier, he and Lee were admonishing each other about this, both pleading reconnaissance as an excuse, when "gallant little A. P. Hill" dashed up and ordered them both out of harm's way.[18]

Even Toombs, who led his brigade through the Seven Days, was pleased with the result: "We have utterly defeated and broken up and demoralized McClellan's army." They also garnered an immense and badly needed store of weapons. "Lee has amazed and confounded his detractors by the brilliancy of his genius," said the *Richmond Whig;* "He has established his reputation forever." President Davis was conscious beforehand of "struggling against almost certain defeat," but now with Lee's victories, he was sure the South could win independence. Toombs had to complain: the leadership was "without skill or judgment"; the men had won only "by dint of dead hard fighting." "If we had had a general in command we could easily have taken McClellan's whole command and baggage. . . . It was Manassas and Shiloh all over again, barren victories without results when everything was in our power."[19] But Davis, who knew the inside story, told Varina: "Had all the orders been well and promptly executed" (notably, Jackson's), Lee would have dispersed McClellan's army, and it "would never have fought us again." McClellan "showed capacity," he said, "but there is little cause to laud a general who is driven out of his intrenchments by a smaller and worse armed force than his own. . . . If our ranks were full we could end the war in a few weeks. . . . Our success has been so remarkable that we should be grateful, and believe that even our disappointments were ordered for our gain."[20]

"Our army is greatly reduced," he said in his laconic way. The cost of the Seven Days was fearful; at Gaines's Mill alone, almost nine thousand fell. One was Maj. Roberdeau Wheat, of the Louisiana Tigers, who had brought his father, a friend of Polk's, to meet the president shortly before.[21] Davis, had already lost "a youth of my family" at Manassas. Now one of his "dearest friends," Brig. Gen. Richard Griffith, who had been his adjutant in the Mississippi Rifles, fell wounded at Savage Station. Varina tells, as doubtless Jeff told her, how he "leaned over him and said, 'My dear boy, I hope you are not seriously hurt.'" But Griffith, grasping his hand, "said, 'Yes, I think fatally; farewell, Colonel,'" and died. William Barksdale, another Davis friend, took over his brigade.[22]

Griffith's regiment, the Twelfth Mississippi, had arrived in Virginia just as Davis was leaving the field of Manassas. He had spoken to it of the victory and of his sorrow for "relatives and friends of the fallen" on both sides. Davis, who thought caring for enemy wounded "the crowning grace of the knightly soldier," said forcibly then, a private recalled: "I wish to impress this upon your mindes. allways be Kinde to your prisoners; fight the enemy with all the power that God has given you, and when he surrenders remember that you are Southern Gentlemen and treat him with courtesy and kindeness. Never be haughty to the humble nor humble to the haughty."[23]

Davis acted on his own advice. With the humbly placed, like the boy guard, he was humility itself. He once "*blushed* very perceptibly" when he mistook the age of a young recruit, and "fearing that he had hurt my feelings . . . hastily said: 'Oh, excuse me; I beg your pardon. It was a long time before I had whiskers myself.'"[24] The day after Manassas, a soldier, seeing him on a porch, "hailed him, with, 'Is that President Davis?' and he, in his inimitably bland way replied, 'Yes, sir,' and added, 'walk up, gentlemen, out of the rain.'" The boy wanted a commission, and Davis promised, doubtless moved especially by the fact that the boy stammered and was cross-eyed. Then the friend who was with him was "dumbfounded" to hear the boy ask, "*Can I rely upon you, Mr. President?*" To this doubt of his word, Davis, "in a manner no man on earth could imitate or use, quietly and gently said, '*You can.*'"[25]

With the froward, however, he was likely to be froward. The army was not short on prima donnas. When Col. Andrew Jackson Grigsby, "as caustic as he was daring," came to Davis, raging because Jackson had picked someone else to head the Stonewall Brigade, their interview ended in a shouting match. Gen. Sterling Price "exploded spectacularly" when Davis appointed another to the Trans-Mississippi command he had come to ask for. Making the ink bottles jump as he pounded the desk, he vowed to resign. Davis icily accepted, with a deprecating remark. But the next day, "subordinating his pride to his sense of duty," he cajoled Price into staying in the army.[26]

When Gen. Humphrey Marshall claimed his appointment was a special "compact" and took umbrage at the advancement of others, Davis wrote him a severe letter. But it was also patiently explanatory, and ended "With best wishes for yourself personally." When Marshall came to the office to complain, Davis's sense of humor saved the day. Although he was very busy, he listened courteously as Marshall read at great length from his letter book. When Davis asked to see a letter, he discovered that the corpulent general would invariably fall asleep while he was silently reading, enabling him to get on with his work. This scene was repeated for days, until Marshall finally gave up. So there was no confrontation.[27]

Varina says Davis was "excitable, but not petulant, easily persuaded where to yield did not involve a principle." Stephen Mallory thought Davis's "naturally irascible and excitable nature" was controlled by "long mental discipline," and so "rarely led him into inconsiderate action." Lee was like him in this: not "invariably amiable," but with temper held under "habitual self-command."[28] Others who knew Davis intimately insist that "his real nature was gentle," that wrath was "far from him." Burton Harrison, who worked with him every day and lived in his house, expressed his character this way: "Mr. Davis was an aristocrat, reticent, stately, courteous . . . of an undaunted courage and rare singleness of purpose. . . . Though a stranger, judging from appearances only, would have thought him cold and austere, he was of the tenderest sensibility; a brief acquaintance was enough to inform any one of how gentle and kindly he really was."[29]

After the battles of the Seven Days, President Davis thanked his troops for "the series of brilliant victories." Only an eyewitness could appreciate their "gallantry," as their attacks drove the enemy "more than 35 miles," compelling "him to seek safety under cover of his gunboats." They had "done enough for glory." But they must not relax, "your one great object being to drive the invader from your soil and carry your standards beyond . . . the Confederacy, to wring from an unscrupulous foe the recognition of your birthright, community independence."[30] This aim drove Davis relentlessly. And these were not idle words; counter-invasion was coming.

On July 13, 1862, Capt. Charles Minor Blackford saw Davis talking with Generals Lee and Jackson on the steps of the Confederate White House—Lee "elegantly dressed in full uniform . . . by far the most magnificent man I ever saw"; Jackson "poorly dressed," shoulders "stooped," one "lower than the other," his cap "pulled down over one eye, much stained by weather and without insignia." "Davis looks like a statesman. His face is pale and thin but very intellectual and he had a graceful manner and easy bearing. He was dressed in a black suit and left a pleasing impression on anyone looking at him." Blackford was sure from the way the three shook hands in parting and the way Jackson "got on his old sorrel horse" and galloped away "in a deep brown and abstracted study" that he "had been ordered to move." He had.[31]

Jackson went up to meet a Union army swarming down and whipped Gen. John Pope at Cedar Mountain. Lee gambled on his hunch that McClellan would not attack Richmond from his James River base, and took most of his army to join Jackson. As soon as he heard that McClellan was moving north to Pope, he brought up all the rest, except for two brigades at Richmond. With Jackson, he smashed the Federals at a second Battle of Manassas and drove into Maryland. Asking Davis's approval, Lee said this was "the propitious time" to "afford her an opportunity of throwing off the oppression to which she is now subject."[32]

Davis had fretted over the ruthless military takeover in Maryland. He thought her people would rise to support the Confederate army. He sent Lee an outline proclamation explaining why he was there. It asked the state to give up "the design of subjugating a people over whom no right of dominion has been ever conferred either by God or man" and make a separate peace. Although Lee found "sympathy" in Maryland, he was soon forced to say, "I do not anticipate any general rising." And there was none. But he told Davis that, if successful there, he would go on to Pennsylvania, "unless you should deem it unadvisable."[33] McClellan discovered Lee's plans through a lost dispatch and fought him to a standstill at Sharpsburg, Maryland, near Antietam Creek, on September 17. Far from defeated, but still facing two-to-one odds and unable to feed his army, Lee fell back into Virginia, bringing a treasured horde of captured arms.[34]

Davis left the name of the state blank in his proclamation, so that Generals Braxton Bragg and Edmund Kirby Smith could use it too. They were invading Kentucky even as Lee fought. Smith, coming out of the East Tennessee mountains, had already won a battle at Richmond, Kentucky, on August 30, and pushed on to the Ohio River, throwing Cincinnati into panic. He and Bragg had worked out details, but the grand strategy was by Beauregard (which explains J. E. Johnston's strange remark in May about sending him to Ohio). Maj. Gen. Don Carlos Buell of the Union knew the grand strategy by September 18, from a captured copy, but by then it had been greatly altered by circumstances.[35]

With the Memphis and Charleston railroad lost, Bragg had to improvise a route for his infantry—from Tupelo down to Mobile and then back northeast to Chattanooga—but he joined Smith before Buell could cut the road. He had meant to trap Buell in Middle Tennessee, but having to wait for cavalry, artillery, and wagons to come cross-country, he could not move against him until August 28. Then Buell had simply retreated to Nashville, his supply base, and not daring to attack the city, Bragg had crossed the Cumberland River east of there and invaded Kentucky.[36]

Bragg and Smith dutifully invited Kentuckians to their standard. Lexington, home of John Hunt Morgan, went wild with enthusiasm, but the people did not rise en masse as he had predicted. Morgan had promised twenty-five thousand men, but only about two thousand joined, and Bragg said half of these later deserted.[37] One who did come, the horseman Abraham Buford, rode as a brigadier under Forrest until the end. Bragg's jaunty offer to see Breckinridge to his home became a mockery when the Kentuckian never even caught up with him. Van Dorn had detained him in Mississippi, for the invasion of West Tennessee called for by Beauregard's plan. This was not launched until Breckinridge left, and then Van Dorn and Price stopped to retake Corinth first, met defeat, and so ruined this part of the campaign.[38]

Bragg was doing little better. Stopping to capture a garrison at Munfordville, he let General Buell get to Louisville ahead of him, unmolested. At Nazareth, the school where so many Davis girls had gone, he was entertained by the Catholic sisters who were nursing his wounded. Then he went to Frankfort to replace the Union governor with a Confederate one. Buell came looking for his army. Leonidas Polk, second in command, had the bulk of it at Bardstown. He and Hardee were moving east, even while disputing Bragg's orders, when Hardee's men became entangled with a Federal advance unit near the hamlet of Perryville.[39]

The battle of October 8, 1862, was extremely bloody, though neither army was fully engaged. The Confederates, "fearfully outnumbered," clearly won the field that day. Even General Halleck said it was "really victorious, over an army double its size." But neither Bragg nor Buell was willing to renew battle on the ninth. The two armies jockeyed warily until October 13. Then Bragg turned and left the state. All his generals except Smith and Humphrey Marshall agreed to this, shamefacedly, their reasons being lack of men and lack of confidence in Bragg. He retired to Knoxville and then took position at Murfreesboro, Tennessee, which he had sent General Forrest to occupy. He remained there for the rest of the year, confronted not by Buell, whose career was ruined, but by Maj. Gen. William S. Rosecrans.[40] Like Lee, Bragg brought home much-needed arms, but also, unlike Lee, "great herds of beef cattle, sheep and hogs."[41]

"My office work fell behind while I was in the field," Davis wrote Lee on July 5. It was obvious where he preferred to be. In 1864, he was still speaking of his "repugnance to the office of chief, and his desire for the field." The next best thing was to visit the camps and defenses on his evening rides around Richmond. Sometimes he took an aide, but he preferred to go alone. Minnigerode was "convinced" that Davis often used "those lonely rides" as a chance for mental prayer. One time a shot rang out. Davis turned his horse and rode straight at the ambush. A man was found on the roof of a shanty with gold in his pocket, but he was not prosecuted, nor did Davis cease his solitary habit of evening exercise.[42]

He yearned for the field so much that he had started up toward the fighting in September of 1862 when Lee hastily wrote about "great uneasiness for your safety should you undertake to reach me." Not only would Davis feel "the hardships and fatigue of a very difficult journey," he would "run the risk of capture," since Lee was breaking up his lines. He sent Walter Taylor down with this message, but the president had already turned back.[43]

They were always mindful of each other. Davis had renewed in July "my caution to you against personal exposure either in battle or reconnaissance" as "a duty to the cause we serve." He offered his "personal attention" to anything Lee wanted. He and Lee regularly wrote each other in great detail about the army. To help Lee reorganize it after Sharpsburg, Davis got Congress to create the rank of lieutenant general. He asked Lee for "the names of such as you prefer," and Lee said, sending them, "Your own knowledge . . . of the officers will . . . enable you to make the best selection."[44]

The president could not get into the field again until 1864, but he made three long trips to inspect the western army and visits to Lee's headquarters whenever he could. One visit was to review the cavalry in November of 1863. Dr. Minnigerode's son, Charlie, aide-de-camp to Fitz Lee, wrote home: "They are making a great fuss over the President. He attended Mr. Hansborough's church at Orange C. H. [Court House] yesterday. He & Genl. Lee the two greatest men in the Confederacy were side by side. Genl. Pendleton preached a very fine sermon."[45]

Office work was Davis's duty now. He was as meticulous about it as about everything. A staunchless flow of letters shows his attention to every detail of Confederate life, to every suppliant, to every complainant. Take his reply to Mrs. A. J. Sanders. Although confined at home by illness, he had heard her appeal in person and had then sent for the naval contract in question. He could now reassure her about her husband's "honor so justly dear to you" (and doing so, revealed his own): "Nothing was further from my purpose than to question your husband's motive. I had no reason to do so, and if it had been otherwise it was not possible for me to have done so in his absence, to his wife, and in my house." Or see his detailed answer to W. M. Brooks, of Marion, Alabama, on many charges. It was said "that I 'have scarcely a friend and not a defender in Congress or in the army'": "for the sake of the country and its cause I must hope it is falsely so said, as otherwise our fate must be confided to a multitude of hypocrites."[46] In his "terse, chaste, vigorous, classic, Anglo-Saxon English," he reasoned with governors and other politicians, pleading for patriotism and the general good over particular state interest. He threatened or cajoled with but one object—support for the struggle that was determining their life or death as a nation.[47]

"Precise and zealous," a man of "great labor, of great learning," President Davis had to know all the details, whether of finances abroad, crops at home, or the "torpedo service" (use of marine and land mines).[48] He consulted his cabinet and experts of all sorts frequently, allowing "the utmost latitude of opinion and expression." He gave every question a scholarly scrutiny before making up his mind, but once it was made up, he stuck to his decision, unless he saw equally good reason to alter it—"unchangeable," said Stephen Mallory, "when convinced of being right." Critics called this obstinacy; admirers saw it as his strength. His "deep and strong convictions," said one, were built, not on ignorance or refusal to reason, as "obstinacy" implies, but on his "vast knowledge." This gave him "great *power of purpose.*"[49]

He did not fear attack for his strong stands; he expected it. It frequently cut him to the quick all the same. He would produce long-winded explanations, trying to prove that he was right, which often as not he was. He was also trying to smother discontent, as his duty to the country. He would have preferred not to answer, and many times, also "as a duty," bore criticism silently.[50] He wished he could be like Maggie "and learn to let people alone who snap at me, in forbearance and charity to turn away as well from the cats as the snakes." It was hard to practice these Pauline virtues, especially under savage assaults from the unbridled press. In a letter to Varina from prison, contrasting "those who never wore a mask" at this time and "those who never were without one," he spoke again of the need for "patience and forbearance & charity and above all for charity."[51]

Whether "cats" or "snakes," there were plenty of enemies. Foote was described as Davis's "only open assailant" in Congress, to which Davis responded: "not even as fair as that." Rhett was forever reminding people in his *Charleston Mercury* what a sorry president Davis was. Edward A. Pollard was a mouthpiece for malcontents, pouring on Davis through the *Richmond Examiner,* along with John Daniel, a steady stream of abuse. As Ben Hill said, the "*Examiner* hated Mr. Davis with a cordial hatred." "An impartial observer" called their paper "a common sewer of falsehood and infamy."[52] Robert Toombs slipped his choice insults in letters to "Little Aleck" Stephens, and both men opposed Davis openly. He heard rumors that Yancey was the anonymous author of a "a scurvy attack on the Administration." Wigfall had turned on him and was bitterly hatching plots.[53]

Wigfall had been so close to Davis that he had once seen that dignified man flat on his back on the floor, "with two or three of his little children climbing over him." Recently, he had seemed friendly, explaining that the Senate refused Davis's appointment of Thomas Jordan, Beauregard's chief of staff, as brigadier general because of a prewar charge of embezzlement revealed by J. E. Johnston. Davis had said "in that case" he "felt obliged to the Senate for rejecting" him.[54] With his faith in truth and the good will of others, Davis wrote to Wigfall because "you thought Holmes had failed in his duty at Malvern Hill [during the Seven Days]." He was able to defend him in detail, since he had been there, and ended: "I am sure that your fairness needs only to have the facts distinctly pointed out to you." He was urging disinterested charity on a man ruled by his passions. One of them was "intense enmity" to Davis. Wigfall had just voted against making Hardee and Pemberton lieutenant generals, apparently to spite Davis for vetoing a bill of his. These confirmations went through, however, since Davis still controlled the Senate. It was perhaps to get Wigfall's vote for Holmes, just named to the same rank, that Davis pleaded "justice" for him, and his "peculiar fitness" for his new command, the Trans-Mississippi Department.[55]

As it turned out, Holmes showed a peculiar unfitness. Davis soon had to send Kirby Smith to take over, leaving Holmes only the district of Arkansas (Magruder taking Texas, and Richard Taylor, Louisiana). After Holmes's health failed in 1864, Davis brought him to command reserves in North Carolina.[56] He never uttered a word of blame: "I am sure you would sacrifice yourself at any time." Davis's support for the faulty Holmes and his attempt to mollify Wigfall toward him were typical. Lubbock says: "While others would be intolerant and very exacting during our struggle, he would be the apologist of many who failed in their duty, treating delinquents with compassion and leniency." "[We must] judge charitably of each other, and strive to bear and forbear," Davis wrote in 1863, "however great may be the sacrifice and bitter the trial." Man can only strive for success, "and leave the rest to Him who governs all things."[57]

It is true that Holmes was an old friend, but Davis treated people who were not, even those who were hostile, the same way. He wrote his "regret" to Humphrey Marshall over a wound someone had given to "your soldierly sensibility," assuring him it was all a mistake, trusting his service would again "be pleasant to yourself as well as useful to your country." His honeyed words went for naught. Marshall resigned and became the only Kentucky enemy Davis had in Congress.[58] Davis made his severe critic T. R. R. Cobb a brigadier general. The most obvious case was that of the cantankerous D. H. Hill. He was commanding at Richmond in 1863, when Davis made him a lieutenant general and sent him to the Tennessee army. Maj. Gen. Robert Ransom says:

> an intimate personal friend of Mr. Davis rather criticized the President for what he considered an unwise and too magnanimous act, remarking that the "President certainly knew that Hill was no

> friend of his and was insubordinate, and had by losing his order in '62, thwarted the plans of General Lee in Maryland." Mr. Davis answered, " . . . it is not proven that he was to blame in reference to the lost order. Besides, men are not perfect, and I can have no personal resentment to true, brave men who are such fighters as all know Hill to be, no matter what their feelings may be to me individually." . . . This is only one instance among many refuting the unjust assertion [of his] visiting personal animosity upon those . . . who were not his personal admirers.[59]

Hill became really bitter against Davis later that year and remained unreconciled until 1886, when Davis wrote him a "kind letter." Hill had asked for a "frank, fair statement" of his case, and he replied to Davis: "You understand the situation fully and you understand fully the sensitive feelings of a soldier. I leave the matter in your own hands, trusting to your sense of justice." He could "never forget," he said, that Davis had received "all the shafts of malice intended for our people." Davis wrote, at Hill's death, less than three months before his own: "a more pure vigilant and gallant soldier did not serve the Confederate cause."[60]

Davis always thought he was acting with justice, as he explained in great detail to the North Carolina governor, Zebulon B. Vance. Those who had no call to resent his justice thought so too. Davis said he pitied "the wretch" whose "personal jealousy" or malignity made him "incapable" of justice. Basil Duke pointed out that even if Davis were not "purely impersonal," still, "his nature was too frank and noble to cherish small resentments, and it is more probable that he refused what some men asked because he thought them unworthy or incompetent, than because he bore them malice."[61]

Naturally those deemed unworthy thought it was malice. Davis managed only to exacerbate the resentment of Maj. Gen. G. W. Smith. Recovering from his paralysis, Smith had been given command of the Richmond–North Carolina area in August 1862. When passed over for the new grade of lieutenant general (he had proven inept in the field), he complained to the War Department. He had been persuaded several times not to resign and had served as interim secretary of war before he wound up his five-month complaint sounding much like his good friend J. E. Johnston: his duties were "higher, more important and more difficult than those of a corps commander"; he would not serve under those "recently my juniors. There is no alternative left me but to resign." Davis endorsed this "remarkable paper": "If the alternative of resignation or appointment as Lieutenant General is presented as a claim founded on former relative rank . . . it will only be proper to accept the resignation, as to admit the claim would be in derogation of the legal power of the Executive and in disregard of the consideration due to service rendered in battle" (promotions had gone to Jackson, Longstreet, Hardee, and Polk). The president was not going to be intimidated or to have his appointive right questioned.[62]

Davis's coldly logical decision made G. W. Smith a personal enemy, if he was not one already. He fled first to Beauregard at Charleston, and then to Georgia, that other cave of Adullam. Gov. Joseph E. Brown gave him command of state troops as a major general. Disaffection with the government (i.e., Davis) was finding two centers: one geographical, largely political, in Georgia; one military, having no local habitation, unless it was Beauregard's headquarters (Colonel Chesnut said he was treated more like a Yankee spy than the president's aide), but swirling in the correspondence of disgruntled generals.[63]

A central sulker in the Georgia cave arrived there late in 1862. The volcanic Toombs, after continually erupting on the peninsula, had challenged D. H. Hill to a duel; Hill had refused; Toombs had denounced him "as a poltroon." A little later, Toombs, after being arrested and released, had led his men to glory on the field at Sharpsburg; then, in a skirmish, his left hand had been "shattered by a rifle-ball." Lee spoke of his brigade's "distinguished gallantry," but did not recommend him for promotion. Toombs resigned and went to Georgia.[64]

Jeff Davis, ignorant that Toombs said he was a "poor fool" who wanted to drive him from the army, told a Georgian of his regret "that General Toombs should have become alienated from me" for not promoting him. He explained what had initially overcome "my reluctance to placing a civilian in so high a command": the complaint about too many West Point men ("though I did not recognize its justice"), Toombs's "distinguished" civil abilities, and his "high promise as a soldier" (in the Florida wars). Although disposed "in his favor," Davis said, "I had gone so far as my sense of duty permitted." He was "almost exclusively dependent" on military reports, and they did not recommend Toombs. Davis told Reagan, who was urging the promotion, that both Lee and Magruder "objected to his advancement." But neither Reagan nor Davis ever told Toombs this. The onus was left on Davis; Toombs was sure he had acted out of spite.[65]

This was not the only time Davis's silence of honor kept him from putting the blame on the proper person. He suffered agonies over having to tell a close friend of his dismissal. The order from the man's superior was marked "private," so Davis felt he could not mention it. "All I could do," he told Varina, "was to make the poor fellow too mad with me to ask an explanation." He had said curtly, "You have, I believe, received your orders; I can suggest nothing but obedience." The friend was devastated, but so was Davis, who went home and shut himself in his room. This sacrifice of feeling doubtless fed rumors of his harsh, abrupt manner, though Lubbock insists he was customarily "as polite and affable to . . . his messenger boy as to the officer of highest rank."

The messenger, in fact, said Davis was "one of the most lovable men I ever knew." Davis's sanguine nature led him to end his letter to the Georgian expecting, "when time shall have soothed the irritation now felt by General Toombs, he will do me justice and no longer attribute to unworthy motives my having selected others for the promotion to which he judged himself entitled." How little he knew Robert Toombs![66]

Toombs and G. W. Smith and Linton Stephens, the vice president's brother, used to sit and "abuse [Davis] by the hour." This triumvirate, along with Aleck Stephens, who had also come to the cave, conferred with Georgia's Gov. Joseph E. Brown on how best to thwart "Davis and his Janissaries (the regular army)." Toombs was sure they were undermining liberty, and Congress was "the Junto" that Davis was manipulating for some "crowning iniquity, the Lord knows what."[67] Conscription and martial law were the main issues, especially the suspension of habeas corpus. But this last was a false issue, because Davis had to have a vote of Congress to impose it, and it was always strictly limited in time and place.[68]

Howell Cobb was also back in Georgia, but as "a loyal Davis man." He had asked to be transferred to his own state after being disgraced by the collapse of his soldiers in a Maryland battle. Richard Taylor says Davis sent him "to counteract Joe Brown." And another Georgian, Sen. Benjamin Harvey Hill, was becoming "Hill the faithful," whose support Davis would one day call "firm as marble."[69] Toombs, having called Davis everything from "malignant wretch" to "scoundrel," hit a new low when he wrote to Aleck Stephens,

> Of course in adopting the proposed course towards Davis I am fully aware of the nature of the contest. We shall both fight under the same flag. *Vae victis* [woe to the conquered],—with this difference: I shall avow it and he will quote scripture, say "God bids us do good for evil" and thus "clothe (his) naked villany in old odd ends stole forth from holy writ and seem a saint when he plays the devil."

This was doubly ironic in that Davis's faith was genuine, and Toombs used the Bible brilliantly as a weapon but had no use for religion until the end of his life.[70]

Happily oblivious of what was going on behind the scenes in Georgia, Davis kept trying to prevent "discord" in the army, knowing it could only "impair its efficiency and otherwise work evil to the public service." Lee, who felt the same way, prevented a duel between A. P. Hill and Longstreet and tried to calm a verbal fight of Hill and Jackson, without much success. He had his own differences with Jackson, but they were short-lived.[71] Longstreet, who resented Lee for taking Johnston's place, was given to questioning his orders. He was truly a disruptive force in the army, but his ability in battle screened this fact, apparently even from Lee. D. H. Hill was extremely critical of Lee, argued about orders, and once became so vexatious that the usually compliant Lee wrote Davis, asking that Hill be removed from his command. Davis had to smooth ruffled feathers on both sides. In general Davis left the Army of Northern Virginia to Lee entirely.[72] When three death sentences in the Stonewall Brigade were referred to him, however, the president seized the opportunity to commute them all. He was scarcely known to let one stand that came under his eye. Even Lee thought he was too lenient.[73]

It was the western army that demanded Davis's attention. In November 1862, when Joseph E. Johnston reported himself well enough for duty, there was the problem of what to do with a full general. After Lee's splendid handling of the Virginia army, no one thought seriously of giving it back to Johnston. Another full general, Bragg, headed the other major army and sat expecting attack at Murfreesboro. Davis decided to try again the theater command that he had invented for Sidney Johnston. This one would stretch from the Blue Ridge Mountains up to, but not beyond, the Mississippi River. It included Bragg's army, troops in East Tennessee, Lieutenant General Pemberton's Mississippi–East Louisiana Department, the forces at Mobile, and, by special order, Atlanta. Johnston was to oversee the whole area, shift troops about as needed through the interior lines, and, if necessary, take personal charge of an army. Chattanooga, in the northeast corner, was a lopsided choice for headquarters, but it signified that city's importance as a rail center.[74]

On the day he received his assignment, J. E. Johnston sent General Cooper a complaint about the number and arrangement of troops, with a strategic plan to correct this, involving forces not his. Louis Wigfall had already urged this plan on Secretary of War Randolph. Wigfall became "virtually" Johnston's "political chief of staff," said John B. Hood, who knew him very well. Before long, Johnston was asking Wigfall to "help me out of my present place," hinting that he wanted his Virginia army back: it was "hard to lose that command for wounds in battle and to receive a nominal command."[75]

Varina, as innocent as Jeff, went to see the Johnstons just before they left Richmond, not knowing that Lydia gossiped about her, much less that she had just said to her husband, "[Davis] hates you & he has power & he will ruin you." The general had replied, "He could. I don't care. My country." Varina says that Johnston "seemed ill and dispirited," and "in answer to a hope expressed by me that he would have a brilliant campaign, he said, 'I might if I had Lee's chances with the army of Northern Virginia.' "[76]

Wigfall had become transmitter of discontent for a small group of men, mostly military, who thought they knew better than Davis what to do with the armies. The strands that bound them together crisscrossed.

Johnston's friend Wigfall had been aide-de-camp to Beauregard, then to Longstreet. Longstreet and Johnston admired each other. Johnston even persuaded G. W. Smith to suppress criticism of Longstreet in his report on the Battle of Seven Pines.[77] He sent Longstreet his likeness. Longstreet was now telling Johnston that he still had the "hearts" of "your old army . . . more decidedly than any other leader [viz., Lee] can ever have," and assured him that its command "will fall to you before Spring." The Wigfalls and the Johnstons had lived together in Richmond after the Seven Days, the wives specially bonded by common spite toward Varina Davis. Now Longstreet told Wigfall not to quarrel with Jefferson Davis, because "we think that all our hopes rest upon you."[78]

Their hopes were for concentration and advance—a strategy offensive rather than defensive. They had been voiced in 1861 by Johnston, Beauregard, and G. W. Smith at Fairfax and were still nursed by them, Longstreet, Bragg, and others. Bragg had embodied the hopes in Kentucky; Beauregard was the group's voice; Wigfall, its trumpet. For convenience, the group might be called "the cabal." Mary Chesnut used the word in 1864.[79] Davis used the word long years after the war, when he finally learned of the group's existence and spoke of its "venom." "I have known none of their conspiracy against me personally and officially from an early period of the war, the misfortune is that it was not then discovered." It was only a loose-knit attempt at influence; for Aleck Stephens never was able to organize an opposition party for it to work through.[80]

The cabal was what led Wigfall to break with Davis. First he backed a demand that Beauregard (at his own suggestion) be restored to the Army of Tennessee, replacing Bragg (who had disappointed cabal hopes in Kentucky). Davis would not hear of it.[81] Then Wigfall became embroiled in a dispute over use of Theophilus Holmes's troops. One fact the cabal completely ignored was that Davis wanted concentration and advance as much as they did. He had told Johnston in 1861 that his "one great object" was to get enough men "to take the offensive." He wrote to Holmes in October 1862, "concentration . . . is so obviously desirable that it is needless even to state it." As he said later, "We cannot hope at all points to meet the enemy with a force equal to his own, and must find our security in the concentration and rapid movement of troops." "Our very existence" depended on using the soldiers "anywhere and everywhere."[82]

What Davis did not share with the cabal was a reckless disregard of consequences. Johnston and Wigfall wanted him to order Holmes summarily to bring his whole force from Arkansas to Mississippi so as to "crush" Grant, who was aiming at Vicksburg. Surely nothing could have pleased Davis more than to defend his own home in this way. But to do it would risk losing the whole Trans-Mississippi, and Davis did not think, as the others did, that to regain it later would be a simple matter. (Johnston said he was "dreaming of" sending Holmes back later to retake Missouri while he himself marched "to the Ohio.") Davis carefully said concentration should "be determined after the freest communication between the Generals, so that each shall possess exact information in regard to the condition of the others." This they certainly did not have: Johnston thought Holmes had fifty-five thousand men, whereas he had at less than half that number.[83]

Holmes was never given a peremptory order. Secretary of War Randolph told him, "When necessary you can cross [the Mississippi River] . . . with such part of your forces as you may select." Davis wired him through Cooper, to throw, if feasible, "say . . . 10,000 men, across the river at Vicksburg." As he told Lee, Holmes was to reinforce Pemberton, "if it can be safely done."[84] But Holmes said it could not, not with his own troops. Instead, he ordered Maj. Gen. Thomas Carmichael Hindman to take his eleven thousand or more men and cross the river. Hindman "protested and objected" and decided to attack Prairie Grove, in the northwest corner of Arkansas, before obeying the order. His corps met defeat there on December 7 and "simply evaporated." This is why no troops were ever sent.[85] Yet Johnston later claimed that his plan to bring Holmes over "was not adopted, nor noticed": Davis had canceled Randolph's order to Holmes, preventing reinforcement of Pemberton and causing Randolph to resign, "to the great injury of the Confederacy." This charge has been repeated down to the present day as another example of Davis's "pig-headedness" (Wigfall's term) and lack of vision.[86]

Davis did object to Randolph's telling Holmes to come over and take command: "The withdrawal of the commander . . . would have a disastrous effect and was not contemplated by me." (Arkansas and Indian Territory were in turmoil.) Davis had in mind "cointelligent action on both sides" of the Mississippi River, with troops dispatched "as circumstances might require." He did not want Randolph changing the command structure he had just worked out, especially without telling him. Davis was commander in chief, Randolph his appointee and "adviser." He told him he was used to "free conference"; "consultation" would avoid "much which is disagreeable"; orders should be sent through "the established channel." Evidently there was other friction: "the appointment of commissioned officers is a constitutional function which I have neither power nor will to delegate." On November 15, 1862, Randolph resigned "without notice." "No loss," said Bragg when he heard.[87]

This was when Davis appointed G. W. Smith as interim secretary. Wigfall called on Davis, to suggest for the permanent place James Alexander Seddon, Johnston, or Smith. Davis and his cabinet had hit upon exactly the same list in the same order (a remarkable instance of Davis's candor, for all three supported cabal ideas). Davis did not tell

Wigfall he had offered Seddon the post, since he was sworn to secrecy until Seddon replied. Next day, the papers announced Seddon's acceptance. When Davis heard that Wigfall was in the Senate denouncing him, he sent Reagan to explain, but Wigfall would not listen. Their friendship was ended, and Wigfall "continued his opposition until the fall of the Confederacy."[88]

Jeff Davis wrote to General Lee on December 8, 1862, "I have been very anxious to visit you, but feeble health and constant labor has caused me to delay until necessity hurries me in an opposite direction." On the tenth, he stepped onto the cars at Richmond, bound for Chattanooga, Tennessee. If he had known what was pending, he might not have gone; for the day after he left, General Burnside began his Virginia assault against Fredericksburg. Davis told Lee he felt he had "to go out there immediately," to raise troops and "arouse all classes to united and desperate resistance." Mississippi's Governor Pettus had called for him. His old friend Sen. James Phelan had said that enthusiasm in their state was "a cold pile of dead ashes" but would spark anew if only Davis would "plant your own foot upon our soil [and] unfurl your banner at the head of the army." This was not mere flattery. Reuben Davis said that from the moment Jeff Davis returned from Buena Vista on crutches, there was a never a time "when he did not stand first in the hearts of Mississippians."

Davis reported to Lee that the outnumbered Pemberton had fallen back (before Grant, coming down from Tennessee), "but I have the most favorable accounts of his conduct as commander, and trust God may bless us, as in other cases seemingly as desperate, with success over our impious foe." He would feel "increasing anxiety" for news from Lee. He had left Preston Johnston to forward dispatches, taking Custis Lee with him. J. R. Davis went too, no longer aide-de-camp but a brigadier general under Lee.[89]

Only the week before, J. E. Johnston and Lydia had also gone toward Tennessee, grumbling and pessimistic. "Nobody ever assumed a command under more unfavorable circumstances," wrote the general; and Lydia, "How dreary it all looks, & how little prospect there is of my poor husband doing ought than lose his army." He had legitimate worries: his territory was large, his troops sparse, his rail lines rickety and roundabout. He did not tackle his problems; he complained about them. And he had no intention of trying to make Davis's ideas work. "It is like being on the shelf with the responsibilities of command," he told Wigfall, "responsibilities which I cannot possibly meet." He was sure, as on the peninsula, that his plan was better than the government's, and so "I did nothing."[90] He disobeyed his first instructions: to use the prerogative for which his command had been created and shift some troops from Bragg to Pemberton. He said it would take a month; send Holmes. Holmes said it would take him a month. Meanwhile, Bragg had sent a thousand men on his own.[91]

When Davis got to Chattanooga, he found Johnston ailing, so he went on to Murfreesboro to inspect Bragg's force, now called the "Army of Tennessee." He found the troops he reviewed "in fine spirits and well supplied." He promoted John Hunt Morgan to brigadier general for his astonishing capture of a vastly larger Union force at nearby Hartsville on December 7. He was entertained at a pleasant house named Oaklands. He could hobnob with old friends Polk and Hardee.[92] Bragg was thought to be Davis's friend. He acted more like Johnston's. In a letter highly critical of Davis, he told Johnston how he asked "that you be assigned to the whole command in the Southwest, with plenary powers" (Wigfall's idea, to include Texas and Arkansas), and how he sent Polk to Richmond to advance the idea.[93] Instead, Polk urged Davis to *replace* Bragg with Johnston! Intrigue was beginning to undercut the Army of Tennessee. Mutterings of discontent were heard from top to bottom. Hardee felt it strongly, having seen in Bragg's Kentucky maneuvers "grave, unpardonable errors." Far from calling for Johnston, however, he stated to a Davis aide that "a competent successor" would be hard to find: "Bragg has proved a failure, it is true, but . . . have we any body who will do better? I confess this has been a strong reason in restraining me from speaking out boldly."[94]

Davis had been generous about Kentucky. He admitted "bitter disappointment," but he said to Kirby Smith, who was vexed over the retreat, that Bragg explained "in a direct and frank manner" and "evinced the most self denying temper in relation to his future position." This attitude, a sure winner with Davis, Bragg also voiced to Johnston, afraid Davis meant to give his command to Smith: "Whenever and wherever I am in the way of a better man, let me be put aside. I only ask to serve the cause where I can do it most good." Davis had spoken before to Bragg of "your long trials and the self-denial with which you have labored to support the cause." Following a journalistic attack, he said, "You have the misfortune to be regarded as my personal friend, and are pursued therefore with malignant censure by men regardless of truth and . . . incapable of conceiving that you are trusted because of your known fitness for command, and not because of friendly regard." Although others might "excite more enthusiasm," he now told Kirby Smith, "all have their defects." He was not going to abandon a man whom he knew to be a patriot, a fine organizer, and, especially, a fighter, because of one failure.[95]

Davis's faith in Bragg seemed to be fully justified on December 31. Rosencrans, learning that both Forrest and Morgan were away, came out of Nashville to destroy him. Bragg's fierce attack, led by Polk and Hardee, caught the Federals off guard. It doubled the Yankee right wing back on itself against the Nashville turnpike and the Stone's River and swept the field, but for one salient. Bragg won a startling victory that day with less than half the Federal numbers and wired Richmond: "God has granted us a happy New Year." Then occurred probably the most glaring example of what was wrong with Bragg's generalship. He stopped. He relaxed. He expected Rosecrans to retreat. Nothing at all happened on that New Year's Day of 1863 except burial of the dead and dressing of the line. When Bragg decided on January 2 to complete his victory, he found it crumbling in his hands. The Union troops had set up a fearful artillery concentration at the very spot where Bragg ordered Breckinridge to attack. The Kentuckians were "almost decimated." The whole army was shaken. Polk and others advised retreat. Bragg was for holding, until shown evidence of the enemy strength; then he felt compelled to withdraw. His army went in good order, unpursued, and took position some twenty-five miles southeast, in a hilly section of Middle Tennessee. Here the smoldering fire of resentment against Bragg burst into flame.[96]

Jeff Davis missed the battle because he left Murfreesboro on the night of December 14. Rosecrans reported he was there when Polk, in one of his four priestly acts in uniform, married General Morgan to a local girl that night, but this is doubtful.[97] At Chattanooga, a wire told the president of a full-scale Federal attack at Fredericksburg on the thirteenth, but nothing of the outcome. "You can imagine my anxiety," he wrote Varina. He relieved it by thoughts of home:

> Kiss the children for their loving Father. They can little realize how much I miss them. Every sound is the voice of my child and every child renews the memory of a loved one's appearance, but none can equal their charms, nor can any compare with my own long-worshipped Winnie.
>
> She is na my ain Lassie
> Though fair the lassie be
> For well ken I my ain lassie
> By the kind love in her eye.

The news made J. R. Davis anxious to get to his brigade. It made Johnston write to Wigfall: "What luck some people have. No one will ever come to attack me in such a place."[98]

By the time Davis and Johnston reached Jackson, Mississippi, they knew Fredericksburg was another stunning victory for Lee. With "merry popping" of their rifles, Barksdale's Mississippi brigade had held up E. V. Sumner's crossing of the Rappahannock for a whole day then had withdrawn through the town and joined other Confederates on the heights behind to hurl the whole invading force back across the river with outlandish losses. By comparison, few Southerners were killed.[99] But one was the "brave, noble, & lovely" T. R. R. Cobb, as Alexander called him. On December 26, Davis stood before the Mississippi legislature and pointed out that this was the fourth attempt by the enemy to take Richmond "as proof that the Confederacy has no existence." The capital, "under God," would continue to "stand safe behind its wall of living breasts."[100]

Davis, the eternal optimist, and Johnston, the eternal pessimist, had come to address another enemy objective, control of the whole Mississippi River. The general had already pronounced ill-planned the fortifications both at Vicksburg and at Grenada, where Pemberton was facing Grant. Varina warned Jeff by letter not to let Johnston "do as he pleases out there," because his "disaffection to you" was common Richmond gossip, but Davis paid little heed. The circuitous long way they had to come from Chattanooga—through Atlanta and West Point down to Montgomery and Mobile, then back up to Meridian and over to Jackson—must have renewed Johnston's despair over shifting troops about as Davis wanted. He "asked the President to take me out of a position so little to my taste." But Davis, blinded by his own spirit, which looked on daunting obstacles as though they were not (witness Buena Vista and Abbeville) talked him into staying.[101] Davis knew troops could be shifted, since he had finally insisted that Johnston send a division of Bragg's to Vicksburg. On December 29, these men helped the garrison hurl back an attack by Sherman, whom Grant had sent to test the Yazoo River route from the north. This defeat at the battle of Chickasaw Bluffs forced Grant to seek some third way to the city, his own simultaneous thrust toward Grenada having been stopped by ruin of his supply lines and his depot at Holly Springs by Forrest and Van Dorn.[102]

Before it was known that Vicksburg was safe, Davis had gone twenty miles closer, to Bolton's Depot. He went to visit Joseph and his family nearby at Fleetwood, "a poor place" to which they had moved a month before. Varina sent love to "dear little Lize" and to Jeff, Christmas messages from his children, who "know I am going to be mean to them because you are not here to give them money." Jeff apparently had not the heart to go down to ravaged Davis Bend. After he left, Joseph sent Thornton Montgomery there to bring out more of their people, to live and work at his Fleetwood and at Jeff's plantation three miles away, both in Hinds County.[103]

The people Davis addressed in Jackson knew that his own family was involved when he spoke of the North's waging war "with a malignant ferocity and with a disregard and a contempt of the usages of civilization entirely unequaled in history." It only pointed up the "difference between the two peoples" North and South. "Our enemies are a traditionless and homeless race," from Oliver Cromwell on down, persecutors of others and "disturbers of the peace of the world." They had singled out Mississippi for "the direst vengeance of all. 'But vengeance is the Lord's,' and beneath His banner you will meet and hurl back these worse than vandal hordes."[104]

He admitted for the first time that recognition was probably not coming: "'Put not your trust in princes,' and rest not your hopes on foreign nations. This war is ours; we must fight it out ourselves. And I feel some pride in knowing that, so far, we have done it without the good will of anybody." At the thought that Mississippi might be subjugated, "every impulse of my heart dragged me hither," ready "to sleep in her soil." But now, seeing the "superior morality of our troops," he could leave with "a lighter heart," relying on "their valor and the assistance of God" to save it. So he tried to spark the "dead ashes."[105]

After wiring Seddon twice to hurry guns to Vicksburg, Jeff Davis began his long journey home, speaking at nearly every stop along the way. At Mobile, he commissioned Dr. Cartwright as medical inspector and learned of General Magruder's princely exploit in recapturing Galveston, Texas. At Montgomery, where Pa had a place with the commissary, he surely saw the Howells, devoted as he was to them. He reached Richmond by rail on January 5, 1863. He had "traveled better than twenty-five hundred miles" and "done as much as any man" to assure that no enemy soldier "now stood within fifty air-line miles" of any of the announced Yankee objectives: Richmond, Chattanooga, and Vicksburg.[106]

He was of course exhausted. He had started out unwell and was already saying by December 15, "[I] feel somewhat the want to rest." But there was little hope of that in Richmond. The very night of his return he had to address serenaders who welcomed him to the White House with Capt. J. B. Smith's Silver Band. He told the Virginians that their soil was "consecrated by blood which cries for vengeance against the insensate foe of religion as well as of humanity." He told not only of victories, but also of devastation, down to the very "means of subsistence," and of base indignities: "Every crime which could characterize the course of demons has marked the course of the invader." There were even attempts to make the slaves revolt: "For what are they waging war? They say to preserve the Union. Can they preserve the Union by destroying the social existence of a portion of the South? Do they hope to reconstruct the Union by striking at everything which is dear to man?" He brought forth "cries of 'Good! good!' and applause" with this: "If the question was proposed to you whether you would combine with hyenas or Yankees, I trust every Virginian would say, Give me the hyenas."[107]

Other matters kept him too anxious for either collapse or repose. Strange tidings followed him home. Bragg had turned at bay before his attackers—not the Union army, but his own. The *Chattanooga Rebel* had said his "retrograde movement from Murfreesboro was against the advice of his general officers," and he had "lost the confidence of his Army." He asked his commanders to reply to this, saying, "I shall retire without a regret if I find I have lost the good opinion of my generals." They had indeed advised the retreat, but they now advised his resignation. "Why General Bragg should have selected that tribunal, and have invited its judgment upon him, is to me unexplained," wrote Davis. He asked J. E. Johnston to go to Tullahoma at once and solve the mystery.[108]

It was a pretty clear case to those on the scene. Generals Polk, Hardee, Breckinridge, Cheatham, McCown, and Cleburne wanted to get rid of Bragg. Kentuckians even wanted Breckinridge to challenge him to a duel. A soldier spoke of "hatred expressed against him." The mystery came from Bragg's peculiar sense of honor, compounded of pride and humility. He sent out his query, a blunt attempt to "save my fair name" from "the deluge of abuse," at a time when his supporters—and there were many in the army—were not there to reply. Saying, "Be candid with me," he offered his enemies an opening, and they took it: "You do not possess the confidence of the army." Even his staff said he should "ask to be relieved."[109]

But Johnston wrote to Davis of Bragg's "great vigor & skill," saying his operations "have been conducted admirably. I can find no record of more effective fighting in modern battles than that of this army in December" (the first day at Murfreesboro). "While . . . you regard General Bragg as brave and skillful," the fact that generals want "a commander with fewer defects, cannot, I think, greatly diminish his value." Johnston knew Hardee and Polk wanted him to take Bragg's place, and he said: "I am sure that you will agree with me that the part I have borne in this investigation would render it inconsistent with my personal honor to occupy that position." To Wigfall he said it would be "injustice" and "would not look well . . . would expose me, injure me." He told Davis "no one in this army" (i.e., Polk or Hardee) should replace him. Davis had asked Johnston "to decide what the best interests of the service require." His answer was: "General Bragg should not be removed."[110]

Polk asked Davis to order Bragg to Richmond as inspector general. This perhaps gave Davis his next idea. He wired Johnston, through Seddon, to take personal command (which he had technically anyway) and to keep Bragg as "an organizer and administrator under you." "You certainly do not realize the popular dissatisfaction . . . nor the distrust and discontent unfortunately pervading all ranks of the army toward him." This, coming from the man who had sustained Bragg after Kentucky (and Sidney Johnston and Lee under censure) can indicate only one thing—Davis wanted Bragg out of the command. He had told Johnston, "though my confidence in General Bragg is unshaken, it cannot be doubted that if he is distrusted by his officers and troops, a disaster may result which, but for that cause, would have been avoided." If Johnston ruled out Polk, Hardee, and himself, "you will perceive how small is the field of selection." So he argued, "I do not think that your personal honor is involved [neither did Polk], as you could have nothing to gain by the removal of General Bragg." Still, "You shall not be urged by me to any course which would wound your sensibility or views of professional propriety. I will expect to hear further from you on this subject." But he did not.[111]

So matters rocked along for about a month, a month in which Bragg's report on the battle of Murfreesboro, excoriating some of his generals, "raised a storm in Congress," and Gen. Henry Heth told Davis that he and Kirby Smith had decided in Kentucky "that General Bragg had lost his mind." Davis laid aside his scruples and ordered Johnston in no uncertain terms to assume command and send Bragg to Richmond for conference. Johnston "simply refused." He had a double excuse: "Should the enemy advance," Bragg would be "indispensable" and "Mrs. Bragg's critical condition." Elise had been allowed to pass through the lines after Yankees ruined their plantation: "my wife driven forth destitute, and my negroes, stock, and all movables carried off." She was now at Winchester, Tennessee, "at the point of death" from typhoid fever.

Davis made one more effort to discover what was going on. He sent Preston Johnston to inspect the army. The aide's real report must have been oral; his written one is noncommittal; but it was useless. As soon as Elise had fully recovered, on April 10, Johnston put himself on the sick list: "General Bragg is therefore necessary here." Davis had met someone more obstinate than himself. By then, he was sick too. The question was swallowed up by subsequent events. Bragg stayed.[112]

Destruction of plantations below New Orleans—among them the Braggs' near Thibodaux—was only the latest reason why Southerners called Ben Butler "Beast" or "Spoons." Davis had mentioned to his serenaders in Richmond the Yankees' "stealing of silver forks and spoons," reminding him of Butler. With "his dishonors thick upon him," he was receiving "the plaudits of the only people on earth who do not blush to think he wears the human form."[113] Davis told Congress on January 12, 1863, that he had been waiting since the previous August for the promised "explanation" by the United States of Butler's murder of William Mumford in New Orleans. Since their silence tacitly admitted Butler's guilt and their sanction of it, "I have accordingly branded this criminal as an outlaw, and directed his execution in expiation of his crimes if [captured]." Davis had also protested General McNeil's murder of "seven prisoners of war in cold blood" in Missouri, and General Milroy's threat of death to civilians in Virginia, but he had "faint hope" that they would be repudiated. "Those who have obtained temporary possession of power in the United States" were "fast making its once fair name a byword of reproach among civilized men."[114]

Then Davis told Congress of "the most execrable measure recorded in the history of guilty man," one by which "several millions of human beings of an inferior race, peaceful and contented laborers in their sphere, are doomed to extermination, while at the same time they are encouraged to a general assassination of their masters." This was "a proclamation, dated on the 1st day of the present month, signed by the President of the United States, in which he orders and declares all slaves within ten of the States of the Confederacy to be free, except such as are found within certain districts now occupied in part by the armed forces of the enemy." If any "commissioned officers" were captured attempting to execute this order, Davis, unless Congress decreed otherwise, would deliver them to the state involved, to be tried by its laws as "criminals engaged in exciting servile insurrection." Enlisted men, however, as "unwilling instruments," would be merely prisoners of war.[115]

Davis quoted and cited the many admissions by Lincoln "that he was utterly without constitutional power" to issue this proclamation of partial emancipation. The members of his Republican Party had concealed their purpose by the "perfidious use" of just such "solemn and repeated pledges." This was "the complete and crowning proof" of the "uses to which [they] intended from the beginning to apply their power." The "despotism" from which the South had escaped was "now apparent to the most skeptical." But happily, "This proclamation is also an authentic statement by the Government of the United States of its inability to subjugate the South by force of arms," showing other nations "our just claims to formal recognition." One thing was sure: "a restoration of the Union has been rendered forever impossible."[116]

XV

The Year of Our Lord 1863

For President Jeff Davis, 1863 began bad, stymieing Bragg's victory at Murfreesboro and raising a tempest in his army. The Richmond weather kept pace. It snowed from January to April. In February it was ten below; the James River froze. The anniversary of Davis's inauguration and Washington's birth was "the ugliest day I ever saw," J. B. Jones told his diary. Wind howled "furiously," snow was "nearly a foot deep, and the weather very cold." All this did not bode well for the president's chronic neuralgia and bronchitis. And indeed, he told Clement Clay on March 10 that "ill health has prevented" earlier reply to a letter. That may be why Judah Benjamin signed his proclamation on February 27 naming March 27 as a day of fasting and prayer, proper to "a people who acknowledge the supremacy of the living God": "Prostrate yourselves in humble supplications to Him," with "devout thankfulness for signal victories," and with "prayer to Almighty God that he will . . . scatter our enemies [and] set at naught their evil designs."[1]

Colonel Gorgas excused his armorers, saying *laborare est orare* [to work is to pray], but Davis went to St. Paul's for the service. Maybe he took Mary Chesnut with him. She tells how the Davises would pick her up to go to church. Once she told the president, as he walked her home, how she wished she had grandchildren (the Chesnuts were childless), so she could give them her prayer book and tell how he carried it for her. She and James had rooms across from the White House now, and two Preston girls visiting. Even in crowded quarters, Mary entertained. At one of her parties, Davis came in quietly alone. Wigfall's daughters stayed seated and turned their backs on him. Someone whispered, "The Wigfalls are trying to snub Jeff Davis!" Mary rushed over to repair the slight, while others "stood up to receive the head of the Confederacy." As for her: "I was proud to receive him in my house—for himself, Jeff

Davis." She had not always felt so. She had said cutting things about his military ambition earlier. But her prejudice had long since dissolved in parlor and dinner table conversations. She was ready to take on all comers in his behalf. The Davis charm worked quickly on one of the Preston girls. After breakfast at the White House with the president and his staff, she went away ready to "fight for him to the death."[2]

Varina was not at the party where Jeff was snubbed, because she and Margaret Howell had been called to Montgomery, Alabama, to their sick father. On the sixteenth of March, William Burr Howell died. Jeff wrote to Ma, "I should be with you . . . to share if it may not be to alleviate, your anguish." Varina was there in his place, and "when you are sufficiently composed . . . you will tell me how I can serve you, and surely will not hesitate to believe that my best efforts are always at your command." He signed himself, "Your son."[3]

The Howells' own sons were widely scattered. Joe was in parts unknown. Becket was at Gibraltar, a marine first lieutenant on the *C. S. S. Sumter,* sitting under the blockade that ended that cruiser's brilliant career. He followed Raphael Semmes into the *Alabama,* and by war's end was a captain. Jeffy D., underage, had joined an army unit, but he was soon to be a midshipman in the navy.[4] Billy had fled to Georgia from New Orleans with his wife, Minnie, whose English father, Dr. William T. Leacock, rector of Christ Church, was then exiled from the city by General Butler, along with others, and their churches closed, for refusing to pray for the president of the United States.[5] Varina mentions Billy in a letter, so at least this son was probably there when William Howell was buried in Montgomery's Oakwood Cemetery.[6]

Priscilla Cooper Tyler, refugee wife of President Tyler's son Robert, came into town to call on Varina. She found her "extraordinarily gracious, affectionate"—"I really thought her one of the most charmingly entertaining persons I ever met with." This bears out Mary Chesnut on Varina—"so brilliant indeed, so warmhearted, and considerate toward all who are around her. After . . . the spice and spirit of her conversation, away from her things seem flat and tame." A Tyler grandson, Lt. William G. Waller, nephew to these Tylers, married Varina's sister Jennie before the year was out. In due time, Robert (and probably Priscilla) and their daughter, Letitia, who had raised the first flag, were buried near Pa in Oakwood Cemetery.[7]

Margaret stayed with Ma, who was very ill, but Varina went home when Jeff became ill too. Before leaving, she bought a fat leather volume entitled *Elegant Extracts, or Useful and Entertaining Pieces of Poetry for Young Persons.* She had cried over being away from the children. They were always in their parents' minds. Maggie was growing up with a "full loving heart." A soldier recalled how "a beautiful girl child at your gate in Richmond kissed me because I looked tired and hurt."[8] Jeff Jr., described by his mother as "beaming, blustering, blooming, burly and blundering as ever," had a pony, and his own little Confederate major's uniform. Once Virginia Clay had to tone him down, as he sat a Newfoundland dog like a horse, shouting "Bully for Jeff!" When he played army, Varina wrote, putting "his sword over his 'soldier' [shoulder]," Joe, then seventeen months, "instantly wheels and calls out 'March' quite plain." She told his godfather, Clement Clay, that Joe was "as pretty as was Maggie in her babyhood, and so very gentle & loving."[9] Before long, she was bragging on baby Billy, now a toddler, as "an unusually fine boy . . . very active and very good. I think his mind is like his dear Fathers." That father gave himself at least an hour every night to relax with his family. He customarily had prayers with the children, his "perfectly modulated" tones probably enhancing the beauty of the prayer book language, for there was a special service for families. When company prevented this, little Joe would still insist on saying his prayer at his father's knee.[10]

That "resonant voice" had been put to quite a different use on April 2, crying out to a mob of women and boys from a dray pulled across a Richmond street, "You say you are hungry and have no money. Here is all I have; it is not much, but take it." Davis turned out his pockets and said, "We do not desire to injure anyone, but this lawlessness must stop." The mob had begun by seizing food but then had looted jewelry and clothing stores. The mayor had "read the Riot Act, and as this had no effect he threatened to fire on the crowd." This was when Davis appeared. He was met "at first with hisses from the boys, but after he had spoken some little time with great kindness and sympathy, the women quietly moved on, taking their food with them." They milled around, were given food that day and the next by the city, and finally dispersed when the City Battalion marched down Main Street. So ended "the famous misnamed bread riot."[11]

By the time Varina got back to Richmond, Jeff had no voice at all. J. B. Jones reported him on April 22, "dangerously ill—with inflammation of the throat." This "recent attack" had "commenced with fever, and was followed by bronchitis," Jeff told Joseph on May 7. As in 1858, the infection involved his eyes, and it was rumored that he might lose the sight of the other one this time. Jones was alarmed: "Total blindness would incapacitate him for the executive office. A fearful thing to contemplate!" The War Department clerk felt relieved on May 6 when Davis sent over, from his White House office, fifty-five letters that he had read, with several endorsed "in his own hand"—"So he has not lost his sight." Jeff told Joseph he had not missed any "official duties" except, since he could not talk, "personal interviews." Now "the cough only remains," and "my present debility is no doubt due to confinement and anxiety." It took him several more weeks, however, to recover.[12]

There was anxiety aplenty. Richmond had been so threatened earlier that Lee had sent two divisions under Longstreet to secure the lines to the southeast. On May 3, in the midst of Davis's illness, Stoneman's Federal cavalry, sent by Maj. Gen. Joseph Hooker to cut Lee's communications, swung within three miles of the capital. Mary Chesnut, who fled to Varina's for the night, saw Davis come downstairs in the morning "feeble and pale" and watched her husband and Custis Lee load his pistols for him. Then they all rode off, Davis in Dr. Garnett's open carriage. The president "exhibited the finest spirits," said J. B. Jones, enjoying the "zeal of the old men and boys" marching out with muskets. But there was no fight this time. Stoneman veered off. A month later, Custis Lee was appointed to head a brigade formed of Richmond citizens. His father needed every regular soldier.[13]

For the whole northeastern front, Gen. Lee had less than half the men of Hooker. The Union general boasted that he would destroy Lee's army. In the midst of thick woods called the Wilderness, he gathered ninety thousand men around a great house and clearing known as Chancellorsville. Against this concentration Lee could bring no more than thirty-six thousand. With supreme audacity, he divided even these. He threw a skeleton force on the enemy left, kept only two divisions with himself in the center, and sent the bulk of his army under Stonewall Jackson all the way around to Hooker's right. Jackson, concealed by the dense thicket, achieved almost total surprise and smashed that wing back to the middle. Jubal Early, Pendleton, and Barksdale, whose brigade was "nearly destroyed" by overwhelming numbers, kept the left busy while Lee safely linked his men with Jackson's. Lee wired the president on May 3, "We have again to thank Almighty God for a great victory." Three more days, and "Fighting Joe" Hooker had fled north of the Rappahhanock River.[14]

The victory at Chancellorsville was the "supreme moment of [Lee's] life as a soldier," but it cost almost too much. The large loss of life was bad enough, but one man, Davis said, was "a host in himself." Returning in the dark from a reconnaissance, such as Davis and Lee warned each other against, Stonewall Jackson was shot by his own men. He was recovering from the amputation of his left arm when pneumonia ensued, brought on, so Pendleton reported, by Jackson's having himself wrapped in a wet sheet. Lee said that his own "right arm" was lost. On Sunday, May 10, he told Jackson's chaplain, "I wrestled in prayer for him last night, as I never prayed, I believe, for myself." On that day Jackson died. The poetic cadence of his delirious last words lodged forever in the Southern memory: "Let us cross over the river, and rest under the shade of the trees."[15]

In Richmond, Jeff and Varina too had watched and prayed all night. The body came down by train on the eleventh, the coffin "wrapped in a handsome flag Mr. Davis had sent for the purpose." It was the new national flag just adopted, the Stainless Banner, a pure white field, with Beauregard's battle flag in the corner. Jeff made the effort to go with Varina to the governor's mansion on Capitol Square "to take a last look," as she says, "at the patriot saint."[16] But the next day he had to ride in a carriage, "looking thin and frail," as Jackson's body was borne through the streets and back to the square. Then twenty thousand persons viewed, through the glass of the coffin, "the hero's face," with its "expression of shining calm." Davis, suffering from more than illness, had let a tear drop on Jackson's corpse. He said to someone trying to talk business, "You must excuse me. I am still staggering from a dreadful blow." Lee, who also shed tears, had said, as Jackson worsened, "God will not take him from us, now that we need him so much. Surely he will be spared to us." The devout Jackson himself had believed "that his Heavenly Father still had a work for him to do." The prayers of Davis, Lee, the whole army, the whole country for Jackson's life had received the answer— "No."[17]

Lee rebounded: "Any victory would be dear at such a cost. But God's will be done." With Davis too sick to come to him, he went to Richmond to talk about plans. From May 14 through 17, presumably in the upstairs office next to Davis's bedroom, they thrashed out with the cabinet a general Confederate strategy. Lee won his way for his own army; he would take the battle to the enemy. He wrote back to Davis, "I cannot express the concern I felt at leaving you in such feeble health, with so many anxious thoughts for the welfare of the whole Confederacy weighing upon your mind. I pray that a kind Providence will give you strength to bear the weight of care it has thought good to impose upon you."[18]

Davis replied, "My health is steadily improving. And if we can have good news from the West, I hope soon to be quite well again." He was still looking "sickly," however, when a visiting Prussian, Justus Scheibert, saw him in mid-July. It could not have occurred to Davis, or to anyone else, that his constant debility might be caused by anemia; no one had yet made any connection between malaria and parasites in the blood. There was sufficient anxiety, however, to down anyone. For good news did not come from the West, nor yet from the East.[19]

The staggering blow of Jackson's death came just as Davis was reeling from another: a Union army was loose in Mississippi. Adm. David D. Porter (a camel-buyer for Davis in 1856) ran enough boats past the batteries at Vicksburg one moonless night to supply General Grant below and ferry him across the river. Chased away from Grand Gulf, where he wanted to land, Grant merely marched down the right bank six miles farther, while Confederate forces (at one point a company of local planters) could give only pitiful harassment. He crossed into Mississippi at an undefended spot named Bruinsburg.[20]

Farther down on the west, Gen. Nathaniel Banks was rendering the whole Louisiana countryside "a desert," his greed fed by cotton bales, the rancor of his men appeased by burned and desecrated churches. This, and Lt. Gen. Richard Taylor, kept Banks too busy to make his planned attack on Port Hudson, a bastion on the left bank. This was bad news for General Pemberton: it meant Grant could defy his orders to help the Banks attack and concentrate on Vicksburg.[21]

President Davis thought it imperative to hold both places, especially Port Hudson, to secure the way to Texas and the crucial border trade with Mexico. Grant, too, saw both the river towns as vital, both to the South and to his aims. He quickly marched north and east from his bridgehead at Bruinsburg, scattering everything put in his path, and took possession of Jackson, in the middle of the state, on May 14. Where was Pemberton? Where was Johnston?

Pemberton had wired Johnston on May 1 that Grant was across the river. Johnston had approved his troop dispositions but stayed in Tennessee, ailing. On May 9, Seddon ordered him in no uncertain terms to go to Mississippi and take charge. He got to Jackson just as Grant did and wired Seddon: "I am too late." Pemberton was then in front of Vicksburg with less than eighteen thousand men. Johnston told him to attack Grant "if practicable"—"Troops here could cooperate." Neither one realized the size of Grant's force, or his ability. He had by now almost fifty thousand men in Mississippi, and he had decided to chance cutting loose from his river base and living off the country. But nothing else was left to chance; it was organized all the way back to Memphis.[22]

When Johnston saw twenty-five thousand men coming at Jackson on May 14, he took his six thousand and rode the rails north toward Canton. Then came many confused and delayed dispatches between Johnston and Pemberton. Pemberton was reluctantly obeying a Johnston order to hit Grant's supply line to the river when a second order came: move on Clinton (just west of Jackson); Johnston was moving there too. (He was actually moving to Canton. Was it a tragic mistake in spelling?) Against his will, Pemberton reversed directions and came up on, not the rear of a detachment, as he was led to expect, but the bulk of Grant's army, marching at him.

Grant too had Johnston's dispatch, from a spy. He had immediately gone out to meet Pemberton, leaving Sherman to destroy Jackson. Seeing he could not get back to his prepared line, Pemberton took position at a strong point known as Champion's Hill. Here, against Grant's thirty-five thousand (and more coming), the Southerners put up "one of the most obstinate" fights of the war, said a Union man. But they could not stand. They suffered badly in the retreat and were lucky to get into the Vicksburg fortifications, built on the land side over many months for just this contingency. Johnston, seeing "you must ultimately surrender" if the heights on the north were taken, sent word to evacuate at once, "if it is not too late." Pemberton and his generals refused to abandon the city they had been given to hold. Anyway, it *was* too late; Grant was already investing Vicksburg.[23]

The battle at Champion's Hill (Baker's Creek), raged only a couple of miles from Fleetwood, where Joseph Davis housed five women refugees and his servants. He had already protested thefts at the place to the Union general, whom he knew, describing three of his ladies as "invalids" and himself as "a 'non combatant' in my 79th year." He never got an answer. After the battle, Yankee soldiers came rummaging through even the women's sickrooms, ransacking trunks and desks, stealing anything of value. By the end, Joseph said, they had "carried off most of the negroes, stock of horses, mules, oxen, wagons, carriages, and other property."[24]

Having ruined Jackson and the rails all around it, Sherman was leading his troops to Grant when he stopped at a house near Bolton to get a drink. In the wreckage strewing the yard he saw a copy of the United States Constitution with "Jefferson Davis" written on the flyleaf. He was on the plantation Joseph had bought for Jeff. When a staff officer heard Fleetwood was near, he went there, and, as Sherman baldly said, "took a pair of carriage horses."[25]

The next day, a squad came to Fleetwood under orders from Gen. Peter J. Osterhaus to "leave no board unburned." Joseph was given half an hour to get out. Warned beforehand, he had sent Lise and his niece, Anna Miles, into Jackson. Eliza and the widowed Martha Harris (one of the orphans he had raised) were too sick to travel. He managed to get them, Martha's daughter, Margaret, and some furniture, into the yard, where soldiers broke into trunks that others had missed and stole jewels and silver. The "worse than vandal hordes" that Davis had deplored were upon them. The torches were lit. Then a Confederate uniform was spotted behind the house. It was Capt. Joe Mitchell, alone, coming to check on his grandfather, but the Yankees fled, burning only outbuildings. Fleetwood was safe for the moment, but Jeff's house was sent up in flames. Eliza and Martha were so distraught that Joseph sent them to his friend Cox, near Clinton. Lise came back to Fleetwood, so her grandfather would not be alone.[26]

Grant sat before Vicksburg all through June, his every assault bloodily repulsed. The defenses, though seven miles long and scantily manned, were never breached. Grant kept his huge army reinforced and supplied from bases on the river now. He fortified his line in back as well as in front, expecting attack from Johnston. In Richmond, the tension became almost unbearable. Jeff Davis had never intended Pemberton to be bottled up: "My purpose [was] an attack on Grant when in the interior, by combined forces of Johnston and Pemberton.

Thus alone was a complete victory to be expected."[27] He wrote to Lee on May 31: "Genl. Johnston did not, as you thought advisable, attack Grant promptly, and I fear the result is that which you anticipated." He confessed he could not avoid reproachful thoughts, but "it would be unkind to annoy you" with them. "All the accounts" of Pemberton "fully sustain the good opinion heretofore entertained." In his frustration, Davis had been heard to cry, "If I could take one wing and Lee the other, I think we could between us wrest a victory from those people."[28]

"Those people" was Lee's own term for the enemy, and he was out to wrest a victory all by himself. His wing in the east was moving north. On June 15, he telegraphed Davis, "God has again crowned the valor of our troops with success." Early had taken Winchester, in the Shenandoah Valley. Chancellorsville had dispirited "those people" and had raised Southern hopes that "a single direct blow, aimed at the vitals of the North" might win independence. It was for this that Lee was on the march. He also hoped to feed his army, to draw the enemy out of Virginia, and to relieve pressure on Vicksburg.[29]

Everyone had approved this offensive at the May meeting, except John Reagan. (The vice president also disapproved, but apparently was not there.) Reagan was convinced that Lee should send his army to save Vicksburg and merely feint to the north. Other appeals for Lee at Vicksburg caused Davis to recall the cabinet. But after long conference, the plans were unchanged: Johnston was to reinforce Pemberton, and Lee to march north. But Reagan still "felt so strongly that we had made a great mistake," that he could not sleep. In the middle of the night he sent a note to Davis, who promised to reconvene the cabinet again on Monday. On Sunday, however, when they met informally in Davis's office, Reagan saw he had no support, so he gave up. But all this shows, he says, contrary to the slander that Davis "was self-willed and arbitrary and would not accept the advice of others," how willing he was to reconsider even closed questions.[30]

Hanging in suspense between Lee's risky move and Johnston's inertia, Davis had other stresses to bear as well. Yancey suddenly accused him of "personal dislike," though until now he had been "entirely unaware" of "enmity"—a testimony to Davis's deep wish to avoid strife. Both he and Davis denied personal animosity, though Yancey admitted harboring resentment against Davis for over a year. He had fought him so hard in the Senate, over the issue of a supreme court, that Ben Hill had thrown an inkwell at him. At a champagne breakfast for Henry Foote and J. E. Johnston, Yancey had toasted Johnston as "the only man who can save the Confederacy." R. B. Rhett, a Davis enemy, was his close friend.[31]

These two masters of the English language were about to achieve amity, when Davis showed their letters to Clement Clay, "your noble personal friend," Yancey called him, "who would not flatter Caesar for his crown." Clay was blunt, all right. Davis discovered that it was he who had set Yancey off, blaming Davis entirely in a squabble they had over an Alabama postmastership. Clay had told Yancey:

> He is a strange compound which I cannot analyze, although I thought I knew him well. . . . He will not ask or receive counsel, and, indeed, seems predisposed to go exactly the way his friends advise him not to go. I have tried harder than I ever did with any other man to be his friend, and to prevent his alienating me or other friends, I have kept my temper and good will towards him longer than I could do with any other than an old and cherished friend.[32]

This says as much about the vituperative Clay as it does about Davis. If he wanted to "prevent discord," he had a strange way of doing it. He expressed "surprise" that Davis denied hostility and told Yancey how Davis had spoken ill of him. "Some of my friends think he will *show his friendship* to me by trying to have me defeated next fall, if I run for the Senate. It would argue more friendship for me than he has expressed to me of you. . . . The more I see of [Davis] the less I understand him."[33]

Yancey, however, aware of Davis's "former personal friendship and good deeds," seemed eager for reconciliation. He was mortally ill. He asked Clay "whether Davis appeared desirous of holding on to my regard or no?" And Clay answered: "Yes! I was surprised to find him unwilling . . . to have you believe him unfriendly." Then he nearly undid things again by adding: "I can see no motive . . . but to prevent making you an enemy."[34] Yancey may never have seen this, however. Soon after, he called out to a son just arriving at his home near Montgomery: "I am dying; all is well; it is God's will." He was forty-eight. They laid him in Oakwood Cemetery, not far from William Howell. He left Davis "a spy glass once the property of Genl. Washington," and Davis told his widow how he valued this proof of "the kind feelings of my former associate and friend, the distinguished patriot and statesman."[35]

The animus of Clay toward Davis showed in L. Q. C. Lamar's remark that their wives, on opposite sides of a parlor, were like two men-of-war firing at each other. The Clays, besides, were intimate friends of the Wigfalls and the J. E. Johnstons, and kin by marriage to Davis's bitter foe, James Hammond of South Carolina. Clay was indeed defeated in the next election, but, ironically, it was because he was considered the president's friend. Davis overlooked his role as sower of discord and offered him several posts, which he refused, before sending him off, grumbling that he was "not suited," to Canada. Clay admitted to Wigfall: "[Davis] professed to be my friend & never to have been otherwise, & I am now satisfied that I have misunderstood his feelings toward me."[36]

Public policy brought tension too. General Lee, even while moving north, wrote Davis that with enemy superiority "in numbers, resources, and all the means and appliances for carrying on the war . . . we have no right to look for exemptions from the military consequences." "We should not . . . conceal from ourselves that . . . the disproportion" in men "is steadily augmenting." He asked Davis not "to discourage any party whose purpose is peace." Civilian peace talk was emerging now, and Lee's military argument gave it weight, but Davis refused to consider it. Vice President Stephens, writing from "Liberty Hall, Ga.," offered to go North and to see about prisoner exchange and peace. Davis immediately wired, "Please come here."[37]

He hoped Stephens, a personal friend of Lincoln's, might move him, but not toward peace. Davis had no idea of giving up the fight. He gave Stephens verbal instructions and spelled out for him carefully in writing: "Your mission is simply one of humanity, and has no political aspect." He wanted him to address "the unheard-of conduct of Federal officers in driving from their homes entire communities of women and children, as well as of men."

> My whole purpose is in one word to place this war on the footing of such as are waged by civilized people in modern times, and to divest it of the savage character which has been impressed on it by our enemies, in spite of all our efforts and protests. War is full enough of unavoidable horrors . . . [to] demand of any Christian rulers who may be unhappily engaged in carrying it on to seek to restrict its calamities and to divest it of all unnecessary severities. You will endeavor to establish the cartel for the exchange of prisoners . . . to prevent for the future what we deem the unfair conduct of our enemies in evading the delivery of the prisoners who fall into their hands . . . and by detaining them sometimes for months in camps and prisons.[38]

Davis had explained in 1850 that only a "savage foe" destroys private property; "cultivated nations" march army against army "and fight battles to decide issues." He complained to Lincoln now, in a letter for Stephens to deliver, of violation of "all the rules of war" in destroying "even agricultural implements" and "standing crops" of helpless noncombatants, to produce "starvation." This went on everywhere.[39] Davis well knew this ferocity personally and not only toward himself and Joseph. His brother had just written, "The enemy robbed Sister Anna of most of her property"—Locust Grove had been looted and partly destroyed. Stephens got as far as Newport News with Davis's letter, but his request to go to Washington was termed "inadmissible." "We were stigmatized as insurgents," says Davis, "and the door was shut in our faces." The date was July 3, 1863.[40]

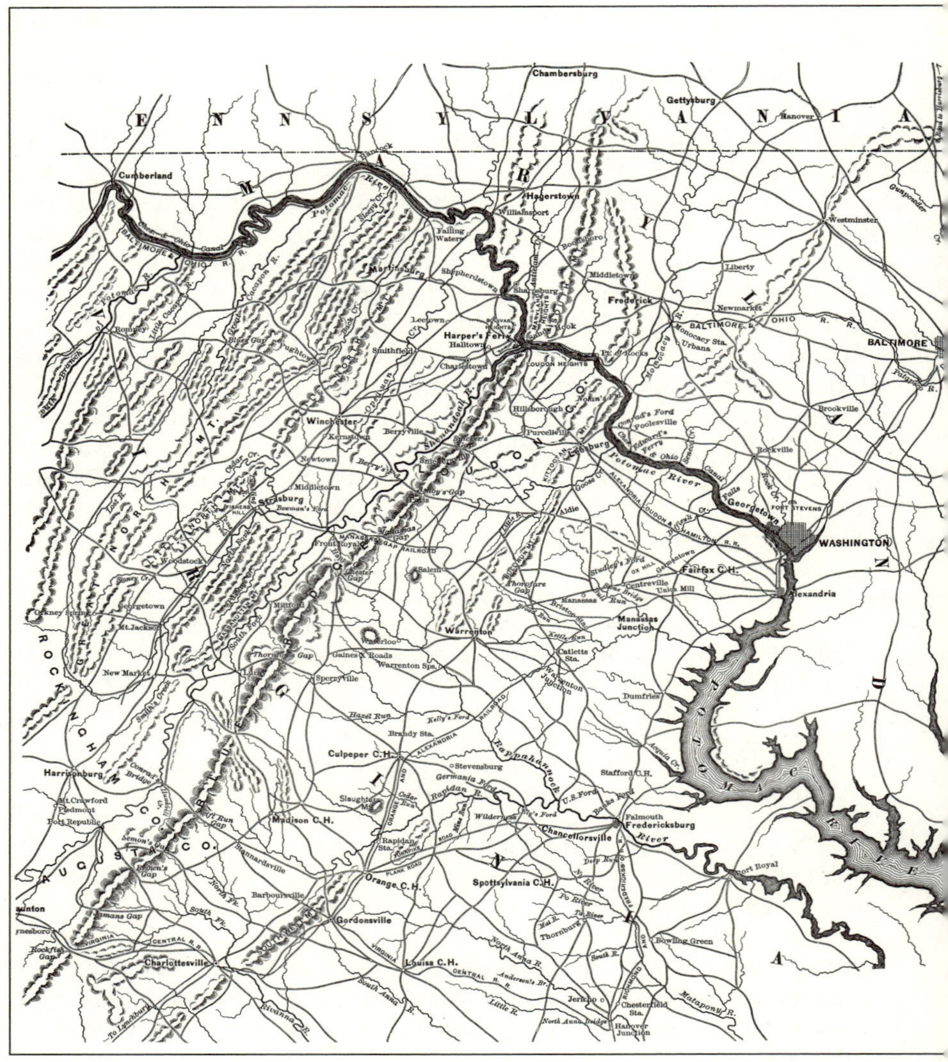

Northern Virginia, Maryland, and Gettysburg

Battle was raging at Gettysburg, Pennsylvania, but it was "war only upon armed men," as Lee's general orders of June 27 read. "We cannot take vengeance for the wrongs our people have suffered without lowering ourselves . . . and offending against Him to whom vengeance belongeth." Plenty of people back home were hoping that Lee *would* take vengeance, but General Pendleton noted the great "forbearance" of the army, after all the Yankee "outrage." So did many others. Davis told Congress of the "striking contrast." Lee's men were forbidden to enter private homes. Ewell punished men for stealing vegetables. General Early, indeed, requisitioned hats, shoes, and money (which he spent on provisions) from the town of York and rather gleefully burned ironworks owned by Thaddeus Stevens (who advocated ravaging the South), but these were legitimate war measures. His men did not molest private property or people, and in one town, they helped put out a fire.[41]

Invading Pennsylvania, Lee had wanted a diversion by Beauregard in Virginia, but when Davis asked it, Beauregard declined. Lee wanted to hit the enemy army off guard, piecemeal, as it came up after him, but the barefoot condition of the Southern army ruined his plan. General Heth, hearing of shoes in the town of Gettysburg, sent a brigade in to get them and tangled with what proved to be the edge of the main Federal army, under its new head, Gen. George Gordon Meade. Lee had only just heard from a spy that that army was anywhere near. His eyes and ears, Stuart's cavalry, coming another route, had let the Yankees get between them and had not yet joined.[42]

Once it began, fighting became unstoppable. Lee could not choose his ground as planned and had to attack with only part of his army. His men carried all before them that first late afternoon of July 1, except the crucial and already fortified Cemetery Hill, behind the town. Cemetery Ridge, however, running south, to the Confederate right, with commanding heights at the end named Round Top and Little Round Top, was still empty. Meade kept filling that ridge all night with soldiers. Lee ordered Longstreet to attack "very early" the next day from the right and drive some Federals from a lower ridge, back toward the town. "Longstreet is a very good fighter when he . . . gets everything ready," Lee mused, "but he is *so slow*."[43]

It was four o'clock in the afternoon before Longstreet was ready. The delay "gave the enemy time to be all up and protected by earth works," said Pendleton. According to Gov. John Carroll of Maryland, Lee told him after the war that "if Longstreet had obeyed his orders . . . we would have gained the victory at Gettysburg." When the attack finally came, its fury chased the Federals, toward not the town but the upper ridge to which Meade was still rushing troops. Some poured into Little Round Top just in time to keep men of Gen. John Bell Hood, already wounded, from seizing it.[44]

Meade's hold was so precarious that he was on the verge of retreat when at midnight Capt. Ulrich Dahlgren brought a captured dispatch: it was from Davis to Lee, saying Beauregard was not coming. Thus assured that his rear was safe, Meade held on desperately to the heights. The next day, July 3, another attack ordered for morning was delayed by Longstreet until afternoon. Pickett's division led a charge that reached the heights but then fell back. When the Fourth of July dawned, Meade still held his ridge. Lee held the rest of the field and an opposing height. Both armies were so shocked by losses that neither renewed the battle.[45]

Lee waited the whole day to see if Meade would move; then, as at Sharpsburg, neither defeated nor victorious, he began to withdraw from enemy territory. He explained to Davis that the enemy, though "much shattered . . . can be easily reinforced," while he could not. He expected attack every night, and dug in, but "the enemy made no effort to follow except with his cavalry." Persistent rain and flooded rivers were the enemy now. Slowly, painfully, but "in perfect order," says Early, Lee led his men back into the Shenandoah Valley still intact, still the Army of Northern Virginia. In August, to counter Meade's infantry moving south, it took position on the line of the Rapidan River, from which it had set out.[46]

Young Col. Arthur James Fremantle of the Coldstream Guards had been on his way to visit Lee's army when he stopped in Richmond on June 17. Benjamin, "a stout dapper little man," had taken him to tea at the White House. Fremantle found the president's face "emaciated, and much wrinkled," but his features good, "especially his eye, which is very bright, and full of life and humor." "He looked what he evidently is, a well-bred gentleman. Nothing can exceed the charm of his manner, which is simple, easy, and most fascinating." Fremantle, who had come all the way from the Rio Grande, noted in his journal: "many people have remarked to me that Jefferson Davis seems in a peculiar manner adapted for his office"—"a brave man and a good soldier . . . the only man who . . . was able to control the popular will. People speak of any misfortune happening to him as an irreparable evil too dreadful to contemplate." Gorgas noted on July 2, when Davis's physician was alarmed about him, that his death "would indeed be the most serious calamity that could befall us."[47]

Fremantle brought firsthand news from Mississippi. This must have been welcome; it was hard to tell what was happening there. He had seen reinforcements coming to Johnston and thought he must now have "nearly 25,000." Later, Bragg sent Breckinridge's division of over five thousand, two other infantry regiments, and a brigade of cavalry. The men Fremantle saw were "in excellent spirits . . . and clamoring to be led against *only* double their numbers."[48]

J. E. Johnston was not their man. He was unmoved by Seddon's order, "You must hazard attack," even when Seddon offered to take the responsibility and urged, "It is better to fail nobly daring, than, through prudence even, to be inactive." Johnston never thought like this. He wanted all the odds in his favor. Mary Chesnut relays the story of a South Carolina bird hunt when the other hunters came home with full bags and Johnston with an empty one: "He was too fussy, too hard to please . . . too much afraid to miss and risk his fine reputation for a crack shot." The others "shot right and left—happy-go-lucky," but Johnston never fired at all because "the exactly right time and place never came."[49]

It is true that in Mississippi he never even had the "only" one-to-two odds that his men asked. And if he concentrated his few on one spot in Grant's far-flung line, Grant could easily overmatch him. Grant had so many men that he had put Sherman in a second line, facing out, specifically to meet Johnston, saying he "was about the only general on that side whom he feared." (He does not say why.)[50]

Lee kept Davis up-to-date on all his moves and plans.[51] Johnston kept him largely in the dark, mostly arguing with Seddon about his authority and how many men he had. When the siege of Vicksburg had its "disastrous termination," Davis complained that, though "painfully anxious," he had been "without information from you as to any plans proposed or attempted to raise the siege. Equally uninformed as to . . . Port Hudson, I have to request such information in relation thereto as the Government has a right to expect from one of its commanding Generals in the field."[52] This was a little unfair of Davis. Johnston had expressed in many ways what he said on June 15: "I consider saving Vicksburg hopeless." He had explained to Seddon that Grant had more reinforcements than he had men; he was "without hope of doing more than aid to extricate the garrison." To this end, he was moving cautiously toward Grant's lines, looking for a weak spot, when on July 3 he sent a message in to Pemberton that he "hoped" to create a diversion on July 7, during which they could try to break out. The men were too weak for this anyway, from hunger and sleeplessness under the ceaseless bombardment. But Pemberton never saw the message until it was shown to him as a prisoner: it had been intercepted. He and his generals agreed to ask for terms while there was time to avoid unconditional surrender, and they were paroled with their men on the Fourth of July. This meant they could fight again when exchanged. Pemberton's parole ordered him to report to Johnston. He saluted as he did so but refused to shake the offered hand.[53]

Across the river, on the day of surrender, General Holmes, in accord with Davis's wish to draw men away from Grant, tried to recapture Helena, Arkansas. He was defeated, just as Taylor had been when he attacked the Union camp at Milliken's Bend a month before. On the lower Mississippi, Port Hudson was on July 4 still making spirited resistance to a tardy siege by Banks, but the garrison gave up when they heard that Vicksburg had fallen.[54]

Davis had hung impaled on double anxiety, official and personal. He knew "every other family" around Vicksburg, and his adoptive niece, Julia Porterfield, was in the city. As he said later, he had given Johnston the defense of his home, family, and friends, showing that he did not "deprecate [his] merits." Joseph had told him that Johnston apparently "intends to surrender the Country" but then had telegraphed on Johnston's behalf: "Can the army of Genl Bragg be sent?" Jeff had already told Joseph on May 7 that this was "impossible without ruin to the Confederacy. I have spared no effort and am still striving to give aid to the defenders of my home, but that is not my only duty."[55]

Johnston, reversing his former stand, had wanted Bragg to come, but still believing it "would involve yielding Tennessee" had refused to order him: "It is for the Government to decide." He had, however, persuaded Governor Pettus as well as Joseph to appeal to Davis, who found Pettus's wire "discouraging." It showed "no reliance on efforts to be made with the forces on the spot," and withdrawing "thirty thousand troops" would dismember the eastern Confederacy. But he had again asked Bragg and Beauregard if they could possibly spare more men, and had sent Gen. G. J. Rains with "submarine and sub terra shells," his inventions in which Davis set great store.[56] Seddon reported he had "drained resources even to the danger of several points" and was "too far outnumbered in Virginia to spare [any there]." "I have done all which was in my power," Davis said, having called for militia and even plain citizens to turn out. It was not enough. It was becoming clear that the South simply did not have enough men. The weight of Union numbers, wielded by inventive and ruthless generals, was beginning to crush the Confederacy.[57]

Long before this, Davis had been "urged by friends to send a force of men to protect" Brierfield but had said he could not "use public means to preserve private interests," Reagan relates, and it was the same when "all his books and papers were in danger of destruction" in Hinds County. But, thinking perhaps of the "family letters running back to the time when I was a schoolboy," including Knox Taylor's love letters to him and his to Varina, he did finally send one wagon for his personal papers. It arrived too late.[58]

He had urged Joseph to bring his family to Richmond, but Eliza was too feeble, and Joseph did not feel he could leave his "people." As Jeff said, "the faithful deserve to be saved from the fate to which the Yankees would consign them." They were forcing black men by brutal means into the army, labor, or noisome refugee camps. Many of the Davis slaves ran away, but many stayed. Admiral Porter made Isaiah Montgomery his cabin boy, put Thornton in the navy, and persuaded Ben and his wife to go live at Cincinnati. With enemy occupation bringing confiscation laws and the Emancipation Proclamation, Joseph could care for only those who stayed with him willingly. In the end, he still had about forty.[59]

Gen. J. E. Johnston appeared at Fleetwood on the morning of July 4 with the news of Vicksburg's fall. Sherman was coming after him, fast. The whole family, black and white, made haste to follow him toward Jackson, piling necessities on a wagon that he gave them with its team and teamster. Joseph and Lise in their mule-drawn carriage, and the servants in ox carts, or driving the stock, inched along through Johnston's retreating army to Clinton, where they joined Eliza and Martha Harris and Margaret. Cox decided to take his family away, too, and left his home in charge of a friend, Robert Melvin. Johnston did not defend Jackson, though he had said losing it would "lose Mississippi." Fighting only a rearguard action, he took his army thirty miles east, and Sherman chose not to pursue. Beyond Jackson, the Davis ménage became true refugees, camping along the roadside and cooking over campfires. Finally they crossed the state line into Choctaw County, Alabama, and found refuge on a farm where Eliza, steadily growing worse, could be cared for. They were out of harm's way for the time, but their property was not.[60]

Sherman did a more thorough job of wrecking and burning Jackson this time, destroying in the process an irreplaceable stock of railroad engines and cars, an "injury" from which, Davis said in 1865, "we have never recovered." He blamed it on Johnston's failure to repair the bridge over the Pearl River while he had time. Sherman's men also did a more thorough job on the Davis belongings. When Joseph sent Cox and Joe Nicholson back to see about Fleetwood, all they could find were a few books lying about the yard. The house with its contents had been burned, the silver dug up and stolen.[61]

At Clinton, Yankees became wildly excited when a runaway slave told them that Jeff Davis's things were stored at Cox's place. Cox, however, had failed to tell Robert Melvin this. The poor man repeated in vain to the swarming bluecoats that this was not the Davis plantation. They held him "with the most shocking imprecations" at triple bayonet point while furniture was slashed, boxes were "torn open and emptied." "Books and papers were . . . scattered through the wood for miles; fine carpets were cut to pieces." A "walnut card table" and "a small writing case (Rosewood I think)" were literally torn apart, Melvin wrote to Jeff Davis: "every thing useful or ornamental was plundered and destroyed . . . they appeared to exult more in some walking sticks than anything else except the wine." This went on from Saturday, July 18, through Monday noon, when Gen. Hugh Boyle Ewing came with a wagon and took what he wanted, including much that belonged to Cox and Melvin, "but it was useless to remonstrate." One cherished item was saved, the marble bust of Jeff and Varina's first child, Samuel Emory Davis. Melvin claimed it as his; "otherwise it would have been broken to pieces and the fragments sent North as trophies." To vent their "petty malice," however, "the soldiers" found "your Excellency's likeness" in a book, and this they "stabbed as often as they could find a piece of the paper large enough to receive the point of a knife."[62]

Davis's response was typical. Justus Scheibert was with him when a lady was lamenting the destruction of his "famous library." Davis said that he demanded sacrifice of every Confederate, and so "had not a word to waste about such trifles, but if he pitied anything, it was his poor Negroes, who had been living at his home for generations and had now been driven off . . . to misery and ruin. He said that he had a personal interest in every one of them."[63]

The consequence of Yankee vandalism was not trifling for Franklin Pierce. General Sherman, to whom General Ewing turned over Davis's letters, sent some back to people he knew, thinking they might be intimidating. There was reason to fear. George W. Jones, though a diplomat for the United States, had found himself in prison in 1861 because of a letter to Davis, which Seward had opened illegally. Sherman's soldiers had already made off with Pierce's letters, so they could not be returned to him. One surfaced at the North just in time to ruin Pierce for good.[64]

The ex-president was all for the Union, but he wrote his wife, "I will never justify, sustain, or in any way or to any extent uphold this cruel, heartless, aimless unnecessary war." He opposed just as firmly Lincoln's violations of civil rights, and thought the Emancipation Proclamation showed, his biographer says, "that the true purpose of the war was to wipe out the states and destroy property." In 1863, Pierce came out of retirement to give the Fourth of July speech for the Democrats of Concord, New Hampshire. He warned against "arbitrary, irresponsible power" and said only "peaceful agencies" could achieve "the great objects" of the Constitution. His arguments were called treasonous in the press and were undercut, even as he spoke, by rumors of a great victory at Gettysburg.

Nathaniel Hawthorne, who was sitting on the platform, had just dedicated to Pierce his new book, *Our Old Home*. The very day it came out, there appeared a captured Davis letter, written by Pierce in 1860, deploring "the madness of northern abolitionism" and predicting that, if war came, there would be fighting in northern streets between "those who respect their political obligations" and those who were moved only by "fanatical passion" about slavery. Most New Englanders already thought Pierce what Harriet Beecher Stowe called him, "that arch traitor," and this was the last straw. Emerson and others bought *Our Old Home*, but they cut out the dedication. (Hawthorne said to withdraw it would be "poltroonery.") Pierce fell so low that he was not even asked to be a pallbearer at the funeral of Hawthorne, his best friend.[65]

All that fatal first week of July, racked by illness and anxiety, but working right on, Davis had grief to bear as well. J. R. Davis came through Gettysburg alive, but his brigade was cut to pieces. Another nephew, Capt. Isaac Stamps of the Twenty-first Mississippi, and Davis's friend Barksdale, "out in front of the whole line" leading the charge, both died of wounds on the second day. Barksdale's brigade went to a West Point comrade of Davis and Lee's, Col. B. G. Humphreys. Isaac Stamps had married Humphreys' daughter, Mary Elizabeth. She was staying now at the White House. As the twenty-eight-year-old widow lay prostrate with sorrow, Varina lavished on her and two little daughters all her nursing skill and motherly warmth. The Davis children helped, causing Mary to say they had "the finest natures that I ever saw." She was soon up and asking her uncle for a pass through the lines. She interviewed Isaac's companions, in Richmond hospitals, then went and found his body and brought it to Richmond. After a funeral at St. Paul's, she took it for burial to Rosemont, where his parents, Lucinda and William Stamps, still lived. His stone reads: *Dulce et decorum est pro patria mori.*[66]

That was Isaac's very sentiment. Mary knew, from many letters of men who were with him, that he had said he "had rather die on the battlefield in defense of [my family] and my country than to live and see it subjugated." He sent Mary the sword his Uncle Jeff had given him. She related all this in a letter to Davis:

> Were it not, my dear Uncle, that I knew you wanted to hear all about "the dear boy," it would be sufficient apology to say that it comforts me to write you about it. . . . you will forgive me for leaning, along with my country and as a part of it, upon your great heart. . . . You can lean only upon its God, and through Him, our common Father, I hope to repay a part of your tenderness to me."[67]

Davis propped up many another during the war. Lee was one. Lee was also prop to him. "You were required in the field and I deprived myself of the support you gave me here," said Davis; "I need your counsel." Lee, in return, had asked *him* for military advice. "I hesitate to express an opinion, but as you request it," Davis began, and went on to give an informed, succinct summary.[68] Davis had recently written Lee about the military situation in every part of the Confederacy, implicitly asking advice and mentioning the desire of some to remove unsuccessful officers. Lee's reply thanked him for "uniform kindness" and for all his help to the army. Then he spoke of "discontent in the public journals" and how losing the confidence of one's troops meant disaster "sooner or later." He had been forced south of the Rapidan: "We must expect reverses, even defeats. They are sent to teach us wisdom and prudence." But then he said, "The general remedy for the want of success in a military commander is his removal." (Wigfall and Clay were saying he should resign.) Citing his shortcomings and decreasing bodily powers, Lee asked Davis to "to take measures to supply my place" with "a younger and abler man."[69]

Davis, reminded of the "senseless clamor" against Sidney Johnston, assured Lee that nothing required "a greater effort of patience than to bear the criticisms of the ignorant."

> I admit . . . that an officer who loses the confidence of his troops should have his position changed . . . but when I read the sentence, I was not at all prepared for the application you were about to make. Expressions of discontent in the public journals furnish but little evidence of the sentiment of an army. . . . Were you capable of stooping to it, you could easily surround yourself with those who would fill the press with your laudations . . . rather than detract from the achievements which will make you and your army the subject of history and object of the world's admiration for generations to come.
>
> But suppose, my dear friend, that I were to admit . . . the points which you present, where am I to find that new commander who is to possess the greater ability which you believe to be required. I do not doubt the readiness with which you would give way to one who could accomplish all that you have wished, and you will do me the justice to believe that if Providence would kindly offer such a person for our use, I would not hesitate to avail of his services. My sight is not sufficiently penetrating to discover such hidden merit if it exists, and I have but used to you the language of sober earnestness, when I have impressed upon you the propriety of avoiding all unnecessary exposure to danger because I felt our country could not bear to lose you. To ask me to substitute you by some one in my judgment more fit to command, or who would possess more of the confidence of the army or of the reflecting men in the country is to demand for me an impossibility.[70]

Lee bowed, thanking him for "your kind and partial consideration of my feeble services." He was "willing to serve . . . in any capacity," the lower the better.[71]

Davis held himself more expendable than Lee: "If a victim would secure the success of our cause, I would freely offer myself." (He was used to offering himself as "a reasonable, holy, and living sacrifice" to God at every communion service.) Davis was sure that "many of those most assailed" would be willing victims too "if their sacrifice could bring such reward," probably meaning Pemberton and Bragg. He referred more than once to Bragg's "self-denying nature." He had pointed out how much Pemberton had "forfeited" to come South and how "unjust and ungenerous" it was to suspect him because of Northern birth.[72]

Davis threw himself into protection of others he had appointed from the North, and they were many. He rejected indignantly J. E. Johnston's suggestion that "the arrival of Genl. [Samuel Gibbs] French [who was from New Jersey] will produce discontent among the troops."[73] Against suspicion, even by Varina, of his aide-de-camp, Joseph Ives, a New Yorker, he maintained "thorough conviction as to his fidelity."[74]

Ives was not only Northern, he was also Roman Catholic, making him doubly suspect in the largely Protestant South, and making Davis support him all the more, as he did his Catholic cabinet member, Stephen Mallory. Davis, besides being naturally for the underdog, was well known for pro-Catholic leanings. Varina had even been heard to say that church was where she "ought to be." Their Episcopal Church was called Protestant, but its liturgy, creed, calendar, and priesthood bore the stamp of its Romish origin.[75] Jeff's sister Amanda and her five daughters, including Malie, had become Catholic, as had his friend Northrop, and he never forgot his childhood years at St. Thomas school.[76] He admired the Irish-born Confederates, Bishop Patrick Nieson Lynch of Charleston, who had held a service of thanksgiving for secession, and Father John Bannon, "the fighting chaplain" of Missouri troops. He commissioned Lynch to the Papal States in 1864, and sent Bannon to Ireland, where he slowed, but could not stop, its stream of soldiers into the North.[77] Davis never passed a Sister of Charity in the streets without raising his hat in "involuntary reverence," especially for their hospital work. When he and Varina had to leave Richmond, it was with the sisters and a priest that they left their valuables.[78]

Everyone was condemning Pemberton, from the War Department diarist who suspected all Northern officers of treason, to Mississippians who could not forgive him for surrendering. Davis was certain of his loyalty and had his own ideas about what caused the fall of Vicksburg: "want of provisions inside, and a general outside who wouldn't fight." Gorgas, to whom he said this, had found the city's fall "incredible. . . . Why an effort was not made to cut through is not yet known." He thought the president "bitter against Johnston."[79]

Davis had just documented for the general, every step of the way, how he had never believed in or executed his theater command, only bickered ceaselessly about his authority. Davis, answering Johnston's "persistent repetition" of untruths, only implied in this letter his failure as a field general—"mistakes" would have been overlooked "if acknowledged." Elsewhere Davis was explicit: Vicksburg and Port Hudson had fallen "without one blow on his part to relieve either," and he had not tried to defend Jackson. He relieved Johnston now of responsibility for Tennessee (which he claimed he did not have anyway) and left him in command where he was. But he was through with him: "My confidence in General Johnston's fitness for separate command was now destroyed."[80]

Johnston told Louis Wigfall that the letter proved Davis's "ill feeling towards me—for which certainly I have given no cause," and Lydia frenziedly wrote Charlotte that it was full of "such insults as only a coward or a woman could write. I wish it could be published along with his pious proclamations. . . . I feel that nothing can make me forgive either of [the Davises]. . . . I could almost have asked God to punish them." She urged Johnston to resign. Instead, he told a friend: "I took great pleasure in setting him right, for which doubtless he is Christianly thankful."[81]

Davis had his own sarcasm, over a newspaper letter written by one of Johnston's staff members, Dr. D. W. Yandell, using confidential material, extolling Johnston, and accusing Pemberton of disobedience: "It is needless to say that you are not considered capable of giving countenance to such efforts at laudation of yourself and detraction of others." Davis's spleen still showed in postwar years: "The letter was stopped and Dr. Y. ordered to the trans Missi. Dept. where his services might not be diverted from their proper channel." Johnston also got in a late lick: he had thought Davis "incapable of an absurdity too gross to have been committed by the government of any other civilized nation"—expecting a general to command two armies at once.[82]

Davis told Pemberton, under assault from Johnston, that he knew all about "the misrepresentation of which malignity is capable." He ordered a court of inquiry to "develop the real causes of events" in Mississippi. Johnston thought he was out to get him. He called a Davis letter to him a "piece of impudence." But all the while, Davis was saying, "As the misfortunes have already come upon us, it would afford me but little satisfaction to know that they resulted from bad generalship and were not inevitable." He even admitted his aim—"the destruction of Grant's army"—for which he had given Johnston so many troops might have failed because "it was unattainable." The court never got to decide, because just as it began sitting in Atlanta, Rosecrans advanced on Bragg and all officers were required "at their posts."[83] When Davis went out to Bragg in October, he took Pemberton along, hoping to get him a place. Bragg was willing to accept him, but other officers flatly refused. So this lieutenant general voluntarily stepped down to lieutenant colonel of artillery (his first Confederate rank) and helped defend Richmond.[84]

The Fourth of July, 1863, ended an idyll for the Army of Tennessee. All year it had sat on some of the most beautiful land in its name state, with little for Davis's friends to do except watch Rosecrans. The only real activity occurred when Bragg sent the cavalry afar. Wheeler was repulsed at Fort Donelson; Forrest chased Col. Abel Streight through north Alabama to Rome, Georgia; Morgan raided all the way into Ohio and was captured.[85] A few skirmishes aside, the others spent their time drilling and partying. Hardee, whom Polk called "the beau of the army," held reviews, horse races, banquets, dances, and "a tournament," especially for his grown daughters, who were visiting: he loved "to have a bevy of ladies around him." Polk's corps tried to keep the merry pace, and even Bragg joined in, animosities seemingly forgotten.[86]

It was not all frivolity. Religious enthusiasm, with its revivals and conversions, swept through the men in Tennessee, as it did in Virginia.[87] With the officers this most often involved Episcopal clergy. Bishop Polk would not hold services, but he got others to, notably his chaplain-surgeon, Dr. Charles Todd Quintard, and Stephen Elliott, his "dearest friend," the bishop of Georgia. Colonel Fremantle saw nearly three thousand men drawn up to hear the scholarly Elliott preach, with "Bragg, Polk, Hardee, Withers, Cleburne, and endless brigadiers" listening. Quintard gave one "extempore sermon" that led to "a long and very delightful conversation with General Hardee about confirmation."[88]

Bragg was "a God-fearing man," but not a churchman. The Reverend Dr. Quintard knew this, and knew his duty; he also knew Bragg's reputation—"so stern and so sharp." But when he heard that Bishop Elliott was coming, he screwed up his courage and went to Bragg's tent, only to be scared off by a sentry who would admit no one "except for a matter of life and death." The next day he went back saying, "It *is* a matter of life and death." He got in, warned by the sentry: "He is not in a good humor." "I stammered out that I wanted to see him alone." Impossible, Bragg said; but finally he dismissed his secretaries "saying to me rather sternly, 'Your business must be of grave importance, sir.' "

> I was very much frightened, but I asked the General to be seated, and then, fixing my eyes upon a knot-hole in the pine board floor of the tent, talked about our Blessed Lord, and about the responsibilities of a man in the General's position. When I looked up after a while I saw tears in the General's eyes and took courage to ask him to be confirmed. At last he came to me, took both my hands in his and said: "I have been waiting for twenty years to have some one say this to me, and I thank you from my heart. Certainly I shall be confirmed."

He was baptized conditionally and confirmed by Elliott on June 2, with his staff, Polk and his staff, and Colonel Fremantle there. Afterward, he wrote to Quintard: "I feel renewed strength for the task before me."[89]

That task became very trying before the month was out: withdrawing his army safely as Rosecrans moved against him. He intended giving battle, but as the Union army began outflanking him, he decided merely to spar with it and try to reach Chattanooga, which he did intact, foiling Rosecrans's expressed intention of "crushing" him. It was July 4 when he put the Tennessee River safely between himself and the enemy.[90]

Bragg's mind was not at ease about his commander in chief. He expected censure for retreating. Someone had had to reassure him in March that "The President is decidedly your friend," whereas his enemies Polk and Hardee could assume that. Perhaps because all three had tried to dislodge him, Bragg cemented his friendship with Davis's enemies of the cabal. He wrote to Johnston, "I feel most acutely for you," and lamented to him and to Beauregard how much they all had to put up with from the government, which was so wrong, and they so right.[91] He thought that a government man was at the moment endangering "the great point of most importance," Atlanta. When he complained, Davis coldly replied, "You will endeavour to make the dispositions necessary to remove the inadequacy for defense of which you speak."[92]

All the same, Bragg must have known that Davis approved of him. He had written about the "victory" of "your glorious army" at Murfreesboro and was "happily fully aware" that they were both determined to win "the unequal struggle in which we are engaged." Now, in the emergency, though other places needed bolstering too, Davis rounded up for Bragg every man he could. He sent Hardee to second Johnston in Mississippi, but he left his corps with Bragg, and he ordered D. H. Hill west, to lead it. He told Hardee to organize the parolees from Vicksburg, hoping they would be exchanged in time to help.[93] Buckner brought Bragg five thousand men, when Burnside, with twenty-four thousand, ran him out of Knoxville. Breckinridge and W. H. T. Walker both brought divisions. Davis even got Lee to send Longstreet with two divisions, though Lee had to stand on the defensive to do it. The president was always having to rob Peter to pay Paul, but he had effected a concentration to warm the heart even of the cabal.[94]

It was two months before Rosecrans dared follow the Confederates into the labyrinth of mountains around Chattanooga. Then by threatening the vital railroad to Atlanta, he flanked Bragg out of the city. Davis told Lee he was "disappointed." Bragg knew what he was doing. He was laying for Rosecrans, who thought him in full retreat. "Your success must depend on fighting the enemy in detail," Davis had written. Twice Bragg ordered attack on fractions of the Union army isolated in coves; twice his subordinates failed him, first Hill and Hindman, and then Polk.[95]

Both armies were still converging when they clashed on the west side of Chickamauga Creek. Bragg's carefully planned tactics again went awry through faulty execution, but, as Polk pointed out to exonerate himself, in the end it did not matter. Bragg won on September 19 and 20, says a modern writer, "one of the greatest victories of Anglo-American history." Bragg, on the field from start to finish, ordered the attack that Longstreet pressed through to rout the Federal right and the charge that finally broke the stubborn defense of Gen. George Thomas on their left. Davis's opinion of Bragg's fighting ability was handsomely confirmed.

In his new fervor, Bragg paid homage "to Him who giveth not the battle to the strong."[96]

Two days later an implosion began that rocked the Army of Tennessee. Bragg asked Polk why he had disobeyed orders. His crucial dawn attack on the second day was delayed, as Bragg put it later, for "*five precious hours,* in which our independence might have been won." He found Polk's reply insufficient, preferred charges, suspended Polk, and also Hindman (for earlier disobedience), and sent them to Atlanta. Polk bellowed with indignation and began collecting depositions. The trouble was that D. H. Hill, who was to initiate attack, never got Polk's order to do so.[97]

Polk wrote to Davis, asking for Lee to replace Bragg; Longstreet wrote the same to Seddon; they both appealed to Lee directly. Davis was way ahead of them. He had offered the command to Lee early in September. Lee had not said no or yes, but he had made it clear he did not want it. He declined now, in his roundabout way. Polk countercharged Bragg with "the most criminal negligence" in not pursuing Rosecrans after the battle.[98]

At Polk's instigation, eleven generals and one colonel signed a petition to Davis on October 4, saying that their great victory was being rendered fruitless by "complete paralysis." Unless the army got reinforcements and a new commander, it "may deem itself fortunate if it escapes from its present position without disaster." This petition was apparently never presented. Davis, summoned by telegrams from Chesnut, was already on the way to Bragg's headquarters, telling Lee he hoped "to be serviceable in harmonizing some of the difficulties existing there."[99]

Davis had wired Bragg that, to preserve "confidence," he should have pointed out Polk's error and taken no further action. He wanted him to countermand his order, which would only bring on recrimination. Controversy "could not heal the injury sustained." "It must be a rare occurrence if a battle is fought without many . . . failures, but for which more important results would have been obtained." (Bragg thought he could have driven all the way through Chattanooga if Polk's attack had started on time.) To expose errors, said Davis, merely "works evil to the cause for which brave men have died, and for which others have the same sacrifice to make."

Davis the peacemaker must have roiled Bragg's peace of mind with this: "The opposition to you both in the army and out of it has been a public calamity in so far that it impairs your capacity for usefulness." Davis had hoped "the great victory" would harmonize the army and make the country appreciate its general, but now those "predisposed to censure you will connect the present action with former estrangement" (Bragg seemed to be getting even with Polk for the winter before). Davis's ending perhaps buoyed Bragg a little: "I may be mistaken as to what is the wisest course . . . You have a much better knowledge of the facts . . . I fervently pray that you may judge correctly, as I am well assured you will act purely for the public welfare."[100]

Poor Davis was trying to calm a cyclone that had been building since Shiloh. Bragg and Polk had always despised each other. Bragg had referred to "Polk's mob"; Elise called him "our vain glorious Bishop." Now Bragg told Davis that Polk's "flagrant" disobedience was "but a repetition of the past"; Polk said Bragg, after the battle, "let down as usual . . . but a repetition of our old story."[101]

The army cheered for the president with "a great shouting" as he appeared October 9 at the head of the generals, "riding a very fine black horse." He found his trust again rewarded when Bragg agreed to drop charges and take Polk back. But Polk would not go back, so Davis got Hardee, disgruntled with Johnston anyway, to exchange with Polk, as Bragg suggested. (D. H. Hill had not lived up to "expectations" as head of Hardee's corps and had been sent back east, where he stayed on the shelf a long while, largely through his own recalcitrance.)[102]

Davis called the senior generals together and asked opinion "on their military conditions and future operations." He later expressed "surprise" at the idea he asked their opinion of Bragg, as Longstreet says he did. With his regard for the feelings of others, he would never have done that with Bragg there, and he already knew it from Polk's letter. Longstreet and others simply seized the opportunity to ask for Bragg's removal.[103] From his Missionary Ridge headquarters, they could all look down into the Chattanooga breastworks and see Rosecrans's army. To Bragg's officers, it was a visible display of his incapacity: there sat "the beaten enemy," gathering strength, all because "the fruits of the victory" had been lost on the day after Chickamauga. Gen. John B. Gordon thought this way too, then. But he concluded after careful investigation that an immediate assault on Chattanooga "must have failed," so that Bragg's decision "was not only pardonable, but prudent and wise." (The commanders after Sharpsburg, Perryville, and Gettysburg had all failed to follow up the battle, for the same basic reason—staggering losses. Bragg lost nearly a third of his men.)[104]

Davis had asked Bragg to overlook the "errors and failures" of his generals. He evidently expected them to do the same for him. But "the painful fact" became "manifest in the council," he reminded Bragg years later, "that there was not the harmony and subordination essential to success. . . . You had previous to the meeting requested to be relieved, and the answer to that request had been delayed. The conference satisfied me that no change for the better could be made in the commander of the army." "I found then as on other occasions that your views . . . rested on facts." (Seddon said Davis did not think Bragg "a great General," but "better than any with whom he could replace him. That is . . . Johnston or Longstreet.")[105] Davis helped Bragg reorganize his army, hoping it would quell the mutiny, though he finally balked at removing any more generals. "Kind personal relations" were not essential to an army, he said, but "gentle means" would "turn aside" discontent. Bragg promised "forbearance but firmness." Davis hoped others would have some of Bragg's "self-sacrificing spirit." He asked "My dear Hardee" to lay aside "personal considerations" and help restore "a proper feeling" in the army: "I rely greatly upon you." Judging others by himself, he asked "self-denial" for "the holy cause" from the army at large and "cheerful support of lawful authority."[106]

Then he headed southwest, visiting the munitions center at Selma, Alabama, and Hardee at Demopolis, getting his consent to the swap with Polk.[107] Across the Mississippi line, northeast of Meridian, he found his brother Joseph grieving at Lauderdale Springs. Eliza had died a few weeks before. She had at least had the care of a surgeon friend there, and of Episcopal Bishop William Green, also a refugee. Joseph was dauntless. He was planning with Lise to get in a spring crop. Jeff could not stay. He had to inspect the defenses of Mobile, always in danger of attack as the South's main port on the Gulf Coast.[108]

As Davis rode the rails back northeast, he was joined at Montgomery by Bedford Forrest. If he had heard of the dressing-down the cavalryman had given Bragg, refusing to serve longer under him, he chose to ignore it. As the cars rattled toward Atlanta, Davis gave Forrest what he wanted, an independent command as major general. He also pried loose from Bragg a nucleus of Forrest's old troopers around which to recruit it in northern Mississippi and West Tennessee.[109]

From Atlanta, Davis still begged Bragg's officers not to "allow personal antipathies or personal ambition to impair their usefulness." Both these factors were impelling Longstreet that very way. He had expected, coming west, to replace Bragg. He now obeyed him or not as he saw fit. Sounding as if he were the one in charge, he had written the secretary of war about his proposal for a move against Burnside at Knoxville. Bragg had first approved, then stopped it.[110] Longstreet now held command of the left (west) of Bragg's siege line. His duty was to keep the Yankees from using the road to Chattanooga from their rail center at Bridgeport, Alabama. Davis, regretting "that the rains have interfered" with Longstreet's plan to seize the center, alerted Bragg on October 29 to "beat the detachment" about to cross the Tennessee River there. Longstreet did attack these troops, but he countered Bragg's orders with his own ideas and lost not only the engagement, but entire control of this Federal supply line, which Bragg had successfully, and devastatingly, held until then. From Savannah on November 1, Davis wired his "bitter disappointment."[111]

As at Vicksburg, the vigor of Gen. U. S. Grant was more to blame than faint Confederate effort. Bragg's investiture of Rosecrans (then Thomas, who replaced him October 19) was so tight that Grant, arriving in Chattanooga, saw "but two courses" open to his army—"to starve" or "to surrender or be captured." He had gotten there October 23 by a tortuous back road over the mountains, the only one open. But once in charge, he had sent pontoon boats down the river by night to Brown's Ferry and secured the river road before Longstreet knew what was happening. When Hooker led the detachment successfully from Bridgeport to Chattanooga, breaking Bragg's blockade, it was the turning point of the whole campaign. Grant immediately called Sherman to come. Before long he had full supplies and a full army.[112]

Longstreet's idea of wresting Knoxville from Burnside came from an elaborate cabal strategy outlined earlier by Beauregard. Lee also wanted the rail line through the mountains recaptured because he wanted Longstreet back. Davis, knowing this, had tentatively suggested to Bragg that "you might" send Longstreet to Knoxville, if "the operations on your left" did not work out. After the fiasco there, Bragg decided to send him. (Grant supposed Davis had ordered this move while in Tennessee and mocked his "superior military genius.")[113] Now Longstreet went with misgivings and kept calling for more troops. Bragg finally sent more, leaving him with forty-three thousand men. Grant, with seventy-five thousand, was just about to burst out of Chattanooga. Bragg thought, however, that his position was impregnable. "Well, it *was* impregnable," Grant later mused.[114]

Grant had laid careful plans to crack it, all the same. He had details of "Bragg's position and works," brought by an engineer who "absconded to the Federal army."[115] Hooker easily took Lookout Mountain on the Confederate left, but on the right, at the end of Missionary Ridge, Sherman ran into Cleburne, under Hardee, and was beaten. To create diversion for him in the center, Grant told Thomas to take the rifle pits at the foot of the ridge. Suddenly he turned in anger: "Thomas, who ordered those men up the ridge?" In a grand mix-up of orders, some were clambering straight up. Without anyone's quite knowing how, other Yanks followed the first, reached the top after fierce fighting, and turned on the Southerners some of their own guns. Bragg and Hardee tried to rally the men, but Bragg saw "a panic which I had never before witnessed." William Bate's brigade, however, stood firm enough to cover the retreat from the left of the ridge, and Cleburne not only retired the right in good order, but also assured the safety of the whole army by smashing the pursuit at Ringgold, Georgia. The Confederates took refuge just below there, at Dalton, even as Longstreet suffered repulse at Knoxville and wandered off to winter in the mountains.[116]

Braxton Bragg wired Cooper on December 1, "I shall relinquish command tomorrow." He told Davis, "I fear we both erred" in retaining him "after the clamor raised against me." Davis immediately put Hardee in Bragg's place. But Hardee wired back: "feeling my inability to serve the country successfully in this new sphere of duty, I respectfully decline the command if designed to be permanent." For Davis, this was a terrible blow. He had tried to pull up the Army of Tennessee by his own bootstraps—expecting of everyone his disinterested patriotism, expecting soft words to cure deep, caustic wounds. He often misjudged men because he always expected the best of them, and they did not always have it to give. Now even Hardee, his old friend, failed him. Hardee's "secret," confided in the very midst of the disaster—"I am engaged to be married"—may have been a factor, but he had said long before about responsibility for an army, "I would not bear it if I could."[117]

Davis, unrealistically, in his desperation, reached out to the one he trusted most. He asked Lee to go to Dalton. Lee knew about failed expectations, having written Davis about his army after Gettysburg, "I am alone to blame, in perhaps expecting too much of its prowess & valour." But once more, Lee made his excuses about going west. He belonged to the Army of Northern Virginia. There was nothing left for Davis but a bitter cup. On December 16, he called Gen. Joseph E. Johnston to head the Army of Tennessee.[118]

XVI

Double-quick Downhill

"Not mine, O Lord, but thine; not mine, O Lord, but thine," over and over as he walked his room, back and forth, back and forth, "the livelong night." Mary Chesnut heard the steps in the drawing room below where the April breeze lifted the lace curtain and the gaslight flared. There was "no sound but the heavy tramp of his foot overhead," the whole White House "as silent as death."

The words had first fallen from Jefferson Davis's lips that afternoon. Stress having robbed him of sleep and appetite, Varina had brought dinner to the office. She was just uncovering her basket when a servant burst in from home, saying they must come at once. At the White House, Varina went into "wild lamentation." It was Joe. His skull was cracked and both legs broken. An army officer who had been passing the house when the accident occurred had run in. He was rubbing Joe with camphor and brandy, noting even as he did so his beauty. He saw the face of the president, kneeling down by his "little man," holding the insensible hands: "such a look of petrified . . . anguish I never saw." As Davis watched the boy die, "his pale, thin, intellectual face, already oppressed by a thousand national troubles [was] transfixed into a stony rigidity . . . speechless, tearless." Someone came with a message. Jeff stood holding it, staring at Varina, and said, "Did you tell me what was in it?" He tried to write a reply but suddenly cried out, "I must have this day with my little child." "Somebody took the despatch to General Cooper," says Varina, "and left us alone with our dead."[1]

She had left all the children "quite well, playing in my room." In no time, Joe was down on the high back gallery, had "climbed over the connecting angle of a bannister and fallen to the brick pavement below." No one saw him fall; it was some time before he was found. Barefoot little Jeff, kneeling beside him, cried out to a neighbor, who rushed over, "I have said all the prayers I know how, but God will not wake Joe."[2] Mary Chesnut called him "the good child of the family, so gentle and affectionate." To Varina, Joe had become "the most beautiful and brightest of my children," the one most like his father: "Joe is as manly as ever and makes me think of you." He was that father's "greatest joy in life." Gorgas noticed how "very much attached to his children" how "very caressing toward them" Davis was: "this is a heavy sorrow to him."[3]

Burton Harrison, so like a son to the Davises, took charge of the funeral. Mary Chesnut saw the five-year-old laid out, "white and beautiful as an angel—covered with flowers," and "Catherine, his nurse, lying flat on the floor by his side, weeping and wailing as only an Irish woman can. . . . Cheap—that. Where was she, when it all happened?" (The Davises never blamed Catherine.) Mary even hinted at foul play: "Who will they kill next, of that devoted household?" (There had earlier been an attempt to burn the White House.) As Mary left, she met a little girl with a handful of snowdrops: "Put these on little Joe," she said. "I knew him so well."

Thousands of children who did not know Joe brought flowers to his grave next day in Hollywood Cemetery. "The dominant figure" haunting Mary was "that poor old gray-haired man. Standing bareheaded, straight as an arrow, clear against the sky." Varina stood "back in her heavy black wrappings, and her tall figure drooped." Mary would not say it, but Varina was heavy with her sixth child, and in her seventh month. Harrison spoke of her "passionate grief," of Davis's "terrible self-control." It was Sunday, May 1, 1864. On Monday, the president was back in the office.[4]

Necessity for work was a solace. Later, in the enforced idleness of prison, Jeff told Varina he was still waiting "with patience for the grace to say—not mine, but Father, thy will be done; in all thy chastening I see the evidence of love, and not knowing why, yet know that it is well and is so ordered." Dr. Minnigerode had brought him "a twig from a shrub growing over the grave of my bright and beautiful . . . that little mound in which was laid so much of my tenderest love and highest hope of earthly things. The promises which find their fulfilment in a in a [*sic*] better world were mingled with the memories of my buried hope."[5]

There were only three Davis children in the nursery now, but there was still the fourth child, Jim Limber. Mary Chesnut had written on February 16, "Saw in Mrs. Howell's room the little negro Mrs. Davis rescued yesterday from his brutal negro guardian . . . dressed up in little Joe's clothes and happy as a lord. He was very anxious to show me his wounds and bruises, but I fled." Davis said the "negro woman . . . claimed that the boy's mother had left him to her," and Varina says she had "beaten him terribly." "Mr. Davis, notwithstanding his absorbing cares, went to the Mayor's office and had his free papers registered to insure Jim against getting into [her] power" again.[6]

Jim became "a fierce ally of the Hill cats." These "gentlemen's sons," living up near the White House, had a traditional bicker with the "Butcher cats," sons of the "working class" at the foot of the hill—"a hereditary hate" going back "nearly a hundred years." "A shower of stones and bricks" was likely to come at any time. There were also "set battles," which the Butcher cats usually won. This was all fine until Jim Limber came home with "blood pouring over his face from a scalp wound." Then Jeff Davis the peacemaker decided to walk down the hill and treat with the Butchers. After his steep climb back up, he amusedly told Varina their response: "President, we like you, we didn't want to hurt any of your boys, but we ain't *never* going to be friends with them Hill cats."[7]

Little Joe's death was like a portent. One year from the day, Mary Chesnut noted: "The Confederacy has double-quicked downhill since then."[8]

For Jeff Davis, downhill had begun in December, with the appointment of J. E. Johnston to head the Army of Tennessee. Like accepting Joe's death, it involved a surrender of will. He also felt it "imprudent," because Johnston had already proved "deficient in enterprise, tardy in movement, defective in preparation and singularly [wasteful of] supply and transportation." But Polk had said it was the "general desire" and a "duty"—"magnanimity, perhaps, may require it at your hand." He had also urged "magnanimity" on Johnston: if he would just offer to "waive" the past, for the public good, Polk was sure Davis would receive it "in the best spirit." Silence met this appeal. Davis rose to the occasion anyway. "I committed the error of yielding . . . against my own deliberate convictions."[9]

He gave Johnston an army "designed to recover the State of Tennessee from the enemy." The general knew this policy, but he "made no attempt to advance," complaining of "deficiencies and difficulties" that he was "unable to overcome." By April, frustration with the Army of Tennessee, sitting on its hunkers at Dalton, Georgia, was one of the things ruining Davis's sleep.[10]

Another appointment brought severe criticism on Davis. He called Braxton Bragg to him as military advisor, or, Varina says more exactly, as "Chief of Staff." Lee was Davis's advisor to the end. Davis may have meant to use at the top level, as Polk advised, Bragg's "peculiar talent—that of organization and discipline" when he ordered Johnston in vain to send him to Richmond the year before. Army men there thought that Bragg, with his "quick decided spirit" would "*assist*" Davis in "military matters," said Gorgas—something he thought he needed. "The President is not endowed with military genius . . . but who would have done better?"[11]

Richmond was always one of the "three main strategic objectives" of the United States Army. Bragg had just arrived when a cavalry assault came in the first week of March. In the repulse, Col. Ulrich Dahlgren, whom Varina remembered as a "fair-haired boy" in "black velvet suit and Vandyke collar," was killed.[12] On his body were orders to burn the city and release the Northern prisoners. Gen. Fitz Lee brought these captured papers to Davis in his private office, where he was conferring with Judah Benjamin. Davis read the orders aloud, "making no comment" until "he came to the sentence, 'Jeff. Davis and *Cabinet* must be killed on the spot,'" when he laughingly said, "'That means you, Mr. Benjamin.'" The banter shows how close Davis and his Jewish cabinet member had become.[13]

Some called him "Mr. Davis's pet Jew." He called himself "a personal friend." The Davises had always had Jewish friends, like Mordecai and the DeLeons.[14] Varina was so close to Martha Levy that she could say, "I wish you would turn Christian so that you might thank God with me" (for her first letter from Jeff in prison). Both Davises were devoted to the witty, cultivated Benjamin, who, in any case, wore his Jewishness lightly. He had a French Catholic wife and daughter.[15]

He was a favorite butt, especially for Foote, who was to denounce Benjamin and Davis in his book as "fiendish" and "monstrous public criminals." But Foote was notorious as a slanderer and an anti-Semite, of whom there were not a few in the South. When one complained about a Jew's signing a fast day proclamation, Davis answered that, first, it was only a formality, and, second, he was bound by the Constitution "as it is." Perhaps, he said, it should have specified "the Saviour of mankind," but it acknowledged only "God."[16]

Enemies could certainly point out that Benjamin's State Department had not attained its main objective—recognition for the Confederacy. One lady said "Dear old Dudley Mann" might as well come home and do what he was good at—escorting her to parties. Probably the blame lay more with the acumen of Charles Francis Adams (Seward's man in Great Britain) and the duplicity of Napoleon III than with Benjamin and his envoys. Nothing could swerve Davis from his conviction of Benjamin's worth. The secretary was by now preparing messages to Congress, for which Davis simply did not have time, and probably other papers as well.[17]

In the Dahlgren case, the majority of the cabinet, and Bragg, insisted that Davis live up to his repeated threats "for violation of the usages of war." The orders showed a clear case, and he should execute one-tenth (Bragg said all) of the captured troopers. Public support for this was "unanimous." Benjamin recalls the "heated" discussion in which

"Davis alone" argued that these men "had been received to mercy . . . as prisoners of war, and as such were sacred; and that we should be dishonored if harm should overtake them." Only his "unshaken firmness" saved them. According to Reagan, Davis said that "if we had known [their plans] and could have shot them with arms in their hands, it would have been all right," but "in an emphatic manner [he] said that he would not permit an unarmed prisoner to be shot; and so the matter ended."[18]

Sen. Louis Wigfall had led the cry for Johnston's appointment in December. He had earlier suggested to Clay that "Davis's mind is becoming unsettled," because he faulted Johnston for Vicksburg but not Lee for Gettysburg. He raged against Lee's "utter want of generalship" and told the Chesnuts he wanted "to hang Jeff Davis." In default of this, he outlined to Johnston and others, in spring of 1864, his plan to hamstring the president: refuse to confirm his appointments, blame him for all military setbacks, restrict his power, and ruin public confidence in him by belittling him. First he got Congress to have printed the Vicksburg report of J. E. Johnston, who was the "polar star" of his campaign. His "supposed popularity" was a fortress from which to hurl "poisoned arrows at you," explained a Davis admirer.[19]

Clay, once more friendly with Davis after his godson Joe's death, "tried to dissuade Wigfall from his ruinous course." But Wigfall would not be dissuaded. To James Hammond he mocked Davis as "a captain who pipes his crew to prayers & not to the pumps" and said his "vanity" was "excessive." Infuriated that Davis had replaced Abraham Myers with Alexander Robert Lawton as quartermaster general, he said it was because Myers's wife had called Varina "an old squaw." This gossip was by then two years old, and Davis did not operate that way.[20] Lawton saw how he took "great care . . . to be informed before acting," discussed matters "entirely with reference to . . . the 'cause,' " and never "exhibited either undue temper or ill will against" anyone, even when pain forbade him "to sit at ease a moment." Davis told the Senate that his "own observation" of Myers showed him the need for an officer "better qualified to meet the pressing emergencies." The wounded veteran Lawton, a general, as the post now required, had been prewar president of a railroad, and rails were the crucial concern of the department. Wigfall could not block Lawton's confirmation, or get Davis censured, or prevent the appointment of Bragg, though he tried.[21]

Wigfall's counterpart in the House was Foote. Just as Wigfall wanted, he ridiculed Davis, blamed him for everything from nonpursuit after Manassas to defeat at Missionary Ridge, and said if the South must have a dictator, he preferred Lee. An expert on the Congress says, "The strident voices of Foote and Wigfall must not be considered as representative" of either chamber (yet somehow they always are). Although they were loud, and Davis had lost strength in the 1863 elections, he won almost every important vote in both Senate and House until very late in 1864. Of his vetoes, only one was ever overturned, and that was a minor one in 1865, on franking newspapers to servicemen.[22]

Foote stood ever ready to attack Davis appointees, and as the new Second Congress met in May, he moved on Christopher Memminger. Confederate finances were indeed "hopelessly snarled" and inflation was staggering, in spite of the loan from Emile Erlanger and Company of Paris, but Congress was as much to blame as the secretary of the treasury.[23] Memminger had already offered to resign, and he did so in June. Appointing the popular George Trenholm, whose banking house handled Confederate finances at home and abroad, could not save the situation, though Davis thanked him, as he resigned a year later, for reviving credit and increasing resources.[24]

"I warned you," he reminded Trenholm, "that our wants so far exceeded our means that you could not expect entire success and should anticipate censure and perhaps the loss of financial reputation: I can never forget the lofty patriotism with which you replied that if you could promote your country's welfare you would not count the personal sacrifice which might be involved." Davis had found a kindred spirit. "All for the cause . . . nothing for myself," he had said to Ben Hill, puzzled how people could endanger it for "personal grievances": "I have but one enemy to fight . . . our common enemy. I may make mistakes, and doubtless I do, but . . . God knows I would sacrifice my life, much more my opinions, to defeat that enemy." In Lubbock's eyes, Davis showed "more self-abnegation than any human being I have ever known."[25]

Scarcity of goods as well as money plagued the Confederacy, although blockade-running had become a fine art. The government was now requisitioning half the cargo space and trading Europeans cotton for food, medicine, shoes, and "the sinews of war." This supplied the army with weapons, but both soldiers and civilians were beginning to be pinched for food. Lee was faced with desertions caused by the reduction in rations. Part of the shortage was blamed on profiteers, called speculators. On these, Davis lavished contempt, and they in return, along with croakers who predicted ruin, made him, a friend said, "one of the best abused men in the Confederacy."[26] Other people resented conscription, exemption, impressment of goods, the tax in kind, restrictions on the cotton trade, or the brief suspensions of habeas corpus. Congress and the cabinet approved all these measures, but Davis got the blame. In Georgia, Stephens and Brown even tried, unsuccessfully, for secession and separate peace. Ben Hill told Davis, "The people of Georgia sustain you" as "the only way to sustain the cause." He had become "the embodiment" of the Confederacy. To Varina, "He used to say with a sigh, 'If we succeed, we shall hear nothing of these malcontents; if we do not, I shall be held accountable by the majority of friends as well as foes. I will do my best, and God will give me strength to bear whatever comes to me.' "[27]

Shortages touched military strategy. In January, Howell Cobb had written Davis from Dalton, Georgia, that unless Johnston showed strength by retaking Tennessee farmland, his army would starve, and the South would face a war of attrition it could not win. He told his wife the move would be made "within six months." Davis wanted the move at once, to catch the enemy off guard. He discussed plans by Hardee, Beauregard, Longstreet, Polk, and the Kentucky generals-in-exile. They were finally distilled into one plan for advance which Bragg sent to Johnston on March 12.[28]

Davis had been spoiled by proximity to Lee. He expected Johnston, with a fraction of the opposing army, to whip the enemy and advance. Bragg, as chief of military operations, told Johnston, "We must . . . run some risk": strike now, while "the enemy is not prepared for us." Johnston said he would move when "relative forces . . . warrant it." Bragg sent some troops and promised more from three directions, but they never met Johnston's ideal number (whatever that was). Meanwhile, Grant was steadily increasing his strength; he had at least one hundred thousand soldiers, the odds hovering two-to-one in his favor.[29]

The country through which Johnston was to slash his way to the farmland was mountainous, and his transport, shaky. He was not even thinking of trying it, though he teased Richmond by pretending to agree. He did not consult Davis "as commander of the army," he said, because "I could not [do so] without adopting the course he might advise," which would be asking "him to command for me." When Davis finally sent General Pendleton to prod him into action, Johnston proposed a plan "without the hazard of ruin involved in the other." It kept the fighting "this side the Tennessee [River]" (but somehow ended with the old cabal dream, "press [the enemy] back to the Ohio"). Bragg, Davis, and Pendleton agreed that this was "now perhaps the best that can be done." "Now" was April 21. Johnston never did attack. He had decided that the right policy—his own all along—was to wait for the enemy to attack him, then counterattack.[30]

Meanwhile, in February, Sherman had, in his own words, cut "a swath of desolation fifty miles broad" across Mississippi from Vicksburg to Meridian. The latter "no longer exists." Once again, Joseph Davis and Lise Mitchell had been right in his path, fleeing in rickety wagons. They had gone to Hinds County to retrieve what they could, and Joseph had rounded up as well his forty blacks, out of the three hundred and fifty-five he had once owned. Since December of 1863, blacks of the United States Army had occupied Davis Bend, renamed the Home Farm, with Brierfield house as headquarters. Grant planned to make the Bend "a negro paradise." Thousands were drawn into Sherman's lines, with healthy males "mostly being obliged to enlist as soldiers" at Vicksburg; only the indigent went to Davis Bend. "I never saw such degradation," said an emissary of the Cincinnati Contraband Relief Commission, writing from "Jeff Davis Mansion." He noted that slave quarters at the Hurricane showed Joseph Davis to be "a man of system, great order, and large wealth." That man was now on the road, searching for Gen. Leonidas Polk, who was also trying to get out of Sherman's way. When Joseph found his camp, Polk advised him to flee to Georgia, but he decided to take refuge at Tuscaloosa, Alabama, instead.[31]

Sherman was planning to sweep on through Alabama and capture Selma or Mobile, or both. He waited at burned-out Meridian for his cavalry, coming from Memphis under Brig. Gen. William Sooy Smith. Polk had gotten his supplies and rolling stock out of Meridian just in time and taken his tiny army to Demopolis, Alabama, where he wired for help. Johnston argued with Davis for a week before sending Hardee as ordered; then Davis suddenly ordered him back. To everyone's mystification, Sherman had begun marching west. Sherman himself was mystified: where was Smith?

The mystifier was Forrest. He had harried Smith, with less than half his numbers, into turning tail for Memphis. Sherman's announced aim, "to destroy General Forrest," was a mockery. But his main purpose, "to paralyze the rebel forces," was not. By the time he had ravaged his way back to Vicksburg, he had torn up Mississippi so thoroughly that he felt free to go with his twenty-thousand–man corps and take command against Johnston in Georgia.[32]

For three years now, North had battered South without being able to crush it. On March 12, 1864, U. S. Grant was made the first full lieutenant general since Washington and general in chief of all Union armies. He was to devise the defeat of the Confederate States. He worked out with his usual thoroughness a plan made possible by his ample resources, one the South could never have dreamed of. He would launch offensives from five different directions at once. The one under Gen. Nathaniel Banks, to take Mobile, never got started. Banks was first to secure Shreveport, up Louisiana's Red River. He never got there either. His troops were too busy gobbling cotton and destroying plantations. A unit "from Sherman's army," says Richard Taylor, burned "nearly every house on the road" for forty miles. Taylor defeated Banks at Mansfield and worried him so on his retreat that he was lucky to get back to New Orleans.[33]

By then the other four offensives were well under way. Having given the main western one in Georgia to Sherman, his most trusted lieutenant, Grant himself took charge in the East, where three of the five assaults were to mesh. Maj. Gen. Franz Sigel would attack up the

Valley of Virginia; Ben Butler would move up the James River from Fortress Monroe to Bermuda Hundreds; Meade, under Grant, would come down on Lee at the Rapidan River with a huge army. The prize was the Confederate capital.[34]

So it was no ordinary business that drew Jeff Davis to his office the day after his son's funeral: "[We were] encompassed so perfectly that we could only hope by a miracle to overcome our foes," Varina says. Within the week, Grant's synchronized attacks erupted. Sigel was stopped by Breckinridge halfway up the valley and trounced at New Market May 15, with the help of cadets from the Virginia Military Institute. Butler came on, menacing a lifeline to Richmond that traversed the Department of North Carolina–Southern Virginia. Here Beauregard had just taken command. After two years of defensive victories at Charleston, he had his chance to get back in the field. So did Jeff Davis. "Soldiers! [My position] debars me from sharing your danger," he had recently lamented, but "my heart has accompanied you in every march." When the fighting came close, at Drewry's Bluff, Davis was there.[35]

Drewry's Bluff was the strong point on the James River between Richmond and the Bermuda Hundreds peninsula five miles below, where Butler lodged successfully, threatening the railroad to Petersburg. Beauregard, "too unwell" to get to the front yet, had worked out a semigrand strategy: let Lee draw into the Richmond defenses and send him fifteen thousand men. (He "always was devising operations for somebody else," said Davis.) He would beat Butler, then together they would whip Grant. The president knew that Lee was locked in battle with Grant against enormous odds and that being trapped in Richmond was just what he was trying to avoid. He went down to talk to Beauregard.[36]

They had last met the fall before, when Davis stopped at Charleston, coming back from his western trip—met officially, not socially. Beauregard had declined the dinner in Davis's honor: "my relations with the President being strictly official, I cannot participate in any act of politeness which might make him suppose otherwise." Davis had praised the commandant of Fort Sumter (Bishop Stephen Elliott's son) instead of Beauregard. He did say, "Let us trust to our Commanding General," but did not say his name. He had not named Elliott either, but Beauregard said it was worse than if Davis "had thrust a fratricidal dagger into my heart! he has *killed* my *enthusiasm* in our holy cause!" So he wrote to his great admirer, the novelist Augusta Jane Evans, adding, "May God forgive him—I fear I shall not have charity enough to pardon him." He actually thought Davis was jealous of him. He wrote, "The curse of God must have been on our people when we chose him!"[37]

Unconscious of all this, Davis now explained that he could not pull Lee back. He approved, however, a Beauregard plan of battle, promising

Ransom's troops from Richmond. Before this Battle of Drewry's Bluff, it was (ironically, in view of cabal ideas) Davis who wanted concentration and Beauregard, dispersal. Davis's idea was to bring Maj. Gen. Chase Whiting up from Petersburg right away; Beauregard wanted him to stay there and attack from the rear during the battle. Davis thought his own plan was agreed on, and told Lee so, but Beauregard was telling Whiting he "need not" obey orders from Richmond. The result was, Davis wrote, "instead of executing my order and bringing Whiting up" beforehand, Beauregard had "put Butler between our forces and lost the victory which ought to have been won."[38]

Davis was on the field; firing was hot; his staff were afraid he would be struck. They asked Reagan to get him off, but he would not leave. He knew he was not "necessary," he explained later, but "it was very inconvenient to ride off under fire." Beauregard stopped a drive begun by Ransom, to wait for the sound of Whiting's guns. He wired him, "Remember Dessaix at Marengo and Blucher at Waterloo," but Whiting was suffering a crisis of nerves and never attacked. Butler was not destroyed, as Davis had hoped, but he did have to retreat to his peninsula. He had failed to capture any point or break the railroad. His cavalry kept breaking other lines, but they were before long repaired.[39]

Immediately, Beauregard had a new idea: let Lee send troops to him and retire south of the Chickahominy. Lee and Davis, surrounded by the wildest excitement, calmly and seriously wrote to each other about this, in their usual sedate prose. Davis left the decision to Lee, who asked that Beauregard send troops to him instead. The "decidedly Frenchy" general again showed himself a patriot, despite his words to Augusta Evans. He sent them. In proposing what he did, he cannot have realized what kind of fighting was going on north of Richmond.[40]

Four days before, wading "in mud and gore" at a parapet, with the enemy just on the other side, some of Lee's men had fought for over sixteen hours without rest or food, piling up their dead in heaps behind the ditch in which they stood, while the enemy "fired ceaselessly through every opening." This was the worst carnage so far, giving the spot its name, the Bloody Angle; but the struggle was that intense everywhere. Lee's genius was being put to its greatest test.[41]

On the day his other drives started, Grant had crossed the Rapidan, with a more than a two-to-one advantage. Lee's decision to fight him there, says Henry Heth, proved Lee "the most belligerent man in his army." Knowing he could not confront him head-on, Lee allowed Grant to cross the river and head into the tangled Wilderness, aiming to hit him on the move. Lee took great risks. His lines gave and bent, but they always snapped back. He inflicted heavy losses. This Battle of the Wilderness occupied May 5 and 6, 1864. When it was over, "Lee's army was still there, and Grant's had been repulsed at all points."[42]

But Lee's army was not all there. It was minus some ten thousand casualties, and Longstreet had been wounded by his own men. The Federals had lost over seventeen thousand. They could afford this; Lee could not. As Alexander says, Grant "understood arithmetic" and "deliberately set out to play" the numbers game. As part of it, he made sure that the South would never get its prisoners back. To prevent exchange, he made Ben Butler the agent. "We swallowed our pride & offered exchanges" anyway, says Alexander, but "pretenses were always made to evade them." On August 18, Grant wrote to Butler: "It is hard on our men . . . not to exchange them, but it is humanity to those left in the ranks to fight our battles. . . . If we commence a system of exchange . . . we will have to fight on until the whole South is exterminated. If we hold those caught, they amount to no more than dead men. At this particular time, to release all rebel prisoners North would insure Sherman's defeat, and would compromise our safety here." His campaign, Alexander says, was "practically one of extermination—to reduce our numbers at all costs." Grant's plan worked. Gen. Samuel Cooper began guarding army returns like state secrets, lest the enemy find out how weak the South really was.[43]

In the night of May 7, Grant tried to get at Richmond by a left-end sweep. Lee beat him to Spottsylvania Court House, entrenched, and fought him at the Bloody Angle. Although he was near disaster at this salient, twice taken and retaken, Lee proved, says Alexander, that "we simply could never be driven off a battle field, & that whatever force Grant brought, his luck would have to accommodate itself to that fact."[44]

Grant accommodated by continually trying to flank Lee, to provoke him to attack in the open. But Lee resisted, fortified, and kept himself between Grant and Richmond, while both men waited for reinforcements from the Bermuda Hundreds front and jockeyed for position.[45] Meanwhile, Jeff Davis was seeing to the city itself. He had Custis Lee heading the civilian brigade, Ransom the regulars, Pemberton about to take the artillery, and Bragg on tap, but Davis felt the responsibility was his. He was "constantly on the field." On May 11 he had telegraphed the elder Lee: "sorely pressed by enemy on south side . . . now threatened by the cavalry . . . I go to look after defence. . . . May God have you in His holy keeping."[46]

Soldiering might have diverted Davis's grief over Joe, but grief opened afresh. The cavalry he went to meet was under Maj. Gen. Philip Sheridan, sent to cut Lee off from Richmond and especially "thrash hell out of" Jeb Stuart. While deflecting Sheridan's ten thousand troopers with his forty-five hundred, Stuart was shot through the abdomen and borne into Richmond. Davis, so attentive to the wounded with constant hospital visits, went to him: "He was so calm, and physically so strong, that I could not believe that he was dying, until the surgeon . . . told me he was bleeding inwardly, and that the end was near." "Mr. Davis came home," says Varina, "and knelt with me," praying "that this 'precious life might be spared to our needy country.'" The answer once again was "No." "Beauty Stuart," thirty-one years old, loved by all but an unmusical few, had minstrel-like sung at Chancellorsville, "Old Joe Hooker, would you come out the Wilderness?" to the tune of his theme song, "Jine the Cavalry." Now he tried to join in the hymn "Rock of Ages," which he had asked for. He died repeating "God's will be done." Davis followed the body in the rain from Stuart's parish church, St. James, to Hollywood Cemetery. Dr. Minnigerode read the committal service, just as he had done for little Joe less than two weeks before. Stuart also had a five-year-old lying there, his daughter Flora, who had died the previous autumn.[47]

The enemy was almost as near as in 1862, but with cavalry raids all around, and her baby expected in June, Varina stayed this time. Davis felt full confidence in Lee. He rode out to see him every day. The darker Lee's reports were, the more cheerful Davis became, Varina says; he had "a childlike faith in the providential care of the Just Cause by Almighty God." But he had been worried by tales of Lee's trying to lead his men into battle, though they always turned his horse back. Perhaps Stuart's death prompted him to write Lee, as he thanked him for "glorious deeds" on May 15: "I have been pained to hear of your exposure of your person. . . . The country could not bear the loss of you, and, my dear friend, though you are prone to forget yourself, you will not, I trust, again forget the public interest dependent on your life." Lee obeyed his commander in chief. "Lee to the rear!" was heard no more.[48]

On June 1, Lee finally attacked, between Old and New Cold Harbor. Sheridan was there. His "magazine guns" cut down Col. Laurence Keitt and almost his whole new South Carolina regiment of "near a thousand men." The next day, Lee entrenched and, without repeating carbines, reversed the casualty rate when Grant attacked him on June 3. Grant lost thirteen thousand men, almost all in the space of an hour. He had vowed "to hammer continuously" in his "attrition" policy, and "to fight it out on this line," but he "brought his ponderous hammer down upon the little anvil," says Henry Kyd Douglas, "and the hammer was shivered to pieces." He soon left this line, crossing the James River to the south side. In thirty days, he had spent sixty thousand men and was no nearer Richmond than he had been, "except geographically." Lee was still in his way.

Beauregard was also in his way. Again he saved the railroad and Petersburg. Undismayed by his losses, Grant then besieged the town. If his country continued to support his policy, "the science of war reduced to a sum in mathematics," said Douglas, "the outlook for the Confederacy was hopeless."[49]

"Hopeless" was not a Jeff Davis word. "If hope had not lighted the thorny path of duty," he said later, "conscience required that path should be followed wherever the same might lead." Without hope, says Varina, he could not have spoken, as he always did, "words of hope to the soldiers"—"he was too sincere." Historians "will doubtless write," General Alexander says, that "the time had now fully arrived for President Davis to open negotiations for peace." He was condemned right now by certain people for not doing so. But by peace, they meant "reconstruction"—reunion with the North—which was all Lincoln offered, and this, to Davis, was "degradation."[50] He bore condemnation in silence. He had voiced desire for peace in "almost every message I ever sent to Congress" and was putting some hope, though faint, in the Northern peace movement. His fellow Democrats were running George McClellan against Lincoln, and Davis had sent Clay and others to Canada to help elect him president. Then there might be an honorable peace offer. It was his thorny duty, however, to make the South into a free country.[51]

Gov. Zebulon Vance was fighting a move by W. W. Holden in North Carolina for a *separate* peace. Davis had been "unwilling to injure" Holden earlier by talk of treason, "if there be no foundation." Now he told Vance, "to propose peace is to invite insult." The enemy Congress forbade any terms "except absolute, unconditional subjugation or extermination," and Lincoln's "repeated rejections of all conference with us" seemed to "shut out all hope that he would *ever* treat with us, on *any* terms." The South would simply have to whip the enemy "out of his vain confidence in our subjugation. Then and not till then will it be possible to treat of peace."[52]

Davis knew the mind of the South better than his critics. "Both the army and the people at that time would have been very loth to recognize that the cause was hopeless," says Alexander. "In the army, I am sure, such an idea was undreamed of. . . . any end but the last ditch would have seemed to them a breach of faith with the dead we had left on every battlefield." This Davis, above all men, understood.[53]

While scorning a private peace mission to him, Davis, to leave no stone unturned, told his trio in Canada to feel the way toward talks with the Lincoln government. Horace Greeley put out the feeler for them. In his reply, Lincoln used the terms "the whole union," "abandonment of slavery," and, for the Confederate States, "the armies now at war against the United States." So Davis's analysis to Vance was true. There was no meeting. Lincoln perhaps replied at all only because his country was rocked by the losses in Grant's campaign and the approach of Jubal Early to Washington.[54]

Lee sent Early on June 13 to save Lynchburg from Maj. Gen. David Hunter. Early ran him out of the valley, kept on across the Potomac, fought the battle of Monocacy, and reached the outskirts of Washington, scaring the Yankees into drawing some troops off Lee, which was the intent. Hunter was under orders from Grant to "make all the Valley . . . a desert." He had already destroyed food and farm tools and burned the Virginia Military Institute and many private homes. When he slipped in behind Early and burned some more, Early told Chambersburg, Pennsylvania, to pay indemnity or be burned itself. It called his bluff and was put to the torch. Early finally retired to the valley, having secured Lee's supply line. Davis told him later that he and Lee knew his force was inadequate, and it was "glory enough" that he had done so well.[55]

Defense in the East was magnificent, but hope for a positive victory lay with the Army of Tennessee. Davis, sorely tried by Johnston's failure to launch an offensive, hoped on, through May and into June. He had sent Johnston one of the best fighters in the Southern army, Lt. Gen. John Bell Hood, to take D. H. Hill's corps. He had picked Hood in 1855 for the elite Second Cavalry, had seen him in action during the Seven Days, and knew Lee's high opinion of him. Hood, his left hand already paralyzed from his Gettysburg wound, had lost his right leg at Chickamauga. While he was waiting in Richmond for his cork leg from England to arrive on a blockade-runner, he and Davis had become friends.[56]

Hood had close ties to Wigfall and G. W. Smith, but he and Davis had a lot in common, including admiration of Sidney Johnston. In temperament, both were religious, tenderhearted, and "a little oppugnant." Hood kept in his pocket a Bible his mother had given him. Although not a member, he attended St. Paul's with the Davises. As Davis gave the crippled general an arm down the steps after church, some boys said, "That's jolly of the President. If it wasn't Sunday we'd cheer." As soon as he could mount his horse, Hood went with Davis on his afternoon rides and later remarked on this "opportunity to become well acquainted with this extraordinary man . . . his wonderful nerve and ability."[57]

It was early 1864 then, and Davis confided to Hood his plan for an aggressive campaign in Georgia. Hood said, "Mr. President, why don't you come and lead us yourself? I would follow you to the death." Flattery aside, Hood obviously understood what Davis wanted. At first his letters back from Georgia echoed Johnston: the army *could* take the offensive, *if* they had enough men. But on April 13, he wrote Bragg that he had tried to get Johnston "to move forward," but he would "not consent." "I regret this exceedingly, as my heart was fixed on . . . regaining Tennessee and Kentucky." One historian saw a plot to supplant Johnston with Hood in these letters (and his idea has reverberated ever since). But other generals wrote similar letters, and Hood asked to go back to Lee if there were no advance.[58]

On May 7, Johnston lost even the possibility of initiative. Sherman began sporadic attacks. Davis had ordered to Dalton "almost all the available military strength of the south and west," hoping, with "the whole country," for "a decisive victory." While the first attacks were being repulsed, Polk was on the way east with nineteen thousand men. When he reached the Western and Atlantic Railroad, Johnston's lifeline to Atlanta, he was ordered to halt at Resaca, fifteen miles below Dalton. Hood was there. As they rode the cars together up to Johnston's headquarters, he made a strange request. Would the bishop baptize him? Dr. Quintard was too busy in Atlanta to come.[59] Quintard's talk with Hardee the spring before had borne fruit at Dalton: He was confirmed on April 20 and told his wife, "I am so glad. . . . I am trying hard to lead a godly life. In time I hope to conquer the old Adam."[60] Polk did baptize Hood, and on August 10, under bombardment in Atlanta, Quintard presented him for confirmation to Bishop Lay of Arkansas. In the three months between these two ceremonies, the fate of the Confederacy was being decided.[61]

In this interval, Quintard received from the battle area what remained of Lieutenant General Polk's body. On June 14, a Parrott shell had passed through him from left to right. Four copies of Quintard's booklet of prayers, "Balm for the Weary and Wounded," in his breast pocket were now "saturated with his blood." Two days before, Polk had written his name in one and inscribed the others to Hardee, Hood, and J. E. Johnston; Lydia, hearing about Hood, had asked him to baptize her husband also, and he had done it the night of May 17, at Adairsville.[62]

Adairsville, thirty-one miles south of Dalton, was the third stopping-place for the Army of Tennessee in eleven days. Johnston had at first refused to believe that Sherman's main attack was not coming at the fortifications he had spent five months preparing. Finally he had realized that Sherman was slipping unseen down the western side of Rocky Face Ridge toward an undefended gap leading to Resaca. Reluctantly, he gave up Dalton on May 13, and proved at Resaca that he was willing to fight. But he kept changing his mind there, costing one regiment a hundred needless casualties. When he heard that Federals were crossing a river in his rear, he abandoned the battlefield in the night and slipped six miles south to Calhoun—the very place he would have picked to defend, he said, if only Bragg and Davis had not put the army at Dalton. But when he got there, he found no place to make a stand. Adairsville did not suit him either. He took his army on down the railroad by night, after another leapfrog move by Sherman.[63]

At Cassville, he meant to outfox and fight Sherman, but everything went wrong, and there never was a battle. The army had to move again by night down the tracks to the next town. And so it went, back and back, night after night, with Sherman pacing them on the west, always trying to cut the railroad. Once he swung out to reach Atlanta another way, but found Johnston confronting him at New Hope Church and

Dallas. Bloody battles for four days forced him back to the railroad, which was his lifeline, too.[64]

Now Johnston seemed to have reached his ideal spot, with mountains astride the rail line, dominated by Kennesaw, but he termed the position "very hazardous." It was on the height nearest the enemy, Pine Mountain, that Polk was killed reconnoitering. Quintard sent his body on from Atlanta for a funeral in St. Paul's Church in Augusta and interment in the chancel. The president got Bishop Elliott's invitation too late to go. He spoke of how "very near" they had been as cadets and, years later, of "the glorious holy Bishop Polk." Hardee and Johnston, who were with Polk, had been much moved by his death.[65] Johnston called it "the calamity"; the whole army grieved, for whatever the opinion of him as a general, Polk as a man was greatly beloved.[66]

A. P. Stewart inherited Polk's corps, and the war went on. It began to resemble the fierce struggle in the East. Sherman sent waves of men to death against Johnston's breastworks around Kennesaw, and the defenders became "broken down and exhausted," while "our dead and wounded were piled indiscriminately in the trenches." Sherman found he could no more crack Johnston's entrenched line than Grant could crack Lee's, and like Grant, he finally slipped once more around the end. On July 3, Johnston began abandoning Kennesaw for positions he had prepared in its rear. Soon his back was to the Chattahoochee River, and Sherman was in sight of Atlanta.[67]

This made Davis "more apprehensive," but "at this distance I cannot judge . . . the best method of averting calamity." He had stripped others of men until there were no more to send: "[We] are dependent on your success." Other crises cried for attention. He had to order reserves to Mobile, wire Chesnut (now a general heading South Carolina reserves), "Charleston is in great danger," and alert Lee, "the expedition is spoken of on the streets. Shall it *proceed*? . . . If not *stop it as* you deem best." This was a joint sea and land action to release the prisoners at Point Lookout, Maryland, and was indeed aborted, which was well, for the prisoners had been moved.[68]

Cavalry operations added to Davis's anxiety. John Hunt Morgan, who had escaped his Ohio prison, raised Southern spirits by raiding Kentucky, but then dashed them by retiring to the Tennessee-Virginia mountains in defeat. Sherman ordered a special task force out of Memphis (again) to hunt Forrest, who was about to attack his railroad from Nashville. Against this force, Forrest, outnumbered and out-equipped as usual, won his greatest victory at Brice's Cross Roads, Mississippi. Sherman was happy just to have kept him "away from us," but he ordered yet another task force specifically "to pursue and kill Forrest."[69]

Then came frightful news: the *Alabama* had been sunk in battle off Cherbourg, France, on June 19, with Beckett Howell aboard. He and others, including the wounded Captain Semmes, were rescued by an English yachtsman in the *Deerhound*, to whom Congress and President Davis in due time expressed the country's thanks. But the great Confederate destroyer of Northern commercial ships around the world was gone. To recoup somewhat that loss, John T. Wood slipped the CSS *Tallahassee* through the blockade early in August and cruised up the Atlantic coast. Before he rejoined Davis's staff at the end of the month, he had disposed, one way or another, of thirty-three vessels.[70]

The president had not been down sick for a whole year now, under all these anxieties (so they were not the cause of his illnesses). If he lost a day or two near end of June, it was from an accident. Having "learned to ride before he can remember," Davis delighted in mastering the most fractious steeds. His favorite, Kentucky, could not be mounted by anyone else. He had a little white Arabian and "will not admit that he is vicious," said Preston Johnston, "although he bites and kicks at everybody, because he eats bread out of his hand." On an evening ride, "the Arabian . . . became restless and backed over a precipice about twenty feet high. The President was dismounted at about halfway down" and his back, leg, and head were bruised. "Escape from serious injury was almost miraculous," said Johnston: "The horse turned a complete somersault and was much strained." The Arabian was rusticated to the Chesnut plantation, Mulberry, where Sherman's men got him in the end.[71]

On June 27, Varina gave birth at the White House to her sixth child, a girl. Jeff stood as godfather when she was christened and named her Varina Anne.[72] Varina protested, "my name is a heritage of woe," but she said it to Mary Chesnut, who would know how to take this Byronic allusion—lightly. There was laughter in all their exchange; it had made them the best of friends. "I generally let out my crazy bone to you," she had written, "so I must tell you how exquisite my little baby is. In pink she looks like a little rosebud. It is the only point upon which I feel not very sane." General Lee himself pronounced the baby "a remarkably fine one." "Varina Anne" on Jeff's tongue soon became "Winanne," and then "Winnie." The mother's nickname became the baby's name for life, but right now she was stuck with "Pie Cake," from her nurse.[73]

Davis had not much leisure to enjoy this latest treasure, or anything else, though he thanked a British journalist for a "fox-hunting novel." On Sunday, July 10, Ben Hill reached Richmond from Georgia, on a mission from Johnston, Governor Brown, and Wigfall. (He and Charlotte, on the way to Texas, had left two daughters in Atlanta with Lydia.) Davis was besieged with "delegations, petitions, and letters" urging him to replace Johnston with someone who would hold Atlanta. He treated this "clamor," as he had that against Sidney Johnston and Lee, by ignoring it. He had given in to it once only, in *appointing* J. E. Johnston, an exception he now regretted. Benjamin, who witnessed the abuse of

Davis from people "ignorant of the facts," had written Slidell: "it is a spectacle really sublime to observe the utter abnegation of self . . . the entire willingness to leave his vindication to posterity."[74]

Davis had just sent Bragg to get the facts about Georgia, but Hill, straight from the Kennesaw line, could tell him better. Hill had been asked to urge Davis in writing to send "Morgan or Forrest with five thousand men" onto Sherman's supply line (Johnston specified, below Dalton), after which Johnston "thought he could defeat Sherman and probably destroy his army." But when Hill realized that retreat from Atlanta toward LaGrange and Montgomery was being considered, which would involve, as he "explained at length to Gen. Johnston—the fate of the Confederacy," he decided to go to Davis instead "and lay all the facts before him." These were: 1) Johnston could not use his own cavalry for this action (though he had over nine thousand); 2) He could neither attack Sherman nor avoid retreat; 3) He could hold Sherman north of the Chattahoochee long enough for others to attack the supply line. (But Hood had said Sherman would "cross the Chattahoochee river very rapidly" if they left the Kennesaw line.)[75]

Davis "took up the facts one by one," says Hill. "Long ago" he had ordered Morgan to attack in Sherman's rear "directly from Abingdon," Virginia; but Morgan "insisted" he could recruit horses and men if he went "through Kentucky and around Nashville." Davis had "allowed him to have his own way," and now he was back defeated, "with only 1800 men" and few horses. As for Forrest, Davis had told Brown on June 29 that he was "now operating on Sherman's lines," but then the pursuers sent by Sherman had tangled him up. Davis read to Hill urgent cries for help from Maury at Mobile and S. D. Lee in Mississippi. The latter wired that "A. J. Smith had left Memphis with fifteen thousand men" (sent by Sherman, yet again, "to punish Forrest and the people"). Lee "had only seven thousand men *including* [italics mine] the commands of Forrest and Roddy . . . but anyhow, with or without [reinforcements] . . . he should meet Smith and whip him too. 'Ah! there is a man for you' said Mr. Davis."[76]

> After . . . showing how utterly Gen. Johnston was at fault as to the number of troops in the different [cavalry] commands, the President said, "How long did you understand Gen. Johnston to say he could hold Sherman north of the Chattahoochee river?" "From fifty-four to sixty days" I said, and repeated the facts on that subject. . . . Thereupon the President read me a dispatch from Gen. Johnston announcing that he had crossed or was crossing the Chattahoochee river![77]

Johnston had handled his army well under extreme pressure. In retrospect, Hardee admired the clean way he had abandoned position after position. At the time, however, Hardee said he and Hood "would prefer to go [into Atlanta] whipped rather than not to fight at all." He had told Johnston of "our desire to fight" and said to his wife, "the sooner . . . the better." Davis told Ben Hill he made "his great mistake" (appointing Johnston), because his backers claimed he would defeat the enemy. If he meant to "draw Sherman in the interior and then destroy him why did he not leave . . . Polk where he was, and at the proper time order him into Sherman's rear?" Polk had suggested this three months before, but Johnston (backed by Bragg) had vetoed it.[78]

Davis knew high command changes "usually work evil, if done in the presence of the enemy." He told Hill, "The idea of having to remove Gen. Johnston now was a terrible one." He had to consider replacements, however. "He thought Hardee the best man probably but he would not accept the command."[79]

> Mr. Davis, with an earnestness and feeling I think I never saw him manifest on any other occasion said, "Oh! I would rather risk Joe Johnston than any of them. There is not a better fighter in the army if he will only fight. . . . His great defect is a want of confidence. It is constitutional. . . . They say I dislike him. It is not true. If he would only whip Sherman as I know he can do . . . I would help crown him with immortal honors forever.

Perhaps this was what caused Hill to wire Johnston on July 14: "You must do the work with your present force. For God's sake, do it."[80]

The cabinet had already voted Johnston's removal, Seddon told Hill, but Davis, seeing it "very hazardous," would not agree if he thought Johnston would fight. Atlanta was crucial: a rail and munitions center; the key to powder and ammunition works at Augusta; and the supply base, not only for Johnston, but also for Lee in Virginia.[81] On July 12, Davis wired Lee: "*Genl. Johnston* has *failed* . . . strong indications that he will *abandon Atlanta*. . . . It seems necessary to *relieve him* at once. . . . What think you of Hood for the position?" Lee wired back, "Hood is a good fighter, very industrious on the battle field, careless off." He did not know how he would do if given "the whole responsibility." He had a "high opinion of his gallantry, earnestness & zeal. . . . May God give you wisdom to decide in this momentous matter."[82]

July 15: Bragg wired from Atlanta, "I cannot learn that [Johnston] has any more plan for the future than he has had in the past"; July 16: Davis asked Johnston "your plan of operations . . . specifically," and Johnston replied, "It is mainly to watch for an opportunity to fight to advantage. We are trying to put Atlanta in condition to be held a day or two by the Georgia militia, that army movements may be freer and wider." A day or two? Freer and wider? This telegram, said Davis, "overcame my objections" to removal. Seddon recalled, the "unanimous opinion" was "that [Johnston] did not intend to fight a battle," which was "indispensable for the Honor and success of our cause."[83]

On July 17, Cooper wired Johnston: "as you have failed to arrest the advance of the enemy . . . and express no confidence that you can defeat or repel him, you are hereby relieved from the command of the Army." He was to turn it over to Hood who had "temporary rank of general under the late law." Johnston sneered back: "Confident language by a military commander is not usually regarded as evidence of competency." As to "the *alleged* [italics mine] cause of my removal," he compared his campaign to that in Virginia and said he had done much better. He really believed he was removed because Davis hated him. Those who thought Davis acted from "personal hostility or dislike," said Hill, were merely "small, in contrast."[84]

Although Johnston later said he could have held Atlanta "forever," he had warned Wigfall on June 28 that it was risky to leave his daughters there. On July 11, he had told Lydia to send the girls "at once" to safety in Macon, ninety-three miles south. "The machinery, government stores, and wounded" were then already on the cars. As soon as Johnston was relieved, he and Lydia went to Macon. Virginia Clay was keeping the girls. Seeing the general at church, she gave him a kiss to show publicly her sympathy over his removal.[85]

In the army, which idolized Johnston, reaction ranged from dismay to shock.[86] Hood tried to get him to pocket the order and direct a battle for Atlanta, but he refused. Hood, Hardee, and A. P. Stewart together asked Davis to suspend his order "until the fate of Atlanta shall be decided." That would only make the case "worse than it was before," said Davis; the "public good" was at stake, "and to each of you I confidently look for the sacrifice of every personal consideration." For Hardee, this was asking almost too much.[87]

Gen. John Bell Hood, disciple of Lee and Jackson, delivered the "manly blows" that Davis wanted—northwest at Peachtree Creek, and east at the Battle of Atlanta. A Northern general found one of his plans "very bold . . . very brilliant," but they all frayed. Tactical mishaps, more than numbers, defeated him. He suffered more losses than the South could stand. But he "had stopped Sherman cold on two fronts." Sherman had to try another end run. Hood met him July 28 at Ezra Church. Confederates lost this battle to stubborn entrenched fighting and repeating rifles. But still they had kept Sherman out of the city. All during August he sat, lobbing artillery shells in. His cavalry, sent to destroy Hood's communications, failed. Howell Cobb saved Macon. Sherman then moved his whole army south and beat Hardee's isolated corps on the rail line at Jonesboro, and again at Lovejoy's Station, forcing Hood to evacuate Atlanta on September 2.[88]

On August 3, Hardee had wired Davis: "I rely on your kindness to relieve me from an unpleasant position." He was "unwilling to serve under Hood." It seems he had wanted the command after all and was cut to the quick when a youngster was promoted over his head. Knowing Hardee's worth, which he pointed out to Hood, Davis had soothed, "no wound was intended."[89] On August 17, Hardee had written his young wife, Mary, refugeeing in Macon: "General Johnston is mistaken in saying that the President's dispatches to me were insulting. . . . I see nothing in the tone or language . . . of which I can complain. . . . I would not have been passed over had he supposed that [I would accept]." Although the Johnstons were "good friends," he did not want her "influenced so much" by them, especially Lydia: "She is devoured by a bitter feeling of hatred which is inconsistent with her Christian character . . . I hope you will not imitate her . . . you ought to be charitable." Davis "does not refuse to relieve me," but "he appeals to my patriotism to remain." "For the good of the cause . . . I am willing to make any sacrifice."[90]

Hardee stayed. But a month later, Hood, blaming him for all the army's failures, asked Davis to relieve Hardee and to come to Georgia. When Davis got to Palmetto Station, southwest of Atlanta, on September 25, the army cheered him, but some muttered about wanting Hood out and Johnston back, or Beauregard. Davis had hoped anew that Hardee, "sustained by a Divine Wisdom and power," would help "save our country from the impending calamity." But Hardee insisted on leaving and was assigned the South Carolina–Georgia–Florida department.[91] Davis brought Beauregard to head the Military Division of the West, putting him over Hood and Richard Taylor, who had taken S. D. Lee's place when Lee took Hood's corps. This was one more try at the theater idea, "ahead of its time," and now beyond the country's capacity. At least Beauregard, with his Napoleonic flair, suited it better than Johnston had.[92]

Davis had answered a cry for reinforcements on September 5, "No other resource remains." It never occurred to him that this meant the end. "Brave men have done well before against greater odds than ours, and when were men ever braver? . . . We are fighting for existence; and by fighting alone can independence be gained. . . . But do I expect it? Yes, I do. (Renewed cheering.)" This was at Augusta. Everywhere on this trip he tried to woo the exempts and absentees into the army. He was castigated for revealing its weakness. He even tried the Trans-Mississippi again. The response was never enough. Charles Francis Adams, the Northern leader, said Davis made "no fatal mistakes . . . did the best possible with the means. . . . Merely the opposing forces were too many and too strong for him."[93]

What to do next was the question Davis thrashed out with his generals at Palmetto and Augusta. Sherman had emptied Atlanta of its people, including the "old and feeble." He wrote: to any complaint of "my barbarity and cruelty, I will answer that war is war and not popularity seeking." He made the city into a military camp that could not be attacked. But his lifeline could. Davis decided that Hood would march northwest of Atlanta to ruin the rail line back to Tennessee. Sherman would have to come out in pursuit and might be brought to decisive battle. This all went as planned. Sherman, scratching his head over Hood's crazy move, followed all the way to Gaylesville, Alabama. By now it was late October.[94] On the way, he wired Grant that since he could not protect his supply line from "the whole batch of devils" on it, he thought he would just tear it up himself and "strike out with wagons" for Savannah: "I can make the march, and make Georgia howl."[95]

Hood had new plans too. Davis had told him to either battle Sherman or harry him. Instead, Hood headed for Middle Tennessee, planning to whip anyone Sherman sent after him, take Nashville, go through Kentucky to join Lee, beat Grant, then finish off Sherman when he came to help Grant. When told of the plan on November 6, Davis still hoped "you may *first beat* [Sherman] in detail, and subsequently, *without . . . danger to the country in your rear,* [italics mine] advance to the Ohio river." But Hood dared not risk battle, and Beauregard loved the Napoleonic sweep of the plan. The only change he made was to keep Wheeler's cavalry and send Forrest to Hood. Rain and high water delayed the campaign for weeks; it was November 21 before it was under way. By then Sherman had burned Atlanta and started for the sea.[96]

Coming back from Georgia in October, Jeff Davis, Lubbock, and Custis Lee stopped for a few hours with the Chesnuts in Columbia, South Carolina. Davis kissed Mary at the gate and sat chatting with her on the front porch until small boys drove them in by calling, "Come here and look! [This man] looks just like Jeff Davis on a postage stamp." "An immense crowd" came to the house for a speech. Davis extolled "the heroism" of Southern women and told the men to fight with "unconquerable spirit." Afterward, "he was thoroughly exhausted, but we had a mint julep ready for him." Sally "Buck" Preston, whose love affair with Hood had filled Mary's diary for months, kissed him for praising Hood, Davis "all the while smoothing her down on the back from the shoulders, as if she were a ruffled dove." A man, "with the air of a connoisseur," said: "Jeff Davis will do. I like that game look the fellow has." A preacher friend "gave our thoughts a voice," says Mary, as he "prayed God to bless the President—to save him!" Her gourmet dinner sent the party off in style. But while Mary concocted desserts on the back porch, Custis Lee, perched "on the bannister with a cigar in his mouth . . . told me many a hard truth for the Confederacy and the bad time which was at hand."[97]

There was one other bright spot in the bad time closing around them—Christmas. Varina made sure the feast was kept with everything from turkey to plum pudding. The children were ecstatic over a life-sized spun-sugar hen on a nest with blancmange eggs (where her chef got the sugar, she does not say). Jeff Jr., tasting his father's cupful of brandied eggnog on the Eve, announced: "Now I just know this is Christmas." There was the whispered excitement of secret homemade gifts—for the children's stockings, balls of hard-wound rags covered with kid from old gloves, and "teetotums made of large horn buttons and a match which could spin indefinitely." Someone made big Jeff a pair of monogrammed chamois gauntlets. Varina got "a few of Swinburne's best songs bound in wall-paper." Orphans from the "Episcopalian Home" brought baby Winnie a straw hat they had plaited. Varina had her young people make the decorations for the orphans' tree, and "our man servant, Robert Brown" made "a sure enough house" to be a prize for "the most orderly girl." Margaret Howell painted a mantle piece and a fire on the hearth, and Ma made linens for twig-and-pasteboard beds. The girl who won it was so awed, she could only hug it in silence. They were all in "the basement of St. Paul's Church" then, on Christmas night. In his enthusiasm, the president got up to help distribute gifts from the tree "but worked such wild confusion giving everything asked for . . . that we called a halt, so he contented himself with unwinding one or two tots from a network of strung popcorn . . . and taking off all the apples he could when unobserved, and presenting them to the smaller children."[98] Perhaps the nerve pain in his head (following a tooth extraction) made it so hard to sit still. More likely, he was thinking of Joe. One year later to the day Varina wrote: "Last Christmas we had a home—a country—and our children—and yet we would not be comforted for our 'little man' was not."[99]

It was October of 1864 when the president returned from Georgia. He found before long that he had lost control of the Western army. "How little I had to do with the series of blunders in that quarter," he later confided to Varina. He was "as much amazed as everybody else at that strange manoeuvre of Hood's," wrote Pendleton at the time, "and shocked to find he had left all Georgia at Sherman's mercy."[100] Davis recollected wrongly that a wire from Beauregard November 24 was "certainly the first information I had of the purpose to march the army into Tennessee" (it probably said the march was under way), but indeed, as Hood said later, "I know sir you were in no way responsible." On the last day of November, Hood fought a Pyrrhic stalemate at Franklin; he went on to beseige Nashville and met shattering defeat there in December. The remnant of his army got south through freezing weather safely, thanks to the rearguard brilliance of S. D. Lee and Forrest, and found refuge at Tupelo, Mississippi, January 10, 1865. Hood asked to be relieved and was. In his farewell, he thanked his men for the campaign and said it was his "conception" alone. Taylor took over Hood's troops, and Beauregard visited Tupelo. They sent four thousand men to help

Maury hold Mobile, beleaguered since Admiral Farragut had damned the torpedoes (mines) and captured the Bay in August. Only a cadre of Hood's men got back into the fight later in North Carolina.[101]

The collapse of the Army of Tennessee shook the Confederacy. Sherman was free as a bird. "Until we can repopulate Georgia, it is useless to occupy it," Sherman had written, "but the utter destruction of its [rail]roads, houses, and people will cripple their military resources." Grant had taught him in Mississippi to do without a supply line and to eat out the countryside. He had taught himself the techniques of vandalism. When he started southeast from Atlanta in November, he had bottled up the few Confederate troops by feints at Augusta and Macon, leaving no one to fight but meager cavalry and militia. Davis wired frantic orders to obstruct his way to no avail. Sherman left a bare, burned wake through the state and took Savannah on December 21, 1864, just after Hood's defeat, chasing Hardee and his little army to Charleston.[102]

Blame for all these disasters fell on Davis: if only he had not removed Johnston. . . . He had to bear the "odium" for Tennessee, noted J. B. Jones, because he could not publish Beauregard's December 6 letter, which "would exculpate" him. There was talk of supplanting him, but he was personally "well-nigh invulnerable." He had lost strength in Congress, however.[103] It assailed Seddon so that he resigned. Breckinridge, whom Davis called to the War office, forced out Northrop, even though an investigation led by Foote had again exonerated him. The new commissary general, Isaac Monroe St. John, fed Lee better because Breckinridge got the trains to run. But it was Northrop's methods he followed—they were "as perfect," said a major, "as any that could have been devised." Failure had been due to enemy action, breakdown of transport, and lack of money, rather than to Northrop himself. Davis always praised his "energy, fidelity and good conduct," his "extraordinary capacity."[104]

Wigfall, back from Texas, tried to get rid of Benjamin, but the censure vote was a tie, and Davis refused to let him resign. Wigfall thought him the architect (as he was) of the plan Davis had outlined to Congress: instead of impressing slaves for labor, take them into the army noncombat, but arm them if necessary, and grant freedom for faithful service. Davis said privately "we are reduced to choosing whether the negroes shall fight for us or against us." All else was academic. When Wigfall said he would never make a "Santo Domingo of his country," he was expressing the outrage of many, including R. M. T. Hunter, Foote, Rhett, Cobb, and J. E. Brown. But his friend Johnston was urging the move.[105] Davis also had the backing of Lee and most of the army. On March 13, 1865, a compromise law squeaked through, but it was too late. A few companies "paraded in Richmond"; a few men saw combat.[106]

Wigfall persuaded the Senate, however, that Davis had bridled Johnston and Beauregard in 1861. It asked restoration of both to their former commands. It also passed a bill creating a "general-in-chief of all Confederate armies." Although it was obviously designed to undercut him as commander in chief, Davis let it become law and appointed Lee to the post on February 6, 1865. Soon after, Lee recalled Johnston to the army.[107] All this wrought little change between Lee and Davis. They consulted as always, the stress causing a temper flare only once each. But there were no "armies" left, only fragments, except for the Army of Northern Virginia; and all it could do was thwart Grant at Petersburg at a fatal cost in irreplaceable men.[108]

Abraham Lincoln had beat McClellan for president in November, thanks in part to the capture of Atlanta and the failure of Clay's Canadian venture. In January 1865, he let F. P. Blair take Davis an unofficial peace overture. The upshot was a shipboard conference at Hampton Roads on February 6, with Lincoln and Seward for the North, and Stephens, Hunter, and John A. Campbell for the South. "The conference ended without result," said Lincoln. That was because he insisted on referring to a "common country" and demanded unconditional surrender. Davis insisted on "two countries." To him, that was the whole point of the four-year struggle.[109] If there were not two, as Varina said, "you had no authority in the matter." Davis had roused "enthusiastic applause" by telling his audience in Augusta, "Never, never have I sought [peace] on any other basis than independence."[110] He wrote later, "I do not know how anyone could have expected me, under the trust which I held from the people . . . to surrender [the war aims] . . . while the army defiantly held its position in the field." If they had, he would have resigned "in shame and mortification" in favor of someone "fit for such a service." But the people backed him now. He was carrying out their wishes and "the wishes of our army," says Alexander.[111] Lubbock vowed that giving up would have been seen "by the army and the people as . . . pusillanimity or treason."[112]

With neuralgia in his shoulder making him "so feeble he should have remained away," Davis sparked a surge of patriotism by an impassioned speech in Richmond's African Church on February 6, the night the peace commissioners came back with Lincoln's ultimatum of "unconditional submission." Hunter and Benjamin spoke. Ben Hill went to LaGrange to rouse the people of Georgia to fight on. Robert Toombs, though still growling at him, backed Davis against surrender. Even the *Richmond Examiner* did.[113] Army units and states pledged devotion. Lee put out "Order No. 2": "The choice between war and abject submission is before us"; "brave men . . . cannot barter manhood for peace, nor the right of self-government for life or property." Congress itself issued a manifesto: war until independence. But Stephens termed Davis's speech "little short of dementation." He went back to Crawfordville for good.[114]

Stephens's pessimism was justified. Grant was squeezing the Confederacy ever tighter. Sheridan whipped Early out of the Valley of Virginia, stripped it of even a crow's ration, and came to join Grant at Petersburg.[115] Sherman, brazenly giving up South Carolina to special vengeance, marched through the state northward from Savannah. "Every night the entire horizon was illuminated by burning houses!" Ladies who survived the "quivering, molten ocean" of flame in Columbia could only compare it to medieval pictures of hell. Mary Chesnut and the Johnstons, who had fled to Columbia from Macon, had by then removed to Lincolnton, North Carolina. But it was not safe, either. Sherman forced Beauregard and Hardee out of Charleston and pursued them up the state. In North Carolina, if anywhere, a stand had to be made.[116]

The hope of real resistance had fallen along with Wilmington, the last eastern port for blockade-runners. Where were supplies to come from? Braxton Bragg, commanding in North Carolina since November, on Lee's recommendation, was blamed for this disaster and for the resultant death of General Whiting. Bragg had been left without a place in Richmond by Lee's elevation to overall command (as planned by its promoters), and now Lee gave J. E. Johnston the command of all North Carolina forces. This Bragg found "painful in the extreme." He asked to be relieved but was not. "My position is both mortifying and humiliating," he wrote to Davis, "but the example of your more trying one warns me to bear it with resignation." He served under Johnston.[117]

Lee's elevation, Bragg's discomfiture, and, above all, the recall of J. E. Johnston, were indeed seen as humiliations of Jeff Davis. " 'Tray, Blanche, and Sweetheart, bark at him,' " said J. B. Jones. Through it all he moved with aplomb. Lee's promotion was a "nominal dignity."[118] He would give the Trans-Mississippi to Bragg, who could bring the troops Smith had never sent.[119] Although Davis had written out a very long explanation for Congress of why he could not reappoint Johnston, he decided not to send it and allowed Lee to appoint him, salving his conscience with the thought that Lee would control him. When Davis's old friend Sen. Gustavus Henry wrote him a consoling letter, Davis replied: "I regret that you should have thought it necessary to speak of a sacrifice of feeling on my part. . . . Those who are controlled by personal feeling in such matters are . . . unworthy to hold a public trust. I am sure I am not of that class and deem it due to myself so to answer." His judgment on the "military qualities" of officers was "mainly based upon official information"—"any opinion heretofore formed by me on facts, must be changed by other facts."[120]

Johnston was in a temper: "he was only put back to be the one to surrender." But when told that Lee really wanted him, he forgot jealousy and swore to serve under him like a "Knight of old." As for

Davis, however: "I have a most unchristian satisfaction" over his "state of mind"—"To me it is sufficient revenge."[121] When Beauregard fumbled with the troops in North Carolina, Lee used rumors of his ill health to justify putting Johnston over him. He was "a good soldier" and yielded gracefully. Johnston was one too. He thought there was no hope, but when Lee said to fight Sherman, he did. If Sherman and Grant met, Lee was done for.[122]

Burying past quarrels, Johnston, Bragg, and Hardee joined forces to wallop the enemy. Even D. H. Hill had gotten back into the fight. At Bentonville, March 19, Johnston directed a ferocious attack, led in person by Hardee ("with his knightly gallantry," Johnston said), and stunned a part of Sherman's army. Two days later Hardee was again leading the charge when his only son, Willie, sixteen, whom he had just allowed to enlist, fell mortally wounded. It was all in vain. Davis magnanimously spoke of being "gratified" by Johnston's "success," hoping it was "only the first of the good tidings" from him, but Johnston had to retreat before a whole new corps brought in through Wilmington. "To confront our 12,000 effectives, as they are erroneously called," Bragg wrote Davis, "Sherman now has . . . not less than 50,000."[123]

He was blunt. "I fear you are not allowed to see the whole truth . . . I see disasters, disorderly retreats, and utter confusion on our front. . . . You should not permit yourself to hope even for any result here. . . . no one is so blind as not to see the inevitable result." Davis was. He saw the situation but calmly considered possibilities and lectured Bragg about "great generals" whose "boldness of conception and rapidity of execution" beat a stronger enemy. "The President is very pertinacious," Lee observed; someone less polite called him "obstinate as a mule." Perhaps there were personal as well as state reasons for clutching the hope of victory. As he told Bragg on April 1, 1865: "We both entered this war at the beginning of it; we both staked everything on the issue, and have lost all which either public or private enemies could take away." On this same day, Lee attacked Grant at Fort Stedman and failed. Grant, not waiting for Sherman, put everything into a knockout blow that night and broke Lee's lines.[124]

Jeff Davis was in his place at St. Paul's on Sunday, April 2, kneeling for the antecommunion, when he "was called out of church to receive a telegram." The packed congregation saw him rise, deathly pale but absolutely calm, and go out "with his usual quick military tread." The message was, Lee's army would evacuate its lines, including Richmond, that night. He walked down the hill to the executive offices, ordered up Ewell's defense force, and saw to the packing of official papers. Then he walked home that fine spring day. Ladies ran out of their houses to ask if the city were to be given up. They were content, they said, if it would help the cause. Their "affection and confidence . . . were more distressing to me than complaint and unjust censure would have been."[125]

At the White House, there were so many things to take care of, and Varina was not there. He had sent her and the children south in the nick of time. Their housekeeper "promised to take care of everything," he wrote to her, "which may mean some things." "Everybody seemed afraid of connexion with our property. . . . Count on nothing as saved which you valued, except the bust," which had been put "where it should never be found by a Yankee," along with "the painting of the heros of the Valley." Davis managed to send "a large easy chair" to Mrs. Lee, "remembering even then her invalid condition." "You don't know how I value *the chair* you sent me," she wrote.[126]

With the president were his courier, William Davies (who remembers his lighting up a cigar), Robert Brown, Lubbock, and his nephew David Bradford. Clement Clay suddenly appeared and found Davis, amid piles of clothes and papers, packing his valise. Clay had made it back from Canada by the skin of his teeth, his blockade-runner having grounded and burned. He had insisted on struggling to Richmond, to report to Benjamin with his papers. There was no time for that. Davis wrote his wife, "Called off on horseback to the depot, I left the servants to go down with the boxes and they left Tippy." Finally, Davis and his aides, Clay, and the cabinet except for Breckinridge were on the cars and, by eleven that night, on the way to Danville.[127]

There, in the Sutherlin home, while Lee retreated, still fighting, Davis wrote, at a small marble-top table, a proclamation "To the People of the Confederate States of America." Only much later did he call it "over-sanguine." He was expecting Lee's army any day.[128] The people would endure, he had written, if not "deserted by their leaders." Now he confessed that the loss of Richmond was an "injury," but they had preserved it through four years of war—a feat "usually regarded as the evidence to mankind of separate national existence." The enemy imagined its fall "would be the signal for our submission to their rule," but it would be "unworthy of us" to falter now. The army would continue "a struggle the memory of which is to endure for all ages and to shed an increasing luster upon our country." With "confidence in your spirit and fortitude," he announced:

> it is my purpose to maintain your cause with my whole heart and soul . . . I will never consent to abandon to the enemy one foot of the soil of any one of the States of the Confederacy. . . . [If] compelled to a temporary withdrawal . . . again and again will we return, until the baffled and exhausted enemy shall abandon in despair his endless and impossible task of making slaves of a people resolved to be free.
>
> Let us not, then, despond, my countrymen; but relying on the never-failing mercies and protecting care of our God, let us meet the foe with fresh defiance and with unconquered and unconquerable hearts.[129]

A few days later at Greensboro, official word reached Davis of Lee's surrender. It broke him so visibly that everyone withdrew from the room, leaving John Taylor Wood alone with him and his silent tears. After trying in vain to rally Johnston and Beauregard to the fight, he led the cavalry southwest, expecting Johnston to send troops after him. He had plucked up heart enough by then to talk to Burton Harrison "of men and books, particularly of Walter Scott and Byron; of horses and dogs and sports; of woods and fields . . . of roads and how to make them; of the habits of birds," in fact, he seemed "singularly equable and cheerful." It was not until they reached Abbeville, and he alone "seemed to think a longer resistance practicable," that the full implications of Lee's surrender, and Johnston's, hit him. He staggered from the room on Breckinridge's arm, seeing the "ruin, both material and moral," that the Confederacy's fall would bring, "the long night of oppression." Basil Duke tells this scene: "I will venture to say that nothing he has subsequently endured, equaled the bitterness of that moment."[130]

In that bitterness he had to go on, to leave all troops at Washington-Wilkes, overtake Varina in the woods, be captured at Irwinville and sent to prison at Fortress Monroe.

JEFFERSON DAVIS AND THE CONFEDERATE GENERALS.

Commander in chief Davis with generals (left to right) Hill, Hood, Stuart, Jackson, Lee, Longstreet, J. E. Johnston, Beauregard, and A. S. Johnston (in portrait); at top left, Virginia capitol; center, C.S. great seal. A photographer's fantasy from *Life and Reminiscences of Jefferson Davis.*

Lt. Gen. William J. Hardee, C.S.A., a friend of Davis's from the 1850s. Courtesy Alabama Department of Archives and History.

Judah Philip Benjamin, who held three successive cabinet posts in the C.S.A., a good friend of Jeff and Varina Davis's. Courtesy Library of Congress, image LC-USZ62-13690. ▶

▲ John H. Reagan in 1861, when he became C.S. postmaster general and Davis's friend for life. Original owned by Mrs. May Reagan Orr Mathes. From Ben H. Proctor, *Not without Honor: The Life of John H. Reagan* (Austin: University of Texas Press), 1962.

◀ Alexander H. Stephens, vice president of the Confederate States of America, c. 1859. Photograph by Mathew Brady. Courtesy Library of Congress, cracked glass negative LC-BH832-582.

Louis T. Wigfall, C.S. senator, first friend then bitter enemy of Davis's. From Louise Wigfall Wright, *A Southern Girl in '61.*

Robert Augustus Toombs, secretary of state, then brigadier general, C.S.A.; inveterate foe of Davis's. Photograph by Mathew Brady. Courtesy National Archives.

Benjamin H. Hill, firm Davis supporter in Congress, both U.S. and C.S.. Courtesy Library of Congress, scratched glass negative LC-BH826-3691.

Varina Banks Howell Davis, a famed Washington hostess, c. 1860. Photograph by Mathew Brady. Courtesy Museum of the Confederacy, Richmond, Virginia.

President Davis's aides-de-camp and secretary (the obscure names are, clockwise from right: Joseph R. Davis, John Taylor Wood, Burton N. Harrison, G. W. Custis Lee); only Lubbock is anachronistic. From *Life and Reminiscences of Jefferson Davis.*

Francis Richard Lubbock, 1862, a close friend of Davis's later, portrait by W. H. Huddle. Courtesy Texas State Library and Archives Commission.

Mary Boykin (Mrs. James) Chesnut, through merriment and tragedy, Varina Davis's friend, carte de visite c. 1860. Courtesy South Caroliniana Library, University of South Carolina, Columbia.

William Lowndes Yancey, the "fire-eater," friend or foe to Davis? Courtesy Library of Congress, image USZ62-36284.

The "spare, resolute, and rather pleading face" of Jefferson Davis as U.S. secretary of war, c. 1853. Daguerreotype. Courtesy Museum of the Confederacy, Richmond, Virginia.

Davis as U.S. Senator, c. 1859, after illness had cost him the sight of his left eye. Photograph by Mathew Brady. Courtesy National Archives.

Jefferson Davis and Wife, detail, 1867, Montreal, Quebec, Canada, by William Notman. Just after his release from prison: he was "a shadow of his former self," but his "eye still beams with fire." Courtesy Notman Photographic Archives, McCord Museum of Canadian History, Montreal, photograph 1-28149.

Davis's face: a reporter noted at his release "the mingled look of sweetness and dignity for which it was ever remarkable." Detail of photograph by Notman, 1867. Courtesy Museum of the Confederacy, Richmond, Virginia.

Jeff Jr., Maggie, and Billy Davis with their cousin, Joseph R. Davis, and Robert Brown (standing), their servant and protector, Montreal c. 1865. Courtesy Museum of the Confederacy, Richmond, Virginia.

Samuel Emory Davis (1852–1854), first child of Jeff and Varina, marble bust. Photograph by Robin Belesky. Courtesy Beauvoir, the Jefferson Davis Home and Presidential Library.

Richmond White House, back gallery, showing corner where Joseph Evan Davis, aged 5, fell to his death in 1864. Photograph by Katherine Wetzel. Courtesy Museum of the Confederacy, Richmond, Virginia.

Jim Limber (James Henry Brooks) c. 1865. Ambrotype. Courtesy Museum of the Confederacy, Richmond, Virginia.

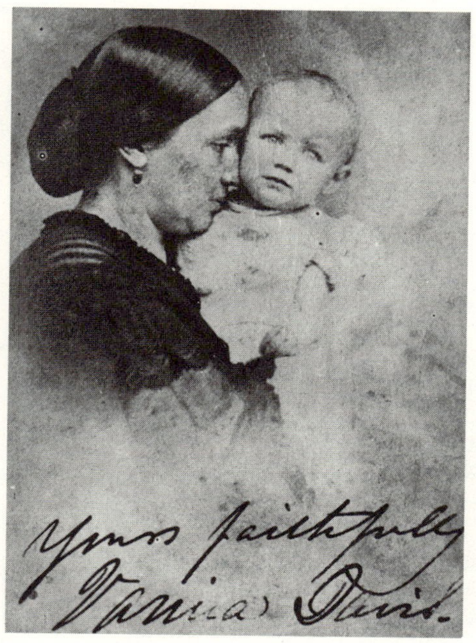

Varina Davis and Winnie ("Pie Cake"), late 1865: "she keeps me from freezing, out in the cold world." Courtesy Transylvania University Library.

Jefferson Davis at the time of his election as president. Courtesy Museum of the Confederacy, Richmond, Virginia.

First White House of the Confederacy on Bibb Street, Montgomery, Alabama, June 3, 1901. One of the ladies is Virginia Clay. Courtesy Cameron F. Napier and the First White House Association of Alabama.

Virginia (Mrs. Clement C.) Clay, who sent Davis in prison "a picture of herself in evening dress." Courtesy Alabama Department of Archives and History.

Jeff Davis and Clement C. Clay, c. 1875, at Mosser's Gallery, Memphis, Tennessee. From Ada Sterling, *Belle of the Fifties*.

Fortress Monroe, Virginia, 1861. Lithograph. Courtesy Casemate Museum.

Inset photograph of Fortress Monroe, showing moat and casemates with walkway on top where Davis was taken for exercise from solitary confinement, 1865–1866. From *Life and Reminiscences of Jefferson Davis*.

XVII

Prisoners

Varina Davis was alone. There were plenty of people at the rail of the steamer *Clyde*, but Jeff was gone. She did not cry. He had told her not to. Not until she got to the cabin. The children, however, were loud. She had watched the boat bear Jefferson Davis and Clement Clay across Hampton Roads toward Fortress Monroe, her husband standing tall among the foreign-born soldiers.

Virginia Clay had stayed in her cabin. As the bereft Davis family came from the deck, she heard Jeff Jr. vent the grief and frustration of them all. A soldier said, "Don't cry, Jeff. They ain't going to hang your pa," and he sobbed back, "When I get to be a man, I'm going to kill every Yankee I see!" Virginia tried to comfort the eight-year-old. His tone changed to "manly tenderness" as he said, "My papa told me to keep care of you and my Mamma!"

Whatever coolness there had been between Varina and Virginia evaporated now in the presence of the enemy. Resistance made them instantly one, and the wit of each buoyed them both through the severe trials that began immediately, as policewomen stripped them, looking for "treasonable papers.""Oh, 'Ginie! What humiliation!" Varina wept. Virginia had been her saucy self, mocking the suspicion, twirling her pistol (remarkably not confiscated), and making the detective unhook and then rehook her clothes, saying, "I've heard that white maids are as good as black ones." Her repartee kept Union officers at bay. Varina muttered behind one of them, "Puss in boots!" and the friends were able to laugh instead of cry. Captain Hudson, from whom the Davises had lately saved Jim Limber, came demanding Varina's shawl as "part of Mr. Davis's disguise." The ladies decided to fox him. Varina held out both their shawls, telling him to choose. But he outfoxed them. He took both shawls, went ashore, and got Varina's maid to identify hers. Colonel Pritchard had already confiscated her waterproof, under Stanton's order to bring to Washington "the woman's dress in which Jeff. Davis was captured."[1]

Varina said that Hudson had told her if she did not give him the shawl, he would "take everything I had." His men did that anyway. As Jeff Davis later said, "the trunks of my family were broken open and robbed of every article tempting to the sight, including the clothes of my infant daughter, photographic albums, medals, etc. etc." A Confederate half-dollar, one of only four ever struck, which Davis had carried through the war as a pocket piece, fell to the thieves. Varina was particularly upset over losing the children's clothes, but they did not get little Jeff's "Confederate gray" major's uniform. He snatched it up and ran to his mother, who somehow managed to save it.[2]

In vain Varina tried to get a doctor for her "exceedingly ill" sister Margaret. In vain she begged the captain of an "English Man of War" anchored nearby to give her passage to England. Jeff, "not knowing the Government was at war with women and children," had already asked that she be allowed to board some other vessel in the Roads, or to go where she had friends. His captors had refused.[3] Burton Harrison, from his cell at Old Capitol prison, asked F. P. Blair to get passports for Varina, but that request too was in vain. She told Blair how the captors had separated Jeff from her suddenly without saying "we were to meet no more"—"a refinement of cruelty worthy of savages." When she realized it, she had begged to be imprisoned with him, then to send him a message, but her requests were denied.[4]

Nelson Appleton Miles, brevet major general of volunteers, came aboard and "summoned" the two wives. General Grant had picked him for commandant of Fortress Monroe as one "who will by no possibility permit the escape of the prisoners." He had personally given him "special orders." Miles was a war hero, from Massachusetts, twenty-five years old."He was not respectful, but I thought it was his ignorance of polite usage," Varina wrote later. He gave them no news of their husbands, only saying ominously that "'Davis' had announced Mr. Lincoln's assassination the day before it happened, and he guessed he knew all about it." Virginia was more tolerant of Miles because he promised to write her about Clement, but he soon returned the Bible she had sent in to him, because she had written a note on the flyleaf commending "my precious husband" to God. This, and Miles's remark to Varina, gave a hint of what was going on inside Fortress Monroe.[5]

The prisoners there were held incommunicado. So were these on the ship, except that Miles agreed to forward some letters, from Varina to Blair and Seward, and from Virginia Clay to her old friend Joseph Holt. Davis was counting on the old friendships, too; he had asked to see Blair and Seward, with no luck. Later on, a sailor slipped forbidden newspapers to Virginia Clay, but this was not a kindness. Varina's "agony of mind" nearly caused her to faint as she read: "We hope soon to see the bodies of those two arch traitors, Davis and Clay, dangling and blackening in the wind and rain!"[6]

As the *Clyde* took "the females" south, in keeping with Stanton's orders, Varina needed all the courage of her dragoon grandfather Kempe, and all the Christian faith taught by her mother, his daughter. The "old transport-ship, hardly seaworthy," ran into a "fearful gale." Varina had to hold her nursing baby all night to keep her from being bruised, tend three other spirited children, and care for two sick ladies; her sister Margaret worsened, and Virginia Clay fell ill. Varina was both "chambermaid and nurse." But Robert Brown was with her. He had refused to go ashore with the female servants. Davis had given him charge of the family, and he more than met the obligation. "I could not tell you what he has been to me," Varina was soon writing Jeff. "He even nursed the baby and washed for her. Billy is his pet, but he watches over all." The trouble also brought to light "the good hearts of my children"—"little Jeff and I did the housekeeping," and Maggie helped Robert with Pie Cake. There were also good hearts among the Union officers and the crew, who helped in various ways, though the soldiers again robbed the trunks. After anchoring a day at Charleston, where ice and milk revived the sick, they all were put ashore at Savannah, still an occupied city.[7]

No provision was made for them. They were not allowed a carriage. "We trudged up to the hotel," says Varina, "quite in emigrant fashion, Margaret with the baby and Robert with the baggage; I, with Billy and Jeff and Maggie" and the parcels. Suddenly a knot of Southern men recognized them, swooped up the children and "bore them on their shoulders into the Pulaski House." Soon "gifts of flowers and fruit" began arriving, and by night they were holding a regular levee at the hotel. Virginia Clay was not under restraint; she soon left for Macon and Huntsville.[8]

Officially, the Davis family also were "at perfect liberty," but when Davis's friend Gen. Hugh Mercer took Varina to see the Federal district commander, she found herself at liberty to pay her expenses but not to leave Savannah or to write letters except through army channels. "Houses were thrown open to me," but she remained at the hotel, so friends would not be intimidated by the detectives watching her. "I am proud of your self denial," Jeff said when he heard. She did accept visits, and clothes for the children. "I have been always led to suppose that your stay there was voluntary," Jeff was soon to write, but "the logic of events has led to the conclusion that you too have been a prisoner."[9]

Li' Pie Cake suffered through the whooping cough, and Varina with her, in the heat and the confinement of hotel rooms. Then the Catholic Sisters of Charity of Our Lady of Mercy found Varina an Irish nurse for Li' Pie, the "sweet-tempered, kind" Mary Ahearn. They also took Maggie as a student at their St. Vincent's Academy, and they let young Jeff come recite his lessons. They had searched out Varina, bringing her "all the money they had in the world," five gold dollars, but she would not take those. Presumably she did not refuse the five hundred and twenty-two dollars that General Hardee sent to her in August. He was living on his wife's Alabama plantations now and had sold some cotton. At the same time, he tried to help Davis by writing to Seward.[10]

Varina lived in her room, only "walking out late at night, with Robert for protection." (He had verbally whipped the hotel servants into shape, after one was rude to her.) But "I could not keep my little ones so closely confined." When they went out to play, soldiers made Billy "snatch apples off the stalls, if Robert lost sight of him for a moment." They would reward him by singing, "We'll hang Jeff Davis on a sour apple-tree." Finally Varina was wounded "to the quick" when Billy told her: "You thinks I'se somebody; so is you; so is father; but you is not; so is not any of us, but me. I am a Yankee every time."[11]

A negro sentinel once turned his gun on Maggie "to shoot her for calling him 'uncle.' " ("My brain burns when I think of the brute levelling his musket at my little, gentle child," wrote Davis.) Women talked in the street of whipping Billy, and little Jeff "was constantly told that he was rich; that his father had 'stolen eight millions,' etc." In the hotel parlor, an officer's wife "told him his father was 'a rogue, a liar, an assassin, and that means a murderer, boy; and I hope he may be tied to a stake and burned a little bit at a time with light-wood knots. . . . Your father will soon be hanged, but that death is too quick.' " The boy ran crying to Varina, his face "purple with mortification." "I commended Jeff's gentlemanly conduct in making no reply," but it all made her "frantically nervous," and she "prepared the children to go where they would not see such indignantly patriotic and prophetic females."[12]

It was Robert who "pled with me to send them away" and Ma, now living in Georgia, who rescued them. The elder Margaret Howell had become "a stout old lady with a handsome, but rather determined face, and pretty, old-fashioned gray curls falling behind her ears." Now in her sixtieth year, she took Billy, Jeff, and Maggie—aged three, eight, and ten—and set sail for New York, bound for Canada. Robert went with her. When someone asked if Jeff Davis were a gentleman, Robert "held up Billy, and said, 'Don't you see his *blood*—did you ever see a child like that belong to common tackies?' " (Varina called Billy as a baby "exquisitely lovely"; he had been a "special pet" of James Chesnut's.)[13] When a man on shipboard spoke ill of Davis in the children's hearing, Robert said, " 'Then you tell me I am your equal? You put me alongside of you in everything?' The man said, 'Certainly.' 'Then,' said Robert, 'take this from your equal,' and knocked him down. The captain was appealed to . . . justified Robert, and required an apology of the levelled leveller."

Varina later sent her sister Margaret to Montreal, escorted by J. R. Davis (who had been paroled at Lee's surrender), "to take care of my devoted mother, who is now too old and delicate to be left alone." She had meant to go herself, with Li' Pie and Mary Ahearn, after a new Federal commander allowed her to move to the farm of George Schley near Augusta. But when she heard that if she left the country, she could never come back, "no matter what befell Mr. Davis," she sent Margaret instead.[14]

What befell Jeff Davis after he was taken from her had already made Varina hysterical. Virginia Clay was "startled" to learn "that Mr. Davis, saddened, ill, strengthless, as we knew him to be, had been put in chains. . . . Not a soul in the South but was horrified." The news turned Varina's life into a nightmare. She shut herself in her room and "had to be kept under opiates for a week." This was at the end of May. On June 1, "shocked by the most terrible newspaper extras . . . which represent my husband to be in a dying condition," she wrote to Dr. Craven, whose name she had seen in the papers as the post surgeon attending him. She said nothing about chains, but calmly, piteously asked about his sleep, his eyes, his food. "If you are only permitted to say he is well, or he is better, it will be a great comfort to me, who has no other left . . . the uncertainty is such agony!"[15]

There was no answer, no word of any kind, except in the newspapers. On June 6, she loosed her tumultuous emotions on F. P. Blair:

> Shame—shame upon your people! While a felon's gyres were being fastened upon a soldier, and honest gentleman, did not the limb which was shrunken from a wound received in defence of your country arrest the work of his tormentors? They need have taken no precaution against his suicide. He never has taken aught which was not his own. His life is his wife's, his children's, his country's, his God's. . . . They may kill but can never degrade him.[16]

Seeing "in the daily journals" that "the agony inseparable from defeat and imprisonment" was "heightened . . . by chains and starvation," she cried out to Craven a second time:

> Can it be that these tales are even in part true? That such atrocities could render him frantic I know is not so. I have so often tended him through months of nervous agony, without ever hearing a groan or an expression of impatience, that I know these tales of childish ravings are not true . . . Is he ill—is he dying? . . . With a blaze of light pouring upon . . . eyes always sensitive to it; chains fettering his emaciated limbs; coarse food, served . . . in the most repulsive manner, without knife, fork, or spoon, "lest he should commit suicide,"—hope seems denied to me; yet I cannot reconcile myself to that result, which for many years must have been

> his gain. Will you only write me one word to say that he may recover? . . . Can it be that you are forbidden?[17]

It was. She wrote to Craven again on July 2: "Still no word of comforting response. . . . I am not capable of the '[still] yet brave despair,' which I know is required in my hopeless position." She daily gave "Thanks to God, that he has raised you up a 'present help' in my husband's time of trouble." "The numberless harrowing statements which daily agonize me" always mention the doctor as "ministering to his necessity," and "your wife and little daughter" too. "A heart . . . overflowing in earnest, constant prayers for you . . . is all I have to offer."[18]

As Varina's nightmare went on through July and August, she sought relief in reading. *Our Mutual Friend* by Charles Dickens was being serialized in *Harper's New Monthly Magazine.* She reported to Jeff in due time that it was "clever a little—but evidently written for money." She dipped into Clay's favorite, *Anatomy of Melancholy* by Robert Burton, but found it the "dirtiest book . . . scientifically filthy." She much preferred Elizabeth Barrett Browning and the "misty style" of Charlotte Yonge.[19]

She had *Christian's Mistake,* by "the author of *John Halifax, Gentleman,"* which novel had "charmed" her when it came out in 1856. She recommended *Pilgrim's Progress* to Martha Levy. Then she said, "Don't let us read any more except every day books—Miss Braddon's or Miss Somebody's who does not feel down deep for the fine fibers." She had already cried herself all the way to "burning tearless eyes." She was "worn out with the heartsickness of hope deferred . . . oh how I realize every hour that 'the tender grace of a day that is dead can never come back to me' . . . I do so long for the touch of his vanished hand."[20]

Varina's greatest relief was putting her own pen to paper. Besides gushing her feelings to friends, she sent thanks to Octavus Cohen for seven hundred dollars raised by the people of Savannah. Clutching every straw, she wrote highly eloquent appeals for help to Montgomery Meigs, George Shea, Seward again, and Horace Greeley. Meigs, Davis's protégé of days gone by, now U.S. quartermaster general, answered only through the Savannah commandant and spoke of the "guerrillas" who had "murdered" his eldest son during the war as "Mr. Davis's assassins." There was no help there.[21]

She loosed her indignation on Shea: "Falsely accused of every baseness and inhumanity which could disgrace mankind without a shade of proof, a brave soldier, a devoted patriot . . . lies in prison awaiting the next veer in popular opinion" (which Salmon Chase had said would decide Davis's fate). "Mr. Stanton's assertion that he knew of no ill treatment is disgusting. What is his standard of decency?" Besides all this, "Quidnuncs are polluting with their unhallowed gaze the precious records of my few happy hours" by publishing "garbled extracts from my husband's letters, and mine." She asked Seward to get the letters back. They were the only record her children had of their father's love and "constant unpremeditated exhibition of his moral rectitude."[22]

She appealed to Greeley, editor of the *New York Tribune:*

> How can the honest men and gentlemen of your country stand idly by to see a gentleman maligned, insulted, tortured and denied the right of trial by the usual forms of law? . . . With all archives of our government in the hands of your government, do they despair of proving him a rogue, falsifier, assassin and traitor—that they must in addition guard him like a wild beast, and chain him for fear his unarmed hands will in a casemated cell subvert the government? Shame, shame—he is not held for the ends of Justice but for those of torture. . . . Is no one among you bold enough to defend him?[23]

Benjamin wrote to his sister from Havana, "We are all in intense anxiety on the subject of our honored and noble chief." The Confederates there thought Davis's trial was being deliberately delayed "so as to give time" for an "assassination . . . by the tortures inflicted on him in prison." "No nobler gentleman, no purer man, no more exalted patriot ever drew breath; and eternal infamy will blacken the base and savage wretches who [intend] to wreak a cowardly vengeance on his honored head."[24]

On September 4, Varina received a letter. This is how it read (with some peculiarities noted):

> Fortress Monroe Va[25]
> 21 Aug. "65
>
> My dear Wife, I am now permitted to write to you, under two conditions viz: that I confine myself to family matters, and that my letter shall be examined by the U. S. Atty. Genl. before it is sent to you.[26]
>
> This will sufficiently explain to you the omission of subjects on which you would desire me to write. I presume it is however permissible for me to relieve your disappointment in regard to my silence on the subject of fulure ["t" uncrossed] action towards me, by stating that of the purpose of the authorities I know nothing.
>
> To morrow it will be three months since we were suddenly and unexpectedly separated, and many causes prominent among which has been my anxiety for you and our children have made that quarter in seeming duration long, very long. I sought permission to write to you that I might make some suggestions as to your movements and as to domestic arrangements.
>
> The first and most important point has in the mean time been so far decided by the journey of the older children that until a key is furnished to open what is now to me unintelligible I can only

speak in very general terms, in regard to your future movements. It is to be inferred that you have decided and I think wisely not to return to our old home, at least in the present disturbed condition of society. Thus you have the world before you but not where to choose, as the loss of our property will require the selection to be, with a view to subsistence. Should I regain my liberty before our "people" have become vagrant there are many of them whose labor I could direct so as to make it not wholly unprofitable. Their good faith under many trials, and the mutual affection between them and myself make me [interlined] always solicitous for their welfare and probably keeps them expectant of my coming. Should my fate be not to return to that country you can best be advised by Brother Jos: as to what and how it should be attempted, if any thing may be done [previous ten words interlined]. Always understand however that I do not mean that you should attempt in person to do any thing in the matter. I often think of "old Uncle Bob" and always with painful anxiety. If Sam. has rejoined him he will do all in his power for the old man's comfort and safety.[27]

The Smith land had better be returned to the heirs. No deed was made and the payments were for moveable effects ["property" crossed out, "effects" interlined] and for interest; their right to the land which alone remains ["property is" canceled, last four words interlined] therefore clearly revives [interlined over canceled "and"] since I am now unable to make the payment which is *I believe* due, and shall be unable [last thirteen words interlined] to fulfil the engagements hereafter to mature; therefore [written over another word] the sooner the case is disposed of the better.[28] Please write to my Brother for me in such terms as you can well understand I would use if allowed to write to him myself.

In like manner please write to my Sisters.

I asked Jeff: V. when he & I parted, to join you as soon as he could and to remain with you; he could render you much assistance as well by his intelligence as his discretion. Have you heard from [written over "of"] him?[29] The servant reported by the newspapers to be with the children in New York, is I suppose Robert, indeed so hope.

Ellen came ashore, and it must have embarassed you greatly under the circumstances to lose her before you could get another.[30] Jim. reported here that he knew where we had buried a large sum of gold at or near Macon. This I heard after he had gone and in such manner as created the impression that he had [interlined] gone on the same ship with you. The ready conclusion was that he had returned with assurances of zeal and fidelity to you and expecting [last four words interlined] to find an opportunity to [extra "to" crossed out] rob your trunks [comma and "and" crossed out]. This [capital written over small "t"] greatly disturbed me until I found that he had gone by way of Raleigh. Then remembering his complaint that he was not to be ["to be" interlined] furnished with transportation from here; another explanation of his fiction was afforded more creditable at least to his cunning.[31] I have the prayer book you sent, but the memorandum placed in it was withheld. The suit of dark grey clothes has also been received. It was like you in moments of such discomfort and annoyance as those [written over an erased "that"] to which you were subjected, to be careful about my contingent and future wants. Some day I hope to be able to tell you how in the long, weary hours of my confinement, busy memory has brought many tributes to your tender and ardent affection. The confidence in the shield of Innocence with which I tried to quiet your apprehensions and to dry your tears at our parting, sustains me still. If your fears have proved more prophetic than my hopes, yet do not despond—"Tarry thou the Lord's leisure; be strong, and He will comfort thy heart."[32] Every day twice or oftener I repeat the prayer of St. Chrysostom and assemble you all, each separately noted, on the right is Winnie, then Polly, Big-boy, Billie ["ie" crowded, written over an erasure], then L. P. held by Aunty and sometimes, as affection numbers the line, "the Little-man" is found between his Brothers. x x x x x _ _ _ _ _.[33]

I daily repeat the hymn I last heard you sing, "Guide me" etc. It is doubly dear to me for that [word smudged] association. The one which follows it in our Book of Common prayer is also often present to me. It is a most beautiful lesson of humility & benevolence.[34]

I have had here fresh occasion to realize the kindness of my fellow man. To the Surgeon [last two words written over an erasure] and the Regtal. Chaplain [last two words written over erasure which began "Rev. Mr."] I am under many obligations.[35] The officers of the Guard and of the Day have shown me increased consideration, such as their orders would permit.[36] The unjust accusations which have been made against me in the newspapers of the day might well have created prejudices against me. I have had no [last two words written over previous "no"] opportunity to refute them by proof [last three words interlined] nor have I sought to do so by ["such" crossed out] statements of chronological and other easily to be verified facts which [written over "as"] I might perhaps have been induced [written over an erasure] to make under other circumstances [last three words written over an erasure]; & can therefore only attribute the perceptible change to those good influences which are always at work to confound evil designs. Be not alarmed by speculative reports concerning my condition. You can rely on my fortitude, and God has given me much of resignation to His blessed [ink blot on "b"] will.

If it be His pleasure to reunite us, you will I trust find that His Fatherly correction has been sanctified to me, and that even in exile and obscurity I should be content to live unknown, quietly to [last three words interlined] labor for the support of my family; and thus [added at end of line] to convince those who have misjudged me, that self seeking and ill regulated ambition are not elements of my character.[37]

Men are apt to be verbose when they speak of themselves and suffering has a rare power to develop selfishness; so I have wandered from the subject on which I proposed to write and have dwelt upon a person whose company I have for some time past kept so exclusively that it must be strange if he has not become tiresome.

Under the necessity before stated, and during our separation, you will have temporarily [interlined] to select a place of abode where you will not be wounded by unkind allusions to myself, where you will have proper schools for the children and such social tone, moral and intellectual, as will best conduce to their culture. As well [smudged] for yourself as for them you should endeavor to find a healthy location. To you a cold climate has been most beneficial, such also will best serve to strengthen the constitution of the children; and though the mind may hold mastery over the body, yet a strong frame is a great advantage to a student, and still more to him who in the busy world is called upon to apply his knowledge. If the news gatherer has rightly concluded that the children were on their way to Canada, I suppose it must have been under some intermediate [interlined above an obliterated word] arrangement. You will sufficiently understand the necessity for your presence with them and you must not [squeezed in at end of line] allow your affectionate solicitude for me to interfere with your care for them.

It has been reported in the news papers that you had applied for permission to visit me in my confinement; if you had been allowed to do so the visit would have caused you disappointment at the time, and bitter memories afterwards. You would not have been allowed to hold private conversation with me and if we are permitted to correspond freely in relation to personal matters, not connected with public affairs, it will be a great consolation, and with it I recommend you to be content.

Your stay in Savannah has been prolonged much beyond my expectation and I fear beyond your comfort. I do not know whether you are still there, but hope your whereabouts may be known at Washington and will ask that this letter may there receive the proper address.

Have the articles belonging to *you personally* and which were seized at the time of our capture been restored? You are aware that I have had no opportunity to present the case, and therefore you have had the unusual task of attending to it yourself. Money derived from the sale of your jewelry and the horses presented to you by Gentlemen of Richmond could hardly be put on the same footing with my private property, and as little could they be regarded as public property, the proper subject of capture in war. The Heads of Executive Departments accustomed to consider questions of law and of fact, would I supposed take a different view of the transaction from subaltern officers of the Army— — —.[38]

You will realize the necessity of extreme caution in regard to our correspondence. The quid nuncs if they hear you have received a letter from me will no doubt seek to extract something for their pursuit, and your experience has taught you how little material serves to spin their web. Have you been sick? On the 21st of July little Maggie appeared to me in a most vivid dream, warning me not to wake you etc. etc. You know how little I have been accustomed to regard like [written over erasure] things. Here such visions have been frequent, nor have they always been without comfort.

I am reluctant to close this first letter to you after so long an interval; but am worried that I may be abusing a privilege, as what I write is to be read by those to whom the labor will not be relieved by the interest which will support you.

If my dear Margaret is with you give to her my tenderest love, she always appears to me associated with little Winnie. Kiss the Baby for me, may her sunny face never be clouded, though dark the morning her life has been.

My dear Wife, equally the centre of my love and confidence, remember how good the Lord has always been to me, how often he has wonderfully preserved me, and put thy trust in Him.

Farewell, may He who tempers the wind to the shorn lamb, whose most glorious attribute is mercy, guide and protect and provide for my distressed family; and give to them and to me that grace which shall lead us all to final rest in the mansions where there is peace that passeth understanding.[39]

Once more farewell, Ever affectionately

your Husband
Jeffn. Davis

"His mind dominated his body in so great a degree," says Varina, "that he was able to endure nearly what he pleased." Nothing could embody that fact better than this letter. On the day he wrote it, Dr. Craven reported to General Miles that he was "suffering severely from erysipelas in the face and head, accompanied by the usual prostration attending that disease . . . his condition denoting a low state of the vital forces." In a high fever, with the "cloud of erysipelas covering his whole face and throat," a carbuncle on his left thigh "much inflamed," and his spirits "exceedingly dejected . . . by anxiety for his wife and children," he produced this ten-page composition of perfect composure, deliberate in style and elevated in tone. Only the loose handwriting, the many strikeovers, erasures, and afterthoughts, show his illness. Craven was finding in him "all the evidence of an iron will." It had probably kept the past three months from shattering him completely. He said nothing to Varina here about his suffering, had said nothing to his captors when "put upon the tug-boat with a high fever upon him."[40]

As the two "State prisoners" had stepped off the tugboat from the *Clyde* onto Engineer's Wharf that May 22, 1865, General Miles, with a hold on Davis's arm and Colonel Pritchard, in charge of Clay, had escorted them through "files of men in blue." "Arriving at the casemate which had been fitted up into cells for their incarceration, Mr. Davis was shown into casemate No. 2 and Clay into No. 4, guards of soldiers being stationed in the cells numbered 1, 3, and 5, upon each side of them." There were guardrooms with locked doors between cell and fort proper. In each were two sentries and an officer "whose duty is to see his prisoners every fifteen minutes." Also, inside each small cell paced two sentinels with loaded muskets. On a shelf above Davis's iron cot, reported Charles Dana, "a lamp is constantly kept burning." The iron-barred window of the stone room was just above a moat eight feet deep and one hundred twenty-five feet wide with perpendicular sides. While Davis was there, two soldiers fell in and drowned. Across the moat "on the counterscarp" was "a strong line of sentries," another "on the parapet overhead," while a third was in the road, to prevent "all access to the vicinity of the casemates."[41]

On May 24, Dr. Craven was called to attend Davis. He found him "a mere fascine of raw and tremulous nerves—his eyes restless and fevered, his head continually shifting from side to side for a cool spot on the pillow . . . extremely despondent, his pulse full and at ninety . . . his head troubled with a long-established neuralgic disorder." Already, the day before, the day after his arrival, he had borne what Dr. Craven called "a trial severer, probably, than has ever in modern times been inflicted on any one who had enjoyed such eminence."[42]

Toward sundown on May 23, Capt. Jerome Titlow entered the cell with two blacksmiths and a pair of leg irons. Dana, an assistant secretary of war, had brought Miles an order from Stanton to "place manacles and fetters" on Davis and Clay whenever he thought it "advisable." Although General Halleck, the area commander, "seemed opposed to it," Miles ordered Titlow to iron Davis. What happened next is unclear in details but perfectly clear in bare fact. "Yesterday I directed that irons be put on Davis' ankles, which he violently resisted, but became more quiet afterward," Miles reported to Dana. Davis said the account by Craven (who was not there) "could not have been written by anyone who either knew the facts," or had "a just idea of what his conduct would be under such circumstances."[43]

Captain Titlow's own account, despite some errors, is probably the most reliable. He found the prisoner sitting on his cot, "reading his Episcopal Prayer Book [Bible: prayer book not yet allowed]." He announced that he had "an unpleasant duty." Davis, seeing the irons, argued that fetters could not be required for his security and asked to see Miles or to telegraph President Johnson. Titlow: "My duty is to execute this order and it is folly for you to resist." Davis: "I shall never submit to such an indignity. . . . Let your men shoot me at once." Then, says Varina's account, "He faced round with his back to the wall and stood silently waiting." Titlow goes on:

> [His] quiet manner led me to think he would not resist. I then said, "Smith, do your work." As the blacksmith stooped to place the clasp of the shackle round his ankle Davis struck him a violent blow that threw him on the floor. He recovered and at once made for Davis with his vice and hammer and would have struck him if I had not caught his arm. . . . A moment after that I saw Davis and one of the sentinels struggling, both having hold of the musket . . . The next instant the sentinel had wrenched the musket from Mr. Davis's hands. I then ordered the soldier to his post and reprimanded him for leaving. I now saw there would be trouble, so I ordered the officer of the guard to go out and get four of the best men. . . . As the men advanced Davis struck the . . . foremost man, but all four instantly closed on him and shoved him on the cot. Davis showed unnatural strength; it was all the four men could do to hold him while the blacksmith riveted the clasp round his ankle. . . . The other clasp was locked on with a brass lock, the same as is used on freight-cars.[44]

The blacksmith wrote: "I forged the irons and put them on Mr Davis I reveted them on his angles not boot. Yes he resested: we laied him on cot while puting them on he saied he would as soon be shot." Varina adds a detail that only Jeff could have told her: "He could not see the blacksmiths . . . but feeling one he kicked him off from him." Then, Titlow says, "Davis lay perfectly motionless. Just as I was going out Davis raised from his cot and threw his feet to the floor, and with the clanging of the chains he gave way. I will say here that it was anything but a pleasant sight to see a man like Jefferson Davis shedding tears, but not one word had he to say."[45]

Not one word had he to say then, not even to Varina, and not many in the years ahead. As in the Georgia woods, he had braved death and found instead, humiliation. He perhaps remembered Black Hawk's phrase for his ball and chain: "extremely mortifying." If, as a newspaper said, the iron entered his soul, it was transmuted by what it found there. Others said he was chained so "the iron might enter into the soul of his people"—that he "was vicariously suffering indignities" for the South. Two hours later, Davis was in command of himself. Captain Titlow came in, saying, "You can't rest well that way." He offered to unlock the fetters to allow him to undress, "if you will give me your word of honour that you will give no more trouble." Davis replied, "'Captain, I assure you there will be no more trouble. I was very much exasperated . . . never expected to be subjected to such an indignity.' I then unlocked the shackle, he taking off his clothing and locking it again himself." Davis evidently approved Titlow's conduct; for Varina told the officer in 1891 of the "kind regard, which my husband always cherished to the end of his life for you."[46]

The most Davis would say about the shackling, sixteen years later, was this:

> Bitter tears have been shed by the gentle, and stern reproaches have been made by the magnanimous, on account of the needless torture to which I was subjected, and the heavy fetters rivetted upon me, while in a stone casemate and surrounded by a strong guard; but all these were less excruciating than the mental agony my captors were able to inflict. It was long before I was permitted to hear from my wife and children, and this, and things like this, was the power which education added to savage cruelty."[47]

Craven not only failed to answer Varina's letters, he did not even tell Davis he had received them. Davis wrote on September 15 about "the painful solicitude I have felt and feel concerning you and our children." He thought of them "by day and by night" but was "ignorant of all which has occurred to you since we were so suddenly separated." He spoke later of "the torturing anxiety with which day after day I prayed to know what was passing with you." Dr. Craven spoke of this suffering, but he did not relieve it by a word about the letters. He did, however, try to reassure his patient in a general way and to engage him in conversation: "whatever could give his mind a moment's repose was in line of his cure."[48]

These talks proved so fascinating to the officers of the day, who had to go with Craven into the cell, that they began to join in. Everyone, says Craven, was struck by Davis's "wonderful" memory and "apparent universality of knowledge." At first, officers, even Craven, were ordered not to shake hands or offer any other courtesy to Davis, and "the brutality" rankled. Some of them told Clay that Davis was "petulant, irascible, and offensive in manner . . . [though] able, learned, high-toned, and imposing." By September, Davis had seen "a steady growth of that kindness on the part of the officers which my position rendered it proper for them to show: and so much depends upon the manner with which an unpleasant thing is done" that this had brought "material relief." Davis rejected Craven's statement that he was "most kindly and considerately treated by officers and men" but not that he enjoyed the conversations. One officer loaned him a novel to read; one was amazed by his knowledge of dogs; one became so obliging that the prisoner warned, "Don't overstep your orders, Mr. Day; don't overstep your orders."[49]

When Dr. Craven recommended exercise to Davis as "the best medicine," he experienced the "first thrill of sympathy for my patient." Davis uncovered his ankles, saying, "I cannot even stand erect. These shackles are very heavy." They had "abraded broad patches of skin." He could take only the feeblest exercise "with great pain, while they were on," unless perhaps Craven could pad them.

Dr. Craven said it was his complaint and threat to resign that got action, that Miles wanted fame for "having [Davis] crucified." But it was equally the work of forces far beyond the prison walls. Even the

Republican leader, Thurlow Weed, wrote Stanton: "I could not believe the accounts of Ironing Davis. . . . If true, it is a great error. . . . The fact—if fact it be—is even less revolting than the details. The World is with us. But this wholly unnecessary severity with a *State* Prisoner will lose us a great advantage." Varina says the Union general in Savannah assured her that such a deed "could not have been perpetrated." The public outcry was so great that Stanton ordered Miles on May 28 to remove the irons.[50]

Even with the fetters gone, Davis could only pace his small cell. It was two months before he was allowed outside it. Other severities that Varina had heard of were all too true. His "soldiers' rations" were passed through the bars in a "revolting" manner, the bread shredded through a soldier's hands "to see that it contained no 'deadly weapons.'" Coffee came "in the same cup, unwashed, in which his soup had been served the day before." He "decided to eat no more than would barely sustain life." Craven knew the diet of heavy bread and beef was unsuitable and got permission to supply the sick man from his own kitchen. Craven's wife and daughter Anna took charge, beginning with tea and toast. "Like the good Samaritan," Davis told Varina, "they gave me relief and proved that I had not passed the limit of humanity." Without the "benevolence" of "the Dr. and the Ladies . . . my captivity would soon have ended in death." He thought "their own good hearts have caused them to reject the base slanders and false accusations made against me."[51]

One of the things they sent him was a spoon, for which he learned many new uses, saying it was, for example, "the best peach-peeler ever invented." He was denied other utensils, said the newspapers, "lest he should commit suicide." "A needless precaution," said Craven, and Davis commented, "not so accounted for to me or by me; if he knew of such a pretext, I did not." He labeled "false" the imputation that he had seized the guard's musket with suicide in mind; his resistance was "from a sense of right & duty; though desperately, it was calmly quietly made." Where Craven's book has him saying that if the government took his life, it "would be the greatest boon they could confer," he objects: "somebody's idea no doubt but not mine."[52]

From every tray, guards stole the spoons as souvenirs. When he retained one in the cell, they stole the napkins. Davis said he was "like him of old who fell amongst a certain class of people [delicately avoiding the biblical word *thieves*] and was succored by the good Samaritan." One night, while chained, he found himself grabbing the hand of a guard who was trying to take from around his neck the cross-medal of St. Benedict, given to him for protection of soul and body when "much exposed on the battlefields about Richmond and Petersburg." Varina, who had "persuaded him to wear [it]," says he called the officer, and he "punished the man, I *suppose*."[53] Another guard had spotted this medal and said, "I want that." Davis had replied, "Come and take it."

And that was the end of that.[54] His briarwood pipe was stolen. Afraid his meerschaum would go the same way, he gave it to Craven. At least he had the use of his tobacco—both pipe and chewing—from his valise.[55]

It proved otherwise with clothes. General Miles had custody of his valise and small trunk. When Davis arrived, he was stripped of his clothing (and pocket contents) and given another suit. He had had no change of outer garments since (neither had Clay, even later). This was bad enough, given Davis's military neatness (he had carried his clothesbrush with him in the woods of Georgia), but one day Craven found him "out of sorts, very ill-tempered," because Miles, who "seemed to think a change of linen twice a week enough," had not sent even that much underwear. If the object in "doling out his clothes, as though he were a convict in some penitentiary . . . were to degrade him, it must fail. None could be degraded by unmerited insult heaped on helplessness but the perpetrators."[56]

Such attempts to degrade were many. Clay, who shared them all, except the chains, described one: "I have never been allowed retirement from sight, actual or potential, of my guards; having to bathe and do all the acts of nature in view of the guard, if they chose to look at me." For highly private souls like Clay and Davis, it was torture enough never "to have one moment to myself," as Davis put it. The gaze of the men in the guardroom and the "unceasing tread," coughing, and audible breathing of the guards in the cell had rendered Davis's nights "very tedious and haggard." As one guard deliberately squeaked his boots going by, Davis got up from his cot to pace the floor, "mad as a caged lion," the guard wrote. They had already had words, though it was forbidden. As they passed each other, Davis suddenly grabbed him by the throat in a grip so tight that he could not use his musket, or breathe. When the officer of the guard rattled his sword on the iron bars, "then old Jeff let loose of me and went back to his bed. I tell you I was weak in the knees . . . He was a spunky old cuss."[57]

Miles finally ordered the cell guards to stand at ease, but still there was no relief from noise. The guardroom unit changed every two hours, with stomping, the sound of rifle butts and swords trailing on the stone floor, the clang of iron doors, and, what irked Davis most, "loud calling of the numbers of relief sentinels." The arched roof of the casemate made it "a whispering gallery in which all sounds were jumbled and repeated," Davis said to Craven. "The torment of his head was so dreadful, he feared he must lose his mind. Already his memory, vision, and hearing, were impaired." "For, say three months," Davis told his wife, "two hours consecutive sleep were never allowed me." Clay spoke of "this frequent, periodical, and irregular disturbance of my sleep" as "one of the tortures of the Spanish Inquisition."[58]

Craven said that having guards in the cell "was counteracting every effort for quieting the nerves of the patient." Miles was willing to believe this about Clay, saying (ungrammatically): "*Unlike Davis* [italics mine], his confinement seems to affect his nervous system." In June, he removed Clay's cell guards and permitted him walks in the open air. "The case of Davis is different," said Miles with perhaps unconscious irony, "as I think him to be as strong as he was the day he entered the fort." It was not until late July that Davis got these measures of relief. But there was still the adjacent guardroom, and still on September 10, Clay was saying: "During the one hundred and twelve days of my imprisonment here I have never enjoyed one night's unbroken sleep."[59]

Dampness from the moat beneath and ten feet of earth on top made the stone cell, Clay noted, like a "living tomb." Davis and Craven discussed the effect on health, especially the production of "mephitic vapors" supposed to cause malaria. Also, "He had but the remains of one eye left, and the glaring, whitewashed walls were rapidly destroying this." Further damage was being done by the small type in his Bible and prayer book, which were "seldom out of his hand while alone." But for two months there was nothing else to read. The worst thing was the perpetual light from the lamp over his cot, frazzling nerves as well as sight. Even the blind eye was sensitive to light. Davis began to imagine that this was a torture devised by someone who knew that his habit had been "through life never to sleep except in total darkness." Miles got permission to remove the lamp, but he never did. He only allowed it to be screened at night.[60]

In October, Jeff wrote to Varina, "My sight is affected but less than I would have supposed," if told "that I was at short intervals to be aroused and the expanded pupils thus frequently subjected to the glare of a lamp." Finally, Varina thought to put her skillful needle to work. By February she had contrived a black broadcloth visor to cover his face down to the mouth and shut out "every ray of light." "I am so triumphant about my shades for your eyes. . . . Would God I could so cover your 'defenseless head.' "[61]

Knowing Varina's extravagantly emotional nature, Jeff was careful to point out how much better off he was than he might be, or else he concealed his suffering entirely, as in his first letter. She was never fooled, and she reacted as he feared she would—by making his sufferings her own:

> It was mistaken kindness in you to refrain from telling me how unwell you were. Do you not know that I could take my death warrant from your lips better than joyful tiding from another . . . I see in the papers accounts of every pang. Why not tell your poor helpless wife in your own sweet kind way the worst . . . I wake and weep, watch and pray to be granted strength to wait, to possess my soul in patience so that I may tarry the Lord's leisure and be strong—like Jacob I have struggled with the Lord, like him if

> I come out triumphant it will be withered, and changed by this great suffering—[62]

She told him later how in Savannah "I nearly lost my mind for some weeks . . . but, when you were better, so was I." Now the newspapers were upsetting her again, and she asked Miles on September 14 to "telegraph how Mr. Davis is": "Rumors . . . have caused me great suffering." Stanton's office furnished a reply.[63]

This made Jeff think Varina had not received his letter of August 21. He got permission to write again, and this time, in his careful, exact manner, he told her what she wanted to know. The carbuncle had been "slow and painful," the erysipelas began "in the nose," but "was arrested before ascending to the eye, it reappeared and was arrested as before. There was the great physical prostration usual in such cases, and some fears that the disease would extend to the brain," probably giving rise "to the report which has caused your alarm." "The Surgeon who attends me is both kind and skillful. I am deeply indebted to him and can assure you" that under his care, nothing "which is needful will be wanting." "Be not disturbed," he said in his next letter, "by the unwarranted statements of those newsgatherers who would earn their living by coining the tears of the afflicted."[64]

Jeff did not mention the dejection of spirits that went with this serious infection—"despondent and dull," said Craven, "a very unnatural condition for him." Always, he tried to buoy her up:

> Endeavor to be cheerful and hopeful. Have confidence in my ability to resist both physical and mental burthens, under the supporting grace of our Heavenly Father, who sends His comfort to alleviate every affliction. Let us accept His dispensation as that which is best, though our blindness should not be able to perceive the good designed, and thus we can with patience and resignation meet whatever fate is decreed to us. . . . Farewell, my loved Wife, remember that you cannot diminish my griefs by sharing them and strive to preserve the tone both of your mind and body by cultivating cheerful views of all things and charitable feelings towards all men.[65]

Varina needed buoying. She told Mary Chesnut, "I bleed inwardly—and suffer more because not put in the surgeons' hands as one of the wounded—I never report unfit for duty. . . . What do I do all day long? I dream . . .'sweeter to rest together—dead—Far sweeter than to live asunder.'" About Jeff's first letter, she said to Mary Ann Cobb: "He writes in such a spirit of pious resignation and trust in God's faith with those who rest their dependence upon Him that he has comforted me greatly."[66]

Dr. Craven was coming to "a sincere personal sympathy and respect" for his patient. He had pulled him through the malarial attack he was suffering when he came, exacerbated as it was by the ironing and the surroundings. He had tried to relieve numbness and "nervous debility" by prescribing "friction" and "the stimulants so urgently needed by his condition." "In docility and strict adherence to whatever regimen was prescribed, Mr. Davis was the model patient of my practice . . . and obeyed every direction, however irksome, disagreeable, or painful, with military exactness."[67]

There was usually "no pointed disease, but general prostration." Chronic fatigue from four years of stress and weeks on the road evading pursuit had caught up with him. Close imprisonment itself was wearing down a man used to daily walks and long horseback rides. It was "solitary confinement," a punishment regarded then as too severe even for "the greatest criminal." But that is what the North held him to be: "The Great Criminal." Not one person from the outside world had been allowed to visit him yet, not his minister, not a lawyer. Hostile eyes were fixed on him every minute. (It was rumored that Miles let a chosen few, like Stanton, peep at him through the bars.) The prisoner remained "very feeble."[68]

After two months, Craven finally procured for him reading matter and exercise. Davis was furnished an enemy paper, the *New York Times*, and books from the post library. Soon he was rereading George Bancroft's *History of the United States*, marking it with his fingernail, "as a pencil was denied him,"[69] and making "comparative reflections" on the biographical "sketches" in "Allison & McCauley & Clarendon."[70]

Exercise was to be an hour's walk daily on the ramparts above the casemates. It was dependent on General Miles's leisure, since he had to accompany Davis with an armed escort. Miles never failed to say "something so offensive and irritating as to render the exercise a painful effort." Craven recalled one day when the "wasted invalid . . . suddenly forgetting his bonds" was "ablaze with eloquent anger": Miles had charged John C. Calhoun with dishonesty. Davis was so weak that the first walk had to be cut short, but "breathing air not drawn through iron bars was a glorious blessing."[71]

One day on the ramparts he passed Clement Clay, under similar guard. He thought Clay looked as if he were "suffering severely," and asked Craven about him. This prompted the doctor to note that "sickness, as a general rule, is sadly selfish," but that Davis was "an exception"—"despite a certain exterior cynicism of manner, no patient has ever crossed my path, who, suffering so much himself, appeared to feel so warmly and tenderly for others." In fact, Davis told Varina, "When Mr. Clay was quite sick I earnestly desired to be with him," probably thinking of the time Clay had cared for him in illness. He spoke of this again later, noting Clay was said "at such times to become sadly dejected." They were not allowed to converse, but Clay managed to send his love to Varina and the children. Twice Davis slipped him messages on minute scraps of paper. One read: "If you get this, say I've got the tobacco and will give you a puff."[72]

Davis found Clay "much changed. Hair and beard quite grey." Clay had begun a letter "in contemplation of death," which Miles was to give his wife in that event, but "my nerves were so shattered by loss of sleep that I could scarcely write." This deprivation had destroyed by September "reasonable hope of living," as he described the "ingenious and refined torture" to Virginia, expecting to smuggle the letter out. But the very next day his guardroom was cleared of men, and he slept for six whole hours without waking.[73]

The guardroom of the ex-president was never cleared. The noise, the "stone coffin" cell, where crumbs he put out for a mouse molded, the forced insomnia and aching eyes, made him say at one point that he must "go crazy or blind or both." Just having "a human eye riveted on you in every moment" was "a maddening, incessant torture." Craven (or Halpine) has him say that it was beginning "to prey on my reason," but the precise Davis corrected this to "mind—memory—thought." In this highly nervous state, of course the prisoner had no appetite. Having begun with not much flesh to lose, he had lost all he could "while still preserving life." Craven reported to Miles: "He is evidently breaking down," and urged his removal to better quarters. He did not want the celebrated prisoner to die on his hands: "the world would form unjust conclusions" and "pass them into history."[74]

Davis did not want to die, either. He wanted a trial, to exonerate himself and the Cause. The "odious, malignant and absurd insinuation" that he was behind Lincoln's assassination was always on his mind. He heard now of another accusation: treason. He knew both were false and thought he could prove it. He asked to see counsel. But his confinement was military; he could see no one. He repeatedly spoke to Craven about having to defend himself, but he said if it was trial in a military court, he would not bother: the predetermined verdict would make it simply "foregone murder." Charles O'Conor, a New York lawyer who offered to defend him, agreed: it was disguised "assassination."[75]

These were the days when Gen. David Hunter—burner of the Valley of Virginia—presided over the "military commission" trying the accomplices of John Wilkes Booth for the murder of Lincoln. Lincoln had appointed Joseph Holt as judge advocate general specifically to develop this type tribunal, which could try civilians without being hampered by legal niceties like habeas corpus. Seizure of papers from the wives was probably an attempt to implicate Davis and Clay. Burton Harrison's incarceration certainly was. Holt spoke of his "revolting guilt"—"an assassin at heart." In solitary confinement worse than that at Fortress Monroe, he was kept in the Washington Arsenal where the trial was, while the commission tried to snare him into some damaging admission about Davis. It was useless, however, as he had nothing to reveal.

Finally, after his own duel with insanity (cramped in total darkness, with an eye "perpetually looking" at him), he was transferred to Fort Delaware, still in solitary. Frank Lubbock and Preston Johnston were there, both in the same fix. They never even saw one another. Four Booth acquaintances were hanged on July 7. "President Johnson is very quick on the trigger," remarked Davis.[76]

Charles O'Conor, who had known Davis in Washington, was the first and most eminent counsel to volunteer his services, but he was not the only one. Another New York lawyer offered, and the Mississippi bar sent word to Davis that a committee of three stood ready to defend him. It was Varina, however, who lit the fires, in her outspoken, not to say brash, challenge to the honor of Northern men. "Let me implore you to cry aloud for justice for him," she wrote Horace Greeley, "if the means used to slay him do not succeed before [his trial]."[77]

This struck a spark from the humanitarian Greeley, especially as he "could not believe the charge" of complicity in Lincoln's assassination. He took Varina's letter to the New York attorney George Shea, who then consulted leading Republicans, Henry Wilson, John A. Andrew, Thaddeus Stevens, and Geritt Smith among them. They all agreed "that Mr. Davis did not by thought or act participate in a conspiracy against Mr. Lincoln." But there were other charges in the wind, and Shea did not want to undertake Davis's defense without being sure of his ground. Varina told him that "living in closest friendship with Mr. Davis," she knew "a great deal" about "his official conduct" and where she had no personal knowledge, could tell him where to look.[78]

One of the places was Canada. Confederate documents were secreted there, possibly sent by Varina with her mother, as she later sent the president's letter books in the false bottom of her sister's trunk. Shea went to Montreal with J. R. Davis, saw John C. Breckinridge and "the official archives," and came back convinced that he might confidently defend Jefferson Davis against all charges.[79]

Judge Adv. Gen. Joseph Holt thought otherwise. Virginia Clay was leaning on this old friend, as on a rotten reed. Holt never answered her appealing May letter, and with good reason. He was the one who had goaded President Johnson into issuing his fatal Proclamation, frenetically insisting that he had proof of the guilt of Davis and Clay, although he had no written evidence. The same testimony that hanged the conspirators incriminated Davis and Clay, and Holt's chief prosecutor, John A. Bingham, told the military commission, "Jefferson Davis is as clearly proven guilty of this conspiracy as is John Wilkes Booth." Clay told Virginia that he had committed no crime, as "God bears me witness," and but for the accusation, would be paroled: "I am made to suffer to save them from the reproach of injustice." Joseph Holt's malice kept this charge hanging over the heads of both prisoners. He refused Malie Brodhead's request to see her Uncle Jeff because of "the number and atrocity of the crimes alleged" against him "and the overwhelming proof of his guilt believed to exist." As Davis said, they were held "under all the rigors of a condemned convict . . . revolting to the spirit of justice" that held men innocent until tried.[80]

On October 2, Davis's jailers, finally admitting "grave fears that his health would give way," transferred him to a drier cell on the second floor of Carroll Hall, an officers' barracks. "The world does move, after all," said he. For a while, the change helped. There was a coal fireplace and a rough screen to hide the commode and wash basin; the cell was loftier, airier; it was wood instead of stone. But wood reverberates. Davis soon realized that he was more nervous than before. The light still burned, the guards made their commotion every two hours, and eyes were fixed on him from three places instead of one—the bars of the guardroom door, the glass panel of another door, and a window on the gallery. He was in "a morbid condition" now, and it took much less to keep him awake. "I have endeavoured to overcome the distraction and annoyance this constant passing causes in the day, and to resist its disturbing effect at night; the success has not, however, been commensurate with the effort."[81]

Davis later wrote, "The tramp of sentinels on three sides of the room was a far greater infliction than their eyes, and Dr. C. was so well aware of this that he *offered* matting to deaden the sound, and criticised the failure to accept his offer." The colonel who inspected the cell September 29 said that matting would be laid, but it was not put down until five and a half months later. By that time, Davis was in such "a state of high nervous excitability" that it did little good.[82]

So there was no real amelioration. Iron will or not, the prisoner's appetite and general health steadily declined. After five months, he was still weak, nervous, insomniac, and "wasting away," and after nine, "not improving." He felt the continual perturbation of thought was impairing his ability to defend himself in the trial he kept hoping for. At times he thought his enemies were trying to get rid of him, so as not to hold a trial at all.[83]

The future looked only dark. Cut off from everyone, alone in the midst of enemies, he trained his sight another way. What he found there enabled him to endure without despair a year of torment in the Carroll Hall cell.

XVIII

An Unseen Hand

On November 3, 1865, Jefferson Davis wrote to Varina: "Jno. Mitchel has been released. He was permitted to take leave of me, through the grates, and offered to write to you." John Mitchel was the only other prisoner at Fortress Monroe besides Davis and Clay. He had come to say goodbye. This journalist, styled by Varina "the Irish patriot," who had escaped British imprisonment, had brought three sons to the Confederate army, two of whom were killed. He had worked for Richmond newspapers before going to the *Daily News* in New York, where he was arrested for no stated reason on June 6. He was just as arbitrarily freed on October 30.[1]

Mitchel did write to Varina, putting the best face on things. "When I bade [Davis] good bye he was in morning *deshabille,* and looked haggard, but I assure you when he dresses to go out he looks as well, steps as firmly and holds his head as high as ever he did on Capitol Square." After Davis was given "a good dry room," Mitchel could see the improvement in health "as we met in our walks." (He and Clay had also been moved to Carroll Hall.) He felt sure that Varina would soon welcome her husband home, "not much worn in body, and not one whit bowed down in spirit." "But for the present a magnanimous public requires to be feasted with daily bulletins describing his suffering and humiliation."[2]

Dr. Craven told Mitchel that Davis's "health is at present pretty good." But Jeff was writing to Varina, "I have not been out to walk lately, on account of a series of boils or a carbuncle with a succession of points which rose in my right arm pit and which has prevented me from putting on my coat since the day I last wrote to you [October 20] until a few days back."[3]

Of course he could not go out without his coat—meaning suit coat, for he had no topcoat—not because it was cold, but because he could not leave the room unless properly attired. Decorum was a means of self-respect under conditions of extreme indignity. One day, precious as the hour away from his cell was, he turned around and went back in, because he saw a crowd of ladies craning to see the famous political prisoner on display, "as though he were the caged monster of some travelling menagerie." Fresh air and exercise at this price "he could not consent to purchase." It was humiliating enough to walk with Miles under the bayonets of a guard. (Steps were later built from gallery to ramparts, to avoid the sightseers.)[4]

Davis gave a key to his prison demeanor, on the natural level, when he said:

> I am not of Cato's creed, and do not hold that it is man's wisdom to equal the swallow, but man's dignity [written very large over an erasure] to bear up under trials, under which the lower animals would sink. Resolution of will may not, according to Father Timon, prolong indefinitely our earthly existence, but will do much to sustain the tottering machine beyond the observer's calculation.

Self-preservation was a duty owed to his manhood, and not to that alone. When Varina urged him, "Keep up your strength . . . eat and sleep if you can for your wife and children, who so love you, so reverence and admire you," he replied: "All the motives you enumerate are ever before me, and others of which you are less apt to think, furnish the strongest inducement to desire life and strength to vindicate my conduct; at least to posterity and for my family. Be hopeful, trust in the 'faithful Promiser.'" In the Cato letter he said, "I look forward to the day when I shall see my Winnie again, and again with our beloved little ones live the life of which the world knew not, and which was more than all beside, to me."[5]

He assured her: "To all the trials mental and physical to which I am subjected I will oppose all the moral power I possess that my life may be prolonged . . . and my power to meet any future ordeal be as great as possible." The ordeal expected was his day in court, yet he wrote to Varina on November 22, "It is six months since we parted and I know no more of the purpose in regard to me than I did then. Measured by painful anxiety for you and your helpless charge those months are to me many, many years."[6]

His army life had given him his basis for survival—the self-discipline learned there and maintained through all the years since. He used to tell Varina about the exhausting dragoon marches with nothing to eat but cold flour. "When speaking of these hardships," Varina recalls, "he took occasion to impress upon me the necessity of requiring our children to eat whatever was set before them without attaching importance to it." But he would not allow things on his table that grownups could eat but they could not: "If it is impossible for adults to deny themselves . . . it is unreasonable to expect children" to do so. A colleague in Pierce's cabinet remembered Davis as "exceeding temperate both in eating and drinking." On fast days in the Confederacy he ate nothing at all and stayed in seclusion. According to Winnie, "Generally he said, 'Take no thought of what ye shall eat. There are so many higher joys than eating.'" His phrase from the Sermon on the Mount indicates that more than abstract willpower was involved. For gluttony, the sin opposed to temperance, "he entertained no mercy"; it was in his eyes "a disgrace."[7]

Under the almost unbearable constraint of solitary confinement, Davis, instead of seeking relaxation, laid upon himself further strictures, physical and emotional. Self-denial was his interior defense against collapse. He was hardly able to digest enough to live, but when Varina proposed sending delicacies, he did not want them: "remember that care for food or for raiment was never one of my sins." When she told him not to eat pork, in alarm over "this shocking German disease Trichinia [trichinosis]," he replied: "Your caution against *pork meat* is one easily observed, as I have so little disposition to eat meat of any kind that but for the adverse opinion of the Doctor I should at least during Lent have continued to abstain entirely." He never ate more than two meals a day. "Breakfast . . . about nine; dinner about four; and tea [supper] would be sent if I desired it." He did not desire it, for a very special reason, which will soon appear.[8]

"Our kind neighbors sent me . . . a bunch of cigars and a bottle of brandy. A reminder of the big glass of julep," Davis wrote, and Varina later mentioned getting the same for him. But when Craven prescribed the stimulant, he "always had much trouble to persuade him" to take it. Varina had once admonished him, "Don't get into the way of smoking too much as you do when troubled," and evidently she did so again. He was always troubled now but answered her: "As [the cigars] have been smoked your caution came too late. I took them in small doses and no injury, but some good was the result." He was well supplied. Someone had sent him "a thousand cigars," and another man who knew "the depressing weariness of incarceration" sent, with his prayers, a large box of tobacco to "help while away the weary hours." But where Craven has Davis say he "hoped to become tranquil" through smoking his pipe, Davis wrote in the margin, "bah!"[9]

Physical discipline was bedrock on which to raise a higher rampart, the one against feelings: "natural affections and excitements are only safe to those who are not unnaturally restrained." Refusing to indulge them kept him from the self-pity that made Aleck Stephens sometimes dissolve in tears, though his imprisonment had been far more lenient, and he was by now released (as was Reagan). Davis thought "complaint diminishes capacity to bear." He wrote to Varina:

> It is true that I did not wish you to know entirely the rigors of my imprisonment and regret that you should have learned them; it is true that my strength has greatly failed me, and the loss of sleep has created a morbid excitability; but an unseen hand has sustained me and a peace which the world could not give and has not been able to destroy, will I trust uphold me to meet with resignation whatever may befal me.

Not his iron will, but a heroic faith was to save him. All his prison letters show it.[10]

The sharpest assault on feeling came with the thought of Varina and the children: "It requires all the self control of which I am possessed to think calmly of my separation from you and them. In vain would I summon the conviction that our sufferings are blessings in disguise if my pen were allowed freely to run on the subject of which my heart and mind are most full." Varina asked for little Joe's dates, to send to friends wishing to place a headstone at his grave in Richmond: "I cannot even remember the age of Pie—without prompting. My dear, have we not been sorely afflicted? But with you I could bear anything—when I could 'see thy fond and fearless smile hope revived again.'" Jeff replied, "1859 & 1864 must be the years," and suggested the family Bible. Searching his mind for the precise time, he faltered. It "was Saturday preceding the meeting of Congress—Pardon me I cannot"—then three little x's and a strange star above the line, corresponding to nothing. "The saddest effect" of the "broken sleep" and the maddening daytime distraction of passing sentinels was "impaired memory," but "I have not sunk under my trials, am better than a fortnight ago and trust shall be sustained under any affliction which it may required of me to bear." He even called "the restraint" of censorship "perhaps fortunate"—"one of the pressures upon feelings which it is necessary for me to control by every means within my power." He did not dare "express my feelings towards you and the children as was my habit."

> There is in all my trials one from which I shrink. . . . There is an unseen hand which upholds me save when my thoughts are concentrated on those objects of my dearest love and greatest solicitude. Perhaps He will give me that strength hereafter.[11]

Maggie nearly broke through the barriers. "Little Polly's voice pronouncing Father, is still in my ear, unchanged, and so it will remain until I hear her in an altered voice, or cease to hear. But of my feelings it is not my purpose to write." Thoughts he could pull up short, but he found himself invaded where he had no control.

> In the broken sleep which I get, you and the children frequently visit me. . . . Little Polly comes oftenest . . . but I will not trust myself to write as I feel about her. May the Lord guide and protect

> you all, and so lead us by His grace that however separated now we may be united in Him and as His own at last be gathered into the same bundle, when He shall divide the tares from the wheat.[12]

> To use your expressive phrase I am hungry for the children's little faces and have habitually to resist the power of that and other tender feelings which may not be gratified. I strive to suppress those memories which would give these bonds additional power to inflict pain, and to look only to those hopes of which man cannot deprive me. . . . Feeling the necessity for this suppression of longing affection and for the constant interposition of judgement to control it, makes me afraid to dream, and I have found two preventives generally effectual—first, to take no tea, that is no food in the evening—second, to sit up very late and read the dullest book in my possession. But as long as your dreams continue to be pleasant, I do not warn you off of that fairy land.[13]

Even awake, he was in danger:

> On the night of the thirtieth [of January 1866] I was sitting before the fire because I could not sleep and had a startling optical illusion, such you know as were common in fever; but to my vision, I saw little Pollie walk across the floor and kneel down between me and the fire in the attitude of prayer, I moved from consequent excitement and the sweet vision melted away. I have not called it a dream because not conscious of being asleep, but sleep has many stages, and that only is perfect sleep which we call Death.[14]

"The dullest book" was part of the discipline: "Would like to read the same books with you," he wrote Varina, "but under present circumstances this would be difficult and objectionable. Difficult because I have little field for selection and objectionable because entertaining books, poetry and romance would excite, whereas my effort is to keep sentiment subdued and to live in the region of driest fact." Being limited by the post library was a help. He read in the first year, besides historical works already noted, Irving's *Washington* ("better even than I used to think"), Alison's *Marlborough* ("graphic and interesting," compares it to Macaulay's), Humboldt's *Cosmos*, and a work on military tactics.[15]

He would read novels (called romances), however, when supplied, like the two handed him by Federal officers, *The Gayworthys* and *The Diary of Kitty Trevyllian*—evidently the latest thing. Varina sent one called *The Quadrilateral.* Davis criticized its attempt to show "the inconsistencies of human nature," which "Sir Walter Scott alone has succeeded in doing"; besides, "We have as much in real life as anyone can need." "The horse is the best character in the book. . . . Do you recollect 'old Duke' the horse I rode in the Pawnee campaign? He might have stood for the portrait, except that even in extreme age he was not gentle."[16]

One contemporary novel, recommended by Varina and sent him by a friend, masqueraded as history. It was entitled *Chronicles of the Shönberg-Cotta Family by Two of Themselves.* There was no author on the title page. The reader plunged directly into sixteenth-century diaries that revealed little by little startling contrasts between the Catholicism of the day and the liberating ideas of a family friend, Martin Luther. Jeff soon realized that, as in *The Gayworthys,* "the characters are only what in pharmacy is called a carrier, and . . . the purpose is . . . to present religious opinions." As he started it, he said, "My eyes cause me to read at intervals," otherwise, he would have been "tempted to read through it without intermission."

The theological debate in the dialogue, especially on the workings of God's providential will in human life, was of "thrilling interest." Perhaps he saw himself in Luther, grieving over his dead child and pursued with a price on his head, or in Fritz, languishing in prison. But in the end, the overdrawn picture—a faultless Luther, convents called graveyards, the cry "I am no more a monk. I am a Christian"—palled. He told Varina he was "much pleased with the book," but he could not help feeling "that the object with which it was written created severity it seemed to me injustice towards the Priests and Nuns. If they had been so bad, their training could hardly have produced the high characters presented, the heroes and heroines of the reformation. Those I knew from close association appeared to me very good."[17]

That happy association made him sure that his precious Pollie was now in the right place. Varina had sent the children to Canada because of "an offer" of convent schooling. "I chose the Convent of the Sacred Heart near Montreal," she told Jeff, "because in convents purity is enjoined as a duty even in the idlest conversations between children, and the necessity of confession keeps them true, and then means were not needed to put her there. The Catholics, God bless them, have been everything to me." Jeff reassured her, "My own experience does not lead me to expect that proselytism will be attempted on a child of Protestant parents."[18]

Jeff Jr. was in an Anglican school, Ma wrote, "the Queens endowed college" near Lennoxville. The archbishop of Halifax, who favored Confederates, later offered to educate both children. Varina wrote to Jeff, "God has been very good to us. The Catholic clergy have been so good to me I love the sight of one." He replied: "I am deeply impressed by the kindness of the Bishop, and that of the Priests who have so nobly shown their readiness to do their Master's work in relieving the afflicted, and protecting the fatherless. They have sent thus, the sweetest solace to one, in the condition of him who went down from Jerusalem to Jericho. Yes, I feel with you, that God has been very good to us." He told Varina she was right to insist that Maggie and Jeff "strictly conform" to the discipline in the schools, which "so well accords with our own views": "Fortitude and self abnegation so essential to success and happiness are seldom possessed by those who were indulged in childhood."[19]

All these things moved him to a discourse on religion that reveals why he chose the Anglican over the Roman church.

> Living souls devoutly offering praise to God present spirituality supreme over matter; and it is perhaps therefore, that the simple singing of an excited congregation of "Methodists," has stirred in my heart a deeper devotional feeling than the noble ceremonial of the High Mass. . . . All modes of Christian worship are in themselves good, they are the different kind of roads suited to the great variety of travellers, and why not to the different mood of the same traveller, if by such diversion he may the more certainly reach the end of his journey. I do not mean such separation as would lose the right of communion with the church chosen. . . . So without abandoning mon premier amour [my first love], I rest my hopes with more satisfaction and security on another organization. The catholicity of St. Paul suits me well.
>
> According to Northrop none but the Papists can be saved, according to Mx all the Papists must be condemned; so between these sectarians both honest and talented, the Lamb of God was sacrificed in vain. How much better to hope that, though the flocks be scattered on a thousand hills they are all cared for by the one great Shepherd, who will seek every sheep that is lost without inquiring from which flock it is astray.
>
> When the Lord shall open the many mansions of His Father's house to receive his own, I would that we should be there together, but more oh! most I would, that we should all be there.

A Good Friday collect in his prayer book asked, for infidels and heretics: "so fetch them home, blessed Lord to thy flock, that they may be saved . . . one fold under one shepherd, Jesus Christ our Lord."[20]

In this letter he called Luther "a benefactor of mankind," but added, "while his protest against the sale of indulgences is most gratefully remembered, there is much in his subsequent career to be covered with the mantle of charity." It was here that he spoke, too, of finding not all prelates as pure as his teachers at St. Thomas. He could never forget, however, "the heroic spirit" of Catholic priests in all ages—"far be it from me to disparage the light which shines brightest in the storm that extinguishes the others. But the heroism that in the face of earthly peril continues in the line of duty to God, may have something of earth mingling with the truthful courage which commands esteem."[21]

In contradiction to these reservations, Davis wore around his neck at that very moment, besides his St. Benedict medal, the one already known as "Miraculous," struck just thirty-three years before, from the vision of a French Sister of Charity, still living, who would one day be known as Saint Catherine Labouré. Nor were these all: thin woven laces over his shoulders held on his breast and back the little cloth panels of a French scapular. Both these distinctly Roman Catholic channels of blessing had been sent to him by the Sisters of Charity who had cared for his family in Savannah. He already loved the sisters for nursing the wounded. "No lives in the whole world could be more beautiful," he told Craven; "if it had been possible" to elevate his "respect for woman," the sisters "would have done so." And there was yet another blessed item: someone worried about his safety had given him the brown scapular of the Discalced Carmelites, signifying peace, salvation, and protection in danger. All these devotional means he wore in prison and preserved to the end of his life.[22]

Before long, the reigning pope, Pius IX, looked out at him from a photograph in a large wooden frame, carved at the top with the papal tiara. Such a gift, said a great niece, was "never before conferred on any but crowned heads." On the broad white border, the Holy Father had written, *Venite ad me omnes qui laboratis, et ego reficiam vos, dicit Dominus.* This was already familiar to the Episcopalian as one of the "Comfortable Words" in the communion service: "Come unto me all ye that travail and are heavy laden, and I will refresh you. *St. Matt.* xi. 28."[23]

Davis and Pope Pius were not strangers: in 1863, they had exchanged letters in which each prayed for the other. Davis had thanked the pontiff for enjoining peace and charity on all Americans, through his archbishops in New York and New Orleans. He had assured him that Southerners always prayed for "the wicked war" to end: "we desire no evil to our enemies, nor do we covet any of their possessions, but we are only struggling to the end that they shall cease to devastate our land . . . and that we be permitted to live at peace with all mankind, under our own laws." Davis had made Dudley Mann "Special Envoy" to deliver this letter. After seeing the papal secretary of state, Cardinal Antonelli, and the pope himself, Mann held in his hands a reply addressed to "Illustrious and Honorable Sir, Jefferson Davis, President of the Confederate States of America." Mann took this to be recognition of the Confederacy: "The hand of the Lord has been in it, and eternal glory and praise be to his holy and righteous name." Judah Benjamin assured him it was only a polite formula with no meaning because no diplomatic action followed. But the notion became widespread. Even Robert E. Lee, pointing to his own portrait of Pius IX, told a visitor after that war that he was "the only sovereign . . . in Europe who recognized our poor Confederacy."[24]

The picture arrived, said Davis, "to cheer and console me in my solitary captivity" which was "most needlessly rigorous, if not designedly cruel; when the invention of malignants was taxed to its utmost to fabricate stories to defame and degrade me in the estimation of mankind."

In the photograph, the pope's left hand is next to a crucifix and his right touches his pectoral cross. These hints of Christ's passion were picked up by the Davises years later, when Pope Pius had lost his own nation, the Papal States, and remained by choice a prisoner in his palace. They hung a circlet of real thorns over this portrait on the wall of Jeff's study. Varina used the same symbol to assuage her children's grief over their father's suffering in Fortress Monroe: she told them it was "a crown of thorns, and glory."[25]

Crucifixion was the major focus in another devotional item Davis had, *The Imitation of Christ*, by Thomas à Kempis. His copy is lost, but we know what it was like from the people who saw it—a very worn and coverless 1861 edition, three inches by four and a half, 360 pages, in an eighteenth-century translation from the Latin by Richard Challoner, an English Roman Catholic bishop. Davis gave it to Mrs. Eliza Ogden Violett in 1879. She wrote in it: "Mr. Davis told me he had used this book continually during his imprisonment in Fortress Monroe," and "The marginal notes and marks were made by Mr. Davis."[26]

The only actual note preserved reads "Nov., 1865, great comfort in this." It was written across the corner of a page entitled 'Of the Day of Eternity and of the Miseries of This Life.' That "most clear day" is contrasted with 'this our day . . . bitter and tedious': "Good Jhesu, when . . . shall I be with thee in thy kingdom . . . ? I am left poor and exile in the land of enemies where are daily battles and greatest misfortunes."[27]

Many marks are recorded, however, by or in passages, whose themes echo in his letters. *Imitation:* "[Without God] is nothing done on earth"; "He hath a great and wholesome purgatory that patiently receiveth wrongs . . . that laboureth in all wise to hold his flesh under the spirit"; "Put thee to patience more than to consolations and to bear the cross more than to gladness"; "for all is done for our help, whatever he suffereth to come to us." Jeff to Varina: "The best source of patience is the assurance that the world is governed by infinite wisdom and that He who rules, only permits injustice for some counterbalancing good of which the sufferer cannot judge"; "The ways of Him who doeth all things well are inscrutable to man. Let us learn to say, 'not mine, but Thy will be done' "; "May the Lord . . . give you that grace which sanctifies every trial and cheers the thorny way with the blessed hope that it was chosen by Him as that which would best bring us to His fold."[28]

Imitation: "This word, 'deny thyself and take thy cross and follow me' seemeth a hard word to many men: but . . . in the cross is perfection of holiness: . . . Take thy cross therefore and follow Jesu and thou shalt go into life everlasting." In another place: "at least suffer patiently if thou canst not suffer joyfully." Jeff to Varina: "Let us train our hearts to feel that these are afflictions given to direct us in the way that leads to eternal life. Thus if we may not with joy accept the severe discipline, we may at least bear it with resignation." *Imitation:* "the more that the flesh is thrown down by affliction, the more the spirit is strengthened by inward grace." Jeff: "It is difficult for me to [think of the baby as walking and talking] and be patient. I am sustained by a power I know not of."[29]

Davis had constant reminders of the passion of Christ: imprisonment, bonds, mocking, false accusation, the scourging of continual noise (like being flayed, he said), enemies trying to engineer his execution. He had claimed many times that he would "if necessary, give my life" for the Cause. Now his *Imitation* told him to "bear thy cross and desire to die on the cross; and if thou be fellow in pain [with Christ] thou shalt be fellow in glory." He marked a prayer beginning, "Lord . . . my willing desire is to offer me unto thee perpetually in oblation, so that I may be thine everlastingly." Sacrifice in spirit was one thing; Davis was in mortal danger. So was St. Paul when he wrote, "I have suffered the loss of all things, and do count them but dung, that I may win Christ" and know "the fellowship of his sufferings, being made conformable unto his death." At this place in his Bible, Davis turned down the corner of the page.[30]

The lesson for Evening Prayer on September 24 said the innocent Christ "suffered for us, leaving us an example, that ye should follow his steps." Two days later, Davis wrote to Varina, attributing Southern "defections of the higher class" not "so much to treachery and deceit as to timidity and avarice." Some were trying to avoid responsibility by "their censure, their accusation or their avowed hostility to the man" whom they had made president, "and who by performing the duties of that station has been rendered the object of special vengeance."

> If one is to answer for all upon him it most naturally and properly falls. If I alone could bear all the suffering of the country and relieve it from further calamity, I trust our Heavenly Father would give me strength to be a willing sacrifice; and if in a lower degree some of those who called me (I being then absent) to perform their behests, shall throw on me the whole responsibility; let us rejoice at least in their escape, expecting for them a returning sense of justice, when the stumbling blocks of fear and selfishness shall have been removed from their path.[31]

"Simple and modest," Davis was called. Nothing could show it better than this unselfconscious toss of such an offer into the middle of a long paragraph about charity for others. It is so offhand it would seem accidental, except that he offered himself again, five months later:

> The suffering of all nearest and dearest to me deaden the pain I should otherwise feel because of my own condition. Oftentimes the question occurs to me, would the spirit of vengeance be satiated by my sacrifice so that my family and country men would then be left in peace? If so, I trust my past life will bring others to the

> conclusion that is embodied [in] the mental answer I have so often made, and that those who would mourn me longest, would least expect or desire me to shrink from the purchase.

Just before this he had heard rumors of a rescue attempt and feared "evil consequences to our people." He hoped that "those who might be willing . . . to risk themselves for me" would "do me the justice to remember, that I would much rather be a sacrifice for the country than that it should be sacrificed for me." "If thou puttest thee forward, as thou oughtest to do," reads *The Imitation*, "to suffer and to die . . . thou shalt find peace."[32]

There was one man in the United States anxious to give Davis his chance to imitate Christ, Joseph Holt: "No sufficient atonement" had been made for Lincoln's assassination. "The wretched hirelings of Davis" (meaning Booth's accomplices) had been condemned, indeed, but Davis himself "should be put upon his trial before a military court." Holt's prosecuting attorney, John Bingham, had called Booth only the tool by which Davis "inflicted the mortal wound."[33]

Clement Clay had surrendered in order "to exculpate Mr. Davis" ("most outrageously accused," said Benjamin), as well as himself, from the assassination charge, "preferring death to living with that brand on me." Holt was now in thrall to a gang of liars, and when Clay saw the evidence that he knew to be absolutely false, he told Virginia in alarm to get him released: "*My life depends upon it, I fear* . . . Judge Holt is determined to sacrifice me *for reasons given you*." Holt, who had once lived in Vicksburg, "had pledged himself to the South" and then gone over to the enemy. He knew "the estimate Mr. Davis and I have of his defection, and would fain get us out of the way!"[34]

This Holt was in a position to do. He attacked the two men relentlessly and in the vilest terms through his Bureau of Military Justice. He had never allowed them advice of counsel. He passed along to Stanton everything evil told him about Davis and Clay. By now, the members of Andrew Johnson's cabinet (including Stanton) were beginning to realize how thin their case was, but Holt continued to insist that Davis be tried. Matters came to a head when the new "Radical" Republican Congress wanted to know why there had been no Davis trial. When Johnson, on advice of Stanton and Attorney General Speed, withheld his evidence, the House Judiciary Committee called Holt before it in April of 1866. He presented eight new witnesses to testify against Davis, and was so sure of them that he offered to have them return for cross-examination. This was his undoing.[35]

The judge advocate whom he sent for the witnesses, Col. L. C. Turner, found one too many. A man named Campbell (whose real name was Joseph A. Hoare) said, "I can't stand it any longer," and told Turner how they had all been rehearsed in lies by one Sanford (or Sandford)

Conover (alias James Watson Wallace, real name Charles A. Dunham). Then another witness confessed. A little probing brought the whole house of cards down. Conover had suborned not only these, but most of the witnesses upon whose testimony the Lincoln conspirators had been convicted. W. W. Cleary, Clay's former secretary, who was in Canada, was also accused in Johnson's proclamation, on Holt's hearsay evidence. He had immediately refuted, point by point, in the *Toronto Leader*, the "preposterous and stupidly contrived falsehoods" and had sent his exposé to Johnson. But Johnson "allowed the charges," says Cleary, "to stain the records of the government for nearly three years."[36]

Holt allowed Conover to escape, but he was later apprehended, convicted of perjury, and suborning of perjury, and sentenced to ten years in jail. But Holt still insisted that Davis's guilt was a "matter of solemn record" and kept trying to put him before a military court. The Judiciary Committee also decided that he and others were probably "privy to" the assassination plot and should be tried anyway. God "knowing my inmost heart will acquit me where man blind man seeks to condemn," Jeff had said. With a "dusty cloud of falsehood and injustice" still enfolding him, he wrote to Varina: "I am supported by the conscious rectitude of my course, and humbly acknowledging my many and grievous sins against God, can confidently look to his righteous judgement for vindication in the matter whereof I am accused by man."[37]

Davis, ready to be offered, though doggedly hopeful, was encouraged to self-abandon from another direction:

> I have lately read the "Suffering Saviour" by the Revd. Dr. Krumacher and was deeply impressed with the dignity, the sublime patience of the model of Christianity as contrasted with the brutal vindictiveness of unregenerate man; and with the similitude of the portrait given of the Jews to the fierce prosecutions which pursued the Revolutionists after the restoration of the Stuarts. One is led to ask did Sir Hy. Vane and the Duke of Argyle imitate the more than human virtue of our Saviour or was their conduct the inspiration of a conscience void of offence in that whereof they were accused.

"Conscience void of offense" is straight from the "Prayer for grace to reform and grow better" in the prayer book family service. Friedrich Wilhelm Krummacher, whose *Der leidende Christus Ein Passionsbuch* was published in English in 1856, does not mention Sir Henry Vane and Archibald Campbell, Earl and Marquess of Argyll, both of whom were beheaded for treason in the reign of Charles II of England. Krummacher, trying to combat the rationalism that would reduce Jesus to a mere human teacher of ethics, stresses the "mysterious transfer" by which Christ offered himself willingly in the place of all sinners as an atonement and emphasizes its effect more than its imitation. It is Davis who made the connection between the British adherents of a lost cause and Christ's superhuman virtue.[38]

He was just reading Lord Macaulay's history, where the Scottish Argyll dies saying his cause "was the cause of God" and writing to his wife how "good and gracious to me" God had always been. Samuel Pepys tells how Sir Harry Vane expected to be "at the right hand of Christ," and how a man called him "martyr and saint." Surely in the back of Davis's mind is his own possible immolation. Krummacher does mention the sweetness of Christ's self-sacrifice for those who are "led on similar paths . . . of suffering and disgrace."[39]

Davis had pondered "the more than human virtue of our Saviour." He once described for Craven the agony in Gethsemane, where Christ under "the burden of the sins of mankind," cries out, "Take away this cup from me." Then "faith reasserts her ascendancy" with "Not my will, but thine be done." Another scene of "consolation" Davis described was "Abraham on the hill of Jehovah jireh," being saved from sacrificing Isaac. "The words Jehovah jireh [God will provide]" had sustained him too, he said, when encompassed with "troubles that seemed hopeless of extrication." In both scenes, an angel comforts "the obedient heart."[40]

Craven says Davis "was fond of . . . comparing text with text; dwelling on the divine beauty of the imagery." "The Psalms were his favorite portion of the Word, and had always been. Evidence of their divine origin was inherent in their text," which plumbed every emotion. "There was no affectation of devoutness," said Craven, who was convinced ever "more deeply" of his sincerity. "There were moments . . . in which Mr. Davis impressed me more than any professor of Christianity I had ever heard. There was . . . a clear, almost passionate grasp in his faith; and the thought would frequently recur, that belief capable of consoling such sorrows as his" was evidence of "a reality—a substance—which no sophistry of the infidel could discredit."[41]

Davis's own letters reveal not only that he read the Bible, but how he read it. Devotions were part of his careful discipline. To Varina's "tell me how you live all day," he answered:

> In the morning as soon as dressed I read the morning prayer (family) sometimes adding a chapter of the new Testament and a Psalm. After breakfast read, at this time Bancroft's History of the United States. Soon after 11—read the morning service, on Sundays, Wednesdays & Fridays, add the Communion service, the Collect, Epistle and Gospel and the Litany. In the afternoon read whatever book occupies me and when Genl. Miles comes, go out to walk say, for an hour on the parapet. In the evening read the Service as appointed. Family prayers at night. To the morning & evening service a *modified* form of the prayer for a person going to sea and of the prayer for a person under affliction are always added.[42]

"The Psalter and Lessons for the day will give us that daily reading in common which you suggest," he said later, but not at the same hour, as she wanted, because he had no way to tell time. "When in the casemate I constructed on the floor of the embrasure a partial dial, here [Carroll Hall] it is not practicable." Still, he would know that she was "uttering the same words, engaged with the same thoughts." On November 27, he quoted from the prayer book version of Psalms 120 and 121, appointed for Morning Prayer that day: "Woe is me that I am constrained to dwell with Mesech," and "The Lord [shall] preserve thee from all evil." "My Bible—Prayer Book and a Dictionary of the Bible are my endless resource."[43]

> Sunday morning. 3. Dec. 65—The bright sun and mild temperature welcomes the blessed day of rest; which calls the redeemed to meet together, and rejoice that their Saviour has risen again, and sitteth in the place prepared for the faithful.
>
> Deprived of the opportunity to assemble with the members of the church, there is left to me the spirit communion with those I daily and nightly summon to meet together in His name who is ever present, and thus I have read the morning service, including the lessons both of the Dominical and Calendar day. How full they are of Providences—Holy innocence closes the mouths of fiercest beasts and triumphs over the crafts and subtelties of wicked men; conscious sinfulness silences those who came to arraign a guilty mortal, and entrap the Righteous judge; repentance working deliverance to an oppressed and dispersed people; the prayers of the church affecting the miraculous preservation of one apostle from the fate which had a short time before fallen upon another.[44]

These reassurances came at a good time. "Having no communication with the outer world, except with you," with no inkling of his future, he was tempted to despond. But Sunday was always the "Glorious day which gave the last proof of the Redeemer's divinity and the first guarantee of man's justification and mediatorial protection." As he read the service, he thought how "the same words were prompting the same thoughts" to Varina and hoped she was at the church, in "that union of prayer the value of which can only be realized by those who have been deprived of it. Although God is omnipresent, and his love enables us to look up to him with trust; though we are taught that the lonely sinner is sought after by the good shepherd . . . the heart even in it's least expressible feeling profits by communion with those who sympathize."[45]

He had been in solitary confinement for six months, no one in his cell but his keepers. Suddenly, one day in December, there was Dr. Minnigerode. The Church had come to him.

> I cannot describe my meeting with Mr. Davis. . . . He knew nothing of my coming, and it was difficult to control ourselves. . . . The

> noble man showed the effect of the confinement, but his spirit could not be subdued . . . not a sign of any humiliating giving way to the manner in which he was treated; he was above that. He suffered, but was willing to suffer in the cause of the people who had given him their confidence, and who still loved and admired and wept for the man that so nobly represented the cause which in their hearts they considered right and constitutional.

Dr. Minnigerode had himself suffered cruel political imprisonment in his youth. He knew how much Davis needed him. He had been trying to get there since May, but Andrew Johnson had never answered his petition. Finally, some Richmond ladies told him to try Stanton, who was an Episcopalian. A request through Stanton's priest got him permission to see Davis as "his pastor and spiritual advisor." Four months later, he was *still* the only friend who had been allowed to see the prisoner. Miles kept Minnigerode waiting all of Sunday this trip, checking his permit, but the next day gave him six hours with Davis.[46]

> At last the question of the holy communion came up. . . . He was very anxious to take it. He was a pure and pious man, and he felt the need and value of the means of grace. But there was one difficulty. Could he take it in the proper spirit—in the frame of a forgiving mind, after all the ill-treatment he had been subjected to? He was too upright and conscientious a Christian man "to eat and drink *unworthily*," *i.e.*, not in the proper spirit, and as far as lay in him, in peace with God and man.

Davis asked time "to search out my heart" about forgiveness, so as to "make no mistake." Minnigerode says, "I left him to settle that question between himself and his own conscience."[47]

Dr. Minnigerode would have known the answer, had he seen the letters passing between husband and wife. Davis honestly confessed, "the unmanly, wanton outrages upon my helpless Wife and children are the hardest for me to forgive." "Torture of myself, indignity and danger to myself I can meet and bear, would that my helpless family were spared." When he heard that little Maggie always left the table in tears after her "grace"—"That the Lord would give father something which he could eat . . . and bring him back to us with his good senses," he remarked that since his loved ones could neither share nor diminish his suffering, "I greatly preferred that they should not know of it." And he went on, "Our injuries cease to be grievous in proportion as Christian charity enables us to forgive those who trespass against us, and to pray for our enemies."[48]

He tried to put forgiveness into action. Rising from his knees one night about ten o'clock, after praying to go to his rest "in peace, charity, and good will," he offered a chair to his guard, saying *"My good young soldier, you must be tired."* The guard wrote to him about it twenty-three years later. As 1865 ended, Davis claimed, "After faithful self examination it is permitted me to say, I have not done to others as they do unto me."[49]

His frayed nerves showed in this letter. The day before, an officer sent by Miles to confiscate a long piece of red tape asked Davis if he had any use for it, and he burst out: "The ass! Tell the damned ass that it was used to keep up the mosquito net on my bed. I had it in the casemate and he knew it. The miserable ass!" Miles sent the remark and the tape to headquarters with a sarcastic note and was commended for his zeal (evidently rumors of rescue were abroad). "I struggle, not always successfully, against my temptations," Jeff wrote Varina a little later, "and often feel how much communion with you would aid my efforts to walk in the way of the Fathers commandments."[50]

Jeff had to struggle against Varina's feelings as well as his own. He made excuses for a woman whose "defection has evidently pained you," though "you will no doubt be surprised that I should be her apologist." "Our adversity may like a furnace be proving our friends," he told his wife, but "if it be ordained that we shall be restored to each other, we shall be better able to forgive those who have been false, than they will be to enjoy their treachery."

It was his suffering that tried Varina most: "You did not spare me, for I heard it all . . . in the public prints"; "I shudder when I think . . . in what spirit promulgated . . . God forever bless those who have been kind to my precious Prisoner—and forgive those who have insulted his helplessness, for I cannot."[51] He answered:

> Less than yourself can I claim to be superior to the feeling of resentment for injuries wantonly or maliciously inflicted. I did not mean so much by invoking you to possess your soul in patience. Our heavenly Father merciful to our infirmities cannot require of us superhuman virtues. Our Litany joins together forgiveness of our enemies and the change of their hearts. . . . The instinct of self preservation involves resistance to aggression, but it's highest development is freest from vengeance & cruelty. Revelation teaches us to hope for forgiveness if truly repentant; magnanimity compels us to accept the declaration made [by others] . . . and both combine to exclude from the heart the spirit of persecution, both lead us to forget, rather than to cherish memories of wrong; so that as soon as the wicked cease from troubling and permit the wounds to heal, the heart fired with grateful love of the Lord, has a mantle of charity broad enough to hide the offences committed against it.

He jokes about "the dull channel into which my letter was running," but he takes up the theme again later, referring Varina to "the parable of the King who took an account of his servants." "When we shall pass into the future state of pure intelligence so as to judge not by external signs but by the inner motives how different men will appear to each other from the estimates of their carnal life. May it not be that we shall then find our most earnest efforts at self examination brought us but to a poor knowledge of ourselves."[52]

Varina was too passionate for such calm appraisal. In "acute agony" over the "publication and republication . . . of the shackling scene" earlier, she had written Jeff, "The Saviour . . . did not faint in Gethsamane" because he "was a God." "I pray for patience . . . but I do not find like St Steven the power given to me to fall (while being stoned,) asleep in Jesus. You are better where you are than here—happier." He answered, "Our heavenly Father . . . does not chasten us in anger but in love and mercy. His instruments may be vengeful and unjust, as were those who murdered St. Stephen, but he looked beyond the rough rod to the hand of the just and passionless Father who held it, and though we may not attain to, we should imitate that example."[53]

On Christmas Day, 1865, grieving over her loneliness and the graves of their little sons, Varina broke down: "while you love me, while you exist nothing is too hard to bear—But if anything happens to you—I cannot I cannot." She retorts to his discourse:

> You think I do not understand the kind of forgiveness which we are to exercise—I do not if it is required of me to pray for those who despitefully use you—I can accord pity to one who would . . . torment a helpless woman . . . but for those who willingly afflict you and torture you with bee stings . . . because you are in their power I cannot find in my heart one prayer . . . I do not want the person so annoying you . . . to go to Heaven—and I cannot help saying so even if it is not religious—It is a great sorrow to hate—and a very intense feeling when the object so detested is powerful—and the sufferer powerless—Where was I straying too far, too far for a Christian upon whom God has laid his hand heavily, even if it is in love—and mercy inscrutable.

She told him a tactless friend had sent her from Washington "a description of the terrible thirst for your blood. . . . She puts into words things that to dream of curdles my blood."[54]

Calm as always, Jeff replied, "I will be glad when you are removed beyond the reach of the brutal cruelty of such statements and suggestions. . . . They are crosses which you cannot bear. . . ." Gently but firmly, however, he pressed on about forgiveness:

> The requirements of the Lord are never beyond the range of possibility; for He knows our infirmities and judges of our motives. These man cannot know, and is therefore forbidden to judge. We

hope & pray for God's forgiveness on the ground of true repentance, and as we cannot tell in the case of those who trespass against us, whether the repentance is true or feigned, we are bound to accept the seeming. That is possible, is it not easy, for virtue far short of the God like or saintly examples of the Redeemer and the first Christian martyr?[55]

His "consolatory remarks about that wretched letter of mine" seemed to win her over: "I felt your strong arm around me and was still." She would try "to 'put on the whole armor of righteousness' . . . against those who encompass us with snares." But Varina was never calm for long: " 'How long, how long till I can see thy face'? All my words seem so faint when I express my love in them. All prayers seem so weak when I strive with God . . . my precious good Husband. . . . if I have ever offended you, and I have been often willful, and irritable, oh forgive your poor old wife for her great love's sake—It is such a comfort to me to tell you that I beg your pardon for everything . . . and how grateful I am to God that I am your wife—may love you as much as I please—."[56]

"My dear Winnie," he replied, "it is not for me to forgive you, but to ask for your forgiveness. We are all weak, erring, willful, sinful creatures, I should have been less so than you being older and stronger, but in justice I feel that it was the reverse, and that it is I who have to ask because I love much that much may be forgiven." He was always mindful "my omitting and committing sinfulness." He said twice a day, "We have left undone those things which we ought to have done; And we have done those things which we ought not to have done." In his *Imitation of Christ,* Davis crossed out some words proper only to a priest (showing his frequent use) in a preparation for communion. In this he prayed for those who 'have in anything wronged me, grieved me, or abused me' and "for them that I have troubled . . . to the end, blessed Lord, that we all may be pardoned."[57]

When Dr. Minnigerode came back to the cell, "I found Mr. Davis with his mind made up. Knowing the honesty of the man, and that there would be, could be, 'no shamming' . . . I was delighted." "Simply and solemnly [Davis] held out his hand and said: 'Doctor, I am ready now. I forgive as I hope to be forgiven. As God knows my heart, I am in charity with all men.' "

Then came the communion—he and I alone, no one but God with us. It was night. The Fortress was so still that you could hear a pin fall. General Miles, with his back to us, leaning against the fireplace in the ante-room, his head on his hands, not moving; the sentinels ordered to stand still . . . [a] solemn communion scene . . . telling upon both of us, I trust, for lasting good.[58]

"Thank God that Mr. Minnegerode administered to you the blessed Sacrament of his body and blood from which you have been so long debarred," Varina wrote. After one such visit, Davis said, "I received the sacrament with comfort to my longing soul." He was grateful for the priest's "prayers and judicious conversations." "I went whenever I could to see my beloved and martyred friend," said Minnigerode, "and precious were the days and hours spent with him. I loved that lowly, patient, God-fearing soul."[59]

Minnigerode's coming was timely, because Davis's only other comfort, the visits of Dr. Craven, became short and infrequent, and then stopped, all because of a coat Craven had ordered for Davis because he had none. Riled by attacks in the press—"those who choose to falsify my conduct have as safe a task as slanderer could desire"—Jeff wrote Varina: "You say the papers tell you every thing, but I warn you that the things they tell are not realities. The example you give will illustrate, the 'new overcoat' I have *not* received." He was in his sarcastic mood: "The matter being of such public importance as to have been followed in its progress through the tailor's shop, and down the Bay, the journals may give you the future history before it is known to me." Southerners leapt to pay for it when they heard, and Northerners raised a howl over pampering the prisoner. On Christmas Day, 1865, Craven was relieved of duty at Fortress Monroe.[60]

"Do not make to yourself causeless anxiety," Jeff told Varina, "but the rather patiently wait . . . believing that an unseen hand is directing our fortune according to the omniscience and infinite mercy which guides and governs all things." It was like a prophecy. Dr. George Cooper, the regular army surgeon who replaced Craven, was thought to be "the blackest of Black Republicans." It turned out he was married to "the damnedest Rebel out," and, though brusque in manner, as sympathetic to Davis as his predecessor. And Dr. Craven, mustered out of the army in January, put together, with Charles G. Halpine, his book, *Prison Life of Jefferson Davis,* "absolutely the first statement in his favor—if so it can be regarded—which the Northern press has yet given to the world."[61]

The unseen hand did not deal so obviously with the falsifiers, but it was there. "Nothing could have made me willing to adopt assassination," Davis claimed. In due time, common sense and confessions of the perjurers forced the United States to see that it had no case, though that was never admitted publicly. At the moment, however, Jeff warned Varina, "The bitterness which caused me to be so persistently slandered will probably find vent in congressional speeches, and test all your christian fortitude." And the slander came, even before Congress met, in a speech by Schuyler Colfax. "My own dear Winnie fear not what man can do, it is God disposes—Now I am shut up and slander runs riot to destroy my fair repute, but any investigation must redeem my character." Colfax, a Radical who was to be Speaker of the House, charged Davis and Lee with deliberate cruelty to prisoners of war. Davis called the speech "an extraordinary accumulation of reprehensible innovations." He feared that "retrospective legislation" would "bring it to bear upon an anticipated trial"—namely his.[62]

The charge had already involved him in the trial of Capt. Henry Wirz, a disabled soldier who had commanded directly the stockade of prisoners at Camp Sumter, Andersonville, Georgia. It was seen as "a sure thing to get at Jefferson Davis."[63] The military court that accused Wirz of cruelty and murder suppressed favorable evidence and refused to hear some of his witnesses. When trial testimony disagreed with dates in the indictment, the court simply altered them. Wirz's counsel, Louis Schade, pointed out the irregularities to President Johnson, but he was ignored. False testimony caused a doctor who had worked with Wirz to call the trial "one grand stupendous farce." While it was going on, the "Specification" of "Charge I" was changed to include the name, "Jefferson Davis." He had conspired with Wirz, it said, "maliciously, traitorously, and in violation of the laws of war, to impair and injure the health and destroy the lives . . . of large numbers of Federal prisoners."[64]

The building of Camp Sumter in March of 1864 came about because prisoners had piled up in Richmond after the North terminated exchange, and Lee asked their removal: there was a shortage of food, and he was skittish about having them at his back, especially after the Dahlgren raid threatened their release. Sumter was at first a healthy place. It was enlarged once, but vast numbers of Federals kept surrendering—Johnston would send thousands at a time. The constantly compressed living space was the chief cause of a large death rate, along with dearth of medicine, shelter, and sanitation (though no one knew its connection with disease), the corn meal and bacon rations (indigestible to Yankees), the prevalent diarrhea and dysentery, and despair over nonexchange. When the war ended, the North wanted someone punished.[65]

Wirz was singled out and condemned by one of Joseph Holt's military commissions in a trial that a present-day lawyer finds "worse than a miscarriage of justice . . . a national disgrace." It was not just Wirz who was on trial, but the whole South, as Holt made clear to President Johnson: Captain Wirz, rather "a demon than a man," represented in "murderous cruelty and baseness" the "inner and real life" of "the rebellion," the "hellish criminality and brutality of the traitors who maintained it. . . . For such crimes human power is absolutely impotent to enforce any adequate atonement." He recommended, however, starting with Wirz. The Swiss immigrant was hanged on November 10, 1865.[66]

General Miles noted that Davis "carefully preserved" reports of evidence in the Wirz trial, as well he might, given Holt's thirst for atonement. This was the charge that sent George Shea to Canada in search of records in January of 1866. He found out how Davis absolutely refused to retaliate for Northern abuse of prisoners and how he was attacked for his stand. In fact, he was assailed repeatedly for his "undue clemency and care" for captives by the *Examiner*. When that paper's cry of "Hoist the black flag" was taken up by some in cabinet and Congress, Davis "answered hotly": "I would not fight with a rope around my neck, and I will not ask brave men to do so. As to the torture of prisoners . . . no people have the right to demand such a deed at my hands." Even John Hunt Morgan could not get him to do more than threaten reprisal for the shameful treatment of him and his men in the Ohio penitentiary, much to Morgan's disgust. Shea came home fully convinced of Davis's innocence on the charge of cruelty and persuaded influential Republicans of it. They began to complain, through Greeley's *Tribune*, of their government's treatment of its own prisoner: Davis should be either tried or released.[67]

Davis had no direct connection with Andersonville, but he had been "painfully affected" by the death rate and tried to think of some way to arrest it. Varina overheard Lee telling him, "Their sufferings are the result of our necessities, not of our policy. Do not distress yourself." John W. Daniel said Davis "would have turned with loathing from misuse of a prisoner." Benjamin was so incensed over "the infamous accusation" of cruelty that he wrote a refutation to the *London Times*. When Davis himself read in Dr. Craven's book, "into whose souls the iron of Andersonville has entered," he wrote in the margin, "bah, rather into whose ears the slander," and "oh! the power of falsehood." Beside "cruel treatment," he put "paltry" (trashy, worthless). He wrote to a friend in later years, "It would be impossible to frame an accusation against me, more absolutely and unqualifiedly false."[68]

Capt. Justus Scheibert, seeing Davis in July of 1863, found him complaining bitterly "that he could not effect the exchange of prisoners." This was, said Benjamin, "one of the most fatal blows." Davis sent "a statement of the mortality prevailing" at Andersonville (without effect). He let prisoners take a petition to Washington (their return unheeded causing despair and death). He offered to buy contraband medicine from the United States to be dispensed by their surgeons: "Incredible as it may appear," he later wrote, "it is nevertheless strictly true that no reply was ever received to this offer." In August 1864, Davis offered to give up both sick and well prisoners without "equivilents" (though some were sent), but ships to take them did not arrive until November. The stone wall Davis had met was Grant's decision to abandon his prisoners. It was "a part of the system of attack upon the rebellion," Butler explained, "to destroy it by depletion, depending upon our superior numbers to win the victory at last."[69]

Wirz hung helpless in this concatenation of circumstances before he was hanged at the Washington Arsenal. Tales of his cruelty appalled him so that he wrote President Johnson, "I sometimes almost doubt my own existence." A voice within assured him, "if men hold thee guilty, God does not." He was suffering so much from both disgrace and gangrene in his old wound that he asked but one thing, and that quickly: "death or liberty." His own Swiss consul, believing the tales, calling him "the detestable tool of monsters in human form," asked Johnson instead to give him "solitary confinement for life." Johnson had already ordered the execution. Gen. J. D. Imboden, who knew of Wirz's efforts to help his prisoners, said he was sacrificed "to the bloody Moloch of 1865." "That poor victim," said his attorney.[70]

Wirz was more than that. "If condemned to death, I shall suffer without a murmur," he wrote Johnson; "In life or death, I shall pray for you." Capt. Richard Bagley Winder, quartermaster for Camp Sumter, had the cell opposite Wirz's at Old Capitol Prison. The night before the hanging, Wirz told him that the civilians he had seen coming to his room had offered to commute his sentence if he would implicate Jefferson Davis, but he had spurned them. They had then gone to his confessor, Father F. E. Boyle, and to Louis Schade, with the same offer. These men told Wirz the next morning, and said he answered (exactly as he had told Winder) that he knew nothing at all about Davis: "If I knew anything of him, I would not become a traitor against him, or anybody else, even to save my life." "His last words were that he died innocent," said Schade, "and so he did." Father Boyle said the same. Davis and thirteen others had been accused of conspiring with Wirz; not one was ever tried on this count. Wirz had become what Davis was willing to be, a sacrifice that spared others. "My life is demanded as an atonement," he wrote on the morning of his death; "I am willing to give it, and hope that after a while, I will be judged differently from what I am now."[71]

Northern readers about this time could guffaw over a "Burlesque Life of Jeff. Davis." The frontispiece showed "Jefferson Davis making her toilet" in a hoop skirt, putting on a bonnet. At the end, a full-page close-up of a gallows showed a hanged figure, hooded and bound, boots and spurs visible under a hoop frame on which crows perched, and in the background the United States capitol (where Wirz's trial was held). The caption was "End of the book and end of Jeff. Davis." Perhaps the guard who sketched a hanged man on the wall of Davis's cell was inspired by this, or by a cartoon showing "Davis as a hyena in an iron cage playing with a human skull" while "the noose around his neck connected with a high gallows [is] about to be drawn taut."[72]

Davis, like Wirz, "was vicariously suffering indignities" for the sake of the South. But his passion was not to be, like Wirz's, over quickly. All those captured with him, all other state prisoners, and all those accused with Wirz were freed within a year, "except Jefferson Davis." (Jeffy D. Howell, indeed, kept being picked up, but he finally got away to Canada.) Davis was puzzled to "find the rule of discrimination," but he was not bitter. He eschewed "the proverb" about misery loving company: "I would that like one of old it were for me to say—I alone am left." And, virtually, he was.[73]

Dr. Cooper's first report on his new patient noted "considerable nervous irritation, and insomnolency. He is . . . more affected by mental than bodily ailments." He was anxious over his family, and he could see no way out of his close confinement: "My days drag heavily on, to what I have no means to direct or to foresee." Outside, the Radicals were gaining power. On New Year's Day, 1866, he wrote, "A heavy burden of oppression rests upon me and the prospect before is gloomy in the extreme."[74]

Against despair, General Davis manned his outer works—the almost monastic round of daily prayer. When "in imagination" he gathered "our family group . . . with one accord to make our common suplication," "each member" stood before him with "distinctness and life." The Bible was a big gun. Thinking how "I sought to keep [the children's] hearts free for the pure pulsations of universal Christian love," he brought up a parable: "Bad, bad was the hand that came to scatter tares upon that virgin field where no evil weed had grown. Should your pious prayers be heard, in that home life for which you hope, we will endeavor to cultivate our crop so as at last to separate the bad without serious diminution of the good." In the face of "a cruel desire for my destruction," advising Varina to "remember that the end is not yet," he quoted Psalm 35: "A fair inquiry will show how 'false witnesses have risen up against me and laid to my charge things that I knew not of.'" Another time:

> In the selections for the morning service of this day I have found comforting promises, and fold them to my breast close mingled with the love which neither misfortune nor suffering nor distance nor inevitable separation can darken or deprive of its warmth. Warned by a sad experience against such calculations as would make hope sanguine and expectation swift, I will yet hope though in patience and strive to find adequate protection beneath the shield of the conviction, that all things are ordered in wisdom and mercy and love, that I may fully feel "even so Father for it is thy will."[75]

General Davis had a hidden, inner line of defense as well. "I have been reading 'thoughts on personal religion' by Dr. Goulburn. His instructions as to Prayer have impressed me particularly. . . . It is no small encouragement to a sinner striving for a better state, to find those who have . . . won the crown of glory, had passed through such tribulation as he is beset with." The military metaphors of this Anglican divine must have appealed to Davis. The "good soldier of Jesus Christ" is to strive for "holiness" by "control over every appetite" and prayer "without ceasing." "Heaviness of spirit" calls for "heroic endurance," like Christ's in Gethsemane—"a great means of spiritual advancement." To "battle" for years with one's besetting sin (like "temper or vanity"), to bear "a shower of needle arrows" (say, Davis's annoyances) "steadily poured in upon us day by day," is "a far better discipline of humility than sublimer trials." The soldier is to "break his way to the heavenly country through the serried ranks of his spiritual foes," advancing from vocal prayer, through meditation, to recollection, won by ejaculations (like "Thy will be done"): "Forward, then, warriors of the Cross."[76]

All this seems to describe what Davis already does. "In His name who is ever present," he summons the family to vocal prayers. He gives Varina the fruit of his "recent reflection" on whether it is right to "mingle earthly with devotional love":

> the New Testament appears to me as a light leading the natural affections to the hallowed and exalted condition in which they become vessels of honor bearing incense acceptable to the Creator. Our Saviour in the agony of the Cross remembered the temporal need of his Mother. The Apostle whom He loved sums up the duties of the Christian in the sentence, Love one another.

Another meditation, on St. Peter's denying Jesus and then dying for him, yielded this: "The timid though he shrunk, may have looked at the sufferer with longing love from the outer court. True at such a time it availed not, yet it might for other trials be all one wants." The last phrase links the scene to himself, as Goulburn advises for this kind of mental prayer. Goulburn on St. Peter might be speaking of Davis: when God "changes our whole plan of life," we must "lie still and let another gird us"; not by action, but by a death thwarting self-will did Peter glorify God; "to love God is to embrace His Will"; suffering is "the highest of all vocations."[77]

Goulburn is writing for those who feel called beyond "mere respectability" to "saintliness": "Make your heart a little sanctuary in which you may continually realize the Presence of God," driving away "vain thoughts." In his *Imitation*, Davis marked: 'Come, heavenly sweetness, and let all impurity fly from thy face' and "when shall I, Lord, have mind on thee alone? . . . when wilt thou be to me all in all?"[78]

Father Boyle said Wirz, submitting "to his persecutors," "died in the peace of God and praying for his enemies." In *The Imitation of*

Christ, Davis marked, 'When shall I enjoy . . . a peace both within and without, a peace everywhere firm?' There was none without; within was a different matter. In acceptance of suffering, he found the peace that the *Imitation* promised. He wrote of it in the very letter that made him a "willing sacrifice." A few weeks later, he wrote:

> Be not downcast. We must meet cheerfully whatever affliction it may be God's will we should bear. Misfortune should not depress us, as it is only crime which can degrade. Beyond this world there is a sure retreat for the oppressed . . . to deny that . . . every event tends to what is right, is to question the wisdom of Providence . . . ever trusting in the mercy of God, I prayerfully hope that we shall be reunited in this world, but humbly strive with becoming resignation to say, Father thy will be done. . . . Let us trust in Him whose wisdom cannot err and whose power cannot fail to effect His will . . . cherish hope, and cultivate cheerfulness as conducive thereto . . . Daily and nightly my prayers are offered for you, and there is a peace which tells me they are heard.[79]

"Dear Saintly Husband," Varina exclaimed,

> If I deserved like you God's immediate presence in my heart, perhaps I might like you possess my soul in patience. . . . But I am not full of love and forgiveness. I may become so when you cease to suffer. While in Savannah, I prayed God to take you to himself. I repined that you had not died at your capture. Now I thank God that you were spared . . . for your heart has become the "temple of the Holy Ghost, the Comforter"—and should your sufferings destroy you, it cannot be long before I come to you. But I must not talk of this until God sends also to me "the Comforter" . . . may the virtuous self sacrificing life which you have led be your shield as Christianity has been the banner under which you have fought & suffered. . . .

And Jeff: "If my self love, not to say sense of justice, would have resisted the reckless abuse of my enemies; I am humbled by your unmerited praise, it teaches me what I ought to be."[80]

Davis had the seclusion so helpful to prayer: "Separated from my friends of this world, my Heavenly Father has drawn nearer to me, His goodness and my unworthiness are more sensibly felt, but this does not press me back, for the atoning Mediator is the way, and his hand upholds me." But there was a terrible difference: isolation "affords abundant opportunity for turning the thoughts inward," but "my prison life does not give me the quiet of solitude." "I am in the condition to give the highest value to quiet, it being the thing never allowed to me by day or by night." Whatever recollection he achieves is bought by supreme effort.[81]

He marks in *The Imitation:* 'I am willing in mind to be above all things but by the flesh am obliged against my will to be subject to them.' The distraction is at times almost unbearable: "The sentinel has stamped with such noise back and forth in front of me, that I must cease from the effort to write until another and more quiet walker comes on, and I recover from the effect produced by the attempt to write under such difficulty." He could only "summon patience against [interruptions] as evils from which it will be a virtue to extract good." (Goulburn calls this "the path not of sanctity only, but of peace.") Three months later: "If my letter seems disjointed and obscure do not infer any physical ill. . . . The tramping and creaking of the Sentinels' boots disturb me so as to render it difficult to write at all." His grim humor did not desert him: "There is no occasion now to make Frankensteins, like ready made clothing they wait in abundance for customers. When Roberts grew angry with Byron you know he charged him with being miserable because of a soul of which he could not get rid."[82]

Somehow, Davis achieves recollected prayer: the "unseen hand" gives "a refuge that man cannot invade." He speaks of how God knows "my inmost heart," of how He hears "best the words most secretly uttered," of "prayers often, very often, in every day and every night." "Sometimes shut out from observation [the mind] turns inwards with a force before unknown and sees more in darkness than it did in light. Let us be happy the lord reigns, and in due time we shall know wherefore things were done." He quotes poetry to the same point: "As darkness shows us worlds of light / We never saw by day." When he says, "May angels watch over you," he reveals his constant state: "I pray, pray, pray— — —[.]"[83]

He still speaks to Varina of reunion, but he seems to be looking beyond her, to "the mansion prepared for the blessed followers of the Son." "The peace which lifts above the troubles of this world and opens the view of the world to come attend you; and may our merciful Father restore us to each other that we may gather our children around us and calmly prepare for the final summons, aiding and sustaining each other in the works both for time and Eternity until that last call shall be given."[84]

Hints of death abound: "Teach [baby Winnie] how her Father loved her when she was too young to remember"; "The lessons of these times will . . . better prepare us for that valley which lies beyond the hill of life"; "Our paths are widely separated but I hope they are converging towards that home where sorrow enters not, where there are no partings, where the wicked cease from troubling and the weary, weary are at rest." Even when he says, "Let us trust that [God] will find it expedient to give us our heart's desire in this world," he warns Varina to prepare for "the worst." His caution is well founded. General Grant says, "Everyone supposed he would be tried for treason if captured, and that he would be executed."[85]

He is ready. His abandon approaches the "ask nothing and refuse nothing" of St. Francis de Sales that Goulburn quotes. His eyes are on "hopes which live beyond this fleeting life" and justice.

> Blessed hope that we are to be judged by Him who bore every human affliction for our salvation, and having felt all the emotions of human affection, can sympathize with those who suffer, and pardon the errors of our better nature. Who that reflects on man's judgement can fail to look out from its corruption and weakness, with desire to meet the judge who cannot err? Often has it occurred in the world's history that fidelity has been treated as a crime and true faith punished as treason. So it cannot be before the Judge to whom all hearts are open from whom no secrets are hid.[86]

Early in 1866, Varina is allowed to go to Canada. As Good Friday approaches, Davis tries to prepare his beloved Pollie: she is thankful that her prayer "has been partly granted in giving your Mother to you" and it is right to hope that "the other part," his own "restoration to you," will be too,

> but if it should be otherwise, you must receive the dispensation will [*sic*] all possible contentment, remembering that all things are ordered by infinite wisdom and unfailing love. It is hard to accept our crosses as needful corrections and rejoice in the pain they give; but we have for our instruction the example of our blessed Saviour who when suffering agony greater than a mere human could bear, still prayed that he might be spared the affliction only if such should be the will of his Father in Heaven.

"With all my prayers," he adds for her sake, "I mingle the entreaty that we may be reunited if it be good in our Father's sight. . . . And oh! may it be His will."[87]

But he does not think it is. He is convinced the Radicals have the power to hang him.

XIX

Varina

Civil war was raging under the Capitol dome as Congress convened in December 1865, Republicans lined up against each other. The speech of Schuyler Colfax had been the opening gun. The battle was over what should be done with, or to, the Southern states. Moderates were for President Andrew Johnson's plan of Reconstruction, to restore the Union; Radicals were for keeping the states out of the Union, and ruling them as conquered provinces. Thaddeus Stevens marshaled Radicals in the House, and Charles Sumner, in the Senate.[1]

Jefferson Davis saw a likeness to the French Revolution, when "the most violent passions were developed after the strife had ceased, for then the blood shedding passed from the cruel sword to the more cruel gown, from the necessities of the battle field to the vindictiveness of the party." So did the British minister who said Sumner was "very like Robespierre"—"remorseless." On January 16, 1866, Sumner resolved that Davis and Clay should be tried "before a military tribunal or court-martial." It looked as if Joseph Holt would get his way.[2]

Davis was in the midst of a letter to Varina when he heard this and said, "you can no longer cherish the hope which was formerly indulged."

> Strengthen your heart for the high responsibilities imposed on you & go forward on the path of duty, accepting every providence with the comforting assurance that it must be right. Truth is powerful and the common sense of justice recoils, after the paroxism of passion subsides, from continuance in wrong doing. Then I say, of the final result of any proceeding against me, be hopeful; my conduct has been too public, too consistent to be perverted, after slanderers are confronted by true witnesses.

Luckily for Davis, the Senate was cool just then to Sumner's proposals. This one was never implemented.[3]

Varina's hope, wildly indulged in every letter, was to come to Jeff in prison, and its springs were very deep. "How fresh and soft [is] the touch of your 'vanished hand,' how musical and sweet rings still within my heart 'the sound of a voice that is still.' " When a "literal" rendition of Homer's *Iliad*, "divested of [Alexander] Pope's swelling, rhyming translation," roused her to "a pitch of high enthusiasm," she quoted parts to Jeff. One suggested his own plight: Iphidamas "slept the brazen sleep assisting his fellow-countrymen, unhappy man! far from his young wedded virgin."

> When I read of the heroic, and good, you are my exemplar better than man can depict, seven times tried in the fiery furnace—brighter than refined gold. . . . I bless God for every hour that I have borne your spotless name, and fervently trust, and expect that He will reunite us . . . My Jeff, my first and only love . . . infinitely dearer in your sorrow and your waning strength than you were in your power, and youth, I am in life & death / Your devoted Wife.[4]
>
> My quivering longing heart . . . has throbbed for you alone since it could feel a woman's love. The all absorbing love of my whole life seems so poor a tribute to your worth.
>
> Some times it seems to me that I must see my children or die—But then the stronger dearer love comes to bid me stay & hope to see you . . . But one clasp of your hand, one look out of your sweet kind true eyes would make me feel that the sufferings were not commensurate with the reward . . . no misfortune can make you other than my best exemplar of every heroic and Christian virtue.[5]

At times, "I can see no way out of our troubles"; at others, hope for permission to see him springs: "God knows & he can touch mens hearts—as he made water to flow out of the rock." But "If we are not to be reunited, may God take me to himself." Jeff cries out: "Seldom has a Wife and a Mother been more sadly tried, and I can do nothing to relieve or sustain you. Let not your solicitude for me interfere with any practicable arrangement. . . . We are powerless to aid each other and must bow to the fate which tears us apart."[6]

Not Varina! "I have appealed again and again to go to you, but never an answer." Hearing that Andrew Johnson thought her plea to him "not in the proper spirit," she humbly wrote, "I have never desired to be either defiant or rude to you. . . . I will take any parole, do anything, if you will only let me see him." Over and over she tells Jeff, "Do not discourage me from coming. . . . It is my only hope of peace, to be near you."[7]

He does discourage her, though every pain, every thought "brings to me the want of your presence." The commotion and insomnia keep him dyspeptic, and his old enemy, neuralgia in the head, returns. "Sometimes [it] renders me almost blind—during the paroxism," though he has a mixture of chloroform and aconite for relief and spirits of camphor for "the milder attacks." Still he tells her, in every way he can, not to come, not even to want to. In his very first letter he warned that "bitter memories" would follow. She retorted: "my bitterest [will be] that I have not been able to help you." "The reports of your rapidly failing health make my blood stand still." She sent a remedy for dyspepsia: lemon rind, "bitter orange peel," soda, and cayenne pepper in brandy—"a teaspoonful after *each* meal."[8]

The bitterness is his now. He has to wrestle with the thought of his trial and possible execution, a topic he has avoided, in order to spare Varina. Finally, on January 28, he tells her she will have to "leave me, for the present, out of all your plans." If she can go to Canada only "as an exile, then so go,"

> and may our Heavenly Father strengthen your heart for the difficult task of filling the place of both parents to our children. Tarry thou the Lord's pleasure and let us always remember that all He does is right and that hereafter it will be given to us to comprehend his ways and say all was well. . . . If in reading this it seem to you hard, so was the struggle in which I spent the night and the cheerless anguish with which I met the coming day.

Pain forces him to stop writing, but the next day he rebounds: "29th. Lord 'cause me to hear thy loving kindness in the morning, for in thee do I trust.'" He ends "affectionately praying for our reunion in peace and safety."

The hint of death, however, remains an undercurrent. She must train the children in "self denial, self-reliance and perseverance," so they will be "a comfort and support to *your* [italics mine] old age." "How gladly would I shield you from every pain, your own love will tell you; that love which caused you to interpose your body to shield mine when I refused to surrender," but she must look at "the realities we have to meet," so as to "bear disappointment if it should come at last." Even visiting Fortress Monroe would not be "the picture your imagination paints." He invites her to look elsewhere: "my dear Wife lift up your heart in the confidence that all our afflictions are to fit us for a better state, and to secure to us a reunion which shall never cease."[9]

But Varina will not hear of his death: "anything but this—I cannot bear this. Even Heaven does not console me for the prospect." She is the one offering comfort now, in her determination that he shall live. He is still "my rock of defence and haven of refuge." "Dearly beloved protector of my youth, joy of all the sentient years of my life, be not 'bowed down by anxiety for your wife and children' . . . My spirit is with you—I clasp you—soothe your pain, tell you of my devotion nightly—May God keep my precious treasure—My Lover, Husband, benefactor, guide, strength and honor, my only love."[10]

"My ark is ever tossing driven before the storm, if however without and within all is dark perhaps like Noahs Pitch, the very gloom will contribute to our good in the end." If they survive, she will "build an altar to the Lord in our household, and there sacrifice earthly affections, and creature enjoyments, as offerings meet for repentance."

> I find myself all unconsciously making conditions with God—Give me my Husband, and I will bow to everything else—and I start back affrighted—heart sick for fear of punishment . . . Dear beloved, saintly Husband, hope—and expect—as I do. If I could come to you my sensibilities would be so deadened by joy that I should see everything pleasant; because you were there.[11]

Hope has been sparked by Virginia Clay. On January 28, 1866, Jeff reported that she was still there, and "daily visits her Husband. I am indebted to her for . . . comestibles and for a photograph of herself in evening dress." She had gotten access to the prison at the end of December and sent word to Davis that she would see him too, but she was never allowed to. Knowing his fondness for coffee, she sent him a pot in which to make his own. His comment was, "I have followed directions not with the best success, indeed, I am led to doubt whether cooking was designed to be my vocation." (He had wrenched off the top by mistake.) "I do so envy Mrs. Clay," cried Varina, "I do so long—agonise to go and do likewise—May the good Father give me the bread I so pray for before long."[12]

President Johnson was always courteous to Virginia, but she had gotten entry to the prison only after many interviews and a letter from General Grant, who even asked for Clay's parole, because of his "manly surrender." Grant told her that, if it were in his power, " 'I would release every prisoner unless—' (after a pause) 'unless Mr. Davis might be detained awhile to satisfy public clamor.' "[13]

"Public clamor" was the excuse Johnson gave her for his 1865 proclamation and his detention of both men. She thought him terrified of the Radicals. He once told her Stanton had "been here an hour clamouring for the blood of Davis and Clay!" Because Stanton's War Department would tell her nothing, Johnson let her borrow in "complete secrecy" his copy of the report on Clay written by Joseph Holt. She was so horrified at his "venomous malice" that she sat up all night making a copy, and when she returned the report, she got Johnson to promise he would never put Clay or Davis before a military commission. She had been told that Johnson "might be moved, if at all, by his heart rather than by his head," and in the end, Virginia charmed the permit from him. She was, as Lubbock said, "handsome, spirited," and Johnson, contrary to appearances, had a good bit of gallantry about him.[14]

It was on her second visit to the prison that Dr. Cooper startled her with: "My wife is the damnedest Rebel out, except yourself, Madam!"

The wife turned out to be a Virginian who told her, "There is nothing under heaven you would do for Mr. Davis or Mr. Clay that I will not do." The record of her kindness is in the items that Jeff Davis gave her as his only means of thanks—a pair of oval cufflinks, a small gold ring, a scarf.[15]

He also repaid the attentions of Dr. Craven's daughter, Anna ("Sweet girl your kindness is gratefully remembered"), by sending her one of his prayer books. They never met, but seeing her on horseback, he saluted her from the ramparts and told Varina he would give her "your fine saddle" if he could. Varina procured for her "an exquisite bleeding heart in red enamel & gold with your monogram and hers, in pearls, hanging on a pure fine chain—opening for hair—very exquisite and peculiar—I will send to Mr Speed to send to you for her." Two weeks later, Davis wrote, "The locket has not reached me." No more is known of it.[16]

Clay and his wife soon had the run of the fort. Davis spoke rather wistfully of this but was glad "that so much of relief has been accorded to one of us." Virginia tried to cheer him with messages on twisted paper lighters, which she sent him with a "segar or two," and Davis would slip notes to Clay about friends to contact outside, or the attempt "to degrade the lost cause in his person." Virginia also brought him "a *robe de chambre,*" and Clay a pillow, from a Southern "fair" in Baltimore.[17]

By now, Andrew Johnson and Virginia were calling each other "dear friend." On January 11, she wrote a "most powerful appeal" to him, sounding much like Varina: Clay was dying, "resigned to God's will"; she was "not such a Christian"; "My husband is . . . my all." But she could not get Clement released on parole, though by now Johnson and even some of the Radicals admitted his innocence. Such were the times.[18]

Her work on Johnson's heart, however, may have helped toward Varina's release. General Grant had urged Johnson to let Mrs. Davis "go where she pleases"—except to Washington or Fortress Monroe. At last on January 23, there came a note from Attorney General James Speed: "I am directed by the President to say that you can go to your children in Canada whenever it may suit your convenience."[19]

Varina does not rush off. She is waiting to decide "my future course" until "Dobbin" (Preston Johnston), long since released, can bring her word from Montreal, where he and his wife have been "most kind and attentive to Maggie." His uncle William Preston has told him to be sure the Davis family there lack nothing. But Dobbin, who would not take the loyalty oath "until I know the Prest's wishes," is busy bringing his own family home to Louisville, Kentucky. He reports all well in Canada, but apparently by letter only.[20]

Varina is also waiting for Burton Harrison. He has telegraphed her first thing, January 16, on release from Fort Delaware, where he has been "suffering vicariously for the alleged treason of his chief." That chief, who "once hoped to have been of service to him," sends him "regret that his faith to me should have brought him so much evil." Lubbock also offered Varina his services when freed in November, but he went home to Texas by a northern route. Reagan tried to get him and the president released earlier, or at least to see the latter, but failed. Now he speaks of Davis "very affectionately" when he stops to see Varina on his way to Texas. He tells her about seeing Mallory in his Fort Hamilton prison and conferring with Charles O'Conor in New York about Davis's defense.[21]

Varina's protector, George Schley, has died, and she is now visiting Howell and Mary Ann Lamar Cobb. So when Harrison comes, it is to Macon, Georgia. The "dear, enthusiastic boy," Varina writes Jeff, "tells many touching, and many funny stories of Johnston and Lubbock. . . . The former wrote poetry all over the walls of his cell—the latter darned his socks, and cleaned his room, and looked as gentlemanly as he could. *When I see you,*" she says pointedly, "I shall tell you many of them. . . . *I do not despair of seeing you.*"[22]

Varina begins to find, "manifested to me in trust . . . everywhere the love of our people." Little children come "to kiss Pie and ask for 'dear, dear Mr. Davis.'" She refuses, knowing he would want her to, "scores" of donations that people long "to confer as a relief to their feelings for you." But she weeps over the letter in which Benjamin Humphreys, now governor of Mississippi, sends her money "contributed spontaneously" for her at the polls, and apparently accepts it. "Dear Burrow [Howell Cobb] scarcely will let me go from him without money—urges it with tears coursing down his face—says 'Do let me comfort myself so.' But I do not now need it. My wants are few. . . . My simple mourning dress and linen collars would not be relinquished if I had Queen Elizabeth's wardrobe."[23]

She feels otherwise when she goes to a dinner party. "I was quite taken aback by the velvet dresses, and headdresses. . . . As the splendor dawned upon me, I felt blacker, and plainer, and more separated . . . and choked up and went blind . . . and won the palm for impassibility, I have no doubt." The host's brother sitting near her, a young man with an empty sleeve, "tread so softly and reverently over the grave of our cause, tears arose in his eyes, and his hand and lips trembled *when a silent toast* was drunk, that I should have been glad to . . . cry outright for both. I would not go through it again for a great many rewards. . . . I cannot be distracted from trouble by such things—a contrary temper I presume." She ends: "I never should have known how inexpressibly dear you are to me if your misfortunes had not been so great. I thank God it is I who share them with you."[24]

After dinner, she finds how inexpressibly dear Jeff is to all. When gentlemen and "pretty well-dressed women" come, one presents "her little boy to me, upon whose head your 'hand had rested.' The boy said,

'I hope, dear Mrs Davis, I shall be good enough to deserve it hereafter. I pray for him, we all do.' I choked, and said nothing—they did not seem to expect it."[25]

It is the same when she and Harrison start off the next day for Atlanta, with "free passage" on the train. She meets Maj. Charles Henry Smith, a quiet state senator, better known as popular humorist "Bill Arp," and he turns out to be "a great admirer" of Jeff. Heading into Mississippi toward New Orleans, "many people came and spoke lovingly of you and kissed our baby." "It was not only of old that the blood of the martyrs could become the seed of the church. The feeling is bitter about your imprisonment." At Holly Springs, acquaintances come to see her, "warm and devoted as ever." Jeff has told her of "the beautiful letter" from ladies there to Andrew Johnson "in my behalf," hoping to "relieve your anguish by showing that those for whose cause I suffer are not unworthy of the devotion of all which I had to give." L. Q. C. Lamar ("my true hearted friend"), riding down with Varina to Canton to see J. R. Davis, sends Jeff "much love, and sympathy" and makes Varina laugh so, "I forgot for a time my griefs."[26]

The devotion appears in the least expected ways. Varina can hardly persuade merchants to take pay. She cannot "force money upon" a porter who says, "Tell your good gentleman for me that I have admired him ever since I knowed him," and offers to "work for you all" free. Varina has heard nothing from Robert Brown, but Benjamin has been "astounded" by a visit from him: "dressed up like a gentleman, wore kid gloves, etc. etc., but [still had] his respectful and quiet demeanor." He has gone to Europe with a "bizarre character" named Cornell ("Colorado") Jewett, with "the express understanding" that he is "to go back to his master" as soon as Davis is free. If "not deteriorated" by the trip, says Jeff, "he could both serve and protect." Meanwhile, Varina accepts the services offered gratis by a tall mulatto named Frederick Maginnis, who admires Davis. "I recollect Frederick very well," says Jeff, "first met him at Manassas, and had a very favorable opinion of him." He was Beauregard's servant all through the war.[27]

Jeff notes a "petition in my behalf by seven thousand ladies of Richmond and vicinity," which has "refreshed my burdened heart as the shower revives a parched field." "If it avail nothing elsewhere, it has been a blessing to me . . . I pray that He who judges the heart of man . . . will requite their goodness." "Providential requital of deeds in kindness done" reminds him how a Federal officer has just told him the story of Lt. Jefferson Davis rescuing his mother as a child. He says to Varina, "Was I not rewarded by the instrumentality of that man who saved my little daughter from the negro sentinel in Savannah?"[28]

Davis has been hurt that no one has answered, since he cannot, the "libellous assertion" by Colfax about prisoners of war: he should have been "scoffed by the multitude as the home bred sentiment of fair play demanded." Davis realizes it is difficult for "men of truth" to speak boldly now, "but [I] think it probable that Genl. Lee like myself did not know how he had been referred to by Mr. Colfax," otherwise, he would have surely "exposed a statement so utterly devoid of truth . . . unless indeed he considered it too absurd for belief." Varina dutifully gets in touch with the general, who is now president of Washington College. Lee knows nothing personally of Andersonville and has "never seen" Colfax's speech. In any case, "I doubt whether I should have thought it proper to reply." He thinks "silence and patience . . . the true course"; controversy will only continue "excitement and passion." He assures her, however, "I have felt most keenly the sufferings and imprisonment of your husband" and he has consulted others "as to any possible mode" of helping him. "He enjoys the sympathy and respect of all good men," and "the exhibition of the whole truth" in his trial "will, I trust, prove his defense and justification."[29]

Privately, Lee refuses the cruelty charge; publicly he speaks about prisoners only when summoned by Congress. He tells Jubal Early, who has written a public letter about Davis, how "pained" he has been at attempts "to cast odium upon Mr. Davis," but "*we shall have to be patient* and suffer for awhile at least." "At present, the public mind is not prepared to receive the truth."[30]

The whole Lee family suffers with the Davises. "Mrs. Lee seems to have opened her whole heart to me—all of her girls too," says Varina. To Jeff, as soon as he was jailed, Mrs. Lee wrote:

> If you knew how many prayers & tears had been sent to Heaven for you & yours, you could realize that you were not forgotten. . . . Oh why did you delay & fall into the hands of those whose only desire is to humiliate & destroy you? The only consolation I can now offer you besides our deep attachment & remembrance of you, is contained in the words of my favorite hymn which I have transcribed for you. As a Christian I feel confident that you have fortitude "to bear the cross & *despise* the shame" & even to *pray* for your persecutors.[31]

Jeff will not see this letter for four more months, but even when feeling most alone—"the unfortunate have always been deserted and betrayed"—he can sense what is going on. "The multitude are silent, why should they speak save to Him who hears best the words most secretly uttered. My own heart tells me the sympathy exists, that the prayers from the family hearth have not been hushed."[32]

He knows his people well. In Canada, "Billy kneels at Ma's knee and prays that God will take his Father out of 'prison at' night and morning," and Maggie is praying, as she tells him later, "for Precious Mother and you." In the South, as the little boy in Macon said, they are "all" praying for him. Another young boy, Willie Gorgas, stands at attention, in silent tribute to "his father's friend," as his boat passes Fortress Monroe. Preston Johnston has written his wife from Fort Delaware, "One chief concern with me is for the Prest. I pray for him often, often."[33] A Virginian tells Davis, as soon as allowed, how "my little household" has daily offered "prayers for you and yours." A South Carolinian assures him of "unceasing prayers to Our Heavenly Father that 'you may be saved from your enemies and from the hand of all that hate you.'" A Georgia captain in his own prison has prayed for "our uncomplaining, dignified, heroic, vicarious sufferer." Out in Texas, Reagan is teaching "my little children to pray, for your health and safety" and freedom. Wade Hampton sums it up: "Every true heart at the South feels that you are vicariously bearing the griefs of our people, & from every corner of our unhappy & desolate land constant prayers go up to Heaven for your deliverance."[34]

By March 18, 1866, Varina has reached New Orleans and is telling "My Precious old Husband" that she has not written because "so constantly occupied" and "when I go to my room for the night my little tyrant can't have a light so I must grope my way in the dark." "The baby is your child and every thing must be pitch dark, and quiet."

> It is impossible to tell you the love which has been expressed here for you. . . . People sit and cry until I am almost choked with effort to be quiet. But it is a great consolation to know that a nation is mourning your suffering with me and to be told hourly how far above reproach you are—how fair is your fame. . . . But for your rigorous imprisonment I fear you would never have been beloved as you are now—at least People would not have found out as your poor old wife knows—all your noble nature.

"The Confederates are nearly all here," and send "you grateful messages of kindness"—J. U. Payne and generals, including "warm hearted" Dick Taylor. "I never saw so many old friends in one place before." She goes to church where Dr. Leacock, back from exile, preaches. "I pray for you—long for you—and love you more hour by hour." "I will tell you all about this *when I see you* [italics mine]."[35]

Steamboats vie for the honor of carrying her. She chooses the *Stonewall* and goes to Vicksburg to see Lise Mitchell and Joseph Davis. He has tried to provoke Gen. Winfield Scott to a duel for an insult to Jeff in his recent autobiography. But Joseph is eighty-one, and Jeff does not want him involved: "Tell my dear old lion hearted Brother that such depraved assaults can only excite my contempt" and should his. "Scott did not ask for satisfaction," Jeff explained later, "which was perhaps rather hoped for than expected." (The general was nearing eighty himself and would be dead before the year was out.)[36]

To Varina, Jeff indulges the disdainful and sarcastic tone he reserves for attackers. "It is known I am not allowed to vindicate myself, and it is a sad evidence of public depravity that [slander] can go unrebuked by all who deserve to be called men." He can excuse the "bald falsehood" of Scott, who "probably did not know" he was not guilty of "repudiation," and only brought it up in connection with the book's claim of Davis's "persecutions" later. The "repudiation" claim originated with "that poor little ingrate Walker who had never received any thing but benefits from me, and had repaid them with treachery and injury (being one of the rare occasions on which he took any heed of his debts)." "He was most actively engaged in Missi. politics," and "must have known it to be false when he went to England to publish it." This was his old friend, Robert J. Walker, who had gone to Washington, become an abolitionist Free-Soiler, and sided with his native North in 1861. Sent to England in 1863, he had gotten a dirigible and showered London with leaflets denouncing Davis as a repudiator in order to destroy Confederate credit abroad.[37]

Going up the Mississippi River from New Orleans, with scenes of her whole life so awfully changed, must have moved the impressionable Varina, but she says only, "We passed our home in the night." She does note "a large number of Negroes (discharged soldiers) 'going to Davis Bend' with pistols, trinkets and calico to sell there." Brierfield is still the Home Farm and Freedmen's Bureau headquarters. The Hurricane is long since leased out piecemeal, mostly to the Davises' own former slaves. Ben Montgomery has signed a contract on shares with Joseph (an arrangement Varina found "a rope of sand" in Georgia)—and been threatened with arrest for it.[38]

When "nearly penniless" in Tuscaloosa, Joseph asked for pardon, but he has not received it. He has written a long letter to President Johnson, asking his land back, but has had no answer. (Others on the Bend get their property back in 1865; Joseph not till 1867.) The old affection between Joseph and his "people" leads them to come to him for help in their many quarrels with the Federal overseers. Jeff expects that his own servants ("poor things") will come up to Vicksburg to see Varina and the baby, and they do. "They were very glad to see me—but talked like proprietors of the land. William told me they are getting along very well—'but twas n't like old times.' *But they have all changed.*"[39]

She sends twenty dollars to Old Uncle Bob, knowing Jeff's anxiety about him. They had left him and his wife, Rhinah, rocking chairs, flannels, and "an extraordinary number of blankets," but the Yankees have taken away everything, saying Bob must have stolen it. Jeff "feared that our negroes would be disturbed . . . but could not have imagined that they would be driven away from their home by those pretending to be their especial advocates." Even not knowing of his "truth," "fidelity" and "piety," "what a beast he must have been who turned old Uncle Bob out of his house to find where he could a shelter for the infirmities of more than a hundred winters." "Were we in proper position, to bring the case to the notice of the authorities I cannot believe such conduct would be tolerated."[40]

Sanguine as usual, he thinks that the "chief of the Bureau" (Gen. Oliver Otis Howard) "would probably" get his deputy to "remove the evils." But this deputy, Col. Samuel Thomas, has in fact been quarreling bitterly with Ben Montgomery and with Joseph, who charges him with trying to exact "a bribe" for return of his lands. Thomas is soon found innocent but he is recalled. When Jeff hears all this, he says,

> Brother Joe. cannot protect the negroes . . . and will only involve himself in controversy most unequal and vexatious. I wish he would employ an agent who would have less personal feeling. . . . Poor creatures they may well cry out to be saved from their "friends" so self called. If they could bring an officer of the Bureau before a civil court, the law making them competent witnesses would have the protective effect which was its chief recommendation, when we used to discuss the question in the olden time.[41]

Jeff has had much to ponder in Varina's letters from Georgia. She has found "chaos," with blacks wandering about and dying from want. "I feel so sorry for the poor things." "Shocking as it seems to you and to me, extermination, first by want, and improvidence, next by amalgamation is their . . . not very distant fate." "Gentlemen are shot down all over the country by the colored soldiers. Murder and theft are rampant. Every man sleeps upon his arms." "I think for many years . . . at the South it will be unsafe for men with families to cultivate in isolated spots like ours." "Emissaries" are preaching insubordination and murder. "I thank God on my knees for the cloud which directed me the day I sent my poor little boys away from danger."[42]

"Like you I feel sorry for the negroes," Jeff replies. He thinks things would settle down

> by the operation of the ordinary laws governing the relation of labor to capital if they were let alone. But interference by those who have a theory to maintain by the manufacture of facts must result in evil, evil only and continually. At every renewal of the assertion that the Southern people hate the negroes my surprise is renewed, but a hostility not now or heretofore existing between the races may be engendered by just such influences.

When Varina reports on a speech by Aleck Stephens that makes whites look like oppressors, he responds: "No southern man can be excusable for arguing against the *non existant* intolerance on the part of the whites towards the blacks."[43]

He thinks if only the case were put "fully and truly" to Andrew Johnson, he could, with "his knowledge of the negro character" and the former "kind relations," remedy the disorders. "However wisely conducted the transition of the negro from his state of dependence to that of self control, must involve serious difficulties." Davis only hopes "resolute will, calm temper and practical sense," will extract good from "unavoidable evil" and "save enough from the wreck to prevent the country from lapsing into desert." He said long before, "Brother Joe should not I think return to the river place. All is changed, he will be troubled beyond his strength," though his "right to the comparatively little which remains can hardly be controverted."[44]

Joseph has told Johnson that the Freedmen's Bureau is "demoralizing the negroes, robbing and defrauding them," and Johnson, after many such complaints, has promised "a thorough investigation." So Jeff's estimate of him, so different from the year before, is not far off. Southern esteem for the president is rising generally. In February 1866, Johnson vetoes the bill to continue the bureau, and his veto is sustained. But in July, Congress will override him, beginning the revolt that leads to his impeachment.[45]

Joseph indeed does not return to the land, but controls matters as best he can from Vicksburg. He and Lise are living at Shamrock, the home of Florida's adopted daughter, Julia Porterfield, recently widowed. From Varina's report of her visit, one would never guess that she and Joseph were once at odds:

> Lise . . . seemed overflowing with love for you, her "dear good gentle Uncle." Then came in Brother Joe . . . about as well as any old gentleman of his age that I ever saw and as bright. . . . He has a rockaway and two mules in which Jack drives him to and fro—he likes the excitement of being in a little town. . . . I begged him to come to me in Canada in the summer, and stay with me which he promised to do—when I trust in God you may see him. He was quite out of money and I gave him four hundred dollars—and your Griffith dressing gown as he had none. He was very affectionate and begged me to stay with him longer. I read the largest part of your letters to him, and he seemed delighted, comforted and very grateful—full of love for you. But who of our people is not excepting only Joe Johnston, Beauregard and Jordan—the meanest and basest of mankind.[46]

Thomas Jordan, Beauregard's chief of staff, showed his colors October last, in *Harper's New Monthly Magazine.* His article, "Jefferson Davis," is a compendium of charges begun during the war and continued ever since: failure to ship out cotton and supply arms, personal malignity (especially against Beauregard and Johnston), removing Johnston ("the feather that broke the camel's back"), "passionate prejudices," favoring incompetents (Benjamin, and most of all, Northrop, that "unhealthy brain"), being "deaf as an adder" to military plans of "superior men of independent mind" (e.g., Beauregard), imperious and obstinate, "constantly" interfering in minor matters while neglecting essentials, swayed "alone" by "personal passions," his incompetence in every field making him "a patricide and a moral suicide," his hand "surely guiding the Southern cause to utter ruin."[47]

But an article in the British *Quarterly Review* has meantime called Davis, as Jordan puts it in his disputing footnote, "a wise statesman, to whom was mainly due such successes as the Confederates achieved." Jordan says the *Review* article attributes "the failure of the Southern people to win independence [to] 'the great superiority of the North in numbers and resources.'" He answers that Frederick the Great overcame even greater disparity by "not squandering [his resources] habitually by division," as Davis did. In 1868, Frank Alfriend showed these cases to be so different that the parallel had "no value," but the comparison has been repeated to this day. (Ironically, Varina was about to send Davis "Frederick the Great and some other hard fact cultivators, if indeed any history can be called so.")[48]

Davis's reaction at the time was:

> I have not seen Jordan's critique and I am at a loss to know where that game was played and was lost by my interference. If the records are preserved they dispose summarily of his romances past, passing and to come. Be not distressed by the conduct of those who wilfully misrepresent. . . . If those whom I have served turn against me theirs is the shame, and time will make them feel it. . . . Every one who has acted must have made mistakes, and the frank acknowledgement of his errors will be the best defence. . . . Let him who has changed his theory confess it, let him whose opinions are unchanged conform his action to the changed circumstances, and both classes may preserve their integrity and live and work in harmony.[49]

Northrop found the article "filled with wanton false-hoods," and he claimed in later years that "Jordan wanted revenge, on *you*, for not making him a brigadier, on *me*, for forcing the decision that he was an imposter, with Bgds sanction." This drew the haughty tone from Davis: "that contemptible fellow, Jordan, whose meanness was exhibited in his malignant publication against us when we were in prison."[50]

Meanness seems in the air now, and Davis seems more sad than angry. "A Senator who I have from my childhood remembered with affection," he finds "voluntarily joining in the detraction which my misfortune not only permits but seems to excite." And James Buchanan, in his just-published book, *Mr. Buchanan's Administration on the Eve of the Rebellion,* has twisted the truth about their relations in 1860.

Davis at the time thought people "unjust" when they "ascribed to him vindictiveness as his absorbing trait." "Censure so unreasonable has pursued the old man . . . that I had come to remember the good to the exclusion of the evil, I wish he had left me that pleasure." The effect of all this slander on Davis may be seen in his remarks about "my early friend Hugh Mercer," who is charged by the United States with murder: "He cannot be guilty and surely must be acquitted, but to one of his gentle, generous nature, it is a sad blow to be even thus unjustly accused." Mercer is indeed found innocent.[51]

Davis, however, has to suffer on in ignorance and silence: "In regard to the action to be taken in my case I have like the weary Knife grinder no story to tell." In his *Imitation* he marks: 'It is good . . . that men have an evil or imperfect opinion of us, even when we do and intend well. These things are often helps to humility, and defend us from vainglory. We better turn to God, our inward witness, when outwardly we are despised of men.' But he cannot live always on such a plane. Thoughts of impending death drag him down. "When the shadows fall darkest upon me," he writes Varina, "then the brightness of your unfaltering devotion is most conspicuous and then most I feel how much more you gave than I deserved. May our heavenly Father reward you according to your deserts and bless our children *for your sake* [italics mine]. . . . [I] feel that it is vain and worse than vain to struggle with a fate to which it is my duty both to bow and seek to reconcile my tenderer self."[52]

She cannot do anything for him, will "meet wounding repulse" if she tries, and "be exposed to the prying curiosity and heartless vulgarity of the scavengers of the press, who cater to the unmanly malice which has so long and unscrupulously assailed me." Even if she comes, "new trials, to which I may say nothing would induce me to subject you, would await us here. . . . May our Heavenly Father give us patience under our affliction & sanctify it to our good."[53]

Varina pays no attention. She will never be reconciled to his death, or to being kept from him. As soon as the trip to Vicksburg "to find what had been left to us" discloses "nothing to recover," she sets out for Canada, but her real aim is Fortress Monroe. She takes her entourage—Harrison, Frederick Maginnis, Mary Ahearn, and baby Pie—by steamboat to Louisville, "without expense." Here Dobbin and his wife give her the news from Montreal, and William Preston offers to educate Jeff Jr., but is "kindly refused." Taking the mail boat to Cincinnati as "guests," her party goes from there by rail—"sleeping cars, and every comfort"—to New York.[54]

Waiting for a permit to see Jeff, which Andrew Johnson has "intimated" will be there, she writes from the New York Hotel on April 12: "Keep heart, dear love, look forward. We will be happy yet, so very happy." She has had a visit from the Craven family: "God bless them [for their care] in your hour of extreme agony." She has seen Charles

O'Conor and is "well satisfied with his course." Malie Brodhead and she have had "a nice cozy time" together. "Dick Taylor" has visited, "affectionate as a brother & son." But it has been "over ten days," and there is no sign of a permit. She gives up and leads her crew to Montreal.[55]

Virginia Clay meanwhile has laid siege to Johnson: "If I called once at the White House . . . I called fifty times." Letters from politicians have done no good, not even Virginia's confrontment of Johnson: "Who *is* the President of the United States?" With his every step "opposed or attacked," he will promise to help and then not do it. Finally she goes to his office at eight o'clock on the evening of April 17, and after waiting hopefully for three hours, angrily demands, "Are you going to give me that paper? I will not go until you do!" "Without further demur," he writes out a note. Clement Clay is free.[56]

Clay, not allowed to "take leave" of Davis, tries to effect "some enlargement" of his imprisonment, but he cannot. In Huntsville, Clay finds desolation—his plantation burned, his mother dead, the Freedmen's Bureau in his office, its chief living in his house. He never really recovers. Nothing, as he once wrote Stanton, can "ever compensate for the crucifixion of soul to wh[ich] I am subject"—"neither life nor liberty is valuable with a dishonored name." And the "incubus" of a "disgraceful charge" still lies upon him.[57]

Clay's release, writes Jeff, is "the happiest event for me [here]," but his heart is in Canada: "I have thought in the night season of the joy which your meeting with our children would give to all and prayed that the Lord would give you strength to dismiss for the time repining on account of my absence, and grace to accept the dispensation with the christian humility which murmurs at nothing which He ordains . . . the judge of all the earth cannot do wrong." Of the children, "tell me as much as you can."[58]

Varina has relayed stories from Ma all along, as when Jeff Jr. tried to get out of learning a hymn by saying "he had never been allowed to read poetry on Sunday." Now, in he comes, "a little boisterous . . . and much grown. The only change I see is that he has learned to fight . . . fought a boy sixteen for pretending to believe that you were in petticoats at your capture"—the fiction, as Davis said, "conceived in a desire to humiliate." Reagan called it a "foolish and wicked charge," meant to make "the Confederate cause odious." Cartoonists in mockery have turned Varina's shawl and waterproof coat into a sunbonnet, petticoat, and hoopskirt in which Davis flees through piney woods, clutching a bowie knife and a bag of gold, while a noose dangles above. One caption sniggers: "How 'Jeff' in His Extremity Put His Naval Affairs and Ramparts under Petticoat Protection."[59]

The real Jeff has sent a message to the "dear warm hearted boy," with his "open brow and truthful eye": "I often repeat that hymn [unidentified] remembering that he does so likewise, and hope it may all be realized to him, and to us all both in time and eternity." When Varina reads him this, the nine-year-old covers his face and sobs, "the dear, dear fellow, will I ever see him again?"—one of his "English expressions," Varina explains. "He has just come to say 'do tell my darlin' Father that your ownself heard me read a piece in my spellin' book.' "[60]

She finds Maggie "fat, but not rosy." Jeff, who has called her "our nervous, confiding little daughter," thinks a picture shows her "too thin," and fears she studies too much. He calls her letter, which he has answered, "a sweet, graceful image of her honest, affectionate heart."[61]

It is Billy ("Beedley" or "Button") he has worried over most, "haunted by the suspicion that Betsy treated him harshly when an infant. . . . When he is numbered in the little group of prayer, my heart *usually* starts compulsively as though he appealed to me for protection." Again and again he mentions this. "Billy's bright and inquiring face is often, very often before me." Varina finds "our beautiful Billy—immensely grown—fat as a little possum—and so sweet and loving to his 'Mudder.' Put both his little hands on my face, and . . . said immediately, 'where is Fader—is we agoing to see Fader, say Moder, say.' "[62]

Although Jeff claims, "I cannot be sad if those far dearer to me than myself are happy," he is fighting despair. "You can imagine," he writes, "how one shut out from all direct communication with his friends dwells upon every shadow and longs for light." He tries not to complain that the birds "are tuneful while 'I so weary fu' o' care' " (quoting Burns's "The Banks o' Doon"). Death is always in mind: the "sweet memory" of Varina's "loving care . . . will cheer the few days which can at most remain of a checkered life."[63]

But he can never be downed for long. "Good may come out of evil." "The hope which belongs to consciousness of innocence . . . sustains me still." Next to this, the approval of Southerners, is, Varina reports, "the greatest of earthly consolations," "whatever may be the form or the end of the afflictions."[64]

Bitter humor is a sort of refuge. Congress's finally looking into his case after his "many months . . . in close confinement [solitary]" is "probably the new reading of the constitution, and the exemplification of civil rights." The maddening stomp of boots he counters with: "It is well for you that my writing is not in characters representing sounds; and now having pointed out to you one thing in it which is well, I rest on that triumph." "Air and exercise" are all he needs, Dr. Cooper says: "It was the want which Cowper's bird had, and hardly has bird more usually sought for air and motion than I did, when I had Byron's 'heritage of woe.' " The allusions, conveying how bad off he really is, are to William Cowper (pronounced Cooper, like the doctor), "On a Goldfinch Starved to Death in a Cage," and Byron, whose lines go on: "to rob the heart within of rest!" Yet this is the very letter in which Davis proclaims it "man's dignity to bear up," and tells Varina, "Do not be distressed about my health . . . the change is so slow that I expect to be on hand like MaCawber."[65]

Dr. Cooper sees him more like the bird: "wasting away gradually," under "high nervous excitability," with "a tendency to vertigo." A rumor comes to Montreal that Davis is dying. Varina telegraphs Andrew Johnson, "Can I come to him? Can you refuse me? Answer." On April 26, 1866, after checking with Stanton, "The President directs that Mrs. Varina Davis be permitted to visit her husband . . . as freely and as often as may be consistent with his safekeeping . . . so long as Mrs. Davis may desire to continue her visit." So long as she desires? "Oh for any valid excuse to be with you always."[66]

The moment so yearned-for arrives, and is a shock. After waiting in a cold anteroom for six hours with baby and servants, Varina is shown to Carroll Hall. "Through the bars of the inner room I saw Mr. Davis's shrunken form and glassy eyes; his cheek bones stood out like those of a skeleton. Merely crossing the room made his breath come in short gasps, and his voice was scarcely audible." Sending the baby by Frederick to "the casemate assigned to me," she is "locked in" with Jeff and begins to realize why he has warned her away.[67]

The crude furnishings and the way the food is "slopped" in serving is all "very offensive" to "fastidious taste." "The bed was so infested with insects as to give a perceptible odor to the room." Aleck Stephens took some glee in hunting down and killing his bedbugs at Fort Warren, but Varina says that Jeff "could not imagine what annoyed him so at night, and insisted it was some cutaneous affection." She finds the passing of the three sentinels by doors and window make her so nervous she can "scarcely keep my eyes still," and their tramp is "torture." She realizes later it has made Jeff so sensitive to noise that the very shifting of a foot in the guardroom keeps him awake, and the lamp still burns "brightly all night in his room."[68]

Varina finds Jeff "bitter at no earthly creature." He has only "supreme contempt for the petty insults inflicted hourly upon him by General Miles," who refuses to provide clothing from his trunk or let Varina assist him on walks (he will not accept support from Miles). Miles's "economy of titles" ("Davis" or "Jeff") offends her. He abruptly calls out "shutting up time," when she and Jeff are enjoying a visit too much. One time Miles says something so "insulting" that Davis leaps at his bars, hissing, "But for these, you should answer to me, now." Varina tries "sincerely to propitiate" Miles at first. "We excused much" because his "opportunities to learn the habits of refined people were said to have been few, and his sectional feeling was very bitter." He sees Frederick one day carrying "white napkins, silver table furniture, and delicate viands" to Carroll Hall, as Varina tries to tempt the appetite of "my husband . . . slowly dying in my sight." Miles says "This fort shall not be made a depot for delicacies . . . for Jeff Davis. I shall have to open your packages." Varina blows up and dares him to, and he backs down. From then on it is war between them.[69]

Her sole aim in the war is to stop Jeff's "slow sinking into death." Johnson is enough alarmed to send a cabinet member, Hugh McCulloch, to check on him. To McCulloch, who enjoys his conversation, he seems not "suffering in health" and "neither depressed in spirits nor soured in temper." Although "indisposed to say much about himself," Davis does admit to McCulloch, when pressed, that he was "treated barbarously" for "two or three months." He notes ironically, "my present quarters . . . are such as a prisoner charged with high treason ought not to complain of." His habitual reticence, which makes his doctor say that "it is with difficulty I can discover from him when he is more unwell than usual," is ruining Varina's battle plan.[70]

She sends Johnson a letter by McCulloch but inserts a note from Cooper to correct his impression of health. She asks Johnson for "a quiet dark room" for Jeff and "the freedom of the post—*both of night and day*, so that his mind and body may have *natural rest*. I think you know that his parole would secure to you his person even if the gates were wide open." Two weeks later, with no answer and Jeff "too weak to walk without tottering," she writes again, telling Johnson of "premonitory symptoms of his spring attack [of malaria] which he cannot stand in his present emaciated condition. I plead with you for the life of my Husband."[71]

Johnson has already asked Dr. Cooper for a full report. It confirms what Varina says and goes beyond, describing deranged digestion, "vertigo, severe facial and cranial neuralgia," "uneven and irregular" gait, and the erysipelas that "quickly affects the right eye (the only sound one he has)." The "want of sleep" has affected his "nervous system": "slight noises which are scarcely perceptible to a man in robust health cause him much pain . . . the description of the sensation being as of one flayed and having every sentient nerve exposed to the waves of sound."[72]

Since nothing seems "to give relief," on May 24 Varina goes to see Johnson. He says he must "mollify the public." She points out there would be no necessity for that, "but for his proclamation." His excuse is that he "was in the hands of wildly excited people." She reminds him of the perjuries and the fact that John Wilkes Booth had left him his calling card (if it had been Davis, she says, he would be dead by now). She asks the president to make a "retraction" of the assassination charge "as public as his mistake" and is astonished to hear him say, "*I would if I could, but I cannot.*" Just then Thad Stevens barges in and threatens him "in such a manner as would have been thought inadmissable to one of our servants," she says. "I tried not to hear." When he leaves, the president breathes, "I am glad you saw a little of the difficulty under which I labor." He asks whether Davis has "thought of asking pardon." Varina answers, "No, and I suppose you did not expect this," which he admits. Johnson finally promises to do "everything I can," short of a retraction. Varina goes away "sorry for a man whose code of morals I could not understand."[73]

Even as she meets with Johnson, Davis is signing his "parole of honor" not to escape. By the president's order, he may now roam the grounds of the fort from sunrise to sunset, and finally, after the lapse of a whole year, consult his attorneys, Charles O'Conor and George Shea. Meanwhile, Dr. Cooper's report is raising a tempest in the press. General Miles, "a man as cruel as he is ignorant, and unmanly" in Varina's eyes, is about to be swept away. The *New York World*, a Democratic paper, quotes Cooper to show the systematic breakdown of Davis by "one of the worst tortures known to humanity," the enforced "insomnia," called by a "grand inquisitor" "the most exquisite and victorious of all he had ever essayed." The *World* asks "prompt exposure" and punishment of the torturer, lest "the American people" be held "accomplices." The *Richmond Times* agrees (for the "honor of the nation"), and the *New York News* asks release on parole.[74]

Miles struggles: "I have endeavoured to do my duty and have acted in implicit obedience to my orders. The gross misrepresentations made by the press infringes severely upon my honor and humanity." "Surgeon Cooper is entirely under the influence of Mr. and Mrs. Davis, the former of whom has the happy faculty that a strong mind has over a weaker to mold it to agree with its views and opinions. Surgeon Cooper's wife is a secessionist and one of the F. F. V.'s of this State." Not the "waves of sound," he argues, but Davis's age and diseases and "the disappointment of his hopes and ambitions" make him "nervous and excitable." "Since Mrs. Davis's appearance at this place there has been a determined effort made that as he could not be a hero to make a martyr of him." He asks another medical opinion and gets a glowing report from the surgeon general, but it does no good. It is obvious who has made the martyr.[75]

On January 9, 1866, John B. Hood writes Stephen D. Lee that Davis is the "greatest man of America—the martyr of modern times." Earlier, shortly before his own death from "prison hardships," Edward F. Morehead writes a poem entitled "The Prisoner":

Aye, chain the captive Eagle!
Debar him from the sun!
Ye well can brave his fury,
Now that your might has won!

But most we sigh & sorrow
For him whose noble breast,

In dungeon darkness suffers
Far more than all the rest.

Miles "is relieved from duty at Fortress Monroe" on August 29, and Gen. Henry S. Burton takes over. But this is not a reprimand, as Miles thinks. He is made colonel in the regular army and becomes, in due time, its general in chief.[76]

Davis must still go back to his cell at night and suffer his broken rest, while Miles remains. He can, however, eat his meals, still provided by Mrs. Cooper, with Varina and Pie in their casemate apartment. Appetite, digestion, and "muscular strength" fluctuate. The malaria strikes and is held at bay with quinine. Over and over in his weekly reports, Dr. Cooper speaks of his patient's "debility." (As noted before, he cannot suggest malaria-produced anemia, since the effect on the blood is unknown.) Varina's dreary battle to recruit Jeff's strength goes on.[77]

One great help is that friends may now visit. Gen. John B. Gordon throws his arms around the president and bursts into tears on seeing his condition. He finds him "self poised and unbending." Preston Johnston, Wade Hampton, William Preston, and others come, sit on candle boxes to dine, and toast "in silence the glorious dead and less happy living heroes." Gordon toasts Davis and Lee together: "the complement of each other." Dick Taylor visits.[78]

When Emily Virginia Mason comes on the Fourth of July, Davis presents her a typical note: "Your ancestors live in the memory of their country men for their resistance to the dogma of the divine right of kings; you will be gratefully remembered for obedience to the commandments of your Divine Master, in this that you visited his children when sick and in prison, relieved the needy and comforted the afflicted." She sends "a piece of grass gathered by his own hand on the ramparts" to a friend.[79]

After Miles leaves, General Burton assigns the Davises four rooms and a kitchen on the upper floor of Carroll Hall. They set up housekeeping, with Pie, Mary Ahearn, Frederick, and a cook named Julia. Now people come "bringing wine and delicacies," stay to dinner, and leave by the evening boat. The bishop of Montreal sends green chartreuse, and "to this powerful digestive stimulant the little Mr. Davis ate was due." It is also medicine for the weak "walls of his heart." Varina sits with fingers on his pulse and (with dreadful irony) wakes him up to sip the liqueur, because Dr. Cooper thinks that sleep too long and sound "might prove his death."[80]

Catholic clergymen friends visit: fiery, Irish-born Confederates, Bishop Lynch of Charleston and Father Matthew O'Keefe, whom Davis knew in Lee's army and who comes nearly every day from Norfolk. From the prisoner's own church come Minnigerode, Bishop Will Mercer Green, and Harrison's uncle from Maryland, Dr. William Francis Brand, who has a school. William Pendleton, back as rector in Lexington, Virginia, has "the painful pleasure" of a visit, bringing news of his vestryman, R. E. Lee. He can never tell of this visit, or of what Davis suffered "as the representative of the Southern people," without "a flashing eye and faltering voice." His daughter wants a handkerchief as a memento, but since Davis has only two, he sends her instead "a little book of sacred verses, 'The Changed Cross,'" bearing "marks of constant use."[81]

And "Reverend Mr. Barton" brings a letter from another devoted heart, John C. Pemberton. Davis was afraid he had done him an "injustice" (when forced by "fault-finders" to send him out of Richmond), but Pemberton feels none; on the contrary, he had tried hard to overtake Davis at the end in order "to share your fortunes."

> I hope and believe, it is unnecessary for me to say . . . how deeply I have felt the wrongs which have been done you. I can never forget the uniform kindness and consideration with which you honored me even to your own prejudices and which manifested itself most, when I was most under the ban. . . . we can only hope that a speedy trial—which we know you earnestly desire, and which can only result to your high honor—may restore you to health and to such freedom as we now possess.[82]

Clement Clay, on a trip east about his property, braves the scene of his own torment to give the prisoner what cheer he can. Davis has learned with "sincere gratification," that Franklin Pierce has been confirmed in the Episcopal Church—"a true hearted gentleman, an honest statesman . . . of pure principles, of clear head, consistent conduct and nice honor, I am . . . happy to believe that he still remembers me with friendship." Wanting to show at his trial that "his people had only asserted a right—had committed no crime," Jeff has lately been wishing Frank could help with constitutional questions. Now they can discuss these, as Pierce visits the prison several times. Davis marks one of the days, in his best penmanship, as "made bright by a visit of my beloved friend and ever honored chief."[83]

But Davis is growing "weaker, more nervous," Varina writes; "his fevers return daily—and he is so patient, so uncomplaining—so entirely quiescent in this death in life—It breaks my heart." When she looks at Jeff "beatified by such holy resignation, slowly dying away from his little ones to whom I could offer no higher example," she tells Reverdy Johnson, "I feel it is a bitter cup and doubt if my Father wills that we should drink it." Much as she admires Jeff's resignation, she does not share it. "Patience has not had its perfect work with me as it has with your Brother," she tells Jeffy D. Her restive spirit must ever be working for his release.[84]

In August, she pursues Charles O'Conor from New York to Lake George (and on impulse goes on to see the children for two days). The attorney's prediction of release on parole makes her feel "so young and happy." When it does not come, she tries Horace Greeley again: "Those who represent him as being well, and about as strong as he used to be, stay a few moments, and are deceived by his spirited self controlled bearing. A slight illness would kill him, for he is patched up by the most excessive care upon his part and mine. . . . I hoped much from the exposure of the suborned testimony against him, but it brought no fruits." Andrew Johnson has at least allowed seven more lawyers to consult Davis, Burton Harrison among them. The secretary has sworn not to marry Constance Cary until the chief is free—a risky vow, since Varina tells him no one can "see Mr. Davis' way out of this living tomb."[85]

The prime task is to get jurisdiction switched from military to civil. Although the courts have been restored, a petition for trial or release on bail has been denied. As a state prisoner, Davis is still at the mercy of the president, but he will not appeal to Johnson: "to ask for a pardon was a confession of guilt." But others will. Governor Humphreys sends Robert Lowry and G. M. Hillyer to tell Johnson, "we regard Mr. Davis as the embodiment of the Southern people . . . he is suffering for us all." When Johnson cries, "Don't you see, don't you see, don't you see Gentlemen, that I can't do anything," one of them replies, "No Mr. President . . . I can't see it." "You could pardon [him] who is made to suffer for us all, and who is no more culpable than the humblest of his . . . followers." Dick Taylor talks to President Johnson for three hours. Howell Cobb stresses that Davis is "their representative man" and pleads on behalf of "a million sympathizing souls": "turn the captive loose."[86]

His attorneys express Davis's "ardent desire for an immediate trial," but hearings are put off, first to October and then to spring. Varina writes Greeley that this "postponement will destroy him." She tells Ma, "Jeff grows hourly weaker, more exhausted; he has now to cling to the banister, and to use his stick in descending the steps—and staggers much in walking." It looks as if "his life will be spent in prison": "I am too grieved, too agonized to talk of this. God knows what we shall do—what we can do."[87]

Fortress Monroe "is a wretchedly dull place," she says, though Pie, "the sweetest, brightest child I ever saw," is "as much company for us as a grown person." Varina starts a quilt of silk squares: "my first symptom of the sere and yellow leaf." She is "reading a little, but do not remember. . . . Sewing a little, but rip it out, knitting a little, but ravel it." They are cheered in the fall by visits from Malie Brodhead and J. R. Davis and Harrison, who has been to Europe to see Connie. The poet John Reuben Thompson, editor of the Confederate *Index* in England, arrives with a message from Thomas Carlyle: Davis has "more of the heroic in him than any other actor in the drama" and is "one of the very few great and good men now on this planet."[88]

Hero-worship certainly springs in young Mary Day, visiting her brother in the apartment below. "Back in Ohio," she had been singing "Hang Jeff Davis on a Sour Apple Tree." She expects almost "hoofs and horns" and is "speechless with amazement" as she meets him: "thin, strong features framed with gray locks—one eye faded a little more than the other, but both lightened with a smile that was almost angelic! And the most arresting of all was a quality in his voice that seemed to go directly to one's heart." She makes good friends of all the family. When she comes to say goodbye, she finds the president alone with Pie, playing at "building blocks." She tries to tell him how her feelings have changed, but she cannot, "for fear of weeping"—his fate has "not yet been decided." But he understands, stoops, and kisses her forehead, "saying 'Daughter,' with that voice of his!" He walks her to the stairs, then, putting his hands on her head, "gave me a parting blessing such as I never before heard in my life. Of course I ran down the steps sobbing aloud." She never forgot. She wrote Varina when Davis died and received this in reply: "Your memory of my dear Husband is that of most people who could discern the grace of God which reigned in his heart."[89]

"Jeff suffers so much when I go, is so wretchedly lonely," Varina says, that she cannot leave to visit the children until Mary Stamps comes in December for a long stay. Seeing O'Conor in New York gives Varina such hope that she goes on to Washington: "I do not know my dearest, most precious love, that I can do any thing." She cannot, but her trip makes one thing clear: "I ought to go away from home sometimes to know how rich I am. You seem a thousand feet high compared with the rest of the world. I seem to feel sanctified by our last long kiss . . . [and] your love gives me confidence to do anything except risk your displeasure. Am I not a foolish old girl—but then I am not a frisky one." "When I get in your 'l'arms' again, I shall never willingly leave you again."[90]

In Canada, Varina finds her mother still the cheerful center of her family. Becket has come from England, and Jeffy D. is still there, "a very good boy and steady." She brings books from Jeff for Ma and Margaret Howell, and a prayer book for little Jeff. "When he saw [it], he shed tears, and said, 'this book will be worth all the world to me'; he has never opened the money which you put in—says he 'cannot bear to move it.' " Billy is charmed with Varina's stories about Jeff and wants to "see how he looks," so she plans to take him back with her. "I shall cheerfully abide by your decision," she says, sensing Jeff may disapprove, "as every thing of you and from you seems to bring a kind of peace and comfort to me in many troubles." He does object: he will not have Billy in prison. But he does not mind her bringing her sister, or Malie's coming for Christmas with her two boys, despite his nerves. Indeed, Varina writes Dobbin, "He is always calm and quiet" (the mark of a humble man). Christmas for Varina just has to be "a little nice," even though "I feel ashamed of troubling you dear Banny about such trifles." Frederick is "to engage some suet against I come," and to "get five pounds of raisins, ditto currants, a barrel of apples" and to have Julia chop them all fine, and make also "a pound and a sponge cake and . . . a batch of [sweet] potato pies."[91]

This is all very well, but hanging over her husband are reckless claims of murder and cruelty and a formal charge of treason. John C. Underwood, a district judge, has permitted the following language in the May grand jury indictment: Davis "most wickedly, maliciously, and traitorously" waged war against the United States, "not having the fear of God before his eyes" but "seduced by the instigation of the devil." Mary Lee called his charge to the jury "the most false and vindictive" thing "I ever read," and his dispensing justice, "a perfect *farce*." Underwood has already denied one motion for release on bail. It is in his court that the Davis lawyers must plead.[92]

Horace Greeley, prompted by Varina and perhaps a bad conscience (Conover, perjurer par excellence, was Canadian correspondent for his paper), repeatedly tells the government in his *New York Tribune* to "repair an obvious wrong." He sends George Shea to get Northern signers for a petition to Johnson saying either try Davis or free him. Gerrit Smith, a backer of John Brown, signs it, offers to put up bail (as Greeley has), and writes the president: "I deem [Davis's] very long confinement in prison without a trial an insult to the South, a very deep injustice to himself, and a no less deep dishonor to the Government and the country."[93]

Meanwhile, Dr. Craven and the writer Charles Halpine have brought out a book that exposes the rigors of that confinement to public view. Johnson finally inquires of his new attorney general, Henry Stanbery, what steps he should take, "if any," for "a speedy, public, and impartial trial." He is told that the first one is to give over the prisoner "to civil custody." He is still in deep political trouble, however. Davis remarks to Robert Lowry, "I shall not be surprised if President Johnson is tried for treason before I am." This proves, as Lowry says, almost prophetic. Johnson is accused of treason (and leniency toward Davis) in the first attempt to impeach him, two months later (a try that failed).[94]

By then, January of 1867, the legal ice jam in Davis's case has begun very slowly to move. Chief Justice Salmon P. Chase tells George Shea that he must file his writ of habeas corpus with Judge Underwood. His court will not meet until May, a full year after Davis's indictment for treason. This means more tedious months of military prison, but the plea, if heard, will bring the change to civil courts.[95]

While waiting, Varina goes to Charleston in March to visit the Trenholms and has a reunion with Mary Chesnut. Then she goes to Baltimore to see about her "decayed teeth" and, "pale with fright, but plucky to all outside appearances," suffers through many extractions. But first she has seen Ex-Governor Pratt of Maryland about getting Jeff freed.[96]

She has had a run-in with Joseph Holt's sister-in-law Nannie Wickliffe Yulee, whose husband, David, once a friend of Davis's, has also been a "political prisoner." Nannie thinks Virginia Clay "too fierce": all Southern ladies should "submit" and "have pleasure." Varina objects: "How can we be comforted," with "mourning, and want and poverty" all over the "prostrate" South? Then Mrs. Yulee settles "down in her double chin" and says that God is keeping Varina's husband in prison to influence her character: "when you please Him He will change his condition. So I quietly said that God . . . I thought chastened whom he loved, and I could wait as could you."[97]

Then Varina learns that John W. Garrett, president of the Baltimore and Ohio Railroad, is a "warm personal friend" of Stanton. Immediately, she asks him "to go to Washington *with her*," as he tells it. Thinking this "impolitic," he offers to go alone and report back to her. Hugh McCulloch, "thunderstruck," assures him it is "useless to see Mr. Stanton," but Stanbery, anxious to avoid "an early trial," wants him to go. Garrett does see Stanton, who exhibits "much anger" at the thought of releasing Davis. Telling him that Johnson only awaits his order, Garrett argues that Davis's "death in prison would be most embarrassing to the United States." "Our discussion was long, and often sharp." Finally Stanton gives in. Garrett takes the news to Stanbery; he summons O'Conor to talk terms; O'Conor and Varina send for Greeley to guarantee bail bond; "and thereupon the release of Mr. Davis was arranged." Varina's own courage and daring have brought her long vigil near its end.[98]

"Unless Underwood kick, the deed will be done," O'Conor writes. To everyone's surprise, the judge grants the writ of habeas corpus. The president orders General Burton to "have the body of Jefferson Davis" in Richmond, before the Circuit Court for the District of Virginia, "on the second Monday in May, 1867," which will be the thirteenth. Burton Harrison goes down to Fortress Monroe on May 10 to spend with Davis "the last night of his sojourn in the bastile. It was the second anniversary of our capture."[99]

The next day he and the Davis household, along with General Burton, federal marshals, Dr. Cooper, and attorney Robert Ould, start up the James River on a steamboat, almost like "a pleasant party on an outing." Davis greets with a "serene smile" people coming from Norfolk to say goodbye. "At every landing," Harrison tells, they find "an enthusiastic little group." At Brandon, ladies (his cousins) come aboard and manifest with "kissing and embracing and tears . . . their devotion to the leader who was beaten." Jeff tells Varina he feels like "an unhappy ghost" returning to Richmond.[100]

At the Richmond landing, Varina takes up the tale: "Mr. James Lyons and his beautiful wife" have come for her; the men take another carriage; "mounted police" have to open a way for them; there is "a sea of heads" from the wharf all the way to Spotswood Hotel, men and women, black and white; windows and roofs are crowded; every head is bared; ladies are "shedding tears." When they reach the hotel, where the same rooms they had in 1861 are ready for them,

> the crowd opened and the beloved prisoner walked through; the people stood uncovered for at least a mile up and down Main Street. As he passed, one and another put out a hand and lightly touched his coat. As I left the carriage a low voice said: "Hats off, Virginians," and again every head was bared. This noble sympathy and clinging affection repaid us for many moments of bitter anguish.[101]

The Radicals have literally made the South into conquered provinces now—five military districts under martial law. Gen. John A. Schofield is over Virginia. General Burton's courtesy prevails: "There are no sentinels, no guards—no stranger would suppose that the quiet gentleman who receives his visitors with such peaceful dignity" was lately secured by "so many battalions," Harrison writes Connie. The next day is Sunday, and "after service, half the congregation from St. Paul's" comes to welcome "the State prisoner," bringing "flowers and bright faces of welcome to him who has suffered vicariously for the millions."[102]

O'Conor explains to Davis the simple procedure he has worked out with the district attorney for court the next day. Once more the men are anxious, the women "in an agony of prayer," over Underwood. He may just decide "to punish the whole Confederacy through their representative man" by refusing bail and clapping Davis in "the town jail." The hundred-thousand–dollar bond is ready: twenty-five thousand each, pledged by Greeley, Smith, and Cornelius Vanderbilt, and twenty-five hundred each, by ten Virginians.[103]

The day arrives. Varina stays at the hotel with friends as Jeff is taken to the Custom House that was once his office. Again, cavalry and police have to open a way through dense crowds. Dr. Minnigerode, riding with Davis, sees him "greatly touched" by the sympathy, "especially [of] the colored people." Newsmen are struck by Davis's pallor and his wearing of a heavy overcoat and green kid gloves on such a "sultry" day. He moves slowly, black felt hat and cane in hand, "as one wanting strength." "He wears a full beard and mustache," now "silvered," the *Richmond Enquirer* reports, and his face, "haggard and careworn, still preserves . . . the mingled look of sweetness and dignity for which it was ever remarkable." "His eye still beams" with fire, as "in the old time, and he seems every inch a king."[104]

"Enthroned with a king," is just how Harrison feels when invited to join Davis in the dock. As the prisoner came into the packed courtroom, "every head reverently bowed to him," George Davis writes to his son. He finds Davis "the shadow of his former self, but with all his dignity and high, unquenchable manhood . . . and a stranger would have sworn that he was the judge and Underwood the culprit." Davis takes no notice of the dignitaries, though even General Schofield is there. He stands "erect, looking steadily upon the judge, but without either defiance or fear," says Minnigerode. "The way he conducted himself just showed the man whom no distress could put down nor a glimpse of hope could unduly excite. He had seen too much and had placed his all in higher hands than man's."[105]

O'Conor asks for bail, since the government does not now intend to "prosecute the trial." After a moment of dread, says Harrison, the court hears, " 'bail should be allowed'—such joy and relief." As the bondsmen come up to sign, Davis exhibits "much cheerfulness" and shakes their hands, meeting Greeley for the first time. Then comes the word: "The marshal will discharge the prisoner." "Deafening applause" and "huzzahs and waving of hats" go on until the judge's gavel dismisses the court.[106]

As the commotion follows Davis into the street, he asks Harrison "to convey him as rapidly as possible" to the Spotswood. "I did so in triumph. . . . Our carriage was beset with a crowd frantic with enthusiasm, cheering, calling down God's blessings, rushing forward to catch him by the hand and weeping manly tears of devotion to 'our President.' I shall never see such joy in a crowd again and some of the faces I saw thro' the tears in my own eyes." Minnigerode was with them and recalled the "negroes with their tender affection, climbing upon the carriage, shaking and kissing his hand and calling out 'God bless Mars Davis.' "[107]

At the hotel, Harrison takes Davis up the stairs. The corridor is "full of friends waiting to congratulate him, but everybody held back with instinctive delicacy as he went in to his wife." When the secretary and the priest go in, "Mr. Davis turned to me: 'Mr. Minnigerode, you who have . . . comforted and strengthened me with your prayers, is it not right that we now once more should kneel down together and return thanks?' There was not a dry eye in the room." Harrison finishes the scene: "The door was locked and we knelt around a table, while the rector offered a prayer of thanksgiving; every one of us weeping irrepressibly, for God had delivered the captive at last, and with him we were all liberated!"[108]

XX

Sad Wandering

Harrison was liberated indeed: he could now marry Connie Cary, which he did in November. Jefferson Davis, however, was only "reprieved, not free"—a prisoner, bailed to appear at the next session of court. But his release certainly brought to the Confederate world "great jubilee." That was Judah Benjamin's phrase from London.[1]

From Canada, Beverley Tucker wrote that after "your manly and Christian endurance of an *unchristian* imprisonment . . . millions of hearts" would praise God "for your deliverance." A matron in Virginia whose household had been praying for Davis every day told Varina that the faces of her children "were radiant—& we could hear the cry from one to the other—'the President is released'" and she herself was so happy "that for the first time for four years I feel . . . willing to put on colours." Another Virginia lady asked a kinsman, "Are you not delighted that our dear President is free?"; she could "never be grateful enough to God for delivering him from his cruel persecutors." Messages came from Joseph, from Pierce and Lee and Reagan, from James Mason and Randolph Stevenson, a surgeon at Andersonville. In New Orleans, S. B. Elder put his "ecstasy" into a poem: "Look up, dear land! Look up! . . . Thy king has left his tomb . . . Let thy sweet voice bid him rejoice / Who bore all ills for thee."[2]

As the reality of release sank in, Jeff and Varina could think of only one thing—their children. On the very first day, late in the afternoon, they went to Hollywood Cemetery and laid flowers on little Joe's grave. Their mental search for his dates had been wasted; the tablet read only, "Erected by the little boys and girls of the Southern capital." Then immediately, they began their journey toward the living. When they reached New York City, Harrison took charge of "the chief" and "conveyed him away forcibly," out of the "continued excitement" that was making him "nervous and weakened," to Charles O'Conor's country estate, while Varina and Margaret Howell stayed in town to see a final performance by the tragedienne Adelaide Ristori. Frank Pierce offered "Genl. D." his cottage on the New Hampshire coast in August, but Davis wanted to go straight to the children and Mrs. Howell in Montreal.[3]

Who can say what embracing his little ones meant to this man? He wrote to Varina, before she could bring baby Winnie to Fortress Monroe, "Please give expression . . . to my feelings for my little Pollie Big Boy and Button . . . Kiss 'ittie Pi. Davy' for me tell her until she understands how dearly I love her and how I long to hold her in my arms." Almost every prison letter has such references. But the protracted nervous suffering rendered him so sensitive now that he could hardly stand the noise and disorder of their presence. People's voices "sounded like trumpets in his ears," and "the motion and life about us drove my husband wild with nervousness." He and Ma would get off to themselves to chat "in loving accord," says Varina, while "the noisy ones remained with me." She was suffering too: "difficulties seemed mountain high, the trees and flowers sheltered and bloomed for others . . . [but] not for me or mine."[4]

Jeff's slow recovery was helped along by a leisurely trip up the St. Lawrence River and across Lake Ontario to visit James Mason. There were many Confederates living in Canada. Mason, Jubal Early, Sidney Winder, and Charles J. Helm were escorting Davis as his boat arrived at Toronto. On shore was the British colonel, George T. Denison: "I was so astonished at the emaciation and weakness of Mr. Davis, who looked like a dying man, that I said to a friend near me, 'They have killed him.' " Denison had gotten a crowd to the wharf to cheer, and he went on to Niagara with the party. He tells how Davis, seeing the United States flag across the river, said, "Look there Mason, there is the gridiron we have been fried on"—an allusion to the real St. Lawrence, probably prompted by coming up his river and by reading about him (roasted on a gridiron) in Butler's *Lives of the Saints*, which Davis had at Fortress Monroe.[5]

Mason's granddaughter, who had known Davis in Richmond, and who was to be so struck by his silent grace at table, sobbed uncontrollably when she saw how he looked. His friends wanted, of course, to hear about his personal frying on "the gridiron," but he was "always disinclined to speak of injuries inflicted upon himself," Varina says, "and had a nervous horror of appearing to be a victim." Whenever the name of General Miles came up, for instance, he would simply fall silent and change the subject. A Canadian noticed how reticent and reclusive he was.[6]

He may have scorned pity, but he knew he had offered himself. He thought the offer had been refused. He wrote to an old friend on July 20: "The consolation which I derived from the intense malignity shown to me by the enemy was in the hope that their hate would, by concentration on me, be the means of relieving my countrymen. That hope has been disappointed, and the worst fears which I entertained as the consequence of a surrender of the armies without terms . . . have been fully realized." He was watching the "systematic persecution of the conquerors" work "the destruction of the South. My trust in earthly powers is lost, but . . . God is just and omnipotent. His ways are inscrutable." He argued that good had often come from what seemed "unmitigated evil."[7]

In the pending trial for treason, Davis might yet have to make good the proffer of his life. But there were other modes of sacrifice. "The trammels of the courts in Richmond," for instance, prevented his engaging in business, and, as he told Joseph, "I have no capital to put in." All he possessed at this time, besides small items, was a "lot"—the "only property real or personal" not stolen by "the Enemy." "As long as this trial is hanging over him, of course," noted Robert E. Lee, "he can do nothing." To a congenial offer, presidency of Randolph Macon College in Virginia, he answered, "I cannot risk the fortunes of any institution by becoming connected with it until the odium cast upon me has been removed."[8]

He had discussed his financial situation somewhat with Mason, who, with Benjamin, and Colin McRae in 1865, had from England paid Varina his back salary. Legal fees were taken care of: the attorneys were serving gratis; McRae had set aside English Confederate funds for his defense; and, at Col. Robert Lowry's urging, Mississippi, under Governor Humphreys, had voted money for it. The ladies of the state had also collected about four thousand dollars for Varina and the children. Many things were provided to the Davises free, like their house in Montreal.[9] But all these were stopgaps; what of the future?

They had no home, no prospects, no focus. Joseph had decided to sell Hurricane and Brierfield to Ben Montgomery and his sons, Thornton and Isaiah, while Jeff was in prison. For once he was not sanguine: "Unless the negroes exceed my expectations, they will never complete the payments." But he had to agree to it. The sudden release from the pressure of imprisonment left the Davises without focus, in Varina's graphic phrase, "floating uprooted."[10] Their aim in life became to anchor somewhere; but they would float, often apart, for years to come. Jeff had to find a way to make a living; but one after another, his plans were doomed to failure.

Perhaps as a start, when he returned to Montreal, he got his letter books out of the bank vault, intending, "while the events were fresh in his mind, to write a history of the Confederacy." Varina was to help. As they looked over the messages, however, and came to his telegram to Lee dated April 9, 1865, they could suddenly see "all the anguish of that last great struggle . . . our gaunt, half-clothed and half-starved men" with nothing left but "their honor." Jeff "walked up and down distractedly, and then said, 'Let us put them by for awhile, I cannot speak of my dead so soon.'" Lee, too, had been gathering material for a book, but he was never able to get it started. Varina had told Jeff, however, that it was to be published in America and Europe and earn Lee ten thousand dollars. Davis was "most glad," especially for "the benefit to the cause of truth." He hoped other generals would follow suit, so as to "enable the careful historian by comparison and correction hereafter to give a just relation of the events of the war. When the passions of the hour shall have so far subsided as to permit reason to resume her judgement seat it will be more practicable than it was during active hostilities."[11]

In the fall, the Davises moved to Lennoxville, though it meant living in a "poorly kept" hotel, to be near schools for both Jeff Jr. and Billy, now almost six. Varina's mother went down to Bennington, Vermont, to visit a Southern friend. She wrote back how beautiful it was there, how "quiet and ladylike" the little girls were, how, when her trunk was lost, "I had made up my mind to freeze this winter and say nothing about it" (but then the trunk was found). Her one sad note was "the forlorn condition" of her own family, which weighed her "to the earth." She sent "much love" to Jeff and "love to the Stotesburys."[12]

This was a Southern family who had befriended her on her arrival in Canada. They had just moved to Lennoxville, where the son and Jeff Jr. both attended Bishop's School. Nearby, at Rock Grove, lived a large family of parentless children named Cummins, shepherded by the eldest sister, twenty-four-year-old Jennie. The five little Stotesburys would join them of an "evening, and as Jennie" played the piano, sing "folk songs, the current ballads, and the war songs of the South." One had in the refrain, "we'll fight for you, Jeff Davis, along the Southern shore," and often the man himself would smile his enjoyment, though he liked best a harmonized "Whip-poor-will" song. According to Stephen Cummins, "The noise of the village irritated Mr. Davis in his nerve-racked condition," and the family "spent most of the time at 'Rock Grove.'" "I wish to emphasize," says Cummins, that "though Mr. Davis was suffering ill health . . . I never heard him utter a bitter word concerning the causes that had brought about his condition." If the young people "gave expression to our feelings" against the North, "he would stop us gently and tell us not to feel or speak with bitterness, for only by kindly feeling and speech could the whole nation be rebuilt." He likewise restrained a Confederate, soliciting Canadian funds for the Southern Hospital Association, from "exposing the terrible wrongs that the carpet-baggers were inflicting on the South." This young man, like him, had been imprisoned on a false charge, and Davis was afraid he would use "strong language" that "the enemies of the South" could then turn against her. "I was so overpowered by his Christian patriotism that I curbed my own desires to hold up Radical devilism to public scorn."[13]

Cummins relates that on their last visit to Rock Grove, "Mr. Davis turned to his wife and said, 'Varina, what is the most valuable thing I have left in the world?' She answered, 'Why, Jeff—your Bible.' He said, 'Yes, my Bible.' And shortly after he sent it to my sister Jennie." On a flyleaf in the tooled leather volume, then or earlier, Davis had written three verses. One was: "In all their affliction he was afflicted, and the angel of his presence saved them. / Is. LXIII." There was a marker in the book of Job. A page corner was turned down at the third chapter of Philippians: "I press toward the mark . . . For our conversation is in heaven."[14]

While in prison, Jeff had worried about Ma's overworking and about the effects of the climate on her. She was now "old," Varina says (sixty-one), and "exceptionally weak." When she came down with typhoid fever, Varina could scarcely fetch her back from Vermont to Montreal before she died. In her, "Mr. Davis lost his dearest friend." This was a tragic, as well as material, loss for them both, after all Ma had done, and it "deepened our gloom."[15]

It foreshadowed things to come. Already, even sadder circumstances had swallowed up a companion of happy days. Alexander Dallas Bache had furnished invaluable maps to the Union army and navy, been vice president of the Sanitary Commission, and had used his West Point training, as Lee invaded Pennsylvania, to help fortify his native Philadelphia. Friends blamed his collapse many months later on this exertion. The diagnosis, however, was "softening of the brain." Varina heard late in 1865 that he had become "a drivelling idiot" who jabbered "unintelligibly." He died February 17, 1867. A eulogist attributed to him, "more than to any other man," the "scientific progress of the nation."[16]

Ever darker stretched the shadow of death. The next year saw Howell Hinds killed trying to stop a fight between friends on the streets of Old Greenville, Mississippi, where Jeff had known him as a boy. Franklin Pierce, whom even the caustic Toombs called "the best gentleman" among the presidents, died October 8, 1869. Davis's aide-de-camp, Joseph Ives, also died that year. The next year bore away sister Anna and brother Joseph and Robert E. Lee and, finally, Old Uncle Bob, aged one hundred fourteen. In 1871, James Mason died. Then came almost unbearable grief: William Howell Davis—Billy—died in 1872.[17]

There was no let-up in the sorrow: Jeff's sister Lucinda and Mary Custis Lee and Hardee all died in 1873. Jeffy D. Howell was swept away in 1875. In that same year, Richard Taylor lost his young wife, Mimi, while Davis was visiting New Orleans. Standing at the coffin with Dick, he bent to kiss the cold brow and was overwhelmed suddenly, perhaps with the thought of Sarah Knox lying so, or of the two little Taylor sons whose death had hastened Mimi's, or his own recent dead, or simply the whole horror of the war that had swept everything away. He burst into tears. "His example completely unnerved me for the time," says Taylor, "but was of service in the end. For many succeeding days he came to me, and was as gentle as a young mother with her suffering infant." Whatever he had done for Davis, he said, "was repaid ten thousand fold."[18]

Davis's thoughts of death swirled under events like an underground current, breaking to the surface now and then. God might claim at any time the offered life. Jeff wrote: the children "can scarcely be old enough to take care of themselves when I shall go hence forever." His *Imitation of Christ* encouraged these thoughts: "blissful is he that hath the hour of his death ever before his eyes and that every day disposeth himself to die." And so did the family prayers, presumably still said nightly: "Make us ever mindful of the time when we shall lie down in the dust, and grant us grace always to live in such a state that we may never be afraid to die." The time seemed possibly at hand in the fall of 1867. Davis heard that the father of an executed Union spy was coming to kill him. The father came, and Davis met him with, "Then you are the man who has come to assassinate me?" His bold confrontation turned into a bitter joke when the man said that he only wanted Davis to certify that the spy was his son so he could get a pension from the United States. Davis refused since their descriptions did not tally and was disgusted when the man wanted him to lie about it. There were other death threats through the years.[19]

Davis had been in Richmond when Ma died on November 24, 1867. He had to appear in court the next day. He wanted a trial, insisting to the end of his life that his actions were not treason and he could prove it. He said once to J. W. Jones, with "flushed cheek and flashing eye, 'Oh, if they had only dared to give me the trial for which I begged. . . . then would I have shown . . . that in making war upon us . . . the North was the . . real 'traitor' to the Constitution.' " Ben Hill said he was "most anxious" to show "the innocence of his people; or, in himself, expiate their guilt by an ignominious death!" But now he was left hanging in suspense: "The case was continued till spring."[20]

Although the Minnigerodes had also invited him, Davis was staying at the home of his attorney, Judge Ould. General Lee came to see him there. Someone took their picture together, seated at a marble-top table, looking solemn, as all before the camera in those days did (except Judah Benjamin). Lee had his full grizzled beard; Davis had shaved his prison one down to chin whiskers. Lee was in Richmond to testify before the grand jury preparing a fresh indictment against Davis, even though the Yankee Gerrit Smith was calling the treason charge "dishonor" to the nation and "a great wrong." The jury tried to get Lee to throw responsibility for overt acts of war on the president, but Lee said that since they always agreed, he would have done what he did whether they had consulted or not. Davis appreciated this as "the highest reach of moral courage and gentlemanly pride." It was six months now since his release, and Lee was able to write Mary that he "looks astonishingly well, and is quite cheerful. He inquired particularly after you all." Lee also said, "Mr. Davis was prevented from attending [Rooney's wedding] by the death of Mrs. Howell."[21]

Margaret Louisa Kempe Howell's funeral was held in Christ Church Cathedral, Montreal. There was no Jeff to comfort Varina, but there were sisters Margaret and Jennie and two of her brothers, William and his family, and Becket, who had come from England long since. Jeffy D. had gone to sea: "I fancy I see poor Ma as she stood in the door the day I left and said, 'I'll not say Good bye, my son, but God Bless you!'" He adored Ma, took an ivory miniature of her with him, and after she died, kept his promise to her to be confirmed. The others buried her in Mount Royal Cemetery. At her grave, then or later, was one bright touch of her native South—a Confederate battle flag.[22]

After the interment, Varina, worried about Jeff, left the children with Margaret and Mary Ahearn and went to him. His North Carolina friends Robert and Minnie Ransom, feeling for his "severe affliction" in Ma's death, wanted him to visit them and let them educate Maggie free in Minnie's school. But he and Varina instead went to see the Charles Howards in Baltimore. To avoid winter in Canada, they sailed to Cuba in time for Christmas, and then took ship for New Orleans, and what was left of home.[23]

In Montreal, when Davis had appeared—"tall, very thin," black-suited, with "slender yellow cane"—at a theater benefit for the Southern Relief Association, "the entire crowd" had leapt to its feet cheering while the orchestra struck up "Dixie." In New Orleans, there could be no such outbursts because of enemy occupation. But the emotion was there. The St. Charles Hotel was so crammed with people that no one could get through. One man climbed a pillar to reach Davis on a balcony and "seized him in his arms, the tears pouring over his face." The typical tribute had to be a silent handclasp from "hearts too full for utterance." But one Methodist minister looked up to heaven and improved on the Bible: "Now, Lord, let thy servant depart in peace, since I have seen his salvation."[24]

Then Davis went to see, probably for the last time, his dear Anna at Locust Grove, where "three generations assembled to welcome their revered kinsman." Anna's granddaughter Nannie Davis Smith, then in her twenties, remembered "the graceful courtesy with which he escorted her to the head of her table," his "whitened" hair, his "military bearing." Nannie went with Uncle Jeff and Aunt Varina (who fancied her as "a quirky little thing") to visit Lucinda Stamps and her family at Rosemont, then on to Vicksburg, where they found Joseph, going on eighty-three, "very feeble, but cheery." Jeff was getting pretty old himself, for those days; he would soon turn sixty. They hoped "to find our property available there." They were unable "to get a dollar," Varina wrote, "but Mr. Davis paid nearly an hundred to support our superannuated old negroes . . . suffice it to say we came back with no hopes for our children's future save those we have in God's promises."[25]

In Jackson, the young people, said one of them, "dared not make a demonstration," but Davis "had suffered much, and we longed to do him honor." They warned Governor Humphreys that they planned to "storm" the mansion to see him, and he sent answer: "Storm on, young ladies; I am ready." It was a quiet, informal reception that he held, in an atmosphere of "deep emotion." Davis refused other invitations, saying to Col. George H. Young of Waverly plantation that he would not "embarrass my friends" by staying with them, because of a false rumor "that the people have conferred with me as to armed resistance." "The desolation of the country has made my visit sad, but the heroic fortitude with which our people bear privation, injustice and persistent oppression fills my heart with pride. It cannot be that so noble a race and so fine a country can be left permanently subject and a desert."[26]

There was one more family visit, to Susannah Davis—"salt of the earth," Jeff said—widow of his brother Isaac, at Canton. Her son was the favorite nephew, Joseph Robert. He was trying to farm:

> This year I made contracts, with about twenty-five or thirty of my former slaves, selecting the best men and women, on the share system, giving them one third and one half of the crops, and I furnishing land, meat, corn, team, houses and farming implements, and the result is, I have lost several thousand dollars and the negroes will not have enough to buy winter clothes. . . . If it was possible, I would sell out and let [them] go where they are fast hastening, to the devil. You have no idea of the improvidence . . . of the negro in his present condition.[27]

This was a common experience then. Even black Ben Montgomery had trouble keeping labor. He was trying to get out of his contract with Joseph E. Davis, whose reaction, however, was the opposite of his nephew's. As Jeff had predicted, Ben could not meet the mortgage payment. It was scarcely his fault in 1867. There were cutworms and army worms, and a devastating flood, so powerful that it created a new river channel, cutting the peninsula neck and making Davis Bend into Davis Island. The elder Joseph Davis forgave Montgomery the current debt and kept the contract in force.[28]

At the end of 1868, it was the same story, but Joseph kept hoping. Jeff did not: "The proposition of Ben and his sons to abandon their contract was preposterous, after having had all its benefits, without having met its obligations." He thought the property too large for their "administrative capacity"—"by themselves, I have not expected them to effect anything permanent or important." Although they never paid the principle, and seldom the interest, the blacks held the land for thirteen years more, until Jeff Davis and Joseph's heirs reclaimed it in court.

The Montgomerys always remained friendly, writing to Varina long after Jefferson Davis died.[29]

The Davises were back in Lennoxville by April 16, 1868. The Lee daughters Mary and Agnes saw them in Baltimore and reported Davis well but "changed a great deal." He was scheduled to appear again in the Richmond circuit court on his birthday, June 3, but his lawyers took care of things, and he did not have to go. The case was again postponed. On June 27, he had a nasty fall, tumbling all the way down the stairs with little Winnie in his arms, managing somehow to deposit her on a landing, but striking his head on each step and arriving "insensible" at the bottom. On coming to, "his first question," Varina says, "was for the baby, and the next was a request that I should not see him die." She goes on, in her dramatic way, "He lay on the verge of eternity for many days," but his actual injuries were the concussion and two broken ribs.[30]

On July 6, Varina confided to Mary Ann Cobb, "Mr. Davis's soul is wearing out his body—inactivity is killing him, and since his accident his difficulties, cough, and physical exhaustion have increased. I feel sure that he would recuperate if he could once get something to do, but it is fearful to hold your earthy hopes upon an if." "Quite feeble from the effects of the fall," Jeff dictated through her a letter to Howell Cobb the same day: "I have decided to go to Liverpool to see what may be done in establishing a commission house, especially for cotton and tobacco." "An English man" had proposed a partnership, and Davis wanted Cobb to get promises of shipments from the South. Varina wrote a postscript, telling Burrow that if only he could send "guarantees of cotton," they might see their way out of "the wretched sense of idle dependence which has so galled us." The shock was great three months later when Cobb dropped dead in a New York hotel. Varina found it hard to console Mary Ann, since they themselves "cannot become reconciled to his loss." "My memory conjures a thousand tender recollections of him as I write, and I can only pray that you may be able to say, 'not my will but thine, Oh Lord, be done.'" The proposed business never came to be.[31]

Jeff's physician "insisted on an entire change of climate and scene," and so, with four children and at least one servant (Mary Ahearn), the Davises sailed from Quebec with English friends in the liner *Austria* on July 26, 1868. They were bound for a land they had known all their lives through history, poetry, and fiction. One result of the enforced idleness of Fortress Monroe, had been the resumption of their old habit of reading aloud: if Varina was not there, Margaret Howell would read to Jeff every evening till midnight. They had begun to replace their vandalized library. Besides the four-volume *Lives of the Fathers, Martyrs, and Other Principal Saints* by the English Catholic priest Alban Butler, they had acquired the ten-volume *History of England* by James Anthony Froude, George Ellis's *Specimens of Early English Metrical Romances,* and *The Albert N'yanza* by Samuel White Baker (the latest thing, in two volumes, on the English search for sources of the Nile), as well as an *Iliad* in English verse and works on Arabella Stuart. They also had a huge *Dictionary of the English Language* by Joseph E. Worcester, with its British definitions, pronunciation, and spelling. England "did not look at all strange to us," said Varina, and Ireland, the land of her grandfather James Kempe, seemed to welcome her as they sailed past.[32]

They landed at Liverpool and received a hearty reception, for this had been the Confederate center in England. Commander James D. Bulloch, who had procured for the South the invaluable cruisers *Alabama, Florida,* and *Shenandoah,* still lived there. Judah Benjamin wrote immediately from London to Davis: "I rejoice at the prospect of seeing you . . . dear Mrs. Davis and the little ones." Liverpool was his bailiwick; within two years he would be appointed Queen's Counsel for Lancashire. He was noted for his generosity to all "who wore the gray" and was devoted to Davis. "God knows what I have suffered," he had written Varina, since "the horrible news that my beloved and honored friend was in the hands of the enemy." How tender must have been the meeting of these three, who had all been through so much since their parting. Varina noticed that "much of the well-remembered music of his voice had fallen silent," but he was "always entertaining and cheery."[33]

A friend from Virginia, Georgianna Walker, whose husband had been a Confederate agent in Bermuda, talked with Varina "twelve hours almost without stopping." She had never seen Jeff "so attractive and charming," she wrote in her diary, "so placid and calm and gentle" without "the weight of a nation upon his Soul." English as well as Confederate homes opened to the Davises. The ardent supporter of the South Alexander James Beresford Hope and his wife, Lady Mildred, invited them to Bedgebury Park, Kent. But, as Varina told Mary Ann Cobb, "It costs so much to dress even decently that I . . . never accept any invitations . . . I feel hourly the necessity of pinching at every turn."[34]

In any case, "It was quiet we sought." They settled the boys in school at Waterloo, a Liverpool suburb, and went to see Wales, homeland to the Howells and the Davises. Then Varina stayed with the Walkers at Llandudno, on the coast, while Jeff went to London on business. He stopped on the way, at Lord Shrewsbury's invitation, at Alton Towers, Staffordshire. "These people do not seem to feel their grandeur, so I am quite at ease," he wrote Varina, finding the gardens and grounds "more beautiful than anything I could have imagined."[35]

Suddenly they were "very near the valley of death." Varina recalled,

> I was summoned to see [Billie] die with typhoid fever of a kind called gastric. I found him quite delirious, with black lips, and fighting everything in deadly fright. The Dr. gave me no hopes at all but I prayed without ceasing and poured brandy down his

> throat after he ceased to be able to swallow; and after three weeks had elapsed he became convalescent; he is considered a perfect wonder and is getting fat and rosy . . . what a miracle his recovery has been.

Her nursing exhausted her so much that she could not sit up and threw her into "a low nervous condition." Luckily, Margaret Howell arrived. Davis was there, but "knocked up," with October cold exciting his neuralgia. "I fear his health is permanently broken," Varina told Mary Ann Cobb; "he is at times much of an invalid. I . . . pray to go first if it must be that we are to be parted. Twenty years difference asserts itself when the younger of the two is middle aged, and I am in terror whenever he leaves me. Pray for me."[36]

Jeff's heart trouble, which she had noted at Fortress Monroe, "had not decreased" by the next year, and their English physician, Maurice Davis, "ordered him up to Scotland." Nothing could have pleased Jefferson Davis more. James Smith (a Scots Confederate) invited him. He roamed happily, seeing "from every bracken-bush and fern" Sir Walter Scott's "knightly figures" starting up "in all their panoply of triumphant immortality." He found *The Lady of the Lake* "the most perfect guide book I have ever followed," though he also had *Black's Picturesque Tourist Guide of Scotland.* "You will recollect," he wrote Maggie, "the scenery described in the first canto of the Poem, and it is with special pride that the course taken by the stag is pointed out to visitors." Along with a copy of the poem, he sent Varina from "Ellen's Isle" in Loch Katrine "leaves and flowers" and "moss pulled from a rock . . . where Duncan's widow stood when her 'husband's dirk gleamed in her hand.' "[37]

Charles Mackay, poet and editor, took him around Edinburgh; to Abbottsford, the home of Scott, whose manuscripts "were to me the most interesting"; and along "the Tweed, the Ettrick, and the Yarrow," and to St. Andrews to visit "Mr. Blackwood, the proprietor of your favorite magazine," he told Varina. From there Jeff sent her three harebells picked "on the ground dedicated to the 'Royal game of golf.' " Everywhere, he plucked a significant sprig to send: a "little daisy" where "the Heart of Bruce" lay buried, a harebell near "the Tomb of Scott," "another . . . from Arthur's seat," a "little white flower" from the spot where Scott's character Marmion stood "enraptured with the beauties" of the scene, "two white flowers" where the body of murdered "Earl Douglas" fell down from Stirling Castle ("It is wonderful . . . how thoroughly Scott's descriptions have entered into the minds of the people hereabouts as History"), and "leaves of box" gathered "at the little garden . . . of Queen Mary [of Scotland] when she was a child." There were wild flowers "from the grave of Rob Roy" and heather from "the field of Culloden." At this site of Bonnie Prince Charlie's defeat in 1746, "Mr. Chambers . . . of the *Miscellany*" showed him "where the clans were posted, where they fought and fell." "Tell Winnie I have a flower, Folks or Fox glove, picked for her at the mountain on which the Folks or Fairies are said to dance; they were not dancing when I was there."[38]

At the Alloway cottage of Robert Burns, he found the poet's nieces had been waiting for him ever since hearing he was in Scotland. If all the copies of Burns and Scott were lost, said Mackay, Davis would be their "living record." There were also shipyards and industries to see. Everywhere the reception was heartwarming. One seafaring man said, "I'd like fine to ha'e a grip o' yer haund"—which Davis gave. This was reported by Blackwood's daughter, who liked "the straightforward, manly uprightness of his character, which was apparent in everything, and withal the charm of his manner, a mixture of dignity and simplicity. . . . His fine figure was seen to great advantage on horseback, and he looked like a cavalry officer all over." Blackwood went his daughter one better: "I could mount and draw a sword for him at a moment's notice."[39]

After seeing Fingal's Cave and procuring "some relics and views" at Iona, "where in the dark ages Christianity found a nursing mother," Davis and Mackay ended their visit with a stay at Inverlochy Castle as guests of Lord and Lady Abinger. She was the niece of an old acquaintance, Gen. John B. Magruder. There were fires in the fireplaces daily, Jeff wrote Varina, "and the air is bracing and most tonic. I tried Salmon fishing yesterday and go out Grouse shooting to day—with such evidence you will be relieved of anxiety for my health." Miss Blackwood had noted his "pale drawn face," but by now a reporter had found him "considerably bronzed." The doctor's prescription was a good one; no more is heard of heart trouble for a long while. Varina said he had recovered "partially, but never again was robust."[40]

Before the Scottish trip, the Davises had crossed over to France and gladdened the hearts of Dudley Mann and other Confederates in Paris. Emily Mason was teaching in a fashionable school. The William Gwins were living in style at Neuilly and entertained the Davises lavishly. At one party, Emily and the others, knowing Davis's "wonderful memory and wide reading," tried to stump him on quotations. He "entered merrily into the spirit of it" and got every one, until Emily tripped him with something from "early childhood."

At a New Year's dinner given by the John Slidells, there was much to celebrate. On Christmas Day, 1868, Andrew Johnson, in one last defiant act before yielding the presidency to Ulysses S. Grant, had issued a general proclamation of amnesty. The so-called Rebels could no longer be prosecuted, only disqualified for public office.

Davis's lawyers had meanwhile argued that penalties in the Fourteenth Amendment overrode the treason charge. When Judges Underwood and Chase could not agree, the case was thrown to the Supreme

Court, but the Court never ruled on it. Instead, under Johnson's proclamation, "a nolle prosequi was entered and [Davis] was finally discharged." But, as Varina points out: "the accusation of complicity in assassination was never withdrawn, and the epithet of 'traitor' was hurled at his head by every so-called orator, patriot, or petty penny-a-liner in the North."[41]

Gwin's American colony in Mexico had failed—fortunately, since the French had pulled out, leaving the Emperor Maximilian to his fate. His execution in June of 1867 had forced many Confederate refugees to flee anew, among them Magruder, John Perkins, Jr., now in Paris, and Thomas Drayton. Most of these Confederates finally went back home. Mann and Slidell never did. The New Yorker Slidell, a Southerner since 1810, said he would never live under "the hated stars and stripes." In 1870, he followed his good friend, Napoleon III, into exile in England, and died there the next year. Mann told Davis, "I shall, I think, die rejoicing, that I belonged to so upright, and honorable, and glorious a country. Loving her with all my heart . . . I continue resolute in my purpose never to adopt or accept another." He stayed expatriate in France.[42]

Jeff Davis, ever the soldier, visited in France the cavalry headquarters, the Ecole Polytechnique (the French West Point), and the fortress of Vincennes. Military reviews were held in his honor. Thanks perhaps to Slidell's intimacy with the imperial family, a staff officer came inviting the Davises to audiences with the emperor and empress. Probably Varina was disappointed at not meeting Eugenie, the reigning queen of fashion and a woman of real spirit like herself. (The *Gaulois* said Varina's "heroism is equal to the harshness of her destiny.") But Jeff insisted on declining. He felt that Napoleon III had not been sincere with him. But Varina got to see the royal pair "at mass and kneeling by them was their beautiful boy, the little Prince Imperial . . . so like our own little William."[43]

"How did Billy like his gun?" Davis wrote in January. "I picked from a large number and thought it the prettiest and the best. Caution him about firing it as a fragment of the cap might fly off laterally and do harm to one by his side." Varina had gone back to England, while Jeff stayed with Mann at his Paris apartment, 17 Boulevard de la Madeleine. "Here . . . we worshipped together . . . the Redeemer of the human race," Mann recalled, and "I felt that He was . . . *with us* to encourage us to patiently bear His Cross and to *bless us* in preparation for . . . Eternity." The lonely widower, whose only son lived in the United States, tried to get Davis to buy Mont Po, his country place near Chantilly, and settle in France. Through the years he addressed him as "My ever dearest Friend," "My Best and Dearest of Earthly Friends." But France was no place for Jeff Davis.[44]

> My opinion of Paris as a place for education has not changed for the better, but rather for the worse. The tone cannot be delicate where living objects and inanimate representations so glaringly offend against decency; and it is to be doubted whether the many advantages found here for intellectual cultivation counterbalance the demoralizing influences.

It was the large crowds attracted to shop windows by "prints of nude women and toys expressive of amorous passions" that shocked him.

> The population which remunerates for such work and the exhibitions of such types of general sentiment cannot be favorable to the cultivation or preservation of *modesty*. This would no doubt be regarded as fantastic or rustic, perhaps barbarous; but I am thankful my wife was reared beyond the contact of these "refinements," and many others of which I forbear to make mention to you.[45]

Davis was fond of kissing pretty women, but that was just Southern gallantry; he also kissed the ugly ones. The word his contemporaries use more than any other to identify him—unless it be "integrity"—is "purity." Sergeant Wolff, who knew him in Mexico, spoke of "the purity of his character." Lubbock loved his conversation, because it was "so chaste," and called him a "pure" man. Minnigerode, who "knew more of his inner life" than "perhaps any other man," testified that Davis was "always pure": "his whole being loathing an impure thought, anything low or corrupting . . . he was 'pure in heart,' and lived conscientiously in the sight of God. All his habits bore the stamp of that."[46]

Varina was also offended by lewdness, but presumably it was she who had persuaded Jeff by April to let Maggie go to a convent school in Paris. He was still "very reluctant," but he committed his precious child to Dudley Mann's care. All the Paris friends petted Maggie, but she was "the happiest thing you ever saw"—and doubtless Jeff with her—when the Davises' doctors in England decided a few months later that, because of back trouble, she should not go back to France. Varina decided to hire an English governess and "will myself give her music lessons."[47]

Davis visited Pere-Lachaise cemetery while in Paris, finding the tomb of Abelard and Heloise and "much to excite historic memories and sad reflections." He little dreamt that one day Judah Benjamin would lie there and perpetuate in this unlikely place the memory of the Confederate States of America. After a trip to Switzerland, which cured his persistent cough, Davis rejoined Varina in London.[48]

Colonel Fremantle, now Sir Arthur, returned Davis's Richmond hospitality by taking him to his club, to the Tower of London, and to the House of Commons. Benjamin lavished on Davis what attention he could between trips to France to see his wife, Natalie, and his daughter, Ninette. There was dinner at his club and at the Middle Temple, his legal center and home, where Cowper and Tom Moore and Thackeray had been members. Benjamin was about to be a famous author himself. *A Treatise on the Law of Sale of Personal Property, with Reference to the American Decisions, to the French Code and Civil Law* became a classic English work, internationally acclaimed. His "exceptional success" at the English bar, says Varina, "did not astonish us."[49]

Benjamin had one long talk with Davis about the Confederacy, but only one. "In speaking of his grief over our defeat, he said that his power of dismissing any painful memory had served him well," says Varina. He wished the like for Davis. He advised him not to publish the answer he had written to the old charge of repudiation, brought up yet again by an English book. He had already argued the point many times and found that "people will not listen to reason," said Benjamin. His lucid presentation of the matter shows why his voice was strong in the Confederate government. Davis "wisely accepted the advice."[50]

When Jeff came back from Scotland, he brought a "wooden bank" to little Winnie, a "wood ball" to Billy, and a prayer book with wood cover to Jeff Jr., all with "scenes of Glasgow." Doubtless there was something for Pollie too. Wherever he was, his thoughts turned to his family: "Kiss my dear children" over and over; "May God have you all in His holy keeping ever prays your ever affectionate Husband"; "My dear Winnie [Varina], I have missed you in all ways and at all times. . . . Well, well, let us pray it will all be well until it is better. . . . God bless and preserve you."[51]

Both parents were bent on getting a good education for the children, Varina more with an eye to their proper place in society, Jeff more for acquiring character. He had in mind their "future usefulness," but "the lessons in Arithmetic etc. etc. though important are less valuable than those which it is less ostensibly the purpose to teach. These latter ones make impressions never to be wholly effaced, and determine whether the boy will grow to be a man who deserves success, and by his character commands respect where he is most intimately known." "If they have the radical virtues and love one another, the clouds which darken the morning of their life may be but the harbinger of a sunny day."[52]

When in Georgia, Varina had written about baby Winnie, "She is not pretty, but a blessed child to me—she keeps me from freezing out in the cold world." She was always precocious. Now, at five and a half, she was quoting from Byron's "Isles of Greece" and Tennyson's "Charge of the Light Brigade" (her parents' influence) and talking about "his Holiness the Pope" (Mary Ahearn's) and naming all the countries of Europe. Jeff feared, from the "extraordinary conversations" Varina reported, "that her brain has been too much excited. She is too old for her years, pray keep her back" (so that she can study better later). The child treasured the hand-colored engraving of a guardian angel that hung by her bed. She was willing to give up dollhouse, tea set, and candy for Christmas if only she could have a child's Bible just published with pictures. Varina saw that she got all four.[53]

Billy, the child with "perhaps the gentlest ways," was just now turning eight. Among his treasures were a harmonica, playing cards, a wooden top, a rubber ball, odd chessmen in a cigar box. "The poor little fellow," the father told Pollie, "was a sad and weeping boy," as he returned to school, but was "quite happy" once he got there. In fact, he was "jolly as a sand boy," he soon wrote, telling about fireworks for Guy Fawkes Day and the Confederate flag he was drawing.[54]

Neither parent seemed quite to know what to do with Jeff Jr. "My generous, headlong 'Big-boy' may not meet your wishes in his progress at school," Jeff told Varina, "but habits of study may be gradually acquired if not too eagerly pressed at first, and time is often gained by waiting." Varina had summed up his case long before in her trenchant way: "Ma says he is growing so pretty, and tall—and so good, and gentlemanly—thank God, thank God—who showeth mercy through our Lord Jesus Christ." There were things more important than learning: "Jeff is morally unchanged, which is very much to us." As Jeff Sr. said, "The big boy has not improved much in his writing, but the warm heart was not to be hidden or hushed by his want of skill clerkly." Varina reported a letter from him "full of tenderness for you as usual." Now almost thirteen, he was still taking up for the South; when young Theodore Roosevelt visited his school, "sharp words ensued."[55]

Maggie was the better student. Davis commended her for "progress in your studies," but he dwelt more on spiritual than mental nurture. He treasured her desire to please him by being thought "incapable of doing wrong" and told her to extend this "to all the relations of this life and above all to those you bear to your Father in Heaven." "My dear little Pollie must try always to understand what is right and give her heart to do it." She should obey rules, just "because it is your duty" and because otherwise, "God to whom all secrets are known would be offended."

Davis is always looking, on behalf of them all, toward "the mansions of bliss, prepared before the foundations of the Earth were laid. How small, how poor are the contentions and objects of this world, when compared with the Eternity to which we are hastening. There oh! Father let us be gathered together, loving there as we loved here, save the earthly imperfections & fears."[56]

It was like death to go off and leave them all after so short a reunion. "We are to sail at one o'clock today and before this reaches you my eyes will have turned with loving looks to the place where my treasure is. . . . Give my tenderest love to all our children. When I awoke this morning the sorrowful realization that I could not have my morning kiss came upon me . . . little darlings." Only the necessity of providing for them could have torn him away. Varina had to struggle with her own emotion as they parted, which Jeff suddenly realized in her "failure to look back." He had wished "to run after you and see you in the cab. . . . Poor little Billy looked so confused that I could imagine his asking you, what will happen next?"[57]

Davis was sailing for America to see what he could find to do. He had no quarrel with those who wanted to stay away, but he would never be happy outside the South. He told the children that no matter where born, they were Mississippians, like their parents. He thought now it was "the part of fidelity to watch [be awake, attentive] and wait for the morning," though "the night may seem long." It was still dark over Mississippi. He went there, after attending to business in Baltimore, with Joseph and Lise, who had come to meet him. The business was two railroad possibilities, which collapsed, and a meeting with a man from an insurance company wanting to engage him. Of the latter he was dubious. The man could not show "the condition of the company and its mode of transacting business"—"He says he lost his satchel." Taking the sea route because "Brother Joe is so feeble," they left for New Orleans on October 15, 1869.[58]

Joseph and Lise went on to Vicksburg, but Jeff lingered in the city, where he had a good visit with his niece Mary Stamps. "Molly," as he called her, had asked him to pray for her, and so he had thought of her "without intermission for years." Closer than the family tie, or even her being "a good angel" conferring "happiness amid the horrors of a prison," was a common bond of spirituality. He was "not willing to see you cover the light within you by that awful bushel: the routine of business. Have you not a life apart from the throng with which you move along?"[59]

Molly, who had lost two little girls as well as Isaac, had two children left to support, and she was struggling to establish a school, so as not to be dependent on her father, Benjamin Humphreys. When she showed Davis her shawl, torn up by a servant whom she had discharged, he asked Varina to buy her a new one in London—"I think she called it Lama lace, but it did not look like wool, nor quite like lace." Under Varina's response seethes the jealousy that her passionate love aroused, when Jeff showed even so innocent an attention to another woman: "I do not remember Mary Stamps' shawl in the least, but have purchased one for her of Lama lace—they are expensive things, and now not much worn. Shall I send it to her, or what shall I do with it?"[60]

To Molly, Davis confided a new sadness—"the tone to which I see a proud, honorable people reduced." Her father had described for him "the political condition of the state, of which I will only say it could hardly be worse." By now, Humphreys, known for his "knightly honor," had been forcibly ejected from the governor's mansion and replaced by a Union general, Adelbert Ames. Davis's friend C. E. Hooker had been forced out as attorney general. Recent elections had given Republicans complete control of the state. "I have lived for the fame of our people," Davis wrote to Molly, "and looked in the darkest hour to posterity to right the wrongs to which we were coerced to yield; if we consent, thus becoming parties to our own degradation, I shall die hoping that our posterity spurn the example and pass over our memory." Perhaps he was reassured when people came "for hours," secretly and silently, "for the Yankees were with us still," to press his hand at Colin Tarpley's home in Jackson, showing "the hearts of the people were with him." Afterward, he sat around the fire with the family, telling "in his charming way of his visit to Scotland," said Sue Tarpley, "altogether like himself before the storms of war." Recalling his "quiet heroism," "his kind and gentle face," she wondered how some could "call him cold and indifferent." Her father said, "Mr. Davis is the grandest man I ever knew."[61]

Memphis, a river and cotton town like Vicksburg, known jocularly as the capital of Mississippi, should have suited Davis, but he never seemed more than "tolerably comfortable" there. Perhaps it was the climate. He found exposure to the sun in summer "positively sickening." He blamed his age—"old animals do not bear heat as well as young ones"—but a young doctor living there had called the sun "murderous" and found dust "half a foot thick" in summer, and in winter, mud three feet deep. "The musketoes are so large and furious that you have to use *iron musketo bars*." This was a joke, but not much of one. The mosquitoes, though no one knew to blame them, furnished Memphis such severe epidemics of yellow fever as to reduce it for twelve years from a city to a tax district. Davis noticed "flakes of soot" falling and advised against light carpets. In the spring, a damp cool spell succeeded heat, "and thus my old enemy neuralgia was aided in an assault."[62]

Perhaps it was the circumstances. "At an earlier period of my life," Davis told Winnie on her sixth birthday, quite as if she were a grown-up, he would have found "very charming" the "kind efforts to make me feel at home." He had written Varina already, "Tell Winnie Anne I am trying to get 'a good home and to stop wandering about' as she advised." But he had to live in a hotel the whole first year without his family. It was another year before they rented a house, and even after that they were often "wandering about." Perhaps it was his job: "If I had been trained to such employment it would no doubt be more congenial."[63]

Memphis, thanks in part to Yankee trading during the war, was a thriving business center, and that is why Davis was there. He put up at the Peabody Hotel and met with men of the Carolina Life Insurance Company. After he was "satisfied of the solidity of the institution and the character of the Directors," he was "unanimously elected President of the Co. with a salary of twelve thousand dollars per annum and travelling expenses." This was handsome remuneration for those days, yet he felt the position beneath those of soldier, planter, and statesman: "I have compounded with my pride for the material interest of my family." He was, therefore, "not a little annoyed" when "some kind friends whose zeal outran their discretion" got up a purse for him. He assured them "that my salary would suffice."[64]

Friends in Baltimore and New Orleans disapproved of his going into business. Some still urged on him the more fitting "Vice Chancellorship, that is the Presidency of the University of the South at Sewanee, the college Bishop Polk labored to establish," but "they are too poor to pay a salary which would support us." He was sorely tempted: it was "more congenial to my tastes," and his friends Bishop Green (the chancellor) and Josiah Gorgas and others were there. But this sacrifice of inclination would allow Varina, he thought, to choose the best schools for the children and the best climate in which to settle—England, Baltimore, or Memphis. (The company was considering relocation in Baltimore, and Dr. Brand had an Episcopal school near there.) He would not say which, for his whole aim was "your greatest contentment"; she begged him to choose: "whatever will render you the happiest will be the most acceptable to me."[65]

In six months, Davis was out of debt, but he was never affluent. He was always helping someone else. Out of his penury two years earlier, he had sent twenty dollars, tobacco, and clothes to Col. George St. Leger Grenfell, suffering even more than he from Joseph Holt's malice, at dread Dry Tortugas. He felt obligated to needy nieces, sending Mary Stamps three hundred dollars, and allowing others to draw on his account with J. U. Payne. Varina said it was like "throwing the hatchet after the helve," "a sinking fund in the literal sense." He said, "I can work and fast and wear shabby clothes and walk wherever I have to go, but this does not furnish a fund sufficient for the half it would please me to do for others." This regret he felt to the end of life. Three months before his death, he wrote on an appeal from "a desolate girl" for aid, "poverty is a two fold misfortune, would that mine bore only on myself."[66]

With the Radical victory in Mississippi, Davis felt "all is lost . . . [in] our beloved state. I have not been so depressed by any public event . . . since the surrender of the Confederate Armies." He might even have known that the winner, James Alcorn, had called him earlier a "miserable, one-eyed, dyspeptic, arrogant tyrant . . . . Oh, let me live to see him damned in the lowest hell." Even as Jeff wrote, Varina was telling him how she dreaded "the return to America as a country in which we are to live and die, more for you . . . than for myself. . . . I turn sick with the thoughts of what you will undergo while you see the ideal people of your life's long love change into a mere temporizing people of expedients.

This death in life is the most harrowing of all sorrows." She asked God to "do all for you which in these long years I have blindly & madly tried to do, and send his ministering angels to bear you up under your many trials."[67]

The death of the Confederacy weighed heavily in other ways. No sooner had Davis arrived in Memphis than the body of Maj. Gen. Patrick Ronayne Cleburne passed through. Buried in Polk's Ashwood churchyard after the battle of Franklin, it was now on the way to Helena, Arkansas. "As we laid him down on the steamer's deck," says Gen. James Ronald Chalmers, "around him stood Jefferson Davis, Isham G. Harris, and the few Confederate generals then in Memphis." One of Cleburne's soldiers asked if he might kiss the coffin. "Mr. Davis nodded a silent assent." As he did so, crossing himself and praying, "not a word was said; but each hat was involuntarily lifted . . . and silent tears stole down . . . manly cheeks."[68]

Nathan Bedford Forrest, Chalmers's commander, was one of the generals living there. Davis had thanked him for "kind personal feeling" when he sent Varina a captured flag in 1864, and he had been planning to "rally on Forrest" when captured. Probably they saw one another on this occasion, but the only recorded meeting was when Davis happened to be back in town in 1877, after he had moved away. He heard Forrest was gravely ill and hurried to his bedside. The general roused enough to speak to him. He died the next day, saying "*I trust not in what I have done, but in the Captain of my salvation.*" The profane and violent general had been conquered by his wife's prayers two years before and joined her Cumberland Presbyterian Church. Davis was a pallbearer. Riding in a carriage behind the body to Elmwood Cemetery, he praised Forrest highly to Gov. James D. Porter but admitted that he saw his full worth only after his campaign in the fall of 1864, having been "misled" earlier by "the generals commanding in the Southwest," who rated him only a "partisan raider."[69]

Forrest, like Davis, had looked to railroads and insurance for a living and had failed at both. Davis threw himself into his work at Carolina Life, hiring many ex-generals as agents—his former aide William M. Browne, who became the firm's secretary, John S. Preston for Virginia, Dabney Maury for Tennessee, Bragg in New Orleans (for a short time), and Hampton, a vice president in Baltimore. Asthma prevented Clay from taking Alabama, so Davis hired Maj. W. T. Walthall. The insurance business was booming in 1870. Pendleton, passing through Memphis, found Davis "working very hard" at it.[70]

But in 1873, the same panic that ruined Forrest's company overtook Carolina Life. While Davis was in the East arranging to save the firm by a move to Baltimore, the managers sold it out from under him to Southern Life of Memphis. He felt betrayed and powerless—another grief, another humiliation, another monetary loss. Unable to "save those for whom we acted," and unwilling either to censure the company publicly for failing its clients, or to be held responsible, Davis resigned. "[I] felt like a seaman who last leaves the wreck."[71]

All the while, Jeff and Varina kept their sights on what they so longed for—"I have missed you dreadfully and wish we had a quiet home"—but it was long in coming. In late summer of 1870, Davis accepted an invitation from Sidney Lanier and fled the Memphis heat for Lookout Mountain. Returning from a horseback ride, he found Robert Toombs sitting on the porch of his cottage: Toombs and his wife had been given a room there by the unknowing Northern hotel-keeper. Toombs thought Davis was coming to call and was all hospitality. Davis embraced Julia tenderly, as if it were the old days in Washington. Such was the healing power of adversity.[72]

Davis went on to White Sulphur Springs in West Virginia, where he saw Mary Chesnut, Dr. Brand, and James Mason, the latter in "visible and rapid decay." Then he went to England to fetch Varina. She was sick, so he sailed back alone, and she followed later, leaving Maggie with Aunt Margaret and her new Alsatian husband, Carl de Wechmar Stoess. This Liverpool importer, a consul for the Kingdom of Bavaria, was "irreproachable," Varina admitted, but she was "wretched" because there was no "romance" in the match.[73]

After putting Billy and Jeff Jr. in Dr. Brand's school near Baltimore, she and Winnie and Mary Ahearn finally reached Memphis, and home in the Peabody Hotel. As Jeff wrote Tom Drayton, "We are too poor to keep house." He had told friends collecting money for a dwelling to give it to Confederate soldiers. It was not until the next Christmas that he and Varina finally had their own place, and then rented, at 129 East Court Street.[74]

Jeff had been "overwhelmed," as he started back from England that October of 1870, in the "bitter" waters of his brother Joseph's death. Reaching Baltimore, he was greeted with the shocking news that Lee too had just died. On November 3, in Richmond, he addressed the first meeting of the Lee Monument Association, then being organized by Jubal Early and others. As he came forward, "Every person in the house rose to his feet, and there followed such a storm of applause as seemed to shake the very foundations of the building." Although it was in the First Presbyterian Church, "cheer upon cheer echoed" from the soldiers and sailors assembled. They presented, Davis began, "a pleasing though melancholy spectacle." "Hitherto . . . men have been honored when successful," but here, "companions in misfortune" had gathered to honor "one who, amid disaster, went down to his grave." "It is as much an honor to you . . . as to him . . . [for] you show yourselves competent to discriminate between him who enjoys and him who deserves success." Long before, Davis had rejected success as "the vulgar test of merit";

now this applied to Lee, and to him as well. R. L. Dabney had recently said, "It is only the atheist who adopts success as a *criterion* of right." Other likenesses in these "friends until the hour of his death" appeared as Davis spoke: "I never in my life saw in [Lee] the slightest tendency to self-seeking." "Self-denying—always intent upon the one idea of duty—self controlled to an extent that many thought him cold. His feelings were really warm." Davis spoke of the "nice sense of honor" and the "magnanimity" of this "gallant gentleman" in not blaming others. "When the monument we build shall have crumbled into dust, his virtues will still live, a high model for the imitation of generations yet unborn." Davis spoke of Mary Custis Lee, offering her "the consolation of a Christian": "Our loss is not his, but he now enjoys the rewards of a life well spent and a never wavering trust in a risen Saviour."[75]

Davis's own faith was soon to be jarred, but its foundation was firm. Picture a Protestant president kneeling down before a Catholic priest to ask his blessing. That was Davis in Memphis, when introduced to a Dominican who had been at St. Rose's, though not when he was. About this time, he wrote to Varina:

> I am sorry you do not commune in the Church, it is a help to the Peace which passeth understanding, and the heart when most bruised is most ready to receive the messenger. To receive worthily could not have meant when one was *worthy*, to sup with the Lord, if so they who first took the sacrament did it to their damnation, for they all fled from Him in the hour of the trial.[76]

By December 5, 1869, Jeff was a communicant at St. Lazarus, the parish that Memphis Confederates had formed in response, it was said, to Sherman's attendance at Calvary Church, and so-named because "we were licked by the dogs." Through the next four years, Davis served as vestryman, senior warden, and delegate to diocesan conventions. He gave a silver communion set to Holy Innocents' Church in nearby Arlington.[77]

Naturally Davis became a good friend of the St. Lazarus rector, Dr. John Thomas Wheat, whose son Rob had introduced them long before. Dr. Wheat had lost another son at Shiloh, and his living son, Leo, was namesake and godson to Leonidas Polk. Leaving Davis's home one day, he observed to Robert Ransom: "If that man were a member of the Romish Church, he would be canonized as a saint, and his sufferings . . . should forever enshrine him in our hearts as our vicarious sacrifice."[78]

When they got the house on Court Street, Varina and Jeff brought the boys and Maggie, now also at school in Baltimore, home to live. Ransom tells of "the bright, fair-haired Willie" rushing into the dining room, wanting dinner for "half a dozen or more about his size" whom he had corralled in the streets to help him work. "With great cheerfulness and an expression of pride and satisfaction, Mr. Davis aided in preparing for his fine boy's guests," and put them all at ease. Sometimes Billy liked to sit silently in his father's office and watch him work. When Varina missed him, Jeff would say, "You will not grudge me our grave little gentleman's company when you know how I enjoy his presence." But it all ended on October 16, 1872. This time, Varina's prayers and care did not avail. Diphtheria took William Howell Davis away in his eleventh year.[79]

"The loss was great, and is irreparable." Those had been Jeff's words to Ma when George Howell died at about the same age, some twenty years before. He said then, as now of Lee, "The loss is our's, not his." "The creator" had required of George "but a brief probation," and long years could not have brought "a more desirable end." The long years since then had taught Davis even more about eternal purposes, but he could not help being "bowed down at the loss of the object of my highest earthly hope." "Dear little bright boy," he had called Billy. He wrote to a friend, "May God spare you such sorrow as our's."[80]

XXI

The Cause

"The loss of each child left him the more bleak," thought a kinswoman, "the suffering more incised." When Mary Custis Lee died, Davis wrote to Custis, "A bitter experience has taught me how vain are the words of consolation in such sorrow as yours . . . the loss is ours, the gain is hers." Weighed down with his own sorrow, Davis had to bear through the next months the collapse of the Carolina company, much of the time alone. Varina, "suffering from a latent nervous affection," even before Billy's death, took Winnie and Mary Ahearn to Canada in the summer of 1873, for cool air and the benefit of change.[1]

The other children were in Lexington, Virginia, with Preston Johnston. In August, Davis went to see them, sending Varina en route "some sprigs of grass" from little Joe's grave in Richmond. He found Maggie "quite happy" in the midst of Dobbin's large family, and Jeff Jr. enrolled in Virginia Military Institute. He pronounced this only son left of his four "improved by his military dress and training." Proudly he spoke of "Jefferson 'a wearing of the gray.'"[2]

Dobbin held the chair of History and English Literature at the college that had been renamed Washington and Lee. Custis Lee had succeeded his father as president. Dobbin had taken the previous year off to begin writing a biography of his own father, Albert Sidney Johnston, and resigned the next year in order to finish it. Confederates were beginning to feel the importance of presenting their side of things, to combat one-sided accounts being published in the North.[3]

Some had early seen the need. Father Abram Ryan in 1865 raised a weekly *Banner of the South* at Augusta, Georgia, and printed in it his poems, "The Conquered Banner" and "The Sword of Lee." In Charlotte, North Carolina, Gen. D. H. Hill had gathered material from 1866 to 1869 into his periodical *The Land We Love*. Baltimore held two fiery apologists: Albert Taylor Bledsoe (friend of Davis at Transylvania and West Point), editor of the *Southern Review* since 1867, and the historian William Hand Browne, who through *Southern Magazine* had taken the torch from Hill.[4]

There had been books too. While the president was still in prison, Bledsoe wrote *Is Davis a Traitor, or Was Secession a Constitutional Right Previous to 1861?* A laudatory, careful, and well-written *Life of Jefferson Davis* by Frank H. Alfriend, last editor of the *Southern Literary Messenger,* had appeared in 1868. He had errors about the Mexican War, Davis said, but he "labored to present me fairly."[5]

In 1867, E. A. Pollard had put together, from his yearly journalistic accounts of the war, *The Lost Cause,* called by D. H. Hill "libel upon history." This and his *Life of Jefferson Davis, with a Secret History . . . [and] Intrigues of his Administration* not only blamed the president for Southern failure, but also held up both him and his wife to ridicule. "That misnamed 'Historian,'" Davis called him later, "that vile scavinger." At this time, he merely said, "I never knew the creature personally, and only heard of him as a malignant who kept out of service by the exemption [of editors]. . . . So his false statements in regard to me individually may have the palliation of ignorance." He thought of suing, but Benjamin dissuaded him.[6]

Alexander Stephens's *Constitutional View of the Late War between the States,* more sedately anti-Davis, was a learned political defense of the South. Davis thought it "very valuable for dates and quotations but his egotism causes many obliquities & more than improbable statements."[7]

Still, numerous records were "scattered and perishing in private hands." To gather these, Dabney Maury, Braxton Bragg, and seven other Confederate officers had started the Southern Historical Society in New Orleans on April 15, 1869. Bragg presided and was later president. Beauregard and Dick Taylor joined in time to be counted founders, and among the many others were James Phelan, a very close Davis friend, and a young Episcopal deacon named John N. Galleher. Hood became vice president for Louisiana; Lee, for Virginia. In 1873, the society met at White Sulphur Springs and decided to move to Richmond and publish their findings. When Davis visited his children, he was on the way back from this gathering, presided over by Beauregard. Hardee had come up from Selma, Alabama, but was confined to his bed by cancer, fast advancing. Surely Davis went to see him. In the fall, on his way home, William Joseph Hardee died.[8]

To the Southerners assembled at the White Sulphur, Davis announced that they were "more cheated than conquered": "We were told the war was merely carried on to maintain the Union. . . . Would there have been a surrender if we had expected what has followed?" Lee had reputedly said to Rosecrans at the Springs in 1868 that if he had foreseen what would be done to the South, he would have cut his way through to the mountains from Appomattox. Davis himself had said Lee "anticipated conditions that have not been fulfilled." A mutual friend told him later that Lee "died of a broken heart," with "every pledge broken, every promise falsified."[9]

Ben Hill said Davis was absolutely right, that enemy promises had caused "malcontents" to undermine the government until "we were . . . cheated into surrender." Hill had already shown this, in his "Notes on the Situation," written against the military bills just after Davis's release. How "horrible to all honorable minds" it was, he had said, that the Radicals were imposing new terms *after* the surrender. If these were carried out, sorrowing pilgrims would wend their way to see Davis's cell, "where 'the last defender of Constitutional government in America' was oppressed, insulted, and chained."[10]

Defeat did not mean "we were necessarily wrong," Davis went on; he was sure "the great Creator" had approved the Confederacy. Perhaps "our chastisement" was "designed to lead to the triumph of the principles for which we struggled." Those principles must be maintained by the children of the dead who had "fought for the truth." The Northern press raised "a perfect howl" over this speech, echoed by "the weak-kneed" in the South, who called Davis "imprudent" for saying anything at all. "A strange doctrine," Jubal Early shot back: "Are not all our acts, sayings, customs, &c., the constant theme of misrepresentation, perversion and abuse" in the press of the North? Should not our children know what we fought for? "If we cannot have political independence, let us have independence of thought at least."[11]

Early, now elected president of the Southern Historical Society, made the main address. It was like an echo of Davis's, and a presage of all the years to come: those who believed that "justice, right and truth" are eternal could see that it was "better to deserve success than to achieve it"; Southerners were no "rebels and traitors" as the Yankees would have it, but the true upholders of "the government founded by our fathers"; they had caused "the battle-fields . . . to blaze with a glory unsurpassed" until "compelled to yield" to "immense numbers and physical power." This speech "kicked up a great muss" in the North, but prompted one German-born New Yorker to offer Early his "flying-mashine" to "bombard cities" in the next "civil war" against "hungrey, corrupt, fiendist brute yankee rule": "[I] hate the swindling magots of humbugging Yankees like a good Christian must hate the Devil!"[12]

The society voiced its finds in various periodicals before beginning its own *Publications* in 1876. But the South's history needed a more durable format. After Davis's address on Lee in 1870, Preston Johnston had written him:

> When I see how steady is the trust and affection reposed in you by the great mass of the Southern people, I feel that you owe it to

> yourself not to die without vindicating the truth of history. It has rarely been the lot of a man who has acted great deeds to be able by education and circumstances to tell the story of them. What is needed is . . . a *narrative of facts* and of your reasons for action. . . . I do not believe any man ever lived who could dare to tell in the light more fully what was done in the dark, than you can . . . your motives will add honour to your acts. Let me beg of you therefore not to put off, too long, publication.

William B. Reed, a Davis lawyer who was also a historian, offered to help him with "the duty of history to the 'lost cause.'" Davis could furnish "the actual truth as you and you alone know it," and "anything known to come from you will be believed at home and abroad." He reminded Davis that Lee had intended to write, "and *he is gone*."[13]

The gale of controversy that was to swirl from Confederate writings had begun as a breeze, with Jordan's attack on Davis in prison. In Canada, Davis had felt an ominous stirring when he got a letter from Joseph E. Johnston, who had just heard of the paper Davis (he said Benjamin) wrote about him in 1865. Davis had sent it, not to Congress as intended, but privately to Mississippi, by Ethelbert Barksdale. There T. J. Wharton had borrowed it and read it to Governor Humphreys and a few others, "under the seal of confidence." But then he had let Humphreys's secretary take it to read, and this man had exposed the document which Davis thought securely hidden. Now Johnston wanted a copy in order "to defend myself."[14]

Davis told Johnston he was "certainly inaccurate" in saying it was a public "series of attacks." It was not public, and, as Davis wrote Wharton, "part of the duty of the Executive" was to form opinions on army commanders, and this "could hardly be denominated an attack, except by one whose . . . egotism reversed the relation of the parties." Johnston said his description "was not inaccurate." So, they were at each other again. Davis's sense of justice made him authorize Wharton to send Johnston a copy. But Barksdale, who had the paper safely back, refused.[15]

No one was ever able to get a copy until Davis himself asked for it in 1874, and then Barksdale only grudgingly sent one, with many warnings not to let it out. So Johnston had only "an abstract from memory," furnished by Humphreys and another, for his *Narrative of Military Operations*, published later that same year. He answered "The Unsent Message" in the last chapter, and he lashed back at Davis all the way through the book. "That he should do all in his power to defend his own reputation was natural," wrote George Davis. "But that . . . he should have permitted himself so unnecessarily, and so vindictively to assail yours, is to me a matter of astonishment." He found him on one point "unjust, ungenerous, and unmanly." The breeze was picking up to a wind.[16]

After the demise of the Carolina, in "the absence of any business offer," Davis began to ponder the best place to live "in view of the purpose to write on the causes and events of the War." Some material was drifting in. When Capt. John L. D. Hillyer heard that the president was "preparing a history," he wanted to send "my memory of some of the facts" about Andersonville: "I knew Wirz, and I know his innocence." To counter an attack by Beauregard in the *Southern Review* earlier, Davis, through his former aide Browne, had asked Braxton Bragg for a recollection and had written one for Bragg. The general did not want to write publicly, but he was apparently helping Major Walthall in Mobile on a "contemplated history of the Army of Tennessee"—exactly what Jeff had once told Varina was "due to truth." He wrote to Walthall, "Genl. Bragg has left you but I hope did not take his records and letters with him." Davis proposed to Dobbin working together, and the next year, Varina urged Dobbin to start the book, "or he will never begin."[17]

Right now, Davis had to put his mind to making a living. He told Varina that self-respect was "likely to be all we shall retain" from the Carolina business. He lost his whole investment of fifteen thousand dollars and had to sell other insurance and stocks to pay a loan secured by his shares. He knew he was "seriously injured as a business man" by the Carolina collapse, but he would find some way to "earn the worth of my labor." About the same time, he learned that an Alabama iron and coal company in which he had invested was failing. "The tide of my fortune is at lowest ebb," he sighed to Varina. "But do not despond." In Memphis, "alone in this big house," he was thinking about selling the fine furniture that Varina had brought recently from Richmond, in order to "raise some money." They talked about leaving Memphis but did not.[18]

They were trying to establish a home there, and for them, that meant books. Jeff had picked up *Half-Hours with the Best Authors*—from Froissart to Bulwar-Lytton—in four tooled half-leather volumes (secondhand), Mark Twain's *Roughing It* (just off the press), Froude's *Short Studies on Great Subjects*, and King's *Antique Gems*, the last doubtless for Varina: "I so love the sheen of cunning goldsmith's work," the "dancing lights," colors and forms of jewels, though "I do not care to wear them." She later bought herself Billing's *Science of Gems*. Some nostalgia must have accompanied his 1870 birthday endorsement of *Sights and Secrets of the National Capital* by John B. Ellis. (He had the book in his room when he died.) From England he had brought *The Liturgy Compared with the Bible* by Henry Bailey, and *The Christian Year* by John Keble. The latter had been a gift from one lady to another, but after the donor met Davis, she asked her friend to give it to him, so that he might "think of both of us when he reads it, and pray for us." A lady came to call in Memphis and picked up the book Davis was reading: "I found 'Schlegel on Dramatic Art.'" She also found a "butler" in attendance. It was Robert. Davis had seen him in New Orleans and brought him to Memphis. Now it had a flavor of home indeed.[19]

Old friends came to see the president—Lamar and Reagan and George W. Jones. He went with Jones to New Orleans, being cheered along the way, but he would not start on Sunday until his minister persuaded him to. The Clays came. Virginia loved life in Memphis and spent much time there. Clement lived mostly among his books in Alabama, still suffering from his imprisonment, impoverished and dejected. He and Davis, however, looked like a smart set of twins, with cloaks and hats and visages just alike, when a Memphis photographer sat them side by side. Davis went to visit Clay more than once in his farmhouse in Gurley valley: "That lovely cove is in my memory like a dream land. . . . How often have I recalled the happy hours . . . around your broad chimney place."[20]

James Phelan, a lawyer with "quick wit and winning manner," to whom Davis said, "God bless you, my dearest friend," now lived in Memphis. This meant for Davis only another blow: Phelan died in May of 1872. The Davises also knew there Brig. Gen. Marcus Joseph Wright, and Col. Peter Turney, who had raised the first Tennessee infantry regiment even before the state seceded. Isham G. Harris, the governor who had followed Tennessee troops everywhere—who was with Sidney Johnston at his death and with Hood on his bitter retreat—Davis referred to as "a fearless and truthful man" and "a personal friend of mine."[21]

Davis was in the Memphis Confederate Historical Association with Col. Charles Wesley Frazer, whose little daughter, Virginia, grew up to write an article about the president, as well as a poem in which she called him "a living sacrifice."[22]

Another who would one day write about him, Elizabeth Avery Meriwether, "delicately" offered aid which he refused—"I am in no present want, and feel confident that some opportunity will be offered me to earn a subsistance." His "lofty spirit" seemed to her unsubdued, his eyes full of "fire and force," his impulses "pure and good." But he would never laugh at funny stories, she said, only "indulge in a grave smile," in contrast to how "jolly" Varina was. Mrs. Meriwether, already an author and editor, had met Joseph Davis when both were refugees in Alabama in 1863.[23]

Maj. Minor Meriwether was the engineer for Forrest in his post-war railroad venture, until they fell out. Elizabeth might have fallen out with the Davises, but for soothing words from Jeff. She imagined he thought ill of her for her "unpopular convictions," but he replied, "You are quite mistaken." He had never measured his opinions "by the numbers who concurred in them" and "could not depreciate one who boldly held to creed against the many headed monster thing." As to *the* creed, he gingerly explained that Varina's "personal attachment" made her regret "your disbelief of things which she considers essential both to temporal and eternal welfare, and the truths by which men should live, for which men should be willing to die." Varina's "regard is better worth than mine," and Elizabeth had "mistaken a pained love for . . .'disapproval.'"[24]

Varina was quite as devout as Jeff, but less contemplative, more the doer. She was the Martha and Jeff the Mary in her painting of the sisters of Lazarus. For St. Lazarus' Church, where she was a communicant by 1870, she got the ladies to give "brooches, rings, chains, and gifts" to make a "chalice, paten and flagon." When St. Lazarus merged with Grace Church, she had this communion service sent in memory of Dr. Wheat to the parish in North Carolina where he had gone.[25] For a church raffle, she made "a wonderful *Quilt*" of "matchless beauty," to commemorate "the glorious, overpowered, Southern cause," prompting the compliment: "a woman of the most extraordinary genius." She did give Maggie the contemplative classic *The Imitation of Christ* in the same translation that Jeff treasured.[26] Varina had a way of hiding her piety, as well as her immense intelligence, behind her jollity, though Lamar asked Jeff "if I did not think you 'the most intelligent woman I had ever seen.'" She was evidently as popular with the clergy of Memphis as she was with most men. Dr. George White, rector of Calvary Church, gave her a large prayer book; Dr. Boyle, at St. Lazarus after Dr. Wheat, gave her De Vere's *Americanisms;* Dr. Quintard, now bishop of Tennessee, inscribed *The Manual of Family Devotion* to "Mrs. Davis with God's blessing"; and Father Thomas Burke presented her with *Catholic Legends.*[27]

Dr. Luke Blackburn, a Kentucky friend who came to Memphis in 1873 to fight a yellow fever epidemic, became the Davises' physician. In January of 1874, he helped Varina in her campaign to send Jeff to England by advising "a sea voyage." Varina thought the trip would improve his strength: "I cannot live without hope of being with you to my journey's end." But he, having gotten as far as New Orleans, had "a severe struggle," feeling "I should not leave you." His feet had been swelling, and he had a bad cough. She feared the water "now settled in other parts" would pass "to your heart"—"then what would become of me. Only and dear love, think of this and go—go at once . . . I am perfectly wretched about you—oh, do go—please do not linger."[28]

Davis insisted he was all right, but he had his heart examined by one of Beauregard's doctors, the noted Samuel Choppin, who assured him that "there was no organic defect" and that the foot-swelling probably came from a liver "derangement." From a swelling in his head, not connected "with any thing else," Dr. Choppin drew off "about seven ounces" of water, but "all is well," Jeff reported, "no possible danger." Varina sent down a recipe for tonic that Mary Stamps was to concoct: chopped burr artichoke leaves in whiskey. "It is intensely bitter but is a specific for dropsy . . . will you take it for me—will you do it because

I love you to distraction?" In the end, he took it, and he also sailed on the SS *Alabama* (doubtless musing ironically on the name), saying, "I hope thus to remove one of your anxieties, and am sorry so little is in my power for the fulfilment of my obligation to bear your burdens."[29]

The separation brought forth tender phrases and pet names. Varina: "I wore your dear letter near my heart as I used to do . . . sweet dear love—good night . . . your old Waafe"; "my dear old precious darling blessed Bannie. I am, as ever devotedly, your own Winnie." Jeff: "My heart has been sad for want of its only sunshine . . . across the seas I send you immeasurable kisses and oceans of love"; "Sweet Wife, I . . . am so lost without you . . . Blessings ever attend you dear Waafe ever prays your old Bann." But Jeff's solitary nature also spoke: "The loneliness of the ship suits me so well that I am not anxious to reach the port." ("Eschew thou noise and the press of men as much as thou mayest," said his *Imitation.*) In Liverpool he lay on a sofa before the fire on their anniversary night in "the luxury of being alone with my love and living over the happiest of our married days." Margaret and Carl Stoess were surprised to find him there when they came in at midnight. He had not noticed the passage of time.[30]

While there, he also stayed with Georgianna and Norman Walker. He called on the manager of the Royal Insurance Company to see about representing them in the South and met a rude shock. The New York agent said "the animosity at the North was so great against *me individually*" that to hire him would affect their business. Jeff felt this "dread of the Yankees" might ruin his chance of English employment and said, almost facetiously, "I could hunt or fish or chop and hoe," but that would not support them. "God guards the sparrow, and will I pray keep watch over my dear Wife and children."[31]

Then Frank Lubbock came. Together they visited Shakespeare's home on the way to London, where Dr. Maurice Davis pronounced his old patient "better than when he first saw us." He found "now as then weak action of the heart, but says it results from debility and will end with improvement of the general health." In March, the two friends crossed the English Channel for a visit with Dudley Mann. He had survived the Franco-Prussian War with its revolt by the Commune, its siege, and the occupation of Paris by the Germans, though his cat had not ("victim on the 103rd day of the siege" to a "human, or rather inhuman, appetite," he wrote). Lubbock knew Davis's "constant habit" was to go to church, and on Sunday he called for him at Mann's, 51 Rue du Luxembourg, only to find that they would read the Episcopal service there. Mann had sworn never to set foot in the Paris church again after the priest refused to pray for the Confederacy. When Davis and Lubbock later went to the chapel of Les Invalides, the disabled veterans there "could but painfully remind me of our neglected braves and their unprovided orphans," Davis wrote Varina; "It is well that virtue is its own reward." The next Sunday, he and Lubbock went to mass at La Madeleine.[32]

Jeff was "sadly" oppressed by separation from Varina. He at least could see her friends: Emily Mason and her guest, Sarah Knox Wood, his niece and godchild, the Slidell daughters (married to highborn Frenchmen), and Mary Lee (the daughter) who sent affection. Mann wanted to keep Davis in France so badly that he offered to turn his country place into a horse farm. It was all of seven acres, and Jeff quipped to Varina; "What a wild herd we could have on that domain!" Mann thought Varina would like Chantilly, since Orleanist royalty lived there. "So impossible is it for our best friends to comprehend the measure of our requirements," Jeff sighed. Shop windows reminded him of "the sad want of money." "Dear Winnie, I reproach myself with the trouble you are bearing alone. . . . I have, however, done as you wished . . . beloved, honored, trusted, sweet, sweet wife . . . God bless and keep you all."[33]

Although he tried hard, in both England and France, to find employment, "I have met disappointment in all my business attempts." A sad shadow of the old irascibility appears in "It is not always possible to be good natured under the remarks which ignorance and cupidity dictate . . . the ignorance of our section is truly astonishing." The British have "*a secret dread of displeasing the Yankees* which presents an obstacle to my success." "The English seem to think every thing in our county is dependent on New York . . . it is hard to avoid melancholy." But "from each overthrow of a hope, I rise proud in the consciousness that my sin is the love of my country and . . . my suffering is for virtue's sake." He used an agent because he felt he owed it "to our people if not to myself," in view of "the dignity conferred upon me," not to "run round begging for employment." "Dear old wife, I hear you say—we can fast, we can toil in secret, but *we can not crawl in public.*" His last hope was a company to buy Southern land for emigrants, but this too faded away. Finally, he took off for Scotland with Lubbock, and then for home.[34]

Jeff came back with health "much improved," the cough "less frequent and less violent," though swelling of feet had "not entirely disappeared." "In these days of our hard fortune," he had written home, "we must consent to be submissionists. When we can, we will try to find a more congenial home than Memphis." Meanwhile, Varina had moved the family into a cheaper house at 98 Court Street. Only "my own little Pollie and my dear little sunbeam Winnanne" were at home now. Maggie had had a member of the Rhett family "more than spooney" about her, which gave her father considerable pause. But Varina was "ready with Excalibar in the shape of ridicule," and she evidently ran him off.[35]

Jeff rewarded Varina's "fidelity and love" through "many trials" with the gift of a an enormous gilt-edged Bible in tooled leather, on February 26, 1875, marking "thirty years of married life." The year to come meant only more trials. Within a month, Davis was writing to Preston Johnston, "Do me the kindness to withdraw Jeff. from the Institute and send him to Memphis." The boy had spoken earlier of V. M. I. as his "penitentiary," but he had seemed proud of "the Corps" when reporting that "the 1st Va Reg. . . . refused to drill against us." In this happy letter, he told "my own dear Father" how his friends in Richmond "all sent a great deal of love." "Miss Mattie Ould, the belle of R., kissed me for my Father, but you may judge I was very glad to get it . . . & particularly as it was for your sake . . . my dear Father . . . tell me all about yourself for you know *that* interests me more than anything else. . . . Your loving / Boy / Jeff." The tone, so typical of him, must have made doubly hard Davis's admission to Johnston, of "the pain which seems ever to rest where he is." He spoke of him as "an *uneducated* boy" and hinted at "dissipation." "This is, my dear friend, a sad conclusion to my hopes for the only Son left to me, and I would he had permitted me to drink of a less bitter cup."[36]

Other cups were waiting, bitterer still.

Varina had had a boisterous letter from Jeffy D. when "At Sea" in the SS *Pelican.* His laughter "that Ma used to say sounded like an empty barrel with the bung out" roared at her description of Jeff Jr.: "I never thought he'd be hung for beauty, but he used to show evidence of something more to be desired by far, i.e., a big, honest heart. Encourage him in the idea of coming to me if he ever runs away. You know it runs in our blood." Then, soberly, "If he does, I guarantee he will be glad to return." It had been seven years since Jeffy D. left Montreal for "a life of adventure." It had been anything but the "careless, romantic sort of Existence" he had imagined. He had had "to ram my hands in my pockets, and biting my tongue & lips, run away to some other part of the ship" to keep from hitting "those above me" for their "taunts and insults." "However, it is all over now."[37]

But it was not all over. Four months later he told how he had won command of a vessel "over the heads of some 75 or 100 applicants." But then they had gotten him dismissed through "an absolute lie," after complaining that he had been "in the 'Rebel Navy' and they had been loyal." He felt like "sliding down the hill . . . but thanks to my native stubbornness, I am still clinging tooth and toenail." "I tremble for poor little Jeff when he comes to encounter the rude buffets of life." "My friends here, God bless them! have stood by me." They had good reason. Jefferson Davis Howell was known in California as a "courteous and chivalric gentleman." As a passenger early that year, he had risked his life to save the ship from breaking up on the rocks. "His daring" attracted the attention of another steamship line, and he was made captain of the *Pacific,* plying between San Francisco and Seattle.[38]

In 1875, Davis asked the boy, not yet thirty, to make his home with them, and he promised to come when he could. William Howell had gone out to join his brother and look for work. From him came the telegram, November 12, answering one from Davis: "Reliable died on raft from exhaustion sunday night body lost." The *Pacific* had been rammed by a sailing vessel in a gale. Davis had heard the news in New Orleans, and while wiring William, had written to Varina in Memphis: "Our dear boy was strong in body and in heart. . . . Too true to his trust to leave his ship while there was anything for the Capt. to do, he would see the danger and provide for it by constructing a raft." That was exactly what happened. Jeffy D. got all his passengers off safely, and then, "the last man to leave the ship," swam to the raft, with an old woman clinging to him. An account, evidently from survivors, says that with the sea "running mountain high," Howell, knowing "that once from his support he was lost forever . . . acted as everyone was sure he would act, and at the cry of a perishing woman plunged in to her assistance, sacrificing his own life."[39]

Jeff wrote, "The pride I felt in the gallantry and success of our boy as a Sailor is both humbled and rebuked." A different sort of "pride in him and bitter grief contended in Mr. Davis's heart as long as he lived," Varina says: he held up Jeffy D. "as his model of a Christian hero." With "our son only" left, "every prop" torn from his old age, Davis "sought constant occupation to still his grief."[40]

He was on the Gulf Coast shortly after this, where "the moaning of the winds among the pines and the rolling waves of the Gulf . . . made me wish to lay me down and be at home until this trial is past." He inspected "the lots you long ago selected" there, "now overgrown." "I then went on to Mrs. Dorsey's, but she had left. . . . Beauvoir is a fine place, large and beautiful house, and many orange trees yet full of fruit." ("Mrs. Dorsey" was Sarah Anne Ellis of Natchez, well known to Jeff "from her infancy" and Varina's "old schoolmate," now a renowned writer, whose husband, Samuel A. Dorsey, had just died.) Not only the loss of Jeffy D., but the failure of every hope was beginning to tell: "Everything is to me like an ignis fatuus, save that my pursuit does not bring me to a relieving precipice."[41]

One failed hope was Brierfield. With no other prospect for income, Davis had begun action before his European trip to recover it before the legal time ran out. On his return, he found that "Lize and Joe Mitchell . . . have denied my claims and pleaded an estoppel." He had not only to contest Joseph's will, of which he was an executor, but actually to prove his ownership, which till then no one had doubted. Ben Montgomery testified that Davis was to reclaim Brierfield whenever he wished. But the legal tangle was tight, and the court ruled against him. He would have kept Varina out of it, "had the other party been fair & truthful," but he had asked her, though "free to decline," to write a deposition. This brought one bright note: his lawyers declared it "*the best instrument of the kind they ever saw.* So much for a poor old Waafe, who might in happier days . . . have been a writer whose name would have gone down to future ages." He appealed the case.[42]

Davis had already inspected some mines in Arkansas and made a trip to Texas, where he had offered to him presidency of the Agricultural and Mechanical College, and of a prospective railroad. He wrote Varina, "I have declined the first and nobody has power to offer the second." He had toyed with the college idea, but Varina's dread of "our Texas hegira," and other things, made him finally refuse it. Lubbock had met him in Galveston and taken him to church (he arrived on Sunday). Then he rode with him by special train all the way to Dallas: "It was like a triumphal procession; never before or since has such an outpouring of the people been seen." At Houston, where he spoke at the state fair, "the old men grew wild at his magnificent tribute" to the veterans of the Texas Revolution. Survivors of the Confederacy's Davis Guards cried as they shook his hand. A huge crowd waited for hours in the rain at Austin because cheering people at every stop had delayed the train by calling him out to the platform. Thousands there told him individually "how they honored and loved him." And there, at the grave of Albert Sidney Johnston, his friends discreetly withdrew and left him alone. They saw him stand in silence. When he rejoined them, Lubbock says, "his eyes were moist with tears."

At Dallas, there was "one continuous ovation" and floral arches with mottos like "God Bless Jeff Davis." Mothers brought their children "to have him lay his hands upon [them]." A parade with Southern martial airs and "waving banners" led the way to a dinner, with speeches. Gen. Richard Montgomery Gano said Davis represented "the great Confederacy," but they were honoring him, not "for his devotion to a lost cause, but . . . [for his] moral worth and purity, worthy of emulation." Gano also announced the death of John C. Breckinridge, which had just occurred.[43]

When Davis said before that "truth crushed to earth would rise again," he had been charged with inciting sedition. He laid that lie to rest in Dallas by sounding a note that became dominant with him: devotion to the South, but unity under the American flag. "I marched many years under its folds. . . . I could not go against it. It was borne against us in violation of the Constitution. It should have been laid away during the war and used by neither side. God grant that it may never again wave over a battlefield of divided Americans!" With both blue and gray standing before him, he said, "I grew up in the blue; but . . . I love the gray best." Continued enmity came not from "honorable warfare" but from "outrages that shocked humanity." There was "no hostility" now, only "a generous rivalry" in doing their duty. "I trust we shall always have peace; but if we must have war, let both go together and stand side by side."[44]

In his military idealism, he claimed that "the brave [i.e., soldiers] could always find common ground," but he soon found otherwise. He had made the Houston fair a great success, and other cities, in Indiana, Illinois, and Iowa, offered tempting sums for his appearance. But Northern veterans raised such a furor that he canceled the engagements, though he needed the money. The "tide of unreasoning prejudice against me . . . [in] the erroneous belief that I instigated [the War]," kept him from even visiting his old friend Crafts J. Wright near Chicago.[45]

He did not have to cancel in Missouri. He went from city to city, speaking to ten or fifteen thousand people at a time. Jeff Jr. was with him and "behaved generally in a quiet, decorous manner." His father noted, he "hardly remembers any thing as far back as Memphis." From Kansas City, they went off to inspect a mine in Colorado, on a snowy stagecoach journey that made him think of Varina's love of cold weather, "and, as I have done under all circumstances, [I] wished you were with me." "Take good care of your dear self for my sake." He himself had started the trip feeble from illness but was now "decidedly improved."[46]

There was one more fair to attend, at Fairview, Kentucky, near the site of his birth. The log house was still there, and a very old lady showed him just where his crib and his mother's bed had stood. His reception was beyond his expectation, he wrote Varina: "a wild burst of affection—exceeding anything I ever had before. I do sadly regret your absence . . . bearded men who have served in battle, melt into tears and vainly try to express their love."[47]

Meanwhile, J. E. Johnston's "bitter tirade against" Davis was circulating, and Henry S. Foote had brought out his *Casket of Reminiscences*, sneering at him and exalting Johnston. Foote was in such bad odor that he could be lightly brushed away. He had been arrested in January 1865, trying "to pass our lines" to the enemy, and was censured by the House. He did get to the North in April, before Lee's surrender, and asked "to atone" by preaching return to the Union, but he was threatened with arrest for treason and fled to Canada. On the way, he had told the newspapers that "U. S. prisoners were designedly treated with inhumanity" on a plan approved by the cabinet and that Northrop was "a most wicked and heathen wretch" who wanted to starve them. "Erroneous," Mallory had said from prison. "What a hell of malice this world is," said Northrop.[48]

Johnston, however, had prestige, and had to be answered, or so Davis's friends thought. Dudley Mann wrote: "Johnston has . . . been accepted as the champion of your revilers"; Davis had "no alternative" but "to take pen in hand . . . in the interests of truthful Confederate history." Mann's son Grayson, who lived in Savannah where Johnston did, had tried to dissuade him from publishing the *Narrative*, "as it is believed to be extremely vulnerable," and Wade Hampton had pleaded with him not to "throw discredit on our cause" by this book.[49]

Davis merely pointed out to Varina Johnston's "usual malignity and suppression of the truth." He said, "Hood is quite excited and anxious for *others* to fight Johnston. *Says* he will make a reply . . . . We shall see, what we shall see." Hood did collect evidence, for Johnston had attacked him brutally. He had just completed his answer when he, his wife, and his eldest child, ten years old, all died of yellow fever in New Orleans. Beauregard chivalrously raised enough money to publish the disgraced general's book, *Advance and Retreat,* to benefit his ten other children left orphans.[50]

Perhaps Beauregard did so partly because Johnston's *Narrative* had raised his ire too, ending "one of the firmest friendships of the war." He began his own reply, especially about Manassas, with the help of Jordan and another admirer, but as he worked slowly, a new enemy reared his head. William Preston Johnston published his biography of his father, and controversy over Shiloh erupted. Davis was drawn into it by a speech in which he glorified Sidney Johnston and spoke of a "cipher dispatch, being his plan of battle." Beauregard insisted that *he* had planned the Shiloh battle. Seeing he would have to speed up his answer to both books, he hired a fellow Creole, the lawyer Alfred Roman, to finish off his "Reminiscences" in a third-person format that would allow praise of himself and attacks on "Davis and other enemies." Roman was the man for this job, being son-in-law to the old Davis antagonist Robert Barnwell Rhett, who lived with him. The title page of *Military Operations of General Beauregard* lists Roman as author, but the preface, signed by the general, says "written from notes and documents furnished by me." Roman said, "I did all I could . . . to make of you a great Captain and at the same time a great man and a great patriot."[51]

The *Narrative* lost J. E. Johnston another friend, G. W. Smith, who thought he had been made a scapegoat. He published an article and a book, *Confederate War Papers* (more critical of Davis than Johnston), and answered fully in 1891, with *The Battle of Seven Pines.* Johnston also lost, through death in February 1874, his "true, faithful friend," Louis T. Wigfall. He had a new friend, however—William Tecumseh Sherman. Sherman (while denigrating Davis) praised Johnston in his 1875 *Memoirs* and on its back flyleaf, which advertised the *Narrative.* Johnston corrected Sherman about the Atlanta campaign in *The Annals of the Army of Tennessee,* sniping at Hood along the way. But he was proud of his commendation from Yankees. He served as an honorary pallbearer for Sherman, an active one for Grant and McClellan.[52]

In November 1875, Davis was planning to go to the National Railroad Convention in St. Louis. Dr. Gwin was trying to get him hired as lobbyist for a Texas rail line, but evidently this failed, like every other prospect. A libel earlier on his survey of rail routes as secretary of war had a happy issue, however, when Davis wrote to Andrew A. Humphreys, who had served under him then. Humphreys, a distinguished Yankee general and now chief of engineers, replied: "The sight of your handwriting . . . brought back vivid recollections of the brightest part of my life." He sent a positive refutation of the libel, with a promise to back it up publicly if necessary.[53]

Davis finally found employment: "President of American Branches" of the Mississippi Valley Society, a London company, "*non trading*, but designed to encourage direct trade and investments of English capital in our section," he explained to Major Walthall. He also said, "I wish my time was not occupied by other matters and that we could go earnestly and immediately to work on the memoir." Walthall had been helping him collect material for many months now, and they had talked to both Appleton and Turnbull Companies about publishing the book. But for most of 1876, he was too tied up by business and family affairs to make a start.[54]

On New Year's Day, 1876, at St. Lazarus Church, he gave away his precious Pollie in marriage to Joel Addison Hayes, Mississippian by birth, member of an esteemed Nashville family, and "a devoted Churchman." Happily, Maggie and he were to stay in Memphis, where Addison was cashier in a bank.[55]

Right after this, Davis found himself under violent public attack. There was a bill before the House to remove "all disabilities" under the Fourteenth Amendment that still barred some Confederates from holding office. On January 6, 1876, James G. Blaine amended it to read: "with the exception of Jefferson Davis." Immediately, John Preston vowed that if this passed, Kentucky would not join the centennial celebration "of American freedom," and Stoddard Johnston termed it "an insult" that "every honorable Southern man will resent."[56]

Blaine had tried to exclude Davis before. This time he waved the trial record of Henry Wirz as "the bloody shirt." He smeared Davis as "the author, knowingly, deliberately, guiltily, and willfully, of the gigantic murders and crimes at Andersonville," which he could have stopped "by a wink of his eye." It was weak "to allow Davis to go free and hang Wirz." James Abram Garfield then castigated Davis for retaining over the prisoners the notorious General Winder, his "intimate and favorite friend." (Davis said Winder was "a gallant man and a good officer . . . utterly incapable of cruelty"; they had "little other than official" acquaintance.) Davis was "the conscious author . . . of the terrible work at Andersonville," Garfield concluded; "do not ask us to restore the right to hold power to that man . . . still unaneled, unshrived, unforgiven, undefended. [Great applause.]"[57]

He was not undefended. Even Northerners in the House, Samuel S. Cox and Gen. N. P. Banks, took his side. Ben Hill had risen and with his great eloquence showed the falsity of the charges. "Not one single man ever mentioned the name of Mr. Davis in connection with a single atrocity" at Wirz's trial, though "really Mr. Davis was the man intended to be tried through him." Hill brought out that officer's refusal to implicate Davis: "What Wirz . . . would not say for his life the gentleman from Maine says to the country to keep himself and his party in power." Just before this one could read in the *Washington Gazette:* "Americans will regret that Wirz was not American born, for he showed . . . that men can and dare die for honor."[58]

Judge James Lyons, "goaded by rage, disgust and mortification at Blaine's vile attack upon you," which Blaine "knew to be utterly false," repeatedly wrote Davis, "I beg you to answer." The "unprincipled demagogue" who "aspires to the Presidency . . . has not merely slandered you, but the entire South." "You alone can give such a reply as the whole world will listen to, and learn the truth from."[59]

Davis answered his friend with irony: "To remove political disabilities which there was not legal power to impose, was not an act of so much grace as to form a plausible pretext for the reckless diatribe of Mr. Blaine." "The Southern people have . . . forgiven much"; "if it be less so among their invaders, it is but another example of the rule that the wrongdoer is less able to forgive." "By gross misrepresentation . . . to revive the worst passions of the war" was inexcusable, but he was not going to answer: "I have been so long the object of malignant slander and . . . unscrupulous falsehood . . . that though I cannot say it has become to me matter of indifference, it has ceased to excite my surprise," even in this extreme case.[60]

Dr. Luke Blackburn, "anxious that you and the noble cause . . . should go down to history, clear and correct, not bleared and mutilated," wanted Davis to write to J. Proctor Knott, chairman of the Judiciary Committee. He did, but he merely asked that others be granted amnesty "on the condition of my exclusion." Knott found Davis's "chivalrous self abnegation . . . perfectly consistent with the genuine dignity and manliness" of his whole career. He told him the peaceable tone of his letter had disappointed "your ignoble traducers."[61]

Blaine crowed that everyone who asked pardon had received it, but Robert Toombs had "contemptuously" refused to ask. "Pardon for what?" Toombs once said; "I have not pardoned you all yet." Davis also had "declined" to sign a petition for pardon at Fortress Monroe, and so "remained subject to the inexcusable privations and tortures which Dr. Craven has but faintly described." He had said to Knott: "It may be proper to state that I have no claim to pardon, not having in any wise repented, or changed the convictions on which my political course was founded, as well before, as during, and since the war between the States." Davis and Toombs of one mind at last![62]

Davis went a step further in 1882: "Our cause was so just, so sacred, that had I known all that has come to pass, had I known what was to be inflicted upon me, all that my country was to suffer, all that our posterity was to endure, I would do it all over again." Toombs was never "forgiven"; Davis, not for one hundred years. In 1977 a Senate resolution by Mark Hatfield of Oregon began the process that restored his full citizenship.[63]

Blaine's attack rebounded. It prompted George Shea to publish his letter to the *New York Tribune*, giving the North his own evidence of Davis's innocence. It caused the Southern Historical Society to devote two numbers in its first volume of *Papers* to "Treatment of Prisoners."[64]

The South felt that "in the person of Mr. Davis the whole question of the rightfulness of the cause" was on trial. "The banner . . . went down in blood and tears, but was never furled by his hands," wrote Methodist Bishop Charles B. Galloway. "Had he ever apostatised or even compromised" or "plead for pardon on the ground that he had . . . misguided his people, the South would have spurned him"; but he showed "unfaltering faith in these words: 'We do not fear the verdict of posterity.'" "He was always ready to follow his principles to their logical conclusion," said John W. Daniel, "to die, if need be, rather than disguise or recant them." He had preserved "the independent and unshamed spirit" of his people by fighting to the bitter end. He was still fighting, now with words. William Browne, afraid the people were "forgetting principle," wanted to come "renew and strengthen my faith by converse with its greatest, and most earnest apostle." "Heroic consistency" was making Davis the rallying point for devotion to the Southern cause.[65]

In March of 1876 in New Orleans, Davis addressed fellow veterans of the Mexican War, deploring their lack of pensions but reminding them that, having done "duty for duty's sake," they had something not "to be measured in this world's goods, self respect and a good name." He wished for them "that kind future which the good Father promises to those who love Him." When a bill for Mexican War pensions came up later, he asked a friend in Congress "silently to allow the malignants to impose . . . the condition of my exclusion."[66]

But when a vote came in 1879, and Senator Hoar of Massachusetts called Davis a traitor, moving that "no pension shall ever be paid" him, Southerners were anything but silent. Lucius Lamar, Isham Harris, Generals John B. Gordon, Matt Ransom, and John T. Morgan, and others in the Senate cried out indignantly, Lamar saying that Davis was "selected for dishonor as the representative of the South." Francis Wolff of the Mississippi Rifles, a captain in the Confederate army, regretted in a letter that "party prejudice & passion could center on so good a man. . . . To call him traitor is an insult to the whole South . . . his Cause & ours are in common." Even an Ohio senator wondered whether "the punishment of the Southern people ought to be vicarious in the person of Jefferson Davis." Senator Hoar charged, as if it too were a crime, that Davis told his people to remember the past: "He glories in 'the lost cause.'" Hoar's motion passed by one vote, but the amendment to which it was attached failed, and the pension was voted with no restrictions. Davis never applied for his.[67]

A meeting of the Mississippi Valley Society was the occasion of Davis's fourth trip to England. This time he had Varina on his arm. They embarked on the SS *Memphis* at New Orleans, leaving Jeff Jr. with Margaret. "Dear boy, I am very anxious about him," Davis wrote her. "A Father's prayers will be fervently offered for you all." It was hard to part from them, but "fate has left me little power to do as I would." Winnie went with her parents, for they intended European schooling for her. She was now twelve. Varina was fifty, and feeling it. Her physical changes were preying upon her temperament, always volatile. Even before the shock of her brother's death, she was having "sudden attacks" of "partial suffocation," followed by "intense pain in the head," variously attributed to "nervousness," or "functional disturbance of the heart," or "of the brain." Davis had worried about her health for years and asked his girls to take care of her, especially not to upset her. Once, after Billy died, he wrote to her: "God grant you may be well and that no harm has come to my dear children. I could not bear another great misfortune." She was "suffering very much" from excitement and neuralgia, and "extremely weak," as they left in May of 1876, but her husband hoped for improvement "when we meet the cool air of the Sea."[68]

Varina's passions often controlled her: "When I am ill at heart I am wild"; "I am like a wild animal about trouble, [and lick] the lance which rankles in my heart." A foreigner who met her just as the Confederacy was collapsing called her "the tigress." Her great warmth and generosity had its counterpart in great animosity and resentment. She had written a caustic letter about her sister Margaret when Jeff was in England before, telling him to leave her home. But Varina was also mercurial, blowing cold as abruptly as she blew hot. Perhaps soothed by Jeff's defence of Margaret, Varina spent some time with her and Carl this trip, though after Jeff had left for home, she complained mightily about them both.[69]

The trip was dismal. Davis was finding the Valley Society shaky, his trust in people betrayed again, and Varina was "for several weeks seriously ill, so much so that I have but seldom left her room." He had to send Winnie by someone else to the Misses Frielanders' school in Carlsruhe, Germany, with her friend Pinnie Meredith. Jeff went one weekend to see them. To keep "the dear little girl" Pinnie "from any mortification," he had proposed saving enough money to keep her in school "by abstinence from smoking." This dire step was apparently unnecessary: he enjoyed his pipe in Mann's chimney corner briefly before being summoned home by the Brierfield suit in November. On shipboard, he read Thackeray's novel *The Newcomes*, finding it "more powerful but less agreeable" than *Pendennis.* Varina, not well enough to go, stayed under the care of Dr. Maurice Davis. On Christmas Eve, sad that "an ocean rolls between," Jeff wrote: "God grant that our sacrifice may be blessed by the restoration of your health." But it was almost a year before she was up to the voyage across.[70]

By June of 1877, Maggie was able to write her mother, "Father has gained his suit about Brierfield *in every particular.*" But he did not have possession; the defendants demanded a review of the decision. Maggie also boasted of her "pretty fat little baby . . . named Jefferson Davis and called Jeffie D." "I should have advised that [the] dear boy be not encumbered with the prejudice which attaches to my name," wrote the grandfather; "force has triumphed over right and the wrong doers hate me with the intensity which would have been more pardonable if I, not they, had been the invader of the soil, and the destroyer of the inheritance." But perhaps before the boy he grew up, "those who risked all and lost all save their honor, to preserve . . . constitutional liberty . . . may not be therefor condemned."[71]

As if to counter Maggie's happy note, the Mississippi Valley Society evaporated for lack of capital soon after Davis returned. There was nothing for it but to start in earnest on the book. Jeff told Varina of going "up and down" the Gulf Coast, looking for a place "to get books and papers together" but not buying a house for "fear of your not liking it." He sent greetings from Sarah Dorsey, "your warm friend," who was "living in her fine house with her cousin, Mrs. Cochrane [Cochran], nee Ogden."[72]

On February 1, Davis had written Maggie: "Mrs. Dorsey offered to take me as a boarder for fifty dollars a month, the rent of the cottage included. . . . This arrangement . . . leaves me at liberty to make any change which may be more satisfactory to your Mother." He had told Winnie about his square pavilion, with one of the four galleries "closed so as to make a chamber & dressing room" and the original center room as "my library and office. Robert is with me and sleeps in the dressing room." There too was "your Brother Jeff" who "occasionally writes for me. . . . I dictate daily for 3 or 4 hours, for a book of reminiscences of my public career. Mrs. Dorsey acts sometimes as my amanuensis and Maj. Walthall assists in compiling and hunting up authorities." The book was under way.[73]

He could not have found a more congenial spot or a fitter amanuensis for writing about the Cause. Beauvoir he described for Winnie, far off in Carlsruhe: the yard was "shaded by live oaks, magnolias, cedars, &c, &c. The sea is immediately in front, and an extensive orange orchard is near"; its "flowers perfume the air for some distance." In the six hundred acres beyond, he found a clear brook, "its banks lined with a tangled wood of sweet bay, wild olive and vines. Then comes a vineyard, then a railroad, and then stretching far far away a forest of stately long-leaved pine . . . where the winds sigh . . . a sad yet soothing sound." As for Mrs. Dorsey, "You can hardly remember her, she met us in Baltimore."[74]

The beautifully educated Sarah Dorsey, a devoted Confederate, had been at home in the most cultivated salons of Europe. She knew Carlyle, Herbert Spencer, the Rosettis, and the learned dean of Westminster, Lynulph Stanley. She could speak French, German, Italian, and Spanish. She knew Sanskrit, Greek, Latin, and Anglo-Saxon. She had published five novels, with another about to appear. She wrote a treatise on "Aryan Philosophy."[75]

Her major work, and the most Southern—"I write for the South"—was *Recollections of Henry Watkins Allen,* a biography of her friend who had become governor of Louisiana, after being crippled in battle, and had died in exile in Mexico, saying he could "not ask pardon for what I don't consider a crime." He had sent mementos to Sarah by John Perkins, Jr., the man who had burned Somerset to keep Grant from doing it. The Dorseys' houses, which *were* burned by Grant, were very near it in Louisiana, across from Davis Bend. Jeff Davis had often been at their Elkridge, famous for its mock tournaments, and Sarah had been "in the habit of visiting" Brierfield and the Hurricane "intimately 'avant le deluge.' "[76]

Davis and Sarah had much besides memories to make them close. Her chief wartime hero was Leonidas Polk, for whom she had devised a banner, after that of St. Constantine: "We are fighting the Battle of the Cross against the Modern Barbarians." Bishop Polk had approved her plan (nullified by the war) to form an order of deaconesses, "a Sisterhood of Mercy." She had always taught religion to her slaves; her first published work, in the *New York Churchman,* was about arranging church music for them. Writing of the chivalric Welsh nature of Henry Allen, she might almost have been describing Davis, and her conversations with Allen suggest what later ones at Beauvoir were like—literary, philosophical, and, above all, religious. After dabbling in other beliefs, Sarah was ready to say to the New Orleans Academy of Science: "I am a Christian by race, education, preference, and philosophic conviction. . . . I care only for the truth." She and Davis got along famously.[77]

Not all were happy with this fact. When Varina saw in the newspaper that Sarah was taking Jeff's dictation for the book, she went into an extended huff. It was not that she thought there was anything improper between them, but *she* had always been his amanuensis, ever since the first days of their marriage. Now she was being left out of the great project. Impropriety probably never occurred to the two principals. As Sarah wrote to Dudley Mann, "Mr. Davis feels a sort of responsibility towards me from having been so closely connected in the bonds of dearest amity with my father and his family. He has always kept a kind of over-sight of me." She hoped Beauvoir would always be "at least *one* of his homes." He insisted on paying her rent and board, and extra when family members came, "which was a large part of the time." Others lived at Beauvoir, and many paid extended visits, but the situation made some people gossip, encouraged by Varina's aloof stance.[78]

Her phrases were as loving as ever: "Believe me, darling . . . intense longing to be with my precious old Banny. / Your old Winnie." And his to her: "Dearest, Waafe, love of many years"; "I send you the kisses of youth"; "misfortune has left us the richest treasure, a love which has grown as all else decayed." If not tied up in the courts, he would "follow the yearning of my heart, and go to you." Jeff Jr. wrote "darling Mother" how his father had said "you were a woman worthy the worship of any son."[79]

But Varina was hurt: "I see . . . that you have called your book 'Our Cause.' I have so often hoped . . . that you would . . . tell me of its plan and scope, and of its progress—but I know I am very far off—and—'and things.' " Jealousy enraged her against Sarah Dorsey: "When people here ask me what part of your book she is writing . . . I feel aggravated nearly to death." She had not mentioned her to Jeff "for I felt too angry . . . to be reasonable." She would not answer Sarah's letters inviting her to Beauvoir: "I do not desire ever to see her house—and cannot say so and therefore have been silent. Nothing on earth would pain me like living in that kind of community in her house. I am grateful for her kindness to you and my children, but do not desire to be under any more obligation to her." Margaret had egged her on: "I never liked Mrs. Dorsey . . . I think she is manish . . . You will not go there if anything I can say will prevent it."[80]

But then Maggie's baby, Jefferson Davis Hayes—"a bright and beautiful child" to his grandfather—died in late June. Sarah Dorsey fixed up the pavilion cottage that was the western twin to Davis's in her front yard and invited the bereaved couple to the coast. At first Margaret refused to go, but finally she did, probably persuaded by her brother, whom she loved. He and Mrs. Dorsey were "boon comrades." In time, Sarah's kindness won Maggie over, and she urged her mother also to go down.[81]

When Varina finally came home from England, in October of 1877, she naturally went to Memphis to be with Margaret, who was still grieving. Sarah kept trying to attract her to Beauvoir, but she turned a cold shoulder. "Do not—please do not let Mrs. Dorsey come to see me," she wrote Jeff. "I do not wish to be uncivil and embarrass you, and I would certainly do so against my will." Jeff and Jeff Jr. went up to Memphis together to fetch her, but she would not go back with them. "I take refuge in mocking," she once said, of her violent moods. She did so as she revealed to Connie Harrison what one of the troubles was: "I dearly love people. . . . Mr. Davis inclines to the 'gentle hermit of the dale' style of old age—so behold we are a tie. . . . In the course of human events I shall go down to Mr. Davis's earthly paradise temporarily."[82]

In July 1878, she suddenly appeared at Beauvoir. The Reverend W. C. McRacken, who was there with Dr. Leacock, remembers a large party that Sarah gave that month, where Varina "reigned supreme with queenly dignity" as guests arriving from New Orleans were "presented to her." She had apparently made up her mind to accept the situation, for she stayed, not "temporarily," but permanently. Sarah wrote Dudley Mann in August how Varina suffered from "the heat of this semi-tropical climate," though she and Davis throve on it. The two women had been trained in the ways of politeness. They forced themselves to be civil, but Varina never forgave Mrs. Dorsey for being so much comfort and help to Jeff. Her jealousy rankled and grew.[83]

Jeff Jr. now had a job in Addison's bank and was in love with a local girl, though Sarah Dorsey's niece, Mary Ellis, was carrying the torch for him at Beauvoir. Davis had hoped Mary's "cultivation and habit of reading" would counteract the influence of "the slangy girls of Memphis." Although he once spoke of the boy as "my lame duck," he recognized the "manly, genial temper which made him a general favorite."[84]

"Noisy as usual, but always affectionate and anxious to serve," was the way he described him. Varina had reported him working steadily, thinking up wild projects, and "quite well, and, but for breaking a looking glass, quite happy—he & I are so superstitious." His father, chagrined at his missing the point (unstated) in a letter from Varina, wrote to her, "I went to my room in order to be alone, with my sympathy in your wounded love and mortified pride. My dear, we do not understand the boy, and I fear never shall. Let us however hold fast to all which is good in him, and there is much." Their bewilderment was about over. The "good in him" caused Jeff Jr. to tend to a man with yellow fever, as Memphis was hit by its worst epidemic ever in 1878. His family evidently thought, not knowing about the *Aëdes aegypti* mosquito, that this was what gave him the yellowjack.[85]

His parents were agonized by worry: "our misery may be imagined, it cannot be described." Quarantines of New Orleans and Memphis prevented their going to him, though his father said that he "would willingly die to save him." Only Walthall, who belonged to Dr. Blackburn's volunteers, known as the Howards, could get through and nurse him.[86]

Shortly before, Bishop Green's son, a priest tending his flock, had died of fever, and Davis had written, "We have learned in sorrow how to feel with you. God knows how to measure, and how to temper such chastisement. . . . To human sight, 'the proper place for man to die, is where he dies for man.' Such was the end of your noble Duncan." Already, he had said, "the dread scourge" surrounded them, but "a merciful Providence has thus far spared us [and] our children. . . . We ask your prayers for further safety."[87]

Davis himself was now in "constant prayer." On October 16, three days before frost signaled the end of the plague, Jefferson Davis Jr. passed away. He was twenty-one. Addison paid for a decent, private burial (more than many yellow fever victims got) and later had Billy's body moved to the same plot. It was more than a month before the father could summon courage to write to Winnie: "What is unusual in that disease, Jeff retained his faculties to the last. In Christian faith he received the comforts of our church, and peacefully his spirit passed from those who loved him here, but may we not hope to a love better worth than ours."[88]

But to Addison he said, "I am crushed under such heavy and repeated blows. I presume not God to scan, but the many and humble prayers offered . . . are hushed in the despair of my bereavement." Speaking of their sorrows the year before, on their anniversary, he had said to Varina: "We have drained the goblet to its dregs." Now they had drunk the dregs themselves.[89]

XXII

The Hero

After so many prayers, the death of Jeff Jr. pushed Davis close to despair. He felt "shadows as dark as ever fell on man" and rather welcomed what Northrop called the "atrocious pain" of neuralgia, as distraction from "less endurable" ills. He wrote to Winnie: "I have bowed to the blows, but in vain have sought for consolation. So many considerations, not selfish, plead for his longer stay on earth that I only shut my eyes, to what it is not permitted me to see, and stifling the outward flow, let my wounds bleed inwardly." Fortitude alone made him able to pray at the end of this letter, "May God have you in his holy keeping."[1]

He had noted long before that ill might follow, "did the Lord always grant our purest prayers when and as they are offered." This humility brought him to the end of life still able to say, this time to Maggie, "God bless and shield you, my beloved child, is [my] fervent prayer." Simple trust in the depth of desolation is what Goulburn and à Kempis call perfection. The offer of his life made so long before seems accomplished in this death to himself. It is not surprising to find that he "especially loved" the biblical book of Job.[2]

Another death seemed as unreasonable as Jeff Jr.'s—that of the Confederacy. Frank Stringfellow, cavalryman and spy in the bid for independence and now Episcopal priest, wrote to Davis, puzzling over how to "harmonize" these facts: "we were right" and "God permitted our overthrow." Davis wrote, "I have often times combatted the idea . . . that the failure of our righteous cause rendered doubtful the government of the world by an overruling providence." They might not have wisely used a victory; "the distant future" might bring good "consequences" from "our present losses." And had not their overthrow shown "how faithless, dishonest, and barbarous our enemies were," and proven "that we were more right than even our own people generally knew?" "The inimitable principles for which we contended must live, or republican government perish from among us." On the flyleaf of his *Christian Year* he had copied an opinion that "religious truth" for John Keble rested more on "faith and love" than on argument. It was the reason of faith that he gave Stringfellow: "Perhaps the furnace to which we have been subjected was necessary for our purification." He said later, he could not believe "that the cause for which our sacrifices were made can ever be lost." "Resting on the imperishable basis of truth, [it] must, in the fullness of time, be vindicated." Davis himself had been subjected to a furnace; his faith rested on truth; it lived.[3]

"Stifling the outward flow," nine days after he penned the expression, on December 6, 1878, he addressed veterans of the Army of Northern Virginia at their banquet in New Orleans. The people of the North had contributed greatly to relief during the yellow fever epidemic, rather altering his view of them: "The heart would be dead to every generous impulse that would try to stimulate in you now a feeling of hostility." It was only their "standard bearers whose hearts were filled with malignity." Davis stimulated instead, memory of the Cause, "the honor in which you maintained it," the fraternity of men who "stood up and faced the foe one to five" and "manfully held the line." "Trained to truth and duty, tried in temptation, and tempered by distress, they came forth the pure gold from the forge," he said—again the allusion to purification by fire.[4]

For a while he could not work on his own vindication of the Cause. Varina would find him sitting "silent in his wordless grief." He counted over the few pitiful mementos he had of Jeff Jr., to be "looked at, as long as I live." "Occasionally, he would say, 'I do not know why I suffer so much, it cannot be long before I am reunited to my boy.'" He wrote Northrop that he "soon must follow" his son: "May he who rules unite us in a better land, where the tears will be wiped away which Earth has no power to dry." On June 3 he noted to a friend that he had attained the biblical three-score years and ten, and to another a year later: "According to the ancient standard I have passed my allotted time, and cannot expect to stay much longer."[5]

At least his book was started. But the loss of all records except his letter book, showing only items sent, had "greatly increased the difficulty of writing with the exactness which is not only desirable, but necessary." He was always very precise. Northrop said, "Your memory is so accurate that I hesitate to inform or amend," but Davis did not depend on that.[6]

He and Walthall probed the memory of everyone they could think of—even Beauregard, though not J. E. Johnston. And Beauregard got Jordan to send a memoir that Davis used. St. John had already sent a full account of his brief tenure as commissary general; Gorgas contributed a detailed summary on ordnance; Pemberton was happy to oblige with his facts; and many others furnished military reports or answered specific points. William Polk, asking Davis's help on his biography of his father, offered "Genl. Polk's letter and dispatch book."[7]

Jubal Early and Preston Johnston were willing helpers, doing some research in Washington. Burton Harrison should have been, but a strange silence met Davis's repeated call for dispatches to dovetail with his letter book. This correspondence, "of a private and confidential nature" from "Genls. in the field," Davis had kept separate in his own office. When he left Richmond, Micajah Clark and John T. Wood had packed it up and brought it out with Harrison's files, already boxed. All these papers were successfully hidden and then sent to Harrison in New York City. He had put them in storage without going through them.[8]

Lee had applied for his dispatches when intending his own book and been disappointed. Suddenly one of his letters appeared in *Scribner's Magazine.* Davis knew that it was from his private file, and that there were no copies. He sent Walthall to New York to see Harrison about it. Together they called on Col. Charles Colcock Jones, Jr., a New York lawyer from Georgia, who had persuaded Harrison in 1870 to let him take the collection to his house in Brooklyn. Now Jones gave Harrison back his other papers and his trunk with the confidential letters—only most of them were missing. They were missing until *Lee's Dispatches* came out in 1915. The mystery of their whereabouts was not solved until 1988.[9]

Captured archives and other papers sold (improperly, many thought) by John T. Pickett, were held by the United States government. At first it was impossible, then just extremely difficult, for a Southerner to gain access to them. He would be, said Davis, "fortunate if *politely* refused." But when Confederate general Marcus J. Wright was appointed to gather Southern documents for *The War of the Rebellion . . . the Official Record,* he gave Davis an entree to all these papers. This proved invaluable, for Davis finished writing before they were published.[10]

Seeing one account of Manassas, Davis quoted Twiggs on Monterey: "I wonder if I was there." It made him the more anxious to get official records, so as to arrive at the truth. He had another problem: "few are willing to bear testimony about anything." Robert Ould and Isham Harris were like this. Seddon and Benjamin were reluctant, but in the end, they furnished important witness. Pendleton on artillery and Bulloch on ships both came too late to use.[11]

Many were dead who might have helped, like Hardee and Lee. Bragg had dropped as if shot while crossing a Galveston street in 1876. Walthall tried to obtain his papers from Mrs. Bragg, but she was hoping to sell them to the government, as Preston Johnston had done his. Davis still referred to Bragg as "that true man and gallant soldier." He referred to Hood in the same words, except that "man" became "friend." He had said the memory of Hood, as of Hardee, was "personally dear"; he never said that of Bragg.[12]

Hood and Richard Taylor both died in 1879, the latter first, giving Hood just barely time to write that Taylor, whose *Destruction and Reconstruction* came out that year too, had "fallen into the popular error that the President ordered me into [Tennessee]," when he could have asked Davis, "and ascertained the truth." Davis said "delicacy probably prevented him" and caused "so grave a mistake"; he found the whole passage "much in error." Taylor was fiercely independent. When Winnie, at age one, rebuffed a man who said, "Come, Pie, I love your Father," Varina commented: "She is like Dick Taylor—she won't shine with a borrowed light."[13]

Northrop opined that Davis wrote "history"; Hood and Taylor "spoke truth"; "the rest are tissues of fables." "Semmes was able, but he writes like a parvenue on a mound." Davis answered that Taylor would never willingly do him "an injustice." Indeed, he wrote in his book: "all who enjoy the friendship of Jefferson Davis love him as Jonathan did David." All the same, he printed another piece of misinformation that reflected on Davis—the story about not running out the cotton in 1861.[14]

Johnston's *Narrative* of 1874 stirred up this whirlwind. If only Davis had seized the cotton crop and sent it abroad in a fleet of steamers to establish credit and buy arms, the South would have won; his failure caused its fall. Both Memminger and Trenholm had answered this "silly reflection" on the government (Davis called it) as soon as Johnston made it, through letters to the *Charleston News and Courier.* They concluded that it was, in Trenholm's words, "an absolute impossibility." Memminger said Johnston was like "our fore-father Adam in casting the fault of a general calamity on some other person"; besides, he had the facts wrong. But evidently Taylor did not see these letters, or Beauregard either, who in 1878 and again in 1881 took all the credit for the proposal. The charge, enshrined in the books of all three generals, has been perpetuated. Davis felt bound to confront its repetition in 1889, when he furnished new testimony, from Bulloch, to its falsehood.[15]

For a long time, Davis would not answer "the malignant fictions with which the press has teemed." He saw that "the passion of the hour" made "abuse of me, the test of merit." As he told Crafts Wright, truth was crushed "so deep below the light of reason in the Northern mind, that justice to me from them is hopeless." "I who have been for so many years the target for all manner of abuses, realize what you cannot, the impossibility of silencing my slanderers. Disprove the assertion, they will only reassert it the louder and add to the first a multitude of fictions to support it." One day, "all this vituperative fabrication will only be remembered as matter of shame, and to that happier time we must fain be content to refer the matter."[16]

He recognized, however, that truth had to be defended, since only the knowledge of it could bring reconciliation with the North. When General Wilson published an article on his capture in the *Philadelphia Times* in 1877, he concealed his own contempt for it by getting Walthall to write a reply. The *Times* refused to print it. Harrison sent Davis a correction in detail of Wilson's "blunders as to facts." Reagan was incensed—"parts of it are so outrageous"—and wrote a refutation that Davis approved. The *Times* did print this one, but answered it by Pollard's *Lost Cause.*[17]

Southerners were bitter at Wilson for reviving yet again the question of Davis's attire. Crafts J. Wright, the Yankee lawyer friend, now wrote on the legal aspects, hoping to get "the captured garments restored" and "the exhibit stopped" (they were "paraded," Davis had said). The derision in songs and cartoons was enhanced by a hoopskirted figure of Davis in P. T. Barnum's American Museum. In a futile attempt to stop the lies, Davis had had a photograph taken in the suit he had been wearing. Bishop Green and Gorgas thought "this likeness" was "the best that has ever been taken of you."[18]

Davis finally broke "the rule of silence" when a newspaper article by R. M. T. Hunter, "The Peace Commission of 1865," was reprinted in the *Southern Historical Society Papers,* which Davis wanted to be "a repertory of trustworthy data." He had looked forward to Hunter's promised account of the Hampton Roads Conference while in Fortress Monroe, since he was then blamed for its failure by another commissioner, John A. Campbell. Now Davis saw in Hunter's article, not exoneration, but attack.[19]

Davis was so sensitive, and so at one with the Confederacy, that he took criticism of public policy personally. Even Preston Johnston had to defend things in his *Life of Gen. Albert Sidney Johnston.* Harrison once said that remarks to Davis had to be "all praise," but Jubal Early felt free to fuss at him. Davis was ingenuous: he had thought it "improbable" that Stephens blamed him for Hampton Roads (he did), and imagined that, though "most appreciative of himself," he was "not unfriendly to me." Davis had spoken "kindly" of Hunter, who backed him until he proposed blacks in the army. Everyone had thought them "in perfect accord." When Hunter imputed to him not only failure of the Conference, but also unworthy motives, Davis felt betrayed and lashed out.[20]

In answering Davis's answer, Hunter made the exchange personal indeed. The extreme irony of his saying Davis was unwilling to sacrifice himself was lost, since his letters from prison were unknown, but when Hunter accused him of cowardice and "insensibility," he had already gone too far. Early said Hunter's answer "did him more harm than any one else." In the old days, Davis might have challenged Hunter for accusing him and his aides of a betrayal of confidence. Now he could only fight with scorn—in expressing which, when roused, he was a past master—and letters from the aides. It was "almost incredible," said Lubbock: "Of all men he is the last to whom such imputation could attach." It was after the conference, Davis said, that his faith in Hunter was first "impaired"—when he had tried to get him to treat for peace without independence. But Davis never knew till now that Hunter had secretly maligned him, or that "there was a cabal in the Senate" to supplant him with Hunter. Still, when J. William Jones offered him new ammunition, Davis decided not to use it, because he felt sorry for Hunter.[21]

Varina had her own view: "I did not care for Mr. Hunter, but you did." He "was a hypocrite to those who believed him true. You, if you were mistaken, acted honestly, out of . . . faith, and self-sacrifice." "You have not been a conciliatory man in your manners always, and the vain and dishonest men who could not bend you to their wills, do not like you." (Davis admitted he could not "conciliate men" with "private ends to serve" or those who wanted to teach him about things on which he had "labored exhaustingly" and of which they were "profoundly ignorant.") She advised him not to answer again because "there is nothing to answer—but dirty little flings" (but he did). "Forgive the advice if you do not like it because I love you."[22]

She took up two painful points: the first in importance was Hunter's saying Lee really despaired of victory but would not tell Davis so. Ives had brought Davis Lee's opinion that he would fail through lack of supplies at Petersburg, Varina reminded him. "You went down to him at once and he said Ives had mistaken his meaning." (But Lee had said this to Congress in secret session.)[23]

Then there was Judge Campbell's attack earlier. Varina had told him in New Orleans in 1866 that after Davis had gotten him appointed to the Supreme Court and then protected him when he resigned and came South, his obligation "should have restrained his tongue" when Davis was in prison. She evidently knew nothing of Campbell's intriguing for an armistice behind Davis's back and plotting with Lincoln when Richmond fell to get the legislature to surrender both Virginia and the army—a plan aborted only because Stanton refused it. But apparently Davis knew: "The last time I met Judge Campbell on the street in N.O. he hesitated as if about to speak, I looked over his head and passed on. I want no controversy with any one, but, hating treachery, must repel a traitor."[24]

Varina was still in Memphis when she wrote that letter, and at Beauvoir, Sarah Dorsey was entertaining for Jeff. She kept a firm hand on her rural salon. At one party, Davis was in conversation on the gallery with three clergymen—Dr. Leacock (retired from Christ Church, and serving the Redeemer at Biloxi), Mr. Kramer (from Christ Church), and a Mr. McRacken, also from New Orleans, who said, "We could have listened gladly" all night. But Sarah saw them "doing nothing" and brought out the card table. Soon McRacken found himself "hopelessly beaten": "The game was euchre, and Mr. Davis had it all his own way"—"the most accomplished player I ever saw."[25]

In the daytime, Davis would work in the pavilion at his book and his huge correspondence: "All sorts of people write to me about all supposable matters and if I don't answer they generally write again." His health remained good ("Minnie [Leacock] Howell says she never saw me 'so fat' ") except for continued swelling in his feet, once a sprained toe, and the ever-present cough. Mrs. Dorsey kept him in Havana cigars, and Jubal Early, in "Lone Jack" smoking tobacco.[26]

Robert was still there to take care of him and of the horses. To Lucius Northrop, Davis confided his great pleasure in "the first horse I have owned since the war . . . a creole filly with some appearance of blood, but no pedigree, she walks well, has a light elastic trot and when broken will suffice for our sandy roads and my short trips in search of air and rest from reading and writing." He would ride out in the evening to visit the neighbors, especially Dr. Leacock, who lived on the next place with his daughter Minnie and her children. Her husband, William Howell, had never come back from California.[27]

Northrop, lame from his bad knee, resided alone with his wife, his four living children being grown, on a farm near Charlottesville, Virginia. He and Davis had quarreled as their country fell, but Davis had asked their friend, Theophilus Holmes, to assure him "that he was not sent adrift." Northrop had written condolence at Billy's death. Then in 1878, he answered a request for "memoranda" and spoke of "your noble treatment of my son in Memphis." This began a long exchange in which they discussed everything from Beauregard to purgatory.[28]

Northrop had named his place for the latter: "Minor Orcus." Purgatory was his "sweet hope." Davis agreed to hope for it too, "lest we go further and fare worse"—that is, "if we do not meet in Paradise." They exchanged health tips, though Davis, "remembering that you are an M. D.," felt something like "the Presbyterian who went to Rome to instruct the Holy Father." They reminisced about dragoon days, and Northrop told about his horses, prompting from Davis: "I like a horse such as Genl. Z. Taylor described as his preference . . . 'big when lying down.' "[29]

It was one of the joys of a quiet life, after so much turmoil, to be in touch with old friends. Army friends were still the best. Davis addressed them, and most men, in military fashion, by last name only, though he often called C. J. Wright "Crafts," or "dear Friend," and even sometimes signed off, "affectionately yours." He always wrote fully and openly to Wright, superintendent of the Marine Hospital at Chicago, begging to differ with him about Stanton, Seward, and Sherman.[30]

Gen. Thomas F. Drayton, who had been with them as "one of the '28" at West Point, had not met much success, in the war or after. He had found his ancestral lands at Hilton Head confiscated or ruined, had plowed a hard row farming in Georgia, where one of his seven children lived, had tried selling insurance, and now lived in Charlotte, North Carolina, where it was "as much as I can do to make ends meet." He wrote frequently and feelingly to Davis, always as "Dear Jeff." All the old friends talked about visiting each other, but they never did.[31]

But Davis could ride his filly just up the coast and see William Harney who lived at Pass Christian when not in St. Louis, a retired brevet major general. It was the wrong army, of course, and after the war he had hobnobbed with Sherman and Grant. But the early friendship seems to have blotted out all that. He was at Beauvoir when he told about throttling the wolf at Fort Winnebago. Davis reminisced happily about the old days for a man writing Harney's biography in 1878 and cited that book in his own.[32]

Theophilus Holmes, who had been in Lee's class at West Point, wrote Northrop (who called him "the old paladin") that he was "contented and happy," with "3 beautiful well bred well behaved" grandchildren. Speaking of mutual friends, he said: "As for Jefferson Davis I look upon him as the great sacrifice of the age, his and not Lee's name should fill the hearts of the Southern people; for he was the embodyment of the Confederacy—pure true generous and brave. May God forever bless him, here and hereafter."[33]

Sarah Dorsey, and many others, saw Davis like this, too. She was determined not "to share in the ingratitude of my country towards a man who is in my eyes the highest and noblest in existence." She wrote Dudley Mann that if he really decided "to come to America in order to be near him, you can come to me, *sans cérémonie*. The first desire of both of us will be to make this noblest of men as happy as we can."[34]

The chief thing she did to that end was to sell him Beauvoir. He paid the first installment on February 19, 1879. She had already willed it to him, as well as her plantations in Mississippi, Louisiana, and Arkansas, but she did not tell him, knowing he would forbid it. She had no children, only brothers and a sister who had repaid her lifelong generosity, she said, with "ingratitude." Although reduced to "comparative poverty" by the war—land poor, as the saying goes—she could at least assure Davis of a home and the possibility of income. The catalyst to all these arrangements was her discovery that she was suffering from cancer.[35]

Raven-haired, considered by some beautiful, as famous for her housekeeping as her conversation, Sarah Dorsey at fifty was "frank, eager, and artless as a child." Tradition says she taught Sunday school. The *New York World* noted in its obituary her international literary repute. It termed her "ardent, faithful, unchanging" friendship for Carlyle and Allen and Davis "hero worship in its highest, best, and most unselfish form." Sarah had bowed out of her place as amanuensis and her very home when Varina came, after nursing her through a brain fever that followed Jeff Jr.'s death. Davis told Pollie that Varina "said no one had ever so nearly approached the skill of your Grandma." But he could see that rancor remained, and quoted: "The sick man knows the Physician's step, but when he is well cannot remember his face."[36]

It was Sarah who was sick now. "With the utmost composure," she underwent surgery in New Orleans, her first question on coming out of the chloroform being whether the ladies nursing her had been served refreshments. It was no use. At the end of June 1879, Davis went to the St. Charles Hotel to be at her side, along with "Mrs. Cochran and Mrs. Prentiss" and Minnie Howell.He wrote detailed bulletins back to Varina, just as if her contempt for Sarah did not exist. Varina filled Maggie in: Mrs. Dorsey had not "left one bone of me upon another to anyone in New Orleans. She told Major Walthall I was crazy. . . . Her death was caused by cancer of the womb and she sank under the flooding."[37]

For Jeff, the scene was played out on a different level altogether. "She had been for some days expecting death," he wrote Walthall. "She said she was at peace with the world and feared not to meet her God." He described for her first cousin, Kate Ferguson, whom he had also known a long time, Sarah's last days:

> Too stoical to complain, too brave to fear death, she suffered more pain than could be known to those around, save by the expression of her face and the wasting of her form. Her mind remained clear. . . . She received "the communion" [from Dr. Leacock and Mr. Kramer] with a few devoted friends, and to the last seemed more anxious for those who loved her, than for herself. After she was unable to speak . . . I repeated to her the beatitude "Blessed are the pure in heart, for they shall see God." She nodded her head several times, to mark her hope and consolation from the promise.

Davis was one of the small company that took her body by steamboat to Natchez for burial in her family cemetery. The very words he had repeated to her are chiseled in stone above her grave, preceded by "Confiding in the promise." Sarah died unreconciled to only one person, her sister, who had accused Davis of impurity.[38]

All the while, Jeff was taking care of Varina too: "Your suffering has been ever on my mind & heart. God grant that you may have found relief from the prescription of Dr. Choppin" (which he had procured in New Orleans). The letter ends, "With tenderest love." Varina told Maggie she could barely walk: "my feet are big as an elephant's." She also said, "It is very bitter to me, bitterer than death a thousand times," that Davis had asked Walthall to write up Sarah's death for the newspapers, singing her praise, "when he knows she has abused me."[39]

Actually, Davis only said, "write an obituary notice," but he did tell Walthall, "You know more than most others how self sacrificing she was, how noble in sentiment, how grand in intellect." To Sarah's cousin he spoke of "her noble soul in which there was neither hatred nor malice, her devotion to truth, her sublime patience under injury," while "over the whole shone the halo of a life spent in efforts to do good . . . to her 'to die was gain.'" "I should be as mean as some of her kin, if I did not feel grateful for many kindnesses and deeply grieved at her death," he wrote to Varina, on the very day, but she could never see beyond the cloud of her passion.[40]

"Your father returned . . . with a carbuncle in his side two inches across very red & suffering greatly" (he had never mentioned it). He seemed as much, "if not more, overcome" than when his children died, "and it is very pitiful to me because I cannot share his sorrow." Sarah's will was read on July 15, with Davis named "my sole heir, executor and administrator." "The family are very outrageous, and I hear going to contest the will bitterly," said Varina to Maggie; "Be very careful . . . to speak kindly of Mrs. Dorsey. *Reasons when we meet.*" Although in a new rage over being cut out, if Jeff should die, in favor of Winnie, Varina did not want the will invalidated.[41]

The sister and brothers, and a half-brother, Mortimer Dahlgren, openly insinuating "more than Platonic relationship," charged Davis with undue influence and Sarah herself with insanity. Insanity was in her family. Her namesake grandmother had died lunatic in the house where Sarah was born; her father had killed himself when she was nine years old. Davis knew this family intimately. That goes far to explain why he stuck to his arrangements with Sarah in the face of Varina's extreme displeasure. She was one of those threatened and insecure people whom he had sheltered throughout his life. "He has always kept a kind of oversight of me and now that I am left entirely alone and desolate in the world, he is kinder and more considerate than ever," Sarah had written Mann. When facing death, she told Davis he had given her "comfort, support, sympathy, and truest affection," and "I leave here thanks and blessings, which I will repeat before the throne of God."[42]

Davis answered the public slander by Dahlgren (first cousin to the one who had aimed to kill him) in a private letter. The circuit court ignored gossip and dismissed the bill; the family appealed; the Supreme Court upheld the lower one. But the legacy was almost empty. "There has been a vast exaggeration as to the value of the estate," said the legatee. He hoped barely "to liquidate the claims against the estate." He had to sell some of the far-off land to pay the taxes, and now he had the upkeep of Beauvoir, "never a source of income."[43]

Sarah's medical bills "were a heavy draft on her small revenue, and my own means are not large," he told Kate Ferguson. But he deeded to Mary Ellis right away the plantation that Sarah had merely asked him to will to her. He had no money to pay the Frielanders' school for Winnie and had to ask "that Addison will arrange it in some way from Memphis." Shortly after this, he regained possession of his own unprofitable Brierfield. Now *he* was land poor.[44]

With Jeff still grieving over Sarah, and Varina still nettled over his grief, they set themselves to finish the book. Varina had always seen the writing as "bitter, *bitter work*." It was "the weary recital of the weary war . . . a splendid but heartbreaking record of cherished hopes now blasted. . . . The graves give their dead and they stalk before us all gory and downcast," along with "noble men living, yet dead, in that they are hopeless." Jeff told Northrop, "The oranges are shining golden on the trees, and our pine knot fires soar in the chimneys, in their light I try to bury my unhappiness." He would finish the "memoirs," he said to Kate Ferguson, who came often to Beauvoir, "and then, and then—."[45]

Gradually Varina and Jeff settled back into their old loving ways. James Redpath, an editor of *North American Review*, who visited in 1888, thought they seemed like honeymooners. Visitors came singly and in huge groups, and Varina had to entertain them all. One of them found her "handsome, as well as strong-minded," and "like her husband, ever dignified, gracious and tactful." Maggie, now with a daughter named for Varina, came periodically. When Walthall disappointed Davis's blind trust, a Judge Tenney was sent to help with the book and had to be put up for weeks.[46]

Margaret Stoess brought her children from England and stayed six months. Father Ryan would come over from Mobile, where he was rector at St. Mary's. He wrote to Bishop Lynch and to Fathers Hamilton and Whelan for "some data" on Andersonville. He offered to stay at Beauvoir and help—"a service of love for the cause and reverence for yourself"; "there is no one living that gives you a heart-loyalty . . . more sincere than mine." His offer, and one from Kate Ferguson, were declined. The book suffered already from too many helpers, apparent in the rather disjointed form.[47]

"*Your* work & *our* defense," the poet-priest told Davis, "ought to be . . . the 'Sacred Scripture' of our Confederacy. And you ought to be *almost inspired* to give to the world of false policies the doctrines of deathless Principles." That is just what Davis tried to do in his first volume. In his preface, he adroitly crams lifelong political beliefs into a nutshell. He exposes "perversion of truth" about the South, warns "the people" about losing "their liberties" to "usurpations of the Federal Government," and looks to the next generation for "the blessed work" of restoring, not from the present "polluted" stream, but from original fountains, "the pristine purity and fraternity of the Union." He hopes that his reader "will admit that the South stands fully acquitted" of initiating the war, of its "cruel manner," and its sad physical "and yet sadder moral results." His hope was realized in one reader at least: "Your vindication of yourself and your people is complete."[48]

Since that was his aim, stated more than once, the book was a success. But he expected "little favor with this generation." In a political assessment, rare for him now, he thought "our people," after "sacrifices and heroic deeds unsurpassed in any age," were "ready to surrender their birthright for less than a mess of pottage." They were "like the ship which, having braved the storm, goes down in calm." This may be one reason why, though practically assured of it, if his disabilities were removed, he did not want political office.[49]

The Rise and Fall of the Confederate Government appeared in June of 1881 in two "cumbrous" volumes that "sold at a dear rate." The publishers, D. Appleton and Company of New York, demanded cash in advance from agents selling the book. They offered Davis royalties on a cloth-bound edition, but they printed their leather-bound one first, and when his returns did come, they deducted the sums they had advanced to Walthall and Tenney, with interest. In the end, Davis told Virginia Clay, his profit amounted to something like zero divided by two.[50]

Appleton's, whom Davis thought laggard, made the excuse later that "many book buyers in the North would not have it and many in the South were too poor to buy it." The man who noted this announcement said, "This is for many reasons unfortunate. Mr. Davis is one of the most remarkable men of the nineteenth century, and no one who is not familiar with his own expression of himself can rightly claim to know him." "Few men living have the faculty of expressing themselves with more force and clearness than he." "As an exposition of the Constitution [the book] will be assigned to the front rank," predicted a Texas man, who found it also "a most luminous military history." "A wonderful and gracious Providence . . . spared you to write that book."[51]

It seemed anything but luminous to generals who were Davis's enemies. G. W. Smith sneered, "cheap glittering generalities." Beauregard said, "Pooh! he stinks in my nostrils," and told Roman to make him look even worse in their book. But Col. Benjamin S. Ewell, West Point graduate and adjutant to J. E. Johnston, "found the accounts of the battles the best and clearest he had seen, from any source." Dabney Maury heard "on all sides" of the book's "great success" and predicted it would "last for our vindication as long as the war between the States shall be remembered."[52]

Longstreet and Billy Mahone, who had turned Republican, attacked it in the *New York Herald.* The *Atlantic Monthly* ended a scornful review with a piece of doggerel by James Russell Lowell about Davis's hands "drippin' red." His invaluable historical record had met, in a worldly sense, with failure. "Mr. Davis, as a failure," said Longstreet, "is the marked success of the nineteenth century." Perhaps the president was consoled when Bishop Wilmer wrote him, about his own book, "[It] will be much abused, for which I thank God. The crown of thorns from some hands is to me a crown of glory."[53]

Davis had gone to Montreal in May to see about getting his book published in England, where it came out on June 3. He sent Varina some leaves from Ma's grave: "It is in the most beautiful part of the cemetery, but it is unmarked and unprotected. Both must be done and I would attend to it now if I had the money. . . . Our loved ones are widely scattered."[54]

In August, he and Varina went to retrieve their living loved one, Winnie. Jeff had wanted to bring her home four years before, but Varina had said the climate "where you desire to live" was too bad, and good education there, "impossible." Emily Mason fetched Winnie, now a scholar and a musician, from Carlsruhe to Paris. There, Varina wanted her to have French and art and singing lessons—she had an "exquisite" voice, "so sympathetic"—but she studied only French. Jeff was living on advances from Jacob Payne, his lifelong friend and factor. He found Li' Pie, at seventeen, grown tall and slim, with blonde hair darkening. Her large, expressive blue eyes (which, like his, looked grey to some) made her face "serious, yet happy."[55]

Varina reveled in city life, visiting a Sèvres exhibit that revived "the longing of my life to create something which would live after me." Jeff, attacked by "acute rheumatism," fled to the "brighter climate" of Chantilly and the home of Dudley Mann, whom Varina described to Winnie as one of the "most generous & refined of gentlemen, and one who loves your Father better than his life, he is inexpressibly dear to us & has been for thirty years." She sent him, by Jeff, "all the love which I can feel for the most stainless of men."[56]

Soon Varina was asking her husband to come in and be "rejuvenated" by a Paris doctor. "Not for me like the Eagle to renew my youth," he muttered. He advised "cheerfully yielding" to "the natural and inevitable decay of all earthly things." His preoccupation with death proved less morbid than hers with health. Her hovering over Winnie always produced new, if not imaginary, ills. He joked: surely she could find a better American than French patent medicine, but "I have not 'the face to be shaved' by either." He was not "obstinate," however, he would listen to her doctor but probably not take his prescription: "I prefer to die a natural rather than an experimental death."[57]

Davis had obviously recovered his spirits. Even late in 1879 it was he who said, "Dear Wife, do try to look on the best side of life." On his Canadian trip, he quipped that the "we" someone used meant "the both all three." He lamented now that "no Frenchman could ever design an equestrian statue properly"—"brave little Joan" of Arc could not reach her stirrups—and he termed Rubens's work the "eternal deification of Marie de Medici." Back home at Beauvoir, which they reached late in December 1881, Davis made "many witty and wise comments" on current topics through the years to come. He held bantering conversation with Winnie and Varina, and with Maggie by letter. He even bantered with the cat. Knowing she hated corn meal, he would offer her a piece of hoe cake not cooked to suit him, and say, as she turned up her nose, "Yes, Barbara, you are right; it is neither good for man nor beast."[58]

Winnie tells this story, and many another spiced with his amusement. She obviously relished his company. They walked the beach hand in hand, rode horseback and read books together. One night, she read *Ben Hur* to him "from ten o'clock until daybreak," and then "left him still absorbed in the novel—indeed he did not go to rest until he had finished it." (He was always a night owl, "never an early riser.") They would read the Bible and talk about it. Varina wrote beside a note in Winnie's: "by my blessed pious child who 'searched the scriptures' all her short and holy life." Her father told Winnie "often" that Job "contained much of the finest poetry in the language." He would defend, with "professional pride," the Roman soldiers at the Crucifixion, preferring St. John's "eye witness" account to St. Luke's, because there they offered Jesus vinegar in mercy rather than mockery: "It is not like a soldier at any period of the world's history to taunt or revile a helpless person, least of all one who suffers silently."[59]

Always the idealism. He wrote to Kate Ferguson: "You ask me not think of you as 'romantic,' if to be intense, to go out of oneself, to rise to the pure ether which floats above the petty strifes of petty men be romantic, I wish so to think of you." This is part of the reason he was hero to many men, women, and children, as well as to Sarah Dorsey. Asked at about age nine if she had seen any great people in Europe, Winnie replied, "I never saw anyone like my father. My father is a great man. He has done great things!" "The dear child!" Davis said when he heard; "I never knew that she thought of such things." Ben Hill held up Davis and Lee together to the Southern Historical Society as "heroes in spite of defeat," great "in the face of fortune" because of "qualities in themselves."[60]

The family went to church at St. Mark's in Mississippi City. Winnie played the organ and Varina taught Sunday school. Later they went to the Church of the Redeemer at Biloxi. (Hurricane Camille, 1969, destroyed everything but its bell tower and the Davis pew.) Both churches claim Davis as vestryman and delegate to diocesan conventions. Sometimes he would attend the Methodist camp meeting held on the shore. He still said his silent grace at table, still had family prayers.[61]

Winnie was confirmed on Easter Day, 1884, in nearby Mobile by Bishop Wilmer of Alabama, who had known Davis since Richmond days and once ended a letter to him: "with veneration." He invited the family to stay overnight, but only the ladies did; Davis was "not well enough to go."[62]

He was seldom seriously ill, but he felt the infirmities of age—rheumatism, especially in the foot "broken at Buena Vista," sciatica, trouble with dentures. He suffered his usual debility, neuralgia, and occasional fevers. Once, when he jumped in the middle of a dog fight and stopped it, he was bitten badly on the hand. He would tell Northrop, "I feel myself going down hill." But Varina said, "He never lost his handsome figure, never stooped, never grew bald; his voice never changed nor did the elasticity of his step become heavy. He gained enough flesh to make him look like a well-preserved man of sixty."[63]

His old discipline served him well. His clothes, even if threadbare, were "well-fitting, refined," and "scrupulously clean" and neat. Custis Lee sent him a fine English dressing gown, but he would never come to the table without being fully clothed, even when ailing, out of respect for Varina. He had his "exercise stone" of about two hundred pounds on a cedar stump by the Beauvoir front steps. As he went out every morning to give his dogs a run on the beach, throwing them sticks out into the surf, he would lift the stone to keep up his muscle strength. He was never feeble. Winnie remembers how, at eighty years old, "he rose with . . . alacrity to offer his seat to a young visitor," and then "gave him his courteous attention."[64]

The visitors still came constantly, to be entertained by his conversation and perhaps a julep on the gallery. There he had his favorite rocker, and benches for sitting or stretching out, all made by him. He had helped to construct a boat. In the evening came backgammon or euchre games, played with zest, as if for money; or Winnie at her piano would perform for him light airs, Southern songs, or the Chopin piece that he loved. Books for his "omnivorous" reading spilled out of the shelves in the back parlor all over the house. Sometimes Davis would read aloud to the ladies, while perhaps they sewed, Varina on some piece like "Thy Will Be Done," sort of needlepoint, which she stitched in wool and finished by outlining the letters in metallic beads. She had it framed for the mantel in Jeff's bedroom.[65]

There was never much money at Beauvoir, but Davis never seemed to mind, until deep in debt at the end. He told Varina they were "not rich" but not "going to the 'poor 'ouse.'" When Northrop said, "North and South alike worship only the dollar, and the sensualities of life," Davis's reply was: those "who never look at the rack to see [if] there is fodder in it . . . the world denounces as impracticable, crabbed men"; "they are not the blessed in this world." He expected people like Kate Ferguson not "to measure your friends by the degree of their success in gathering worldly goods."[66]

On his eightieth birthday he could send only a small donation to the Church of the Redeemer: he was "poorer than an average fisherman." When the Bethel Baptist Church of Fairview, Kentucky, asked him to donate his father's home place to them, Micajah Clark and others had to buy it for him before he could do so. But an admirer said, "Poverty is his priceless crown"—it showed he was not venal. His example, a resolution at his death pointed out, would "teach Southern youth that not worldly success but duty done . . . and the being every inch a man in evil report as in good report . . . are the real goals of the Christian gentleman."[67]

Benevolences, however, went on as always. Having advanced money for years to his widowed niece, Lucy Boyle, Jeff made sure finally that she would not lose Locust Grove. He tried to get a loan for Julia Porterfield, grieving that he could not help her himself: "all I have to offer her is my prayers." He and Varina found an orphan to shelter, Bettie Tillman, in return for services. They offered a home to both Becket and William Howell. Brother Billy was about to accept with joy when he died in California. Becket came to oversee Brierfield, which was always in difficulties, but died after a few months.[68]

The Davises refused all offers of help themselves and managed even to keep that Southern mark of gentility, servants—sometimes ("so we go up, up, up, & so we go down, down, down," said Varina, about to lose some). Robert Brown, loved, loving, and pampered, "does what he pleases, when he wants." Once he "got mad about the horses & left," but came back. He stood with the family at Davis's grave and lived with Maggie until he died.[69]

Varina always hated the Gulf Coast heat, but the climate at least nurtured her precious garden. She created one patterned on the Confederate flag and kept the house filled with "roses & lilies & daffydowndillies." The roses were "so splendid they look unnatural," and "I could pick 500 a day if I wished." She kept the table supplied with "every kind of vegetable & melons."[70]

Still, the place was to her forever dull, "isolated as the island of Elba," except when some intriguing guest like the young Oscar Wilde came. The Irish poet and "aesthete" had bought *The Rise and Fall,* and he admired the South so much that he said Davis was "the man I would like most to see." It was arranged that he should stop off for the night as a lecture tour took him from New Orleans to Mobile. Davis retired early, explaining next day, "I did not like the man," but the ladies, enchanted, talked to him past midnight. Varina made a pencil sketch of his face. He inscribed a copy of his new *Poems* to her and a large photograph of himself to Davis, "in all loyal admiration."[71]

Varina stuck it out at Beauvoir, unwilling ever to leave Jeff alone. The "gentle hermit" was in his "paradise." Winnie would hear him humming about his room; a visitor noted his "quietly cheerful laugh." He loved the relative seclusion and quiet, raising his sheep and peacocks, and the scuppernongs for wine, sitting in contemplation by the lagoon behind the house, or gazing out to sea.[72] "Nature teaches us to expect to be alone as the time draws nigh for our departure hence forever," he said. "The only change" that Varina ever saw in him was, he grew "more and more tender and gentle."[73]

Davis's patience had been made perfect in suffering—almost. Privately, the old temper was nearly gone, but it could still be provoked by unjust public censure of himself or the South. Perfection would have been to let the charges go unanswered, but no other virtue is so hard. Sometimes he flamed out in print.[74]

Davis came back from France, December 1881, to find himself under attack. It was a running fight from then on, to the end of his life. The Reverend General Pendleton urged him to the fray (against J. E. Johnston): "You have . . . to defend the truth, and therein my prayers are with you." But the blunt General Early said, "Do you think it necessary to defend yourself against [your subordinates]? If you do, I don't." Davis did bear silently many "utterly scandalous and inexcusable" misstatements through the years, causing a *New York World* reporter to praise his "magnanimity" to enemies. In one case he himself pointed out his "forbearance." If he said nothing in early 1882, it was because friends, even unknowns, had parried the blow.[75]

"Poor Johnston has ruined himself at last," Ben Hill wrote—"he will lie." "I can never believe him again." Drayton said: "Joe has gone mad in his old age." He told Davis that Johnston had charged him, in an interview with Frank Burr of the *Philadelphia Press*, "with having made way with $2,500,000 of Gold belonging to the Confederacy." Johnston had hinted this already in his *Narrative*, but he tried to charge Burr with "breach of faith." Johnston knew better than any man living, said Burr, that his statements would be published and the article was actually "a very temperate" version of their conversations.[76]

Drayton was "outraged" that he had "dared to couple *thief*, with your honest name," but he warned "Jeff" as "our Representative man of the 'Lost Cause'": Johnston's "crazy attack upon *you*, must not be repeated upon *him!!!* 'Our Lord when he was reviled, reviled not again.'" Davis said many friends wrote "under the fear that I would reply" to Johnston's "absurd mendacity" (Burr even invited him to), but he was told the attack was "very beneficial to me."[77]

Maury had written him: "If our enemies really desire to split the 'solid South' they have adopted the wrong means—for this vile slander has rallied us to you." It rallied even admirers of Johnston. As Hill said, "The whole Southern people are your defenders." Any true Southern man would "prefer a word of approval from [Davis's] lips to a crown of gold from the best of his detractors," declared Preston Johnston. He had been so near to Davis that "no veil to his character was possible, even if he had wished it," and "he has left upon my mind an ineffaceable image of knightly purity . . . a standard and ideal for myself and my countrymen."[78]

In 1884, William T. Sherman retired from the army and took to public speaking. In November, probably echoing Blaine's *Twenty Years in Congress* which had just come out, he told a veterans' post that Davis was "a conspirator" who had wanted power to control the whole United States; had the South won, "you would be slaves." Furthermore, he had seen Davis's signature on a letter threatening to "turn Lee's army against any State" trying to secede from the Confederacy. "Unqualifiedly false," answered Davis: let Sherman produce his evidence "or wear the brand of a base slanderer." Sherman could not produce it, and he did not answer. Instead, he got his "historical statement" printed as an executive document to the Senate—"spread the vile mass on the files," as Davis put it. Then it became "a duty" to his people as well as himself to expose the "picturesque prevarication" and to defend Sidney Johnston, Hampton, and even Grant. (In April 1885, Davis refused to "disturb" Grant's "closing hours" by making any public statement about him; instead he said he "would, if it were in my power" comfort him.) In a letter to J. T. Scharf of the *Baltimore Sun*, Davis built up his proof against Sherman step by step, from witnesses who exposed lie after lie, and concluded: "he stands pilloried before the public and all future history as an imbecile scold or an infamous slanderer." "What a terrible letter," said Northrop's wife, "and he has such a sweet face."[79]

It created "a sensation." Scharf gave it to the Associated Press, and on October 1, 1886, it appeared simultaneously all over the country. Mann read it even in Paris: "your mind has lost nothing of its original vigor." Paul Hamilton Hayne wrote a sonnet to the occasion. Early had no quarrel with this answer, but he accused Davis of "cruel and unusual punishment": "You have not only scalped 'Tecumseh,' but . . . flayed him alive." The *Richmond State* declared that Davis's convictions had relit "his eye with the old-time flash"—it was victory in defeat. From Texas came: "We rejoice in having had you for our leader and are prouder of you every day." To a Yankee who asked if Davis were not in "his dotage now," J. William Jones answered: "If you think so, suppose you read his recent reply to General Sherman." Sherman "declined" a rebuttal.[80]

Even as the battle raged, Confederates in Alabama and Georgia got a chance to greet Davis in person. Ben Hill, keeping his cheer in extreme pain, praying constantly, "Thy will be done," had died from tongue cancer on August 16, 1882. Davis had written him, "I have suffered in your suffering and fervently prayed for your relief." A statue to Hill was to be unveiled in Atlanta now, and his good friend Henry W. Grady knew he would want Davis, "of all men," to be there. He told Davis, "Nothing that you could have asked him . . . would have been refused." Davis came. Fifty thousand people streamed into Atlanta from North and South, "to do honor to those two exponents of all that is true and noble and chivalrous in Southern manhood," said Grady's *Atlanta Constitution*. After the formal orations, Davis spoke briefly: during the war, Hill had asked nothing but given much; after the war, he had selflessly defended Davis against Blaine. Grady had introduced the president with a sort of apotheosis: "This outcast . . . is the uncrowned king of our people," his palace, "the millions of brave hearts in which your dear name and fame are forever enshrined" and "generations yet unborn shall . . . hold your memory sacred." "With dauntless courage" Davis had borne for them, "in obscurity and poverty . . . the obloquy of defeat." "The resurrection of these memories that for twenty years have been buried in our hearts, have given us the best Easter we have seen since Christ was risen from the dead."[81]

This was the tenor of the whole 1886 tour, which had begun in Montgomery the week before. Varina and Margaret had to stay at Beauvoir with a sick child, so only Winnie went with Davis. It was for her sake that he had agreed to go at all. Crowds hailed their special railway car at every stop, and by the time it reached the first Confederate capital, it was filled with flowers and "a thousand other tokens of love." It was night when they arrived, and raining, but thousands were cheering and crowding up to the carriage, while artillery boomed out above "the constant discharge" of fireworks and small arms. They were escorted by the Montgomery Greys and Blues to the tune of "Dixie" through the "half-wild populace," "under a perfect archway of fires" from colored lanterns and "brilliant electric sparks," to the Exchange Hotel. As the president alighted, a set piece spelled out, "Welcome, Our Hero!"[82]

Upstairs, ladies "in their adoration of Mr. Davis" banked the room where he had stayed in 1861 with flowers and strewed his pathway, voicing their acclaim, throwing their arms about his neck. Ex-governor Thomas Watts, friend and once attorney general, embraced him. Frank Burr reported to the *New York World* that Davis "seemed overwhelmed" and "kept constantly bowing his head." When called to the gallery where Yancey had proclaimed, "The man and the hour have met," he was able to say only, "With a heart full of emotion I greet you again," before "the crazy brass band" struck up "Dixie" inside the hotel and drowned him out.[83]

The next day, more people, "more music and fresh hurrahs," in fact, "an ovation," accompanied Davis all the way up the broad avenue to the capitol. As he neared the spot where he had taken the oath of office twenty-five years before, the crowd "broke into the wildest cheers." Winnie sat with the family of Gen. John B. Gordon, the chief speaker. Frank Burr noticed that she resembled her father "in quite a degree," having his "sharp eye." He noted tears in hers as "she saw for the first time how [the Southern people] loved and honored him." Virginia Clay was there (alone, for Clement had died January 3, 1882), and Letitia Tyler, who had raised the first flag, and Varina's niece, Lizzie Waller. Almost prevented by the shouting that greeted him, Davis told the people they had fought "that war which Christianity alone approved—a holy war for defense," and that he could see "the spirit of Southern liberty is not dead." This roused such "long and continued applause" that by the time he got to Savannah, he had to deny that he wanted "to bring on another war."[84]

The third day at Montgomery was calmer. "Sacred duties" occupied him—laying a cornerstone beside the capitol for a monument to Alabama's war dead and decorating the soldiers' graves in Oakwood Cemetery. Since extemporary remarks were known to get him in trouble, Davis had written out his monument speech. But he said the same things he always said (his enemies claimed he learned nothing): "We have no desire to feed the fires of sectional hate," but we believe "in the righteousness of our cause and virtue of those who risked their lives to defend it. (Long applause and cheers.)" He did sound a new note. "A chivalrous people," with rights not yet fully restored, had resumed their "obligations as citizens": "I am proud of you, my countrymen . . . and pray God to give you grace to suffer and be strong."[85]

"The old man looks well, don't he?" a veteran had said the night before, seeing Davis at a play to benefit the monument. How he held up, constantly on the go and shaking hundreds of hands, was "a mystery to everyone." And it was after this that he made the arduous Atlanta trip. On the way there, he had to greet crowds at every stop and hear plaudits like the one by which Georgia welcomed him: "One who has ever borne the cross as becomes a hero. (Cheers.)" It was here, at West Point, that Gordon called Winnie "the daughter of the Confederacy . . . the war baby of our old chieftain." Then, after Atlanta, the chief and his baby went down to Savannah for the centennial of the Chatham Artillery and rededication of the monument to Gen. Nathanael Greene. The sides of Davis's railway car bore banners that read: "Buena Vista" and "He Was Manacled for Us." "All the South is aflame," wrote Burr.[86]

Davis added to the flame in Savannah. He forgot his promise not to speak ad libitum. He reminded the enormous crowd that when Greene, from Rhode Island, helped Georgians win independence from England, their cause was "state sovereignty." "Is it a lost cause now? Never! . . . Truth crushed to earth will rise again . . . clothed with all the majesty and power that God gave it, and so the independence of these states . . . won in 1776 . . . can never die." At this, "there was a mighty surge in the crowd," and Davis came near being crushed by his admirers. What did he mean? He had said on the way to Atlanta, the Cause "is not lost. It will live again," but once there, he had praised only Ben Hill's peaceful methods of resisting Reconstruction. It was the Southern equipoise: fidelity to principle within a framework that denied it—like not asking pardon but still living in America. A year later he said: "The truths we fought for shall not encourage you to ever fight again . . . keep your word in good or evil. . . . If the Union is ever to be broken, let the other side break it."[87]

In Savannah, Davis visited the Sisters of Mercy who had been so kind to his family in 1865. There "the chivalry and beauty of Southern society" attended a dance in Winnie's honor. She was fast becoming a general favorite. Bishop Wilmer could hardly get to her for "her well-wishers." He thought that seeing "her dear father" so honored would "illuminate her whole life." In Atlanta, she had again been introduced to a cheering throng as "The Daughter of the Confederacy," and so she was called ever after.[88]

Bishop Will Mercer Green also wrote Davis how glad he was that Winnie could see "how truly you are loved by all our people." He thanked God for "such just and long-due honors" to Davis, "insufficient as they were to repay you for what you had done and suffered." A few months later, "the very night before his death, he asked for 'The Life of President Davis' [by Alfriend] and said to his children, 'He is a noble man, and every one should read that book that he may know how to live!' "[89]

Davis had become, not just "the martyr," but "the Hero of the Lost cause." A Virginian called him this, fighting a duel for him in 1880. After felling his opponent, he "pressed to his lips," in token of this, Davis's name, engraved on a cane he had given him. The man who told Davis this story said, "Your silent endurance—your king-like bearing has won an undying admiration. . . . We recognize you as [the Cause's] most splendid example of unselfish patriotism."[90]

Enjoying "a new lease of life" from his tour, though it brought on bronchitis, Davis went to Fairview, Kentucky, in November for the dedication of the site for the Bethel Baptist Church. He designated his gift of land, "a thank offering to God."[91]

His religious tolerance was pinked the next year in a running fight with a Methodist. Lubbock got him into this. Prohibition had replaced abolition as the humanitarian cause of the day, and Texas was locked in battle over whether its constitution should forbid "the manufacture and sale of intoxicating liquors." Davis hesitated a long time, knowing Reagan was on the prohibition side, but finally wrote Lubbock a letter saying, "To destroy individual liberty and moral responsibility would be to eradicate one evil by . . . another . . . more fatal." Drunkenness was the evil and should be made a crime. If juries would not convict for that, then laws against liquor itself "would be a dead letter." Charles B. Galloway, a Southern Methodist bishop in Mississippi, said publicly that Davis was opposing "the reform of the age" and that his name was "the shibboleth of the saloons." Davis grieved that Galloway had "left the pulpit" for the "rostrum," to "plead the higher law of prohibitionism" instead of the free will and "brotherly love taught by the meek and lowly Jesus whom we adore." They exchanged fire for months. Prohibition was defeated in Texas.[92]

While these shots were still whizzing in October of 1887, Jeff, Varina, Margaret, and Winnie arrived (with what poignant memories?) in Macon, Georgia. It was no sad little ambulance that brought them this time, but a special train running "under triumphal arches" through "indescribable" enthusiasm. "Flowers covered us," said a reporter, and at every stop, veterans "stormed the train and took him by assault." They were headed for "a grand reunion" that drew, along with Davis's presence and a state fair, fifty thousand people. A torchlight parade led the Davis family to the home of their hosts, Capt. and Mrs. Marshall Johnson.[93]

The Johnsons had invited their Episcopal rector, James Winchester, to dinner. He was impressed by Davis's "reverence" and his scholarly conversation about the Bible, which caused the priest to go on studying Hebrew and Greek. Years later, when the cleric called on the invalid Mrs. Johnson, their conversation "naturally turned to Mr. Davis." "I stressed his firm belief in the Bible and urged upon her the Scriptural and Apostolic rite of confirmation," which she had never received. Being now a bishop, Winchester confirmed her right there: "It was the influence of Mr. Davis that brought her this blessing." His faith was not only well known, but also a means of grace to others.[94]

The veterans were supposed to march in formation to the Johnson home to see Davis, but they became "too impatient . . . jumped over the fence and came running and shouting all the way to greet their old chief," bearing "tattered battle flags" saved from capture. Davis's eyes were "shining with a pride in them too great for words," when suddenly he collapsed. Varina called it "heart failure." After a few days' bed rest, he insisted on going to the fairgrounds, where he and Varina stood like royalty to receive one by one, first orphans, then other children, then adults. He addressed the soldiers briefly, and they once more rushed forward, shouting. He had to be whisked away in a carriage, back to bed. Newspapers reported him "desperately ill" and Bishop Galleher of Louisiana, a veteran himself, offered to come "minister to you." But Davis was tougher than he looked, and he was soon back at Beauvoir.[95]

The Reverend Mr. McRacken had been talking to Galleher on a New Orleans street the year before, when he saw an expression "of heartfelt, almost reverential love" come over his face. He expected to see some example of "pure, exalted womanhood," but when he turned, it was "a tall man in gray, Mr. Davis." "I thought that no ordinary man could bring such an expression to the face of a strong man like Bishop Galleher," wrote McRacken; "Mr. Davis must have been a prince among men." Gen. Thomas T. Munford thought so. He sent him, "with a soldier's love and admiration," his "Brigade Head Quarter's Flag . . . never surrendered": "Give my love to Mrs. Davis and tell her this treasure cost the lives of over 500 men of *my old Regiment* alone . . . and she must see that the old Flag which was never sullied goes down with our Chief."[96]

Davis may have been a prince among men, but he was "Bampa" to his grandchildren (Varina, in a strange turnabout, became "Bannie"). By 1884, Margaret had given him three—Varina ("Daughtie"), Lucy, and

Jefferson Addison (William Davis, named for Billy, came later). After she took them away to Colorado, chosen because of her husband's lung trouble, she brought them to Beauvoir for visits—never often enough or long enough for her father. Once she reported to Addison: "Daughtie manages 'Bampa' perfectly he is only too willing—She says where you hat Bam come Bam & takes him to walk every day if he goes ahead of her she says wait Bam I come—if he goes behind she clucks to him & calls him like a puppy . . . Father think it very funny." He gave her a lamb "& she is to have its fleece every year & all its lambs when it has any." When the grandson grew big enough, Davis showed him how to "put the soldiers in line of battle" and invented the game of "Johnnie Arcoley," which they played on the backgammon board. Davis gave him, before he could read, a *Life of David Livingstone.* Once when the boy "screamed like a hawk" because his stuffed dog was missing at bedtime, Davis got out of his own bed to go look for it in the rain (and found it)—one of what Winnie calls the "thousand little sacrifices of time and inclination he daily made," never "as though it cost him anything."[97]

With such beguiling interludes, Davis began again to write, publishing in the *North American Review* in 1886, "The Indian Policy of the United States," and the next year, "Life and Character of the Hon. John Caldwell Calhoun." This tribute gave him the chance to praise his political hero's "purity" and to quote him on the evil of a Union by force. He also wrote for the same journal two articles not published until 1890. One was "The Doctrine of State Rights," in which he did "justice to the motives which actuated the soldiers of the Confederacy . . . for no . . . devotion can sanctify service in an unrighteous cause."[98]

The other was "Robert E. Lee." He first outlined Lee's career, using the passive voice to hide his own part in the general's advancement, and then grew personal, speaking of Lee's humor, his "true greatness" attained by attention to detail, and his self-sacrificing nature, "the crowning glory of man." The only "defect" he could find, "probably," was that Lee sometimes suggested rather than commanded (which he regularly did himself). He said it might explain why Lee found no food at Amelia Court House on the retreat from Petersburg. Lee had said the failure to execute his order was "fatal." Pollard ("that scandal monger," Davis called him) had blamed "the authorities at Richmond," and his statement was copied by many. Davis thought he had refuted this charge in *Rise and Fall* by showing that Lee's order was never received. He may have brought it up now because A. L. Long's *Memoirs of Robert E. Lee* renewed the question.[99]

Davis's last article was "Andersonville and Other War-Prisons," a final answer to what R. B. Winder called "a most diabolical" scheme to "degrade" the South "before the whole world," while covering up cruelty in Northern prisons ("our national honor was assailed," said another). But it was more. "I have often felt with poignant regret that the Southern public have never done justice to the martyr Major Wirtz [sic]," Davis wrote Louis Schade. He wanted "to do something to awake due consideration for his memory." Davis brought exhaustive testimony and argument to both these matters, only he did not paint Wirz's trial "as black as it was," in his desire that the sections be reconciled. One of the "other" prisons was his own. When the *North American Review* would not let him call Nelson Miles "a heartless vulgarian," he withdrew his article and gave it to *Belford's Magazine*, which printed it in two parts, posthumously. Belford also published his *Short History of the Confederate States*.[100]

Davis had offered to let the editor of the *North American Review* alter one word "provided the change does not involve the waiver of State sovereignty." He did not trust him after seeing "the mutilated condition in which my reply to Lord Wolseley appeared." This reply to the adjutant general of the British army was the final salvo of his final battle. Sir Garnet Wolseley had begun it two years before, praising and criticizing Lee in a newspaper article, and pitying him for being so trammeled: "If Gen. Washington had had a Mr. Davis over him, could he have accomplished what he did?" Davis had slashed back, deriding the "style of a sensational novelist," showing errors of fact, defending Lee, answering such tired charges as nonpursuit after Manassas, and ending with a sneer: the English general had previously attracted interest only by "the unrealized hope that he would save Gen. Charles Gordon from impending sacrifice [at Khartoum, Egypt]." Wolseley had returned fire as he reviewed for the *North American* the first volume of *Battles and Leaders of the Civil War* (with four articles by Davis enemies). It was the old tale about not running out the cotton. The octogenarian Davis demolished it in killing language: Wolseley had "a tone of authority that, viewing his capacity, amuses, and, viewing his record, amazes."[101]

Winnie assisted her father in his literary labors. She helped Varina copy his memorandum on the Battle of Monterey (stolen by Sherman's men and on loan from the "innocent holder" who wanted it "verified"). At the end she wrote a poem, referring to herself as one "who spellbound hears these stories of the past." Love of history and heroism led her to write "An Irish Knight of the Nineteenth Century," on Robert Emmet, the ill-fated leader of her great-grandfather, James Kempe. It was her second work published (privately, by her parents), her first being a newspaper poem addressed to the pines of Beauvoir. Her third was "Serpent Myths," in the *North American Review*.[102]

Winnie had entered New Orleans society at Mardi Gras, 1884, as lady-in-waiting to Mary Lee, Queen of Comus (which she herself would be in 1892). Her charm brought her many invitations to visit as far north as New York. On one trip, she met Joseph Pulitzer and his wife

Kate, née Davis, who embraced her as a distant cousin and later took her with them several times to Europe. While visiting in Syracuse at the home of Dr. Thomas Emory, son of the old Davis friends, Winnie met Alfred Wilkinson. He was a state-rights Democrat, but grandson of an abolitionist, and both her parents were shocked when they learned that she wanted to marry him. But Fred came asking for her hand and won over the reluctant Davis. He gave his consent. Other Confederates were not so charitable; they were very angry. When Winnie realized this, she put off the wedding. She sailed for France with the Pulitzers, though Varina "almost had to force her to go," hoping for relief from her months of "slow fevers." Before she could "bring back the light which goes out when she goes away," as her father said, the question of his feelings was settled forever.[103]

On November 3, 1889, Davis was "preparing to leave for Brierfield, for an absence of ten days or a fortnight." He planned to go up to Diamond Place to see Florida, whose husband and nephew had recently died. "Your poor old father went off . . . positively refusing to let me go though I urged it very much," Varina told Maggie. He wanted her to care for some guests who had arrived. "I did not mind so much . . . as he was well." He could barely lift the exercise stone that day. He caught the train at the Beauvoir stop. At New Orleans there was freezing rain as he took the steamboat to Vicksburg, then back down to Davis Bend, where, through the bitter cold night, he was driven three miles in an open cart from the landing to the house. Varina had once asked Lise, now reconciled after the lawsuit, to let her know "if he is at all ill. He . . . will forbid you to telegraph if you tell him you mean to do it." Lise was not at Brierfield this trip, and it was four days before the plantation manager thought to wire Varina. Davis had been lying all that while in the throes of bronchitis, refusing to let him summon a doctor.[104]

On November 12, in a high fever, he wrote, with wavering lines:

> My deerst
> If I can get to the landing I will go down on the Leathers to morrow. Lest you should hear alarming I write to say I have suffered much but by the help of the Lord [here a sort of cross or ampersand]
> Nothing is as it should be, and I am not able even to look over the place
> With best wishes to all the household
> I am as ever
> Your Husband

Across the end of the envelope, Varina wrote, "My darlings last letter to any one—." The next morning he forced himself, at the request of the manager's daughter, to scrawl in the child's "memory book" his last written words: "May all your paths be peaceful and pleasant, charged with the best fruit, the doing good to others."[105]

The *Leathers* was a steamboat belonging to his friend Tom Leathers, who ran several. When Varina got the telegram, she started up the Mississippi on another of them. When the two came abreast, she transferred to Jeff's. When the boat paused at Bayou Sara, two physicians came on board and diagnosed acute bronchitis and malaria. At New Orleans, Jacob Payne, his son-in-law, Justice Charles E. Fenner, Edgar H. Farrar, and his wife, Lucy (Mary Stamps's daughter), were all waiting for them in "a cold spitting rain," with Dr. Stanford E. Chaillé, who pronounced the patient too sick to travel. He was "struggling for breath like a dying man," said Varina. Four medical students carried Davis on a stretcher bed to an ambulance that took him to the Fenner home at First and Camp Streets. It was soon surrounded by muffled silence; carriages were even rerouted. Crowds gathered, seeking news of his condition, flowers and telegrams began to arrive.[106]

"His fortitude and patience were almost divine," says Varina, though of course he wanted to go home and not trouble Mrs. Fenner. Nannie Davis Smith came to help, along with Bettie Tillman and a practical nurse. Nannie had been taking dictation from him at Beauvoir for an autobiography. He lay there thinking about West Point, Sidney Johnston, and Polk, saying, "I seem to remember more every day." He wanted to go on with it, and told Dr. Chaillé, "It may seem strange to you that a man of my age should desire to live, but I do." But, as always, "If it is God's will, I must submit." One morning he said to Varina, "I want to tell you, I am not afraid to die."[107]

That day "the most patient of patients" rallied and ate a lamb chop. "I'm afraid I shall have to agree with the doctors for once," he said, "and admit I am a little better." Nannie says, "We thought his splendid constitution would triumph," but "suddenly a violent ague seized him—the beginning of the end." When Varina tried repeatedly to give him medicine, he waved her gently off: "Pray excuse me, I cannot take it." Although "unable to speak" after this, "he remained perfectly conscious." When the doctors "sought to make him more comfortable, he turned himself without assistance" onto his right side, laid his cheek upon his hand, closed his eyes, "and fell asleep," so quietly that it took the watchers a while to realize that he would not wake. It was forty-five minutes into the morning of Friday, December 6, 1889.[108]

XXIII

Afterward

It was the quietest possible death. He had been preparing for it a long time. "The departure of the spirit was gentle and utterly painless." It was the "happy death" expected by those who wore the cross of St. Benedict, and Jefferson Davis wore his "always."[1]

He would not let Varina telegraph the children: "Let our darlings be happy . . . I may get well." But Maggie had seen in the papers how ill he was. She got as far as Fort Worth but missed connections and arrived too late to see him alive. She fainted twice in the carriage on the way to the grave.[2]

Winnie, bundling up illustrated French journals for his Christmas present, wrote to him from Paris December 5, "broken-hearted" that he was sick, though a telegram assured her he was "convalescent": "My dearest . . . I cannot get reconciled to the idea of my having, no matter how unwittingly, left you while you were ill." "Dearest darling Father, when as now, I want to tell you how much I love you I grow bewildered . . . [unable] to express to you the devoted love and tenderness of which my heart is and always will be full for you, my darling Father." Still not well herself, and unhappy over her blighted romance, Winnie broke down completely at the news of his death. Kate Pulitzer took her to the Grand Hotel in Naples; Fred came over to see her; but nothing seemed to interest her anymore.[3]

Varina, of course, was overwhelmed and had to be given sedatives. But she was a strong woman in every way, and by late morning, she was able to watch by the corpse, lying coffinless. The gentlemen friends helping to lay it out had noticed a scar on his hand, and Jacob Payne told how, in the early days at Brierfield, Davis had gone after whatever was robbing his cornfield and met a bear, and while it fastened on his left hand, he had killed it with his bowie knife.[4]

Remembering was the order of the day. George W. Jones was "past 85 years old" and full of tales. One was how he tracked down in Iowa, with the help of the law, a photograph album stolen from Varina's trunk at Fortress Monroe. On hearing that Davis was gravely ill, he had set out immediately from Dubuque. Slow trains delayed his arrival till the morning of the death.[5]

Jeff lay dressed in the suit of Confederate gray given him by Jubal Early, who had visited Beauvoir often on his way to share with Beauregard the doubtful honor of drawing tickets for the New Orleans lottery. At the head of the body were crossed palm leaves and a sheaf of wheat—symbols of victory and life. At first, Varina would allow no one but Dobbin and the family into the parlor. But she made an exception for Jones. This friend from youth told reporters: "I never saw Mr. Davis looking more life-like. His face had none of the characteristics of the dead."[6]

Varina also let Miles Cooper view the body, an ex-slave who used to send them fruit from his farm in Florida. Having hurried to the Fenner house, he was "crushed" to find Davis already dead and asked only to look upon him once more. "It was pitiful to hear the sobs and wails of the old man," said a reporter. The only others who got in were two sisters from the St. Alphonsus convent, bringing orphans to pray for "their honored father, Jefferson Davis." This theme of "*pater patriae*" (father of his country), also sounded in speeches and proclamations.[7]

Around midnight, Varina had to give up Jeff to the public. A hearse took the body, in a copper coffin with full-length glass cover, to the city hall. Among the pallbearers were a nephew of Judah Benjamin (E. B. Kruttschnitt) and Edgar Farrar, whose family "venerated as well as adored" Davis as their "hero"—"the stoic, the saint perhaps, the soldier." In a council chamber swathed in black and drooping with flags of both the United and the Confederate States, President Jefferson Davis, surrounded by flowers, bronze howitzers, stacked arms, and a military guard of honor, lay in state for five days. The arrangers could not resist a modern touch: from the black frame around his portrait, "a myriad of electric lights brightly sparkle."[8]

"Fully 10,000 persons . . . young and old, male and female, white and colored and of all nationalities" passed by on the first day. The doors were open from ten in the morning to ten at night. By the fifth day, an estimated one hundred and fifty thousand people had seen him. Many were crying, the unknown as well as intimate friends like Jones and Mrs. John Wheat, the rector's widow, who had come all the way from North Carolina. "Tottering" at age eighty-four, she faltered, and was helped by a one-armed man who, it turned out, had known her son Rob.

At midnight on the first day, the glass coffin cover was unscrewed. Maggie had finally arrived and had come for her last look, on the arm of Joseph R. Davis. Then as Farrar, "representing Mrs. Davis," watched,

Orin Frazer, a sculptor from Atlanta, made the death mask. Henry Grady had sent him, with family permission, intending to use the model for a statue of Davis. Before the month was out, Grady himself would lie dead, at the age of thirty-nine.[9]

The whole city, the whole South, was going into mourning for Davis: "He has always been the hero of his people—their best beloved," said the *Times-Democrat.* Church bells tolled all the first day. Black wound the pillars and festooned the fronts of stores and public buildings. Schools and businesses closed on Friday and would for the funeral, along with the courts, the cotton exchange, and the medical school of Tulane University. Flags were at half-mast everywhere, even on British ships, and on steamboats, including the *Leathers;* but not at the restored nation's capital.[10]

Mayor Joseph Shakespeare wired the War Department of Davis's death, but the flag was not lowered for this former secretary, as was customary. (L. Q. C. Lamar, when secretary of the interior, had gotten into trouble for honoring in this way Jacob Thompson, another Confederate ex-secretary.) The present war secretary said, rather ambiguously, that his non-action was in "the spirit of peace and good will"; he hoped it did not add to the sorrow of Davis's "many friends." " 'Many friends!' " burst out Thomas Riley Markham, a chaplain addressing Army of Tennessee veterans, "Aye, the South is his friends." Let the official try " 'to dwarf and minimize our cause' . . . in the person of our hero"; but let the telegrams and proclamations, "the draped Southern homes," the spontaneous gathering of the people to New Orleans, the services to coincide with the funeral all over the South "make answer." "Millions of attesting voices," said this Presbyterian preacher, would tell "to all time" how the people "from Maryland to Texas . . . delight to honor" Davis. His chains have "the martyr ring" and "in our keeping would be held as Christians hold the wood of the cross."[11]

"Cities and States," he noted, were "contending for the honor of giving his remains a resting place." Richmond, Montgomery, Atlanta, Macon, Memphis, Kentucky, and Mississippi put in their reasoned claims. But New Orleans wanted him. The Metairie Cemetery Association offered a "mound" opposite that of the Army of Tennessee, where the equestrian statue of Sidney Johnston stood. That army and Lee's men vied for the honor of sepulture. Veterans of each met and drew lots, and the Army of Northern Virginia won. Its monument at Metairie, guarded by the effigy of Stonewall Jackson, held a number of marble vaults within its mound of turf. Davis had spoken at the founding of both these monuments. Varina, torn many ways, agreed to have the body laid there for the time being, pending her final decision.[12]

As Davis had wanted, the Confederate organizations planned the funeral, supervised by Preston Johnston, now president of Tulane University. He headed the mayor's committee on arrangements. Other old friends were on hand—Tom Drayton, Ethelbert Barksdale, Robert Lowry (now governor of Mississippi), J. Stoddard Johnston (Sidney's nephew), and Virginia Clay (now married to David Clopton), Lubbock and Reagan and Thomas Watts, John B. Gordon (governor of Georgia), and Robert Brown. Out of the far past came four members of the First Mississippi Rifles. Mrs. Braxton Bragg, now a resident of New Orleans, waited in the parlor of the city hall with Varina for the funeral to begin.[13]

Varina had sent to Beauvoir for the sword Davis wore as an infantry lieutenant. Somehow he had held onto it through thick and thin. It lay on the casket with the palms and a cross made of white flowers. Crosses bloomed all around in many sizes. One, of rosebuds, camellias, hyacinths, and forget-me-nots, from Confederates of Missouri, was eight feet tall. It was topped by a ten-foot display from the Army of Tennessee Association. Ladies and florists had created doves, crowns, anchors, hearts, pillows of roses, and Confederate flags. They were all outdone by a five-foot urn woven of immortelles, with its bowl holding roses and lilies, decorated with "a blazing cross of coral honeysuckle" and "a Latin inscription" (it was from the Jesuit College). Dallas sent "a massive ship" of flowers, with "The Lost Cause" and "Ship of State" flying from the masthead. "The Louisiana Historical Association, of which Mr. Davis was chairman," and the Lee Memorial Association, sent great floral chairs. A lighthouse, symbolizing the Constitution, was lettered: "Davis, a guide and light for his people." The *Times-Democrat* reporter thought the most tasteful and delicate design was that chosen by several donors, showing "gates ajar"—two gates made of flowers, standing half open, crowned by such slogans as, "To the hero of our fathers." More telling of grief and love than all these were innumerable bouquets carried simply in hand and left "without a word or a card." "Some brought violets they swept gently across the glass lid, carrying them away again as cherished souvenirs."[14]

At last it was time for the ceremonies, set for noon, December 11. The doors of the city hall had to be opened at seven to accommodate the thousands still coming. "The body, notwithstanding the very warm and exceptionally oppressive weather of the past week, was remarkably well preserved. The countenance presented an expression of 'rapturous repose.'" The flowers, too, were "as fresh as when gathered," "not a leaf had turned." Mrs. Wheat came again, and "her sobs were audible all over the room." Father Darius Hubert, French Jesuit chaplain to the First Louisiana, a "faithful follower and friend," stood silently praying "long and fervently." "Gradually the look of pain wore away and was replaced by a glow of joy." He was one of the last to look upon "the still, white face" before the metal lid covered the glass.[15]

Varina and Maggie, with other black-swathed ladies, including Elise Bragg and two daughters of Leonidas Polk, looked out from the parlor windows onto the portico, as Louisiana artillerymen brought the body, now draped in Munford's Confederate battle flag, to the catafalque where clergymen of all denominations waited, Rabbi I. L. Leucht among them. The vast crowd in Lafayette Square, where Davis's voice had resounded after Buena Vista, heard the prayer book service begin: "I am the resurrection and the life, saith the Lord." Bishop Galleher gave a short eulogy, speaking of Davis's "knighthood" and saying: "Fearless and unselfish, he could not well escape the life-long conflicts to which he was committed. Greatly and strangely misconceived, he bore injustice with the calmness befitting his place. He suffered many and grievous wrongs, suffered most for the sake of others, and those others will remember." Father Hubert, whose voice trembled, prayed, "in the name of my broken-hearted comrades," that he who was their "constant exemplar" might now find "justice and mercy," and that they might "with him one day love and bless and praise Thee forever more." The *Times-Democrat* reporter thought this "the most affecting portion of the entire service."[16]

Bells had tolled and minute guns had fired throughout, and they went right on as "the bands struck up a funeral march." Soldiers hoisted their burden down the steps and onto a black-draped caisson surmounted by six upright Napoleon guns, cannonballs, crossed muskets, and furled national flags and pulled by six black horses, each led by a soldier. Paced by muffled drums, the procession of parade marshals on horseback, uniformed military, police, and fire department units, students, brass bands, captains of British steamships, units from clubs and trade unions, and dignitaries from the whole South soon stretched farther than eye could reach, taking seventy minutes to pass a given point and over three hours to reach Metairie. Officials and ladies rode, but "the staunch old veterans marched all the way," bearing aloft their own flags, furled in crepe.[17]

Beauregard, as the ranking general, was asked to ride in the lead carriage, but he refused: "I am no hypocrite." It was a response worthy of Jeff Davis, who had decided not to speak at the dedication of Lee's recumbent statue in Lexington when he heard J. E. Johnston was to preside, and had withdrawn material from the *North American Review* because their publication of General Miles "puts me in company I do not care to keep."[18]

In "the prettiest cemetery in the South," the marble column with Stonewall Jackson's statue was wound to the top with laurel and oak leaves. The mound at the foot was banked with the flowers from city hall, and veterans, as they filed around it, cast fresh-cut ones on the tomb ready for "the hero of the Lost Cause." General Gordon stood by the bier "with bowed head," thinking what "a glorious heritage" it was "that this Southland has produced so grand a vicarious sufferer," that "no blemish is found in his private character." Many a cheek was wet when the choir sang, after the Episcopal service, "In my hand no price I bring, Simply to thy cross I cling . . . When mine eyelids close in death . . . Rock of Ages, cleft for me, Let me hide myself in thee." As a bugle sounded "Taps," and cannon boomed "the parting salute," the sun, setting behind a purple cloud, lit the "curling upper rim" with "a border of flaming gold." "The dead soldier had found his temporary resting place." "Thus was broken another cord," said the *Times-Democrat*, "that bound the living, throbbing heart of the South to the dead but loved and unforgotten past."[19]

Varina felt dead herself for a while, but then she remembered the autobiography that Jeff had started. The least she could do was make sure he too was loved and unforgotten. Starting with it as a base, she drove herself mercilessly, with Nannie Smith and others to help, and finished her *Memoir* in less than a year—all sixteen hundred thirty-eight pages of it. James Redpath, the Scottish abolitionist who had been converted to a Southern sympathizer by knowing the Davises, saw to it that Belford's company published it in 1890. The Davis luck held: with but few copies sold, Belford's went out of business.[20]

Varina began calling herself "V. Jefferson Davis," a style that Winnie, and even Maggie, took up. Winnie was unable to return until summer. In the fall, she let Varina drive Fred Wilkinson away, on the grounds that he could not support her properly. Although the lovers met once at the Pulitzers' later, they never married—each other or anyone. Varina and Winnie began to wonder what to do next. They suffered from the Beauvoir climate and were afraid to live there with no man on the place, but they could not afford living elsewhere.[21]

Joseph Pulitzer, that man of busy brain and large heart, solved their dilemma. He hired both of them for his *New York World*. They would draw regular salaries and write articles, but they could write for others too. It meant living in New York, but this did not displease either of them, as they were both cosmopolitans at heart, and Winnie "had literary ambitions." In time, she published, as Varina Anne Jefferson Davis, two novels: *The Veiled Doctor* and *A Romance of Southern Seas*. The move displeased many in the South so much that Margaret finally had to write a soothing explanation. It also meant disposing of Beauvoir in some way, but that was not done until 1902. Varina sold it to the United Sons of Confederate Veterans, as a free home for veterans and a memorial to Davis, his family, and the Lost Cause.[22]

Varina settled the question of a permanent resting place for her husband's body by accepting the offer of Richmond, filed early by Fitz Lee. This infuriated Mississippians, who had applied quite as early, but something about their offer had displeased her, and she thought Beauvoir (the only place Davis himself had mentioned) too low-lying. Mary Lee wrote Varina, however, that all Virginians rejoiced in her decision. The last weekend of May 1893, was chosen for the translation of the remains to Hollywood Cemetery. Varina could not make the trip to New Orleans. She was now sixty-seven, had heart trouble, was quite large, and walked with difficulty. The two daughters went down with Addison Hayes to accompany the body back to Richmond on a special train.[23]

After lying in state at Howard Memorial Hall (now Confederate Museum) on New Orleans's Camp Street, Davis rode alone with a military guard in a dark red observation car, almost entirely glass. Robert Brown wept at the Beauvoir stop to see on the track and platform the tribute of rhododendron blooms. From then on, at each of the many stops, car and coffin were banked with flowers and crowds boarded the train. Even where there was no stop, even at night, the passage was hailed and guns crashed in salute. At Montgomery and Atlanta, with bells of all the churches tolling, huge processions of citizens and soldiers escorted the caisson-borne coffin to the capitol building, where for hours the president was honored once more by tens of thousands passing by. In Atlanta, he lay near Ben Hill's statue, under a Confederate flag of blossoms in a heart of roses. In Montgomery, the door lintels held the words "Monterey" and "Buena Vista," and over Davis's portrait was "He suffered for us."[24]

Varina was waiting in Richmond. The funeral train pulled in at three in the morning, and from then till three in the afternoon, Davis lay in state at the capitol. His copper coffin had been placed inside a new one of oak in New Orleans, the cedar one being returned to the Metairie vault and the marble slab put in place. Jubal Early, in gray as always, called on Varina that morning and rode with her "under the burning sun" in the long military procession to Hollywood Cemetery. Frank Lubbock was there. James Jones, who had been in the guard of honor in Raleigh, drove once more for the president's wife. She had selected an oval plot, large enough to hold the whole family. (Little Joe, lying near, and the three other sons from far away, were soon moved to it.) During the service, Varina sat in her carriage under the tree until Jeff's casket began to be lowered into the earth; then she went forward. Her widow's weeds did not hide the shudder that shook her body then.[25]

Thoughts of "the Great Heart that had gone" and "my dead Hero," she embodied in images. She had "Deo Vindice"—the motto from the Confederate great seal—put at the foot of the marble border around Jeff's body. His grave (and eventually hers) became overgrown with English ivy—the symbol of undying remembrance. Jeff had told the Southern Historical Society, "The highest quality of man is self-sacrifice," and had said, "It is our duty to keep the memory of our heroes green." ("Yet they belong not to us alone . . . they belong to America.") Varina and Maggie together erected a monument for him in 1899. On the pedestal front is an outline of Davis's prewar career, and on the back: "the most consistent of American soldiers and statesmen," and "Blessed are they which are persecuted for righteousness' sake, for theirs is the kingdom of heaven." Maggie later added a tribute to her mother on one side, and on the other, for both parents: "Lord keep their memories green."[26]

For the bronze statue that tops the pedestal, the widow and daughter engaged a well-known Austro-Hungarian sculptor, George Julian Zolnay, a member of Varina's circle in New York. In a vain effort to combat slander, they ordered Davis depicted in his suit worn at the capture. Zolnay modeled it mostly on the photograph made thirty years before. But beyond that, he wanted to depict Davis's "spiritual and mental qualities"—"It is the . . . reflection of the soul which counts." He said of the South, "It was the strength, the heroism, never the pathos that appealed to me." For Maggie, the figure became the "kingly presence" of her father, as he was "in the gray light" of that 1865 dawn, "guarding all that remains of those he held dear."[27]

In New York, Varina and Winnie lived in hotels, and when it got too hot, they went to Narragansett Pier, Rhode Island, where they had friends. The Pulitzers had a home here and often entertained them. Winnie had for years been subject to low fevers. Her health was poor as 1898 began, and she made her will, leaving Beauvoir and nearly everything else to Varina, not forgetting "dear old nurse Mary Ahern" and her cousin Nannie D. Smith, for whom she had once made a whimsical and beautifully painted scrapbook. Travel was thought therapeutic, and she sailed for Egypt. In May she returned, by way of Italy and France, still "far from well."

Winnie always remained the darling of the veterans. Although she went as far as Texas to please them—and moved Lubbock to tears by throwing her arms around his neck, crying "my childhood's friend"—she did not much like being "The Daughter of the Confederacy." In July, Varina sent her in her place to a gathering in Atlanta. Winnie was drenched in a sudden shower and took a chill, but she insisted on greeting all the old soldiers. On September 7, Varina wrote to Connie Harrison from the Rockingham Hotel in Narragansett, "My Winnie is the most suffering person not to be dying that I ever saw. She has now been over six weeks *violently* seasick without any relief night or day. . . . She has wasted away dreadfully but she bears everything with fortitude and patience I have never seen equalled except by her father." But she *was* dying. She succumbed to "malarial gastritis" on September 18, at the age of thirty-three.[28]

Her funeral was held in Richmond at St. Paul's. The Pulitzers paid the expenses; Burton Harrison came; Fred Wilkinson was seen there. Winnie was buried at Hollywood as "The Daughter of the Confederacy" with full military honors—"a rare thing for a woman to have"—while Varina, unable to stand, sat on a chair with Maggie's arms around her. She and Winnie had been very close. Maggie, the only child left out of six, was thought to be "more like her father than her mother," but that only made her the more fiercely loyal. She defended Varina's actions and rebuked those who thought they did not get along. She presented to posterity the names and dates of her four brothers, so early cut off, in a memorial tablet at St. Paul's. Winnie has a large bas-relief "portrait tablet" there by George Zolnay, made for the United Daughters of the Confederacy. It bears the same inscription as Sarah Dorsey's tomb: "Blessed Are The Pure In Heart For They Shall See God." Zolnay's most striking sculpture is the angel that droops gracefully in mourning over Winnie's grave.[29]

There is a plaque to Varina, too, in St. Paul's, and she, too, was buried from there. She lived until 1906, long enough to ride in an automobile. She told Maggie, "I am going to die. . . . Don't you wear black. It is bad for your health and will depress your husband." At the Majestic Hotel on October 16, the end came. She had around her Maggie with two children, Kate Pulitzer, Carrie Phelan Beale (a cherished friend), and one other. Mary Lee, who chanced to be in New York, said she had "lost one of the dearest & oldest of friends," and came to the service held in the room for "your darling mother." Then Varina had, as she had wanted, "a strictly military funeral," all the way from the army escort through the streets of New York (ordered by General Grant's son), joined by Confederate veterans with their flag, and a band playing "Dixie" as well as a dirge, to the three-volley salute at Hollywood by the Richmond Howitzers, and taps. James Jones was there at the cemetery, sobbing. On the casket, draped with a Confederate flag, Carrie cast, at the very end, roses, Varina's favorite flower. She had been, as Mary Lee said, "one of the most interesting personalities" of the era.[30]

Within three years, Maggie's ashes were buried in Colorado Springs, but her urn in due time passed through St. Paul's to Hollywood. The large double monument there, covering Addison too, is inscribed with words that were also Varina's last: "Lord, in Thee have I trusted, let me never be confounded."[31]

Maggie and her children had been with Varina on Easter Sunday, 1898, when St. Paul's unveiled its Tiffany window to Jefferson Davis. It was in line with "pew 63" of the middle aisle, where the family used to sit. Across the church was the window to Lee, depicted (lower half) in Egyptian dress as the young Moses leaving the court of Pharaoh, and (upper half) as Moses on the Mount. Davis is St. Paul. The figure in the window is not the short, dark figure associated with Paul, but a tall, thin, light-bearded one, with the graceful hand seen in Davis photographs. He stands before King Agrippa and Princess Berenice in chains, and the legend reads: "This Man Doeth Nothing Worthy Of Death Or Of Bonds. Acts 26.31." The upper section, "suggested by the sixth verse of the Twenty-third Psalm," depicts torch-bearing "angels of

Goodness and Mercy," and the inscription is: "Let Me Be Weighed In An Even Balance That God May Know Mine Integrity. Job 31.6."[32]

Davis's favorite hymns were sung: "Guide Me, O Thou Great Jehovah," "How Firm a Foundation," and "For All the Saints." A warrior theme runs through the last. The sermon, by "The Rev. William M. Dame, of Baltimore, a former 'Richmond Howitzer,'" was "The Title of This Man to This Memorial." He showed why men would remember Davis and how, in Southern hearts, "he will forever have his own peculiar sacred place." But he asked what right his name had to be enshrined in the house of God "where nothing must intrude that is not distinctly His." His answer was: "In the devout conviction of devout men this man is worthy to be numbered with God's saints. A saint of God? Yes! Why not?"[33]

T. C. DeLeon wrote, "His wildest admirer has never claimed that Jefferson Davis was a saint." But Dr. Wheat did, and Lubbock said, "We all know such as he make up the kingdom of heaven." Many, like Galleher, pictured him entering heaven. Others, like the Richmond committee at his death, held up "his stainless probity and glad self-sacrifice" as "an example and an inspiration forever."[34]

Dr. Dame said, "Our thinking is full of mistaken and unreal conception of God's saints"—they are not "faultless men, but just the reverse" (and he named Moses, David, Peter, and Paul). They were "men in whom was good mingled with evil, but who hated the evil and sought to have the good prevail." "Was not the man, Jefferson Davis, one . . . in whom God signally declared His wonderful conquering grace and virtue?" (Minnigerode said his very faults made Davis "the humble petitioner for grace" and "he was preserved from self-deception or spiritual pride.")

Dame told the story he had from the "saintly" Minnigerode about Davis's communion in prison. "Not many of us can quite understand how horribly he suffered," his "soul so sensitive to honor" quivering under "an unutterable burden of shame and wrong." When Davis said then, "I forgive as I hope to be forgiven," he was uttering "the Divine spirit of the Master," and before him "many of the best of God's saints might stand uncovered." St. Paul's Church, where he came regularly "to get his soul strong . . . is the shrine where Jefferson Davis' memorial ought to be." He had won an immortal name, but here he would be known simply as "a man who glorified God." The sunlight through this window would remind onlookers that Davis's name was "shining in eternal light" and written in "'The Lamb's Book of Life.'"[35]

Not all would go so far, but very few, aside from his inveterate enemies, would quibble with John Daniel's assessment (quoting Carlyle), "a veritable man, 'terribly in earnest,'" or with the summation of Jefferson Davis that George Davis made: "He was the most honest, truest, gentlest, bravest, tenderest, manliest man I ever knew."[36]

Others would remember best, however, as Fitz Lee did, that as "the ship of the new republic," with cordage "rent" and breakers "dashing against her," "began to settle and sink . . . the captain was seen standing calm, heroic, resolute, grand in all the glory of a man, grasping with a firm hand the helm as she sank down, down, in the sea of eternity."[37]

Davis at age 80 in New Orleans. Photograph by Washburn. Courtesy Museum of the Confederacy, Richmond, Virginia.

The Davis plot, Hollywood Cemetery, Richmond: left, graves of Maggie and Addison Hayes (unidentified sculpture); right, Winnie, with Zolnay marble; the four boys—Sam, Jeff, Joe, and Billy—are buried on the periphery. Courtesy Museum of the Confederacy, Richmond, Virginia.

Davis in suit worn at capture, photographed in 1869, model for statue on his grave by George Julian Zolnay. From Francis Miller, *Photographic History of the Civil War,* 1912. Courtesy Auburn University Libraries.

Jefferson Davis window, St. Paul's Episcopal Church, Richmond, Virginia, lower half: "This man doeth nothing worthy of death or of bonds. Acts 26.31." Courtesy St. Paul's Episcopal Church.

Davis's death mask, made from original by Orin Frazer, presented to Beauvoir 1970 by W. A. Hohlweg on behalf of D. S. Belnap. Courtesy Beauvoir, the Jefferson Davis Home and Presidential Library.

"Thy Will be done" hand-worked for Jeff by Varina in colored wool. She directed it to be put on his bedroom mantle, when giving it to the First White House Association, Montgomery, Alabama. Author's collection.

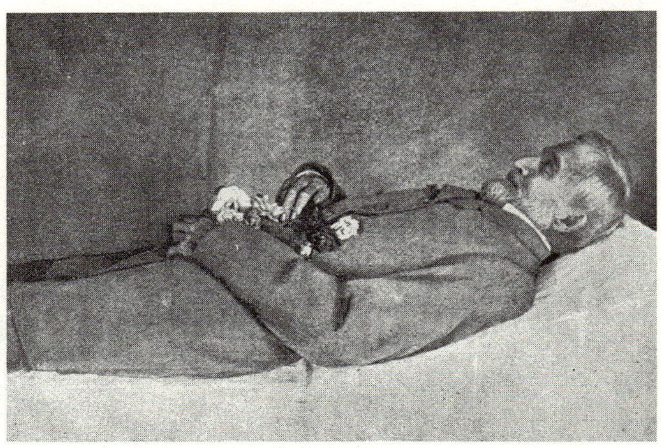

"I never saw Mr. Davis looking more lifelike": Davis in death, 1889. From *Life and Reminiscences of Jefferson Davis.*

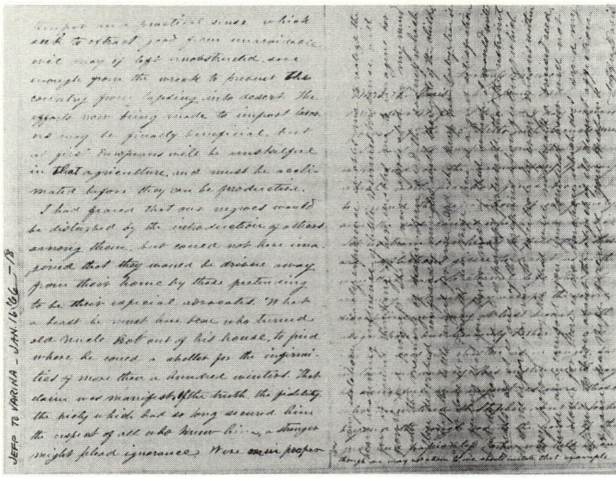

JEFF TO VARINA – JAN. 16 '66 – 18

[illegible] I had feared that our negroes would be disturbed by the introduction of others among them, but could not have imagined that they would be driven away from their home by those pretending to be their especial advocates. What a beast he must have been who turned old Uncle Bob out of his house, to find where he could a shelter for the infirmities of more than a hundred winters. [illegible] might plead ignorance. Were [illegible]

A letter from prison: Jefferson to Varina Davis, January 16, 1866, pages 1 and 4, showing crosshatch on 1 with his abbreviated signature, upper right corner. Courtesy Transylvania University Library.

Nelson Appleton Miles, major general U.S. volunteers, Davis's jailer: "a Beast—a hyena—& only twenty-five too," said Varina. Courtesy Library of Congress, image LC-B8172-2044.

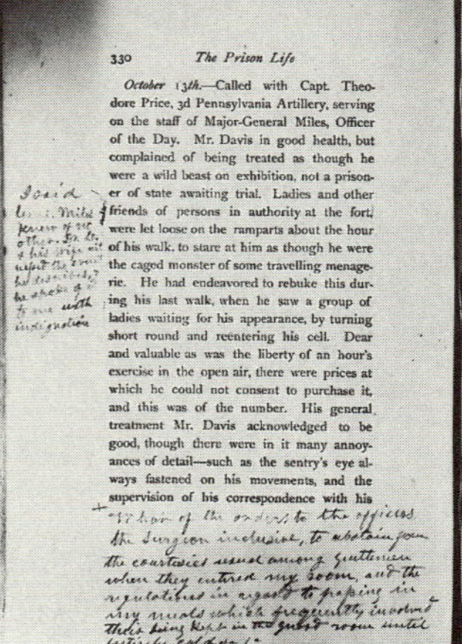

330 *The Prison Life*

October 13th.—Called with Capt. Theodore Price, 3d Pennsylvania Artillery, serving on the staff of Major-General Miles, Officer of the Day. Mr. Davis in good health, but complained of being treated as though he were a wild beast on exhibition, not a prisoner of state awaiting trial. Ladies and other friends of persons in authority at the fort were let loose on the ramparts about the hour of his walk, to stare at him as though he were the caged monster of some travelling menagerie. He had endeavored to rebuke this during his last walk, when he saw a group of ladies waiting for his appearance, by turning short round and reentering his cell. Dear and valuable as was the liberty of an hour's exercise in the open air, there were prices at which he could not consent to purchase it, and this was of the number. His general treatment Mr. Davis acknowledged to be good, though there were in it many annoyances of detail—such as the sentry's eye always fastened on his movements, and the supervision of his correspondence with his

+ [illegible] of the orders to the officers, the Surgeon inclusive, to abstain from the courtesies usual among gentlemen when they entered my room, and the regulations in regard to passing in my meals which frequently involved their being kept in the guard room until entirely cold.

of Jefferson Davis. 331

wife—unworthy of any country aspiring to magnanimity or greatness.

The following letter will be read with interest as giving a most graphic view of what the prisoner's wife and family had to endure from his quitting them on board the *Clyde*, in Hampton Roads, down to the day of its date; certain parts, (reflecting upon individuals by name,) I have taken the liberty to strike out, but the remainder of the letter is as written: see p. 333

Mill View (near Augusta, Ga.), October [illegible], 1865.

Colonel John J. Craven,

Chief Medical Officer, Fort Monroe, Va.

My Dear Colonel,—Though you remain irrevocably dumb I am sure you hear me, and in addressing you I feel as if writing to one of my oldest and most reliable friends. Every letter from my husband comes freighted with good wishes for you, and thanks for all your kindness to him in his hours of anguish and solitude. Can you doubt that my prayers for you, and appreciation of your goodness, have been even greater than his, for I could do nothing but pray? Mr. Davis sent me a carte

Pages from *Prison Life of Jefferson Davis* (1866) by John J. Craven, M.D., with Davis's marginal notes; "see p. 333" refers to "stars of omission," which conceal not names, but Craven's failure to tell Davis of his wife's letter, which follows here. Courtesy Tulane University Library.

Sarah Anne Ellis (Mrs. Samuel W.) Dorsey, portrait artist unknown. Courtesy Beauvoir, the Jefferson Davis Home and Presidential Library.

Davis at Beauvoir, on porch of east pavilion rented from Mrs. Dorsey, where he began writing *The Rise and Fall of the Confederate Government.* Courtesy Beauvoir, the Jefferson Davis Home and Presidential Library.

Jeff Davis Jr., in 1878, just before his death from yellow fever at age twenty-one. Courtesy Beauvoir, the Jefferson Davis Home and Presidential Library.

Winnie Davis in her twenties, "The Daughter of the Confederacy." Courtesy Beauvoir, the Jefferson Davis Home and Presidential Library.

On the porch at Beauvoir house, 1885: Varina Hayes, Maggie Davis (Mrs. J. A.) Hayes, Jefferson Davis holding Lucy Hayes, Varina holding Jefferson Addison Hayes (later Hayes-Davis), with servant. Courtesy Beauvoir, the Jefferson Davis Home and Presidential Library.

Appendix A

J. E. Johnston to J. Davis, on Rank

(From Varina Howell Davis, *Jefferson Davis, Ex-President of the Confederate States of America: A Memoir by His Wife* 2:144–53 [see text chapter 12]; variant in *War of the Rebellion: Official Records*, 4, 1:605–8)

Headquarters, Manassas, September 12, 1861.

Sir: I have had the honor to receive through the War Department a copy of the proceedings of Congress on August 31, 1861, confirming the nominations made by the President of the Confederate States of five Generals of the Confederate Army and fixing their relative rank.

I will not affect to disguise the surprise and mortification produced in my mind by the action taken in this matter by the President and by Congress. I beg to state further, with the most profound respect for both branches of the Government, that these proceedings are in violation of my rights as an officer, of the plighted faith of the Confederacy, and of the Constitution and laws of the land. Such being my views, lest my silence should be deemed significant of acquiescence, it is a duty as well as a right on my part, at once to enter my earnest protest against the wrong which I conceive has been done me. I now and here declare my claim that, notwithstanding the nominations made by the President, and their confirmation by Congress, I still rightfully hold the rank of first General in the armies of the Southern Confederacy. I will proceed briefly to state the grounds upon which I rest this claim.

The act of the Confederate Congress of March 6, 1861, section 8, amended by that of March 14, 1861, section 2, creates the grade of Brigadier-General as the highest rank in their service, and provides that there shall be five officers of that grade. The fifth section of the last-named act enacts "That in all cases of officers who have resigned, or who may within six months tender their resignation from the army of the United States, and who have been or may be appointed to original vacancies in the army of the Confederate States, the commissions issued shall have been one and the same date, so that the relative rank of officers shall be determined by their former commissions in the United States Army held anterior to the secession of the Confederate States from the United States."[1]

Under these laws, on May 13, 1861, R. E. Lee and myself were nominated as Brigadier-Generals in the Confederate States Army. Samuel Cooper had been nominated to the same grade and confirmed a few weeks previously.

The nominations of myself and R. E. Lee were confirmed by Congress promptly. Each of the three had resigned his commission in the United States Army in accordance with the terms of the law. The other two had resigned colonelcies, but the commission which I had resigned was that of a Brigadier-General. It is plain, then, that under these laws I was the officer first in rank in the Confederate Army. Two or three days afterward, on May 16th, Congress, by the second section of its act of that date, enacted, "That the five general officers provided by existing laws for the Confederate States shall have the rank and denomination of 'General' instead of 'Brigadier-General,' which shall be the highest military grade known to the Confederate States. They shall be assigned to such commands and duties as the President may specially direct, and shall be entitled to the same pay," etc.

I conceive, and I submit to the careful consideration of the Government, that this section of the act last cited operated in two ways: 1. It abolished the grade of Brigadier-General in the Confederate Army. 2. It at once, by the mere force of law, raised the three officers already named to the rank and denomination of "General" in the army of the Confederate States. The right, therefore, which I claim to my rank is founded on this act. Congress by its act, the President by his approval of it, at once made us Generals. It is clear that such likewise was the construction of both branches of the Government, else why were not nominations made then? It was a time of flagrant war. Either we were Generals, or the army and country were left without such officers. Our former grade had been abolished.[2] We were not Brigadier-Generals, we were nothing, and could perform no military duty, exercise no command. I think it clear that I was a General by the plain terms of the law. It is plain from the action of the President and Congress that such was their construction, as I was at once ordered to Harper's Ferry to take command in the valley of Virginia, and the President soon after placed three Brigadier-Generals under my orders. In hurrying to assume the command in the valley of Virginia, I did not wait for my commission to be sent to me. I did not doubt that it would be made out, for I was persuaded that it was my right, and had no idea that there was any purpose of withholding it. I remained two months in the valley, too earnestly engaged in the public service to busy myself particularly in my personal interests. But when the emergencies of the campaign required me to march to Manassas, and to act with another general officer, I appreciated the importance and the indispensable necessity of not leaving the question of rank open or doubtful between us. With this view I transmitted a telegraphic despatch to the President on July 20th, inquiring, in the simplest and most direct terms, what my rank was. He replied that I was a General. The battle of Manassas ensued on the next day. The President came in person to participate in it, but reached the scene of action soon after the close of the struggle. The morning after the battle he announced his purpose to elevate General Beauregard to the rank of General. He returned to Richmond the ensuing day. The nomination was made immediately on his return, and was promptly confirmed by Congress. General Beauregard then became a General and ranked me unless I was such by virtue of the act of Congress on May 16th, already referred to. Yet from the time of General Beauregard's appointment to the day of the renewed nominations I continued to act as the commanding General of the "Army of the Potomac," under the authority of the President and of the Department of War. Thus it appears that I have the sanction of the President to my claim of rank under the act of Congress. In addition to this, my rank was expressly recognized by Congress also in the resolutions adopted by that body returning the thanks of Congress to General Johnston, to General Beauregard, and to the officers and soldiers of the army for the victory of Manassas.

Thus stood matters when the recent nominations were made. But one additional name was offered—that of A. S. Johnston. His commission in the army of the United States had been that of Colonel. I as resigning the higher rank in that army, was, by the provisions of the act of Congress of March 14, 1861, and the plighted faith of the Government of the Confederate States, the General first in rank in their armies. By that act and that of May 16, 1861, the rank would stand thus: J. E. Johnston, S. Cooper, A. S. Johnston, R. E. Lee, G. T. Beauregard. [A footnote by Varina, here omitted, contains a letter of Davis to his wife, which is in chapter 12 of the text.]

I held, and claim to hold, my rank as General under the act of May 16, 1861. I was a General thenceforth or never. I had the full authority of the constitutional Government of the Confederate States to sustain me. Heretofore those who disputed my authority as General have done so because they denied the existence of the Government whose officer I claimed to be. Now that Government joins the hostile power in denying my authority. When I sent back the missives of the Government of the United States, because they ignored the Government which I served and acknowledged, I little thought that one of the acts of that Government would be to ignore me as its officer, by trampling upon its own solemn legislative and executive action. The nomination seeks to annul the irrevocable past, and to make me such only from the 4th day of July. The present, and so far as human legislation may operate, the future, may be controlled by Congress. Human power cannot affect the past. Congress may vacate my commission and reduce me to the ranks. It cannot make it true that I was not a General before July 4, 1861.[3]

The effect of the course pursued is this: It transfers me from the position first in rank to that of fourth.[4] The relative rank of the others among themselves is unaltered. It is plain that this is a blow aimed at me only. It reduces my rank in the grade I hold. This has never been done heretofore in the regular service in America but by the sentence of a court-martial as a punishment and as a disgrace for some military offence. It seeks to tarnish my fair fame as a soldier and as a man, earned by more than thirty years of laborious and perilous service. I had but this—the scars of many wounds, all honestly taken in my front and in the front of battle, and my father's revolutionary sword. It was delivered to me from his venerable hand without a stain of dishonor. Its blade is still unblemished as when it passed from his hand to mine. I drew it in the war, not for rank or fame, but to defend the sacred soil, the homes and hearths, the women and children, ay, and the men of my mother, Virginia—my native South. It may hereafter be the sword of a general leading armies, or of a private volunteer. But while I live and have an arm to wield it, it shall never be sheathed until the freedom, independence, and full rights of the South are achieved. When that is done, it may well be a matter of small concern to the Government, to Congress, or to the country, what my rank or lot may be.

I shall be satisfied if my country stands among the powers of the world free, powerful, and victorious, and that I as a general, a lieutenant, or a volunteer soldier, have borne my part in the glorious strife, and contributed to the final blessed consummation.

What has the aspect of a studied indignity is offered me. My noble associate with me in the battle has his preferment connected with the victory won by our common trials and dangers. His commission bears the date of July 21, 1861, but care seems to be taken to exclude the idea that I had any part in winning our triumph.

My commission is made to bear such a date that my once inferiors in the service of the United States and of the Confederate States shall be above me. But it must not be dated as of July 21, nor be suggestive of the victory of Manassas.

I return to my first position. I repeat that my rank as General is established by the acts of Congress of March 14, 1861, and May 16, 1861. To deprive me of that rank it was necessary for Congress to repeal these laws. That could be done by express legislative act alone. It was not done, it could not be done by a mere vote in secret session upon a list of nominations.

If the action against which I have protested is legal, it is not for me to question the expediency of degrading one who has served laboriously from the commencement of the war on this frontier, and borne a prominent part in the only great event of that war, for the benefit of persons neither of whom has yet struck a blow for this Confederacy.

These views and the freedom with which they are presented may be unusual, so likewise is the occasion which calls them forth.

I have the honor to be, most respectfully,

Your obedient servant,
J. E. Johnston, *General.*

Appendix B

Proclamations by Davis for Days of Prayer

Proclamation for May 16, 1862 (issued May 3) (From James D. Richardson, ed., *A Compilation of the Messages and Papers of the Confederacy* 1:227–28):

To the People of the Confederate States of America

An enemy, waging war in a manner violative of the usage of civilized nations, has invaded our country. With presumptuous reliance on superior numbers, he has declared his purpose to reduce us to submission. We struggle to preserve our birthright of constitutional freedom. Our trust is in the justice of our cause and the protection of our God.

Recent disaster has spread gloom over the land, and sorrow sits at the hearthstones of our countrymen; but a people conscious of rectitude and faithfully relying on their Father in Heaven may be cast down, but cannot be dismayed. They may mourn the loss of the martyrs whose lives have been sacrificed in their defense, but they receive this dispensation of Divine Providence with humble submission and reverend faith. And now that our hosts are again going forth to battle, and loving hearts at home are filled with anxious solicitude for their safety, it is meet that the whole people should turn imploringly to their Almighty Father and beseech his all-powerful protection.

To this end, therefore, I, Jefferson Davis, President of the Confederate States of America, do issue my proclamation, inviting all the people to unite at their several places of worship on Friday, the sixteenth day of the present month of May, in humble supplication to Almighty God that he will vouchsafe his blessings on our beloved country; that he will strengthen and protect our armies; that he will watch over and protect our people from the machinations of their enemies; and that he will, in his own good time, restore to us the blessing of peace and security under his sheltering care.

Given under my hand and the seal of the Confederate States, at Richmond, on the third day of May, A.D. 1862.

Jefferson Davis

The other proclamations were for the dates following (all in Richardson on page numbers indicated in parentheses):

June 13, 1861 (issued May 28) (103–4)
November 15, 1861 (issued October 31) (135)
February 28, 1862 (issued February 20) (217–18)
September 18, 1862 (issued September 4) (268–69)
March 27, 1863 (issued February 27) (324–25)
August 21, 1863 (issued July 25) (328)
April 8, 1864 (issued March 12) (412–14)
November 16, 1864 (issued October 26) (564–65)
March 10, 1865 (issued January 25) (567–68)

Appendix C

Devotional Material Used by Davis in Prison

Prayer of St. Chrysostom:

ALMIGHTY God, who hast given us grace at this time with one accord to make our common supplications unto thee; and dost promise that when two or three are gathered together in thy Name thou wilt grant their requests; Fulfil now, O Lord, the desires and petitions of thy servants, as may be most expedient for them; granting us in this world knowledge of thy truth, and in the world to come life everlasting.

Hymns

Hymn #177 (first two stanzas of four):

GUIDE me, O thou great Jehovah, / Pilgrim through this barren land; / I am weak, but thou art mighty; / Hold me with thy powerful hand.

Open now the crystal fountains / Whence the living waters flow; / Let the fiery, cloudy pillar, / Lead me all my journey through.

Hymn #178 (three stanzas of six):

WHENE'ER the angry passions rise, / And tempt our thoughts or tongues to strife, / To Jesus let us lift our eyes, / Bright pattern of the Christian life.

To do his heavenly Father's will / Was his employment and delight; / Humility and holy zeal / Shone through his life divinely bright.

Thy fair example may we trace, / To teach us what we ought to be; / Make us, by thy transforming grace, / O Saviour, daily more like thee.

Prayers from Book of Common Prayer *(1850)*

1) "For a Person under Affliction [italics for substitution of other forms]: O MERCIFUL God, and heavenly Father, who hast taught us in thy holy Word that thou dost not willingly afflict or grieve the children of men; Look with pity, we beseech thee, upon the sorrows of thy *servant,* for whom our prayers are desired. In thy wisdom thou hast seen fit to visit *him* with trouble, and to bring distress upon *him.* Remember *him,* O Lord, in mercy; sanctify thy fatherly correction to *him;* endue *his* soul with patience under his affliction, and with resignation to thy blessed will; comfort *him* with a sense of thy goodness; lift up thy countenance upon *him,* and give *him* peace; through Jesus Christ our Lord."

2) "For a Person, or Persons, going to Sea: O ETERNAL God, who alone spreadest out the heavens, and rulest the raging of the sea; We commend to thy Almighty protection, thy *servant,* for whose preservation on the great deep our prayers are desired. Guard *him,* we beseech thee, from the dangers of the sea, from sickness, from the violence of enemies, and from every evil to which *he* may be exposed. Conduct *him* in safety to the haven where *he* would be, with a grateful sense of thy mercies; through Jesus Christ our Lord."

A Dictionary of the Holy Bible . . . (New York: American Tract Society, 1859), 534 pp., very worn, endorsed "Jefferson Davis 1865" (Jefferson Davis Book Collection, Old Capitol Museum of Mississippi History).

Bibles and prayer books, from Museum of the Confederacy inventory and photocopies (sent to author 1984 by Cathy Carlson and Charlene S. Alling):

Bibles (King James Version):

1) Black leather, given by Davis to his attorney, George Shea, whose child, "M. Ritter Shea," gave it to the museum.

2) Gold-tooled leather, gilt-edged leaves; given to the museum by "S. S. Cummins"; identified (evidently by him) as "Fort Monroe Bible" given "to Miss Jennie Cummins of 'Rock Grove'"; inscribed to her on the flyleaf, "as a token of sincere regard and esteem of her friend," signed "Jeffn. Davis / Lennoxville / 17 July 1868." On a blank page opposite the frontispiece, Davis wrote these verses:

> In all their affliction he was afflicted, and the angel of his presence saved them. / Is. LXIII.

> In this was manifested the love of God toward us, because that God sent his only begotten son into the world, that we might live through him. / I. John IV.
> And whosoever will, let him take the water of life freely. / Rev. XXII.

(Pictured on the cover of *Confederate Veteran,* March 1929; accompanying article by Virginia Fraser Boyle, pp. 89–93.)

3) Red leather, inscribed in Davis's hand: "Jefferson Davis Jr from Fortress Monroe" ("Jr" squeezed in at end of line); in another hand, on flyleaves: *Book of Common Prayer* collect for feast of St. Michael and All Angels and a litany "To our Guardian Angel" in Latin.

Book of Common Prayer:

1) Identified as "Given Jeff by his father while at Fort Monroe" (see text, chapter 19).

2) *The Book of Common Prayer . . . according to the Use of the Protestant Episcopal Church in the Confederate States of America;* inscription says this is the "first edition . . . procured under great difficulties and embarrassments . . . presented to / His Excellency / Jefferson Davis"; Davis's signature is at the top of the title page. This is one of the few surviving copies. Only one edition of three (London, 1863) reached North Carolina; the others were captured running the blockade. (Joseph Blount Cheshire, *The Church in the Confederate States: A History of the Protestant Episcopal Church in the Confederate States,* 99–103, and see 61–63, 138–44.) Davis had two prayer books in prison. He gave one to Anna Craven; this is presumably the other.

Book of Common Prayer, 1850, C.S.A., and 1928 are identical except for "Confederate" replacing "United" and a few phrases in the earlier one, some of which are reflected in Davis's letters: "Grant us patience under any affliction thou shalt see fit to lay on us, and minds always contented with our present condition"; "Keep us temperate in our meats and drinks."

Preface to the Notes

Sources for facts, and even opinions, are here. Direct quotations are designated "quot." or "quots." Books, articles, and manuscripts are identified at first use, with full data in the bibliography. If the use is only incidental, full data is in the pertinent note. "Text," "page," and "Note" always refer to this work, "p." and "n." to others, except in "Ed. Note" and "Descr. Note."

Short titles that are not mere truncations are listed in abbreviations below, as are code names for frequently used items. For example, "Rowland" stands for Dunbar Rowland's ten volumes of letters, papers, and speeches, *Jefferson Davis, Constitutionalist* (his other works are under "D. Rowland," to distinguish from those of his wife, Eron, "E. Rowland"); "Rosenstock" for the Jefferson Davis Book Collection, Old Capitol Museum of Mississippi History, Mississippi Department of Archives and History (purchased from Fred Rosenstock); *Memoir* for [Varina Howell Davis] *Jefferson Davis, Ex-President of the Confederate States of America: A Memoir by his Wife.*

The Papers of Jefferson Davis (*Papers*), variously edited and still in progress, uses marginal numbers for each item in volumes 1 and 2, with volume and item joined by a colon (also revised edition of 1 and reprint of 2). Publishing practice has since adopted the same device to join *volume* and *page*, which *Papers* uses after volume 2 (so, in this text, *Papers* 3:5 means volume 3, page 5). To avoid confusion, I add an extra colon between volume and *item* number in Papers 1 and 2 (*Papers* 2::5 means volume 2, item 5), and where needed, use "p." to designate page within the item. The single colon is used before *unnumbered parts* of 1 and 2, like Appendix (*Papers* 1:App. 4).

Davis made notes in *Prison Life of Jefferson Davis* by John J. Craven (1866), always the primary source for this subject, but they were not fully published until 1987, by Edward K. Eckert, in *"Fiction Distorting Fact": The Prison Life, Annotated by Jefferson Davis* (here, "Eckert"), providing a new primary source. Every page cited in these notes from Craven has been checked in Eckert for Davis's comments; no reference means no comment. Eckert forces reevaluation of *Prison Life* by denying Craven's authorship and calling it a "creative fantasy" of Charles G.

Halpine. The reality of Craven's narrative is confirmed by some of the very notes that Eckert prints, by Davis letters from prison, and by Halpine's letters in Eckert's introduction, which speak of Davis's "real conversations with Dr. Craven." This author accepts Craven's fundamental text, recognizes that Halpine added much, and depends largely on Davis's annotations to tell the difference. For a full discussion, see Felicity Allen, "Martyrdom or Mythmaking? Prison Life of Jefferson Davis in a New Light" (in bibliography).

Life and Reminiscences of Jefferson Davis will be found under the title; for though John W. Daniel is often listed as editor, his name appears on the title page only as author of the "Introductory." All references to Heitman, *Historical Register* (of U.S. Army) mean volume 1, and those to *Official Records* (*O. R.*) mean series 1, unless otherwise stated.

Definitions of English words are from Webster's dictionary, which will not be cited except for special reason; Oxford ones, where used, are cited as *OED* and *Shorter OED* (see bibliography). Dumas Malone's 1934 edition of the *Dictionary of American Biography* (*DAB*) is the one used, unless a later date is specified. No page numbers are cited for reference works arranged alphabetically (unless for special reason) or in other books so arranged, e.g., Ezra J. Warner's *Generals in Gray*, and the biographical volumes of *The South in the Building of the Nation*, 11 and 12. The *Holy Bible* is cited from the Authorized (King James) Version unless otherwise noted. The Episcopal *Book of Common Prayer* (*BCP*) is cited from contemporary editions.

Abbreviations do not repeat those in Webster's *New Collegiate Dictionary* and *The Chicago Manual of Style*. Acronyms keep straight the three prominent Johnstons: ASJ, JEJ, WPJ (see abbreviations). "JD" and "VHD" distinguish Jefferson and Varina. The many other Davises are always identified by initial or name; for the children, see the editorial note.

Where no other source for an object or place is listed, the reader may assume personal knowledge of the author. "Unknown" means of course "to author"; someone else may know it.

Abbreviations and Short Titles

A.A.G.	acting adjutant general
abol.	abolition(ists)
acct.	account
ADAH	Alabama Department of Archives and History
ADC	aide-de-camp
adj.	adjutant
AHS	Alexander Hamilton Stephens
A.I.G.	acting inspector general

AJ	Andrew Jackson
ALA	University of Alabama collections
ANV	Army of Northern Virginia
appt.	appoint, etc.
arr.	arrive(d)
art.	artillery; article
ASJ	Albert Sidney Johnston
ass.	assistant; association
att. gen.	attorney general
b.	born; buried
bapt.	baptized; Baptist
Battles and Leaders	Robert U. Johnson and Clarence C. Buel, *Battles and Leaders of the Civil War*
BCP	*Book of Common Prayer*
Benj.	Judah P. Benjamin
Bgd.	Beauregard
Bgd.	T. Harry Williams, *P. G. T. Beauregard, Napoleon in Gray*
BNH	Burton Norvell Harrison
Bragg	Don C. Seitz, *Braxton Bragg, General of the Confederacy*
Breck.	Breckinridge
Breck.	William C. Davis, *Breckinridge: Statesman, Soldier, Symbol*
brig.	brigadier
bsp.	bishop
Buch.	James Buchanan
cal.	calendar
cav.	cavalry
cem.	cemetery
Chesnut	Mary Boykin Miller Chesnut, *Mary Chesnut's Civil War*
comm.	command, etc.; commission, etc.; commissary; committee; community
Conf.	Confederate; Confederacy
Conf.	James D. Richardson, ed. *A Compilation of the Messages and Papers of the Confederacy*
"Conf. Treasury"	Clark, M. H. "Departure of President Davis and Cabinet from Richmond, Va., and the Last Days of the Confederate Treasury and What Became of Its Specie"
Conf. Vet.	*Confederate Veteran* (periodical)
Cong.	Congress, etc.
const.	constitution, etc.
corr.	correspondence

C.S.(A.)	Confederate States (of America)
C. W.	Civil War
d.	died; death; daughter
DAB	*Dictionary of American Biography*
dem.	democracy, etc. (cap.: Democrat, etc.).
descr.	describe, etc.
Eckert	Edward K. Eckert, *The Prison Life, Annotated by Jefferson Davis*
ed.	edit, etc.
encl.	enclosed, etc.
Encycl. Brit.	*The New Encyclopedia Britannica*
endrs.	endorse, etc.
eng.	engineer, etc.
Eur.	Europe, etc.
ev.	evening
Ewell	Percy Gatling Hamlin, *"Old Bald Head" (General R. S. Ewell)*
Fleming Collection	Walter L. Fleming Collection, New York Public Library
hdq.	headquarters
Hill	Benjamin H. Hill, Jr. *Senator Benjamin H. Hill of Georgia: His Life, Speeches and Writings*
Hoyt	*Hoyt's New Cyclopedia of Practical Quotations*, edited by Kate Louise Roberts.
H.R.	House of Representatives
ident.	identity, etc.
I.G.	Inspector General
inscr.	inscribed; inscription
Inventory	Inventory of Davis Family Artifacts, Museum of the Confederacy
itin.	itinerary
JD	Jefferson Davis
JEJ	Joseph Eggleston Johnston
JEJ	in *A Memoir of the Life and Public Service of Joseph E. Johnston Once Quartermaster General of the Army of the United States, and a General in the Army of the Confederate States of America;* Craig Symonds, *Joseph E. Johnston: A Civil War Biography.*
jnl.	journal
Jnl. Miss. Hist.	*Journal of Mississippi History*
LBN	Lucius Bellinger Northrop
LC	Library of Congress
legis.	legislature

Letters	Hudson Strode, *Jefferson Davis: Private Letters, 1823–1889*
lit.	literature, etc.
Longs.	Longstreet
Marg.	Margaret
MBC	Mary Boykin Chesnut
MC	member of Congress
MDAH	Mississippi Department of Archives and History
mem.	memoir, memorial, etc.
Memoir	*Jefferson Davis, Ex-President of the Confederate States of America: A Memoir by His Wife*
Montg.	Montgomery, Alabama
mg.	morning
mon.	monument
mov't.	movement
MVC	Mississippi Valley Collection
N. Am. Rev.	*North American Review*
natl.	national
N. O.	New Orleans, Louisiana
nom.	nominate, etc.
Northrop	Jerrold Northrop Moore, *Confederate Commissary General: Lucius Bellinger Northrop and the Subsistence Bureau of the Southern Army*
OED	*Oxford English Dictionary*
off.	officer(s)
O. R.	*War of the Rebellion: Official Records*
ord.	ordnance
org.	organize, etc.
Pemb.	Pemberton
Pemberton	John C. Pemberton [Jr.], *Pemberton, Defender of Vicksburg*
Pendleton	Susan P. Lee, *Memoirs of William Nelson Pendleton, D.D.*
pic.	picture(d)
PM(G)	Postmaster (General)
PMHS	*Publications of the Mississippi Historical Society*
Polk	William M. Polk, *Leonidas Polk, Bishop and General*
poss.	possibly
prob.	probably
procl.	proclamation
Prov.	Provisional
publ.	published, etc.
Q.	Quarterly
QM(G)	Quartermaster (General)

quot(s).	quotation(s), quoted
recoll.	recollections
recomm.	recommend, etc.
reminisc.	reminiscences
repr.	represent(ative)
res.	resolution
res'd.	resigned
Rosenstock	Jefferson Davis Book Collection, Old Capitol Museum of Mississippi History, MDAH
Rowland	*Jefferson Davis, Constitutionalist: His Letters, Papers and Speeches*, edited by Dunbar Rowland
RPR	reprint edition
SAR	Sons of the American Revolution
SAED	Sarah Anne Ellis Dorsey
S.C.V.	Sons of Confederate Veterans
SHS	Southern Historical Society
SHSP	*Southern Historical Society Papers*
So.	South; Southern
soc.	society
TRANSYL	Davis collection, Transylvania University
TULANE	Davis collection, Tulane University
U.C.V.	United Confederate Veterans
U.D.C.	United Daughters of the Confederacy
unident.	unidentified
USMA	United States Military Academy (West Point)
VHD	Varina Howell (Mrs. Jefferson) Davis
vet.	veteran
"Capture"	"The True Story of the Capture of Jefferson Davis"
West Pt.	West Point
Wirz Trial	Mildred Lewis Rutherford, comp., *Andersonville Prison and Captain Henry Wirz Trial*
WPJ	William Preston Johnston
Yancey	John Witherspoon DuBose, *The Life and Times of William Lowndes Yancey . . .*
ZT	Zachary Taylor

Notes

Chapter I Capture

1. Varina Howell Davis, *Jefferson Davis, Ex-President of the Confederate States of America: A Memoir by his Wife* 2:648, quot. (ref. perhaps to *Romeo and Juliet* 3.2.92: "Upon his brow shame was ashamed to sit").

2. John J. Craven, *Prison Life of Jefferson Davis,* 28, quot. (see preface to notes); Strode, *Jefferson Davis, Tragic Hero,* 230, 526; J. William Jones, *The Davis Memorial Volume,* 650–51.

3. VHD, *Memoir* 2:645–46; *Recollections of Alexander H. Stephens, His Diary,* ed. Myrta Lockett Avary, 114–24; *A Belle of the Fifties, Memoirs of Mrs. Clay of Alabama,* ed. Ada Sterling, 260–62. For Germans, see Ella Lonn, *Foreigners in the Union Army and Navy,* 406–35 and App. C, 666–72 (663: 4,136,175 foreigners in U.S. 1860; 3,903,672 in North).

4. Ovid L. Futch, *History of Andersonville Prison,* 59–60; A. Dudley Mann to JPB, Nov. 11, 1863 (James D. Richardson, *Conf.,* 2:589, quot.; see 589–95, 601, 455, 562–63; also Philip Tucker, "Confederate Secret Agent in Ireland . . . ," *Jnl. of Conf. Hist.* 5:69–70). Ella Lonn, *Foreigners in the Confederacy,* 73–81.

5. Craven, *Prison Life,* 24–29 (quot. on 24). This book uses "Fortress Monroe" (rather than Fort) because JD does.

6. Sterling, *Belle,* 379 (quot.), 64, 322; Virginia Clay-Clopton [m. David Clopton after Clay's death], "Clement Claiborne Clay," 74–76, 82; Clay in *Dictionary of American Biography;* Jefferson Davis, *The Rise and Fall of the Confederate Government* 1:206–7, quot.

7. JD, *Rise and Fall* 1:221–25; Edward A. Pollard, *The Lost Cause . . . ,* 88–90 (excerpts from Clay's speech).

8. JD, *Rise and Fall* 2:611–12; JD corr., Mar. 14 and Apr. 14, 27, 29, 1864 in Rowland 6:204–6, 226–27, 236–37; JD to C. W. Frazer, 1880 (ibid. 8:529–30); JD corr., 1886 (ibid. 9:501–10); Frazer to Duke et al., Nov. 1, 1886 (*Calendar of the Jefferson Davis Postwar Manuscripts,* 255–56); W. W. Cleary [Clay's sec. in Canada], "The Attempt to Fasten the Assassination of President Lincoln on President Davis and other Innocent Parties," 313, 322–25; J. G. Randall, *The Civil War and Reconstruction,* 615–16, 683; James F. Rhodes, *History of the United States* 5:315–42. See also Stephen Z. Starr, *Colonel Grenfell's Wars,* 132–51.

9. VHD to JD, Nov. 13, 1865, MS, ALA, quot; Cleary, "Attempt," 313. Varina once faced down a slave who had scared the overseer (VHD, *Memoir* 1:478–79).

10. BNH, "Capture of Jefferson Davis," 226–60, and note by JD on 250. Other firsthand sources are by the Davises, Lubbock, Reagan, Mallory, the cav. leaders, M. H. Clark, as well as those in W. T. Walthall, "The True Story of the Capture of JD" and A. J. Hanna, *Flight into Oblivion.* Hanna's maps and clear trace of Davises' separate itineraries are invaluable. Town known in Ga. as "Washington-Wilkes" (Wilkes the county) will be called that, to avoid confusion with D. C.

11. VHD, *Memoir* 2:589–97; Susan P. Lee, *Pendleton,* 401–4.

12. JEJ, *Narrative,* 396–407, 410; JD, *Rise and Fall* 2:676–85 (quots. on 681, 682), 689; JD, Memorandum of conversation *re* JEJ, Oct. 6, 1876, MS, TULANE

(précis in *Cal. of JD MSS,* 51–52); see *SHSP* 3:103, 107: depots readied for JEJ's retreat through S. C.

13. JEJ, *Narrative,* 399–414 (knew JD disapproved; quots. on 402, 412); JD, *Rise and Fall* 2:687–88, quots; Stephen R. Mallory, "Last Days of the Confederate Government," Part 2, 242 ("Heaven" quot.). JEJ later did not even ask JD's consent (Reagan memorandum in Rowland 6:569). Grant had refused to discuss peace terms, saying the president "alone" had "such authority" (Douglas Southall Freeman, *R. E. Lee: A Biography* 4:8–9).

14. Quots.: JEJ, *Narrative,* 411–14; Walthall, "Capture," 106; JD, *Rise and Fall* 2:695; JD to "a friend," May 1865, in Robert McElroy, *Jefferson Davis, The Unreal and the Real* 2:502 (JD said the same to E. H. McCaleb [*SHSP* 29:5]).

15. JD, *Rise and Fall* 2:693; *Memoirs of General William T. Sherman by Himself* 2:349–50, quots.; *Personal Memoirs of U.S. Grant* 2:497, quots.; JEJ, *Narrative,* 411–12, 415 (quot.); R. Taylor, "The Last Confederate Surrender," 318.

16. JD, *Rise and Fall* 2:694 and 682 (quots.), 689, 692–96; JD, "Autobiography" (*Papers* 1::1, p. lxiii, JD quot.); Freeman, *R. E. Lee* 4:156, shows Lee with 7,892 infantry on Apr. 9; for JEJ's conditions, see *Conf. Soldier,* 322–23; Rowland 6:559–60, JEJ, *Narrative,* 398–403, 409–10.

17. JEJ, *Narrative,* 411–12; JEJ to J. C. Breck., Apr. 25, 1865, in *Conf. Soldier,* 322–23, quot. (calls JD et al. "civil functionaries"); JD quots. in Rowland 9:358 and 8:54, and from *Rise and Fall* 2:697 and 693.

18. VHD to JD, "Washington [Ga.] 9-o'clock Monday morning [May 1865]" (Rowland 6:589, quot.; mil. areas, in CSA as in USA, called Depts.); *The Private Mary Chesnut: The Unpublished Civil War Diaries,* ed. C. Vann Woodward and Elisabeth Muhlenfeld, 242, 244, 259, quots. ("country"="nation," then "countryside").

19. J. H. Reagan in Jones, *Davis Memorial,* 338 (JD quot.); Strode, *Tragic Hero,* 506, and passim.

20. VHD, *Memoir* 2:198n (he said he was "Jim Limber . . . in his every-day clothes"; "Jeems Henry Brooks in his best suit on Sunday"); VHD to JD, Apr. 19, 1865 (Rowland 6:550, quot.); VHD to JD, Apr. 28, in Eron Rowland, *Varina Howell, Wife of Jefferson Davis* 2:412, quot.; Tucker Hill, *Victory in Defeat: Jefferson Davis and the Lost Cause,* 34 (VHD's note with pic.: "A great pet in the family and known as Jim Limber"; the text will use this name).

21. Hanna, *Flight,* 209–12, 219–23, 242; Jones, *Davis Memorial,* 344 (quot. from G. Davis address); G. Davis to JD, Nov. 9, 1889 (Rowland 10:163, quot.).

22. Trenholm-JD corr., Apr. 27–28, 1865 (Rowland 6:564–65, quots.); Trenholm to JD, Apr. 30, 1870 (ibid. 7:268–69, quots.); Hanna, *Flight,* 58, 190–92, 238–39.

23. BNH, "Capture," 235–38 (quots.: 238 and JD n. on 236; see JD, *Rise and Fall* 2:694); *SHSP* 29:4–5 (1st JD quot., in address of E. H. McCaleb, June 3, 1901); Hanna, *Flight,* 194–208; Pierce Butler, *Judah P. Benjamin,* 362, 363–74 (Benj.'s trials), 395, 398 (Eng. bar).

24. Mallory to JD, May 2, 1865 (Rowland 6:586, quots.); Mallory, "Last Days," Part 2, 247; Hanna, *Flight,* 136, 242–43 (imprisoned, threatened with trial for piracy and treason, until Mar. 1866).

25. Basil W. Duke, *Reminiscences,* 385–90; W. C. P. Breckinridge and Duke to Walthall, Apr. 3 and 6, 1878 (Rowland 8:151–54 and 156–60); Clark, "Conf. Treasury," 318–22 (sum on 320; see Rowland 8:162; $40,000 more paid to soldiers in Washington-Wilkes). Clark shows disposition of all C.S. gold and silver coin brought from Danville ($327,022.90); Va. bank specie ("about $230,000") was handled by bank officers under the same escort but was never mixed with C.S. coin; all paper money burned by Reagan (Rowland 8:113–15). For rest of story, see Hanna, *Flight,* 108–16; also *SHSP* 32:157–63.

26. Basil W. Duke, *History Morgan's Cavalry,* 574–78, quot.; Duke, *Reminisc.,* 386–87; JD, *Rise and Fall* 2:695–96; W. C. Davis, *Breck.,* 528; Hanna, *Flight,* 104–6, 230–35.

27. Jones, *Davis Memorial,* 408 and 583 (Lubbock quots.); F. R. Lubbock, *Six Decades in Texas,* 326 (quot.), 329, 548–51; Hanna, *Flight,* 72–73; Reagan, *Mem-*

oirs, 109–10, 209; Lubbock in *DAB.* See Lubbock-JD corr., 1862–64, in Rowland 5, 6.

28. Reagan, *Memoirs,* 252 (quot.; JD "thoughtful, prudent, and wise"), 41–47, 51, 60, 126; AHS, *Recollections,* 501 (children now in Texas; Reagan did not know this till Sept. 1); Lubbock, *Six Decades,* 654 (quot.), 1–12, 69, 123–24.

29. H. P. Beers, *Guide to the Archives of the Government of the Confederate States of America,* 63 (WPJ appt'd. A.D.C. Apr. 19, 1862; Wood, Jan. 1863); Royce Gordon Shingleton, *John Taylor Wood,* 141. Affection, e.g., from WPJ to JD, 1888, and from Wood, 1878 (Rowland 10:83 and 8:240). For early acquaintance, see text below, chaps. 4 and 5.

30. Rowland 6:563 fn.1; Richardson, *Conf.,* 1:200 (BNH has no rank, but is called "Col.": see Beers, *Guide to C.S.A.,* 62, *Conf. Soldier,* 17, Rowland 6:562, 564); [Constance Cary] Harrison, *Recollections Grave and Gay,* 69, 206 (quots.).

31. VHD, *Memoir* 2:617; BNH, "Capture," 226–28.

32. JD to Burt, Apr. 23, and to VHD, Apr. 24, 1865 (Rowland 6:562, 564; JD, Nov. 3, MS, TRANSYL: "Armistead always was pure gold"); VHD, *Memoir* 1:409, quot.; BNH, "Capture," 242–43. For the Davises and Burts in 1850: see Strode, *Letters,* 59.

33. BNH, "Capture," 243, n."i" by JD, quot.; VHD to JD, Apr. 28 1865 (Rowland 6:566, quots.). The Burt home, a typical white-columned house, is still standing.

34. BNH, "Capture," 227, 245; AHS, *Recollections,* 111; Jones, *Davis Memorial,* 402–4 (Billy's age wrong); (Catherine:) JD to VHD, Sept. 26, 1865, MS, TRANSYL, and *Chesnut,* 601, 609; *Papers* 1:App. 4, Chart 14; Elizabeth Wright Weddell, *St. Paul's Church, Richmond, Virginia* 1:281.

35. VHD, *Memoir* 1:576 and 2:610; J. Thomas Scharf, *History of the Confederate States Navy,* App., 819–20, 773–81; Hanna, *Flight,* 6, 31–33, 61–63; JD to VHD, Apr. 5, 1865 (Rowland 6:533). Scharf, 779 n.1, says Howell lieut. in Raphael Semmes's "naval brigade," but that was of his sailors, not middies (Semmes, *Memoirs of Service Afloat,* 809–23).

36. Hanna, *Flight,* 33–34; VHD to JD, Apr. 13, 1865 (Rowland 6:544: quots. on Clay and Chesnut); VHD, *Memoir* 2:610–12, quots. (incl. Preston and Hood); J. B. Hood, *Advance and Retreat,* 158–59, quot. See Ruth Ketring Nuermberger, *The Clays of Alabama,* 262–65; *Chesnut,* 783, 428, 596, 755, 762, 764n; Preston and Hood in Warner, *Gens. in Gray.*

37. Hanna, *Flight,* 34–35, 61–63; VHD to JD, Apr. 19, 1865 (Rowland 6:550). See also *SHSP* 32:157–63.

38. Scharf, *Hist. C.S. Navy,* 778–79, quot.; Hanna, *Flight,* 61–63; VHD to JD, Apr. 24, 1865 (Rowland 6:551); VHD, *Memoir* 2:616–17 (see JD, *Rise and Fall,* 704); Semmes, *Service Afloat,* 822–23, quot. (parole wording).

39. VHD, *Memoir* 2:616, quot.; BNH to [?], May 2, 1865 (Rowland 6:587–88, quots.). For Toombs on JD, see *Correspondence of Robert Toombs, Alexander H. Stephens and Howell Cobb,* ed. U. B. Phillips, 595; see also Myrta Lockett Avary, *Dixie after the War,* 57–61.

40. VHD to JD, Apr. 28, 1865 (Rowland 6:566, quot.); VHD, *Memoir* 2:577, quot. (see JD note "i" in BNH, "Capture," 243).

41. VHD, *Memoir* 2:577; JD to Gorgas, Mar. 29, 1865, quot. (MS, marked "Private," Davis Papers, ADAH; Gorgas endorses it with an order for 50). Tucker Hill, *Victory in Defeat,* 24 (pic. "1855 Colt New Model Pocket Pistol and case" with label by VHD.). JD owned a Colt, but it was a very large 1851 model (seen at Mus. of Conf., 1986).

42. Tucker Hill, *Victory in Defeat,* 24; VHD, *Memoir* 2:577, 575, quots.; VHD in *Chesnut,* 467–68: "One can die but once."

43. JD to People of C.S.A., Apr. 4, 1865 (Rowland 6:529–31); Davis corr., Apr. 5–May 3 (ibid., 532–89 passim); Duke, *Hist. Morgan's Cav.,* 574; Reagan in *Life and Reminiscences of Jefferson Davis by Distinguished Men of his Time,* 261 (JD quot.).

44. Manly Wade Wellman, *Giant in Gray: A Biography of Wade Hampton,* 186–89; Hampton to JD, Apr. 19 and 22, 1865 (Rowland 6:552–54, quots.).

45. W. C. P. Breck. to Walthall, Apr. 3, 1878 (Rowland 8:154, quots.); Jones, *Davis Memorial*, 478, quot.

46. JD, *Rise and Fall* 2:689–90, 694; Mallory, "Last Days," Part 2, 246–47; Walthall, "Capture," 106–9; W. C. P. Breck. to Walthall, Apr. 3 and May 3, 1878 (Rowland 8:151–54 and 187–93); Dibrell to JD, Apr. 3, 1878 (ibid., 149–51).

47. Quots.: VHD to JD, Apr. 28, 1865; "Monday morning," [May 1] and n.d. (Rowland 6:566, 589 and 590).

48. VHD to JD, n.d. (ibid., 590); JD to VHD, Apr. 23, 14, 1865 (ibid., 559, 545, 562).

49. VHD to JD, Apr. 19, "9-o'clock Monday morning," 1865 (Rowland 6:551, 590).

50. JD to VHD, Apr. 23, 1865 (ibid., 561); VHD to JD, Apr. 28 (ibid., 566).

51. JD to VHD, Apr. 14, 1865 (Rowland 6:545); VHD to JD, Apr. 19, 24, n.d. (ibid., 549–51, 590).

52. Clark to VHD, Oct. 6, 1890, in VHD, *Memoir* 2:586–87, quots.; JD, *Rise and Fall* 2:689–90, 700; BNH, "Capture," 229; Hanna, *Flight*, 94, 110–17; *Life and Reminisc.*, 349–53 (JD refused to "seek his own personal safety in flight"; always disapproved word *flight*: e.g., Eckert, 47).

53. Hanna, *Flight*, 22, 20, 47–48; Jones, *Davis Memorial*, 395; Avary, *Dixie after War*, 51 (quots. from Mrs. W. T. Sutherlin).

54. *BCP* (1850): table for finding date of Easter; VHD, *Memoir* 2:627–28, quots.; Hanna, *Flight*, 44, errs in saying Easter is Apr. 17.

55. Hanna, *Flight*, 55–56 (Stoneman quot.); H. A. Tupper to J. W. Jones, Dec. 25, 1889, in Jones, *Davis Memorial*, 400, quots.; W. Stanley Hoole, *Vizetelly Covers the Confederacy* (Tuscaloosa, Ala.: Conf. Publ. Co., Inc., 1957), 141–42, 147; *SHSP* 29:5, quot.

56. Duke, *Hist. Morgan's Cav.*, 575, and *Reminisc.*, 385, quots.

57. Duke to Walthall, Apr. 15 and 6, 1878 (Rowland 8:171, 158–59, quots.).

58. JD to VHD, Apr. 23, 1865 (Rowland 6:560, quots.); VHD to JD, Apr. 28 (ibid., 566); Benj., J. C. Breck., Mallory, G. Davis, and Reagan to JD, Apr. 22–24 (ibid., 569–85; Reagan quot. on 585); Richard Weaver, *The Southern Tradition at Bay: A History of Postbellum Thought*, ed. George Core and M. E. Bradford, 115, quot.

59. JD, Inaugural Address, Feb. 22, 1862 (Rowland 5:202, quots.); Shingleton, *John T. Wood*, 155; Duke to Walthall, Apr. 15, 1878 (Rowland 8:171, quot.). JD, *Rise and Fall* 2:694–95, does not mention Abbeville (see 681). JD on Washington in *Papers* 2::67 (p. 272), 111.

60. Dibrell to WPJ, Apr. 9, 1878 (Rowland 8:161–62, quots.); JD to Walthall, July 12, 1877 (Rowland 7:560); Rowland 6:564, 8:151, 189–90, 250–51; L. H. Stout, "Reminiscences of General Braxton Bragg," 18; *Confederate Chronicles of Tennessee* 2 (1987): 184 n.25 (Bragg and wife captured in Ga. May 9).

61. Duke to JD, Apr. 13, 1878 (Rowland 8:168–69, quots.; see 158: Same to Walthall, Apr. 6); BNH, "Capture," 259 (JD quot.); Reagan, *Memoirs*, 212 (JD quot.).

62. JD in Senate, May 15, 1850 (*Papers* 4:107, quot.); JD, *Rise and Fall* 2:681, quot.; Reagan, *Memoirs*, 212 (JD quot.). Duke to Walthall, Apr. 6, 1878 (Rowland 8:158); Clark, "Conf. Treasury," 321 (col. 2). For another faithful band, see Rowland 10:60–62.

63. Quots.: text above, page 13; VHD, *Memoir* 2:616; JD to VHD, Apr. 23, 1865 (Rowland 6:559–62).

64. Lubbock, *Six Decades*, 569–70, quots.; BNH, "Capture," 250, JD in note "l"; Reagan, *Memoirs*, 217–18 (JD quot.).

65. Reagan, *Memoirs*, 214, quot.; BNH, "Capture," 249, 250 n. l, 257 (For Thorburn, see 252 was a friend of Wood). See also Hanna, *Flight*, 79, 96–97; JD, *Rise and Fall* 2:700. VHD sent "Kindest regards to Robert and thanks for faithful conduct" (Rowland 6:567; see *Chesnut*, 555).

66. BNH, "Capture," 250–53, quots.; Lubbock, *Six Decades*, 570–71; Reagan,

Memoirs, 218; *The Wartime Journal of a Georgia Girl, 1864–65,* ed. S. B. King, Jr., 202, quot.; WPJ to Walthall, July 14, 1877, in Jones, *Davis Memorial,* 405, quot. "Irwinville" (without "s") is the spelling (maps and *Conf. Vet.,* Oct. 1907, 438). A small park marks the spot of capture (1997).

67. BNH, "Capture," 252 (quots. in JD n. "m," 253–56; brackets in text), 257–58; JD, *Rise and Fall* 2:698 (Taylor and Forrest gave up May 8; Smith, May 26). "Tea"=light evening meal; dinner early afternoon (e.g., Nuermberger, *Clays of Ala.,* 220).

68. Hanna, *Flight,* 70–72, 80–81 (Smith quot.; had tried to interest Max. in joint action against U.S.); JD to VHD, Apr. 23, 1865 (Rowland 6:561, quot.); JD to Smith, July 14, 1863 (Rowland 5:552–54, quot.; sorry "so little aid"). On C.S. and Max., see VHD, *Memoir* 2:449, William Preston in Warner, *Gens. in Gray,* and Justus Scheibert, *Seven Months in the Rebel States,* ed. William Stanley Hoole, 12–13.

69. JD quots.: Rowland 7:444–45; note "m" in BNH, "Capture," 252–53; Rowland 8:53; *Rise and Fall* 2:701 (Jones "a free colored man, who faithfully clung to our fortunes"). Donation of stolen spurs to Mus. of Conf. ("Annual Report, 1987/88," 12, 14) shows *Conf. Vet.,* Oct. 1907, 447 to be in error. Dragoon: text below, chap. 4.

70. JD, *Rise and Fall* 2:701–2, quot. See Rowland 7:441–49 and 8:176–77. Variants on "defiant answer": Rowland 7:445; "'Running at the Heads,'" 345 [single quotation marks omitted hereafter]; *Conf. Vet.,* Oct. 1907, 448. "Raglan" and shawl: BNH, "Capture," 255; Rowland 8:54 and 176–77; VHD, *Memoir* 2:648–49; Sterling, *Belle,* 266–67; *The Private Chesnut,* 257 (also 251–52). See William Garrett Piston, *Lee's Tarnished Lieutenant,* 33; AHS, *Recollections,* 110.

71. WPJ to Walthall, July 14, 1877, in Jones, *Davis Memorial,* 406, quots. (see Rowland 7:448n; James Jones in *Conf. Vet.,* Oct. 1907, 448; Walthall, "Capture," 118). Deep South cold rainy mornings in May known to author.

72. BNH, "Capture," 258, 227–28; JD, *Rise and Fall* 2:702–3, quots. (see Rowland 8:175–78). On VHD's money and horses, see Lubbock in Jones, *Davis Memorial,* 409; Lubbock, *Six Decades,* 573.

73. JD, *Rise and Fall* 2:701 (ref. to Virgil *Aeneid* 3.57); quot. from Wilson's broadside (photocopy seen 1985 in Old Capitol Mus. Miss. Hist., MDAH); Hanna, *Flight,* 84, 55 (Stanton quot.); JD to C. J. Wright, Oct. 13, 1877, and Feb. 4, Apr. 18, 1878 (Rowland 8:35, 77, 176). See Note 25 above for real value of specie.

74. Strode, *Tragic Hero,* 223; Clark, "Conf. Treasury," 321; VHD to Shea, July 14, 1865, in McElroy, *JD* 2:543, quot.; Reagan in *Life and Reminisc.,* 262; JD to C. J. Wright, Feb. 4, 1878 (Rowland 8:77); Reagan, *Memoirs,* 209–10, 214. An Inventory of the Davis Family Artifacts, Mus. of Conf., Richmond, lists the bills among items "taken from Davis at his capture" (author's typescript from Cathy Carlson, Feb. 17, 1984).

75. Lubbock to Walthall, Aug. 2, 1877, in Jones, *Davis Memorial,* 409, quot.; Reagan, *Memoirs,* 219, quot. Even servant, Robert Brown, had "clothes taken from him by the Federals at our capture" (VHD to JD, Sept. 14, 1865, MS, ALA).

76. Lubbock, *Six Decades,* 571–73, quot. He was still indignant in 1881 and took "a parting shot at the Michigan robbers" who had appeared in print: "I presume they think it a good joke that they were enabled to rob women and children" (Rowland 9:43).

77. Hanna, *Flight,* 104, 152–53, 136 (quot.), 243; Richardson, *Conf.,* 1:76, 115–16, 120–21, 181–87.

78. Lubbock to Walthall, Aug. 2, 1877, in Jones, *Davis Memorial,* 408–9. A Lt. Barnwell did escape with Wood; they and Thorburn and his servant (who had ridden off earlier) were the only ones not made prisoner: see Lubbock, *Six Decades,* 573; BNH, "Capture," 257–58; Hanna, *Flight,* 96–97, 132.

79. Lubbock, *Six Decades,* 572, quots.; Lubbock to Walthall, Aug. 2, 1877, in Jones, *Davis Memorial,* 409, quots.

80. Quots.: BNH, Memorandum to JD, Sept. 1877 (Rowland 7:589); JD to Walthall, May 20, 1876 (ibid., 515); WPJ to same, July 14, 1877, in Jones, *Davis Memorial*, 407; JD to C. J. Wright, Apr. 18, 1878 (Rowland 8:176).

81. Lubbock, *Six Decades*, 572; Jones, *Davis Memorial*, 401–2; Strode, *Tragic Hero*, 221 (Wood quots.).

82. Craven, *Prison Life*, 139–40. JD said in Danville, "I don't reckon I shall need anything very long" (Mrs. Sutherlin in Jones, *Davis Memorial*, 395).

83. JD to C. J. Wright, Oct. 13, 1877 (Rowland 8:35, quot.; 53: it was "a carbine, which led me to believe . . . he would probably miss"); JD to Walthall, May 20, 1876 (ibid. 7:515, quot.); Walthall, "Capture," 112.

84. JD to Walthall, May 20, 1876 (Rowland 7:515, 2 quots.; VHD says significantly, May 23, 1865, "he was taken alive" [ibid, 21]); VHD, *Memoir* 2:579, quot.

85. JD to C. J. Wright, Oct. 13, 1877 (Rowland 8:35, quot.; "God's will" also in JD to Green, Aug. 18, 1875 [7:445] and in Walthall, "Capture," 111; cf. Matt. 6:10 and 26:36–45); JD to Cong., Mar. 13, 1865 (Richardson, *Conf.* 1:551, quot.). See chaps. 16 and 17 below for son and prison. Civilization: e.g., Raimondo Luraghi, *The Rise and Fall of the Plantation South* (New York: New Viewpoints, 1978); H. A. Scomp in *Conf. Vet.*, June 1907, 253.

86. *Early Fathers from the Philokalia*, ed. E. Kadloubovsky and G. E. H. Palmer, 215 (also: "A humble man is never hurried, hasty, or perturbed"); Hanna, *Flight*, 58; Mallory, "Last Days," Part 2, 240–42 ("his usual quiet, grave way"; "low, even tone") and Part 1, 107, quots.

87. BNH, "Capture," 238–42, quots. ("regret and grief" over Lincoln), 236 n. "h" by JD (on Cooper); JD to C. J. Wright, May 11, 1876 (Rowland 7:512–14, quots.; see ibid. 9:34–34, and Craven, *Prison Life*, 123); Cooper in Warner, *Gens. in Gray*.

88. Duke, text above, pages 13–14; Mallory quots. in Frank H. Alfriend, *The Life of Jefferson Davis*, 636; BNH, "Capture," 257, quot.; The Rev. H. A. Tupper to J. W. Jones, Dec. 25, 1889, in Jones, *Davis Memorial*, 400–401, quots. (and Avary, *Dixie after War*, 60; ref. to Job 13:15). JD's insouciance was so great that Tupper said, "I really believe [he] wishes to be captured," but that was clearly not the case.

89. Craven, *Prison Life*, 140 (quot.), 258–60. See John 18:8.

90. "Running at the Heads," 346, quots.; Reagan in *The Annals of the War*, 150, quot.; Samuel P. Hillhouse to wife, Sept. 30, 1862 (*Conf. Vet.*, May–June 1989, 19, quot.); Ishbel Ross, *First Lady of the South: The Life of Mrs. Jefferson Davis*, 249 (VHD quot.).

91. VHD, *Memoir* 2:641–42, quots.; "Running at the Heads," 346, quot.; BNH, "Capture," 258–59. See *Conf. Chron. of Tenn.* 2 (1987): 182, for list of prisoners, incl. V.'s teamsters, Morgan's men; and 173–79.

92. McElroy, *JD* 2:505–6; JD, *Rise and Fall* 2:703; VHD, *Memoir*, 2:644n, quot. See Beverly Tucker to JD, July 1, 1867 (Rowland 7:117–19), Chester Forrester Dunham, *The Attitude of the Northern Clergy toward the South, 1860–65*, 172–80, and text below, chaps. 17–19.

93. JD, *Rise and Fall* 2:703–4, quots.; Walthall, "Capture," 117, quots. See Rowland 9:396–98. William Hanchett, *The Lincoln Murder Conspiracies*, 82–83, and Ridley, *Battles and Sketches*, 459, show regret in South over assassination.

94. VHD, *Memoir* 2:643 n., quot. (ref. to Gal. 3:6). Other details in Michael B. Ballard, *A Long Shadow: Jefferson Davis and the Final Days of the Confederacy* (Jackson: Univ. Press of Miss., 1986), 150–51.

95. Reagan, *Memoirs*, 221–22, quot.; JD, *Rise and Fall* 2:703–4; Lubbock, *Six Decades*, 575. Wheeler had been prevented from following JD with his cav. from Charlotte, to "defend him or die in the effort" (*Life and Reminsc.*, 311–12).

96. Sterling, *Belle*, 246–56, quots. Benj. H. Hill, Jr., *Senator Benjamin H. Hill of Georgia*, 273–93. Mansion, now Bellevue, is kept by LaGrange Woman's Club (brochure; visits). Hill and Mallory were arrested here and sent to Fort Lafayette, N. Y., as "political prisoners"; Wigfall escaped (*Hill*, 45–47; *The War of the Rebellion:*

A Compilation of the Official Records of the Union and Confederate Armies, 2, 8:640). For Burton's *Anatomy of Melancholy*, 1621, see *A Literary History of England*, ed. Albert C. Baugh, 596–98.

97. *Belle of '50's*, 256–57, quots. The soldiers were the 4th Mich. Cav.; Col. Pritchard had been given the honor of escorting his prisoners.

98. Ibid., 258, quots.; AHS, *Recollections*, 99–101, 105–6, 109, 110–11, 115 (quots.); King, *Wartime Jnl. Ga. Girl*, 256, quots. (citing letter from Augusta).

99. Sterling, *Belle*, 259–60; AHS, *Recollections*, 110–15.

100. Ibid., 114 and 116, quots.; JD, *Rise and Fall* 2:704; BNH, "Capture," 259.

101. VHD, *Memoir* 2:642 and 645n, quots.; James S. Allen, *Reconstruction: The Battle for Democracy, 1865–76*, 225–27 (quot. from Sherman's orders, Jan. 16, 1865; this was "the most advanced outpost of the revolution" [50]); AHS, *Recollections*, 116, quots. Hudson a "drunkard, thief, liar" (JD in Rowland 7:445).

102. Sterling, *Belle*, 260, quots. (see VHD, *Memoir* 2:645n); Scharf, *Hist. C.S. Navy*, 805–6; R. Semmes letter in Walthall, "Capture," 102–3.

103. Wheeler quoted in McElroy, *JD* 2:522–23; Wheeler in *Life and Reminisc.*, 312–13; AHS, *Recollections*, 119; Sterling, *Belle*, 261.

104. Dunham, *Attitude of Northern Clergy*, 173, 174, and 177, quots. For non-recognition of the C.S.A. and Southern claims, see Richardson, *Conf.* 1:341–42 and text below, passim.

105. Hanchett, *Lincoln Murder*, 62–67 (Holt quots. on 63; a defense lawyer said mil. comm. had already judged defendants guilty and sat merely to decide punishment); Lubbock, *Six Decades*, 573, quot.; McElroy 2:522–23 (Wheeler quot.).

106. Lubbock, *Six Decades*, 577–88 (quots. on 577, 584); Reagan to J. W. Jones, Jan. 10, 1890, in Jones, *Davis Memorial*, 466, quots.; Psalm 26 quot. from *BCP* (1850). Stephen Elliott, 1st Episc. bsp. of Ga., also asked to share JD's imprisonment, feeling insulted by his treatment (Richard Hooker Wilmer, *The Recent Past from a Southern Standpoint*, 240–41).

107. AHS, *Recollections*, 118–20 and 123–24, quots.; Dunham, *Attitude of Northern Clergy*, 178 quot. 179: Unitarian *Christian Examiner* of Boston demands life of JD and "wretched accomplices" as "just and necessary forfeit to the law."

108. JD, *Rise and Fall* 2:704, quots.; VHD, *Memoir* 2:647, quot.; C. C. Harrison, *Recoll.*, 228–37.

109. Sterling, *Belle*, 261; VHD to JD, Sept. 14, 1865, MS, ALA, quots. (JD speaks of his "parting charge" to Robt. in letter to V., Sept. 26, MS, TRANSYL).

110. Quots.: Sterling, *Belle*, 262; VHD, *Memoir* 2:648 and 704n; VHD to Craven, June 14, 1865, in Craven, *Prison Life*, 143.

111. Quots. from text above, page 1; Weddell, *St. Paul's* 2:480–81, 398 and 1:133–34, 233.

112. Lubbock *Six Decades*, 650 (quots. from V.'s descr.: eyes "a decided blue, with large pupils"; also height); Other features from photographs, paintings, and firsthand accounts; Don Quixote in Winnie Davis, "JD in Private Life," 9 ("blue eyes" on 5; many call them grey; perhaps changed with colors worn). Gold still shines in locks of JD's hair (seen at Old Courthouse Mus., and in "relic room" at First White House of the Confederacy).

113. Quots.: *Chesnut*, 84; VHD, *Memoir* 1:200; W. H. Russell in *Richmond in Time of War*, ed. W. J. Kimball, 6. (Friend and foe:) Lubbock in Jones, *Davis Memorial*, 349–50; Carl Schurz in Hudson Strode, *Jefferson Davis, American Patriot, 1808–1861*, 252.

114. Semmes, *Service Afloat*, 818, quots. (as natural for Yankee to hate Davis as for cat to arch back); Johnson in H. R., May 29, 1846 (*Papers* 2::218, quot.).

115. Dunham, *Attitude of Northern Clergy*, 176 (quot. from Rev. E. S. Atwood of So. Congregational Church, Salem); Hanchett, *Lincoln Murder*, 67 (Hunter quot., which caused Reverdy Johnson of Md. to leave the defense of Mary Surratt).

116. *Life and Reminsc.*, 339 (quot. from C. C. Jones, Jr.); Virginia Clay-Clopton,

"Clement C. Clay," 75, quot. (ref. to Edmund Burke, *Reflections on the Revolution in France* [*Hoyt's Cyclopedia of Practical Quotations*, ed. Kate Louise Roberts, 108]).

117. Dunham, *Attitude of Nor. Clergy*, 198 (quot. from Quint sermon entitled, "The Southern Chivalry, and What the Nation Ought to Do with It"; some mean by "the chivalry" only fire-eaters, but Quint means the "Southern Gentleman": see 94–95 and n.).

118. "Gentleman" and "chivalry" in *OED; Papers* 2::11 n.2; Benj. to Clay, Jan. 22, 1863, in Marietta Minnigerode Andrews, *Scraps of Paper*, 235–36, quots.

119. *Hill*, 117, quot.; *Doctor Quintard, Chaplain C.S.A. and Second Bishop of Tennessee: Being his Story of the War*, ed. Arthur Howard Noll, 92–94; Lonn, *Foreigners in Conf.*, 447, quot.; JD to C. J. Wright, May 11, 1876 (Rowland 7:512, quot.). Polk was both line off. and Episc. bsp. of La. (William Stevens Perry, *Bishops of the American Church Past and Present*, 75).

120. W. C. P. Breck. to Walthall, Apr. 3, 1878 (Rowland 8:152–53, quot.); Ridley, *Battles and Sketches*, 599–601, quots. (464: his diary says JEJ's troops "would sacrifice everything except honor").

121. G. P. R. James, *The History of Chivalry*, 28, 19, quots.; Truth: see Reagan, *Memoirs*, 220–21; Semmes, *Service Afloat*, 818.

122. James, *Hist. of Chivalry*, 33, quot.; Wilmer, *Recent Past*, 49, quot. ("chivalry of spirit . . . forbade unkindness"). Edward Mayrick Goulburn, *Thoughts on Personal Religion*, 311: "Perfect love would involve perfect courtesy" (read by JD in 1865).

123. Quots.: Nannie Davis Smith, "Reminiscences of Jefferson Davis," 180; *Papers* 2::203 Ed. Note, 89 (p. 347), 95; Alfriend, *Life of Davis*, 73; John W. Daniel in Jones, *Davis Memorial*, 297.

124. Phillips, *Corr. of Toombs*, 595, 608, 612; Reagan, *Memoirs*, 214–15 (Toombs and JD quots.); *Chesnut*, 318, quots. Toombs thought JD free "to go anywhere," up to the Chattahoochee (not knowing JEJ had caused surrender beyond); JD (Craven, *Prison Life*, 136) and C. J. Wright (Rowland 8:110) thought him not "liable to capture" at all. Toombs later escaped to Cuba, then Europe (Hanna, *Flight*, 228–29).

125. JD, *Rise and Fall* 2:764, 191, and 611, quots.; Richardson, *Conf.* 1:73–74 (quot. *re* Bgd.). See AHS, *Recollections*, 139–40: "no foul stigma" on South's "escutcheon"; "Let us be able to say . . .'We have lost all but honour.'"

126. Lubbock, *Six Decades*, 609 (quot. from paraphrase of 1875 JD speech); JD in Senate, Aug. 5, 1850 (Rowland 1:470, quot.); JD, *Rise and Fall* 2:562, quot.; Jefferson Davis, "Robert E. Lee," 66, quot. Walker "from the pages of old Froissart" (Richard Taylor, *Destruction and Reconstruction*, 22–23).

127. JD to Lee, July 31, 1862, in VHD, *Memoir* 2:543–45, quot. (see Jefferson Davis, "Andersonville and other War-Prisons," Part 2, 337–38); JD to C.S. Cong., Dec. 7, 1863 (Richardson, *Conf.* 1:381, quots.).

128. Benj. to Mann, Aug. 14, 1862 (ibid. 2:312–13, quot.); Lonn, *Foreigners in Conf.*, 75 (Benj. quot.). See also Butler, *Judah P. Benj.*, 249–50, 341.

129. *SHSP* 6:162–63 (quots. from certificate, La. Div., July 10, 1878). Apparently, Soc. of ANV also enrolled JD (Rowland 8:39–40).

130. Jones, *Davis Memorial*, 342, 530, quots.; Galleher to JD, Nov. 3, 1887 (*Letters*, 552, quot.; on Gen. S. B. Buckner's staff; Episc. bsp. of La., 1880–91: see William Preston Johnston, *The Life of Gen. Albert Sidney Johnston*, 727; Perry, *Bsps. of Am. Church*, 263).

Chapter II Home

1. *Papers* 1:App. 4, Chart 4 (rev. ed.) (JD b.: "1807/08"); JD to [C. J. Wright], June 3, 1878, MS, TRANSYL (in JD's hand; signature missing). JD also said he served the government from age 16 (*Papers* 4:206).

2. Strode, *Patriot*, 3 (only source in which "Finis" occurs; author indebted to Herman Hattaway for this point); *Papers* 1::15–353 ("F" appears erratically in army records Nov. 1824–May 1833), 528 (will), also 361–63 Ed. Notes; Hollywood Cem., Richmond, Va., base of JD statue, 1899.

3. Jane C. Davis in *Papers* 1:App. 4, chart 3 (Rev. Ed.). Latest birth date assigned is 1762, in Alfred F. Ganier's application to SAR (author's copy, courtesy SAR).

4. *Papers* 1:App. 4, Chart 4; N. D. Smith, "Reminisc. of JD," 178–79 (quots., incl. JD to Anna, Apr. 3, 1851); JD to VHD, Nov. 3, 1865, MS, TRANSYL, quot. (elsewhere Ann).

5. "The Birthplace of Jefferson Davis," 486–87.

6. Will T. Hale and Dixon L. Merritt, *A History of Tennessee and Tennesseans* 2:486. Background sources: Harriette Simpson Arnow, *Seedtime on the Cumberland;* John D. Wright, Jr., *Lexington, Heart of the Bluegrass*, 1–45; John M. Blum et al., *The National Experience*, 143–47; Sister Mary Ramona Mattingly, *The Catholic Church on the Kentucky Frontier, (1785–1812)*, 32–33.

7. Sibley, "JD Recalls the Past," 170; *Papers* 1::5 n. 6, App. 3, pp. 490–94, 496, 497, 500–502, 504, 506–7; Walter L. Fleming, "The Early Life of Jefferson Davis," 153 (says Evan crossed river about where JD did in 1865).

8. Original gravestone for Samuel Emory Davis from Davis Bend (now at Beauvoir) has agreed date of death, July 4, 1824, and "Aged 66," making birth date 1758, contrary to JD in VHD, *Memoir* 1:3–5, 32 (see *Papers* 1:App. 4 n. 11). Gravestone moved 1940 (Frank E. Everett, *Brierfield: Plantation Home of Jefferson Davis*, 17–18).

9. George White, *Statistics of the State of Georgia*, 607–14; Janet Harvill Standard, comp., *The Battle of Kettle Creek: A Turning Point of the American Revolution in the South*, 19; Kenneth Coleman, *The American Revolution in Georgia*, 1–15, 71–72, 224–25; Fleming, "Early Life," 153–54.

10. JD in VHD, *Memoir* 1:4–5; N. D. Smith, "Reminisc. of JD," 182; Fleming, "Early Life," 154 and nn.8 and 9 (land grants: 120 A. from Wilkes Co. and 287 1/2 A. in Washington Co.; see Coleman, *Am. Rev. in Ga.*, 217–20: latter standard Ga. grant). J. Hayes-Davis shows 1000 A. from S. C. (SAR application; author's copy, courtesy of SAR; see *Papers* 1::5 n.11).

11. VHD, *Memoir* 1:3; T. C. DeLeon, "The Real Jefferson Davis in Private and Public Life," 77–78; Fleming, "Early Life," 153–54.

12. J. G. M. Ramsay, *The Annals of Tennessee . . .*, [Charleston: Walker and James, 1853], 217, quot. (mounted men distinct from cav.: see Henry Lee, *Memoirs of the War in the Southern Department* 1:148); White, *Statistics of Ga.*, 607–10 (quots. on 610); Standard, *Battle of Kettle Creek.*

13. JD to VHD, Oct. 20, 1865, MS, TRANSYL, quot.; *Papers* 1:App. 4, Chart 4. Confused refs. in W. Williams Colbert to JD, Sept. 5, 1889 (Rowland 10:135) may be clue to later life of half brothers.

14. Standard, *Battle of Kettle Creek*, 49–52 (Samuel Davis in list of "Kettle Creek Heroes," 57 [battle]:) 1, 4, 6, 11–14, 24–25; Fleming, "Early Life," 154 and n.8.

15. JD, "Autobiography" (*Papers* 1::1, p. liii, quot.; see VHD, *Memoir* 1:4); N. D. Smith, "Reminisc. of JD," 182, quot.; Quot. from marker at Beauvoir cem. erected after 1940; (Lincoln Co. was not formed until 1796 [White, *Statistics of Ga.*, 381]).

16. White, *Statistics of Ga.*, 513–14, 623–24; Charles C. Jones, Jr., *The History of Georgia* (Boston: Houghton Mifflin, 1883), 2:376–416, 451–61; Henry Lee, *Memoirs* 1:67–71; Coleman, *Am. Rev. in Ga.*, 120–21, 127–29, 133–34, 143–44; White, *Hist. Coll. of Ga.*, 685–86.

17. White, *Statistics of Ga.*, 513–14; White, *Hist. Coll. of Ga.*, 685; Jones, *Hist. of Ga.*, 2:454–58, 473–89; Henry Lee, *Memoirs*, 1:147–48, and 2:86–95, 99–111 (quots. from 94n and 101n).

18. Standard, *Battle of Kettle Creek*, 3, 6–7, 10, 21; Henry Lee, *Memoirs* 2:110–17 and nn.

19. Henry Lee, *Memoirs* 1:148–52 and n., 1–2 and n.; Douglas Southall Free-

man, *George Washington: A Biography* 5:112. Ironically, Henry Lee was late in life nearly killed by a mob, after surrendering to militia (Freeman, *R. E. Lee* 1:14–16).

20. JD in Senate, Aug. 13, 1850 (Rowland 1:489, quot.); JD endorsement in Rowland 8:52; JD, Speech at Macon, Ga., Sept. 28, 1864 (ibid. 6:341, quots.); Arnow, *Seedtime,* 299–300.

21. JD quoted in Jones, *Davis Memorial,* 292; JD, Speech at Dem. Convention, Portland, Me., Aug. 24, 1858, paraphrase (Rowland 3:285, quot.); JD to C. J. Wright, May 11, 1876 (ibid. 7:512, quot.). See ibid. 4:301 for same sentiments in 1860.

22. Quots.: JD in VHD, *Memoir* 1:17 and 4–5; Sibley, "JD Recalls the Past," 171 (variant on restive horse story).

23. Fleming, "Early Life," 156; "Birthplace of JD," 486–87, quots. (see Rom. 12:13; VHD, *Memoir* 1:5n); N. D. Smith, "Reminisc. of JD," 182; Jones, *Davis Memorial,* 44 (JD quot.); Herman S. Frey, *Jefferson Davis,* 8 (pic. of improved house). House shown at Centennial Exposition, Nashville, 1896, stored in Richmond, lost track by 1923 (Fleming, as above; see McElroy, *JD* 1:3: still missing in 1937).

24. JD in VHD, *Memoir* 1:4, 15; "Birthplace of JD," 486; Fleming, "Early Life," 154–55; Henry H. Cook to [VHD] Feb. 17, 1890, explains Cook relationship to Greene, MS, TULANE; see *Cal. JD MSS,* 293–94.

25. Fleming, "Early Life," 155 (quots., Mrs. E. M. D. Anderson); Sibley, "JD Recalls the Past," 171 (JD quot.); Anna Farrar Goldsborough, "Varina Howell Davis," 12, quot.

26. Strode, *Patriot,* 7–8; *Papers* 4:App. 2, p. 402, quot.; (also 1:App. 4, Chart 4 [Rev. Ed., 1991]; though rejected ibid., 1971 ed.; see 1::2 n.3 and 363 n.34); Arnow, *Seedtime,* 346–47, quot.; Craven, *Prison Life,* 356 (JD quot.).

27. Mattingly, *Catholic Church,* 179 (quot. from Rev. David Rice), 195 (Badin quot.), 185, 188–93 (2d Badin quot. on 191).

28. VHD, *Memoir* 1:17 (JD quot.); Goldsborough, "Varina Howell Davis," 14–15, quots.

29. Mattingly, *Catholic Church,* 173 (Badin quots.), 172 (quot.), 115, 118, 105 and n.7; "Slavery" in *Columbia Encyclopedia* and *The Universal Standard Encyclopedia;* Eugene D. Genovese and Elizabeth Fox-Genovese, "The Religious Ideals of Southern Slave Society," *Ga. Hist. Q.* 70 (1986): 2–4, 9–11; Robert William Fogel and Stanley L. Engerman, *Time on the Cross: The Economics of American Negro Slavery,* 15–20, 29–32.

30. Arnow, *Seedtime,* 249 and n.7, 293 and n.44, 245 (quot.), 389; JD in U.S. Senate, May 17, 1860 (Rowland 4:327–28, quots.).

31. Fleming, "Early Life," 157–58, 161 (dates the move 1811; date in text from hist. marker). In 1822, S. Davis still owned these two slaves, and also "Bob and his wife Farah, Charles, Jim Pemberton" (*Papers* 1::9 n.7).

32. Blum et al., *Natl. Experience,* 166–68; David King Gleason, *Plantation Homes of Louisiana and the Natchez Area,* vii, 44, 48–49; Hist. marker near Franklin, La.: "In 1810, Samuel Davis . . . acquired a tract of land fronting on Bayou Teche for 14 acres and running back to the depth of 40 acres . . . built a home, not now standing" (photograph, courtesy of the late Miriam Patrick); VHD, *Memoir* 1:6 (JD quot.).

33. R. W. Jones, "Some Facts Concerning the Settlement and Early History of Mississippi" (*PMHS* 1:86; quot. from A. R. Kilpatrick); "Wilkinson County Guide and Map," 10. Feliciana not divided "East" and "West" until 1824 (*Papers* 1::363 n.1).

34. Fleming, "Early Life," 158 (quot. from Mrs. E. M. D. Anderson); Gleason, *Plantation Homes of La.,* 83 (date Rosemont c. 1815); Frey, *JD,* 10.

35. *Papers* 5:132 (called Rosemont by 1855); Fleming, "Early Life," 158; JD in VHD, *Memoir* 1:7, 5; Sibley, "JD Recalls the Past," 171 (2 quots., paraphrasing JD).

36. VHD, *Memoir* 1:6 (JD quot.); "Joseph Emory Davis" in *Mississippi, Com-*

prising Sketches of Counties . . . and Persons, ed. Dunbar Rowland, 2:630–32 (see "Old Greenville," ibid. 803, and *Papers* 3:117 n.10); D. Rowland, "Mississippi's First Constitution and its Makers," *PMHS* 6:90, quot.

37. Tombstones, Locust Grove Cem.; Fleming, "Early Life," 162; *Papers* 1:App. 4, Chart 6 and nn., Chart 8 and nn.53 and 55; *Papers* 1::363 n.26 and 526 n.1 (Ben Davis married Smith's niece); W. A. Evans, *Jefferson Davis, His Diseases and His Doctors* . . . , 3; M. E. Hamer to Fleming, Feb. 19, 1908, MS, Fleming Collection (Ben Davis studied in Phila.)

38. *Jnl. Miss. Hist.* 28 (1966): 237; Robert Lowry and William H. McCardle, *A History of Mississippi*, 592; *Papers* 1::9 n.12, 19 n.8, App. 4, Chart 7 (Rev. Ed.), and 2::3 n.4.

39. VHD, *Memoir* 1:8–9 n, quots.; *Papers* 1:App. 4, Charts 4 and 8, and 1::528 n.5 (Rev. Ed.).

40. Fleming, "Early Life," 162, quot.; VHD, *Memoir* 1:8, 18–20 (JD quots.).

41. JD in Senate, June 14, 1860 (Rowland 4:514, quot.); JD in Senate, Jan. 26, 1858 (ibid. 3:138, quot.); Eron Rowland, *Andrew Jackson's Campaign against the British* . . . , 140–41, 249; J. F. H. Claiborne, *Mississippi, as a Province, Territory and State* . . . , 228, 483–526. Allies also in D. Rowland, *History of Mississippi, The Heart of the South* 1:463–64.

42. Claiborne, *Miss.*, 315–24 and 320n (Isaac in Miss. Terr. Vols.; ensign below 2d lieut.; diff. numbers for slain here and in D. Rowland, *Hist. of Miss.* 2:458–59); *Horseshoe Bend* pamphlet by Natl. Park Service; E. Rowland, *AJ's Campaign*, 74 and n.1, 96–103 (quots. on 98–99), 102 n.1; Jones, *Davis Memorial*, 448 (JD quot.).

43. Claiborne, *Miss.*, 325–26; *Horseshoe Bend* pamphlet by Natl. Park Service; D. Rowland, *Military Hist.*, 8–9.

44. E. Rowland, *AJ's Campaign*, 141–47; D. Rowland, *Military Hist.*, 9; D. Rowland, *Miss.* 2:870–71; *Papers* 4:214 n.3; Ibid. 1::19 n.1; Ibid., n.8 (son Samuel vol. as pvt. soldier, but we have Isaac's rec., and 2 bros. were commended by AJ [Jones, *Davis Memorial*, 292], Samuel must be the one besides Joseph).

45. Quots.: JD in Jones, *Davis Memorial*, 448; JD in VHD, *Memoir* 1:6–7; JD in H. R., Feb. 6, 1846 (Rowland 1:34). With three brothers "under arms," the one ordered to stay home must be Benjamin.

46. E. Rowland, *AJ's Campaign*, 141–47, 246, 247 (quot.); D. Rowland, *Military Hist.*, 9–10; Marquis James, *Andrew Jackson, The Border Captain*, 186 (commands 7th Military District).

47. James, *AJ Border Captain*, 208, 213; D. Rowland, *Military Hist.*, 13; E. Rowland, *AJ's Campaign*, 249, 146, 245, 250–51.

48. Ibid., 299–300, 318–19, 321, 324–25, 332–34, 342, 344–45; D. Rowland, *Military Hist.*, 10–11 (AJ quot.); JD in H. R., Feb. 6, 1846 (Rowland 1:34); JD, Eulogy on the Life and Character of AJ (*Papers* 2::67, p. 275, quots.); Jones, *Davis Memorial*, 292 (JD quot.). JD also quoted AJ in Miss. speeches, 1851 and 1857 (*Papers* 4:185 and 6:138).

49. D. Rowland, *Military Hist.*, 11, 9; E. Rowland, *AJ's Campaign*, 398–99, quot.; JD to Lise Mitchell, Feb. 7, 1884 (*Papers* 1::19 n.1, quot.; "my love for him . . . a sentiment than which I have none more sacred"); VHD, *Memoir* 1:46–49; *Papers* 2::20 n.8; E. Rowland, *Varina* 1:20. For Joseph at Greenville, see *Papers* 1::19 n.1, 2::71 n.58.

50. JD, Speech at Fayette, Miss., July 11, 1851, paraphrase (*Papers* 4:184; quots.); JD to Joseph Davis, Jan. 26, 1847 (ibid. 3:114, quot.); Greenville, Hinds, etc., in D. Rowland, *Miss.*, 801–3, 967, 870; Greens and Jacksons: ibid., 798, 953–54, 966; and James, *AJ, Border Capt.*, 55–57, 62–64, 66–71.

51. Most plausible date for JD at Greenville is 1815–16; natural inference is that he lived with Joseph (*Papers* 3::117 n.10 and 4:214 n.2), but see D. Rowland, *Miss.* 2:802. Time and age at trip variously given, VHD, *Memoir* 1:8–9, 15 (left without "mother's knowledge," so author assumes from his home); Sibley, "JD

Recalls the Past," 172; *Papers* 1::3 n.3; JD to VHD, Dec. 2–3, 1865, TRANSYL; but book at St. Thomas reads: "Jefferson Davis arrived July 10, 1816" (V. F. O'Daniel, *The Father of the Church in Tennessee* [Washington, D. C.: The Dominica, 1926], 147), and school took boys only "8 to 16" (Frey, *JD*, 17).

52. VHD, *Memoir* 1:8–11 (JD quots.).

53. VHD, *Memoir* 1:11–12 (JD quots.); James, *AJ, Border Capt.*, 287–89, 358–59, 105–6 and plate facing 124 (true pic. of 1st Hermitage, rarely shown correctly); *Landmarks of Tennessee History*, ed. William T. Alderson and Robert M. McBride, 7–8. Jacksons raised 3 nephews and a friend's son, and were guardians of several other children.

54. VHD, *Memoir* 1:11 (JD quots.); A. S. Colyar, *Life and Times of Andrew Jackson, Soldier-Statesman-President* 1:90–98, 70, 252; James, *AJ, Border Capt.*,161–63, 267, 273–75.

55. Strode, *Tragic Hero*, 315–16, quot.; JD to W. B. Tebo, Aug. 22, 1849 (Rowland 1:246 (quots.)).

56. VHD, *Memoir* 1:11–12 (JD quots.); James, *AJ, Border Capt.*, 219, 161–63, 122–27; Colyar, *Life and Times of AJ* 1:58–59, 90–98, 190, 196–97; E. G. W. Butler to JD, Sept. 20, 1885 (Rowland 9:393, AJ quot.).

57. James, *AJ, Border Capt.*, 288 (AJ quot); VHD, *Memoir* 1:11–12 (JD quots.); Sibley, "JD Recalls the Past," 171–73 (JD quot.). AJ adopted (1813) and raised an abandoned Indian baby, Lincoyer: see James, 168–69, 288, 311, 357; Colyar, *AJ* 1:101–2 (d. at 17 of consumption); James Parton, *Life of Andrew Jackson* 1:439–40.

58. VHD, *Memoir* 1:12 (JD quot.). For school, see *Papers* 1::3 n.1; Mattingly, *Catholic Church*, 83–84; Frey, *JD*, 12, 15–18. O'Daniel, as in Note 51, 149–50, thinks "Hynds" near "Davis" may be Howell, giving "probable" reason for trip: indeed, no other presents itself; called "classmate" and "schoolmate" (Rowland 5:329 n.1, 6:59 n.1) which could mean plantation school. JD calls him "a very near friend," 1856 (*Papers* 6:52; see n.1).

Chapter III School

1. Mattingly, *Catholic Church*, 80–88; "Historic Saint Rose Priory" (printed material, n.p., n.d., courtesy Sister Aloysius, O.P., Nashville, Tenn.). School closed 1828 (*U.S. Dominican* 17:3, 7); church replaced 1855; again in use 1983 (conversation with Rev. Chris Allegra, O.P.).

2. Frey, *JD*, 17, quots.; VHD, *Memoir* 1:13–15 (JD quots.). Another priest treated him like "a near relative"; see *Papers* 1::2 n.7. Charles was probably one of the Greens of Jefferson Co., Miss.: see above chap. 2 and Note 50).

3. O'Daniel, *Father Church* (as above, chap. 2, Note 51), 152, quot.; VHD, *Memoir* 1:13–14 (JD quots.)

4. JD to VHD, Oct. 20, 1865, MSS, TRANSYL, quot.; JD to VHD, Dec. 30, 1865–Jan. 1, 1866, ibid., quot.

5. Quots.: JD to VHD, Dec. 30, 1865–Jan. 1, 1866, Oct. 20, 1865, and Feb. 17–19, 1866, MSS, TRANSYL (Maggie and Jeff Jr., aged 10 and 8, are to "resume French"). Latin: Virgil *Aeneid* 6.26: *Hic opus, hic labor est* ("this [the escape] indeed is a task; this indeed is a toil" [*Hoyt*, 364]).

6. VHD, *Memoir* 1:15–17 (JD quots.). JD "astonished and overcome" at reception; he had forgotten at school "all family attachments" (Sibley, "JD Recalls the Past," 174–75).

7. VHD, *Memoir* 1:19–20 (JD quots.); JD in Senate, Dec. 17, 1850, seconding testimonial to Harmanson, in H. R. from La. (*Congressional Globe*, 31st Cong., 2d sess., 69–70, quots.; "strict" in etymological sense of "drawn close, tight," hence, "intimate"). Latin paradigm to decline word for "this" begins *hic, haec, hoc*. Jefferson College opened as academy 1811; became mil. school 1829 (D. Rowland, *Miss.*, 961–63).

8. VHD, *Memoir* 1:20–21, 17–18 (JD quots.).

9. Quots.: Eliza Davis to JD, Nov. 17, 1834 (*Papers* 1::439); Winnie Davis, "JD in Private Life," 3–4; Sibley, "JD Recalls the Past," 173 (WPJ); N. D. Smith, "Reminisc. of JD," 178; A. R. Lawton in *Life and Reminisc.*, 196; W. H. Davies in ibid., 41. For women, see *Chesnut*, 84; VHD, *Memoir* 1:191.

10. Sibley, "JD Recalls the Past," 173–74 and 171 (WPJ quots.); N. D. Smith, "Reminsc. of JD," 178; *Chesnut*, 84 (MBC quot.). N. D. Smith says Jeff slept at Locust Grove in the swinging baby bed, now labeled "Cradle of Jefferson Davis" at Conf. Mus., N. O., but actually made for a Smith son born in 1817 (original record cited in Wilbur E. Meneray to author, Aug. 6, 1985).

11. Craven, *Prison Life*, 236, quots. (paraphrase of JD); R. W. Jones, "Some Facts Concerning the Settlement and Early History of Mississippi," *PMHS* 1 (1898): 88 (quots. from A. R. Kilpatrick).

12. Winnie Davis, "JD in Private Life," 3–5, quots.; *Papers* 2::18 n.104, p. 108 (JD quot., 1857); JD to Mrs. S. W. Ferguson, Sept. 5, 1879, quot. (MS, Fleming Collection).

13. Papers 1::9 n.7 (quot. from Stamps to JD, July 3, 1874); Ibid.:App. 4, Chart 12 (Rev. Ed.); VHD, *Memoir* 1:22 (JD quot.); JD, Remarks on Death of Quitman, Jan. 5, 1859 (Rowland 3:464; lessons after Q. arr. in Miss. [Dec. 1821: J. F. H. Claiborne, *Life and Correspondence of John A. Quitman* (New York: Harper and Brothers, 1860) 1:68, 70]; so JD did not leave for college before 1822, despite G. W. Jones in VHD, *Memoir* 1:27).

14. S. E. Davis to JD, June 25, 1823 (*Papers* 1::5, quots.; JD letter lost); Ibid., n.8.

15. VHD, *Memoir* 1:22–27 (JD quots.). Time at Transyl. in dispute: see G. W. Jones in *Life and Reminis.*, 107, 109; Jones, *Davis Memorial*, 54. He evidently entered as freshman 1822 (see *Papers* 1::124 and Note 13 above); qualified as soph. and as jr. by early fall; being classified as such in Jan. and June 1824 (*Papers* 1::6 nn.2, 7). He would have been sr. in fall 1824, but Joseph did not want him to graduate at "seventeen" (1825)—more evidence of 1808 birth date (VHD, *Memoir* 1:34; *Papers* 1:10).

16. VHD, *Memoir* 1:27–29 (quots. from JD, Jones, and Peters); Margaret Newman Wagers, *The Education of a Gentleman: Jefferson Davis at Transylvania, 1821–1824*, 9–10 (1824 curriculum; "natural philosophy"=physics), 37. Fleming, "Early Life," 173, 171: diff. curriculum, says JD had French at Transyl. with Constantine Rafinesque, a famous naturalist; but French not in either curriculum; he (and Mentelles) did teach French privately (Wright, *Lexington*, 32, 33). For Peters, see *Papers* 6:501.

17. *Papers* 1::24 n.7; Fleming, "Early Life," 172. Socinians and Unitarians, from 16th c.: no church or sacraments, only "delegated divinity" for Christ, morality the essence of religion—"salvation by character"—from European Transylvania (Williston Walker, *A History of the Christian Church* [New York: Charles Scribner's Sons, 1918], 451–53, 494–95, 576–78).

18. William Kavanaugh Doty, "The Reverend James Moore, First President of Transylvania University" (*The Transylvanian*, June 1907), 412–15; Wagers, *Education of a Gentleman*, epigraph to Part 2 (Holley quot.).

19. *Papers* 1::5 n.8; VHD, *Memoir*, 1:26 (JD quot.); Fleming, "Early Life," 169–70, quot.; Wagers, *Education of a Gentleman*, 10 (quots.), 24, 26, 29; WPJ, *Gen. ASJ*, 8 (ASJ quot.).

20. Wagers, *Education of a Gentleman*, 25, 28 and 10, quots.; VHD, *Memoir* 1:23–27 (JD quots.; ref. to Mark 5:12–13). Mr. Bishop taught philosophy and history, became president Miami Univ. in Ohio (JD thought Kenyon) (Fleming, "Early Life," 170–71). David Atchison was from Frogtown, Ky. (*Columbia Encyclopedia*).

21. Fleming, "Early Life," 170–71 (quots. from bsp. and student); Wagers, *Education of Gentleman*, 28, 36.

22. Fleming, "Early Life," 172 (church papers lamented "no Savior in Transylvania"); Wagers, *Education of a Gentleman*, 5, 8 (Holley accused of teaching morality

and beauty rather than "Christ Crucified"); Jones, *Davis Memorial*, 346–47 (Geo. Davis quots.).

23. KJV at First White House (given by VHD who directed its placing); *The New Testament: The Authorized English Version; with . . . Various Readings from the Three Most Celebrated Manuscripts of the Original Greek Text* by Constantine Tischendorf (Leipzig: Bernhard Tauchnig, 1869), flyleaf signed by JD; note: "Taken from his bedroom" (Jefferson Davis Book Collection, Old Capitol Museum of Mississippi History, MDAH). Codex Sinaiticus a 4th c. Greek MS.

24. JD to VHD, Nov. 3–4, 1865, MS, TRANSYL, quot. Other refs. to Greek and Latin in text below, passim.

25. Quots.: Lubbock, *Six Decades*, 655–56; JD in VHD, *Memoir* 1:24; James, *AJ, Border Capt.*, 358.

26. Quots.: transcript of audiotape, "JD" (Rosemont); A. H. Garland in *Life and Reminisc.*, 154; Unident. clipping in J. B. Price to JD, Sept. 1, 1889 (Rowland 10:133–35 n.2).

27. Quots.: VHD, *Memoir* 1:32, 29 (from JD and Peters); Wagers, *Education of Gentleman*, 9–10, n.16.

28. JD to Allen, July 24, 1840 (Rowland 1:4–5; quots.); JD, Speech at Oxford [Miss., July 15, 1852] (*Papers* 4:286–89, quots.).

29. *Papers* 1::7 and n.2 (quots.); VHD, *Memoir* 1:28–29 (quots.), 25; Fleming, "Early Life," 173–74; Wagers, *Education of a Gentleman*, 12–13 (Jones quot.).

30. Wagers, *Education of Gentleman*, 13; JD to Wm. L. Marcy, Feb. 10, 1851 (*Papers* 4:158–59 [quots.] and nn.); VHD, *Memoir* 1:29–31, quots. Ficklins: see Eliza Davis letter, 1840 (*Papers* 1::534); their brick house still stands at corner of Limestone and Clay, now put to commercial use.

31. Wagers, *Education of a Gentleman*, 15, 24–26 (Jones quots.), 37 n.59; VHD, *Memoir* 1:28 (Jones quots.; Peters: "I never heard him reprimanded . . . for misconduct of any sort" [29]). For JD and Clays, see *Papers* 4:107 and n.8.

32. Quots.: Wagers, *Education of Gentleman*, 25–26; Jones in *Life and Reminsc.*, 109; VHD, *Memoir* 1:29 (Peters); JD, Speech at Natchez, June 10, 1847 (*Papers* 3:182). JD told of swimming a river, rifle in hand (Sibley, "JD Recalls the Past," 169). On the Donelson nephews, see *Papers* 5:176; James, *AJ, Border Capt.*, 358.

33. Lewis Sanders, Jr., to JD, Nov. 30, 1839 (*Papers* 1::530, quots.); VHD, *Memoir* 1:30, quots. "Card"=newspaper art., editorial, or personal. JD pistols were seen in 1984 in Old Capitol Mus., MDAH. JD never fought duel in Lexington, "as far as we know" (Wagers, *Education of Gentleman*, 30, 13).

34. S. E. Davis to JD, June 25, 1823 (*Papers* 1::5, quots.); Ibid.:App. 4, Chart 13 and n.124 (Mary Ellen d. Mar. 2, 1824; 1824 birthdate of 2d daughter suggests childbed death).

35. VHD, *Memoir* 1:32–33; Stamps to JD, July 3, 1874 (*Papers* 1::9 n.7; father "had the [six] Negroes in the crop" at son Samuel A.'s place above Vicksburg [see 2:3 n.4], fell out with him, "took his Negroes to Vicksburg, bought a Boat and Shipped them with himself" to Davis Bend).

36. JD to Susannah Gartley Davis, Aug. 2, 1824 (*Papers* 1::9, quots.); S. E. Davis to JD, June 25, 1823 (ibid.::5, quot.); VHD, *Memoir* 1:32, quots.

37. JD in VHD, *Memoir* 1:33–36, quots.; JD to Amanda Davis Bradford, Aug. 2, 1824 (*Papers* 3:App. 3, p. 455, quot.).

38. *Papers* 1::24 (quots.) and nn.3, 6, 14; Wagers, *Education of Gentleman*, 38.

Chapter IV Army

1. JD to Calhoun, July 7, 1824 (*Papers* 1::8, quots.; and nn.2, 3, 5); JD in Senate, Feb. 15, 1859 (Rowland 3:559–60, quot.). See Stephen E. Ambrose, *Duty, Honor, Country: A History of West Point*, 25, 79.

2. Ambrose, *Duty, Honor,* 72; *Papers* 1::14 n.2 (see Rev. Ed.); Ibid.::11 Descr. Note and 74 n.6; VHD, *Memoir* 1:34–36 (JD quots.). On arithmetic, see William M. Polk, *Leonidas Polk, Bishop and General* 1:50–51.

3. Walter L. Fleming, "Jefferson Davis at West Point," 252–54; Ambrose, *Duty, Honor,* 64–66, 4 (see 71); *Papers* 1::30 n.2; *Polk* 1:54. On French math texts, see Freeman, *R. E. Lee* 1:63 n.10.

4. Elizabeth Stoddert Ewell to Benjamin Ewell, Aug. 1828, in Percy Gatling Hamlin, *"Old Bald Head" (General R. S. Ewell),* 4–5, quots.; *Papers* 1:110, 119, 21; Fleming, "JD at West Point," 256–57; Ambrose, *Duty, Honor,* 83.

5. VHD, *Memoir* 1:37 (JD quot.); *Papers* 1::116 ("Record of Delinquencies"), 118 n.1, quots. (demerit system explained).

6. *Papers* 1::11 (quot.), 48, 51, 65, 66, 84, 26 (quot.), 118, 55, 62; VHD, *Memoir* 1:51 (quot. from cadet).

7. VHD, *Memoir* 1:48–51, quots.; see *Papers* 1::19, 33 and n.1.

8. VHD, *Memoir* 1:51, 36.

9. JD, Speech, July 9, 1858 (Rowland 3:280, quot.); JD, Address, Apr. 6, 1883 (ibid. 9:206, quot.); JD in VHD, *Memoir* 1:36–37; WPJ, *Gen. ASJ,* 1, 9, 10.

10. WPJ, *Gen. ASJ,* 11 (quots. from Bartlett and JD), 72, 721, 728.

11. Quots.: Polk to Mother, Aug. 27, 1823, in *Polk* 1:52; Freeman, *R. E. Lee* 1:54; J. B. Hood, *Advance and Retreat,* 8.

12. WPJ, *Gen. ASJ,* 11 and 13 (JD quots.), 4, 5, 8, 76, 144, 162, 164; *Register of Graduates and Former Cadets of the United States Military Academy,* "Class of 1826."

13. WPJ, *Gen. ASJ,* 152, 24 (ASJ quot.).

14. VHD, *Memoir* 1:51, quot.; WPJ, *Gen. ASJ,* 723, 727, 4 (quot. from J. S. Chambers).

15. Ibid., 53 (quot. from Mrs. Geo. Hancock), 9 (quots.); Winnie Davis, "JD in Private Life," 3, 4 (JD quot.; Laurence Sterne, *The Life and Opinions of Tristram Shandy, Gentleman,* vol. 2, chap. 12).

16. *Polk* 1:55 (Polk quots.), 51–52 ("lofty self-respect kept him from secret evasions of his duty"); McElroy, *J.D.* 1:19, quot.

17. JD to E. L. Drake, 1877 (Rowland 8:28, quot.); JD, Address, Mar. 7, 1876 (Rowland 7:507, quot.).

18. WPJ, *Gen. ASJ,* 164 (ASJ quot., 1848), 728 (quots. from Col. J. W. Avery), 72, 90, 149, 155; Reagan, *Memoirs,* 165, quot. (see, e.g., N. D. Smith, "Reminisc. of JD," 179). "Honest" prob. still connoted "honorable," from Latin *honestus.* It comes through the French, where *honnête homme* meant "gentleman."

19. Jones, *Davis Memorial,* 272 (quot. from John W. Daniel); Ibid., 419–20, and *Life and Reminsc.,* 231 and 230 (quots. from the Rev. Charles Minnigerode); JD to Lucinda Davis Stamps, June 3, 1829 (*Papers* 2:App. 3, p. 718, quot.).

20. JD in Senate, Feb. 23, 1859 (Rowland 3:576, quot.); [Unknown] to JD, Nov. 25, 1858 (ibid., 360–62, quots.); Jones, *Davis Memorial,* 478 (quot. from *New Orleans Times-Democrat*).

21. Minnigerode in *Life and Reminisc.,* 227; JD, Address, Mar. 7, 1876 (Rowland 7:499; ref. to *Hamlet* 3.1.58: allusion fused with text typical of JD).

22. Twiggs to Jesup, Feb. 7, 1835 (*Papers* 1::451, quot.; JD under Twiggs 1829–31: see 146 Desc. Note, 149 Descr. Note and n.4, 267); JD, Address, July 10, 1878 (Rowland 8:232, quot.); JD in Richardson, *Conf.* 1:209, quot.

23. WPJ, *Gen. ASJ,* 5–10 (Eaton quots. on 10; became ASJ's friend for life); JD in Rowland 9:206; VHD, *Memoir* 1:37 (JD quot.); JD in Rowland 8:232.

24. JD to Joseph Davis, Jan. 12, 1825 (*Papers* 1::19, quots. [italics omitted] and n.13; Descr. Note: letter stolen by U.S. soldier from JD plantation, 1863); Polk to Father, n.d., in *Polk* 1:62–63, quot.; see 59 and 61).

25. Rowland 7:458 n.1, 512; VHD, *Memoir* 1:38–40; Jones, *Davis Memorial,* 57; *Register USMA,* "Class of 1825"; Fleming, "JD at West Point," 255; Bache in *Col. Encycl.* (Benjamin Franklin's "great-grandson"; JD errs: "grandson").

26. JD to Joseph Davis, Jan. 12, 1825 (*Papers* 1::19, quot.); Ibid.::34 and nn.; Proceedings of a General Court Martial, Specification 2d (ibid.::36, quot.). Benny Havens' and the Falls: ibid.::35 n.12, 36 n.16; Fleming, "JD at West Point," 261–63; Morris Schaff, *The Spirit of Old West Point, 1858–62,* 199–201 (famous song with refrain beginning, "Oh! Benny Havens, oh!").

27. *Papers* 1::34–42 (quots. on pp. 37, 40; Hays in 34 n.3). For Hays, who res'd. 1826, see ibid.::34 n.3.

28. VHD, *Memoir* 1:52, quots. (doubtless from JD). See Schaff, *Spirit of Old West Point,* 153, on furloughs. JD had leave Aug. 7–20, 1826; color guard appt. Aug. 30; listed "sick" Aug. 31 (*Papers* 1::61–63). LaSere: ibid. 2::222 n.11. Variant on the fall by Thomas Drayton, classmate and friend, in Jones, *Davis Memorial,* 560.

29. *Papers* 1::63 and n.1, and App. 5, p. 531 (quot.; 530–33: JD "sick" only 6 other times in 4 years); JD to VHD, Oct. 11–12, 1865, MS, TRANSYL, quot.; ASJ in *Register USMA,* "Class of 1826." Lee came June 1825 (Freeman, *R. E. Lee* 1:48).

30. *Polk* 1:70–78 (quots.). The other cadet bapt. was W. B. Magruder, not to be confused with John B., who entered later that year. *BCP* (1830) (quot. from "Ministration of Baptism, to such as are of riper years . . ."; Mg. Prayer rubric has "all kneeling" for confession).

31. WPJ, *Gen. ASJ,* 721, 243 (ASJ quot.), 720 (quots., incl. ASJ, from address of Col. Munford, 1871) and see 724–25. Author finds no evidence for Fleming's word, often copied, that JD and ASJ "soon followed" Polk in kneeling ("JD at West Point," 265); see WPJ, 721: ASJ still saying to Polk 1839: "if I could be convinced."

32. JD to Stephen Elliott, July 8, 1864 (Rowland 6:284, quot.); JD to W. M. Polk, *Polk* 1:326, quot.

33. Evans, "JD, His Diseases," 1–2; Charles Pettit McIlvaine in Perry, *Bsps. of Am. Church,* 65, quot. (bsp. of Ohio 1832); JD to McIlvaine, Sept. 16, 1850 (Rowland 1:578, quots.). Conjecture on thoughts based partly on JD letters while ill 1865.

34. Sibley, "JD Recalls Past," 175–77 (quots. from WPJ; see nn. 13 and 15 for JD's aid to Hopkins in 1859 and to Thomas S. Twiss, a math prof.).

35. *Papers* 1::68–87, 90, and nn., 81 n.6; Fleming, "JD at West Point," 264 (JD quot.). All the boys involved were Southern except four, one of whom was Davis's friend Wright.

36. VHD, *Memoir* 1:52–54, quots; *Papers* 1::102, 103, 35 n.6. The laboratory was at this time in "The Academy," a building that also housed the chapel, library, classrooms, and adj.'s office (Freeman, *R. E. Lee* 1:56).

37. VHD, *Memoir* 1:53 and 567 (quots.), 2:301–2; *Papers* 1::37, p. 40 (JD quot.). "The Children in the Wood" is title in *Reliques of Ancient English Poetry* by Thomas Percy.

38. *Register USMA,* "Class of 1831"; *SHSP* 17:191 (JD quot.); Robert E. Lee [Jr.], *Recollections and Letters of General Robert E. Lee,* 267–68, quot.; Gilbert E. Govan and James W. Livingood, *A Different Valor,* 14–15 (quot.); Freeman, *R. E. Lee* 1:55, 74. The fistfight story, told by a Yankee soldier, is in James A. Bethune to W. L. Fleming, June 2, 1908 (MS, Fleming Collection).

39. Fleming, "JD at West Point," 264 n.35; *Papers* 1::78, 80. See Schaff, *Spirit of Old West Point,* 77, 282: formed the "habit of truth-telling"; "dear old Alma mater, Fountain of Truth."

40. *Polk* 1:81–83, 86, 88 (quot.), 89. Graduates expected (before 1838) to serve a year; all got promissory "brevet" rank of 2d lieut.; dependent on vacancy in regular places for permanent rank; had to wait sometimes for years; many allowed to resign, in order to reduce number (Ambrose, *Duty, Honor,* 32, 70–71, 85, 117; *Papers* 1::122 n.5).

41. *Papers* 1::77 n.16 (Drayton), 102 n.8 and 317 (Gardenier), 447 (Holmes), 447 (and n.10), 455 (p. 368) and 462 (Izard); *Register USMA,* "Class of 1828," Ambrose, *Duty, Honor,* 93, and VHD, *Memoir* 1:54 (Church); *Papers* 1::75 n.16, and

Rowland 7–9, passim (Wright). Others on frontier: B. W. Kinsman, Robt. Sevier; in C.S.A.: Hugh Mercer, Gustave Rousseau, John B. Magruder; see W. H. C. Bartlett in VHD, *Memoir* 1:40–41.

42. Quots.: Winnie Davis, "JD in Private Life," 9, 4; James Campbell in *Life and Reminisc.*, 133; N. D. Smith, "Reminisc. of JD," 180; VHD, *Memoir* 2:918 and 1:41–42 (JD uses "classmates" loosely; both ASJ and Polk in class ahead).

43. *Papers* 1::121–123, 124 (JD to Winfield Scott, quots.), 126 (see n.6: Cooper adj. gen. for JD as both U.S. sec. of war and pres. of Conf.); Ibid. 3:251 (6th Inf.).

44. Janet Sharp Hermann, *Joseph E. Davis: Pioneer Patriarch*, 78–79, 91; *Papers* 1::534, 361 and n.8, 439.

45. R. Jackson to Mrs. Eliz. Watson, July 18 [1828] (*Correspondence of Andrew Jackson*, ed. John Spencer Bassett, 3:415–16, quot.; see n.); Alderson and McBride, *Landmarks of Tenn. Hist.*, 9. The Jacksons knew that Rachel's divorce had been granted by N. C. legis., but not that the final decree was held up in court, so there was no moral guilt, but legal fault. They remarried in 1794 (Leona Taylor Aiken, *Donelson, Tennessee: Its History and Landmarks*, 272).

46. Sibley, "JD Recalls Past," 173 (JD quots., paraphrase); Marquis James, *Andrew Jackson*, 164–75 (quot. from Rachel; ref. to Ps. 84:10; AJ thought slander killed her).

47. *Papers* 1::19 n.3, Rev. Ed., 362 n.12, 363 and n.1; Ibid.:App. 4, Charts 8, 6, 4, 11; Samuel A. et al. in chap. 2 above; VHD, *Memoir* 1:48.

48. *Papers* 1::123 (quot.) and n.3, 138 and n.2, 144, 152 (see 1::5 and n. 4); McElroy, *JD* 1:20–21 (JD quots.). McElroy seems to place the story at Fort Crawford.

49. VHD, *Memoir* 1:55; Russell F. Weigley, *History of the United States Army*, 171; WPJ, *Gen. ASJ*, 17–18, 21, 13, 48 (quot.); JD to VHD, Oct. 20, 1865, MS, TRANSYL, quot.

50. WPJ, *Gen. ASJ*, 21–24 and 47, quots.; *Papers* 1::301 n.7; Weigley, *Hist. U.S. Army*, 170; JD to VHD, Dec. 30, 1865–Jan. 1, 1866, MS, TRANSYL, quot.

51. *Papers* 1::142 and n.2 (see front end paper map), 144–55, 168, 173–290 (duties May 1829–June 24, 1831; quot. in 178; see esp. 264 n.11, 212 n.8); VHD, *Memoir* 1:81–82 and 72–73, quots.

52. VHD, *Memoir* 1:81, quots. VHD seems to connect JD's pneumonia with building a sawmill, but the only "sick" Return is Mar. 1833 at Fort Crawford (*Papers* 1::352), and the only record *re* a sawmill is his supervising one already built, July–Aug. 1831 (ibid.::272 and n.2). Author takes stories from V., who doubtless had them from JD, but places and dates from *Papers*. The two sources cannot be harmonized entirely. The confusion has misled many, as noted in "The Northwestern Career of Jefferson Davis" by M. M. Quaife (1923). It was righted considerably by P. L. Scanlon in "The Military Record of Jefferson Davis in Wisconsin" (1940). Bruce E. Mahan's *Old Fort Crawford and the Frontier* (1926), not primarily about JD, is a full and accurate history that sheds much light.

53. *Papers* 1::239 (see 222, 234), 159–60, 190, 156–58, 172, 254, et al.; JD to James D. Butler, Feb. 22, 1885 (Rowland 9:345, quot.); VHD, *Memoir* 1:59–60, 76 (quot.).

54. VHD, *Memoir* 1:77–79, quots.; *Papers* 1:192, 205, 211, 215.

55. VHD, *Memoir* 1:67–69, 138 (quot.; refs. here hopelessly confused: rescue of boy may belong to JD's dragoon service); JD to VHD, Feb. 3–4, 1866, MS, TRANSYL.

56. VHD, *Memoir* 2:305, 1:66–67, 99 (Chippewa the Indian "court language"), 264; JD to VHD, Oct. 11–12, 1865, MS, TRANSYL, quot.; Winnie Davis, "JD in Private Life," 5, quots. In First White House is a woven "slipper case," VHD's note says, made for JD by "Wisconsin Indians."

57. Winnie Davis, "JD in Private Life," 2, quot.; *Chesnut*, 531, quots.; VHD, *Memoir* 1:80, quots.

58. H. Montgomery, *The Life of Major-General Zachary Taylor*, 33, quot.; Holman

Hamiliton, *Zachary Taylor: Soldier of the Republic* (hereafter called vol. 1), 77, 79. Snelling was the northernmost post in the area, at junction of St. Peter's and Miss. Rivers.

59. VHD, *Memoir* 1:113, 31 (quots. on 122, 129–30; see 201–2 for Gaines's peculiar speech); *Papers* 1::267, 268; WPJ, *Gen. ASJ*, 29–32; JD in Rowland 9:184. Gaines and Scott swapped command of east and west, the only departments, every 2 yrs. (Weigley, *Hist. U.S. Army*, 170).

60. *Papers* 1::267 n.8, 268, 278; WPJ, *Gen. ASJ*, 24–25, 144 (JD quots.). For WPJ, see also VHD, *Memoir* 1:96–97.

61. *Papers* 1::272, 274, 277; Hamilton, *Zachary Taylor* 1:119 (quot. from traveler), 112; Mahan, *Old Fort Crawford*, 243; VHD, *Memoir* 1:74; JD to Lucinda Stamps, June 3, 1829 (*Papers* 2::32 n.11 and App. 3, p. 718).

62. VHD, *Memoir* 1:97–101 and 104 and n., quots. The French were mostly Canadian *voyageurs*.

63. Hamilton, *Zachary Taylor* 1:112, 118–19; T. C. Reynolds to JD, Jan. 4, 1883, and JD to Reynolds, Jan. 5 (Rowland 9:198–200, JD quot.); Jones, *Davis Memorial*, 52–53 (Harney quots.).

64. Mahan, *Old Fort Crawford*, 245–49; VHD, *Memoir* 1:63–64 (quot.), 73; Quaife, "Northwestern Career of JD," 7 (quots.).

65. McElroy, *JD* 1:22–23 (quot.); Hamilton, *Zachary Taylor* 1:102–3 and n.12. In the story ZT is laughing, not indignant.

66. Rowland 2:582 n.1; *Papers* 1::264 n.10 (JD quot.; Trelawny a friend of Shelley and Byron). Heitman, *Hist. Register*, wrongly gives birthplace as La.: see Harney in *The South in the Building of the Nation* 11, and Rowland 2:175. Dabney Maury tells a hair-raising story of Harney's prowess in *Recollections of a Virginian in the Mexican, Indian, and Civil Wars*, 43–44.

67. VHD, *Memoir* 1:74 and 64 (quots.), 73; *Papers* 1::264 n.10 (JD quot.); Hamilton, *Zachary Taylor* 1:117. (Hunting:) ibid., 119, and Mahan, *Old Ft. Crawford*, 251. The army issued a "whiskey ration" (actually rum), and as comm. off., JD once had "115 14/100 galls whiskey" charged to his account (*Papers* 1::417).

68. *Papers* 1::212; Quaife, "Northwestern Career of JD," 8, quots. (see 6); *Papers* 1::271 n.1, 231 and n.9); Ibid.:: 271 (quot. from Marsh Diary; "Bill" prob. means itemized list); JD described the Stockbridge tribe in 1851 (*Papers* 4:157 and n.7).

69. *Papers* 1::149 n.4 (Twiggs made lt. col. of 4th Inf.), 278, 237 n.4, 272 and n.2 (cf. Hamilton, *Zachary Taylor* 1:114), 282, 287 (assigned to Dubuque, Oct. 11, 1831), 291 n.2 (JD quot.), 294 (Morgan quots.) and n.6.

70. *Papers* 1::303, 316; Jones in *Life and Reminisc.*, 107–9, quot.; VHD, *Memoir* 1:58–59; *Papers* 1::163 n.3, suggests JD on leave; but the "sergeant" with him renders this unlikely.

71. *Papers* 1::313, 317, 322 and n.4; VHD, *Memoir* 1:96, quot.; Joseph Davis to JD, July 9, 1832 (*Papers* 1::328, quots.). Preston's childhood name "Willie" or "Will" (WPJ, *Gen. ASJ*, 155, 122).

72. Hamilton, *Zachary Taylor* 1:81–90 (quots. on 89–90 from ZT to [Gen. T. S.] Jesup, Dec. 4, 1832; Morgan d. Apr. 4; ZT arr. May 7); Mahan, *Old Ft. Crawford*, 166–71.

73. WPJ, *Gen. ASJ*, 33–45 (quots. on 36, 37); Hamilton, *Zachary Taylor* 1:87–99 (quot. on 94); VHD, *Memoir* 1:138–43 (JD quot. on 140). See also Mahan, *Old Ft. Crawford*, 165–78; *Papers* 1::334 n.6 and App. 2, p. 486 n.14. Dodge col. Mich. vols. 1832 in Heitman, *Hist. Register;* but maj. gen. Mo. militia in *DAB*.

74. JD to P. Howard, June 20 [1887] (Rowland 9:569, quot.); VHD, *Memoir* 1:133; G. W. Jones in *Life and Reminisc.*, 110–11; Hamiliton, *Zachary Taylor*, 91–94. JD ref. to 1832 also in letter to Buch., *Papers* 1::322 n.4, p. 242; the earlier *staff* duty prob. explains why JD "Joined Co. August 18," not *arrived* then (ibid::332); ZT arrived in May but was not at his post until Aug. 4 (Hamilton, 87, 97). Date confusion may explain absence of Black Hawk War in JD record, *Register USMA*.

75. Hamilton, *Zachary Taylor* 1:95 (JD quots. on Wisc. Hgts.); WPJ, *Gen. ASJ*, 38 (quot.), 36 (U.S. off. acting with militia); Sibley, "JD Recalls Past," 170 (JD quot.); *Papers* 6:133 n.7 (JD quot.).

76. *Papers* 1::332; VHD, *Memoir* 1:141–42 (JD quots.). Black Hawk taken Aug. 27; surr. to the Indian agent Gen. Street at Ft. Crawford (*Papers* 1::334 n.6 and 386 n.3).

77. *Papers* 1:App. 2, p. 486, n.15; 1::334 and nn.2, 5; VHD, *Memoir* 1:142 (quots.); *Papers* 1::386 (quots. from Black Hawk, *Life*, dictated by him 1833; ref. to ball and chain at Jeff. Barracks). Army also used flogging, branding, and tar-and-feathers: see ibid.::385, nn.2, 4.

78. *Papers* 1::386 and 334 n.2; Sibley, "JD Recalls Past," 170 (quot. from WPJ-JD conversation). Indian leaders known as "Lions of the West" ("Black Hawk at Fort Monroe" in *Tales of Old Fort Monroe*); names in *Papers* 1::335.

79. Pipe, donated by Jefferson Hayes-Davis 1965, in Casemate Mus.; "Black Hawk at Fort Monroe" in *Tales of Old Fort Monroe;* Mahan, *Old Ft. Crawford*, 176–78; *Papers* 1::334 n.6.

80. WPJ, *Gen. ASJ*, 47, quot.; *Papers* 1::339–43.

81. Mahan, *Old Ft. Crawford*, 177–78, 198–200; VHD, *Memoir* 1:84–89 (quots. from JD and Jones, who gives wrong date); Jones in *Life and Reminisc.*, 111–15, quots. (right date: "cold winter of 1832–33," after war and treaty); JD to Jones, Aug. 8, 1882 (Rowland 9:183–85, quot.).

82. *Papers* 1::349 and n.2, 350, 353, 354, 404 and n.1, 366 (quot. from JD letter, July 24, 1833), 375; VHD, *Memoir* 1:149. Dodge had left militia to be maj. in U.S. army, heading Mounted Rangers which evolved into 1st Dragoons (*Papers* 1::370 n.2; Weigley, *Hist. U.S. Army*, 159). On Mason, see *Papers* 1::375 n.8.

83. VHD, *Memoir* 1:149 (JD quot.), 145–146 (quots.); *Papers* 1::357–60, 353 n.3, 361 n.4, 362 n.6; Wright, *Lexington*, 43–45 (Clay quot. and last quot.). Three family members wrote to JD at this time expressing concern over the cholera (*Papers* 1::361–363).

84. *Papers* 1::367, 369–385, 387–390 (JD also post adj. Oct. 2–21), 392–394, 397; [John] Doran to JD, June 11, 1886 (ibid.::367 n.3, quots.); Hamlin, *Ewell*, 12 (jacket trim); VHD, *Memoir* 1:90 (JD quot.).

85. *Papers* 1::372, 373; D. Bradford to JD, June 18, 1834 (ibid.::419, quot., and see 395 nn.20–22); WPJ, *Gen. ASJ*, 47–53. "Uncle" and "Aunt" used for favorite servants, as still in the South for close friends of parents.

86. *Papers* 1::397 and n.4 (quots.); VHD, *Memoir* 1:155–56, quot. (see 198).

87. Mason to Jesup, Aug. 30, 1834 (*Papers* 1::421 and nn.; JD had qm. and comm. duties: see also 424–38, 440, 442, 446); VHD, *Memoir* 1:149, 153–54 (quots. and Doran letter). Creeks and Cherokees were 2 of the Five Civilized Tribes forced to move from the East to what is now Oklahoma, some Cherokees not until 1838 ("Cherokees" and "Creeks" in *Universal Encycl.*).

88. VHD, *Memoir* 1:155–56, quots.; Winnie Davis, "JD in Private Life," 8, quot. ("Hoe cakes" consisted of corn meal, water, and salt); *Papers* 1::420 and n.6, 421, 424; Weigley, *Hist. U.S. Army*, 160 (on this march, June 18–Aug. 16, 1834, heat reached 114 degrees in the shade).

89. JD in Senate, June 11, 1850 (Rowland 1:359–60, quots.); VHD, *Memoir* 1:27–28 (Jones quots.); *Papers* 1::401–3; Dodge to Jones, Apr. 18, 1834 (ibid.::409, quot.).

90. *Papers* 1::458 (quots. from JD's "Defense," p. 381); G. A. McCall [Gaines's ADC] to Arbuckle, Jan. 22, 1834 (ibid.::449, quot.), 507; *Papers* 1::455, p. 363, quot.

91. *Papers* 1::454 (p. 358, quots.), 458 (p. 381, quot.) n.28. After the War between the States, JD, charged with treason and unable to secure a trial, refused to ask pardon, and said the North, not the South, had violated the Const. and the original concept of the Union.

92. *Papers* 1::454–458, 471 (quots. on pp. 378, 379, 366, 382 n.28, 381, 358, 398).

93. *Papers* 1::454–458 (quots. on pp. 377, 375, 380, 361; see also p. 360 on health); Goldsborough, "Varina Howell Davis," 17–18.

94. *Papers* 1::447, 456 and nn. 20, 21, 459–464, 467, 469, 472; LBN in *Biographical Dictionary of the Confederacy*, ed. Jon L. Wakelyn.

95. LBN in *DAB;* Jerrold Northrop Moore, *Confederate Commissary General: Lucius Bellinger Northrop*, 1, 7–8, quots.; *Papers* 1::459–61. LBN and JD often speak of horses in corr., 1878–87, Rowland 8 and 9.

96. *Papers* 1::467; JD to LBN, Mar. 17, 1879 (Rowland 8:369, quots.); VHD, *Memoir* 2:303; *Lalla Rookh* in *Oxford Companion to English Literature* (Oxford: Clarendon Press, 1946). For Kingsbury, Bowman, Trenor, see *Papers* 1::213 n.2, 455 n.20, 440 n.3.

97. VHD, *Memoir* 2:918, quots.; LBN to JD, Apr. 17 and May 14, 1879 (Rowland 8:379–80, 390, quots.; "Vindegres" prob. mistake for Verdigris [River]: see *Papers* 1:front endpaper map).

98. JD to LBN, Apr. 25, 1879 (ibid. 383–84, quot.). Wm. Whistler was lt. col. 7th Inf. at Ft. Gibson in 1834 (Heitman, *Hist. Register*, 95, 1026); at Green Bay when major in 2d Inf. (WPJ, *Gen. ASJ*, 19).

99. LBN to JD, May 14, 1879 (Rowland 8:390, quots.); JD to LBN, Apr. 25 (ibid., 383–84, quots.; ref. to 1 Cor. 13:13). Whistler retired as col. of 4th Inf., 1861; d. Dec. 4, 1863 (Heitman, *Hist. Register*, 1026).

100. JD to LBN, Apr. 25, 1879 (Rowland 8:383, quots.); VHD, *Memoir* 1:94–96 (quots. from either Col. H. L. Dousman or "Mrs. McRee": punctuation confused; see JD in Sibley, "JD Recalls the Past," 177). Dousman agent of Am. Fur Co. (Mahan, *Old Fort Crawford*, 142).

101. JD to Mason and Arbuckle, Mar. 1 and 2, 1835 (*Papers* 1::465, 466); Arbuckle to R. Jones, Mar. 10 and May 12 (ibid. ::470, 476 (quot. in Encl. 2); LBN to JD, Dec. 15, 1879 (Rowland 8:433, quots.).

Chapter V Marriage

1. Arbuckle to McCall [ADC to Gaines], May 12, 1835 (*Papers* 1::477, quot.). See ibid.::480, 486, 492 (asks forward to Washington; effective June 30).

2. G. W. Jones to JD, Dec. 9, 1880 (Rowland 8:532–33, quots. from ZT's friend, Col. Dousman, friend); Hamilton, *Zachary Taylor* 1:81–82, 97, 101. 75, 57 (Knox b. Mar. 6, 1814; see *Papers* 1::484 and n.4); *Papers* 1::443 n.2.

3. Walter L. Fleming, "Jefferson Davis's First Marriage," 32–35, quots.

4. *Papers* 1::443 n.2, 483 n.8 (ZT "gave his consent"). For JD's movements, see chap. 4 above.

5. Hamilton, *Zachary Taylor* 1:21–25, 115–16 (Scott quots.); Silas Bent McKinley and Silas Bent, *Old Rough and Ready: The Life and Times of Zachary Taylor*, 15–26; JD, Speech, 1852 (Rowland 2:174, quots.).

6. JD, Speech (to Conf. vets.), July 10, 1878 (Rowland 8:234, quot.); JD in Senate, Aug. 5, 1850 (ibid. 1:470–71, quots.; notes this in T. J. Jackson, ibid. 9:166–67; Dabney Maury also speaks of it in *Recoll.*, 57, 59, 71–72); H. Montgomery, *The Life of Major-General Zachary Taylor*, 462, quot.

7. Fleming, "JD's First Marriage," 32 (quot. from cousin); Mahan, *Old Fort Crawford*, 138–39 (and pic. facing p. 129); Hamilton, *Zachary Taylor* 1:37, xvi (under 1823 and 1831), 72, 81–82.

8. G. W. Jones to JD, Dec. 9, 1880 (Rowland 8:532–33, quots.). See Fleming, "JD's First Marriage," 29–30 (5 diff. false "elopements"); Quaife, "Northwestern Career of JD," 16–18.

9. Hamilton, *Zachary Taylor* 1:101 (ZT quot.). Jones, *Davis Memorial*, 449–50 (JD, 1888, rejects "baseless scandal of a romantic elopement" in *Appleton's Cyclopedia of American Biography*).

10. Sibley, "JD Recalls the Past," 177 (quot. from WPJ-JD conversation). The incident is in chap. 4 above.

11. Fleming, "JD's First Marriage," 32 (quot. from cousin), 27 (Mary's father was Gen. J. M. Street); *New York Times*, Oct. 20, 1906 (Betty Taylor quotes Knox, in letter signed "D. B. C."); VHD, *Memoir* 1:95; see *Papers* 1::332, 343, 347 (JD in MacRee's co.). MacRee also sp. McRee and McCree.

12. *Papers* 1::443, n.16 (says only extant letter, but see VHD in 2::20 Descr. Note); Lynda Lasswell Crist, "A Bibliographical Note: Jefferson Davis's Personal Library: All Lost, Some Found," 189–90 (a soldier "took a packet of letters with the name of Davis' first wife on it").

13. JD to Sarah Knox Taylor, Dec. 16, 1834 (*Papers* 1::443, quots.; ellipsis concerns "wretch"; he calls her "Knox" in summarized passage; "friends"="family"; French: "goodbye my dear, very dear, friend, goodbye; "au Recrire" prob. "till we write again," an analogy of "au revoir").

14. VHD, *Memoir* 1:161–62, quot.; Eliza Davis to JD, Nov. 17, 1834 (*Papers* 1::439, quots.). "Wild horse" may be one JD bought because nobody else could ride him (Sibley, "JD Recalls the Past," 173); VHD descr. one in VHD, *Memoir* 1:194–95.

15. Fleming, "JD's First Marriage," 27, 31, 32–33 and n.14; *New York Times* letter (as in Note 11 above), quot.; S. Knox Taylor to Mother, June 17, 1835, in Hamilton, *Zachary Taylor* 1:106, quot; VHD, *Memoir* 1:162.

16. William H. Samson, ed., *Letters of Zachary Taylor from the Battle-fields of the Mexican War*, xii; Fleming, "J D.'s First Marriage," 33, 27.

17. *Papers* 1::469, 470; Ibid.:App. 1, p. 475; VHD, *Memoir* 1:162 (JD quot.); WPJ, *Gen. ASJ*, 52, quot. (res'd. Apr. 24, 1834), 53 (quot. from Mrs. Geo. Hancock).

18. Fleming, "JD's First Marriage," 31, 33 n.14; Hamilton, *Zachary Taylor* 1:59, 74, 106; Sarah Knox Taylor Davis to Mother, June 17, 1835 (ibid., 106, quots.). This Elizabeth Taylor m. John Gibson Taylor, a second cousin (*New York Times* letter [as in Note 11 above]).

19. Fleming, "JD's First Marriage," 32–33 (quots. from cousin) and n.14 (bond; see *Papers* 1::484); Hamilton, *Zachary Taylor*, 1:106, 107, 22. JD's handmade "wedding vest" of ecru silk, decorated in a random trapunto design, is at Beauvoir.

20. Hamilton, *Zachary Taylor*, 107; VHD, *Memoir* 1:162; Fleming, "JD's First Marriage," 33 (quot. from cousin); Samson, *Letters of ZT*, x (J. T. Wood b. Fort Snelling, Aug. 13, 1830).

21. D. Clayton James, *Antebellum Natchez*, 267; S. Knox Taylor to Mother, June 17, 1835, in Hamilton, *Zachary Taylor*, 1:106, quots. (from MS: see n.18).

22. Hamilton, *Zachary Taylor* 1:107; *BCP* (1830) (quot. from "Solemnization of Matrimony"); *Bishop Whipple's Southern Diary, 1843–44*, ed. Lester B. Shippee, 121–31, quots. Joseph Davis mentions "timber sales to passing steam vessels" in 1850 (*Papers* 5:123 n.6).

23. Everett, *Brierfield*, passim, and endpaper maps (his 25 mi. tallies with JD in Rowland 9:406, though VHD, *Memoir* 1:47 and 187, has 36); James T. Currie, *Enclave: Vicksburg and her Plantations, 1863–1870*, map on 84; Currie, "Freedmen at Davis Bend, Apr. 1864," nn.5, 8, 13, 14 (ident. landowners); Refs. in Davis corr.

24. Eliza Davis to JD, Nov. 17, 1834 (*Papers* 1::439, quots.); Ibid.::328 n.2 and Strode, *Patriot*, 101; Everett, *Brierfield*, 14.

25. Everett, *Brierfield*, 10; VHD, *Memoir* 1:192–93, quots.

26. VHD, *Memoir* 1:192–93, quots. (ref. to Gen. 6:19–20); Everett, *Brierfield*, 47–48.

27. VHD, *Memoir* 1:193, quots.

28. Portrait at Rosemont (guide there mentioned following art., but said portrait by Benj. West, 1824); Sara E. Lewis Flanary, "William Edward West in New Orleans

and Mississippi," 1015 (Fig. 4: portrait of Joseph, "c. 1818"), 1010–12 (Wm. E. West in Europe 1823). Benj. West left Am. 1760, d. in Eng. 1820; Strode, *Patriot*, caption says, portrait 1824 in N. Y. "by Raphael West," but this son of Benj. was in U.S. only 1800–1802 (George C. Groce and David H. Wallace, *The New-York Historical Society's Dictionary of Artists in America, 1564–1860* [New Haven: Yale Univ. Press, 1957], 674–76).

29. Eliza portrait (provenance unknown) at Rosemont. The only ref. to one of Samuel is in Fleming, "Early Life," 155 n.12: cites JD as saying "1823 or 1824" by "*English* artist named West" (italics mine); Fleming says "unable to locate." An *American* Wm. West (*not* Wm. E.) painted in Phila. 1823, when Samuel Davis was there (Groce and Wallace, *N. Y. Hist. Soc. Dict.*, 674–76; *Papers* 1::5).

30. Everett, *Brierfield*, 10–13, quots.; VHD, *Memoir* 1:193–94; *Papers* 1::328 n.2, p. 248, and 3:119 n.16; Flanary, "William Edward West," 1011 (caption to Plate 2; workshop uses).

31. Everett, *Brierfield*, 12 and 14 (quots.), 19; *Papers* 1::328 n.2, p. 248, quots.

32. Everett, *Brierfield*, 14–15 (many illegible stones), 151 n.7 (Mrs. Wallace; see VHD, *Memoir* 1:6); *Papers* 1:App. 4, Chart 11 and Chart 9 (Rev. Ed.; David Bradford, Jr., and Isaac's son Lewis Davis). One illegible stone may be for Joseph's 1st wife, d. between 1823 (birth of last child) and 1827 (when Joseph remarried), ibid., Chart 5, see 1971 ed., App. 4, n.25; Samuel buried there 1824 (Davis Bend gravestone, now at Beauvoir).

33. H. R. Howard, *The History of Virgil A. Stewart, and . . . Execution of . . . Murrell's Associates in . . . Mississippi during the Summer of 1835 . . .*, 227, quot.; Reuben Davis, *Recollections of Mississippi and Mississippians*, 197–98; Robert M. Coates, *The Outlaw Years*, 239–42, 280–83; Gwin to Van Buren, Aug. 15, 1835, in Miles, *Jacksonian Democracy*, 126–27, quot. (Miles treats plot as fact).

34. R. Davis, *Recoll. of Miss.*, 41 (see Henry S. Foote, *Casket of Reminiscences*, 261).

35. The official "Proceedings at Livingston," in *Hist. V. A. Stewart*, 221–62 (quot. on 235); Augustus Q. Walton, *A History of . . . John A. Murel, the Great Western Land Pirate; . . . Plan of Exciting a Negro Rebellion . . .* (Athens, Tenn.: George White, 1835); Robert M. Coates, *The Outlaw Years: The History of the Land Pirates of the Natchez Trace* (New York: Literary Guild of America, 1930), 169–301, esp. 280–96; James Lal Penick, Jr., in *The Great Western Land Pirate: John A. Murrell in Legend and History* (Columbia: Univ. of Missouri Press, 1981) says plot a fiction; ignores witness to its reality in, e.g., Howard, 223–25, 228–29, 235–37, and crucial evidence in "Proceedings." See Edwin A. Miles, "The Mississippi Slave Insurrection Scare of 1835" (*Journal of Negro History* 42 [Jan. 1957]: 48–60), an objective study.

36. *Chesnut*, 211–12, quots. (see 198, 209, 218; the murderers were pampered servants; so was Nat Turner who massacred whites in Virginia: see Clement Eaton, *Freedom of Thought in the Old South*, 92).

37. *Chesnut*, 245, 564, quots.; Louise Wigfall Wright, *A Southern Girl in '61*, 15; Ulrich Bonnell Phillips, *Life and Labor in the Old South*, 164; Parton, *Life of AJ*, 678, quot. Strong sense of propriety in blacks: see, e.g., *Chesnut*, 464: one refusing to "wait on pine tables."

38. JD, Speech to Dem. meeting, Oct. 19, 1858 (Rowland 3:337, quots.); VHD, *Memoir* 1:163 (Everett, *Brierfield*, 26, says twenty). "The haze of bitterness" which "still remains to cloud the true picture of slavery in the South" (1930) came from the ignorance of the Northern pamphleteers (Coates, *Outlaw Years*, 236 and n.2).

39. Phillips, *Life and Labor*, 339, 352–53; Fogel and Engerman, *Time on the Cross*, 52–57.

40. Hurricane originally 5,000 A. (VHD, *Memoir* 1:48); Brierfield: 1,290 A. (*Papers* 3:414, in 1846 tax rpt.; other estimates: 4:364, 6:549, 666; Everett, *Brierfield*, 77, 24); Hurricane: c. 2,960 A. (ibid., 24). Both in "large planter" category

(Warren I. Smith, "Land Patterns in Ante-Bellum Montgomery County, Alabama" [*Alabama Review*, July 19, 1955], 200).

41. VHD, *Memoir* 1:163, quots. See *New York Times* letter (in Note 11 above), and *Papers* 1::9 n.7.

42. JD to VHD, Oct. 20, 1865, MS, TRANSYL, quots.; *Papers* 1::9 n.7; "Diary of a Mississippi Planter, Jan. 1, 1840, to Apr., 1863," ed. Franklin L. Riley, 332, quot. See Bassett, *Corr. of A J* 6:239–40.

43. See, e.g., Joseph Davis to JD, Jan. 19 and Feb. 19, 1838, and Apr. 16, 1847 (*Papers* 1::518, 521; 3:165) and JD to VHD, Aug. 21, 1865, MS, TRANSYL; also *Chesnut*, 535, 33–34, 53, 462–63 (with scenes of intimacy between the races).

44. JD to W. J. Blackburn, July 13, 1888 (Rowland 10:75, quot.).

45. Jefferson Davis, "The Doctrine of State Rights," 218, quots. "*Service for life*, on condition of protection and support, is the *essence* of American slavery" (Samuel Seabury, *American Slavery Distinguished from the Slavery of English Theorists, and Justified by the Law of Nature* [New York: Mason Brothers, 1861] 202, and see 194, 197–203; 189–96 shows legal protection).

46. JD in Senate, Mar. 8, 1850 (Rowland 1:315, quots.). U.S. Const.: slaves "Persons" only (Art. 1, Sec. 9 and Art. 4, Sec. 2). JD to C.S. Cong., Nov. 7, 1864: distinguishes "service" as "property" and relation to state as person (Richardson, *Conf.* 1:493–94). See Fulkerson, *Random Recoll.*, 131–32; *Bishop Whipple's Diary*, 183; *Cong. Globe*, 31st Cong., 1st sess., App., 282 (Senator Butler of S. C.: feeling "would revolt" at master killing slave); Lonn, *Foreigners in Conf.*, 472.

47. VHD, *Memoir* 1:164, quots.; S. Knox Taylor Davis to Mother, Aug. 11, 1835 (*Papers* 1:App. 1, p. 475, quots.); Hamilton, *Zachary Taylor* 1:65, 68–69 (quots. from ZT letter), 37. "The fever" dreaded, but diff. in malaria, yellow, typhoid, and typhus unknown; new theories of separate kinds discussed by Dr. F. E. Gordon, "On Continued Fevers," in the *New-Orleans Medical and Surgical Journal*, 1853.

48. Mosquito transmission discovered 1897 (V. S. LeQuire, M. D., to author, Dec. 19, 1986); VHD, *Memoir* 1:164, quot.; J. M. Da Costa, *Medical Diagnosis with Special Reference to Practical Medicine* . . . [1866], 687, quot. ("Periodical Fevers" all due "to that poison"). Inspecting site for prison 1864, Dr. Isaiah H. White found some "decaying vegetable matter" apt to produce "malarious diseases," but no "vegetable mould" in the soil "to engender malaria" and "no marshes or other source of malaria" (quots. in R. Randolph Stevenson, *The Southern Side; or Andersonville Prison*, 54, 52, 61).

49. VHD, *Memoir* 1:164, quot.; Sarcophagus, Locust Grove Cem., West Feliciana Parish, La., quot.

50. "Quinine" in *Universal Encycl.;* JD to Cartwright, Sept. 23, 1851 (*Papers* 4:225); VHD, *Memoir* 1:165, quots.

51. Knox's effects are at Rosemont; Fleming, "JD's First Marriage," 35; *BCP* (1830) (quots. from the Order for the Burial of the Dead). Knox was an Episcopalian; *BCP* assumed.

52. WPJ, *Gen. ASJ*, 53–55, quots.

53. *Papers* 1::493; VHD, *Memoir* 1:165–66, quots. This is the only mention of JD's drawing; he studied it at West Point: see *Papers* 1, facing p. 37.

54. JD to VHD, Dec. 30, 1865–Jan. 1, 1866, MS, TRANSYL, quots. (The quot. "plague . . . famine" from Litany in *BCP.* Author assumes Cuba to be scene because of ref. to the cathedral and high mass. JD had not yet been to Europe but might have seen these in N. O.). See chap. 3 above for earlier attempt to become Catholic.

55. VHD, *Memoir* 1:166, quots. VHD jumbles them, but JD made 2 distinct trips to Washington; 1st: after Nov. 17, 1835—before Apr. 8, 1836 (*Papers* 1::493, 496), when he met Tyler (1836) (VHD, *Memoir* 1:255; Rowland 2:262) who did not return till 1840 (Robert Seager, 2, *and Tyler too: A Biography of John and Julia Gardiner Tyler*, 115, 121, 127 [lowercase "a" was a deliberate play on Tyler's designation when he ran for vice president]); 2d: 1837–38, well attested (see text below).

56. Seager, *and Tyler too*, 110–15, quots. (res'd. Feb. 29, 1836; "chalice" ref.

to John 18:11 or Matt. 26:39, 42, or Ps. 75:8); VHD, *Memoir* 1:255–58; Strode, *President,* 60, 62, 192.

57. Geo. E. Payne to JD, Apr. 1, 1875 (Rowland 7:420, quot.; Payne was his factor, i.e., cotton broker and banker, 1838–44: see *Papers* 1::525 n.8); Warren County, Miss., tax rolls, 1836, 1838, 1839, 1841 (*Papers* 2:App. 3, p. 719 and 3:455; only ages 5 to 60 taxable). Census: 1840: 40 slaves (JD "only free person" there: points up his claim to safety); 1850: 72; 1860: 113 aged "four months to 104" (ibid. 1::531; 4:364; 6:App. 1, 667).

58. VHD, *Memoir* 1:176–77, quots. Southern gentlemen generally wait to be asked before sitting in another's home. This friendship not unique: see WPJ, *Gen. ASJ,* 248; obelisk in Canton, Miss., erected by W. H. Howcott to loyal servants of "Harvey Scouts" in C. W., and to "my faithful servant and friend Willis Howcott, a colored boy of rare loyalty . . . whose memory I cherish with deep gratitude."

59. Aiken, *Donelson,* 281–83; Alderson and McBride, *Landmarks of Tenn. Hist.,* 20; Fogel and Engermann, *Time on the Cross,* 210–12; VHD, *Memoir* 1:179–80, quots.

60. VHD, *Memoir* 1:163, quots.; Blum et al., *Natl. Experience,* 231; Jones in *Life and Reminisc.,* 121 (quot.), 118; Van Benthuysen to JD, Jan. 16, 1838 (*Papers* 1::517; see 395 n.7); JD in Senate, Feb. 27, 1849 (ibid. 4:16, quot.; see 17 n.6 for Catlin; exhibit helps date JD's visit).

61. JD to Joseph Davis, Jan. 2, 1838 (*Papers* 1::516, quots.); JD to G. W. Jones, Feb. 9, 1839 (ibid.::527, quot.); Jones in *Life and Reminisc.,* 119–20, and VHD, *Memoir* 1:167–68, quots. Linn: see *Papers* 1::527 n.14, and *Life and Reminsc.,* 107–9; Jones delegate from Wisc. Terr., 1837–39 (Rowland 1:2 n.2).

62. Jones in *Life and Reminsc.,* 119 (quot.) and in VHD, *Memoir* 1:166; Joseph Davis to JD, July 9, 1832 (ibid., 328, quot.); VHD, *Memoir* 1:169–70, quots.

63. VHD, *Memoir,* 169; Nathaniel Hawthorne, *The Life of Franklin Pierce,* 13–14, quots.; Jones, *Davis Memorial,* 272 (Daniel quots.); VHD, *Memoir,* 523–24 (JD quot.). By 1858, JD regarded Van Buren, in contrast to Pierce, as "a very corrupt man" (*Papers* 3:375).

64. JD to W. L. Marcy, Dec. 31, 1845 (*Papers* 2::121, quots.); Hamilton, *Zachary Taylor* 2:20, quot.; Bradford to JD, June 18, 1834 (*Papers* 1::419); DeLeon, "The Real JD," 79. See *Papers* 2::7; 3:173 n.10; 4:300, 301 n.3. JD, as Sec. of War, expected army personnel "to refrain entirely from" politics; any found guilty was to "be promptly dismissed" (Rowland 3:106).

65. Roy Franklin Nichols, *Franklin Pierce: Young Hickory of the Granite Hills,* 98; JD, "The Doctrine of State Rights," 211, quots.; JD, "Autobiography" (*Papers* 1::1, p. lx, quot.); JD, Speech, June 9, 1852, paraphrase (*Papers* 4:263, quot.; says met Pierce 1837–38 session; Nichols [97] has 1836–37). Va. Clay found Pierce "a genuine Southerner" (Nuermberger, *Clays of Ala.,* 113–14).

66. JD to "Gentlemen" [of Portland, Me.], Aug. 14, 1858, MS, TRANSYL, quot.; VHD, *Memoir* 1:90 (JD quots.); JD in Senate, July 31, 1850 (Rowland 1:431–32, quots.).

67. JD, Speech, June 9, 1852, paraphrase (*Papers* 4:263, quots.); JD to Lowndes Co. Citizens, Nov. 22, 1850 (ibid., 143, quot.); Blum et al., *Natl. Experience,* 226–32, 251–53; Miles, *Jacksonian Democracy,* 124–27 (Gwin quot.); Penick, *Great Western,* 151–53; VHD, *Memoir* 1:419, quot.

68. JD, Speech, June 9, 1852, paraphrase (*Papers* 4:263–65, quots.; Calhoun saw "a direct and dangerous attack" in the petitions [ibid., 63]); Claiborne, *Miss.,* 419, quots.

69. Senate res., Jan. 10, 1838 (*Papers* 4:64, quot.; date in n.5); JD, Speech, June 9, 1852, paraphrase (*Papers* 4:263–64, quots.). "Most Northerners, too, regarded the abolitionists as irresponsible fanatics" (Blum et al., *Natl. Experience,* 253).

70. Nichols, *Franklin Pierce,* 99, 103; "William J. Graves" in *National Cyclopae-*

dia of American Biography 12:206–7; *New Orleans Picayune*, Dec. 7, 1889, p. 2, col. 3 (Jones quots.; duel wrongly dated 1839); JD to Jones, Feb. 9, 1839 (*Papers* 1::527, quot.; and nn.6, 7, 10). See John Lyde Wilson, *The Code of Honor, or Rules for the Government of Principals and Seconds in Duelling* (Charleston, 1838) in Jack K. Williams, *Dueling in the Old South*, 87–104; also 76, 48; the choice of rifles was unusual.

71. Graves in *Natl. Cycl. Am. Biog.* 12:206–7; Williams, *Dueling*, 98, 96–97 (also 101, 103); JD to Willison Hughey, Mar. 7, 1838 (*Papers* 1::522, quots.); Personal Property Tax Roll, Warren Co., Miss., 1845 (ibid. 2::75); Tucker Hill, "Victory in Defeat," 19 (quots. from JD to C. E. Hooker, Dec. 18, 1878; and pic. of Staudenmayer). See above, chap. 3, Note 33.

72. Williams, *Dueling*, 74–78, 72, 24–25, 48–49, 95 (quot.); WPJ, *Gen. ASJ*, 54 (ASJ quot.).

73. Ibid., 70–80 (quots. on 80, 76). Sam Houston did narrowly escape a duel with ASJ (ibid., 121–22).

74. Ibid., 76–80 (quots. on 76, 78), 85; Wilson, *Code of Honor*, in Williams, *Dueling*, 95–98 (Huston could have declared his honor satisfied after the first shot; that he did not indicates how seriously he felt insulted).

75. *Papers* 2::26, pp. 151–52 (quots. from "Capt." Davis, paraphrase), p. 143 (quots. from *Sentinel*); for Robins, see Ed. Note and 2::1 n.4; Bradford, 2::21.

76. *Papers* 2::26, pp. 152–53, quots. (Guion: 1::75 n.15); R. Davis, *Recoll. of Miss.* 79, quot. JD's near-duels in text below passim; Joseph's challenge of Scott in chap. 19 (only one known to author).

77. VHD, *Memoir* 1:178, quot.; Wilson, *Code of Honor*, in Williams, *Dueling*, 92–93; JD and Quitman to Public, July 10, 1845 (*Papers* 2::72, quot.). For 1858, see chap. 11 below. JD, as sec. of war, ruled an army discharge "not *technically*" honorable because of a duel (*Papers* 6:App. 1, 402 under Jan. 18, 1856).

78. *New Orleans Picayune*, Dec. 7, 1889, p. 2, col. 3 (Jones quot.); Van Benthuysen to JD, Jan. 16 and Apr. 18, 1838 (*Papers* 1::517 and 523, quots.). For JD Van B., see Hanna, *Flight*, 109 and *Papers* 6:App. 1, 518, under Nov. 29 (1856).

79. JD, "Autobiographical Sketch" (*Papers* 2:App. 1, p. 697, quot.; his oft-quoted remark, "seldom leaving the cane brake in which I lived" [Rowland 7:453] refers only to 1836); JD to G. W. Jones, Feb. 9, 1839 (Rowland 1:2–4, quots.); Goldsborough, "Varina Howell Davis," 5, quots.

80. JD to Allen, July 24, 1840 (*Papers* 1::533, quot.); JD to Jones (as in Note 79 above); (Other travel and meetings:) Rowland 1:539, 10:18–19 (AJ), *Papers* 1::513, 526, 533, 535,2::5, 7, 12, 8, 9; Davis Bend families in Note 23 above; J. E. Davis to Rev. J. W. Kerr, Dec. 26, 1866, quots. (MS copy in Kerr, "Memorial of John Perkins"; author's collection, courtesy Mary M. McGavock).

81. Quots.: JD to Joseph Davis, Aug. 25, 1855 (*Papers* 5:117); "J. E. Davis" in *South in Bldg. of Nation* 11; ZT to JD, Apr. 20, 1848 (*Papers* 3:308); A. R. Lawton in *Life and Reminisc.*, 200. Hospital: *Papers* 6:249 (see 260 n.2) and M. E. Hamer to Fleming, Dec. 18, 1907, MS, Fleming Collection (Joseph imported German steam doctor: see *William Johnson's Natchez: the Ante-Bellum Diary of a Free Negro*, ed. William R. Hogan and Edwin A. Davis, 146 n.60).

82. VHD, *Memoir* 1:202–3, quots.; *Papers* 1:App. 1, p. 477 n.2 (built 1838); Walter L. Fleming, "Jefferson Davis, the Negroes, and the Negro Problem," 6 ("cat and clayed"=logs chinked with clay).

83. VHD, *Memoir* 1:172, quot.; JD to G. W. Jones, Feb. 9, 1839 (Rowland 1:2–4, quots.); JD to Allen, July 24, 1840 (*Papers* 1::533, quots.; see nn.2, 5). Demosthenes' famous denunciation of Philip of Macedon gave English the common noun *philippic*.

84. VHD, *Memoir* 1:172 (quot.), 257 (Tyler); JD to Joseph Davis, Jan. 2, 1838 (*Papers* 1::516, quot.); ZT to JD, July 27, Aug. 16, Sept. 18, 1847, and Apr. 20, 1848 (*Papers* 3:202–4, 208, 223, 307–9); Hamilton, *Zachary Taylor* 1:155.

85. Joseph Davis to JD, e.g., Jan. 19, Feb. 19, Aug. 27, 1838 (*Papers* 1::518,

521, 525; last also about horses seen in Ky.); JD, Speech at Augusta, Me., Sept. 29, 1858, paraphrase (Rowland 3:310–11, quots.).

86. VHD, *Memoir* 1:172–73, quot. (see letter, 1839, in *Papers* 1::530: "Your close application to business . . . of planting"). In 1860 Brierfield was worth $100,000, with income more than $20,000 a year (Everett, *Brierfield*, 63); JD's "personalty" valued at $125,000 (*Papers* 6:667 under Sept. 4).

87. JD, Eulogy on the Life and Character of Andrew Jackson, June 28, 1845 (*Papers* 2::67, quots. on pp. 278, 281; allusion to Gen. 3:17–19, 23); Marsh in chap. 4 above. AJ became Presbyterian after retiring in 1837, but he had already been reading 3 Bible chaps. a day for 43 years (Aiken, *Donelson*, 288–92; Hale and Merritt, *Hist. of Tenn.* 2:523–26).

88. JD, Speech, Jan. 8, 1844 (*Papers* 2::18, pp. 72, 73; refs. to Luke 16:19–31 and Gen. 8:8–11); Jones, *Davis Memorial*, 56–57 (quot.) and *Papers* 1::447 n.10 (Izard d. 1836 in Seminole War, age 26); Ibid.::5 n.10; JD, Speech, May 26, 1851, paraphrase (Rowland 2:80, quot.).

89. VHD, *Memoir* 1:171–73, quot.

90. Crist, "A Bibliog. Note," 188; Everett, *Brierfield*, 45–46 and floor plan, after p. 22 (see 25 n.3 on spelling of name); Poetry, 1-vol. ed., 1843, and *Works of Tobias Smollett*, n.d. (inscr. "Davis / Briarfield") at Beauvoir (Mrs. T. J. Fulks and T. M. Czekanski to author, Oct. 19, 1984 and Dec. 19, 1988); Scott's *Tales of My Landlord*, 1826, the travel book (inscr. "captured in Jefferson Davis privet library . . . by Christian Stausser [?] May 14") and *Dictionary*, 1843 (inscr. Mar. 21, 1845 and "Davis/Brierfield") in Rosenstock; VHD, *Memoir* 1:192, quots.

91. Hermann, *Pursuit of a Dream*, 12–13, 30–31 (quot.); JD to VHD, Jan. 26–28, 1866, MS, TRANSYL; VHD, *Memoir* 1:174–76, 479 (quot.); David D. Porter, "Discipline in the Navy" (*N. Am. Rev.* 150:412).

92. JD to VHD, Oct. 20, 1865, MS, TRANSYL, quots.

93. Hermann, *Pursuit of a Dream*, 3–4; VHD, *Memoir* 1:49–50 (quot.), 171; Everett, *Brierfield*, 15 (epitaph quot., ref. to Matt. 5:5).

94. Quots.: 1 Cor. 6:20 (and 7:23; see Acts 20:28), Eph. 6:5–9 (see also Col. 4:1). R. Taylor, *Destruction*, 210: fidelity of slaves during War testified "the kindness of the master and the gentleness of the servant," and all the "falsehood in 'Uncle Tom's Cabin' . . . can not rebut it."

95. VHD, *Memoir* 1:179, 174–75; Hermann, *Pursuit of a Dream*, 17–21 (Ben also handled the mail, though the steamboat captain complained because he was black).

96. Jones, *Davis Memorial*, 137, quots.; M. E. Hamer to Fleming, Dec. 18, 1907, MS, Fleming Collection; JD letters in *Papers* 6: 246–49, 259 (see 614, 615); Strode, *Patriot* 333–34; Hermann, *Pursuit of a Dream*, 16, quot. See Cartwright in Kelly and Burrage, *Dict. of Am. Med. Biog.*, 125–26, and his art., "Alcohol and the Ethiopian . . ." (*The New Orleans Medical and Surgical Journal*, Sept. 1853).

97. J. A. Orr, "Trip from Houston to Jackson, Miss. in 1845," *PMHS* 9:177, quot.; Roberta Seawell Brandau, *History of Homes and Gardens of Tennessee*, 228–34; Conversation with Gordon Cotton, Old Courthouse Mus., Vicksburg, and visit to King David Church, 1984. Cf. F. L. Olmsted, *The Slave States*, ed. Harvey Wish, 172; Claiborne, *Miss.*, 472; John B. Boles, ed., *Masters and Slaves in the House of the Lord: Race and Religion in the American South, 1740–1870*, (n.p.: Univ. of Ky. Press, 1988), esp. Blake Touchstone, "Planters and Slave Religion in the Deep South," 99–126.

98. *Polk* 1:103, 108–9, 114, 120, 127–28, 133–34, 136–37, 150–52 (quots.; pic. of church), 194; Trezevant Player Yeatman, Jr., "St. John's, a Plantation Church of the Old South" (typescript in author's collection). Episcopalians still hold services at Ashwood on Pentecost.

99. Christ Church hist. marker; *Papers* 2::6 and n.8, 58 and n.7 (Page later married Jeff and Varina), and 1 n.4 ; the Rev. Robert Saul (rector of Christ Church, Vicksburg) to author, Feb. 26, 1987; *Chesnut*, 818.

100. M. E. Hamer [Lise Mitchell] to Fleming, Dec. 18, 1907, quots. (MS, Fleming Collection; see Fleming, "JD and Negro Problem," 8); *Bishop Whipple's Diary*, 36, quot. ("blacks who are truly religious will not hear him"); VHD, *Memoir* 1:180, quots. Slave preachers: Howard, *Hist. V. A. Stewart*, 227 ("greatest scoundrels"); Freeman, *R. E. Lee*, 1:111–12 (Lee notes they lead 1831 rebellion); King, *Wartime Jnl. of Ga. Girl*, 101–2, 137 (approves some; see also 169).

101. Hamer to Fleming (as in Note 100 above), quot.; *Papers* 2::2 n.4; Ibid.::58 n.8.

102. E. Rowland, *Varina* 1:23, 25; *Papers* 2::20 n.8 (11 children; 3 died in all); VHD, *Memoir* 1:191, 187–88; *Papers* 1::5 n.10, 1::362 n.11, 2::2 n.4, 2::21 nn.4–7, 3:98 n.5.

103. VHD to Marg. K. Howell, Jan. 3, 1847 (*Letters*, 45, quot.). The Briars: visit, 1984; pics. in Harnett Kane, *Natchez on the Mississippi*, and Mary Wallace Crocker, *Historic Architecture in Mississippi* (Jackson: Univ. Press of Miss., 1973); date from Kerr, "Memorial"; Perkins living there 1833 (James, *Antebellum Natchez*, 142); Howell may have bought it 1839 (Hogan and Davis, *Wm. Johnson's Natchez*, 263).

104. VHD, *Memoir* 1:187–89; *Papers* 2::20 nn.6, 8; James, *Antebellum Natchez*, 248–49.

105. Ross, *First Lady*, 7; R. A. Howell to Marg. K. Howell, Nov. 29, 1836, quots. (MS, Wm. B. Howell folder, MDAH). E. Rowland (*Varina* 1:107) says Varina spent "several winter terms" at the school.

106. Strode, *Patriot*, 126 n.1, quot.; VHD, *Memoir* 1:188–90, quots. Great-heart is in *The Pilgrim's Progress from this World to that which is to Come* by John Bunyan.

107. VHD, *Memoir* 1:188, 190–92 (quots.; ref. to Alfred, Lord Tennyson, "The Lady of Shalott" 3.91; note Latin word for baggage); *Papers* 1::363 n.20. JD was then 35, Marg. Howell, 37. Her mother of course did know the brother (see text above, chap. 4).

108. VHD to JD, Feb. 8, 1866, MS, ALA, and VHD, *Memoir*, 1:191 (2 quots. from each, alternately); Ibid., 192–93, 189 (quot.; i.e., everybody who was anybody in Natchez; paper was "central organ of the Whig party" [*Papers* 2::137 n.17]).

109. Quots.: VHD to JD, Jan. 22, 1866 and Dec. 7, 1865 (MSS, ALA), Apr. 17, 1859 (*Letters*, 107), and Oct. [1], 1865 (MS, ALA). Much of this material appears in *Letters*, but highly edited.

110. Ross, *First Lady*, 7, 19 (engagement ring is in Smithsonian Mus. of Hist. and Technology [*Smithsonian*, June 1978, 22–23] the presentation now is assumed); VHD, *Memoir* 1:197; VHD to JD, Feb. 8, 1866, MS, ALA, quots. "Musical and sweet" voice; thought in youth "I had given you [all]" but "How dearer is the old Husband" (VHD to JD, Oct. 23, and Oct. [1], 1865, ibid.).

111. VHD to JD, Oct. 23, 1865, MS, ALA, quot.; E. Rowland, *Varina* 1:67. "Romaunt"="romance" (medieval tale); "tendir & trewe" in old Scottish poem (*Hoyt*, 100). VHD later owned a handsome ed. of *Specimens of Early English Metrical Romances*, ed. George Ellis (Rosenstock).

112. Quots.: JD to Varina B. Howell, Mar. 8 and 15, 1844, and n.d. (*Papers* 2::20, 21, and App. 2, p. 705). The French means "Good night, my dear angel, I am your [JD]."

113. JD to Varina B. Howell, Mar. 8, 1844 (*Papers* 2::20. quots.).

114. Ibid. (Ages:) Joseph Davis, e.g., 27 yrs. older than Eliza; Luther Smith 21 yrs. older than Anna (*Papers* 1:App. 4, Charts 5 and 8).

115. Quots.: JD to Varina B. Howell, Mar. 15, June 22, Sept. 6, and Nov. 22, 1844 (*Papers* 2::21, 29, 41, 49). "Blessed . . . expect nothing" ref. to "The Eighth Beatitude," coined by Alexander Pope in a letter to John Gay, Oct. 6, 1727 (*Hoyt*, 244).

116. Quots.: JD to Varina B. Howell, n.d., Mar. 15, June 22, and Sept. 6, 1844 (*Papers* 2:App. 2, p. 704; ibid.::21, 29, 41).

117. JD to Varina B. Howell, Nov. 22, 1844 (ibid.::49, quot.); JD in Senate, Aug.

5, 1850 (Rowland 1:471, quot.); *Letters*, 25 Ed. Note; JD to Varina B. Howell, Dec. 11, 1844 (*Papers* 2::55, quot.).

118. JD to Varina B. Howell, Jan. 31, 1845 (précis in *Papers* 3:App. 3, p. 456); VHD, *Memoir* 1:199, quots.

119. VHD, *Memoir* 1:199 (quot.), 200 and n.; E. Rowland, *Varina* 1:99, quot.; Ross, *First Lady*, 18–19, quot. V.'s embroidered mull pettiskirt, 41" long, borrowed from cousin, in Old Capitol Mus. of Miss. Hist., MDAH; jewels, gift of grandmother Kempe, in Smithsonian Mus. of Hist. and Technology (Victorian Parlor of the First Ladies area) (Ross, *First Lady*, 19; *Smithsonian*, June 1978, 22–23).

120. VHD, *Memoir* 1:200, quots.; E. Rowland, *Varina* 1:102.

121. Quots.: *Bishop Whipple's Diary*, 195; VHD, *Memoir* 1:200–202 ("the uncle, I think, of the poet and aesthete, Oscar Wilde"); E. Rowland, *Varina* 1:114. Wilde, former att. gen. of Ga., was then teaching law in Univ. of La. (Louise Manly, *Southern Literature from 1579–1895*, 178–79).

122. VHD to JD, Nov. 7, 1865, MS, ALA, quot. VHD was then harbored with 4 other women by the George Schley family (ibid. and Strode, *Tragic Hero*, 259). Refs.: "Love's Young Dream" by Thomas Moore (*Hoyt*, 475); "arise . . . blessed" adapted from Prov. 31:28.

Chapter VI Plantation and Politics

1. JD to "Miss V. B. Howell. Present." [i.e., at the Hurricane], n.d. (*Papers* 2::App. 2, p. 705, quots.; brackets in text). Letter to Knox Taylor in text above, chap. 5.

2. VHD, *Memoir* 1:475 (*re* 1852) and 203, quots.

3. E. Rowland, *Varina*, 64; J. D. Howell to W. F. Howell, in Strode, *Patriot*, 139–40; VHD *Memoir* 1:475. Alligators were numerous in Mississippi swamps: see, e.g., Hogan and Davis, *William Johnson's Natchez*, 258, 271, 410, 412.

4. Quots.: VHD, *Memoir* 1:203–4; VHD to JD, Oct. [1], 1865, MS, TRANSYL; VHD to JD, Apr. 28 (*Letters*, 159).

5. JD to Marg. K. Howell, Apr. 25, 1845 (*Papers* 2::60, quots.).

6. VHD to JD, Apr. 7, 1878 (*Letters*, 476–77); VHD, *Memoir* 1:474, quot.; VHD to John J. Craven, Oct. 10, 1865, in Craven, *Prison Life*, 347, quots.; VHD to JD, Apr. 10, 1859 (*Letters*, 106); VHD to Marg. K. Howell [1845] (*Papers* 2::App. 2, p. 714, quot.).

7. VHD, *Memoir* 1:254, quot. (this vol. abounds in the private jokes); JD to Marg. K. Howell (as in Note 5 above).

8. JD to V. Howell, Feb. 25, 1845 (*Papers* 3:App. 3, p. 456, quot.); Rowland 6:537, 549 and, 551, quots.; Ross, *First Lady*, 205–6.

9. Winnie Davis, "JD in Private Life," 5; VHD, *Memoir* 2:302–3. VHD calls novel "The Handley Cross Hounds," but she may mistake it, as she does the main character ("Jorax" for "Jorrocks"); Robert S. Surtees had a novel named *Handley Cross* (Baugh, *Lit. Hist. of England*, 1277). For Byron and Sterne, see text passim.

10. VHD, *Memoir* 2:303–4, quots. (later, "Clough's 'Poems of Patriotism' were great favorites": JD's copy "marked all through"); Winnie Davis, "JD in Private Life," 5–6, quots.

11. VHD, *Memoir* 2:302–5, quots.; Mrs. Hezekiah Sturges, "Recollections of Jefferson Davis," 10; Chippewa: chap. 4 above. Editions dating 1812 to 1853 of Livy, Thucydides, Homer, French grammar, R. C. Trench's *Study of Words*, an *Abridgement of Ainsworth's Dictionary* are at First White House, also a German dictionary (probably later). VHD owned, 1874, *Americanisms: The English of the New World* by M. Schele De Vere (Rosenstock).

12. VHD, *Memoir* 2:304–5 and 1:193, quots.; VHD to JD, Nov. 13, 1865, MS, ALA, quot.

13. VHD to Marg. K. Howell, Jan. 3, 1847 (*Letters*, 45, quot.). William Francis Howell was then between 12 and 13 years old (*Papers* 2::20 n.8).

14. JD to Hugh R. Davis (Lucinda's son by 1st marriage), Apr. 17, 1842 (*Papers* 3:455) and to George E. Payne, Feb. 14, 1845 (*Papers* 6:675); VHD, *Memoir* 1:173–74 (JD quot.); VHD to JD, Oct. [1], 1865, MS, ALA, quot. (ref. to Matt. 6:34; Eccl. 11:1; Luke 16:19–31); VHD to JD, Feb. 26, 1866, MS, ALA, quot.; VHD to JD, June 16, 1871 (*Letters*, 350, quot.).

15. JD to V. Banks Howell, Mar. 15, 1844 (*Papers* 2::21, quot.); Ibid. 1::5 n.10 (Everett, *Brierfield*, 17, and A. Ganier, SAR appl., name other places for death); Joseph Davis to JD, Dec. 30, 1846 (*Papers* 3:100, quot.). Bradford wrote affectionate letters to Jeff; one speaks of his reputation for rage (ibid. 1::363, 419).

16. JD to V. Banks Howell, Mar. 15, 1844 (*Papers* 2::21 and nn.6 and 7); Ibid. 1:App. 4, Chart 11 (Rev. Ed.). The others were children of Mary and Charles Mitchell (ibid., 362 n.11), and Joseph Davis Nicholson, whose parents died at Hurricane (ibid. 2::4 n.5).

17. VHD, *Memoir* 1:479, 174, and 178, quots.; Jones, *Davis Memorial*, 500 (quot. from Samford); Fleming, "JD and Negro Problem," 9, quot. (brackets in text).

18. VHD, *Memoir* 1:178 and 480 (quots.), 538; Duke, *Reminisc.*, 342, quot.; Goldsborough, "Varina Howell Davis," 5, quot. JD's sense of humor: VHD, *Memoir* 1:173, 175–76; his patience was not always appreciated: 177–78.

19. Winnie Davis, "JD in Private Life," 10, quot.; JD to VHD, Dec. 30, 1865–Jan. 1, 1866, MS, TRANSYL, quot.; JD to VHD, Mar. 13–14, 1866, ibid., quot.

20. JD in Senate, July 12, 1848 (*Papers* 3:355, quots.); JD, May 16–17, 1860 (Rowland 4:327–28, quots.); "Chivalry," 5, *OED.*

21. Shippee, *Bishop Whipple's Diary*, 32, quot. JD to Conf. Congress, Nov. 7, 1864 (Richardson, *Conf.* 1:496); VHD, *Memoir* 1:480 quot. (ref. to I Cor. 13:4). See G. F. R. Henderson, *Stonewall Jackson and the American Civil War*, 66–67 (Southerners would not tolerate "cruelty"; brutality rare.).

22. *Chesnut*, 818–19 (quot.) and n.7. Dr. Lord, a Yankee, stayed through Vicksburg siege of 1863, went then to S. C., where Sherman burned his church; returned to Vicksburg after War (*The Private Chesnut*, 251; Hist. marker, Christ Church; conversation with Gordon Cotton, 1984).

23. "Confirmations," Parish Register, St. Paul's Episc. Church, cited in John S. Lewis to Strode, Nov. 12, 1954 (Strode Papers, Univ. of Ala.) and guide at Rosemont, 1984; Miss. a missionary district 1843; Polk bsp. of La. (Perry, *Bsps. of Am. Church*, 69, 75, 111).

24. JD to VHD, Oct. 11–12, 1865, MS, TRANSYL, quot.; *Papers* 1::362 n.12; Obit of "Mrs. Annie E. Smith, relict of the late Luther L. Smith," *New Orleans Picayune*, Aug. 27, 1870, RPR in [Jackson, Miss.] *Semi-Weekly Clarion* (typescript in Samuel Davis subject file, MDAH).

25. Ross, *First Lady*, 13; VHD to JD, Apr. 12, 1866 (*Letters*, 244); VHD to Marg. K. Howell, Sept. 5, 1845 (*Papers* 2::83, quots.); Same to same, n.d. (ibid., App. 2, p. 714, quot.). See Phillips, *Life and Labor*, 301–2.

26. VHD to Marg. K. Howell, Jan. 5, 1847 (*Letters*, 46, quots.).

27. VHD, *Memoir* 1:179, quots. (also 193: women given "fancy plaid linsey or calico dresses" as "consolation for a death in their families").

28. VHD, *Memoir* 1:477 (quot.), 190; JD note, n.d., n.p., MS, TRANSYL, quot. (*Papers* 6:App. 1, 592, dates it "[1858–60?]"; this time seems as likely); Ibid. 2::18 and n.7 (JD quot.; see 2::17). "Tea" and "julep": JD to VHD, Feb. 3, 1866, and July 29, 1881, MSS, TRANSYL. Quitman describes a typical day, which includes juleps, in Kane, *Natchez*, 221–22.

29. Quots.: Robert Dabney Calhoun, "The John Perkins Family of Northeast Louisiana," 72; JD to VHD, Sept. 26, 1865, MS, TRANSYL (ref. to Acts 24:25); VHD to JD, [Nov. 21, fragment], MS, ALA.

30. JD, "Autobiog. Sketch," (*Papers* 2:App. 1, p. 697, quots.; *Papers* 2::11, 12; VHD, *Memoir* 1:196. Prentiss, b. in Me., came to Miss. 1829; d. 1850 in N. O.; a Vicksburg lawyer and famous duelist (*Papers* 1::518 n.16; Baldwin, *Flush Times*, 144–62; see Fulkerson, *Random Recoll.*, 69, 106–9; *Chesnut*, 126).

31. Rev. Luther Rice Burrows to Fleming, May 25, 1908, quot. (typescript in Fleming Collection); Reuben Davis, *Recoll. of Miss.*, 165–66 and 193, quots. A newspaper found Prentiss "bold, figurative, declamatory"; JD, "more classical and chaste" (*Papers* 2::13).

32. JD to J. D. Smith, Dec. 6, 1872 (Rowland 7:335, quots.); JD, Speech at Oxford [Miss., July 15, 1852] (*Papers* 4:281, 285–86, quots.; "Good . . . report" echoes 2 Cor. 6:8; "No one . . . has a right to refuse his attention to public affairs").

33. *Vicksburg Sentinel,* June 28, 1845 (*Papers* 2::65); JD, Eulogy on the Life and Character of Andrew Jackson (ibid.::67, quots.); Hale and Merritt, *Hist. of Tenn.* 2:523–26; Bassett, *Corr. AJ* 6:414–15 and n.

34. Quots.: JD, Eulogy of AJ (*Papers* 2::67, p. 279); JD, in Senate, Feb. 24, 1851 (Rowland 2:40–41; see 30, and JD, "Doctrine of State Rights," 211–15); JD in H. R., Mar. 16, 1846 (*Papers* 2::164, p. 514). See also JD, "Life and Character of the Hon. John Caldwell Calhoun," 252–54; *Papers* 4:187–88; Blum, et. al., *Natl. Experience,* 222–26; Randall, *Civil War,* 31–33.

35. JD in Senate, Feb. 11, 1851 (Rowland 2:19, quot.); VHD, *Memoir* 1:207–8, quot.; Charles M. Wiltse, *John C. Calhoun, Nationalist, 1782–1828* (hereafter: *Calhoun* 1), 132–37; JD, Speech Mar. 16, 1846 (*Papers* 2::164 and Ed. Note); JD, Remarks [in Senate], Apr. 14, 1848 (ibid. 3:296–301).

36. *Papers* 2::14 n.10 (quots.), 13 Ed. Note (bonds), 18 n.102, p. 105 (C.S.A.); JD, "Autobiog. Sketch" (ibid.:App. 1, pp. 697–98, quots.; see p. 702); JD to R. S. Guernsey, Apr. 9, 1870 (Rowland 7:266–68, quots.).

37. *Papers* 2::14 (quots. from *Vicksburg Sentinel*), 18 (quots. from JD speech), 32 (quot. from a letter) (and see 17). Calhoun had withdrawn his name, but it was not known until Jan. 29 (Charles M. Wiltse, *John C. Calhoun, Sectionalist, 1840–1850* [hereafter: *Calhoun* 3], 147–48).

38. James Elliott Walmsley, "The Presidential Campaign of 1844 in Mississippi," *PMHS* 9:181–82; Claiborne, *Miss.*, 437, 452; *Polk* 1:36–37; Rowland 1:73 n.1; *Papers* 2::18 n.69, 27 n.8, 31 n.6.

39. Walmsley, "Pres. Campaign of 1844," *PMHS* 9:188 (Prentiss quot.), 189, quot.; R. Davis, *Recoll. of Miss.*, 193; *Papers* 2::30 (quots. from *Port Gibson Herald,* July 4, 1844).

40. R. Davis, *Recoll. of Miss.*, 101–2, 120–24 (Foote quot.); *Papers* 2::18 n.38 (esp. p. 86).

41. *Papers* 2::30, 28 n.15; WPJ, *Gen. ASJ,* 77–78, 91–98, 118–30 (sec. of war 1838–40).

42. *Papers* 2::34, 32, and 27 (quots. from *Holly Springs Guard, Jackson Southern Reformer,* and *Vicksburg Sentinel*); R. Davis, *Recoll. of Miss.*, 196–97 and 324, quots.

43. *Papers* 2::69 nn.23, 24, 34 (see 73 n.5, and 71 nn.31, 36); Ibid.:: 18 n.103; Claiborne, *Miss.*, 427–28; R. Davis, *Recoll. of Miss.*, 112, quots. (leader must be "above reproach").

44. *Papers* 2::48 n.8 (JD quot.), and Ed. Note, and 71; JD to Mrs. Virginia Ritchie, Sept. 3, 1875 (Rowland 7:454, quots.); VHD, *Memoir* 1:205–6, quot.; Rowland 1:13–22 (quots. from *Sentinel* and from letter [ref. to Matt. 13:46]; also contains JD to *Sentinel,* July 5, 1845, and Briscoe Bill).

45. VHD, *Memoir* 1:196–98 and 161, quots.; VHD to Marg. K. Howell, Sept. 5, 1845 (*Papers* 2::83, quot.); Florida D. McCaleb to JD, Oct. 15 [1838?] (ibid. 1:App. 1, p. 477); Ibid. 2::22 n.4 (Jane Davis d. Oct. 1845). VHD, *Memoir* here seems to say illnesses began 1844, but same passage speaks of Jane Davis's death; a letter July 1, 1845, mentions "ill health" (*Papers* 2::67, p. 265), but none does in 1844.

46. Statewide Election Returns, Nov. 3–4, 1845 (*Papers* 2::96; tally in n.12); Ibid., 97, 18 nn.98, 99; VHD to [Marg. K. Howell], Nov. 14, 1845, quot. (MS, Old Courthouse Mus.; addressed "W. B. Howell" but written to Ma: "Kiss dear Father"); For cavalier bestowal of rank in Miss., see ibid.::11 n.2.

47. *Papers* 2::97 n.8, 99 and n.7; VHD to [Marg. K. Howell] (as in Note 46 above),

quots.; JD to Wilson Hemingway, Nov. 11, 1845 (*Papers* 2::98, quots.); VHD, *Memoir* 1:207–15, quots.; *Papers* 2::101; Joseph D. Howell to Marg. K. Howell, Nov. 21, 1845 (ibid., 103). Memphis convention: Wiltse, *Calhoun* 3:235–40.

48. Joseph D. Howell to Marg. K. Howell, Nov. 21, 1845 (*Papers* 2::103, quots.); VHD, *Memoir* 1:209–14, quots. ("His letters were all lost during the war").

49. VHD, *Memoir* 1:215–17, 269, 97–98, quots.; Blum et al., *Nat'l. Experience*, 197, quot. and map; JD to Varina B. Howell, June 22, 1844 (*Papers* 2::29, quots.).

50. VHD, *Memoir* 1:217–20, quots. JD speaks of their "very severe trip," with "the weather intensely cold," Dec. 16, 1845 (*Papers* 2::109).

51. Wiltse, *Calhoun* 3:220, 242 (Calhoun had res'd. as sec. of state; resumed Senate seat Dec. 22, 1845); VHD, *Memoir* 1:220–25, quots.; G. W. Jones in *Life and Reminisc.*, 121, quot. (story also in *New Orleans Daily Picayune*, Dec. 4, 1889, p. 1, Dec. 7, p. 2, and Jones, *Davis Memorial*, 51; he was in D. C. as territorial surveyor-general).

52. Sterling, *Belle*, 78–81, quots.; Jones in *Life and Reminisc.*, 109 (quot.), 115–17; VHD, *Memoir* 1:115–16, quot.; Dodges in *DAB* (represented Wisc. and Ia. Terr.).

53. JD, *Rise and Fall* 2:616; Claiborne, *Miss.*, 435–36; VHD, *Memoir* 1:221, 224; Ibid., 25, 281, quots.

54. *Papers* 2::18 n.102, 130 n.7, 231 n.3; VHD, *Memoir* 1:260–62 (quots.), 38 (JD quot.); A. D. Bache in Heitman, *Hist. Register*, and *Col. Encycl.* (also U.S. supt. of weights and measures; later pres. Am. Ass. for the Advancement of Science and of Am. Philosophical Soc.; founder and 1st pres. Natl. Academy of Sciences).

55. VHD, *Memoir* 1:262–64, quots. Survey of coast for defense, begun after War of 1812, was slow until Bache took it 1843 (Weigley, *Hist. U.S. Army*, 163–64; Bache in *Col. Encycl.*; see Rowland 2:11).

56. *Papers* 2::105; Shippee, *Bsp. Whipple's Diary*, 156, quots. (he visited 1844). Evidence of JD tobacco in *Papers* 4:238; Hanna, *Flight*, 120; "Lone Jack" seen at Beauvoir. ZT and James M. Mason chewed, among others (Hamilton, *Zachary Taylor* 1:117; *Chesnut*, 520).

57. *Papers* 2::104, 109 (and n.3); Ibid.::111 (quots. from paraphrase of JD speech), Ed. Note, and n.9 (quots. from abol. speech); Ibid.:App. 1, pp. 702–3 (last JD quot., n.d.); Ibid.::114 n.7 (quot. from Adams; d. Feb. 23, 1848). See VHD, *Memoir* 1:244–45 for variant of Adams's remark and vivid descr. of him; also 255.

58. *Papers* 2::112, 114, Ed. Note (quot. from Smithson's will) and n.11, 194, 195 Ed. Note and n.2; Ibid.:App. 1, pp. 702–3; Ibid. 3:263 n.1; Bache in *Col. Encycl.*; VHD, *Memoir* 1:225, 49–50 (mistakenly calls both Owens "Robert Dale").

59. *Papers* 2::192 and Ed. Note, 130 n.15; VHD, *Memoir* 1:248–52, quots. ("fire-bell": T. Jefferson's term for "a geographical party" (*Papers* 4:28); VHD to Marg. K. Howell, Apr. 3, 1846 (*Papers* 2::176).

60. *Papers* 2::226 and Ed. Note; VHD, *Memoir* 1:252–53, quots. *Papers* 2::226 Descr. Note disputes VHD on the rpt., but JD himself said: "I drew and championed the report which exonerated him. Mr. Webster never forgot that act" (ibid.::130 n.15).

61. VHD, *Memoir* 1:253, quots.; *Papers* 2::130 n.15 (JD quots.); Ibid. 6:226 n.2.

62. VHD, *Memoir* 1:259–60, 226–27 and 253–57 (quots.), 574 (254: Tyler "a tall thin gentleman, with a large, hooked nose, steady gray eyes, iron-gray hair, and a certain benevolent, bland toleration of manner, like a general in mufti among his troops").

63. VHD to Marg. K. Howell, Apr. 3, 1846 (*Papers* 2::176, quots.); Same to [same], Nov. 14, 1845, quot. (MS, Old Courthouse Mus.).

64. VHD to Marg. K. Howell, Apr. 3, 1846 (*Papers* 2::176, quots.); Same to same, Jan. 30 (ibid.::130, quots.; the night before, Jeff's "very bad earache" kept her from going to see "a celebrated juggler").

65. VHD, *Memoir* 1:225, quots.; JD, "Life of Calhoun," 258, quots.; *Papers* 2::137.

66. Wiltse, *Calhoun* 3:247–51, quot.

67. JD, Speech on the Resolution to Terminate the Joint Occupation of Oregon, Feb. 6, 1846 (*Papers* 2::137, quots. on pp. 458, 459).

68. Ibid., pp. 462–63 and 460, quots.; Wiltse, *Calhoun* 3:70, quot.

69. Wiltse, *Calhoun* 3:257, 152 (quot.), 151, 153 (quot. from Ashbel Smith, citing Peel to Abolitionists at World Convention in London), 154 (quot. from Abel Upshur to Calhoun), 170; JD, Speech Feb. 6, 1846 (*Papers* 2::137, p. 460).

70. Ibid., 454 and 453, quots.; JD, Remarks on and Substitute for the Bill to Protect the Rights of American Settlers in Oregon, Apr. 17, 1846 (*Papers* 2::187, quots. on pp. 555, 554; his subst. bill rejected); Ibid., p. xxxviii; Wiltse, *Calhoun* 3:265.

71. Justin H. Smith, *The War with Mexico* 1:xxii (map); Wiltse, *Calhoun* 3:273–76; Blum et al., *Natl. Experience*, 271–72. Taylor did not move until Mar. (Hamilton, *Zachary Taylor* 1:171).

72. Twiggs to JD, May 4, 1846 (*Papers* 2::196, quot.; brackets in text; see n.2); Robert Selph Henry, *The Story of the Mexican War*, 47; J. Smith, *War with Mex.* 1:149–50 (ZT quot.). Hardee (later Conf. gen.) was soon released (Rowland 1:449; Oliver Otis Howard, *General Taylor*, 126).

73. Grady McWhiney, *Braxton Bragg and Confederate Defeat*, 59–61 (quot. on 60); Seitz, *Bragg*, 6, quot.; Ambrose, *West Point*, 140; Hamilton, *Zachary Taylor* 1:181–90; Wiltse, *Calhoun* 3:282–84.

74. John G. Poindexter to J. Thompson and JD, May 11, 1846 (*Papers* 2::201, quot.); JD, Amendment (rejected) to Bill, May 11, 1846 (*Papers* 2::200, quot.); JD "To a Gentleman in Vicksburg," May 12, 1846 (*Papers* 2::203 and Ed. Note, quots.). The Oregon crisis was not resolved until June 18.

75. JD "To a Gentleman" (as in previous note), quots.; *Papers* 2::225 and n.9; Ibid.::134, 146, 166, 188, 189, 191, 205, 208.

76. JD, Speech on Harbors and Rivers Bill, Mar. 16, 1846 (ibid., 164 and Ed. Note, quots.; Dem. 1844 platform against internal improvements); Ibid., n.51.

77. JD, Speech (as in Note 76 above; quots. on pp. 513–15; "surprised" [504] appropriations treated like spoils); Wiltse, *Calhoun* 3:235–36.

78. JD, Speech (as in Note 76 above, quot. on p. 515) and n.51; Wiltse, *Calhoun* 3:262–64, 266–72, 235–36, 245–46 (quot. on 246).

79. *Papers* 2::171, 172 and n.9, 179 (quot. on p. 543), 180 and Ed. Notes, 202 n.2. Polk consulted JD, who recomm. Bennet Riley to head the mounted regt., but he was not appt'd. (ibid., 207 and nn.2 and 4).

80. *Papers* 2::230 and n.7; JD, First Reply to William Sawyer, ibid., 216 (quots. on p. 617), Ed. Note, and n.7 (Sawyer quot.), n.9. The fort, renamed for fallen comm. of 7th Inf., Maj. Jacob Brown, was nucleus for Brownsville, Texas (ibid., 196 n.5).

81. VHD, *Memoir* 1:243; *Papers* 2::217 Ed. Note (Sawyer quot.); First Exchange with Andrew Johnson, May 29, 1846 (ibid., 218, quots.). See sketch of Johnson, ibid., 142 n.13.

82. *Papers* 2::218 (n.7: Burt a disciple of Calhoun; m. to his niece); Remarks . . . Second Exchange with Andrew Johnson, May 30, 1846 (ibid.::220, quots.); Ibid., n.13 (*Intelligencer* quot.); VHD, *Memoir* 1:244, quot.

83. *Papers* 2::217 Ed. Note; Speight et al. to Polk, June 3, 1846 (ibid.::222); Ibid.::18 n.104; Ibid.::211 and 225, quots. from Quitman and Pontotoc.

84. VHD to Marg. K. Howell, June 6, 1846 (*Papers* 2::224, quot.); JD to VHD [June 22, 1846], quots. (MS at the Briars, copied by author, 1984; date from précis in *Papers* 3:457; ref. unknown).

85. VHD to Marg. K. Howell, June 6, 1846 (*Papers* 2::224, quots.); JD to People of Miss., July 13, 1846 (*Papers* 3:3, quot.); R. Davis, *Recoll. of Miss.*, 212; *Papers* 2::239 (elected June 18); Ibid.::241, 253, 254, and 3:3 (rec'd. comm. July 1 and orders from Adj. Gen. July 3).

86. JD, Autobiog. Sketch (*Papers* 2:App. 1, p. 700, quot.); Ibid.::239 n.12 and 172 (quot.) and n.9; JD to Thomas Ritchie, July 2, 1846 (ibid., 2::252, quot.); Ibid.::241 and n.5 and 3:18; Ibid. 2, p. xxxix. Scott was now maj. gen. and gen.-in-chief (Heitman, *Hist. Register*, 1:20; *Papers* 1::124 n.2).

Chapter VII Fame

1. JD, Speech on Oregon, Feb. 6, 1846 (*Papers* 2::137, pp. 461–62, quot.; ref. to Scott, *The Lady of the Lake,* canto 5, stanza 5, lines 96–97); VHD, *Memoir* 1:284, quots. The 2 tactics books in use were Winfield Scott's (revised 1835) and William Duane's *Handbook for Infantry* (*Papers* 1::124 n.2; Weigley, *Hist. U.S. Army,* 170–71).

2. VHD to Marg. K. Howell, June 6, 1846 (*Papers* 2::224, quots.); JD to Lucinda Stamps, July 8 (ibid.::255, quot.).

3. VHD at Hurricane, Dec. 1846 (*Papers* 3:97, 100); at Natchez, July, Oct. 1846, late Feb.–June 1847 (ibid., 14 Descr. Note, 54–55, 121 n.12, 123 n.4, 170, 178 Descr. Note); at Brierfield, Dec. 1846–early Feb. 1847 (ibid., 96–97, 100, 119 and n.12, *Letters* 45–46); in La., n.d. (N. D. Smith, "Reminisc. of JD," 179).

4. VHD, *Memoir* 1:284–85, quots. (for Jim Green, see also *Papers* 3:95 n.1); Ibid., xxxi. The vol. regts. enlisted for 12 mos. (Henry, *Story of Mex. War,* 83–84).

5. *Papers* 2::253, 254, 239 n.12 and 3:9–10 n.1; JD to People of Miss., July 13, 1846 (ibid., 3–9, quots. on 3); Ibid. 2::239 and n.27 and 48 n.10; Ibid. 3:30 n.11; JD to VHD, July 18 (ibid. 11 and Ed. Note). Whig eds. said Tom Robins engineered JD's election over Whigs Bradford and McClung; one apologized when Robins challenged him to a duel (*Papers* 2::239 n.19; 1 n.4, p. 5).

6. Francis A. Wolff [1st Miss. sgt. maj.] to W. T. Walthall, May 15, 1879, MS, TULANE, quot.; *Papers* 3:11 Ed. Note, quot. See R. Davis, on Bradford ("chevalier Bayard") and McClung ("too highly strung," "died by his own hand") in *Recoll. of Miss.,* 88–89, 137–41, 198, 213–19. Sterling, *Belle,* 15: McClung "wild and untameable," famous as duelist. Known as "Death's Ramrod," he was said to have killed between 14 and 30 men (Dueling exhibit, Old Capitol Mus. of Miss. Hist., MDAH; seen, 1984).

7. *Papers* 3:11–13 (JD to Walker, July 22, 1846 and nn.1, 3, and 4); Same to same, Aug. 24 (ibid., 17–18); Henry, *Story of Mex. War,* 85.

8. JD to Walker, Aug. 24, 1846 (*Papers* 3:18–19; 178 of his men were sick [n.9]; "Land" ref. to Gen. 13:14–17, Num. 14:8). See J. Smith, *War with Mex.,* 205–7, and Henry, *Story of Mex. War,* 74–78, 85–86. "Lighters" were boats of shallower draft than ocean-going steamboats.

9. JD to VHD, July 18, 1846 (*Papers* 3:11, quots.); JD to VHD, July 29, MS, TRANSYL, quots. (this letter almost unique in having two excisions); JD to VHD, Aug. 16 (*Papers* 3:16, quot.; last phrase from I Cor. 9:25).

10. JD to VHD, Aug. 16, 1846 (*Papers* 3:16, quot.); ZT to JD, Aug. 3 (ibid., 14–15, quots.); Henry, *Story of Mex. War,* 138, 141, 144; *Papers* 3: xxxi.

11. WPJ, *Gen. ASJ,* 132–36, 232, 142 (quot.); Henry, *Story of Mex. War,* 83 (ASJ served ZT without formal rank or pay); *Papers* 3:21 Ed. Note; J. Smith, *War with Mex.* 1:492–93 n.8 ("Field Div." meant temporary).

12. Henry, *Story of Mex. War,* 140; Twiggs in Heitman, *Hist. Register;* J. Smith, *War with Mex.* 1:143; JD to Crosman, Sept. 3, 1846 (*Papers* 3:20–21 and n.1); *Papers* 2::207 n.4 (Riley quot.).

13. Maury, *Recoll.,* 43; Harney in Heitman, *Hist. Register;* J. Smith, *War with Mex.* 1:266–76 (Harney, 268–69); Freeman, *R. E. Lee* 1:203–12. Harney alone survived massacre of his sleeping men in Florida, ran 40 miles for help, came back, captured and hanged most of the guilty Seminoles (Maury, 43–44).

14. Nathaniel Cheairs Hughes, Jr., *General William J. Hardee: Old Reliable,* 27–31; McWhiney, *Braxton Bragg,* 63; JD in H. R., May 28, 1846 (*Papers* 2::216, 217).

15. R. Davis, *Recoll. of Miss.,* 220, quot.; *Papers* 2::50 n.13; Ibid. 3:14 n.3; Ibid. 2::203 and 8 n.7; Ibid. 3:134 n.7 (quot. from Corwine; see Rowland 2:187–88).

16. For Rogers, see text below; Russell to JD, Nov. 24, 1847 (*Papers* 3:247–48); (Griffith:) *Papers* 3:9 n.1, 4:240 n.11, 5:152, Warner, *Gens. in Gray,* and Madison McAfee to JD, Apr. 20, 1853 (Rowland 2:208); *Papers* 3:32–35.

17. VHD, *Memoir* 1:352 (Estes quots.); Wolff to Walthall, May 15, 1879, MS, TULANE, quots.; JD to VHD, Dec. 10, 1846 (*Papers* 3:95); Posey to G. H. Gordon,

Feb. 19, 1847, in Mrs. John W. Day, "Brigadier General Carnot Posey [C.S.A.]," (*United Daughters of the Confederacy Magazine*, Aug. 1988), 26, quot. ("repulsive"=repellant; they "admired and respected each other"; see also *Papers* 3:74 n.9).

18. JD to Addison [Hayes], July 19, 1880, MS, MVC; George H. Hise to JD from Cal. State Prison, Dec. 25, 1853 (Rowland 2:340–41); *New Orleans Daily Picayune*, Dec. 7, 1889, p. 2, col. 6 (quot. from "Mr. Mills"; for Ward, see *Papers* 5:App. 1, 218, June 10). Other letters, e.g.: *Papers* 4:394, 400, 5:255, 415 (see 3:33 n.34) and Rowland 7:451–52. VHD says they gave him comfort "to the last hour of his life" (VHD, *Memoir* 1:480).

19. Wolff to Walthall, May 15, 1879, MS, TULANE, quots. (incl. quots. from JD to Wolff, Feb. 23, 1848).

20. VHD, *Memoir* 1:288–89 quots.; JD, "Autobiography," *Papers* 1:lv; Henry, *Story of Mex. War*, 87–88; Winnie Davis, "JD in Private Life," 10 ("his sterling honesty"). JD distinguished "public property, the proper subject of capture in war" from private, which was not (JD to VHD, Aug. 21, 1865, MS, TRANSYL).

21. Return of killed and wounded, Sept. 21, 1846 (*Papers* 6:675); JD, Additional Rpt. [on Monterey] (ibid. 3:37, quot.); Ibid., 140, 143 and n.25, 81, 84 n.7; VHD, *Memoir* 1:323, 352–53 (Estes quots.; has "Estis," but see Rowland 7:415–16), 285 (quot. on Joe); Hughes, *Gen. Hardee*, 42 n.2; *Papers* 3:17 n.3. JD had noted AJ's care for men and "small loss" (ibid. 2::67, p. 270).

22. Wolff to Walthall, May 15, 1879, MS, TULANE, quots. (Quitman called 1st Miss. "best drilled regiment on the whole line"); Joseph Davis to JD, [Oct.] 7, 1846 (*Papers* 3:56, quot.).

23. *Papers* 3:21 Ed. Note (and map after p. 19), 102; Wolff to Walthall, May 15, 1879, MS, TULANE, quots.; Henry, *Story of Mex. War*, 142–44. Wolff thought JD and ZT met here for first time "since Davis stole his gal"—showing how widespread was the slander, even among his own men, and still uncorrected in 1879 (see text above, chap. 5).

24. Henry, *Story of Mex. War*, 138, 144, 146–49 (quots.); *Papers* 3:map after p. 19; McWhiney, *Braxton Bragg*, 61–63 (quot.), 67–68; J. Smith, *War with Mex.* 1:226–31, 252–53; McKinley and Bent, *Old Rough and Ready*, 167; Wolff to Walthall, May 15, 1879, MS, TULANE.

25. Wolff to Walthall, May 15, 1879, MS, TULANE, quots.; Hamilton, *Zachary Taylor* 1:210; Joseph D. Howell to Mother, Sept. 25, 1846, MS, MDAH, quot.; JD, Speech at Vicksburg [Nov. 10] (*Papers* 3:81, quots.); Russell to JD, Sept. 26 (ibid., 48, quot. from JD). Wolff calls grey horse "Pompey"—an error repeated by J. Smith, *War with Mex.* 1:252, and by others; it was Tartar: see VHD, *Memoir* 1:311.

26. Quots.: JD, Memorandum on the Battle of Monterrey [*sic* throughout] (*Papers* 3:102); JD to Jenkins, Nov. 16, 1846 (ibid., 87); J. L. McManus to JD, Oct. 18 (ibid., 67.).

27. Russell to JD, Sept. 26, 1846 (*Papers* 3:48, quots.); Ibid. 30 n.11; WPJ, *Gen. ASJ*, 138 (McClung quot.); JD, Memorandum (*Papers* 3:102–3); JD, Speech at Vicksburg (ibid., 82, quot.; Wolff, as in Note 24 above, mistakes where McClung wounded); R. Davis, *Recoll. of Miss.*, 214, quot.

28. WPJ, *Gen. ASJ*, 138–39 (quots. from JD's account; see 141); JD, Memorandum (*Papers* 3:103, quot. *re* door); Russell to JD, Oct. 18, 1846 (ibid., 71, quot.); J. Smith, *War with Mex.* 1:253–55, map on 240 (see "Remarks," 499–501 n.10). "Stone building" also called "tannery" and "distillery."

29. Henry, *Story of Mex. War*, 150–51; JD to A. G. Brown, Sept. 20, 1847 (*Papers* 3:229, quots.); JD, Speech at Vicksburg [Nov. 10, 1846] (ibid., 82, quot.). For other action this day: ibid., 35–36, 43 n.7, 70 n.5, 76 n.6, 229–31.

30. JD, Speech at Vicksburg (*Papers* 3:82, quot.); Joseph D. Howell to Marg. K. Howell, Sept. 25, 1846, MS, MDAH, quots.; [1st Lt.] S. A. D. Greaves to JD,

Oct. 18, 1846 (*Papers* 3:65, quots.; see 66 n.9 and 110 n.41); Ibid., 41, 64, 106–7, 231–32, 242–43.

31. JD, Autobiography (*Papers* 1::1, pp. lv–lvi, quots.); JD, Memorandum (ibid. 3:106–7); JD to A. G. Brown, Sept. 20, 1847 (ibid., 231–32); C. T. Harlan to JD, Oct. 17 (ibid., 243). JD told of this dangerous withdrawal in Senate, Aug. 5, 1850 (Rowland 1:463–64; and of whole campaign, 436–73).

32. J. Smith, *War with Mex.* 1:258–59; JD, Autobiography (*Papers* 1::1, p. lvi, quots.); WPJ, *Gen. ASJ*, 142–44 (quots. from WPJ and JD). JD, Memorandum on Capitulation of Monterrey (*Papers* 3:57–61). ASJ was discharged with ZT's thanks Oct. 1 (Rowland 1:458).

33. *Papers* 3:21–23 (quot.), 61 n.3, 108, 110–12; Henry, *Story of Mex. War*, 153, 164–65; J. Smith, *War with Mex.* 1:259–60; Heitman, *Hist. Register*, 949 (quot. from Cong. res.); Joseph Davis to JD, [Oct.] 7, 1846 (*Papers* 3:55–56, quot.); JD, Autobiography (*Papers* 1::1, pp. lvi–lvii, quot.). See Rowland 7:502.

34. *Papers* 3:62 n.1 (JD quot.); VHD, *Memoir* 1:308–9 (quots. from ZT rpt. and Joseph D. Howell to mother, Oct. 13); Same to same, Sept. 25, 1846, MS, MDAH, quots. Conf. Mus., N. O., has JD's saddle and portmanteau and a ".58 caliber" Miss. rifle. Uniforms are red shirts, white pants, panama hats, in Fritz Kredel and Frederick P. Todd, *Soldiers of the American Army* [Chicago: Henry Regnery Company, 1954] under "Texas Rangers and Mississippi Rifles, 1846" [n.p.]: no stripes here or in *Papers* 3:frontispiece and 99 n.13.

35. Henry, *Story of Mex. War*, 103–6; Joseph D. Howell to Mother, Oct. 13, 1846, in VHD, *Memoir* 1:307–9, quots. R. Davis says strictness made JD "somewhat unpopular" at first, but after his men found him "fearless in action . . . they almost idolized him" (*Life and Reminisc.*, 210).

36. JD, Speech at Vicksburg [Nov. 10, 1846] (*Papers* 3:79 and 83, quots.); McWhiney, *Braxton Bragg*, 92, quot.; J. Smith, *War with Mex.* 2:48.

37. VHD to JD, [Sept. 1846] (*Papers* 3:53, quot.; "warrant by Dr. W. R. Holt" may show need for JD at home); VHD, *Memoir* 1:310–11, quots.; *Papers* 3:xxxii–xxxiii and 74 Ed. Note.

38. JD-Peyton correspondence, Nov. 1, 3, 1846 (*Papers* 3:77–78, quots. and nn.); JD to John Jenkins, Nov. 16 (ibid., 88 and 86, quots.; and nn.); Ibid., 29 n.3 and 84 n.6; JD to Peyton, Nov. 14 (ibid., 84–85, quots.). JD's rough draft says position of regts. proves claim "ridiculous" (ibid., Apr. 1, 401).

39. JD to Jenkins, Nov. 16, 1846 (*Papers* 3:88, quot.); Ibid., 78 n.1 (quots. from Peyton to Campbell, Nov. 5); Joseph Davis to JD, [Oct.] 7 (ibid., 55, quot.; and n.5); Corr. of JD and Wm. H. Bissell, Feb. 22–27, 1850 (ibid. 4:79–82, 85–86 and nn.; Bissell col. of 2d Ill. in Mex. War; now Dem. in H. R.; "warrants for their arrest" had been issued).

40. Ibid. 3:30–31 nn.11–12 (but see Rowland 1:81: McClung disclaims credit); Willis and Rogers to JD, July 25 and Aug. 6, 1847 (ibid. 5:App. 2, 475, quots. from précis; for Rogers, see 3:46 n.3). For battle rpts. on this point, see *Papers* 3:25–52, 62–63, 67–68, 75–76, 403–4.

41. JD to John Jenkins, Sept. 21, 1847 (*Papers* 3:233–35, quots.; see nn.: anti-JD quots. in n.9); Officers of 2d Miss. Regt. to JD, July 16 (ibid., 193–94, quot.); JD to Officers, Aug. 19 (ibid., 215–16); Ibid., 30 n.11 (McClung quot.; JD recomm.); Ibid. 5:App. 1, 301, Jan. 21, quot. See R. Davis, *Recoll.*, 217–19: McClung insane at the end.

42. Joseph Davis to JD, [Oct.] 7, 1846 (*Papers* 3:55–56, quots.); Ibid., 96 n.11; Strode, *Patriot*, 172–74; VHD, *Memoir* 1:311–12, quots.; JD, Speech at Vicksburg (*Papers* 3:81, quots.); Ibid., 95 n.1.

43. *Papers* 3:xxxiii; JD to VHD, Dec. 10, 1846 (ibid., 93–95, quots.); Joseph Davis to JD, Dec. 16 (ibid., 96–97, quot.; and see same to same, Dec. 30, ibid., 100); JD to Joseph Davis, Jan. 26, 1847 (ibid., 116, quot.).

44. JD to VHD, Dec. 10, 1846 (*Papers* 3:93–95, quot.; text has "creaturis").

45. Ibid., quots. (MacRees in nn.4–6; see *Letters* 45–46); JD, Statement on

Tenería (*Papers* 3:App. 1, p. 401, quot.); JD to Varina B. Howell, Sept. 6, 1844 (ibid. 2::41, quot).

46. JD to VHD, Dec. 10, 1846 (*Papers* 3:94); JD, Autobiography (ibid. 1::1, pp. lvi–lvii; notes ZT moved supplies in "large india-rubber bags" which, when emptied, could hold water for a desert march); Samson, *Letters of ZT,* 179–80; Henry, *Story of Mex. War,* 159–71, 183–89, 193–95; J. Smith, *War with Mexico,* 1:349–63; Howard, *General Taylor,* 225–29.

47. *Papers* 3:xxxiii; ZT to James Buchanan, Aug. 29, 1847 (Samson, *Letters of ZT,* 180, quot.); ZT to R. C. Wood, Apr. 4 (ibid., 94–97); Howard, *General Taylor,* 228 (Scott quot.); Hamilton, *Zachary Taylor,* 1:226 (quot. from ZT to Wood, Feb. 9), and see p. 444; *Papers* 3:114–15, 4:306.

48. Henry, *Story of Mexican War,* 194–98 (ZT quot.); J. Smith, *War with Mexico,* 1:357–58, 362 (quot.); *Papers* 3:xxxiii; Ibid. 2::207 n.4; JD to Joseph Davis, Jan. 26, 1847 (ibid., 3:114–16 and n.4): Harney and Bragg in Heitman, *Hist. Register* (see Rowland 2:175). Sherman is T. W., not W. T. of C. W. fame.

49. JD to Joseph Davis, Jan. 26, 1847 (*Papers* 3:114–16, quots.). See Samson, *Letters of ZT,* 115; it was on this proposed march that ZT would have used the bags spoken of in Note 46 above and in Rowland 7:502–3.

50. ZT to Buch., Aug. 29, 1847 (Samson, *Letters of ZT,* 182–83); Hamilton, *Zachary Taylor* 1:227–32; JD to VHD [Feb. 8] (*Papers* 3:118, quot., and nn.).

51. Henry, *Story of Mexican War,* 243; VHD, *Memoir,* 1:337–38 (quots. from Estes): JD letter, Sept. 24, 1847 (*Papers* 3:236–37, quots.; see Rowland 2:174); Montgomery, *Life of Taylor,* 358 (quot.), 263, 273–74; Maury, *Recollections,* 29, quot.

52. Quots.: WPJ, *Gen. ASJ,* 152–54; Maury, *Recoll.,* 29; JD, Senate speech, Aug. 5, 1850 (Rowland 1:472).

53. VHD, *Memoir* 1:338–40 (quots. from Estes), 316–17, 354n; Montgomery, *Life of Taylor,* 309; Henry, *Story of Mex. War,* 243–45. See J. Smith, *War with Mex.* 1:382–83, 385–87; Rowland 1:468–69, 472; *Papers* 3:122–63, 406–8; McWhiney, *Braxton Bragg,* 87.

54. J. Smith, *War with Mex.* 1:384 (quots.), 386–88, 555 n.5; Howard, *General Taylor,* 246–47 (Santa Anna quot.); Hamilton, *Zachary Taylor* 1:233; *Papers* 3:237 and n.3 (Crittenden quot.) and 123 n.3; Ibid., 160 n.1 (Rogers quots.); Rogers to JD, Mar. 6, 1847 (Rowland 1:174–75); Major Bliss m. Betty Taylor the next year (Samson, *Letters of ZT,* xii–xiii).

55. McWhiney, *Braxton Bragg,* 54 (quot.), 61, 74–75, 79–80 (see Weigley, *Hist. U.S. Army,* 172, 184; J. Smith, *War with Mex.* 1:450–51 n.6); Montgomery, *Life of Taylor,* 254, quot.; *Papers* 3:127 n.17, 182, 183 n.5; JD, Autobiog. (*Papers* 1::1 p. lvii, quots.).

56. VHD, *Memoir* 1:340–41 (quots. from Estes); JD, Rpt. on Buena Vista, Mar. 2, 1847 (ibid., 319–21 and 327, quots.); *Papers* 3:147 n.10; JD, Deposition in Court of Inquiry [on Col. W. A. Bowles of 2d Ind.], Apr. 1847 (Ibid., 3:166–67; see also Rowland 2:13–14); McWhiney, *Braxton Bragg,* 80–83 (2d Ky. also moved left); J. Smith, *War with Mex.* 1:389–91.

57. VHD, *Memoir* 1:321 (quots. from JD rpt.), 342–44 (quots. from Estes), 350n, 316–17,; JD, Speech at Natchez, June 1847 (*Papers* 3:184); (Wound:) Ibid., 122–23 (dressing "in the saddle" in n.2 here appears a newspaper invention), Ibid. 1::1, p. lix. Regt. members praised JD for staying with them when wounded (*Papers* 3:163, 153–54); he commended others for it (VHD, *Memoir* 1:331).

58. VHD, *Memoir* 1:343 and 353 (quots. from Estes; mistakenly says 6 cannon), 321–22 (quots. from JD rpt.); McWhiney, *Braxton Bragg,* 83 (Bragg quot.); Montgomery, *Life of Taylor,* 282. See Smith, *War with Mex.* 1:558 n.13 for Bragg.

59. VHD, *Memoir* 1:322–23 (quots. from JD rpt.), 335–36 (quots. from Estes; JD vouched for this incident); JD in Rowland 3:341–42; JD to Wm. A. Buck, June 21, 1859 (ibid. 4:57, quots.; JD sketched here the "V" formation, as seen in *Papers*

3, facing p. 224); JD, Address to Mex. War Vets., Mar. 7, 1876 (Rowland, 7:504, quot.).

60. VHD, *Memoir* 1:345 (quots. from Estes), 323–24 (quot. from JD rpt.)

61. VHD, *Memoir* 1:345–47 (quots. from Estes), 324 (quots. from JD rpt.); JD, Address to Mex. War Vets. (Rowland 7:504, quot.; "lace" = gold or silver braid). Inf. usually formed a hollow square to meet cav. attack, or at least an angle facing out, not in (JD to Buck, as in Note 59 above). Enemy estimated "tenfold" and "five times greater" (*Papers* 3:155, 157). JD by now had probably no more than 200 men (see refs. in Notes 55, 56 above).

62. VHD, *Memoir* 1:324 (quot. from JD rpt.), 347–48 (quots. from Estes); *Papers* 3:136, 138 n.13; Montgomery, *Life of Taylor*, 283.

63. *Papers* 3:147 n.10, 159–60 and nn.; VHD, *Memoir* 1:324–25, 348–49; Montgomery, *Life of Taylor*, 283–85; Henry, *Story of Mex. War*, 250–52.

64. Montgomery, *Life of Taylor*, 285–86 (quots. from ZT rpt.), 338–39 (quots.); McWhiney, *Braxton Bragg*, 84–85 (Bragg quot.), 90–93 (ZT quots.; see Seitz, *Bragg*, 9); VHD, *Memoir* 1:325 (quot. from JD rpt.). Bragg did pass ZT's post (disputed): used perimeter of field to avoid ravines (maps in McWhiney, 81, and *Papers* 3:endpaper); see *Papers*, 3:149 n.30 for 3rd Ind..

65. JD in Senate, Aug. 5, 1850 (Rowland 1:471, quot.); ZT to Wood, Apr. 4, 1847 (Samson, *Letters of ZT*, 97, quot.).

66. VHD, *Memoir* 1:326 (quot. from JD rpt.), 332; JD, Autobiog. (*Papers* 1::1, p. lix, quots.); JD to VHD, Feb. 25, 1847 (ibid. 3:122–23, quot.). JD wounded "severely," rather than "slightly" or "dangerously" (Rowland 1:175–77): a "compound comminuted fracture of the os calcis which became infected" (Evans, *JD, Diseases and Doctors*, 4).

67. *Papers* 3:149 n.32; VHD, *Memoir* 1:332–33, 316–18 (Crittenden quot.; her "Captain Eustis" on 332 is not in 1st Miss. roster: see *Papers* 3:9–10); Jones, *Davis Memorial*, 92.

68. VHD, *Memoir* 1:326–27 (quots. from JD rpt.), 352 (quots. from Estes); JD, Address to Mex. War Vets., Mar. 7, 1876 (Rowland 7:504, quot.; ambulance was a wagon: *Papers* 3:149 n.32); Howard, *General Taylor*, 280–81.

69. Montgomery, *Life of Taylor*, 287; *Papers* 3:123 n.4 (quots. from J. D. Smith letter); VHD, *Memoir* 1:327–28 (quots. from JD rpt.); Jones, *Davis Memorial*, 93 (quot. from Claiborne). JD's rpt. is "on narrow strips of age-browned paper," in Conf. Mus., N. O. (Strode, *Patriot*, 180 n.2).

70. VHD, *Memoir* 1:333 (ZT quot.), 359 (quot.); JD in Senate, Aug. 5, 1850 (Rowland 1:470–71, quots.; similar ref., 3:213); ZT to Wood, July 13, 1847 (Samson, *Letters of ZT*, 112); ZT to JD, July 27 (*Papers* 3:198–204), Aug. 16 (208, 214), Sept. 18 (223), Feb. 16, 1848 (270), Apr. 20 (304, 311).

71. Howard, *General Taylor*, 123, quot.; Montgomery, *Life of Taylor*, 269, 287, 333, 335, 337; *Papers* 3:127 nn.17, 19. JD says ZT refused to abandon field because "My wounded are behind me, and I shall never pass them alive!" (ibid., 375). Mex. murder of wounded: e.g., Henry, *Story of Mex. War*, 155 n.22; *Papers* 3:124, 129; VHD, *Memoir* 1:343; Montgomery, 342. ZT notes (ibid., 341) some murders by Americans as "unfortunate exceptions." Joe Howell rescued a wounded Mex. about to be killed by a Tenn. soldier, "the coward" (to Mother, Sept. 25, 1846, MS, MDAH).

72. Marg. K. Howell to W. B. Howell, Mar. 6, 1846, MS, MDAH; *Papers* 2::20 n.8; Joseph Davis to JD, Feb. 13, 1847 (ibid. 3:119, quot.); VHD, *Memoir* 1:576–77 and 333, quots.

73. Montgomery, *Life of Taylor*, 290–91 (ZT quot.); James K. Polk to JD, May 19, 1847 (*Papers* 3:175–76; quot. in n.1); Ibid. 2::18 n.102, p. 104. See JD to Walker, June 20 (ibid. 3:186–87).

74. JD, Autobiog. Sketch, *Papers* 2:App. 1, p. 700 ("I did not believe that Congress had the power": "not delegated"; *Statutes at Large* cited in n.28); JD to Polk, June 20, 1847 (ibid. 3:185–86, quots.); JD to Walker, June 20 (ibid., 186–87, quot.); VHD, *Memoir* 1:247, quot.

75. *Papers* 2::222; Ibid.::18 n.104, p. 107 (quots. from Q. to wife); JD to Joseph Davis, Jan. 26, 1847 (ibid. 3:115, quots.); JD, Memorandum (ibid., 104, quots.; and see 82, 90).

76. Montgomery, *Life of Taylor,* 373; Henry, *Story of Mex. War,* 367 (Quitman maj. gen. and gov. of City of Mexico); McWhiney, *Braxton Bragg,* 85–88 (Bragg quot. on 87) 93, 96–97, 99, 101–2, 104, 107–8.

77. Jones, *Davis Memorial,* 102 (ZT quot.; Colquitt: army thought JD's regt. "saved the day"); Lubbock, *Six Decades,* 565, quot.

78. VHD, *Memoir* 1:353–56, quot.; JD, Speech at N. O., June 10, 1847 (*Papers* 3:181–82, quots.; and Ed. Note); Rogers to JD, Aug. 6 (précis in *Papers* 5:App. 2, p. 475); JD, *Rise and Fall* 2:390, quot.

79. VHD, *Memoir* 1:357–58; JD to Calhoun, May 28, 1847 (*Papers* 3:180); Reception in honor of 1st Miss. Regt., June 15 (Rowland 1:74–84, all quots. from *Natchez Weekly Courier,* except JD speech); JD, Speech at Natchez, June 15 (*Papers* 3:183–84 [quots. from paraphrase] and Ed. Note; ref. to Vergil *Aeneid* 2.5–6; author indebted to Ward S. Allen for ident.).

80. Quots.: VHD, *Memoir* 1:358; Reception . . . June 15, 1847 (Rowland 1:84); JD to VHD, May 27, 1847 (*Papers* 3:178).

Chapter VIII United States Senator

1. J. Smith, *War with Mex.* 2:Conspectus, xii-xiii; Montgomery, *Life of Taylor,* 314–16 (quot. from Pike); *Selections from the Southern Poets,* ed. William Lander Weber, xli, 130–34 (quots. from O'Hara) and 210n; C. W. mon., e.g., Perryville and Auburn, Ala. JD is also in "The Siege of Monterey" by William C. Falkner of Miss. (1851) (*Papers* 2::41 n.5).

2. VHD, *Memoir* 1:225–26, quots.; JD to Stephen Cocke, July 15, 1847 (*Papers* 3:192 and n.1: Speight died May 1); Same to Brown, Aug. 15 (ibid., 207–8).

3. ZT to JD, July 27 and Sept. 18, 1847 (*Papers* 3:198–204, 217–23; quots. on 203, 218–19); ZT to Wood, June 23 (Sansom, *Letters of ZT,* 109, quot.). "General" Davis (ZT:) *Papers* 3:198, 200, 208, 217, 268, 270, 304, Rowland 1:208, 210; (others:) ibid. 2:177, 349 Endrs., and 9:416, VHD, *Memoir* 1:542, Ridley, *Battles and Sketches,* 77.

4. ZT to JD, July 27, 1847 (*Papers* 3:203, quots.; last word printed "dectine").

5. *Papers* 3:App. 2, p. 414 (real estate tax roll, Dec. 1846; prob. 636 A. of "backland" should be added [see 120 and 122 n.19]); Joseph Davis to JD, May 13 and Apr. 16, 1847 (ibid., 173 and 165, quots.); Ibid., App. 2, p. 449 (Personal Property tax roll, Sept. 1848, cited [slaves and cattle]); VHD, *Memoir* 1:194–95. Joseph wrote to Jeff in detail from Ky. about horses in 1838 (*Papers* 1::525).

6. ZT to Wood, July 13, 1847 (Samson, *Letters of ZT,* 112, quot.); VHD, *Memoir* 1:359, quot.; VHD to [Marg. K. Howell, summer 1847] (*Letters,* 48, quot.). See ZT to JD, July 27 (*Papers* 3:198–99). Dr. Charles Mitchell, widower of Joseph's daughter Mary, lived nearby in La. (ibid. 2::2 n.4).

7. JD to Stephen Cocke, July 15, 1847 (*Papers* 3:192, quots.); ZT to JD, Sept. 18 (ibid., 223, quot. from Mitchell); JD to Officers of 2d Miss. Regt., Aug. 19 (*Papers* 3:215–16); ZT to John Jenkins, Sept. 21 (ibid., 235, quot.).

8. JD to Brown, Aug. 15, 1847 (*Papers* 3:207–8); Joseph Davis to JD, May 21 (ibid., 176); ZT to Wood, Oct. 27 (Samson, *Letters of ZT,* 144, quot.); JD to VHD, Sept. 30, (*Papers* 3:238, quots.; for Thompson and Roberts, see 240 n.8).

9. Ibid., 226 n.2 (rpt. and quot. from *Vicksburg Weekly Sentinel,* Sept. 29, 1847); ZT to Wood, Oct. 27 (Samson, *Letters of ZT,* 145, quot.); JD to Brown, Oct. 3 (*Papers* 3:241, quots.).

10. JD to VHD, Sept. 30, 1847 (*Papers* 3:238–39, quots.; "miserabile" [lamentable] a jocose turn on "mirabile dictu" [wonderful to relate]; Eliza: see ibid., 240 n.4); Ibid., nn.1, 2; *Letters,* 53. Visitor prob. Dr. M. W. Philips of Hinds Co., who

loved to talk about his experimental planting: see *Papers* 4:176–77, Rowland 2:179–82, and Riley, "Diary of Miss. Planter."

11. N. D. Smith, "Reminisc. of JD," 179, quots.; *Papers* 3:App. 2, p. 419 (med. bill for Carroll, 1847), 4:239 (bills for Carroll, 1851) and 241 n.16 (see also 6:App. 1, 543, Mar. 17).

12. JD to VHD, Sept. 30, 1847 (*Papers* 3:238, quot.); Ibid. 1:App. 4, Chart 11 and nn.; Everett, *Brierfield*, 35–41, 46, Plate after p. 22; VHD to Marg. K. Howell, Jan. 3, 1847 (*Letters*, 45, quot.: the children "so *very* destructive, so very unruly that I do not like to let them come").

13. VHD to Marg. K. Howell, [summer 1847], Oct. 17 and Nov. 12 (*Letters*, 48–49, 53, 54, quots.; ref. to John Dryden, *Alexander's Feast*, 4.2; off. was Lt. R. K. Arthur: see *Papers* 3:9 n.1 and 33 n.33). VHD, *Memoir* 1:215–16, quot. (descr. route here and *Letters*, 54; northern in text above, chaps. 5–7).

14. *Papers* 3:xxxv (arr. Nov. 25; White House Dec. 9; appts. Dec. 14; election Jan. 11); Ibid., 250 n.1; JD to Cocke, Nov. 30, 1847 (ibid., 249); Ibid., 254 n.1.

15. JD to P. W. Tompkins, Dec. 25, 1847 (ibid., 253, quots.); JD to Crittenden, Jan. 23, 1848 (ibid., 262); Ibid., 246 n.2.

16. Miles, *Jacksonian Dem. in Miss.*, 164, quot.; *Papers* 2::18 n.38, 1::5 n.10, 2::26 Ed. Note; R. Davis, *Recoll. of Miss.*, 144–53; Williams, *Dueling in the Old South*, 17, 55 (quot.); Dueling Exhibit, Old Capitol Mus. of Miss. Hist., MDAH (seen, 1984).

17. JD to Howell Hinds, Sept. 30, 1856 (*Papers* 6:51–52, quots.; see 53 n.8: Foote and Quitman fight); Wiltse, *Calhoun* 3:325–26; Mem. by A. W. Venable, in letter to JD, Aug. 8, 1874 (Rowland 7:395 n.1, quot.; names witnesses to fight); Wilson, *Code of Honor*, in Williams, *Dueling in Old South*, 99 (#2, #3), 94 (#3).

18. ZT to JD, Sept. 18, 1847 (*Papers* 3:223, quot.; "your crutch," Feb. 16 and Apr. 20, 1848 [270, 304]); Rowland 2:240 and 10:156 (quots. *re* Scott). Foote: see *Papers* 2::18 n.38, and JD in Rowland 2:125–32, 138–71.

19. JD to VHD, Apr. 18, 1848 (*Papers* 3:303, quots.); JD to VHD, Jan. 3–4 (quots. from typed copy of excerpts provided author by Lynda Crist: see ref. and précis in *Papers* 5:App. 2, 475–76).

20. Quots.: VHD to Marg. K. Howell, June 6, 1846 (ibid. 2::224); JD to VHD, Sept. 30, 1847 (ibid. 3:238–39); JD to VHD, Sept. 6, 1844 (ibid. 2::41; ref. unknown).

21. VHD to Marg. K. Howell, Jan. 1848 (*Letters*, 56–57, quots.; cameo "white on a deep lead-colored ground"). VHD visited Diamond Place in Dec. and Locust Grove in Jan. (letters in Index to ALA, pp. 29–30). Her jewels at Smithsonian include a cameo bracelet (*Smithsonian*, June 1978, 22–23).

22. JD to VHD, Jan. 3–4, 1848 (as in Note 19 above), quots. (shows Joseph not to blame for trouble over house, as often claimed; see also Everett, *Brierfield*, 38).

23. JD to VHD, Jan. 3–4, 1848 (as in Note 19 above), quots.; VHD to JD, Oct. 23, 1865, and Apr. 17, 1859 (*Letters*, 193 and 107, quots.). VHD later spoke of the suffering and "doubt" of this time as "my clouded youth" (ibid., 227–28).

24. JD to VHD, Jan. 3–4, 1848 (as in Note 19 above), quots.; JD to VHD, Apr. 18 (*Papers* 3:302–3, quots.; mentions previous corr.). By "sensibility," JD means his tender feeling for her ("Sense and Sensibility" in *The Oxford Anthology of English Literature*, ed. J. B. Trapp et al. [New York: Oxford Univ. Press, 1973], 1:2286–87).

25. Quots.: VHD to JD, Feb. 2, 1866 (*Letters*, 227–28); JD to VHD, Apr. 18, 1848 (*Papers* 3:303); VHD to JD, Jan. 24, 1849 (ibid. 4:7–8); JD to VHD, May 27, 1847 (ibid. 3:178). For her trip to Washington, see ZT to JD, July 10, 1848 (Rowland 1:209–10).

26. JD, Remarks on the Ten-Regiment Bill, Jan. 3 and 5, 1848 (*Papers* 3:254–56 and 260, quots.; Ed. Note); VHD, *Memoir* 1:363–69; Henry, *Story of Mex. War*, 384, 365. Mex. City fell Sept. 14, 1847.

27. JD, Remarks on 10-Regt. Bill, Jan. 5, 1848 (*Papers* 3:257–61); JD in Senate,

Feb. 8, Feb. 3, Mar. 17 (ibid., App. 2, 428; 263–65; 277–88); Ibid., 262 n.8, quots.; Henry, *Story of Mex. War*, 386–88, 390, 393 n.35.

28. JD, Remarks on the Cumberland Island Dam Bill, Apr. 14, 1848 (*Papers* 3:295–301, quots.; n.7). See also VHD, *Memoir* 1:369–75.

29. *Papers* 3:316 n.1 (Calhoun quot.); Ibid., 313–14 Ed. Note; Wiltse, *Calhoun* 3:341–42, 325 (quot. on Hale); JD, Remarks on the Protection of Property, Apr. 20, 1848 (*Papers* 3:314–15, quots.); Quots. from Garrison in *Universal Encycl.* and Blum et al., *Natl. Experience*, 253, and from Isaiah 28:15, 18.

30. Blum et al., *Natl. Experience*, 253 (and see JD in *Papers* 4:37 and n.), 275, 274; Wiltse, *Calhoun* 3:311, 293, 296, 283–84, 315, 327–28; Hamilton, *Zachary Taylor* 2:270–71.

31. Blum et al., *Natl. Experience*, 275; Wiltse, *Calhoun* 3:337, 293 (quots.), 345; *Papers* 3:332 Ed. Note.

32. JD, Speech on the Oregon Bill, July 12, 1848 (*Papers* 3:332–38, quots.). JD seems to overlook prohibition of slavery in the Northwest Territory by the congress of the Confederation in 1787 (Blum et al., *Natl. Experience*, 124; pointed out to author by Hutch Johnson); but see *Papers* 4:20 and n.4, and 4:28.

33. Wiltse, *Calhoun* 3:295, quot.; JD to People of Miss., Sept. 25, 1851 (Rowland 2:90, quots.); JD, Speech on Ore. Bill, July 12, 1848 (*Papers* 3:332–38 and 357, quots.). See JD on "extension" in *Rise and Fall* 1:6–7, and Rowland 1:262–63. *Southern Review*, July 1869, 97: Seward said South meant to force slavery on the North, but nobody believed him, "not even Mr. Seward himself."

34. JD, Speech on Ore. Bill, July 12, 1848 (*Papers* 3:355–56, 363–64, quots.; see Rowland 1:285 for this argument in 1850). In 1850, out of the 347,525 slaveowners in the United States, 345,792 owned less than 100; most, between 1 and 10; only 11, more than 500 (Randall, *Civil War*, 60).

35. JD, Speech on Ore. Bill, July 12, 1848 (*Papers* 3:355, 362–64, quots.). JD said on Feb. 14, 1850, that the "present condition of Jamaica" and San Domingo showed the error of liberating blacks "before God, in his wisdom, designed it should be done" (Rowland 1:300).

36. JD, Speech on Ore. Bill, July 12, 1848 (*Papers* 3:363, 359–60, quots.; see 363–64 for alternate ideas). On slave and free, and Northern idea that blacks "would soon be made to die out," see "Chivalrous Southrons" in *Southern Review*, July 1869, 116–17, 118.

37. JD, Speech on Ore. Bill, July 12, 1848 (*Papers* 3:360–63, quots.); JD in Senate, Mar. 8, 1850 (Rowland 1:316–17, quots.; ref. to Rev. 18:13). Sons of Noah in Gen. 9:18–10:32; slaves in Lev. 25:44–46.

38. JD, Speech on Ore. Bill, July 12, 1848 (*Papers* 3:354–69, quots.). See JD in 1849: ibid. 4:27.

39. JD, Speech on Ore. Bill, July 12, 1848 (*Papers* 3:354–69, quots.). Abraham and Lot: Gen. 13:5–11; JD quoted v. 9 in his speech.

40. Wiltse, *Calhoun* 3:349–57 (quot. on 357); JD, speech at Holly Springs, Miss., [Oct. 25], 1849, paraphrase (*Papers* 4:49, quots.); Ibid., 28; 3:373 n.48.

41. Wiltse, *Calhoun* 3:296, 344, 357–58 (Calhoun quot.); *Papers* 3:358 (JD quot.).

42. VHD to Marg. K. Howell, Nov. 26, 1847 (*Letters*, 56, quots.); ZT to JD, July 10, 1848 (Rowland 1:209–10); JD to VHD, Apr. 18 (*Papers* 3:303); Ibid., xxxvi and App. 2, 447 [Aug. 9].

43. VHD to JD, Jan. 24, 1849 (ibid. 4:7, quot.; cholera in N. O. and Vicksburg [14 n.8]; for link of fruit and cholera, see 1::363).

44. Hamilton, *Zachary Taylor* 1:249–54; *Papers* 3:271 n.7; ZT to JD, Apr. 20, 1848 (*Papers* 3:304–11, quots.).

45. ZT to JD, July 10, 1848 (Rowland 1:208–11, quot.). John M. Morehead, former gov. of N. C., presided over Whig convention of 1848 (Hamilton, *Zachary Taylor* 2:90).

46. ZT to JD, July 10, 1848 (Rowland 1:208–9, quots.).

47. *Papers* 3:202, 209, 212, 268–69, 305 (letters to JD), and Samson, *Letters of ZT*, 14, 102–4, 108–9, 113–14, 130, 137, 162–64 and n.1, 161 (quot., June 25, 1848); (Parties:) ibid., 102–3, 143, 153–54; Howard, *General Taylor*, 295–96; Hamilton, *Zachary Taylor* 2:97.

48. JD to Walker, June 29, 1847 (*Papers* 3:190–91, quots.); ZT to JD, July 17 (ibid., 201, quot.; brackets in text); ZT to J. S. Allison, Apr. 22, 1848 (Hamilton, *Zachary Taylor*, 80, quot.; and see 133 on Dems.); Wiltse, *Calhoun* 3:369–71, quot. ZT thought Whigs now embodied Jeffersonian principles better than Dems. (to JD, Sept. 18, 1847 [*Papers* 3:221]).

49. Hamilton, *Zachary Taylor* 2:92–94; Sansom, *Letters of Z T*, 108, 114, 118, 180, 184–85, and *Papers* 3:199–200, 305–6; ZT to JD, Apr. 20, 1848 (ibid., 306, quot.); ZT to Wood, July 20, 1847 (Sansom, 119, quot.); ZT to JD, Sept. 18 (*Papers* 3:219, quot.; ref. to Matt. 6:14–15). See chap. 18 below.

50. (JD quots.): letter, Apr. 12, 1848 (*Papers* 3:292); speech, 1849 (Rowland 1:239); speech, May 1860 (ibid. 4:304); speech, June 13, 1848, paraphrase (*Papers* 3:327–29). Campaign: ibid., 52 n.1, 374–91, app. 2, 449 (Sept. 26, Oct. 6).

51. Cass in *DAB* and *Papers* 3:392 n.5; JD, Speech at Jackson [Miss.], Sept. 23, 1848 (ibid., 385, quot.); JD to Hugh R. Davis, June 4 (ibid., 325, quots.); Ibid., 21 Ed. Note.

52. JD to Barksdale and Jones, Dec. 27, 1851 (Rowland 2:113, quots.; see also 2:137); *Calhoun* 3:325–26; Paul D. Escott, *After Secession: Jefferson Davis and the Failure of Confederate Nationalism*, 21–22, 33; JD to Woodville Citizens, Oct. 23, 1848 (*Papers* 3:390, quots.).

53. "General Cass's Nicholson Letter," *Washington Union*, Mar. 17, 1852 (Rowland 2:109–17); JD in Senate, May 16–17, 1860 (Rowland 4:304–305, quots.); *Papers* 3:276 n.13 (Miss. vote: Cass, 26,537; ZT, 25,992); Ibid., 4:79 n.6, quot. JD on Cass: *Papers* 3:391–92 and 4:53–54, 76–78; on ZT, ibid., 49–50. The veto power was an issue in the campaign.

54. Wiltse, *Calhoun* 3:364–70 (Polk quot. on 369; quot. on 370); Blum et al., *Natl. Experience*, 277; George W. Julian, *Political Recollections, 1840 to 1872*, 60, quot.; JD to [Simon Cameron], July 26, 1847 (*Papers* 3:196–97, quots.; see 4:28: T. Jefferson's "fire bell at night" was "a geographical party"). JD was also suggested for Dem. v. p. (*Letters*, 55).

55. JD to Marcy, Nov. 30, 1847 (*Papers* 3:250, quots.; Whitney was Eli's son [n.2]); JD to [Lt. Col.] Geo. Talcott, Nov. 7 (ibid., 245, quot.); JD to Marcy, Aug. 12, 1848 (ibid., 374 [quot.] and n.2; for rifles of 1st Miss., see 174–75, 197–98, 206, 241 and Rowland 1:89–91); JD to Marcy and Marcy to JD, June 29 and July 16, 1847 (ibid., 87–89); JD to Polk, Mar. 28, 1848 (*Papers* 3:289–90, quot.).

56. (Comms., e.g.:) *Papers* 3:245 n.19, 414–21, 427; (Bounty lands, e.g.:) ibid., 421, 422, 425, 427 and 4:317, 319, 322; (Pensions, e.g.:) ibid., 325, 328, and 5:242; (Hospital:) ibid. 3:421, 423; Ibid. 4:322, Feb. 23 (Rogers quot.; see text above, chap. 7).

57. JD to Polk, Apr. 13, 1848 (*Papers* 3:293–94); Twiggs in Heitman, *Hist. Register;* Jeanne Twiggs Heidler, "The Military Career of David Emmanuel Twiggs," 134–35, 149–50; *Papers* 3:App. 2, 448, 436.

58. Moore, *Northrop*, 26–36; JD to J. K. Polk, June 23, 1848 (Rowland 1:205–6, quots.); JD to Marcy, May 5 (*Papers* 3:316–17 and nn.; also App. 2, 424, 425, 439, 446, 447, and 5:App. 2, 476); Calhoun and Butler to Polk, July 6 (ibid. 3:331–32 and Descr. Note).

59. Ibid.:xxxvi; JD to Crawford, May 15, 1849 (ibid. 4:21 and n.3); Cass in *DAB*. On Smithsonian, see JD, Jan. 12, 1849 (*Papers* 4:3).

60. Seating Chart, Senate, 1850 (ibid., after 152); JD in Senate, Feb. 11, 1851 (Rowland 2:19, quot.); Wiltse, *Calhoun* 3:372 (quots.), 377–88 (quots. on 387), 541 n.9.

61. *Papers* 4:xxxi–xxxii (see also 18 n.3 and JD comm. rpt., Rowland 1:224–25); Hamilton, *Zachary Taylor* 2:135, 150; McElroy, *JD* 1:111, quot.

62. JD to J. T. Crittenden, Jan. 30, 1849 (*Papers* 4:8–9, quot.); Hamilton, *Zachary Taylor* 2:102, 137–38, 144–45; Paraphrase of JD speech, [Oct. 25], 1849 (*Papers* 4:48, quot.; see nn.6–7 and Wiltse, *Calhoun* 3:395).

63. JD to J. T. Crittenden, Jan. 30, 1849 (*Papers* 4:8, quots., and nn.1–2); JD to Polk and Marcy, and from Jones, Jan. 1849 (ibid.:App. 2, 312; see also 357); Comm. rpts., Feb. 28, Mar. 2 (ibid. 5:App. 2, 477); George Bibb and Thomas Leonidas Crittenden in *South in Bldg. of Nation*, 11.

64. *Papers* 4:xxxii; JD, Speech at Jackson, May 7, 1849 (ibid., 19–20, quots.; Ed. Note; 51 n.13); JD to Malcolm D. Haynes, Aug. 18 1849 (ibid., 26–44, quots. on 37, 41, compares "partial assurance" not to attack slavery in the states to "the wooden horse of the faithless Greeks"; ref. to Virgil, *Aeneid*).

65. JD to Haynes, Aug. 18, 1849 (ibid., 26–44, quots.; "eyeservice" on 41–42; ref. to Eph. 6:6; Col. 3:22). JD called the novel issue of sin, "the glamour of ethical illusions" (*Rise and Fall* 1:14). On "political heresy," see "Chivalrous Southrons," 114, 104.

66. Quots.: JD to Cocke, Aug. 2, 1849 (*Papers* 4:25; ref. to Matt. 7:13–14); JD to Searles, Dec. 20 (ibid. 53); JD, Speech at Convention [June 18] (Rowland 1:236–43; refs. to Matt. 7:24–25; Ex. 20:24 and Lev. 19:5; 2 Macc. 1:18–33; he also alluded to Luke 16:19–31: "rise from the dead . . . not believe").

67. *Papers* 4:25, 13; Ibid. 120 n.7 and 1::363 n.20; Ibid. 2::2 n.4; JD to VHD, Oct. 14, 1849 (ibid. 4:47, quot.; 46 Ed. Note); JD to Kingsbury, Dec. 15 (ibid. 52, quots.; Ed. Note; he refers, e.g., to *Peter Simple* by Frederick Marryat [n.2]); Ibid., 120 n.8.

68. VHD, *Memoir* 1:409 (1848 date here a mistake); VHD to Marg. K. Howell, Jan. 6, 1850 (*Letters*, 59, quots.). See also *Papers* 4:121 n.9.

69. VHD to Marg. K. Howell, Jan. 6, 1850 (*Letters*, 59–60, quots.; 58 Ed. Note); Hamilton, *Zachary Taylor* 2:136, 26, 173 (Bliss bvt. lt. col and ZT's private sec.). ZT urged JD to visit Mrs. T. and Betty at Baton Rouge in Aug. 1847 (no evidence that he did), and sent greetings from Betty 1848 (*Papers* 3:214, 270–71).

70. Hamilton, *Zachary Taylor* 2:150 (Seward quots.), 149; Samson, *Letters of ZT*, 169; JD quots. on ZT: Rowland 1:470, 472 and *Papers* 3:236. Betty "charming and popular" (Howard, *Gen. Taylor*, 324).

71. ZT to JD, Feb. 16, 1848 (*Papers* 3:270, quot.; ref. to Ps. 90:10, "threescore years and ten"; he was then 63); ZT to JD, July 10 (Rowland 1:210, quot.). JD tried to get Dems. to nom. ZT (*Papers* 3:292).

72. Strode, *Patriot*, 223 (quot. from ZT friend); Knox T. quot.: see above, chap. 5; Hamilton, *Zachary Taylor* 2:175–80, 278–86, 297–301; Blum et al., *Natl. Experience*, 277–78, 281; Rowland 1:307, 391–94, 502–4 (faults in Cal. bill).

73. JD in Senate, Jan. 29, 1850 (*Papers* 4:67, quot.) and May 15 (107, quots.); Ibid. 2::22 n.13 (Clay quot.). For a Clay-JD clash, see ibid. 4:170–72 and Rowland 2:62–66.

74. *Life and Reminisc.*, 16 (JD quots.; see JD, *Rise and Fall* 1:17n, and *Papers* 4:32); Hamilton, *Zachary Taylor* 2:279–80 (Clay quot.); JD in Senate Feb. 13, 1850 (Rowland 1:279, quots.). Tex. accepted $10 million for its northwest area; slave trade, but not slavery, abolished in D. C.; Cong. could not interfere with *interstate* slave trade (Blum et al., *Natl. Experience*, 270, 281, 278).

75. JD in Senate, June 27, 1850 (Rowland 1:373–74, quots.); JD, Mar. 14 (*Papers* 4:87, quot.); JD to *Washington Union*, May 18 (Rowland 1:347, quot.). On 1821 Mo. Compromise line, at 36°30'N., see Blum et al., *Natl. Experience*, 203–5.

76. Blum et al., *Natl. Experience*, 281; Randall, *Civil War*, 123–25 and n.3, 166–69; JD, *Rise and Fall* 1:16–17; JD in Senate, Feb. 13, 1850 (Rowland 1:268, quot.; see also *Papers* 4:33, 36–37).

77. *Papers* 4:162 n.7; "Speech of Mr. Davis . . . [on] Slavery in the Territories," Feb. 13–14, 1850, in *Pamphlets relative to Jefferson Davis from Boston Public Library;* Wiltse, *Calhoun* 3:457–58, 460–65 (quots. incl. Calhoun); VHD, *Memoir* 1:458 ("lordly" quot.); Blum et al., *Natl. Experience*, 205 (T. Jefferson quot.).

78. VHD, *Memoir* 1:457–58 (quots., incl. Benton and Calhoun; errs in saying C. not there Mar. 4); Wiltse, *Calhoun* 3:465–71 (quots. on 471; Benton on 477); Randall, *Civil War,* 122–23; *Masterpieces of American Poets,* ed. Mark Van Doren [Garden City, N. Y.: Garden City Publishing Co., Inc., 1936], 666 ("Ichabod" on 160); Blum et al., *Natl. Experience,* 281 (quot. on Sumner).

79. Wiltse, *Calhoun* 3:471–72, 474–79 (Webster quot. on 477); VHD, *Memoir* 1:462–63, quots. VHD promised Ma a strand of Calhoun's hair, and told of the D. C. funeral (*Letters,* 60). See JD on Webster's oration in "Life and Character of Calhoun," 260, and *Rise and Fall* 1:17.

80. VHD, *Memoir* 1:463, quot. The Scott quot. is "The Lady of the Lake," canto 3, stanza 16, lines 3–4, which JD used *re* Calhoun, June 27, 1850, in Senate debate (Rowland 1:375), and also in *Rise and Fall* 1:17; but this author finds no separate eulogy such as VHD describes here (repeated by Strode, *Patriot,* 222).

81. L. C. Loan Record, Jan. 3–Sept. 30, 1850 (*Papers* 4:173–75, quots.); VHD to JD, Jan. 25 [1850] (ibid. 62, quots., and nn.; *Letters,* 58, prints this letter as 1849 from Natchez).

82. VHD to Marg. K. Howell, May 18 and 20, 1850 (*Letters,* 61–62, quots.); Hamilton, *Zachary Taylor* 2:24–25, 171–72, 387, 396; VHD to JD, [June] 14, 1850 (from Easton) (*Papers* 4:119–20 and nn.).

83. JD in Senate, Feb. 11, 1858 (Rowland 3:213, quots.); JD, Feb. 27, 1849 (ibid. 1:225; quot. paraphrasing ZT; see Howard, *Gen. Taylor,* 320–21, 336, 340); Hamilton, *Zachary Taylor* 2:294–97, 388–89 (quot.; see also Howard, *Gen. Taylor,* 346–47 and 367–69; says ZT *laid* cornerstone).

84. VHD to Marg. K. Howell, July 10, 1850 (*Letters,* 62–63, quots.). The Woods and ZT's brother, Col. Joseph Taylor, were there (Montgomery, *Life of Taylor,* 426). "Mrs. Taylor would not permit her husband's corpse to be embalmed" (Hamilton, *Zachary Taylor* 2:394).

85. Hamilton, *Zachary Taylor* 2:387–92 (quots.), 224; Howard, *Gen. Taylor,* 373; Montgomery, *Life of Taylor,* 449, 429. Hamilton (1:22, 113; 2:24, 397) insists ZT did not belong to Episc. Church, but he came from a strongly Anglican family and was probably baptized as an infant. On his religion, see ibid., 241, and Samson, *Letters of ZT,* 13, 17, 21 (also 71, 89, 95, 117, 137).

86. Samson, *Letters of ZT,* xxv (quot. from July 10 procl.); Hamilton, *Zachary Taylor* 2:394, 26–27 (quot.; other Wood d., Blandina, was prob. in La.), 386, 396–98 (quot.), 400 (place of burial now called ZT Natl. Cem.).

87. ZT to R. C. Wood, Sept. 27, 1847 (Samson, *Letters of ZT,* 135, quot.); JD to [Marg. K. Howell], July 18, 1850, MS, TRANSYL, quots. (also *Papers* 4:123 and nn.; "After life's fitful fever, he sleeps well": *Macbeth* 3.2.23); *Papers* 2::20 n.8.

88. *Papers* 4:123 n.2 (quot.); Ibid., 120 n.8; Ibid., App. 1, 362, 370, 363, 367; JD speech, Aug. 5, 1850 (Rowland 1:436–73; "aspersions" on 441–42); Rowland 1:542–43. Gaines d. June 6, 1849 (Heitman, *Hist. Register*).

89. Quots.: Rowland 1:565–67, see *Papers* 4:App. 1, 371, 557–60, 567–68.

90. VHD, *Memoir* 1:412–13, quots. (her 1848 date wrong); Freeman, *R. E. Lee* 1:303–8 (time uncertain); Hamilton, *Zachary Taylor* 2:368–69 (the exp. failed in May 1850); Rowland 7:283 (JD quot.). The Davises and Lee were all here only 1849–50: see *Papers* 4:59 n.2 and Ray Broussard, "Governor John A. Quitman and the Lopez Expeditions of 1851–1852," 108. "Filibuster" came to mean Cong. debate only in 1882 (*Shorter OED*).

91. JD to Marg. K. Howell, Sept. 15, 1850 (*Papers* 4:132, quot.).

Chapter IX Victory in Defeat

1. *Papers* 4:xxxv; VHD to JD, [June] 14, 1850 (ibid., 119, quot.); VHD to [Marg. K. Howell], Nov. 14, 1845, quot. (MS, Old Courthouse Mus.); VHD to JD, Feb. 23, 1866, MS, ALA, quot.

2. E. Rowland, *Varina Howell* 1:19; Strode, *Patriot,* 196–97, 248–49; *Wm. Johnson's Natchez,* (Sprague and Howell:) 65 and n.3 quot. (also 94, 124, 126, 127, 130, 134, 142, 166, 171, 173, 188, 202, 215, 216), (shooting, etc:) 255–56, 260, 263, 265 and n.9, 279, 294, 308 (a Garnet Howell also in Natchez [91], but W. B. named several times); Rowland 1:191; *Papers* 4:120 n.5, quot.; *Papers* 2::20 n.8 (Wm. was 16; Becket, 10; Marg., 8; Jane [n. d.]; JD, 4; Joe back by 1852 [83 n.6, p. 331]).

3. VHD, *Memoir* 1:177, 474 (quots.); Everett, *Brierfield,* 49, 55 (E. says Pemberton died in 1852).

4. VHD, *Memoir* 1:465; *Papers* 4:xxxv, 134–35 Ed. Note (136 n.2: Quitman calls legis. for Nov. 18); "Protest against the California Bill," Aug. 13, 1850 (Rowland 1:502–4, quots.); JD, Speech at Raymond [Miss.], Oct. 26, paraphrase (*Papers* 4:135–36, quots.); JD, Speech at Benton, [Miss.], Nov. 2, paraphrase (ibid., 136–37, quots.; n.1).

5. *Papers* 4:xxxv, 134–35 Ed. Note, and App. 1, 373–74; JD to VHD, [Dec.] 5 (ibid. 5:App. 1, 480, quot.; says "Nov."; this date from 4:xxxv); JD to Lowndes Co. Citizens, Nov. 22, 1850 (ibid., 138–45, quots.). JD on South as minority, Rowland 1:589, 594, 596; on "British emissaries" using "false pretext of philanthropy to mask their unholy designs to kindle the fires of civil war," ibid. 247–49; also 4:73, 107–8.

6. *Papers* 4:xxxv, xxxiii; JD in Senate, Jan. 10, 1850 (Rowland 1:253, quot.); JD to W. R. Cannon, Jan. 8 (*Papers* 4:56, quot.); JD to S. Cobun et al., Nov. 7 (Rowland 1:592–93, quots.).

7. Resolutions of the Miss. Legis., Dec. 19, 1850 (date when read in Senate) (Rowland 1:600–603, quots., incl. earlier request for instruction and reply; passed and signed Nov. 30).

8. JD, Remarks [in Senate], Feb. 12, 1851 (Rowland 2:22–28, quots.).

9. *Papers* 4:85 n.11, xxxvi, and 76 nn.1, 3; F. L. Claiborne to JD, May 25, 1850 (ibid. 5:App. 2, 479, quots.); JD in Senate Jan. 30, 1851 (Rowland 2:14–17, quots.); JD, Feb. 27, 1849 (*Papers* 4:14–17, quots.; nn.3, 4, 6, 8, 9; after Catlin mortgaged and lost his Indian paintings, the Smithsonian acquired them 1879). Natl. Gallery not opened until 1941, with a Smithsonian trustee (D. E. Finley, "Intro." in *Masterpieces of Painting from the National Gallery of Art,* ed. Huntington Cairns and John Walker [New York: Random House, 1944]).

10. JD in Senate, Feb. 18 and 24, 1851 (Rowland 2:28–43, quots.).

11. JD in Senate, Feb. 18, 1851 (Rowland 2:30–31, quots., incl. that from Quitman); Broussard, "Gov. Quitman and Lopez," 115.

12. *Papers* 2::18 n.104, p. 107; Hamilton, *Zachary Taylor* 1:200–201, 224–25, 368–70; Broussard, "Gov. Quitman and Lopez," 108–18; *Papers* 4:272–73 nn. 13, 16; *Christ Church, Nashville, 1829–1929,* 82, and Henry, *Story of Mex. War,* 294 (see Major "Bob" Wheat in Terry L. Jones, *Lee's Tigers: The Louisiana Infantry in the Army of Northern Virginia* [Baton Rouge: Louisiana State Univ. Press, 1987], passim); *Papers* 4:26 n.2.

13. *Papers* 4:xxxvi, 176 n.1, 237 (quots. from JD account with Payne and Harrison, Mar. 3 and 10, 1851; and see 12–13, Wm. Ziegler to JD, Feb. 25, 1849); Everett, *Brierfield,* 39 and 41 (VHD quots.), 44–49, and floor plan after 22; Cameron Freeman Napier, *The First White House of the Confederacy, Montgomery, Alabama,* 9. See *Papers* 2::60 n.1, p. 246.

14. JD to J. E. Heath, Jan. 12, 1851 (*Papers* 4:152 and nn.; see Howell to JD, Jan. 31, 1853 [Rowland 2:185]); "Mother" to "My dear Child," Apr. 7, 1851, quots. (MS, MDAH; Marg. is with VHD).

15. JD to VHD, May 8, 1851 (*Papers* 4:181, quots.); Ibid., xxxvi–vii and 183 Ed. Note; R. Davis, *Recoll. of Miss.,* 316.

16. Lowry and McCardle, *Hist. of Miss.,* 321, quot.; *Papers* 2::18 n.38, p. 84; Foote and JD in Senate, June 27 and Sept. 16, 1850 (Rowland 1:369–86 and 543–46); R. Davis, *Recoll. of Miss.,* 315–21, quots.; Marg. K. Howell to W. B. Howell, Mar.

6, 1846, MS, MDAH, quot.; JD, *Rise and Fall* 1:19–20. See JD to Yulee in *Papers* 4:218–19; Quitman in text above, chap. 7.

17. JD to J. A. Pearce, Aug. 22, 1852 (*Papers* 4:300, quot.; 301 n.3); Ibid., xxxvii; JD to H. Hinds, Sept. 30, 1856 (ibid. 6:50–51, quots.; see also ibid. 53 n.4, Rowland 2:37, and JD, *Rise and Fall* 1:21n).

18. JD to LBN, Apr. 25, 1879 (Rowland 8:384, quot.); Robert E. May, *John A. Quitman: Old South Crusader*, 261–62; JD to D. L. Yulee, July 18, 1851 (*Papers* 4:218, quot.); R. Davis, *Recoll. of Miss.*, 317–18, quots.

19. *Papers* 4:xxxvii–viii and back endpaper map; Ibid., 222 n.2; VHD, *Memoir* 1:469, quot.; Evans, "JD, Diseases and Doctors," 4; Riley, "JD and His Health," (Pt. 1) 198–99; JD to [Dr.] S. A. Cartwright, Sept. 23, 1851 (*Papers* 4:225, quot.); Ibid., 223 n.2. Quitman res'd. Sept. 6; JD en route Sept. 9–15; nom. Sept. 16.

20. JD, *Rise and Fall* 1:20; E. Barksdale to JD, Sept. 19, 1851 (*Papers* 4:222, quots.); Lowry and McCardle, *Hist. of Miss.*, 322, quot.; *Papers* 4:219 n.1 and 223 n.2.

21. JD to Yulee, July 18, 1851 (*Papers* 4:218, quot.); JD in Senate, May 16, 1860 (Rowland 4:288, quot.); JD to Cocke, Dec. 19, 1853 (ibid. 2:335, quot.; n.1: res'd. Sept. 23); JD, *Rise and Fall* 1:20, quot.; JD to Wilkinson, Sept. 17, 1851 (Rowland 2:86).

22. VHD, *Memoir* 1:469, quot.; JD to Cartwright, Sept. 23, 1851 (*Papers* 4:224–25, quots.; n.3). Dr. Harris D. Riley, Jr., says this descr. is "entirely compatible with herpes simplex keratitis [inflammation of the cornea]" caused by "type 1" of the virus, not to be confused with the "genital herpes" of "type 2." Type 1 also causes fever blisters; JD was rpt'd. at the time to have "fever blisters on his eye" ("JD and His Health," 198–99).

23. VHD, *Memoir* 1:469–70, quots. (incl. Quitman's); *Papers* 2::18 n.104; JD in Senate, Feb. 12, 1851, and Jan. 5, 1859 (Rowland 2:25 and 3:463–68, quots.) and to Miss. Legis., Nov. 16, 1858 (ibid., 354, quot.).

24. JD, *Rise and Fall* 1:20, quot.; VHD, *Memoir* 1:470, quots. (her 3 weeks, picked up by many, is wrong; it was 2: see *Papers* 4:xxxviii); Ibid., 225 n.4; JD, Speech at Athens [Miss.], paraphrase [Oct. 27, 1851], ibid., 231–32, quots., nn.1, 3 (quot. from A. M. Clayton); Ibid., 233 n.2 (total vote, 57,717).

25. Quots.: JD to Stephen Cocke, Dec. 19, 1853 (Rowland 2:335); JD in Senate, May 16, 1860 (ibid. 4:288); JD in Senate, Mar. 3, 1851 (*Papers* 4:171 and see 293–97).

26. Quots.: JD in Senate, Aug. 15, 1850 (Rowland 1:506–8); JD, Speech at Fayette [Miss.], July 11, 1851, paraphrase (*Papers* 4:186–87); JD to Yulee, July 18 (ibid., 218–19; ref. to Joseph Addison, *Cato* 4.4: "Content thyself to be obscurely good. / When vice prevails and impious men bear sway, / The post of honor is a private station" [*Hoyt*, 372]). See Rowland 2:84–85.

27. Quots.: JD to Tarpley, Dec. 19, 1855 (*Papers* 5:149); Petition . . . [by] citizens of Wilkinson county [printed Nov. 19, 1850] (Rowland 1:589–90); James Blair et al. to JD, Nov. 11 (ibid. 2:87; he had to decline their invitation to a dinner for him [*Papers* 4:138]).

28. JD to Clayton, Nov. 22, 1851 (Rowland 2:108, quots.; ref. to *The Lady of the Lake*, canto 5, stanza 6, lines 21–22). The charge of disunion was "one of those perversions of truth which, least of all others, he felt able to forgive" (paraphrase of JD speech, Rowland 2:122).

29. *Papers* 6:141 ("sorrow" at the vote, but "no sullen submission"); JD, speech, Jan. 8, 1852, paraphrase (Rowland 2:117–25, quots.); C. D. Fontaine to JD, July 13, 1853 (ibid., 235, quot.).

30. R. Davis, *Recoll.*, 320, quots.; R. Davis to JD [Nov. 1851] (*Papers* 4:232–33, quot.); *Papers* 4:237 n.9.

31. VHD to Parents, Oct. 28, 1851 (*Letters*, 63–64, quots.); VHD, *Memoir* 1:474–76 (quots., incl. JD and gardener); VHD to Marg. K. Howell, Mar. 4, 1852 (*Letters*,

65, quots.); *Papers* 5:App. 2, 481, under Jan. 5, 1852; Everett, *Brierfield,* 49, 52; *BCP* (1830), quots. from "Solemnization of Matrimony."

32. Everett, *Brierfield,* 44–45; VHD to Marg. K. Howell, Mar. 4, 1852 (*Letters,* 65, quot.); Philips to JD, Jan. 12, 1853 (Rowland 2:179–82, quots.); *Papers* 2::60 n.1, pp. 246–47, and 17 n.10. For overseers, see 4:293 n.3; 5:42 n.22 and 117–18 and n.1; 6:130 n.1.

33. JD to People of Miss., Jan. 26, 1852 (Rowland 2:132–38); E. Barksdale to JD, Dec. 28, 1851 (*Papers* 4:234–36, 237 nn.6, 9); JD to Barksdale and Jones, Feb. 2, 1852 (ibid., 241–49 and nn.1, 10; quot. on 249) and Feb. 16 (Rowland 2:138–71; quot. on 157).

34. JD to W. D. Chapman, Oct. 13, 1853 (Rowland 2:274, quot.; and see JD to LBN, Apr. 25, 1879 [ibid. 8:384]); Inge to JD, June 1, 1854 (ibid. 2:363, quot.; also, Foote in Cal.); A. G. Brown to JD, May 1, 1852, said "thrashing" Foote was like "Kicking a *pole cat*" (*Papers* 4:255), and see 5:14; Ibid. 4:251 and n.6, 252, 253–54, 301 n.5 and 5:37 n.8 and App. 1, 311, under Feb. 15, 1854.

35. May, *John A. Quitman,* 270–95; Lowry and McCardle, *Hist. of Miss.,* 322; Barnwell to JD, Oct. 20, 1851 (*Papers* 4:227, quot.); *Papers* 4:xxxviii, 272 n.1, and Rowland 4:305.

36. JD, Speech at Jackson, June 9, 1852 (*Papers* 4:258–71; quots. on 259); Blum et al., *Natl. Experience,* 282.

37. JD, Speech June 9, 1852 (*Papers* 4:260–62 and 271, quots.); Ibid., 272–73 nn.9–17; Broussard, "Gov. Quitman and Lopez," 119, 118 (and see May, *Quitman,* 252).

38. JD, Speech at Jackson (*Papers* 4:269–70, 259, 266, and nn.); JD, Speech at Oxford [Miss.], [July 15, 1852] (ibid., 275–90, quot. on 276; see nn.1–3); Rowland 2:171.

39. JD, Speech at Oxford (*Papers* 4:279–80, quots.; doubtful words were deleted or transposed; n.15); Blum et al., *Natl. Experience,* 279 (Seward quot.); JD in Senate, Jan. 12, 1849 (Rowland 1:219, quot.).

40. JD, Speech at Oxford (*Papers* 4:286–89, quots.).

41. *Papers* 4:xxxix and 301 n.2; Ibid., App. 1, 398–99 (quots. from speeches of July 19, 20, and [24], 1852).

42. VHD to JD, July 25, [1852] (ibid., 291–92, quots.; n.2), VHD to Marg. K. Howell, Mar. 4 (*Letters,* 65, quots.).

43. Ibid., 292; (Friends' children:) Ibid. 3:19 and 191, 4:219, 257; Marg. K. Howell to [W. B. Howell], Aug. 20, 1852 (*Letters,* 67, quot.); VHD to [parents], June 14, 1850 (*Papers* 4:120 n.2, quot.); JD to VHD, Mar. 13–14, 1866, MS, TRANSYL, quot. (Le Roy=the king; "old one"=the devil [*OED*]).

44. JD to James Pearce, Aug. 22, 1852 (*Papers* 4:300, quot.); Ibid., xxxix and 302 Ed. Note; Cartwright to JD, Oct. 16 (ibid., 302–4, quots.). Ship Island is c. 15 mi. off Biloxi. Quinine prob. aggravated JD's eye condition and digestive troubles (Riley, "JD and His Health," Part 2, 264–65).

45. Conversations with Drs. V. S. LeQuire and Emil Wright, Jr.; "Neuralgia" in *A Dictionary of Medical Science,* ed. Robley Dunglison [Philadelphia: Henry C. Lea, 1874] (types analysed, some of Cartwright's treatment mentioned; also severing nerve—still the only remedy known); Riley, "JD and His Health," Part 2, 262–64, 266 ("tic"); Craven, *Prison Life,* 153, quot.; *Papers* 4:xxxix (see 307 n.1)

46. *Papers* 4:App. 1, 400 (Oct. 29 speech); Nichols, *Franklin Pierce,* 216 and n., 214, 217–23. See Jones, *Davis Memorial,* 51.

47. Pierce to JD, Dec. 7, 1852 (Rowland 2:177–78, quots.); Nichols, *Franklin Pierce,* 221–23, 227.

48. Pierce to JD, Jan. 12, 1853 (Rowland 2:178–79, quots.); Nichols, *Franklin Pierce,* 86, 106, 109, 124–25, 171–72, 224–25; JD to Charles G. Greene, Feb. 13, 1853 (*Papers* 5:5, quot.; Greene transmitted their letters, to avoid public notice [Rowland 2:178]); JD to Cocke, Dec. 19, 1853 (Rowland 2:335–36, quots.); JD, *Rise and Fall* 1:22, quots.

49. *Papers* 4:304 n.1 (quot. from JD to Cartwright, Jan. 20, 1853) and 301 n.2

(quot. from VHD to Marg. K. Howell, May 25, 1852); Ross, *First Lady*, 68; JD to VHD, Sept. 15, 1865, MS, TRANSYL, quot.

50. *Papers* 2::5 n.5, 16 n.3 and 5:6 n.6; T. J. [here, "I."] Durant to JD, Jan. 22, 1853, and JD to Durant, Feb. 17, 1853 (Rowland 2:183–84 and *Papers* 5:5–6 and n.6; also 2::50 n.19); VHD to JD, July 25, 1852 (ibid. 4:291, quot.); VHD to Marg. K. Howell, Apr. 29, 1854 (*Letters*, 78, quot.).

51. JD to Joseph Davis, June 11, 1855 (*Papers* 5:111, quots., incl. Joseph to Ma; 1852 seems only year possible); Marg. K. Howell to VHD, Jan. 27 and Feb. 22, 1852, MSS, MDAH, quots.; Joseph Davis to JD, June 12 [1855] (*Papers* 5:112, quots. from Endrs., see n.6: Joseph planned to prevent Howells' access to his estate; did same to Laughlin children [ibid 2::5 n.5]); JD to VHD, June 14, 1875 (*Letters*, 413, quots.).

52. Recomm. of JD in WPJ, *Gen. ASJ*, 183, R. Davis, *Recoll. of Miss.*, 330, and Rowland 2:187; JD, Speech, Oct. 2, 1857, paraphrase (*Papers* 6:141, quots.); JD to Cocke, Dec. 19, 1853 (Rowland 2:336, quot.); VHD, *Memoir* 1:477, quot.; *Papers* 5:4 n.1, xxxvii. Terms "sec. of war" and "war dept." in use until 1947.

53. Corwine to JD, Mar. 10, 1853 (Rowland 2:187, quots.); JD to R. F. W. Allston, Apr. 15, 1853 (ibid., 203, quot.); Brown to JD, Jan. 1, 1853 (*Papers* 5:3–4, quots.).

54. JD to VHD, Apr. 17, 1853 (*Papers* 5:10–11, quots.; nn.9, 13; "Le man" surely a variant of "li' man," not the archaic word for "sweetheart" which n.2 makes it); VHD, *Memoir* 1:533; Malie Brodhead to VHD, May 7, MS, MDAH, quots. (W. B. Howell folder).

55. JD to VHD, Apr. 17, 1853 (*Papers* 5:10, quot.); VHD, *Memoir* 1:532–33; W. E. Starke to JD, June 8, 1853 (*Papers* 5:19–20); Samson, *Letters of ZT*, xiii, x; Heidler, "Twiggs," 150, 161 (N. O. had been his Div. HQ, and Twiggs spent much time on coast; E. Pasc. very near Mobile).

56. Quots.: JD to Cocke, Dec. 19, 1853 (Rowland 2:336); JD to Lowndes Co. Citizens, Nov. 22, 1850 (*Papers* 4:145); JD in Senate Aug. 6, 1850 (Rowland 1:474); JD to W. R. Cannon, Dec. 13 (*Papers* 5:52–53); JD to Eli Abbott, Apr. 17 (ibid., 9).

57. JD to Cocke, Dec. 19, 1853 (Rowland 2:334–37, quots.).

58. See McRae to JD, Jan. 30, 1855 (Rowland 2:440), James Phelan to JD, July 19, 1853 (*Papers* 5:34–37), and summary of corr. under Mar. 12 (ibid., App. 1, 164); Tarpley to JD, May 6, 1853 (ibid., 14, quots.); R. Davis to JD, Jan. 10, 1854 (ibid., 55, quots.); Ibid., 15 n.9, 36–37 and nn.7, 8, 53 n.5, 55 and n.2.

59. JD to Cocke, Dec. 19, 1853 (Rowland 2:336–37, quot.); JD to W. R. Cannon, Dec. 13 (*Papers* 5:53, quot.).

Chapter X War Department Days

1. JD to W. R. Cannon, Dec. 13, 1853 (*Papers* 5:53, quots.); JD to Cocke, Dec. 19 (Rowland 2:336, quot.).

2. JD, War Dept. rpts.: ibid. 2:292–333 (1853), 389–418 (1854), 552–71 (1855), and 3:68–98 (1856).

3. JD to Meigs, Apr. 4, 1853, and Aug. 2, 1855 (ibid., 194–95 and 486, quot.; see also *Papers* 5:App. 1, 413–14 [under Mar. 6, 1855], 6:App. 1, 536 [under Feb. 6, 1857], 546–47 [under Aug. 6]).

4. Meigs to JD, Dec. 27, 1856 (ibid., 522–23 [under Dec. 20], quot.); *Life and Reminsc.*, 33–34 (Meigs quot.).

5. JD to Buch., Feb. 2, 1857, and June 2, 1860 (Rowland 3:110 and 4:458–59); JD in Senate, June 12, 1860 (ibid., 502–4); JD to Floyd, Jan. 23, 1858 (*Papers* 6:167–69 and nn.); Ibid., App. 1, 647–49 (under Mar. 28, 1860). See ibid., 88–91 and nn.46–51, and Index to 5 and 6, under Meigs, Capitol, Capitol dome, Capitol extension, Washington Aqueduct, Post Office Dept., Patent Office (all were completed 1863–68).

6. JD to Meigs, Apr. 4, 1853 (Rowland 2:195, quot.; see *Papers* 6:181–82 and App. 1, 589–90, under Dec. 14, 1858); JD to A. Etex, Aug. 10, 1855 (ibid. 5:116: but see, to Meigs, June 18, 1859 [6:257] and corr under May 24, 1858 [App. 1, 573–74]); JD in Senate, June 21, 1860 (Rowland 4:533–39, quot. on 538). See Davis-Meigs corr., *Papers* 6:436–37 under Mar. 5, 1856.

7. JD to Meigs, Jan. 15, 1856 (ibid., 6–7 and n.4); Sturges, "Recoll. of JD," 12–15 (quots. from Thomas Crawford and Sumner; see pic. and caption on 8; unclear who added eagle head and feathers); *We, the People: The Story of the United States Capitol, its Past and its Promise* (Washington: U.S. Capitol Hist. Soc., 1985), 4, 46–50, 54, 57.

8. *Washington: City and Capital*, 810; *Papers* 5:48–49 and n.1 and App. 1, 159–60 (under Mar. 9, 1853); JD to Meigs, July 25, 1860 (ibid. 6:360–61 and nn.); Sturges, "Recoll. of JD," 15–17 (name restored 1909).

9. JD in Senate, Jan. 31, 1849 (Rowland 1:222, quot.); JD, 1853 Rpt. (ibid. 2:310–20; see also 565–70 and other Rpts., as in Note 2 above; *Papers* 6:103–8, 201–2 and nn., and App. 1, 664 [in Senate June 28, 1860]); JD to Stevens, Apr. 8, 1853 (Rowland 2:199–201); Stephen W. Sears, *George B. McClellan: The Young Napoleon*, 36–41; *Papers* 5 and 6, front endpaper maps.

10. Blum, et al., *Natl. Experience*, 333, 409 map, 418–21, 290 (Gadsden, 1854); JD to Fillmore, Feb. 21, 1851 (*Papers* 4:167, quot.).

11. E. G. W. Butler to JD, July 16, 1883 (Rowland 9:216; cites M. C. Butler of S. C., putting Calhoun, JD, and Joel R. Poinsett in same class); McElroy, *JD* 1:173 (McClellan quot.).

12. *Papers* 5:xxxviii; *Letters*, 88 (servants); VHD, *Memoir* 1:532 (says Becket 10, but *Papers* 5:42 n.22 says b. 1840), 550–51; W. B. Howell to JD, Jan. 31, 1853 (Rowland 2:184–87); *Papers* 6:App. 1, 497 (under Aug. 22, 1856), 519 (under Dec. 9).

13. See App. I in *Papers* 5 and 6 (e.g., Pensions: 6:649 [under Mar. 28, 1860] and 573 [May 20, 1858]; see ibid., 4:58 n.4, 5:97 n.3); Ibid., xxxviii–ix (sec. of navy June 1–15 and Oct. 4–14, 1853); JD Rpt. 1856 (Rowland 3:76).

14. VHD, *Memoir* 1:563, quot.; Rowland 2:441 (quot. from Mrs. H. A. Bartlett); Ibid. 305–6, 408, 557, and 560 (JD rpts.), and 4:440; *Papers* 6:App. 1, 579 (June 7, 1858), 590 (Dec. 15), 608 (Mar. 3, 1859), 662 (June 15, 1860).

15. *Papers* 5:App. 1, 163, 266 (Scott to JD, Nov. 8, 1853) and 6:App. 1, 509 (same to same, Nov. 3, 1856 [under Oct. 30]), 645–46 (corr. under Mar. 20, 1860; see ibid., 575 and 601); Rowland 2:559–60 and 4:17–21; Howard, *General Taylor*, 338; JD to Anderson, Jan. 20, 1850 (*Papers* 4:57–58, quot.; see nn.); VHD, *Memoir* 1:560–61, quot.; JD to J. B. Weller, Feb. 6, 1857 (*Papers* 6:App. 1, 535–36); *Washington: City and Cap.*, 882 (Soldiers Home still there 1937).

16. H. Johnson to JD, Oct. 20, 1854 (Rowland 2:385–86); T. J. Johnston to JD, Nov. 7, 1855 (*Papers* 5:App. 1, 465, quot.); C. E. Hooker to VHD, Sept. 26, 1899, MS, TRANSYL (Smith quot.; Smith in Warner, *Gens. in Gray:* West Pt. class of 1853).

17. VHD, *Memoir* 1:567 (Campbell quot.), 2:908 (JD quot.), 1:566 (quots. *re* "outlaw"); JD letters *re*: Smith in *Papers* 4:App. 1, 372–73 and 6:App. 1, 539, corr. under Feb. 19, 1857 (2 quots.); Kate Lee Ferguson to Fleming, Oct. 4, 1907, quots., MS, Fleming Collection.

18. *Life and Reminsc.*, 30–31 (quot. from E. V. Murphy); Autograph book in permanent Davis exhibit, White House of Conf. (seen, 1986). JD asks pay etc.: *Papers* 6:App. 1, 553 (Dec. 23 1857), 649 (Mar. 28, 1860), 653 (May 11), 663 (June 23); asks appt., 516 (under Nov. 19, 1856); 615 (Aug. 1, 1859, Treas. Dept. clerk thanks JD for many kindnesses).

19. Dickins to JD, Oct. 27, 1851 (*Papers* 4:229–30, quots.); *New Orleans Daily Picayune*, Dec. 7, 1889, p. 2, col. 4 (W. B. Lee quot.); VHD, *Memoir* 1:543, 566 (quots.) and McPherson to JD, May 7, 1886 (*Cal. JD MSS*, 247; see 77).

20. VHD, *Memoir* 1:564–65 (both stories, with quots.); JD to Robert McClelland,

Jan. 5, 1856 (*Papers* 5:App. 1, 284, quot.; see 287 under [1853?]: inquires into treatment of an asylum inmate).

21. VHD, *Memoir* 2:921, quot.; Winnie Davis, "JD in Private Life," 1–2. Corporal works: to provide for the needy, harbor the harborless, visit the sick, ransom captives, bury the dead; spiritual: to counsel the doubtful, instruct the ignorant, admonish sinners, comfort the sorrowful, forgive all injuries, bear wrongs patiently, pray for the living and dead (*Manual of Prayers for . . . Catholic Laity* [Baltimore: John Murphy Co., 1888 RPR 1916], 22).

22. Nichols, *Franklin Pierce,* 77, 150 ("Frank"), 76, 57, 257, 86–87, 97, 123 (quot.), 124, 291, 94, 212–13 (Mex.; see 161–63), 524–27 (Mrs. Pierce d. 1863; Hawthorne, 1864; Pierce, 1869), 529 (Julian Hawthorne on Pierce's personality). JD on Pierce, e. g., *Rise and Fall* 1:25; *Papers* 4:263–66; Rowland 2:238, 488.

23. Winnie Davis, "JD in Private Life," 2–3, quots.; JD in Senate, Feb. 29, 1860 (*Papers* 6:283, quots.).

24. JD to Joseph Davis, Aug. 30, 1857 (*Papers* 6:136, quots.); JD to VHD, July 20 (ibid., 129, quot.).

25. Quots.: JD to VHD, May 27, 1853 (*Papers* 5:17; "our dear le man"; "full of love for my Wife and child"); VHD, *Memoir* 1:534; JD to VHD, July 12, 1853, MS, TRANSYL (day of month, blurred here, from *Papers* 5:xxxviii); JD to VHD, Aug. 28, 1853 (*Papers* 5:43–44).

26. Quots.: VHD to Marg. K. Howell, July 26 and 30, 1853 (*Letters,* 72–73); Same to same, Mar. 3, 1854 (ibid., 75); A. Campbell to JD, Aug. 20, 1853 (*Papers* 5:39–40 and 42 n.16; n.23: LBN up from S. C. to see a Baltimore M.D.; see Moore, *Northrop,* 37); VHD, *Memoir* 1:534; W. B. Howell to JD, June 17, 1854 (*Papers* 5:73).

27. Quots.: VHD to Marg. K. Howell, Jan. 1854 (*Letters,* 75); Same to same, Mar. 26 and Apr. 29 (ibid., 76 and 77–78); JD to Wood, [June] (*Papers* 5:68). Becket brought measles home from school in May, but Sam was already sick in Mar. (ibid., App. 1, 315–16, corr. under Mar. 2; *Letters,* 76).

28. VHD to Marg. K. Howell, Apr. 29, 1854 (*Letters,* 77, quot.); Eckert, lxii n.233; *Papers* 5:App. 1, 354–55 (June 28); VHD to W. B. Howell, July 1854 (*Letters,* 78–79, quot.); W. B. Howell to JD, June 17 (*Papers* 5:72–73, quot.; nn.1, 2); Ibid. 2::20 n.8.

29. *Papers* 6:App. 4, Chart 14 (see 5:93 n.10); VHD to JD, Dec. 25–28 and Sept. 14, 1865, MSS, ALA, quots.; *Letters,* 78–79 (miniature); Keith A. Hardison to author, Mar. 15, 1988, and Thompson, "Beauvoir," n.p. (bust of Sam at Beauvoir); VHD, *Memoir* 1:534–35, quots.

30. Joseph Davis to JD, Aug. 27, 1838 (*Papers* 1::525); Ibid.::456, p. 372 (quots. from LBN); VHD, *Memoir* 1:524, quot. Erudition: see e.g., J. W. Forney (ibid., 528–29); J. Campbell in *Life and Reminisc.,* 134–35. On details, etc., see JD on geodetic surveying and on furnishing Senate "retiring room" (Rowland 1:551–53; 4:39–41).

31. VHD, *Memoir* 1:563–64, quots.; Samuel [Mason] Cooper to JD, July 4, 1877 (Rowland 7:559, quots.; not "Jr." as here: see *The Private Chesnut,* 118 n.8); Fitz Lee, "Sketch of the Late General S. Cooper," 271–72; JD to F. Lee, Apr. 5, 1877 (*SHSP* 3:274, 275, quots.); Cooper in Warner, *Gens. in Gray* (10 yrs. older). Cooper did ask "consideration" of his son for USMA (*Papers* 5:App. 1, 311).

32. VHD, *Memoir* 1:572, quot.; LBN to JD, Mar. 3, 1855 (*Papers* 5:App. 1, 333 [under Apr. 13, 1854], quot.); Corr. with Crosman et al. (ibid., 316–17 [under Mar. 6, 1854] and ibid. 6:App. 1, 443 [JD Endrs. under Mar. 15, 1856]); Ibid., 468, corr. under May 2, 1856 (quot. from JD to Delafield).

33. JD to Crosman, Oct. 17, 1853 (Rowland 2:274–75, quots.); JD to R. B. Marcy, May 16 (*Papers* 5:16, quot.); JD to Hitchcock, June 3 (ibid., 18, quot.); JD, *Rise and Fall* 1:24 and n.; JD to S. Earl, Nov. 24, 1856 (*Papers* 6:App. 1, 517; see ibid. Nov. 21 from C. Gray).

34. Odie Faulk, *The U.S. Camel Corps: An Army Experiment,* 18–20, 24–25, 28 (Wayne's full rpt. in Rowland 2:288–91); JD in Senate, Mar. 3, 1851 (*Papers* 4:167–

70, all quots.; nn.5 and 6; see also his res., after 152, and App. 1, 380–81, corr. under [Jan. 21], 1851); VHD, *Memoir* 1:526. *Grande Dictionnaire,* Vol. 2 (Paris, 1852), signed by JD, is in Rosenstock.

35. Faulk, *U.S. Camel Corps,* 34–57, 59–68, 75–81; JD to Wayne and Porter, May 10 and 16, 1855 (Rowland 2:461–62 and 464–66; with camel lore); JD to Wayne, July 5, 1856 (ibid. 3:52); JD to [sec. of navy] Dobbin, Apr. 11, 1856 and to Porter, June 26 (Rowland 3:26–27 and 47–48 [quot.]); JD to E. DeLeon, June 18 (*Papers* 6:26–27 and nn.). See also corr. under Aug. 4, 1853 (ibid. 5:App. 1, 238), Mar. 31 and July 10, 1854 (327, 357), Mar. 22 and Apr. 11, 1855 (418–19, 424–26), Jan. 3 and May 28, 1856 (6:App. 1, 385–89, 476).

36. Faulk, *U.S. Camel Corps,* 83–91 (use; see 98–117, 142–50), 69–70, 79, 120, 125–27, 139–41, 154–70, 174–75, 180–82, 186); Rowland 3:93–95.

37. VHD, *Memoir* 1:526; JD, War Dept. rpt., Dec. 3, 1855 (Rowland 2:561); Faulk, *U.S. Camel Corps,* 123, 152–53; JD, "Autobiography" (*Papers* 1::1, p. lx); *New Orleans Daily Picayune,* Dec. 7, 1889, p. 2, col. 4 (W. B. Lee quot.). Wayne designed a uniform for the Camel Corps, never produced (Randy Steffen, *The Horse Soldier, 1776–1943: The United States Cavalryman* 2:28 and Fig. 111 on 32).

38. JD, "Autobiography," *Papers* 1::1, p. lx, quots.; Tactics and rifles in text below; (Carriages:) Rowland 3:79–80, *Papers* 6:App. 1, 429 (corr. under Feb. 29, 1856) and 495 (from H. K. Craig [Chief of Ord.], Aug. 15), and William E. Birkhimer, *Historical Sketch of the Organization, Administration, Matériel, and Tactics of the United States Army* [James Chapman, 1884, RPR New York: Greenwood Press, 1968], 254–55.

39. JD, *Rise and Fall* 1:23, quot.; (Casting guns:) Rowland 3:80–81 (see 2:329–30); *Papers* 5:App. 1, 412 (corr. under Feb. 27, 1855), 6:93 nn.22, 23 App. 1, 459–60 (under Apr. 11); and Birkhimer (as in Note 38 above), 283–84; VHD, *Memoir* 1:569–70.

40. JD corr. with H. K. Craig (Chief of Ord. [*Papers* 5:41 n.6]): ibid., App. 1, 431 (under, May 10, 1855), 6:391 (under Jan. 5, 1856), 413 (under Feb. 6), 446 (Mar. 24) and Rowland 3:81; VHD, *Memoir* 1:525, quot.

41. Rowland 2:446–48, 450–52; 3:85–86, and *Papers* 5:124–25 and nn.3, 4. For Mordecai, see ibid., 41 n.8; for Delafield, James L. Morrison, Jr., *"The Best School in the World": West Point,* 40.

42. JD, War Dept. rpt., 1854 (Rowland 2:410–12, quots.); JD, War Dept. rpt., 1855 (ibid., 562, quot.; see *Papers* 5:App. 1, 431, under May 10, 1855); Rowland 2:411, 563, 3:81–83; *Papers* 6:App. 1, 413 (under Feb. 6, 1856), 416 (under Feb. 11), 452 (JD to Weller, Mar. 31), 468 (under May 2), 495 (Aug. 15); see also ibid. 5:App. 1, 334–35 (under Apr. 21, 1854) and JD to Wise, Oct. 6, 1856 (Rowland 3:62–64).

43. *Papers* 6:App. 1, 478, 479 (from Craig, June 5 [quot.] and 11, 1856); also ibid. App. 1, 480 (under June 13, 1856), 509 (Oct. 24), and 5:App. 1, 405 (Jan. 29, 1855).

44. Rowland 2:411–12, 563, 3:83; *Papers* 6:App. 1, 527 and 533 (Jan. 3 and 26, 1857); Ibid. 5:App. 1, 398 (Jan. 6, 1855), 404–6 (Jan. 26, 29, Feb. 2), 6:App. 1, 492 (Aug. 1, 1856), 509–10 (Craig rpt. under Oct. 30). Inventions for breechloading and rifling cannon were offered in 1857 (ibid., 532 and 537).

45. *Papers* 5:xxxix and 6:xlvi; JD, 1855 Rpt. (Rowland 2:562–63; quots.); *Papers* 5:App. 1, 431, under May 10; T. Hill, "Victory in Defeat," 19 (JD quot. with pic. of Staudenmayer, which was seized 1865 and kept by U.S. [Rowland 7:403–5 and n.1]). See pistol-carbine in Randy Steffan, *The Horse Soldier, 1776–1943* 2:54, figure 127.

46. JD, War Dept. memo, Nov. 7, 1856 (*Papers* 6:55, quots.); VHD, *Memoir* 1:525–26, quots; Steffan, *Horse Soldier* 2:34 (quot. on JD), 35, 68, figs. 107, 112, 121, 124, 125, 127.

47. JD, 1854 Rpt. (Rowland 2:412); *Papers* 3:17 n.3; Weigley, *Hist. U.S. Army,* 170–71; Hughes, *Gen. Hardee,* 45, 49, 40 and n.49. Cooper wrote a militia manual

(ibid., 24–25, and F. Lee, "Sketch of Cooper," 272). JD in Senate 1860 descr. all tactics books in use (Rowland 4:427).

48. JD to Roy, Feb. 29, 1880, in T. B. Roy, "Gen. Hardee and Military Operations Around Atlanta," 377, quots.; JD in Senate, Aug. 5, 1850 (Rowland 1:449, quot.); Hughes, *Gen. Hardee,* 36, 23, 31–34.

49. JD to A. Vattemare, May 5, 1855 (*Papers* 5:103 and n.4); See text above and Note 34; Hughes, *Gen. Hardee,* 42–50 (quots. on 49–50); *Papers* 5:App. 1, 341 (under May 18, 1854); Brevet Lieut.-Col. W. J. Hardee, *Rifle and Light Infantry Tactics* (name on title p.; quot. in 2:223).

50. Scott, *Infantry Tactics* (New York: Harper and Bros., 1857), quot.; Note 49 above; JD to Lippincott and Co., Mar. 13, 1860 (Rowland 4:207, quot.); Inventory, p. 5.

51. Winnie Davis, "JD in Private Life," 9, quots.; Sumner in Heitman, *Hist. Register;* JD to Buch. [ambassador to Eng.], Apr. 4, 1854, and Sumner to JD, Oct. 6 and Mar. 1, 1855 (Rowland 2:349, 380–81, 444–45).

52. Hughes, *Gen. Hardee,* 23–24, 36, 44–45, 52 (quot.) and n.5; *Papers* 5:App. 1, 341 (under May 18, 1854), 362 (Aug. 1), 432 (under May 15, 1855); see 6:55–56 (JD expert on cav. equip.; concern for horse); Steffen, *Horse Soldier* 2:22, 35, 38, 66, and fig. 112.

53. Rosalie Carter, *Captain Tod Carter of the Confederate States Army,* 27 (quot. from *The Rebel,* Mar. 26, 1863); Schaff, *Spirit of Old West Point,* 37, 60; Hughes, *Gen. Hardee,* 4–7, 56–57, 60–68 (quot. on 63), 73 n.9, 80, 35 (Aztec: also Twiggs, Bgd., JEJ, Pemberton, et al.), 19, 23, 37, 39, 40 (children with sister-in-law in St. Augustine).

54. VHD, *Memoir* 1:529, 535–38 (quots.); Sears, *McClellan,* 3.

55. Ibid., 12, 13, 23–24, 35–36, 42–49 (quots.), nn.29–30; *Papers* 6:App. 2, 678–79, corr. June 19, Aug. 27, Sept. 30, 1854; Ibid. 5:124–25 and nn.3,4 (war ended Sept. 1855), App. 1, 427–29 (under Apr. 23, 1855); Ibid. 6:xlvi, App. 1, 393–96 (under Jan. 10, 1856), 569 (under May 10, 1858).

56. *Papers* 6:505 (corr. under Oct. 3, 1856; see also 515, Nov. 13); Steffan, *Horse Soldier* 2:53, 58 and fig. 131 (JD's "woolen yarn" for girth adopted 1859 in place of McClellan's leather); Sears, *McClellan,* 47–48, quot.

57. JD in Senate, June 6 and 11, 1850 (Rowland 1:356–57, 357–61; see *Papers* 4:App. 1, 337–38 [under Feb. 20], 355 [under June 27], 377 [under Dec. 10]); Ibid. 5:8 n.1; JD, 1853 Rpt. (Rowland 2:303–5); JD, 1854 Rpt. (ibid., 392–94, quots.).

58. JD, 1855 Rpt. (Rowland 2:553–54, quot.); Steffan, *Horse Soldier* 2:34, quot.; *Papers* 5:119 n.16 and 4:App. 2, 405; JD to Joseph Davis, Aug. 25 (ibid. 5:118, quot.). In 1861, the distinction among U.S. mounted troops was lost; all became "cavalry": see Jubal Anderson Early, "Comments on the First Volume of Count of Paris' Civil War in America," 140–41.

59. WPJ, *Gen. ASJ,* 184–85, quot.; *The Memoirs of Henry Heth,* ed. James L. Morrison, Jr. (hereafter: *Heth Memoirs*), 124 (Cooper quot.); JD, *Rise and Fall* 1:24, quot. See JD in Rowland 2:448–50. Some officers had to be chosen from civilians: *Papers* 5:119 n.16, App. 1, 416 (corr. under Mar. 14, 1855), Early, "Comments," 142.

60. Early, "Comments," 142–45 (full roster, 1st and 2nd Cav. off., plus later rank U.S.A. and C.S.A.); Sumner, JEJ, and Emory in Heitman, *Hist. Register; Papers* 5:App. 1, 172, 204, 235, 303–4, 377, 397; JD to Floyd, June 15, 1859 (ibid. 6:App. 1, 613, quot.); Rowland 6:272 n.1 and VHD, *Memoir* 2:906–7 (Ransom).

61. R. Taylor, *Destruction,* 232, quot. (ZT said this "more than once"); WPJ, *Gen. ASJ,* 166–69, 185–86.

62. Lee to JD, Feb. 2, 1850 (*Papers* 4:App. 1, 336); Freeman, *R. E. Lee* 1:319, 326, 349–50 and nn.59, 60; Schaff, *Spirit of Old West Point,* 232, quots.; R. E. Lee in Heitman, *Hist. Register;* Ibid. 2:594–97 (org. of army in 1848 and Mar. 3, 1855).

63. *Papers* 5:App. 1, 411 (under Feb. 24, 1855); M[ary] C[ustis] Lee to JD, [June 30] 1854 (ibid., 355); Fitzhugh Lee and William Henry Fitzhugh Lee in Warner,

Gens. in Gray. Fitz was son of R. E.'s brother, Sydney Smith Lee and wife, Anna Mason, whose sister Sarah was Cooper's wife (De Leon, *Belles,* 437; R. E. Lee [Jr.], *Recoll. and Letters,* 361–62); for Rooney, ibid. 38 and n., and *Growing up in the 1850s: The Journal of Agnes Lee,* ed. Mary Custis Lee deButts, 6 and n.8, 16 and n.28.

64. Early, "Comments," 140–45, quots. (incl. from Count of Paris); J. Campbell in *Life and Reminisc.,* 133, quot.; JD in Senate, Feb. 10, 1858 (Rowland 3:186, quot.); JD, Feb. 26, 1859 (ibid. 4:24–29). For O'Hara (not in Early), see *DAB* and Heitman, *Hist. Register;* Fitz Lee (ibid.) appt'd. later. See Richard M. McMurry, *John Bell Hood and the War for Southern Independence,* 15–20.

65. WPJ, *Gen. ASJ,* 183–84, quots.; JD in Senate, Feb. 10, 1858 (Rowland 3:175–99; see also Feb. 11, pp. 200–14). Rpts. listed in Note 2 above.

66. Steven E. Woodworth, *Jefferson Davis and his Generals,* 11, quot.; Senate debate, June 5 and 7, 1860 (Rowland 4:450–58, 460–64, quots.); *Papers* 6:App. 1, 632 (corr. under Feb. 4, 1860).

67. "Department of Interior" in *Universal Encycl.;* JD to Pierce, Dec. 16, 1854 (*Papers* 5:94–95, quots. and Scott quot., and nn.; App. 1, 377–78, under Oct. 11); JD to McClelland [sec. of interior], Jan. 27 and Apr. 27, 1855 (ibid., 99–100, 102, and nn.); L. U. Reavis, *The Life and Military Services of Gen. William Selby Harney,* 249–51.

68. JD in Senate, Mar. 3, 1849 and Feb. 11, 1858 (Rowland 1:233–34 and 3:210, quots.); JD to Cocke, Jan. 6, 1856 (Rowland 2:586, quot.). See *Papers* 6:App. 1, 599–600 (under Jan. 31, 1859); Craven, *Prison Life,* 280.

69. JD, Rpt., 1853 (Rowland 2:294, quot.); JD, 1856 (ibid. 3:71, quot.).

70. JD, Rpts., 1854, 1855 (Rowland 2:390–94, 554); JD to P. H. Bell [Gov. of Tex.], Sept. 19, 1853 (ibid., 265–66).

71. JD to Harney, Dec. 26, 1855 (Rowland 2:583, quots.); Reavis, *Life of Harney,* 247–58; Sturges, "Recoll. of JD," 12; *Papers* 5:App. 1, 371–72 (under Sept. 12, 1854), 402–3 (under Jan. 23, 1855), 419 (under Mar. 22), 101 n.4; *Heth Memoirs,* 124–29; JD in Senate, Feb. 10, 1858 (Rowland 3:190–91, quot.).

72. JD to Harney, Dec. 26, 1855 (Rowland 2:583–84, quots.); Harney to JD, Mar. 8, 1856, in Reavis, *Life of Harney,* 261–65 quots.; *Heth Memoirs,* 92, quot.; JD in Senate, Feb. 10, 1858 (Rowland 3:191, quot.; see Reavis, iv). On Indians, see JD, Rowland 1:550, 565–67; *Papers* 4:156–58.

73. *Papers* 5:95 n.2 and front endpaper map; JD, Rpt., 1856 (Rowland 3:71–76, quots.); JD, 1853 (ibid. 2:297–306, quot. on 305; see 1855 rpt., ibid., 557); Ibid., 395; JD in Senate, Feb. 10, 1858 (ibid. 3:176–77); Weigley, *Hist. U.S. Army,* 191. JD repeatedly asked for the concentration (Rowland 2:295–96, 391–92), but seems not to have been heeded: see *Papers* 6:235 (1859).

74. JD, War Dept. rpt., 1854 (Rowland 2:397–406, quot. on 397; staff and command plans, compares French, Eng., and Ger. armies); JD, 1856 (ibid. 3:76–77, quot.; see 2:556–57); *Papers* 6:App. 1, 529 (under Jan. 13, 1857, quot.), 568 (under May 5, 1858), 575 (in Senate, June 8; under May 25); Morrison, *"Best School,"* 142.

75. Bragg in Heitman, *Hist. Register;* McWhiney, *Braxton Bragg,* 35–38 (quot.), 94–95, 106–7, 129–40 (letter to John, 130–34; quot. from Bragg to JD, May 4, 1853, on 136).

76. Bragg in Heitman, *Hist. Register;* McWhiney, *Braxton Bragg,* 137 (Sherman quots.), 139–40 (quots. from 1856 letter, with part from Seitz, *Bragg,* 17). Birkhimer (as in Note 38 above), 134, says Co. C, 3d Art., *not* dismounted 1851; says nothing about rifled guns; nor does JD; see his ideas: Rowland 2:556, 3:80; *Papers* 5:96–97.

77. *Papers* 5:App. 1, 279 (under Nov. 30, 1853; see JD to Emory, June 15, 1859 [ibid. 6:255–56 and nn.3,6]); Twiggs in Heitman, *Hist. Register.*

78. *Papers* 2::254 n.2; Ibid. 5:App. 1, 291, 319–20, 327–28 (corr. under Jan. 7, Mar. 9, Mar. 31, 1854); JD to Wool, Apr. 14 (ibid., 63–64, quot., and nn.); Same

to same, Jan. 12, Aug. 18, Dec. 13 (Rowland 2:342–43 [and n.1], 374–76 [quot.], 419–27).

79. Inge to JD, Oct. 16 (*Papers* 5:87–88, quots. and n.1; see 64 n.5; 477 [1849, Jan. 6]; 3:164); McWhiney, *Braxton Bragg*, 96–97 (Bragg quot.; see 86–87); R. Wood to JD, 1859: Wool's "meaness, and duplicity" (*Papers* 6:250).

80. JD to Wool, Aug. 18, Dec. 13, 1854 (Rowland 2:374–76, 419–27, quot. on 427); Ibid., 469–70, 553, 555; *Papers* 6:App. 1, 515–16 (Nov. 15, 1856); Ibid 2::254 n.2. Other Wool faults: *Papers* 5:App. 1, 368 (Aug. 24), 371 (Sept. 5), 389 (Dec. 6). Other corr. on Wool: Ibid., 385 (Nov. 13); Ibid 6:398–400 (Jan. 14, 1856).

81. Ibid. 5:App. 1, 454 (Sept. 17, 1855), 6:App. 1, 545–46 (corr. under July 12, 1857); JD to N. R. Stimson, Dec. 14 (ibid., 165–66, quots.; Wool quots. in n.4); Cooper to JD, July 24 (Rowland 3:119–21; explains non-delivery; Endrs.: "About Wool's sword or rather his falsehood. J.D.").

82. Davis-Scott letters, 1853–56: Rowland 2:221, 228–31, 357–59, 460, 472–82, 486–89, 491–525, 572–82, 590–603, 3:1–25, 36–39, 43 (quots.: 2:476, 230, 481); (other corr.) Ibid. 2:452–58, 470, 510–11, 527–44, 547–48, 550–52; 3:66–67, 108; *Papers* 5:143 (and n.2); 6:102. Docs. in Senate Ex. Doc. No. 34, 34th Cong., 3rd Session.

83. VHD, *Memoir* 1:555, quot.; Corr. in Note 82 above; Corr. in *Papers* 5:App. 1, 196 (under May 3, 1853), 342 (under May 22, 1854), 414–15 (under Mar. 8, 1855), 441–43 (under July 17; see also 470 under Dec. 3), 6:App. 1, 393 (under Jan. 8, 1856), 409–10 (under Jan. 31); JD in Senate May 11, 1858 (ibid., 569); (Harney:) Ibid. 5:App. 1, 301 (under Jan. 22, 1854), 446 (July 31, 1855); Nichols, *Franklin Pierce*, 385–87.

84. Quots.: JD to Scott, Dec. 20, 1855 (Rowland 2:573); Scott to JD, May 21, 1856 (ibid. 3:36); JD to Scott, May 27 (ibid., 43).

85. Scott to JD, Jan. 31, 1856 (Rowland 2:592, quot.); JD to Scott, Feb. 29 (ibid. 3:2, quots.); Nichols, *Franklin Pierce*, 385; AJ to A. J. Donelson, July 14, 1818 (Bassett, *Corr. of AJ* 2:382, quot.; see 409). Scott said "no challenge" (Rowland 3:15), but see Hale and Merritt, *Hist. of Tenn.* 2:337.

86. *Papers* 5:26–27, App. 1, 180 (under Apr. 7, 1853), 196 (under May 3, at end), 371 (under Sept. 12, 1854), 374 (Sept. 27), 389 (under Dec. 8); Rowland 2:304–5, 332–33; WPJ, *Gen. ASJ*, 730; *Papers* 6:App. 1, 517; Ibid. 5:105, quot.

87. Morrison, *"Best School,"* 32; Schaff, *Spirit of Old West Point*, 50–52; *Heth Memoirs*, 48, quot.

88. Schaff, *Spirit of Old West Point*, 94–95 (quots.), 68–69 (Church); Hughes, *Gen. Hardee*, 55; Morrison, *"Best School,"* 25, 39–40, 44–52, 59–60, 142–46, 151. Friends: text above, chap. 4; VHD, *Memoir* 1:54; *Papers* 6:59 n.7, App. 1, 451 (under Mar. 29) and 564 (Feb. 9); Crist, "Bibliog. Note," 191.

89. Morrison, *"Best School,"* 114–25; *Papers* 6:30 n.4, 59 n.8, App. 1, 529 (under Jan. 13, 1857), 583–84 (under July 17, 1858), 643–44 (under Mar. 14, 1860); Ambrose, *Duty, Honor*, 141–46; Rowland 4:204–7, 441–47, 464–86, 519.

90. Marg. G. Howell to [W. B. Howell], Oct. 29, 1854, MS, MDAH, quot.; Schaff, *Spirit of Old West Point*, 232, quot.; *Papers* 5:xli; Ambrose, *Duty, Honor*, 141; Freeman, *R. E. Lee* 1:327 (quots.), 369, 372 (Lee quot.).

91. (Lee on Scott:) Ibid., 289, *An Irishman in Dixie: Thomas Conolly's Diary of the Fall of the Confederacy*, ed. Nelson D. Lankford, 71, and R. E. Lee [Jr.], *Recoll. and Letters*, 147; Ibid., 10 (*Lady of Lake*); *Letters*, 249–50; (Custis:) deButts, *Growing up in 1850s*, 33, 37, Warner, *Gens. in Gray*, and G. W. C. Lee to JD, 1878, in *SHSP* 5:224 ("My dear Friend"). For another Davis-Lee likeness see text above chap. 2.

92. Freeman, *R. E. Lee* 1:330–31 (see Lee quots. on 328, 350, 368, 369–70, 374); (Hymn:) VHD, *Memoir* 2:494; M. M. Andrews, *Scraps of Paper*, 205; and *Hymns suited to the Feasts and Fasts of the Church*, #144 (bound with *BCP* [1850]).

93. Author's copy of print and ident., courtesy Joseph Dandridge Logan, 3; *Papers* 6:59 n.13 (see App. 1, 545, June 29, 1857); Ibid.:xlv; VHD's *BCP* (stolen

in Miss. 1863, found on rubbish heap in Mich. 1975), at Beauvoir; "The Order of Confirmation," *BCP* (1850).

94. JD to Buch., June 19, 1857 (Rowland 3:116–18, quots.); JD to French, Nov. 9, 1856 (*Papers* 6:58, quots.; n.1; see also Dec. 12, 1860 [376–77] and App. 1, 672–73, corr. under Dec. 19); Ibid., 494, corr. under Aug. 14, 1856 (see 529 [under Jan. 13, 1857], 30 n.3); Rowland 3:113–15; Morrison, *"Best School,"* 57, 116–17.

95. *Papers* 6:xlvi, and App. 1, 502 (Delafield to JD, Sept. 21, 1856).

96. *Papers* 5:42 n.16 (Margaret quots.; see ill. and map after 76), App. 1, 386 (corr. under Nov. 19, 1854), xli; Ibid. 6:114–15, quots.; Ross, *First Lady*, 79, 92 (quot.).

97. VHD to Marg. K. Howell, Jan. 1854 (*Letters*, 74, quot.); VHD, *Memoir* 1:547–59; Ross, *First Lady*, 79; *Papers* 6:110 n.4, quot.; Marg. K. Howell to W. B. Howell, Oct. 29, 1854, MS, MDAH, quots.

98. VHD, *Memoir* 1:549–51; *Papers* 3:262–63 and n.3; Rowland 3:44 and n.1. Marg. K. Howell to W. B. Howell, Oct. 29, 1854, MS, MDAH; Calhoun, "John Perkins Family," 82–83, 88 (quot. from obit.); Sterling, *Belle*, 29–31; VHD, *Memoir* 1:222; Nichols, *Franklin Pierce*, 259, 383–84.

99. Mann in *DAB* and in *Register USMA* (under "Non-graduates," Class of 1827); Mann to JD, Dec. 19, 1884 (*"My Ever Dearest Friend": The Letters of A. Dudley Mann to Jefferson Davis, 1869–1889*, ed. John P. Moore [hereafter: Moore, *Mann Letters*], 93); VHD, *Memoir* 1:556–57 (quot.; ref. to 1 Cor. 13:4 and 1 and 2 Sam.).

100. Sturges, "Recoll. of JD," 9–11, quots.; *Papers* 5:xli. Adelina Patti, gave concerts 1851–55, managed by pianist Strakosch (David Ewen, *The New Encyclopedia of the Opera* [New York: Hill and Wang, 1971]); Ole Bull was a Norwegian violinist (*Col. Encycl.*).

101. 9. *Papers* 6:149–50, 159, 241; Julian, *Political Recoll.*, 147–50 (quot. from Owen Lovejoy); Nichols, *Franklin Pierce*, 21–22, 25, 106–7, 124–25, 225, 243, 528.

102. Marg. K. Howell to W. B. Howell, Oct. 29, 1854, MS, MDAH, quot.; Chronology in *Papers* 5 and 6 (1853–57; concert by Sigismund Thalberg, Dec. 16, 1856); VHD, *Memoir* 1:540 and 559, quots. See *Papers* 5:119 n.13 for house.

103. VHD, *Memoir* 1:541–43 (quots.), 572. See DeButts, *Growing Up in 1850s*, 64 and n.87: Capt. Smith Lee was in Perry's expedition.

104. VHD, *Memoir* 1:559 (quot.), 2:749 and n. (quot.); JD to J. A. Hayes, July 19, 1880, MS, MVC, quot.; JD to Marg. D. Hayes, Apr. 26, 1889 (*Letters*, 556, quot.); Same to same, May 23, 1866, MS, TRANSYL, quot.; VHD to JD, Aug. 31, 1857 (*Papers* 6:App. 1, 548, quot.). See Strode, *Patriot*, 287 n.1 for footnote to dog story.

105. *Papers* 1:App. 4, Chart 14; VHD, *Memoir* 1:571 (quot.); Nichols, *Franklin Pierce*, 497; VHD to Marg. K. Howell, Jan. 31, 1857 (*Letters*, 82, quot.; illness named); JD to A. Campbell [Jan. 22] and n.3 (*Papers* 6:102–3); Ibid.:App. 1, 531 (corr. under Jan. 20: illness called "neuralgia").

106. VHD to JD, Apr. 17, 1859 (ibid., 244, quots.); VHD to Marg. K. Howell, Jan. 31, 1857 (*Letters*, 82, quot.); Same to same, May (ibid., 88–89, quot.); *Papers* 6:xlvii, 59 n.13.

107. JD to VHD, July 20, 1857 (*Papers* 6:130, quot.); JD to Pierce, Mar. 2, 1857 (ibid., 109); Same to same, Apr. 4, 1858 (ibid., 173, quots.); VHD to JD, Apr. 17, 1859, and Aug. 31, 1857 (ibid., 244 and App. 1, 548, quots.).

108. Nichols, *Franklin Pierce*, 425–69 (quot. on 427); JD to Cannon, Dec. 7, 1855 (*Papers* 5:141, quots.); JD to Ellsworth, June 5, 1856 (ibid. 6:25–26).

109. Ibid.; JD to T. J. Hudson, Nov. 25 [1855] (*Papers* 5:137–39); JD to Tarpley, Dec. 19, 1855 (ibid., 147–49, quots., nn.4, 5); Ibid. 6:4 n.2 (caucus vote, 50–35). R. Davis, *Recoll. of Miss.*, 351–52, and William E. Dodd, *Jefferson Davis*, 152–53, err *re* this election. On not campaigning, see Nichols, *Franklin Pierce*, 208, 427–28; *Papers* 3:App. 3, 455; *Hill*, 48.

110. Nichols, *Franklin Pierce*, 508–9 (trip, Nov. 1857–spring 1859), 529–30

(quot.); *Papers* 6:4 n.2 (see App. 1, 540–41, corr. under Mar. 3). Stick now at First White House, Montgomery, Ala.

111. J. R. Tucker in *Life and Reminisc.*, 161, and A. H. Markland in Rowland 9:571; (minutiae): *Papers* 6:App. 1, 522, 507, 512, 517, 486, 492 (from gutta percha to complaints of cadets bathing nude); Ibid. 2::18, p. 73 (quot. from JD speech, 1844); Sterling, *Belle*, 69, quot.

112. *Papers* 6:421, 505, front endpaper map, 5:386–87; Mary B. Poppenheim et al., *History of the United Daughters of the Confederacy*, 2 vols. in 1 (Raleigh: Edwards and Broughton Co., 1956) 87; *Life and Reminisc.*, 32–33 (quot. from Maj. W. B. Lee).

Chapter XI Struggles for Health and the South

1. JD to Cocke, Jan. 6, 1856 (Rowland 2:585, quots.; n.3: "never sought an office"); (Purity:) Schaff, *Spirit of Old West Point*, 232, R. Davis, *Recoll.*, 324, Reagan in *New Orleans Daily Picayune*, Dec. 7, 1889 (p. 2, col. 5) and in Jones, *Davis Memorial*, 340, and Charles Marshall in *Life and Reminisc.*, 246; Allen Tate, *Jefferson Davis, His Rise and Fall: A Biographical Narrative* [New York: Milton Balch and Company, 1929], 94, quot.

2. Quots.: JD to Buch., July 23, 1855 (Rowland 2:474); *Papers* 6:110 n.4; Jones, *Davis Memorial*, 225; Long, "JD," 20 (Prescott d. 1859).

3. JD to Buch., Apr. 7, 1853 (Rowland 2:197, quot.; see same to same, Feb. 2 and 18, 1857 [ibid. 3:110 and *Papers* 6:App. 1, 538]); Buch. to JD, Mar. 16, 1850 (Rowland 1:319–21); VHD, *Memoir* 1:223, quots.

4. JD, *Rise and Fall* 1:26–31 (quots. from bill); W. C. Davis, *Breck.*, 100–119; Randall, *Civil War*, 128–35, 150–54; JD in Senate, Feb. 8, 1858 (*Cong. Globe*, 35th Cong., 1st sess., 619; see *Papers* 6:159–60, 219–20); James M. McPherson, *Battle Cry of Freedom*, 121–25, 145–49.

5. JD in Senate, May 17, 1860 (*Papers* 6:322–23, quot.; and see 122–23, 220).

6. Randall, *Civil War*, 135–39, quots.; McPherson, *Battle Cry*, 145–49 152–53; VHD, *Memoir* 1:577; JD to E. V. Sumner, Feb. 15 and May 23, 1856 (Rowland 2:603–4 [quot.] and 3:40–41); *Papers* 6:39–42, 46–47 and nn. (quot. 40 n.1), and App. 1, 418–20 (corr. under Feb. 15); JD, 1856 Rpt. (Rowland 3:97–98, quot.).

7. JD speeches, Oct. 2, May 23, and Nov. 7, 1857, paraphrases (*Papers* 6:141 [quots.], 122–23, and 158–59); JD in Senate, Jan. 26, 1858 (Rowland 3:142–48, quot. on 147; see also 181–83 and 352–56).

8. David Donald, *Charles Sumner and the Coming of the Civil War*, 227–39, 243 (quot. from F. Lieber), 214–15; VHD, *Memoir* 1:557–58, quots.

9. Donald, *Chas. Sumner and C. W.*, 278–347 (last Sumner quot. on 312), 144 (quot.), 306–7 and n.4; *Cong. Globe*, 34th Cong., 1st sess., App.:529–44 (Sumner, 530–31 [quot.], 543; see Douglas, 546; Butler, 625); Randall, *Civil War*, 139–40; McPherson, *Battle Cry*, 149–52; Wilson, *Code of Honor*, in Williams, *Dueling*, 99; Brooks and Butler in *South in Bldg. of Nation*, 11.

10. Brooks in H. R., July 14, 1856 (*Representative American Orations*, ed. Alexander Johnston, 2:289–90, quots.; see 294); Donald, *Sumner and C. W.*, 299–307 (some exceptions; see also Randall, *Civil War*, 140); McWhiney, *Braxton Bragg*, 144 (Bragg quot.); May, *John A. Quitman*, 317 (Quitman quot.).

11. S. C. citizens to JD, Sept. 17, 1856 (*Papers* 6:App. 1, 501) and JD reply, Sept. 22 (ibid., 44, quot.); Ibid., xlvi.

12. McPherson, *Battle Cry*, 60–62, 151–52 (quot. from Rep. organizers), 126–30, 138–44, 153–56; Randall, *Civil War*, 134; Wiltse, *Calhoun* 3:371 (see 425 on abol. control in North).

13. JD, Speech at Jackson, Nov. 4, 1857 (*Papers* 6:159, quot.); JD, at Miss. City, Oct. 2 (ibid., 148–51, quot.; see also App. 1, 548, Sept. 5); (Walker:) *Papers*

2::18 n.102 and 64 n.31; Claiborne, *Miss.*, 415–23; McCardle, *Hist. of Miss.*, 174; Rowland 1:346–49.

14. "Kansas" in *Universal Encycl.;* Robert Selph Henry, *The Story of the Confederacy*, 25.

15. *Papers* 6:xlvii, 114–15; VHD to Marg. K. Howell, May 1857 (*Letters*, 88–89, quots.)

16. VHD to Marg. K. Howell, May 1857 (*Letters*, 88–90, quots.); *Papers* 6:xlv–vi (did not visit Brierfield 1856); Ibid. 5:117–18, 122–23; Ibid. 6:49 n.3. David Brodhead, was then senator from Pa. (ibid. 4:120 n.7).

17. VHD to Marg. K. Howell, May 1857 (*Letters*, 90); JD, Speech at Vicksburg, May 18 (*Papers* 6:117–19); JD, at Jackson, May 29 (ibid., 120–25, quots. and Ed. Note; ref. to Gen. Cambronne at Waterloo [ibid. 5:9 n.2]).

18. *Papers* 6:xlvii and App. 1, 545 (June 5 and 13, 1857); VHD to W. B. Howell, Aug. 9 (*Letters*, 93); JD to VHD, July 20 and 27 (*Papers* 6:129, and App. 1, 546, quots.).

19. Quots.: JD to Pierce, July 23, 1857 (*Papers* 6:131); JD to VHD, July 20 (ibid., 130); VHD to JD, Aug. 31 (*Letters*, 94–95). For the coastal lots, see ibid., 93, and *Papers* 6:App. 1, 547–48, under Aug. 14). JD sold some La. property, July 21, and bought, with others, over 10,000 A. of Ark. land. Oct. 2 (ibid., 546, 549).

20. Ibid., xlviii; JD to Joseph Davis, Aug. 30, 1857 (ibid., 137, quot.; and nn.4 and 1; see App. 1, 549 for speech).

21. JD to VHD, Aug. 23, 1857 (*Letters*, 94, quot.; "Lassie wi' the Lint-White Locks" [*Poems and Songs of Robert Burns*, ed. James Barke, 634–35]); VHD to W. B. Howell, Sept. 27 (*Letters*, 95, quots.); *Papers* 6:xlviii.

22. JD, Speech at Miss. City, Oct. 2, 1857, paraphrase (*Papers* 6:137–55, quots. on 143–153; see JD speech, App. 1, 550, Oct. [10]; for Walker, 132 n.1).

23. Ibid., xlviii, *Papers* 6:162 n.1 (see 155 n.6); JD, Speech at Jackson, Nov. 4, 1857, paraphrase (ibid., 157–62, quots. on 161).

24. JD to Payne and Harrison, Nov. 16 and 23, 1857 (ibid., App. 1, 550 and 163, quots.); Ibid. 164 nn.3–5, and 547, Aug. 6 (crop approx. 500 bales, prob. yielding c. $20,000; hoped for 15 cents a lb., got 10). For Ark. land, see Note 19 above.

25. *Papers* 6:xlviii; VHD to Marg. K. Howell, Oct. 1857 (*Letters*, 96, quots.) and Dec. 16 (ibid., 97); JD to C. C. Clay, May 17, 1859 (*Papers* 6:252, quot.).

26. Ibid., xlviii–xlix and App. 1, 554, under Jan. 4, 1858; Ibid., 99–101, and 102 n.13; Claiborne, *Miss.*, 427–46 (see also JD letter, *Papers* 6:201–2 and n.9).

27. JD speeches, Dec. 19 [1857], Jan. 7 and 26–27 and Feb. 8, 10, and 11 [1858] (Rowland 3:123–214 [quot. on 153]); WPJ, *Gen. ASJ*, 730 (after ASJ, JD had rec. P. F. Smith and R. E. Lee), 213 (quots. from JD in Senate), 195–240; ASJ in Heitman, *Hist. Register*, quot.

28. JD in Senate, Feb. 10–11, 1858 (*Cong. Globe*, 35th Cong., 1st sess., App.: 53–62, quots. on 62).

29. Quots.: JD to Buch., Feb. 18, 1858 (*Papers* 6:App. 1, 565); JD to Sparke, Feb. 19 (ibid., 169–70); Marg. K. Howell to W. B. Howell, Oct. 29, 1854, MS, MDAH.

30. Quots.: JD to Cocke, Dec. 19, 1853 (Rowland 2:335); JD to Joseph Davis, Aug. 25 and Sept. 22, 1855 (*Papers* 5:118 and 123); Atchison to JD, Feb. 26, 1856 (ibid. 6:12); Drayton to JD, Apr. 9, 1858 (Rowland 3:216).

31. *Papers* 6:170, quot.; n.1; VHD, *Memoir* 1:574–76, quots.; Riley, "JD and His Health," 197–99; Derrick Vail in *Better Homes and Gardens Family Medical Guide*, ed. D. G. Cooley [New York: Meredith Press, 1966], 547–49.

32. VHD, *Memoir* 1:576–79, quots.; Hughes, *Gen. Hardee*, 57. For Napiers, see also Sterling, *Belle*, 115–17, and *Papers* 6:li (JD managed a ball for them 1859); for Sumner, ibid. 1::382 n.4.

33. G. W. Jones to JD, Dec. 9, 1880 (Rowland 8:533, quots.).

34. Nuermberger, *Clays of Ala.*, 122–23, 320, 184 (quot. from VHD letter);

Sterling, *Belle,* 64, 68–69 (quots.), 153; Clement Eaton, *Jefferson Davis,* after p. 146 (pic. of *carte de visite* with quot.); Clay-Clopton, "Clement Claiborne Clay," 74–75.

35. VHD, *Memoir* 1:579–83, quots. (see 652: Buch. on Seward's style meant "to inflame"). Seward in Ga. Jan.–June 1819 (*Papers* 6, 284 n.7); 1860, said African "a pitiful exotic . . . incapable of assimilation" (Long, "JD," 14); slashed 1865, not fatally, by Booth accomplice (Hanchett, *Lincoln Murder,* 54–57).

36. VHD, *Memoir* 1:582, quots. Although she says "appropriation," there was in a Coast Survey this session only a res. and 1 other ref. (*Cong. Globe,* 35th Cong., 1st sess., 936–37, 1059; 1021–23); neither shows JD there; funding vote was June 12, after JD returned (App.:568, 601). JD's major speech for Survey, to prevent transfer to navy, was Feb. 19, 1849 (ibid., 30th Cong., 2nd sess., App.:204–12; VHD, *Memoir* 1:526–28); see also *Papers* 4:App. 1, 321–22, and Rowland 2:11.

37. *Papers* 6:xlix, 171 n.8; JD to F. Bostick, May 14, 1858 (Rowland 3:228 and 230, quots.; see 353–56; *Papers* 6:588); *Cong. Globe,* 35th Cong., 1st sess., 1869–99 (see 1758–1855 for previous debate; 1799, 1899 for "pair off"); Randall, *Civil War,* 159–60 (bill May 4; rejection Aug. 2).

38. VHD, *Memoir* 1:581–82, quots. (time sequence differs from that in text); *Papers* 6:199–200 and n.1 (see App. 1, 622, under Dec. 20, 1859: tries to prevent another duel).

39. JD in Senate, Dec. 20, 1849 (Rowland 1:249, quot.; see VHD, *Memoir* 1:426–31 and n.); JD, Speech to Miss. legis., [Nov. 11], 1858 (Rowland 3:356–57, quots.; dated from *Papers* 6:588); Alex. Johnston, *Repr. Am. Orations* 3:34–46 (Seward quot.); JD on white labor, Rowland 4:48–50.

40. JD in Senate, Feb. 8, 1858 (*Cong. Globe,* 35th Cong., 1st sess., 619, quots.), JD to Pierce, Apr. 4 (*Papers* 6:173–74, quots.); *Papers* 6:xlix; JD in Rowland 3:339, quot.; VHD, *Memoir* 1:582, quot.; *Papers* 6:171 n.1 (quot. from reporter); JD in Senate, May 11–June 12 (Rowland 3:218–70).

41. Butler, *Judah P. Benj.,* 99–101 ("terrible in sarcasm"), 117, 178 (Bayard quot.); Louis Martin Sears, *John Slidell,* 100–102, 6; *Cong. Globe,* 35th Cong., 1st sess., 2780–82 (June 8, 1858; Benj. quot.), 2822–23 (June 9; quots., Pearce, JD, and Benj.). For anger in others, see W. C. Davis, *Breck.,* 114–18; Nuermberger, *Clays of Ala.,* 135, 138–39, 157; *Papers* 6:237 Ed. Note.

42. JD in Senate, Jan. 19, 1859 (Rowland 3:395, 398 [quot.; ref. to *Merchant of Venice* 1.1.93–94]). RR debate: Rowland 3:363–460, 501–15 (Dec. 14, 1858–Jan. 25, 1859); *Papers* 6:App. 1, 561–63 (under Jan. 27, 1858), 583 (July 14); Jones, *Davis Memorial,* 158–59.

43. McElroy, *JD* 1:202–3 (JD quot.); JD in Senate, Jan. 26, 1860 (Rowland 4:167, quot.; and see exchange with Collamar, 236–38).

44. JD to Pierce, Apr. 4, 1858 (*Papers* 6:172–74, quots.); VHD, *Memoir* 1:587, quot. (and anecdotes).

45. *Papers* 6:172 and 252 (JD quots.); Rowland 3:218, 223, 228 (still unable to read in May); JD, Remarks on death of Henderson, June 5, 1858 (ibid., 261–63, quots.; see text above, chap. 7).

46. JD to Comm., July 1, 1858 (Rowland 3:270, quots.); JD, Speech to Miss. Legis., Nov. 16 (ibid., 340, quots.; see also 280, 295, 306); *Papers* 6:xlix; VHD, *Memoir* 1:584, quot.; JD to A. C. Halbert, Aug. 22 (*Papers* 6:205).

47. Rowland 3:271–73 (quots. from rpt. in *Boston Post* of extemporary speech; JD complained of mis-reporting [*Papers* 6:204–7 and nn.]; see JD on slave trade and British search, ibid., 183, 187 n.1, and Rowland 4:65–68, 361–63).

48. JD, Speech, July 9, 1858, paraphrase (Rowland 3:274–81, quots.; see also Jones, *Davis Memorial,* 153–62, "musical voice"); *Papers* 6:202 n.2. For the other speeches, see ibid., xlix–l, 214–23, and Rowland 3:284–315. On hope in the people, see Rowland 1:433 and *Papers* 6:230.

49. JD, Speech at Belfast, Me. [Sept. 2, 1858], paraphrase (Rowland 3:291–92, quot.); VHD, *Memoir* 1:587–88, quots.; James R. Winchester, "Jefferson Davis,

Communicant," 727 (knew theology and "held orthodox views"). The Nicene Creed, with Apostles' Creed, embodied the belief of Epsic. Church: "Resurrection . . . and the Life of the world to come" (*BCP* 1850).

50. *Papers* 6:App. 1, 581 (June 18), 584 (July 27 and Aug. 8); VHD, *Memoir* 1:585–90, quots.; Merle M. Odgers, *Alexander Dallas Bache: Scientist and Educator, 1806–1867,* 7, 40, 59–60, 190–92; Strode, *Patriot,* 309; JD in Rowland 3:233, quots. (ibid. 1:480: "chain and compass" less accurate).

51. VHD, *Memoir* 1:590–91, quots. (says visit 3 weeks, but *Papers* 6:Chronology, l, shows 5 days in Sept.; "Ah, che" from *Il Trovatore* 4.2; 1st perf. 1853 [Ewen, *Encycl. of Opera,* 11, 704]); Odgers, *Alexander D. Bache,* 40, 99–100 (quots. on Bache), 204–5.

52. VHD, *Memoir* 1:592 and 587, quots.; *Letters* 205, quot. (from ALA fragment [Nov. 1865?]); Odgers, *Alexander D. Bache,* 191–97 (Bache quots.); *Papers* 6:225–26 and nn. Comet found June 2, 1858, by Giovanni B. Donati (*Universal Encycl.*).

53. *Papers* 6:Chronology, l, 226 n.2; Ibid. 5:App. 1, 386 (under Nov. 19, 1854); VHD, *Memoir* 1:593–94, quots.; Everett in *Universal Encycl.* (many other posts; ran for v. p. with John Bell 1860); Odgers, *Alexander D. Bache,* 149–50.

54. *Papers* 6:Chronology, l; VHD, *Memoir* 1:594–641 (Cushing and JD speeches from *Boston Morning Post,* Oct. 12, 1858; quots. on 603–19). Thought of blacks as inferior "universal" in 18th century (Taney in Randall, *Civil War,* 153); in 19th, "nearly as intense in the North as in the South" (Blum et al., *Natl. Experience,* 253–57).

55. David Donald, *Charles Sumner and the Rights of Man,* 156–57; M. A. DeWolfe Howe, *The Life and Letters of George Bancroft* [1908 RPR Port Washington, N. Y.: Kennikat Press, 1971] 2:134; Rowland 4:234 (Wilson of Mass. and Bayard of N. J.); Donald, *Chas. Sumner and C. W.,* 29; Abraham Lincoln, *Complete Works . . .*, ed. John G. Nicolay and John Hay (New York: Century Co., 1907) 1:187 ("We cannot then make them equals"; see Long, "JD," 14; McPherson, *Battle Cry,* 127–28).

56. VHD, *Memoir* 1:620 (JD quots.).

57. VHD, *Memoir* 1:623–24 and 627–28 (JD quots.; see JD in Eckert, 92); Douglas in Senate, May 20, 1856 (*Cong. Globe,* 34th Cong., 1st sess., 545, 546, quots.). See Donald, *Chas. Sumner and C. W.,* 133–34, 184, 228–33, 263–64, 367. The man in Sumner's ref. (2 Kings 8:13; he omits "great") immediately betrayed and murdered his king.

58. Donald, *Chas. Sumner and C. W.,* 264 (Sumner quot.; taken from J. Q. Adams [153–54]); JD in Senate, May 8 and 16, 1860 (Rowland 4:286, 253, 252, and 290, quots.; said also 1853 [2:237]). Montesquieu invented "higher law" than God (David Brion Davis, *The Problem of Slavery in Western Culture* [Ithaca: Cornell Univ. Press, 1966], 404–6).

59. JD, Speech at Jackson, July 6, 1859 (Rowland 4:63, quots.; see Donald, *Chas. Sumner and C. W.,* 230, 286, 354–56, 367–68); VHD, *Memoir* 1:608–41 (quots. on 628 and 611; ref. to Matt. 21:12 or Mark 11:15; also cites 2 Cor. 6:8, Job 39:25, I Cor. 3:13–15). Rep. control: VHD, *Memoir* 1:631; *Papers* 6:224 n.3; Rowland 4:277.

60. VHD, *Memoir* 1:641–42; Hardee to VHD, Aug. 15, 1858 (Rowland 3:282–83, quot.); Hughes, *Gen. Hardee,* 65–66.

61. *Life and Reminisc.* 309; JD, Speech at Palace Garden, New York City, Oct. 19, 1858 (Rowland 3:332–39, quots. on 338–39; italics omitted).

62. VHD, *Memoir* 1:642, quot.; *Papers* 6:207 n.3 (quot. from *Eufala [Ala.] Spirit of the Times;* and see n.4 and 224 n.3; see JD in *Life and Reminisc.,* 138–39).

63. JD, Speech to Miss. legis., [Nov. 11], 1858 (Rowland 3:339–60, quots.; ref. to Job 13:15; date from *Papers* 6:588); Randall, *Civil War,* 150–54.

64. Alex. Johnston, *Repr. Am. Orations* 2:46; James M. McPherson, *Abraham Lincoln and the Second American Revolution* [New York: Oxford Univ. Press, 1991], 3; *The Civil War in the United States by Karl Marx and Frederick Engels,* ed. Richard Enmale, Intro., ix, xiv; JD, Speech (as in Note 63 above), 358 and 360, quots. JD

spoke against "this revolution" of "a higher law" in 1860 (*Cong. Globe*, 36th Cong., 1st sess., 546–47).

65. *New Orleans Daily Picayune*, Dec. 7, 1889, p. 2 (quots.)

66. Carol Bleser, *The Hammonds of Redcliffe* [New York: Oxford Univ. Press, 1981], 18 (Hammond quot.; see Wiltse, Calhoun 3:369); John Witherspoon DuBose, *The Life and Times of William Lowndes Yancey*, 585 (Kennedy quots.); JD and Green in Senate, Jan. 20, 1859 (Rowland 3:444, 447–48, 459–60 [quot.]).

67. Quots.: *New Orleans Daily Picayune*, Dec. 7, 1889, p. 2 (Murphy); *Papers* 4:62 (VHD); JD to Hale, "Saturday" (They agreed to have the remarks "erased"; John Parker Hale Papers, 1822–85, N. H. Hist. Society MS collection, Concord N. H.); DuBose, *Yancey*, 585 (opponent); *Life and Reminisc.*, 134 (Campbell).

68. See, e.g., Rowland 3:376–95, 4:7–9, 121–39 (this dispute ends in laughter); JD to Pierce, Jan. 30, 1860 (Rowland 4:185, quots.). See JD, July 1859 (ibid., 73) on slavery as "only question."

69. (JD on Cuba:) Speech Jan. 8, 1852 (Rowland 2:123–25; defends Lopez), letter 1855 (*Papers* 5:138), speeches 1857 (ibid. 6:118, 121, 143–45), 1858 (Rowland 3:313), 1859 (ibid. 4:79–85), 1860 (ibid., 526; see 497–99); see *Papers* 5:72 n.12 and 109–10 nn.5, 6; (on slave trade:) Rowland 1:284–85; *Papers* 4:154–55 (see 261); Rowland 4:48, 65–70, 260–61, 520–29.

70. May, *John A. Quitman*, 270–95, 328–50 (d. July 17, 1858, during recess of Congress); JD, Remarks on Death of Quitman, Jan. 5, 1859 (Rowland 3:467–68, quots.; refs. to Thomas Gray, "Elegy written in a Country Churchyard," 36, and *Macbeth* 3.2.23; last unknown: also in Henderson eulogy [263]).

71. JD to Marg. K. Howell, Mar. 28, 1859 (*Papers* 6:241–42, quot.); Ibid. n.5, 248 n.6, 242 n.6 (quot. from J. Roach), App. 1, 600 (Feb. 1); Rowland 3:459, 468–69, 472; VHD to Marg. K. Howell, Mar. 1 (*Letters*, 102).

72. *Papers* 6:App. 1, 608 (Mar. 20, 1859); JD to W. B. Howell, Apr. 18 (ibid., 246, quot.); JD to Cartwright, Apr. 25 (ibid., 248–49, quot.).

73. VHD to Marg. K. Howell, Apr. 25, 1859 (*Letters*, 108–9, quots.); *Papers* 6:242 n.5, 256 (loss "very heavy") and JD to W. B. Howell (as in Note 72 above).

74. JD to W. B. Howell, Apr. 24, 1859 (*Papers* 6:247, quots.); Ibid., 250 n.5 and 248 n.5; VHD to JD, Apr. 3 (*Letters*, 105, quot.; see also *Papers* 6:250, 615–16 [Aug. 22 and 25]); JD to J. L. M. Curry, June 4 (ibid., 253–54 and n.10); Riley, "JD and His Health," Part 1, 200–201.

75. JD to Clay, May 17, 1859 (*Papers* 6:251, quot.); JD to Emory, June 15 (*Papers* 6:256, quot.); Ibid., li, 247, 248 n.8, 257 n.11, 259 (quot.).

76. Ibid., lii and Rowland 4:61–88 (Speech July 6, 1859); H. Chetwood to VHD, July 13, 1858 (*Papers* 6:App. 1, 582–83; *re* Jeffy D.; 242: still with Davises, Mar. 1859); Marg. K. Howell to JD, [July] 14, 1859 (Rowland 4:116–18, quots.; month from *Papers* 6:614).

77. JD to Marg. K. Howell, Mar. 28 (*Papers* 6:241, quot.); VHD, *Memoir* 1:566 and 538, quots.

78. Marg. K. Howell to JD, [July] 14, 1859 (Rowland 4:116–18, quots.; refs. to Matt. 25:7 and 22:11–12). See Ben to Mas Jeff, Aug. 1 (ibid., 92–93). The Rev. John Cumming publ. *The End . . .* and *Lectures on the Apocalypse* in 1855 (*Papers* 6:614), also *Infant Salvation, the Baptismal Font, the Communion Table*, which W. B. Howell gave his wife in 1862 (Beauvoir book list, sent to author by Pat D. Fulks, Oct. 19, 1984); ads for 3 new Cumming books in Craven, *Prison Life*, 1866 (back matter, p. 6).

79. Wood to JD, May 1, 1859 (*Papers* 6:250, quot.); VHD to Marg. K. Howell, Apr. 25 and "May" (*Letters*, 109 and 110, quots.); VHD to JD, July 2 (ibid., 111, quots.).

80. Joseph Davis to JD, June 21, 1859 (*Papers* 6:258 and n.1; for trip, see App. 1, 612 [under June 7] and 615, July 15); VHD to JD, Apr. 3 (*Letters*, 105); *Papers* 6:259 n.5; JD to Pierce, Sept. 2 (Rowland 4:93, quots.).

81. JD to J. P. Heiss, Oct. 13, 1859 (*Papers* 6:263, quot., and Descr. Note); JD

to C. J. Faulkner, Oct. 13 (ibid., App. 1, 617, quot.). Illness mentioned Sept. 12, 16, Oct. 17 (ibid., 616, 618); spoke in Miss. Nov. 6 and 17 (ibid., lii).

82. JD to Woolfson, Jan. 6, 1860 (ibid., App. 1, 625); Ibid., liii; Craven, *Prison Life,* 68 ("not so" in Eckert, 23, seems to refer only to lessons *re* vision), 148 ("sight of one eye lost . . . other seriously impaired"); VHD, *Memoir* 1:198; Sterling, *Belle,* 69; W. H. Russell in Kimball, *Richmond in Time of War,* 6.

83. JD to Anna E. Carroll, Feb. 27, 1860 (*Papers* 6:App. 1, 638); Ibid., 299, 303, 318, 356, 358, and Rowland 4:266–69, 274, 275, 404.

84. Rowland 3:494; Nuermberger, *Clays of Ala.,* 122 (Clay quot.; see Donald, *Chas. Sumner and C. W.,* 264), 139 (press quot.); JD to Pierce, Jan. 30, 1860 (Rowland 4:185); *Papers* 1:App. 1, Charts 1, 14; Ibid. 6:after 72 (Senate seating chart 1859), liii, 59–60 n.13, 174 n.9; Clay to JD, May 23, 1859 (ibid., App. 1, 611, quot.).

85. Quots.: VHD to JD, Apr. 17, 1859 (*Papers* 6:244; he sat pouting in her lap, having just snatched away Maggie's "frock"); VHD to Marg. K. Howell, "May" (*Letters,* 110–11); VHD to JD, July 2 (ibid., 111; Maggie is "pestiferous, honorable").

86. Quots.: JD to Marg. K. Howell, Mar. 28 (*Papers* 6:241); JD to W. B. Howell, July 17 (ibid., App. 1, 615); JD to Pierce, Jan. 17 (Rowland 3:498).

87. McPherson, *Battle Cry,* 153, 169, 202–13 (the "Six"; quots. from preacher and Thoreau on 209–10); JD in Senate, Dec. 8, 1859 (Rowland 4:99–110, quots. on 107–8, 99); Freeman, *R. E. Lee* 1:389, 394–403; Randall, *Civil War,* 172 (6 of his 18 men hanged later).

88. *Papers* 6:269 n.5, 208 n.1, lii–liii (see 267–68); McPherson, *Battle Cry,* 204–7, 211 (Unionist quot.); JD, *Rise and Fall* 1:41; VHD, *Memoir* 1:647; Randolph in Warner, *Gens. in Gray.* Some said Seward caused Brown's raid by "irrepressible conflict" speech (McPherson, *Battle Cry,* 211), but see JD in Rowland 4:104–5.

89. JD, *Rise and Fall* 1:42–44; Rowland 4:203–4, 250–82, 348–61, 367–71; JD in Senate, Feb. 29, 1860 (*Papers* 6:278–84); JD to L. P. Connor et al., Oct. 7 (Rowland 4:541, quots.). Alexander H. Stephens, *A Constitutional View of the Late War between the States* 1:408–17, and Eaton, *JD,* 113–14, give other views of JD res.

90. JD, *Rise and Fall* 1:83–85; JD in Senate, Feb. 29, 1860 (*Papers* 6:282); JD, July 6, 1859 (Rowland 4:75, quots.); Randall, *Civil War,* 152–55; Julian, *Political Recoll.,* 41–43; Victor B. Howard, *Religion and the Radical Republican Movement, 1860–70* (Lexington: Univ. Press of Kentucky, 1990), 3.

91. This and next paragraph based on: Howard, *Religion* (as in Note 90 above); W. W. Sweet, *The Story of Religions in America;* Dunham, *Attitude of No. Clergy;* D. B. Davis, *Problem of Slavery* (as in Note 58 above); James H. Moorhead, *Am. Apocalypse;* Robert L. Dabney, *Defence of Virginia;* Elizabeth Fox-Genovese [and] Eugene D. Genovese, "The Divine Sanction of Social Order . . ." (*Jnl. of the Am. Academy of Religion* LV/2: 211–33); Genovese and Fox-Genovese, "Religious Ideals" (as above chap. 2, Note 29); Mark A. Noll, *A Hist. of Christianity in the U.S. and Canada* (Grand Rapids: William B. Eerdmans Publ. Co., 1992); C. Gregg Singer, *A Theological Interpretation of Am. Hist.* (Phillipsburg, N. J.: Presbyterian and Reformed Publ. Co., 1981).

92. Nikolai Velimirovic, *The Prologue . . . Lives of the Saints,* trans. by Mother Maria (Birmingham [Eng.]: Lazariea Press, 1985) 1:84, quot.

93. "Humanitarian" in *OED* (humanity as "object of worship" traced to Comte; under "Humanism," a quot. from Coleridge 1812 shows line from orthodoxy through Arianism "to direct Humanism," which in *Webster* (Unabridged) is "substituting faith in man for faith in God." Unitarians (ibid.) saw man progressing "onward and upward forever."

94. Cartwright, "Alcohol and the Ethiopian," 157, quot.; Meade to JD, Jan. 21, 1862 (Rowland 5:187, quot.).

95. Wood, *Life of St. John's Parish,* 68 (quot. from Bsp. Wilmer of Ala.).

96. Giddings in H. R., Feb. 26, 1858 (*Cong. Globe,* 35th Cong., 1st sess.,

App., 65–68, quots.; Dred Scott an "absurdity"; these ideas reappear in Sumner's speech, text below). On new religion as utopian, see quots. in Blum et al., *Natl. Experience,* 239–43, and chap. 3 above, Note 17.

97. Keitt in H. R., May 24, 1858 (*Cong. Globe,* 35th Cong., 1st sess., App., 404–9, quots.; "inconcussible": "that cannot be shaken" [OED]). On N. T. support for slavery, see Dabney, *Defence of Va.,* 140–41, 146–208. The Genovese arts. in Note 91 above find Keitt's position "overwhelmingly confirmed by modern scholarship."

98. Blum et al., *Natl. Experience,* 240, 257; Walter L. Fleming, *Civil War and Reconstruction in Alabama,* 21–24; Sweet, *Story of Religions,* 428–44, 454–55, 486; Dunham, *Attitude of Northern Clergy,* 14 (R. C. quot.), 18–21. For Episc., see also Charles Blount Cheshire, *The Church in the Confederate States.*

99. McPherson, *Battle Cry,* 209 (Parker quot.; Brown on God, ibid. and 203); Donald, *Chas. Sumner and C. W.,* 350 (Sumner quot.), 18 (quot.); see 166–67, 170, 259–60, 341, 353, 356, 373); *Chesnut,* 245, quot.

100. Unitarians: G. W. Stearns (Howard, *Religion* [as in Note 90 above], 16), Parker (ejected, formed own church), T. W. Higginson (*Universal Encycl.*), and S. G. Howe's wife, Julia Ward, who "preached" (*Col. Encycl.*); Transcendentalists (see Singer, *Theolog. Interpret.,* 54–59): F. B. Sanborn and Higginson (later) (McPherson, *Battle Cry,* 204; *Universal Encycl.*); Gerrit Smith had private sect, for which he wrote *The Religion of Reason* (Rowland 7:73 n.1 and *Col. Encycl.*).

101. Donald, *Chas. Sumner and C. W.,* 353–57 (quots. from speech), 16 and 19–20, 372–73 (Adams quot.) (on revenge, see 347, 341 and n.3, 352–54); Donald, *Chas. Sumner and Rights,* xxxv, Index; JD to Cartwright, June 10, 1849 (*Papers* 4:22, quots.). "Slave" from "Sclavi" (Slavs), spared death by Charlemagne, a Christian (Jubal Early letter in *Southern Historical Monthly* 1 [1877]: 175).

102. JD, Speech, July 15, 1852 (*Papers* 4:280, quot.); *BCP* (1850); JD in Senate, May 8, 1860 (Rowland 4:280, 276, quots.); JD to Cartwright, June 10, 1849 (*Papers* 4:23, quots.).

103. JD to Pierce, Sept. 2, 1859 (Rowland 4:93–94); Pierce to JD, Jan. 6, 1860 (*Letters,* 113–14, quot.; see W. H. Winder to JD, May 18 [*Papers* 6:App. 1, 654]); Nuermberger, *Clays of Ala.,* 173 (Yancey quot.). See Dwight Lowell Dumond, *The Secession Movement, 1860–1861,* 36–37.

104. J. R. Davis to JD, Dec. 13, 1859 (*Papers* 6:264); JD to E. De Leon and to J. R. Pease, Jan. 2 and Feb. 10, 1860 (ibid., 270–71; 272 nn.2, 3; 276–77 and n.2); VHD, *Memoir* 2:925, quot.; JD, *Rise and Fall* 1:207 (Clay quot.); Clay to JD, Oct. 30, 1875 (Rowland 7:460).

105. JD to Pierce, Jan. 30, 1860 (Rowland 4:184–85); Eaton, *JD,* 115–17; *Papers* 6:295 Ed. Note; Davis-Douglas debate in Senate, May 16–17, 1860 (Rowland 4:283–340, esp. 299–301, 293, 335–40); Dumond, *Secession Movt.,* 33–34, 43–54; Fleming, *C. W. in Ala.,* 13; *Papers* 6:342–43 n.32.

106. JD to Pierce, June 13, 1860 (Rowland 4:496, quots.). See Rowland 4:196, 210–12, 229, 300–301, and John Eddins Simpson, *Howell Cobb: The Politics of Ambition,* 126–27.

107. Dumond, *Secession Movt.,* 77–96, 112; JD, *Rise and Fall* 1:49–53, 207; VHD, *Memoir* 1:685 (Breck. quot.).

108. JD, "Doctrine of State Rights," 216 (Phillips quot.); JD, *Rise and Fall* 1:49–53; JD, Speech July 9, 1860 (*Papers* 6:358–59, quots.); *Papers* 6:liv–lv, 364–67, 295 Ed. Note, App. 1, 667–68 (Sept. 21–Nov. 3); McPherson, *Battle Cry,* 216–21, 232; Donald, *Chas. Sumner and C. W.,* 363.

109. Dumond, *Secession Movt.,* 102, 158; JD, *Rise and Fall* 1:57–70; JD to Rhett, Nov. 10, 1860 (*Papers* 6:368–70, and n.4); Ibid., App. 1, 669–71 (under Dec. 10); VHD, *Memoir* 2:3n, quot.; Randall, *Civil War,* 200–204; JD to VHD, Feb. 3–4, 1866, MS, TRANSYL.

110. JD to French, Dec. 12, 1860 (*Papers* 6:376, quot.); To Our Constituents, Dec. 14 (ibid., 377, quots.; and n.1; see App. 1, 669–71, and Rowland 8:460–61);

Dumond, *Secession Movt.*, 155–64, 168, 192–93, 196, 198; JD to VHD, Feb. 3–4, 1866, MS, TRANSYL, quot.

111. WPJ, *Gen. ASJ*, 271 (ASJ quot.); Dodd, *JD*, 196–97; McPherson, *Battle Cry*, 252–54; William Y. Thompson, *Robert Toombs of Georgia*, 150, quot. See JD to Pettus, Dec. 26, 1860 (Rowland 4:559–60) and Clay in JD, *Rise and Fall* 1:207–9.

112. JD to Rhett, Nov. 10, 1860 (*Papers* 6:370, quot.); McPherson, *Battle Cry*, 235; JD to Pettus, Jan. 4, 1861 (Rowland 4:565, quots.). On treatment of S. C., see Rowland 4:570–81: JD gets rpt. read and praises "Christianity" of his friend Barnwell.

113. McPherson, *Battle Cry*, 265–66; JD, *Rise and Fall* 1:212–20 (see 54–55, and Appendices G and I); JD to VHD, Feb. 3–4, 1866, MS, TRANSYL, quot. (JD charitable towards Buch., though told he was vindictive and dishonorable [see *Papers* 4:226], until "made painfully aware" Buch. was using him to restrain "others").

114. JD, *Rise and Fall* 1:220, 221–24 (quot. on 222), 230–31 (see also 55–57), 200–209 (last quot. on 202). Clay (ibid., 207–9) ans. "conspiracy" charge made in *Am. Cyclopedia 1875;* JD called it "shallow nonsense" (Rowland 9:483); and see Clay, ibid. 7:459–61.

115. JD to Pierce, Jan. 20, 1861 (Rowland 5:37–38, quots.); JD, Speech, Nov. 16, 1858 (ibid. 3:358, quots.); VHD, *Memoir* 1:697. Leaving "the flag he loved" "cost [JD] the keenest suffering and sorrow" (BNH interview, ALA typescript). Friends, e.g., Pierce, Bache, Harney, Geo. Jones, Emory and Anderson; family: Malie Brodhead, and Howell kin of VHD. (*Papers* 6:259 n.3; *Letters*, 37).

116. JD, *Rise and Fall* 1:220–21, 226 (quot.; gave "little attention" to rumor of arrest); VHD, *Memoir* 2:3n and 1:696–98, quots.; Joseph Davis to JD, Jan. 2, 1861 (Rowland 4:561–62; another false rumor had JD "severely wounded" by Andrew Johnson).

117. VHD, *Memoir* 1:687–96 (quots. from speech), 698–699 (other quots.); Gilmer, Memoir [*re* org. of Conf. govt.], May 1880 (Rowland 8:462, quot.). On coercion, see JD, ibid. 3:355, 4:548, 543–53. He scorned use of Declaration to defend John Brown (ibid. 4:108; and see 171, 230–33).

Chapter XII President

1. JD to C. J. Wright, Feb. 12, 1876 (Rowland 8:493; see 9:473); VHD, *Memoir* 2:8, 12 (quot.); Pettus to JD, Dec. 31, 1860 (under Dec. 20, 1859) (*Papers* 6:App. 1, 623–24); Duke, *Reminisc.*, 340, quots.; JD, *Rise and Fall* 1:239–40 (J. Chesnut quot.). See Arthur James Fremantle, *Three Months in the Southern States*, 213–14.

2. McElroy 1:265 (JD quot.); JD, *Rise and Fall* 1:230, quots. (only says "precautions . . . to prevent"; see William C. Davis, *Jefferson Davis: The Man and His Hour*, 302–3). George T. Denison, *Soldiering in Canada*, 70, says JD named Cobb 1882; no hint in Horace Montgomery, *Howell Cobb's Confederate Career*, 22–26, or Simpson, *Howell Cobb*, 146–47; see William Y. Thompson, *Robert Toombs of Georgia*, 160–63.

3. JD to Stringfellow, June 4, 1878 (*Letters*, 483, quots.); VHD to Fleming, Dec. 20, 1905, in Ross, *First Lady*, 413, quots.; VHD, *Memoir* 2:12, quots.; JD to W. M. Brooks, Mar. 13, 1862 (Rowland 5:218–19: wanted to be "a General in the army.").

4. VHD, *Memoir* 2:6–8, quots.; Blum et al., *Natl. Experience*, 298 map. JD had helped Pettus get arms: Rowland 4:201–2, 559–61; *Papers* 6:App. 1, 622–24 (under Dec. 20, 1859); McElroy, *JD* 1:261–62; R. Davis, *Recoll. of Miss.*, 408–9.

5. JD, *Rise and Fall* 1:227–31; WPJ, *Gen. ASJ*, 251; VHD, *Memoir* 2:9–12, quots. (refs. to Luke 23:34 and 2:14); JD to J. T. Scharf, Sept. 23, 1886 (Rowland 9:473, quot.). JD, "Life of Calhoun," 258: war evil unless for honor and rights.

6. VHD, *Memoir* 2:10–11 (JD quot.); Dumond, *Secession Movt.*, 210, 212. Simpson, *Howell Cobb*, 146–47; Montgomery, *Howell Cobb's Conf. Career*, 25.

7. *Chesnut*, 6, 142; Burton J. Hendrick, *Statesmen of the Lost Cause: Jefferson Davis and his Cabinet*, 191; Pleasant A. Stovall, *Robert Toombs: Statesman, Speaker, Soldier, Sage*, 216–18.

8. JD, *Rise and Fall* 1:237–40 (quots. from Miss. and La. men; but see T. R. R. Cobb in *SHSP* 28:282); Richardson, *Conf.* 1:30. These sources and those in Note 2 above, and F. M. Gilmer's in Rowland 8:461–63 show JD was not a dark horse (as said in *SHSP* 36:141–45).

9. VHD, *Memoir* 2:18–19, quot.; Richardson, *Conf.* 1:30; JD to VHD, Oct. 20, 1865, MS, TRANSYL, quot.

10. Quots.: JD to Pierce, Jan. 20, 1861 (Rowland 5:38); *Charleston News and Courier*, Dec. 12, 1889, p. 2, col. 1 (from W. T. Thompson; photocopy, Fleming Collection); JD to C. J. Wright, Feb. 12, 1876 (Rowland 7:493–94; see also 8:69).

11. JD to Stringfellow, June 4, 1878 (*Letters*, 483), quot.; (see also *Papers* 1::1, lxii); Jones, *Davis Memorial*, 341 (Reagan quot.); JD to Pettus in McElroy, *JD* 1:267–68, quot. JD preferred "active service as commander-in-chief of the army," meaning *of Miss.*, not of C.S.A. (Clayton in JD, *Rise and Fall* 1:237; see *SHSP* 29:5; Reagan, *Memoirs*, 109; Denison, *Soldiering*, 71: "command of an army," not *the* army).

12. VHD, *Memoir* 2:19; JD, *Rise and Fall* 1:230; Sue Tarpley Carter, "President Davis as I Knew Him," 209, quots. For Tarpley, see, e.g., *Papers* 5:12–15 and nn., 147–49.

13. VHD, *Memoir* 2:22–23 (quot. from eyewitness; see JD on 33); Strode, *Patriot*, 405–6; W. P. Chilton to JD, Mar. 28, 1886 (Rowland 9:418); Bronze plaque at RR station, Auburn, Ala.; date, Feb. 16, 1861.

14. Fleming, *C. W. in Ala.*, 13 (quots.), 41–42; DuBose, *Yancey*, 27–34, 151–52; Stovall, *Toombs*, 177–78 (Yancey quot.); JD in Senate, May 16, 1860 (Rowland 4:337–38, quots.; see *Papers* 6:342, nn.224, 225).

15. DuBose, *Yancey*, 152–55; Chilton to JD, Mar. 28, 1886 (Rowland 9:418); Wood, *Life of St. John's Parish*, 48 (quots. from Mary P. Watt); JD, Speech Feb. 16, 1861 (Rowland 5:49, quot.). See Gilmer on Yancey in Rowland 8:461–63.

16. Winnie Davis, "JD in Private Life," 10, quot.; *New York Times*, Feb. 10, 1865 (JD quot.); VHD, *Memoir* 2:8–10; Rowland 10:124 (quot. from clipping in letter to JD, June 22, 1889); McElroy *JD* 2:723 (AHS quot.). On his responsibility, see Rowland 9:473.

17. "Montgomery Alabama" (photographs publ. for S. H. Kress and Co., Montg., by L. H. Nelson Co., Portland, Me., 1906); *The Way It Was, 1850–1930: Photographs of Montgomery . . .* (Montg.: Landmarks Foundation of Montg., 1985), 105–28, 153 (Market St. now Dexter Ave.); visits by author.

18. Wood, *Life of St. John's Parish*, 47–49; Strode, *Patriot*, 408–12 and n.1; *Journal of Confederate History* 7:117; "A Contemporary Account of the Inauguration of Jefferson Davis," ed. Virginia K. Jones, 273–74, quots. The Bible and JD's chair now at ADAH.

19. JD, Inaugural Address, Feb. 18, 1861 (Rowland 5:49–53, quots.; ref. to I Kings 8:39 or Psalm 44:21; JD said in Senate, Jan. 10: "But God, who knows the hearts of men, will judge" [25]). See JD, *Rise and Fall* 1:258–63 and App. K, 640–75 (C.S. and U.S. Const. side by side).

20. T. R. R. Cobb, Feb. 18, 1861, in *SHSP* 28:283, quots.; Rod Gragg, *The Illustrated Confederate Reader* (New York: Harper and Row, 1989), 60 (quots. from eyewitness); Wood, *Life of St. John's*, 49; V. K. Jones, "Contemporary Account," 273–75 (quots.) and n.7; DuBose, *Yancey*, 157–58 (Harris in H. R.). AHS had taken oath Feb. 11, his 49th birthday (AHS, *Recollections*, 62).

21. JD to VHD, Feb. 20, 1861, in VHD, *Memoir* 2:32–33, quot.

22. DuBose, *Yancey*, 587–90; VHD, *Memoir* 2:37–39; JD, *Rise and Fall* 1:242, quots. (See Stovall, *Toombs*, 23, 33, 38–39, 59, 220–21, and Hendrick, *Statesmen*, 188–93.) Clay-Clopton, "Clement C. Clay," 76–77; Nuermberger, *Clays of Ala.*, 183–87; *Chesnut*, 706.

23. JD, *Rise and Fall* 1:242; Reagan, *Memoirs*, 109–10 (on P. O. comm. in H. R. [65]; P.O. Dept. in C.S.A.: 124–35, 150, 156–59, and Henry, *Story of Conf.*, 91–93); Scharf, *Hist. C.S. Navy*, 29–30 and n.1; JD to VHD, Nov. 3–4, 1865, MS, TRANSYL, quot.; Butler, *Judah P. Benj.*, 36–45, 118–19, 139–40.

24. VHD, *Memoir* 1:409–12, quots. See Stovall, *Toombs*, 6, 24, 45, 126–27, 358–59, and Thompson, *Robert Toombs*, 8–11, 57–58, 125–26.

25. VHD, *Memoir* 1:412; J. Campbell in *Life and Reminisc.*, 133, quot.; Stovall, *Toombs*, 8–9, 45–46, 106, 184–85, 205–8, 364–65; Thompson, *Robert Toombs*, 8–9, 18–19, 80, 109, 153, 184–87; *Papers* 5:App. 1, 232 (under July 20, 1853), and 6:App. 1, 391 (Jan. 7, 1856).

26. Thompson, *Robert Toombs*, 42–44, 49–50, 58, 62, 71–87, 97–98, 104–9, 121; (Army:) *Cong. Globe*, 35th Cong., 1st sess., App., 451; Rowland 3:176, 185, 197, 559–62, 4:402, 422–23, 443, 448, 512–14.

27. JD to Gaskill, Sept. 21, 1853 (Rowland 2:277–79); Thompson, *Robert Toombs*, 91–92, 116, 146–59; *Papers* 6:App. 1, 542 (under Mar. 12, 1857); Ibid., 670–71; Stovall, *Toombs*, 202–15. See ibid., 43, 371–72 and VHD, *Memoir* 1:410. AHS had his own room in Toombs's Georgia home (visit, 1986).

28. VHD, *Memoir* 1:410–11, quot.; Stovall, *Toombs*, 91, 184–85; Montgomery, *Howell Cobb's Conf. Career*, 25–26; AHS, *Recollections*, 11–12, 62; Thompson, *Robert Toombs*, 158 n.7; Rowland 10:6, 20; Laura A. White, *Robert Barnwell Rhett: Father of Secession*, 194–200 (and see *Private Chesnut*, 122).

29. White, *R. B. Rhett*, 194, 196–97; JD, *Rise and Fall* 1:244; Richardson, *Conf.* 1:55 and n.1, 57, 76, 2:83; Sandor Szilassy, "America and the Hungarian Revolution of 1848–49" [*The Slavonic and East European Review* 44 (Jan. 1966)], 186 n.38, quot. (Mann had repr. U.S. in Vienna, Paris and Trieste [185 and n.34], and in Bremen [*DAB*]); Moore, *Mann Letters*, 83; Randall, *Civil War*, 463 and n.10.

30. Richardson, *Conf.* 1:55–56; JD, *Rise and Fall* 1:263–66 and App. L (see *Papers* 6:372); Randall, *Civil War*, 204–6; Sterling, *Belle*, 144 (Tyler quot.); Elizabeth Tyler Coleman, *Priscilla Cooper Tyler and the American Scene, 1816–1889*, 120, 135–36, 142–43, 145.

31. Randall, *Civil War*, 222–27 (Lincoln quots. on 224); Shingleton, *John T. Wood*, 14 (Wood quot.; see 5–6); Const. of U.S.A., Art. 2, sect. 1; JD, *Rise and Fall* 1:266–80 and App. L (Seward quot. on 677); Moore, *Mann Letters*, 83–86 (not "civil" war: 2 countries involved).

32. JD, *Rise and Fall* 1:301–8 and App. K, 640–47 (Const. for Prov. Govt. of C.S.A., Art. 1, Sect. 1, and Art. 3); Richardson, *Conf.* 1:56–58; William C. Harris, *Leroy Pope Walker: Confederate Secretary of War*, 56–71.

33. Fitz Lee, "Sketch of Cooper," 272–73; JD to Fitz Lee, Apr. 5, 1877 (*SHSP* 3:274–76, quots.); JD, *Rise and Fall* 1:308–9. Duke, *Reminisc.*, 343: Cooper's "eminent and acknowledged ability."

34. VHD, *Memoir* 2:8–10, 33; Simpson, *Howell Cobb*, 146, 149–50; Richardson, *Conf.* 1:56–57; Harris, *Leroy P. Walker*, 57 and n.4, 72–76, 79–80; JD, *Rise and Fall* 1:304–5, 311–16; Josiah Gorgas to JD, monograph (Rowland 8:308–36, esp. 309–12); Semmes, *Service Afloat*, 75–88 (quot. on 79); JD in *Life and Reminsc.*, 428–33, quot.

35. Schaff, *Spirit of Old West Point*, 94–95, quots. (see 232 on JD); (Huse:) Rowland 8:311, Harris, *Leroy P. Walker*, 84–86, and Charles S. Davis, *Colin J. McRae: Confederate Financial Agent*, 40–45; (Gorgas:) Warner, *Gens. in Gray*, and Rowland 8:308 n.1.

36. Collins in Heitman, *Hist. Register;* (Ives:) *Letters*, 300–302, *Chesnut*, 423 and nn.6, 8, *Papers* 6:App. 1, 664 (Sept. 3, 1860 [under June 28]; see June 26), and Beers, *Guide to C.S.A.*, 63.

37. Hardee in Heitman, *Hist. Register;* Hughes, *Gen. Hardee*, 67–74; T. B. Roy, "Sketch" of Hardee (Hardee Papers, ADAH); *Conf. Soldier in C. W.*, 344 (appt. dates in C.S., as in U.S., were retroactive); McWhiney, *Braxton Bragg*, 150–55.

38. R. C. Wood, Jr., in Heitman, *Hist. Register;* WPJ, *Gen. ASJ*, 509; *O. R.*

10 (Part 1): 6–7; Holland, *Morgan and His Raiders*, 73–83, 102–3; R. Taylor, *Destruction*, 15–17, quot.; Shingleton, *John T. Wood*, caption on 7, 15–19 (quot. on 16), 25.

39. *Conf. Soldier in C. W.*, 347, 369, 344, 350; R. Davis, *Recoll. of Miss.*, 404–5; Jones in *Life and Reminsc.*, 121–22. See Rains and F. Lee in Warner, *Gens. in Gray;* Van Dorn in *Papers* 6:App. 1, 471 (May 15, 1856); Longstreet, ibid. 5:App. 1, 456–57 (under Oct. 2, 1855); Magruder, ibid., e.g., 39 and 41–42 nn.12–14.

40. J. T. Headley, *The Illustrated Life of Washington*, 214, quots.; Mercer et al.: Warner, *Gens. in Gray* (Holmes also in Heitman, *Hist. Register*).

41. T. Harry Williams, *P. G. T. Beauregard: Napoleon in Gray*, 44–49; JD to Floyd, Jan. 19, 1858 (*Papers* 6:App. 1, 558, quot.); Bgd. in Warner, *Gens. in Gray;* Floyd, ibid.; Morrison, *"The Best School,"* 127; Thompson, *Robert Toombs*, 152. Bgd.'s line rank was capt.; res'd. Feb. 20 (Heitman, *Hist. Register*).

42. Bgd. in Warner, *Gens. in Gray;* Williams, Bgd., 49–56; JD, *Rise and Fall* 1:212–14, 216, 219, 289.

43. JD, *Rise and Fall* 1:266–81 and App. L (quots. on 280, 273, 274, 276–77 [Welles, italics omitted], 281), 290–91 (force against Sumter "really an act of war"; see JD in Rowland 2:323); McPherson, *Battle Cry*, 267–72; *The Private Chesnut*, 56, quots.

44. JD, *Rise and Fall* 1:274 (quot.), 278, 280–89 (quot. on 287), 293, 297 (quot.); JD to Prov. C.S. Cong., Apr. 28, 1861 (Richardson, *Conf.* 1:70–74, quot. on 73); Williams, *Bgd.*, 56–61; Wright, *Southern Girl*, 43–50; Henry, *Story of Conf.*, 29–33.

45. JD to Prov. C.S. Cong., Apr. 29, 1861 (Richardson, *Conf.* 1:74–75, quots.; see Rowland 5:112–13); Randall, *Civil War*, 360, 366; JD, "Doctrine of State Rights," 219, quot.; JD, *Rise and Fall* 1:292, quots. (and see 297); AHS, *Const. View* 2:39–40 ("self-defence"), 370–72 (Lincoln's Procl. in full).

46. AHS, *Const. View* 2:370–75 (quot. on 372; see 397–412, 416, 419–21); JD to Prov. C.S. Cong., Apr. 28, 1861 (Richardson, *Conf.* 1:75 and 79, quots.); McPherson, *Battle Cry*, 274–75.

47. JD to VHD, Feb. 20, 1861, in VHD, *Memoir* 2:33, quot.; Ibid., 34 (quot.), 36, 40; Napier, *First White House*, brochures, visits (house moved 1921); Ross, *First Lady*, 108–9, 112–13 (Russell quots.); Strode, *President*, 20, 12–13. For "clever," see *OED;* Phillips, *Life and Labor*, 366 n.2.

48. Strode, *President*, 20; Quots. from Mary P. Watts in "Order of Service" at dedication of mem. tablet to JD in St. John's, 1925 (Tenn. State Library) and Wood, *Life of St. John's*, 49–50. Original hand-carved JD pew bears ceramic number "115."

49. Ross, *First Lady*, 109, quots.; *The Private Chesnut*, 18–19, quot. (dated by eds. Mar. 2, but V. arr. Mar. 4: Napier, *First White House*, 2).

50. Ross, *First Lady*, 109, 117; Nuermberger, *Clays of Ala.*, 177, 185, 198; VHD to C. C. Clay, May 10, 1861 in *Heroines of Dixie: Spring of High Hopes*, ed. Katherine M. Jones, 29, quot.; *The Private Chesnut*, 12 n.5; Conversation with Mills Thornton, July 1992.

51. *The Private Chesnut*, 11 and n.2, 19 (also, e.g., 34–40, and *Chesnut*, passim); Beers, *Guide to C.S.A.*, 63; *Papers* 6:374 n.30; Phillips, *Corr. of Toombs*, 706. Browne often called English: both countries then under one rule.

52. Chesnut in Warner, *Gens. in Gray; The Private Chesnut*, 55–60 (quot. on 57); *Chesnut* 35–51 (quot. on 44); Simpson, *Howell Cobb*, 151; Ross, *First Lady*, 112 (Russell quot.); Alvy L. King, *Louis T. Wigfall, Southern Fire-Eater*, 29–35, 118–21; Wright, *Southern Girl*, 35–50.

53. AHS, *Const. View* 2:376–80, 382–95 (secession dates; see Randall, *Civil War*, 254 n.1); John B. Jones, *A Rebel War Clerk's Diary*, ed. Earl Schenck Miers (hereafter: Miers, *Jones Diary*), 19, 21; JD, *Rise and Fall* 1:339–40; JD to C.S. Cong., July 20, 1861 (Rowland 5:112); Henry, *Story of Conf.*, 46; F. Lee, "Sketch of Cooper," 274.

54. Miers, *Jones Diary*, 21 and 22 (quots.), 19; Thomas Robson Hay, "Lucius B. Northrop: Commissary General of the Confederacy," 6.

55. VHD, *Memoir* 2:74–75; Thompson, *Robert Toombs*, 171; JD to C. J. Wright, May 11, 1876, and to VHD, Dec. 7, 1865 (Rowland 7:514 and MS, TRANSYL, quots.); King, *Wigfall*, 128–29; Wright, *Southern Girl*, 54–55 (quot. from Mrs. Wigfall).

56. King, *Wigfall*, 129; Kimball, *Richmond in Time of War*, 30–31; Henry, *Story of Conf.*,46–48; Wright, *Southern Girl*, 55 (quot. from letter, May 30, 1861).

57. King, *Wigfall*, 126–35; Wigfall in Warner, *Gens. in Gray;* JD to C.S. Cong., Nov. 18, and to Letcher, Sept. 13, 1861 (Rowland 5:167 and 131, quots.); *Heth Memoirs*, xxxiii, quots. (see xxxix, 149–96, and Warner, *Gens. in Gray*).

58. AHS, *Const. View* 2:378–80, 384–87; JEJ in Warner, *Gens. in Gray;* Govan and Livingood, *Different Valor*, 28–39; Jeffrey N. Lash, *Destroyer of the Iron Horse: General Joseph E. Johnston and Confederate Rail Transport, 1861–1865*, 6–15.

59. Freeman, *R. E. Lee* 1:515–16; VHD, *Memoir* 2:138–40 (quots. from JEJ dispatches and JD endrs., July 24 and 29, 1861; see *O. R.* 2:1007, Freeman, *Lee's Lieuts.* 1:112, and Symonds, *JEJ*, 126).

60. Quots.: JD to Custis Lee, June 18, 1883 (*Letters*, 527); JD, "Robert E. Lee," 60; Lee to Mary C. Lee, July 12, 1861, in R. E. Lee [Jr.], *Recoll. and Letters*, 36. Freeman complains of Lee's "empty title" (*R. E. Lee* 1:516–18, 527–30), but Lee was signing dispatches as "General, Commanding" (*O. R.* 2:239, 959, 925).

61. JD to J. Lyons, Aug. 30, 1878 (Rowland 8:257, quots.); VHD, *Memoir* 2:150n; *Papers* 6:App. 1, 665 (June 28); JD in Senate, June 13, 1860 (Rowland 4:510–14). T. S. Jesup, QMG since 1818, died June 10 (Heitman, *Hist. Register*).

62. Freeman, *R. E. Lee* 1:411–12 (quot. from Lee to Custis Lee, Apr. 16, 1860; says re. QMG appt., but that was May); Craig L. Symonds, *Joseph E. Johnston: A Civil War Biography*, 45, 88–91 (seems to confuse line and bvt. rank); JEJ in Heitman, *Hist. Register* (the bvts. here are explained in Freeman, *Lee's Lieuts.* 1:715; and see 143).

63. *Papers* 6:App. 1, 644–45 (under Mar. 15, 1860), 5:App. 1, 440 (under July 11, 1855); Robt. Ransom to Walthall, Mar. 23, 1879 (Rowland 8:370–71, quots.; R. had been in 1st Cav. [Heitman, *Hist. Register*]); Freeman, *R. E. Lee* 1:411 and n.23, 458, 527, 607; Symonds, *JEJ*, 51, 76–78, 88 (JEJ quot.).

64. Twiggs in Heitman, *Hist. Register*, in Warner, *Gens. in Gray*, and in *Conf. Soldier in C. W.*, 347; Heidler, "Mil. Career of Twiggs," 197–217, 224–44; JD to T. A. Moore, Sept. 26, 1861 (Rowland 5:136–37).

65. Freeman, *R. E. Lee* 1:414–29, 433–42; R. E. Lee in Heitman, *Hist. Register;* R. E. Lee [Jr.], *Recoll. and Letters*, 24–28; Heidler, "Mil. Career of Twiggs," 198, quot.

66. Pendleton to JD, May 11, 1861, in Kimball, *Richmond in Time of War*, 7, quot.; Pendleton in Warner, *Gens. in Gray;* Rowland 6:227 n.1 (West Pt. 1830, res'd. 1833, ordained 1838); JD, *Rise and Fall* 1:358, 300; Henry, *Story of Conf.*, 50–51. See *Papers* 5:App. 1, 311 (Feb. 14, 1854).

67. *Polk* 1:316–24 (quots. on 319 from letter, June 10, 1861; see Polk to Elliott, 323–24, and JD to Polk, 316–17).

68. *Polk* 1:263–77, 283–85, 288 (quot.), 292–99 and (App. to chap. 7), 300–13; Cheshire, *Church in C.S.*, 13–38 (formed July 3, 1861, in Montg.; see *Polk* 1:327); JD, Address, July 10, 1878 (Rowland 8:230, quot.).

69. *Polk* 1:320–26 (Polk quots. and last JD quot.), 191–236, 286–92 (Polk quots. on 291, 292; see Butler, *Judah P. Benj.*, 250: burning of houses urged); Rowland 5:160 n.1; JD, Address, July 10, 1878 (ibid. 8:230, quots.). On Polk's case, see Cheshire, *Church in C.S.*, 46–49.

70. JD to Polk, May 22, 1861, in *Polk* 1:316; Henry, *Story of Conf.*, 49–54; Williams, *Bgd.*, 66–77; JD, *Rise and Fall* 1:340. On who thought of sending JEJ: ibid., 344–48, 367–71; Lee to JD, Rowland 5:177; LBN to JD, ibid. 8:145–46; Freeman, *R. E. Lee* 1:531, 536–37, 540.

71. JD, *Rise and Fall* 1:359, quot.; *Chesnut*, 113, 114; JD to Bgd., July 18, 1861 (Rowland 5:111, quot.).

72. Bowman, *C. W. Almanac*, 60; JD, *Rise and Fall* 1:348; JD to Bgd., July 18, 1861 (Rowland 5:111, quot.; see also 110–11); Freeman, *R. E. Lee* 1:535–40; R. E. Lee [Jr.], *Recoll. and Letters*, 37; J. R. Davis in *Conf. Soldier in C. W.*, 358.

73. JD, *Rise and Fall* 1:348–50, 359 (quot. on 350; see Symonds, *JEJ*, 368).

74. JD Paper, Feb. 18, 1865 (Rowland 6:493); JEJ, *Narrative*, 38–39, 41–42; Jubal Anderson Early, *Jubal Early's Memoirs: Autobiographical Sketch and Narrative . . .*, 34–36 (see Early in Rowland 8:104); Bradley T. Johnson, *A Memoir of the Life and Public Service of Joseph E. Johnston . . .*, 49–52; Williams, *Bgd.*, 71, 76–79.

75. JD, *Rise and Fall* 1:349–52, 382 (Lay quot.); Lay to Walthall, Feb. 13, 1878, précis in *Cal. JD MSS*, 72–73 (JD quot.); Walthall-Chesnut corr., Feb. 7, 10, 24, 1879 (ibid., 121–26); *The Private Chesnut*, 102, quot. (Col. C. angered by claim JD "too late").

76. JD, *Rise and Fall* 1:351–52; Early, *Memoirs*, 27; McElroy, *JD* 1:321–22; *Fighting for the Confederacy: The Personal Recollections of General Edward Porter Alexander*, ed. Gary W. Gallagher (hereafter, under Alexander), 54–58; Quots. from Leven B. Lane, Jr., obituary (Marion, Ala., paper, Sept. 11, 1861, RPR in *Demopolis Times*, n.d.; clipping courtesy Nancy Rankin McKee).

77. JD to Bgd., Apr. 27, 1878 (Rowland 8:185–86, quots.); JD, *Rise and Fall* 1:352–65 (quots. 354–56 from a Jordan letter); Alexander, *Fighting for Conf.*, 554–59 (names "Crazy Hill," which JD does not).

78. JD, *Rise and Fall* 1:356 (quot.; see JD in *O. R.* 2:986, 987), 365 (quot. JD to Bgd., Aug. 4, 1861); JEJ, *Narrative*, 56, 63–65 (indicates pursuit impossible, as does Early, *Memoirs*, 40–46).

79. Williams, *Bgd.*, 95 (Bgd. "liked to fight"); Rowland 2:145, quot.; R. Davis in *Life and Reminsc.*, 211, quot.; Thompson, *Robert Toombs*, 172–74, quot. (and n.75), 176; Stovall, *Toombs*, 234–35; Rowland 2:214 n.1; Eckert, 65 (quots. from Craven text and JD note).

80. Harris, *L. P. Walker*, 98–122 (quots. on 113, 114, 121); Walker in Warner, *Gens. in Gray;* Freeman, *Lee's Lieuts.* 1:116; Miers, *Jones Diary*, 29, quots.

81. Butler, *Judah P. Benj.*, 240 (Benj. att. gen. and ad interim sec. of war till Nov. 15); Thomas Bragg in *South in Bldg. of Nation*, 11 (gov. N. C. 1854–58; U.S. Senate 1858–61).

82. JD, *Rise and Fall* 1:230–31 and 2:4–5; JD to C. J. Wright, Feb. 12, 1876 (Rowland 7:493–94); JD, Inaugural Address, Feb. 22, 1862 (Richardson, *Conf.* 1:185, quot.); An Act [of Prov. C.S. Cong.], May 6, 1861 (ibid., 104–10; quot. on 105); McElroy, *JD* 1:180; Rowland 3:286, 471, 474.

83. JD to Lincoln, July 6, 1861 (Richardson, *Conf.* 1:115–16, quots.). *Savannah:* ibid., 102–3; JD, *Rise and Fall* 2:10–14 (also the ship *Jefferson Davis* later).

84. Ibid., 11–14, 580–608 (quots. on 584, 594 [JD to Lincoln, July 2, 1863]; 1st cartel, Feb. 14, 1862 [587]); Jones, *Davis Memorial*, 605–6 (JD quots. from T. H. Watts, att. gen. 1862–63; ref. to Esther 7:9–10; see Rowland 5:375; *Conf. Vet.*, Feb. 1910, 68; Randall, *Civil War*, 506). See JD in Rowland 9:171–73.

85. JD, *Rise and Fall* 2:588–91, quot.; Christopher Losson, *Tennessee's Forgotten Warriors: Frank Cheatham and His Confederate Division*, 200.

86. JD in Senate, Jan. [28], 1860 (Rowland 4:169, quot.); VHD, *Memoir* 2:163, quots.; *Chesnut*, 80–91, 100–122; Strode, *Tragic Hero*, 186; JD to VHD, Jan. 17, 1870, quot. (ALA typescript).

87. Quots.: JD in Senate, Jan. [28], 1860 (Rowland 4:169); Minnigerode in *Life and Reminisc.*, 231, VHD to JD, Feb. 23, 1866, MS, ALA (the man was an express agent).

88. Williams, *Bgd.*, 39–45, 71–75 (quot. on 73; Lee rejected 2nd plan; JEJ, another [77]); Bgd. to Wigfall, July 8, 1861, in Wright, *Southern Girl*, 71–72.

89. JD Paper, Feb. 18, 1865 (Rowland 6:492, quot.); Jones, *Davis Memorial*,

341 (Reagan quot.; see BNH in Rowland 7:552; Freeman, *Lee's Lieuts.* 1:112–13; *Chesnut* 608); VHD, *Memoir* 2:150n; Ross, *First Lady,* 94.

90. JEJ to JD, May 17, 1855, MS, ALA, quot.; Govan and Livingood, *A Different Valor,* 26 (JEJ quot. 1860; Wood not ident.); (JD to JEJ quots.:) *O. R.* 2:973–74 (bracket in text), 976–77, and Rowland 5:119–20.

91. JEJ, *Narrative,* 64 and 54, quots. (see 63); VHD, *Memoir* 2:91; Lay (as in Note 75 above) and Alexander, *Fighting for Conf.,* 54 (see Jones in *Memorial,* 453, and Early, *Memoirs,* 27).

92. B. T. Johnson, *JEJ,* 54 (quot. from boy); H. T. Childs, "Turney's First Tennessee Regiment" (*Conf. Vet.,* Apr. 1917, 165, quot.); JD, *Rise and Fall* 1:350 (358: field very extensive). JD said, 1874, JEJ's account "only excusable on the score of his ignorance of the closing events of the battle" (*Letters,* 397).

93. JEJ, *Narrative,* 59, quot.; Freeman, *R. E. Lee* 1:579–631; *Heth Memoirs,* 151–62 (quots. on 160); Wise in Warner, *Gens. in Gray.*

94. Freeman, *R. E. Lee* 1:602, quot.; JD, "Robert E. Lee," 60–61, quot.

95. W. H. Taylor, *Gen. Lee,* 27–34, 47 (quot. from JD to Taylor, Jan. 31, 1878; JD seems not to know about Pollard); *Heth Memoirs,* 156; Edward A. Pollard, *The First Year of the War,* 169–70.

96. R. E. Lee [Jr.], *Recoll. and Letters,* 37–53 (JD quot. on 53; ref. to James 1:24); JD to J. H. Savage, July 3, 1880 (Rowland 8:478, quot.).

97. Williams, *Bgd.,* 96–98 (Bgd. quot.); White, *R. B. Rhett,* 216–17; Quot. from *Whig,* Aug. 27, 1861, in Kimball, *Richmond in Time of War,* 24.

98. JD to Bgd., Aug. 4 and Oct. 30, 1861 (Rowland 5:120–21 and 156–57, quots.); Williams, *Bgd.,* 105–6; *O. R.* 2:484–505 (Bgd. Rpt. with JD Endrs., quot. on 504).

99. Williams, *Bgd.,* 106–8 (for plan, see 74–75); Lee to JD, Nov. 24 (Rowland 5:176–77); JD to Chesnut, Oct. 30 and Nov. 11 (ibid., 157 and 164–66, quots.; Chesnut's letter in *O. R.* 2:509–11). Cooperation: see, e.g.: JD to JEJ, Feb. 28, 1862, and to G. W. Smith, Nov. 22, 1861 (Rowland 5:208–10 and 174–75).

100. JD to JEJ, Nov. 3, 1861 (*O. R.* 2:511–12, quot.); JEJ to JD, Nov. 10, in JD, *Rise and Fall* 1:363, quot. (and see 362); JEJ, *Narrative,* 59 and 64, quots.; B. T. Johnson, *JEJ,* 56, 59 (says JD blamed JEJ; he did not in *Rise and Fall* 1:352–84).

101. Rowland 8:104 (Early quot.; says no lack of supply, as do LBN and JD, ibid. 9:346–48); JD to Ed. of *Courier Journal,* May 5, 1887 (ibid., 540–55). See JD-LBN corr., 1878 and 1879 (Rowland 8:146 and 337): JD says "an afterthought and an absurdity"; the strong U.S. position was "reason given to me"; see *O. R.* 2:977. Author heard JD charged with this orally in 1976.

102. JD to JEJ, Sept. 5, 1861 (Rowland 5:135–36, quots.).

103. WPJ, *Gen. ASJ,* 247–48, 273 (res'd. Apr. 10, 1861; left Apr. 25: see 261–62, 267), 277–91 (JD quot. on 291), 266 (Scott offer; see 67); JD, Address, 1878 (Rowland 8:232, quot.); Richardson, *Conf.* 1:129 (ranking recomm. by sec. of war).

104. JEJ to Cooper, July 24, 1861, in VHD, *Memoir* 2:139, quots. (italics omitted); Symonds, *JEJ,* 126 (JEJ quots.; for his temper, see 157, and Alexander, *Fighting for Conf.,* 82).

105. JEJ to JD, Sept. 10, 1861, in VHD, *Memoir* 2:142, quot. (italics omitted); JEJ to JD, Sept. 12, ibid., 144–53 (quots. on 153, 145, 151, 152; see full text in appendix A above); VHD to W. L. Fleming, Dec. 20, 1905, in Ross, *First Lady,* 413, quot.

106. JD to Van Dorn and G. W. Smith, e.g., in Rowland 5:153–56; JD, War Dept. Rpt. 1854 (ibid. 2:397–406, quot.); Richardson, *Conf.* 1:129 (see 392–94: JD to Senate 1864).

107. Cooper, ASJ, Lee, JEJ, Bgd. in Heitman, *Hist. Register; Chesnut,* 608, quot.; JEJ to JD, Sept. 12, 1861, in VHD, *Memoir* 2:144–53 (quots. on 151, 152; his ranking keeps Cooper in first place). See J. A. Bethune to Fleming, June 12, 1908, MS, Fleming Collection; Richard M. McMurry, "'The *Enemy* at Richmond': Joseph E. Johnston and the Confederate Government," 5–8.

108. JD to JEJ, Sept. 14, 1861, in VHD, *Memoir* 2:154, quot.; Ibid., 155, quot.; JEJ, *Narrative*, 73, quot. See appendix A above and nn.

109. JD to VHD, n.d., in VHD, *Memoir* 2:150n, quots. (see JD to Lyons, Aug. 30, 1878 [Rowland 8:257]); *O. R.*, 4, 1:164, quot.

110. Early to Fitz Lee, May 14, 1877 (Rowland 7:554–55, quots.; and see F. Lee to JD on 554).

111. JEJ, *Narrative*, 73, quot.; VHD, *Memoir* 2:158 (quot. from unident. 1880 letter; Wright ident. from corr. with JD in Rowland 8).

112. Letters of both Johnstons in Symonds, *JEJ*, 220–21, and Govan and Livingood, *Different Valor*, 173, 175, 225, 227, 230–31, 337, 338, 347 (and see 380); JD to VHD, Apr. 26, 1874 (*Letters*, 397, quot.; "memory" *re* relative rank JEJ and Lee).

113. JD Paper, Feb. 18, 1865 (Rowland 6:491–503); JD to G. A. Henry, Apr. 21 (ibid., 557); BNH undated interview, quot. (ALA typescript from BNH Papers, LC); JD to Mercer, Jan. 15, 1863 (Rowland 5:417). See, e.g., John B. Gordon, *Reminiscences of the Civil War*, 133–34, and B. T. Johnson, *JEJ*, 251–69.

Chapter XIII The Chief Executive

1. Newsletters of Mus. of Conf., 1985 to 1988; VHD, *Memoir* 2:198–201, quot.; Samuel J. T. Moore, Jr., *Moore's Complete Civil War Guide to Richmond*, 148–50; Visit, 1986 (the author was graciously given a tour of the house, then being restored, by Tucker Herrin Hill).

2. House refs. as in Note 1 above; VHD, *Memoir* 2:199; Ross, *First Lady*, 134–35; Sterling, *Belle*, 170, quots.; T. C. DeLeon, *Belles, Beaux, and Brains of the '60s*, 71.

3. *Chesnut*, 595 and 504, quots. Many others remembered Jeff's prayers with Joe: Pryor, *Reminisc. of Peace and War*, 249–50; Amelia G. Gorgas to W. L. Fleming in Fleming Papers; Mrs. Pattillo to JD, Rowland 9:529; C. C. Harrison, *Recoll.*, 181–82; Vandiver, *Gorgas Diary*, 96.

4. Beers, *Guide to C.S.A.*, 62 (2 previous secretaries); *Mus. of Conf. News*, No. 2, summer/autumn, n.d., and *Mus. of Conf. Journal*, summer, 1987, 8–9, and winter/spring, 1988, 6–7.

5. *Heth Memoirs*, 163, quots. (JEJ's letter "a scorcher"; JD's reply, "forcible"). Heth mistakes year and child, but confirms Dec. as Wm.'s birth month (see *Papers* 1:App. 4, Chart 14, n.138, and rev. ed., Chart 13, n.148).

6. VHD to Marg. K. Howell, June 1861 (*Letters*, 124, quots.); *Gache*, 180, quot. (says Cath. governess, but see DeLeon, *Belles*, 73). These servants and Betsy and Robert in JD letters, Aug. 21 and Sept. 26, 1865, MSS, TRANSYL; see *Chesnut*, 555, 601, 609, 535; others in Rowland 9:231–32; Hanna, *Flight*, 109, 117.

7. *Papers* 2::60 n.5; C. C. Harrison, *Recoll.*, 69; *Moore's Guide*, 149.

8. Janet Sharp Hermann, *Joseph E. Davis: Pioneer Patriarch*, 97–100; Strode, *President*, 146–47 (Eliza quots.).

9. VHD, *Memoir* 1:258; Coleman, *Priscilla C. Tyler*, 147–48, 143; Weddell, *St. Paul's* 1:170, quot.; Johns in Perry, *Bsps. of Am. Church*, 87 (asst. to Meade); T. R. R. Cobb, Jan. 18, 1862, in *SHSP* 28:290, quot.

10. Quots.: Hermann, *Joseph E. Davis*, 100; VHD, *Memoir* 2:161 (incl. *Examiner*); Strode, *President*, 147 (Eliza); C. C. Harrison, *Recoll.*, 127. Social life: ibid., 55–96, 116–206; Pryor, *Reminisc. of Peace and War*, 235–36, 228, 264; *Chesnut*, passim; Sterling, *Belle*, 168–77; DeLeon, *Belles*, passim, esp. 66–70; Ross, *First Lady*, e.g., 118–37, 170–76.

11. VHD, *Memoir* 2:160–62, quot.; Sterling, *Belle*, 174–77; *Chesnut* 553–54 (quot.), 549–50, 423 n.6.

12. C. C. Harrison, *Recoll.*, 172–77 and 129–30, quots.; *Chesnut*, 536–40, 423 n.8, 528–32 (quots.); DeLeon, *Belles*, 116–19, 217–32; Emory M. Thomas, *Bold*

Dragoon: The Life of J.E.B. Stuart, 281–82 (differs from *Chesnut* account), 290–95 (d. in May).

13. JD to LBN, Apr. 9, 1879 (Rowland 8:376, quot.; see 9:189); VHD, *Memoir* 2:138–44; Rowland 5:141–43, 146–49, 150–51.

14. G. W. Smith, "Council of war at Centreville ["Fairfax" in his text]" (*O. R.* 5:884–87); Symonds, *JEJ*, 130–31, quot.; JD, *Rise and Fall* 1:312, 440–42, 445–54; JD to M. J. Wright, Oct. 15, 1880 (Rowland 8:506–12); JD to JEJ, Sept. 5, 1861 (ibid. 5:135, quot.; also July 13 [*O. R.* 2:976–77]). JD tells Cong., Nov. 18, of conflict from Chesapeake Bay to Ariz. (Rowland 5:166). Gorgas: "darkest period," no arms imported till "about" Dec. (ibid. 8:315; see 308–16, 318, 327–28).

15. JD, War Dept. rpts. (Rowland 2:295–96, 391–92); JD to Vance and Holmes, 1862 (ibid. 5:354–55 and 386–88); JD to Gov. Flannigan of Ark., July 15, 1863 (ibid., 564, quot.); JD, letters of Mar. 13 and July 11, 1862 (ibid., 216–17 and 293, quots.). See also Feb. 18 (ibid., 195–97) and to Cong. Feb. 25 (Richardson, *Conf.* 1:189–91).

16. Lyons to Walthall, Aug. 20, 1878 (Rowland 8:256); JD to JEJ, Sept. 8, 1861 (ibid. 5:129–30, quots.); G. W. Smith, "Council of war" (as in Note 14 above). See JD to JEJ, Nov. 10, 1861, and Mar. 6, 1862 (Rowland 5:161–63 and 211–12); to Smith, Oct. 10 and 24, 1861 (ibid., 138–41 and 149–50).

17. G. W. Smith, "Council" (as in Note 14 above; "signed in triplicate," Jan. 31, 1862; later dated Oct. 1, 1861; see G. W. Smith, *Confederate War Papers. Fairfax . . .*); JD, *Rise and Fall* 1:449–54; JD to M. J. Wright, Oct. 14, 15, 1880 (Rowland 8:503, 506–12; see corr. Mar.–Dec. 1882 [9:156–57, 178–79, 183, 185–88, 192–93, 196–97], and *SHSP* 34:128–43).

18. JD to Bgd., Oct. 20, 1861 (Rowland 5:146–49); *Conf. Soldier*, 338.

19. Reagan, *Memoirs*, 161, and Rowland 5:138n (Smith acting sec. of war, Nov. 17–20, 1862).

20. JD to Bgd., Oct. 16, 20, 25, 1861 (Rowland 5:143, 148–49, 151, quots.); Williams, *Bgd.*, 101–5, 113–14 (Bgd. quot.), 109–10.

21. S. Foote, *C. W.* 2:322, map (numbers in 1863); JD to Bgd., Oct. 20, 1861 (Rowland 5:148).

22. Thomas Lawrence Connelly and Archer Jones, *The Politics of Command . . . Confederate Strategy*, 50; WPJ, *Gen. ASJ*, 292, 336, 343–44 (quots. from ASJ to Benj., Dec. 25, 1861; see 346); Stanley F. Horn, *The Army of Tennessee: A Military History*, 74. Compare number in Thomas L. Livermore, *Numbers and Losses in the Civil War in America: 1861–1865* [Bloomington: Indiana Univ. Press, 1957], 43; *Polk* 2:63; Horn, 441 n.6; Williams, *Bgd.*, 116 and n.10; Hughes, *Gen. Hardee*, 86; Connelly and Jones, *Politics of Command*, 94; Woodworth, *JD and His Gens.*, 53: all agree ASJ drastically outnumbered.

23. Cooper and Pike in Warner, *Gens. in Gray;* Rowland 1:118 n.1; *Jefferson Davis and the Confederacy*, ed. Ronald Gibson (Dobbs Ferry, N. Y.: Oceana Publications, Inc., 1977), 77–201 (Treaties with Indian Tribes, July 10–Dec. 21, 1861).

24. Randall, *Civil War*, 326–29 and nn.; Twiggs in Warner, *Gens. in Gray* (the 4 gens. listed); Reavis, *Harney*, 361–92 (quots. on 390, 383). Harney in Heitman, *Hist. Register* (res'd. 1863).

25. *Conf. Soldier*, 337; *Polk* 2:14, 33–35, 67, and 1:334–49 (quots. on 338–39, 335; Bledsoe, 56 n.2); Calhoun, "John Perkins Family," 84–85. Memminger church membership deduced from *Chesnut*, 574, 739. "Presbyter"="priest."

26. JD to A. Y. P. Garnett, Jan. 22, 1885 (Rowland 9:337–38, quot.); *Polk* 2:19–25; *O. R.* 4:179–87; JD, *Rise and Fall* 1:385–403 (quot. on 392). Woodworth, *JD and Gens.*, 37–41, thinks JD indecisive, but see *Polk*, as above.

27. *Polk* 2:23–28; *O. R.* 4:191–94 (ASJ quot.); WPJ, *Gen. ASJ*, 299–305, 311–12, 518; Henry, *Story of Conf.*, 70–75.

28. WPJ, *Gen. ASJ*, 518 (quot.), 311–12, 302–3, 306–18 (quots. on 316), 328–48, 425; Buckner in Warner, *Gens. in Gray;* Hughes, *Gen. Hardee*, 80–83, 92; Lubbock, *Six Decades*, 314–25, 326–27 (quot.), 329.

29. WPJ, *Gen. ASJ*, 329–33 (quot.), 338–39, 348, 328 (quot. from Munford; see 317); ASJ to Cooper, Oct. 17, 1861 (*SHSP* 3:128–29); *Polk* 2:15, 34–35, 59; Horn, *Army of Tenn.*, 58, 60 (JD quot.), 69. See JD, *Rise and Fall* 2:20–22; to JEJ (Rowland 5:163); to Polk, Feb. 1862 (*Polk* 1:348); also Butler, *Judah P. Benj.*, 246–47, 257.

30. WPJ, *Gen. ASJ*, 297–305, 316, 334, 390; All those named in Warner, *Gens. in Gray;* JD, *Rise and Fall* 1:399–402 (ex-gov. Morehead was in prison); W. C. Davis, *Breck.*, 280–90; McPherson, *Battle Cry*, 296.

31. WPJ, *Gen ASJ*, 316, 379–82 (Ky. admitted to C.S.A. Dec. 10, 1861), 518; W. C. Davis, *Breck.*, 296–97, 347; Henry, *Story of Conf.*, 192.

32. Horn, *Army of Tenn.*, 57 (quot.), 75–79; Hughes, *Gen. Hardee*, 85–86; WPJ, *Gen. ASJ*, 309–17, 303–4, 362–63, 407–17, 343–46, 425, 490.

33. Ibid., 378, 357, 394–406; *Polk* 2:63–65, quot.; Henry, *Story of Conf.*, 77–79.

34. JD, *Rise and Fall* 2:18–23; Horn, *Army of Tenn.*, 70; J. J. Crittenden in Rowland 1:220 n.1; Gens. Geo. and T. L. Crittenden in *South in Bldg. of Nation*, 11. See George in R. Carter, *Capt. Tod Carter*, 11 ("Drunk all the time"); Seitz, *Bragg*, 100–101; Warner, *Gens. in Gray; Conf. Soldier*, 347.

35. *Polk* 2:62, 64; Ridley, *Battles and Sketches*, 78 (ASJ quot.; number here and 67), 42–63 (Buckner quots.), 68–73 (ASJ quot. on 68); WPJ, *Gen. ASJ*, 416–17, 423–76, 550–51; Henry, *Story of Conf.*, 77–87, 102–4 (N.C.). Numbers in Ridley, and in WPJ (e.g., 443, 469, 474, 478–82) are far fewer than in Livermore, *Numbers and Losses* (as in Note 22 above), 78 and n.4; see also *Conf. Soldier*, 62.

36. Richardson, *Conf.* 1:181–92 (JD quot. on 188); [Sallie B. Putnam], *Richmond during the War: Four Years of Personal Observation* (1867; RPR 1983 [Time-Life Books]), 106–7; *Conf. Vet.*, June 1907, 280; Williams, *Bgd.*, 98, 107.

37. JD, 1845 (*Papers* 2::67, p. 272, quot.); Henry, *Story of Conf.*, 212, 88; *The Virginia State Capitol* (n.p.: 1983) and visit 1986; Richardson, *Conf.* 1:183 (JD quot.). See JD in *Letters*, 555, and "Doctrine of State Rights," 205; and Lonn, *Foreigners in Conf.*, 96.

38. Quots.: Jones, *Davis Memorial*, 318 (from Alfriend); R. Davis, *Recoll. of Miss.*, 429–31; Richardson, *Conf.* 1:184–88 (from JD).

39. VHD, *Memoir* 2:180 (quot.), 183 (quot. from unident. letter, Feb. 22, 1862); Richardson, *Conf.* 1:188 (JD quots.); Headley, *Ill. Life of Washington*, 476–77. For others deeply affected, see Jones, *Davis Memorial*, 318, 324, 590. Henry, *Story of Conf.*, 163, notes "the martyrdom of heading the Confederacy."

40. Jones, *Davis Memorial*, 318 (quots. from Alfriend); JD to Polk, Feb. 7, 1862, in *Polk* 1:348, quot.; WPJ, *Gen. ASJ*, 515 (quot. from *Mobile Register;* see R. Taylor, *Destruction*, 232–33).

41. WPJ, *Gen. ASJ*, 510–15 (quots.), 496 (Tenn. quot.; see 490–92 and Ridley, *Battles and Sketches*, 71–73, 80–81); JD, *Rise and Fall* 2:36–48 (quots. on 38). Other contemporary opinions in Duke, *Hist. Morgan's Cav.*, 118–19; Hamlin, *Ewell*, 74; *Pen and Sword: The Life and Journals of Randal W. McGavock*, ed. Herschel Gower and Jack Allen [Nashville: Tennessee Historical Commission, 1959], 615.

42. WPJ, *Gen. ASJ*, 511–12, quots.; Hughes, *Gen. Hardee*, 95 (Hardee quot.). Bragg's wife said he should "*urge*" JD either to come or to appoint Bragg or Bgd. (McWhiney, *Braxton Bragg*, 207).

43. JD to ASJ, Mar. 12, 1862, in WPJ, *Gen. ASJ*, 517–18, quots.; Woodworth, *JD and Gens.*, 94. ASJ's rpts. so far (Ridley, *Battles and Sketches*, 68–69; WPJ, 516–17) dealt only with Nashville and beyond. On Bragg, see McWhiney, *Braxton Bragg*, 178–84.

44. WPJ, *Gen. ASJ*, 488–89 (quot.), 515–16 (JD quot.; and see 213, 228, 231, 234, 243–45); *Polk* 2:102–3 and 34, quots.; Ridley, *Battles and Sketches*, 68 (see 56–60); JD to Cong., Feb. 25 (Rowland 5:204, quot.).

45. Gower and Allen, *Pen and Sword* [as in Note 41 above], 603, 611 (quots.

from 1862 diary; and see 79, 602, 617–18); Ridley, *Battles and Sketches,* 42–51; JD, *Rise and Fall* 2:28, quot. See Tilghman in Warner, *Gens. in Gray.*

46. WPJ, *Gen. ASJ,* 513 map, 509–10, 515–17 (quot. from ASJ), 520–21; Ridley, *Battles and Sketches,* 68–69; Hughes, *Gen. Hardee,* 93–98.

47. WPJ, *Gen. ASJ,* 518–21 (quots. from ASJ to JD, Mar. 18, 1862), 491 (ASJ quot.; see 514: "a battle and a victory," and 551–52). See Bragg, ibid., 548; Hughes, *Hardee,* 94–95.

48. WPJ, *Gen. ASJ,* 522 (quots. from aide, and from JD to ASJ, Mar. 26, 1862). These plans (see also ibid., 539, 516, 540–41, and Ridley *Battles and Sketches,* 68–69) contradict the claim that concentration was Bgd's. idea and that ASJ, "close to mental collapse," planned to move "away from" Bgd. (Connelly and Jones, *Politics of Command,* 98).

49. McWhiney, *Braxton Bragg,* 136–40, 153–54 (Elise quot.), 190–92 (quot. from T. Bragg; Benj.: Bragg's "noble and self-sacrificing spirit"; see 185–86, 178), 197–98 (quots. from Benj. and Bragg); JD to G. W. Smith, Oct. 29, 1861 (Rowland 5:155, quot.); *Conf. Soldier,* 344.

50. *Polk* 2:83, quot.; Williams, *Bgd.,* 122–24, 118, 120; Seitz, *Bragg,* 86–96; WPJ, *Gen. ASJ,* 548, 542 (Bgd. quot.).

51. *Polk* 2:82–84; WPJ, *Gen. ASJ,* 539, 544, 548 (Bragg quots.); Seitz, *Bragg,* 95; Horn, *Army of Tenn.,* 119; McWhiney, *Braxton Bragg,* 217.

52. WPJ, *Gen. ASJ,* 527–39, 541–42 (Bragg wants to attack earlier; see McWhiney, *Braxton Bragg,* 208–11), 576–80, 590–91; *Polk* 2:77–82; Seitz, *Bragg,* 104–5, 110. See Horn, *Army of Tenn.,* 116–19.

53. WPJ, *Gen. ASJ,* 543–44, 548–72, 290 (quots. on 554, 569, 290); *Polk* 2:84–100; McWhiney, *Braxton Bragg,* 212–27.

54. WPJ, *Gen. ASJ,* 549–51, 567, 573, 580–639; Duke, *Hist. Morgan's Cav.,* 142–44, quots. (and see 136, 141); Ridley, *Battles and Sketches,* 85–86 (quot. from Bgd. to Cooper), 86–95. Grant tried to deny this surprise and defeat (*Memoirs* 1:362, 364–65), but see also Henry, *Story of Conf.,* 117–18, and Rowland 9:379.

55. Duke, *Hist. Morgan's Cav.,* 151, quot.; WPJ, *Gen. ASJ,* 597–615 (quots. on 604, 612, [from Harris:] 613–14); Grave in Texas State Cemetery, Austin, and hist. marker at Ney home. On the charge, see *O. R.* 10 (Part 1): 569; W. C. Davis, *Breck.,* 306–7; McWhiney, *Braxton Bragg,* 240, 242.

56. WPJ, *Gen. ASJ,* 640, 544, 688–89, 694–718, 734 (quots. from "In Memoriam" by John. B. S. Dimitry; "interest"=profit or advantage; for Dimitry, see DeLeon, *Belles,* 115–16); Henry, *Story of Conf.,* 476; Strode, *Tragic Hero,* 303. The gens. were Bgd., Bragg, Buckner, Taylor, Longstreet, Gibson, Hays, Hood.

57. Ridley, *Battles and Sketches,* 85–86 (Bgd. quot.), 88–89; *O. R.* 10 (Part 1): 570 (Hardee quots.); *Polk* 2:107 (Bgd. quot.); Seitz, *Bragg,* 113 (Bragg quots., Apr. 8); Robert Selph Henry, *"First with the Most" Forrest,* 79–81; *Conf. Soldier,* 84–85.

58. *O. R.* 10 (Part 1): 569 (Hardee quots.); Fremantle, *Three Months,* 148 (quots., citing Polk); Bragg quots.): Rowland 9:561; Seitz, *Bragg,* 111; WPJ, *Gen. ASJ,* 553 (see Bragg on 633; Harris and Polk on 631; McWhiney, *Braxton Bragg,* 241).

59. Seitz, *Bragg,* 113–22; McWhiney, *Braxton Bragg,* 260–61, 247 (Bgd. quot.); Richardson, *Conf.* 1:211; WPJ, *Gen. ASJ,* 633 (Bragg to War Dept.).

60. JD to Cong., Apr. 8, 1862 (Richardson, *Conf.* 1:209, quots.; "no purer spirit, no more heroic soul"; see JD, *Rise and Fall* 2:67–70); JD at Metairie Cem., N. O., Apr. 6, 1883 (Rowland 9:207, quot.).

61. WPJ, *Gen. ASJ,* 658 (JD quot.; see 731–32); LBN to JD, Oct. 7, 1879 (Rowland 8:421, quot.). Others: R. Taylor, *Destruction,* 19, 231–33; Bragg in *Gen. ASJ,* 633; R. L. Gibson, ibid., 635; Moore, *Mann Letters,* 79.

62. Freeman, *R. E. Lee* 1:628 (JD quot.); Frank E. Vandiver, *Their Tattered Flags: The Epic of the Confederacy,* 140, quot.; JD, Nov. 3, 1870 (Rowland 7:285, quot.); VHD to Fleming, Dec. 20, 1905, in Ross, *First Lady,* 413, quot.

63. Ross, *First Lady,* 144; Weddell, *St. Paul's* 1:15–48, 54–56, 81, 250, 480–81 (from Westphalia), 243 (Minnigerode quot.) 2:291–92, 590, 379 (pews; 1:200

and 50: lent by owners); *Chesnut*, 585, 794; Strode, *President*, 141–42 (quot. from visitor). See Craven, *Prison Life*, 314.

64. Meade to JD, Jan. 21, 1862 (Rowland 5:188, quot.); Jones, *Davis Memorial*, 417–18 (Minnigerode quot.); WPJ, *Gen. ASJ*, 724; VHD, *Memoir* 2:269 ("His religious convictions had long occupied his thoughts").

65. VHD, *Memoir* 2:33, quot.; Henry, *Story of Conf.*, 106, 63, 77, 96–97, 103; Richardson, *Conf.* 2:117–28, 133–37, 147, 153–65; JD in Rowland 5:196, quot.; Wilfred Buck Yearns, *The Confederate Congress*, 37, 140–42; Butler, *Judah P. Benj.*, 252–53.

66. Yearns, *Conf. Cong.*, 46–48; Montgomery, *Howell Cobb's Conf. Career*, 48–49, quot.; T. R. R. Cobb, Jan. 24, 1862, in *SHSP* 28:290 and 289, quots.; Thompson, *Robert Toombs*, 179, 176; *Conf. Soldier*, 351, 357 (both Cobbs brig. gens. 1862).

67. Yearns, *Conf. Cong.*, 38, 47, 108, 221, 224, 226; Clay to JD, Apr. 21, 1862, with n. by Yancey and JD Endrs., MS, ADAH, quots.; DuBose, *Yancey*, 677–79, 667–68, 748 (claim that JD resented an earlier letter [650–53] not borne out by his reply [Rowland 5:231–32]); Nuermberger, *Clays of Ala.*, 207.

68. *Papers* 2::18 n.38, pp. 85–86 (Foote in Tenn. after 1859); WPJ, *Gen. ASJ*, 513, 496; Ridley, *Battles and Sketches*, 80–81; Yearns, *Conf. Cong.*, 140–42, 220; Rowland 8:380; White, *R. B. Rhett*, 219–20, 224–26; T. R. R. Cobb, Mar. 16, 1862, in *SHSP* 28:291. See Woodworth, *JD and Gens.*, 150.

69. Hamilton J. Eckenrode, *Jefferson Davis: President of the South*, 168; Freeman, *Lee's Lieuts.* 1:123–30; Henderson, *Stonewall Jackson*, 151–59; JD to JEJ, Feb. 14, 1862 (Rowland 5:192–93); Yearns, *Conf. Cong.*, 141–42, 145, 47; *O. R.*, 4, 1:954, 1005; Randolph in *Conf. Soldier*, 369.

70. *SHSP* 17:191 (quot. from Early; see VHD, *Memoir* 2:320); Vandiver, *Their Tattered Flags*, 129–30; Freeman, *R. E. Lee* 2:25–29; King, *Wigfall*, 137–38 (n.5: U.S. law a year later); JD, *Rise and Fall* 1:506, quot. (see 506–14); Yearns, *Conf. Cong.*, 65–67, 108 (see *O. R.* 4, 1:997–98); Richardson, *Conf.* 1:215–16.

71. Freeman, *R. E. Lee* 2:4–5 (quot. on 5), 44–46, 50–57, 61–66; T. R. R. Cobb, Mar. 16, 1862, in *SHSP* 28:291, quot.; Walter H. Taylor, *Four Years with General Lee*, 37–39, quot.; JEJ-Lee corr., May 8, 1862 (*O. R.* 11 [Part 3]: 499–501, JEJ quot.; and see Taylor, *Four Years*, 518) JD in Rowland 6:454, quot. (see JD to Lee, 453). Henry (*Story of Conf.*, 105) and Freeman (2:6–7) say Lee had no authority, but his dispatches, Mar. 18–June 1, 1862, prove otherwise (*O. R.* 11 [Part 3]: 384–567).

72. *The Wartime Papers of R. E. Lee*, ed. Clifford Dowdey and Louis H. Manarin, 434, 530–33, 596, 807, 811–12; W. Taylor, *Gen. Lee*, 216–17, 222; *SHSP* 17:191–92 (JD quots.); Rowland 5:308, 501, 502, 512, 6:304; JD in 9:555, quot., paraphrasing Lee; Undated BNH interview, quot. (ALA typed copy from LC).

73. *Conf. Soldier*, 17, 358; Beers, *Guide to C.S.A.*, 62–63; Rowland 5:197 n.1, 6:431–32 (duties: 5:279–80, 346–47; 6:462 Endrs.).

74. Freeman, *R. E. Lee* 1:641; *Papers* 6:App. 1, 664 (June 27 and Aug. 31, 1860); Arthur Marvin Shaw, *William Preston Johnston*, 70–73; Browne in Warner, *Gens. in Gray; Chesnut*, 327, 428, 455; JD to J. Chesnut, May–Oct. 1862 (Rowland 5:247, 295, 354, 355, 359).

75. Yearns, *Conf. Cong.*, 61–67; JD to Cong., Feb. 25, 1862 (Rowland 5:204–5; see also 141–42, 146–47).

76. JD to JEJ, Mar. 4, May 10 and 26, 1862 (Rowland 5:210–11, 242–43, 251–52; also to Lee, 274–75, and Lee to JEJ [*O. R.* 11 (Part 3): 488, 491]); Govan and Livingood, *Different Valor*, 78, 83–88, 116; Symonds, *JEJ*, 133–38, 141, 157–58 (JEJ quot.); B. T. Johnson, *JEJ*, 79, quot.

77. JD to JEJ, May 10, 1862 (Rowland 5:243, quots.; see also 208–10); B. T. Johnson, *JEJ*, 79, quot.; Symonds, *JEJ*, 133–38 (quots.; JEJ would demand specific instructions, then fail to carry them out), 145; JD to JEJ, Feb. 14, Mar. 4,

1862, and to M. J. Wright, Oct. 14, 1880 (Rowland 5:192–93, 210–11 and 8:503); JEJ, *Narrative*, 87–90; James I. Robertson, Jr., *The Stonewall Brigade*, 66–67.

78. JEJ, *Narrative*, 96–99, 104–6; B. T. Johnson, *JEJ*, 77–78; Freeman, *Lee's Lieuts.* 1:134–36; JD to JEJ, Mar. 15, 1862 (Rowland 5:222; see 211–12, 214); JD, ibid. 6:493–94, 8:502–3; JD, *Rise and Fall* 1:462–68; Lash, *Destroyer of Iron Horse*, 39–40, 27–34 (see sources in nn.29–31, esp. JD-LBN letters, Rowland 8 and 9).

79. Thompson, *Robert Toombs*, 177–78; Toombs to AHS, Sept. 22 and [30?], 1861 (Phillips, *Corr. of Toombs*, 575, 577, quots.); Stovall, *Toombs*, 246, 239–42 (Toombs quots.). The Peaks of Otter is in western Va.

80. JD, *Rise and Fall* 1:466–67; JD to M. J. Wright, Oct. 14, 1880 (Rowland 8:502–3); Freeman, *R. E. Lee* 2:12–16; *C. W. Almanac*, 90–93; McPherson, *Battle Cry*, 454–60.

81. Freeman, *R. E. Lee* 2:13–23, 31–32, 43 (JEJ had 55,000 at most); Early, *Memoirs*, 58; Alexander, *Fighting for Conf.*, 74; JD, *Rise and Fall* 2:84; *C. W. Almanac*, 93, quot. (under Apr. 3).

82. JD, *Rise and Fall* 2:86–88; Freeman, *R. E. Lee* 2:21–22, 34–35 (and see 16–17); JEJ to Lee, Apr. 30, 1862 (*O. R.* 11 [Part 3]: 477); McPherson, *Battle Cry*, 373–77; Scharf, *Hist. C.S. Navy*, 152–221.

83. JEJ, *Narrative*, 116, quots.; JEJ-Lee corr., Apr. 22–May 1, 1862 (*O. R.* 11 [Part 3]: 455–56, 473, 477, 485, quots.; see also 464, 469); Freeman, *R. E. Lee* 2:41–44; JD, *Rise and Fall* 2:92–100; JD to JEJ, May 1, 1862 (Rowland 5:239–40, quot.); Magruder tells how he bluffed McClellan: Fremantle, *Three Months*, 35–36.

84. Weddell, *St. Paul's Church* 1:160–61; VHD, *Memoir* 2:269; Strode, *President*, 243; Minnigerode in Jones, *Davis Memorial*, 418, quots. (echoing I John 1:7 and Luke 24:49); *BCP* (1850) (quots. from "Private Baptism" and of those "Able to Answer for Themselves"). Conf. *BCP* not yet in print (Cheshire, *Church in C.S.*, 98–103; Weddell, 248).

85. *The Civil War Diary of General Josiah Gorgas* (hereafter: *Gorgas Diary*), ed. Frank S. Vandiver, 11; Amelia G. Gorgas to Fleming, Mar. 16, 1908, in typescript, Fleming Collection; Minnigerode in Jones, *Davis Memorial*, 418–19, quot.; *BCP* (1850): The Order of Confirmation (quots.) and rubric at end, communion service Exhortations, Articles of Religion 25.

86. VHD, *Memoir* 2:269, quots. (cf. Col. 4:7); *The Diary of Edmund Ruffin*, ed. William Kauffman Scarborough (Baton Rouge: Louisiana State Univ. Press, 1976) 2:460, quot. (see xxx–xxxii, 306–7, and White, *R. B. Rhett*, 241).

87. Wigfall to Clay, May 16, 1862, in Nuermberger, *Clays of Ala.*, 195, quots. (see 24); Eckenrode, *JD*, 291 (quot. from *Examiner*, May 19; see Dabney, *Pistols and Pointed Pens*, 54); Miers, *Jones Diary*, 73–74; LBN to JD, Apr. 21, 1878 (Rowland 8:180).

88. King, *Wigfall*, 135–40 (see *Chesnut*, 106; Rowland 5:210–11, 242–43); JD, *Rise and Fall* 2:93–94; Richardson, *Conf.* 1:227–28, quots.; appendix B above.

89. JD to VHD, May 16, 1862, in VHD, *Memoir* 2:272–74, quot. (V. was in N. C.). "The office seekers are welcome to the one I hold" (Rowland 5:218–19).

90. *Hymns*, #144, quots.; VHD, *Memoir* 2:494 (quot.), 249–50, 823; Dorsey, *Recoll. of H. W. Allen*, 84–116; Scharf, *Hist. C.S. Navy*, 278–302; JD, *Rise and Fall* 2:210–31; Henry, *Story of Conf.*, 128–30; Ralph W. Donnelly, *The History of the Confederate States Marine Corps*, 121, 13 (Algiers); Strode, *President*, 239–41; John D. Winters, *The Civil War in Louisiana*, 85–104.

91. Hermann, *Joseph E. Davis*, 101–5 (JD quots.; Hermann, *Pursuit of Dream*, 39, has diff. account); JD to C. R. Dickson, June 12, 1862 (Rowland 5:274). See Shingleton, *John T. Wood*, 216, n.15; Yearns, *Conf. Cong.*, 166–67, 131–32.

92. VHD, *Memoir* 2:268–69, quot.; (Composite quot.:) VHD to JD, May 1862 (*Letters*, 125, through "Husband") and May 19, MS, TRANSYL ("peace": Phil. 4:7; also Communion service blessing, *BCP*); JD to VHD, May [17?], in Strode, *President*, 247, quot.

93. Shingleton, *John T. Wood*, 41–53 (Wood quot. on 42); Wood to VHD, May

[15], 1890, précis in *Cal. JD MSS,* 295. See JD in VHD, *Memoir* 2:323. V. sheltered Lola (Mrs. J. T.) Wood and children in Raleigh (VHD to JD, May 19, 1862, MS, TRANSYL).

94. Rowland 4:89 n.1, 3:40 n.1; Gorgas, ibid., 8:311–12, 322–23. On capital, see Rowland 8:216; Vandiver, *Their Tattered Flags,* 55–56, 137; Grant, *Memoirs* 2:425.

95. Lee to JEJ, May 12, 1862 (*O. R.* 11 [Part 3]: 511); JD to JEJ, May 17 (ibid. 524, quots.); JD to VHD, May 16, in VHD, *Memoir* 2:272–73, quots. (ref. to *Romeo and Juliet* 2.2.1); Reagan, *Memoirs,* 139 (Lee quot.; JD tells JEJ to fight).

96. Gustavus W. Smith, "Two Days of Battle at Seven Pines (Fair Oaks)," 222; Reagan, *Memoirs,* 137; JD, *Rise and Fall* 2:101–4; JD to JEJ, May 17, 1862 (*O. R.* 11 [Part 3]: 524, quot.); JD to VHD, May 19, in VHD, *Memoir* 2:275, quot. See map in chapter 14.

97. Reagan, *Memoirs,* 138, quot.; JD to VHD, May 19, 1862, in VHD, *Memoir* 2:275 (quots.), 280; G. W. Smith, "Two Days of Battle," 224–25; JD, Paper Feb. 18, 1865 (Rowland 6:495); JD, *Rise and Fall* 2:119–22 (Lee quot. on 120); Freeman, *R. E. Lee* 2:58–66 (map on 59: RR station near Seven Pines, Fair Oaks, gives Yankee name for battle).

98. Reagan, *Memoirs,* 137–39; JD to JEJ, May 1, 1862 (*O. R.* 11 [Part 3]: 484); see Rowland 5:527, 6:53, 258, 415, 417, 425, 464, 480, 544; JD, *Rise and Fall* 2:93–94, 98; Toombs to AHS, May 17 (Phillips, *Corr. of Toombs,* 594–95, quots. hard on JD too).

99. JD to Stringfellow, June 4, 1878 (*Letters,* 482, quots.); JD to VHD, June 3, 1862, in VHD, *Memoir* 2:294, quot. (may mean Bgd.; but see JD in Rowland 6:494–96).

100. JD to Lee, June 2, 1862 (*O. R.* 11 [Part 3]: 569, quot.); JD, *Rise and Fall* 2:122–24, quots.; JD to LBN, Apr. 24, 1879 (Rowland 8:382, quot.; JEJ's "blunders" and "ignorance"; 6:495: battle "disastrous" despite JEJ's "gallantry").

101. James Longstreet, *From Manassas to Appomattox,* 85–100; G. W. Smith, "Two Days of Battle," 224–25, 238, 241–42, 244–46. "Masses" on enemy "fractions": see McWhiney, *Braxton Bragg,* 311.

102. JD to VHD, June 2, 1862, in VHD, *Memoir* 2:291–92, quots. (JEJ feared spine injury [not so]; JD saw musket ball wound in shoulder [accurate]; shrapnel had also broken some ribs; see Alexander, *Fighting for Conf.,* 88).

103. JD to VHD, June 3, 1862, in VHD, *Memoir* 2:293; JD to VHD, June 11 (ibid., 310, quot.; italics omitted); D. H. Maury's Reminis. in B. T. Johnson, *JEJ,* 305, quot. (on jealousy of Lee see *Chesnut,* 799); JD, *Rise and Fall* 2:124, 129, 131; *O. R.* 11 (Part 3): 568–69, 571. Lee named the ANV, Freeman, *R. E. Lee* 2:77 and n.6).

104. JD, *Rise and Fall* 2:128–29, quot.; Smith, "Two Days of Battle," 261 (says paralyzed only after Lee took over; but see JD, 121; Alexander, *Fighting for Conf.,* 88; Henderson, *Stonewall Jackson,* 132; Smith had imagined JD's dislike 1857 [Mahan to JD, *Papers* 6:App. 1, 551–52]); JD to Smith, Nov. 22, 1861 (Rowland 5:174–75 ["my feelings" not involved] see 149–50, 154–56).

105. JD to VHD, June 2, 3, 1862, in VHD, *Memoir* 2:292–93, quots. (see Smith on 288); Reagan, *Memoirs,* 141–42; H. W. Cleveland to JD, Nov. 25, 1887 (Rowland 9:603).

Chapter XIV Commander in Chief

1. Freeman, *R. E. Lee* 1:472–74, 500–509, 529–35, 2:1–23, 30–74; *Wartime Papers,* 181; Henry, *Story of Conf.,* 436–37.

2. Henry, *Story of Conf.,* 130–31, 123, 151; Vandiver, *Their Tattered Flags,* 190; Robert C. Black III, *Railroads of the Confederacy* (1952, RPR Wilmington: Broadfoot Publ. Co., 1987), 143–45, maps on 6 and 141.

3. Henry, *Story of Conf.*, 476, 103–4, 69; Arthur W. Bergeron, Jr., *Confederate Mobile*, 37–39; JD, *Rise and Fall* 2:79–81 (Lee's arrival date wrong: see Freeman, *R. E. Lee* 1:608); Scharf, *Hist. C.S. Navy*, 663–69; George Linton Hendricks, *Union Army Occupation of the Southern Seaboard, 1861–65*, front map and 67; T. Drayton in Warner, *Gens. in Gray*.

4. Sears, *McClellan*, 192, 195–201; Freeman, *R. E. Lee* 2:79–88 (quot. on 86); Lee to JD, June 5, 1862 (*Wartime Papers*, 184); Longstreet, *From Manassas*, 112–14.

5. Alexander, *Fighting for Conf.*, 91 (2 quots.), 93; JD, "Robert E. Lee," 62–63 (Lee quot.; see JD, *Rise and Fall* 2:130–32, 152, and WPJ to JD in Rowland 10:83). See Vandiver, *Their Tattered Flags*, 139–40, 141; Ben Hill in *SHSP* 14:497.

6. JD, Address, Apr. 25, 1882 (Rowland 9:167, quot.); Freeman, *R. E. Lee* 2:81–83; Shaw, *WPJ*, 75 (quots. from WPJ letter, June 2); Strode, *President*, 243 (quots. from niece); Lawton in *Life and Reminisc.*, 196, quots.; JD to VHD, June 23, in VHD, *Memoir* 2:314, quots.

7. JD to VHD, June 23 and 13, 1862, in VHD, *Memoir* 2:314 and 312, quots. (see Williams, *Bgd.*, 156); Hay, "Lucius B. Northrop," 8 (LBN quot.); Seitz, *Bragg*, 129–32 and n.; JD to Bragg, June 14, and to Pettus, June 19 (Rowland 5:279 and 282).

8. *Chesnut*, 80 and Rowland 8:381 (JD quips *re* Bgd.); JD to VHD, June 13, 1862, in VHD, *Memoir* 2:312–13, quot.; JD to WPJ, June 14 (Rowland 5:279–80, quot.).

9. JD to Bragg, June 20, 1862 (Rowland 5:283); JD to E. K. Smith, Oct. 29, in McWhiney, *Braxton Bragg*, 327; Pickens-JD corr. in Rowland 5:274–76; *Conf. Soldier*, 340; Williams, *Bgd.*, 156–67, 171 (faults JD for sending order over Bgd's. head, but JD had proved 1855 that a govt. had this right [Rowland 2:495–99]).

10. JD to VHD, June 13, 1862, in VHD, *Memoir* 2:311–13, quots. (and quot. from text); JD to VHS, June 12 (*Letters*, 128, the quot. "God grant"); JD to VHD, June 2 and 3, in Ross, *First Lady*, 150, 151, quots.

11. JD to VHD, June 13, 1862, in VHD, *Memoir* 2:311–13, quots. ("Spare us" from the Litany in *BCP*); Polly to My dear Father, Aug. 28 (*Letters*, 128: "Billy is so sweet—he is growing so fast and laughs so loud").

12. Hermann, *Joseph E. Davis*, 103–7; Hermann, *Pursuit of Dream*, 38–40; Currie, "Freedmen at Davis Bend," 124 (quot. from 1864 letter).

13. Hermann, *Joseph E. Davis*, 106; Hermann, *Pursuit of Dream*, 40, 56; Everett, *Brierfield*, 75–77; VHD, *Memoir* 2:267, quots. from text and JD letter (and see 11). "After us, the deluge" attributed to Louis XV of France (*Hoyt*).

14. Joseph Davis to JD, Aug. 23, 1862 (*Letters*, 126–27; see ibid., 341); Hermann, *Joseph E. Davis*, 106 (quot.), 108–13, 115.

15. Miers, *Jones Diary*, 83–87 (battles and dates on 86); JD, *Rise and Fall* 2:130–58 (Lee quot. on 132; see VHD, *Memoir* 2:309n, Lee in *O. R.* 11 [Part 3]: 617, and JD Endrs. on 618); Freeman, *R. E. Lee* 2:92–119, 122–219.

16. Undated interview with BNH, quots. (ALA typescript from LC); D. H. Hill, "Lee's Attacks North of the Chickahominy" in *Battles and Leaders* 2:352 (quot.), 361; *Pendleton*, 194–95 (quots. from letter, June 28, 1862); Alexander, *Fighting for Conf.*, 99 (quot.), 107; Miers, *Jones Diary*, 87, quot.

17. Geo. Davis in *Life and Reminsc.*, 220–21, quot.; JD, *Rise and Fall* 2:140, 144–46 (spelled "Frazier's"), 149; Pendleton to JD, Dec. 6, 1880 (Rowland 8:528; cites JD letter to him).

18. VHD, *Memoir* 2:324, 317 (quot.; see Miers, *Jones Diary*, 86, and cf. *Chesnut*, 413); Reagan, *Memoirs*, 189 (at Mechanicsville: see *Chesnut*, 411 and C. C. Harrison, *Recoll.*, 72–74); JD, *Rise and Fall* 2:144, quots. (see Freeman, *R. E. Lee* 2:182–85); Jones, *Davis Memorial*, 438–39 and 453–54, quot. (JD's own account, Frayser's Farm).

19. Toombs to AHS, July 14, 1862 (Phillips, *Corr. of Toombs*, 600–601, quots.);

Strode, *President,* 286 (quot. from *Whig*), 278–83; Interview with BNH (as in Note 16 above), quot.; William B. Franklin, "Rear Guard Fighting during the Change of Base" in *Battles and Leaders* 2:366–82; D. H. Hill, "McClellan's Change of Base and Malvern Hill," ibid., 383–95.

20. JD to VHD, July 6, 1862, in VHD, *Memoir* 2:322–23, quots.; *Wartime Papers,* 213. Lee confirms JD's analysis: see ibid., 211–22; Freeman, *R. E. Lee* 2:231–34; also Alexander, *Fighting for Conf.,* 94–120.

21. VHD, *Memoir* 2:323 (quot. from July 6 JD letter); *Conf. Soldier,* 379 (but see Freeman, *R. E. Lee* 2:157); Charles L. Dufour, *Gentle Tiger: The Gallant Life of Roberdeau Wheat,* 191, 194–96, 127, 149, 152.

22. JD, *Rise and Fall* 1:357, quot. (see 2:141 for Griffith); VHD to Mrs. R. Griffith, May 8 [1864], quot. (copy at Old Courthouse Mus.); VHD, *Memoir* 2:316n, quots.; Rowland 2:571–72 and n.1 and Freeman, *Lee's Lieuts.* 1:588.

23. JD, *Rise and Fall* 2:146, quot.; Wm. L. Allen to VHD, Dec. 3, 1891, MS, TULANE, quots. See JD, May 26, 1862, in *O. R.* 11 (Part 3): 546–47. For 12th Miss. during Seven Days, see *Conf. Soldier,* 100.

24. Jones, *Davis Memorial,* 468 (quots. from letter of S. A. Ashe, Dec. 18, 1889).

25. VHD, *Memoir* 2:118–19 (quots. from J. H. Shepard [to VHD, Feb. 11, 1890: ident. in *Cal. JD MSS,* 291]); Alexander, *Fighting for Conf.,* 76 (describes boy; diff. locale).

26. Robertson, *Stonewall Brigade,* 162–63, quot.; Woodworth, *JD and Gens.,* 150–52, quots.

27. JD to Marshall, Oct. 6, 1862 (Rowland 5:348–51, quot.; and see 219–20); Duke, *Reminisc.,* 142–44 (mistakes reason for visit: see Marshall in Warner, *Gens. in Gray; Conf. Soldier,* 366).

28. Quots.: VHD, *Memoir* 2:921; Mallory, "Last Days," Part 2, 248n; W. Taylor, *Gen. Lee,* 156–57. See Freeman, *R. E. Lee* 3:357, 359; Alexander, *Fighting for Conf.,* 389–90.

29. Minnigerode in Jones, *Davis Memorial,* 417, quots.; Interview with BNH (as in Note 16 above), quot. See Geo. Davis in *Life and Reminisc.,* 290–91.

30. JD to the Army of Eastern Va., July 5, 1862 (Richardson, *Conf.* 1:229–30, quots.).

31. *Letters from Lee's Army,* ed. Charles Minor Blackford III, 86–87, quots.

32. JD, *Rise and Fall* 2:312–32; *Wartime Papers of Lee,* 224–306 (quots. from Lee to JD, Sept. 3, 1862, on 292–94); Henry, *Story of Conf.,* 172–79.

33. JD, *Rise and Fall* 2:460–68, 333–34 (quot. from Lee procl. based on JD's [Rowland 5:338–39]); *Wartime Papers,* 294–310 (quots. from Lee to JD, Sept. 7 and 4, 1862, on 298, 294).

34. JD, *Rise and Fall* 2:335–43; *Wartime Papers,* 311–24; Early, *Memoirs,* 92–161, 403n; Alexander, *Fighting for Conf.,* 126–54; W. Taylor, *Gen. Lee,* 87–139; D. H. Hill, "The Lost Dispatch," in *Land We Love* 4:273–78; Henry, *Story of Conf.,* 181–90 (map on 184).

35. Rowland 5:338–39; Horn, *Army of Tenn.,* 162–65; Williams, *Bgd.,* 163–64, 169–70; Connelly and Jones, *Politics of Command,* xii, 103–6, 140; *O. R.* 16 (Part 2): 543–45 (see 977, 985–86).

36. Horn, *Army of Tenn.,* 165–67; McWhiney, *Braxton Bragg,* 266–74, 282–83; Don Carlos Buell, "East Tennessee and the Campaign of Perryville," in *Battles and Leaders* 3:31–41. Horn mistakenly says Bragg aimed only at Tenn.: see McWhiney; Seitz, *Bragg,* 154, 159–62, 166–67; Rowland 5:313.

37. James A. Ramage, *Rebel Raider: The Life of General John Hunt Morgan,* 98–106, 119–26; *O. R.* 16 (Part 2): 763; McWhiney, *Braxton Bragg,* 295–99, 322–23; Seitz, *Bragg,* 173–74, 206–7 (see Rowland 5:346).

38. Buford and Van Dorn in Warner, *Gens. in Gray;* McWhiney, *Braxton Bragg,* 281–82, Horn, *Army of Tenn.,* 165–68, 172–75; W. C. Davis, *Breck.,* 325–29.

39. Seitz, *Bragg,* 178–79; McWhiney, *Braxton Bragg,* 283–310; *Land We Love* 4:77; Anna Blanche McGill, *The Sisters of Charity of Nazareth, Kentucky* (New

York: Encyclopedia Press, 1917), 161 (see 130–31); Horn, *Army of Tenn.*, 168–72, 176–80.

40. Seitz, *Bragg*, 197–203 (quot., Bragg to Cooper), 206; *Polk* 2:114–59; Hughes, *Gen. Hardee*, 123–35; Ridley, *Battles and Sketches*, 142 (Halleck quot.); S. Foote, *C. W.* 1:744, 773–74; Buell, "E. Tenn. and Perryville," in *Battles and Leaders* 3:46–51; Joseph Howard Parks, *General Edmund Kirby Smith*, 198–243.

41. Horn, *Army of Tenn.*, 188, quot. See Miers, *Jones Diary*, 111; *O. R.* 13:906.

42. JD to Lee, July 5, 1862 (Rowland 5:290, quot.); Rowland 6:346 (JD quot., paraphrase of speech); W. H. Davies in *Life and Reminisc.*, 41–42; *Chesnut*, 159, 503; Minnigerode in Jones, *Davis Memorial*, 416, quots.; JD to C. J. Wright, May 11, 1876 (Rowland 8:514). See WPJ in Sibley, "JD Recalls Past," 170, 174, but also Miers, *Jones Diary*, 502.

43. Lee to JD, Sept. 9, 1862 (*Wartime Papers*, 303, quots.); W. Taylor, *Gen. Lee*, 119–20, 125n.

44. *Wartime Papers*, passim, e.g., 304–11, 600–603, 646–47; JD to Lee, July 5 and Sept. 28, 1862 (Rowland 5:290 and 345, quots.; also, e.g., 384–86, 496–98, 501–3 and 6:319–21); Freeman, *R. E. Lee* 2:418–19 (Lee quot.). On org., see Alexander, *Fighting for Conf.*, 104 and Freeman, *Lee's Lieuts.* 2:237–38.

45. S. Foote, *C. W.* 3:260, 263 (1864), 2:6–20, 815–26; 3:604–10. (trips west: Dec.–Jan. 1862–63; Oct.–Nov. 1863; Sept.–Oct. 1864); Andrews, *Scraps of Paper*, 148 (quots.), 92; *Pendleton*, 306–7 (date from *Wartime Papers*, 625). JD visits, 1864: *Atlanta Jnl. and Const.*, Apr. 19, 1990, p. A-3 (art. on a Va. house) and Freeman, *R. E. Lee* 3:368.

46. Rowland 5 and 6, passim (see Frank Vandiver, "Jefferson Davis—Leader without Legend," 8); JD to Mrs. Sanders, June 11, 1863 (Rowland 5:511–12, quots.); JD to Brooks, Mar. 13, 1862 (ibid., 218, quots.).

47. Jones, *Davis Memorial*, 456, quot. (see *Life and Reminisc.*, 45; but also Vandiver, *Their Tattered Flags*, 35). JD letters, e.g.: to govs., Rowland 5:334–37, 342–43, 360, 377–78, 492–93, 6:338–40; to Ark. sens. and reprs., ibid. 5:460–63. Most relate to armed services; some prob. written by others at his direction: see ibid. 6:462 Endrs.; Butler, *Judah P. Benj.*, 329–33.

48. Vandiver, *Their Tattered Flags*, 26, quot. (see 32–33, 174–75); Reagan in Jones, *Davis Memorial*, 340, quot.; JD to C. J. McRae, Sept. 8, 1863 (Rowland 6:42–43); JD to People of C.S., Apr. 10 (ibid. 5:460–73); G. J. Rains to Walthall, June 21, 1879 (précis in *Cal. JD MSS*, 142–43, quot.; JD an expert on torpedoes: see Rowland 6:407 and Rains in Warner, *Gens. in Gray*).

49. Garland in *Life and Reminisc.*, 152–57, quots. (but see AHS in S. Foote, *C. W.* 3:94); Mallory, "Last Days," Part 1, 104, quot.; Reagan, *Memoirs*, 120–22, 162 (see JD in Rowland 5:217; Symonds, *JEJ*, 145).

50. S. Foote, *C. W.* 3:95–96; VHD, *Memoir* 2:162–63, 551; JD letters, Rowland 5:216–19, 254–62, 457–60, 6:193–97, 403–6; JD Paper, Feb. 18, 1865 (ibid., 492, quot.).

51. JD to VHD, May 16, 1862, in VHD, *Memoir* 2:274, quot.; JD to VHD, Mar. 13–14, 1866, MS, TRANSYL, quot. (see Col. 3:12–14). On press, which JD refused to muzzle: Fremantle, *Three Months*, 154; Strode, *Tragic Hero*, 18; "Close of American War," 130.

52. Eckert, 66, quots.; Hendrick, *Statesmen of Lost Cause*, 191–92; White, *R. B. Rhett*, 224–26, 230–33; Dabney, *Pistols and Pointed Pens*, 49, 56; *Cong. Record*, 44th Cong., 1st sess., 1876, Vol. 4, pt. 1, p. 350 (Hill quot.); Shingleton, *J. T. Wood*, 216 n.15, quots. *Examiner* "one of J. E. J.'s strikers" (JD in Rowland 8:382).

53. Toombs to AHS, Mar. 24 and July 14, 1862, Mar. 2 and Nov. 2, 1863, Mar. 16, 1865 (Phillips, *Corr. of Toombs*, 592, 601, 611, 630, 660); JD to Bragg, Aug. 5, 1862 (Rowland 5:312, quot.); King, *Wigfall*, 139, 172–73, 192–95, 211; Symonds, *JEJ*, 178–81, 222–26.

54. Wright, *Southern Girl*, 29, quot.; JD to LBN, Mar. 3, 1885 (Rowland 9:348–49, quots.: says Jordan's rank "a nullity"; but see Warner, *Gens. in Gray*, and *Conf.*

Soldier, 364). See JD in Rowland 8:424 and 9:392; M. J. Wright to JD, Sept. 18, 1885 (précis in *Cal. of JD MSS,* 241–42).

55. JD to Wigfall, Oct. 11, 1862, in Wright, *Southern Girl,* 88–89, quots. (see JD, *Rise and Fall* 2:142–44); King, *Wigfall,* 157–59; Hood, *Advance and Tetreat,* 73, quot. Symonds, *JEJ,* 178–79; Yearns, *Conf. Cong.,* 222–29, 234–35; *Conf. Soldier,* 342.

56. *Conf. Soldier,* 345 (Holmes and Taylor), 344 (Smith), 347 (Magruder); Rowland 5:265 n.1.

57. JD to Holmes, Nov. 19, 1863 (ibid. 6:85, quot.); Jones, *Davis Memorial,* 349 (Lubbock quot.); JD to R. W. Johnson, July 14, 1863 (Rowland 5:548, quots.). See JD to Holmes, Rowland 5:356–57, 439–41; to E. K. Smith, 85–87; to Garland and others, 457–63 ("Hindman" a misprint for "Holmes" on 459); Kavanagh to JD, 590–92; Reynolds to Harris, 6:154–55.

58. JD, *Rise and Fall* 2:144; JD to Marshall, Mar. 11, 1863 (Rowland 5:446–47, quots.); Marshall in Warner, *Gens. in Gray;* Yearns, *Conf. Cong.,* 58; *O. R.* 16 (Part 2): 755, 763–65, 851.

59. T. R. R. Cobb in *SHSP* 28:295, 298 (see 292–93 on D. H. Hill); Hal Bridges, *Lee's Maverick General: Daniel Harvey Hill,* 189, 192–95; VHD, *Memoir* 2:363n (Ransom quot.; see Freeman, *Lee's Lieuts.* 2:421 for Ransom). On Hill: ibid., vols. 1–3, passim; Montgomery, *Howell Cobb's Conf. Career,* 68 (Cobb calls him "a self-conceited, heartless and cruel ass").

60. D. H. Hill to JD, Oct. 30 and Nov. 8, 1886 (Rowland 9:498–500, quots.; JD's half of the corr. is missing); Hal Bridges, *Lee's Maverick General,* 275–76 (JD quot.).

61. JD to Vance, Feb. 29, 1864 (Rowland 6:193–97; see also 346); JD, Nov. 16, 1858 (ibid. 3:349, quots.); Duke, *Reminisc.,* 343, quot. See Watts in Jones, *Davis Memorial,* 605–7; JEJ in Freeman, *Lee's Lieuts.* 1:126; Rowland 5:145, 417, 436–37, 438, 475.

62. Freeman, *Lee's Lieuts.* 2:53–54, 145, 419–27 (JD quots. on 425), 493, 3:317; Bridges, *Lee's Maverick,* 163–65; *Conf. Soldier,* 17; Ibid., 344–45 (others made lieut. gen.: E. K. Smith, Pemb., and Holmes; wrong date for Smith: see Warner, *Gens. in Gray*).

63. Freeman, *Lee's Lieuts.* 2:426; G. W. Smith in Warner, *Gens. in Gray;* Williams, *Bgd.,* 100, 112; Connelly and Jones, *Politics of Command,* xii, 50–61, 85; *Chesnut,* 469. (Adullam:) ibid., 437; R. Taylor, *Destruction,* 26–27 (1 Sam. 22:12).

64. Thompson, *Robert Toombs,* 182–206 (quot. on 194); Ulrich B. Phillips, *The Life of Robert Toombs,* 245, quot.; *Wartime Papers,* 321 (Lee quot.). See Toombs letters in Phillips, *Corr. of Toombs,* 601, and Stovall, *Toombs,* 242.

65. Stovall, *Toombs,* 242 (Toombs quot.); JD to D. W. Lewis, Sept. 21, 1863 (Rowland 6:43–44, quots.); Reagan, *Memoirs,* 215–16, quots.; Phillips, *Corr. of Toombs,* 608, 611, 614.

66. VHD, *Memoir* 2:163–64, quots.; Lubbock, *Six Decades,* 655, quot.; *Life and Reminisc.,* 41 (quot. from W. H. Davies); JD to Lewis, Sept. 21, 1863 (Rowland 6:44, quot.).

67. H. W. Cleveland to JD, Nov. 25, 1887 (Rowland 9:603, quot.); Hendrick, *Statesmen of Lost Cause,* 425; Toombs to AHS, July 14, 1862, and Mar. 16, 1865 (Phillips, *Corr. of Toombs,* 601 and 660, quots.; see 592, 595).

68. Toombs to W. W. Burwell, Aug. 29, to AHS, Nov. 2, 1863, and Ben Hill to AHS, Mar. 14, 1864 (Phillips, *Corr. of Toombs* 628–31, 634–37); Phillips, *Life of Toombs,* 246–49; (Habeas corpus:) Yearns, *Conf. Cong.,* 150–60, and JD to Gov. Moore of La., 1862, to Holmes, 1863, and to C.S. Cong., 1864 (Rowland 5:243–45, 439–40 [see 458; also 357], and 6:164–69).

69. Montgomery, *Howell Cobb,* 77, quot. (army career 70–98; see 87: Browne to Cobb, Jan. 21, 1863); R. Taylor, *Destruction,* 211, quot.; *Hill,* 227 (JD quots.).

70. Toombs quots. in Thompson, *Robert Toombs,* 208, and Phillips, *Corr. of*

Toombs, 608 (see 611); Toombs to AHS, Nov. 2, 1863 (ibid., 630, quot.; ref. to *Richard III,* act 1, sc. 3, lines 335–38); Thompson, 224, 235 (e.g.), and 256.

71. JD to E. K. Smith, Nov. 19, 1863 (Rowland 6:86, quots.); Alexander, *Fighting for Conf.,* 157–58; Freeman, *Lee's Lieuts.* 1:664–68, 2:129–30, 147–48, 164–65, 322–23, 393–94, 510–14, 568–70; Bridges, *Lee's Maverick,* 155–61.

72. *Wartime Papers,* 228, 289; W. Taylor, *Gen. Lee,* 107–10; Bridges, *Lee's Maverick,* 142–51, 168–69, 181–90.

73. Freeman, *Lee's Lieuts.* 2:498–99; Lubbock, *Six Decades,* 655; Stevenson, *Southern Side,* 471; Reagan, *Memoirs,* 164; Robertson, *Stonewall Brigade,* 179. See JD to Lee (Rowland 5:427, 6:143, 208–9, 326); to A. P. Hill and Bgd. (188, 204); to Speed (326, 333); G. W. C. Lee to Lee (5:428), Early to JD (8:139); JD in Rowland 6:311, 315–16, 324: will not "intervene," but wants time given "to prepare for death."

74. JD Paper, Feb. 18, 1865 (Rowland 6:496–97); Henry, *Story of Conf.,* 215; *O. R.* 20 (Part 2): 423–24 and n. (Orders to JEJ, Nov. 24, 1862); *Conf. Soldier,* 334 (E. Tenn.), 345 (Pemb.); Eckenrode, *JD,* 205.

75. JEJ to Cooper, Nov. 24, 1862 (*O. R.* 20 [Part 2]: 424; see JEJ to Wigfall in Wright, *Southern Girl,* 105, 107); Hood, *Advance and Retreat,* 73, quot. (said *re* 1864); King, *Wigfall,* 171, 160–64; JEJ to Wigfall, Jan. 26, 1863, in Wright, 121–23, quot.

76. VHD, *Memoir* 2:413, quots.; Symonds, *JEJ,* 180, 220–21 (quots. from Lydia to Charlotte Wigfall, Aug. 2, 1863; her phrase, "I said then" indicates remarks in Nov. 1862; Govan and Livingood [*Different Valor,* 28, 227 and nn.] say 1861).

77. Connelly and Jones, *Politics of Command,* xii and passim; King, *Wigfall,* 153, 173; Longstreet, *From Manassas,* 100; Symonds, *JEJ,* 172–74 (*re* Seven Pines), 178–81.

78. Longs. to JEJ, Oct. 5, 1862, in Bridges, *Lee's Maverick Gen.,* 145, quots.; Wright, *Southern Girl,* 80–83, 89–90 (quot. from Longs. to Wigfall, Nov. 7).

79. Connelly and Jones, *Politics of Command,* 52–61 (others Floyd, the Prestons, Hampton, W. P. Miles; called "western concentration bloc"), see 85–86, 103–6, 120–21, 140, 148; Williams, *Bgd.,* 181–82; *Chesnut,* 673.

80. JD to Marcus J. Wright, Aug. 17, 1882 (Rowland 9:186; also on 349); JD to LBN, Apr. 24, 1879 (ibid. 8:381, quots.; *re* JEJ, Bgd., Jordan); AHS to H. V. Johnson, Apr. 8, 1864, précis in *Cal. JD MSS,* 227–28; Yearns, *Conf. Cong.,* 226.

81. Connelly and Jones, *Politics of Command,* 58, 85–86, 120; Williams, *Bgd.,* 164–65; Eckenrode, *JD,* 181.

82. JD to JEJ, July 13, 1861 (*O. R.* 2:977, quot.); JD to Holmes, Oct. 21 and Dec. 21, 1862 (Rowland 5:357 and 388, quots.); JD to Ark. men, Mar. 30, 1863 (ibid., 460–63); Randolph to Holmes, Oct. 20 (*O. R.* 13:890).

83. S. Foote, *C. W.* 2:11–12; Connelly and Jones, *Politics of Command,* 121, quot.; JEJ to Wigfall, Dec. 15, in Wright, *Southern Girl,* 104–5, quots. (see also 121); JEJ, *Narrative,* 148; Symonds, *JEJ,* 190–91. See JD in Rowland 6:497, 87.

84. Randolph to Holmes, Oct. 27, 1862 (*O. R.* 13:906–7, quot.); Cooper to Holmes, Nov. 11 (ibid., 914, quots.); JD to Lee, Dec. 8 (Rowland 5:383–84, quot.; leaves final decision to gen. on the scene: see also 311, 426). Cooper says, Dec. 3, Holmes "peremptorily ordered" (*O. R.* 17 [Part 2]: 777): contradicted, ibid., 753, 765–66, and quots. in text, and Symonds, *JEJ,* 191.

85. Henry, *Story of Conf.,* 216–17, quot.; S. Foote, *C. W.* 2:46–52; Robert L. Kerby, *Kirby Smith's Confederacy,* 34–37, quot.

86. JEJ, *Narrative,* 148–50, quots.; King, *Wigfall,* 176 (Wigfall quot.). JEJ's version reappears ibid. 161, in B. T. Johnson, *JEJ,* 94, Hendrick, *Statesmen of Lost Cause,* 325, Govan and Livingood, *Different Valor,* 163, S. Foote, *C. W.* 1:785–86 (somewhat modified by 2:11–12), McWhiney, *Braxton Bragg,* 339, Vandiver, *Their Tattered Flags,* 182, Symonds, *JEJ,* 183 (but not 191), and W. C. Davis, *Jefferson Davis,* 485.

87. Randolph to Holmes, Oct. 27, 1862 (*O. R.* 13:906–7); JD to Randolph, Nov.

12, 14, 15 (Rowland 5:369, 371–72, 374, quots.); Kerby, *Kirby Smith's Conf.*, 41, 37; Seitz, *Bragg*, 210 (Bragg quot.); Randolph in Warner, *Gens. in Gray* (his illness: may bear on case); Miers, *Jones Diary*, 118, 120 (Nov. 13, 15).

88. Freeman, *Lee's Lieuts.* 2:420; Reagan, *Memoirs*, 161–62, quot.

89. S. Foote, *C. W.* 2:5–7 (Phelan quots.), 25–26; JD to Lee, Dec. 8, 1862 (Rowland 5:384–86, quots.); R. Davis in *Life and Reminisc.*, 210, quot.; John C. Pemberton [Jr.], *Pemberton, Defender of Vicksburg*, 62–63; VHD, *Memoir* 2:367; T. R. R. Cobb, Nov. 17, 1862, in *SHSP* 28:299.

90. S. Foote, *C. W.* 2:7 (quots. from JEJ and Lydia); JEJ to Wigfall, Jan. 8, 1863, in Wright, *Southern Girl*, 106–8, quots. (see same to same, ibid., 104–5, and in McWhiney, *Braxton Bragg*, 386–87).

91. JEJ to Cooper, Dec. 6 (*O. R.* 20 [Part 2]: 441); JEJ, "Jefferson Davis and the Mississippi Campaign," 473–74; Symonds, *JEJ*, 190–91; *O. R.* 17 [Part 2]: 769, 773.

92. S. Foote, *C. W.* 2:7–8; JD to VHD, Dec. 15, 1862 (*Letters*, 128–29, quot.); McWhiney, *Braxton Bragg*, 344; Alderson and McBride, *Landmarks of Tenn. Hist.*, 273.

93. Bragg to JEJ, Jan. 11, 1863, in Seitz, *Bragg*, 254–55, quot.; King, *Wigfall*, 161.

94. McWhiney, *Braxton Bragg*, 323–27; Hughes, *Gen. Hardee*, 60, 152–54, 127, 134–35 (quots. from Hardee to WPJ, Nov. 19, 1862). See *O. R.* 16 (Part 2): 903, 905: in Ky., Bragg wants what Hardee does, but cannot effect it.

95. Quots: Peter Cozzens, *No Better Place to Die: The Battle of Stones River*, (Urbana: Univ. of Illinois Press, 1990), 11; JD to E. K. Smith, Oct. 29, 1862, in McWhiney, *Braxton Bragg*, 327; Bragg to JEJ, Jan. 11, 1863, in Seitz, *Bragg*, 254–55; JD to Bragg, Aug. 5, 1862 (Rowland 5:312–13).

96. Rosecrans to Halleck, Dec. 24, 1862, (*O. R.* [Part 2]: 218–19); Horn, *Army of Tenn.*, 196–210 (Bragg quot. on 205); Ridley, *Battles and Sketches*, 148–58 (quot. on 154); McWhiney, *Braxton Bragg*, 349–73; Bragg to JEJ, Jan. 11, 1863, in Seitz, *Bragg*, 254–55 (blames JD, but in rpt. blames Breck. [W. C. Davis, *Breck.*, 351]); Cozzens, *No Better Place to Die;* Judith Lee Hallock, *Braxton Bragg and Confederate Defeat*, map on 15.

97. JD to Seddon, Dec. 15, 1862 (*O. R.* 20 [Part 2]: 449–50); Rosecrans to Halleck, Dec. 15 (ibid., 179); *Polk* 1:327–28, 2:169–70 (does not mention JD). Ramage, *Rebel Raider*, 134, says JD not at wedding. Duke, *Hist. Morgan's Cav.*, 322: "commander-in-chief" here prob. means "commanding general."

98. JD to VHD, Dec. 15, 1862 (*Letters*, 128–29, quots.; ref. to "O This is No My Ain Lassie" [Barke, *Poems and Songs of Robert Burns*, 627]); JEJ to Wigfall, Dec. 15, 1862, in Wright, *Southern Girl*, 106, quot.

99. Henry, *Story of Conf.*, 208–13; Alexander, *Fighting for Conf.*, 166–87 (quot. on 170; Whitworths "made a loud 'pop'" [Castel, *Decision in West*, 109]); James Dinkins, "Griffith-Barksdale-Humphrey Mississippi Brigade and its Campaigns" (*SHSP* 32:267–74).

100. Alexander, *Fighting for Conf.*, 177, quot.; T. R. R. Cobb in *SHSP* 28:298–301; JD, Speech Dec. 26, 1862, in S. Foote, *C. W.* 2:15, quots. (see 13).

101. S. Foote, *C. W.* 2:front endpaper map, 8–18; W. C. Davis, *JD*, 492 (quots. from VHD letter); JEJ to Wigfall, Jan. 8, 1863, in Wright, *Southern Girl*, 108, quot. (and see 104–6).

102. JD to Seddon, Dec. 15, 1862 (*O. R.* 20 [Part 2]: 449–50); McWhiney, *Braxton Bragg*, 340–41, 344–45; Horn, *Army of Tenn.*, 192; S. Foote, *C. W.* 2:17–18, 60–79.

103. S. Foote, *C. W.* 2:endpaper map; Hermann, *Joseph E. Davis*, 114–15 (1,500 A. bought for JD "early in 1863"; see 110–12 for Fleetwood); VHD to JD, Dec. 18, 1862, MS, TRANSYL, quots.

104. S. Foote, *C. W.* 2:13–15 (quots. from JD speech to Miss. legis., Dec. 26, 1862; ref. to, Deut. 32:35, Rom. 12:19, Ps. 146:3).

105. S. Foote, *C. W.* 2:14–16 (quots. from JD speech to Miss. legis., Dec. 26, 1862; ref. to Ps. 146:3).

106. JD to Seddon, Dec. 23 and 31, 1862 (Rowland 5:388–89); JD to Cartwright, Dec. 31 (ibid., 389; see 395 and n.2); Strode, *President*, 324 (see Ross, *First Lady*, 178); Foote, *C. W.* 2:18–20 (quots.), 56–59 (and see JD to Magruder, Rowland 5:424).

107. JD to VHD, Dec. 15, 1862 (*Letters*, 129, quot.); JD speech, [Jan. 5], 1863 (Rowland 5:390–95, quots. from newspaper rpt.).

108. McWhiney, *Braxton Bragg*, 374–79 (all quots.; but Bragg also said, "I shall die in the traces"; JD asks JEJ for "the advice which I need").

109. Ibid., 374–78, all quots. (see 377 n.10 for supporters; also 380–83); Seitz, *Bragg*, 256, 271–80.

110. McWhiney, *Braxton Bragg*, 379–80 (quots. from JEJ-JD corr.; see Seitz, *Bragg*, 276–77), 382–87 (quots. from JEJ to Wigfall).

111. McWhiney, *Braxton Bragg*, 384–85 (Seddon quots.), 379 (JD quots.); JD to JEJ, Feb. 19, 1863 (*O. R.* 23 [Part 2]: 640–41 [quots.], 613–14); *Polk* 2:198–203 (JEJ's feeling "morbid" and "misplaced"). Seddon wanted Bragg simply removed (Eckenrode, *JD*, 201; see King, *Wigfall*, 165–66: Wigfall thought JEJ *wanted* Bragg's place "but did not want to appear to want it"). Poss. JEJ still hoped for ANV.

112. McWhiney, *Braxton Bragg*, 387–88 (quots.) and n.31; *Heth Memoirs*, 168, quot.; Seitz, *Bragg*, 289 (JEJ quots.), 207–8; Bragg to JD, Nov. 24, 1862 (*O. R.* 20 [Part 2]: 423, quot.); *Polk* 2:200–203; Strode, *President*, 385.

113. Kerby, *Kirby Smith's Conf.*, 22–24 and map on 101; McWhiney, *Braxton Bragg*, 141–44; Miers, *Jones Diary*, 437, quot.; JD speech, [Jan. 5], 1863 (Rowland 5:392, quots.).

114. JD to Cong. (ibid. 5:396–415, quots. on 408–9); JD, *Rise and Fall*, 2:589–91; *Conf. Vet.*, Feb. 1910, 68 (see Rowland 5:375); (Milroy:) Freeman, *R. E. Lee* 2:482, *Lee's Dispatches: Unpublished Letters of General Robert E. Lee to Jefferson Davis . . .*, ed. Douglas Southall Freeman, with additions by Grady McWhiney, 70–71; see Fremantle, *Three Months in So. States*, 214.

115. JD to Cong., Jan. 12, 1863 (Rowland 5:409, quots.) On "extermination": Wilmer, *Recent Past*, 223–24; Cartwright, "Alcohol and Ethiopian," 161–63; J. R. Davis to Shea, 1867, in *Calendar of Confederate Papers*, ed. Douglas Southall Freeman, 475–77 (pleads for Freedmen's Bureau to "save the negro from starvation").

116. JD to Cong. (Rowland 5:409–11, quots.). See Donald, *Chas. Sumner and C. W.*, 388 (Sumner urged this in 1861); Randall, *Civil War*, 477–98 (a "war measure"), 502–3 (shows, instead, adverse effect on recognition).

Chapter XV The Year of Our Lord 1863

1. Miers, *Jones Diary*, 152, 162, 167 (quots.), 172, 173, 177–80, 185; Dabney, *Pistols and Pointed Pens*, 99; JD to Clay, Mar. 10, 1863 (Rowland 5:445–46, quot.); Richardson, *Conf.* 1:324–25, quots. See appendix B.

2. Vandiver, *Gorgas Diary*, 27, quot.; Weddell, *St. Paul's* 1:199–200; *Chesnut*, 429–30 and n.2, 433 (quots.; church also 549, 571, and see 55, 585), 32 (on JD:) 56, 83, 85, 108, 109 (adverse mil. comment restored, which MBC deliberately had left out), 318, 439–40, 498, 532, 607–8, 609–10, 623–24, 627, 649–52, 673, 799.

3. Ross, *First Lady*, 178; JD to Marg. K. Howell, Mar. 19, 1863, quots. (from MS, ALA, and Strode, *President*, 377).

4. (Joe:) *Papers* 2::83 n.6; (Becket:) Donnelly, *Hist. C.S. Marine Corps*, 94–95, 147–50; *Conf. Soldier*, 420, 442; Scharf, *Hist. C.S. Navy*, 786–89, 796–97, 820; (Jeffy D.:) Ibid., 779 n.1.

5. *Papers* 2::83 n.18, 6:246 n.7, and JD to VHD, Oct. 11–12, 1865, MS, TRANSYL; Hodding Carter and Betty Werlein Carter, *So Great a Good: A History of the Episcopal Church in Louisiana,* 93–96, 132–42 and pic. facing 144.

6. VHD to JD, [Mar.] 28, 1863 (MS, Adele Davis Papers, MDAH); W. B. Howell gravestone and Oakwood Cemetery brochure (courtesy James W. Little, S.C.V.).

7. Ross, *First Lady,* 178; Coleman, *Priscilla Cooper Tyler,* 147–48 (quots.), 98, 76, 175 (Priscilla d. in Montg.); *Chesnut,* 429, quot.; Weddell, *St. Paul's* 1:204, 207; Oakwood brochure (as in Note 6 above; only Robt. and Letitia listed).

8. *Elegant Extracts* (London, 1805), inscr. Montg., Apr. 1863; VHD to JD, [Mar.] 28, 1863 (MS, Adele Davis Papers, MDAH); VHD to JD, Dec. 18, 1862, MS, TRANSYL, quot.; H. W. Cleveland to JD, Mar. 3, 1888 (Rowland 10:39, quot.).

9. VHD to Clay, May 10, 1861, in K. M. Jones, *Heroines of Dixie: Spring,* 29 (quots. *re* Jeff Jr. and Joe); *Chesnut,* 566; VHD, *Memoir* 2:649 and pic. facing 650; T. Hill, "Victory in Defeat," 34; Sterling, *Belle,* 276, quot.; VHD to JD, Sept. 22 [1860], ALA typescript, quots.

10. VHD to Mrs. Griffith [May 1864], quot. (copy in Old Courthouse Mus.); DeLeon, *Belles, Beaux and Brains,* 66; *Chesnut,* 532, quot.; *BCP* (1850): "Forms of Prayer to be Used in Families." Prayers mentioned in JD to VHD, Aug. 21 and Sept. 15, 1865, MSS, TRANSYL; see VHD, *Memoir* 2:498; for Joe, see above, chap. 13, Note 3.

11. T. H. Watts in Jones, *Mem. Vol,* 606, quot.; VHD, *Memoir* 2:373–76 (quots. from unnamed source: only this one says *JD* threatened to fire on crowd; it seems out of character); Pryor, *Reminisc. of Peace and War,* 238–39 (quots. from letter); Miers, *Jones Diary,* 183–85. See Vandiver, *Gorgas Diary,* 29, JD in *Letters,* 522; and *Gache,* 159–61.

12. Miers, *Jones Diary,* 188, 190–92 (quots.), 193, 198, 201–2 (quots. *re* letters; see corr. in Rowland 5:474–82); JD to Joseph Davis, May 7, 1863, in Strode, *President,* 395–96, quots. (see also 389–93); JD to J. E. Brown, May 20 (Rowland 5:490); Vandiver, *Gorgas Diary,* 33, 40.

13. Freeman, *R. E. Lee* 2:483, 499–500, 556, 559; S. Foote, *C. W.* 2:243, 262–64, 268, 314; *Chesnut,* 477–78, quot. (says "no troops" in city, but see Foote, *C. W.,* 252 and 254 map; Miers, *Jones Diary,* 198–200 (quots.), 231–33; (G. W. C. Lee:) *Conf. Soldier in C. W.,* 353; JD, *Rise and Fall* 2:664–65.

14. S. Foote, *C. W.* 2:261–316 (Lee quot. on 307); *Wartime Papers,* 449–72; Freeman, *R. E. Lee* 2:506, 508–42; Alexander, *Fighting for Conf.,* 194–217 (quot. on 212) Henry, *Story of Conf.,* 240–51.

15. Freeman, *R. E. Lee* 2:542, quot.; S. Foote, *C. W.* 2:314–19; JD, *Rise and Fall* 2:364–65, quot.; R. L. Dabney, *Life and Campaigns of Lieut. Gen. Thomas J. Jackson,* 682–725 (quots. on 716, 725, 723); *Pendleton,* 269 (had just seen son "Sandie," Jackson's A.A.G. [Henderson, *Stonewall Jackson,* 642, 681; losses on 717]; see M. M. Andrews, *Scraps of Paper,* 108–9).

16. VHD, *Memoir* 2:377–83 (quots. on 382; says they watched: prayer assumed: see 500); Lee to Seddon, May 10, 1863 (*Wartime Papers,* 483); Devereaux D. Cannon, Jr., *The Flags of the Confederacy: An Illustrated History* [Memphis: St. Lukes Press and Broadfoot Publishing, 1988], 16–20, 51–52, and figs. 13, 46 (this flag now at Mus. of Conf.).

17. Miers, *Jones Diary,* 207, quots.; M. M. Andrews, *Scraps of Paper,* 109; *Pendleton,* 274; Dabney, *Life of Jackson,* 728–32 (quot. on 730; buried Lexington, Va.), 725 (Lee quot.), 713 (quot., Jackson paraphrase; see 719); see 726–28 on questions raised by his death.

18. Lee to G. W. C. Lee, May 11, 1863 (*Wartime Papers of Lee,* 484, quot.); Lee to JD, May 20 (ibid., 487, quot.; to Mrs. Lee: "I suppose he cannot feel better as long as this uncertainty hangs over Vicksburg" [499]; see JD, May 20, in Rowland 5:490); Freeman, *R. E. Lee* 3:18–20.

19. JD to Lee, May 26 (Rowland 5:497, quot.); Scheibert, *Seven Months in Rebel States,* 128, quot. The parasite in the blood causing malaria (with consequent ane-

mia) was not identified until 1880 ("Malaria" in *The New Encyclopedia Britannica* 7:725).

20. Henry, *Story of Conf.*, 252–54; *Papers* 6:26–27 and n.2; Winters, *C. W. in La.*, 188–96; S. Foote, *C. W.* 2:323–44; Sarah A. Dorsey, *Recollections of Henry Watkins Allen*, 159–71.

21. S. Foote, *C. W.* 2:389–95; T. Michael Parrish, *Richard Taylor: Soldier Prince of Dixie*, 264–80; Carter and Carter, *So Great a Good*, 144–45; Winters, *C. W. in La.*, 212–241; Kerby, *Kirby Smith's Conf.*, 92–110 (quot. on 110); Ulysses S. Grant, "The Vicksburg Campaign," 501, 515.

22. Grant, "Vicksburg Campaign," 493–507; JD, *Rise and Fall* 2:397–405 (JEJ quots. on 404–5); *Pemberton* 126–35; Dorsey, *Recoll. of H. W. Allen*, 123, 130, 182–212, 397–420 (1863 diary); Winters, *C. W. in La.*, 166; Kerby, *Kirby Smith's Conf.*, 20, 155–68 (see Yearns, *Conf. Cong.*, 136); S. Foote, *C. W.* 2:323–63.

23. JD, *Rise and Fall* 2:404–410; Dorsey, *Recoll. of H. W. Allen*, 198, 210–22, 228–32; S. Foote, *C. W.* 2:365–380 (battle number on 370; quots. on 375, 379); Grant, "Vicksburg Campaign," 507–517; S. H. Lockett, "The Defense of Vicksburg," in *Battles and Leaders* 3:482–92; JD corr. Mar. 16–May 14, 1863 (Rowland 5:426, 447, 451, 475–76, 479–88); Ibid. 6:2–11; *Pemberton*, 59–60, 99–100, 132–168, 289–319 (cf. JEJ, *Narrative*, 172–90); Govan and Livingood, *Different Valor*, 197–205.

24. Hermann, *Joseph E. Davis*, 116–18 (quots. from Joseph to Andrew Johnson, Sept. 22, 1865); Margie Riddle Bearss, *Sherman's Forgotten Campaign: The Meridian Expedition*, 64–65 (Fleetwood on map). U.S. Army practice to destroy private property: order of Apr. 1863 cited in Richardson, *Conf.* 1:380–81; firsthand accounts in Dorsey, *Recoll. of H. W. Allen*, 149–50, 165–67, 397–420; also 238, and army rpts. on 196, 205, 207.

25. *Memoirs of General William T. Sherman by Himself* 1:321–23, quots. (cites only mil. destruction, but see Fremantle, *Three Months*, 104–11). May (not July: see text below) shown by dates on stolen letter (*Papers* 4:297) and book (Rosenstock) and fact that Joseph still has horses.

26. Strode, *President*, 409–10 (quot. from Lise Mitchell); Hermann, *Joseph E. Davis*, 69, 117–19, 123 (Cox: 103 and *Papers* 4:293 n.6; Harris: *Papers* 6:App. 1, 545 [June 14], 616 [Sept. 29]); S. Foote, *C. W.* 2:15 (JD quot.).

27. S. Foote, *C. W.* 2:379–89, 406–15 (see 79 and Lockett, as in Note 23 above); *Pemberton*, 171–72, 178–224; Dorsey, *Recoll. of H. W. Allen*, 222–26; Strode, *President*, 410 (quot. from JD to Joseph Davis, 1863; see JD to JEJ, May 18 [Rowland 5:489]).

28. JD to Lee, May 31, 1863 (Rowland 5:501–3, quots.; see Lee to JD, May 28, in Freeman-McWhiney, *Lee's Dispatches*, 98); VHD, *Memoir* 2:392, quot. (see 494).

29. Freeman, *R. E. Lee* 3:18–52 ("people," e.g.: 25, 166); Lee to JD, [June] 15, 1863 (Freeman-McWhiney, *Lee's Dispatches*, 102–3, quot.; Ibid., 104 n.3 (quot. from summary); Early, *Memoirs*, 240–52.

30. Reagan, *Memoirs*, 150–53, 120–22 (quots.); AHS, *Recollections*, 350.

31. DuBose, *Yancey*, 744–45 (Yancey to JD, May 6, 1863, quots.), 745–49 (corr. June [misdated "July"] 11 and 20); Ibid., 739–43, and *Hill*, 212; Symonds, *JEJ*, 179, quot.; White, *R. B. Rhett*, 96, 191.

32. JD to Yancey, May 26, 1863 (Rowland 5:498); Corr. in DuBose, *Yancey*, 744–49 (quot. from Yancey to JD, [June] 11, 1863, on 749); Clay to Yancey, June 30 (ibid., 749–51); Same to same, May 2 (ibid., 743–44, quot.).

33. Clay to Yancey, June 30, 1863, in DuBose, *Yancey*, 749–51, quots. Clay wrangled so with another C.S. agent in Canada that they had to separate (Nuermberger, *Clays of Ala.*, 238).

34. Yancey to JD, [June] 11, 1863, in DuBose, *Yancey*, 749, quot.; Yancey to Clay, July 1, in Nuermberger, *Clays of Ala.*, 209, quot.; Clay to Yancey, July 25, in DuBose, *Yancey*, 752, quots. (July 15?: see n.38).

35. Ibid., 734–35 (Yancey quot.); visits to Oakwood and brochure (as in Note 6 above); JD to Mrs. Yancey, Dec. 16, 1863 (Rowland 6:133, quots.; spyglass given Yancey by Ladies' Mt. Vernon Ass.; his cousin a regent [Dubose, *Yancey*, 30–31]). See W. P. Chilton to JD, 1886, in Rowland 9:416–18.

36. *Chesnut*, 559 (see 654 and n.1; 774; for VHD's dislike of Va. Clay, see Lankford, *Irishman in Dixie*, 48); Wright, *Southern Girl*, 21–22, 178–79, 185–86; King, *Wigfall*, 176–77; Nuermberger, *Clays of Ala.*, 198, 218–28, 231–33 (quots. from Clay to Wigfall, Apr. 29, 1864), 263 (Hammond: also Sterling, *Belle*, 212–19 and *Private Chesnut*, 109, 121, 122).

37. Lee to JD, June 10, 1863 (*Wartime Papers of Lee*, 507–9, quots.; see 530–31); Escott, *After Secession*, 187–95; AHS to JD, June 12, 1863 (Richardson, *Conf.* 1:339–41); JD to AHS, June 18 (Rowland 5:525, quot.). Liberty Hall, near Crawfordville, Ga., still stands (*Atlanta Jnl. and Const.*, Dec. 15, 1985).

38. JD to AHS, July 2, 1863 (Richardson, *Conf.* 1:341–43, quots.; see ibid., 375–77); JD, "Andersonville" (Part 2), 337–43. Offenses: *O. R.* 23 (Part 2): 858–59; Hendricks, *Union Army Occupation*, 7; JD, *Rise and Fall* 2:312–15, 588–89. Exchange: ibid., 580–88, 591–96; Early, *Memoirs*, 287–98; Benj. in *SHSP* 6:185.

39. JD in Senate, Sept. 26, 1850 (Rowland 1:563, quot.); JD to Lincoln, July 2, 1863 (Richardson, *Conf.* 1:343–44, quots.); JD, *Rise and Fall* 2:606; Rowland 5:392–93 and 6:12; Vandiver, *Gorgas Diary*, 73; WPJ, *Gen. ASJ*, 360–61; Fremantle, *Three Months*, 104–11, 199–200, 228–31; *Pendleton*, 304–8; Pryor, *Reminsc. of Peace and War*, 245–47; Early, *Memoirs*, 299; Hendricks, *Union Army Occupation*, 4–5, 10–19.

40. Strode, *President*, 419–20 (quot. from Joseph, June 23, 1863); *Papers* 1::526 n.1; JD, *Rise and Fall* 2:595, quots.

41. *Wartime Papers*, 477–80, 533–34 (quot.; see 530–31); Dorsey, *Recoll. of H. W. Allen*, 417; Wright, *Southern Girl*, 137; Fremantle, *Three Months*, 111, 237–46 (but see 279–80); *Pendleton*, 278–82 (quots. on 280); JD to Cong., Dec. 7, 1863 (Richardson, *Conf.* 1:381, quot.); Early, *Memoirs*, 255–65.

42. W. Taylor, *Gen. Lee*, 216–17; Williams, *Bgd.*, 182–83; Freeman, *R. E. Lee* 3:48–49, 60–67; *Heth Memoirs*, 172–75; Alexander, *Fighting for Conf.*, 227–33; Walter H. Taylor, *Four Years with General Lee*, ed. James I. Robertson, Jr., 90–96.

43. Early, *Memoirs*, 270–72, quot. (see 276); Freeman, *R. E. Lee* 3:71–85, 161; *Pendleton*, 282–84, 288 (Lee quot., from Early); W. Taylor, *Four Years with Lee*, 99–102. Whole battle: *Wartime Letters*, 474–75 (maps), 569–75, and Fremantle, *Three Months*, 251–73.

44. Alexander, *Fighting for Conf.*, 218, 233–43; Pendleton to JD [1880?] (Rowland 8:578, quot.); Early to JD, May 30, 1877 (ibid. 7:545, quot.; has Carroll letter to Fitz Lee); W. Taylor, *Four Years with Lee*, 96–102; *Pendleton*, 284–93; S. Foote, *C. W.* 2:489–514.

45. Alexander, *Fighting for Conf.*, 244–67, 275 (Dahlgren: 246–47; Freeman, *R. E. Lee* 3:140 n.37); W. Taylor, *Gen. Lee*, 194–212; W. Taylor, *Four Years with Lee*, 102–10; S. Foote, *C. W.* 2:510–79. For later controversy over Lee's orders, see William Garrett Piston, *Lee's Tarnished Lieutenant: James Longstreet and His Place in Southern History*, 95–150.

46. Alexander, *Fighting for Conf.*, 267–75; *Wartime Papers*, 544 (Lee to JD, July 8, 1863, quot.), 583 (quot.); *Pendleton*, 295–99; Early, *Memoirs*, 279–86; Fremantle, *Three Months*, 273–88, 296–97, 300–301.

47. Fremantle, *Three Months*, 205–14, quots. (his travels, 16–205); Vandiver, *Gorgas Diary*, 47, quot.

48. Fremantle, *Three Months*, 111–126 (quots. on 126; see JEJ, *Narrative*, 507); *O. R.* 23 (Part 2): 846–49 and 853; Rowland 5:482–85 (JD corr. May 7–13, 1863); Henry, *Story of Conf.*, 262; W. C. Davis, *Breck.*, 364–66.

49. Seddon to JEJ, June 16 and 21, 1863, in JEJ, *Narrative*, 512–14, quots. (202–3: JEJ sneers at Seddon's "wild spirit" and says "no hope of saving the place by raising the siege"; 173, 187: excuses inaction by sickness, but Yandall [Rowland

6:4, 12] and Fremantle [*Three Months*, 117, 125] both remark his energy); *Chesnut*, 268, quots. (story from her uncle, the host).

50. JEJ, *Narrative*, 197–200, 202 n.1 (numbers), 508–9; Sherman, *Memoirs* 1:328–29 (Grant quot.); S. Foote, *C. W.* 2:414–17, 388 (approx. 31,000 vs. 71,000; other numbers in Sherman; Symonds, *JEJ*, 211–12; W. C. Davis, *Breck.*, 364–66).

51. Lee to JD, June 7–25, July 4–31, 1863 (*Wartime Papers*, 502–66, plus many to Seddon, which JD would see; others in Freeman-McWhiney, *Lee's Dispatches*, 100–11 and Rowland 5:508–9 [will change plans "if you think differently"]; see JD to Lee, June 6–July 28, ibid., 505, 508, 512, 526–27, 540, 573–74, 578–80)

52. Rowland 5:491–534 (12 items, JD to JEJ, May 22–July 2; none JEJ to JD; but 2 quoted in JEJ, *Narrative*, 197–98, and Seddon-JEJ corr., 198–202, 508–9); JD to JEJ, July 8 (Rowland 5:540, quots.).

53. JEJ, *Narrative*, 200–204, quots. (see corr. on 506–16); *Pemberton*, 180–237, 243–45, 281–88 (see *Battles and Leaders* 3:492; Rowland 8:346–48); Dorsey, *Recoll. of H. W. Allen*, 226–27, 231–32; S. Foote, *C. W.* 2:410–15, 424–27, 606–14, 622–23.

54. *Pemberton*, 202–4, 216–17; Kerby, *Kirby Smith's Conf.*, 130–34, 113–15; S. Foote, *C. W.* 2:405–6, 596–97, 601–6, 614–15; Henry, *Story of Conf.*, 261–65. See JD to E. K. Smith, July 2, 1863 (Rowland 5:534).

55. VHD, *Memoir* 2:412, quot.; JD, Paper, Feb. 18, 1865 (Rowland 6:496–97, quot.); Hermann, *Joseph E. Davis*, 120–22 (quots. from Joseph, June 14 and 22, 1863, and from JD, May 7; see Strode, *President*, 419–20). See JD to Bragg, May 22, 23 (Rowland 5:492, 493).

56. JEJ, *Narrative*, 199–200 (quots.), 506–7; JD to JEJ, July 15, 1863 (Rowland 5:562–63); JD to Pettus et al., June 20 (ibid., 527–28, quots.); JD to Bragg and to Bgd., June 25 (ibid., 531–32); JD to Rains, June 3 (ibid., 504, quot.; see Bergeron, *Conf. Mobile*, 69, 73; Milton F. Perry, *Infernal Machines: The Story of Confederate Submarine and Mine Warfare* [Baton Rouge: Louisiana State Univ. Press, 1965], 42–43).

57. Seddon to JEJ, June 5 (Rowland 5:558, quot.); JD to McRae, June 13 (ibid., 519, quot.). On militia et al., see ibid., 485, 489–91, 499, 513, 519, 563.

58. Jones, *Davis Memorial*, 431 (Reagan quots.; see also Reagan, *Memoirs*, 210–11); Crist, "A Bibliog. Note," esp. 190, 189, 188 n.3; *Papers* 2::20, Descr. Note; *Letters*, 10 Ed. Note; JD to Philip Phillips, July 13, 1874 (Rowland 7:384, quot.; asks him to recover papers; see 403–6: "seized in Hinds Co., Missi." with "library").

59. Hermann, *Joseph E. Davis*, 119–20, 125–28 (JD quot.); Hermann, *Pursuit of Dream*, 40–45, 66; *SHSP* 32:370; *O. R.* 52 (Pt. 2): 332; Currie, *Enclave*, xix–xxiii, 34, 42–48; Randall, *Civil War*, 480–82, 494–98. For treatment of blacks in S. C. Sea Islands, see Hendricks, *Union Army Occupation*.

60. Hermann, *Joseph E. Davis*, 122–24; Sherman, *Memoirs* 1:330–32; Robert Melvin to JD, [July 22] 1863, in *Mississippi in the Confederacy: As They Saw It*, ed. John K. Bettersworth, 210–12 (date from Crist, "A Bibliog. Note," 192 n.9); JEJ, *Narrative*, 202 (quot.), 205–10.

61. JD, Paper, Feb. 18, 1865 (Rowland 6:497–98). Foote, *C. W.* 2:620–21; Lash, *Iron Horse*, 77–80; JD, Paper Feb. 18, 1865 (Rowland 6:498, quot.; see ibid. 8:224–25, 241–42); JEJ, *Narrative*, 252; Hermann, *Joseph E. Davis*, 125 (see Crist, "A Bibliog. Note," 193 n.13).

62. Melvin letter (as in Note 60 above), quots.; Ewing in Ezra J. Warner, *Generals in Blue: Lives of the Union Commanders*. Bust now at Beauvoir. Crist, "Bibliog. Note," traces some papers (188), says "4 large libraries" were dispersed: of Davis brothers, Amanda Bradford, and Martha Harris; see also *Cal. JD MSS*, 223, 274; *Papers* 3:49, 108, 239; 4:47; 5:81; Rowland 4:120, 7:384, 403–6, 9:408, 485–86; Hermann, *Joseph E. Davis*, 128; (Lise's rare Audubon saved by a servant). Other items: Rowland 8:518–19; JD to [Crafts J. Wright], June 3, 1878, MS, TRANSYL.

63. Scheibert, *Seven Months in Rebel States*, 127, quots.

64. Crist, "Bibliog. Note," 191–93; G. W. Jones in Rowland 8:531 and 2:2n; Ibid. 4:118–20.

65. Nichols, *Franklin Pierce*, 519–23, 525 (quots. on 522, 520; Hawthorne d. 1864); Randall Stewart, *Nathaniel Hawthorne: A Biography* (New Haven: Yale Univ. Press, 1948), 229–33 (Stowe quot.); Pierce to JD, Jan. 6, 1860 (Rowland 4:118–19, quots., see 9:562–64).

66. Miers, *Jones Diary*, 234–39; Rowland 5:346 n.1, 501, 505, 573–74; S. Foote, *C. W.* 2:508–9, quot. (see 505–6); Barksdale and Humphreys in Warner, *Gens. in Gray; Papers* 5:135 nn.13, 14; *Letters*, 133, Ed. Note; Strode, *President*, 450–51 (quot. from Mary); Weddell, *St. Paul's* 1:213; *Papers* 1::362 n.12 and App. 4, nn.19, 85; Isaac Stamps gravestone, Rosemont ("Sweet and fitting it is to die for one's country)."

67. Mary Elizabeth Humphreys Stamps to JD, Aug. 16, 1863 (*Letters*, 133–35, quots.). The sword is preserved at Rosemont.

68. JD to Lee, Aug. 2, 1863 (Rowland 5:583–84, quots.).

69. JD to Lee, July 28, 1863 (ibid., 578–80); Lee to JD, Aug. 8 (ibid., 585–87, quots.); Freeman, *R. E. Lee* 3:144–47; King, *Wigfall*, 171–72.

70. JD to Lee, Aug. 11, 1863 (Rowland 5:588–90, quots.; see S. Foote, *C. W.* 2:656–59). See JD in Rowland 5:587–88 *re* the press.

71. Lee to JD, Aug. 22, 1863 (*Wartime Papers*, 593, quots.).

72. JD to Lee, July 28, 1863 (Rowland 5:580, quots.); *BCP* (1850), quot. (see Romans 12:1); JD, *Rise and Fall* 2:412, quot. (see Seitz, *Bragg* 401; Rowland 5:155, 9:515–16); JD to Brooks, Apr. 2 (ibid. 5:464–65, quots.; see 581–82); *Pemberton*, 21, 244–48 (see Henry, *Story of Conf.*, 264).

73. JD to JEJ, June 11, 1863 (Rowland 5:511, quot.); French in Warner, *Gens. in Gray* (Northerners besides those named earlier: Blanchard, C. Clark, Frost, Gardner, Gracie, B. R. Johnson, M. L. Smith, Pike, Ripley, C. H. and W. H. Stevens).

74. *Chesnut*, 423, 492, 796; Alexander, *Fighting for Conf.*, 89–90; JD to Cora S. Ives, Apr. 25, 1869 (*Letters*, 301–2, quot.).

75. *Chesnut*, 531, 276–77; *Gache*, 143–48, 160–61, 166, 195–96, 204, 180 (V. quot.; Gache: "You are well aware of the sentiments of our worthy President"); Hendrick, *Statesmen of Lost Cause*, 364–65; *BCP* (1850) and Perry, *Bsps. of Am. Church*, ix–xlii.

76. McGill, *Sisters of Charity*, 130–31; *Papers* 2::21 n.6, 29 n.17; Moore, *Conf. Comm. Gen.*, 27–28. Other Catholic friends: G. W. Jones (Rowland 8:533), Lubbock (*Six Decades*, 23) and prob. Harney (Reavis, *Harney*, 39–44, 138–39, 242, 468).

77. Lonn, *Foreigners in Conf.*, 75–81; S. Foote, *C. W.* 3:794; Richardson, *Conf.* 1:451, 2:470–73, 641, 659; Tucker, "Conf. Secret Agent," *Jnl. of Conf. Hist.* 5:55–85 (quot. on 55).

78. Craven, *Prison Life*, 289–90, quot. (JD, in Eckert, 107, rejects only a remark by Lynch; see *Gache*, 147–48, 151); JD to VHD, Apr. 23, 1865 (Rowland 6:561); N. D. Smith, "Reminisc. of JD," 178.

79. Miers, *Jones Diary*, 192, 193, 266, 336, 376, 432; *Chesnut*, 332, 375, 387, 469, 474, 694; Dorsey, *Recoll. of H. W. Allen*, 118–19, 195–96, 218; Fremantle, *Three Months*, 112, 116–17; B. T. Kavanaugh to JD, Aug. 13, 1863 (Rowland 5:590–92); Vandiver, *Gorgas Diary*, 48–50, quots. (see JD to Pettus, July 11 [Rowland 5:542]).

80. JD to JEJ, July 15, 1863 (Rowland 5:556–63, quots.; never interfered: see Cooper cited ibid. 7:270); JD, Paper Feb. 18, 1865 (ibid. 6:497–98, quots.); Seitz, *Bragg*, 321 and Symonds, *JEJ*, 219 (keeps Miss.-Ala. and part of West Tenn.). See JEJ-JD corr. in JEJ, *Narrative*, 229–52, and Rowland 6:24–25.

81. Govan and Livingood, *Different Valor*, 227–28 (quots. from Lydia and JEJ to Wigfalls); Symonds, *JEJ*, 221 (JEJ quot.).

82. JD to JEJ, Aug. 1, 1863 (Rowland 5:582–83, quot.; see 6:1–13); JD to Walthall, Nov. 23, 1874 (ibid., 7:408, quot.; see 6:402; 7:421; 9:370–71); JEJ, *Narrative*, 242–43, quot.

83. JD to Pemb., Aug. 9, 1863 (Rowland 5:587–88, quots.; see also 578, 596, and *Pemberton*, 303); Govan and Livingood, *Different Valor*, 229–30, quot.; JD to J. M. Howry, Aug. 27 (Rowland 6:17, quot.); JD telegram, Sept. 10 (ibid., 29, quot.).

84. JD to Bragg, June 29, 1872 (ibid. 7:320–22; see Chesnut to JD in *O. R.* 52 [Part 2]: 545); *Polk* 2:277; JD to Pemb., Mar. 11, 1864 (Rowland 6:203); *Pemberton*, 258–64; *Conf. Soldier*, 345.

85. Fremantle, *Three Months*, 136–72; Seitz, *Bragg*, 304, 309; Henry, *Story of Conf.*, 287–91, 296–97; Ramage, *Rebel Raider*, 160–78.

86. *Polk* 2:203–10 (quots. on 204); Hughes, *Gen. Hardee*, 150–56; R. Carter, *Capt. Tod Carter*, 26–30 (Hardee's "rollicking spirit").

87. William W. Bennett, *A Narrative of the Great Revival Which Prevailed in the Southern Armies* [1877, RPR Harrisonburg, Va.: Sprinkle Publications, 1989], 69, 229 (1862), 242–64, 265–311; J. William Jones, *Christ in the Camp, or Religion in the Confederate Army* [1887, RPR Harrisonburg, Va.: Sprinkle Publications, 1986], 190–91, 212–23, 230–46.

88. *Pendleton* 293–94; *Land We Love* 4:127–31, 2:129; *Polk* 1:209–15, 327–28, 2:204–5, 207–8 (quot.; see Rowland 6:284 n.1; Wilmer, *Recent Past*, 208–42); Fremantle, *Three Months*, 137, 140–41, 144, 147–48, 153–54 (quot.), 157; Noll, *Dr. Quintard*, 11–12, 18, 54, 69–86 (quots. on 76).

89. Noll, *Dr. Quintard*, 95 and 77–80, quots.; Fremantle, *Three Months*, 162. Bragg was a friend of Bsp. Otey of Tenn., who had brought Quintard to the ministry (Noll, 5; McWhiney, *Braxton Bragg*, 117); see ibid., 96, 254; WPJ, *Gen. ASJ*, 547; *O. R.* 22 (Part 1): 446–47; *Gache*, 58.

90. Ridley, *Battles and Sketches*, 604–5; Horn, *Army of Tenn.*, 234–38; Hallock, *Bragg and Defeat*, 15–27 (Rosecrans quot. on 23; he had 82,000 to Bragg's 55,000; see Miers, *Jones Diary*, 260–61).

91. Hallock, *Bragg and Defeat*, 22–23; J. B. Sale to Bragg, Mar. 5, 1863, in Seitz, *Bragg*, 285, quot.; Bragg to JEJ, June 22 (ibid., 308, quot.; see Bragg to Bgd. and JEJ, 321–23 and 255–56); Connelly and Jones, *Politics of Command*, 129–33, 139–40.

92. Bragg to [Cooper], July 22, 1863, in Seitz, *Bragg*, 322, quot. (addressee Lee here, but see Hallock *Bragg and Defeat*, 39 n.26); Bragg-JD corr., July 22 (*O. R.* 52 [Part 2]: 511–12, JD quot.).

93. JD to Bragg, Jan. 15 and June 17, 1863 (Rowland 5:418 and 523–24, quots.; see *Polk*, 287); Henry, *Story of Conf.*, 483; Rowland 5:547–48, 568–71, 597, 6:15, 19, 20, 25–28, 35–37 (others needing aid, e.g.: 5:584–85, 598); Hughes, *Gen. Hardee*, 157–63; S. Foote, *C. W.* 2:690.

94. JD, *Rise and Fall* 2:427–29; S. Foote, *C. W.*, 690–91; Freeman, *R. E. Lee* 3:165–67; JD to Lee, Sept. 16, 1863 (Rowland 6:35–37); JD, *Rise and Fall* 2:428–29; Connelly and Jones, *Politics of Command*, 132–36. JD also asked for militia of Ga., Tenn., and Ala.: Rowland 5:578, 6:19–27, 32–34, 42.

95. Henry, *Story of Conf.*, 304–7; Ridley, *Battles and Sketches*, 605, 205–6 (see Seitz, *Bragg*, 404–5); JD to Lee, Sept. 16, 1863 (Rowland 6:35–37, quot.); JD to Bragg, Sept. 10 and Oct. 29 (ibid., 30 [quot.] and 70; also 23 and 5:597); *Conf. Soldier*, 199–202; D. H. Hill in *Land We Love* 4:281–83; S. Foote, *C. W.* 2:691–94.

96. S. Foote, *C.W.* 2:710–57; *Polk* 2:274, 289; Glenn Tucker, "The Battle of Chickamauga," 47, quot.; *Conf. Soldier*, 202–9; Hallock, *Bragg and Defeat*, 66–70, 75–77; *O. R.* 30 (Part 2): 38 (Bragg quot.; Eccles. 9:11).

97. Hallock, *Bragg and Defeat*, 88–108 (see Hindman on 145); *Polk* 2:240–52, 257, 280–84 (Bragg quot.); *O. R.* 30 (Part 2): 54–65, 47–48, 67–77; Bridges, *Lee's Maverick*, 208–16, 231–32,.

98. *Polk* 2:274–77, 288–90; Lee to Longs., Oct. 26, 1863, in Longs., *From Manassas*, 469n; Lee to JD, Sept. 6, 1863 (*Wartime Papers*, 596); JD to Lee, Sept. 8 (*O. R.* 29 [Part 2]: 702); Polk to JD, Oct. 6 (*O. R.* 30 [Part 2]: 67–68, quot.).

99. Bridges, *Lee's Maverick*, 234–37; *O. R.* 30 (Part 2): 65–66, quots.; Ibid. 52 (Part 2): 677–78, 517, 535, 538, 540; D. H. Hill to JD, Oct. 30, 1886 (Rowland 9:498–99); JD to Lee, Oct. 5, 1863 (ibid. 6:56, quot.).

100. JD to Bragg, Sept. 30 and Oct. 3, 1863 (Rowland 6:53–56, quots.); D. H. Hill to JD, Oct. 30, 1886 (ibid. 9:498, citing Bragg). See *Polk* 2:284.

101. McWhiney, *Braxton Bragg,* 205, 216, 255 (Elise quot.), 262–63, 275–76, 300–12, 326–28; Seitz, *Bragg,* 112 (Bragg quot.), 289–94, 379 (Bragg to JD, quot.); *Polk* 2:88–96, 290 (Polk to JD quot.); Hughes, *Gen. Hardee,* 124–35, 150; Hallock, *Bragg and Defeat,* 78, 92.

102. Blackford, *Letters from Lee's Army,* 216, quots.; Rowland 6:57–58, 60–72 (JD quot. on 60); *Polk* 2:282–86; Hughes, *Gen. Hardee,* 158–59 and n.2, 162–65; *O. R.* 30 (Part 2): 292–313, 148–53; Hallock, *Bragg and Defeat,* 94–97; Bridges, *Lee's Maverick,* 227–28, 239–40, 246–72.

103. Horn, *Army of Tenn.,* 287–88 (JD quots.; says Longs. "unexpectedly" brought up opinion of Bragg); Longs., *From Manassas,* 465. S. Foote (*C. W.* 2:815–17), Strode, *President,* 480, and Symonds (*JEJ,* 246), believe JD; most others believe Longs. (but see Hallock, *Bragg and Defeat,* 96–99); Buckner is ambiguous in *O. R.* 31 (Part 3): 660–61.

104. *Polk* 2:270, 271, 274, 286; Hallock, *Bragg and Defeat,* 98–99, 109–10; *O. R.* 30 [Part 2]: 65 (quots. from petition, Oct. 4, 1863); Gordon, *Reminisc. of C. W.,* 213–16, quots.; Hallock, *Bragg and Defeat,* 78.

105. JD to Bragg, Oct. 3, 1863, and June 29, 1872 (Rowland 6:55 and 7:321, quots.); Wright, *Southern Girl,* 160 (Seddon quot.). On JD's options, see Hallock, *Bragg and Defeat,* 99; Woodworth, *JD and Gens.,* 242; Vandiver, *Their Tattered Flags,* 253.

106. Quots.: JD to Bragg, Oct. 29, 1863 (Rowland 6:69–71); Bragg to JD, Oct. 31 (*O. R.* 52 [Part 2]: 557); JD to Hardee, Oct. 30 (Rowland 6:72); JD to Army of Tenn., Oct. 14 (ibid., 61–62). Org. of army: Losson, *Cheatham,* 115–19 and *O. R.,* as above, 546.

107. S. Foote, *C. W.* 2:819–20; Gorgas, Notes (Rowland 8:323–24); Hughes, *Gen. Hardee,* 162–63.

108. Hermann, *Joseph E. Davis,* 124–25, 128 (Eliza d. Oct. 4); Nash K. Burger, "The Rt. Rev. William Mercer Green, First Episcopal Bishop of Mississippi," 20; JD to Polk, Oct. 23, 1863 (ibid. 6:62); S. Foote, *C. W.* 2:770–71, 819–20. Foote pictures Eliza living, but Jeff's visit was between Oct. 17 and 23 (*O. R.* 52 [Part 2]: 545–47).

109. S. Foote, *C. W.,* 812–13, 820; Henry, *"First with the Most" Forrest,* 198–201; Hallock, *Bragg and Defeat,* 100–102; Forrest to Cooper, Aug. 9, 1863 (*O. R.* 23 [Part 2]: 955–56); JD to Forrest and to Bragg, Oct. 29 (Rowland 6:64–66, and n.1); *O. R.* 52 (Part 2): 529, 557, 572.

110. JD to Bragg, Oct. 29, 1863 (Rowland 6:68–69, quot.); Longs. to Lee, Sept. 5 (*O. R.* 29 [Part 2]: 699); Longs., *From Manassas,* 469n (Lee to Longs.); Hallock, *Bragg and Defeat,* 96, 107–8, 121–22; Longs. to Seddon, Sept. 26, in *Polk* 2:274–75.

111. Hallock, *Bragg and Defeat,* 122–25; JD to Bragg, Oct. 29 and Nov. 1, 1863 (Rowland 6:69–71 and 73, quots.); Longs., *From Manassas,* 468–77; Alexander, *Fighting for Conf.,* 304–6, 309–11; Bragg to JD, Oct. 29 and 30 (*O. R.* 52 [Part 2]: 555–56).

112. Grant, *Memoirs* 2:26–39 (quot. on 27; see Bragg in *O. R.* 30 [Part 2]: 36–37); Sherman, *Memoirs* 1:347, 350–62; Longs., *From Manassas,* 472–77; Henry, *Story of Conf.,* 316–19, map on 305.

113. Seitz, *Bragg,* 387–91 (JD quots. on 388); Connelly and Jones, *Politics of Command,* 139–40; Longs. to Buckner, Nov. 5 (*O. R.* 52 [Part 2]: 559–60); Lee to Longstreet, JD, and S. Jones in *Wartime Papers,* 602–6, 617–18 (see Rowland 6:35–37); Grant, *Memoirs* 2:85–87 (the ridicule is much repeated, lately in Hallock, *Bragg and Defeat,* 125–27).

114. Seitz, *Bragg,* 390–95; S. Foote, *C. W.* 2:837–42 (others give diff. numbers); *Battles and Leaders* 3:693n (Grant quot.).

115. Lonn, *Foreigners in Conf.,* 245, quots. (this "Frenchman," Nocquet, mentioned *SHSP* 11:53 and 13:376, but not as deserter). Grant also had C.S. code (Alexander, *Fighting for Conf.,* 310).

116. Grant, *Memoirs* 2:75–85; Joseph S. Fullerton, "The Army of the Cumberland at Chattanooga," in *Battles and Leaders* 3:725–26 (Grant quot.); Ridley, *Battles and Sketches*, 255–58 (Bragg quot.); Alexander, *Fighting for Conf.*, 322–32; Henry, *Story of Conf.*, 324–25.

117. Seitz, *Bragg*, 400–401 (Bragg quots.); Hardee to Cooper, Nov. 30, 1863 (*O. R.* 31 [Part 3]: 764–65, quot.); Hughes, *Gen. Hardee*, 178 and 85, quots. (see also Hardee on 87 and Bragg on 149; 188: Hardee m. Mary Lewis, Jan. 13, 1864). See VHD, *Memoir* 2:451.

118. JD to Lee, Dec. 6 (Rowland 6:93; see 128); Lee to JD, July 31 and Dec. 7 (*Wartime Papers*, 565 [quot.] and 642; and see ibid., Lee to Stuart, Dec. 9); JD to JEJ and to Hardee, Dec. 16, 1863 (Rowland 6:132; Polk takes Army of Miss.).

Chapter XVI Double-quick Downhill

1. VHD, *Memoir* 2:496–97, quots. (words repeated by day; at night assumed; ref. to Matt. 26:39, Mark 14:36, Luke 22:42); *Chesnut*, 601–2 and 609, quots.; Vandiver, *Gorgas Diary*, 96; *Richmond Sentinel*, May 31, 1864 (quots. from officer's letter, May 3; illegible word at ellipsis); JD to VHD, Aug. 21, 1865, MS, TRANSYL ("little man").

2. VHD, *Memoir* 2:496–97, quots.; *Richmond Sentinel* (as in Note 1 above; Joe fell 15 feet; *Richmond Daily Dispatch*, May 2, implied the cause was a 15- to 20-foot ladder left at porch); *Chesnut*, 601, quot.; White House visit, 1986 (author indebted to Tucker H. Hill for showing spot of the fall).

3. Quots.: *Chesnut*, 601; E. Rowland, *Varina* 2:361 (from letter, VHD to JD); VHD, *Memoir* 2:497; Vandiver, *Gorgas Diary*, 96.

4. C. C. Harrison, *Recoll.*, 181–82 (incl. BNH quots.); *Chesnut*, 601–2 and 609, quots. (see 545, 547; Miers, *Jones Diary*, 327); Weddell, *St. Paul's* 1:230; Rowland 6:238–39 (items show JD at work May 2), 267. Catherine remained in the Davises employ; JD was 55; Varina Anne Davis was b. June 27, 1864 (*Papers* 1:App. 4, Chart 14).

5. JD to VHD, Feb. 17–19, 1866, MS, TRANSYL, quots. (JD, Apr. 21–23, speaks of "effort" as a comfort).

6. *Chesnut*, 568, quot.; JD to W. M. Green, Aug. 18, 1875 (Rowland 7:443, quot.); VHD, *Memoir* 2:198n, quots. (see 645 n).

7. VHD, *Memoir* 2:198n, quots. Henry Heth speaks of his "battles with the butcher cats" and the 100 years (*Heth Memoirs*, 231).

8. *Chesnut*, 796, quot.

9. JD, Paper, Feb. 18, 1865 (Rowland 6:498–99, quots.); Seddon to Walthall, Feb. 10, 1879 (ibid. 8:350–51); Polk to JD, Dec. 8, 1863, and to Harvie [of JEJ's staff], Jan. 3 [1864] in *Polk* 2:293 and 295–96, quots.

10. JD, Paper, (Rowland 6:500, quots.); JD to JEJ, Dec. 23, 1863, and Jan. 14, 1864 (ibid. 6:135–37, 149); McMurry, "'The *Enemy* at Richmond,'" 18–29; Robert D. Little, "General Hardee and the Atlanta Campaign," 18–20.

11. Seitz, *Bragg*, 410; VHD, *Memoir* 2:450, quot. (see Rowland 9:553); Hallock, *Bragg and Defeat*, 163–66. (Lee:) Rowland 6:344, 9:272–73, 555; Freeman-McWhiney, *Lee's Dispatches*, 169–77, 283–84, 371–72, 165 n.1; *Wartime Papers*, 639, 687–88, 699–700; *Polk* 2:201–3, quot. (see 291–92); Vandiver, *Gorgas Diary*, 89 and 165, quots. (see 158).

12. Thomas L. Connelly, *Civil War Tennessee: Battle and Leaders* (Knoxville: Univ. of Tennessee Press, 1979), 53, quot. (see Rowland 9:522); Seitz, *Bragg*, 410–11; VHD, *Memoir* 2:462–72 (quot. on 472).

13. "The Kilpatrick-Dahlgren Raid against Richmond," comp. by J. W. Jones, 515–60 (quots. from F. Lee on 553; see also *SHSP* 3:219–21). Other firsthand evidence in Vandiver, *Gorgas Diary*, 85, 89; [Benjamin F. Butler] *Butler's Book*,

1051–52; Miers, *Jones Diary,* 346–47; Seitz, *Bragg,* 411; Wright, *Southern Girl,* 166–67. Joseph George, Jr., in "'Black Flag Warfare': Lincoln and the Raids against Richmond and Jefferson Davis" (1991), concludes orders were genuine.

14. *Chesnut* 288, quot. (see 542); Benj. in *SHSP* 6:183 (quot.), 186–87; VHD, *Memoir* 1:535–36; *Papers* 5:39, 41, 124–25, 6:26–27, 270–73; DeLeon, "The Real JD," 77.

15. E. Rowland, *Varina* 2:467–68, quot. (465 n.1 and Ross, *First Lady,* 266, wrongly ident. Martha as "Mrs. Phillips," who was her sister Eugenia: see *Chesnut,* 423 and n.7); VHD, *Memoir* 2:207–8; Reagan, *Memoirs,* 163; Butler, *Judah P. Benj.,* 239–40, 328–33, 340–41, 369, 34–36.

16. Foote, *Casket of Reminisc.,* 236, 240, quots.; Bertram Wallace Korn, *American Jewry and the Civil War* (Philadelphia: The Jewish Publication Society of America, 1951), 177–84; JD to J. W. C. Watson, Mar. 8, 1865 (Rowland 6:512, quots.). For attacks see Lonn, *Foreigners in Conf.,* 336, Miers, *Jones Diary,* 72, 326, 496, and *Chesnut,* 288–89.

17. Richardson, *Conf.* 2:passim; S. Foote, *C. W.* 3:98–101; Pryor, *Reminisc. of Peace and War,* 264 (quot. from a letter); Butler, *Judah P. Benj.,* 267–89, 299–324, 339–42, 396 (on writing for JD, see also Beers, *Guide to C.S.A.,* 63; *Chesnut,* 498; see Rowland 7:235 for JD paper wrongly ascribed to Benj.).

18. Seitz, *Bragg,* 410–11; Reagan, *Memoirs,* 182, quots.; Benj. to *London Times* [1865] in *SHSP* 6:186–87, quots.; Butler, *Judah P. Benjamin,* 348; JD, *Rise and Fall* 2:504–8; Miers, *Jones Diary,* 346.

19. Nuermberger, *Clays of Ala.,* 221 (Wigfall to Clay, Aug. 13, 1863, quot.); King, *Wigfall,* 172–73 (quot. on Lee), 176, 179–95 ("star" on 184); *Chesnut,* 498, quot. (see 607–8); McMurry, "'The *Enemy* at Richmond,'" 15–16, 25; T. J. Wharton to JD, Jan. 24, 1868 (Rowland 7:236, quots.).

20. Nuermberger, *Clays of Ala.,* 232–33; King, *Wigfall,* 187–95 (quots. on 194, 192), 177–78 (quot.); Yearns, *Conf. Cong.,* 233–34; Miers, *Jones Diary,* 229, 233, 259, 328; W. C. Davis, *JD,* 537–38.

21. Lawton in *Life and Reminisc.,* 199, quots. (see 196–97); JD to Senate, Jan. 27, 1864 (Richardson, *Conf.* 1:392–94, quot.); Black, *Railroads of Conf.,* 99–100, 105–6, 168–69; Lawton in Warner, *Gens. in Gray;* Eckenrode, *JD,* 280. See *O. R.* 32 (Part 1): 318–22.

22. *SHSP* 50:20–23; Yearns, *Conf. Cong.,* 49–59, 144 (quot.), 224–27, 232, 234–35 (veto; also 115), 268 n.37, and see 132, 156–60.

23. Yearns, *Conf. Cong.,* 184–217, 229–30 (quot.); Vandiver, *Their Tattered Flags,* 94–96, 166–67, 177–78, 230–35, 242–43, 270–71; C. S. Davis, *Colin J. McRae,* 34–59.

24. JD to Memminger, June 21, 1864 (Rowland 6:275–76); JD to Cong., Nov. 7 (ibid., 389–92); JD to Trenholm, Apr. 28, 1865 (ibid., 565); Stephen R. Wise, "Greyhounds and Cavaliers of the Sea: Confederate Blockade Running . . ." (*Jnl. of Conf. Hist.* 4 (1989): 61–76).

25. JD to Trenholm (as in Note 24 above, quots.); Hill, Address Feb. 18, 1874 (*SHSP* 14:497–98, JD quots.); Lubbock, *Six Decades,* 655, quot.

26. Yearns, *Conf. Cong.,* 132–39; JD to H. V. Johnson, July 22, 1864 (Rowland 6:297–98, quot.); Vandiver, *Their Tattered Flags,* 233, 238–39, 271, 172–80, 282–84, 318–19 (n.24); Wise, "Greyhounds" (as in Note 24 above), 74–76; *Wartime Papers,* 659–60; JD in Richardson, *Conf.* 1:328 and Rowland 6:40–41, 342–43, 359–60; Howell Hinds to JD, Oct. 11, 1863 (ibid., 60, quot.).

27. Phillips, *Life of Robt. Toombs,* 246–49; Miller, *Photo. Hist.* 7:197; Louis Pendleton, *Alexander H. Stephens,* 311–18; Escott, *After Secession,* 203–5; Hill in *SHSP* 14:497–98, quot.; David B. Parker, "Bill Arp, Joe Brown, and the Confederate War Effort," 83 and passim; Dorsey, *Recoll. of H. W. Allen,* 12, quot.; VHD, *Memoir* 2:574, 164 (JD quot.).

28. Montgomery, *Howell Cobb's Conf. Career,* 108–9, quots.; JD to Longs., Mar.

7 and 25, 1864 (ibid., 199–201, 209–11); JD, *Rise and Fall* 2:547–51; Hughes, *Gen. Hardee*, 180; Connelly and Jones, *Politics of Command*, 141–52, 162; Longs., *From Manassas*, 544; Seitz, *Bragg*, 414–19; JEJ, *Narrative*, 291–301; Hood, *Advance and Retreat*, 266.

29. Seitz, *Bragg*, 416–19 (Bragg to JEJ, Mar. 7 [quots.] and Mar. 12), 421 (JEJ quot.). Wide variety in numbers: ibid., 427–31; JD, *Rise and Fall* 2:551; JEJ, *Narrative*, 298–302, 574; McPherson, *Battle Cry*, 744; S. Foote, *C. W.* 3:320; Symonds, *JEJ*, 259–60; Castel, *Decision in West*, 108–16 (lists several categories of inf., with art. and cav. separately, which may explain variety).

30. Horn, *Army of Tenn.*, 242, map on 280, 309–11; Govan and Livingood, *A Diff. Valor*, 139 (JEJ to Wigfall, Nov. 1863, quots.); Seitz, *Bragg*, 415–22, 427–32 (JEJ quots.); *Pendleton*, 314–20, quot.; JD, *Rise and Fall* 2:549–52; Castel, *Decision in West*, 30–33, 37–38, 73–78, 100–104.

31. S. Foote, *C. W.* 2:937 (Sherman quot.); Bearss, *Sherman's Forgotten Campaign*, passim (Sherman quot. on 192); *O. R.* 32 (Part 1): 173–79; Castel, *Decision in the West*, 43–53; Sherman, *Memoirs* 1:386–92, 398–401; Hermann, *Joseph E. Davis*, 128; Hermann, *Pursuit of Dream*, 44–53 (Grant quot. on 46); Currie, "Freedmen at Davis Bend," passim (quots. on 126, 121, 122, 124; Davis slaves in n.10); Currie, *Enclave*, 36–37.

32. S. Foote, *C. W.* 2:920–38; Henry, *"First with the Most" Forrest*, 217–33; Herman Hattaway, *General Stephen D. Lee* (Jackson: Univ. Press of Mississippi, 1976), 108–10; JEJ, *Narrative*, 281–82; Bearss, *Sherman's Forgotten Campaign*, 177, 188, 191, 204, 209–10, 329–30 n.12; Sherman, *Memoirs* 1:386–95 (quots. on 394); *O. R.* 32 (Part 1): 254–60; Hughes, *Gen. Hardee*, 194–96.

33. William Glenn Robertson, *Back Door to Richmond: The Bermuda Hundred Campaign, Apr.–June 1864*, 13–14; Heitman, *Hist. Register*, 19; S. Foote, *C. W.* 3:3–61, map on 63, 77–90; Winters, *C. W. in La.*, 325–79; R. Taylor, *Destruction*, 193–94, quots.; Parrish, *Richard Taylor*, 317–54.

34. McPherson, *Battle Cry*, 722; S. Foote, *C.W.* 3:13–24, 126–27; J. F. C. Fuller, *Grant and Lee: A Study in Personality and Generalship*, 206–13. See Alexander, *Fighting for Conf.*, 511–12. Army will be called Grant's in text; Meade had field command.

35. VHD, *Memoir* 2:496 (quot.), 508–19; Early, *Memoirs*, 369–70; Williams, *Bgd.*, 164–67, 173–79, 185–96, 199–209, 219; Bradley T. Johnson, "Case of Jefferson Davis," 185 (quot. from JD, Address to Armies of C.S., Feb. 10, 1864).

36. Robertson, *Back Door*, 78, 150–52, 68 (quot.), 76–77, 83, 149–50, 153 (usage then was "Hundreds"); JD to LBN, Jan. 19, 1879 (Rowland 8:337, quot.); Freeman, *R. E. Lee* 3:333, 373 (JD knew plans: e.g., 265–68, 339–42); JD, *Rise and Fall* 2:525. Actual numbers: ibid., Alexander, *Fighting for Conf.*, 347–48; W. Taylor, *Four Years with Gen. Lee*, 136–37.

37. Williams, *Bgd.*, 198–202 (Bgd. quots.; on A. J. Evans, see 160, 171); *Charleston Daily Courier*, Nov. 3, 1863 (Rowland 6:73–78, JD quot.; see 8:381); *Chesnut*, 493n. Alfred Roman, *Military Operations of General Beauregard*, 168, gives variant version of events.

38. Robertson, *Back Door*, 153–54 (see Bragg on 151), 170–72, 176–78; JD, *Rise and Fall* 2:508, 510–13; JD to Lee, May 15, 1864 (Rowland 6:253; see 252–58); Williams, *Bgd.*, 217–18 (Bgd. quot.); JD to LBN, n.d. (Rowland 8:194, quot.; see 337, 417–18, 420–21).

39. JD, *Rise and Fall*, 2:513–14; Reagan, *Memoirs*, 190–91, quots.; Williams, *Bgd.*, 220 (Bgd. quot.); Robertson, *Back Door*, 194, 205–6, 209–15, (cav.:) 95–106, 160–69. On Whiting, see also Freeman, *Lee's Lieuts.* 3:492 (battle, 478–93); Alexander, *Fighting for Conf.*, 393–94.

40. JD to Lee, May 20, 1864 (Rowland 6:256–58; see JD to LBN, ibid. 8:337–38, and JD, *Rise and Fall* 2:514–15); Lee to JD, May 23 (Freeman-McWhiney, *Lee's Dispatches*, 194–97 and n.7); T. R. R. Cobb in *SHSP* 28:287, quot.; Robertson, *Back Door*, 219–22.

41. Freeman, *R. E. Lee* 3:325 (quots.), 329; Alexander, *Fighting for Conf.*, 373–80; JD, *Rise and Fall* 2:516.

42. Alexander, *Fighting for Conf.*, 347–63; *Heth Memoirs*, 181–85, quot.; Douglas, *I Rode with Stonewall*, 263–67, quot.; W. Taylor, *Four Years with Gen. Lee*, 124–29.

43. Alexander, *Fighting for Conf.*, 359–65, 346–48 (quots.); JD, *Rise and Fall* 2:598–600 (Grant quot.); *Butler's Book*, 592–606; Taylor, *Gen. Lee*, 232, 262, 292, 293; Cooper in *SHSP* 7:290. See also Rowland 7:494–95; *O. R.*, 2, 8:153, 175–76, 801, 803–4; Page, *True Story*, 107–8; VHD, *Memoir* 2:538; Blakey, *Gen. Winder*, 166; Marvel, *Andersonville*, 154–56, 221.

44. Henry Kyd Douglas, *I Rode with Stonewall*, 267–71 (faults Grant rpts.); Alexander, *Fighting for Conf.*, 345 (quot.), 365–86; W. Taylor, *Four Years with Gen. Lee*, 129–33; Freeman, *R. E. Lee* 3:298–326.

45. Alexander, *Fighting for Conf.*, 387–91, 395–98; Freeman, *R. E. Lee* 3:340–72 (map 376: same battle sites as 1862, with a new Cold Harbor).

46. Miers, *Jones Diary* 231–36, 273–74, 343–45, 363, 372–74; Pemb. in *Conf. Soldier in C. W.*, 345; Thomas, *Bold Dragoon*, 290–91; Alfriend, *Life of JD*, 550, quot.; JD to R. E. Lee, May 11, 1864 (Rowland 6:250, quot.; see also to Ransom, 265).

47. Thomas, *Bold Dragoon*, 288–96 (quots. from Sheridan and Stuart); Lubbock, *Six Decades*, 654; JD, *Rise and Fall* 2:508–10, quot.; VHD, *Memoir* 2:498–503, quots.; *Moore's Guide to Richmond*, 39; Alexander, *Fighting for Conf.*, 209 and Bobby Horton, "Homespun Songs of C.S.A.," Vol. 2 (audiocassette). Stuart critics in Starr, *Colonel Grenfell's Wars*, 110–11.

48. VHD, *Memoir* 2:493–94, quot.; JD to Lee, May 15, 1864 (Rowland 6;253, quots.); *Pendleton*, 326, quot.; Freeman, *R. E. Lee* 3:287–88, 313, 318–21 (all 4 incidents precede May 15).

49. Freeman, *R. E. Lee* 3:380, 387; Alexander, *Fighting for Conf.*, 398–407 (quots.), 417–33 (see also 414); S. Foote, *C. W.* 3:14, 212 (Grant quots.); Douglas, *I Rode with Stonewall*, 272–74, quots.; W. Taylor, *Four Years with Gen. Lee*, 135–37; McPherson, *Battle Cry*, 739–43.

50. JD to VHD, Nov. 3, 1865, MS, TRANSYL, quot.; VHD, *Memoir* 2:494, quots.; Alexander, *Fighting for Conf.*, 433, quot.; JD speech, 1864 (Rowland 6:347, quots.). JD on hope: Richardson, *Conf.* 1:287–88, Rowland 5:201, 203, 394–95, 548, 6:84–85, 344, 346–47, 351, 353, 549.

51. JD to Vance, Jan. 8, 1864 (Rowland 6:144, quot.); JD, *Rise and Fall* 2:611–12; Clement Claiborne Clay in *DAB;* Nuermberger, *Clays of Ala.*, 231–33; Butler, *Judah P. Benjamin*, 346; Escott, *After Secession*, 194–205, 216–17; Larry E. Nelson, *Bullets, Ballots, and Rhetoric: Confederate Policy for the United States Presidential Contest of 1864* (Tuscaloosa: Univ. of Alabama Press, 1980).

52. JD to Vance, Jan. 8, 1864, and July 24, 1863 (Rowland 6:143–46, and 5:576–77, quots.; see 9:329–33); E. Barksdale to Walthall, Aug. 3, 1878 (ibid. 8:247–48). See VHD, *Memoir* 2:454–55; Yearns, *Conf. Cong.*, 174–75; Escott, *After Secession*, 200–203.

53. Alexander, *Fighting for Conf.*, 433–34, quots. See J. L. M. Curry in *Life and Reminisc.*, 148 and John M. Gibson, *Physician to the World: The Life of William C. Gorgas* (Tuscaloosa: Univ. of Alabama Press, 1989), 24.

54. JD, *Rise and Fall* 2:610–12 (Lincoln quots.); Clement Claiborne Clay in *DAB;* Randall, *Civil War*, 615–17; S. Foote, *C. W.* 3:465–69.

55. Early, *Memoirs*, 371–405, 474 (JD quot.); Douglas, *I Rode with Stonewall*, 276–87 and nn.; *SHSP* 8:215–16; *Pendleton*, 341, 344–49; Charles C. Osborne, *Jubal: The Life and Times of General Jubal A. Early, CSA*, 299–300 (Grant quot.); JD in Rowland 6:337, 385.

56. Rowland 6:346; JD to Lee, June 9, 1864 (ibid., 269–70); McMurry, *John Bell Hood*, 14–16, 46–51, 60–62, 77, 83, 86, 88–89; JD, *Rise and Fall* 2:121, 138; *Wartime Papers*, 489; Hood, *Advance and Retreat*, 66–68.

57. McMurry, *John Bell Hood,* 23, 29, 32–33, 80, 170, 180–81, 196; King, *Wigfall,* 171; Miers, *Jones Diary,* 341, quot.; *Chesnut,* 442, 566–67 (quot. from boys), see 527, 559; Hood, *Advance and Retreat,* 8, 66–67 (quot.).

58. *Chesnut,* 565 (Hood quot.); Hood, *Advance and Retreat,* 67, 92–95 (quots.); Eckenrode, *JD,* 276–80, 295, 299–300, 302–6; McMurry, *John Bell Hood* (1982), 86–89 and n.25 (plot sometimes involves JD), 95–98 and n.12. See Seitz, *Bragg,* 505; Stout, "Reminisc. of Bragg"; McMurry, "'*Enemy* at Richmond,'" 30; Thomas Robson Hay, "Davis, Bragg, and Johnston in the Atlanta Campaign" (plot impossible); Hallock, *Bragg and Defeat* (1991), 191–202; Castel, *Decision in West* (1992), 356–57, 423–24.

59. Ridley, *Battles and Sketches,* 306; JD, *Rise and Fall* 2:551, quots.; S. Foote, *C. W.* 3:320–29; *Polk* 2:324–29; Noll, *Dr. Quintard,* 96.

60. Ridley, *Battles and Sketches,* 422; Noll, *Dr. Quintard,* 97 (96: errs *re* Hardee's bapt.); Hardee to Mary [Lewis Hardee], June 5, 1864, quot. (copy in Hardee Papers, ADAH).

61. *Polk* 2:329, 338–39; McMurry, *John Bell Hood,* 102–3, map on 104; Noll, *Dr. Quintard,* 100; Castel, *Decision in West,* xii; Henry, *"First with the Most" Forrest,* 305; Little, "Gen. Hardee and Atlanta," 19–20.

62. Noll, *Dr. Quintard,* 97–98, quot.; *Polk* 2:330, 339, 345–50, 362–63 (quot.; see 328–29, 321); Castel, *Decision in West,* 276; Irving R. Buck, *Cleburne and His Command,* ed. Thomas Robson Hay, 223; Losson, *Cheatham,* 151; Johnston, *Narrative,* 337. Details differ in all these accounts.

63. JEJ, *Narrative,* 276–335; Ridley, *Battles and Sketches,* 295–302, 307–8; S. Foote, *C. W.* 3:320–38; Hughes, *Gen. Hardee,* 198–203; Losson, *Cheatham,* 143–48; McMurry, *John Bell Hood,* 102–7.

64. JEJ, *Narrative,* 320–36; *Polk* 2:330–33, 351–57; Hood, *Advance and Retreat,* 95–124; Horn, *Army of Tenn.,* 327–30 and n.50; McMurry, *John Bell Hood,* 107–9 and n.40; Ridley, *Battles and Sketches,* 303–9. JEJ blames Polk and Hood, who dispute him, for Cassville; Horn and McMurry believe Hood. Castel, *Decision in West,* 589–90 nn.100–102, adduces new evidence.

65. JEJ, *Narrative,* 336–39, quot.; Henry, *Story of Conf.,* 381 map (Pine Mtn.), 385–86; Noll, *Dr. Quintard,* 98–99; JD to Elliott, July 8, 1864 (Rowland 6:284, quot.); JD, Speech, 1882 (ibid. 9:164, quot.); *Polk* 2:346–50, 358–70, 328–29 (Polk and JD: 1:316–17, 320, 326, 345, 348).

66. Ridley, *Battles and Sketches,* 310–11 (JEJ quot.); Curry, *Civil Hist. of C.S.,* 178; Fremantle, *Three Months,* 139–40, 144–48, 165–67, 240n; Losson, *Cheatham,* 151–52.

67. Horn, *Army of Tenn.,* 332–38 (quots. from defenders); Ridley, *Battles and Sketches,* 311–19; JEJ, *Narrative,* 345–46. See Hood, *Advance and Retreat,* 97; Castel, *Decision in West,* 332–34.

68. JD to JEJ (quots.), and to Watts, July 7, 1864 (Rowland 6:283); (see Sharf, *Hist. C.S. Navy,* 551, 556–58); JD to Chesnut, July 8 (Rowland 6:286, quot.; see 238–39); JD to Lee, July 8 (ibid., 285, quots.; italics=code: see Horn, *Army of Tenn.,* plate facing 401); Shingleton, *John T. Wood,* 116–18.

69. Ramage, *Rebel Raider,* 194–98, 211–26 (Morgan heads Dept. of W. Va. and E. Tenn.); Henry, *"First with the Most" Forrest,* 280–307 (quots. on 307; see map on 218.

70. Semmes, *Service Afloat,* 750–68, 777–86 (*Ala.* career, 400–750); S. Foote, *C. W.* 3:380–89; JD to J. Lancaster, Mar. 1, 1865 (Rowland 6:490; transmits Cong. thanks); Shingleton, *John T. Wood,* 118–41, 207–8; see JD in Rowland 6:366–67, 418–21).

71. Sibley, "JD Recalls the Past," 171, 173–74 (WPJ quots.; Rowland 6 shows no JD corr. for June 30–July 1); *Chesnut,* 607 (date differs), 763, 785, 787; De Leon, *Belles,* 424–25. JD asks help in getting "an Arabian of great value" through blockade in 1862 (Rowland 5:297).

72. *Papers* 1:App. 4, Chart 14; Ross, *First Lady,* 203; Weddell, *St. Paul's Church*

1:281 (bapt. Mar. 19, 1865; other sponsors, Maggie Howell and "Mrs. Lyons"), 2:369, 590.

73. VHD to MBC, Apr. 7, 1865, and Nov. 20, 1864 in *Chesnut,* 786 and 675, quots. (see also 666–67; ref. to Byron, "Lara" 1.2); Lee to Wife, Sept. 5, 1864 (*Wartime Papers,* 851, quot.); N. D. Smith, "Reminsc. of JD," 179; Burchenal, "Yankee Girl," 17; T. Hill, "Victory in Defeat," 34.

74. JD to F. Lawley, July 8, 1864 (Rowland 6:285, quot.; see Strode, *President,* 429); JD, *Rise and Fall* 2:556–59, quots.; Reagan to JD, Feb. 7, 1878 (Rowland 8:78–79); King, *Wigfall,* 196–97; Butler, *Judah P. Benj.,* 340–41 (quots. from Benj., Dec. 9, 1863).

75. JD to Bragg, July 9, 1864 (Rowland 6:286); Ben Hill to Walthall, Oct. 12, 1878, MS, TULANE, quots.; JEJ, *Narrative,* 362–63, 352; JD-JEJ corr., July 8 and 11, 1864 (*O. R.* 38 [Part 5]: 868–69, 875–76; see [Part 3]: 619–20, 30 [Part 2]: 21). RR lines were quickly repaired: S. Foote, *C. W.* 3:319, 337, 357, 520, 521; Castel, *Decision in West,* 562–63; Horn, *Army of Tenn.,* 473 n.12.

76. Ben Hill to Walthall (as in Note 75 above), quots. (Roddey led cav. [Warner, *Gens. in Gray*]); JD to Brown in JEJ, *Narrative,* 361, quot.; Henry, *"First with the Most" Forrest,* 286–307 (quots. on 307; see 306, 307–27, 343, 345, 348). Morgan was in Richmond early 1864, but others seem not to have known JD approved Ky. raid (Ramage, *Rebel Raider,* 206; Holland, *Morgan and His Raiders,* 294, 298, 302–4, 311–12, 318–19).

77. Ben Hill to Walthall (as in Note 75 above), quot.; JEJ, *Narrative,* 347 (crossed July 9). JEJ thought S. D. Lee had 16,000 (Hill and *O. R.* 38 [Part 5]: 868–69). See 1864 summaries by Seddon and Hill: ibid. 52 (Part 2): 693–95 and 704–7.

78. JEJ, *Narrative,* 366; Hardee to Mary [Lewis Hardee], June 19 and June 5, 1864, quots. (copies in Hardee Papers, ADAH); Little, "Gen. Hardee and Atlanta," 19–20; Ben Hill to Walthall (as in Note 75 above), quots. (cf. Rowland 6:346); Losson, *Cheatham,* 140–41. See Alfriend, *Life of JD,* 566–72.

79. JD to Bragg, Oct. 29, 1863 (Rowland 6:71, quot.); Ben Hill to Walthall (as in Note 75 above), quots.; Roy, "Gen. Hardee and Atlanta," 376–78 (JD quot., 1880: Hardee "old reliable" had "previously declined").

80. Ben Hill to Walthall (as in Note 75 above), quots.; Ben Hill to JEJ, July 14, 1864 (*O. R.* 38 [Part 5]: 879, quot.). See Seddon to Walthall, 1879 (Rowland 8:349–54); Hill, 1874, in *SHSP* 14:498: "agony" in JD's face, etc.; Hill did not advise removal, as some charged. One was Alexander, who knew JD was not "prejudiced" against JEJ (*Fighting for Conf.,* 468).

81. Ben Hill to Walthall (as in Note 75 above), quot. (Atlanta:) JD, *Rise and Fall* 2:556–57; Oladowski in *O. R.* 38 (Part 5): 864–65; Seitz, *Bragg,* 322–23; JEJ, *Narrative,* 332; JD to Lyons, Rowland 7:517–18 (also states his whole position, confirming Seddon and Hill).

82. JD to Lee, July 12, 1864 (ibid. 6:291–92, quot.; also July 13; italics=coded words); Lee to JD, July 12 (*Wartime Papers,* 821–22, quot.; advises all cav. on line; "must risk much" to save city).

83. Quots.: Bragg to JD, July 15, 1864 (*O. R.* 38 [Part 5]: 881); JD-JEJ corr., July 16 (ibid., 882–83); JD to Seddon, Aug. 18, 1874 (Rowland 7:396); Seddon to JD, June 17, 1872 (ibid., 320). G. W. Smith, head of Ga. militia, said it could not have held Atlanta 24 hours (Hood, *Advance and Retreat,* 147).

84. Quots.: Cooper to JEJ, July 17, 1864 (*O. R.* 38 [Part 5]: 885); JEJ to Cooper, July 18 (ibid., 888); Ben Hill to Walthall, (as in Note 75 above). See *O. R.* 38 (Part 3): 620; B. T. Johnson, *JEJ,* 290; *Chesnut,* 730 (see 616, 622–24); John P. Dyer, *The Gallant Hood,* 253.

85. King, *Wigfall,* 197; JEJ, *Narrative,* 350, quot. (see Castel, *Decision in West,* 538); Wright, *Southern Girl,* 178–79 (quots.), 181–86.

86. T. J. Walker, "Reminiscences of the Civil War," ed. Russell S. Bailey, in *Confederate Chronicles of Tennessee* 1 (June 1986): 60–62; JEJ, *Narrative,* 367–69; S. Foote, *C. W.* 3:420–24.

87. Hood, *Advance and Retreat,* 125–28; Corr. between Gens. and JD, July 18, 1864 (Ridley, *Battles and Sketches,* 321–22, and Rowland 6:295–96, quots.).

88. JD to H. V. Johnson, Sept. 18, 1864 (Rowland 6:336–38, quot.); Hood, *Advance and Retreat,* 190 (quot. from Gen. F. P. Blair [Jr.]); Dyer, *Gallant Hood,* 253–70 (quot. on 261–62); Castel, *Decision in West,* 365–414, 425–43, 458–75, 485–507, 509–25; S. Foote, *C. W.* 3:422–24, 472–92, 520–30; Montgomery, *Howell Cobb's Conf. Career,* 122–23.

89. Hardee to JD, Aug. 3 (quot.) and Aug. 6, 1864, and JD to Hardee, Aug. 4 (quot.) and Aug. 7 (copies in Hardee Papers, ADAH); Hardee to Cooper, Apr. 5, 1865, in Roy, "Gen. Hardee and Atlanta," 338, quot.; JD corr. Aug. 5–Sept. 16 (Rowland 6:305, 307, 334–35); S. Foote, *C. W.* 3:423; Hood, *Advance and Retreat,* 162, 249. In 2d Cav., Hardee had been maj., Hood 2d lt.

90. Hardee to Mary, Aug. 17, 1864, quots. (copy in Hardee Papers, ADAH; Hardee 48, she 26 [gravestones, Live Oak Cemetery, Selma, Ala.]; see Hughes, *Gen. Hardee,* 243–45 and quots. from Johnstons in Ross, *First Lady,* 211).

91. Hood, *Advance and Retreat,* 168, 171, 183–92, 205–6, 248–55; JD to Hardee, Sept. 16 (Rowland 6:334–35, quots.); JD to Roy, 1880, in Roy, "General Hardee," 376–78. See *Chesnut,* 652–53.

92. JD to Hood, to Seddon, to Bgd., Sept. 28, Oct. 2, Nov. 1 (Rowland 6:344–45, 348–49, 368); Frank Vandiver, "Jefferson Davis—Leader without Legend," 11, quot.; Williams, *Bgd.,* 239–42; *Conf. Soldier,* 345–46 (Taylor's Dept. is Miss.-Ala.-E. La.).

93. Hood, *Advance and Retreat,* 245 (JD quot.); JD speech, Augusta, Ga. (Rowland 6:356–61, quots. from rpt. Oct. 10; other speeches, 341–56); JD to E. K. Smith, Sept. 29 (ibid., 348); Escott, *After Secession,* 219 and n.42; Long, "JD," 7 (Adams quot.). See Gen. F. P. Blair in Hood, 190; Lee in *Wartime Papers,* 433, 868; Castel, *Decision in West,* 446.

94. JD, *Rise and Fall* 2:563–69 (and map after 764); Hood, *Advance and Retreat,* 229–42, 253–64; Horn, *Army of Tenn.,* 369 (Sherman quots. *re* Atlanta), 374–78; JD to H. V. Johnson, Sept. 18, 1864 (Rowland 6:336–38); JD to LBN, Sept. 25, 1879 (ibid. 8:415–19; plan in detail); S. Foote, *C. W.* 3:618, map.

95. Sherman to Grant, Oct. 9, 1864 (*O. R.* 39 [Part 3]: 162, quots.; see Grant, *Memoirs* 1:347–48, and S. D. Lee to Walthall, July 20, 1878, MS, TULANE).

96. Horn, *Army of Tenn.,* 378–83 (Sherman left Nov. 16); Hood, *Advance and Retreat,* 94, 263–81 (JD quot. on 273); plan formed Oct. 15–16, approved by Bdg. Oct. 21, proving false Sherman's claim that JD's speeches, Sept. 28–Oct. 5, tipped him off to Hood's Tenn. move (*Memoirs* 2:344–50), as do his own dispatches: see S. Foote, *C. W.* 3:610–11.

97. *Chesnut,* 644–52 (quots. 650–52; see 698; see Index for Hood-Preston romance); Dyer, *Gallant Hood,* 274–75; JD, Speech (Rowland 6:349–56, quots. from rpt. Oct. 6, 1864; see 444); Elizabeth Muhlenfeld, *Mary Boykin Chesnut: A Biography,* 58, 116, 120, pic. of house after 73.

98. [Varina Davis], "Christmas in Conf. White House," quots. (VHD a "manager" for orphanage; see Rowland 8:520–21). Lower back room of church (which was on a hill) served as parish house until 1923 (Weddell, *St. Paul's* 1:78–79, 192; 2:574–78; orphanage: 1:131, 148, 194–95).

99. VHD to JD, Dec. 25, 1865, MS, ALA, quot. (ref. to Matt. 2:18); Seitz, *Bragg,* 476; *Pendleton,* 378–79; Miers, *Jones Diary,* 460–62 and 464, 472; Rowland 6:418, 439; H. D. Riley, "JD and His Health," 279.

100. JD to VHD, Nov. 3–4, 1865, MS, TRANSYL, quot. (ref. to mil. "operations in Ga. and Ala."); *Pendleton,* 380 (quot., letter Dec. 19, 1864).

101. JD to LBN, Sept. 25, 1879 (Rowland 8:415–19, quot.); McMurry, *John Bell Hood,* 188 (quot., Hood to JD); Hood, *Advance and Retreat,* 198–99, 268–311, 317–37 ("popular error" that JD ordered move); Horn, *Army of Tenn.,* 394–423 (quot., Hood to army); Dyer, *The Gallant Hood,* 285–304; Scharf, *Hist. C.S. Navy,* 551–91; S. Foote, *C. W.* 3:492–508; A. Bergeron, *Conf. Mobile,* 138–51; Hughes, *Gen. Hardee,* 280 n.21.

102. Sherman to Grant, Oct. 9, 1864 (*O. R.* 39 [Part 3]: 162, quot.); Seitz, *Bragg*, 475; S. Foote, *C. W.* 2:936–40, 3:640–54, 711–14; Hallock, *Bragg and Defeat*, 225–27; JD in Rowland 6:407, 410–17 (see 8:376); Grant, *Memoirs* 2:359–76.

103. Dyer, *Gallant Hood*, 305–7; Miers, *Jones Diary*, 474, 476 (quots.; see Seitz, *Bragg*, 474–75), 482; Yearns, *Conf. Congress*, 225–35 (quot. on 228; see 157–60).

104. Miers, *Jones Diary*, 481, 485; Vandiver, *Their Tattered Flags*, 297–98; Hay, "Lucius B. Northrop," 17–21; Moore, *Northrop*, 229, 236–54, 260–67, 270–82; "Resources of the Confederacy in 1865," 107 (quot.), 97–98, 100–101; JD to LBN, Aug. 30, 1880, and Mar. 3, 1885 (Rowland 8:492 and 9:349, quots.; see JD, *Rise and Fall* 1:303 and Alfriend, *Life of JD*, 550n).

105. King, *Wigfall*, 205–9 (quot. on 207); Butler, *Judah P. Benj.*, 348–52; JD to Cong., Nov. 7, 1864 (Rowland 6:394–97); JD to Forsyth, Feb. 21, 1865 (ibid., 482, quot.; impressment on 456).

106. Lee-JD corr., Mar. 10–Apr. 2 (Vandiver-McWhiney, *Lee's Dispatches*, 373–74 and nn.; Rowland 6:513, 526; *Wartime Papers*, 927); Escott, *After Secession*, 240–55 (quot. on 253); *Black Southerners in Gray*, ed. Richard Rollins (Murfreesboro: Southern Heritage Press, 1994), 26–28.

107. King, *Wigfall*, 210–13 (quot.; says JD vetoed bill; not in Richardson *Conf.* 1, and Henry, *Story of Conf.*, 448, says JD "approved" it); *SHSP* 52:190; Richardson, *Conf.* 1:570.

108. JD, *Rise and Fall* 2:631; Yearns, *Conf. Cong.*, 227–28; *Wartime Papers*, 892–93; Freeman-McWhiney, *Lee's Dispatches*, 271–360 passim (also xx); Rowland 6:452–526 passim; Freeman, *R. E. Lee* 3:533–34, 4:55 (see *Letters*, 469–70); W. Taylor, *Gen. Lee*, 252–65.

109. Donald, *Sumner and Rights*, 189; Randall, *C. W.*, 618–24; W. Taylor, *Gen. Lee*, 263; Nuermberger, *Clays of Ala.*, 250–51, 260; JD, *Rise and Fall* 2:612–20 (quot. on 617); AHS, *Const. View* 2:599–619; Grant, *Memoirs* 2:420–23; Rowland 6:465–78 (Lincoln quot. on 478); Hill in *SHSP* 14:498–99.

110. VHD to JD, Feb. 4, 1878 (*Letters*, 468–70, quot.); E. Barksdale to Walthall, Aug. 3, 1878 (Rowland 8:246–47); JD speech, 1864 (ibid., 6:359, quots.).

111. JD to E. L. Drake [1878] in Edwin L. Drake, ed., *The Annals of the Army of Tennessee*, 213, quots.; Alexander, *Fighting for Conf.*, 503, quot. (see Chalmers in Rowland 8:197).

112. Rowland 8:128 (Lubbock quot.); Alfriend, *Life of JD*, 596–97. See *When the World Ended: The Diary of Emma LeConte*, ed. Earl Schenck Miers (New York: Oxford Univ. Press, 1957), 66, 76–77, 85, 90–91; Lankford, *Irishman in Dixie*, 67–68.

113. Miers, *Jones Diary*, 491–96 (quots.); *New York Times*, Feb. 10, 1865, p. 1 (RPR of Richmond papers: Benj., *Examiner*); *SHSP* 4:306; Butler, *Judah P. Benj.*, 350–51; *Hill*, 45, 273–93; Thompson, *Robert Toombs*, 216–17.

114. JD to govs. of N. C. and Fla., Feb. 21, 1865 (Rowland 6:483); Vandiver, *Their Tattered Flags*, 292–93, 299; Pryor, *Reminsc. of Peace and War*, 329 (Lee quot.); Alfriend, *Life of JD*, 605–13; Yearns, *Conf. Cong.*, 180–83; Reagan, *Memoirs*, 172–74; AHS, *Recollections*, 241 (quot.), 85.

115. Fuller, *Grant and Lee*, 238; Early, *Memoirs*, 459–69; Early to *The State* [1888] (Rowland 10:31).

116. Miers, *When World Ended* (as in Note 112 above), xi–xiii, 42–69 (quots. on 67 and 46; see *SHSP* 8:202–14); JD, *Rise and Fall* 2:625–29, 632–34 (and see Rowland 9:22–23); *Chesnut*, 715, 708, 725; Symonds, *JEJ*, 339, 341–42, 345 (map); Hughes, *Gen. Hardee*, 275–80.

117. JD, *Rise and Fall* 2:644–46; Alexander, *Fighting for Conf.*, 503–4, 511; Seitz, *Bragg*, 463–516 (quot. on 513), 522 (quot.); *O. R.* 42 (Pt. 3): 1218; Hallock, *Bragg and Defeat*, 220–52 (see Vandiver, *Gorgas Diary*, 158); Miers, *Jones Diary*, 485, 488.

118. Vandiver, *Tattered Flags*, 295–96; S. Foote, *C. W.* 3:768–70; Symonds, *JEJ*, 341–43; Miers, *Jones Diary*, 484, quot. (paraphrase of *King Lear* 3.6.62); JD, *Rise and Fall* 2:631, quot.

119. Winters, *C. W. in La.*, 415; Hallock, *Bragg and Defeat*, 249–50, 255–56; Rowland 6:427–28, 456–58, 509–11, 521.

120. JD to Phelan, Mar. 1, 1865, and Paper, Feb. 18 (ibid., 491–503); JD to Henry, Apr. 21 (ibid., 557, quots.; see Hood, *Advance and Retreat*, 65–67).

121. *Chesnut*, 725, 729 (quot., paraphrasing JEJ), 730; Symonds, *JEJ*, 343–44 (JEJ quot.); Govan and Livingood, *Different Valor*, 347 (JEJ quots.).

122. Williams, *Bgd.*, 252–53; Lee to Breck. and JD, Feb. 19–23, 1865, and to JD Mar. 14 (*Wartime Papers*, 904–6, 909–10 [quot.], 914–15); JD to Lee, Bgd., and Gilmer, Feb. 18–24 (Rowland 6:481–84); S. Foote, *C. W.* 3:790–92, 798–800.

123. Symonds, *JEJ*, 344–52; Hallock, *Bragg and Defeat*, 250–54; Bridges, *Lee's Maverick*, 269–72; Hughes, *Gen. Hardee*, 275–94 (JEJ quot. on 288); JD to Lee, Mar. 22, 1865 (Rowland 6:520, quots.); Seitz, *Bragg*, 513–22 (Bragg quots. on 522).

124. Seitz, *Bragg*, 521–22 and 524 (quots. from Bragg and JD, Mar. 26 and Apr. 1, 1865); Lee to JD, Mar. 26 (*Wartime Papers*, 916–18); Gordon, *Reminsc. of C. W.*, 393 (Lee quot.); T. R. R. Cobb in *SHSP* 28:284, quot. (but see JD in Rowland 6:338: "my need of assistance . . . thankful for well-meant advice"); Fuller, *Grant and Lee*, 238–39.

125. Minnigerode in *Life and Reminisc.*, 234; JD to VHD, Apr. 5, 1865 (Rowland 6:532, quot.); Weddell, *St. Paul's* 2:591–92; C. C. Harrison, *Recoll. Grave and Gay*, 207, quot.; JD, *Rise and Fall* 2:667–68, quot.; Freeman, *Cal. Conf. Papers*, 250–53. Antecommunion: first part of communion service.

126. JD to VHD, Apr. 5 and 23, 1865 (Rowland 6:532–33, 559–62, quots.; author takes the bust to be of Sam, but there was one of JD [DeLeon, *Belles*, 280], *Heroes of the Valley* unknown); Mary W. Rhodes to JD, Sept. 4, 1881 (Rowland 9:15, quots.; see Freeman, *R. E. Lee* 3:209–10 and house, 262); Mary C. Lee to JD [1865] (*Letters*, 250, quot.).

127. JD to VHD, Apr. 5 and 23, 1865 (Rowland 6:532–33, 559–62; quot. on 533); Davies in *Life and Reminisc.*, 42–43; Lubbock, *Six Decades*, 563; Sterling, *Belle*, 226–27, 241–45; Nuermberger, *Clays of Ala.*, 262–64.

128. John H. Brubaker 3, *The Last Capital: Danville, Virginia, and the Final Days of the Confederacy* (Danville: Danville Mus. of Fine Arts and History, 1979), 19–35, 45, 67–68 (copy preserved here may be one Benj. made for printers; see Rowland 8:70) 71–72; Avary, *Dixie after War*, 49–50; JD, *Rise and Fall* 2:668, 676–78 (quot.); JD to Lee, Apr. 9, 1865 (Rowland 6:541–42).

129. JD to W. Newton, Mar. 3, 1865 (ibid., 503–4, quot.); JD, Procl. ("Address"), Apr. 4 (Richardson, *Conf.* 1:568–70, quots.). See Freeman, *R. E. Lee* 4:3 n.7 (Lee says retreat from Petersburg not "necessarily fatal to our success").

130. Lee, *Recoll. and Letters*, 157; (Quots.:) BNH, "Capture," 239; Duke to Walthall, Apr. 6, 1878 (Rowland 8:158); JD to VHD, Apr. 23, 1865 (ibid. 6:560); JD, *Rise and Fall* 2:681; Duke, *Hist. Morgan's Cav.*, 575–76.

Chapter XVII Prisoners

1. The narrative picks up where chap. 1 left off (maid, Pritchard, and Hudson are there). VHD, *Memoir* 2:648–50; Sterling, *Belle*, 261–67, quots. (McElroy, *JD* 2:705, says garments in Conf. Mus.); *O. R.*, 2, 8:569–71 (quot. on 570; see also 555).

2. VHD, *Memoir* 2:649, quots. (uniform pic. facing 650 and T. Hill, "Victory in Defeat," 34); JD to C. J. Wright, Apr. 18, 1878 (Rowland 8:177, quot.; for an album, see *Life and Reminisc.*, 123–26). Memminger gave JD the 1861 coin, which "reappeared" 1961; in 1995 $1 million was asked for it (*Nashville Tennessean*, Mar. 29, 1995; clipping courtesy Guerry C. McComas).

3. VHD, *Memoir* 2:649, quot. (see Craven, *Prison Life*, 77–78); JD, *Rise and Fall* 2:704–5, quots.; VHD to capt. of the British *Clyde* [not their steamer], May 23, 1865 (Rowland 7:21–22, quot.; husband "sick" when taken).

4. BNH to Blair, May 22, 1865 (ibid., 20–21); VHD to Blair, June 6, in Ross, *First Lady,* 253–54, quots. (Blair did go to see President Johnson [262]).

5. Grant to Halleck and Meade, May 19, 1865 (*O. R.* 46 [Part 3]: 1174, 1175, quots., and see 1191, 1192); Miles in Warner, *Gens. in Blue;* VHD, *Memoir* 2:650, quots; Sterling, *Belle,* 267, quot. (Miles did write in June [292–3]). JD only heard of Lincoln's death 5 days later (Rowland 6:551).

6. Halleck to Miles, May 22, 1865 (*O. R.*, 2, 8:565); Stanton to Halleck, May 21 (ibid., 562); Miles to Dana, May 25 and Dana to Hunter, May 31 (ibid., 573 and 585–86); Sterling, *Belle,* 270 (quots.), 271–72 (Holt, judge advocate general of U.S. Army).)

7. Stanton-Halleck-Miles-Dana corr., May 19–24, 1865 (*O. R.*, 2, 8:559–60, 565–66, 570–71 [quiot.]); JD, *Rise and Fall* 2:705, quot.; VHD to Craven, Oct. 10, in Craven, *Prison Life,* 333–35, quots. (whole letter 331–48; JD put one "X" in Eckert, 121–27); see VHD, *Memoir* 2:650–51, 708–17; VHD to JD, Sept. 14, MS, ALA, quots.

8. VHD to Craven (as in Note 7 above), 335, quots.; Sterling, *Belle,* 274–76, quots. See VHD in E. Rowland, *Varina,* 459–60.

9. VHD to Craven (as in Note 7 above), 337–39, quots.; Stanton to Halleck, May 19 and 20 (*O. R.*, 2, 8:559–60, 561–62); Halleck to Miles, May 22 (ibid., 566, quot.); JD to VHD, Oct. 20 and Sept. 26, 1865, MSS, TRANSYL, quots.

10. VHD to Craven (as in Note 7 above), 339–40; VHD to JD, Sept. 14, 1865 (MS, ALA, quot.); *The Southern Cross* [paper of Savannah diocese], Sept. 16, 1965 (quot. from VHD to W. M. Green *re* money; photocopy in Strode Papers, ALA); Hughes, *Gen. Hardee,* 306. Name of order 1865 and ident. of paper and school from Sr. Charlene Walsh, R.S.M., to author, Mar. 24, 1986.

11. VHD to Craven (as in Note 7 above), 341–42, quots. There was continual public cry for JD's death (Claude G. Bowers, *The Tragic Era: The Revolution after Lincoln,* 11, 17, 22).

12. VHD to Craven (as in Note 7 above), 341–44, quots. (she asked to go to Augusta and was refused; then sent children away); VHD to JD [Dec. 14, 1865] (*Letters,* 215–16, quots.; says sentinel also threatened Jeff Jr.); JD to VHD, Feb. 3–4, 1866, MS, TRANSYL, quot.

13. VHD to JD, Oct. 1, 1865, MS, ALA (quots.); *Papers* 2::16, n.2; Ibid. 1:App. 4, Chart 14; King, *War-Time Jnl. of Ga. Girl,* 160 (quot. *re* Ma); VHD to JD, June 5, 1862, quot. (MS, Davis Family Collection, MDAH); *Chesnut,* 789, quot.; VHD to Craven (as in Note 7 above), 344–47, quots.

14. VHD to Craven, 344–47 quots.; *Conf. Soldier,* 313 (see Rowland 6:528); VHD to JD, Oct. 23, 1865, MS, ALA; VHD to Mrs. H. Cobb, Sept. 9 (Phillips, *Corr. of Toombs,* 668).

15. Sterling, *Belle,* 275, quot.; Ross, *First Lady,* 258, quot.; VHD to Craven, June 1, 1865, in Craven, *Prison Life,* 88–89, quots. (JD, Eckert 31, corrected "has" to "have"). For Craven, see Chester D. Bradley, "Dr. Craven and the Prison Life of Jefferson Davis," passim, esp. 79–88.

16. VHD to Blair, June 6, 1865, in Ross, *First Lady,* 261, quot. (Blair promised to do anything he could).

17. VHD to Craven, June 14, 1865, in Craven, *Prison Life,* 142–45, quots. (JD in Eckert, 53: "Dr. Craven did not reply . . . and though private has published").

18. VHD to Craven, July 2, 1865, in Craven, *Prison Life,* 169–71, quots. (speaks of 3 previous letters; only 2 are printed; "present help" from Psalm 46:1). Craven took pains to assure readers that he was a Unionist and Republican (ibid., 19).

19. VHD to JD, Jan. 22, 1866, MS, ALA, quot.; *Harper's,* Oct. 1865; Ross, *First Lady,* 268 (quots. from VHD; Browning a poetess, Yonge a fiction writer [Albert C. Baugh, *Lit. Hist. of England,* 1403–4, 1370n]).

20. *Christian's Mistake* (New York: Harper and Bros., 1865), signed "VHD / Oct 19th 65 / Mill View" (Rosenstock; author "Dinah Maria Mulock, Mrs. Craik" [Baugh, *Lit. Hist. of England,* 1370n]); *Letters,* 81 (VHD quot., 1856); VHD to M. Levy, [Aug. or Sept.] 1865 in E. Rowland, *Varina,* quots. (refs. to Prov. 13:12 and

Tennyson, "Break, break, break"; Mary E. Braddon wrote *Lady Audley's Secret* in 1862 [Baugh, 1353n]).

21. Ross, *First Lady*, 262–68 (VHD to JD, Nov. 7, 1865, MS, ALA, mentions the $700); *O. R.*, 2, 8:666 (VHD to Meigs, June 17, 1865), 683–84 (quots. from Meigs; does send word that JD's health is better).

22. VHD to Shea, July 14, 1865, in E. Rowland, *Varina*, 456–62, quots. (Shea had talked to Charles O'Conor about JD's defense: see Rowland 7:488n); Ross, *First Lady*, 264 (quot. from VHD to Seward, July 10).

23. VHD to Greeley, June 22, 1865, in E. Rowland, *Varina* 2:462–64, quot. (not "all" archives were held: see text below; but also *O. R.*, 2, 8:848). For Greeley, see Randall, *Civil War*, 92.

24. Benj. to Sister, Aug. 1, in Butler, *Judah P. Benjamin*, 369, quots. JD said, 1888, her "fears that the cruel treatment" would "speedily" bring death were "well founded" (Rowland 10:55).

25. Ross, *First Lady*, 268; JD to VHD, Aug. 21, 1865, MS, TRANSYL, quot. The "Fortress Monroe" heading on all prison letters is hereafter omitted. Ordinarily a reading is simply that arrived at by the author; the reason for brackets, which refer to preceding word unless otherwise noted, will appear later. Comparison of letter in text and in *Letters*, 168–70, reveals the silent omissions, inversions, and insertions that mark all Strode's editing; cf. VHD, *Memoir* 2:703–6 (she is usually more accurate and indicates omissions).

26. Only "inspection" by James Speed required (*O. R.*, 2, 8:719), but JD's letters read by Miles, and those in War Office: see Miles to E. D. Townsend, ibid. 769–70, and JD in Craven, *Prison Life*, 358–59.

27. "Brother Jos:"=Joseph E. Davis. For Sam and Bob see *Papers* 6:136–37. JD speaks of them to VHD, Sept. 15, Oct. 11–12, Oct. 20, 1865, MSS, TRANSYL, and on Apr. 23, says, "The only yearning heart in the final hour [in Richmond] was poor old Sam, wishing for 'Pie Cake'" (Rowland 6:561–62).

28. Smith place: see VHD, *Memoir* 2:704n; *Letters*, 341 (sold 1870). JD Sept. 15, 1865, says, "All incomplete transactions had better be cancelled, as the means which I possessed when they were entered into have been destroyed, and it only is possible to meet the moral obligation" (MS, TRANSYL).

29. Sisters living: Anna (Anne), Lucinda, and Amanda (*Papers* 1:App. 4; wants VHD to "explain the silence on my part" [Sept. 15, 1865, MS, TRANSYL]). It is clearly "V." after "Jeff:" but must be mistake for "D.": see chap. 1 above.

30. Ellen in chap. 1 above. On Robt., see JD in Craven, *Prison Life*, 215, 216: "had attended him through many serious illnesses" and "though a slave, had a moral nobility deserving honor"; JD in Eckert, 80–81, put "*among*" after "was" in: "Robert was the best and most faithful of his race."

31. James (Jim) Jones in chap. 1 above. See *SHSP* 41:21–22, 30; JD in Rowland 8:54; Walthall, "Capture," 118.

32. Psalm 27:16 from Psalter in *BCP* (1850), quoted from memory (it reads "shall" and "thine").

33. Prayer from Divine Liturgy of St. John Chrysostom (Eastern Orthodox Church) in Mg. and Ev. Prayer and the Litany, *BCP* (1850): full text in App. C. (JD cites it, Sept. 15, 1865: "I ask what in His wisdom it may be expedient for us to have" [MS, TRANSYL]). Winnie=Varina, Aunty=Marg. G. Howell (other nicknames in preface). "In my prayers you and the children form the little group, spiritually, assembled in our Heavenly Father's name"; "I daily bring them [the dear children] by memory together and . . . ask petitions for us according to our dear Saviour's promise" (JD to VHD, Sept. 15, 1865, Mar. 22, 1866, MSS, TRANSYL).

34. *Hymns*, #177 ("Guide me, O Thou Great Jehovah") VHD calls "our hymn" (Oct. 1, 1865, MS, ALA); #178 ("Following the Example of Christ") begins, "Whene'er the angry passions rise": see App. C. On *Hymns*, see Cheshire, *Church in C.S.*, 99.

35. Regtal.=Regimental; Pa. Art., replaced Nov. 1 by 5th U.S. Art. (Craven, *Prison Life*, 34, 74; 355, 357). JD named 2 chaplains, Dec. 2–3, 1865, MS, TRAN-

SYL; June 8, Stanton forbade Miles "again to admit Rev. Mr. Chevers . . . to see Mr. Davis" (*O. R.*, 2, 8:647). Mark L. Chevers was 1st post chaplain, 1828–75 (plaque on chapel organ).

36. Off. forbidden to show any courtesy: JD in Eckert, 121; Clay in Sterling, *Belle*, 298; Burchenal, "Yankee Girl," 17; M. B. Clarke, "Puritan Peculiarities," in *Land We Love* 1 (1866): 407.

37. Phrases from *BCP* (1850) prayer, "For a Person under Affliction" (see appendix C.; cf. JD, Nov. 26–27, 1865, MS, TRANSYL: " . . . happier as made better by the chastening correction of the merciful, loving Father"); on accusations of ambition, see McElroy, *JD* 2:533–34, 704 (under 12); *New York Times*, July 20, 1865, p. 4.

38. See chap. 1 above, and JD to VHD, Apr. 5, 1865 (Rowland 6:533). C. J. Wright, a lawyer, said, "rules of war were not observed"; Davis property "not liable to seizure . . . should be returned" (Rowland 8:143).

39. "God tempers the wind to the shorn lamb" was a popular adage (*Hoyt*, 644), but prob. JD knew it from its use in *A Sentimental Journey* by Laurence Sterne, a favorite author (he quoted him in the Senate in 1850 [Rowland 1:318]). "Mansions": John 14:2; "The peace of God, which passeth all understanding" (Phil. 4:7) began final blessing in communion service, *BCP* (1850).

40. VHD, *Memoir* 1:198, quot.; Craven, *Prison Life*, 222–23, 215–17, 219, 268, quots. (see *O. R.*, 2, 8:720); VHD to Shea, July 14, 1865, in E. Rowland, *Varina* 2:458, quot. Craven's book, though it has mistakes, remains a chief source for prison events from May to Dec. 1865 (see JD in *Papers* 1::1, p. lxiv and preface to notes above).

41. Craven, *Prison Life*, 26–29, quots.; *O. R.*, 2, 8:255 and Index ("state or political prisoners" distinct from POWs); C. A. Dana to Stanton, May 22, 1865 (ibid., 563–64, quots.); McElroy, *JD* 2:527; Bradley, "Dr. Craven," 77 n.82; Burchenel, "Yankee Girl," 18.

42. Craven, *Prison Life*, 40–41, 33, quots. On the account here (33–40), JD says in Eckert, 1–12: "fiction distorting fact," "coloring laid on," "Gross misrepresentation no part of the affair truthfully reported." Overblown style is typical of the man who helped Craven write the book: see William Hanchett, *Irish: Charles G. Halpine in Civil War America*.

43. McElroy, *JD* 2:527–30 (Titlow to son; errs in saying Mitchel there); *O. R.*, 2, 8:563–65 (Dana quots., May 22), 570–71 (Miles quot., May 24; hands "unencumbered": JD often mistakenly said "manacled"). Clay said JD "only grew violent when they offered to iron him"; Clay was never ironed (Sterling, *Belle*, 298–99, 293; see Bradley, "Dr. Craven," 77 n.82, showing another Titlow error).

44. McElroy, *JD* 2:527–30 (quots. from Titlow to son); VHD, *Memoir* 2:656, quot.; *O. R.*, 2, 8:564, 570 (Bible and *BCP;* see JD in Eckert, 9); Ibid., 12 ("The sergeant had no musket") seems to deny the struggle; but it is only JD's precision: guards in his room, *not* the sergeant and extra men, had muskets (McElroy, 529).

45. McElroy, *JD* 2:527–31 (quots. from blacksmith and Titlow); VHD, *Memoir* 2:657–58, quot. (gives variant end to scene). M. B. Clarke (as in Note 36 above), 408, rejected tears, as did JD (Eckert, 12), who also put "no" at "eyes filled with tears" in gratitude for removal of chains (ibid., 23). Tears were not, however, thought unmanly: Lee and his men shed them at Appomattox (R. E. Lee [Jr.], *Recoll. and Letters*, 153).

46. *Papers* 1::386 (Black Hawk quot.); *O. R.*, 2, 8:918 (*Richmond Times*, May 26, 1866; ref. to Ps. 105:18 in *BCP*); Stevenson, *Southern Side*, 285, quots.; McElroy, *JD* 2:530 (Titlow quots.); VHD to Titlow, Mar. 18, 1891, quot., in Bradley, "The Shackling of Jefferson Davis," and in Bradley, "Dr. Craven," 90 n.133 (see Titlow here and passim, esp. 75 n.79).

47. JD, *Rise and Fall* 2:705, quot.

48. JD to VHD, Sept. 15, 1865, and Feb. 3–4, 1866, MSS, TRANSYL, quots.; Craven, *Prison Life*, 54–58 (quot. on 56), 61–63 (JD notes in Eckert here not *re* this topic), 184, 219, 363 ("X" here in Eckert, 133). JD had no newspapers until end of

July (*O. R.* 2, 8:710), read unexplained and contradictory stories about children going to Canada (Sept. letter above); on Aug. 21, did not know where VHD was.

49. Craven, *Prison Life,* 264–66 (quots.; JD in Eckert, 98, rejects only cock-fighting), 327–28 (quot.); JD in Eckert, 120–21, quots. (see 129–30 and Note 36 above); Sterling, *Belle,* 299 (Clay quot.); JD to VHD, Sept. 15, 1865 (quots.), and Dec. 2–3 (novel), MSS, TRANSYL; Burchenal, "A Yankee Girl," 17–18 (JD quot.; see 45; her brother, Capt. S. A. Day, VHD calls a gentleman [*Memoir* 2:760–61]).

50. Craven, *Prison Life,* 50–52 and 56–57 (quots.), 65–67; Rowland 9:534–35 (quot., Craven citing); Weed to Stanton, May 29, 1865 (Rowland 7:26, quot.); VHD, *Memoir* 2:658 n., quot. (many still, 1890, do not believe it); Stanton to Miles, May 28, 1865 (*O. R.*, 2, 8:577; Miles's excuse: cell doors being replaced). A similar case in Starr, *Col. Grenfell's Wars,* 279–83.

51. Craven, *Prison Life,* 65–66, 32, 52–53 (also 48–49); Dana to Stanton, May 22, 1865 (*O. R.*, 2, 8:564, quot.); VHD, *Memoir* 2:661n, quots. (see JD in Eckert, 121); JD to VHD, Apr. 8–9, 1866, MS, TRANSYL, quots.

52. Craven, *Prison Life,* 234–35, 223–24, quots. (knife and fork allowed Aug. 25); JD quots. in Eckert, 87, 12 (also rejects "a tempting remedy for neuralgic torture"), 32. The preoccupation with suicide is interesting; Halpine, Craven's coauthor, died by his own hand (Hanchett, *Irish,* 177–78).

53. Craven, *Prison Life,* 223–24, 64 (JD quot.; ref. to Luke 10:30–37); VHD, *Memoir* 2:676n, quot.; medal seen in Casemate Mus., 1986 (man holds cross, "Crux S[ancti] P[atri] Benedicti" on rim; ident. for author by Abbé G. Marc'hadour); Quots. from note on medal by VHD, Nov. 2, 1904 (copy in R. Cody Phillips to author, May 29, 1985); W. C. Matthews to author, July 10; "The Medal or Cross of St. Benedict" (pamphlet of Liturgical Press, Collegeville, Minn.).

54. N. D. Smith, "Reminisc. of JD," 178, quots. (author takes this confused story to refer to same medal).

55. Miles-Halleck corr., Sept. 24, 1865 (*O. R.*, 2, 8:570); JD in Eckert, 13, 14 (rejects pipe scene in Craven, *Prison Life,* 43–44, as "Inaccurate" and "fanciful"; "pillage I had suffered" was reason for gift). This Meerschaum is in Conf. Mus., given by grandson of Craven (see T. Hill, "Victory in Defeat," 27); another is pictured in George E. Hicks brochure, "The Casemate Museum," 2.

56. Leml. Shipman to JD, July 10, 1889 (Rowland 10:126–27); Inventory, p.5; Craven, *Prison Life,* 151, 96–97 (quot., paraphrasing of JD; JD in Eckert, 34, objects to "trunks" ["had but one"] and to "sufferings he was undergoing would do him good with his people (the South)": "not my expression, but the writer's"); Sterling, *Belle,* 297–98 (Clay also robbed).

57. Sterling, *Belle,* 296–97 (Clay quot.; does not see even minister or physician alone); Hugh McCulloch, *Men and Measures of Half a Century,* 411 (JD quot.); Craven, *Prison Life,* 90 and 62, quots. (and see 30–31, 52); Strode, *Tragic Hero,* 242–43 (quots. from Pvt. Elisha Kisner, in newspaper story, which Strode warns may be fabrication).

58. Quots.: JD in Eckert, 32; Craven, *Prison Life,,* 116, 90–91 (paraphrasing JD); JD to VHD, Oct. 11, 1865, MS, TRANSYL.; Sterling, *Belle,* 296 (from Clay; see 294). On the ghastly power of total prevention of sleep, see Aleksandr I. Solzhenitzyn, *The Gulag Archipelago, 1918–1956,* 1–2 (New York: Harper and Row, 1974), 99, 100, 111–13, 182 and n.3, and Josef Cardinal Mindszenty, *Memoirs* (New York: Macmillan, 1974), 98–110, 119 (combined with other torture, it drew from him a false confession).

59. Craven, *Prison Life,* 146, quot.; Miles to E. D. Townsend [War Dept. A.A.G.], July 4 and June 25, 1865 (*O. R.*, 2, 8:695 and 673, quots.; see same to same, 744, Townsend to Miles, 673, and Miles to Smith, 657); Stanton to Miles, July 22, 1865 (ibid., 710–11); Sterling, *Belle,* 296 (Clay quot.).

60. Sterling, *Belle,* 296 (Clay quot.); Craven, *Prison Life,* 91–92, 63 (quots.) 74–76 (corrected by JD in Eckert, 32), 166–68 (JD quots.), 91–92, 214; (on eyes, see also: 67–73, 143, 146–53, 171, and JD in Eckert, 61–62, 23, 25, 53–56); *O. R.*,

2, 8:710–11; VHD, *Memoir* 2:767. Craven says (268) "guards and light" removed; but this rpt. in *O. R.*, 2, 8:740, lacks "and light"; see JD's comments in Eckert, 99.

61. JD to VHD, Oct. 20, 1865, MS, TRANSYL, quot.; VHD to JD, Dec. 25, 1865, and Feb. 2 and 8, 1866, MSS, ALA (quots. from Feb. 8; ref. to *Hymns* #143: "Jesus, Saviour of my soul" by Charles Wesley). She made several masks; black one in Conf. Mus.; see T. Hill, "Victory in Defeat," 26.

62. VHD to JD, Sept. 14, 1865, MS, ALA, quot. She alludes to Luke 21:19 (patience), Ps. 27:16, Gen. 32:24–32 (Jacob's sinew was shrunk and his name changed).

63. VHD to JD, Oct. 23, 1865, MS, ALA, quot.; Craven, *Prison Life*, 64–65; *O. R.*, 2, 8:747 (quots. from VHD's wire; telegram in reply).

64. JD to VHD, Sept. 15 and 26, 1865, MSS, TRANSYL, quots.; Dr. Riley thinks infection prob. "Group A hemolytic streptococcus" ("JD and His Health," 282); erysipelas sometimes fatal (Freeman, *Cal. Conf. Papers*, 556; Rowland 7:394).

65. Craven, *Prison Life*, [Aug. 14–Sept. 11] 214–19, 222–28, 235, 243, 254–56 (JD in Eckert here not *re* health), 266–69 (quot.; JD in Eckert, 99), 275, 291, 308 (describes illness almost exactly as JD does, which shows reality of his book); JD to VHD, Sept. 15, 1865, MS, TRANSYL, quot.

66. Ross, *First Lady*, 270 (VHD quots.).

67. Craven, *Prison Life*, 19, 171, 78, 255, quots.

68. Craven, *Prison Life*, 268, 23, 350 (quots.), 53–54, 269, 330; McCulloch, *Men and Measures*, 411, quot.; Dunham, *Attitude of Northern Clergy*, 177, quot.; VHD, *Memoir* 2:660n.

69. *O. R.*, 2, 8:710–12; Craven, *Prison Life*, passim, 162, 243–45 (see JD in Eckert, 99, 59, 90), 350 (quot.).

70. JD quots. in Eckert, 118 (on Craven, 321–22; JD speaks of the newspapers and the books, Oct. 11–12 and Nov. 3–4, 1865 MSS, TRANSYL). Bancroft, *Hist. of U.S.*, vols. 1–5 (Boston: Little-Brown and Co., 1852–56); Macaulay's *Hist.* (1848–61), Sir Archibald Alison's *Hist. of Europe* (1833–42), and *Hist. of the Rebellion and Civil Wars in England*, 3 vols., by Edward Hyde, Earl of Clarendon (1702–4) (Baugh, *Lit. Hist. of Eng.*, 1327–28, 1326, 787 n.13; see Clarendon in *Chesnut*, 7).

71. VHD, *Memoir* 2:718 n., 760 (quot.); Craven, *Prison Life*, 149–53 (beside "Miles supporting," JD put in Eckert, 56: "say watching" and see 99), 162, 189–90, 204–8 (quots. *re* anger; JD in Eckert, 76–77, rejects some points, but confirms incident by "such was my answer"), 151–54 (quot., paraphrasing JD); JD to VHD, Dec. 2–3, 1865, MS, TRANSYL; *O. R.*, 2, 8:710–12 (first walk July 24; Craven prior dates for walks, 151, are wrong).

72. Craven, *Prison Life*, 189–91, quots. (misdated; on their being separated for speaking French, JD says in Eckert, 70: "not correct," but see Clay in Sterling, *Belle*, 346); JD to VHD, Sept. 26 (in "P.S." written cross-hatch over first page), and Nov. 21–22, 1865, MSS, TRANSYL, quots.; Nuermberger, *Clays of Ala.*, 274; Sterling, *Belle*, 347 and n. (quot.).

73. JD to VHD, Sept. 26, 1865, MS, TRANSYL, quot.; Sterling, *Belle*, 294–97 (quots. from Clay, Aug. 11, Sept. 10, Oct. 16); Nuermberger, *Clays of Ala.*, 274.

74. Craven, *Prison Life*, 315 (quot.), 254–56, 275–76, 166–68 (quots.; JD quot. in Eckert, 62, an "X" on 61, 317 (quot.), 266–69 (quot. on 268; see Eckert 99), 183–84 (quots.), 305–6 (Eckert, 113: by "painfully fretful" JD put, "He always commended my calm resolution, etc."). "Duel with insanity" from incessant noise and light; "not a single moment" for sleep or privacy; "You were always being watched and always in their power" (Solzhenitsyn as in Note 58 above, 180–87).

75. Craven, *Prison Life*, 163–66 (quot.), 79–85 (quot. on 79, paraphrasing of JD), 91, 184, 214–15, 219–20, 224–27, also 122–24, 153 (see Eckert, 60–61, 28–29, 68, 80, 45); O'Conor-War Dept.-JD corr., June 2–17, 1865 (*O. R.*, 2, 8:634, 640, 642, 647, 655–58; see Rowland 7:37); O'Conor to Shea, Aug. 12 (Freeman, *Cal. Conf. Papers*, 450–51, quot.). See W. C. Davis, *Breck.*, 530.

76. *O. R.*, 2, 8:696–700 (quot.), 570–71, 566, 838–40 (Holt quots.), 660, 710 (JD quot.); Holt in *DAB;* C. C. Harrison, *Recoll.*, 228–37 (quot.; cell 4'x 8'), 240–42; Lubbock, *Six Decades*, 580–89; Shaw, *WPJ*, 84–86; Hanchett, *Lincoln Murder*, 70. See Douglas, *I Rode with Stonewall*, 324–33 and Starr, *Col. Grenfell's Wars*, 274–80.

77. McElroy, *JD* 2:536–39; Shea, "JD Letter," 7–8; VHD, *Memoir* 1:555–56; *O. R.*, 2, 8:763, 766; VHD to Greeley, June 22, 1865, in E. Rowland, *Varina* 2:462–64, quots. For JD and O'Conor in politics, see *Papers* 6:276–77 and n.2, and App. 1, 633 (Feb. 6); Lubbock, *Six Decades*, 280.

78. Shea, "JD Letter," 6–11 (quots. on 6, 8); VHD to Shea, July 14, 1865, in E. Rowland, *Varina* 2:456–62, quot. (has letter book, cannot trust it "in the Federal reach").

79. Shea, "JD Letter," 8–11 (quot. on 9); Shea to JD, Jan. 24, 1876 (Rowland 7:488–89); Strode, *Tragic Hero*, 266. From the nature of his escape, Breck. could not have taken C.S. papers to Canada, but someone else might have; many Southerners fled there (W. C. Davis, *Breck.*, 523–44, 548–51, 553–54).

80. Sterling, *Belle*, 271–72, 337–39 and n., 346, (Clay quots.:) 294 and 298; Holt to Stanton, Jan. 18 and Dec. 15, 1866 (*O. R.*, 2, 8:848 and 976–77); Hanchett, *Lincoln Murder*, 71–73 (Bingham quot.; all evidence hearsay), 125–26; Holt, June 30, 1865 (*O. R.*, 2, 8:690, quots.); Craven, 79–80 (JD quot.).

81. Mary W. Rhodes to JD, Sept. 4, 1881 (Rowland 9:15, quot., paraphrasing a Dr. Simmons; Craven, *Prison Life*, 268–69, 275–76, 303–6 (see Eckert, 113), 314–15, 323–24 (JD quot.); VHD, *Memoir* 2:727 (quots. from JD to VHD, not Oct. 11 as stated, but composite from Oct. 20 and Nov. 3–4, and evidently JD's descr. of room "objected to," Nov. 21, and not in MSS, TRANSYL).

82. JD in Eckert, 130, quot.; *O. R.*, 2, 8:755–60, 761, 892–93 (quot.), 894, 897, 900.

83. *O. R.*, 2, 8:846, 897, 892 (quot.), 945 (quot.); Craven, *Prison Life*, 79–85 (see Eckert, 28, 29), 87, 153, 163–66 (Eckert, 60–61), 184 (Eckert, 68), 214–15 (Eckert, 80), 217, 219–20, 225, 317, 359, 361, 363 (Eckert, 133), 368 (Eckert, 136). Cf. Butler, *Judah P. Benj.*, 369.

Chapter XVIII An Unseen Hand

1. JD to VHD, Nov. 3–4, 1865, MS, TRANSYL, quot.; VHD, *Memoir* 2:444 n., quot.; Mitchel in *DAB; Papers* 6:125 and n.13; Lonn, *Foreigners in Conf.*, 154–55 and n.54; Roman, *Military Operations*, 170; Miers, *Jones Diary*, 175; *O. R.*, 2, 8:641, 653, 657, 715–16, 725, 775, 782.

2. Mitchel to VHD, Nov. 1, 1865 (Rowland 7:52–54, quots.). See Craven, *Prison Life*, 152.

3. Mitchel to VHD, Nov. 1, 1865 (Rowland 7:53, quot.), JD to VHD, Nov. 3, 1865, MS, TRANSYL, quot. On Nov. 21–22 (ibid.), he says the "local disease . . . changes the place but keeps the pain."

4. Craven, *Prison Life*, 352, 359–62, 330 (quots.; see JD in Eckert, 121), 189–90, 305; *O. R.*, 2, 8:758.

5. JD to VHD, Apr. 21–23, 1866, MS, TRANSYL, quots.; VHD to JD, Nov. 13, 1865, MS, ALA, quot.; JD to VHD, Nov. 21–22, MS, TRANSYL, quot. In Jan. 24, 1866, letter, ibid., "faithful Promiser" used as title; a "tract" of this name mentioned in Kerr, "Memorial of John Perkins," n.p.

6. JD to VHD, Jan. 24, 1866, MS, TRANSYL, quot.; JD to VHD, Nov. 21–22, 1865, ibid., quots.

7. VHD, *Memoir* 1:155–56 (quots.) and see 432, 2:884 (ref. to Matt. 6:25; see Luke 10:8; Gal. 5:22–23); Winnie Davis, "JD in Private Life," 8–9, quots.; Jones, *Davis Memorial*, 137 (quot. from J. Campbell); Kimball, *Richmond in Time of War*, 75. Chivalry strictly forbade "gluttony and intemperance" (G. P. R. James, *History of Chivalry*, 40).

8. VHD to JD, Nov. 7, 1865, MS, ALA; JD to VHD, Nov. 21–22, MS, TRANSYL, quot. (cf. Matt. 6:25, 28); VHD to JD, Mar. [8], 1866, MS, ALA, quot. (*Letters*, 236; here called fragment); JD to VHD, Mar. 22, MS, TRANSYL, quot.; JD to VHD in VHD, *Memoir* 2:727, quot. (see Craven, *Prison Life*, 327, 363; on date see above chap. 17, Note 81).

9. JD to VHD, Sept. 26, 1865, MS, TRANSYL, quot.; VHD to JD, Nov. 7, MS, ALA; Craven, *Prison Life*, 254–55, quot.; VHD to JD, June 5, 1862, quot. (MS, Adele Davis Collection, MDAH); JD to VHD, Nov. 3–4, 1865, MS, TRANSYL, quot.; VHD to JD, Nov. 27, MS, ALA, quot.; T. Hill, "Victory in Defeat," 27 (quot. from note in box lid); JD in Eckert, 14, quot.; JD had a "quantity of smoking and plug tobacco" and "six boxes of cigars" in his trunk (Hanna, *Flight*, 120–21).

10. JD to VHD, Dec. 7–8, Oct. 20, Sept. 26, 1865, MSS, TRANSYL, quots.; *O. R.*, 2, 8:712; AHS, *Recollections*, 132–33, 151–54, 258, 367–68, 389, 394, 437, 439, 457, 531 and passim (AHS had orderly, saw Reagan daily; released Oct. 12).

11. Quots.: JD to VHD, Nov. 21–22, 1865, MS, TRANSYL; VHD to JD, undated fragment, MS, ALA; JD to VHD, Oct. 20, 1865, Jan. 16, 1866 (memory "now down to zero"), Dec. 7–8, 1865, MSS, TRANSYL.

12. JD to VHD, Nov. 21–22, Oct. 11–12, 1865, and Feb. 17–19, 1866, MSS, TRANSYL, quots. ("If I were a believer in dreams my days would be spent in reviewing the visions of the night" [Oct.]; Feb. quot. begins at "but I"; ref. to Matt. 13:24–30).

13. JD to VHD, Feb. 3–4, 1866, MS, TRANSYL, quot.

14. Ibid., quot. In the family prayer that JD reads every evening, a petition for "refreshing sleep" is followed by: "Make us ever mindful of the time when we shall lie down in the dust" (*BCP* [1850]).

15. JD to VHD, Oct. 20, 1865, MS, TRANSYL, quot.; JD to VHD, Nov. 26, ibid.; JD to VHD, Dec. 2–3, ibid., quots.; McCulloch, *Men and Measures*, 410. Baron F. H. A. von Humboldt (1769–1835) was a German naturalist. For other works, see above chap. 17 and Note 70.

16. JD to VHD, Dec. 2–3, 1865, Apr. 21–23, Feb. 17–19, 1866, MSS, TRANSYL, quots.

17. Quots.: JD to VHD, Dec. 2–3 (1st and last quots.), Nov. 26–27, 1865, Apr. 21–23, 1866, MSS, TRANSYL; *Chronicles of the Schönberg-Cotta Family by Two of Themselves*, 324 (1st ed. 1863; 1866 ed. in Auburn Univ. Library has written in, "fictitious" and "Elizabeth Rundle Charles"; ident. also in ref. in *New York Times*, July 24, 1865). VHD owned two-vol. *Hist. of the Life, Writing and Doctrines of Luther* by M. Audin (London: C. Dolman, 1854) (Rosenstock).

18. VHD to W. M. Green, n.d., quot. (newspaper clipping in Strode Papers, Univ. of Ala.); VHD to JD [Oct. 1], 1865, MS, ALA, quot. (in *Letters*, 181–83 as fragment; author believes this and fragment on 179–80, dated Oct. 1, are one letter); VHD to JD, Oct. 2, MS, ALA; JD to VHD, Dec. 30, 1865–Jan. 1, 1866, MS, TRANSYL, quot.

19. VHD to JD, Oct. 2, 1865, MS, ALA (quoting Ma's letter); VHD to JD, Nov. 27, ibid., quot.; Nuermberger, *Clays of Ala.*, 234; JD to VHD, Dec. 7–8, Nov. 21–22, MSS, TRANSYL, quots. (ref. to Luke 10:29–37).

20. JD to VHD, Dec. 30, 1865–Jan. 1, 1866, MS, TRANSYL, quot. (clearly "Mx" and not "Ma"; "oh! most" written over erasure; refs. to Ps. 50:10, John 10:1–16 and 14:2–3); *BCP* (1850), quots. St. Paul does not use word "catholic"; but voices JD's very hope: God "will have all men to be saved" (I Tim. 2:4).

21. JD to VHD, Dec. 30, 1865–Jan. 1, 1866, MS, TRANSYL, quots. (quots. also in chaps. 3 and 5 above).

22. Joseph I. Dirvin, *Saint Catherine Labouré of the Miraculous Medal* (New York: Farrar, Straus and Cudahy, 1958), xii, 80–119; Craven, *Prison Life*, 289–90, quots. (Eckert, 107, rejects only a remark of Bsp. Lynch); medal and French scapular (few words legible) in Conf. Mus., N. O.; brown scapular in Conf. Mus., Richmond, with inscr. by VHD (inventory: in black leather wallet initialed "JD"; pics. sent author

Oct. 16, 1984, by Charlene S. Alling; author indebted to Sr. Anne Odile C.S.J., for data on all items).

23. Photograph, c. 9"x13" with inscr. attested by Card. Barnardo, Dec. 1866, in Conf. Mus., N. O.; N. D. Smith, "Reminisc. of JD," 178, quot. (she mentions a letter with it: unknown to author); *BCP* (1850), quot. Same pic. with diff. Latin inscr. dated Dec. 9, 1866, at Beauvoir; provenance unknown.

24. JD to Pius IX, Sept. 23, 1863, and appt. of Mann, Sept. 24 (Richardson, *Conf.* 2:570–72, quots.); Mann to Benj., Nov. 11, 14, 21, Dec. 9 (quot.), 12 (quot. from Pius IX to JD) (ibid., 589–604); Benj. to Mann, Feb. 1, 1864 (ibid., 622–24); Rhodes to JD, Sept. 4, 1881 (Rowland 9:16; Lee quot.). Others: H. W. Cleveland (ibid. 10:3–4), Geo. Bancroft (Charles L. C. Minor, *The Real Lincoln* [1904; RPR Harisonburg, Va.: Sprinkle Publications, 1992], 116).

25. JD to *Catholic Universe* [now defunct], Mar. 7, 1878, quot. (copied from clipping at Beauvoir); Crown of thorns at Conf. Mus., N. O.; Meneray to author, Aug. 6, 1985 (ident. crown); N. D. Smith, "Reminsc. of JD," 178; VHD to JD, Nov. 7, 1865, MS, ALA, quot. Strode mistakenly says (*Tragic Hero*, 302; *Letters*, 472) pope wove crown and sent it to JD (poss. because it hung in Conf. Mus. on pope's pic. with no ident., author's inquiry at Vatican fruitless).

26. Mary Lorenz (of Old Cap. Mus. of Miss. Hist., MDAH) to author, Feb. 8, Mar. 29, 1988, and Keith A. Hardison (of Beauvoir) to same, Mar. 15 (book loaned to Beauvoir by MDAH 1941; no trace since; given to MDAH 1911 [sources below and May, *J. A. Quitman*, 110, 352, 353]). Sources (author indebted to Lorenz for 1 and 3): 1) *New Orleans Picayune* clipping, Apr. 14 [1908?]; 2) *Conf. Vet.*, June 1908, 264 (very like 1; Violett quots.; wrong date for gift to her); 3) *Memphis News-Scimitar* clipping, Dec. 15, 1911; 4) McElroy, *JD* 2:616–17. Quots. from these are ident. by single mark ('), those in *Imitation* (1916) (see bibliography), by double ("). JD copy dated from Challoner in *Cath. Encycl.* and 1) (where his date is wrong).

27. Quots. from 1) in Note 26 above and *Imitation* (1916), 196–97.

28. Quots.: *Imitation* (1916), 204, 50, 82 and 84; JD to VHD, Nov. 21–22 and Dec. 7–8, 1865 (cf. Luke 22:42), and Jan. 28, 1866, MSS, TRANSYL.

29. *Imitation* (1916), 87, 221, 89–90, quots.; JD to VHD, Jan. 16, 1866, and Nov. 3–4, 1865, MSS, TRANSYL, quots.

30. *O. R.*, 2, 8:908 (JD must have given Cooper this descr.); JD speech, 1864 (Rowland 6:355, quot.); *Imitation* (1916), 87, 256, quots. (see McElroy, *JD* 2:616); Phil. 3:8–10, quots.; Virginia Frazer Boyle, "Jefferson Davis in Canada," 89.

31. I Peter 2:19–24, quot. (Lesson for 15th Sun. after Trinity in *BCP* [1850]; also reading for Aug. 17; JD always read these); JD to VHD, Sept. 26, 1865, MS, TRANSYL, quots. Headley's *Life of Washington*, 1862, contains this quot. from JD's hero: "I could offer myself a willing sacrifice" (73–74).

32. Jones, *Davis Memorial*, 480, quot.; JD to VHD, Feb. 17–19, 1866, MS, TRANSYL, quot.; JD to VHD, Feb. 3–4, ibid., quots.; *Imitation* (1916), 91, quot.

33. Holt to Stanton, Jan. 18, 1866 (*O. R.*, 2, 8:855, quots.); Hanchett, *Lincoln Murder*, 125–26 (Bingham quot.; see 68). See VHD to Shea, July 14, 1865, in E. Rowland, *Varina*, 456–57, *re* thinks Bingham's charge: "the real assassin *slain before a confession of his accomplices could be made.*"

34. Sterling, *Belle*, 337 and n., quots.; Benj. in Butler, *Judah P. Benj.*, 364, quot.; Clay to A. Johnson, Nov. 23, 1865 (*O. R.*, 2, 8:812–14); Holt in *DAB;* Lowry and McCardle, *Hist. of Miss.*, 594.

35. Sterling, *Belle*, 318–28 and nn.; JD to VHD, Nov. 3–4, 1865, MS, TRANSYL; *O. R.*, 2, 8:812–14, 847–61, 890–92, 931–45, 962–65 (see also 867–69, 876–80, 883–85); Hanchett, *Lincoln Murders*, 62–63, 74–78.

36. Hanchett, *Lincoln Murders*, 26–29, 63–65, 71–74, 78–82 (Campbell quot.); Cleary, "Attempt," 315, 324–25, quots.; *Clays of Ala.*, 278 (Procl. "living, burning lie"); Sterling, *Belle*, 321–28; AHS, *Recollections*, 216.

37. Hanchett, *Lincoln Murder*, 71–74, 78–82 (quots. from Holt and comm.);

David Miller DeWitt, *The Impeachment and Trial of Andrew Johnson, Seventeenth President of the United States: A History*, 136–42; Stevenson, *Southern Side*, 131; JD to VHD, Nov. 3–4, 1865, MS, TRANSYL, quot.; JD to VHD, (Jan. 24, 1866), MS, ALA, quots. (marked "1865," but ident. from internal evidence, MS, TRANSYL of this date), VHD, *Memoir* 2:745.

38. JD to VHD, Oct. 11–12, 1865, MS, TRANSYL, quot.; *BCP* (1850), quot.; F. W. Krummacher, *The Suffering Saviour: Meditations on the Last Days of Christ*, 206, quot. (see xiv–xv, xix–xx, 46, 225). The thought throughout this book is echoed in JD letters.

39. Lord Macaulay, *History of England from the Accession of James the Second*, ed. Charles Harding Firth (London, 1914; RPR New York: AMS Press, 1968) 2:554–58, quots.; *The Diary of Samuel Pepys* [London: J. M. Dent and Sons, Ltd., 1906] 1:256, 259, quots.; Krummacher, *Suffering Saviour*, 304, quot.

40. Craven, *Prison Life*, 256–60, quots. (style here smacks more of Halpine than JD, but there is no mark in Eckert, 95–96; ref. to Matt. 26:36–44; Mark 14:32–41; Luke 22:39–44; Gen. 22:1–18).

41. Craven, *Prison Life*, 193–94, quots. Burchenal ("Yankee Girl," 18) quotes Craven here, saying, "No one could become acquainted with Mr. Davis without soon realizing the deep sincerity of his religious convictions."

42. VHD to JD, [Oct. 1], 1865, MS, ALA, quot.; JD to VHD, Oct. 20, MS, TRANSYL, quot. *BCP* (1850): Mg. and Ev. Prayer distinct from the ones for "Families"; Collect (prayer), Epistle and Gospel (KJV) for Sundays and Holy Days printed in *BCP;* penitential Litany was "To be used after Morning Service" Sun., Wed., and Fri. (as JD does); other prayers mentioned in "Prayers and Thanksgivings upon Several Occasions": see appendix C.

43. JD to VHD, Nov. 26–27, 1865, MS, TRANSYL, quots.; *BCP* Psalter was divided by day of month, trans. by Miles Coverdale for Great Bible of 1541 (S. L. Greenslade, Intro. to *The Coverdale Bible, 1535* [facsimile RPR, Folkestone: Dawson, 1975]), 20–21; Bible readings were appt'd. for each day of both church year and calendar year. For dictionary, see App. C.

44. JD to VHD, Dec. 2–3, 1865, MS, TRANSYL, quot.; VHD, *Memoir* 2:718–19, prints parts, under Oct. 2; but "Dec." is in MS. *BCP* (1850): "Calendar" readings are Isa. 18 and Acts 12; "Dominical" ones, for church year, should be 1st Sun. in Advent (Dec. 3 in 1865), but he descr. Dan. 6 and John 8, which belong to 22nd Sun. after Trinity (Nov. 12). Perhaps he had the date, but missed the season by being without the Church.

45. Quots.: JD to VHD, Dec. 2–3, 1865; Apr. 21–23, 1866; Nov. 26–27, 1865, MSS, TRANSYL. Ref. to John 10:14; Matt 18:12–14.

46. Minnigerode, Address, Dec. 11, 1889 (Jones, *Davis Memorial*, 419–21, quots.); Weddell, *St. Paul's Church* 2:481–86 (M. jailed in 1830s for plotting revolt while at Univ. of Giessen); Minnigerode to Stanton, Nov. 28, 1865, with Endrs. (*O. R.*, 2, 8:818–19, quot.); Ibid., 821, 833–34; JD to VHD, Apr. 8, 1866, MS, TRANSYL.

47. Minnigerode, Address (Jones, *Davis Memorial*, 420–21, quots.); Weddell, *St. Paul's Church* 2:391–92 (quots. from Rev. W. M. Dame, as told him by Minnigerode). First Exhortation in *BCP* (1850) says to examine one's conscience, confess to God, and be "ready to forgive others," for otherwise "Holy Communion doth nothing else but increase your condemnation" (cf. I Cor. 11:26–31). See *The Private Chesnut*, 256.

48. JD to VHD, Dec. 2–3, 1865, and Jan. 28–29, 1866, MSS, TRANSYL, quots. (same sentiment in Feb. 3–4); VHD to Craven, Oct. 10, in *Prison Life*, 340, quot.; JD to VHD, Oct. 20, 1865, MS, TRANSYL, quots.

49. James Cahill to JD, Sept. 3, 1888 (Rowland 10:78, quot.); *BCP* (1850), quot.; JD to VHD, Dec. 30, 1865–Jan. 1, 1866, MS, TRANSYL, quot. (cf. Matt. 7:12; rest of sentence obliterated by X's).

50. Miles to Townsend, Dec. 29, 1865 (*O. R.*, 2, 8:841, encl. rpt. with JD quot.);

Townsend to Miles, Dec. 30 (ibid. 841–42); JD to VHD, Jan. 16–18, 1866, MS, TRANSYL, quot. Clay also called Miles "the ass" (Eckert, xxiv).

51. JD to VHD, Dec. 30, 1865–Jan. 1, 1866, MS, TRANSYL, quots. (ref. to Isa. 48:10); VHD to JD, Nov. 13 and 7, 1865, MSS, ALA, quots.

52. JD to VHD, Nov. 21–22 and Dec. 7–8, 1865, MSS, TRANSYL, quots. Refs.: Luke 21:19; Job 3:17; Matt. 18:23–35; Litany in *BCP* (1850) ("That it may please thee to forgive our enemies, persecutors, and slanderers, and to turn their hearts").

53. VHD to Craven, Oct. 10, 1865, in Craven, *Prison Life*, 430, quots; VHD to JD, Oct. 23, MS, ALA, quot. (ref. to Matt. 26:36 and Acts 7:57–60); JD to VHD, Nov. 3–4, 1865, MS, TRANSYL, quot. (chasten: Ps. 94:12, Heb. 12:5–11, etc.; Stephen: Acts 6–7).

54. VHD to JD, Dec. 25–28, MS, ALA., quots. (cf. Job 19:21).

55. JD to VHD, Jan. 16–18, 1866, MS, TRANSYL, quots. (he changed "is not" to "is it not," to make a question). His "martyr" ref. to her "St. Steven," about whom he would have read on Dec. 26 (Table of Lessons for Holy Days, *BCP*), praying in the Collect, "[that we may] learn to love and bless our persecutors."

56. VHD to JD, Feb. 2, 1866, MS, ALA, quot. (ref. to 2 Cor. 6:7 and Eph. 6:11); VHD to JD, Jan. 22, ibid., quots.

57. JD to VHD, Feb. 3–4, 1866, Oct. 11–12, 1865, MSS, TRANSYL, quots. (cf. Luke 7:47); *BCP* (1850), quot. from Gen. Confession in Mg. and Ev. Prayers; quots. from McElroy, *JD* 2:616 ("and this sacrifice of propitiation" deleted); *Imitation* (1916), 258. JD was already reading *Thoughts on Personal Religion* by Edward Mayrick Goulburn (see below), which urged (146–58) self-examination and frequent communion, unusual at that time.

58. Minnigerode, Address Jones, *Davis Memorial*, 421, quots.; Weddell, *St. Paul's Church* 2:392 (middle quot., from Dr. Dame). Macaulay (as in Note 39 above) said Argyle "forgave, as he hoped to be forgiven."

59. VHD to JD, Dec. 25–28, 1865, MS, ALA, quot.; JD to VHD, Feb. 17–19, Mar. 13–14, 1866, MSS, TRANSYL, quots. (other visits noted Feb. 3–4, Apr. 8); Minnigerode, Address (Jones, *Davis Memorial*, 419, quot.). He could not speak of his 2 visits to others, or take messages to "the outer world" (*O. R.*, 2, 8:818–19, 871–72, 874); see his pass, Nov. 20, 1866, in Weddell, *St. Paul's Church* 2:facing 558.

60. Craven, *Prison Life*, 352–53 (JD in Eckert, 129: "?" and "p. 364" [showing his ed. 1866]), 359–68 (allowed to speak only of health; JD in Eckert, 136: one "X"); JD to VHD, Dec. 2–3, 1865, MS, TRANSYL, quots.; Bradley, "Dr. Craven," 54 (n.22: *New York Herald*, Nov. 8, said coat sent down today).

61. JD to VHD, Dec. 2–3, 1865, MS, TRANSYL, quot.; Sterling, *Belle*, 333 and 350–53, quots.; Craven, *Prison Life*, 369–71, quot.; Hanchett, *Irish*, 143–50; Bradley, "Dr. Craven," 55, 59–60, 67–69, 88–89, 93–94; Eckert, xlii, xliv, xlv–xlvii.

62. JD to C. J. Wright, May 11, 1876 (Rowland 7:514, quot.); VHD, *Memoir* 2:801; JD to VHD, Dec. 7–8, 1865, and Jan. 28–29, 1866, MSS, TRANSYL, quots. (see Lee, *Recoll. and Letters*, 224); Bowers, *Tragic Era*, 85–86.

63. House Executive Document 23, 40th Congress, 2nd Session: Report of Trial of Henry Wirz. Letter from Secretary of War; Mildred Lewis Rutherford, *Andersonville Prison and Captain Henry Wirz Trial*, 3–5, 28–30 (quot. from letter of Louis Schade, Apr. 4, 1867); Lonn, *Foreigners in Conf.*, 273–75 (calls Wirz maj.); William Marvel, *Andersonville: The Last Depot*, 21, 34–38.

64. Glen W. LaForce, "The Trial of Major Henry Wirz—A National Disgrace," 6–9; James Madison Page, *The True Story of Andersonville Prison: A Defense of Major Henry Wirz*, 82, 207, 217; Ovid L. Futch, *History of Andersonville Prison*, 120; J. D. Imboden in *SHSP* 1:192; R. B. Winder to JD, 1888 (Rowland 10:94); Rutherford, *Wirz Trial*, 15–16; Cobb in *Corr. of Toombs*, 668–69; *O. R.*, 2, 8:773–74 (Schade to Johnson), 784–92 (quots. on 789; JD not on 785; altered dates on 791); Stevenson, *Southern Side*, 87–88, 107, 226; Same to JD, June 7, 1867 (Rowland 7:111–13, quot.).

65. Lee to Seddon, Oct. 28, 1863 (*Wartime Papers*, 616–17; see Rowland 6:322); JD, *Rise and Fall* 2:596–98; JD, "Andersonville and Other War-Prisons," passim; *O. R.*, 2, 8:730–36; *Butler's Book*, 610; Stevenson, *Southern Side*, 18–85, 96–99, 102–5, 138–45, 447–62; Arch Frederic Blakey, *General John H. Winder, C.S.A.*, 175–94 (best summary of conditions); Miller, *Photographic Hist.* 7:156–86 (292: germs unknown); Futch, *Hist. of Andersonville;* Marvel, *Andersonville: The Last Depot*, 14–29, passim.

66. Imboden in *SHSP* 1:192; LaForce, "Trial of Wirz," 10, quot.; Holt to pres., Oct. 31, 1865 (*O. R.*, 2, 8:781, quots.); Auger to Adj. Gen., Nov. 11 (ibid., 794). See JD to Lyons, Jan. 27, 1876 (Rowland 7:482), W. E. Woodward (1928), *Meet General Grant*, 343, Randall (1937), *Civil War*, 803.

67. Miles to Townsend, Dec. 25, 1865 (*O. R.*, 2, 8:840, quot.); VHD, *Memoir* 2:550–60 (quots. on 551); JD in Rowland 7:431–32, 8:381–82; Holland, *Morgan and His Raiders*, 295–98; Shea, "JD Letter," 6–15. Shea denied Northern abuse, but see JD in Rowland 7:498, in Eckert, 38, and in *Rise and Fall* 2:606–7; VHD, *Memoir* 2:554–73; Marvel, *Andersonville*, 61, 173, 260 n.20; Rowland 6:504–8, 7:264–65; *"For the Sake of My Country": The Diary of Col. W. W. Ward*, ed. R. B. Rosenburg (Murfreesboro: Southern Heritage Press, 1992), 16–17, 55–70; T. H. Pearce, " 'The Immortal Six Hundred' " (*Conf. Vet.*, Jan–Feb. 1986), 6–23.

68. VHD, *Memoir* 2:559 (Daniel quot.), 573–74 (quot. and Lee quot.; see Lee in *SHSP* 1:120–22); Benj. to VHD, Nov. 16, 1865 (*Letters*, 203, quot.; *Times* letter in *SHSP* 6:183–87); Eckert, 23 (JD quots.; see also 37–38); JD to C. J. Wright, Feb. 12, 1876 (Rowland 7:495, quot.; Gen. Winder "utterly incapable of cruelty" and see 497–98).

69. Scheibert in *SHSP* 19:415, quots. (prisoners have same rations as C.S. soldiers; see, e.g., *O. R.*, 2, 8:617; James H. McNeilly in *Conf. Vet.*, Jan. 1907, 14–16); JD, *Rise and Fall* 2:598–608 (quots. 600–603, 605 [Butler], see Grant on 600); *SHSP* 6:186 (Ben.; quot.), 187–89, 1:187–96; JD to Lyons, Jan. 27, 1876, Rowland 7:481–85; *True Story*, 102–6 (also 42); Schade to JD, Nov. 18, 1888 (Rowland 10:87–89); Stevenson, *Southern Side*, 211–15 (original "cartel"), 217–26, 480.

70. McNeilly in *Conf. Vet.*, Jan. 1907, 14–16; *O. R.*, 2, 8:111, 312–13, 537–38; Wirz to pres., Nov. 6, 1865, in Rutherford, *Wirz Trial*, 39–40, quots. (see also 44, 28–29, 30, 35, 9–12); Page, *True Story*, passim; John Hitz to pres., Nov. 9, 1865 (*O. R.*, 2, 8:792–93, quots.); Ibid., 791; Imboden in *SHSP* 1:187–96 (quot. on 192; Moloch worshipped by human sacrifice); Schade to JD, Aug. 6, 1887 (Rowland 9:589, quot.; see 10:87–89). See R. Taylor, *Destruction*, 216; Douglas, *I Rode with Stonewall*, 326–28; Roy Meredith, *The Face of Robert E. Lee in Life and Legend*, 86; Lubbock, *Six Decades*, 589–90.

71. Wirz to pres., Nov. 6, 1865, in Stevenson, *Southern Side*, 128–30, quots. (and see 124–26); Schade, Apr. 4, 1867 (ibid., 130–37 [quots. on 132, 133]; see *O. R.*, 2, 8:773–74, 793); R. B. Winder to VHD, Jan. 9, 1867 (Rowland 7:86–87; see *O. R.*, 2, 8:730–36, 796–98); Same to JD, Dec. 10, 1888 (Rowland 10:93–95); Boyle to JD, Oct. 10, 1880 (Rowland 8:501–2; confirms Winder and Schade; other priests defended Wirz: *Stevenson*, 126–27; *Ga. Hist.* 71:13–22; *Gache*, 187); *O. R.*, 2, 8:789 (one man, Duncan, was tried on another charge [926–28]); Wirz to Schade, Nov. 10, 1865, in Rutherford, *Wirz Trial*, 38–39, quot.

72. "Life and Adventures of Jeff. Davis" by McArone in *Pamphlets*, quots.; Strode, *Tragic Hero*, 243; George Edmonds, *Facts and Falsehoods Concerning the War on the South*, 259, quots. McElroy 2:705: "a brutal little cartoon" of JD "on the way to be hanged"; (see Bowers, *Tragic Era*, 16, 22; Sterling, *Belle*, 346).

73. Stevenson, *Southern Side*, 285 and 133, quots. (see 286); *O. R.*, 2, 763–64, 814–17, 870, 893 (last political prisoner, Yulee, freed Mar. 25, 1866); Blakey, *Gen. John H. Winder*, 201–4; Simpson, *Howell Cobb*, 174–75; Shaw, *WPJ*, 86–87; C. C. Harrison, *Recoll.*, 243–44; J. D. Howell to VHD, Dec. 18, 1865, MS, TRANSYL; *Letters*, 218, 257; JD to VHD, Dec. 7–8, MS, TRANSYL, quots. (ref. to Elijah in I Kings 19:10, 14); Randall, *C. W.*, 698–99.

74. *O. R.*, 2, 8:846, quot. (see 871, 875); JD to VHD, Dec. 2–3, 1865, Dec. 30, 1865–Jan. 1, 1866, MSS, TRANSYL, quots.; Randall, *C. W.*, 718–24.

75. Quots. from MSS, TRANSYL: JD to VHD, Feb. 3–4, 1866, ("one accord" from Chrysostom prayer: see appendix C); JD to VHD, Dec. 2–3, 1865 (ref. to Matt. 13:24–30; Billy had some bad experience; VHD spoke of "real home life" in a Nov. fragment, ALA); JD to VHD, Dec. 7–8 (Ps. 35:11, from memory: slight misquote); JD to VHD, Mar. 13–14, 1866 (lessons for Mg. Prayer Mar. 14 in *BCP* (1850): Deut. 3 and Luke 3).

76. JD to VHD, Dec. 7–8, 1865, MS, TRANSYL, quot. (ref. to Acts 14:22); Goulburn, *Thoughts* (see Note 57 above; 1st ed., 1861 [ix]): quots. on 127–28 (cf. 2 Tim. 2:3), 317, 46–47, 249, 344, 253–54, 240, 269, 179 (see 170–79, 249–50); on prayer: Part 1, Chap. 4; all of Part 2; Part 3, Chaps. 3 and 8; Part 4, Chap. 12 (draws on à Kempis [113, 271] and Francis de Sales [68–69, 177, 368–69]).

77. JD to VHD, Dec. 2–3, MS, TRANSYL, quot.; JD to VHD, Dec. 30, 1865–Jan. 1, 1866, ibid., quots. (wants=needs; refs. to John 19:25–27; I John 3:23; John 18:15–18, 25–27); Goulburn, *Thoughts*, 271–83, quots. (ref. to John 21:18–19, 13:36–38).

78. Goulburn, *Thoughts*, 59 and 271, quots.; *Imitation*, quot. from 2) of Note 26 above (has "my" for "thy" by mistake"); *Imitation* (1916), 196–97, quot. (here in his copy JD wrote "great comfort").

79. Boyle to JD, Oct. 10, 1880 (Rowland 8:501–2, quots.; he was with Wirz on scaffold); *Imitation* quot. from 2) of Note 26 above; JD to VHD, Sept. 26, Oct. 11–12, 1865, MSS, TRANSYL, quots. The peace of "complete surrender" is "first step in Sanctification"; "brightness" shows "the good soldier" (Goulburn, *Thoughts*, 271, 309, 240).

80. VHD to JD, Nov. 7, 1865, MS, ALA, quots. (refs. to Luke 21:19, I Cor. 6:19, and John 14:26); JD to VHD, Dec. 7–8, MS, TRANSYL, quot. "Holy Ghost the Comforter" from *Te Deum* in Mg. Prayer, *BCP* (1850).

81. Quots.: JD to VHD, Oct. 20, Dec. 7–8, 1865, and Mar. 22, 1866, MSS, TRANSYL. See Goulburn, *Thoughts*, 212–13, 216.

82. *Imitation* quot. from 2) in Note 26 above; JD to VHD, Dec. 30, 1865–Jan. 1, 1866, MS, TRANSYL, quots.; JD to VHD, Mar. 13–14, 1866, quot. ("If my letter . . ."); Goulburn, *Thoughts*, 218–30, quot.; *Frankenstein* by Mary Shelley 1817 (Baugh, *Lit. Hist. of Eng.*, 1196). Wm. Roberts (ed. *Brit. Review*), and Byron had words over a line in *Don Juan* 1.209 (see St. 113: "my soul invincible") (R. G. Howarth, ed., *Letters of Byron* [London: Dent, 1933] 228–30; W. H. Marshall, *Byron, Shelley, Hunt, and the Liberal* [Philadelphia: Univ. of Pennsylvania Press, 1960], 85–89).

83. Quots.: JD to VHD, Dec. 2–3, Nov. 3–4, Oct. 20, 1865; Dec. 30, 1865–Jan. 1, 1866; Feb. 17–19, 1866; Mar. 13–14 (ref. unknown); Dec. 7–8, 1865, MSS, TRANSYL.

84. Quots.: JD to VHD, Dec. 7–8 (ref. to John 14:2–3), Dec. 2–3, 1865, MSS, TRANSYL.

85. Quots.: JD to VHD, Nov. 3–4, 1865; Dec. 30, 1865–Jan. 1, 1866; Mar. 13–14, 1866 (ref. to Job 3:17); Feb. 3–4, MSS, TRANSYL ("expedient" from Chrysostom Prayer: see appendix C); Grant, *Memoirs*, 524.

86. Goulburn, *Thoughts*, 368–69 (quot. from de Sales); JD to VHD, Apr. 21–23, 1866, MS, TRANSYL, quots. (last 2 phrases from 1st collect in communion service; Last Judgment in Apostles' and Nicene Creeds, *BCP* [1850]; see Matt. 25:31–32, 2 Cor. 5:10).

87. Speed to VHD, Jan. 23, 1866 (*O. R.*, 2, 8:870); JD to Marg. Davis, Mar. 23, MS, TRANSYL, quots. Good Friday was Mar. 30; "Lo, I come to do thy will, O God" is in the Epistle (*BCP* [1850]). Goulburn, *Thoughts*, 196, 280–83, 368; and *Imitation* (1916), 71, 84, 90–92, 195: joy in suffering shows love for God; latter, near where JD wrote "great comfort," links it to "crowns of saints in heaven."

Chapter XIX Varina

1. Randall, *Civil War,* 718–24; Bowers, *Tragic Era,* 5–23, 72–73, 85–96; Edmund G. Ross, *History of the Impeachment of Andrew Johnson,* 1–2, 9, 18–20, 30–32, 39–45; Donald, *Chas. Sumner and Rights,* 224–47, 254–68; Allen, *Reconstr.,* 20–23 (in foreword by Richard Enmale), 34–42 (pres. ref. to as "Jefferson Davis Johnson").

2. JD to VHD, Jan. 28–29, 1866, MS, TRANSYL, quot.; Donald, *Chas. Sumner and Rights,* 256 (quot. from Sir F. Bruce; Sumner said, "I never cease to regret that Jeff. Davis was not shot at the time of his capture" [221]); Shea, "JD Letter," 11, quot. (see *O. R.,* 2, 8:869–70; Stevenson, *Southern Side,* 480–88). DeWitt, *Impeachment,* 152, also cf. French Rev.

3. JD to VHD, Jan. 16–18, 1866, MS, TRANSYL, quot.; Donald, *Chas. Sumner and Rights,* 238–41 (this res. not mentioned, but not one of his was then taken up by Comm. on Reconstr.).

4. VHD to JD, Oct. 23, 1865, MS, ALA, quots. (quots. from Tennyson's "Break, break, break" and unident. *Iliad;* mingled ref. to Ps. 12:6, Prov. 17:3, Isa. 48:10, Dan. 3:19–28, Zech. 13:9).

5. Quots.: VHD to JD, Nov. 7 and Sept. 14, 1865, MSS, ALA, Dec. 7, photocopy, ALA.

6. Quots.: VHD to JD, Jan. 22, 1866, and Nov. 13, 1865, MSS, ALA (ref. to Num. 20:10–11); JD to VHD, Dec. 30, 1865–Jan. 1, 1866, MS, TRANSYL.

7. Quots.: VHD to JD, Oct. 23, 1865, MS, ALA; VHD to [A. Johnson] (*O. R.,* 2, 8:874–75; n.d., placed after Jan. 30, 1866); VHD to JD, Sept. 14, 1865, MS, ALA.

8. *O. R.,* 2, 8:871–75, 880–86 (Cooper rpts., Jan., Feb. 1866); JD to VHD, Feb. 17–19, and Aug. 21, 1865, MS, TRANSYL, quots.; JD to VHD, Nov. 26–27, 1865, Dec. 30, 1865–Jan. 1, 1866, and Jan. 28–29, ibid.; VHD to JD, Sept. 14, 1865, Feb. 8 and 2, 1866, MSS, ALA, quots.

9. JD to VHD, Jan. 28–29, 1866, MS, TRANSYL, quots.; JD to VHD, Feb. 3–4, ibid. ("realities" quot.). Refs.: "Tarry": Ps. 27:16 in *BCP* ("pleasure" should be "leisure"); "cause me . . .": Ps. 143:8, KJV (appt'd. for Day 29, *BCP*); "lift up your heart" from *BCP* communion service.

10. VHD to JD, Feb. 8 and 2, 1866, MSS, ALA, quots.

11. VHD to JD, Feb. 8, 1866, MS, ALA, quot. (ref. to Gen., chaps. 6–8; pitch in 6:14).

12. JD to VHD, Jan. 28–29, Feb. 17–19, 1866, MSS, TRANSYL, quots.; Sterling, *Belle,* 307; *O. R.,* 2, 8:841; VHD, *Memoir* 2:750n; VHD to JD, Feb. 2, MS, ALA, quot. ("bread": cf. Matt. 6:11). JD mentions Va. Clay Nov. 21, Nov. 26–27, Dec. 2–3, 1865, Dec. 30, 1865–Jan. 1, 1866, Mar. 13–14, Mar. 22, 1866, MSS, TRANSYL.

13. Sterling, *Belle,* 307–17 (quots. on 316).

14. Ibid., 318–32, 364–66 (quots. on 318, 364, 321, 320, 322, 329; see Johnson note on 344); Lubbock, *Six Decades,* 575, quot.; Bowers, *Tragic Era,* 43–44. Stanton had rudely rebuffed Minnigerode, who asked improved conditions for JD (Jones, *Davis Memorial,* 442).

15. Sterling, *Belle,* 344, 350–54, and 370–71, quots.; Items seen at Beauvoir, 1978, 1984 (Mrs. Cooper's first name diff. in notes at Beauvoir and in Sterling, but both say she cared for JD).

16. Craven, *Prison Life,* 150–51 (see appendix C for the *BCP*), 318; JD in Eckert, 36, quot.; JD to VHD, Sept. 26, 1865, MS, TRANSYL, quot. (Rowland 6:561 for saddle); VHD to JD, Feb. 2, 1866, MS, ALA, quot.; JD to VHD, Feb. 17–19, MS, TRANSYL, quot. Hearing Malie Brodhead failed to visit Anna, in school near her, JD said, "Her claim to attention cannot have been understood" (Nov. 26–27, ibid.).

17. JD to VHD, Mar. 22, 1866, MS, TRANSYL, quot.; Sterling, *Belle,* 347–48, 368–69, quots. Another "dressing gown" (robe) which "500 people sewed on" was "sent to Mr. Davis from a St. Louis fair" (VHD in T. Hill, "Victory in Defeat," 26; see VHD, *Memoir* 2:764–65).

18. Nuermberger, *Clays of Ala.*, 290–92, quots.; Sterling, *Belle*, 318–19, 336–37, 340–44 (Johnson quot.), 354–366 ("Dear Friend" on 362). The struggle between Johnson and the Radicals was now approaching a climax: see Bowers, *Tragic Era*, 99–115.

19. *O. R.*, 2, 8:840–41 (Grant quot.; Dec. 28, 1865), 870 (Speed quot.).

20. VHD to JD, Jan. 22, 1866, MS, ALA, quots. (see Rowland 7:61n); VHD to JD, Oct. 2, Nov. 13, 1865, and Feb. 8, 1866, MSS, ALA; Anastasia White to VHD, Nov. 7, 1865 (*Letters*, 197, quot.); Wm. Preston to VHD, Nov. 1 (ibid., 194–96); Shaw, *WPJ*, 85–89 (WPJ quot.).

21. C. C. Harrison, *Recoll.*, 243, 241 (quot. from H. K. Douglas; see his *I Rode with Stonewall*, 332–33; also Ross, *First Lady*, 286); VHD to JD, Feb. 8, 1866, Nov. 27, 1865 (quot.), MSS, ALA, and Dec. 7, 1865, ALA copy; JD to VHD, Mar. 13–14, Feb. 17–19, 1866, MSS, TRANSYL, quots.; Lubbock, *Six Decades*, 588–92; Reagan, *Memoirs*, 228–34. See *O. R.*, 2, 8:839–40, 816–17, 763–64.

22. VHD to JD, Feb. 23, 1866, MS, ALA, quots. See Lubbock, *Six Decades*, 578–90, *O. R.*, 2, 8:660, and Shaw, *WPJ*, 84–87: both were kept in solitary, read Bible and BCP; Lubbock recited poetry; WPJ later had lit. career (ibid., 268, 278; Manly, *Southern Lit.*, 482).

23. VHD to JD, Feb. 2 and 23, 1866, and Nov. 7, 1865, MSS, ALA, quots.; Humphreys in Warner, *Gens. in Gray* (later deposed by Radicals).

24. VHD to JD, [Mar. 8], 1866, MS, ALA, quots. (cf. *Letters*, 236; dated from other letters and an ALA fragment with "March 8" in VHD's hand). Hosts are Col. and Mrs. Lewis M. Whittle, who have harbored Va. Clay (Sterling, *Belle*, 278–81).

25. VHD to JD, [Mar. 8], 1866, MS, ALA, quots.

26. VHD to JD, Feb. 23, Mar. 8, 1866, MSS, ALA, quots.; VHD to JD, Feb. 2, ibid.; JD to VHD, Oct. 11–12, 1865, Mar. 22 [1866], MSS, TRANSYL, quots. For Smith, see Manly, *Southern Lit.*, 326–29; Wakelyn, *Biog. Dict. of Conf.*; Parker, "Bill Arp and War Effort"); for Lamar, Rowland 8:222 n.1 and *Mississippi Heroes*, ed. D. F. Wells and H. Cole (Jackson: Univ. Press of Mississippi, 1980), 107–42.

27. VHD, *Memoir* 2:756; VHD to JD, Nov. 13, 1865, Feb. 23, 1866 (quots.), and Feb. 2, MSS, ALA; Benj. to VHD (from Paris), Nov. 16, 1865 (*Letters*, 203, quots.); Nuermberger, *Clays of Ala.*, 241, quot.; JD to VHD, Jan. 28–29, and Feb. 17–19, 1866, MSS, TRANSYL, quots. (and see Nov. 21, 1865); Williams, *Bgd.*, 52, 120.

28. JD to VHD, Feb. 3–4, 1866, MS, TRANSYL, quot. See text above, chaps. 4 (rescue) and 17 (sentinel). Va. Assembly also asked Johnson to free JD, Oct. 1865 (Osborne, *Jubal*, 406).

29. JD to VHD, Jan. 28 and Jan. 24, 1866, MS, TRANSYL, quots.; Lee to VHD, Feb. 23, in Lee, *Recoll. and Letters*, 223–24, quot. (italics omitted; ans. hers of Feb. 12; see 179). VHD wrote WPJ earlier *re* reply to slanders (Shaw, *WPJ*, 88).

30. *SHSP* 1:120–22, 178; Lee to Early, Mar. 16, 1866, in Lee, *Recoll. and Letters*, 220–21, quot. (165: hopes asking pardon will enable him to help JD).

31. VHD to JD, [Oct. 1], 1865, MS, ALA, quot. (see also Sept. 14); Mary C. Lee to JD, [1865] (*Letters*, 249–50, quots.; encl. in letter June 6, 1866; hymn missing; cf. Heb. 12:2). Lee expressed to Walter Taylor his suffering over both JD and VHD (Taylor, *Gen. Lee*, 310).

32. *Letters*, 249–50; JD to VHD, Oct. 20, 1865, MS, TRANSYL, quot. Captives in hijacked TWA Flight 847 in Lebanon felt strength from people praying (*Atlanta Const.*, July 3, 1985, pp. 13-A, 12-A); Brig. Gen. James Dozier, rescued from brutal kidnapping in Italy, thanked the people "on the praying end of it" and said "You could sure as hell feel it!" (*Newsweek*, Feb. 8, 1982; telecast seen by author).

33. Quots.: VHD to JD, Nov. 13, 1865, MS, ALA; Marg. Davis to JD, Mar. 14, 1866 (*Letters*, 240); Gibson, *Physician to World* (as above, chap. 16, Note 53), 28; WPJ to wife, July 4, 1865, in Shaw, *WPJ*, 86.

34. Quots.: W. H. Richardson to JD, May 15, 1867 (MS, JD Papers, ADAH); B. G. Wilkins to JD, Aug. 15, 1866 (Rowland 7:73; ref. to *Benedictus* in Mg. Prayer [*BCP* (1850)] or Luke 1:68–71); Diary of Capt. R. E. Park (*SHSP* 3:252); Reagan to

JD, May 21, 1867 (Rowland 7:106–7; see also C. E. Hooker on 79, Culver on 92); Hampton in Strode, *Tragic Hero*, 290 (see *Letters*, 212). See *Chesnut*, 824.

35. VHD to JD, Mar. 18, 1866, MS, ALA, quots. (names many gens.); VHD to JD, Apr. 12 (*Letters*, 243, quot.).

36. *Letters*, 243–44, JD to VHD, Feb. 17–19, MS, TRANSYL, quot.; JD to Walthall, n.d. (Rowland 8:277–78, quot.; Scott, whom Joseph knew, was then in N. O.); *Papers* 1::124 n.2. For book, see Note 37 below.

37. JD to VHD, Feb. 17–19, 1866, MS, TRANSYL, quots.; Winfield Scott *Memoirs* (New York: Sheldon, 1864) 1:148n, quot.; *Papers* 2::18 n.102 and 64 n.31; VHD, *Memoir* 1:183–86 and n. See JD letters (Rowland 7:248–51, 266–68, 473–74); Vagn K. Hansen, "JD and the Repudiation of Miss. Bonds" (*Jnl. Miss. Hist.* 33 [1971]: 105–32).

38. VHD to JD, Apr. 12, 1866 (*Letters*, 244, quots.); James T. Currie, "Freedmen at Davis Bend," 123–29; Currie, *Enclave*, 90–119; Hermann, *Pursuit of a Dream*, 61–106 (see esp. 72 and 82); VHD to JD, Nov. 7, 1865, MS, ALA, quot. (see *Letters*, 199–200).

39. Hermann, *Joseph E. Davis*, 132–51 (quot. on 133; VHD offered Joseph $100 as "he is quite poor" [Sept. 14, 1865, MS, ALA]); Currie, *Enclave*, 115, 121; JD to VHD, Apr. 8, 1866, MS, TRANSYL, quot.; VHD to JD, Apr. 12 (*Letters*, 244, quot.).

40. VHD to JD, Apr. 12, 1866 (*Letters*, 244; see his letter, Aug. 21, 1865,); VHD, *Memoir* 2:10–11 (quot.) and n.; JD to VHD, Jan. 16–18, 1866, MS, TRANSYL, quots. Uncle Bob was 104 in 1860 (Hermann, *Pursuit of a Dream*, 16).

41. JD to VHD, Jan. 16–18, 1866, MS, TRANSYL, quots.; *Letters*, 244 ("bribe"); Hermann, *Pursuit of Dream*, 64–95; Hermann, *Joseph E. Davis*, 140–49; JD to VHD, Jan. 28–29, MS, TRANSYL, quot. (see Randall, *Civil War*, 729).

42. VHD to JD [Nov. 16, 1865?], fragment, MS, ALA, quots. (date from *Letters*, 204, and JD to VHD, Nov. 26–27, MS, TRANSYL); VHD to JD, Nov. 7 and Dec. 25, MSS, ALA, quots. (cloud: see Ex. 13:21). See *Letters*, 199–200, 205, 218, 228, 233, and Richard Weaver, *The Southern Tradition at Bay: A History of Post-bellum Thought*, ed. George Core and M. E. Bradford, 159–70. J. R. Davis says, 1867, Freedmen's Bureau necessary "to save the negro from starvation" (Freeman, *Cal. Conf. Papers*, 475–77).

43. JD to VHD, Feb. 3–4, and Mar. 13–14, 1866, MSS, TRANSYL, quots. VHD herself says of the speech (Feb. 23; MS, ALA): "There are no men in the community so lost to a sense of the obligations of manhood who would not, unarmed as they are . . . protect the inferior race from oppression."

44. JD to VHD, Jan. 16–18, 1866, MS, TRANSYL, quot. (fears, however, "the excitement and blindness of the 'Radicals' "); JD to VHD, Oct. 20 and Oct. 11–12, 1865, MSS, TRANSYL, quots. JD points out Joseph's right to the land, Sept. 26 (ibid.): cf. Allen, *Reconstruction*, 46, 50, 48.

45. Hermann, *Joseph E. Davis*, 137–56 (quots. on 141 from Joseph and Johnson); Hermann, *Pursuit of Dream*, 93, 97–98; David Donald, *The Politics of Reconstruction, 1863–1867* (Baton Rouge: Louisiana State Univ. Press, 1965), 23–25; DeWitt, *Impeachment*, 42, 45–49; Randall, *Civil War*, 731–33.

46. Hermann, *Joseph E. Davis*, 134–37 (for Porterfield and Shamrock, see *Papers* 2::17 n.35); VHD to JD, Apr. 12, 1866 (*Letters*, 244–45, quot.).

47. Jordan in Warner, *Gens. in Gray;* Jordan, "JD," passim, quots. LBN, 1885, calls this "the text on which" JEJ, Bgd., and Imboden preach "hatred" of him and JD (Rowland 9:391); cf. H. Foote, 1860s (*SHSP* 50:20–24, 36–37), and Eckenrode, *JD* (1923), passim, esp. 366.

48. Jordan, "JD," 620n, quots.; "The Close of the American War" (*Quarterly Review*, July 1865), 106–36; Alfriend, *Life of JD*, 575n, quot.; Andrew Lytle, *Bedford Forrest and His Critter Company* (1931, RPR 1984, and Nashville: J. S. Sanders, 1992), 357 (cites Frederick as Jordan does); VHD to JD, Nov. 7, 1865, MS, ALA, quot.

49. JD to VHD, Oct. 20, 1865, MS, TRANSYL, quot.

50. LBN to JD, Jan. 14, 1885 (Rowland 9:327, quots.; see 338–39, 386, 391, 392); JD to LBN, Mar. 3, 1885 (ibid. 348–49, quot.). LBN was in prison June–Oct. 1865 (*O. R.*, 1, 46 [Part 3]: 1276; 47 [Part 3]: 672; 2, 8:782). See Jordan, "JD," 614, *re* gens. on staff.

51. JD to VHD, Jan. 28–29, Feb. 3–4, 1866, and Dec. 30, 1865–Jan. 1, 1866, MSS, TRANSYL, quots.; *O. R.*, 2, 8:871. Noting "unkind criticism" on Buch.'s book (New York: D. Appleton and Co., 1866), JD said, "critics however are not believed to read the books they 'review'" (Dec. 7–8, 1865, MS, TRANSYL).

52. *SHSP* 29:24–25; JD to VHD, Dec. 7–8, 1865, MS, TRANSYL, quot. ("knife-grinder" also in Apr. 21, 1866, ibid.); McElroy, *JD* 2:616 (*Imitation* quot.); JD to VHD, Mar. 13–14, 1866, MS, TRANSYL, quot. "*Knifegrinder.* 'Story! God bless you! I have none to tell, sir.'" ("*The Friend of Humanity and the Knife-Grinder*" in *Poetry of the Antijacobin* [London: J. Wright, 1801], 11–13: parody on Robert Southey [Baugh, *Lit. Hist. of Eng.*, 1116 and n.11]).

53. JD to VHD, Mar. 22, Apr. 8–9, 1866, MSS, TRANSYL, quots. (cf."For a Person under Affliction," appendix C). Clay also told Va. to expect "incivilities" (Sterling, *Belle,* 299).

54. VHD, *Memoir* 2:756–57, quots.; VHD to JD, Apr. 12, 1866 (*Letters,* 243–45, quots.).

55. VHD, *Memoir* 2:757 (1st and last quots.); VHD to JD, Apr. 12, 1866 (*Letters,* 245, quots.; see 246).

56. Sterling, *Belle,* 340–78 (quots. on 354, 340, 361, 373); *The Papers of Andrew Johnson,* ed. Paul H. Bergeron, 10:21–22 (see 241–43, 262–63: Clay "neither afraid or ashamed" to say why he went to Canada).

57. JD to VHD, Apr. 21, 1866, MS, TRANSYL, quot.; Nuermberger, *Clays of Ala.,* 289–97 (quots. on 293, 289–90), 271; Sterling, *Belle,* 281–84, 340–41. The country in N. Ala. "even more thoroughly devastated than in the path of Sherman through Georgia" (Fleming, *C. W. in Ala.,* 255).

58. JD to VHD, Apr. 8–9, 21–23, 1866, MSS, TRANSYL, quots.

59. VHD to JD, Nov. 13, 1865, and Apr. 14–16, 1866, MS, ALA and *Letters,* 246, quots.; JD in Rowland 8:35, quot.; Reagan, *Memoirs,* 220, quot.; Cartoon on sheet music, "The Sour Apple Tree, or Jeff Davis' Last Ditch" (ALA Collection,, Archives, Auburn Univ. Library); McElroy, *JD* 2:704, quot. (703–5 descr. 12 cartoons). See others in Mark E. Neeley, Jr., Harold Holzer, and Gabor S. Boritt, *The Confederate Image* [Chapel Hill: Univ. of North Carolina Press, 1987], 80–92.

60. JD to VHD, Feb. 17–19, and Apr. 8–9, 1866, MSS, TRANSYL, quots.; VHD to JD, Apr. 14–16 (*Letters,* 246, quots.). JD says Jeff Jr.'s ref. "to the Hymn" shows "gentle affection" (Dec. 7–8. 1865); calls him "Big Boy" (e.g., Jan. 28–29, Apr. 8–9, 1866); anxious about him (Dec. 30, 1865–Jan. 1, 1866), MSS, TRANSYL.

61. VHD to JD, Apr. 14–16, 1866 (*Letters,* 246, quot.); JD to VHD, Feb. 17–19, Apr. 21–23 and 8–9, MSS, TRANSYL, quots. Maggie's letter in *Letters,* 239–40.

62. JD to VHD, Jan. 24 and Jan. 28–29, 1866, MSS, TRANSYL, quots.; JD to VHD, Sept. 26, and Nov. 3, 1865, ibid., quots. See also ibid., Feb. 17–19, Mar. 22, Apr. 8, and Apr. 21–23, 1866. Betsy in *Letters,* 88, 96 [1857], and *Papers* 6:130; "Old Betsy" in Ma's letter Apr. 7, 1851, MS, MDAH; she was 100 in 1860 (Hermann, *Pursuit of Dream,* 16).

63. JD to VHD, Apr. 8–9 and 21–23, 1866 (quots.; miscalls Burns "The Bard of Avon"), and Mar. 13–14 (quots., written crosshatch on 1st p.), MSS, TRANSYL.

64. JD to VHD, Apr. 21–23, Feb. 17–19, Apr. 8, and Jan. 28–29, 1866, MSS, TRANSYL, quots.

65. JD to VHD, Apr. 21–23, 1866, MS, TRANSYL (quots.; ref. [besides Cowper]: Byron, "Lara," 1.2 and Dickens, *David Copperfield* [Micawber]); JD to VHD, Mar. 22, ibid. (quot. *re* boots). On JD's unjust imprisonment, see S. Teackle Wallis in *Life and Reminisc.,* 274–308, esp. 304–6.

66. Quots.: Cooper to Miles, Mar. 21, 1866 (*O. R.*, 2, 8:892; see 894–901: rpts. Apr. 4, 10, 18, 25); VHD to Johnson, Apr. 25, 1866 (ibid., 900; Endrss. by Johnson

and Stanton); Townsend to Miles, Apr. 26 (ibid., 901; also to VHD, and see 902); VHD to JD, [Oct. 1], 1865, MS, ALA.

67. VHD, *Memoir* 2:757–59, quots. (see 775, "a walking skeleton," and 771, thigh smaller than a stout man's upper arm; says May 10, but really May 3 [*O. R.*, 2, 8:904–5; see Cooper's rpt. this day]). "I was reduced to little more than a skeleton" (JD, "Andersonville," 163).

68. VHD, *Memoir* 2:759–60, 767, quots. (see VHD to Johnson, May 19, 1866 [*Papers of Johnson* 10:522]); AHS, *Recollections*, 378, 405, 409–10, 473–74.

69. VHD, *Memoir* 2:758–67, quots. "[I] have striven not to feel too bitterly the undue harshness . . . (JD to VHD, Sept. 21, 1866, MS, ALA).

70. VHD, *Memoir* 2:767, quot. (see also 696–702 and Cooper on 771–72); McCulloch, *Men and Measures*, 409–11, quots.; *O. R.*, 2, 8:947 (Cooper quot.; WPJ says same [Shaw, *WPJ*, 75]).

71. VHD to A. Johnson, May 5, 1866 (*Papers of Johnson* 10:477, quot.; see 521 and n.1); VHD to A. Johnson, May 19 (ibid., 521–22, quots.; she has promised not "to make public" Miles's "cruelties").

72. Cooper to Adj. Gen., May 9, 1866 (*O. R.*, 2, 8:908, quots.).

73. *O. R.*, 2, 8:918–19; VHD, *Memoir* 2:768–71, quots. (Stevens ident. by descr. here, that in Bowers, *Tragic Era*, 65–67, 74–75, and pic. in Randall, *Civil War*, 769). See DeWitt, *Impeachment*, 137–48; Hanchett, *Lincoln Murder*, 78–83 (mentions Booth card). Evidence pointed "much *more strongly*" to Johnson than anyone in his "perfectly absurd" Procl. (Beverly Tucker to JD, July 1, 1867 [Rowland 7:117–19]).

74. *O. R.*, 2, 8:910–16 (quots. on 914, 915–16 [from *World*, May 24, 1866]), 917–18 (other quots.); Donald, *Politics of Reconstr.*, 22; VHD to Johnson, May 19 (*Papers of Johnson* 10:521, quot.). See corr. of O'Conor and Reid [Reed] in Rowland 7:26–32, 36–39, 43–44, 56–57, 62–63.

75. *O. R.*, 2, 8:914 and 919 (quots.), 924 (surg. gen's. rpt. June 6; see 925, 926), 955–56, 961 (Miles asks to stay till Oct., then resign, but is refused; see also 909–10), 917 (*New York News*: "the martyr").

76. McMurry, *John Bell Hood*, 88 (Hood quot.); *Cal. JD MSS*, 6–7 (quots. from poem and ident. note); *O. R.*, 2, 8:955 (quot.), 956, 961–62; Miles in Warner, *Gens. in Blue*.

77. Cooper's rpts., May 29–Dec. 26, 1866 (*O. R.*, 2, 8:921, 925, 929–31, 945–56, 962, 965–68, 972–76, 978, 980; quots. on 945, 947; see also VHD, *Memoir* 2:773, 775).

78. Gordon in *Life and Reminsc.*, 270, quot.; VHD, *Memoir* 2:772–73, quot.; Ross, *First Lady*, 409 (quot.), 292 (Index ident. Preston as John, but he was still in Europe [Warner, *Gens. in Gray*]); R. Taylor, *Destruction*, 246–47.

79. JD to E. V. Mason, July 4, 1866 (Rowland 7:72, quot.); Mary Bayard Clarke to VHD, July 14, quot. (pasted in Clarke's *Mosses from a Rolling Stone* [1866; inscr. to JD; Rosenstock]; for Clarke, see F. Allen, "Martyrdom or Myth-making?" 10 and n.19).

80. VHD, *Memoir* 2:773–75, quots.; *Letters*, 256–57; *O. R.*, 2, 8:954–55 (Cooper rpt., Aug. 22: "eats but little"; circulation "languid" [929]; "no prominent lesion . . . gradual wearing away of his whole system" [968]; no rpt. mentions heart).

81. VHD, *Memoir* 2:774; Lonn, *Foreigners in Conf.*, 80–81; (O'Keefe:) *SHSP* 35:176–82 and Rowland 7:87–88; Green to JD, Aug. 14, 1875 (ibid., 441–42, 447–49); C. C. Harrison, *Recoll.*, 69; *Pendleton*, 422–24, 428, 439 (quots.), 435.

82. Pemb. to JD, Aug. 28, 1866 (Rowland 7:74–75, quots.; now on farm in Va.); Vandiver, *Gorgas Diary*, 158 and 165 (quots., Dec. 28, 1864, and Jan. 6, 1865; JD admits Pemb. prone to quarreling but thinks "him a good soldier," makes him field inspector of art. and ord.).

83. Nuermberger, *Clays of Ala.*, 302; JD to VHD, Feb. 3–4, 1866, MS, TRANSYL, quots. (see Nichols, *Franklin Pierce*, 528); Craven, *Prison Life*, 164–65, quot. (2 JD notes in Eckert, 60); Strode, *Tragic Hero*, 295, 306; JD to Pierce, "Present," May 8,

1867, quot. (MS, Franklin Pierce Papers, 1820–1946, N. H. Hist. Society Collection, Concord, N. H.).

84. VHD to R. Johnson, July 19, 1866 (Rowland 7:72, quots.); VHD to J. D. Howell, Nov. 24, 1866, MS, ALA, quot. (ref. to James 1:4). Fevers July 4–Aug. 29 (*O. R.*, 2, 8:945–56). O'Conor to Shea, Aug. 6: finds JD "much weaker," "fear he may sink" (Freeman, *Cal. Conf. Papers,* 465).

85. VHD to JD, Aug. 17, 1866 (*Letters,* 250–51, quot.); VHD to Greeley, Sept. 2, Oct. 16, Nov. 21, 1866 (Rowland 7:75–80; quots. on 75–76); *O. R.*, 2, 8:925; Strode, *Tragic Hero,* 289; Ross, *First Lady,* 286 (quot. from VHD to BNH, Aug. 2).

86. McElroy, *JD* 2:564–577; VHD, *Memoir* 2:777 (JD quot.); Lowry to Claiborne, Aug. 28, 1878 (Rowland 8:268–72, quots.; encl. in Same to JD, Sept. 5; *re* Nov. 1866); R. Taylor to VHD, Nov. 10, 1866 (Rowland 7:79); Cobb to D. E. Sickles, Sept. 12, 1866 (Phillips, *Corr. of Toombs,* 682–84, quots.; expects him to influence Johnson).

87. Rowland 7:155 (quot. from J. T. Brady; see A. Johnson on 161); Strode, *Tragic Hero,* 289, 296; VHD to Greeley, Oct. 16, 1866 (Rowland 7:76–77, quot.); VHD to Marg. K. Howell, Oct. 18 (*Letters,* 252–53, quots.).

88. *Letters,* 252, quot.; VHD to WPJ, Sept. 27, 1866, MS, TULANE, quots. (ref. to *Macbeth* 5.3.23); VHD to J. D. Howell, Nov. 24, MS, ALA; Strode, *Tragic Hero,* 296; Ross, *First Lady,* 286, 292 (Carlyle quots.). See C. C. Harrison, *Recoll.,* 119–23; DeLeon, *Belles,* 203–4, 216–17, 288–89; Weber, *Selections from So. Poets,* 150–57.

89. Burchenal, "Yankee Girl," passim (quots. on 18, 43; VHD on 45; brother Capt. Selden Day in VHD, *Memoir* 2:760, and Craven, *Prison Life,* 369).

90. VHD to Marg. K. Howell, Oct. 18, 1866 (*Letters,* 252, quot.); VHD to JD, Dec. 8, 12, MSS, ALA, quots. ("l'arms" must be Pie's word; Malie goes to Washington with her; Wm. Preston and Gov. Pratt of Md. help).

91. VHD to JD, Dec. 16, 1866, MS, ALA, quots.; VHD to JD, Dec. 12, ibid., and in Strode, *Tragic Hero,* 299 (quot. *re* Billy); VHD to WPJ, Sept. 27, MS, TULANE, quot.; Kadloubovsky and Palmer, *Early Fathers,* 215; Strode, *Tragic Hero,* 299–300. Cooper still notes "nervous excitability" in Mar. 1867 (*O. R,* 2, 8:982).

92. McElroy, *JD* 2:576, 558–59, 578, 568 (JD bail of $1 million was ready); Rowland 7:150–53, quots.; Mary C. Lee letter, May 6, 1866, in Strode, *Tragic Hero,* 279, quots.

93. VHD to Greeley, Sept. 2, Oct. 16, and Nov. 21, 1866 (Rowland 7:75–80; see 10:49, 54–55: JD gives Greeley a "higher motive"—justice [ibid. 10:54–55; see 49]); *O. R.*, 2, 8:931–32; McElroy, *JD,* 2:564–76 (quots., Greeley on 576, Smith on 571); O'Conor to Shea, Aug. 6 (Freeman, *Cal. Conf. Papers,* 465); Shea, "JD Letter," 13–15; McPherson, *Battle Cry,* 204.

94. Craven, *Prison Life* (see Eckert, xv, xlvii–li, liv, lix–lx, lxiv, and F. Allen, "Martyrdom or Mythmaking," 3–4, 28–35, 38–39); McElroy, *JD,* 2:564–76 (quots. on 573 [Johnson], 574 [Stanbery; appt. July 23: *Papers of Johnson* 10:435 n.1]); Rowland 8:271 (JD quot.; see Lowry, Note 86 above); Randall, *Civil War,* 761–63.

95. McElroy, *JD* 2:578. JD's counsel, serving gratis, now includes Shea, O'Conor, BNH, and Wm. B. Reed (see corr., Nov. 1865–May 1867, in Rowland 7:56–57, 81–93, 99–101), Lowry and Hillyer of Miss. (ibid., 82–84, 89–91, 101–3), and Brady (of N.Y.), Lyons, Ould, and Tucker in Richmond (McElroy, *JD* 2:564, 583).

96. Marg. G. Howell to MBC, Feb. 25 [1867] and MBC note (letterbook MS, South Caroliniana Library); VHD to JD, Apr. 9 and Mar. 18 (*Letters,* 267 and 265, quots.). VHD's dentist, Adalbert Volck was a noted artist: see Neeley, Holzer, and Boritt, *Conf. Image,* as in Note 59 above, 43–54.

97. Sterling, *Belle,* 202–3; *Papers* 4:218–19; *O. R.*, 2, 8:762, 844, 848, 893; Rowland 2:445–46; Hanna, *Flight,* 113–20; VHD to JD, Mar. 5, 9, 15 (quots.; ref. to Heb. 12:6), 19, "28th" [typescript], "25th," and "Wednesday," 1867, MSS, ALA (*Letters* ascribes last 2 to Apr.).

98. VHD, *Memoir* 2:777–80 (Garrett quots.). VHD mentions Garrett in her 1867 letters (last 3 in Note 97 above).

99. O'Conor to Shea, May 2, 1867, in McElroy, *JD* 2:578, quot.; Ibid., 579, quots.; *O. R.*, 2, 8:983–86; BNH to Constance Cary, May 13, in C. C. Harrison, *Recoll.*, 263–64, quot. (letters, May 13–18, will be cited hereafter by p. only).

100. Quots.: Strode, *Tragic Hero*, 306; *New York Tribune*, May 13, 1867, p. 1, col. 4 (bust of JD in Richmond store window is "encircled with wreaths of laurel"); BNH in C. C. Harrison, *Recoll.*, 264; VHD, *Memoir* 2:794.

101. Ibid. 2:794–95, quots.; *New York Tribune*, May 13, 1867, p. 1, col. 4; *Moore's Guide to Richmond*, 68–69.

102. Randall, *Civil War*, 756–57 (Johnson vetoed this bill but was overridden, Mar. 23, 1867 [n.7]); BNH in C. C. Harrison, *Recoll.*, 264, quots.

103. BNH in C. C. Harrison, *Recoll.*, 265–66, quots.; B. T. Johnson, "Case of JD," 169–75 (O'Conor cites diff. surety on 173). On Greeley's part and what it cost him: see ibid., 150; McElroy, *JD* 2:566–68. *New York Tribune*, May 14, expects JD to be sent "to the Libby or some other prison."

104. BNH in C. C. Harrison, *Recoll.*, 267; Minnigerode in Jones, *Davis Memorial*, 422–24, quots. ("Bail Bond" facsimile on 423 is Nov.: cf. names in Rowland 7:175); *Moore's Guide to Richmond*, 24; *New York Tribune*, May 14 and 13, quots.; Strode, *Tragic Hero*, 307 (*Enquirer* quots.).

105. BNH in C. C. Harrison, *Recoll.*, 266, quot.; Strode, *Tragic Hero*, 308 (Geo. Davis quots.); *New York Tribune*, May 14, 1867, p. 1; Minnigerode in Jones, *Davis Memorial*, 422, quots. (this is the exact descr. of a "humble man" in Kadloubovsky and Palmer, *Early Fathers*, 215).

106. B. T. Johnson, "Case of JD," 169–76, quots.; BNH in C. C. Harrison, *Recoll.*, 266–67, quots.; *New York Tribune*, May 14, 1867, p. 1, col. 3, quot.

107. BNH in C. C. Harrison, *Recoll.*, 267, quots.; Minnigerode in Jones, *Davis Memorial*, 422, quot.

108. BNH in C. C. Harrison, *Recoll.*, 267, quots; Minnigerode in Jones, *Davis Memorial*, 424, quot.

Chapter XX Sad Wandering

1. Daniel E. Sutherland, *The Confederate Carpetbaggers*, 36–37, 40–41 (BNH lawyer in New York City); VHD, *Memoir* 2:795, quot.; B. T. Johnson, "Case of JD," 175; Butler, *Judah P. Benj.*, 390 (Benj. quot.).

2. Tucker to JD, May 14, 1867, quots. (MS, Davis Collection, ADAH); Anne Rose Page to VHD, May 15, ibid., quots.; Lucy Ashton Harrison to Joseph Prentis Webb, May 24, quot. (typed copy of MS, courtesy Joseph H. Harrison); *Letters*, 270–75; Rowland 7:103–13; Elder poem dated "June 1867," photocopy at Beauvoir.

3. Ross, *First Lady*, 299–300, 285; Quot. from gravestone (which was there by 1866: Avary, *Dixie after War*, 407–8); BNH in C. C. Harrison, *Recoll.*, 268, quots.; Bowers, *Tragic Era*, 149, 152, and Index (Ristori); Pierce to VHD, May 14, 1867 (Rowland 7:103, quot.; "Boon's Head" really "Boar's Head": see Nichols, *Franklin Pierce*, 530).

4. JD to VHD, Jan. 28–29, 1866, MS, TRANSYL, quot.; VHD, *Memoir* 2:797, quots.

5. Denison, *Soldiering*, 68–69, quots.; VHD, *Memoir* 2:797–98; Blakey, *Gen. Winder*, 202–3; W. C. Davis, *Breck.*, 546–71 (Helm had been C.S. agt. in Cuba, see Rowland 7:117, 120); Butler's *Lives:* see below.

6. Strode, *Tragic Hero*, 315–17, 364, 367; VHD, *Memoir* 2:797–98, quot. (see 915 for another silent blessing); George E. Carter, "A Note on Jefferson Davis in Canada," *Jnl. Miss. Hist.* 33:134. See also N. D. Smith, "Reminisc. of JD," 178. Davises never "sought sympathy" or "expressed self-pity" (Goldsborough, "Varina H. Davis," 16).

7. JD to R. H. Chilton, July 20, 1867, in McElroy, *JD* 2:594, quots. (one phrase, "systematic . . ." from Strode, *Tragic Hero,* 320). See Chilton in *Papers* 2::249 n.2, and JD, *Rise and Fall* 2:129, 512. On terms, see John H. Reagan, "Flight and Capture of Jefferson Davis" in *Annals of the War,* 150–51.

8. McElroy, *JD* 2:595 (quots. from JD to Joseph Davis, July 22, 1867), 617 (JD quot. *re* college); JD to J. W. J. Niles, Feb. 15, 1871, MS, ALA, quots. (prob. the lot VHD bought on Gulf Coast 1857: see Strode, *Patriot,* 297–98; VHD, *Memoir* 2:825); Lee to Fitzhugh [Rooney] Lee, Mar. 30, 1868 (Lee, *Recoll. and Letters,* 309, quot.);

9. Benj. to VHD, Sept. 1, 1865 (*Letters,* 170–73); Mason to JD, June 28 and July 13, 1867 (Rowland 7:116–17, 119–20; also 111, 115; he was Conf. "banker" abroad [Vandiver, *Their Tattered Flags,* 232]); Lowry to BNH, May 10 (Rowland 7:101–3); JD to McRae, June 12 (ibid., 113–15); C. S. Davis, *Colin J. McRae,* 81–86; Strode, *Tragic Hero,* 317–18.

10. Everett, *Brierfield,* 87–90 (JD quot.; sale to "be rescinded" if he claimed Brierfield later; see Hermann, *Pursuit of Dream,* 109); Strode, *Tragic Hero,* 298–99; VHD to Mrs. H. Cobb, July 6, 1868 (*Corr. of Toombs,* 700, quot.).

11. VHD, *Memoir* 2:798, quots. (see Rowland 6:541–42); VHD to JD, Feb. 23, 1866, MS, ALA; JD to VHD, Mar. 13–14, 1866, MS, TRANSYL, quots. (but see Freeman, *R. E. Lee* 4:418–19, and *SHSP* 13:551).

12. VHD, *Memoir* 2:799–800; Boyle, "JD in Canada," 91, quot.; Marg. K. Howell to VHD, Oct. 11, 1867, MS, ALA, quots.

13. Boyle, "JD in Canada," incl. a memoir of Stephen S. Cummins (quots. passim); J. G. Ryan to VHD, Feb. 13, 1890 (Rowland 7:121–22, quots.; encl. JD to Ryan, July 19, 1867).

14. Boyle, "JD in Canada," 92 (quots.), 89 (the Bible came to Cummins at sister's death). See appendix C for the Bible and verses (pic. in T. Hill, "Victory in Defeat," 25).

15. JD to VHD, Oct. 11 ("Give my love to her"), Dec. 2–3, 1865, Dec. 30, 1865–Jan. 1, 1866, MSS, TRANSYL; VHD, *Memoir* 2:800–801, quots. (see Rowland 7:133); Ross, *First Lady,* 303–4. JD sends affection and love to Ma, Mar. 13–14, Mar. 23, Apr. 21–23, MSS, TRANSYL; ends letter to her, 1859: "the affection with which I am as ever your Son" (*Papers* 6:242).

16. Odgers, *A. D. Bache,* 174–77, 208–15 (quots. on 210, 208); VHD to JD, Nov. 7, 1865, MS, ALA, quots. The private Sanitary Comm. gave medical care to troops and prisoners (Randall, *Civil War,* 635).

17. *Papers* 6:52 and n.1; Nichols, *Franklin Pierce,* 532; Thompson, *Robert Toombs,* 252 (Toombs quot.); JD to Cora Ives, Apr. 25, 1869 (*Letters,* 301–2); *Papers* 1:App. 4, Charts 8 and 5; Freeman, *R. E. Lee* 4:492; Hermann, *Pursuit of Dream,* 17; Mason in *DAB; Letters* 357 Ed. Note.

18. Ibid., and 420 Ed. Note; *Papers* 1:App. 4, n.19; Hughes, *Gen. Hardee,* 313; R. Taylor, *Destruction,* 136–37, 247 (quots.); Parrish, *Richard Taylor,* 281–84, 480–81 (Mimi was 41). For Taylor and JD, see Rowland 7:79; VHD, *Memoir* 1:94.

19. JD to VHD, [1870 fragment], typescript, ALA, quot.; *Imitation* (1916), 46, quot. (he used "this book continuously . . . in Canada": *Conf. Vet.,* June 1908, 264); *BCP* (1850), quot.; VHD, *Memoir* 2:805–6 (JD quot.); (Other threats:) Rowland 7:130, 133–34 (both 1867), 10:18–19 (1887); *Cal. JD MSS,* 14 (1870); McElroy, *JD* 2:628–29 (1875).

20. *Papers* 2::16 n.2; Freeman, *Cal. Conf. Papers,* 474; VHD, *Memoir* 2:800–802; Jones, *Davis Memorial,* 458, quot.; Hill in *SHSP* 14:488, quot.; JD to R. S. Guernsey, Apr. 9, 1870 (Rowland 7:268, quot.).

21. Minnigerode to JD, Nov. 5, 1867 (Rowland 7:135–36); Jones, *Davis Memorial,* 391 (pic., dated Nov. 25, 1867); Randall, *Civil War,* 343 (Benj.); Freeman, *R. E. Lee* 4:334–37; Smith to Shea, Oct. 21, 1867 (Freeman, *Cal. Conf. Papers,* 474–75, quots.; he again posted bond for JD [McElroy, *JD* 2:597]); JD, "R. E. Lee," 65–66, quot.; R. E. Lee to Mary C. Lee, Nov. 26, 29 (Lee, *Recoll. and Letters,* 286–88, quots.).

22. *Papers* 2::16 n.2; VHD, *Memoir* 2:799; Strode, *Tragic Hero,* 278; W. F. Howell to JD, Nov. 4, 1867 (Rowland 7:133); VHD to JD, Oct. 23, 1865, MS, ALA; J. D. Howell to VHD, May 17, 1874 (*Letters,* 397–98, quot.; and see 289); Scharf, *Hist. C.S. Navy,* 779 n.1, quot.; flag see at Beauvoir (1986) (made by Mrs. B. N. Holtham, Sherbrooke, Quebec, used when Ma's grave "blessed" [n.d.]).

23. Minnie H. Ransom to JD, Nov. 28, 1867 (Rowland 7:137–38, quot.); VHD, *Memoir* 2:803–4.

24. Strode, *Tragic Hero,* 319, quots.; VHD, *Memoir* 2:804, quots. (see Luke 2:29–30); Randall, *Civil War,* 757; Sue T. Carter, "Pres. Davis as I Knew Him," 209.

25. N. D. Smith, "Reminisc. of JD," 180, 179, quots. (real name Anna, b. 1841 [*Papers* 4:App. 2, p. 406]); Ibid. 1:App. 4, Charts 5 and 14; VHD to Mrs. H. Cobb, July 6, 1868 (*Corr. of Toombs,* 699–700, quots.). Cobb, 54, spoke of himself as "a tolerable old man" (Simpson, *Howell Cobb,* 190).

26. Sue T. Carter, "Pres. Davis as I Knew Him," 209, quots.; JD to Young, Feb. 25, 1868, quots. (composite from *Letters,* 287–88, and McElroy, *JD* 2:597).

27. *Papers* 1:App. 4, Chart 9; N. D. Smith, "Reminsc. of JD," 180 (JD quot.); J. R. Davis to Shea, Nov. 3, 1867 (Freeman, *Cal. Conf. Papers,* 475–77, quot.).

28. Rowland 7:286–88, 9:602; Nuermberger, *Clays of Ala.,* 310–11, 314; Weaver, *So. Tradition,* 263–64; James Wilford Garner, *Reconstruction in Mississippi,* 104–7, 111, 182–83, 193–97. Hermann, *Pursuit of Dream,* 131–34, 116–20; Strode, *Tragic Hero,* 371–72.

29. Hermann, *Pursuit of Dream,* 135–38, 211 (claims settled 1881); JD to Joseph Davis, Dec. 26, 1868 (quots., composite from ibid., 139, and Everett, *Brierfield,* 94); Ibid., 96–97, 104–5; Montgomery corr. 1875–1902, in Rowland 7:416, 9:490–91; in ALA: Thornton to VHD 1898; Isaiah to VHD, 1900 (regrets missing "pleasure of seeing you once more [in New York City]" and wishes her "such blessings as this temporal life affords"; also 1902).

30. Mason to JD, Apr. 22, 1868 (Rowland 7:237–41 and n.1 on trial; Lee to Fitzhugh [Rooney] Lee, Mar. 30, 1868 (Lee, *Recoll. and Letters,* 309–10, quot.; see 313 on trial); McElroy, *JD* 2:599–601; N. D. Smith, "Reminisc. of JD," 180, quot.; VHD, *Memoir* 2:805, quots. (says 3 ribs; see JD, Rowland 7:243).

31. VHD to Mrs. H. Cobb, July 6 and Oct. 22, 1868 (Phillips, *Corr. of Toombs,* 699–700 and 704–6, quots.); JD to Cobb, July 6, and P. S. by VHD (Rowland 7:242–43, quots.); Simpson, *Howell Cobb,* 190–91; Strode, *Tragic Hero,* 337.

32. VHD, *Memoir* 2:805–7, quots.; N. D. Smith, "Reminisc. of JD," 180; Strode, *Tragic Hero,* 334–37, 339; Marg. Howell to MBC, Mar. 23, 1867 (MS, S. Caroliniana Library; and see *Letters,* 255); Butler (Baltimore, 1866; "Alban Butler" in *Universal Encycl.*), Froude (London, 1862), Ellis (London, 1848), Baker (London, 1866), Worcester (Boston, 1866): all inscr. "Fortress Monroe," except Baker, which has date, "Jan. 21st 1867" (Rosenstock); *The Iliad of Homer* (trans. by Edward Earl of Derby; [New York: Scribner, 1866]; from Shea, Mar. 11, 1867) and *Life and Letters of Lady Arabella Stuart* by Elizabeth Cooper ("Fortress Monroe" [Beauvoir]); VHD, *Memoir* 2:807, quot.; "Joseph Emerson Worcester" in *Universal Encycl.*

33. Scharf, *Hist. C.S. Navy,* 783–85 and n.1; JD-Bulloch corr., 1880–85, in Rowland 8, 9; see *Letters,* 186; Benj. to JD, Aug. 6, 1868, and to VHD, Sept. 1, 1865 (ibid., 293, 171, quots.); Butler, *Judah P. Benj.,* 381, 387, 389, 395, 402–3 (VHD quot.), 425; *SHSP* 32:171, quot.; VHD, *Memoir* 2:810, quot. .

34. Strode, *Tragic Hero,* 335–37 (Walker quots.; invitations: 343–44, *Letters,* 341–43, VHD, *Memoir* 2:807–8, Ross, *First Lady,* 309); Hope to JD, July 23 [1868] (Rowland 7:122–23 and n.1; see 116, 244–45 ["Edgebury" here, but see Lee, *Recoll. and Letters,* 216]; Hope in McElroy, *JD* 2:724–25); VHD to Mrs. H. Cobb, Oct. 22, 1868 (Phillips, *Corr. of Toombs,* 705, quot.).

35. VHD, *Memoir* 2:807–8 (quot.), 1:43; N. D. Smith, "Reminisc. of JD," 181; JD to VHD, Sept. 4, 1868 (*Letters,* 294, quots.); *The Oxford Illustrated Literary Guide to Great Britain and Ireland,* comp. and ed. by Dorothy Eagle and Hilary Carnell, 6–7, 129, Map 3.

36. VHD to Mrs. Cobb (as in Note 34 above), 705–6, quots. (ref. to I Thess. 5:17; Billy was exhibited to a visiting doctor); VHD, *Memoir* 2:808.

37. Ibid., 808–11, quots. (see 775); (Smith:) *Six Decades*, 602, Strode, *Tragic Hero*, 335–36; Jefferson Davis, "Scotland & the Scottish People. An Address . . . St. Andrew's-Day, 1875," 9–10, quots.; JD to Marg. Davis and to VHD, Aug. 6 and 9, 1869 (*Letters*, 308–9, quots.; misquot. from *Lady of Lake* 6.565–67; see Ed. Note); *Black's Guide* (1868) in Rosenstock, also James Ballantine's *One Hundred Songs*, inscr. to JD, "Edinburgh. 26 August 1869."

38. *Letters*, 304–5 Ed. Note, and 306–13 (JD to VHD and Marg. Davis, July 30–Aug. 26, 1869, quots.); JD, "Scotland," 27, quot.; Culloden in *Universal Encycl.* *Blackwood's Edinburgh Magazine*, noted for satire, supported C.S.A. (Baugh, *Lit. Hist. of Eng.*, 1178–79; McElroy, *JD* 2:370).

39. N. D. Smith, "Reminisc. of JD," 180–81; JD, "Scotland," 12n (Mackay quot.); Strode, *Tragic Hero*, 345–52 (quots. on 346–48; 350: *Glasgow Herald* notes "modesty" as JD's "characteristic"). Cf. descr. by Ransom in VHD, *Memoir* 2:914 (also "excellent swordsman").

40. JD to VHD, Aug. 17, 1869 (*Letters*, 311, quots. and Ed. Note; see 328–29, Mackay to VHD, Dec. 21); Strode, *Tragic Hero*, 346 and 350 (quots. from Miss Blackwood and *Glasgow Herald*); VHD, *Memoir* 2:811, quot.

41. Strode, *Tragic Hero*, 339–41; Avary, *Dixie after War*, 415, quots.; Randall, *Civil War*, 807–8 and nn.; Paul Bagby to JD, Aug. 31, 1867 (Rowland 7:128); William T. Walthall, "The Life of Jefferson Davis," 28, quot.; VHD, *Memoir* 2:801, quot. See B. T. Johnson, "The Case of JD," 145.

42. Claiborne, *Miss.*, 443–46; Octave Aubry, *The Second Empire*, 397–405, 423–24; Magruder and Drayton in Warner, *Gens. in Gray* (see also, e.g., Price, Early, Hindman, Wm. Preston); R. D. Calhoun, "John Perkins Family," 85–88; *Letters*, 299; *U.D.C. Magazine*, Dec. 1987, 46–49; DeLeon, *Belles*, 302; Sears, *John Slidell*, 6–9, 225–26 (quot.), 234–37; Mann to JD, Aug. 30, 1872 (Moore, *Mann Letters*, 32, quot.); Winters, *C. W. in La.*, 426–27; Kerby, *Kirby Smith's Conf.*, 428.

43. JD to VHD, Jan. 17, 1869, MS, ALA; Slidell to JD, Feb. 12 (*Letters*, 298); JD to R. S. Guernsey, Apr. 9, 1870 (Rowland 7:268); VHD, *Memoir* 2:809, quots. (on Napoleon III, see E. C. Wharton to JD, Rowland 10:49–53); Aubry, *Second Empire*, 99, 150–51, 310–13, 592–601; Ross, *First Lady*, 312 (*Gaulois* quot.).

44. JD to VHD, Jan. 27, 1869, MS, ALA, quot.; JD to VHD, Feb. 7 (*Letters*, 296 and Ed. Note); Strode, *Tragic Hero*, 339–41; Mann to JD, Jan. 19, 1872 (Rowland 7:301–3, quots.); Moore, *Mann Letters*, 22, 23 n.29 and 35 (son), 77, 69 (quots.; see passim).

45. JD to VHD, Feb. 7, 1869 (*Letters*, 297, quots.; cf. *Polk* 1:112; see Craven, *Prison Life*, 271).

46. N. D. Smith, "Reminsc. of JD," 180; Wolff to Walthall, May 15, 1879, MS, TULANE, quot.; Lubbock, *Six Decades*, 666, quots. (see 608, 610); Minnigerode in *Life and Reminisc.*, 229–30, quots. See ibid., 246, 321; R. Davis, *Recoll. of Miss.*, 324; Alfriend, *Life of Davis*, 19; Jones, *Davis Memorial*, 340, 346, 350, 416, 419, 520, 578, 581, 623; Strode, *Tragic Hero*, 364; *New Orleans Daily Picayune*, Dec. 7, 1889, pp. 2, 8 (10 refs. to purity); and even Wigfall, in Wright, *Southern Girl*, 159.

47. *Letters*, 470 (VHD finds an actress "an incarnation of lust . . . disgusting in the extreme"); JD to Mann, Apr. 19, 1869 (ibid., 300 and Ed. Note, 299); Marg. Davis to JD, Apr. 30 (ibid., 302–3); VHD to JD, Oct. 2 (ibid., 317, quots.; see 320, 322–23).

48. JD to VHD, Feb. 7, 1869 (*Letters*, 297, quot.) and Feb. 9 from Lausanne (MS, ALA); Robert Douthat Meade, *Judah P. Benjamin: Confederate Statesman*, 379 (buried in wife's plot, 1884; U.D.C. marker, 1938; wife and daughter, pic. facing 57); Strode, *Tragic Hero*, 341–42.

49. Strode, *Tragic Hero*, 337–38; JD to VHD, Nov. 22, 1868 (*Letters*, 294–95); T. Hill, "Victory in Defeat," 29 (invitation presumed from Benj.); Butler, *Judah P.*

Benjamin, 344, 367, 390–400 (called to bar at Lincoln's Inn [383; see 379–81] but lived at Temple [see 388, 394]); VHD, *Memoir* 2:810, quot.

50. Ibid., quot.; Benj. to JD, Dec. 20, 1868 (Rowland 7:246–47, quot.; see JD to ed. of the *Standard*, 248–51); McElroy, *JD* 2:613, quot.

51. Inventory, 8–9, quots. (ball assumed for Billy, others named); JD to VHD, Sept. 4, 1868, and July 27 and Feb. 7, 1869 (*Letters*, 294, 305 and 298 [quots.]; see 295, 296, 303, 306 ["God preserve you all, is the constant prayer"], 307, 308, 310, 312, 324; also kisses to Mary Stamps' children, 322).

52. Ross, *First Lady*, 308, 313–14; JD to Marg. Davis, May 10, 1869 (*Letters*, 303, quot.); JD to VHD, Dec. 7–8, 1865, and Mar. 13–14, 1866, MSS, TRANSYL, quots. ("radical [i.e., root] virtues" prob. means to theological ones, faith, hope, and charity, and/or cardinal ones, prudence, justice, temperance, fortitude).

53. VHD to JD, Dec. 25–28, 1865, MS, ALA, quot.; "Winnie's Table Talk," quots. (typescript, n.d., Strode Papers, ALA; ref. to Guy Fawkes indicates England); VHD to JD, Nov. 1865 fragment, ALA (Tennyson); *Letters*, 364 (Ahearn); Marg. Davis to JD, Nov. 14, 1869 (ibid., 322); JD to VHD, Dec. 4, 1869 (ibid., 328; see 325–26; he worried about her on Nov. 21 and Dec. 2–3, MSS, TRANSYL); VHD to JD, Dec. 22–25 (ibid., 330–31); T. Hill, "Victory in Defeat," 35.

54. DeLeon, *Belles*, 71, quot.; Inventory, 10 (cigar box in T. Hill, "Victory in Defeat," 32); JD to Marg. Davis, May 10, 1869 (*Letters*, 303, quots.); Ross, *First Lady*, 313–14 (quot. from Billy's letter).

55. Quots.: JD to VHD, Apr. 8–9, 1866, MS, TRANSYL; VHD to JD, Dec. 25–28, 1865, MS, ALA; VHD to JD, Apr. 14, 1866 (Strode, *Tragic Hero*, 278); JD to VHD, Oct. 20, 1865, MS, TRANSYL; VHD to JD, Oct. 2, 1869 (*Letters*, 318); T. R. diary in Ross, *First Lady*, 314. T. R. attacked JD later: see Benjamin Sacks, "A Jefferson Davis Sequel" in *Jnl. Miss. Hist.* 51 (1989): 360–65.

56. JD to Marg. Davis, Mar. 23, 1866, MS, TRANSYL, quots.; JD to VHD, Apr. 21–23, ibid., quot.

57. JD to VHD, from "South Hampton," Sept. 25, 1869 (*Letters*, 313–14, quots.; and Ed. Note).

58. JD to VHD, Mar. 13–14, 1866, MS, TRANSYL, quots.; JD in Eckert, 74; Marg. Davis Hayes in *Conf. Vet.*, Jan. 1907, 42; Garner, *Reconstr. in Miss.*, 121–246, 269; JD to VHD, Oct. 11 and 15, 1869 (*Letters*, 318–19, quots.).

59. JD to Mary Stamps, Nov. 10, 1869, Aug. 1870, and Nov. 8, 1871 (*Letters*, 321–22, 345, 353–54, quots.).

60. Strode, *Tragic Hero*, 297–98, 300, 373–75 (see 466–67); *Papers* 5:135 n.14; Gravestone of Sarah Barnes Stamps, 1859–62, Rosemont Cem. (graves of Mildred Maury [d. 1856], and also Mary, "presumed" here in list furnished by Rosemont); JD to VHD, Dec. 4, 1859, and VHD to JD, Dec. 22–25 (*Letters*, 328 and 331, quots.; Shawl at Beauvoir, 1984 (given by Mary's granddaughter); Goldsborough, in "Varina Howell Davis" (describes VHD's jealousy, especially of her grandmother, Mary Stamps).

61. JD to Mary Stamps, Nov. 10, 1869 (*Letters*, 321–22, quots.); Lowry and McCardle, *Hist. of Miss.*, 361, quot.; Garner, *Reconstr. in Miss.*, 209–42 (Hooker: Rowland 7:77–79 and n.1); Sue T. Carter, "Pres. Davis as I Knew Him," 209, quots.; C. Tarpley's exact words used by J. A. P. Campbell in Jones, *Davis Memorial*, 667.

62. JD to VHD, Jan. 17, 1870, MS, ALA, quot.; JD to Winnie Davis, June 27 (*Letters*, 343, quots.; see 367); Nancy D. Baird, "A Kentucky Physician Examines Memphis," *Tenn. Hist. Q.* 37:193–94, quots.; Shields McIlwaine, *Memphis Down in Dixie*, 168–75; Gerald M. Capers, Jr., *The Biography of a River Town: Memphis: Its Heroic Age*, 180–205; JD to Marg. Davis, Oct. 26, 1871, MS, TRANSYL; JD to VHD, May 17, 1870 (*Letters*, 341, quot.).

63. JD to Winnie Davis, June 27, 1870 (*Letters*, 343, quot.); JD to VHD, Nov. 23 and Dec. 25, 1869 (ibid., 324, 330, quots.); Ibid., 323, 345, Ed. Notes on 346, 347, 350, 357; Strode, *Tragic Hero*, 376.

64. Capers, *Biog. of River Town*, 152–58, 183–86; JD to VHD, Nov. 23, 1869

(*Letters*, 323, quots. and Ed. Note); JD to VHD [Nov. fragment], Dec. 4 (ibid., 324–25, 327, quots.).

65. JD to VHD, letters Oct.–Nov., Dec. 25, Dec. 4, 1869 (*Letters*, 319, 321, 323–25, 330, 328 [quots.]); VHD to JD, Dec. 22–25 (ibid., 331, quot.); JD to Gorgas, Jan. 6, 1870 (ibid., 333, quot.); Strode, *Tragic Hero*, 375 (salary $2000; see 341–42 for Brand).

66. JD to VHD, May 17, 1870 (*Letters*, 341); Starr, *Col. Grenfell's Wars*, 271–318 (Davises: 307, 314; see 205–48, 254–66); Strode, *Tragic Hero*, 375, 358; *Letters*, 420; VHD to JD, Jan. 17, 1874 (ibid., 381, quots.; see 383); JD to VHD, June 7, 1871 (ibid., 349, quot.); Quots. from JD Endrs. on envelope, pic. in VHD, *Memoir* 2:922.

67. JD to VHD, Dec. 4, 1869 (*Letters*, 327–28, quots.); Bruce S. Allardice, *More Generals in Gray* [Baton Rouge: Louisiana State Univ. Press, 1995], 18 n.2 (Alcorn quot.); VHD to JD, Dec. 3 (*Letters*, 326–27, quots.).

68. Thomas Robson Hay, *Pat Cleburne: Stonewall Jackson of the West*, 63; Chalmers, Address to SHS, Aug. 1879 (*SHSP* 7:482, quots.; he too was at Franklin).

69. Henry, *"First with the Most" Forrest*, 452, 459–62 (reinterred 1905), 347–65 (1864); JD to Forrest, June 9, 1864 (Rowland 6:270, quot.); *SHSP* 29:5, quot.; *as they saw* [sic] *Forrest*, ed. Robert Selph Henry (1956, RPR Wilmington: Broadfoot Publ. Co., 1991), 179 (Forrest quot.); John Allan Wyeth, *That Devil Forrest: Life of Nathan Bedford Forrest* (1959, RPR Baton Rouge: Louisiana State Univ. Press, 1989), 560–61, quots. See JD, *Rise and Fall* 2:550n. (The gens. were ASJ, Bgd., Bragg, Polk, JEJ, S. D. Lee, R. Taylor).

70. Henry, *"First with the Most" Forrest*, 452, 456–59; Strode, *Tragic Hero*, 363; Rowland 7:288, 334, 264, 265–66, 272; Nuermberger, *Clays of Ala.*, 304–6, 309; *Pendleton*, 458, quot.

71. Strode, *Tragic Hero*, 379–87 (JD quots. on 383; also other causes for failure); JD to VHD, July 12–Sept. 7, 1873 (*Letters*, 363–70); VHD, *Memoir* 2:811–13; Browne to JD, Mar. 24, 1876, MS, TULANE (JD not "in the remotest degree responsible"; So. Life, kept afloat by Carolina funds, had by now sunk; see Lee, *Recoll. and Letters*, 376–77).

72. JD to VHD, June 30, 1871 (*Letters*, 352, quot.); JD to VHD, Aug. 1, 1870 (ibid., 344; 346 Ed. Note); Stovall, *Toombs*, 284–85.

73. JD to Hope, Oct. 6, 1870 (Rowland 7:280, quot.; Mason died 1871 [*DAB*]); *Letters*, 338–41 (quots. from VHD, Mar.–May 1870). For Stoess, see *Papers* 2::60 n.5; Lubbock, *Six Decades*, 597; DeLeon, *Belles*, 70. Pamphlet on Suez Canal by "Chevalier" Stoess, inscr. to JD, 1869, and book signed to VHD, 1877, in Rosenstock.

74. VHD, *Memoir* 2:811–12; Strode, *Tragic Hero*, 341, 358, 366–70, 372, 376; Drayton to JD, Jan. 23, 1871 (Rowland 7:287; JD quot.); Brandau, *Hist. of Homes of Tenn.*, 314.

75. JD to Lise Mitchell, Oct. 24, 1870 (*Letters*, 346, quots.).; Osborne, *Jubal*, 441–42; JD, Remarks to Lee Mon. Ass., (Rowland 7:281–85, quots. from newspaper rpt.; on success: *Papers* 4:285–89, Rowland 8:228); Weaver, *So. Tradition*, 147 (Dabney quot., 1868).

76. Victor F. O'Daniel, *An American Apostle: The Very Reverend Matthew Anthony O'Brien, O.P.* (Washington, D.C.: The Dominicana, 1923), 297, 26–27; JD to VHD, 1870 fragment, ALA typescript, quot. (refs. to Phil. 4:7; I Cor. 11:26–30; Matt. 26:26–28 and 56).

77. Letters of Newton P. Allen and Rev. George A. Fox to author, Feb.–Dec. 1981 (church org. 1866); McIlwaine, *Memphis*, 121–23, 176 (quot.; ref. to Luke 16:20–21). Prob. really named for Lazarus of Bethany (John 11:1–44), "raised from the dead . . . 'South will rise again'" (Allen letter Sept. 10; Canon Fox letter, Apr. 9; Fox says JD's chalice and paten later in Memphis cathedral chapel: "I have used them myself many times").

78. Letters to author, in Note 77 above; Dufour, *Gentle Tiger,* 8, 169, 127; *Christ Church Nashville,* 81–83 (JD "admired ardently" by Wheat), 100–101, 123; VHD, *Memoir* 2:915 (quot. from Wheat).

79. Strode, *Tragic Hero,* 373, 376–77, 380; VHD, *Memoir* 2:916–17, 814 (Ransom quots.; JD quot.; VHD has 1874; but letters of JD, LBN, Maury, Mrs. Lee show it 1872 [Rowland 7:332, 334–35, and ALA typescript]; see *Papers* 1:App. 4, n. 138).

80. Quots.: JD to Marg. K. Howell, July 18, 1850 (*Papers* 4:123); JD to Walthall, Oct. 25, 1872 (Rowland 7:332); JD to VHD, Mar. 22, 1866, MS, TRANSYL; JD to Sarah Helm, Dec. 14, 1872, in W. C. Davis, *JD,* 665.

Chapter XXI The Cause

1. Goldsborough, "Varina Howell Davis," 13, quot.; JD to G. W. C. Lee, Nov. 10, 1873 (Rowland 7:378, quot.; ref. to Phil. 1:21); JD to Hope, May 15, 1873 (Rowland 7:344, quot.); Strode, *Tragic Hero,* 373, 380–86; JD to Lucinda Stamps, Jan. 4, 1873 (*Letters,* 361).

2. JD to VHD, Aug. 12, 24, and 28 (ibid., 365 and 368, quots.: see JD Jr. to VHD, June 19 and Ed. Note, 362); Shaw, *WPJ,* 114–15 (Lee notes WPJ's "wife and six sweet little children" [100]). Ref. combines John Eston Cooke, *Wearing of the Gray* (publ. 1867) and old Irish song (Freeman, *R. E. Lee* 4:554; *Hoyt,* 401).

3. Shaw, *WPJ,* 98–101, 110, 111, 109; Osborne, *Jubal,* 433, 436–38; Weaver, *So. Tradition,* 135–37; Strode, *Tragic Hero,* 386.

4. Ryan in *Cath. Encycl.;* F. V. N. Painter, *Poets of the South* (New York: Am. Book Co., 1903), 109, 235–36 (date from Rowland 8:164); Thomas Stritch, *The Catholic Church in Tennessee* (Nashville: Catholic Center, 1987), 153; Hill in *Gens. in Gray;* Weaver, *So. Tradition,* 116–21, 135–38, 143–47, 153–58, 163–66; Frank Luther Mott, *A History of American Magazines, 1865–1885* (Cambridge, Mass.: Harvard U. Press, 1938), 70, 382–84; W. H. Browne in *South in Bldg. of Nation,* 11; Osborne, *Jubal,* 439.

5. McElroy, *JD* 2:716, 714; Alfriend in *South in Bldg. of Nation,* 11 and Rowland 7:528 n.1; JD to Walthall, Oct. 29, 1875, and Oct. 13, 1877 (ibid., 459 [quot.] and 8:33).

6. McElroy, *JD* 2:731, 755–57; Hill in *Land We Love,* Feb. and Mar. 1868, 272–84 (quot.), 389–91, 442–43; Pollard, *Life . . .* (Phila.: Natl. Publ. Co., 1869); Vandiver, "JD," 3–5; JD to C. J. Wright, Feb. 12, 1876, and to Walthall, Dec. 27, 1875 (Rowland 7:495 and 474, quots.); JD to T. C. Reynolds, Jan. 15, 1870 (ibid., 259, quot.); Ross, *First Lady,* 314–16. Errors noted in Pollard by WPJ (*Gen. ASJ,* 396), Dorsey (*Recoll. of H. W. Allen,* 158), W. A. Irving (Weddell, *St. Paul's* 1:242), JD (Rowland 9:522).

7. JD to Walthall, Oct. 13, 1877 (ibid. 8:33, quots.). See "Chivalrous Southrons" (*So. Review,* July 1869), 113–14, for remarks on AHS book.

8. *SHSP* 18:349–65 ("The Southern Historical Society; its Origin and History"); Ibid. 7:449–50 (quot. from Maury); Maury, *Recoll.,* 251–52 (he says 1868); Perry, *Bishops of Am. Church,* 263 (Galleher priested May 30, 1869); Osborne, *Jubal,* 433–34; Hughes, *Gen. Hardee,* 312–13 (d. Nov. 6).

9. *New Orleans Daily Picayune,* Aug. 24, 1873 (JD quots.; cf. JD in 1877 and 1882, in Rowland 8:54 and 9:162–70); Strode, *Tragic Hero,* 367; JD, Speech Nov. 3, 1870 (ibid. 7:284, quot.); Rhodes to JD, Sept. 4, 1881 (ibid. 9:16, quots.).

10. Hill, Speech Feb. 18, 1874 (*SHSP* 14:487, quots.); *Hill,* 50–52, 730–811 (quots. from "Notes" on 746–47, 804); Haywood J. Pearce, Jr., *Benjamin H. Hill: Secession and Reconstruction* (Chicago: U. of Chicago Press, 1928), 148n ("Notes" publ. June–Aug. 1867).

11. *New Orleans Daily Picayune,* Aug. 24, 1873 (JD quots.); Newspaper clips., Aug. 26–Sept. 5, 1873 (Rowland 7:363–78, in Early to JD, Sept. 5; quots. on 377, 367).

12. Osborne, *Jubal*, 434–38 (quots. from Early Aug. 14; also succeeded Lee as v. p. in Va.); Early to JD, Sept. 5, 1873 (Rowland 7:363–78, encl. clippings; quots. on 368, 369).

13. *SHSP* 18:363; WPJ to JD, Dec. 11, 1870 (Rowland 7:285–86, quot.); Reed to JD, Sept. 18, 1871 (ibid., 296–98, quots.). Mann, writing his own mem., asked JD in 1869 to come "pursue your work" and "compare notes" (Moore, *Mann Letters*, 28).

14. Jordan, "JD" (1865); JEJ to JD, Sept. 30, 1867 (Rowland 7:129–30, quot.; see 6:491–503); Wharton to JD, Jan. 24, 1868 (ibid. 7:234–36, quot.).

15. JD to JEJ, Oct. 23, 1867 (Rowland 7:131, quot.); JD to Wharton, Oct. 23 (ibid., 132, quots.); JEJ to JD, Jan. 6, 1868 (ibid., 234, quot.); Wharton to JD, Jan. 24 (ibid., 236).

16. Barksdale to JD, Jan. 7, 1874 (ibid., 381–82, quot.); JEJ, *Narrative*, 430–65 (quots. on 431 and header) and passim; Geo. Davis to JD (2 letters), Oct. 15, 1880 (Rowland 8:504–6, quots.; points out JEJ errors).

17. JD to VHD, Aug. 28, 1873 (*Letters*, 368, quots.); Hillyer to JD, Dec. 19, 1873 (Rowland 7:380–81, quots.); Bragg to Browne, Feb. 19, 1872, in Seitz, *Bragg*, 132n.; JD to Bragg, June 29, 1872 (Rowland 7:320–22); JD to Walthall, Nov. 23, 1874 (ibid., 408–9, quots.); JD to VHD, Jan. 24, 1866, MS, TRANSYL, quot.; Hallock, *Bragg and Defeat*, 264; Shaw, *WPJ*, 109–10 (with VHD quot.).

18. JD to VHD, July 23 (quot.), Aug. 24 (quot.), 26, 28, Sept. 7 (quots.), 10, 1873 (*Letters*, 365–71); Strode, *Tragic Hero*, 382–88, 376 (VHD had reclaimed some furniture and bought some).

19. Froude at Beauvoir, other books, Rosenstock (all say Memphis, except the religious ones; inscr. in *The Christian Year* from Mrs. Liscombe Clarke); VHD to JD, Feb. 4, 1878 (*Letters*, 471, quots.); Sturges, "Recoll. of JD," 17–18, quots. (Mrs. H. G. Otis of Boston sent Schlegel to JD in prison); Ident. of Robt. assumed from *Letters*, 332, 448.

20. JD to VHD, Jan. 17, 1870, MS, ALA; Jones, *Davis Memorial*, 339; G. W. Jones interview in *New Orleans Picayune*, Dec. 7, 1889, p. 2, cols. 3–4; Nuermberger, *Clays of Ala.*, 302–12 (JD quots. on 312; see JD corr., 1870–75, in nn., and Va. Clay to JD, Rowland 7:398–99); Clay-Clopton, "C. C. Clay," 74, 82 (photograph).

21. R. Davis, *Recoll. of Miss.*, 255–56, quot.; JD to Phelan, Aug. 10, 1870 (Rowland 7:279, quot.); Phelan in Wakelyn, *Biog. Dict. of Conf.* and Rowland 5:353 n.1 (see *Papers* 5:34–35 and n.10); JD to M. J. Wright, Jan. 18, 1875 (Rowland 7:413–14); Childs, "Turney's First Tenn.," 164 and Frazer to VHD in *Cal. JD MSS*, 295; Harris to JD, Dec. 25, 1864, in Hood, *Advance and Retreat*, 306; JD to LBN, Jan. 14, 1880 (Rowland 8:438, quots.); Ibid. 5:303 n.1.

22. Jones, *Davis Memorial*, 483, 646, and 647 (quot. from poem); Boyle, "JD in Canada"; Virginia Frazer Boyle in *South in Bldg. of Nation*, 11; Corr. in Rowland 8:426–28, 529–30 and 9:354, 579–80, 582–83.

23. JD to "Mrs. Merriwether," Sept. 6, 1873 (quots.), and Feb. 17, 1872, subscribes to her "Tablet" (MSS, Meriwether Papers, Univ. of Memphis); Elizabeth Avery Meriwether, *Recollections of 92 Years*, 198, quots. (on JD, 198–202, *Facts and Falsehoods Concerning the War on the South*, under pen name George Edmonds); Hermann, *Joseph E. Davis*, 130–31.

24. Henry, *"First with Most,"* 458–59; JD to "Mrs. Merriwether," Jan. 5, 1876, quots. (MS, Meriwether Papers, Univ. of Memphis; "many-headed"="the herd" in Scott, *Lady of the Lake*, Canto V, lines 828–35). On her irreligion, see Meriwether, *Recoll. of 92 Years*, 30, 32–33, 201, but also 35.

25. Painting (copy of Bernadino Luini) at Beauvoir (*The Cloud of Unknowing* [London: Burns Oates and Washbourne, 1947], 29–36, Martha as active life, Mary as contemplative); Newton P. Allen to author, Aug. 24, 1981; Geo. A. Fox to author, Feb. 19 and July 6; Strode, *Tragic Hero*, 372; St. Luke's, Salisbury, N. C., in "Historic Churches Date Book, Episcopal Edition" (Boston: Colonial Publishing, Inc. [1960]), quots.

26. Mann to VHD, June 20, 1873, in E. Rowland, *Varina* 2:498–501, quots.; Ibid. 1:350–51; Quilt in Mus. of Conf. (1986), presumed this one (T. Hill, "Victory in Defeat," back cover); *Imitation* in Rosenstock (called *Following* . . . , but Challoner trans.; inscr. by VHD, "Feb 18th 1872/Memphis").

27. JD to VHD, Jan. 17, 1870, MS, ALA; Pryor, *Reminisc. of Peace and War,* 81; Geo. A. Fox to author, Feb. 19 and July 6, 1981; *BCP* and *Manual* at Beauvoir; De Vere and *Legends* in Rosenstock. Many men, besides the devoted Benj., BNH, and WPJ, express regard for VHD: e.g., *Papers* 3:204; Rowland 7:386, 467, 9:333, 599, 10:18, 19, 162, 164, 165; *Cal. JD MSS,* 221.

28. (Blackburn:) Rowland 7:485 n.1 (in Natchez before War; see ibid. 8:118–19; may be related to JD: 10:38) and Capers, *Biog. of River Town,* 188–93; JD to VHD, Jan. 5 and 8, 1874 (*Letters,* 376 and 378, quots.); VHD to JD, Jan. 12 and 17 (ibid., 379 and 381, quots.; see 372).

29. Choppin in Kelly and Burrage, *Dict. of Am. Med. Biog.* and Rowland 6:349, 8:260 (here "Chopin"); JD to VHD, Jan. 5, 16, 18, 1874 (*Letters,* 376–82; quots. on 380, 382; ref. to Gal. 6:2; see also 383–84); VHD to JD, Jan. 12 (ibid., 379, quot.). Author indebted to J. David Hagan, M. D., for discussing JD's ailments at this time.

30. Quots.: *Letters,* 376, 391, 385 (2), 392, 388 (Jan. 1–Mar. 15, 1874), and *Imitation* (1916), 16 (Part 1, chap. 20 is "On Love of Silence and to be Alone").

31. JD to VHD, Feb. 17 and 26, 1874, and to Marg. Davis, Feb. 24 (*Letters,* 386–92, quots. on 389; ref. to Matt. 10:29; see 391).

32. Lubbock, *Six Decades,* 601 (quot.), 655–56; JD to VHD, Mar. 15 and 29, 1874 (*Letters,* 392 and 393, quots.); Moore, *Mann Letters,* 23, 29 (address, 35–44); Mann to JD, Apr. 2, 1871 (Rowland 7:290–93, quots.; see also 298–303); Aubry, *Second Empire,* 592–603.

33. JD to VHD, Mar. 29, 1874 (*Letters,* 393–95, quots.). Sarah Wood lived in Germany with her sister, Baroness Blandina von Grabow (Samson, *Letters of ZT,* xi; Hamilton, *Zachary Taylor* 2:27). Moore, *Mann Letters,* 48 and n.37, 44, 41, 42: Slidell daughters and Duc d'Aumale were his neighbors.

34. JD to VHD, Mar. 29 and Apr. 26, 1874 (*Letters,* 394 and 396, quots.; "run round" on 389; agent on 391–92, 394); JD to Mrs. A. S. Ayres, Aug. 15 (ibid., 399–400); Lubbock, *Six Decades,* 602–3. Mann mentions "the Land Company" (Moore, *Mann Letters,* 41–42).

35. JD to VHD, Apr. 13, Mar. 29, and Jan. 26, 1874 (*Letters,* 395, 394 and 384, quots.); JD to Marg. Davis, Feb. 24, MS, TRANSYL (quot. *re* cough); VHD to JD, Mar. 8 (*Letters,* 389–90); JD to VHD, Jan. 8, 1874 (ibid., 377–78; Rhett's 1st name never given; see Ed. Note); VHD to JD, Jan. 12 (ibid., 379, quot. (Excalibur was King Arthur's sword). Last ref. to JD in Europe is May 6, 1874 (*Mann Letters,* 39).

36. Quots. from JD inscr. in Bible, Conf. Mus., N. O. (copied 1978); Shaw, *WPJ,* 115–17 (quots. from JD to WPJ, Mar. 22, 1875, and n.d.; "cup": e.g., Mark 14:36); JD to VHD, Dec. 31, 1873 (*Letters,* 372, quoting Jeff Jr.); JD Jr. to JD, Nov. 2, 1874 (ibid., 402–3, quots.). Mus. of Conf. has his V. M. I. jacket (T. Hill, "Victory in Defeat," 32).

37. J. D. Howell to VHD, May 17, 1874 (*Letters,* 397–98, quots.).

38. Same to same, Sept. 28, 1874 (ibid., 400–401, quots.); Scharf, *Hist. C.S. Navy,* 779 n.1, quots. (traces Howell's career, names 6 ships he commanded); VHD, *Memoir* 2:819–20, quot.

39. W. F. Howell to JD, Nov. 12, 1875, MS, TRANSYL, quot. (telegram, sent before all details known); JD to VHD, Nov. 11 (*Letters,* 421, quot.; for Wm., see 377, 380); Scharf, *Hist. C.S. Navy,* 779 n.1, quots. See also VHD, *Memoir* 2:821–22 and Strode, *Tragic Hero,* 403n.

40. JD to VHD, Nov. 11, 1875 (*Letters,* 421, quot.); VHD, *Memoir* 2:819 and 822–23, quots.

41. JD to VHD, Nov. 18, 1875 (*Letters,* 420–22, quots.); *Papers* 1::1, p. lxiv, quot.; VHD, *Memoir* 2:825, quot.; JD to VHD, Nov. 18, 1875 (*Letters,* 422, quot.; ignis fatuus=will-o'-the-wisp; cf. *Hamlet* 1.4.69–78); Zoe Posey, "Sarah Anne Dorsey:

A Sketch," 2, 3, 5; Charlotte Elizabeth Lewis, "Sarah Anne Dorsey: A Critical Estimate"; Bertram Wyatt-Brown, *The House of Percy,* 124, 163.

42. *Letters,* 371, 377, 379, 381, 383–84, 411–14, 422–23; JD to VHD, Oct. 23, 1874, and Oct. 22, 1875 (ibid., 401–2 and 419, quots.); Everett, *Brierfield,* 97–104 (on estoppel, see also McElroy, *JD* 2:622–23); Hermann, *Pursuit of Dream,* 201–4.

43. JD to VHD, Feb. 22–May 14, 1875 (*Letters,* 407–10; quot. on 409); Strode, *Tragic Hero,* 401–4 (VHD quot. on 403); Lubbock in *Life and Reminisc.,* 188–93, and Lubbock, *Six Decades,* 607–11, quots. (he was then Galveston tax-collector); Gano in Warner, *Gens. in Gray;* Breck., ibid. (d. May 17, 1875).

44. McElroy, *JD* 2:625; *New Orleans Daily Picayune,* Aug. 24, 1873 (quot.); Lubbock, *Six Decades,* 609 (JD quots. in Texas). This speech alone shows there was no sharp postwar cleavage between a "submissive" Lee and a "stubborn" JD, as said in Hesseltine, *Conf. Leaders in New South,* vi–vii, 28–41.

45. Lubbock, *Six Decades,* 609 (JD quot.); Strode, *Tragic Hero,* 406; JD to C. J. Wright, Feb. 12, 1876 (Rowland 7:492–93, quot.). See Geo. W. Jones, ibid., 456–57 and in *Life and Reminsc.,* 127.

46. McElroy, *JD* 2:628–30; Strode, *Tragic Hero,* 407–9 (JD quot.); JD to VHD, Sept. 12–23, 1875 (*Letters,* 415–17, quots.); JD to Redpath, Sept. 6 (Rowland 7:456).

47. JD to VHD, Oct. 9, 1875 (*Letters,* 418, quots.); Strode, *Tragic Hero,* 409.

48. McMurry, *John Bell Hood,* 198, quot.; Foote, *Casket,* passim, esp. 241–45, 154–57 (contradicts *O. R.* below); JD to H. R., Jan. 13, 1865 (Richardson, *Conf.* 1:516, quot.); *SHSP* 52:215–17; Yearns, *Conf. Cong.,* 182; *O. R.,* 2, 8:68–69, 471–72 (quot.), 500, 504, 526, 532, 557, 664 (Mallory quots., the 1st citing Foote); Hay, "LBN: Comm. Gen.," 22 (Foote quot.); LBN to JD, Apr. 17, 1879 (Rowland 8:380, quot.).

49. Mann to JD, Apr. 18, 1874 (Moore, *Mann Letters,* 37–38, quots. from Mann and son; see also 35, 38–42); JEJ, *Narrative,* 430–33; Symonds, *JEJ,* 361 (Hampton quot.).

50. JD to VHD, Jan. 8, 1874 (*Letters,* 378, quots.); McMurry, *John Bell Hood,* 195–203 (d. Aug. 30, 1879; Sherman also acted gallantly); Dyer, *Gallant Hood,* 315–19 (3 sets of twins); Williams, *Bgd.,* 320. Title page of *Advance and Retreat:* "Published for the Hood Orphan Memorial Fund, G. T. Beauregard, New Orleans, La., 1880."

51. Williams, *Bgd.,* 306–10 (quots. on 307, 309; title and Roman quot. on 310; see 313 and WPJ to JD, Sept. 9, 1878 [Rowland 8:276–77]); JD, Speech at Miss. City, July 10 (ibid., 227–37, quot. on 232; does *not* say Bgd. threw away victory, as Williams avers); White, *R. B. Rhett,* 242 (see 241 n.20); Roman, *Mil. Operations* 1:Preface, quot.

52. Symonds, *JEJ,* 363, 365, 370, 380; Smith in Warner, *Gens. in Gray; Battles and Leaders* 2:220–63 (art.); Govan, *Different Valor,* 387 (quot. from Lydia Johnston); B. T. Johnson, *JEJ,* 289; Sherman, *Memoirs* 1:328, back flyleaf, 2:141; JEJ, "The Dalton-Atlanta Operations," 1–13 (other Sherman errors noted in Rowland 9:489 and *Cal. JD MSS,* 50).

53. JD to Walthall, Nov. 21, 1875, and Gwin to JD, Dec. 1, 2, 11 (Rowland 7:465–69); Humphreys in Warner, *Gens. in Blue;* Davis-Humphreys corr., Feb. 15 and 22, 1872 (Rowland 7:303–7, quot. on 305; and see 307–9; also 9:307 for JD at 1874 convention).

54. JD to Walthall, Nov. 14, 1875, and Apr. 5, 1876 (Rowland 7:463–64 and 510, quots.); Same to same, Oct. 29.–Dec. 27, 1875 (ibid., 459, 464–66, 472–74), Jan. 24–Aug. 3, 1876, Feb. 6, 1877 (ibid., 487–88, 492, 496, 507–12, 514–17, 523).

55. VHD, *Memoir* 2:823; *Letters,* 422–24; J. A. Hayes gravestone, Hollywood Cem., Richmond; Wardin, "Belmont Mansion," 6; Winchester, "JD, Communicant," 727, quot.; Strode, *Tragic Hero,* 410.

56. *Cong. Globe,* 44th Cong., 1st sess., 1875 and 1876, 4, pt. 1:224 and 303

(Dec. 15, quot. from Randall bill; Jan. 6, Blaine quot.); J. S. Johnston to JD, Jan. 10, 1876 (Rowland 7:477–78, quots. from Wm. Preston and J. S. Johnston in encls., n.1).

57. McElroy, *JD* 2:632–38; Bowers, *Tragic Era*, 462–64, quot.; *Cong. Globe*, 44th Cong., 1st sess., 1876, 4, pt.1:323–26 (Blaine quots.) and 382–89 (Garfield quots.); JD to C. J. Wright, Feb. 12, 1876 (Rowland 7:495, quots.; see 497–98, 471–72, Stevenson, *Southern Side*, 472–75). Ben Butler waved the first "bloody shirt" (a real nightshirt) in 1868: see Stanley F. Horn, *Invisible Empire: The Story of the Ku Klux Klan 1866–1871* (1939; RPR New York: Haskell House Publ., 1973), 150–51.

58. *Cong. Globe*, as in Note 57 above, 326–28, 408–10, 345–51 (Hill, quots.; debate went on through Jan. 17 [403–13, 420–22, 443–47]); G. W. Alexander to JD, Nov. 12, 1875 (Rowland 7:463, quot. from encl. clipping).

59. Lyons to JD, Jan. 12 and 14 (2), 1876 (Rowland 7:478–80, quots.).

60. JD to Lyons, Jan. 27, 1876 (ibid., 481–85, quots.). JD said when Northerners knew "the whole truth," they would change (ibid., 498); *Conf. Vet.*, July 1907, 296, quoted a U.S. vet. publ. saying Wirz, "specifically ordered by" JD, had killed as many men as a recent assassin, "with cruelties incomparably worse."

61. Quots.: Blackburn to JD, Jan. 15, 1876 (Rowland 7:485–86); JD-Knott corr., Jan. 22, 27 (ibid., 486, 489–90). Strode, *Tragic Hero* (414) says Blaine's version of the bill passed; McElroy, *JD* (2:686) says the bill failed "because [JD] was not excepted."

62. *Cong. Globe* (as in Note 57 above), 324 (Blaine quot.); Manly, *Southern Lit.*, 286 (Toombs quot.); JD to Lyons, Jan. 27, 1876, and to Knott, Jan. 22 (Rowland 7:483 and 486, quots.).

63. JD speech, Apr. 25, 1882 (ibid. 9:164, quot.; see 280–81); *Senate Jnl.*, 95th Cong., lst sess., Res. 16 (became law Oct. 17, 1978 [*Montg. Advertiser*, Oct. 18]).

64. Shea, "JD Letter," title p. (publ. Jan. 24, 1876) and Shea to JD, Jan. 24 (Rowland 7:488–89); *SHSP* 1, Nos. 3 and 4 (quot.; see JD to J. W. Jones, May 15, 1877 [Rowland 7:539–40]).

65. *Charleston News and Courier*, Dec. 12, 1889, p. 2, col. 2 (photocopy in Fleming Collection; 1st and last quots., from Edw. McCrady); Charles B. Galloway, "Jefferson Davis: A Judicial Estimate," 21, quots.; Daniel in Jones, *Davis Memorial*, 266 and 269, quots.; Browne to JD, June 26, 1882 (Rowland 9:174, quots.).

66. JD, Address, Mar. 7, 1876 (Rowland 7:499–507, quots. on 499, 507; cf. I Cor. 2:9); JD to O. R. Singleton, Feb. 17 [1858] in McElroy, *JD* 2:646–47, quot. (see Singleton to JD, May 18, in Rowland 8:201–3, and other corr., 360–67).

67. Debate on Pensioning JD, Mar. 3, 1879, in *Pamphlets*, quots. (condensed from Senate record); Wolff to Walthall, May 15, 1879, MS, TULANE, quots.; *Papers* 3:33 n.34. No JD application known; his and all Conf. land grants from Mex. War annulled 1867 (*Papers* 5:114 n.2).

68. *Letters*, 422–37 (quots. 428–29, from JD to VHD and to Marg. D. Hayes, Apr. 22 and May 25, 1876); *Papers* 1:App. 4, Chart 14; JD to Mann, Aug. 6, 1875 (Rowland 7:427, quots.); JD to VHD, Mar. 15, 1874 (*Letters*, 392, quot.); JD to Marg. D. Hayes, May 25 (ibid., 428–29, quots.; see 426). On VHD's health, 1870: VHD to JD, Jan. ("middle age"; "nervous depression"), JD to Winnie Davis, June 1, and to VHD, Aug. 1 and Nov. 1, MSS, ALA; on same, 1871–74: *Letters*, 351, 371, 376, 378, 387.

69. Strode, *Tragic Hero*, 265 and 286 (VHD quots.), 416–19; Lankford, *Irishman in Dixie*, 48, quot.; VHD to JD, Mar. 8, 1874, and July 2, 22, and Sept. 9, 1877 (*Letters*, 390–91 and 457, 460, 462); JD to VHD, Feb. 17, 1874 (ibid., 386).

70. JD to W. T. Cordner, Dec. 7, 1876 (Rowland 7:520–23); JD to James Phelan [Jr.], Oct. 7 (ibid., 519, quots.); JD to Winnie Davis, Sept. 21 (VHD's "physical pain"), and to VHD, Oct. 29 (quots.) and 31, Nov. 25, Dec. 24 (quot.; "your dreadful pain") (*Letters*, 434–37, 440; see 428, 433 Ed. Notes for Pinnie; 435 Ed. Note; 447, 464, 467 Ed. Note); Moore, *Mann Letters*, 37, 49–56.

71. Marg. D. Hayes to VHD, June 9, 1877 (*Letters*, 455, quots.); JD to Marg. D. Hayes, Mar. 26, MS, TRANSYL, quot.; Strode, *Tragic Hero*, 428.

72. JD to VHD, Dec. 9, 1876, and Feb. 26, 1877 (*Letters*, 439 and 450) and McElroy, *JD* 2:639–40; JD to VHD, Dec. 24, 1876, and Jan. 1877 (*Letters*, 440 and 445–46, quots.; Ogdens and Dorseys both had land across from Davis Bend in La.: Currie, *Enclave*, 84, map).

73. JD to Marg. D. Hayes, Feb. 1, 1877 (*Letters*, 447, quots.; see 448); JD to Winnie Davis, Mar. 17 (ibid., 451, quots.). Book first called *Personal Memoirs of Public Events* (W. C. Davis, *JD*, 674). Bills for transport of books and household goods, and passage for Robert Brown, Feb. 1877, are in Davis-Hayes Papers, MVC.

74. JD to Winnie Davis, Mar. 17 and Apr. 24, 1877 (*Letters*, 451–53, quots.; sends "love to dear Pinnie" in both); JD to Winnie Davis, Mar. 30 (ibid., 474, quot.); Thompson, "Beauvoir" (approx. acreage; RR was LandN).

75. Wyatt-Brown, *House of Percy*, 124, 135, 139–44; SAED in *South in Bldg. of Nation*, 11 (lists her novels, 1867–77); SAED's Anglo-Saxon dictionary by Joseph Bosworth (Rosenstock); Posey, "Dorsey: Sketch," 4, 6–7, 3; Lewis, "Sarah Dorsey," passim.

76. SAED, *Recoll. of H. W. Allen*, 159–67 (quot. on 160), (Allen:) 138–39, 143–46, 233–38, 290–307, 326–29, 335 (quot.), and (Perkins:) 162, 322–23, 364, 410, 417; Evans, "JD, Diseases and Drs.," 12; R. D. Calhoun, "John Perkins Family," 72–75, 83–87; SAED to Walthall, Oct. 26, 1877 (Rowland 8:39, quot.; "before the flood": a turn on "après [after] moi le deluge").

77. Dorsey, *Recoll. of H. W. Allen*, 15, 17–23, 70–71, 37–39, 48–52, 308–24, and see 328–44, 351–62 (SAED did admire Bgd. [65–73], but came to think Pemb. blamed unjustly [218], as JD did); Wyatt-Brown, *House of Percy*, 131, quots.; Lewis, "Sarah Dorsey," n.p.; Posey, "Dorsey: Sketch," 2–5, quot.

78. Strode, *Tragic Hero*, 426–34; Dorsey to Mann, Apr. 25, 1878 (*Letters*, 479, quots.); JD to Mary Negus, Aug. 4, 1879 (ibid., 495–97, quot.); VHD, *Memoir* 2:825–26. People at Beauvoir, besides Mrs. Cochran: Strode, as above; Wyatt-Brown, *House of Percy*, 162, 164, 160; Rowland 8:73–74. Tradition handed down on the coast: "It was all a very proper relationship" (conversation with Lawrence Oden, Sept. 16, 1984).

79. Quots.: VHD to JD, Sept. 9, 1877 (*Letters*, 463); JD to VHD, May 1, June 11, July 15 (ibid., 454, 457, 459, 456); JD Jr. to VHD, May 7 (ibid., 454–55).

80. Quots.: VHD to JD, Aug. 2 and Sept. 9 (ibid., 461 and 462); Marg. D. Hayes to VHD in Wyatt-Brown, *House of Percy*, 163 (thinks Sarah scorns other women because of her intellect).

81. Strode, *Tragic Hero*, 428; JD to VHD, June 11 and July 15, 1877 (*Letters*, 456 [quot.], 458–59; pays rent for Maggie, over Sarah's protest); JD to VHD, May 1 (ibid., 453, quot.). Maggie calls brother "dear old Jeff" in several letters, 1881 (Davis-Hayes Papers, MVC).

82. Strode, *Tragic Hero*, 286 and 429–35 (VHD quots.; ref. to "A Ballad" in Oliver Goldsmith, *The Vicar of Wakefield*, chap. 8); *Letters*, 456–78.

83. *Letters*, 487 Ed. Note; McRacken in *[New Orleans] Times Democrat*, May 11, 1902, quots. (typescript, Fleming Collection); SAED to Mann, Aug. 4, 1878, in Strode, *Tragic Hero*, 435, quot. (author finds no evidence for quarrel scene here and in Wyatt-Brown, *House of Percy*, 164); VHD to Walthall, Sept. 8, 1878 (Rowland 8:276); VHD to Marg. D. Hayes, July 5 and 17, Sept. 21, 1879 (Davis-Hayes Papers, MVC).

84. Ross, *First Lady*, 327–29; JD to VHD, Feb. 26, 1877 (*Letters*, 450, quots.); JD to VHD, Jan. (ibid., 446, quot.); JD to E. L. Sutton, Apr. 22, 1888 (Rowland 10:56, quot.). Mary in Wyatt-Brown, *House of Percy*, 162, and JD to VHD, Feb. 9, 1879, ALA typescript ("wild in her grief").

85. JD to VHD, May 1 and Feb. 26, 1877 (*Letters*, 453 and 450, quots.); VHD to JD, Feb. 4, 1878 (ibid., 470, quot.); Winchester, "JD, Communicant," 727 (story

from Hayes's sister); Capers, *Biog. of River Town*, 187–98 (*Aëdes* found to be carrier 1900).

86. JD to Hayes, Oct. 12 (*Letters*, 488–89, quots.); JD to Winnie Davis, Nov. 27, 1878 (ibid., 492–93); Capers, *Biog. of River Town*, 183, 193–98; McIlwaine, *Memphis*, 167–74.

87. Green to JD, Sept. 23 (Rowland 8:279–80); JD to Green, Sept. 29 (Rowland 8:282–83, quots.; ref. to poem of M. J. Barry, 1844 [H. L. Mencken, *A New Dictionary of Quotations* (New York: Knopf, 1960), 1082]: "proper" should be "fittest").

88. JD to Hayes, Oct. 12, 1878 (*Letters*, 488, quot.); Ross, *First Lady*, 329–30; McIlwaine, *Memphis*, 170–74; VHD, *Memoir* 2:827–28; Medical and funeral bills, and one from Elmwood Cem., Dec. 23, for "removal of William Davis . . . to your Lot $9.00" (Davis-Hayes Family Papers, MVC); JD to Winnie Davis, Nov. 27, 1878 (*Letters*, 492–93, quots.).

89. JD to Hayes, Oct. 18, 1878, MS, ALA, quots. (ref. to Alexander Pope, *The Essay on Man* 2.1); JD to VHD, Feb. 26, 1877 (*Letters*, 450, quot.).

Chapter XXII The Hero

1. Quots.: JD to VHD, Nov. 11, 1878 (*Letters*, 492); LBN to JD, May 1, 1879 (Rowland 8:391); JD to Winnie Davis, Nov. 27, 1878 (*Letters*, 493).

2. JD to VHD, Nov. 21–23, 1865, MS, TRANSYL, quot.; JD to Marg. D. Hayes, Apr. 26, 1889 (*Letters*, 556, quot.); Goulburn, *Thoughts*, 205, 280–81; à Kempis, *Imitation* (1916), 161 (see 85–92, 133–38, 175–76; Matt. 5:48; Heb. 2:9–10; also Jean-Pierre de Caussade, *Abandonment to Divine Providence* [Garden City: Image Books, 1975], 64–74, 95–105: "What we have wanted to do is done in the sight of God"); Winnie Davis, "JD in Private Life," 5, quot.

3. Stringfellow to JD, May 22, 1878 (*Letters*, 480–81, quots. and Ed. Note); R. Shepard Brown, *Stringfellow of the Fourth* (New York: Crown Inc., 1960), passim (see esp. 299 n.107). Quots.: JD to Stringfellow, June 4 (*Letters*, 483; *Imitation* [1916], 223: God's judgments true and incomprehensible); JD inscr. in [Keble], *The Christian Year* (Rosenstock); JD, Speech, 1884 (Rowland 9:281); JD to J. G. Ryan, July 2, 1889 (ibid., 10:126; and see 8:174–75).

4. Jones, *Davis Memorial*, 445–47 (JD quots.).

5. VHD, *Memoir* 2:828, quots.; JD to VHD, Feb. 9, 1879, ALA typescript, quot.; JD to LBN, Mar. 17, 1879 (Rowland 8:369–70, quots.; ref. to Rev. 7:17, 21:1–4); JD to C. J. Wright, June 3, 1878, MS, TRANSYL (see Ps. 90:10); JD to Kate Lee Ferguson, Sept. 5, 1879, quot. (typescript, Fleming Collection). Gorgas wrote, turning 50, "I have 20 years more to live" (Wiggins, *Jnls. of Gorgas*, 228).

6. JD-Walthall-Dorsey corr., Feb. 1877–Mar. 1878 (Rowland 7:523–58, 8:32–40, 69–70, 115–16, 122) and other corr., Mar.–Dec. (ibid., 136–308); JD-Gilmer corr., Mar. 29–Apr. 2, 1880 (ibid., 448–51, quot. on 450; see *Letters*, 482–84); VHD, *Memoir* 2:101; LBN to JD, May 9 [1878: not 1870] (Rowland 7:271, quot.; dated by refs. in letter).

7. JD to Bgd., Apr. 27 (ibid. 8:185–86; Jordan mem. in *Rise and Fall* 1:353–55); Rowland 7:349–61 (St. John; see 8:290), 308–36 (Gorgas), 338–39, 346–48 (Pemb.; see 403–4), 423, 489 (Polk; quot.); (Others, e.g.:) ibid. 59–61 (Chilton), 113–15 (Reagan), 76, 343–44 (G. W. C. Lee), 239–40 (Wood), 370–71 (Ransom), 413–14 (Hayden), 464–74 (Maffitt).

8. Rowland 7:544–45, 554–55, 8:1–25, 61–62, 81–105, 136–41; Ibid. 37–38, 70, 340, 344–46, 359 (see Shaw, *WPJ*, 130–31) JD to Marcus J. Wright, July 18, 1878 (Rowland 8:238, quots.; see Jones, *Davis Memorial*, 456–57); BNH to JD, May 24 (ibid., 547–53).

9. William Harris Bragg, "Charles C. Jones, Jr., and the Mystery of Lee's Lost Dispatches" (1988), 429–62: Jones denied having Lee letters, but he did; finally sold them to W. J. DeRenne, who invited D. S. Freeman to edit them (*Lee's*

Dispatches); dispersed at DeRenne's death, they now repose at Duke, Tulane, and Va. State Library.

10. E. L. Drake [1878] (*Cal. JD MSS,* 118); Walthall-JD corr., Nov. 30–Dec. 7, 1878 (Rowland 8:289–94); Hendrick, *Statesmen of Lost Cause,* 138; W. H. Bragg, "Charles C. Jones," 457–58; JD to C. J. Wright, Nov. 28, 1877 (Rowland 8:54, quot.); Marcus J. Wright to JD, July 16, 1878 (*Cal. JD MSS,* 99); JD to Marcus J. Wright, July 18 (Rowland 8:238–39; see Wright in nn.1, 2, and corr. 403–4, 419–20, 464, 497–98, 502–4, 598). JD wrote 1876–79 (*Papers* 1::1, lxiv–lxv); *O. R.* publ. began 1880.

11. JD to Walthall, Feb. 23, 1878 (Rowland 8:116; Twiggs quot.; but JD used this material in *Rise and Fall* 1:381–82); JD to LBN, Apr. 24, 1879 (Rowland 8:380, quot.); Ibid., 405 (Ould), 437–38 (Harris; also Trenholm's son: 301–3); 7:318–20 and 8:349–54 (Seddon), 7:540–43 and 8:355–57 (Benj.), 514–15, 528–29, and 548–80 (Pendleton), 459–60 and 9:1–4 (Bulloch; see 223–25 and *Cal. JD MSS,* 207).

12. Seitz, *Bragg,* 543–44 (buried, from Christ Church, Mobile, in "Conf. Rest" Magnolia Cem.); Rowland 8:116, 119, 292, 294; JD to C. J. Wright, Dec. 22, 1878, ALA typescript, quot.; JD to LBN, Nov. 1, 1879 (Rowland 8:425, quot.); JD to T. B. Roy, Feb. 29, 1880, in Roy, "Gen. Hardee and Atl.," 377, quot.

13. Hood and Taylor in Warner, *Gens. in Gray;* Hood, *Advance and Retreat,* 273n, quots.; JD to LBN, Sept. 25, 1879 (Rowland 8:417, quots; see 384); VHD to JD, Oct. 1, 1865, MS, ALA, quots.

14. LBN to JD, Sept. 15, 1889 (Rowland 10:138, quots. in "P.S."); JD to LBN, Sept. 25, 1879 (ibid. 8:417, quot.); R. Taylor, *Destruction,* 24, quot. (ref. to 1 Sam. 18–20); Reagan, *Memoirs,* 116. Some Taylor errors noted in Drake, *Annals of Tenn.,* 117–21.

15. JEJ, *Narrative,* 421–24; JD to Carmack, May 8, 1889 (Rowland 10:116, quot.); Letters encl. in Memminger to JD, Nov. 14, 1877 (Rowland 8:41–51; with encl. by him and Trenholm; quots. on 51, 42; see McElroy, *JD* 2:644); Roman, *Mil. Operations* 1:55–64; JD, "Lord Wolseley's Mistakes," [1889] in *Life and Reminisc.,* App., 425–43. See also Williams, *Bgd.,* 63–64; Reagan, *Memoirs,* 111–16; Butler, *Judah P. Benjamin,* 233–36.

16. JD to C. J. Wright, Nov. 28, Oct. 13 and 22, 1877 (Rowland 8:54, 36, 38, quots.). See JD to Walthall, Dec. 17, 1875 (ibid. 7:473–74).

17. Rowland 8:38, 10:106; JD to Walthall, July 12, 1877 (ibid. 7:560); Walthall art. in *SHSP* 5 (Mar. 1878): 97–126; BNH and Reagan in Rowland 7:588–92 and 586–88 (quots.), 565; *The Annals of the War,* 147–59 and 554–89 (arts. RPR from *Times*).

18. C. J. Wright to Walthall, Mar. 30, 1878 (Rowland 8:142–43, quots.); JD to Green, Aug. 18, 1875 (Rowland 7:444, quot.); Neeley, Holzer, and Boritt, *Conf. Image,* 79–96; JD to Mann, Apr. 19, 1869 (*Letters,* 300; see McElroy, *JD* 2:705); Green to JD, Jan. 28, 1878 (Rowland 8:74, quots.).

19. Hunter's art. in *SHSP* 3 (Apr. 1877): 168–76 (Ed. Note: Campbell's in *So. Mag.*); JD to J. W. Jones, Aug. 16, in *SHSP* 4 (Nov. 1877): 208–14, quots. (with Benj. letter and 1865 docs.; see Rowland 7:539–43); JD to VHD, Jan. 24 and Mar. 22, 1866, MSS, TRANSYL. See VHD, *Memoir* 2:742–43 and n.; *Letters,* 203 and 237; Reagan, *Memoirs,* 166–79, esp. 177–78.

20. WPJ to JD, Dec. 7, 1877 (Rowland 8:56–57; and see 37); Ross, *First Lady,* 342 (BNH quot.); Early to JD, Sept. 13, 1882 (Rowland 9:186–88); JD to VHD, Jan. 24, 1866, MS, TRANSYL, quot.; JD to C. J. Wright, Nov. 29, 1878, ibid., quots. (cf. Rowland 9:487); WPJ to JD, Jan. 9, 1878, in *SHSP* 5:225, quots.; Eckenrod, *JD,* 143, 326; Rowland 9:592–93, 602–5 and 10:19–22, 1–16.

21. *SHSP* 4 (Dec. 1877): 303–18 (Hunter quot. on 312); Early to JD, Jan. 28, 1878 (Rowland 8:74, quot.; see LBN, 7:270); *SHSP* 5 (Jan.–June 1878): 222–27 (quots. from Lubbock, JD, WPJ); Jones, *Davis Memorial,* 461–62. Avary, *Dixie after War,* 91, notes Hunter's "hostility" to JD. See Browne in *Letters,* 471 (Hunter's "shuffling timidity").

22. VHD to JD, Feb. 4, 1878 (*Letters*, 468–70, quots.); JD to LBN, Mar. 3, 1885 (Rowland 9:349, quots.). On JD's manner, see Mallory in Alfriend, *Life of JD*, 601–2.

23. VHD to JD, Feb. 4, 1878 (*Letters*, 468–70, quots.). A. S. Colyar to Hunter, Jan. 3, 1878 [misdated 1877] in Drake, *Annals of Tenn.*, 163–64; see JD, ibid., 211–13; Barksdale, ibid., 229–32; and in Rowland 8:246–49. See also Freeman, *R. E. Lee* 4:1–10; Richard D. Goff, *Confederate Supply* (Durham: Duke Univ. Press, 1969), 234–40.

24. VHD to JD, Feb. 4, 1878 (*Letters*, 468–69, quots.); George Duncan, "John A. Campbell" (*Transactions of the Ala. Hist. Soc.* 5 [1904], RPR Montg.: *Ala. Polytechnique Institute Hist. Papers* [2nd Series], 1905), 7 n.1, 29–34; Goff, *Conf. Supply* (as in Note 23 above); Avary, *Dixie after War*, 32–43; JD to VHD, Feb. 16, 1878 (*Letters*, 471–72, quot.), he said to her, "Though we may not judge, we may avoid the goats, when . . . set apart by proofs," Apr. 8–9, 1866, MS, TRANSYL.

25. McRacken, "Three Impressions of JD," quots. (see McElroy, *JD* 2:671); Carter and Carter, *So Great a Good*, 180; Julia Guice, "History—Church of the Redeemer" (Leacock there 1878–80; author's typescript, courtesy Mrs. Guice).

26. JD to Marg. D. Hayes, Aug. 7, 1882 (*Letters*, 522, quot.); Strode, *Tragic Hero*, 429–35 (quot. on 432); JD to VHD, Jan. 29, 1879, MS, TRANSYL, and Feb. 9 and Apr. 7, MSS, ALA; JD to LBN, Mar. 17 (Rowland 8:369); Wyatt-Brown, *House of Percy*, 160; Early to JD, Jan. 28, 1878 (Rowland 8:73). Cigar box by bed, "pocket cigar case," etc., and pipes (Inventory); cigar holder and Lone Jack at Beauvoir; pipe, tobacco items at First White House.

27. JD to VHD, Jan. 12 and 29, 1879, MSS, TRANSYL; JD to LBN, Apr. 9 (Rowland 8:377, quot.); McRacken, "Three Impressions"; Rowland 8:276, 605, and *Polk* 1:165 331; VHD to JD, [Apr. 18, 1878] in *Cal. JD MSS*, 92.

28. LBN to JD, July 1882 (Rowland 9:179–81; had 6 children [ibid. and 191]; see 7:269, 8:348, 378, 419, 422, 426); JD to VHD, Dec. 7–8, 1865, MS, TRANSYL, quot.; LBN to JD, Oct. 23, 1872 (Rowland 7:332); LBN to JD, Mar. 31, 1878 (ibid. 8:145, quots.; Memphis ref. unknown); Ibid. 8–10 (JD-LBN corr., 1878–89; Bgd., e.g., 9:310–13).

29. JD-LBN corr., quots.: Rowland 8:402 (June 22, 1879), 422, 426 (Oct. 7 and Nov. 1), 9:349–50 (Mar. 3, 1885), 8:384 (Apr. 25, 1879; see 278–79). Ibid. 6:536–37 (Apr. 7, 1865): JD assures LBN his comm. still "in force" (as col.?; appt. as brig. not confirmed; but he is brig. in Warner, *Gens. in Gray*).

30. JD to C. J. Wright, Feb. 12 and May 11, 1876, Oct. 13, 1877, Feb. 4 and Dec. 22, 1878 (Rowland 7:492, 512–14; 8:35, 78 [quot.]; last name, e.g., 368, 380, 437; most often, "dear Friend"; once calls G. W. C. Lee "Custis" [174]); Ibid. 7:458 n.1.

31. JD to Wright, Nov. 29, 1878, MS, TRANSYL, quot.; Drayton in Warner, *Gens. in Gray* (successful before War: Rowland 3:216 n.1); G. W. Hughes to JD, Sept. 19 [1854], MS, TRANSYL; Drayton to JD, Jan. 23, 1871 (Rowland 7:286–88); Same to same, Jan. 18, 1886 (ibid. 9:405, quot.; see 29, 33, 356, and 10:122, 164). The JD letters mentioned in Drayton's are not in Rowland.

32. Harney in Warner, *Gens. in Blue;* Oliver Jensen, *The American Heritage History of Railroads in America* (New York: Bonanza Books, 1981), 94–95; VHD, *Memoir* 1:64; JD to L. U. Reavis, Jan. 1878, in Reavis, *Harney*, iv, and JD, *Rise and Fall* 1:418, 420 (see E. G. W. Butler to JD, Rowland 9:268–69, 274–75).

33. Freeman, *R. E. Lee* 1:51, 83; LBN to JD, June 22, 1879 (Rowland 8:402, quots. *re* and from Holmes; LBN thinks Holmes will make it to heaven, though Protestant, because a man of good will "in invincible ignorance"). JD=the Cause: see *Letters*, 398, Rowland 7:103, 10:96, McElroy, *JD* 2:574, Duke, *Reminisc.*, 344, Dunham, *Attitude of Northern Clergy*, 177, *Life and Reminisc.*, 245.

34. Quots.: SAED, Last Will and Testament, in *New Orleans Picayune*, July 16, 1879 (SAED Collection, Beauvoir; Walthall a witness); Same to Mann, Apr. 25, 1878 (*Letters*, 479, quot.; "You who appreciate him so truly").

35. J. W. Thompson, "Beauvoir," n.p. (will signed Jan. 4, 1878); SAED, Will (as

in Note 34 above); McElroy, *JD* 2:653; SAED to JD, Mar. 28, 1879, ALA typescript, quots. (from St. Charles Hotel, facing surgery; leaves him everything; asks him to will some things to family members; "take care of my old servant Phoebe Clark" and "my old horse Rupert"); Dorsey, *Recoll. of H. W. Allen*, 218, quot.; JD to Hayes, Sept. 11, 1879, MS, MVC.

36. Lewis, "Sarah Dorsey" (quot. from Ida Raymond, *Southland Writers* [Philadelphia: Claxton, 1870]); Posey, "Dorsey: Sketch," 6–8 (*World* quots.); Strode, *Tragic Hero*, 440; JD to Marg. D. Hayes, Nov. 8, 1878 (*Letters*, 491, quots.; ref. unknown).

37. Posey, "Dorsey: Sketch," 7 (quot. from *New York World;* Minnie Howell was one of the ladies [*Letters*, 495]); Strode, *Tragic Hero*, 440, 442; JD to VHD, July 2 (quot.) and 4, 1879, MSS, TRANSYL; VHD to Marg. D. Hayes, July 5, MS, MVC, quot.

38. JD to Walthall, July 4, 1879 (Rowland 8:403; mentions the Beatitude); JD to Kate Ferguson, Sept. 5, quot. (typescript, Fleming Collection; Matt. 5:8); Kate Ferguson to Fleming, Oct. 4, 1907, MS, ibid.; JD to VHD, July 2 (priests' names), 4, 9, MSS, TRANSYL (mourners in Posey, "Dorsey: A Sketch," 8); SAED tombstone descr. in catalog of Job Routh private cem. (courtesy Mrs. A. C. Tipton, Natchez, 1984); Wyatt-Brown, *House of Percy*, 166.

39. JD to VHD, July 9, 1879, MS, TRANSYL ([from steamboat] quots.; see July 2, 4, and 9 [from N. O.]); VHD to Marg. D. Hayes, July 5, MS, MVC, quots. "Your mother is yet suffering in her feet, a strange disease for which no remedy has been found" (JD to J. A. Hayes, Sept. 11, MS, MVC).

40. JD to Walthall, July 4, 1879 (Rowland 8:403, quots.); JD to Kate Ferguson, Sept. 5 (Fleming Collection typescript, quots.; ref. to Phil. 1:21); JD to VHD, July 4, MS, TRANSYL, quot.

41. VHD to Marg. D. Hayes, July 17, MS, MVC, quots.; SAED Will (as in Note 34 above), quot.

42. Lewis, "Sarah Dorsey," citing *New Orleans Picayune;* Wyatt-Brown, *House of Percy*, 105–6, 119–22, 165–69, and Wyatt-Brown, *The Literary Percys . . .* (Athens: U. of Ga. Press, 1994), 3–34 (other madness and suicide in family; Kate Ferguson and her aunt Catherine Warfield in chaps. 1 and 2: see JD to Kate, Sept. 15, 1879: Catherine "among my dearest and most honored friends," typescript, Fleming Collection); SAED to Mann, Apr. 25, 1878 (*Letters*, 479, quot.; Mann sent this to JD 1883 to prove the will valid [Moore, *Mann Letters*, 87–88]); SAED to JD, Mar. 28, 1879, ALA typescript, quots.

43. JD to Mary Negus, Aug. 4, 1879 (*Letters*, 495–97, quots.); Strode, *Tragic Hero*, 20–23; Kane, *Natchez*, 251–58 (M. Dahlgren's father, Charles, was SAED's stepfather); McElroy, *JD* 2:654–57.

44. JD to Kate Ferguson, Sept. 5, 1879, quots. (typescript, Fleming Collection); N. D. Smith, "Reminsc. of JD," 182; SAED to JD, Mar. 28, MS, ALA; VHD to Marg. D. Hayes, Sept. 21, MS, MVC, quot.; JD to Hayes, Sept. 11 and Dec. 27, MSS, MVC; Hermann, *Pursuit of Dream*, 211–12 (Brierfield suit, 1881).

45. VHD to Marg. D. Hayes, Sept. 21, 1879, MS, MVC; Strode, *Tragic Hero*, 433, 444 (quots. from VHD); JD to LBN, Nov. 1 (Rowland 8:426, quot.); JD to Kate Ferguson, Sept. 5, quot. (typescript, Fleming Collection); Kate Ferguson to Fleming, Oct. 4, 1907, MS, ibid. JD to Amanda Bradford, Dec. 28, 1879: "I can have but a short time longer to suffer in this world" (MS, Old Courthouse Mus.).

46. Ross, *First Lady*, 345; *Letters*, 467–560 (loving terms, e.g., 468–73, 508, 512–15; Maggie's visits, passim [daughter: *Papers* 4:App. 2, 415]); McElroy, *JD* 2:687; Strode, *Tragic Hero*, 445–48 (quots. on 446); JD to Pendleton, Dec. 1, 1880, in *Pendleton*, 473; Walthall to JD, Feb. 10, 1881 (Rowland 8:592–95).

47. *Letters*, 506 Ed. Note (see 507 and MSS, MVC: letters of VHD and Marg. D. Hayes, Sept. 7 and 16, 1880, Feb. 21 and 25, 1881); Ryan to JD, Nov. 5, 1880 (*Letters*, 503–4, quots.); JD to Kate Ferguson, Sept. 5, 1879 (typescript, Fleming. Collection); W. C. Davis, *JD*, 669–76.

48. Ryan to JD, Nov. 5, 1880 (*Letters*, 503, quots.); JD, *Rise and Fall* 1:v–viii, quots.; W. G. Richardson to JD, Feb. 14, 1882 (Rowland 9:151, quot.). Pendleton also urged "vindication" of "the great cause of Right," and other spiritual aims (ibid. 8:528–29; see 9:17–19).

49. JD to Walthall, Jan. 24, 1876 (Rowland 7:487–88); JD to Pendleton, Dec. 1, 1880 in *Pendleton*, 473, quots. (ref. to Gen. 25:31–34); JD to C. J. Wright, Dec. 8, 1877 (Rowland 8:58); JD to G. W. C. Lee, Apr. 17, 1878 (ibid., 175); VHD, *Memoir* 2:816–18.

50. Strode, *Tragic Hero*, 448–49; VHD, *Memoir* 2:830; JD to Va. Clay, Feb. 25, 1882, in W. C. Davis, *JD*, 678, quots.; Ray M. Thompson, "The Confederate Shrine of Beauvoir" [n.p.]; JD to VHD, May 29 (unident. clippling at First White House), JD to VHD, May 30, June 1, and July 29, 1881 (MSS, TRANSYL), and *Cal. JD MSS*, 124, 131. Trouble with Appleton's went on past JD's death; arbitration finally favored the publisher (Rowland 10:97–98, 108, and docs. from 1892, ALA).

51. W. C. Davis, *JD*, 678; Unident. clipping with J. B. Price to JD, Sept. 1, 1889 (Rowland 10:133 n.2, quots.); Richardson to JD, Feb. 14, 1882 (ibid. 9:151–53, quots.; complains of "Websterian spellings" before seeing publisher responsible; see JD, *Rise and Fall* 2:764, 1:88 and n.: JD also preferred Worcester; see VHD, *Memoir* 2:830).

52. Smith, *Conf. War Papers*, 39, quot. (*re* Manassas); Williams, *Bgd.*, 311–12 (Bgd. quot.); C. Brown to JD, July 23, 1885, MS, TULANE, quot. (Ewell's brother Richard was Brown's stepfather: Ewells in *South in Bldg. Nation*, 11, and Osborne, *Jubal*, 243); Maury to JD, June 11, 1881 (Rowland 8:604, quots.).

53. A. W. Cowper to JD, June 23 (ibid.; on Mahone, see Early to JD, ibid. 9:9); Freeman, *Lee's Lieuts.* 3:769, 772; *Atlantic Monthly*, Sept. 1881, 405–11, quot.; Basso, *Bgd. Great Creole*, 147 (Longs. quot., from *Phila. Press;* see 306–7 on Bgd.); Wilmer to JD, Mar. 11, 1887 (*Letters*, 550).

54. Strode, *Tragic Hero*, 448; JD to VHD, June 1, 1881, MS, TRANSYL; JD to VHD, May 29, quots. (unident. clipping in First White House).

55. VHD to JD, Aug. 2, 1877 (*Letters*, 461, quots.); VHD to Winnie Davis, May (ibid., 506–8); Winnie Davis to VHD, June 20, 1881 (MS, Davis-Hayes Collection [Webb], MDAH); K. Meredith to VHD, Sept. 13, 1880, and VHD to Hayes, Apr. 1, MSS, MVC, quots.; Chiles Clifton Ferrell, "'The Daughter of the Confederacy,'—Her Life, Character, and Writings" (single quots. omitted hereafter), 71; JD to VHD, Feb. 4 (MS, TRANSYL), VHD, *Memoir* 2:756, 927; W. C. Davis, *JD*, 678; VHD to JD, [Oct. 1] 1865, and Aug. 14, 1866, MSS, ALA; Strode, *Tragic Hero*, 449–50; Jones, *Davis Memorial*, 431, quot.

56. Strode, *Tragic Hero*, 450 (VHD quot.); JD to Messrs. A. and M. Heine, Sept. 20, 1881, quots. (MS, Davis-Hayes Family Papers, MDAH [Webb]); VHD to Winnie Davis [June 27, 1881], quots. (MS, ibid. [Webb 2]; dated from internal evidence); VHD to JD, Sept. [n.d.] 1881 (*Letters*, 513, quot.).

57. Strode, *Tragic Hero*, 451 (VHD quot.; on Winnie, see ibid. and 417, 429); JD to VHD, Sept. 22, 1881 (ibid., 514–15, quots.; ref. to a spoonerism c. 1845 by Rev. Domenico Barberi: "without face [faith] you cannot be shaved [saved]"; ident. for author by Abbé G. Marc'hadour).

58. JD to VHD, Dec. 18, 1879 (*Letters*, 499, quot.); JD to VHD, June 1, 1881, MS, TRANSYL, quot.; Winnie Davis, "JD in Private Life," 7 (JD quots.); VHD, *Memoir* 2:830, quots.; Jones, *Davis Memorial*, 461; JD to Marg. D. Hayes, Aug. 7, 1882 (*Letters*, 521–22).

59. Ferrell, "Daughter of Conf.," 72; Winnie Davis, "JD in Private Life," quots. passim (refs. to John 19:28–30 and Luke 23:36; cf. Matt. 27:46–49); Bible at Beauvoir (quot. from VHD's note, at Matt. 15:13, ref. to Acts 17:11). See J. W. Thompson, "Beauvoir" and *Letters*, 535–36 for Winnie's sidesaddle and horse. *Ben Hur: A Tale of the Christ* was by Gen. Lewis Wallace, a member of the mil. comm. that tried Booth conspirators and Wirz (Warner, *Gens. in Blue*).

60. JD to Kate Ferguson, Sept. 5, 1879, quot. (typescript, Fleming Collection);

Meriwether, *Recoll. of 92 Years,* 199, quots. (see Winnie Davis, "JD in Private Life," 1); Hill, Address, Feb. 18, 1874 (*SHSP* 14:491, quots.; see 499–500). Others on JD: Jones, *Davis Memorial,* 263, 520, 578; *Life and Reminisc.,* 117, 172, 228; Goldsborough, "Varina Howell Davis," 4, 11.

61. J. B. Roberts (rector of St. Mark's) to author, Nov. 27, 1984 (JD vestryman 1878–89; all recs. destroyed in Hurricane Camille, 1969 [Norah Linenberger to same, Jan. 4, 1985]); Guice, "History—Church of Redeemer" (typescript, courtesy Mrs. Guice, who copied some recs. before 1969; JD in diocesan recs.); JD to Walthall (1878) (Rowland 8:287); Jones, *Davis Memorial,* 465; VHD, *Memoir* 2:895, 915; L. R. Burrows to Fleming, May 15, 1908 (typescript in Fleming Collection).

62. Wilmer to JD, Apr. 9, 1884 (*Letters,* 533); Same to same, Mar. 11, 1887 (ibid., 550, quot.); VHD to Marg. D. Hayes, Apr. 11, 1884 (ibid., 534, quot.); Wilmer, *Recent Past,* 22–23; Perry, *Bsps. of Am. Church,* 155.

63. LBN-JD corr. in Rowland 8–9, passim, esp. 8:423, 440, 9:349 (quot.), 215 ("serious illness"), 189 (quot.); Davis-Hayes corr. in MVC, 1879–81 (esp. VHD to J. A. Hayes, Nov. 19, 1879, and JD to same, Jan. 17, 1881); Marg. D. Hayes to same, Mar. 6 and (illegible date: #658–59 in microfilm; dog bite); Strode, *Tragic Hero,* 446; JD to VHD, Jan. 12, May 23, Nov. 6, 1879, and July 29, 1881, MSS, TRANSYL; VHD to Mary D. Burchenel, "Xmas 1889" in Burchenel, "Yankee Girl," 45, quot.

64. Winnie Davis, "JD in Private Life," 3–5, quots. (and dogs; see *Letters,* 531; McElroy, *JD* 2:664; Strode, *Tragic Hero,* 446); Clothes at First White House; JD to G. W. C. Lee, Apr. 17, 1878 (Rowland 8:174); Burrows to Fleming, May 25, 1908 (typescript in Fleming Collection) and *Montg. Advertiser and Ala. Jnl.,* Aug. 22, 1987 (stone found in ADAH; curator said, 1996, can be lifted easily when chest-high).

65. Boyle, "JD in Canada," 90; Jones, *Davis Memorial,* 424, 428–41; Furniture at Beauvoir (see ibid., 437; VHD, *Memoir* 2:facing 896; *Life and Reminisc.,* facing 56); Wyatt-Brown, *House of Percy,* 162; Jones, *Davis Memorial,* 428–41; Winnie Davis, "JD in Private Life," passim (quot. on 5), much sheet music in Rosenstock; Ferrell, "Daughter of Conf.," 72; Backgammon board and "Thy Will Be Done" at First White House (VHD stipulated placing of the latter; much of the handwork here and at Beauvoir; hers and Winnie's at Mus. of Conf. [Inventory]).

66. VHD, *Memoir* 2:815, 927; McElroy, *JD* 2:663–64, 695–96; JD to VHD, Sept. 13, 1881 (*Letters,* 512, quots.); LBN to JD, Oct. 7, 1879, and JD to LBN, Nov. 1 (Rowland 8:422, 425–26, quots.); JD to Kate Ferguson, Sept. 5, 1879, quot. (typescript, Fleming Collection); Hayes tended to much business for JD (MSS, MVC, Sept. 1879–Jan. 1882; paid overdue shoe bill, Jan. 1877).

67. JD to Rev. R. G. Hinsdale, June 3, 1888 (*Letters,* 554, quot.; see 447, 522); "Birthplace of JD," 486–87; McElroy, *JD* 2:682–83; Clark to JD, July 11, 1886 (*Letters,* 544); J. W. Godwin to JD, June 22, 1889 (Rowland 10:124, quot. from encl. clipping); Jones, *Davis Memorial,* 592–94 (quot. from res.; poverty on 613, 342).

68. *Letters,* 348–39 and 351; *Papers* 1:App. 4, Chart 8 and nn.; Deed of trust, JD to L. Boyle, Apr. 22, 1884 (Davis-Hayes Family Collection [Adele], MDAH); JD to Porterfield and to Hayes (quot.), Apr. 8, 1881, MSS, MVC; *Letters* 540 Ed. Note; Fleming, "JD and Negro Problem," 23; Tillman MS (by a grandchild), ALA; *Letters* (Wm.:) 537–38, (Becket:) 519–20, 522–23, (Brierfield:) 532–33, 535–37, 541–42, 549.

69. *Life and Reminsc.,* 268; *Letters,* 534, 536, 540; VHD to Marg. D. Hayes, Sept. 7, 1880, MS, MVC, quot.; Strode, *Tragic Hero,* 462 (JD quot.), 523 (at grave); Marg. D. Hayes to J. A. Hayes, June 6, 1880, MS, MVC, quot.; *Letters,* 474, 493, 497 (mutual devotion Robt. and Winnie), 499, 522, 524; Fleming, "JD and Negro Problem," 14.

70. Thompson, "Conf. Shrine"; JD to Marg. D. Hayes, Apr. 26, 1889 (*Letters,*

556); VHD to same, Apr. 11, 1884 (ibid., 534, quots.; see 524 and Jones, *Davis Memorial,* 431); Marg. D. Hayes to J. A. Hayes, June 6, 1880, MS, MVC, quot.; VHD to same, Apr. 1, ibid.

71. Ross, *First Lady,* 350 (VHD quot.; see *Letters,* 540, 422); Ibid., 340–41 and pics. after 148 (VHD's sketch and Wilde inscr.; *Poems:* London: Davis Bogue, 1882 [typescript, ALA]); Strode, *Tragic Hero,* 444, 459–61 (quots. *re* Wilde; n. says photograph at Beauvoir; presumably lost in Hurricane Camille, 1969).

72. Ross, *First Lady,* 351–55; Strode, *Tragic Hero,* 430–31 (VHD quots. from VHD); JD to Marg. D. Hayes, Aug. 7, 1882 (*Letters,* 522; see 515); Jones, *Davis Memorial,* 429, 433; Boyle, "JD in Canada," 90; Winnie Davis, "JD in Private Life," 6; McElroy, *JD* 2:671, quot.; R. M. Thompson, "Conf. Shrine." Bottle of wine made by JD, dated Nov. 4, 1889, at First White House.

73. JD to J. A. Hayes, July 19, 1880, MS, MVC, quot.; VHD to Mary D. Burchenal, "Xmas, 1889," in Burchenal, "Yankee Girl," 45, quot.

74. JD to VHD, Nov. 10, 1879, MS, TRANSYL (promises no "temper"; only latter-year ref.); Goldsborough, "Varina Howell Davis," 5 ("never saw him irritable or angry"); Kadloubovsky and Palmer, *Early Fathers,* 236–37, 240–41. See Drayton to JD in text below.

75. (Quots.:) McElroy, *JD* 2:660–94 (from *World,* 671; see 644–45); Pendleton to JD, Sept. 6, 1881 (Rowland 9:19); Early to JD, Sept. 13, 1882 (ibid., 188; see 537–39); (Defenders) A. F. Smith, BNH, C. J. Wright, Lizzie G. Fisher, M. H. Clark, J. B. Briggs (JEJ admirer), J. F. Wheless (JEJ admirer), T. C. Reynolds, J. S. Johnston, J. W. Jones, F. C. Randolph, James Benagh, D. H. Maury, and E. G. W. Butler (ibid., 24–43, 141–51).

76. Hill to JD and to Burr, Dec. 27, 1881 (ibid. 9:37, 39–40, quots.; "knew he was suspicious, spiteful and jealous, but assumed" truthful); Drayton to JD, Dec. 22 (ibid., 29, quots.; see 33: JEJ "hates" JD); JEJ, *Narrative,* 408–9; VHD, *Memoir* 2:848–81. There was never anything like that much money: see chap. 1 above.

77. Drayton to JD, Dec. 22, 1881 (Rowland 9:29, quots.; ref. to 1 Pet. 2:23); JD to WPJ, Feb. 17, 1882, in Shaw, *WPJ,* 184–85, quots.; Burr to JD, Dec. 19, 1881 (*Cal. JD MSS,* 190).

78. Maury to JD, Jan. 18, 1882 (Rowland 9:144); Hill to JD, Dec. 27, 1881 (ibid., 38, quot.); List in Note 75 above; WPJ to J. R. Davis, Jan. 6, in VHD, *Memoir* 2:878–81, quots. Daniel said, "Not a human being ever believed [it]" (Jones, *Davis Memorial,* 263).

79. Sherman in Warner, *Gens. in Blue;* JD to Scharf, Sept. 23, 1886 (Rowland 9:472–90; quots. on 474–76, 483, 485; exec. doc. in *Cal. JD MSS,* 222–28); JD to N. Walker [of *Boston Globe;* Apr. 3, 1885] (Rowland 9:323, JD's view of Grant disputed by Pendleton and Early [18 and 10:31]); LBN to JD, Oct. 14, 1886 (ibid. 9:495, quot.). See JD, ibid., 358, and in VHD, *Memoir* 2:833–47.

80. Scharf to JD, Oct. 9, 1886 (*Cal. JD MSS,* 253); Moore, *Mann Letters,* 97, quot.; Hayne to JD, Jan. 18, 1885 (Rowland 9:335–37); Early to JD, Oct. 4, 1886 (ibid., 492–95 and n.1, quots. from him and *Richmond State*); T. McRae to JD, Oct. 16 (ibid., 495–96, quot.); Jones, *Davis Memorial,* 457, 357, quots. Other reaction: Rowland 9:307–8, 315–17, 329–33, 350–51, 511; 10:48, 95–97; *Cal. JD MSS,* 216–17, 219–21, 249–52.

81. *Hill,* 94, 97, 102–7 (Hill quot. [also 133], and quot. from JD to Hill), 210 (quot. from *Const.;* unveiling May 1, 1886; Easter, Apr. 25 [*BCP* (1896)]), 116–19, 226–28 (JD and Grady quots.), 131; Grady to JD, Mar. 27, 1886 (Rowland 9:412–13, quot.). Sickness mentioned Dec. 1881 (ibid., 40).

82. Strode, *Tragic Hero,* 478–79; Frank Burr dispatches to *New York World,* Apr. 28–30, 1886 (Rowland 9:419–31; quots. on 419–20).

83. Ibid., quots. on 420, 427, 421.

84. Ibid., 424, 427–29, 448 (quots.; see Grady's defense of JD's outspokenness, 443–44); Nuermberger, *Clays of Ala.,* 315.

85. Burr in *New York World*, Apr. 30, 1886 (Rowland 9:432, 435 [quots.], 437 (cf. 8:235–37: JD speech, 1878); Tate, *JD* (as in chap. 11, Note 1 above), 198.

86. Burr (as in Note 85 above), 438, quots. (431 for play); *Atl. Const.*, May 7, 1886 (ibid., 445–49); Same, May 1 ("hero" quot. from clipping at Beauvoir); Suzanne T. Dolensky, "The Daughters of Jefferson Davis" (*Jnl. of Miss. Hist.* 51:321; Gordon quot.); Strode, *Tragic Hero*, 483, 485 (RR car quots.).

87. *Atl. Const.*, May 7, 1886 (Rowland 9:445–46, quots.; denies wanting war [448]); *Atl. Const.*, May 1, 1886 (quot., JD at Auburn, Ala.; clipping at Beauvoir); JD speech at Atl., May 1 (Rowland 9:442); JD speech at Meridian, May 12, 1887 (ibid., 558, quot.). Cf. speeches 1878 and 1888 (ibid. 8:227–37 and 10:47–48). See W. H. Bragg, "Charles C. Jones, Jr.," 448–49 and n.42 for an incident at this time.

88. *Atl. Const.*, May 7, 1886 (Rowland 9:446–47, quot.); Burr, ibid. 443, quot.); Wilmer to JD, Mar. 11, 1887 (*Letters*, 550, quots.). For Winnie's admirers, see, e.g., Rowland 9:351, 497, 10:48, 161; *Cal. JD MSS*, 253; Strode, *Tragic Hero*, 492.

89. Green to JD, Aug. 20, 1886 (*Letters*, 457–48, quots.; Margaret J. Weber to JD, Feb. 15, 1887 (ibid., 549, quot.).

90. Jones, *Davis Memorial*, e.g., 460, 578; W. H. Payne to JD, June 10, 1880 (Rowland 8:475–76, quots.; duelist Col. Tom Smith, son of wartime gov., "Extra Billy," challenged ed. of *Richmond Whig* for attacking his father and JD; see Payne and Wm. Smith in Warner, *Gens. in Gray*).

91. Burr in Rowland 9:438, quot.; Ross, *First Lady*, 349; "The Birthplace of JD," 486–87; Clark to JD, July 11, 1886 (*Letters*, 544, quot.); McElroy, *JD* 2:682–83. Orphan Brigade vets. formed JD Home Ass. in 1907 and bought back part of land for mem. park; U. C. V. and U. D. C. raised obelisk (1917–1924), like Washington Mon. (*Conf. Vet.*, Oct. 1907, 437–38; *The Building of a Monument*, comp. Anita J. Darnell and William T. Turner [Pennyroyal Area Mus., Inc., 1979]; Strode, *Tragic Hero*, 488).

92. Wendell Phillips in *Universal Encycl.;* JD to Lubbock, July 20, 1887 (Rowland 9:580–82, quots.; see Reagan to JD, July 29, in *Cal. JD MSS*, 269–70); *Open Letters on Prohibition: A Controversy between Hon. Jefferson Davis and Bishop Chas. B. Galloway, D.D.* (Nashville: Publishing House of the Methodist Episc. Church, So., 1893), 1–47 (quots. on 14, 8; letters Aug. 13–Dec. 21); Lubbock to JD, Aug. 6 (Rowland 9:589–91; see Schade, 589, and E. E. Merrill, 595).

93. Strode, *Tragic Hero*, 492–93, and *Letters*, 551–52 Ed. Note, quots.

94. Winchester, "JD, Communicant," 727; Thomas F. Gailor, *The Episcopal Church* [Milwaukee: Young Churchman Co., 1914], 95 (Winchester made bsp. coadjutor of Ark., 1911).

95. VHD, *Memoir* 2:831–32, quots.; Strode, *Tragic Hero*, 493–94; Galleher to JD, Nov. 3, 1887 (*Letters*, 552, quot.; chief of staff to Buckner, idolized ASJ [WPJ, *Gen. ASJ*, 727]). Evans, "JD, Diseases and Doctors," 9–10, denies "heart failure," but does not say what it was.

96. McRacken, "Three Impressions of JD," quots.; Munford to JD, Feb. 22, 1884 (Rowland 9:277, quots., see 10:113–14). Munford col. 2d Va. Cav.; brig. gen. 1864 (*Conf. Soldier in C. W.*, 367).

97. Marg. D. Hayes to J. A. Hayes, Feb. 25 (quots.), Mar. 2, Mar. 12, Aug. 9, 1881, MSS, MVC; *Papers* 4:App. 2, 415–16 (J. D. Hayes b. 1884); DeLeon, *Belles*, 73; *Letters*, 515–59, passim (Addison, 535–36; quots. on 557); VHD note on backgammon board, First White House; *Livingstone* by Annie M. Barnes, inscr. from JD, Mar. 9, 1889 (Beauvoir); Strode, *Tragic Hero*, 502 and n., quot.; Winnie Davis, "JD in Private Life," 4, quots.

98. Jefferson Davis, "The Indian Policy of the United States," *N. Am. Rev.* 143:436–46; A. T. Rice to JD, Apr. 27, 1887 (Rowland 9:540); JD, "Life of Calhoun," 250–51 (quot.), 246, 256; JD, "Doctrine of State Rights," 205, quot.

99. JD, "Robert E. Lee" (quots., 57, 62, 64; see Mallory, "Last Days," [Part 2] 248n); Long, *Memoirs* (New York: J. M. Stoddart and Co., 1887), 412–13 (blames "a railroad official"), 693 (quot. from Lee rpt.); JD to Marcus J. Wright, Jan. 29,

1887 (Rowland 9:521–23, quot.); Pollard, *Lost Cause,* 703, quot.; JD, *Rise and Fall* 2:668–76; Lee, *Recoll. and Letters,* 152 (says supplies "captured").

100. Jefferson Davis, "Andersonville" (*Belford's Mag.,* Jan. and Feb. 1890); R. B. Winder to JD, Dec. 10, 1888 (Rowland 10:95, quot.); W. J. Green to JD, Mar. 22, 1889 (ibid., 102–3, quot.); JD to Schade, Oct. 5, 1888 (ibid., 82, quots.). See Schade, ibid., 87–89 and 9:589; JD to Redpath, Nov. 3, 1889, in *Belford's,* Jan. 1890, 274, quots.; McElroy, *JD* 2:687–94, 710.

101. JD to Redpath (as in Note 100 above), quots. (see 273 Ed. Note); JD to Ed. of *Courier Journal,* May 5, 1887 (Rowland 9:540–55; quots. on 551 [Wolseley], 540, 555). See *N. Am. Rev.* 148 (May 1889): 538–63 (Wolseley, 26 pp.), 149 (Oct.): 472–82 (JD, 11 pp.); and 6 more arts. by W. (also Rowland 10:115–17, 81–82). For W.'s 1884 expedition to Egypt and massacre, see Alan Morehead, *The White Nile* (New York: Harper and Brothers, 1960), 237–75. Bgd., JEJ, Jordan, and Rhett (Jr.) in *Battles and Leaders,* Vol. I.

102. Rowland 1:146 (quots. from JD note and Winnie poem); Winnie Davis to VHD, May 26, 1878 (*Letters,* 480; descr. heroic act); Ferrell, "Daughter of Conf.," 74–75.

103. Ross, *First Lady,* 377 (cf. Ferrell, "Daughter of Conf.," 71 and n.1), 350–58 (son of the Wm. Emorys), 369; Strode, *Tragic Hero,* 456, 494, 498–99, 505; Rowland 10:159–62 *re* Winnie. *New Orleans Daily Picayune,* Dec. 7, 1889, p. 1, col. 4, quots.; JD to Mann, Oct. 23, 1889 (*Letters,* 559, quot.). Winnie's Comus gown at Old Courthouse Museum. See Pulitzer in *DAB* (enrolled in U.S. Army 1864 by a German recruiter about whom JD had protested).

104. JD to Redpath (as in Note 100 above), quot.; VHD to Marg. D. Hayes, Nov. 8, 1889 (*Letters,* 560, quots.); Burrows to Fleming, May 25, 1908 (typescript in Fleming Collection); *New Orleans Daily Picayune,* Dec. 7, 1889, p. 1, col. 5; VHD to Lise M. Hamer, July 9, 1886 (*Letters,* 544, quot.; see 542 and 543 Ed. Note); VHD, *Memoir* 2:928.

105. JD to VHD, Nov. 12, 1889 (quots. from MS and envelope, copied by author, at First White House, July 30, 1978; no longer on display in "relic room"); Quot. from pic. of page in Alice Trainer's memory book (unident. newspaper clipping at Beauvoir); Strode, *Tragic Hero,* 505–6.

106. VHD, *Memoir* 2:928–31; Strode, *Tragic Hero,* 506–8; Ross, *First Lady,* 359 (quots. from VHD letter); Evans, "JD, His Diseases and Doctors," 11–12; Conversation with Lawrence Oden, at Biloxi, Sept. 16, 1984. Fenner on sup. ct. of La. (Jones, *Davis Memorial,* 487); Capt. T. P. Leathers gave JD *50 Years on the Mississippi* by E. W. Gould (Beauvoir).

107. VHD, *Memoir* 2:929–32 and Strode, *Tragic Hero,* 508–11, quots.; N. D. Smith, "Reminisc. of JD," 182.

108. Ibid., quots.; Strode, *Tragic Hero,* 510–12 (1st JD quot.); VHD, *Memoir* 2:929–32 (2nd JD quot.; Dr. C. J. Bickham also attended him); Riley, "JD and His Health" (Part 2), 286 (attributes death to pneumonia).

Chapter XXIII Afterward

1. Quots.: [*New Orleans Daily*] *Picayune* in Jones, *Davis Memorial,* 473 (476: face "showed no trace of suffering"); Pamphlet, "The Medal or Cross of St. Benedict" (patron of happy death), medal and VHD's note on it at Casemate Mus.

2. VHD, *Memoir* 2:930 (JD quot.); *New Orleans Daily Picayune,* Dec. 7, 1889, p. 1, col. 4 and p. 8, col. 3; Strode, *Tragic Hero,* 523.

3. Winnie Davis to JD, Dec. 5, 1889 (*Letters,* 562–63, quots.); VHD, *Memoir* 2:930–31; Ross, *First Lady,* 358, 366–68 (the Pulitzers also had a yacht in the harbor); W. A. Swanberg, *Pulitzer,* 155.

4. Jones, *Davis Memorial,* 475, 473 (body "straightened and bathed" that night, embalmed in morning [from newspapers]); *[New Orleans] Daily Picayune,* Dec. 7,

1889, p. 1, col. 4; *SHSP* 29:5–6 (laying-out and story, told by E. H. McCaleb, June 3, 1901).

5. *[New Orleans] Daily Picayune,* Dec. 4, 1889, p. 1, col. 4, quot.; Ibid., Dec. 7, p. 2, cols. 3–4; G. W. Jones in *Life and Reminisc.,* 123–26 (see Jones' 1874 letters in Rowland 7:385–87, 392–96, 400–403, and Ross, *First Lady,* 346).

6. Strode, *Tragic Hero,* 501–2, 513–14; Early to JD, May 4 and 15, 1889 (Rowland 10:112–13); Ibid. 8:476–77, 9:9, 205–6, 212, 296–97, 308–9, 366–67, 375–76, 380–81, 492–93; Ross, *First Lady,* 352–53, 355; Williams, *Bgd.,* 296–303; JD, *Rise and Fall* 1:372; [*New Orleans*] *Daily Picayune,* Dec. 7, 1889, p. 1, col. 4; Ibid., p. 2, col. 3 (Jones quot.); *Life and Reminisc.,* 77, 84 and pic. opposite.

7. Jones, *Davis Memorial,* 493 (quots. from [*New Orleans*] *Times-Democrat*); *Life and Reminisc.,* 75–78; [*New Orleans*] *Daily Picayune,* Dec. 7, 1889, p. 1, col. 4, quot.; Ibid., p. 8. col. 3 ("father" of Conf.); *SHSP* 14:69 (Latin quot.; see 99–100); T. W. Hall in *Life and Reminisc.,* 354–59 ("another Washington"; see also "Close of Am. War," 125 and A. H. Edey in Rowland 6:508).

8. [*New Orleans*] *Daily Picayune,* Dec. 7, 1889, p. 1, cols. 4–6 (and quot. on lights); Jones, *Davis Memorial,* 494–96, 498; Butler, *Judah P. Benj.,* xxvi; Goldsborough, "Varina Howell Davis," 11, quots.

9. Jones, *Davis Memorial,* 496, 498–502 (quots. from *Picayune;* "a number" of Davis ex-slaves come; sculptor is called "Orion Frazee"; other estimates of number on 512 and in *Life and Reminisc.,* 81); *[New Orleans] Picayune,* Dec. 7, 1889, p. 8, col. 4; Grady in *DAB* (d. Dec. 23).

10. Jones, *Davis Memorial,* 509 (*Times* quot.); *[New Orleans] Picayune,* Dec. 7, 1889, p. 1 (cols. 4–6), p. 2 (cols. 1, 4), p. 8; *Life and Reminsc.,* 79.

11. Rowland 9:360–62, 368, 4:371 n.1 (Thompson, sec. of interior 1857–61; d. 1885) and 8:222 n.1 (Lamar, sec. 1885–87); Jones, *Davis Memorial,* 503, 509–10 (sec. of war quots.), 511–15 (quots. from Markham, quoting sec. of war and a "Dr. Hedges"; see Markham on 501).

12. *[New Orleans] Daily Picayune,* Dec. 7, 1889, p. 2 (col. 2), p. 1 (col. 7); Jones, *Davis Memorial,* 513 (quot. from Markham), 484–85, 504 (Louisville offered the unused ZT grave in Cave Hill Cem.), 481, 508 (quot.), 488–89; Strode, *Tragic Hero,* 513–14; Rowland 9:206–7; *SHSP* 9:216–18.

13. *[New Orleans] Daily Picayune,* Dec. 7, 1889, p. 1, col. 6; Jones, *Davis Memorial,* 490, 547, 559–66 (Drayton last survivor of their West Pt. class); Nuremberger, *Clay of Ala.,* 317 (Va. m. Clopton, justice of Ala. Sup. Ct., 1887); *Life and Reminisc.,* 93–94; Strode, *Tragic Hero,* 521; Seitz, *Bragg,* 544.

14. Jones, *Davis Memorial,* 501, 516–21, and 566–68, quots. ("gates" prob. from Ps. 118:19–20); *Life and Reminisc.,* 81, 84, 95–96. A stone chair, small but lifesize, made to look like living wood and cushioned upholstery, stands in memory of JD "from the Ladies / of / Selma Alabama / May 1893" in the Selma cemetery, where Hardee lies.

15. *Life and Reminisc.,* 84, quot.; Jones, *Davis Memorial,* 514 (quot. from Markham *re* Hubert), 516 (quot. *re* flowers), 526–28 (quots.; Dec. "12th" should read "11th" [see 503]; also there: 3 other priests and Hugh M. Thompson, Episc. bsp. of Miss. [Perry, *Bishops of Am. Church,* 273]); *Gache,* 75, "Commentary."

16. Strode, *Tragic Hero,* 521; Jones, *Davis Memorial,* 542, 527–32 (quots. from *[New Orleans] Times-Democrat;* Leucht also 501; John 11:25 in "The Order for the Burial of the Dead," *BCP*); *Papers* 3:181–83; Flag assumed to be Munford's, but it was removed at the grave; *Life and Reminisc.,* 84, 95).

17. Jones, *Davis Memorial,* 532–34 (quots.), 536–55 (gives route of procession in detail); *Life and Reminisc.,* 88–90.

18. Basso, *Bgd.: Great Creole,* 309–10, quot.; Early to JD, Apr. 1 and May 2, 1883 (Rowland 9:205–6 and 212); JD to Bryce of *N. Am. Rev.* (quot. in *Belford's,* Jan. 1890, 274).

19. *Life and Reminisc.,* 90–98, quots.; Jones, *Davis Memorial,* 570–72 (Gordon quots., said that night to U. C. V.), 536 (quots. from *[New Orleans] Times-Democrat:*

pics. of mon. facing 534, 536; and see 555–58); *Hymns*, #139, quots. (Rock=Christ: 1 Cor. 10:4; cf. Ex. 33:20–23, Num. 20:7–11).

20. VHD to Marg. D. Hayes, [early 1890], MS, TRANSYL (one assistant is "a type writer"); VHD, sketch of own life, n.d., MS, ALA ("dear Husband . . . thought I could do it best—wrote under pressure of grief health succumbed"); Strode, *Tragic Hero*, 527, 407, 497, 501, 509; McElroy, *JD* 2:687–94 (Redpath had left *N. Am. Rev.* for *Belford's;* see 638); Ross, *First Lady*, 364–65, 371–76, 386–87.

21. Ross, *First Lady*, 397, 366–76; VHD to Marg. D. Hayes, [early 1890], MS, TRANSYL; V. Jefferson Davis to "My very dear old Friend," Feb. 19, 1890, and Mar. 28, 1893, MSS, ALA. For Maggie's altered name, see Weddell, *St. Paul's* 2:372 and *Conf. Vet.*, Jan. 1907, 42.

22. Swanberg, *Pulitzer*, 217 and passim; Ross, *First Lady*, 378–80, 382–85, 391, 394–96, 405–6; VHD, life sketch (as in Note 19 above); Marg. D. Hayes to S. D. Lee in *Conf. Vet*, Jan. 1907, 42, quot.; Ferrell, "Daughter of Conf.," 81 (arts. by Winnie), 75 n.3 and 82 n.1 (Harper publ. the novels in 1895 and 1898).

23. Ross, *First Lady*, 380–81; *[New Orleans] Daily Picayune*, Dec. 7, 1889, p. 2 (col. 2: Fitz Lee to Fenner, Dec. 6); *Life and Reminisc.*, 247n, 257–58; (Miss.'s claim:) Marg. D. Hayes, letter, as in Note 21 above, *Picayune*, p. 8, col. 1; Jones, *Davis Memorial*, 481; Mary C. Lee to VHD, July 15, 1891, MS, ALA; Ross, *First Lady*, 374, 381–82, 393; V. Jefferson Davis to ["Friend"], Mar. 28, 1893, MS, ALA; J. T. Ellyson (mayor of Rich.) to Hayes, Apr. 25 (MS, Davis-Hayes Family Papers [Webb 2], MDAH).

24. *[New Orleans] Daily Picayune*, May 29 (Robt. called "Uncle Bob"); *New York Times*, May 28, p. 17, and May 30, quots.

25. *[New Orleans] Daily Picayune*, May 29, 1893; *New York Times*, May 28, p.17; Ross, *First Lady*, 381–82, quot.; Lubbock, *Six Decades*, 639. Jones had wanted to "show my lasting appreciation for my best friend" in 1889, by driving JD's body to the grave (*Davis Memorial*, 467).

26. VHD to Marg. D. Hayes, [early 1890], MS, TRANSYL, quot.; Minnigerode in *Life and Reminisc.*, 224 (quot. from VHD to him); Visit to Hollywood Cem., 1986 (quots. from gravestones; Matt. 5:10); *SHSP* 29:7–8; JD to SHS, Apr. 25, 1882 (Rowland 9:165–66, quots.); Ross, *First Lady*, 418 (Maggie's inscr.; see 395–96).

27. Zolnay to VHD, June 15 [1899], MS, ALA; Same to Marg. D. Hayes, [June 13] (quots.) and canceled checks (VHD to Zolnay and to Henry-Bonnard Bronze Co.), Nov. 9 and 23 (Davis-Hayes Family Papers [Webb 2], MDAH); *Letters*, 300; DeLeon, *Belles*, 75; N. D. Smith, "Reminisc. of JD," 178; Louise Davis, "Zolnay," in *Sunday Tennessean*, Aug. 28, 1988, Sec. F, pp. 1–2 (Zolnay quot.; author indebted to Nashville friends for this clipping); Marg. D. Hayes letter in *Conf. Vet.*, Oct. 1907, 448, quots.

28. Ross, *First Lady*, 378–80, 382–83, 391–92 (quots.); Scrapbook at Old Courthouse Mus.; Lubbock, *Six Decades*, 639 and n.128 (Winnie quot.); Tommie Phillips LaCavera, "Winnie Davis Memorial Hall" (*U. D. C. Magazine*, Feb. 1988), 18–21. Da Costa's *Medical Diagnosis* (1866), 697–98: vomiting distinctive feature of "*gastroenteric* form" of "Congestive Fever" ("malignant, destructive, malarial") (author indebted to Dr. V. S. LeQuire for this ref.). Several of Winnie's books on Egypt are in Rosenstock.

29. Weddell, *St. Paul's* 2:419–25 (quots.), 371–72; Swanberg, *Pulitzer*, 253; VHD to Winnie, *Letters*, passim; DeLeon, *Belles*, 73 (quot. *re* Maggie); *Conf. Vet.*, Jan. 1907, 42; Ross, *First Lady*, 371, 392, 385, 418 (U. D. C. gave angel); Zolnay letters (mentions angel being cast), checks, and L. Davis, "Zolnay," as in Note 27 above.

30. Weddell, *St. Paul's* 2:367–71 ("military" quot. on 371); Ross, *First Lady*, 416–18 (Grant's son [see 388–89]; Carrie [also 395, and Marg. D. Hayes to her, Apr. 6, 1899, ALA typescript]); E. Rowland, *Varina* 2:547, 553–56 (quot.); Mary Lee to Marg. D. Hayes, Oct. 17 [1906], MS, ALA, quots. ("her dear face").

31. Weddell, *St. Paul's* 2:425–26; Hayes monument, Hollywood Cem. (inscr.

quot. from *Te Deum* in Mg. Prayer, *BCP* [1896]; Hayes d. 1919); *Papers* 1:App. 4, Chart 14; Ross, *First Lady*, 416 (VHD quot.; has "not" for "never").

32. Weddell, *St. Paul's* 2:373–95 (quots. on 379, 374, 380–81; Apr. 17 date here, but *BCP* [1896] has Easter Apr. 10), pics. facing 318 and 350, 520–25 (Lee window, 1892: see 1:frontispiece). For hand: see esp. pic. in *Conf. Vet.*, Apr. 1907, 166.

33. Hymns: first 2 in *Hymns* [1850], last written 1864/1868 (*The Hymnal* [New York: Church Pension Fund, 1940], #126, 2d tune); Weddell, *St. Paul's* 2:378 (quot.), 381–95 (sermon; quots. on 381, 394, 382, 390).

34. DeLeon, *Belles*, 64, quot.; VHD, *Memoir* 2:915 (Wheat); Jones, *Davis Memorial*, 530 (Galleher), 583 (Lubbock quot.), 592–94 (quots.). Others: ibid., 441, 465, 523–25, 620–23, 668 and 671; Rowland 9:556; *Hill*, 211; *Columbia [S. C.] Record*, Dec. 11, 1889, pp. 1–2; *Conf. Vet.*, July 1907, 294–95, and Oct., 437; Winchester, "JD, Communicant," 728; *SHSP* 19:416.

35. Weddell, *St. Paul's* 2:390–95, quots. (ref. to Rev. 21:27); Jones, *Davis Memorial*, 416 (Minnigerode quot.). To bear wrongs patiently and to forgive are two of the spiritual works of mercy.

36. Jones, *Davis Memorial*, 263 (Daniel quot.), 343 (Geo. Davis quot.), 605, 669; Mallory in Alfriend, *Life of JD*, 602.

37. Gov. Fitzhugh Lee, Richmond, Dec. 21, 1889, to an assembly asking that JD's body be interred there (Jones, *Davis Memorial*, 592, quots.).

Appendix A J. E. Johnston to J. Davis, on Rank

1. This law (*O. R.*, 4, 1:163–64) would apply, if at all, to JEJ's appt. as brig. gen.; but he did not come directly, but through the state forces of Va.

2. The grade was not abolished. By the "three" JEJ evidently means himself, Lee, and Cooper; but Bgd. and Bragg were also brig. gens. then. If all automatically became full gens. on May 16, 1861, they would have become so; but both were specially appt'd. later (*Conf. Soldier in C. W.*, 343, 344; Bragg in prov. army). See L. P. Walker to JD, Apr. 27, 1861 (*O. R.*, 4, 1:249): rank only designed to give C. S. off. precedence over state off.

3. Only Cooper's commission retained the May 16, 1861, date: ASJ's was May 30; Lee's, June 14; JEJ's, July 4; Bgd.'s, July 21 (Richardson, *Conf.* 1:129). The dating was merely a device for ranking. No one else complained. The word *past*, from the *O. R.* printing, corrects VHD's "part."

4. JEJ had never been first in rank except in his own mind.

Select Bibliography

Unpublished Material

Collections

Alabama Department of Archives and History, Montgomery (ADAH)
- Jefferson Davis Papers
- William Joseph Hardee Papers

University of Alabama (Tuscaloosa)
- W. Stanley Hoole Special Collections Library
  - Jefferson Davis Collection (ALA)
  - Hudson Strode Papers

Beauvoir, The Jefferson Davis Home and Presidential Library, Biloxi, Mississippi
- Rare Books Collection
- Sarah Anne Ellis Dorsey Collection

Casemate Museum, Fort Monroe, Virginia

Confederate Museum (formerly Memorial Hall), New Orleans, Louisiana

First White House of the Confederacy, Montgomery, Alabama
- Davis Papers

University of Memphis (Tennessee), McWherter Library
- Mississippi Valley Collection (MVC)
  - Jefferson Davis–Joel Addison Hayes, Jr. Family Papers, 1864–1882 (microfilm)
- West Tennessee Historical Society Archives
  - Meriwether Family Papers (microfilm)

Mississippi Department of Archives and History, Jackson
- Private Manuscripts, Series Z: Davis and Howell family files
- Jefferson Davis and Family Papers of the Estate of Adele Davis
- William Burr Howell–Jefferson Davis–Joel Addison Hayes, Jr., Family Papers donated by Mrs. Barbara Webb and Accretion Thereto
- Old Capitol Museum of Mississippi History
- Jefferson Davis Book Collection

Museum of the Confederacy, Richmond, Virginia
White House of the Confederacy
"Victory in Defeat" (exhibit of Davis family items)
National Society of the Sons of the American Revolution
Applications of Davis family members
New Hampshire Historical Society Manuscript Collections, Concord
The John Parker Hale Papers, 1822–1885
The Franklin Pierce Papers, 1820–1946
New York Public Library, Astor, Lenox, and Tilden Foundations
Manuscripts and Archives Division
Walter L. Fleming Collection
Old Capitol Museum (Eva W. Davis Memorial), Vicksburg, Mississippi
Davis Papers
Rosemont, Woodville, Mississippi
Cemetery list
Typescript of audio guide tape
University of South Carolina
South Caroliniana Library
Williams-Chesnut-Manning Collection
Tennessee State Library and Archives, Nashville
Transylvania University, Lexington, Kentucky
Jefferson Davis Papers
Tulane University, Howard-Tilton Memorial Library, New Orleans
Louisiana Historical Association Collection of Jefferson Davis Papers

Other

Goldsborough, Anna Farrar. "Varina Howell Davis." Hudson Strode Papers, University of Alabama. Typescript.

Guice, Julia. "History—Church of the Redeemer." Author's collection. Typescript.

Heidler, Jeanne Twiggs. "The Military Career of David Emanuel Twiggs." (Ph.D. diss., Auburn University, 1988).

Horton, Bobby. "Homespun Songs of the C.S.A." Vol. 2. Audio cassette, 1986.

Inventory of the Davis Family Artifacts in the Museum of the Confederacy, Richmond. Author's collection. Photocopy.

Kerr, J. W. "Memorial of John Perkins, Born Somerset Md May 17th A D 1781. Died at the Oaks Columbus Miss. Nov 30th A D 1866." Author's collection. Manuscript.

Lewis, Charlotte Elizabeth. "Sarah Anne Dorsey: A Critical Estimate." (Thesis, Department of English, Louisiana State University, July 1940). Dorsey Papers, Davis Library, Beauvoir. Photocopy.

Posey, Zoe. "Sarah Anne Dorsey: A Sketch." Dorsey Papers, Beauvoir. Typescript.

Wall, Allie Patricia. "The Letters of Mary Boykin Chesnut." (Thesis, University of South Carolina, 1977). Author's collection. Photocopy.

Yeatman, Trezevant Player, Jr. "St. John's, a Plantation Church of the Old South." Author's collection. Typescript.

Printed Matter

Books, Articles, Pamphlets

Aiken, Leona Taylor. *Donelson, Tennessee: Its History and Landmarks.* Nashville: n.p., 1968.

Alderson, William T., and Robert M. McBride. *Landmarks of Tennessee History.* Nashville: Tennessee Historical Society & Commission, 1965.

Alexander, Edward Porter. *Fighting for the Confederacy: The Personal Recollections of General Edward Porter Alexander.* Edited by Gary W. Gallagher. Chapel Hill: University of North Carolina Press, 1989.

Alfriend, Frank H. *The Life of Jefferson Davis.* Cincinnati: Caxton Publishing House, 1868.

Allen, Felicity. "Martyrdom or Myth-making? Prison Life of Jefferson Davis in a New Light." *Journal of Confederate History* 6 (1990): 1–52.

Allen, James S. *Reconstruction: The Battle for Democracy, 1865–1876.* New York: International Publishers, 1937.

Ambrose, Stephen E. *Duty, Honor, Country: A History of West Point.* Baltimore: Johns Hopkins Press, 1966.

Andrews, Marietta Minnigerode. *Scraps of Paper.* New York: E. P. Dutton & Company, 1929.

Andrews, Matthew P., comp. *The Women of the South in War Times.* Baltimore: Norman, Remington Co., 1920.

The Annals of the War, Written by Leading Participants, North and South, Originally Published in the Philadelphia Weekly Times. Philadelphia: Times Publishing Co., 1879.

Arnow, Harriette Simpson. *Seedtime on the Cumberland.* New York: Macmillan Co., 1960.

Aubry, Octave. *The Second Empire.* Philadelphia: J. B. Lippincott Co., 1940.

Avary, Myrta Lockett. *Dixie after the War.* Boston: Houghton Mifflin Co., 1937.

Baker, Raymond F. *Andersonville: The Story of a Civil War Prison Camp.* Washington: National Park Service, 1972.

Bassett, John Spencer. *Correspondence of Andrew Jackson.* 7 vols. Washington: Carnegie Institute of Washington, 1926–1935.

Basso, Hamilton. *Beauregard, the Great Creole.* New York: Charles Scribner's Sons, 1933.

Baugh, Albert C., ed. *A Literary History of England.* 2d ed. New York: Appleton-Century-Crofts, 1967.

Bearss, Margie Riddle. *Sherman's Forgotten Campaign: The Meridian Expedition.* Baltimore: Gateway Press, 1987.

Beers, H. P. *Guide to the Archives of the Government of the Confederate States of America.* Washington, D.C.: U.S. Government Printing Office, 1968.

Bergeron, Arthur W. *Confederate Mobile.* Jackson: University Press of Mississippi, 1991.

Bettersworth, John K., ed. *Mississippi in the Confederacy: As They Saw It.* Jackson: Mississippi Department of Archives and History, 1961.

"The Birthplace of Jefferson Davis." *Confederate Veteran* (November 1907): 486–87.

Black, Robert C., III. *The Railroads of the Confederacy.* Chapel Hill: University of North Carolina Press, 1952. Reprint, Wilmington, N.C.: Broadfoot Publishing Co., 1987.

Blackford, Charles Minor, III, ed., and Susan Leigh Blackford, comp. *Letters from Lee's Army, or Memoirs of Life in and out of the Army in Virginia during the War between the States.* New York: Charles Scribner's Sons, 1947.

Blakey, Arch Fredric. *General John H. Winder, C.S.A.* Gainesville: University of Florida Press, 1990.

Blum, John M., Bruce Catton, Edmund S. Morgan, Arthur M. Schlesinger, Jr., Kenneth M. Stamp, and C. Vann Woodward. *The National Experience.* New York: Harcourt, Brace & World, 1963.

Boatner, Mark. *Civil War Dictionary.* New York: Davis McKay Co., 1959.

The Book of Common Prayer and Administration of the Sacraments, and Other Rites and Ceremonies of the Church, according to the Use of the Protestant Episcopal Church in the United States. New York: New York Protestant Episcopal Press, 1830.

The Book of Common Prayer and Administration of the Sacraments, and Other Rites and Ceremonies of the Church, according to the Use of the Protestant Episcopal Church in the United States of America: Together with the Psalter, or Psalms of Davis. Hartford: C. M. Welles, 1850. Reprint, Thomas Nelson & Sons, 1896.

Bowers, Claude G. *The Tragic Era: The Revolution after Lincoln.* New York: Blue Ribbon Books, 1929.

Bowman, John S. *The Civil War Almanac.* New York: W. H. Smith Publishers, 1983.

Boyle, Virginia Frazer. "Jefferson Davis in Canada." *Confederate Veteran* (March 1929): 89–93.

Bradley, Chester D. "Dr. Craven and the Prison Life of Jefferson Davis." *Virginia Magazine of History and Biography* 62 (1954): 50–94.

———. "The Shackling of Jefferson Davis." In *Tales of Old Fort Monroe.* Fort Monroe, Va.: Fort Monroe Casemate Museum, [n.d.]. Pamphlet of 15 parts.

Bragg, William Harris. "Charles C. Jones, Jr., and the Mystery of Lee's Lost Dispatches." *Georgia Historical Quarterly* 72 (1988): 429–62.

Brandau, Roberta Seawell. *History of Homes and Gardens of Tennessee.* Nashville: Garden Study Club of Nashville, 1936.

Bridges, Hal. *Lee's Maverick General: Daniel Harvey Hill.* New York: McGraw-Hill Book Co., 1961.

Broussard, Ray. "Governor John A. Quitman and the Lopez Expeditions of 1851–52." *Journal of Mississippi History* 28 (1966): 103–20.

Burchenal, Mary Day. "A Yankee Girl Meets Jefferson Davis." *Holland's, the Magazine of the South* (October 1931): 17–18, 43, 45.

Burger, Nash K. "The Rt. Rev. William Mercer Green, First Episcopal Bishop of Mississippi." *Journal of Mississippi History* 12 (1950): 3–27.

Burns, Robert. *Poems and Songs of Robert Burns.* Edited by James Barke. London: Collins, 1955. Reprint, 1964.

Butler, Benjamin F. *Butler's Book: A Review of His Legal, Political, and Military Career.* Boston: A. M. Thayer & Co., 1892.

Butler, Pierce. *Judah P. Benjamin.* Philadelphia: G. W. Jacobs, 1907. Reprint, New York: Chelsea House, 1980.

Calhoun, Robert Dabney. "The John Perkins Family of Northeast Louisiana." *Louisiana Historical Quarterly* 19 (1936): 70–88.

Capers, Gerald M., Jr. *The Biography of a River Town: Memphis, Its Heroic Age.* Chapel Hill: University of North Carolina Press, 1939.

Carter, Hodding, and Betty Werlein Carter. *So Great a Good: A History of the Episcopal Church in Louisiana and of Christ Church Cathedral, 1805–1955.* Sewanee, Tenn.: University Press, 1955.

Carter, Rosalie. *Captain Tod Carter of the Confederate States Army: A Biographical Word Portrait.* Franklin, Tenn.: Athens Advertising, 1978.

Carter, Sue Tarpley. "President Davis as I Knew Him." *Confederate Veteran* (May 1903): 209.

Cartwright, Samuel A. "Alcohol and the Ethiopian; or, the Moral and Physical Effects of Ardent Spirits on the Negro Race, and Some Account of the Peculiarity of That People." *New-Orleans Medical and Surgical Journal* 10 (1853): 150–65.

Castel, Albert. *Decision in the West: The Atlanta Campaign of 1864.* Lawrence: University Press of Kansas, 1992.

The Catholic Encyclopedia. 15 vols. New York: Encyclopedia Press, 1913.

[Charles, Elizabeth Rundle]. *Chronicles of the Schoenberg-Cotta Family by Two of Themselves.* New York: M. W. Dodd, 1866.

Cheshire, Joseph Blount. *The Church in the Confederate States: A History of the Protestant Episcopal Church in the Confederate States.* New York: Longmans, Green, & Co., 1912.

Chesnut, Mary Boykin Miller. *Mary Chesnut's Civil War.* Edited by C. Vann Woodward. New Haven: Yale University Press, 1981.

———. *The Private Mary Chesnut: The Unpublished Civil War Diaries.* Edited by C. Vann Woodward and Elizabeth Muhlenfeld. New York: Oxford University Press, 1984.

Childs, H. T. "Turney's First Tennessee Regiment." *Confederate Veteran* (April 1917): 164–66.

"Chivalrous Southrons." *Southern Review* (July 1869): 96–128.

Christ Church, Nashville, 1829–1929. Nashville: Marshall & Bruce Co., 1929.

Claiborne, J. F. H. *Mississippi, as a Province, Territory and State, with Biographical Notices of Eminent Citizens.* Jackson, Miss.: Power & Barksdale, 1880. Reprint, Baton Rouge: Louisiana State University Press, 1964.

Clark, M. H. "Departure of President Davis and Cabinet from Richmond, Va., and the Last Days of the Confederate Treasury and What Became of Its Specie." In *The Confederate Soldier in the Civil War,* 318–22.

Clay-Clopton, Virginia. "Clement Claiborne Clay." *Transactions of the Alabama Historical Society, 1897–1898* 2 (1898): 74–82.

Cleary, W. W. "The Attempt to Fasten the Assassination of President Lincoln on President Davis and Other Innocent Parties." *Southern Historical Society Papers* 9 (1881): 313–25.

"The Close of the American War." *Quarterly Review* 118 (1865): 106–36.

Coleman, Elizabeth Tyler. *Priscilla Cooper Tyler and the American Scene, 1816–1889.* University: University of Alabama Press, 1955.

Coleman, Kenneth. *The American Revolution in Georgia, 1763–1789.* Athens: University of Georgia Press, 1958.

The Columbia Encyclopedia in One Volume. Edited by William Bridgwater and Elizabeth J. Sherwood. Morningside Heights, N.Y.: Columbia University, 1950.

Colyar, A. S. *Life and Times of Andrew Jackson, Soldier-Statesman-President.* Nashville: Marshall & Bruce Co., 1904.

Confederate Soldier in the Civil War: The Campaigns, Battles, Sieges, Charges and Skirmishes . . . The Foundation and Formation of the Confederacy . . . The Confederate States Navy . . . Eulogy by Fitzhugh Lee. [Louisville: Courier-Journal Job Printing Co., 1895]. Reprint, n.p.: Fairfax Press, n.d.

Connelly, Thomas Lawrence, and Archer Jones. *The Politics of Command: Factions and Ideas in Confederate Strategy.* Baton Rouge: Louisiana State University Press, 1973.

Craven, John J. *Prison Life of Jefferson Davis, Embracing Details and Incidents in His Captivity, Particulars Concerning His Health and Habits, Together with Many Conversations on Topics of Great Public Interest.* New York: Carleton, 1866.

Crist, Lynda Lasswell. "A Bibliographical Note: Jefferson Davis's Personal Library: All Lost, Some Found." *Journal of Mississippi History* 45 (1983): 186–93.

Currie, James T. *Enclave: Vicksburg and Her Plantations, 1863–1870.* Jackson: University Press of Mississippi, 1980.

Currie, James T., ed. "Freedmen at Davis Bend, April 1864." *Journal of Mississippi History* 46 (1984): 120–29.

Dabney, Robert L. *A Defence of Virginia, [and through Her, of the South,] in Recent and Pending Contests against the Sectional Party.* E. J. Hale & Son, 1867. Reprint, Harrisonburg, Va.: Sprinkle Publications, 1977.

Dabney, Virginius. *Pistols and Pointed Pens: The Dueling Editors of Old Virginia.* Chapel Hill: Algonquin Books of Chapel Hill, 1987.

Da Costa, J. M. *Medical Diagnosis with Special Reference to Practical Medicine: A Guide to the Knowledge and Discrimination of Diseases.* Philadelphia: J. B. Lippincott & Co., 1866.

Davis, Charles S. *Colin J. McRae: Confederate Financial Agent.* Confederate Centennial Studies. Tuscaloosa, Ala.: Confederate Publishing Co., 1961.

Davis, Jefferson. "Andersonville and Other War-Prisons." Parts 1, 2. *Belford's Magazine* 4 (1890): 161–78, 337–53 (Microfilm, American Periodical Series 3, Reel 586).

———. "The Doctrine of State Rights." *North American Review* 150 (1890): 205–19.

———. "Life and Character of the Hon. John Caldwell Calhoun." *North American Review* 145 (1887): 246–60.

———. *The Papers of Jefferson Davis.* Vol. 1, 1808–1840, edited by Haskell M. Monroe, Jr., and James T. McIntosh. Baton Rouge: Louisiana State University Press, 1971.

———. *The Papers of Jefferson Davis.* Vol. 2, June 1841–July 1846, edited by James T. McIntosh. Baton Rouge: Louisiana State University Press, 1974.

———. *The Papers of Jefferson Davis.* Vol. 3, July 1846–December 1848, edited by James T. McIntosh, Linda L. Crist, and Mary S. Dix. Baton Rouge: Louisiana State University Press, 1981.

———. *The Papers of Jefferson Davis.* Vol. 4, 1849–1852, edited by Lynda Lasswell Crist, Mary Seaton Dix, and Richard E. Beringer. Baton Rouge: Louisiana State University Press, 1983.

———. *The Papers of Jefferson Davis.* Vol. 5, 1853–1855, edited by Lynda Lasswell Crist and Mary Seaton Dix. Baton Rouge: Louisiana State University Press, 1985.

———. *The Papers of Jefferson Davis.* Vol. 6, 1856–1860, edited by Lynda Lasswell Crist and Mary Seaton Dix. Baton Rouge: Louisiana State University Press, 1989.

———. *The Rise and Fall of the Confederate Government.* 2 vols. New York: D. Appleton & Co., 1881.

———. "Robert E. Lee." *North American Review* 150 (1890): 55–66.

———. *Scotland and the Scottish People. An Address Delivered in the City of Memphis, Tennessee, on St. Andrew's-Day 1875.* Glasgow: Anderson & Mackay, 1876.

Davis, Reuben. *Recollections of Mississippi and Mississippians.* Cambridge, Mass.: Houghton, Mifflin, 1890.

Davis, Varina Howell Jefferson. "Christmas in the Confederate White House." *New York World Sunday Magazine,* December 13, 1896.

———. *Jefferson Davis, Ex-President of the Confederate States of America: A Memoir by His Wife.* 2 vols. New York: Belford Co., 1890.

Davis, William C. *Breckinridge: Statesman, Soldier, Symbol.* Baton Rouge: Louisiana State University Press, 1982.

———. *Jefferson Davis: The Man and His Hour.* New York: HarperCollins Publishers, 1991.

Davis, Winnie. "Jefferson Davis in Private Life." *New York Herald,* August 11, 1895.

deButts, Mary Custis Lee. *Growing Up in the 1850s: The Journal of Agnes Lee.* Chapel Hill: University of North Carolina Press, 1984.

DeLeon, T. C. *Belles, Beaux and Brains of the '60s.* New York: G. W. Dillingham Co., 1907. Reprint, New York: Arno Press, 1974.

———. "The Real Jefferson Davis in Private and Public Life." *Southern Historical Society Papers* 36 (1908): 74–85.

Denison, George T. *Soldiering in Canada: Recollections and Experiences.* Toronto: George N. Morang & Co., 1900.

DeWitt, David Miller. *The Impeachment and Trial of Andrew Johnson, Seventeenth President of the United States: A History.* 1903. Reprint, New York: Russell & Russell, 1967.

Dictionary of American Biography. Edited by Allen Johnson, et al. New York: Charles Scribner's Sons, 1934.

Dinkins, James. "Griffith-Barksdale-Humphrey Mississippi Brigade and Its Campaigns." *Southern Historical Society Papers* 32 (1904): 250–74.

Dodd, William E. *Jefferson Davis.* American Crisis Biographies. Philadelphia: George W. Jacobs & Co., 1907.

Donald, David. *Charles Sumner and the Coming of the Civil War.* New York: Alfred A. Knopf, 1960.

———. *Charles Sumner and the Rights of Man.* New York: Alfred A. Knopf, 1970.

Donnelly, Ralph W. *The History of the Confederate States Marine Corps.* Washington, D.C.: Published by author, 1976.

Dorsey, Sarah A. *Recollections of Henry Watkins Allen, Brigadier-General Confederate States Army, Ex-Governor of Louisiana.* New York: M. Doolady, 1866.

Douglas, Henry Kyd. *I Rode with Stonewall: Being Chiefly the War Experiences of the Youngest Member of Jackson's Staff from the John Brown Raid to the Hanging of Mrs. Surratt.* University of North Carolina Press, 1940. Reprint, Marietta, Ga.: Mockingbird Books, 1974.

Drake, Edwin L., ed. *The Annals of the Army of Tennessee and Early Western History, Including a Chronological Summary of Battles and Engagements in the Western Armies of the Confederacy.* Vol. 1, April–December, 1878 [only vol. printed]. Reprint, Jackson, Tennessee: Guild Bindery Press, n.d.

DuBose, John Witherspoon. *The Life and Times of William Lowndes Yancey . . . .* Birmingham, Ala.: Roberts & Son, 1892.

Duke, Basil W. *History of Morgan's Cavalry.* Cincinnati: Miami Printing & Publishing Co., 1867.

———. *Reminiscences of General Basil W. Duke, C.S.A.* Garden City, New York: Doubleday, Page & Co., 1911.

Dumond, Dwight Lowell. *The Secession Movement, 1860–1861.* New York: Macmillan Co., 1931.

Dunham, Chester Forrester. *The Attitude of the Northern Clergy toward the South, 1860–1865.* Perspectives in American History, no. 6. Philadelphia: Porcupine Press, 1974.

Dyer, John P. *The Gallant Hood.* Indianapolis: Bobbs-Merrill Co., 1950.

Early, J. A. "Comments on the First Volume of the Count of Paris' Civil War in America." *Southern Historical Society Papers* 3 (1877): 140–54.

———. *Jubal Early's Memoirs: Autobiographical Sketch and Narrative of the War between the States.* Great War Stories Series. Baltimore: Nautical & Aviation Publishing Co. of America, 1989.

Eaton, Clement. *Freedom of Thought in the Old South.* New York: Peter Smith, 1951.

———. *Jefferson Davis*. New York: Free Press, 1977.

Eckenrode, Hamilton J. *Jefferson Davis: President of the South*. 1923. Reprint, Freeport, N.Y.: Books for Libraries, 1971.

Eckert, Edward K. *"Fiction Distorting Fact": The Prison Life Annotated by Jefferson Davis*. Macon, Ga.: Mercer University Press, 1987.

The Encyclopedia Britannica. 29 vols. Chicago: University of Chicago, 1993.

Enmale, Richard, ed. *The Civil War in the United States by Karl Marx and Frederick Engels*. New York: International Publishers, 1937.

Escott, Paul D. *After Secession: Jefferson Davis and the Failure of Confederate Nationalism*. Baton Rouge: Louisiana State University Press, 1978.

Evans, W. A. *Jefferson Davis, His Diseases and His Doctors and a Biographical Sketch of Dr. Ewing Fox Howard. Mississippi Doctor* (June 1942): 14–26. Reprint, Biloxi: Jefferson Davis Shrine, Beauvoir House, n.d.

Everett, Frank E., Jr. *Brierfield: Plantation Home of Jefferson Davis*. Hattiesburg: University & College Press of Mississippi, 1971.

Faulk, Odie. B. *The U.S. Camel Corps: An Army Experiment*. New York: Oxford University Press, 1976.

Ferrell, Chiles Clifton. "'The Daughter of the Confederacy,'—Her Life, Character, and Writings." *Publications of the Mississippi Historical Society* 2 (1899): 69–84.

Flanary, Sara E. Lewis. "William Edward West in New Orleans and Mississippi." *Antiques* (November 1983): 1010–15.

Fleming, Walter L. *Civil War and Reconstruction in Alabama*. Columbia University Press, 1905. Reprint, Gloucester, Mass.: Peter Smith, 1949.

———. "The Early Life of Jefferson Davis." *Mississippi Valley Historical Review*, extra number (April 1917). Reprint, *Louisiana State University Bulletin* (June 1917): 151–76.

———. "Jefferson Davis at West Point." *Publications of the Mississippi Historical Society* 10 (1909): 247–67.

———. "Jefferson Davis's First Marriage." *Publications of the Mississippi Historical Society* 12 (1912): 21–36.

———. "Jefferson Davis, the Negroes and the Negro Problem." *Sewanee Review* (October 1908). Reprint, *Louisiana State University Bulletin* (October 1908), 1–23.

———. "The Religious Life of Jefferson Davis." *Methodist Review* (April 1910). Reprint, Louisiana State University Bulletin (May 1910), 32542.

Fogel, Robert William, and Stanley L. Engerman. *Time on the Cross: The Economics of American Negro Slavery*. Boston: Little, Brown & Co., 1974.

Foote, Henry S. *Casket of Reminiscences.* Chronicle Publishing Co., 1874. Reprint, New York: Negro Universities Press, 1968.

Foote, Shelby. *The Civil War: A Narrative.* 3 vols. New York: Random House, 1958–1974.

Freeman, Douglas Southall, ed. *A Calendar of Confederate Papers with a Bibliography of Some Confederate Publications.* Richmond: Confederate Museum, 1908.

———. *George Washington: A Biography.* 7 vols. New York: Charles Scribner's Sons, 1948–1957.

———. *Lee's Lieutenants: A Study in Command.* 3 vols. New York: Charles Scribner's Sons, 1950–1951.

———. *Robert E. Lee: A Biography.* 4 vols. New York: Charles Scribner's Sons, 1949.

Freeman, Douglas Southall, and Grady McWhiney, eds. *Lee's Dispatches: Unpublished Letters of General Robert E. Lee to Jefferson Davis and the War Department of the Confederate States of America, 1862–65.* New York: G. P. Putnam's Sons, 1957.

Fremantle, Arthur James Lyon. *Three Months in the Southern States, April–June, 1863.* New York: J. Bradburn, 1864. Reprint, Lincoln: University of Nebraska Press, 1991.

Frey, Herman S. *Jefferson Davis.* Nashville: Frey Enterprises, 1978.

Fulkerson, H. S. *Random Recollections of Early Days in Mississippi, with a Biographical Sketch of the Author and an Introduction by P. L. Rainwater.* Vicksburg, Miss.: Vicksburg Printing & Publishing Co., 1885. Reprint, Baton Rouge: Otto Claitor, 1937.

Fuller, J. F. C. *Grant and Lee: A Study in Personality and Generalship.* Civil War Centennial Series. Bloomington: Indiana University Press, 1957.

Futch, Ovid L. *History of Andersonville Prison.* N.p.: University of Florida Press, 1968.

Gache, Louis-Hippolyte. *A Frenchman, a Chaplain, a Rebel: The War Letters of Père Louis-Hippolyte Gache, S.J.* Translated and edited by Cornelius M. Buckley. Chicago: Loyola University Press, 1981.

Garner, James Wilford. *Reconstruction in Mississippi.* New York: Macmillan Co., 1901.

George, Joseph, Jr. "'Black Flag Warfare': Lincoln and the Raids against Richmond and Jefferson Davis." *Pennsylvania Magazine of History and Biography* 115 (1991): 291–318.

Gleason, David King. *Plantation Homes of Louisiana and the Natchez Area.* Baton Rouge: Louisiana State University Press, 1984.

Goff, Richard D. *Confederate Supply.* Durham: Duke University Press, 1969.

Gordon, F. E. "On Continued Fevers." *New-Orleans Medical and Surgical Journal* 10 (1853): 145–50.

Gordon, John B. *Reminiscences of the Civil War.* New York: Charles Scribner's Sons, 1903.

Gorgas, Josiah. *The Civil War Diary of General Josiah Gorgas.* Edited by Frank E. Vandiver. Tuscaloosa: University of Alabama Press, 1947.

———. *The Journals of Josiah Gorgas, 1857–1878.* Edited by Sarah Woolfolk Wiggins. Tuscaloosa: University of Alabama Press, 1995.

Goulburn, Edward Mayrick. *Thoughts on Personal Religion, Being a Treatise on the Christian Life in the Two Chief Elements, Devotion and Practice.* 4th American ed. New York: D. Appleton & Co., 1867.

Govan, Gilbert E., and James W. Livingood. *A Different Valor: The Story of General Joseph E. Johnston, C.S.A..* Indianapolis: Bobbs-Merrill Co., 1956.

Grant, U. S. *Personal Memoirs of U. S. Grant.* 2 vols. New York: Charles L. Webster & Co., 1885.

———. "The Vicksburg Campaign." In *Battles and Leaders* 3:493–539.

Hale, Will T., and Dixon L. Merritt. *A History of Tennessee and Tennesseans: The Leaders and Representative Men in Commerce, Industry and Modern Activities.* 8 vols. Chicago: Lewis Publishing Co., 1913.

Hallock, Judith Lee. *Braxton Bragg and Confederate Defeat.* Vol. 2. Tuscaloosa: University of Alabama Press, 1991.

Hamilton, Holman. *Zachary Taylor: Soldier of the Republic and Soldier in the White House.* 2 vols. Bobbs-Merrill, 1941 and 1951. Reprint, Hamden, Conn.: Archon Books, 1966.

Hamlin, Percy Gatling. *"Old Bald Head" (General R. S. Ewell).* Strasburg, Va.: Shenandoah Publishing House, 1940.

Hanchett, William. *Irish: Charles G. Halpine in Civil War America.* Syracuse, N.Y.: Syracuse University Press, 1970.

———. *The Lincoln Murder Conspiracies.* Urbana: University of Illinois Press, 1983.

Hanna, A. J. *Flight into Oblivion.* Richmond: Johnson Publishing Co., 1938.

Hardee, W. J. *Rifle and Light Infantry Tactics; for the Exercise and Manoeuvres of Troops when Acting as Light Infantry or Riflemen.* 2 vols. Nashville: J. O. Griffith & Co., 1861.

Harris, William C. *Leroy Pope Walker: Confederate Secretary of War.* Confederate Centennial Studies. Tuscaloosa, Ala.: Confederate Publishing Co., 1962.

Harrison, Burton Norvell. "Capture of Jefferson Davis: Extracts from a Narrative, written not for publication, but for the entertainment of my children only." In D. Rowland, *Jefferson Davis, Constitutionalist* 9:226–260 (variant, ibid 7:1–19).

Harrison, Mrs. Burton [Constance Cary]. *Recollections Grave and Gay*. New York: Charles Scribner's Sons, 1911.

Hawthorne, Nathaniel. *The Life of Franklin Pierce*. Boston: Ticknor, Reed & Fields, 1852. Reprint, New York: MSS Information Corp., 1970.

Hay, Thomas Robson. "Davis, Bragg, and Johnston in the Atlanta Campaign." *Georgia Historical Quarterly* 8 (1924): 38–48.

———. "Lucius B. Northrop: Commissary General of the Confederacy." *Civil War History* 9 (1963): 5–23.

Hay, Thomas Robson, ed. *Pat Cleburne: Stonewall Jackson of the West* (pp. 13–66) and Irving A. Buck. *Cleburne and His Command* (pp. 67–307). McCowat-Mercer Press, 1957. Reprint, Wilmington, N.C.: Broadfoot Publishing Co., 1991.

Headley, J. T. *The Illustrated Life of Washington*. Chicago: O. F. Gibbs, 1862.

Heitman, Francis B. *Historical Register and Dictionary of the United States Army from its Organization, September 29, 1789 to March 2, 1903*. 2 vols. Washington, D.C.: Government Printing Office, 1903.

Henderson, G. R. R. *Stonewall Jackson and the American Civil War*. New York: Grossett & Dunlap, 1943. Reprint, New York: DaCapo Press, 1988.

Hendrick, Burton J. *Statesmen of the Lost Cause: Jefferson Davis and His Cabinet*. New York: Literary Guild of America, 1939.

Hendricks, George Linton. *Union Army Occupation of the Southern Seaboard, 1861–1865*. Doctoral Dissertation Series. Ann Arbor, Michigan: University Microfilms, 1954.

Henry, Robert Selph. *As They Saw Forrest: Some Recollections and Comments of Contemporaries*. McCowat-Mercer Press, 1956. Reprint, Wilmington, N.C.: Broadfoot Publishing Co., 1991.

———. *"First with the Most" Forrest*. McCowat-Mercer Press, 1969. Reprint, Wilmington, N.C.: Broadfoot Publishing Co., 1987.

———. *The Story of the Confederacy*. Garden City, N.Y.: Garden City Publishing Co., 1931.

———. *The Story of the Mexican War*. Indianapolis: Bobbs-Merrill Co., 1950.

Hermann, Janet Sharp. *Joseph E. Davis: Pioneer Patriarch*. Jackson: University Press of Mississippi, 1990.

———. *The Pursuit of a Dream*. New York: Oxford University Press, 1981.

Hesseltine, William B. *Confederate Leaders in the New South*. Baton Rouge: Louisiana State University Press, 1950.

Heth, Henry. *The Memoirs of Henry Heth*. Edited by James L. Morrison, Jr. Contributions in Military History. Westport, Conn.: Greenwood Press, 1974.

Hicks, George E. *The Casemate Museum: Home of the U.S. Army's Coast Artillery Museum, Fort Monroe, Virginia.* N.p.: Fort Monroe, n.d. Pamphlet.

Hill, Benjamin Harvey. "Address before Southern Historical Society, Atlanta, February 18, 1874." *Southern Historical Society Papers* 14 (1886): 484–505.

Hill, Benj. H., Jr. *Senator Benjamin H. Hill of Georgia: His Life, Speeches and Writings.* Atlanta: H. C. Hudgins & Co., 1891.

Hill, Daniel H. "The Lost Dispatch." *Land We Love* 4 (1868): 270–84.

Hill, Tucker. *Victory in Defeat: Jefferson Davis and the Lost Cause.* Richmond: Museum of the Confederacy, 1986.

Holland, Cecil Fletcher. *Morgan and His Raiders: A Biography of the Confederate General.* New York: Macmillan Co., 1942.

Hood, J. B. *Advance and Retreat: Personal Experiences in the United States and Confederate States Armies.* New Orleans: G. T. Beauregard for the Hood Orphan Memorial Fund, 1880.

Hoole, W. Stanley. *Vizetelly Covers the Confederacy.* Confederate Centennial Studies. Tuscaloosa, Ala.: Confederate Publishing Co., 1957.

Horn, Stanley F. *The Army of Tennessee: A Military History.* Indianapolis: Bobbs-Merrill Co., 1941.

Howard, H. R. *The History of Virgil A. Stewart, and His Adventure in Capturing and Exposing the Great "Western Land Pirate" and His Gang . . . Execution of a Number of Murrell's Associates during Summer of 1835, and the Execution of Five Professional Gamblers by the Citizens of Vicksburg, on the 6th July, 1835.* New York: Harper & Brothers, 1836.

Howard, Oliver Otis. *General Taylor.* Great Commander Series. New York: D. Appleton & Co., 1892.

Hoyt's New Cyclopedia of Practical Quotations. Edited by Kate Louise Roberts. New York: Somerset Books, 1947.

Hughes, Nathaniel Cheairs, Jr. *General William J. Hardee: Old Reliable.* Baton Rouge: Louisiana State University Press, 1965.

Hymns, Suited to the Feasts and Fasts of the Church, and Other Occasions of Public Worship (bound with *Book of Common Prayer*). Hartford: C. M. Welles, 1850.

James, D. Clayton. *Antebellum Natchez.* Baton Rouge: Louisiana State University Press, 1968.

James, G. P. R. *The History of Chivalry.* New York: A. L. Fowle, 1900.

James, Marquis. *Andrew Jackson: The Border Captain.* New York: Literary Guild, 1933.

———. *Andrew Jackson: Portrait of a President.* Indianapolis: Bobbs-Merrill Co., 1937.

Johnson, Andrew. *The Papers of Andrew Johnson.* Vol. 10. Edited by Paul H. Bergeron. Knoxville: University of Tennessee Press, 1992.

Johnson, Bradley T. "Case of Jefferson Davis." In Rowland: *Jefferson Davis, Constitutionalist* 7:138–227.

Johnson, Bradley T., ed. *A Memoir of the Life and Public Service of Joseph E. Johnston Once Quartermaster General of the Army of the United States, and a General in the Army of the Confederate States of America.* Baltimore: R. H. Woodward & Co., 1891.

Johnson, Robert U., and Clarence C. Buel. *Battles and Leaders of the Civil War.* 4 vols. New York: Century Co., 1884–1888.

Johnson, William. *William Johnson's Natchez: The Ante-Bellum Diary of a Free Negro.* Edited by William Ransom Hogan and Edwin Adams Davis. Source Studies in Southern History. N.p.: Louisiana State University Press, 1951.

Johnston, Alexander, ed. *Representative American Orations to Illustrate American Political History.* 3 vols. New York: G. P. Putnam's Sons, 1884.

Johnston, Joseph E. "The Dalton-Atlanta Operations (A Review, in Part, of General Sherman's Memoirs)." In *The Annals of the Army of Tennessee* 1 (1878): 1–13.

———. "Jefferson Davis and the Mississippi Campaign." In *Battles and Leaders* 3:472–82.

———. *Narrative of Military Operations, Directed, during the Late War between the States by Joseph E. Johnston.* New York: D. Appleton & Co., 1874.

Johnston, William Preston. *The Life of Gen. Albert Sidney Johnston, Embracing His Service in the Armies of the United States, Republic of Texas, and the Confederate States.* New York: D. Appleton & Co., 1880.

Jones, J. William. *The Davis Memorial Volume; or our Dead President, Jefferson Davis, and the World's Tribute to His Memory.* N.p.: B. F. Johnson & Co., 1889.

Jones, J. William, comp. "The Kilpatrick-Dahlgren Raid against Richmond." *Southern Historical Society Papers* 13 (1885): 515–60.

Jones, Katharine M., ed. *Heroines of Dixie: Spring of High Hopes.* Indianapolis: Bobbs-Merrill Co., 1955. Reprint, St. Simons Island, Ga.: Mockingbird Books, 1974.

Jones, Virginia K., ed. "A Contemporary Account of the Inauguration of Jefferson Davis." *Alabama Historical Quarterly* 23 (1961): 273–77.

Jordan, Thomas. "Jefferson Davis." *Harper's New Monthly Magazine,* October 1865, 610–20.

Julian, George. *Political Recollections, 1840 to 1872.* Jansen, McClung & Co., 1884. Reprint, New York: Negro Universities Press, 1970.

Kadloubovsky, E., and G. E. H. Palmer. *Early Fathers from the Philokalia.* London: Faber & Faber, 1954.

Kane, Harnett T. *Natchez on the Mississippi.* New York: William Morrow & Co., 1947.

Kelly, Howard A., and Walter L. Burrage. *Dictionary of American Medical Biography: Lives of Eminent Physicians of the United States and Canada, from the Earliest Times.* Longwood Press, n.d. Reprint, New York: Appleton, 1928.

Kempis, Thomas à. *The Imitation of Christ.* Everyman's Library. London: J. M. Dent & Sons, 1910. Reprint, 1916.

Kerby, Robert L. *Kirby Smith's Confederacy: The Trans-Mississippi South, 1863–1865.* New York: Columbia University Press, 1972.

Kimball, William J., ed. *Richmond in Time of War.* Houghton Mifflin Research Series. Boston: Houghton Mifflin Co.,1960.

King, Alvy L. *Louis T. Wigfall: Southern Fire-Eater.* Baton Rouge: Louisiana State University Press, 1970.

King, S. B., Jr., ed. *The Wartime Journal of a Georgia Girl, 1864–1865.* Macon, Ga.: Ardivan Press, 1960.

Kredel, Fritz, and Frederick P. Todd. *Soldiers of the American Army, 1775–1954.* Chicago: Henry Regnery Co., 1954.

Krummacher, Friedrich Wilhelm. *The Suffering Saviour: Meditations on the Last Days of Christ,* with a biographical introduction by Wilbur M. Smith. Edinburgh: 1856. Reprint (abridged), Chicago: Moody Press, 1947.

The Ladies' Hermitage Association. *Andrew Jackson's Hermitage.* Hermitage, Tenn.: Ladies' Hermitage Association, 1987.

LaForce, Glen W. "The Trial of Major Henry Wirz—A National Disgrace." *Army Lawyer,* June 1988, 3–10.

Lankford, Nelson D., ed. *An Irishman in Dixie: Thomas Conolly's Diary of the Fall of the Confederacy.* Columbia: University of South Carolina Press, 1988.

Lash, Jeffrey N. *Destroyer of the Iron Horse: General Joseph E. Johnston and Confederate Rail Transportation, 1861–1865.* Kent, Ohio: Kent State University Press, 1991.

Lee, Fitz. "Sketch of the Late General S. Cooper." *Southern Historical Society Papers* 3 (1877): 269–76.

Lee, Henry. *Memoirs of the War in the Southern Department of the United States.* 2 vols. 1812. Reprint, New York: Burt Franklin, 1970.

Lee, Robert E. *The Wartime Papers of R. E. Lee.* Edited by Clifford Dowdey and Louis H. Manarin. Virginia Civil War Commission. New York: Bramhall House, 1961.

Lee, Robert E. [Jr.]. *Recollections and Letters of General Robert E. Lee.* Garden City, N.Y.: Garden City Publishing Co., 1924.

Lee, Susan P. *Memoirs of William Nelson Pendleton, D.D.* Philadelphia: J. B. Lippincott Co., 1893. Reprint, Harrisonburg, Va.: Sprinkle Publications, 1991.

Life and Reminiscences of Jefferson Davis by Distinguished Men of His Time. Baltimore: R. H. Woodward & Co., 1890.

Little, Robert D. "General Hardee and the Atlanta Campaign." *Georgia Historical Quarterly* 29 (1945): 1–22.

Long, Daniel Albright. *Jefferson Davis: An Address Delivered at Concord, North Carolina, June 3, 1921.* Raleigh, N.C.: Edwards & Broughton Printing Co., 1923.

Longstreet, James. *From Manassas to Appomattox: Memoirs of the Civil War in America.* Reprint, n.p.: Blue & Grey Press, n.d.

Lonn, Ella. *Foreigners in the Confederacy.* Chapel Hill: University of North Carolina Press, 1940.

———. *Foreigners in the Union Army and Navy.* Baton Rouge: Louisiana State University Press, 1951.

Losson, Christopher. *Tennessee's Forgotten Warriors: Frank Cheatham and His Confederate Division.* Knoxville: University of Tennessee Press, 1989.

Louisiana Historical Association. *Calendar of the Jefferson Davis Postwar Manuscripts in the Louisiana Historical Association Collection, Confederate Memorial Hall, New Orleans, Louisiana.* N.p.: Louisiana Historical Association, 1943.

Lowry, Robert, and William H. McCardle. *A History of Mississippi from the Discovery of the Great River by Hernando DeSoto . . . to the Death of Jefferson Davis.* Jackson: R. H. Henry & Co., 1891.

Lubbock, Francis Richard. *Six Decades in Texas or Memoirs of Francis Richard Lubbock.* Edited by C. W. Raines. Austin: Ben C. Jones & Co., 1900.

McCulloch, Hugh. *Men and Measures of Half a Century: Sketches and Comments.* 1888. Reprint, New York: DaCapo Press, 1970.

McElroy, Robert. *Jefferson Davis: The Unreal and the Real.* 2 vols. New York: Harper & Brothers, 1937.

McIlwaine, Shields. *Memphis down in Dixie.* Society of America Series. New York: E. P. Dutton & Co., 1948.

McKim, Randolph H. *A Soldier's Recollections: Leaves from the Diary of a Young Confederate.* New York: Longmans, Green, & Co., 1910.

McKinley, Silas Bent, and Silas Bent. *Old Rough and Ready: The Life and Times of Zachary Taylor.* New York: Vanguard Press, 1946.

McMurry, Richard M. " 'The *Enemy* at Richmond': Joseph E. Johnston and the Confederate Government." *Civil War History* 27 (1981): 5–31.

———. *John Bell Hood and the War for Southern Independence.* N.p.: University Press of Kentucky, 1982.

McPherson, James M. *Abraham Lincoln and the Second American Revolution.* New York: Oxford University Press, 1991.

———. *Battle Cry of Freedom: The Civil War Era.* New York: Oxford University Press, 1988.

McRacken, William C. "Three Impressions of Jefferson Davis." *New Orleans Times-Democrat,* May 11, 1902. Typescript in Fleming Collection.

McWhiney, Grady. *Braxton Bragg and Confederate Defeat.* Vol. 1. New York: Columbia University Press, 1969.

Mahan, Bruce E. *Old Fort Crawford and the Frontier.* Iowa City: State Historical Society of Iowa, 1926.

Mallory, Stephen R. "The Last Days of the Confederate Government." Parts 1, 2. *McClure's,* December 1900, 99–107, January 1901, 239–48.

Mann, A. Dudley. *"My Ever Dearest Friend": The Letters of A. Dudley Mann to Jefferson Davis, 1869–1889,* ed. John P. Moore. Confederate Centennial Studies. Tuscaloosa, Ala.: Confederate Publishing Co., 1960.

Manly, Louise. *Southern Literature from 1579 to 1895: A Comprehensive Review, with Copious Extracts and Criticisms.* Richmond: B. F. Johnson Publishing Co., 1895.

Marvel, William. *Andersonville: The Last Depot.* Civil War America Series. Chapel Hill: University of North Carolina Press, 1994.

Mattingly, Sister Mary Ramona. *The Catholic Church on the Kentucky Frontier (1785–1812).* Washington, D. C.: Catholic University of America, 1936.

Maury, Dabney Herndon. *Recollections of a Virginian in the Mexican, Indian, and Civil Wars.* New York: Charles Scribner's Sons, 1894.

May, Robert E. *John A. Quitman: Old South Crusader.* Baton Rouge: Louisiana State University Press, 1985.

Meade, Robert Douthat. *Judah P. Benjamin: Confederate Statesman.* New York: Oxford University Press, 1943.

Meredith, Roy. *The Face of Robert E. Lee in Life and in Legend.* Rev. ed. New York: Fairfax Press, 1981.

Meriwether, Elizabeth Avery [George Edmonds, pseud.]. *Facts and Falsehoods Concerning the War on the South.* Memphis: A. R. Taylor & Co. [c. 1904].

———. *Recollections of 92 Years.* Nashville: Tennessee Historical Commission, 1958. Reprint, McClean, Va.: EPM Publications, 1994.

Miers, Earl Schenck, ed. *A Rebel War Clerk's Diary by John B. Jones.* Condensed edition. New York: A. S. Barnes & Co., 1961.

Miers, Earl Schenck, ed. *When the World Ended: The Diary of Emma LeConte.* New York: Oxford University Press, 1957.

Miles, Edwin Arthur. *Jacksonian Democracy in Mississippi.* Chapel Hill: University of North Carolina Press, 1960.

Miller, Francis Trevelyan. *Photographic History of the Civil War.* 10 vols. Barnes & Co.. Reprint, New York: Castle Books, 1957.

Montgomery, H[enry]. *The Life of Major-General Zachary Taylor, Twelfth President of the United States.* Philadelphia: Porter & Coates, n.d.

Montgomery, Horace. *Howell Cobb's Confederate Career.* Confederate Centennial Studies. Tuscaloosa, Ala.: Confederate Publishing Co., 1959.

Moore, Jerrold Northrop. *Confederate Commissary General: Lucius Bellinger Northrop and the Subsistance Bureau of the Southern Army.* Shippensburg, Pa.: White Mane Publishing Co., 1996.

Moore, Samuel J. T., Jr. *Moore's Complete Civil War Guide to Richmond.* N.p.: 1978.

Moorhead, James H. *American Apocalypse: Yankee Protestants and the Civil War, 1860–1869.* New Haven: Yale University Press, 1978.

Morrison, James L., Jr., ed. *"The Best School in the World": West Point, the Pre-Civil War Years, 1833–1866.* Kent, Ohio: Kent State University Press, 1986.

Moses, Montrose J. *The Literature of the South.* New York: Thomas Y. Crowell & Co., 1910.

Muhlenfeld, Elisabeth. *Mary Boykin Chesnut: A Biography.* Baton Rouge: Louisiana State University Press, 1981.

Napier, Cameron Freeman. *The First White House of the Confederacy, Montgomery, Alabama.* Montgomery: First White House Association, 1978.

National Cyclopaedia of American Biography. New York: James T. White & Co., 1929.

Nichols, Roy Franklin. *Franklin Pierce: Young Hickory of the Granite Hills.* 2d ed. Philadelphia: University of Pennsylvania Press, 1969.

Noll, Arthur Howard, ed. *Doctor Quintard, Chaplain C.S.A. and Second Bishop of Tennessee: Being His Story of the War (1861–1865).* Sewanee Tenn.: University Press, 1905.

Nuermberger, Ruth Ketring. *The Clays of Alabama: A Planter-Lawyer-Politician Family.* Lexington: University of Kentucky Press, 1958.

Odgers, Merle M. *Alexander Dallas Bache, Scientist and Educator, 1806–1867.* Philadelphia: University of Pennsylvania Press, 1947.

Osborne, Charles C. *Jubal: The Life and Times of General Jubal Early, CSA, Defender of the Lost Cause.* Chapel Hill: Algonquin Books of Chapel Hill, 1992.

Oxford English Dictionary, The Compact Edition of the. 2 vols. N.p.: Oxford University Press, 1971.

The Oxford Illustrated Literary Guide to Great Britain and Ireland. Compiled and edited by Dorothy Eagle and Hilary Carnell. Oxford University Press, 1981. Reprint, London: Spring Books, 1987.

Page, James Madison, with M. J. Haley. *The True Story of Andersonville Prison: A Defense of Major Henry Wirz.* New York: Neale Publishing Co., 1908.

Pamphlets relative to Jefferson Davis from Boston Public Library. 1884. Reprint, Cleveland: Micro Photo, n.d.

Parker, David B. "Bill Arp, Joe Brown, and the Confederate War Effort." *Georgia Historical Quarterly* 73 (1989): 79–87.

Parks, Joseph Howard. *General Edmund Kirby Smith, C.S.A.* Baton Rouge: Louisiana State University Press, 1962.

Parrish, T. Michael. *Richard Taylor: Soldier Prince of Dixie.* Chapel Hill: University of North Carolina Press, 1992.

Parton, James. *Life of Andrew Jackson in Three Volumes.* 3 vols. New York: Mason Brothers, 1860. Reprint, New York: Johnson Reprint Corp., 1967.

Pearce, Haywood J., Jr. *Benjamin H. Hill; Secession and Reconstruction.* Chicago: University of Chicago Press, 1928.

Pemberton, John C. [Jr.]. *Pemberton, Defender of Vicksburg.* Chapel Hill: University of North Carolina Press, 1942.

Pendleton, Louis. *Alexander H. Stephens.* American Crisis Biographies. Philadelphia: George W. Jacobs & Co., 1907.

Perry, William Stevens. *The Bishops of the American Church Past and Present: Sketches, Biographical and Bibliographical, of the Bishops of the American Church, with a Preliminary Essay on the Historic Episcopate and Documentary Annals of the introduction of the Anglican line of succession into America.* New York: Christian Literature Co., 1897.

Phillips, U. B. *Life and Labor in the Old South.* Boston: Little, Brown, & Co., 1939.

———. *The Life of Robert Toombs.* New York: Macmillan Co., 1913.

Phillips, U. B., ed. *The Correspondence of Robert Toombs, Alexander H. Stephens and Howell Cobb.* Vol. 2 of Ninth Report of the Historical Manuscripts Commission. Washington, D.C.: American Historical Association, 1913.

Piston, William Garrett. *Lee's Tarnished Lieutenant: James Longstreet and His Place in Southern History.* Athens: University of Georgia Press, 1987.

Polk, William M. *Leonidas Polk, Bishop and General.* 2 vols. New York: Longmans, Green, & Co., 1894.

Pollard, Edward A. *The First Year of the War.* Richmond: West & Johnston, 1862. Reprint, New York: Charles B. Richardson, 1865.

———. *Life of Jefferson Davis with a Secret History of the Southern Confederacy*. Philadelphia: National Publishing Co., 1869.

———. *The Lost Cause: A New Southern History of the War of the Confederates*. New York: E. B. Treat & Co., 1867. Reprint, New York: Bonanza Books, n.d.

Pryor, Mrs. Roger A. *Reminiscences of Peace and War*. New York: Macmillan Co., 1924.

Quaife, Milo M. "The Northwestern Career of Jefferson Davis." *Journal of the Illinois State Historical Society* 16 (1923): 1–19.

Ramage, James A. *Rebel Raider: The Life of General John Hunt Morgan*. Lexington: University Press of Kentucky, 1986.

Randall, J. G. *The Civil War and Reconstruction*. Boston: D. C. Heath & Co., 1937.

Reagan, John H. "Flight and Capture of Jefferson Davis." In *The Annals of the War*, 147–59.

———. *Memoirs, with Special Reference to Secession and the Civil War*. Edited by W. F. McCaleb. New York: Neale Publishing Co., 1906.

Reavis, L. U. *The Life and Military Services of Gen. William Selby Harney*. St. Louis: Bryan, Brand & Co., Publishers, 1878. Microfilm.

Register of Graduates and Former Cadets of the United States Military Academy. West Point: West Point Alumni Foundation, 1964.

"Resources of the Confederacy in 1865—Report of General I. M. St. John, Commissary General." *Southern Historical Society Papers* 3 (1877): 97–111.

Rhodes, James Ford. *History of the United States from the Compromise of 1850 to the McKinley-Bryan Campaign of 1896*. 9 vols. New York: Macmillan Co., 1912–1936.

Richardson, James D., ed. *A Compilation of the Messages and Papers of the Confederacy*. 2 vols. Nashville: United States Publishing Co., 1905.

Ridley, Bromfield L. *Battles and Sketches of the Army of Tennessee*. Mexico, Mo.: Missouri Printing & Publishing Co., 1906.

Riley, Franklin L., ed. "Diary of a Mississippi Planter, January 1, 1840, to April, 1863." *Publications of the Mississippi Historical Society* 10 (1909): 305–481.

Riley, Harris D., Jr. "Jefferson Davis and His Health." Parts 1, 2. *Journal of Mississippi History* 49 (August, November 1987): 179–202, 261–87.

Robertson, James I., Jr. *The Stonewall Brigade*. Baton Rouge: Louisiana State University Press, 1963.

Robertson, William Glenn. *Back Door to Richmond: The Bermuda Hundred Campaign, April–June 1864*. Baton Rouge: Louisiana State University Press, 1987.

Roman, Alfred. *The Military Operations of General Beauregard.* 2 vols. New York: Harper's, 1884.

Ross, Edmund G. *History of the Impeachment of Andrew Johnson, President of the United States, by the House of Representatives, and His Trial by the Senate, for High Crimes and Misdemeanors in Office, 1868.* Santa Fe, N.M.: Author, 1896.

Ross, Ishbel. *First Lady of the South: The Life of Mrs. Jefferson Davis.* New York: Harper, 1958. Reprint, Westport, Conn.: Greenwood Press, 1973.

Rowland, Dunbar. *History of Mississippi, The Heart of the South.* 2 vols. Chicago-Jackson: S. J. Clarke Publishing Co., 1925.

———. *Military History of Mississippi, 1803–1898.* 1908. Reprint, Spartenburg, S.C.: Reprint Co., 1978.

Rowland, Dunbar, ed. *Jefferson Davis, Constitutionalist: His Letters, Papers and Speeches.* 10 vols. Jackson: Mississippi Department of Archives & History, 1923.

———. *Mississippi, Comprising Sketches of Counties, Towns, Events, Institutions, and Persons, Arranged in Cyclopedic Form.* 3 vols. Atlanta: Southern Historical Publishing Association, 1907. Reprint, Spartenburg, S.C.: Reprint Co., 1976.

Rowland, Eron. *Andrew Jackson's Campaign against the British, or the Mississippi Territory in the War of 1812.* New York: Macmillan Co., 1926.

———. *Varina Howell, Wife of Jefferson Davis.* 2 vols. New York: Macmillan, 1927, 1931.

Roy, T. B. "General Hardee and Military Operations Around Atlanta." *Southern Historical Society Papers* 8 (1880): 337–87.

"'Running at the Heads': Being an Authentic Account of the Capture of Jefferson Davis." *Atlantic Monthly,* September 1865, 342–47.

Rutherford, Mildred Lewis, comp. *Andersonville Prison and Captain Henry Wirz Trial.* Georgia U. D. C. Bulletin, 1921. Reprint, n.p.: 1921.

Samson, William H., ed. *Letters of Zachary Taylor from the Battlefields of the Mexican War, Reprinted from the Originals in the Collection of Mr. William K. Bixby, of St. Louis, Mo.* Rochester, N.Y.: 1908. Reprint, New York: Kraus Reprint Co., 1970.

Scanlon, P. L. "The Military Record of Jefferson Davis in Wisconsin." *Wisconsin Magazine of History* 24 (1940–41): 174–82.

Schaff, Morris. *The Spirit of Old West Point, 1858–62.* Boston: Houghton Mifflin Co., 1909.

Scharf, J. Thomas. *History of the Confederate States Navy, from its Organization to the Surrender of its Last Vessel.* [1887]. Reprint, n.p.: Fairfax Press, 1977.

Scheibert, Justus. *Seven Months in the Rebel States during the North American War, 1863.* Translated by J. C. Hayes. Edited by W. S. Hoole. Confederate Centennial Studies. Tuscaloosa, Ala.: Confederate Publishing Co., 1958.

Seagar, Robert, II. *and Tyler too: A Biography of John & Julia Gardiner Tyler.* New York: McGraw-Hill Book Co., 1963.

Sears, Louis Martin. *John Slidell.* Durham: Duke University Press, 1925.

Sears, Stephen W. *George B. McClellan: The Young Napoleon.* New York: Ticknor & Fields, 1988.

Seitz, Don C. *Braxton Bragg, General of the Confederacy.* 1924. Reprint, Freeport, N.Y.: Books for Libraries Press, 1971.

Semmes, Raphael. *Memoirs of Service Afloat during the War between the States.* 1903. Reprint, Secaucus, N.J.: Blue & Grey Press, 1987.

Shaw, Arthur Marvin. *William Preston Johnston: A Transitional Figure of the Confederacy.* Baton Rouge: Louisiana State University Press, 1943.

Shea, George. *Jefferson Davis: A Statement concerning the Imputed Special Causes of His Long Imprisonment by the Government of the United States, and of His Tardy Release by Due Process of Law; Contained in a Letter from the Honourable George Shea, of New York, One of His Counsel. New York Tribune,* January 24, 1876. Reprint, London: Edward Stanford, 1877. Pamphlet.

Sherman, William T. *Memoirs of General William T. Sherman.* 2 vols. New York: D. Appleton & Co., 1875; also 2d ed. rev. and corr., 1931.

Shingleton, Royce Gordon. *John Taylor Wood: Sea Ghost of the Confederacy.* Athens: University of Georgia Press, 1979.

The Shorter Oxford English Dictionary on Historical Principles. Compiled by William Little, H. W. Fowler, & J. Coulson. 3rd Ed. rev. with addenda by C. T. Onions. Oxford: Clarendon Press, 1933. Reprint, 1968.

Sibley, Marilyn McAdams, ed. "Jefferson Davis Recalls the Past: Notes of a Wartime Aide, William Preston Johnston." *Journal of Mississippi History* 33 (1971): 167–78.

Simpson, John Eddins. *Howell Cobb: The Politics of Ambition.* Chicago: Adams Press, 1973.

Smith, Gustavus W. *Confederate War Papers. Fairfax Court House, New Orleans, Seven Pines, Richmond and North Carolina.* 2d ed. New York: Atlantic Publishing & Engraving Co., 1884.

———. "Two Days of Battle at Seven Pines (Fair Oaks)." In *Battles and Leaders* 2:220–63.

Smith, Justin H. *The War with Mexico.* 2 vols. New York: Macmillan Co., 1919.

Smith, Nannie D. "Reminiscences of Jefferson Davis." *Confederate Veteran* (May 1930): 178–82.

South in the Building of the Nation, The: A History of the Southern States . . . . 12 vols., plus Index. Richmond: Southern Historical Publication Society, 1909, 1913.

Standard, Janet Harvill, comp. *The Battle of Kettle Creek: A Turning Point of the American Revolution in the South.* Washington, Ga.: Wilkes Publishing Co., 1973.

Starr, Stephen Z. *Colonel Grenfell's Wars: The Life of a Soldier of Fortune.* Baton Rouge: Louisiana State University Press, 1971.

Steffan, Randy. *The Horse Soldier, 1776–1943: The United States Cavalryman, His Uniforms, Arms, Accoutrements, and Equipments.* 4 vols. Norman: University of Oklahoma Press, 1977–79.

Stephens, Alexander H. *A Constitutional View of the Late War between the States.* 2 vols. Philadelphia: National Publishing Co., 1868.

———. *Recollections of Alexander H. Stephens, His Diary Kept When a Prisoner at Fort Warren, Boston Harbour, 1865; Giving Incidents and Reflections of His Prison Life and Some Letters and Reminiscences, with a Biographical Study.* Edited by Myrta Lockett Avary. New York: Doubleday, Page & Co., 1910.

Sterling, Ada, ed. *A Belle of the Fifties: Memoirs of Mrs. Clay of Alabama, covering Social and Political Life in Washington and the South, 1853–66.* New York: Doubleday, Page & Co., 1905.

Stevenson, R. Randolph. *The Southern Side; Or, Andersonville Prison, compiled from official documents.* Baltimore: Turnbull Brothers, 1876.

Stout, L. H. *Reminiscences of General Braxton Bragg.* Hattiesburg, Miss.: Book Farm, 1942. Microfiche. Pamphlets in American History, C. W. 46.

Stovall, Pleasant A. *Robert Toombs, Statesman, Speaker, Soldier, Sage. . . .* New York: Cassell Publishing Co., 1892.

Strode, Hudson. *Jefferson Davis. American Patriot, 1808–1861.* New York: Harcourt, Brace & Co., 1955.

———. *Jefferson Davis. Confederate President.* New York: Harcourt, Brace & World, 1959.

———. *Jefferson Davis. Tragic Hero: The Last Twenty-five Years, 1864–1889.* New York: Harcourt, Brace & World, 1964.

———. *Jefferson Davis: Private Letters, 1823–1889.* New York: Harcourt, Brace & World, 1966. Reprint, New York: DeCapo Press, 1995.

Sturges, Mrs. Hezekiah. "Recollections of Jefferson Davis." *Register of the Kentucky State Historical Society* 10 (1912): 9–19.

Swanberg, W. A. *Pulitzer.* New York: Charles Scribner's Sons, 1967.

Sweet, William Warren. *The Story of Religions in America.* New York: Harper & Bros., 1930.

Symonds, Craig L. *Joseph E. Johnston: A Civil War Biography.* New York: W. W. Norton & Co., 1992.

Taylor, Richard. *Destruction and Reconstruction: Personal Experiences of the Late War.* New York: D. Appleton & Co., 1879.

———. "The Last Confederate Surrender." In *The Confederate Soldier in the Civil War,* 318.

Taylor, Walter H. *Four Years with General Lee.* Edited by James I. Robertson, Jr. Indiana University Press, 1962. Reprint, New York: Bonanza Books, n.d.

———. *General Lee: His Campaigns in Virginia, 1861–1865, with Personal Reminiscences.* Norfolk: Nusbaum Book & News Co., 1906.

Thomas, Emory M. *Bold Dragoon: The Life of J. E. B. Stuart.* New York: Harper & Row, 1986.

Thompson, James West. *Beauvoir, the Last Home of Jefferson Davis.* Bowling Green, Ky.: Rivendell Publications, 1984.

Thompson, Ray M. *The Confederate Shrine of Beauvoir, Last Home of Jefferson Davis.* Biloxi: G. C. Hamill & Associates, 1957. Pamphlet.

Thompson, William Y. *Robert Toombs of Georgia.* Baton Rouge: Louisiana State University Press, 1966.

The Universal Standard Encyclopedia, an Abridgment of the New Funk and Wagnalls Encyclopedia. Edited by Joseph Laffan Morse. 24 vols. New York: Standard Reference Works Publishing Co., 1957.

Vandiver, Frank E. "Jefferson Davis—Leader without Legend." *Journal of Southern History* 43 (1977): 3–18.

———. *Their Tattered Flags: The Epic of the Confederacy.* Harper's Magazine Press, 1970. Reprint, College Station: Texas A&M University Press, 1989.

Wagers, Margaret Newman. *The Education of a Gentleman: Jefferson Davis at Transylvania, 1821–1824.* Lexington, Ky.: Buckley & Reading, 1943.

Wakelyn, Jon L. *Biographical Dictionary of the Confederacy.* Westport, Conn.: Greenwood Press, 1977.

Walthall, William T. *The Life of Jefferson Davis. New Orleans Times-Democrat,* 1908. Reprint, Biloxi, Miss.: Beauvoir, the Jefferson Davis Shrine, 1989.

———. "The True Story of the Capture of Jefferson Davis." *Southern Historical Society Papers* 5 (1878): 97–126.

War of the Rebellion, The: A Compilation of the Official Records of the Union and Confederate Armies. Edited by various hands. 128 vols. Washington, D.C.: Government Printing Office, 1880–1901.

Wardin, Albert W., Jr. *Belmont Mansion: The Home of Joseph and Adelicia Acklen.* Nashville: Historic Belmont Association, 1981.

Warner, Ezra J. *Generals in Blue: Lives of the Union Commanders.* Baton Rouge: Louisiana State University Press, 1964.

———. *Generals in Gray: Lives of the Confederate Commanders.* Baton Rouge: Louisiana State University Press, 1959.

Washington: City and Capital. Washington, D.C.: U.S. Government Printing Office, 1937.

Weaver, Richard M. *The Southern Tradition at Bay: A History of Postbellum Thought.* Edited by George Core and M. E. Bradford. New Rochelle, N.Y.: Arlington House, 1968.

Weber, William Lander, ed. *Selections from the Southern Poets.* New York: Macmillan Co., 1905.

Webster's New Collegiate Dictionary, Based on Webster's New International Dictionary. 2d ed. Springfield, Mass.: G. & C. Merriam Co., 1949.

Webster's New International Dictionary of the English Language. 2d ed., unabridged. Springfield, Massachusetts: G. & C. Merriam Co., 1950.

Weddell, Elizabeth Wright. *St. Paul's Church, Richmond, Virginia: Its Historic Years and Memorials.* 2 vols. Richmond: William Byrd Press, 1931.

Weigley, Russell F. *History of the United States Army.* New York: Macmillan Co., 1967.

Wellman, Manly Wade. *Giant in Gray: A Biography of Wade Hampton of South Carolina.* New York: Charles Scribner's Sons, 1949.

Whipple, Henry B. *Bishop Whipple's Southern Diary, 1843–1844.* Edited by Lester B. Shippee. Minneapolis: University of Minnesota Press, 1937.

White, George. *Historical Collections of Georgia . . . Compiled from Original Records and Official Documents.* 3rd ed. New York: Pudney & Russell, Publishers, 1855.

———. *Statistics of the State of Georgia, Including an Account of Its Natural, Civil, and Ecclesiastical History . . . .* Savannah: W. Thorne Williams, 1849.

White, Laura A. *Robert Barnwell Rhett, Father of Secession.* New York: Century Co., 1931.

Wiley, Bell I. *Embattled Confederates: An Illustrated History of Southerners at War.* New York: Bonanza Books, 1964.

Williams, Jack K. *Dueling in the Old South: Vignettes of Social History.* College Station: Texas A&M University Press, 1980.

Williams, T. Harry. *P. G. T. Beauregard, Napoleon in Gray.* Baton Rouge: Louisiana State University Press, 1955.

Wilmer, Richard H. *The Recent Past from a Southern Standpoint.* New York: Thomas Whittaker, 1887.

Wiltse, Charles M. *John C. Calhoun, Nationalist, 1782–1828.* Indianapolis: Bobbs-Merrill Co., 1944.

———. *John C. Calhoun, Sectionalist, 1840–1850.* Indianapolis: Bobbs-Merrill Co., 1951.

Winchester, James R., "Jefferson Davis, Communicant." *The Living Church,* June 8, 1935, 727–28.

Winter, John D. *The Civil War in Louisiana.* Baton Rouge: Louisiana State University Press, 1963.

Wood, Mattie Pegues. *The Life of St. John's Parish: A History of St. John's Episcopal Church from 1834 to 1955.* Montgomery, Ala.: Paragon Press, 1955.

Woodworth, Steven E. *Jefferson Davis and His Generals: The Failure of Confederate Command in the West.* Lawrence: University Press of Kansas, 1990.

Wright, John D., Jr. *Lexington, Heart of the Bluegrass.* Lexington, Ky.: Lexington-Fayette County Historic Commission, 1983.

Wright, Louise Wigfall (Mrs. D. Girard). *A Southern Girl in '61: The War-Time Memories of a Confederate Senator's Daughter.* New York: Doubleday, Page & Co., 1905.

Wyatt-Brown, Bertram. *The House of Percy: Honor, Melancholy, and Imagination in a Southern Family.* New York: Oxford University Press, 1994.

Yearns, Wilfred Buck. *The Confederate Congress.* Athens: University of Georgia Press, 1960.

Newspapers

Atlanta [Ga.] Constitution (1985)
Atlanta [Ga.] Journal and Constitution (1990)
[Marion, Ala.] Baptist Correspondent (1861)
Charleston [S.C.] News and Courier (1889)
Columbia [S.C.] Record (1889)
Montgomery [Ala.] Advertiser (1978)
Nashville Sunday Tennessean (1988)
Nashville Tennessean (1995)
New Orleans Daily Picayune (1873, 1889)
New York Times (1865, 1906)
New York Tribune (1867)
Richmond [Va.] Daily Dispatch (1864)
Richmond [Va.] Sentinel (1864)

Chief Periodicals Sources

Confederate Chronicles of Tennessee

Confederate Veteran (vols. 1–40 publ. January 1893–December 1932; also new series, to present)

Congressional Globe (Washington, D. C.: privately printed, 46 vols., 1834–1873)

Georgia Historical Quarterly

Journal of Confederate History

Journal of Mississippi History

Publications of the Mississippi Historical Society

Southern Historical Society Papers (1876–1910, and new series; 52 vols.)

Index

Page numbers in italics refer to pictures and maps. JD in index refers to Jefferson Davis. CSA refers to Confederate States of America.